SO-CBQ-059

FRANCE

Café Bonaprtte
Rue de
Bonaparte

2nd Revised Edition

Directed by
André Gayot

Contributing Editors
Alice Brinton, Françoise Boisard, François Duipuigrenet Desrousilles,
Heidi Ellison, Jonell Galloway, Odile Granier, Louisa Jones,
Michèle Marion, Sheila Mooney, Brigitte du Tanney

Coordination
Sophie Gayot

Publisher
Alain Gayot

Adapted from the
French-Language Guide

published in French by SPES (Paris)

Paris ▪ Los Angeles ▪ New York ▪ San Francisco ▪ London ▪ Munich ▪ Turin

GAULT&MILLAU

The Best of Chicago
The Best of Florida
The Best of France
The Best of Germany
The Best of Hawaii
The Best of Hong Kong
The Best of Italy
The Best of London
The Best of Los Angeles

The Best of New England
The Best of New Orleans
The Best of New York
The Best of Paris
The Best of San Francisco
The Best of Thailand
The Best of Toronto
The Best of Washington, D.C.
The Best Wineries of North America
Paris, Ile de France & The Loire Valley

LA Restaurants, NYC Restaurants, SF Restaurants
The Food Paper, Tastes Newsletter
http://www.gayot.com

GAYOT PUBLICATIONS

Published by GaultMillau, Inc.
5900 Wilshire Blvd.
Los Angeles, CA 90036
E-mail: gayots@aol.com

Advertising Sales:
Pascal Meiers Communication
10 bis rue Jeanne d'Arc, 94160 Saint-Mandé, France
tel. 01 43 28 20 20, fax 01 43 28 27 27

Please address all comments regarding
France to:
GaultMillau, Inc.
P.O. Box 361144
Los Angeles, CA 90036

ISSN: 1092-986X

Printed in the United States of America

CONTENTS

■ INTRODUCTION 5

What makes Normandy different from Provence? How to discover the true face of France and how to find your way around *our Guide to France*. We've classified the country into seventeen regions, and we've scoured score upon score of cities, towns, villages, and remote hamlets to uncover all the best restaurants and hotels. Whether you're looking for a world-famous restaurant, a romantic resort, or a charming village inn, you'll find it among these thousands of in-the-know reviews. And at the end of each chapter, you'll find sources for regional foods and wines. If you are lost, check in the alphabetical index to find the region, city, or village where a restaurant, inn, or shop you are looking for is located.

■ SYMBOL SYSTEMS 7

Read this short chapter before you go any further. How to decipher the rankings, prices, symbols, and abbreviations.

■ TOQUE TALLY 9

A listing of the very best restaurants in France.

■ PARIS & ILE-DE-FRANCE 11

■ ALSACE 121

■ BRITTANY 131

■ BURGUNDY 145

■ CENTRAL FRANCE 175

This region includes Auvergne, Berry, and Limousin.

■ CHAMPAGNE 193

■ FRANCHE-COMTÉ 203

A savory journey among the maddening, marvelous gauls

Our Guide to France now offers an improved format. Previously, our guide to the restaurants and hotels of France looked something like an encyclopedia of French gastronomy—the entries were all listed in alphabetical order.

Now, however convenient an alphabetical presentation may be in many respects, it ignores a fundamental reality: it puts Angoulême next to Annecy. But what, in fact, do these towns have in common besides the letter A? Annecy in the Alps, Angoulême in Charente are worlds apart, with different histories, landscapes, populations. "Worlds apart? Just a few hundred kilometers... And Angoulême is just as French as Annecy! So why do you say they're so different?"

True, the French adore paradoxes and exceptions to the rule. But leaving aside the wordplay and witticisms that are as essential to a Frenchman as his daily *baguette*, France is as wonderfully diverse as it is deeply united. The *Gaulois* are a complex breed, hard to define or pigeonhole. And though that elusive quality may be irritating, it is also a part of their indefinable charm. No French are more patriotic than Bretons or Alsatians, but even they are attached to the special character that makes them different from, say, the Auvergnats or Provençals.

Life in Lille, obviously, is nothing like life in Nice. Climate and geography play their part: Flanders will never be Provence, and people can't play *pétanque* in the shade of plane trees when they live by the North Sea. Too little sunshine, and no plane trees at all! That's one good reason, but there are others, too. France has been an extraordinary melting pot since prehistoric times. Each wave of immigration or conquest left its legacy of customs, culture, and language. Thank goodness, this diverse heritage still subsists: just listen to the rich range of clipped and rolling accents, the sayings and expressions of French as it is spoken today! Time, fashions, fortunes, and misfortunes have left their mark—a mark that varies from region to region—on houses, churches, châteaux, and palaces. Why do Romanesque sanctuaries in the Limousin differ from those in Ile-de-France? Because Limousin granite is so recalcitrant to the chisel that sculptors were obliged to adopt a sober, unadorned style.

No bouillabaisse in the mountains

It's the same thing with food. You won't find bouillabaisse in the mountain fastness of Clermont-Ferrand, far from the Mediterranean and its abundance of fish.

What you'll discover in these pages is the real France, presented in all its splendid diversity. A France we hope you will enjoy all the more as you ramble through its provinces, provided with keys to understanding the cities and regions you visit. France is a bouquet of rich *terroirs* and of distinctive personalities. We recommend that you take these maddening, marvelous Gauls as they are—but first, arm yourself with a little information!

So we have classified (let's avoid the word "divide") France into **seventeen regions**. The chapters devoted to the most visited ones—*Paris & Ile-de-France; Burgundy; the Loire Valley; Normandy; Provence & the Riviera;* and *the Southwest* (Bordelais, the Basque Country & Western Pyrenees, Gascony & Périgord)—are chockablock with bistrots, top notch restaurants, country inns or gilded palaces. Should you decide however to discover the charms of a less well know France, we will also help you to find your way around: *Alsace; Brittany; Central France* (Auvergne, Berry, Limousin); *Champagne; Franche-Comté; Languedoc-Roussillon & Midi-Pyrénées; Lorraine* with *Western Vosges; the Lyonnais; the North; Poitou, Vendée & Charentes; the Rhône Valley & the Alps.* Each chapter offers an in-depth introduction to the region followed by discerning reviews of restaurants and hotels, and tips on where to find local food specialties and wines. A detailed alphabetical index will help you locate all these establishments quickly and easily.

The rise of a new star

In the French gastronomic world, important events have occured last year: the retirement of celebrated Joël Robuchon in Paris and in neighbouring Switzterland of Freddy Girardet; the undomitable rise of Alain Ducasse who splitting his life in two succeeds both in Paris in the former *hôtel particulier* of Robuchon and in Monaco as well at his famous Louis XV where he first conquered celebrity.

The cook of the year could not be anyone else than Jacques Chibois. This gifted chef has now settled in his own house of La Bastide Saint-Antoine in Grasse in Provence. In this beautiful scenery, he enchants his guests with an exuberant though subtle cooking.

As we take stock after completing our tour of France, it's clear that the overall level of French cooking is higher than when we published our first guide a quarter of a century ago. Since a talented new generation is on its way up, we felt that our former rating system might not reflect their progress. We therefore limited the number of spots at the top of the pyramid—chefs rated 19/20—while opening our pages more and more to young talents eager to show their stuff.

Our Guide to France introduces you to a new, panoramic view of French gastronomy. With this guidebook in hand, you can personally ascertain that at the dawn of the 21st century, dining in France is better than ever!

SYMBOL SYSTEMS

RESTAURANTS

We rank restaurants in the same manner that French students are graded: on a scale of zero to twenty, twenty being unattainable perfection. The rankings reflect *only* the quality of the cooking; décor, service, reception, and atmosphere do not influence the rating. They are explicitly commented on within the reviews. Restaurants ranked thirteen and above are distinguished with toques (chef's hats), according to the following table:

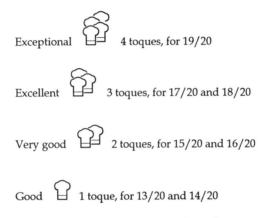

Exceptional — 4 toques, for 19/20

Excellent — 3 toques, for 17/20 and 18/20

Very good — 2 toques, for 15/20 and 16/20

Good — 1 toque, for 13/20 and 14/20

Keep in mind that these ranks are *relative*. One toque for 13/20 is not a very good ranking for a highly reputed (and very expensive) temple of fine dining, but it is quite complimentary for a small place without much pretension.

• In addition to the standard **carte**, or à la carte menu, you will frequently be offered a choice of all-inclusive fixed-price meals called **menus**, which are generally a very good value. Also common in finer restaurants is the many-course sampling menu, or **menu dégustation**, a good (though not always economical) way to get an overview of a restaurant's specialties. Daily specials, or **plats du jour**, are usually reliable, inexpensive, and prepared with fresh ingredients that the chef found at the market that morning.

• At the end of each restaurant review, prices are given—either *A la carte* (**C**) or *Menu* (**M**) (fixed-price meal) or both. A la carte prices are those of an average meal (a starter, a main course, dessert, and coffee) for one person, including service and a half-bottle of relatively modest wine. Lovers of the great Bordeaux, Burgundies, and Champagnes will, of course, face stiffer tabs. The menu prices quoted are for a complete multicourse meal for one person, including service but excluding wine, unless otherwise noted. These fixed-price menus often give diners on a budget a chance to sample the cuisine of an otherwise expensive restaurant.

• When you go to a top restaurant, let the **headwaiter** suggest some possibilities from the menu (you'll find that many maître d's quite often speak English, though they always appreciate an attempt on the diner's part to speak French). Likewise, the **sommelier**'s job is to give diners expert advice on the choice of a suitable wine—regardless of price. Don't be afraid to seek his or her opinion, or to state your budget.

- French law mandates that the **service charge**, 15 percent, always be included in the menu prices. You are not obliged to leave an additional tip, but it is good form to leave a little more if the service was satisfactory.
- The **opening** and **closing times** we've quoted are always subject to change, particularly holiday closings, so be sure to call ahead.
- Many chefs have the bad habit of **changing restaurants frequently**, which means a restaurant can turn mediocre or even bad in just a few days. Chef-owned restaurants tend to be more stable, but even they can decline. A successful owner may be tempted to accept too many diners, which can result in a drop in quality. Should this be your experience, please don't hold us responsible!

HOTELS

Our opinion of the comfort level and appeal of each hotel is expressed in a ranking system, as follows:

Very luxurious

Luxurious

Very comfortable

Comfortable

Very quiet

The prices indicated for rooms and half-board range from the cheapest for one person to the most expensive for two.

Sadly, prices continue to creep up, so some places may have become more expensive than our estimates by the time you visit. If you expect to pay a little more—you may end up being pleasantly surprised!

OTHER INFORMATION & ABBREVIATIONS

✿ A laurel wreath indicates restaurants serving outstanding traditional or regional recipes.

Rms: Rooms
Seas: Season
Priv rm: Private room
Rm ser: Room service

Stes: Suites
Conf: Conference facilities
Air cond: Air conditioning
Pkg: Parking

Half-board: Rate per person for room, breakfast, and one other meal (lunch or dinner)

How to read the locations:

ABBEVILLE	80100
Paris 160 - Amlens 45 - Dieppe 63	Somme

THE CITY	THE ZIP CODE
Kilometers to Paris and nearby major cities	
	The regional department

TOQUE TALLY

Four Toques
19/20

Arpège, *Paris 7th*
L'Aubergade, *Puymirol*
Auberge de l'Ill, *Illhaeusern*
Georges Blanc, *Vonnas*
Michel Bras, *Laguiole*
La Côte d'Or, *Saulieu*
Alain Ducasse, *Paris 16th*
L'Espérance, *Saint-Père-sous-Vézelay*
Michel Guérard, *Eugénie-les-Bains*
Le Louis XV, *Monaco*
Restaurant de Bricourt, *Cancale*
Troisgros, *Roanne*
Marc Veyrat, *Veyrier-du-Lac*

Buerehiesel, *Strasbourg,*
Carré des Feuillants, *Paris 1st,*
Alain Chapel, *Mionnay*
Le Clos de la Violette, *Aix-en-Provence*
Pierre Gagnaire, *Paris 8th*
Le Grand Véfour, *Paris 1st*
Le Jardin des Sens, *Montpellier*
Les Jardins de L'Opéra, *Toulouse*
Ledoyen, *Paris 8th*
Léon de Lyon, *Lyon 1st*
Lucas Carton, *Paris 8th*
Montparnasse 25, *Paris 14th*
La Pyramide, *Vienne*
Guy Savoy, *Paris 17th*
Taillevent, *Paris 8th*
La Terrasse *Juan-les-Pins*
Thibert, *Dijon*
Les Trois Marches, *Versailles*

Three Toques
17/20

Albert-Ier, *Chamonix*
Amat, *Bouliac*
Les Ambassadeurs, *Paris 8th*
Amphyclès, *Paris 17th*
L'Auberge Bretonne, *La Roche-Bernard*
Auberge de la Galupe, *Urt*
Le Bateau Ivre, *Courchevel*
La Belle Otéro, *Cannes*
Jean-Pierre Billoux, *Dijon*

Three Toques
18/20

L'Ambroisie, *Paris 4th*
Apicius, *Paris 17th*
L'Auberge des Cimes, *Saint-Bonnet-le-Froid*
Jean Bardet, *Tours*
La Bastide Saint-Antoine, *Grasse*
Bistrot des Lices, *Saint-Tropez*

Paul Bocuse, *Collonges-au-Mont-d'Or*
Le Bourdonnais, *Paris 7th*
La Bourride, *Caen*
Boyer, *Reims*
Le Bristol, *Paris 8th*
Jean Brouilly, *Tarare*
Café de Paris, *Biarritz*
Le Centenaire, *Les Eyzies-de-Tayac*
Le Cerf, *Marlenheim*
Le Chapon Fin, *Bordeaux*
La Côte Saint-Jacques, *Joigny*
Richard Coutanceau, *La Rochelle*
Le Crocodile, *Strasbourg*
Le Dauphin, *Toul*
Les Élysées du Vernet, *Paris 8th*
Christian Étienne, *Avignon*
Faugeron, *Paris 16th*
La Fenière, *Lourmarin*
Ferme du Letty, *Bénodet*
Les Feuillants, *Céret*
La Flamiche, *Roye*
Gill, *Rouen*
Goumard Prunier, *Paris 1st*
Grand Hôtel du Lion d'Or, *Romorantin*

Le Jardin du Royal Monceau, *Paris 8th*
Jean-Paul Jeunet, *Arbois*
Lameloise, *Chagny*
Laurent, *Paris 8th*
Régis Mahé, *Vannes*
Maximim, *Vence*
Paul Minchelli, *Paris 7th*
Le Moulin de Martorey, *Saint-Rémy*
Le Mungo Park, *Besançon*
L'Oasis, *Mandelieu-La-Napoule*
Georges Paineau, *Questembert*
La Palme d'Or, *Cannes*
Passédat, *Marseille*
Le Pastel, *Toulouse*
Pavillon des Boulevards, *Bordeaux*
Les Plaisirs d'Ausone, *Bordeaux*
Pont de L'Ouysse, *Lacave*
Le Pré Catelan, *Paris 16th*
Les Pyrénées, *Saint-Jean-Pied-de-Port*
Jean Ramet, *Bordeaux*
Bernard Robin, *Bracieux*
La Table d'Anvers, *Paris 9th*
Les Terrasses d'Uriage, *Uriage*
Vivarois, *Paris 16th*

A DISCLAIMER

PARIS
& ILE-DE-FRANCE

A CAPITAL DESTINATION

Despite its name, Ile-de-France is not an island. No spot could be less insular than this province at the heart of Europe, since archaic times a strategic crossroads for culture and commerce between Britain and the Mediterranean, Germany and Spain. Home to some twenty percent of France's inhabitants—that comes to about fifteen million souls—Ile-de-France is the nation's richest, most populous and productive region.

What New York, Chicago, Los Angeles, and Washington are to the United States, **Paris** alone is to France. This single city dominates the nation's government and politics, its industry, business, and finance, its media and communications, its artistic and intellectual life. Paris is the biggest consumer market for everything from vacuum cleaners to theater tickets, and the biggest producer of goods. In recent years, the French government has sought to correct the imbalance between the ever-burgeoning capital and the provinces. "Decentralization" is the order of the day: industries and institutions are offered hefty subsidies to set up their headquarters away from the Paris region. Still, the capital remains a dreamed-of destination for many. Nowhere else in France are jobs more plentiful. To this day, ambitious young provincials still "go up" to Paris hoping to make their name and fortune. Foreigners too, especially from France's former colonies in Africa and Asia, pour into Paris dreaming of a better life. They have put their stamp on the capital, establishing ethnic neighborhoods like the North African quarter of the Goutte d'Or east of Montmartre, the Southeast Asian "Chinatown" around Place d'Italie, and the Black African enclaves of Belleville. Who could recognize the city of the 1950s—the mythical city of An American in Paris—in this multicolored metropolis that is hurtling headlong into the twenty-first century?

Some might be tempted to view Paris, with its sumptuous monuments and historic sites, as a shrine to the glories of past kingdoms and empires. But that is not the whole story. Paris is also a high-energy metropolis, a creative world capital. New urban districts have sprung up. La Défense, on the city's western edge, hosts a major modern landmark, the Arche de La Défense. To the east, the Bercy district is home to the pharaonic national library, the recently inaugurated Bibliothèque de France, as well as the mammoth Palais Omnisports. The city's center has been enriched with the Musée d'Orsay and the expanded Grand Louvre, which now houses an ever greater complement of masterpieces.

A new cathedral for a new town

Cars and trucks from all over Europe rumble into the Paris region via a sophisticated network of high-speed autoroutes. The revamped Métro and regional rapid transit system (RER) cross Paris in just minutes and also serve far-flung suburbs. Bullet trains—the TGV—link the capital to the rest of France and Europe. And a third major airport will soon be built to accommodate the millions of air passengers whose numbers are straining the present kubs of Orly and Roissy Charles-de-Gaulle. Central planners in their Cartesian wisdom have created five *villes nouvelles*, "new towns" complete with schools, parks, and shopping centers, all erected *ex nihilo* in the middle of grain fields. One of them, **Évry**, built on former farmland south of Paris in 1969, even boasts a brand-new (and highly controversial) cathedral designed by Mario Botta.

Since Hugues Capet, count of Paris, was elected King of France in 987 the destiny of Ile-de-France has been shaped by that of the city on the Seine. Royal residences are scattered throughout Ile-de-France, for Hugues Capet and his successors kept their courts on the move: to oversee their lands and subjects; to keep one step ahead of their enemies; and to indulge their passion for the hunt. Even in their present ruined state, the thick-walled fortresses of **Senlis** and **Dourdan**, and the donjon at **Vincennes** (under reconstruction) evoke a feudal age when kings required protection from rivals nearly as powerful as themselves. The Renaissance graces of **Fontainebleau** and **Saint-Germain-en-Laye** mirror a less brutal era, while **Versailles** embodies the brilliance of absolute monarchy at its zenith. With the curious exception of Versailles, most royal châteaux gave onto huge forests teeming with game, where the king could ride to hounds. Even now woodlands covers an astonishing twenty percent of Ile-de-France. The forests of **Fontainebleau** and **Rambouillet**, two of the most splendid in France, count among the region's greatest beauties.

The ire
of the Sun King

Not all of the 3,000 châteaux in Ile-de-France belonged to the Crown. The princely Montmorency and Condé clans, for example, owned vast domains at Ecouen and Chantilly. Their sumptuous dwellings (now home to the Musée de la Renaissance and the splendid Musée Condé, respectively) are set amid gardens and woodlands that impress visitors even today. The seventeenth century was a high-water mark for château construction. The patrician châteaux of **Courances** and **Guermantes** combine brick and stone in a style made popular under Louis XIII; the opulence and classic proportions of **Maisons-Laffitte**, designed by François Mansart in mid-century.

That age dawned in 1661 when Louis XIV attended a *fête* given in his honor by finance minister Nicolas Fouquet, at the latter's new and indescribably luxurious château, **Vaux-le-Vicomte**. Put out by Fouquet's showy splendor (and suspicious of how he had obtained his fortune), Louis had the minister thrown into prison. He then proceeded to hire the same architect, decorator, and garden designer to work on his own royal showplace at **Versailles**. From its completion in 1682 until 1789, Versailles supplanted Paris as the political and artistic capital of the realm. On the eve of the Revolution the château and town counted some 50,000 inhabitants. The Age of Elegance, endures in the eighteenth-century château of **Champs-sur-Marne**, with its Rococo interior (featuring the first dining room ever built for that express purpose) and ravishing *jardin à la française*. The owners of the Renaissance château of **Thoiry** turned the grounds into a wild animal reserve. Visitors drive through the estate (with their windows rolled up...) and watch lions, elephants, monkeys, and rhinos roam free.

The rulers of France, "eldest daughter of the Church," endowed Ile-de-France with a fabulous legacy of religious architecture such as the abbey of **Saint-Denis** where sovereigns are interred, the abbey of **Royaumont**, and the sublime Sainte Chapelle.

Gothic architecture was born in Ile-de-France in the twelfth century. Every nuance of Gothic is represented in the region, from the earliest ogives in the abbey church of **Morienval**, to the vertiginous spires and lacy stonework of the late Flamboyant phase, that grace the church of Saint-Jean Baptiste in **Nemours**. Nowhere else but in Ile-de-France is there such a collection of Gothic cathedrals as those at **Saint-Denis, Paris, Chartres, Pontoise, Senlis, Meaux**...

Just beyond the rose-tinted turrets of Sleeping Beauty's Castle in Disneyland Paris lies the rural **Brie**. A rich agricultural land graced with ancient fortified farms and fine churches, it arcs southward from the town of **Meaux** (famed for Brie cheese and coarse-grain mustard as well as for its splendid architecture) to **Provins**, a well preserved medieval merchant center, once the third largest city in France. And in the wheat-bearing plains of the **Beauce** and of the **Brie** region—still, as always, the breadbasket of France—**Chartres** retains its Gothic serenity despite the throngs of tourists who come to admire the cathedral each year.

While the suburbs of **Asnières** and **Argenteuil**, both close to the capital, are unrecognizable as the arcadian sites painted by Seurat and Monet, **Moret-sur-Loing**, a sleepy town on the edge of the Fontainebleau forest, still bathes in the tender light that Sisley and Renoir captured on canvas. And (in the off-season at least) certain spots of **Auvers-sur-Oise** look much as they did when Cézanne, Pissarro, and Van Gogh planted their easels there.

There are restaurants, *auberges*, and modest eateries aplenty near all the major sites. A few notable exceptions aside (watercress from the Essonne Valley, rabbits and honey from the Gâtinais, cheeses from Meaux, Coulommiers, and Dreux), homegrown foods do not feature prominently in local cuisine. Most ingredients come straight from **Rungis**, the mega-market complex that replaced Paris's Halles in 1969 as the region's supplier of comestibles from France and abroad. There's nothing "provincial" about dishes like the John Dory in curry with melting eggplants cooked to perfection with an oriental twist at Le Régence in Paris, or the beignets de sardines à la ricotta sauce indienne from La Rôtisserie de la Vieille Fontaine in Maisons-Laffitte. Sophistication and virtuosity are key. Paris, of course, is a magnet for ambitious chefs from all over France. From Normandy's legendary Taillevent, who cooked for King Charles V in the 1300s, to Landes native Alain Ducasse, contemporary culinary genius, Paris is the place where chefs prove their mettle and make their name.

Fine food, ancient monuments, thrilling history: the litany is not exhaustive. Still, it should incite you to venture, as Henry James put it, beyond "the wondrous capital, and the wondrous capital alone" to explore the châteaux and cathedrals, the forests and rivers, the urban and rural treasures of Ile-de-France.

(For an in-depth, insider's guide to the City of Light, its restaurants and hotels, shops, nightlife, monuments, and more, consult GaultMillau/Gayot's **Best of Paris**.)

PARIS RESTAURANTS

1ST ARRONDISSEMENT

Postal code	75001

10/20 Joe Allen

30, rue Pierre-Lescot
01 42 36 70 13, fax 01 40 28 06 94
Open daily until 1am. Bar: until 2am, Sun 1am. Terrace dining. Air cond.
Relaxed and casual: American, in short. Come to Joe's when you feel the urge to sink a few beers or dig into a chef's salad, chili burger, barbecued spare ribs, or apple pie. C 170-250.

Armand

6, rue du Beaujolais
01 42 60 05 11, fax 01 42 96 16 24
Closed Sat lunch, Sun, Aug. Open until 11:30pm. Pkg.
A plush, intimate restaurant near the gardens of Palais Royal. Delicious corn crêpe served with warm foie gras and a cream sauce sparked with Sherry vinegar. M 180 (lunch), 250 (dinner).

Gérard Besson

5, rue du Coq-Héron
01 42 33 14 74, fax 01 42 33 85 71
Closed Sat lunch, Sun. Open until 10:30pm. Air cond. Pkg.
A chic conservatory of cuisine bourgeoise. Polished classicism, not innovation, is Besson's signature; his only failing is a tendency to over-complicate (chicken fricassée with sweetbreads and quenelles). Splendid cellar, but too few half-bottles. Delectable desserts. C 550. M 280 (lunch).

11/20 Brasserie Munichoise

5, rue Danièle-Casanova · 01 42 61 47 16
Closed Sat lunch, Sun. Open until 12:30am. Priv rm 20.
A cozy little brasserie that serves good grilled veal sausages and one of the best choucroutes in Paris. Excellent Hacker-Pschorr beer on tap. C 185.

> Some establishments change their **closing times** without warning. It is always wise to check in advance.

11/20 Café Bennett

40, pl du Marché-Saint-Honoré · 01 42 86 04 24
Closed Sat pm, Sun. Open until 7pm. Terrace dining.
The American-style menu features T-bone steak, burgers, and cheesecake, served by two charming *restauratrices*. Ask for a table upstairs, with a view of the arresting new building by Catalan architect Ricardo Bofill. C 180-220. M 69 (lunch), 98 (dinner), 130.

11/20 Café Marly

93, rue de Rivoli · 01 49 26 06 60
Open daily until 1am. Terrace dining.
Here in the Louvre, you may order the most expensive club sandwich in Paris, tuna sashimi, or a well-made *plat du jour*, served in magnificent surroundings. A very dressy crowd of fashion and literary notables has staked out its turf here—you may find yourself sitting next to Karl Lagerfeld! C 200.

Carré des Feuillants ✪

"Alain Dutournier,"
14, rue de Castiglione
01 42 86 82 82, fax 01 42 86 07 71
Closed Sat lunch, Sun, Aug. Open until 10:30pm. Priv rm 14. Air cond.
Authentic ingredients from first-rate producers form the basis of Alain Dutournier's Basco-Béarnaise cuisine. Pheasant consommé dotted with chestnuts; foie gras spread on warm cornbread; savory Pauillac lamb in a tight, sapid jus; a robust garbure (cabbage soup) with duck confit; slow-simmered veal shank that is lacquered on the outside and meltingly tender within—all these dishes brim over with vigorous, exhilarating flavors. The exciting cellar harbors a mother lode of (mostly affordable) Southwestern wines. C 650. M 330 (weekday lunch), 600.

Les Cartes Postales

7, rue Gomboust · 01 42 61 23 40, fax 01 42 61 02 93
Closed Sat lunch, Sun. Open until 10:30pm.
Scores of postcards adorn the beige-and-white walls of this small, pretty, flower-filled restaurant. Yoshimasa Watanabe's dual culinary heritage yields a menu that lists tuna carpaccio or barely cooked brill alongside a sauté of duck and foie gras or a fricassée of langoustines in a chicken jus. Nicely balanced cellar. C 250. M 135.

10/20 Le Caveau du Palais

17, pl. Dauphine - 01 43 26 04 28, fax 01 43 26 81 84
Closed Nov-Apr: Sun. Open until 10:30pm. Terrace dining.
Grilled meats and satisfying bourgeois fare served in a charming Place Dauphine cellar. Good wines sold by the pitcher. C 250-350. M 140.

12/20 Il Cortile

Hôtel Castille, 37, rue Cambon
01 44 58 45 67, fax 01 44 58 44 00
Closed Sun. Terrace dining. Air cond. Pkg. Open until 10:30pm. Priv rm 45.
A lovely Italian restaurant, surely one of the prettiest in town. The rather pricey menu offers clam risotto, gnocchi in Gorgonzola sauce, and beef shanks stewed in Chianti. The flavors need more definition, though, and the cooking can be uneven. C 250. M 195.

L'Espadon

Hôtel Ritz, 15, pl. Vendôme
01 43 16 30 80, fax 01 43 16 33 75
Open daily until 11pm. Terrace dining. Air cond. No pets. Valet pkg.
A bastion of tradition, cautiously opening itself to the new winds of gastronomy, and operated by an earnest chef. Better bets are the pan-roasted langoustines or a "mosaic" of sea bass spiced with mustard seeds. Sumptuous cellar, and the service is sheer perfection. C 800. M 380 (lunch), 600 (dinner).

Fellini

47, rue de l'Arbre-Sec - 01 42 60 90 66
Open daily until 11:30pm. Priv rm 30. Air cond.
Mellow stone walls contribute to Fellini's warmly elegant atmosphere. Appetizing Italian *plats du jour*: fresh pasta with scallops, shrimp and artichoke sauté, calf's liver with a bright lemon sauce. C 230. M 110 (lunch).

Gaya

17, rue Duphot - 01 42 60 43 03, fax 01 42 60 04 54
Closed Sun. Open until 10:30pm. Priv rm 50. Air cond. Valet pkg.
Each day the tide pulls sparkling fresh seafood into this bright and elegant annex of Goumard-Prunier (see below). The catch of the day sometimes features marinated fresh anchovies, pan-roasted red mullet, or tuna with chilis. Be warned, though, that the tab is heftier than you might expect. C 300.

Goumard Prunier

9, rue Duphot
01 42 60 36 07, fax 01 42 60 04 54
Closed Mon. Open until 10:30pm. Priv rm 40. Air cond. Pkg.
Jean-Claude Goumard procures the fattest sole and turbot, the sweetest lobsters and prawns, the briniest sea bass and red mullet from his fishermen friends in Brittany and Roussillon. Nothing interferes with the fresh taste of the sea in dishes like scallop carpaccio with oysters, crab with Sherry aspic, or such seasonal delights as sea urchins or baby eels. The cellar spotlights fine white Burgundies. Little remains, alas, of the restaurant's original décor, designed by Majorelle—the only vestiges, it happens, are in the restrooms! C 500-700. M 295 (lunch exc Sun), 750 (dinner exc Sun).

11/20 Le Grand Louvre

Museum entrance, under the pyramid
01 40 20 53 41, fax 01 42 86 04 63
Closed Tue. Open until 10pm. Priv rm 80. Air cond.
Something is cooking under I.M. Pei's glass pyramid. In contrast with the modern décor, the Louvre's restaurant serves classic cuisine, but not every dish is a masterpiece: good pike quenelles, bland scallop ravioli, cloying fruit gratin. Non-stop service. C 250. M 180.

Le Grand Véfour

17, rue de Beaujolais
01 42 96 56 27, fax 01 42 86 80 71
Closed Sat, Sun, Aug. Open until 10:15pm. Air cond. No pets. Priv rm 25. Valet pkg.
Guy Martin's menu grows more inventive by the day, with such exceptional creations as almond-milk flan in sorrel bouillon, lightly cooked salmon terrine with eggplant aspic, and basil shortbread topped with candied fennel. Hearty Alpine offerings have their place as well (Martin is a native of Savoie): how about a double chop of farm-bred pork swaddled in smoky bacon? As always, the Grand Véfour provides sublime surroundings: carved boiserie ceilings, painted allegories under glass, snowy napery, and fragile Directoire chairs. The service is as elegant as the cosmopolitan clientele. C 800. M 325 (weekday lunch), 750.

A la Grille Saint-Honoré

15, pl. du Marché-Saint-Honoré
01 42 61 00 93, fax 01 47 03 31 64
Closed Sun, Mon, Aug 1-19. Open until 10:30pm. Terrace dining. Air cond.
The Place du Marché Saint-Honoré redesigned by Riccardo Bofill reminds us of Place Beaubourg' Pompidou Museum. But don't let that discourage you from visiting Jean Speyer's Grille, for tasty, imaginative "market cuisine": fragrant crab soup, guinea hen with blackcurrants, smoked haddock with cabbage and chives... Good set meal; affordable wines. C 300-350. M 180.

12/20 Juvenile's

47, rue de Richelieu
01 42 97 46 49, fax 01 47 03 36 93
Closed Sun. Open until 11pm.
We've always felt perfectly at ease in Tim Johnston's hybrid wine-and-tapas bar, where the Queen's English is spoken, and American understood. The premium Sherries that headline the wine list are ideal companions to the Spanish-style bar snacks (chicken wings,

marinated fish, grilled squid, and such) that are the house specialty. But the vineyards of southern Burgundy, the Rhône, and Bordeaux are not neglected; and the menu even sounds a British note with a yummy roast-beef sandwich and nursery desserts. C 145. M 98-128.

Kinugawa

9, rue du Mont-Thabor
01 42 60 65 07, fax 01 42 60 45 21
Closed Sun, May 1, Dec 23-Jan 5. Open until 10pm. Priv rm 100. No pets. Air cond.
Perfect sushi, sashimi, and shabu-shabu, charmingly served in an intimate setting. But the prices cut like a samurai's sword. C 300-500. M 245 (lunch), 510-700.

11/20 Lescure

7, rue de Mondovi - 01 42 60 18 91
Closed Sat dinner, Sun, Aug. Open until 10:15pm. Terrace dining. Air cond.
Tried-and-trusted French fare served in a feverish bistro atmosphere. Sample the hearty veal sauté or duck confit. Game dishes are highlighted in hunting season. C 150. M 100 (wine incl).

Mercure Galant

15, rue des Petits-Champs
01 42 97 53 85, fax 01 42 96 08 89
Closed Sat lunch, Sun, hols. Open until 10:30pm. Priv rm 40.
Careful, classic cooking, fairly priced. The 220 F menu offers very good value, as long as you're fond of pastry: feuilleté of snails and mushrooms, chicken fricasséed in Sherry-like vin jaune, and a "mille et une feuilles" for dessert. Interesting cellar with a wide range of half-bottles. C 390-420. M 220-290.

Le Meurice

Hôtel Meurice, 228, rue de Rivoli
01 44 58 10 50, fax 01 44 58 10 15
Open daily until 11pm. Air cond. Priv rm 180. No pets. Valet pkg.
Rosy nymphs cavort across a ceiling further adorned with gilt and crystal chandeliers, in what is surely one of the city's most sumptuous restaurants. Le Meurice is not all show, however: the food is superb. Marc Marchand eschews pompous cuisine for full-bodied dishes with plenty of rustic flavor: grilled sea bream with fennel chutney, dandelion greens with lamb's brains and a coddled egg, lobster cannelloni in a suave, winy sauce. Faultless service, and a cellar administered by Antoine Zocchetto, an expert sommelier. C 400. M 330 (lunch), 395 (dinner), 150 (children).

Chez Pauline

5, rue Villedo - 01 42 96 20 70, fax 01 49 27 99 89
Closed Sat (exc dinner May-Sep), Sun. Open until 10:30pm. Air cond. Priv rm 15. Pkg.
A traditional bistro that perfectly represents a certain ideal of French cuisine. Robust and full

of frank flavors, the neo-bourgeois dishes are based on uniformly fine ingredients prepared by a veteran chef. Subtlety is not the strong suit here: braises, sautés, and long-simmered stews are André Genin's stock in trade. The cellar holds memorable (and expensive!) Burgundies. We only wish that the dining room were more comfy, and the staff less chilly. C 300-500. M 220.

11/20 Au Petit Ramoneur

74, rue Saint-Denis - 01 42 36 39 24
Closed Sat, Sun. Open until 9:30pm. Terrace dining.
Cheap and cheerful homestyle cooking. M 70.

12/20 Au Pied de Cochon

6, rue Coquillière - 01 40 13 77 00, fax 01 40 13 77 09
Open daily 24 hours. Terrace dining. Air cond. Priv rm 40.
The atmosphere is effervescent at this Les Halles landmark, renowned for serving thundering herds of pigs' trotters (85,000 annually) and a ton of shellfish every day of the year. C 180-340. M 123 (dinner, wine incl), 178.

Le Pluvinel

Hôtel Régina, 2, pl. des Pyramides
01 42 60 31 10, fax 01 40 15 95 16
Closed Sat, Sun, Aug, hols. Open until 10pm. No pets. Priv rm 45. Terrace dining. Air cond.
Chef Hervé Riebbles runs the kitchen in this hotel restaurant, changing the menu according to the season and choosing each ingredient with care. Start with duck foie gras or fresh fenneled crab with roasted apples, followed by scallops or roasted scampi with asparagus in tangerine vinegar, then one of the delicious desserts. The Art Nouveau setting is elegant, and the restaurant faces the Tuileries Gardens. C 270. M 120 (lunch, wine incl), 145 (from 7pm to 9pm), 160, 180, (wine incl).

Le Poquelin ⚜

17, rue Molière - 01 42 96 22 19, fax 01 42 96 05 72
Closed Sat lunch, Sun, Aug 1-20. Open until 10:30pm. Air cond. Priv rm 8. Pkg.
In the red-and-gold dining room where portraits of Molière look down from the walls, chef Michel Guillaumin wins applause from his regular patrons (many from the Comédie-Française across the street) for his renditions of such popular favorites as warm foie gras with prunes and nuts or sweetbreads and scallops with young turnips. Good notices too for his warm apple tart, and a standing ovation for Maggy Guillaumin's cheery welcome. C 280-320.

11/20 Le Relais du Sud-Ouest

154, rue St-Honoré - 01 42 60 62 01
Closed Sun, Aug. Open until 11pm. Pkg.
The Southwest, in all its gluttonous glory: house-made cassoulet, duck stewed with

prunes, confit de canard. All at unbeatable prices. C 160. M 65 (lunch, wine incl), 85 (dinner).

11/20 Au Rendez-Vous des Camionneurs

72, quai des Orfèvres - 01 43 54 88 74
Open daily until 11:30pm.
More cops than truck drivers to be seen here (the criminal division is right nearby), tucking into chicken liver terrine, calf's liver with cranberries, and bitter-chocolate fondant. C 170. M 78 (weekday lunch), 98 (weekdays), 128.

12/20 Restaurant Costes

Hôtel Costes, 239, rue Saint-Honoré
01 42 44 50 25, fax 01 42 44 50 01
Open daily until 12:30am. Terrace dining.
The only reason to come to this restaurant is the extraordinary setting and décor—certainly not the steep prices or the food. Choose to sit in the little armchairs or on the delightful terrace (in summer) of this Italianate luxury hotel, in a nineteenth-century town house just steps from Place Vendôme. You will dine in trendy dishes surrounded by a trendy clientele, and be served by young waiters who don't really look like waiters. C 300-350.

Chez Rosine

12, rue du Mont-Thabor - 01 49 27 09 23
Closed Sun, Mon lunch, Aug. Open until 11pm, Sat 11:30pm. Terrace dining.
Khmer cooking served in a discreetly Asian setting, just behind the Hôtel Meurice. Featured are blue Mekong shrimp, fragrant Cambodian soups, fried ducks' tongues, and grilled catfish with tamarind sauce. Exotic and delicious. C 200-250. M 78-108 (weekday lunch, wine incl), 148 (wine incl), 78 (children).

11/20 Toupary

2, quai du Louvre - 01 40 41 29 29, fax 01 42 33 96 79
Closed Sun. Open until 11:30pm. Priv rm 15. Terrace dining. Air cond. Valet pkg.
Hilton McConnico designed this colorful dining room on the fifth floor of the Samaritaine department store. Along with a splendid view of the Seine, you'll taste essentially classic cooking: cold chayote soup with almonds, lamb with pickled lemons, salmon à la niçoise. C 160-260. M 95 (lunch), 180 (dinner), 45 (children).

11/20 La Tour de Montlhéry

5, rue des Prouvaires - 01 42 36 21 82
Closed Sat, Sun, Jul 14-Aug 15. Open 24 hours.
Here, until the wee hours, you can order up a satisfying plate of stuffed cabbage or warming mutton stew. C 230-260.

Chez Vong

"Aux Halles," 10, rue de la Grande-Truanderie
01 40 39 99 89
Closed Sun. Open until 12:30am. Terrace dining. Priv rm 60. Valet pkg. Air cond.

Excellent dim-sum, steamed scallops, and shrimp with lotus leaves. The gingered lobster lacks spirit, though, and prices are high. C 250-300. M 150 (lunch).

Willi's Wine Bar

13, rue des Petits-Champs
01 42 61 05 09, fax 01 47 03 36 93
Closed Sun. Open until 11pm.
Mark Williamson and Tim Johnston are a witty, wise pair of wine experts, whose cellar holds treasures from all over France and the world. Enjoy them (by the glass, or better, the bottle) along with a good quail salad, tarragon-scented rabbit, or a nice bit of Stilton. If you can't nab a table in the smallish dining room, join the customers sitting elbow-to-elbow at the polished wood bar. C 300-450. M 150 (weekday lunch), 180 (weekday dinner).

12/20 Yvan sur Seine

26, quai du Louvre - 01 42 36 49 52
Open daily until 4am. Terrace dining. Air cond.
Yvan's quayside annex specializes in good seafood, served well into the wee hours. The 138 F prix-fixe meal, which includes wine, is just like the one offered at Le Petit Yvan (see *8th arrondissement*). A cheerful mood prevails in the shipshape dining room; indeed, the ambience gets downright gay as the night wears on! C 240. M 138.

2ND ARRONDISSEMENT

Postal code	75002

Café Runtz

16, rue Favart - 01 42 96 69 86
Closed Sat, Sun, Aug, hols. Open until 11:30pm. Priv rm 44. Air cond.
This is an 1880s Alsatian *winstub* serving rich foie gras, excellent choucroute garnie, and warm potato salad with pork knuckle. Good French Rhine wines; cheeky service. C 180. M 129 (weekdays).

12/20 Canard'Avril

5, rue Paul-Lelong - 01 42 36 26 08
Closed Sat, Sun, hols. Open until 10pm. Priv rm 30.
The menu's just ducky: gizzard salad, confit, and magret de canard feature prominently, alongside a handful of similarly hearty Southwestern dishes. The bargain-priced set meals are sure to quack you up. C 220. M 89-128.

> **Please excuse us... (and the chefs).** *Menus are subject to the winds of change, and the dishes we've described may no longer be available when you visit.*

Le Céladon

Hôtel Westminster, 13, rue de la Paix
01 47 03 40 42, fax 01 42 61 33 78
Closed Sat, Sun, Aug, hols. Open until 10:30pm.
Priv rm 50. Air cond. Valet pkg.
Why is that every time we go, we leave liking
Céladon just a little better than last time? Because
Emmanuel Hodencq, the ever-improving chef,
never ceases to delight us with his resolutely
refined dishes: taste his scallop carpaccio and
truffle terrine, pig trotter roulé with (very unusual) pumpkin-seed oil, subtle John Dory on a
bed of wilted lettuce salad, and Mediterranean-
inspired roasted lamb perfumed with exquisite
confit lemon sauce. Desserts are divine, especially the little pure Arabica coffee tart. Interesting,
eclectic cellar. Lovely setting for a romantic dinner in a brand new décor. C 400-450. M 250, 370.

 ## La Corbeille

154, rue Montmartre
01 40 26 30 87, fax 01 40 26 08 20
Closed Sat lunch, Sun, Aug. Open until 10pm. Priv
rm 30. Air cond. Valet pkg.
An attractive single-price menu is served in the
kitsch surroundings of La Corbeille's upstairs
dining room. We recently feasted on a tasty
celery root salad with gingerbread-coated foie
gras, braised ox jowls and calf's foot, a flawlessly
matured Cabécou cheese, and a yummy walnut
chaud-froid. Not bad for 195 F! C 220. M 125-195,
395 (dinner, wine incl), 100 (children).

 ## Delmonico

Hôtel Édouard VII, 39, av. de l'Opéra
01 42 61 44 26, fax 01 42 61 47 73
Closed Sat, Sun, Aug. Open until 10pm. Priv rm 20.
Air cond. Valet pkg.
With a lightened décor and a brighter atmosphere, this old standby has stepped briskly into
the age of the business lunch. The classic *carte*
lacks originality, but the dishes are deftly turned
out: chicken liver terrine, monkfish in sauce
corail, tiramisù... Pricey cellar; professional service. C 175. M 135.

 ## Drouant

18, rue Gaillon - 01 42 65 15 16, fax 01 49 24 02 15
Open daily until 10:30pm, midnight at Le Café.
Priv rm 50. Air cond. Valet pkg.
The cream of the city's biz and show-biz sets
meet and greet in the Drouant's grand Art Deco
dining room. A master technician, Louis Gron-
dard prepares a menu that lacks only a dash of
personality: red mullet with bone marrow,
Pauillac lamb in an herbal crust, scallop salad
with a lively orange dressing, millefeuille of foie
gras and artichokes. The Café Drouant draws
business lunchers (at noon) and theater-goers (at
night) with reasonably priced bourgeois cooking. C 630. M 290 (lunch), 650 (dinner).

11/20 Gallopin

40, rue Notre-Dame-des-Victoires
01 42 36 45 38, fax 01 42 36 10 32

Closed Sun. Open until midnight. Terrace dining.
Priv rm 15.
The brassy Victorian décor is a feast for the
eyes. The food at Gallopin isn't bad either. Try
the house specialties: rib steak Gallopin and
floating island. Jolly service. C 250. M 150 (dinner).

12/20 Le Grand Colbert

2, rue Vivienne
01 42 86 87 88, fax 01 42 86 82 65
Closed Aug 10-20. Open until 1am. Air cond.
Classic brasserie cuisine (oysters and shellfish,
andouillette ficelle, bœuf gros sel, and poached
chicken) served in a sprucely restored historic
monument complete with frescoes and ornate
plasterwork, brass railings and painted glass
panels. Expect a warm welcome and swift, smiling service. C 160-250. M 160.

 ## Le Moï

5, rue Daunou - 01 47 03 92 05
Open daily until midnight. Air cond. No cards.
At a new address (next door to Harry's New
York Bar), Huguette and her son regale their
patrons with fragrant Vietnamese soups, delicate dumplings, and delicious grilled
lemongrass chicken. Comfortably exotic surroundings. C 150-250. M 80 (weekday lunch,
wine incl).

 ## Pile ou Face

52bis, rue Notre-Dame-des-Victoires
01 42 33 64 33, fax 01 42 36 61 09
Closed Dec 23-Jan 1, Aug. Open until 10:30pm.
Priv rm 16. Pkg. Air cond.
Why fiddle with a winning formula? That's the
philosophy of the young couple who runs Pile
ou Face. The menu continues to showcase fresh
farm produce, served in a red-and-gold setting
with *fin de siècle* touches. Wide-ranging cellar. C
350-450. M 245 (weekday lunch), 280-320 (weekday dinner).

12/20 Rôtisserie Monsigny

"Jacques Cagna", 1, rue Monsigny
01 42 96 16 61, fax 01 42 97 40 97
Closed Sat lunch, Aug 10-20. Open until midnight,
Sun & Mon 11pm. Priv rm 40. Air cond.
Jacques Cagna is the driving force behind this
busy restaurant, where juicy roast lamb and spit-
roasted chicken are served forth by an energetic
staff under the soft music of a piano. C 200. M
160, 100 (after 10pm).

12/20 Le Saint-Amour

8, rue de Port-Mahon - 01 47 42 63 82
Open daily until 10:15pm. Air cond. Pkg.
Impeccable service and fresh, generous
cuisine. The chef offers a 165 F set meal and a
carte that delivers (for example) house-made foie
gras terrine, eels in persillade, and a millefeuille
with blackcurrant coulis. Concise but interesting
wine list. C 280. M 165.

La Taverne du Nil

9, rue du Nil - 01 42 33 51 82, fax 01 42 33 01 35
Closed Sat lunch, Sun, Aug. Open until 11pm. Air cond.
Lusty Lebanese specialties based on first-rate ingredients: lamb with bulghur, marinated grilled chicken, an array of tasty mezes and shish kebabs. The dining room is more attractive than the exterior leads one to expect. C 180-220. M 52-70 (weekday lunch), 90 (weekday lunch, wine incl), 135-182 (wine incl), 65 (children).

12/20 Le Vaudeville

29, rue Vivienne - 01 40 20 04 62, fax 01 49 27 08 78
Open daily until 2am. Terrace dining. Air cond. Pkg.
This glittering outpost of the Flo empire is decked out in 1930's-style brass, glass, and wood. Waiters swoop and swirl amid the good-natured clamor (the crowd is often studded with stars and celebrities), delivering platters of glossy shellfish, prime meats, the popular house foie gras, and attractively priced little wines. A very Parisian choice for a late bite after the theater. C 250-300. M 119 (weekday lunch & Sat, wine incl), 189 (dinner, wine incl), 121 (dinner, after 10pm, wine incl).

3RD ARRONDISSEMENT

Postal code	75003

 L'Alisier

26, rue de Montmorency
01 42 72 31 04, fax 01 42 72 74 83
Closed Sat, Sun, Aug. Open until 10pm. Priv rm 35. Air cond. No pets. Pkg.
An inviting, old-fashioned bistro (ask for a table upstairs) where you can enjoy Jean-Luc Dodeman's deft and clever cooking: cod baked with honey and cumin, lamb's brains in a delicate mussel jus, millefeuille layered with spiced custard and caramel sauce. Another point. C 250. M 150 (weekday lunch), 185.

 Ambassade d'Auvergne

22, rue du Grenier-Saint-Lazare
01 42 72 31 22, fax 01 42 78 85 47
Open daily until 10:30pm. Air cond. Priv rm 35.
Come here for an authentic taste of Auvergne: aged country ham, cabbage and Roquefort soup, and the legendary house aligot (satiny mashed potatoes with cheese). Good desserts—try the mousseline glacée à la verveine du Velay. The cellar holds some little-known Auvergnat wines (Chanturgue, Saint-Pourçain) in a wide range of prices. C 260. M 160, 300 (wine incl).

11/20 Le Bar à Huîtres

33, bd Beaumarchais - 01 48 87 98 92
Open daily until 2am. Priv rm 25. Terrace dining. Air cond.
See 14th arrondissement. C 250-350. M 98-198.

 Au Bascou

38, rue Réaumur - 01 42 72 69 25
Closed Sat lunch, Sun, 3 wks in Aug. Open until 11pm. Terrace dining.
Basque-country native Jean-Guy Loustau (formerly the sommelier of Le Carré des Feuillants) runs this smart address. Menu highlights include scallops with fiery Espelette chilis, tiny squid stewed in their ink and presented with a toothsome risotto, and tender tripe en daube with sweet peppers. Top-notch wines. C 220. M 90 (lunch).

 Chez Nénesse

17, rue de Saintonge - 01 42 78 46 49
Closed Sat, Sun, 1 wk at Feb school hols, Aug. Open until 10pm. No pets.
Nénesse puts on the dog for dinner: he covers the Formica tables of his venerable bistro with tablecloths and flowers! Fresh, flavorful *plats du jour* based on fine ingredients, carefully prepared. Worth a toque. C 180-250. M 85 (weekday lunch).

 Opium Café

5, rue Elzévir - 01 40 29 93 40, fax 01 40 29 93 46
Open daily until midnight. Air cond.
Opposite the Musée Cognacq-Jay (home to an exquisite collection of eighteenth-century art and antiques), this spacious, elaborately decorated dining room—lovely armchairs and banquettes, gleaming chandeliers, gilded details everywhere—is a great favorite with the city's gay crowd. Highlights from the clever and appealing menu include fresh vegetables in a blood-orange sabayon and fragrant braised pork with spices. We like the friendly atmosphere, but the desserts could stand improvement. Brunch is served on weekends. C 200-300. M 110 (weekday lunch), 100-150 (lunch Sat, Sun).

4TH ARRONDISSEMENT

Postal code	75004

 L'Ambroisie

9, pl. des Vosges
01 42 78 51 45
Closed Sun, Mon, Feb school hols, 1st 3 wks of Aug. Open until 10:15pm. No pets. Priv rm 12. Valet pkg.
With its inlaid stone and parquet floors, book-lined shelves, and sumptuous Aubusson

tapestry adorning honey-hued walls, L'Ambroisie has the feel of a beautiful private home, of which Danièle Pacaud is the attentive hostess. Don't expect to see much of Bernard Pacaud, though. He prefers the sizzling sounds of the kitchen to the applause of an appreciative public. His concise *carte* is supplemented by a few *surprises du jour*: marjolaine de foie gras (layered goose liver, truffles, and celery—divine!); flash-cooked sea bass with rosemary-scented artichokes; a majestic poularde en demi-deuil. Each dish is flawlessly finished. Faultless cellar, too, run by Pierre Le Moullac, an exemplary maître d'hôtel–sommelier. C 580-780.

 Baracane

38, rue des Tournelles - 01 42 71 43 33
Closed Sat lunch, Sun. Open until midnight.
Tables fill quickly in this tiny Southwestern enclave, because the cooking is full-flavored and generous to boot. Lentil salad with dried goose breast or cassoulet with duck confit precede delectable desserts. Low-priced regional wines wash it all down. Affable service. C 200-320. M 49-78, 125-220 (wine incl).

 Benoit

20, rue St-Martin - 01 42 72 25 76, fax 01 42 72 45 68
Closed Sat, Sun, Aug. Open until 10pm. No pets. No cards.
Benoit is the archetypal Parisian bistro (and surely one of the priciest): velvet banquettes, brass fixtures, lace curtains, and a polished zinc bar compose a seductive décor. Owner Michel Petit (who is anything but!) continues the lusty tradition begun before the Great War by his grandfather: delicious bœuf à la parisienne, good cassoulet, creditable codfish with potatoes and cream. The cellar is stocked with good bottles from Mâcon, Sancerre, Beaujolais, and Saumur. C 450-550. M 200 (lunch).

11/20 Bistrot du Dôme

2, rue de la Bastille
01 48 04 88 44, fax 01 40 04 00 59
Open daily until 11:30pm. Terrace dining. Air cond.
See *14th arrondissement*. C 210-260.

 Bofinger

3-7, rue de la Bastille
01 42 72 87 82, fax 01 42 72 97 68
Open daily until 1am. Priv rm 80. Terrace dining. Air cond.
Bofinger's stained-glass ceiling, ceramics, marquetry, mirrors, and tulip-shaped sconces compose a magnificent Belle-Époque décor that has long been a landmark in the Bastille quarter. Parisians, provincials, tourists, and celebrities throng in for generous assortments of extra-fresh shellfish and hearty choucroute garnie. The Flo group, which recently took over this thriving enterprise (the restaurant serves 300,000 meals each year!), plans to put the kitchen on a more even keel. Among the *plats du jour* the roasted

lobster, magret de canard, and seasonal game are worth noting. C 200-350. M 169 (wine incl).

11/20 L'Excuse

14, rue Charles-V - 01 42 77 98 97, fax 01 42 77 88 55
Closed Sun, Aug 5-20. Open until 11pm. Priv rm 18. Air cond.
A dainty little candybox of a restaurant, decorated with mirrors, engravings, and posters. Our most recent meal left us perplexed—is the chef slipping, or does he have an excuse? Let's give him another chance... C 280. M 120 (weekday lunch), 165.

11/20 Le Fond de Cour

3, rue Sainte-Croix-Bretonnerie
01 42 74 71 52, fax 01 42 74 02 04
Open daily until 11:30pm, Sat & Sun midnight. Terrace dining. Air cond.
At the back of the courtyard, as the name suggests, you'll find this cleverly decorated restaurant. Olivier Le Cam proposes such options as langoustines with angel-hair pasta, rabbit wrapped in an herbal crust, and chocolate soufflé studded with candied orange peel. C 250.

 Les Fous d'en Face

3, rue du Bourg-Tibourg - 01 48 87 03 75
Open daily until midnight. Terrace dining. Air cond. Pkg.
Generous bistro cooking made even more appealing by expertly chosen wines. Enjoy star anise-spiced salmon, scallops en papillote, and pear tart, in a convivial atmosphere. C 220-290. M 88 (weekday lunch) 175-200 (wine incl).

10/20 Jo Goldenberg

7, rue des Rosiers - 01 48 87 20 16
Open daily until 11pm. Priv rm 60. Terrace dining. Air cond.
The most picturesque of the Goldenberg restaurants in Paris (see *17th arrondissement*). The Central European Yiddish cuisine is served in the heart of the Marais's Jewish district. Prepared foods are sold in the take-out shop. C 150-200.

11/20 Au Gourmet de l'Isle

42, rue Saint-Louis-en-l'Ile - 01 43 26 79 27
Closed Mon, Tue. Air cond. Open until 10:30pm.
The reception is charming, the crowd young and cheerful, the stone-and-beams décor convincingly rustic. More than 40 years of deserved success for one of the city's surest-value set menus priced at 130 F. Lots of à la carte choices too: artichoke "Saint Louis", beef stewed in Marcillac wine, andouillette with kidney beans. C 130. M 85 (lunch).

 Le Grizzli

7, rue Saint-Martin - 01 48 87 77 56
Closed Sun. Open until 11pm. No pets. Priv rm 30. Terrace dining.
At age 95-plus this Grizzli is still going strong, serving lusty specialties rooted in the Southwest: white-bean salad with duck confit, roast baby

lamb, and veal stewed with cèpes. To drink, try the delicious Pécharmant. C 220. M 120 (lunch), 155.

11/20 Chez Léon

11-13, bd Beaumarchais - 01 42 78 42 55
Open daily until 11:30pm. Terrace dining. Air cond.
A favorite with neighborhood hipsters, this Tunisian spot provides solid sustenance—good beef couscous, grilled scampi, crisp brik pastries—at moderate prices. C 150.

 ## Miravile

72, quai de l'Hôtel-de-Ville
01 42 74 72 22, fax 01 42 74 67 55
Closed Sat lunch, Sun, 3 wks in Aug. Open until 10:30pm. Priv rm 35. Air cond. Pkg.
Alain Lamaison's has slimed down his tempting single-price menu, and now offers a complete menu—somewhat expensive. We can vouch for the calf's head terrine with roasted tomatoes, juicy pike perch cooked in its skin, and flaky prune tart showered with lemon zest. Each month brings a fresh selection of recommended wines. C 380. M 240.

 ## Le Monde des Chimères

69, rue Saint-Louis-en-l'Ile
01 43 54 45 27, fax 01 43 29 84 88
Closed Sun, Mon. Open until 10:30pm.
A delightful old "island bistro" run by former TV personality Cécile Ibane. The cuisine is reminiscent of Sunday dinner *en famille*—if, that is, your family included a French granny who was also a marvelous cook! Try the oxtail terrine garnished with sweet-and-sour quince and cherries, or chicken sautéed with 40 cloves of garlic. Yummy homemade desserts. C 300-400. M 160.

 ## L'Orangerie

28, rue Saint-Louis-en-l'Ile - 01 46 33 93 98
Open daily until 12:30am. Air cond.
This elegant dining room adorned with tall mirrors and huge paintings is the "secret garden" of French actor Jean-Claude Brialy, who has owned L'Orangerie for some 30 years. The restaurant reflects Brialy's own urbane refinement, and it is a distinguished choice for after-theater suppers. The actor/waiters recite the selections from the single-price menu, a compendium of full-flavored French classics, which may be escorted by a fine Bordeaux. Only the stiffish tab keeps us from booking here more often... M 400 (wine incl.)

12/20 L'Ostéria

10, rue de Sévigné - 01 42 71 37 08
Closed Sat, Sun, Jul 26-Sep 2. Open until 11pm.
Hidden away behind a non-descript façade in the heart of the Marais, this little Italian restaurant plays host to fashion, film, and show-biz luminaries. They delight in the arugula salad showered with Parmesan shavings, spaghetti in

a lusty seafood sauce, and potato gnocchi lavished with sage-infused butter, all clemently priced. C 150-200.

 ## Le Vieux Bistro

14, rue du Cloître-Notre-Dame
01 43 54 18 95, fax 01 44 07 35 63
Open daily until 10:45pm. Priv rm 30. Terrace dining. Pkg.
Right next to Notre-Dame, an honest-to-god bistro that the tourist crowds have somehow overlooked. Owner Fernand Fleury cultivates a warm, inviting atmosphere; chef Beaudouin Verlaten's prepares a robust menu of vigorous, homestyle favorites. The cellar is a shade too expensive. C 250-320.

5TH ARRONDISSEMENT

Postal code	75005

 ## L'Atlas

12, bd St-Germain - 01 44 07 23 66, fax 01 40 46 06 56
Open daily until 11pm. Air cond. Pkg.
Surprising, slightly cerebral, determinedly modern Moroccan cuisine. The range of options extends beyond couscous and tagines (though a dozen excellent varieties are offered) to such delicacies as lamb with mallow, monkfish with thyme blossoms, and kidneys with sea-urchin butter. Decorated with mosaics and ornamental plasterwork, the dining room is perfectly lovely; so is the service. C 150-350. M 75 (children).

11/20 Le Bar à Huîtres

33, rue St-Jacques - 01 44 07 27 37, fax 01 43 26 71 62
Open daily until 2am. Pkg.
See *14th arrondissement.* C 98-198. M 89 (children).

 ## Le Bistrot d'à Côté

16, bd St-Germain - 01 43 54 59 10, fax 01 43 29 02 08
Closed Sat lunch, Sun. Open until 11pm. Terrace dining. Air cond.
Michel Rostang's popular bistro annex serves up lively specialties that include lentil soup with garlic sausage, codfish fricassée à la lyonnaise, and veal kidney in red-wine sauce. The well-chosen wines are a half-tone too dear—we usually opt for a pitcher of the house red instead. M 119 (lunch), 148, 189.

Les Bouchons de François Clerc

12, rue de l'Hôtel-Colbert
01 43 54 15 34, fax 01 46 34 68 07
Closed Sat lunch, Sun. Open until 11pm. Priv rm 20. Air cond.
Sure, the food is good (snails and gnocchi au pistou, rabbit with foie gras...) but what lures us back again and again is the wine list! Pichon-Longueville '87 for 121 F, Ducru-Beaucaillou '90 for 130 F, or Châteauneuf-du-Pape Domaine de Beaucastel '86 for just 92 F: an irresistible deal for wine buffs. Another point this year. M 117 (weekday lunch, wine incl), 219.

 ## La Bûcherie

41, rue de la Bûcherie
01 43 54 78 06, fax 01 46 34 54 02
Open daily until midnight. No pets. Priv rm 40. Terrace dining. Air cond. Pkg.
Bernard Bosque is built like a Breton buccaneer and has been running his Bûcherie for three decades with great success. Handsome woodwork and modern prints adorn the walls, and there are views of Notre-Dame beyond the covered terrace. The cuisine, classic and understated, reflects the seasons. There's game in autumn; baby eels from January to March; asparagus and morels in spring. Prices are not of the giveaway variety, but the lunch menu is quite attractive. The wine list favors pricey Bordeaux. C 360-680. M 230 (wine incl).

12/20 Campagne et Provence

25, quai de la Tournelle
01 43 54 05 17, fax 01 43 29 74 93
Closed Sat & Mon lunch, Sun, Aug. Open until 11pm, Sat & Sun 1am. Air cond.
Sunny, unhackneyed Southern cuisine. Sample Patrick Jeffroy's cuisine: tasty basil ravioli, sea bream with roasted fennel, and dried cod à la niçoise are so skimpy. All wines are priced under 100 F, and there's a short but sweet 110 F lunch menu. C 270. M 110 (lunch).

11/20 Chieng Mai

12, rue Frédéric-Sauton - 01 43 25 45 45
Closed Aug 1-15, Dec 16-31. Open until 11:30pm. Priv rm 60. Air cond.
Its cool, stylized atmosphere and spicy Thai menu have won Chieng Mai quite a following. Lately, though, we've noted a lack of subtlety in the shrimp soup with lemongrass, baked crab claws with angel-hair pasta, steamed seafood served in a crab shell, and coconut-milk flan. Service is courteous and competent, but the tables are set too close together. C 240. M 122, 173.

 ## Au Coco de Mer

34, bd St-Marcel - 01 47 07 06 64, fax 01 47 07 41 88
Closed Sun, Mon, Aug 10-20. Open until 11pm. No pets.
No, your eyes are not playing tricks: that sandy beach you see is part of the Coco de Mer's exotic décor. The Seychelle Islands inspire the chef's gingery tuna tartare, octopus stewed in coconut milk, grilled pork and duck with tropical fruit. Friendly prices. C 200-250. M 135, 170 (exc Sat lunch).

 ## Dodin Bouffant

25, rue Frédéric-Sauton
01 43 25 25 14, fax 01 43 29 52 61
Closed Sat lunch, Sun. Open until 11pm. Terrace dining. Air cond.
Not a spark of imagination lights the menu, yet patrons continue to crowd into this popular spot for oysters in Champagne sauce, daube provençale, and hot raspberry soufflé. Mostly good-natured service. C 250. M 180, 245 (wine incl).

12/20 Les Fontaines

9, rue Soufflot - 01 43 26 42 80
Closed Sun, Mon, Aug. Open until 10:45pm. Terrace dining.
A charmless corner café that draws a smart Rive Gauche crowd with meat dishes (the boss used to be a butcher), game in season, and even a few fish offerings (lobster salad, salmon crêpes). Excellent wine list; relaxed atmosphere. C 110-220.

12/20 Aux Iles Philippines

9, rue de Pontoise - 01 43 29 39 00, fax 01 44 07 17 44
Closed Sat lunch, Sun. Open until 11pm. Terrace dining. Air cond. No pets.
Nicely crafted Philippine dishes: scrambled eggs with crab on a bed of crispy noodles, glazed pork, and delectable banana cake. C 130-215. M 78 (weekday lunch), 120, 150, 250 (wine incl).

12/20 Inagiku

14, rue de Pontoise
01 43 54 70 07, fax 01 40 51 74 44
Closed Sun, Aug 1-15. Open until 10:45pm. Air cond.
Since we often leave Japanese restaurants as hungry as we came, we ordered a side of sashimi with our Matsu, or big menu. Well, after putting away the assorted fresh raw fish, sushi with avocado, crisp fried hors d'œuvres, pile of fat shrimp, tender beef fillet, and duo of ginger and chestnut sorbets, we waddled out happy and absolutely stuffed! C 200-300. M 88 (lunch), 148-248.

 ## Mavrommatis

42, rue Daubenton
01 43 31 17 17, fax 01 43 36 13 08
Closed Mon. Open until 11pm. No pets. Priv rm 25. Terrace dining. Pkg.
The Mavrommatis brothers have raised the level of Greek cuisine served in Paris by several notches! There are 30 delicious starters (octopus salad, tuna carpaccio, stuffed eggplant, lamb meatballs, etc.), and worthwhile main dishes, too: red mullet grilled in vine leaves, smothered leg of lamb with herbs, or veal with oaten pasta.

Good Greek wines. C 160-240. M 120 (weekday lunch, Sat, wine incl), 140.

 Moissonnier ♕

28, rue des Fossés-Saint-Bernard - 01 43 29 87 65
Closed Sun dinner, Mon, Aug. Open until 10pm.
Despite a page of history that turns because of the departure of Louis Moissonnier, nothing has changed, in this landmark Paris bistro. Ex-Troisgros and Senderens chef Philippe Mayet turns out the same robust Lyonnais specialties. Tasty Beaujolais wines are on hand to slake your thirst. C 280. M 150 (weekdays).

11/20 Chez Pento

9, rue Cujas - 01 43 26 81 54
Closed Sat lunch, Sun. Open until 11pm.
This neighborhood favorite serves generous portions of salt-cured duck with lentils, sausage with butter-braised cabbage, homey chocolate cake and the like, along with astutely chosen wines (offered by the glass or bottle). C 170-240. M 83 (weekday lunch), 104 (dinner).

11/20 Perraudin

157, rue Saint-Jacques - 01 46 33 15 75
Closed Sat & Mon lunch, Sun, last 2 wks of Aug. Open until 10:15pm. Garden dining.
Known to every publisher and professor in the Latin Quarter, this modest eatery provides solid sustenance—roast leg of lamb with scalloped potatoes, bœuf bourguignon, tarte Tatin—in a lively setting. C 125. M 63 (lunch).

12/20 Le Petit Navire

14, rue des Fossés-Saint-Bernard - 01 43 54 22 52
Closed Sun, Mon. Open until 10:15pm.
Anchored not far from the Seine for the past twenty-odd years, Le Petit Navire regales its many regular customers with tapenade, garlicky shellfish soup, grilled sardines, and delightful growers' wines. C 250. M 150.

12/20 Chez René

14, bd Saint-Germain - 01 43 54 30 23
Closed Sat, Sun, Aug. Open until 11pm.
Boiled beef, chard gratin, and coq au vin are served forth by speedy yet attentive waiters at this popular bistro. The tipple of choice here is Beaujolais *au compteur* (you pay for what you drink). C 250. M 153 (lunch, wine incl).

12/20 Rôtisserie du Beaujolais

19, quai de la Tournelle
01 43 54 17 47, fax 01 44 07 12 04
Closed Mon. Open until 11:15pm. Terrace dining. Air cond.
Claude Terrail of the Tour d'Argent (across the road) owns this Lyonnais-style bistro, a nice little place to spend a lively evening with friends over spit-roasted Challans duck, saucisson pistaché, or a salad of boiled beef and lentils. Splendid cheeses and exemplary Beaujolais from Dubœuf. C 230.

12/20 La Timbale Saint-Bernard

18, rue des Fossés-Saint-Bernard
01 46 34 28 28, fax 01 46 34 66 26
Closed Sat lunch, Sun, July 26-Aug 27. Open until 10pm. Priv rm 20. Terrace dining.
We don't think the chef is living up to his potential, but this vivacious bistro still has plenty of appeal. An adorable staff delivers simmered scallops, pork with aïoli, a flaky turnover stuffed with potato and foie gras... Goodly number of wines available by the half-bottle. C 135-255. M 88-132 (weekday lunch), 162-230.

 La Timonerie

35, quai de la Tournelle - 01 43 25 44 42
Closed Sun, Mon lunch, Aug. Open until 10:30pm. Air cond.
Philippe de Givenchy continues to surprise us with his streamlined cuisine, based on simple, unpretentious ingredients: mackerel, pollack, inexpensive cuts of meat, offal, and pork. Another chef would make bistro chow out of foods like these, but Givenchy turns them into great modern dishes. What he does with hogs' jowls and a little red wine, or with a mackerel fillet and a handful of herbs, is pure magic. Desserts follow the same vein: a homey repertoire glorified by virtuoso technique. The cellar is not vast, but it is perfectly à propos, with a fine range of growers' wines. C 350-450. M 240 (lunch).

La Tour d'Argent

15-17, quai de la Tournelle
01 43 54 23 31, fax 01 44 07 12 04
Closed Mon. Open until 10:30pm. Priv rm 60. Air cond. Valet pkg.
Claude Terrail is as savvy as he is charming. He knows that a reputation—no matter how exalted—is not sufficient to survive in the highly competitive world of world-class restaurants. He recently appointed Bernard Guilhaudin to succeed veteran chef Manuel Martinez and infuse some new blood into the Tour d'Argent. Half of the menu is composed by the legendary specialties of this venerable institution such canard au sang—over 800,000 have already been served—and the rest, to which Guilhaudin has added his own creations, such as gougère with spring vegetables and tomato sabayon, pan-fried red mullet with anchovy butter and parsley purée, and Bresse-chicken tourte with tarragon-speckled pan-fried foie gras. Fabled cellar, with thousands of pricey bottles and a few affordable ones, too. A la carte prices are stuck in the stratosphere, but there is a more accessibly priced set lunch. C 950. M 350 (lunch).

12/20 Toutoune

5, rue de Pontoise - 01 43 26 56 81
Closed Mon lunch, Sun. Open until 10:45pm.
The arrival of a chef with a Provençal repertoire infused fresh life into this popular spot. The 158 F single-price menu features fragrant soups, tasty terrines, snails in a garlicky tomato sauce, sea bream with zucchini, and grapefruit gratin

with sabayon sauce. Lively atmosphere. M 108 (weekday lunch), 158.

11/20 La Truffière

4, rue Blainville - 01 46 33 29 82, fax 01 46 33 64 74
Closed Mon, 2 wks in Aug. Open until 10:30pm. Priv rm 40. Air cond.
Candlelight flickers amid the dining room's ancient beams, a Chopin sonata plays softly in the background: the romantic mood is set, and perhaps that's just as well, for it will help you ignore the misfires that mar the kitchen's classic cuisine, and the annoying supplemental charges on the so-called single-price menu (130 F for less than half an ounce of truffles). C 350-450. M 98 (lunch, exc Sun), 140 (dinner, exc Sun), 198.

6TH ARRONDISSEMENT

Postal code	75006

12/20 Chez Albert

43, rue Mazarine - 01 46 33 22 57
Closed Sun, Mon lunch, Aug. Open until 11pm.
Many patrons don't realize that this is a Portuguese restaurant. The menu is mostly French, but the coriander clams, rabbit à la Ranhado, and half-dozen dishes starring salt cod (we like the one with eggs and onions) point clearly to the owner's Lusitanian origins. So does the wine list, with its Douros and Dãos. C 180-200. M 80 (lunch), 135.

Allard

41, rue Saint-André-des-Arts
01 43 26 48 23, fax 01 46 33 04 02
Closed Sun, 1 wk in Aug. Open until 10:30pm. Air cond.
Little has changed at Allard, from the mellow décor to the classic menu (sole meunière, duck with olives, tarte Tatin). This nostalgic ambience continues to charm the cosmopolitan patrons, but we still find the prices too high. Another point. C 250. M 150 (weekday lunch), 200.

11/20 Arbuci

25, rue de Buci - 01 44 41 14 14, fax 01 44 41 14 10
Open daily until dawn. Priv rm 80. Terrace dining. Air cond.
Those in the know dine downstairs at the Blanc Brothers' Arbuci: the food and prices are the same as upstairs, with live jazz to boot, at no extra charge. C 210-280. M 72-98 (lunch), 79-135.

La Bastide Odéon

7, rue Corneille - 01 43 26 03 65, fax 01 44 07 28 93
Closed Sun, Mon, Aug. Open until 11pm. Priv rm 8. No pets.
Gilles Ajuelos impressed us from the start with his sunny Southern cooking. But now his menu

is in danger of becoming a cliché. Provençal cuisine is more than just heaps of herbs and fresh vegetables! Gilles needs to hone his technique, balance his seasonings, learn to choose only prime ingredients... Still, the atmosphere is friendly, prices are moderate, and the wine list offers wonderful Provençal wines. C 230. M 139-180.

Le Bistrot d'Alex ✪

"La Foux", 2, rue Clément - 01 43 54 09 53
Closed Sat lunch, Sun, Dec 24-Jan 2. Open until 10pm. Priv rm 12.
Lyon and Provence (with a penchant for the latter) inspire Stéphane Guini's zestful menu. You're sure to like the pistachio-studded saucisson, fragrant daube de bœuf, and tasty orange flan. Delightful welcome. C 220-250. M 140, 170.

Les Bookinistes

53, quai des Grands-Augustins
01 43 25 45 94, fax 01 43 25 23 07
Open daily until midnight. Priv rm 25. Terrace dining. Air cond. Pkg.
This addition to Guy Savoy's string of bistros sports an avant-garde look that obviously suits the mostly young, mostly Left Bank crowd. Crowded is how you might feel in this elbow-to-elbow eatery, but don't let that diminish your enjoyment of the gnocchi with mussels and spinach, sweetbread fricassée, and gingerbread millefeuille. Snappy service. C 240-260. M 160 (weekday lunch), 180 (dinner Sun).

Bouillon Racine

3, rue Racine - 01 44 07 34 07
Closed Sun. Open until 1am.
Olivier Simon, a talented young Belgian chef, presides in the kitchen of this freshly (and beautifully) refurbished Belle Époque jewel. Not only are the surroundings a feast for the eye, but the *carte* promises a corresponding treat for the palate: tomatoes stuffed with tiny shrimp, mousse of smoky Ardennes ham with juniper aspic, beef braised in beer à la flamande, pheasant à la brabançonne, and buttery Belgian brioche given the French-toast treatment. Tempting list of Belgian beers; brunch served on Saturdays. C 150-200. M 78, 108.

12/20 Brasserie Lutétia

Hôtel Lutétia, 23, rue de Sèvres
01 49 54 46 76, fax 01 49 54 46 00
Open daily until midnight. Priv rm 100. Air cond. Valet pkg.
The no-nonsense cooking is prepared with considerable finesse in the same kitchens as Le Paris (see below). The seafood is attractively priced, and the satisfying bourgeois dishes (veal chop with macaroni gratin, poulet au thym) always hit the spot. Brunch served on Sundays. C 200-250. M 180, 295 (wine incl), 60 (children).

The prices in this guide reflect what establishments were charging at press time.

La Cafetière

21, rue Mazarine - 01 46 33 76 90, fax 01 43 25 76 90
Closed Sun, 3 wks in Aug, end Dec-beg Jan. Open until 11pm. Priv rm. Air cond.
A friendly, open spirit reigns in this restaurant now that it is under the new management of a former employee of Sormani. Customers are encouraged to indulge their cravings, depending on the seasonal products available, but the Vietnamese chef's Italian menu has plenty of interesting offerings. Try the divinely seasoned scampi carpaccio, the risotto with wild mushrooms, or the macaroni and cheese with pancetta. The panna cotta with a Fernet Branca-flavored cream sauce is a true pleasure. Italian wines. C 150-250. M 130 (lunch).

 Jacques Cagna

14, rue des Grands-Augustins
01 43 26 49 39, fax 01 43 54 54 48
Closed Sat lunch, Sun, 3 wks in Aug, 1 wk at Christmas. Open until 10:30pm. Priv rm 12. Air cond. Valet pkg.
Near the Seine, in the refined setting of his wood-panneled sixteenth-century mansion decorated with Flemish paintings, Jacques Cagna keeps turning out the classic dishes that built his success over the years. Sure enough, the products he uses are superb (sea bass from Brittany, fatted chicken from Normandy, lamb from the Pyrénées) but we have known a more audacious Cagna. That's why we give him kudos when he dares adding to his classics, dishes like tiny escargots hidden under ground tomato in a Charentes potato. The wine cellar is superb and has a fine collection of old Ports. C 350. M 280 (lunch), 490.

11/20 **Le Caméléon**

6, rue de Chevreuse - 01 43 20 63 43
Closed Sat lunch, Sun, 1 wk in Jan, 1 wk in Apr or May, 3 wks in Aug. Open until 10:30pm. Pkg.
A pretty and authentic bistro with a different *plat du jour* every day of the week: house-made sausage, stuffed tomatoes, codfish with aïoli. Boring desserts. C 200-250.

12/20 **Casa Bini**

36, rue Grégoire-de-Tours
01 46 34 05 60, fax 01 46 34 07 32
Closed Aug 10-20, 1 wk at Christmas. Open until 11pm. Priv rm 18. Terrace dining.
Anna Bini travels all the way to Tuscany to seek out the best ingredients for her little restaurant. The concise menu of carpaccio, crostoni, pasta, and good daily specials suits her trendy Saint-Germain patrons to a T. Reasonably priced Italian wines. C 220. M 150, 170.

 Le Chat Grippé

87, rue d'Assas - 01 43 54 70 00, fax 01 43 26 42 05
Closed Sat lunch, Mon, Aug. Open until 10:30pm. Air cond.
Well-spaced tables in an intimate setting, where diners tuck into a fine 240 F menu that includes marinated tuna with anchovies, sea bream with tomatoes and ginger, roast rabbit with peppers, and licorice custard with prune coulis. Heartwarming welcome. M 160 (weekday lunch), 200, 240, 325.

12/20 **Le Clocher Saint-Germain**

22, rue Guillaume Apollinaire
01 42 86 00 88, fax 01 42 60 37 75
Open daily until midnight. Terrace dining. Air cond.
Tourists and locals alike fetch up at this pleasant bistro for such hearty regional classics as warm saucisson lyonnais, salmon with green lentils, and silky blancmange embellished with caramel jam. The frisky wines, offered by the bottle or glass, are ideally suited to the bill of fare. For the neighborhood, a pretty darn good deal. C 180. M 72 (lunch, exc Sun), 148.

 Dominique

19, rue Bréa - 01 43 27 08 80, fax 01 43 26 88 35
Closed Sun, Mon lunch, Jul 20-Aug 20. Open until 11:30pm. Terrace dining.
This famed Montparnasse Russian troika—take-out shop/bar/restaurant—steadfastly refuses perestroika when it comes to cuisine and décor. Rostropovitch and Solzhenitsyn have been spotted here, sampling the delicious smoked salmon, borscht, and blinis. And there's vodka, of course, both Russian and Polish. C 250-300. M 98 (weekday lunch, wine incl), 170.

 L'Écaille de PCB

"Pierre et Colette Bardèche," 5, rue Mabillon
01 43 26 73 70, fax 01 46 33 07 98
Closed Sat lunch, Sun. Open until 11pm. No pets. Priv rm 10. Terrace dining.
Marinated sardines with fennel or a salad of finnan haddie and bacon segue into osso buco de lotte à l'orientale, John Dory with coarse-grain mustard, or scallops in a creamy garlic sauce. The cellar is of only middling interest, save for a fine, bone-dry Jurançon from Charles Hours. C 280-350. M 195.

12/20 **L'Épi Dupin**

11, rue Dupin
01 42 22 64 56, fax 01 42 22 30 42
Closed Sat, Sun. Open until 11pm. Terrace dining.
Well-deserved praise has been heaped on young François Pasteau's cooking. A pupil of some of the city's finer chefs, he proposes a menu that includes briefly seared tuna set atop a zesty onion pizza, scallops paired with celery in a fragrant Provençal-style broth, breaded calf's head with saffron potatoes (try it, it's delicious!), and a bouquet of light, inventive desserts. A meal here will set you back only 153 F (plus wine, of course). Remember to book your table in advance, but don't be in a hurry because the service is very slow. M 97 (weekday lunch, wine incl), 153.

12/20 Chez Henri

16, rue Princesse - 01 46 33 51 12
Open daily until 11:30pm. No pets. No cards.
There's no sign outside, since the trendy denizens of the Rue Princesse know just where to find Henri's bistro specialties. The cooking can be uneven, but calf's liver with creamed onions, farm chicken in vinegar, roast lamb, and apple clafoutis are usually good bets. Nervous service; bare-bones cellar. C 220-250.

12/20 Joséphine

"Chez Dumonet", 117, rue du Cherche-Midi
01 45 48 52 40, fax 01 42 84 06 83
Closed Aug. Open until 10:30pm. Terrace dining.
Joséphine draws a crowd of prominent jurists, journalists, and theater folk who appreciate the good cuisine bourgeoise and the fabulous (though pricey) wine list. Chummy atmosphere, animated by owner Jean Dumonet, a former yachting champ. C 300.

Lipp

151, bd Saint-Germain
01 45 48 53 91, fax 01 45 44 33 20
Closed 3 wks in Aug. Open until 1am. Air cond.
Despite often disappointing food (choucroute, bœuf gros sel) and the cruel whims of fashion, this glossy brasserie still manages to serve some 400 to 500 customers a day. And one often catches sight of a powerful politician or a beauty queen ensconced at a ground-floor table, admiring the gorgeous décor. C 280. M 200 (wine incl).

11/20 La Lozère

4, rue Hautefeuille - 01 43 54 26 64
Closed Sun, Mon, Jul 12-Aug 12, 1 wk at Christmas. Open until 10pm. Air cond. Pkg.
You can smell the bracing air of the rural Lozère region in the warming winter soups, herbed sausages, pâtés, and cheese-laced mashed potatoes (aligot) served at this crafts shop-cum-restaurant. C 180-220. M 93 (lunch, wine incl).

La Marlotte

55, rue du Cherche-Midi
01 45 48 86 79, fax 01 44 44 34 80
Closed Sat, Sun, Aug. Open until 11pm. Terrace dining. Air cond. No pets. Pkg.
A rustic, timbered setting softened by madras upholstery and candlelight in the evening. Patrick Duclos crafts a classic repertoire: veal kidney perfumed with rosemary, duck breast with apples, nougat with raspberry jus. Crowded both at lunch and dinner, often with the smart set. C 200.

11/20 La Méditerranée

Pl. de l'Odéon - 01 43 26 02 30, fax 01 43 26 18 44
Open daily until 11pm. Terrace dining.
A trim seafood restaurant moored on the Place de l'Odéon, offering shipshape fish tartare, grilled sea bass, and bouillabaisse. C 200-250.

Le Muniche

7, rue St-Benoît - 01 42 61 12 70, fax 01 42 60 37 75
Open daily until 2am. Priv rm 35. Terrace dining. Air cond.
See *Le Clocher Saint-Germain*. C 250-300. M 99 (lunch), 149.

Le Paris

Hôtel Lutétia, 45, bd Raspail
01 49 54 46 90, fax 01 49 54 46 00
Closed Sat, Sun, Jul 26-Aug 24. Open until 10pm. Air cond. Priv rm 16. Valet pkg.
Philippe Renard reigns in the kitchens of Le Paris, one of the best tables on the Left Bank. Rich, well-defined flavors distinguish his terrine of boiled beef and foie gras, turbot cooked in seaweed and sea salt, and rack of pork braised for 36 hours with truffles and leeks. Note the luscious chocolate desserts, and the excellent 260 F prix-fixe lunch. C 480. M 260 (lunch), 350, 565, 60 (children).

10/20 Le Petit Saint-Benoît

4, rue Saint-Benoît - 01 42 60 27 92
Closed Sun, hols. Open until 10:30pm. Terrace dining. No pets.
The crowded sidewalk terrace is a refuge for fashionable fast-food haters in search of cheap eats: hachis parmentier, bacon with lentils, bœuf bourguignon, roast lamb. C 110.

12/20 Le Petit Zinc

11, rue St-Benoît - 01 42 61 20 60, fax 01 42 60 37 75
Open daily until 2am. Priv rm 8. Air cond.
See *Le Clocher Saint-Germain*. C 260-310. M 168 (wine inc).

12/20 La Petite Cour

8, rue Mabillon - 01 43 26 52 26, fax 01 44 07 11 53
Closed Jan. Open until 11pm, 11:30pm in summer. Priv rm 45. Terrace dining.
Chef Patrick Guyander generally plays it safe, but he sometimes produces a dish with extra dash (duck breast with honey and soy sauce). C 320-370.

11/20 Polidor

41, rue Monsieur-le-Prince - 01 43 26 95 34
Open Mon-Sat until 12:30am, Sun 11pm. No cards.
Familiar and soothing blanquettes, bourguignons, and rabbit in mustard sauce are served in a dining room that time has barely touched in more than a century. C 140. M 55 (weekday lunch), 100.

10/20 Le Procope

13, rue de l'Ancienne-Comédie
01 43 26 99 20, fax 01 43 54 16 86
Open daily until 1am. Priv rm 80. Terrace dining. Air cond.
The capital's oldest café, founded in 1686, restored to its original seventeenth-century splendor, may not be your best bet for a full meal. Tables of tourists feed on unexceptional bras-

serie fare (shellfish, coq au vin). **C** 240. **M** 106 (lunch), 123 (dinner, wine incl), 169, 185.

 Relais Louis XIII

8, rue des Grands-Augustins
01 43 26 75 96, fax 01 44 07 07 80
Open daily until 10:15pm. No cards.
Louis XIII was proclaimed King of France in this luxurious tavern with its beams and polished paneling... And today chef Manuel Martinez from La Tour d'Argent arrives to redefine a most often heavy cuisine. At the best part is that the prices have been halved and the service rejuvenated. On the other hand dishes vary from mediocre to a most acceptable millefeuille of rouget and game hen with wild mushrooms, and a stupendous, shockingly expensive cellar. **C** 600-700. **M** 200, 250 (lunch), 260, 360 (dinner).

12/20 **Le Rond de Serviette**

97, rue du Cherche-Midi
01 45 44 01 02, fax 01 42 22 50 10
Closed Sat lunch, Sun, Aug 1-24. Open until 10:45pm. Priv rm 35. Terrace dining. Air cond.
The owners cosset their clients in a fresh, pretty setting with lively cuisine: red-mullet tart with basil, creamy asparagus soup. The chef sometimes falters (bland saddle of lamb), but on balance he does pretty well. Fair prices. **C** 220-250. **M** 132-250 (lunch), 168, 250.

 La Rôtisserie d'en Face

2, rue Christine - 01 43 26 40 98, fax 01 43 54 54 48
Closed Sat lunch, Sun. Open until 11pm, Sat 11:30pm. Air cond. Valet pkg.
Jacques Cagna's smart rotisserie continues to attract Parisians hungry for rousing bistro food at reasonable prices. Sit down to taste duck pâté, Moroccan-style guinea hen with eggplant, and an iced caramel-walnut vacherin. Very nice welcome by Daniel and Olivier. **M** 135-159 (lunch), 210 (dinner).

12/20 **Santal des Prés**

6, rue du Dragon - 01 45 44 26 35
Closed Sun. Open until 11:30pm. Pkg.
A former Saigonese lawyer defends the cause of authentic Vietnamese cuisine with her delicious "grandmother's" shrimp, duck breast with chilis and glacéed fruit, peppery salmon, and plum duck. **C** 150. **M** 59 (lunch), 87-290, 50 (children).

 Yugaraj

14, rue Dauphine - 01 43 26 44 91, fax 01 46 33 50 77
Closed Mon lunch. Open until 11pm. Priv rm 26. Air cond.
The best Indian restaurant in the city, hands down. We love the refined surroundings, the smiles of the formally suited waiters, and—especially—the rare delicacies culled from every province of the subcontinent. Savor the cumin-spiced crab balls, tender lamb that is first roasted

in a tandoori oven then sautéed with herbs, or cod suavely spiced with turmeric and fenugreek; the subtly harmonized flavors bloom on the palate. **C** 270. **M** 130 (lunch), 180, 220.

7TH ARRONDISSEMENT

Postal code	**75007**

12/20 **Apollon**

24, rue Jean-Nicot - 01 45 55 68 47
Closed Sun. Open until 11pm. Terrace dining. Pkg.
First-rate mezes (chopped olives with saffron, meatballs, brochettes) make this one of the city's top Greek eateries. Chummy service. **C** 180. **M** 79 (lunch), 128 (dinner).

 Arpège

"Alain Passard,"
84, rue de Varenne
01 45 51 47 33, fax 01 44 18 98 39
Closed Sat, Sun lunch. Open until 10:30pm. Air cond. Priv rm 12.
Although he sits now at the top of the Mount Olympus of gastronomy, Alain Passard has not changed his down-to-earth manner. While some others invest time and money in marble floors and gold faucets, he devotes all his efforts to his twelve tables set in an almost spartan décor of wood and etched glass, overseen by a portrait of his ancestor. Some call the restaurant cold and stark, but Passard believes in no gimmicks, no tricks, no show off—in the dining room or his cuisine. Subtle hamornies mark his splendid and delicate compositions, each the result of a reflection about the complementary flavors and textures of the ingredients. If "art cuisine" exists, this is it. Arpège (Arpeggio), a rapid succession of harmonious tones, best describes Passard's virtuosity: spicy fresh ginger melts in the sweeteness of minced apple and sublimates the oceanic scent of sole; crispy suckling pig in a sweet horseradish mousse is glorified by melon sautéed in salt-edged butter. Perhaps one reason Passard's cuisine is so far above the majority of others, is because each dish reflects his considerable thought as well as his respect for the eater. **C** 700-1,000. **M** 320 (weekday lunch), 690.

 Le Bamboche

15, rue de Babylone
01 45 49 14 40, fax 01 45 49 14 44
Closed Sat, Sun, Aug. Priv rm 14.
Wee but wildly charming, David Van Laer's new restaurant (tucked away behind the Bon Marché department store) harbors a solid toque for herb-strewn snail and lentil soup, lamb sim-

mered in spices, and a deeply delectable chocolate-passion fruit millefeuille. The cellar, understandably, is still young. C 250. M 180-240.

12/20 Le Basilic

2, rue Casimir-Périer - 01 44 18 94 64
Open daily until 10:30pm. Terrace dining.
Here's a pretty brasserie across from the stately church of Sainte-Clotilde, where you can count on a warm welcome and a good meal. We can vouch for the saddle of hare en compote, grilled steak with Roquefort, and the fruit gratins offered for dessert. Interesting cellar. C 200.

 ### Beato

8, rue Malar - 01 47 05 94 27
Closed Sun, Mon, Aug, end Dec. Open until 11:30pm.
Sure, the setting and service are still starchy, but Beato's menu has visibly loosened up. Alongside the incomparable scampi fritti, lobster risotto, and noble chop of milk-fed veal, you'll find zuppa di fagioli, bollito misto, and tasty gnocchi with hare. C 300-350. M 145 (weekday lunch).

 ### Au Bon Accueil

14, rue de Monttessuy - 01 47 05 46 11
Closed Sat lunch, Sun, Aug, 1 wk at Christams. Open until 10pm. Terrace dining. No pets.
Unbeatable value. Jacques Lacipière's 120 F market-fresh menu might propose a hearty terrine of calf's foot and kidney, skate with Sherry butter or bœuf bourguignon, and creamy cherry chiboust. A la carte, look for beef fillet à la bordelaise or turbot in an herbal vinaigrette. Just as the sign says, you'll find a friendly welcome. C 250. M 120.

 ### Le Bourdonnais

113, av. de La Bourdonnais
01 47 05 47 96, fax 01 45 51 09 29
Closed Jan 1, May 1, Dec 24-25. Open until 11pm. Priv rm 30. Air cond.
Owner Micheline Coat, a peach of a hostess, greets newcomers as warmly as the politicos and financiers who number among her faithful customers (on the rare occasions when Micheline is absent, however, the ambience is not quite so chic). At lunchtime the 240 F menu (it even includes wine) is a paragon of generosity. The more expensive set meals also give you quality for your dining dollar, with lobster in brik pastry, spiced langoustines, rosemary-scented Lozère lamb, and a vanilla-berry feuillantine. C 450. M 240 (lunch, wine incl), 320 (dinner), 420.

11/20 Café de Mars

11, rue Augereau - 01 47 05 05 91
Closed Mon. Open until 11:30pm, Sun 4:30pm. Bar until 2am.
A menu that provides an engaging mix of American (spareribs, salads) and Mediterranean (breaded mozzarella with arugula, grilled scampi), a jovial atmosphere, and a cosmopolitan crowd account for the Café's continuing success. The staff goes all out to produce a traditional American brunch on Sunday. C 150. M 70 (weekday lunch).

12/20 Clémentine

62, av. Bosquet - 01 45 51 41 16
Closed Sat lunch, Sun, Aug 15-30. Open until 10:30pm. Terrace dining. Air cond. Pkg.
Here's a friendly little bistro with a summer terrace, where the chef produces tasty, unpretentious fare: grilled ham with shallots, corned duck with vegetables, creamy fresh cheese swirled with acacia honey. C 180. M 139.

 ### Écaille et Plume

25, rue Duvivier - 01 45 55 06 72
Closed Sat lunch, Sun, 1 wk in Feb, Aug. Open until 11pm. Priv rm 10. Air cond.
Seasonal game specialties and seafood are Marie Naël's strong points: try the briny salade océane, shark roasted with lemongrass, hare à la royale or, in its short season, Scottish grouse flambéed with single-malt whisky. The dining room is cozy, the Loire wines well chosen. C 260-340. M 180, 195.

12/20 La Fontaine de Mars

129, rue Saint-Dominique - 01 47 05 46 44
Closed Sun. Open until 11pm. Terrace dining. Air cond.
A smiling staff and tasty family-style cooking make this a popular spot. You'll surely relish the warm cèpe pâté, andouillette sausage laced with Chardonnay, or duck breast with cranberries. To drink, look no further than the good Cahors priced at 40 F. C 220. M 85 (lunch).

 ### Chez Françoise

Aérogare des Invalides
01 47 05 49 03, fax 01 45 51 96 20
Open daily until midnight. Terrace dining. Valet pkg.
Chez Françoise is an immense subterranean restaurant, a perennial favorite with hungry parliamentarians from the neighboring Assemblée Nationale. They blithely ignore the prix-fixe specials and opt instead for the pricier à la carte offerings, like duck terrine, roast rack of lamb, poule au pot, and crêpes Suzette. We, on the other hand, usually choose one of the set meals, which are really a good deal (although the cooking can be a mite uneven at times). C 250. M 120 (dinner), 168, 60 (children).

 ### Gaya Rive Gauche

44, rue du Bac - 01 45 44 73 73, fax 01 42 60 04 54
Closed Sun lunch. Open until 11pm. Terrace dining. Air cond. Pkg.
The smart literary set of the Faubourg Saint-Germain quickly staked out their turf at this annex of the Goumard-Prunier seafood empire. They come here to savor ultrafresh fish in such unfussy preparations as a bracing tartare of tuna and John Dory, tiny deep-fried red mullet, and

line-caught sea bass grilled with roasted tomatoes. C 260-360.

 Les Glénan

54, rue de Bourgogne - 01 45 51 61 09
Closed Sat, Sun, 1 wk in Feb, Aug. Open until 10pm. Air cond. Priv rm 20.
Christine Guillard manages Les Glénan with energy and charm, while the kitchen is in the capable hands of Thierry Bourbonnais. His sensitive touch brings out all the delicate nuances of seafood and other seasonal ingredients. The 195 F set meal, which includes a half-bottle of Loire Valley wine, features creamy cumin-spiced tomato soup, grilled sea bream with smothered artichokes, and chocolate-swirled pear shortbread. C 350. M 195 (wine incl).

 Jules Verne

Tour Eiffel, second floor
01 45 55 61 44, fax 01 47 05 29 41
Open daily until 10:30pm. Air cond. No pets. Valet pkg.
Dining in this sophisticated room high atop the Eiffel Tower is a treat in itself. Chef Alain Reix's menu majors in seafood: Chinese-style steamed oysters with roasted tomatoes, scallop carpaccio with asparagus and Parmesan, and fricasséed cuttlefish paired with pan-roasted foie gras are all fine, modern dishes. Superior, surely, to the poached sole immobilized in a sabayon studded with sea snails. Certain offerings have a pleasing Alsatian accent, and the desserts are delicious. Perfect service. C 750-800. M 300 (weekday lunch), 420 & 460 (weekday lunch, Sat), 680 (exc weekday lunch), 720 & 770 (wine incl).

 Kamal

20, rue Rousselet - 01 47 34 66 29
Open daily until 11pm. Priv rm 40. Air cond.
Kamal means lotus, a symbol of purity. Pure pleasure is what we derive from this moderately spicy North Indian fare; you too will savor the tender tandooris, shrimp and lamb curries, red hacked chicken, saffron rice, and naans. M 69 (weekday lunch, wine incl), 85 (lunch), 129.

 Le Divellec

107, rue de l'Université
01 45 51 91 96, fax 01 45 51 31 75
Closed Sun, Mon, Dec 24-Jan 1. Open until 10pm. Air cond. No pets. Valet pkg.
We are still disapointed by Le Divellec which was one of the great seafood restaurant of Paris. The crew will have to steer a simpler and (if possible) less costly course to regain its past grandeur. Classic cellar; well-bred welcome and service. C 700-900. M 290-390 (lunch).

 Le Luz

4, rue Pierre-Leroux - 01 43 06 99 39
Closed Sat lunch, Sun, Aug 11-18. Open until 10pm. No pets. Air cond.
Behind its fresh and tidy façade, this cozy little restaurant offers clever but uncomplicated

seafood, prepared with quality ingredients. Try the tasty fresh cod with roasted vegetables or scallops sparked with orange vinegar, followed by one of the alluring desserts. Varied wine list; professional welcome. C 235. M 155.

12/20 Maison de l'Amérique Latine

217, bd St-Germain
01 45 49 33 23, fax 01 40 49 03 94
Closed Sat, Sun, hols, Aug 4-25. Open until 10:30pm. Priv rm 150. Terrace dining. No pets.
Don't come here looking for churrasco or feijoada—the chef is Japanese and his repertoire is resolutely French (with a barely discernible Eastern touch). Among the menu's highlights are a squab raviolo with shiitake aspic, pan-roasted salmon with sesame seeds and bok choy, and beef tournedos sparked with preserved lemon. The garden is a delightful place to dine, weather permitting. C 320-375. M 195-225 (weekday lunch).

12/20 Le Maupertu

94, bd de Latour-Maubourg - 01 45 51 37 96
Closed Sat lunch, Sun, 1 wk in Feb, 2 wks in Aug. Open until 10pm. Terrace dining. No pets.
Seasonal, market-fresh cooking figures on Le Maupertu's unbeatable 135 F prix-fixe meal. Try the lush millefeuille layered with shrimp and crabmeat, the satisfying daube provençale, and bright-flavored orange and almond terrine. Among the attractive selection of half-bottles in the cellar, you'll find a tasty '93 Chinon from Couly-Dutheuil. C 250. M 135.

 Paul Minchelli

54, bd Latour-Maubourg
01 47 05 89 86, fax 01 45 56 03 84
Closed Sun, Mon, hols, Aug, end Dec-beg Jan. Open until 10:30pm. Air cond. Priv rm 10.
Remember Paul Minchelli? He's the man who "reinvented seafood," stripping away meretricious sauces to reveal pure, virginal flavors. He shipped out of Le Duc, the restaurant he ran with his late brother, and fetched up here, in Art Deco–style premises featuring Norwegian birch, frosted glass, and a huge black bar with a few stools for casual dining. Minchelli's minimalism requires fish of optimal quality. He chooses sea bass that is delectable even in its raw state, just sliced and drizzled with olive oil, or briefly steamed to reveal its briny essence. Depending on what the tide brings in, he might offer lobster (for example) in several different guises. In one winning version, the crustacean is flavored with a touch of honey and chili. Each dish is prepared to order, so service can be painfully slow. C 500.

12/20 L'Œillade

10, rue Saint-Simon - 01 42 22 01 60
Closed Sat lunch, Sun, last 2 wks of Aug. Open until 11pm. Air cond. Pkg.
The single-price menus looks reasonable enough, and the eggplant caviar, duck ballottine, and berry gratin with Champagne sabayon are perfectly decent, but beware of the expensive wine list which could send your bill right through the roof! C 220. M 158.

Le Petit Laurent

38, rue de Varenne
01 45 48 79 64, fax 01 42 66 68 59
Closed Sat lunch, Sun, Aug. Open until 10:15pm.
Sylvain Pommier turns out an impeccable warm scallop salad enriched with chive butter, terrine of sweetbreads and mushrooms dressed with herbed oil, sea bream roasted with mango and lime, guinea hen intriguingly perfumed with lemongrass, and a luscious apple and chocolate confection laced with Banyuls wine. Diligent service in a comfortable, Louis XVI–style setting. And the 185 F menu is one of the better deals on the Left Bank. C 300-400. M 185, 250.

Le Récamier

4, rue Récamier - 01 45 48 86 58, fax 01 42 22 84 76
Closed Sun. Open until 10:30pm. Terrace dining. Air cond. Priv rm 12.
Martin Cantegrit, owner of this elegant establishment, oversees the service of Burgundian classics (jambon persillé, prime rib bourguignon, pike mousse with sauce Nantua) and a few lighter options (John Dory with an herbal emulsion). The clientele—politicians, publishers, media moguls—visibly enjoy tapping the magnificent 100,000-bottle cellar. In summer the terrace spills across a pedestrian zone for fume-free outdoor dining. Expect a hefty tab. C 400. M 230 (lunch Sat, coffee incl).

12/20 Chez Ribe

15, av. de Suffren - 01 45 66 53 79
Closed Sat lunch, Sun, Aug, end Dec-beg Jan. Open until 10:30pm. Terrace dining. Pkg.
Granted, a 168 F prix-fixe meal is not—yet—hard to find, even in Paris, but this frequently changing menu is reliably delicious and well prepared. Possibilities include eggplant gâteau with tomato coulis, rack of lamb with mild garlic, and tiramisù, all graciously served in Belle Époque surroundings. C 220. M 118, 168.

Tan Dinh

60, rue de Verneuil
01 45 44 04 84, fax 01 45 44 36 93
Closed Sun, Aug. Open until 11pm. Priv rm 30. No cards.
Tan Dinh's huge wine list has few equals, even among the city's top restaurants—some say it outclasses the food. But the Vifians are justly proud of their innovative Vietnamese menu, which spotlights light, refined dishes like smoked-goose dumplings, lobster toast, chicken with Asian herbs, and veal with betel nuts. If you resist the cellar's pricier temptations, a dinner here amid the stylish Left-Bank crowd needn't lead to financial disaster. C 350.

Le Télégraphe

41, rue de Lille - 01 40 15 06 65
Open daily until 12:30am. Terrace dining. No cards.
A furiously fashionable restaurant, Le Télégraphe is more society scene than gastronomic mecca. The Art Nouveau setting is lovely indeed, the waiters' attire is ever so chic...and the food? The current chef acquits himself pretty well, but by the time you read this a new face may be at the stoves—the kitchen seems to be equipped with a revolving door! C 280-400. M 125 (lunch), 195.

11/20 Thoumieux

79, rue St-Dominique - 01 47 05 49 75
Open daily until midnight. Priv rm 25-120. Air cond.
Regional favorites from the rugged Corrèze region are Thoumieux's stock in trade: chestnut-studded boudin, milk-fed veal, and the rustic fruit flan known as flognarde. Lively atmosphere. C 230. M 72, 150 (wine incl).

Vin sur Vin

20, rue de Monttessuy - 01 47 05 14 20
Closed Sun, Sat & Mon lunch, Aug 1-20, Dec 23-Jan 2. Open until 10pm. Air cond.
Former sommelier Patrice Vidal has assembled a first-rate cellar made up exclusively of growers' wines, from which he selects a few each week to sell by the glass. They accompany such sturdy bistro standbys as sardine gâteau, salmon trout with Banyuls-wine butter, and apple clafoutis with caramelized cider sauce. Prices are high, however, with no prix-fixe relief in sight. C 300-350.

Le Violon d'Ingres

135, rue St-Dominique - 01 45 55 15 05
Closed Sun, Mon. Open until 10:30pm. Air cond.
Now at the helm of his own ship with no admiral watching over him, Christian Constant, who has left Les Ambassadeurs and set up his own restaurant, is more at ease with his flavorful cuisine, which he constantly refines and simplifies, leaving behind all pomp and circumstance. The ingredients are, as always, superb, and the cooking times are incredibly precise (except in the case of a risotto, which was surely a momentary lapse). The result is nearly perfect cuisine that is rustic yet refined. The prices are almost as low as those in an ordinary bistro: mussels and herbs en papillote are priced at only 70 F, and green pollack and chorizo and white-bean purée with aged vinegar at 85 F. His masterpiece, however, is his marvellous dish of pearly scallops roasted in the shell and topped with a pat of parsleyed, salted butter. The limited dessert menu (four simple choices, including rice pudding) deserves to be expanded, as does

the wine list. The latter is certainly well chosen, however, and includes a true Bandol (1989, from Château Sainte-Anne). In the end, quality counts more than quantity. **C** 250-350. **M** 290.

8TH ARRONDISSEMENT

Postal code **75008**

12/20 **Al Ajami**

58, rue François-Ier
01 42 25 38 44, fax 01 42 56 60 08
Open daily until midnight. Air cond.
Fortunately the menu's perfunctory French offerings are outnumbered by authentic dishes from the Lebanese highlands—assorted mezes, chawarma, keftedes, and sticky pastries. The wines lend a dash of local color to the refined, yellow-and-blue dining room. **C** 180-200. **M** 79 (weekday lunch exc Sun), 99-140.

Les Ambassadeurs

Hôtel de Crillon, 10, pl. de la Concorde
01 44 71 16 16, fax 01 44 71 15 02
Open daily until 10:30pm. Priv rm 140. Terrace dining. Air cond. No pets. Valet pkg.
Eight seems to be the lucky number of Dominique Bouchet, the new chef at Les Ambassadeurs. He was 28 in 1981 when he started at La Tour d'Argent, which he left in 1988 with an 18 rating. For the next eight years, he was away from the Paris food scene, busy running his own restaurant and hotel, Le Moulin de Marcouze, in Mosnac in the Charente region. Laurent Vanhoegaerden, restaurant manager—who will turn 38 in August—welcomes you to the majestic eighteenth-century landmark dining room with its 8-meter ceiling! An intensely modern cuisine without extravagances, a classic cuisine without the frills, is served on twenty well-spread tables: morels with foie gras and wild mushrooms, cooked-to-perfection langoustines with asparagus, roast turbot poached in smoked milk accompanied by a red-oignon jam, and pink-in-the middle lamb. Bouchet is backed up by Christian Felder, a talented Alsatian pastry chef who, believe it or not, is 28. Should we take this as a sign that Dominique Bouchet is once again reaching toward his favorite number, that is to say, 18? **C** 800. **M** 340 (lunch), 620.

11/20 **Aux Amis du Beaujolais**

28, rue d'Artois - 01 45 63 92 21
Closed Sat dinner, Sat lunch Easter-Oct, Sun, hols. Open until 9pm. Air cond. Pkg.
Vigorous French bistro cooking (the menu changes daily) and tasty Beaujolais. Full plates, friendly prices. **C** 150-200.

12/20 **L'Appart'**

9, rue du Colisée - 01 53 75 16 34, fax 01 53 76 15 39
Open daily until midnight. Air cond.
Decked out to look like a private home—living room, dining room, library—L'Appart' is not just an amusing scene, it's also a pretty good restaurant. You'll enjoy the cheese ravioli, pan-roasted cod with meat juices, and French toast with caramel sauce. Brunch is served on Sundays. **C** 190-245. **M** 175 (wine incl) 110, 160, 85 (children).

Astor Madeleine

11, rue Astorg - 01 53 05 05 20, fax 01 53 05 05 30
Closed Sat, Sun. Open until 10pm. No pets. Priv rm 20. Air cond. Valet pkg.
The restaurant of the freshly rehabbed Astor Madeleine hotel is under the supervision of Joël Robuchon. He's put one of his star pupils, Éric Lecerf (a two-toque winner in his previous post), in charge of the kitchen, and we're expecting great things. We'll let you know how he's doing as soon as we've had the chance to sample his wares—watch this space! **C** 400-500. **M** 290 (lunch, wine & coffee incl).

L'Avenue

41, av. Montaigne
01 40 70 14 91, fax 01 49 52 13 00
Open daily until midnight. Priv rm 180. Air cond.
If you book a table in the elegant upstairs dining room, you can mingle with the chic couture and media crowd that flocks into L'Avenue for such stylish specialties as risotto d'escargots au pistou, spiced scampi fricassée, and lemony veal piccata. Shellfish assortments and a good club sandwich are also on hand. Worthy cellar. Considering the classy location in the heart of the Golden Triangle, prices are downright reasonable. **C** 260-460. **M** 175 (weekday dinner).

11/20 **Barfly**

49-51, av. George-V - 01 53 67 84 60
Closed Sat lunch. Open until 1am. Terrace dining. Air cond.
Here's a stylish eatery on the Champs, with a menu that offers sushi, pasta dishes, burgers, spiced chicken breast, and other trendy edibles. A DJ is on hand in the evening to liven things up. Reasonable prices, but the welcome is not exactly warm. **C** 150-200.

Le Bistrot du Sommelier

97, bd Haussmann
01 42 65 24 85, fax 01 53 75 23 23
Closed Sat, Sun, Dec 25, Jan 1. Open until 11pm. Air cond. Priv rm 24.
Crowned "World's Best Sommelier" in 1992, Philippe Faure-Brac naturally encourages his new chef to cook with wine. Thus, the menu features chicken au vin du Jura and rabbit with tiny onions in Chablis. But it's the cellar that captures the wine buff's interest, with bottles from all over France—and the world. A special

prix-fixe dinner brings six courses paired with compatible wines. C 300. M 390 (dinner, wine incl).

12/20 Le Bœuf sur le Toit

34, rue du Colisée - 01 43 59 83 80, fax 01 45 63 45 40
Open daily until 2am. Air cond. Priv rm 24.
From a seat on the mezzanine watch the dazzling swirl of diners and waiters reflected a hundredfold in this mirrored, Art Deco dining room. But don't get so distracted that you can't enjoy the plentiful shellfish platters, juicy steaks, or choucroutes de poissons. C 150-230. M 123 (lunch, wine incl), 169 (dinner, wine incl), 128 (dinner, after 10pm, wine incl).

12/20 Boucoléon

10, rue de Constantinople - 01 42 93 73 33
Closed Sat lunch, Sun, 3 wks in Aug, end Dec-beg Jan. Open until 10:30pm. Terrace dining. No pets.
An address where value goes hand-in-hand with lively, inventive cooking. Here in a quiet district near Place de l'Europe you'll dine happily on ravigote de joue de bœuf (ox jowls in a tangy sauce), lamb sauté showered with juniper-spiced breadcrumbs, and crème brûlée brightened with mango and passion fruit. C 180-250. M 90 (weekdays), 150 (weekdays & Sat dinner).

 ## Le Bristol

Hôtel Le Bristol,
112, rue du Fg-Saint-Honoré
01 53 43 43 00, fax 01 53 43 43 01
Open daily until 10:30pm. Terrace dining. Air cond. No pets. Valet pkg.
Think that hotel dining rooms are boring? The Bristol is out to prove the opposite. The management has put its efforts where its mouth is, by hiring culinary troubadour Michel del Burgo, fresh from Carcassonne, to cook up a lyrical new menu that is strongly influenced by the cuisine of the Southwest of France. A tempting first course is the conserved duck liver, cooked to perfection and served with a quince jelly that melts in the mouth. The spelt risotto is made with extraordinary truffles and a flavorful sauce of meat juices. The scallops, grilled on a wood fire and served with clams in shellfish juice, are deliciously crunchy on the outside. Don't miss the desserts, which compare most favorably with the other dishes. Try the warm chocolate soufflé served with chocolate-honey ice cream. Michel del Burgo well deserved the three toques and 17/20 rating that he had in his previous restaurant, and we are now giving them back to him. Welcome to Paris! C 600-900. M 380.

12/20 Café Terminus

Hôtel Concorde Saint-Lazare, 108, rue St-Lazare
01 40 08 43 30, fax 01 42 93 01 20
Open daily until 10:30pm. Priv rm 250. Air cond. Valet pkg.
A bar/bistro/restaurant in the huge and luxurious Concorde Saint-Lazare hotel. The 198 F menu includes a glass of Champagne and a half-bottle of wine, along with pistachio-studded duck terrine, salmon gratinéed with walnuts, and saffron-spiced banana crumble. Effective, very attentive service. C 300. M 148, 198 (wine incl).

 ## Cap Vernet

82, av. Marceau - 01 47 20 20 40, fax 01 47 20 95 36
Open daily until midnight. Terrace dining.
A kitchen crew trained by Guy Savoy runs this show, producing a fresh, flavorful menu that features a zingy dish of sole with lemon and capers, and rack of lamb en petite marmite escorted by Noirmoutier potatoes and tender carrots. Don't overlook the oyster and raw shellfish bar. C 220-240.

 ## Le Carpaccio

Hôtel Royal Monceau, 35-39, av. Hoche
01 42 99 98 90, fax 01 42 99 89 94
Closed Aug. Open until 10:30pm. No pets. Valet pkg.
Executives in expensive suits are the backbone of Le Carpaccio's sleek clientele. Here, in a spectacular winter-garden setting, they feed on warm octopus salad brightened with preserved lemon, veal garnished with either porcini mushrooms or white truffles, shellfish and assorted fresh vegetables encased in sheer tempura batter, dusky cuttlefish tagliatelle topped with spears of crisp asparagus, and an improbably good raspberry-vinegar gelato. Outrageously priced, these fine dishes (and excellent wines) are served by a rather haughty staff. C 450-550.

 ## Cercle Ledoyen

Carré des Champs-Élysées
01 53 05 10 01, fax 01 47 42 55 01
Closed Sun. Open until 11:30pm. Air cond. No pets. Terrace dining. Valet pkg.
Jacques Grange is the man behind the elegantly spare interior of this spacious restaurant, a favorite haunt of the city's chic and famous. Jean-Paul Arabian oversees the impeccable service, while Ghislaine Arabian does the same for the menu, which changes practically every day. Zesty starters like a gently poached egg in a sea-urchin shell or finnan-haddie terrine with lentils segue into rabbit en pot-au-feu, sea bass with celery root, or old-fashioned blanquette de veau. Irrigated by modest but tasty little wines, they add up to perfectly modern meals at a perfectly moderate price. C 250-300.

 ## Chiberta

3, rue Arsène Houssaye
01 45 63 77 90, fax 01 45 62 85 08
Closed Sat, Sun, Aug. Open until 11pm. Priv rm 45. Air cond. Pkg.
Louis-Noël Richard, the soul of this elegant restaurant, passed away. But as he himself would have been the first to say, "The show must go on." The new chef, Éric Croisel, likes herbs, and knows how to get the best out of them in preparations such as artichoke ravioli with ricotta and coriander, John Dory served on anchovy

tapenade and basil, and lamb sweetbreads à la sariette. The herb theme even carries through to the desserts in such creations as his basil sorbet, which accompanies a mixed-berry soup in a verbena herb tea. C 450. M 290.

 ## Le Clovis

Hôtel Sofitel Arc de Triomphe, 4, av. Bertie-Albrecht
01 53 89 50 53, fax 01 53 89 50 51
Closed Sat, Sun, Aug, Dec 23-Jan 2, hols. Open until 10:30pm. Air cond. Priv rm 70. Valet pkg.
The understated setting of Le Clovis is conducive to doing business, a fact that has not escaped the city's executives. The kitchen produces well-wrought dishes with an occasional bold touch: we're thinking of a salad that combines tiny artichokes and firm pears with bits of chorizo sausage. Or even better, the rosemary-roasted kid with braised fennel. Delicate desserts (try the iced verbena délice). Extensive cellar; attentive service. C 380. M 195 (dinner), 235, 320.

 ## Le Copenhague

142, av. des Champs-Élysées
01 44 13 86 26, fax 01 42 25 83 10
Closed Sun, 1st wk of Jan, Aug, hols. Open until 10:30pm. Priv rm 80. Terrace dining. Air cond. No pets.
This Danish enclave is perhaps the last high-class restaurant on the Champs-Élysées, the last to survive the onslaught of hamburger chains, pizzerias, and other fast-food eateries. In the muted atmosphere of the upstairs dining room, salmon is featured in myriad guises, of course, but there is also smoked eel paired with creamy scrambled eggs, duck à la danoise, and spiced reindeer fillet. And there's plenty of Danish aquavit to wash it all down. Elegant but impersonal service. C 400. M 250 (weekdays, wine incl), 550 (2 per), 80 (children).

 ## La Couronne

Hôtel Warwick, 5, rue de Berri
01 45 63 78 49, fax 01 45 59 00 98
Closed Sat lunch, Sun, Aug, hols. Open until 10:30pm. Priv rm 6. Air cond. Valet pkg.
Posh and conservative: that about sums up both the food and the setting of this well-regarded hotel restaurant. No flaws to be found in the warm salad of lotte and foie gras dressed with Sherry vinegar, rosemary-scented red mullet fillets, or lamb pot-au-feu spiced with star anise (though from the latter we expected more layers of flavor). Courteous reception; stylish service. C 450-510. M 250, 270.

11/20 Drugstore des Champs-Élysées

133, av. des Champs-Élysées - 01 44 43 79 00
Open daily until 2am. Terrace dining. Air cond. No pets.
Believe it or not, the food at this landmark of 1960s chic is not bad at all. The main-course salads, grills, and crisp pommes frites go very well with the noisy, bustling atmosphere. C 150-300. M 59, 85 (weekday, wine incl), 38 (children).

Chez Edgard

4, rue Marbeuf - 01 47 20 51 15, fax 01 47 23 94 29
Closed Sun. Open until 11:30am. Priv rm 35. Valet pkg.
Just because the *gratin* of French politics eats here, don't expect to see Jacques Chirac or Alain Juppé seated across from you. "Monsieur Paul" serves up to 500 meals here each day, and in any case the Parisian powers-that-be are always whisked off to the quiet private rooms upstairs. Downstairs, amid the typically Gallic brouhaha, the rest of us can choose from a wide range of good grilled meats and hearty cuisine bourgeoise, prepared with care and skill. C 220-350. M 195, 250-355 (wine incl).

 ## Les Élysées du Vernet

Hôtel Vernet, 25, rue Vernet
01 44 31 98 98, fax 01 44 31 85 69
Closed Sat, Sun, Jul 28-Aug 22, Dec 22-26, hols. Open until 10pm. Priv rm 16. Air cond. No pets. Valet pkg.
Which way to the Riviera, please? We'd suggest this elegant address just off the Champs-Élysées. Although you won't have a view of the Mediterranean, chef Alain Solivérès brings the perfumes and savors of Provence into the Vernet's glass-roofed dining room. His salt cod with roasted tomatoes, mesclun, and anchoïade beneath a paper-thin chickpea galette is an eloquent dialogue of Southern flavors. Lately the menu has also made incursions into the Southwest, paying homage to that region's fabulous duck, Chalosse beef, and Pyrenees lamb. Desserts? They're exciting indeed: consider the lemon-bergamot soufflé flanked by quince marmalade, ewe's-milk ice cream, and Szechuan pepper—a clever and delicious conceit. Competent, attentive service; exemplary cellar. C 550-650. M 340 (lunch), 390 & 530 (dinner).

 ## L'Étage Baumann

"Baumann Marbeuf," 15, rue Marbeuf
01 47 20 11 11, fax 01 47 23 69 65
Closed Sat lunch, wk of Aug 15. Open until midnight. Priv rm 30. Air cond.
The name is new and so is the refurbished décor, but the menu still features glossy fresh shellfish, colossal choucroutes (topped with fish, or ham shanks, or confit de canard...), and expertly aged meats. We like the chocolate cake, too, and the thirst-quenching Alsatian wines. C 180-200. M 128, 170 (wine incl), 55 (children).

 ## Fakhr el Dine

3, rue Quentin-Bauchart
01 47 23 44 42, fax 01 47 27 11 39
Open daily until 12:30am. Air cond. No pets. Valet pkg.
Delicious Lebanese mezes dazzle the eye as they delight the palate: bone-marrow salad, brains in lemon sauce, spinach fritters, fried lamb's sweetbreads, etc. These tidbits are offered

in batches of 8, 10, 15, or 20, depending on the size of the company and your appetite. C 250. M 120 (lunch), 150-300, 85 (children).

12/20 Finzi

182, bd Haussmann - 01 45 62 88 68
Closed Sun lunch. Open until 11:30pm.
The white-collar crowd that spills out of neighboring offices gladly risks spotting their ties with Finzi's good pasta sauces. Look for lusty Italian hams and salamis, too, and apricot ravioli with custard sauce for dessert. C 230.

Flora Danica

142, av. des Champs-Élysées
01 44 13 86 26, fax 01 42 25 83 10
Closed May 1, Dec 24 dinner. Open until 11pm. Terrace dining. Air cond.
Salmon—smoked, pickled, marinated, or grilled—and delicious tender herring prepared in every imaginable way are the stars of this limited menu. Upstairs, more elaborate (and costly) dishes are served (there's an interesting terrine of foie gras and reindeer). If the weather is fine, ask to be seated on the patio behind the Flora Danica. C 300. M 150 (lunch, exc Sat, beer incl), 525 (2 per), 80 (children).

11/20 Fouquet's

99, av. des Champs-Élysées
01 47 23 70 60, fax 01 47 20 08 69
Open daily until 1am. Priv rm 200. Terrace dining. Valet pkg.
After a bout of bad publicity, Fouquet's is poised for a fresh departure. This listed landmark on the Champs-Élysées has acquired the services of Gérard Salé from the Plaza, and Bernard Leprince of La Tour d'Argent. Snapers en escabèche, and osso buco à l'orange bring back good memories. Impeccable service, something that has disappeared on the the Champs. Here's wishing them luck... C 350-500. M 265.

Pierre Gagnaire

Hôtel Balzac, 6, rue Balzac
01 44 35 18 25, fax 01 44 35 18 37
Closed Sat, Sun dinner. Open until 10:30pm. Air cond.
After the demise of his renowned restaurant (probably too upscale for the industrial city of Saint-Étienne, near Lyon), where he earned four toques, the highest award from GaultMillau, talented chef Pierre Gagnaire has resurfaced on the Champs-Élysées. The former premises of Bice, in the hotel Balzac, have been redesigned in a (to our taste) cold postmodern style with severe blue and gray tones. Tables are well separated, but some of the seats could be more comfortable. A simpler dining room in the back absorbs the overflow of patrons. In his new Paris bastion, Gagnaire proves once again his great artistry. His creations, with their intense flavors, unexpected combinations and extraordinary ingredients, are staggering: John Dory braised in "vadouvan," polenta in "Brocciu," aromatic mesclun (mixed salad greens) with "Tellines,"

etc. (Even a good dictionary may not help in deciphering this menu.) Try the incredible cigale de mer (a rare variety of spiny lobster) in an apple and turnip sabayon, the little squids stuffed with nuts, the grilled "nori" algae and potato quenelles, or the light roasted turbot in shallot juice with melissa leaves. Do not expect the desserts to reach new heights—although they wander off the beaten path, they do not match the grandeur of the main dishes. The succinct, well chosen wine list will help you make a quick choice. The refined and unusual experience of dining here could benefit from more fluid and convivial service. We expect that that will happen as the pieces fall in place. For this stellar culinary voyage, be prepared to pay astronomical prices. A lunchtime plat du jour (130-180 F) at the bar is a more affordable option and does not require a reservation. C 900. M 450 (lunch), 480 (dinner).

Le Grenadin

44-46, rue de Naples
01 45 63 28 92, fax 01 45 61 24 76
Closed Sat lunch, Sun, 1 wk in Jul, 1 wk in Aug. Open until 10:30pm. Priv rm 14. Terrace dining. Air cond.
Pungent herbs and bold harmonies are the hallmarks of Patrick Cirotte's repertoire. His affinity for keen, acidulous flavors shows up in the delicious oysters with alfalfa sprouts and lemony cream sauce, and in a pork tenderloin served with quince compote. But he can also strike a suave note, as in the saddle of rabbit cloaked in a mild, creamy garlic sauce. Desserts don't get short shrift either: the ethereal vanilla millefeuille-minute, wine granita, or spiced fruit croûte tempt even flagging appetites. Mireille Cirotte offers reliable advice on wine (note that Sancerres are the pride of her cellar). C 400-450. M 200-330.

Hédiard

21, pl. de la Madeleine
01 43 12 88 99, fax 01 43 12 88 98
Closed Sun. Open until 10:30pm. Priv rm 12. Air cond. Valet pkg.
Upstairs over their celebrated fine-foods emporium, Hédiard has inaugurated a French colonial-style restaurant where modern dishes (game aspic, herb salad with Parmesan and porcini) vie with bistro cooking (vegetable soup, steak au poivre) for your attention. All starters are priced at 65 F, meats at 120 F. Noble cellar; amateur service. C 260-400.

12/20 Higgins

1, rue Montalivet - 01 42 66 95 26
Closed Sat, Sun, 2 wks in Aug. Open lunch only until 3:30pm. Terrace dining.
Quietly nestled in an arcade a block away from the fashion district, this American-style eatery with a cruise-ship décor will throw you back into the 1930s. Nearly everything here is American, from the waiters to the menu and even some of the wines. Dishes include a bacon cheeseburger

(72 F), eggs Benedict (68 F), guacamole (48 F), and a tasty club sandwich (55 F). If you're still hungry, try a warm brownie or a delicious berry millefeuille. With its outdoor terrace, this is a great spot for lunch, but don't forget to reserve a table in advance. C 150. M 120.

Le Jardin des Cygnes

Hôtel Prince de Galles, 33, av. George-V
01 47 23 55 11, fax 01 47 20 61 05
Open daily until 11pm. Garden dining. Air cond. No pets. Valet pkg.
A jewelbox of a dining room that opens onto a charming patio is an alluring stage for Dominique Cécillon's sun-struck cuisine. All the items on the menu—house foie gras au torchon, pigeon pastilla, red mullet with Provençal vegetables—are very nearly as delicious as they are expensive, and are delivered to your table by a high-class staff. If economy is your aim, head over instead to the hotel's Regency Bar, for a good, light little meal. C 350-600. M 290 (wine incl).

Le Jardin du Royal Monceau

Hôtel Royal Monceau, 35, av. Hoche
01 42 99 98 70, fax 01 42 99 89 94
Closed Sat, Sun. Open until 10:30pm. Priv rm 500. Garden dining. Air cond. No pets. Valet pkg.
You step into another world when you enter the candy-pink dining room, its french windows opening onto manicured lawns and flower beds: a garden that seems to have been brought to Paris by the wave of a magic wand. The same spell holds in the kitchen, where Bruno Cirino conjures up a modern, exquisitely delicate menu with a gracious Provençal lilt. Why not order his spider crab in pistou broth—a marvel of subtlety; follow it with sautéed sole escorted by a superb chard gratin, then indulge in the richness of a banana roasted in its skin, laced with amber rum, and flanked by lush Malaga raisin ice cream. Service is impeccable, and a youthful sommelier provides sound advice on a wine list studded with rarities. C 550-700. M 280, 340 (weekday lunch), 430 (weekday dinner).

Lasserre

17, av. Franklin-D.-Roosevelt
01 43 59 53 43, fax 01 45 63 72 23
Closed Sun, Mon lunch, Aug. Open until 10:30pm. No pets. Valet pkg.
One of the few surviving examples of *le grand restaurant à la française*, Lasserre merits our attention for the ethnological interest it presents. Nowhere else is the service so minutely choreographed, the atmosphere so well-bred (piano music, soft lights, glowing silver...). After a disapointing era, Lasserre has retrieved its standards of quality and food—on the classic side—has greatly improved. Don't forget to look up as Lasserre's retractable roof brings you (weather and visibility permitting) the stars. C 700-1,000.

Laurent

41, av. Gabriel
01 42 25 00 39, fax 01 45 62 45 21
Closed Sat lunch, Sun, hols. Open until 11pm. Priv rm 70. Terrace dining. No pets. Valet pkg.
The economic climate must be warming up! At Laurent this welcome change in the weather has brought smiles back to the waiters' faces, and the *carte*, too, reflects the sunnier trend, with lighter dishes and sprightlier sauces. Philippe Braun executes a menu designed by his mentor, Joël Robuchon, which includes fresh anchovies on a bed of fresh-tasting vegetable brunoise, duck liver set atop black beans fired up with hot chilis, and a superb veal chop set off by tender hearts of lettuce in a savory jus. Now, you may have to sell off a few T-bonds to pay the bill—or else you can do as many of the other high-powered patrons do, and order the excellent prix-fixe menu. Whatever course you choose, sommelier Patrick Lair will advise you on the appropriate wine. C 800-1,000. M 390.

Ledoyen

Carré des Champs-Élysées
01 53 05 10 01, fax 01 47 42 55 01
Closed Sat, Sun, Aug. Open until 10:30pm. Priv rm 250. Air cond. No pets. Valet pkg.
Lille's Ghislaine Arabian has made her mark at the luxurious and oh-so-Parisian Ledoyen. After teaching locals to love Flemish flavors—sauces laced with beer and gin, smoked mussels, gingerbread, and pungent Northern cheeses—she is working wonders outside of her regional register. Thus, while signature dishes like Zeeland oysters with smoked ham and buttermilk, smoked sprats on a potato galette, turbot roasted in beer, or potjevleish (a meaty Flemish terrine) with rhubarb chutney hold their own on the menu, she balances them with, for example, lightly salt-cured salmon poached in milk and served with sorrel hollandaise or roasted sweetbreads marinated with smoked garlic and flanked by melting endives. Such marvels have their price, of course, but we say they're worth it! C 550-850. M 290 (lunch), 520 & 590 (dinner).

11/20 Lloyd's Bar

23, rue Treilhard - 01 45 63 21 23, fax 01 45 63 36 83
Closed Sat, Sun lunch, Dec 24-Jan 2. Open until 10:30pm. Terrace dining.
Lloyd's is a little bit of London in Paris. The clubby dining room, with its dark paneling adorned by horse and hunting prints, is the scene of decent if not exciting meals. Be sure to give our regards to Daniel, a veteran waiter with a rather unpredictable character! C 320. M 185 (dinner).

Lucas Carton

9, pl. de la Madeleine
01 42 65 22 90, fax 01 42 65 06 23
Closed Sat lunch, Aug 2-24. Open until 10:30pm. Priv rm 14. Air cond. No pets. Valet pkg.
In a magnificent Belle Époque dining room warmed by mellow woodwork, Alain Senderens and his chef, Bernard Gueneron, propose a

clever blend of Senderens's most celebrated creations—canard Apicius, foie gras de canard steamed in a cabbage leaf, red-mullet fillets with olives, lemon, and capers—and a (very) few recent inventions. Outstanding among the latter are the pan-roast of frogs' legs and asparagus paired with hot gingered crab and cooling hollandaise sauce; sea bream with thyme-scented potatoes and cuttlefish ravioli; and crisp-crusted veal sweetbreads with crayfish and popcorn. Every recipe is intelligently composed and the execution is invariably faultless. Inspired desserts; legendary cellar. C 1,000. M 395 (weekday lunch).

 ## La Luna

69, rue du Rocher - 01 42 93 77 61, fax 01 40 08 02 44
Closed Sun. Open until 11pm. Air cond.
The tides deposit first-quality fish at La Luna's door, and the kitchen's modern approach to seafood (brief cooking times, light sauces) enhances its natural flavors. The menu changes from day to day, but you could start out with an ultrafresh carpaccio of sea bream and red mullet, then go on to pan-roasted baby lotte sparked with lemon, or skate with a lively sauce gribiche. Summary wine list, though the choices are good. C 350.

12/20 La Maison d'Alsace

3, av. des Champs-Élysées
01 53 93 97 00, fax 01 53 93 97 09
Open daily 24 hours. Priv rm 80. Terrace dining. Air cond.
Since this lively brasserie never closes, any time's a good time for perfect oysters, delicious sauerkraut, and fresh Alsatian wines. Expect a hospitable welcome, whatever the hour. C 200-400. M 123 (weekday dinner, wine incl), 178.

 ## Maison Blanche

15, av. Montaigne
01 47 23 55 99, fax 01 47 20 09 56
Closed Sat lunch, Sun, Aug. Open until 11pm. Priv rm 50. Terrace dining. Air cond. Valet pkg.
Here atop the Théâtre des Champs-Élysées, diners look out on the glittering dome of the Invalides, the shimmering Seine, and the handsome buildings that line the quais. In contrast, the dining room sports a spare, vaguely Californian look. The service, though chilly, is efficient and the cellar ranges wide. So far so good, you say, but how about the food? It's very good indeed: José Martinez's talent shines brightest in dishes that blend simplicity and sophistication: sweet peppers stuffed with lamb's trotters, for example, or duck pie with a snappy herb salad. C 400.

 ## La Maison Porte Bonheur

12, av. de Wagram
01 42 27 69 82, fax 01 44 09 90 70
Open daily until 11:30pm. Air cond.

A blessed change from the surrounding fast-food outlets, this "Lucky House" offers delicate steamed dumplings, fragrant Thai soups and salads, seafood and vegetables grilled on a hot stone, and warming stews served in individual pots. C 200-250. M 65, 85.

 ## Le Marcande

52, rue de Miromesnil
01 42 65 19 14, fax 01 40 76 03 27
Closed Sat, Sun, Aug. Open until 10pm. Terrace dining.
The well-spaced tables in an elegant setting punctuated by paintings are not always crowded. Still, Le Marcande's team is betting on its good 240 F menu and revamped *carte* to attract discriminating diners. Best bets are the hot foie gras on rösti potatoes with onion compote, grilled duck au jus accompanied by wonderful country-style fries, and a high and handsome Saint-Honoré pastry. C 275. M 240.

 ## La Marée

1, rue Daru - 01 43 80 20 00, fax 01 48 88 04 04
Closed Sat, Sun, Jul 26-Aug 27. Open until 10:30pm. Priv rm 32. Air cond. Valet pkg.
Seafood naturally rates top billing at La Marée, a restaurant named for the tide. Cast your eye down the long menu for the langoustines encased in an ideally crisp batter coating, or grilled pike perch poised on a bed of roasted vegetable julienne. To partner the cellar's fabulous Bordeaux, you'll also find a first-rate tenderloin of Charollais beef, roast pigeon, and veal kidney. Precise, classic cooking for a conservative, well-heeled clientele. C 600. M 270 (from 6:45pm to 8:15pm).

 ## Marius et Janette

4, av. George-V - 01 47 23 41 88, fax 01 47 23 07 19
Open daily until 11:30pm. Priv rm 10. Terrace dining. Air cond. Valet pkg.
Not even a fire could destroy the unsinkable Marius et Jeannette, now shipshape again and back afloat with a seaworthy décor of glowing wood and polished brass. A cosmopolitan crowd watches approvingly as waiters flambé fennel-flavored sea bass (270 F per person) and deliver pricey portions of grilled lobster (480 F). Still, ingredients are of pristine quality (note the exquisitely fresh seafood salad), and not every item is stratospherically priced. To drink, try a wine from Bandol or Cassis. C 450. M 300, 120 (children).

 ## Maxim's

3, rue Royale - 01 42 65 27 94, fax 01 40 17 02 91
Closed Sun off-seas, Sun & Mon in Jul-Aug. Open until 10:30pm. Priv rm 80. Air cond. Valet pkg.
Pierre Cardin, owner of Maxim's since 1981, decided that he'd served his last plateful of homard à l'américaine and other such culinary chestnuts. He hired Michel Kerever, a respected Breton chef, to rejuvenate what had become a rather fusty menu. The dining room, thank

goodness, is as glorious as ever: Czar Nicholas, the Duke and Duchess of Windsor, Maria Callas and the other legendary denizens of Maxim's in its heyday would surely feel right at home. Kerever's light, exciting menu features rabbit roasted with rosemary and Noirmoutier potatoes, a pan roast of fresh morels and asparagus, and sole on a bed of artichokes, onions, and leeks. Expect to pay a hefty sum, however, to sup in these historic surroundings. Even the cellar's more modest wines are awfully expensive. C 600-1,000.

L'Obélisque

Hôtel de Crillon, 10, pl. de la Concorde
01 44 71 15 15, fax 01 44 71 15 02
Closed Aug, hols. Open until 10:30pm. Priv rm 140. Air cond. Valet pkg.
To eat at the Hôtel de Crillon without breaking the bank, try its other, less formal restaurant. You'll still benefit from top-notch service and a menu supervised by Dominique Bouchet, the new chef of Les Ambassadeurs (see above). The food is classic bistro fare: traditional joue de bœuf in a wine sauce, sea bream roasted with lemon. Sixteen wines are offered by the glass or half-liter jug. C 300-400. M 270.

Le Patio

Hôtel de Crillon, 10, pl. de la Concorde
01 44 71 15 15, fax 01 44 71 15 02
Open mid May-mid Sep for lunch only until 2:30pm. Valet pkg.
Another way to enjoy the Crillon's atmosphere is to lunch in the flower-filled inner courtyard, which is open in the summertime and when the weather permits it. On offering are such cold dishes as shellfish velouté with asparagus, red mullet atop ratatouille and fruit-of-the-season tart. C 350.

Au Petit Montmorency

26, rue Jean-Mermoz or 5, rue Rabelais
01 42 25 11 19
Closed Sat, Sun, Aug. Open until 10pm. Priv rm 12. Air cond. No pets.
Here is cuisine that flatters one's cravings for rich, generous food. Daniel Bouché coaxes voluptuous flavors out of his superb ingredients; in fall and winter, when the season for truffles, game, and wild mushrooms rolls around Bouché is in his glory, offering grilled cèpes with foie gras spread on toast, warm pigeon pâté, macaroni gratin ennobled with morels and truffles, hare à la royale, or a winy civet of boar flanked by sauerkraut, pears, and chutney. The cellar's venerable vintages are ever-so-tempting, but they'll make the bill even harder to swallow. C 450-800.

12/20 Le Petit Yvan

1 bis, rue Jean Mermoz
01 42 89 49 65, fax 01 42 89 30 95
Closed Sat lunch, Sun. Open until midnight. Priv rm 24. Terrace dining. Air cond.
Yvan's little annex pulls in a lively, friendly crew with an unbeatable all-in menu that features—for example—scrambled eggs with roasted tomatoes, steak tartare (minced by hand, not by machine) flanked by crispy french fries, and a rum-soaked savarin for dessert. Wine and coffee incur no extra charge. It's all served on bistro tables in a colorful, split-level dining room. M 138.

Le Régence

Hôtel Plaza Athénée, 25, av. Montaigne
01 53 67 65 00, fax 01 53 67 66 66
Closed Feb school hols, Jul 21-Aug 10. Open until 10:15pm. Garden dining. Air cond. Valet pkg.
Changes have not spared the Plaza Athénée among top hotels of Paris. Young chef Éric Briffard, trained by Meneau and Robuchon, blends colors and flavors in perfect harmony. This style of cooking should work very well for the Plaza's clientele. For example: a John Dory in curry with melting eggplants cooked to perfection with an oriental twist; finish with a sweet roasted peach with pineapple and lavender syrup. Perfect service. C 550-800. M 310 (weekday lunch), 580.

12/20 Le Relais Vermeer

Hôtel Golden Tulip Saint-Honoré, 218, rue du Fg-St-Honoré - 01 49 53 03 03, fax 01 40 75 02 00
Closed Sat lunch, Sun, Aug. Open until 10pm. Priv rm 200. Air cond. Pkg.
A luxurious restaurant for a luxurious hotel, owned by the Dutch Golden Tulip chain. Don't bother looking for an inventive dish on the menu: there aren't any. And the quality of ingredients has declined of late, judging by the crab millefeuille and the peppery sea bream with artichokes. C 220-350. M 180.

Les Saveurs

Sofitel Champs-Élysées, 8, rue Jean-Goujon
01 43 59 52 41, fax 01 42 25 06 59
Closed Sat, Sun, Aug. Open until 10:30pm. Priv rm 200. Terrace dining. Air cond. Valet pkg.
If you book a table here, you will able to try Didier Lanfray's fresh cooking: vegetable terrine (pressé de légumes) abetted by a truffle infusion, or the bold, full-flavored lotte with green mangos and fresh pasta. Tempting desserts, too, and attentive service. C 210-250. M 165 (wine incl).

12/20 Sébillon Élysées

66, rue Pierre-Charron
01 43 59 28 15, fax 01 43 59 30 00
Open daily until midnight. Air cond. Valet pkg.
As in the sister establishment in Neuilly (see *Paris Suburbs*), excellent but expensive shellfish platters are followed by Sébillon's famous leg of lamb, cooked to rosy tenderness and carved before your eyes. Elegant décor, energetic service. C 245. M 180 (wine & coffee incl).

Shing Jung

7, rue Clapeyron - 01 45 22 21 06
Closed Sat, Sun lunch. Open until 10:30pm. No pets.
Pkg. No cards.
The owner of this modest establishment will try to convince you that Koreans are more generous than their Japanese neighbors. Indeed, a colossal assortment of raw fish, listed on the menu as "medium", comprised sea bream, salmon, tuna, brill, and mackerel. For the same money most Japanese places would serve about one-quarter the quantity. Also on hand are jellyfish salad, barbecued beef strips, a hotpot of vegetables and beef, and stuffed lentil-flour crêpes. Delicious and incredibly inexpensive. **C** 150. **M** 69 (weekday lunch), 75.

 Shozan

11, rue de La Trémoille
01 47 23 37 32, fax 01 47 23 67 30
Closed Sat lunch, Sun. Open until 11pm. Terrace dining. Air cond. Valet pkg.
Show-biz celebrities and fashion honchos have given this new Japanese restaurant their stamp of approval. They settle into the discreetly handsome brown-and-beige dining room to feast on superb sashimi and lightly grilled fish, or the more complex (and most rewarding) ginger-steamed bass with leeks. Meat eaters are not neglected: the beef tenderloin in dashi broth is delectable. Shozan's owners produce sake in Japan, so there is quite a choice on hand for tasting here. **C** 400. **M** 175 (weekday lunch, wine incl).

 Le Stresa

7, rue Chambiges - 01 47 23 51 62
Closed Sat dinner, Sun, Aug, Dec 20-Jan 3. Open until 10:30pm. Priv rm 12. Terrace dining. Air cond. Pkg.
Le Stresa's dining room is always full of press, fashion, and movie people (Sharon Stone was spotted here recently) who love the antipasti drizzled with fruity Tuscan olive oil, the spinach ravioli, calf's liver, and smooth tiramisù prepared by Marco Faiola. Claudio and Toni Faiola seat their guests with a sure social sense of who's up, who's in, who's out. **C** 450.

La Table du Marché

14, rue de Marignan
01 40 76 34 44, fax 01 40 76 34 37
Closed Sat lunch, Sun. Open until 11pm. Air cond. Valet pkg.
The Paris annex of Christophe Leroy's well-known Saint-Tropez restaurant was launched with considerable media brouhaha. Alas, it provides little in the way of warmth, charm, or good food (a grilled vegetable assortment included cold, oily eggplant; the salade de coquillages et vongoles looked more like plain potato salad...). High prices in line with the smart address, but not with the quality of what's in one's plate. **C** 200. **M** 160 (weekdays).

 Taillevent

15, rue Lamennais
01 44 95 15 01, fax 01 42 25 95 18
Closed Sat, Sun, Aug. Open until 10:30pm. Priv rm 32. No pets. Valet pkg.
Refined yet graceful, elegant but never stiff, the tone at Taillevent is set by Jean-Claude Vrinat, a restaurateur whose sole standard is perfection: each detail of the décor and the menu is calculated to provide utter comfort and well-being. While not boldly creative, the kitchen is far from stodgy. Simpler offerings underscore the pristine quality of the ingredients: seared Breton langoustines, for example, in a lightly creamed broth or sea bass anointed with olive oil and accompanied by slow-roasted vegetables. Still, the classic repertoire provides pleasures of its own: why turn down a chance to savor the rich, resonant flavors of a truffled game pie filled with venison, duck and pheasant? The cheese board is exceptional, and desserts invite you to splurge. Incomparable cellar; silken service. **C** 850.

 Chez Tante Louise

41, rue Boissy-d'Anglas
01 42 65 06 85, fax 01 45 65 28 19
Closed Sat, Sun, Aug. Open until 10:15pm. Priv rm 12. Air cond.
The regulars love being pampered in this snug little spot, where a smiling staff serves Michel Lerouet's lightened versions of traditional French favorites. The single-price menu offers great value, and there is a nicely balanced cellar to boot. **C** 320. **M** 190.

 Tong Yen

1 bis, rue Jean Mermoz
01 42 25 04 23, fax 01 45 63 51 57
Closed Aug 1-25. Open until 12:15am. Terrace dining. Air cond.
The quietly attractive dining room, punctuated with fresh flowers, plays host to personalities from stage and screen, who come to enjoy precisely cooked and seasoned Chinese specialties: Peking dumplings, chicken glazed with honey and vinegar, salt-and-pepper shrimp, and the like. To drink, order a cool, white Sancerre. **C** 300-350.

12/20 Le "30"

"Fauchon", 30, pl. de la Madeleine
01 47 42 56 58, fax 01 47 42 96 02
Closed Sun. Open until 10:30pm. Terrace dining. Air cond.
Whoever dreamed up the name (Le Trente—30—is the building's address) of Fauchon's restaurant won't win any prizes for creativity, but the decorator might, for its "Roman fantasy" interior. Mostly classic, with some bold touches of spice, Bruno Deligne's menu lists very good oysters with celery-root purée (but an otherwise tasty turbot was spoiled by indigestible beans). The stupendous pastries are crafted by Sébastien Gaudard. **C** 310-450. **M** 259 (lunch, wine & coffee incl), 245 (dinner).

Chez Vong

"Aux Champs-Élysées," 27, rue du Colisée
01 43 59 77 12, fax 01 43 59 59 27
Closed Sun. Open until midnight. Priv rm 60. Air cond. Valet pkg.
Here's everyone's dream of a Chinese restaurant: embroidered silk, furniture inlaid with mother-of-pearl, lots of little nooks, an air of mystery, and dishes named "quail in a nest of happiness" or "merry shrimps." The cooking is quite well done. Oddly enough, the cellar is rich in fine (and costly) claret. **C 300.**

 ## Yvan

1 bis, rue Jean-Mermoz
01 43 59 18 40, fax 01 42 89 30 95
Closed Sat lunch, Sun. Open until midnight. Air cond. Valet pkg.
Yvan Zaplatilek is café society's darling, but he is also a hard-working chef who gives his customers very good food at moderate prices in a most elegant setting. The menu is primarily French, with an occasional Belgian touch here and there (sole waterzoï, veal kidney braised in dark beer). **C 300. M 178** (weekday lunch), **168 & 298** (dinner).

9TH ARRONDISSEMENT

Postal code	75009

 ## L'Alsaco ☺

10, rue Condorcet - 01 45 26 44 31
Closed Sat lunch, Sun, 1 wk in May, Aug. Open until 11pm. Priv rm 45.
Beyond the unremarkable façade is an authentic Alsatian *winstub*, decked out in traditional painted wood paneling. L'Al- saco serves generous renditions of choucroute garnie, cream and onion tart, and potatoes with melted Munster cheese, which now deserve a toque. To drink, there are Rieslings galore, and a huge cache of clear fruit brandies. **C 150. M 87, 170** (wine incl).

 ## Auberge Landaise ☺

23, rue Clauzel - 01 48 78 74 40
Closed Sun, Aug 10-20. Priv rm 50. Pkg.
In a rustic setting conducive to a hearty tuck-in, Dominique and Éric Morin treat their customers to cassoulet, foie gras, braised duck with wild mushrooms, and good grills. Cooking times are not always spot-on, but the flavors are full and robust. Expensive little cellar; superb Armagnacs. **C 280. M 130** (dinner), **180.**

Looking for a celebrated chef? Refer to the Index.

11/20 Le Bistrot des Deux Théâtres

18, rue Blanche - 01 45 26 41 43, fax 01 48 74 08 92
Open daily until 12:30am. Air cond.
A bistro with a British accent, in an improbable neighborhood. The menu is a pretty good deal, what with its duck liver pâté, saffron-spiced scallops, and iced nougatine with raspberry coulis. **M 169** (wine incl).

 ## Bistrot Papillon

6, rue Papillon - 01 47 70 90 03, fax 01 48 24 05 59
Closed Sat, Sun. Open until 10pm. Air cond.
The cozy ambience fits Jean-Yves Guion's soothing menu, made up of long-standing favorites and some good "market specials." Reliably fine ingredients go into his scallop terrine, herbed duck breast, and iced honey vacherin. Balanced cellar. **C 210-310. M 140.**

 ## La Casa Olympe

48, rue Saint-Georges
01 42 85 26 01, fax 01 45 26 49 33
Closed Sat, Sun, Aug, 1 wk at Christmas. Open until 11pm. Air cond. No pets.
Olympe is at home in the former Casa Miguel, long the city's cheapest deal, with a philanthropically priced 5 F set meal. The current menu reflects Olympe at her best. Her fans fall eagerly onto such warming dishes as cumin-spiced calf's foot sausage, pumpkin soup dotted with mussels, and roast shoulder of Sisteron lamb. Unpretentious wine list. The premises are small (not to say cramped) though prettily painted in warm tones of yellow and burnt sienna. **C 280. M 190.**

 ## Charlot

"Roi des Coquillages," 81, bd de Clichy (pl. de Clichy) - 01 53 20 48 00, fax 01 53 20 48 09
Open daily until 1am. Priv rm 20. Air cond. Pkg.
A fine view of the Place de Clichy, a warm welcome, and attentive service will take your mind off the overbearing Art Deco interior. Sparkling fresh oysters, plentiful shellfish assortments, bouillabaisse à la marseillaise, and lobsters prepared every possible way are the staples here. **C 350. M 169, 185.**

 ## Chez Catherine

65, rue de Provence - 01 45 26 72 88
Closed Sat, Sun, Mon dinner, Aug, 1 wk beg Jan. Open until 10pm.
It's no easy feat to find a decent restaurant up here near the major department stores. But we did it! Catherine's sleek bistro provides well-wrought classics based on excellent ingredients: minted lamb terrine, salmon with lentils, spiced sea-bass fillet, and duck confit merit your close attention. Frédéric tends the cellar of astutely selected growers' wines. **C 180-200.**

12/20 Les Diamantaires

60, rue La Fayette · 01 47 70 78 14, fax 01 44 83 02 73
Open daily until 11:30pm. Air cond.
Greek food cooked by Kurds, served by Armenians to a mostly Jewish clientele in a Lebanese-style setting: the mixture is a whole lot more peaceable than it sounds! Delicious Byzantine mezes, meatballs, and skewered lamb, washed down by tasty Greek wines. C 140-200. M 78 (weekday lunch), 125, 150.

I Golosi

6, rue de la Grange-Batelière
01 48 24 18 63, fax 01 45 23 18 96
Closed Sat dinner, Sun, Aug. Open until midnight. Air cond. Pkg.
Enter this bistro from the Passage Verdeau to discover two levels decorated in a style we can only call "1950s Italian." You can order rabbit with wild thyme, chicken dressed with balsamic vinegar, and nettle risotto, accompanied by irresistible Italian wines assembled by a passionate oenophile. A toque this year. C 120-200.

12/20 Le Grand Café Capucines

4, bd des Capucines
01 43 12 19 00, fax 01 43 12 19 09
Open daily 24 hours. Terrace dining. Air cond.
The waiter won't pull a face if you order just one course—a shellfish assortment, salmon tartare, or a grilled pig's trotter. The extravagant décor is a replica of a Roaring Twenties *café boulevardier*. C 280. M 123 (dinner, after 11pm, wine incl), 169, 185.

Les Muses

Hôtel Scribe, 1, rue Scribe
01 44 71 24 26, fax 01 44 71 24 64
Closed Sat, Sun, hols, Aug. Open until 10:30pm. Priv rm 80. Air cond. Valet pkg.
The muse of interior design was off duty the day the hotel Scribe's basement restaurant was decorated. And the chef's inspiration has its ups and downs too, judging from our most recent visit (overcooked pike perch, a fine lobster fricassée served a few degrees too cool). Good cheese board, and there's an array of alluring sweets. Interesting list of growers' wines. C 300-400. M 270.

L'Œnothèque

20, rue St-Lazare · 01 48 78 08 76, fax 01 40 16 10 27
Closed Sat, Sun, hols, 2 wks in Aug. Open until 11pm. Priv rm 40. Air cond.
Daniel Hallée was the sommelier at Jamin before he opened his restaurant-cum-wine shop. Grand vintages at attractive prices and interesting lesser-known growths partner such market-fresh offerings as baby leeks mimosa, smoked-haddock salad, stewed oxtail with al dente vegetables, and excellent grilled fish. Superb collection of Cognacs. C 350.

Opéra Restaurant

"Café de la Paix," 5, pl. de l'Opéra
01 40 07 30 10, fax 01 40 07 33 86
Closed Sat, Sun, Aug. Open until 11pm. No pets. Valet pkg.
Thanks to the efforts of Christian Le Squer, the cuisine now lives up to the restaurant's opulent Second Empire setting. Suitably luxurious (and delicious) are the cream of cèpes with foie gras and duck cracklings, codfish in a green-olive cream, roast pigeon, and cinnamon-scented roasted figs. Rely on the competent sommelier for help with the wine list. C 340. M 240 (lunch), 345 (wine incl).

12/20 Au Petit Riche

25, rue Le Peletier · 01 47 70 68 68, fax 01 48 24 10 79
Closed Sun. Open until 12:15am. Priv rm 45. Air cond.
The brass trim, mirrors, and woodwork of this nostalgic bistro sparkle and gleam. The cooking is of the honest, satisfying sort: coq au vin de Chinon, calf's head sauce gribiche, sole meunière. Excellent choice of Loire Valley wines. C 250. M 160 (weekday lunch, Sat), 135-175 (weekday dinner, Sat).

Sinago

17, rue de Maubeuge · 01 48 78 11 14
Closed Sun, Aug. Open until 10:30pm.
Wonderful Cambodian cooking is served in this vest-pocket eatery (there's only room for twenty). Savor the amazing crêpe stuffed with saffron-stained pork, fish spiced with coriander and ginger, or broth perfumed with lemongrass and enriched with plump dumplings. C 150. M 55 (lunch).

La Table d'Anvers

2, pl. d'Anvers
01 48 78 35 21, fax 01 45 26 66 67
Closed Sat lunch, Sun. Open until 11:30pm. Priv rm 30. Air cond.
While so many chefs fall back on a "safe," reassuring repertoire of neo-bourgeois and bistro dishes to hide their lack of inspiration, Christian Conticini invents and reinvents flavor combinations with a wizardry that is nothing short of staggering. If you're tempted by the prospect of a real gastronomic adventure, we suggest you trek up to his Table at the foot of Montmartre and prepare for a feast! Choose one of the intriguing "theme" menus (featuring novel vegetables, rare spices, or "just desserts"...), or explore an exciting *carte* that is keyed to the seasons. The options are all so enticing that we usually just close our eyes and pick at random! The astonishing desserts are crafted by Christian's brother, Philippe Conticini. C 500. M 180 (weekday lunch), 250 (weekday dinner).

11/20 La Taverne Kronenbourg

24, bd des Italiens · 01 47 70 16 64, fax 01 42 47 13 91

Open daily until 2am. Priv rm 100. Terrace dining. Air cond.
The last of the *cafés-concerts* on the Grands Boulevards (live music nightly) serves robust, unpretentious brasserie fare: shellfish, pork knuckle with cabbage, sauerkraut, and fine Alsatian wines. C 200. M 140 (wine incl).

 ## Venantius

Hôtel Ambassador, 16, bd Haussmann
01 48 00 06 38, fax 01 42 46 19 84
Closed Sat, Sun, 1 wk in Feb, Aug. Open until 10:30pm. Air cond. Valet pkg.
Changes, changes, changes... Jean-Claude Troisville, from the Concorde Saint-Lazare, tries his best to fill up the large dining room which works well with local businessmen at lunch, but somewhat stale for dinner: so is the food. C 350-450. M 220 (weekday lunch), 180 & 280 (weekday dinner).

 ## Wally le Saharien

36, rue Rodier - 01 42 85 51 90, fax 01 42 86 08 35
Closed Sun. Open until 11:30pm. Priv rm 60. Air cond. No pets. No cards.
Wally has pitched his tent not far from Pigalle, in a setting accented with carved screens, crimson carpets, and Tuareg-style seating. Topping the list of specialties is his Saharan couscous (no broth, no vegetables), but you can also sample mutton with caramelized skin, pigeon pastilla, and honey cake perfumed with orange-flower water. C 200-300. M 240, 150 (children).

10TH ARRONDISSEMENT

Postal code	75010

 ## 12/20 Brasserie Flo

7, cour des Petites-Écuries
01 42 46 15 80, fax 01 42 47 00 80
Open daily until 1:30am. Air cond. Valet Pkg.
The quintessential Alsatian brasserie, Flo is a jewel: nowhere else will you find the same vivacious atmosphere, superb décor, lively patrons, and delicious sauerkraut, best washed down with carafes of frisky Riesling. C 190-250. M 119 (lunch, wine incl), 189 (dinner, exc Sun), 121 (Sun dinner, wine incl).

 ## Le Canard Laqué Pékinois

34, bd Bonne-Nouvelle
01 47 70 31 65, fax 01 44 79 00 21
Open daily until midnight. Priv rm 80. Air cond.
We're usually suspicious of these oversized Chinese affairs, but Le Canard Laqué is a find. Good dim-sum, salads, and sautéed shrimp to

start, followed by tasty roasted items and a most honorable Peking duck. C 120. M 47 (weekday lunch, wine incl), 58-116 (wine incl).

 ## Le Châteaubriant

23, rue Chabrol - 01 48 24 58 94, fax 01 42 47 09 75
Closed Sun, Mon, Aug. Open until 10:15pm. Air cond. No pets.
From the name you'd never guess that this little dining room tucked away near the Gare de l'Est is a noted Italian restaurant. Save for the rotating roster of daily specials, the menu is immutable. Familiar though they may be, the sardine lasagne with eggplant and the millefeuille de filet de veau are still perfectly delicious and courteously served. Tempting desserts; high prices. C 250-350. M 159.

12/20 Aux Deux Canards

"Chez Catherine," 8, rue du Fbg-Poissonnière
01 47 70 03 23, fax 01 44 83 02 50
Closed Sat lunch, Sun, Jul 20-Aug 20. Open until 10:30pm. Air cond.
This is a place for duck: diners may enjoy the salmon rillettes, magret de canard, canard à l'orange, and tasty desserts in this naively charming bistro with great wines to match. C 220.

12/20 Julien

16, rue du Faubourg-Saint-Denis
01 47 70 12 06, fax 01 42 47 00 65
Open daily until 1:30am. Air cond. Valet pkg.
For the pleasure of dining in these exuberant surroundings (vintage 1880), we are willing to put up with mediocre food. But if you stick to the oysters, the cassoulet, or eggs poached in red wine, you'll leave with a pleasant memory. C 150-230. M 119 (lunch, wine incl), 121 (dinner, after 10pm, wine incl).

 ## Chez Michel

10, rue Belzunce - 01 44 53 06 20
Closed Sun, Mon, Aug. Open until 11pm.
Scion of a family of restaurateurs, Thierry Breton was just doing what came naturally when he decided to become a chef. Just as naturally, his preference is for Breton cuisine, the backbone of his original 168 F single-price menu, which draws gourmets from all over Paris. It features a daring andouille terrine with buckwheat crêpes, kig ha farz (an Armorican boiled dinner of hog jowls and country-cured bacon), and buttery rich kouign-aman cake. He's even unearthed a cheap and cheerful Breton vin de pays to wash these good things down! M 168.

La P'tite Tonkinoise

56, rue du Fg-Poissonnière - 01 42 46 85 98
Closed Sun, Mon, Aug-1st wk of Sep. Open until 10pm.
Old Indochina hands come regularly for a whiff of the nostalgia that is virtually palpable here. The chef is a pony-tailed titan, while his wife is indeed a tiny Tonkinoise. Their menu

features crisp egg rolls, grilled shrimp in rice sauce (they're not on the menu, so ask for them), duck breast rubbed with five-spice powder, and a savory chicken wing stuffed with onion curry. C 200-240. M 150 (lunch).

11/20 Le Réveil du 10e

35, rue du Château-d'Eau - 01 42 41 77 59
Closed Sat during school hols, Sun, wk of Aug 15. Open until 8pm, Tue 9:30pm exc during school hols. Pkg.
A hearty Auvergnat welcome awaits in this modest bistro, along with well-chosen wines, house-made terrines, and robust daily specials. C 120.

12/20 Terminus Nord

23, rue de Dunkerque
01 42 85 05 15, fax 01 40 16 13 98
Open daily until 12:30am. Priv rm 12. Air cond.
Part of the brasserie group of which Flo (see above) is the flagship, the Terminus serves exactly the same food as the rest of the fleet. Enjoy the atmosphere, the gay 1925 décor, and look no farther than the sauerkraut, oysters, and grills for a satisfying meal. Nimble service. C 150-230. M 119 (lunch exc Sun, wine incl), 121 (dinner, after 10pm, wine incl), 180 (dinner, Sun, wine incl), 62 (children, drink incl).

11TH ARRONDISSEMENT

Postal code	75011

12/20 L'Aiguière

37 bis, rue de Montreuil
01 43 72 42 32, fax 01 43 72 96 36
Closed Sat lunch, Sun. Open until 10:30pm. Priv rm 50. Air cond. Pkg.
Pascal Viallet is a dab hand with seafood; his repertoire is rooted in tradition but often shows a pleasing contemporary touch. Eclectic wine list; elegant setting overseen by owner Patrick Masbatin. C 250-320. M 135 (weekdays, wine incl), 175, 248 (wine incl).

 ## Les Amognes

243, rue du Fg-Saint-Antoine - 01 43 72 73 05
Closed Sun, Mon lunch, 2 wks in Aug. Open until 11pm. Terrace dining.
Thierry Coué has crossed rich and costly ingredients off his shopping list. The food he serves in his country-style dining room is full of earthy character: warm oysters and leeks ravigote, sweetbreads with cumin-spiced cucumber confit, crêpe stuffed with an eggplant compote redolent of cardamom. The cellar is filled with interesting finds. He deserves another toque. M 180.

 ## Astier

44, rue Jean-Pierre-Timbaud - 01 43 57 16 35
Closed 1 wk end Apr, Aug, Dec 23-Jan 2. Open until 11pm. Air cond.
For 135 F, Jean-Luc Clerc will set you up with a slab of savory chicken-liver terrine, followed by rabbit in mustard sauce or a duo of sea whelks and shrimp, nicely aged cheeses, and rich chocolate mousse for dessert. The bistro atmosphere is good-humored and noisy. Intelligent, wide-ranging cellar. M 135.

12/20 Bistrot Lyonnais

8, rue de la Main-d'Or - 01 48 05 77 10
Closed Sat lunch, Sun. Open until 11pm. No cards.
A genuine Lyonnais bouchon, where you can tuck into terrine beaujolaise, rabbit rillettes, and lots of other regional specialties. Wash them down with a *pot* of Beaujolais. C 65-140.

 ## Chardenoux

1, rue Jules-Vallès - 01 43 71 49 52
Closed Sat lunch, Sun, Aug. Open until 10:30pm. No pets.
In the heart of the old cabinet-makers' district, this graceful corner bistro (a registered Belle Époque building) flaunts its charms of marble, fanciful moldings, and etched glass. It's a setting peculiarly suited to Bernard Passavant's simple, generous cooking: eggs poached in red wine, daube de bœuf à la provençal and the like. Connoisseur's cellar. C 200-270.

Khun Akorn

8, av. de Taillebourg
01 43 56 20 03, fax 01 40 09 18 44
Closed Mon. Open until 11pm. Priv rm 80. Terrace dining. Pkg.
Thai cooking of rare refinement, served in an evocative, exotic setting. The tong-sai (assorted appetizers) set the mood for what follows. The curries are lighter than their Indian cousins, but Thai chilis make their fiery presence felt elsewhere on the menu. C 250. M 129 (lunch), 195-325.

Mansouria

11, rue Faidherbe - 01 43 71 00 16, fax 01 40 24 21 97
Closed Mon lunch, Sun. Open until 11:30pm. Terrace dining. Air cond.
The trendy Bastille crowd comes here for a taste of Morocco: honeyed pumpkin purée, Moroccan crêpes, a light and flavorful couscous, and mellow, long-simmered tagines. Charming reception and service. C 250. M 99 & 135 (weekday lunch), 168, 280 (wine incl).

11/20 Jacques Mélac

42, rue Léon-Frot - 01 43 70 59 27
Closed Mon dinner, Sat, Sun, Aug, end Dec-beg Jan. Open until 10:30pm. Terrace dining. Air cond.
One of the city's most popular wine bars. The countrified menu proposes charcuteries from the Aveyron region, good cheeses, and exemplary wines. C 200.

11/20 **Chez Paul**

13, rue de Charonne - 01 47 00 34 57
Open daily until 12:30am. Terrace dining. Pkg.
This traditional bistro stands out from its
determinedly hip neighbors. Come here for rillettes, rabbit stuffed with chèvre, and chocolate
charlotte. C 200.

 Chez Philippe 😊

106, rue de la Folie-Méricourt - 01 43 57 33 78
*Closed Sat, Sun, Aug. Open until 10:30pm. Air
cond. Garage pkg.*
The menu written in purple ink is nothing if
not eclectic: herrings Bismarck, grilled lobster, a
monumental cassoulet, paella (the best in Paris),
York ham with macaroni au gratin, beef bourguignon, turbot Dugléré, and old-fashioned
braised hare. Great Burgundies at giveaway
prices only add to the gaiety. C 350-450.

 **Le Repaire
de Cartouche** 😊

99, rue Amelot or 8, bd des Filles-du-Calvaire
01 47 00 25 86
Closed Sat lunch, Sun. Open until 10:30pm.
Emmanuel Salabert, an experienced, skillful
chef, presides over this shrine to Southwestern
cuisine. Settle down in the wood-paneled dining
room and sample foie gras steamed in a cabbage
leaf, mussels in a creamy sauce, pork with
prunes and celery, and flaky Landais apple pie
laced with Armagnac. Interesting cellar,
manageably priced. C 230. M 155 (wine incl).

 Le Roudoulié 😊

16, rue de la Vacquerie - 01 43 79 27 46
*Closed Sat lunch, Sun, Aug 1-15. Open until
10:30pm. Air cond.*
Remember to book in advance (especially for
lunch), since Le Roudoulié's charming service,
jolly atmosphere and generous, inexpensive
food have plenty of fans. The menu has a rustic
Southwestern accent: hot duck pâté studded
with cèpes and foie gras, pot-au-feu de canard,
and scallops with oyster mushrooms. C 200-300.
M 65 (weekday lunch, wine incl), 110, 210.

 La Table Richelieu

276, bd Voltaire - 01 43 72 31 23
*Closed Sat lunch, Mon. Open until 11pm. Priv rm
40. Terrace dining. Air cond.*
For fresh seafood, you couldn't do much better
than this bright, comfortable restaurant, where
Daniel Rousseau treats customers to sparkling
shellfish assortments and delicious lobster in
Sauternes with fresh pasta. Tasty desserts
(chocolate millefeuille with morello cherries and
pistachio sauce). C 300. M 149 (exc lunch Sun,
wine incl), 200, 260.

 Thaï Éléphant

43-45, rue de la Roquette
01 47 00 42 00, fax 01 47 00 45 44
*Closed Sat lunch, May 1, 3 days at Christmas. Open
until midnight, Sun 11:45pm. Air cond.*
Filled with flowers, pagodas, and cheerful
waiters, the Thaï Éléphant is not your run-of-the-
mill Asian eatery. The menu is miles long, and
many of the dishes are fiercely fiery (the hottest
are marked with three red elephants). The
shrimp curry is quite fine, and so are the
Fomyang soup and the garlicky pork. For dessert, try the delicious jasmine tart. C 280. M 150
(weekday lunch), 275, 300.

 Le Villaret

13, rue Ternaux - 01 43 57 75 56
*Dinner only. Closed Sun, 10 days in May, Aug, 2
wks at Christmas. Open until 1am. Air cond.*
The former owner of Astier (see above)
launched this engaging bistro, where an oft-
revised menu of scrupulously prepared cuisine
bourgeoise is served with bargain-priced wines.
It's a winning formula! C 200.

12TH ARRONDISSEMENT

Postal code	**75012**

 La Flambée 😊

4, rue Taine - 01 43 43 21 80
*Closed Sun, Aug 3-19. Open until 10:15pm. Terrace
dining. Air cond. Pkg.*
The dining room shows some signs of wear,
but never mind. Michel Roustan warms things
up nicely with his traditional Southwestern
charcuteries, tasty confit de canard with sautéed
potatoes, and excellent warm apple tart. The
good wines are moderately priced. C 250. M 125,
199 (wine incl).

 La Gourmandise

271, av. Daumesnil - 01 43 43 94 41
*Closed Sun, Mon dinner, Aug 3-25. Open until
10:30pm. Garage pkg.*
Gourmand or gourmet, you'll be tempted to
indulge in Alain Denoual's excellent set meals,
the less expensive of which delivers fish terrine
with shellfish fumet, saddle of rabbit confit with
cabbage, and a rich triple-chocolate mousse. A la
carte, the langoustines with a red-tea infusion
and the zippy mango charlotte are both worthy
of note. C 340. M 145, 175, 199 (wine incl), 95
(children).

11/20 **Les Grandes Marches**

6, pl. de la Bastille - 01 43 42 90 32, fax 01 43 44 80 02
*Closed 3 wks in Aug. Open until 1am. Terrace
dining. Air cond.*
Restored around the same time as the Opéra
Bastille was built, this posh brasserie is a fine
spot for a post-performance supper. Oysters and
other shellfish, steaks, and a splendid sea bream

roasted in a salt crust deserve a round of applause. C 260. M 138, 175.

12/20 Le Mange Tout

24, bd de la Bastille - 01 43 43 95 15
Closed Sun, 1 wk in Aug. Open until 11:30pm. Priv rm 18. Terrace dining.
Uncomplicated cooking, served with a smile and a generous hand. Scrambled eggs with morels, skate with capers, andouillette sausage, and clafoutis are the mainstays of a menu rooted in the provinces of France. C 220. M 99.50, 199 (wine incl).

L'Oulette ☺

15, pl. Lachambeaudie - 01 40 02 02 12
Closed Sat lunch, Sun. Open until 10:15pm. Terrace dining.
A charmless cohort of office blocks contributes precious little warmth to the surroundings, but happily, Marcel Baudis can be relied upon to kindle a glow with his spirited Southwestern cooking. He ignited our enthusiasm with a spiced duck pâté, tender Pyrenees lamb with country potatoes, and hefty portion of tomme d'Aspe cheese. The cellar is awash in sturdy wines from the Quercy and thereabouts; the service is most attentive. C 300-400. M 160, 240 (wine incl).

La Plantation

5, rue Jules-César - 01 43 07 64 15
Closed Sat lunch, Sun. Open until 11pm. No pets.
Nouvelle cuisine, Creole-style: blaff de bulots (sea whelks marinated in lime juice and chilis), chicken in pan juices deglazed with pineapple vinegar, and fabulous stuffed crab are expertly handled dishes full of vivid tropical flavors. C 220-300. M 90-100 (weekday lunch), 180 (wine incl), 150-235.

Au Pressoir

257, av. Daumesnil
01 43 44 38 21, fax 01 43 43 81 77
Closed Sat, Sun, Aug. Open until 10pm. Priv rm 40. Air cond. Valet pkg.
Forgotten by most Parisians since the Colonial Exposition closed 60 years ago, the Porte Dorée district is home to a covey of fine restaurants. Le Pressoir numbers among them: chef Henri Séguin cooks with fine ingredients and a generous spirit, shown to advantage in his scallop fricassée with wild mushrooms, codfish brandade with asparagus, or in season a sumptuous hare à la royale. Expensive cellar. C 500-650. M 400.

Le Quincy ☺

28, av. Ledru-Rollin - 01 46 28 46 76
Closed Sat, Sun, Mon, Aug 15-Sep 15. Open until 10pm. Air cond. No cards.
Bobosse, the jovial host, keeps things lively in the dining room, while in the kitchen Jean-Pierre Rouat cooks up zestful bistro dishes rooted in the Berry and Vivarais regions: famously tasty

farmhouse terrine, chicken fricassée, boiled crayfish, and the best stuffed cabbage in town. Delicious Rhône and Loire wines. C 300-400.

Le Saint-Amarante ☺

4, rue Biscornet - 01 43 43 00 08
Closed Sat, Sun, Jul 14-Aug 15. Open until 10:30pm. Terrace dining. No pets.
Tucked in a quiet street near the Opéra-Bastille, a remarkable bistro where lusty food and low prices go hand in hand. Kid terrine, artichokes barigoule, lamb's sweetbreads with mushrooms are washed down with growers' wines priced under 100 F in a crowded, lively setting. C 200 (wine incl).

La Sologne

164, av. Daumesnil
01 43 07 68 97, fax 01 43 44 66 23
Closed Sat lunch, Sun, 1 wk in spring, 2 wks in Aug. Open until 10:30pm, Sat & Sun 11:30pm. Terrace dining. Air cond.
Didier and Virginie Maillet spare no pains to make their patrons feel welcome and well fed. The 155 F menu is most attractive (the offerings change often) and the kitchen highlights game in season. M 155, 210.

Le Train Bleu

Gare de Lyon, 20, bd Diderot
01 43 43 09 06, fax 01 43 43 97 96
Open daily until 11pm. Pkg.
The feast is for your eyes only: an extravagant, colossal, delirious, dazzling décor. The food? Don't miss your train for it... High prices. C 300. M 250 (wine incl).

Au Trou Gascon ☺

40, rue Taine - 01 43 44 34 26, fax 01 43 07 80 55
Closed Sat lunch, Sun, Jul 26-Aug 24, Dec 28-Jan 4. Open until 10pm. Air cond.
Time marches on, but here the mellow décor and familiar menu remain unchanged. Year in, year out, you can order well-cured Chalosse ham, a warm pâté de cèpes in a bright-green parsley jus, truffled chop of milk-fed veal with macaroni gratin, or rich duck and pork cassoulet. A few dishes from the Carré des Feuillants can also be spotted on the list (red mullet with potatoes and marrow, chestnut bouillon with bits of pheasant...). To accompany this robust cooking, Nicole Dutournier recommends wonderful wines from Madiran and Jurançon. C 380. M 220 (weekday lunch), 280 (dinner, wine incl).

11/20 Le Viaduc Café

43, av. Daumesnil - 01 44 74 70 70
Open Sun-Thu until midnight, Fri-Sat 12:30am. Terrace dining.
After browsing around the artisans' shops of the Viaduc des Arts, you can enjoy simple French cooking at this arty café. On offer you'll find salmon tartare, grilled duck breast, and vanilla-scented pain perdu (aka French toast). C 150.

11/20 Les Zygomates
7, rue de Capri - 01 40 19 93 04
Closed Sat lunch, Sun, Aug, last wk of Dec. Open until 10:30pm. No pets.
For starters, there's an earthy salad of pork tongue, followed by grenadier (a firm-fleshed fish) with red-wine butter or pig's tail with morels. The incredible dining room—formerly a butcher shop—is full of *fin de siècle* details. C 200. M 75 (weekday lunch), 130.

13TH ARRONDISSEMENT

| Postal code | 75013 |

L'Anacréon
53, bd Saint-Marcel - 01 43 31 71 18
Closed Sun, Mon, 1 wk in Feb, Aug. Open until 10:30pm. Air cond. No pets.
No-frills surroundings, but the food is full-flavored and unbeatably priced: soy-marinated salmon bundled up in a crêpe purse, veal kidney with mustard sauce and buttery cabbage, light and lively grapefruit gratin. M 120 (lunch), 180 (menu-carte).

12/20 Auberge Etchegorry
Hôtel Vert-Galant, 41, rue Croulebarbe
01 44 08 83 51, fax 01 44 08 83 69
Closed Sun. Open until 10:30pm. Terrace dining.
Come here for hearty Basque food and wines. A cheerful *patron* plates up excellent regional charcuterie, tasty stuffed squid, and generously served quail paupiettes au foie gras. Lots of charm, and a lively atmosphere. C 280. M 135, 210.

Entoto
143, rue Léon-Maurice-Nordman - 01 45 87 08 51
Closed Sun, Mon, 2 wks in Aug. Open until 11pm. No pets. Pkg.
Entoto, or the vegetable kingdom. Spinach, pink lentils with a snap of lime juice, pumpkin, and cracked wheat feature prominently in the generously spiced cuisine of Ethiopia. Meat-eaters will find happiness with lamb's tripe or guinea hen served on a huge crêpe that does double duty as plate and bread. Fabulous coffee. C 150.

La Mer de Chine
159, rue Château-des-Rentiers - 01 45 84 22 49
Closed Tue. Open until 1am. Air cond.
The menu features sautéed ducks' tongues, fried soft-shell crabs (imported from Vietnam), oyster beignets, and gingery carp anointed with

sesame oil. If chop suey is what you want, look elsewhere! C 180. M 64, 72 (weekday lunch).

12/20 Chez Paul
22, rue de la Butte-aux-Cailles
01 45 89 22 11, fax 01 45 80 26 53
Closed Dec 25, Jan 1. Open until midnight. Terrace dining. No pets.
In the heart of the Butte-aux-Cailles district, a corner of old Paris where tourists never go, Chez Paul serves calf's head gribiche, streaky bacon with lentils, sage-scented suckling pig, and other bistro classics. Do stop to admire the magnificent 1930s bar. C 250-290.

Le Petit Marguery
9, bd de Port-Royal - 01 43 31 58 59
Closed Sun, Mon, Aug, Dec 24-Jan 3. Open until 10:15pm. Priv rm 20.
The Cousin brothers aren't sticks-in-the-mud: they're willing to leave the beaten path of bistro fare and offer their patrons crispy ravioli stuffed with langoustines and green apples (delicious!). But they also please their faithful public with down-home favorites delivered by fleet-footed waiters: braised wild mushrooms, terrine de boudin, cod gratin with oysters and asparagus, or compote de coq. The single-price menus help keep costs down. M 165 (weekday lunch, Sat), 205, 450.

Les Vieux Métiers de France
13, bd Auguste-Blanqui
01 45 88 90 03, fax 01 45 80 73 80
Closed Sun, Mon. Open until 10:30pm. Priv rm 16. Air cond.
Onto an austere modern building, Michel Moisan has grafted the most amazing medieval décor of sculpted wood, stained glass, beams, and paintings. What saves all this quaintness from tipping over into kitsch is Moisan's cuisine: pigeon pâté, braised farm chicken with mushrooms, luscious desserts. Amateur service. C 360-460. M 165, 300.

14TH ARRONDISSEMENT

| Postal code | 75014 |

L'Amuse Bouche
186, rue du Château - 01 43 35 31 61
Closed Sat lunch, Sun, Aug 7-20. Open until 10:30pm.
A neighborhood crowd comes here for virtuously priced set meals served in a bright, tiny (just 22 seats) dining room. At lunch there's snail

fricassée, guinea hen with celery-root purée, and dried fruit-and-nut soup spiced with cinnamon. M 140, 168.

 ## L'Angélus

12, rue Joannes (corner of rue Boulitte)
01 45 41 51 65
Open daily until 10:30pm.
The two owners used to be magicians, but there's no hocus-pocus going on in the kitchen. The menu is based on prime ingredients handled with a light touch: try the chicken liver terrine, gutsy andouillette sausage with mustard sauce, and frozen honey nougat. Well-annotated wine list dominated by Burgundy and Bordeaux. M 85-132 (exc Sun, wine incl), 158, 100 (children).

 ## L'Assiette

181, rue du Château - 01 43 22 64 86
Closed Mon, Tue, 1 wk in May, Aug. Open until 10:30pm.
If Lulu's success were due merely to the fact that her prices are high, her customers chic, and her dining room determinedly "working class," it would surely have faded long ago. No, the high and the mighty come here year after year because they love the food. So do we: the ingredients are magnificent and the portions huge. When Lulu puts truffles in a dish, you can see, smell, and taste them! Try her justly famous boudin parmentier, hare civet, mackerel rillettes, and superb sole meunière (it weighs in at 14 oz). But desserts are not her strong suit, as Lulu owns up herself right on the menu! C 300, 480. M 200 (lunch, wine incl).

12/20 Auberge de l'Argoat

27, av. Reille - 01 45 89 17 05
Closed Sat lunch, Sun, Mon dinner, wk of Aug 15. Open until 10pm.
Here's a welcoming, unpretentious little seafood spot, situated across from the Parc Montsouris. Jeannine Gaulon greets diners warmly, while in the kitchen her chef cooks up soupe de poissons, langoustine and artichoke salad, fresh tuna en daube (a bit dry on our last visit), and grilled sea bream. A few meat dishes round out the bill of fare. C 280-300. M 100 (weekday lunch), 180.

11/20 Le Bar à Huîtres

112, bd du Montparnasse - 01 43 20 71 01
Open daily until 2am. Terrace dining. Pkg.
At this popular oyster bar you can, if you wish, order and eat just one oyster—but that would be a shame. Six or a dozen Belons, fines, or spéciales would surely be more satisfying, as are the gargantuan shellfish platters (200 to 600 F). The cooked fish dishes, however, are skippable. C 220. M 98, 198, 89 (children).

12/20 Bistrot du Dôme

1, rue Delambre - 01 43 35 32 00
Open daily until 11pm. Terrace dining. Air cond.
Flipping-fresh seafood is presented with becoming simplicity at this fashionable spot: fea-

tured are crispy fried smelts, tuna with sauce vierge, and lotte in a garlicky cream sauce. A price savvy wine list features all bottles for 99 F, or by the glass at 22 F; merry ambience. C 250.

 ## La Cagouille

Opposite 23 rue de l'Ouest,
12, pl. Constantin-Brancusi
01 43 22 09 01, fax 01 45 38 57 29
Open daily until 10:30pm. Priv rm 20. Terrace dining.
At this *bistro du port,* dishes made from the very freshest fish and shellfish (delivered direct from Atlantic ports) are chalked on a blackboard: depending on the day's catch, they might include tiny squid in a garlicky sauce of their own ink, baked black scallops from Brest, fresh fried anchovies, shad in beurre blanc sauce, herbed brill, mackerel with mustard sauce, or thick, juicy sole. If you are content to drink a modest Aligoté or Quincy, your bill will hover around 300 F. But beware if you succumb to the temptations of the finest Cognac collection in Paris (and maybe the world). C 300. M 150, 250 (wine incl), 60 (children).

 ## Le Caroubier

122, av. du Maine - 01 43 20 41 49
Closed Mon, Jul 13-Aug 18. Open until 10:30pm. Air cond.
Do you like couscous? Here you'll find the genuine article: homemade, hand-rolled, and fragrant with spices. Also on offer are a lively eggplant salad, savory pastillas, and succulent tagines, simmered in the best Moroccan tradition. Heartwarming welcome. C 180-220. M 140.

 ## La Chaumière des Gourmets

22, pl. Denfert-Rochereau - 01 43 21 22 59
Closed Sat lunch, Sun, 1st 3 wks of Aug. Open until 10:30pm. Priv rm 12. Terrace dining.
The Chaumière's friendly, provincial dining room still features faded fabric on the walls, the staff carries on with imperturbable diligence, the wine list remains small, and the house repertoire invariably classic. But in this case, no news really is good news: the flavorful duck terrine, entrecôte bordelaise, and frozen nougat on the 165 F menu attest to Jean-Paul Huc's unfailing consistency and flair. C 350. M 165, 245.

12/20 La Coupole

102, bd du Montparnasse
01 43 20 14 20, fax 01 43 35 46 14
Open daily until 2am. Priv rm 200. Air cond.
This Montparnasse landmark, respectfully restored and run by the Flo brasserie group, survives with its mystique intact. The menu bears Flo's unmistakable stamp: exemplary shellfish assortments, grilled meats, and carafes of sprightly house Riesling are delivered by swift, efficient waiters. C 250-350. M 89 (lunch, exc Sun), 119 (lunch, exc Sun, wine incl), 121 (dinner, wine incl).

Le Dôme

108, bd du Montparnasse
01 43 35 25 81, fax 01 42 79 01 19
Closed Mon. Open until 12:30am. Priv rm 8. Air cond.
   Le Dôme is the capital's top seafood brasserie, with a neo–Art Deco interior, booths that provide cozy comfort and privacy for the high-powered patrons, and an appetizing *carte* prepared by chef Franck Graux. In addition to impeccably fresh oysters and the justly famous lobster salad in a truffled dressing, you can choose bouillon de langoustines aux champignons, turbot hollandaise, sea bass in chive vinaigrette, or bouillabaisse that bears comparison with Marseille's best. Precise, cheerful service, and a cellar filled with bottles that incite you to splurge. C 400.

 ## Le Duc

243, bd Raspail · 01 43 20 96 30, fax 01 43 20 46 73
Closed Sun, Mon, hols. Open until 10pm. Air cond.
   The respectful, minimalist approach to seafood imposed by Le Duc's founders endures even now that the Minchelli brothers are gone. The kitchen continues to handle only impeccable ingredients, heightening their innate goodness with a little sea salt, a dribble of oil, a brief moment on the fire. A recent dinner brought wild Scottish salmon cured for just a few hours in a bed of salt; perfect raw sardines; expertly grilled sea bream; and red mullet enhanced with fruity olive oil. It deserves another point. But why, we wonder, at a seafood restaurant of this caliber is the supply of white wines so woefully low? We spotted one lonely white Bordeaux on the list! C 500-600. M 260.

12/20 Giovanna

22, rue Édouard-Jacques · 01 43 22 32 09
Closed Sat lunch, Sun, Aug. Open until 10pm.
   You, your companion, and sixteen other diners can tuck into perfectly wrought fresh pasta and other fine Italian dishes in this minute trattoria, popular with the show-biz crowd. Don't overlook the osso buco. C 160-220. M 65 (weekday lunch).

 ## Lous Landés   ❍

157, av. du Maine · 01 45 43 08 04, fax 01 45 45 91 35
Closed Sat lunch, Sun, Aug. Open until 10:30pm. Priv rm 12. Terrace dining. Air cond.
   Hervé Rumen's Southwestern specialties range from the robust to the refined. Taste his truffled foie gras au jus de canard, Landais squab flavored with three kinds of garlic, or his world-class cassoulet. Desserts are all you would expect from a former colleague of Christian Constant, and the wine list offers some excellent Cahors and Madirans. Marie-Thérèse, a charming hostess, welcomes guests into the pretty green dining room. C 300-400. M 195, 310.

Looking for a celebrated chef? Refer to the **Index.**

Le Moniage Guillaume

88, rue de la Tombe-Issoire
01 43 22 96 15, fax 01 43 27 11 79
Closed Sun. Open until 10:15pm. Priv rm 30. Terrace dining. Valet pkg.
   The regulars (and they are legion) just love this long-established seafood spot. Fish and crustaceans are handled with skill—and priced to kill, though the set meals provide some relief. Rich cellar, including a reasonably tariffed Menetou-Salon. C 350-400. M 185, 245.

 ## Montparnasse 25

Hôtel Méridien,
19, rue du Commandant-Mouchotte
01 44 36 44 25, fax 01 44 36 49 03
Closed Sat, Sun. Open until 10:30pm. Priv rm 32. Air cond. No pets. Valet pkg.
   Unlike many hotel restaurants which are little more than a convenience for in-house patrons, the Méridien posts a magnetic menu that draws gourmets from all over Paris. The Art Deco interior opens onto a patio, and the well-spaced tables are just what executives desire for their power lunches. Yet even the most intense negotiations come to a halt when the waiter presents chef Jean-Yves Guého's expressively flavorful dishes. This triple-toque winner cooked for years at the Hong Kong Méridien, and it shows in his spiced sole with fried noodles and baby bean sprouts or stupendous suckling pig served in two courses: the rack and leg rubbed with sesame and satay paste, the shoulder and ribs braised with vegetables. A monumental cheese board presents over 150 choice specimens, and the cellar is awash in remarkable growers' wines. C 400-600. M 240 (lunch), 300-390 (dinner).

Pavillon Montsouris

20, rue Gazan · 01 45 88 38 52, fax 01 45 88 63 40
Open daily until 10:30pm. Priv rm 43. Terrace dining. No pets. Valet pkg.
   A walk across the Parc Montsouris at sunset will give you an appetite for a fine feast in this turn-of-the-century greenhouse overlooking the park, once the haunt of the beautiful spy, Mata Hari. New comer Gérard Fouché's deft cooking adds sunshine to this charming spot: taste the excellent tatin of red snapper and zucchini and tapenade. Many other dishes harbor his native Southwestern style. Very expensive cellar, and small tables are balanced by gorgeous desserts, and friendly service. C 255-280. M 180, 265, 100 (children).

 ## Les Petites Sorcières

12, rue Liancourt · 01 43 21 95 68, fax 01 42 79 99 03
Closed Sat lunch, Sun. Open until 10:30pm. Priv rm 14. Terrace dining. Pkg.
   Christian Teule fills up his pocket-sized restaurant with an appealing lunch menu that offers house-made jambon persillé followed by herb-poached cod, cheese, and bitter-chocolate mousse. A la carte choices are more elaborate but no less savory: yummy chicken terrine, sautéed

lotte with sweet peppers, and spiced pear clafoutis. Good wines are available by the carafe. C 160. **M** 120 (weekday lunch), 160 (dinner).

11/20 Pinocchio

124, av. du Maine - 01 43 21 26 10, fax 01 43 21 26 37
Closed Sat lunch, Sun. Open until 11pm. Priv rm 40. Terrace dining. Air cond.
Step past the wooden statue of Pinocchio on the sidewalk, and settle down for some satisfying Sicilian fare: spiced octopus, grilled peppers, lamb-stuffed pansotti, and fragrant bollito misto. C 240. **M** 120 (weekdays, wine incl).

 ### La Régalade

49, av. Jean-Moulin - 01 45 45 68 58
Closed Sat lunch, Sun, Mon, Jul 20-Aug 25. Open until midnight. Air cond.
Don't fail to book your table way in advance, for La Régalade fills up fast. Here's why: Yves Camdeborde (ex-Crillon, no less) serves up first-rate cooking at incredible prices. Regionally rooted but modern in outlook, the menu proposes a sapid terrine of oxtail and leek, potato and lobster gratin glazed with Parmesan, succulent wood pigeon barded with bacon, and such delectable desserts as pan-roasted burlat cherries. Appealing Southwestern cellar. Another toque. **M** 165.

 ### Les Vendanges

40, rue Friant - 01 45 39 59 98, fax 01 45 39 74 13
Closed Sat lunch, Sun, Aug 4-25. Open until 10:30pm. Priv rm 15. Pkg.
Pink napery and antiques lend an old-fashioned charm to the dining room. Guy Tardif cooks up generous classics like pheasant galantine with foie gras, braised beef and vegetables, grilled pike perch with lentils and bacon, and rhubarb-topped shortbread. Son of a charcutier, he also turns out a bang-up andouillette. Interesting cellar, rich in Bordeaux. **M** 150, 200, 100 (children).

 ### Au Vin des Rues ☯

21, rue Boulard - 01 43 22 19 78
Closed Sun, Mon, end Feb, Aug. Priv rm 10. Terrace dining. No cards.
Jean Chanrion's robust Lyonnais-style *plats du jour* are served forth in an authentic bistro setting, and are washed down by jugs of wonderful growers' Mâcons and Beaujolais. C 180-240.

 ### Vin et Marée

108, av. du Maine - 01 43 20 29 50
Open daily until midnight. Air cond. Priv rm 40.
Jean-Pierre Durand's first seafood brasserie (on Boulevard Murat in the sixteenth arrondissement) is so successful that he decided to reprise that winning formula here, in premises that formerly housed the Armes de Bretagne restaurant. Durand brings home expertly chosen fish and shellfish from the market at Rungis, so that lucky diners can feast on ultrafresh Breton shrimp, tiny squid sautéed with mild garlic, sole

cooked in sweet butter, or grilled turbotin. Briny steamed cockles are offered as an amuse-bouche, and for dessert there's a yummy baba au rhum. C 140-225.

15TH ARRONDISSEMENT

Postal code	75015

 ### L'Agape

281, rue Lecourbe - 01 45 58 19 29
Closed Sat lunch, Sun, Aug. Open until 10:30pm. Terrace dining.
Marc Lamic's attractive menu brims with bright ideas and flavors: we gobbled up his delicious confit de canard served beneath a fluffy potato blanket, the tasty turbot roasted with fragrant olive oil, potatoes stuffed with ox tail, and hot pineapple gratin. Down-to-earth prices. C 120.

12/20 Le Barrail

17, rue Falguière - 01 43 22 42 61, fax 01 42 79 93 91
Closed Sat, Sun. Open until 10pm. Priv rm 15. Air cond.
In this attractive spot done up in pastel tones, you make no complaints about the traditional bourgeois cooking. C 250. **M** 99, 130 (lunch), 165, 170.

Bistro 121

121, rue de la Convention
01 45 57 52 90, fax 01 45 57 14 69
Open daily until midnight. Air cond. Valet pkg.
Decorated in a now "dated" "modern" style, but comfortable and bright nonetheless, André Jalbert's bistro is a conservatory of reassuring, traditional French cuisine. You won't leave hungry after feasting on molded anchovies in vinaigrette, veal tenderloin scented with juniper, or the robust game dishes served in season. Attractively priced cellar. C 250. **M** 121, 168 (weekday lunch), 210 (Sat, Sun, wine incl).

12/20 Casa Alcalde ☯

117, bd de Grenelle - 01 47 83 39 71
Open daily until 10:30pm. Terrace dining. Air cond.
A lively *bodega* offering zesty Basque and Spanish fare. Try the excellent pipérade, marinated anchovies, generously served paella, or codfish à la luzienne. The wine list features fine bottles from beyond the Pyrenees. C 210. **M** 155.

This could be the start of something beautiful.

Veuve Clicquot

LA GRANDE DAME
Champagne

Les Célébrités

Hôtel Nikko, 61, quai de Grenelle
01 40 58 20 00, fax 01 40 58 24 44
Closed Aug. Open until 10pm. Priv rm 22. Air cond. Valet pkg.
No rough edges mar Jacques Sénéchal's virtuoso handling of flawless seasonal foodstuffs. His 350 F single-price menu presents (for example) clams marinière with garlic and parsley, a lusty boiled-beef salad rémoulade, grilled fish of the day, and pasta fired up with capers, herbs, and chilis. Flavors are refined yet definite, cooking times are invariably right. As for the cellar, it's beyond reproach: astutely assembled, appealing and, all in all, affordably priced. C 290-390. M 350.

 ## Chen

15, rue du Théâtre
01 45 79 34 34, fax 01 45 79 07 53
Closed Sun. Open until 11:30pm. Priv rm 14. Air cond. Valet pkg.
Inside a shopping mall, aggressively decorated—Chen does not look promising! But the short menu holds lots of wonderful surprises. The fresh, precisely prepared crab velouté with asparagus, dumplings in a fragrant broth, peppery sautéed crab, and exemplary Peking duck may not be cheap, but they're well worth the money. C 250, 300. M 170 (weekday dinner), 230 (weekdays lunch, wine incl).

 ## Le Clos Morillons

50, rue des Morillons
01 48 28 04 37, fax 01 48 28 70 77
Closed Sat lunch, Sun. Open until 10pm.
The French colonial décor of this charming establishment transports you to the tropics. The feeling lingers as you peruse the menu, for Philippe Delacourcelle's repertoire is redolent of exotic spices. Among the original, expertly rendered dishes are sole with sweet lime leaves, calf's liver scented with cinnamon, suavely spiced snails, and gingered veal with puréed almonds. Delectable desserts and a fine selection of wines priced under 100 F complete the picture. He earns another point. C 290-360. C 165, 285.

 ## Philippe Detourbe

8, rue Nicolas Charlet
01 42 19 08 59, fax 01 45 67 09 13
Closed Sat lunch, Sun, Aug. Open until 11pm. Priv rm 55. Air cond.
Philippe Detourbe's customers never need to wonder about their bill, since the two moderately priced set meals do the figuring for them. Among the adroitly prepared dishes we've noted lately are cassolette of snails with bacon and mushrooms, grilled red mullet on a bed of ratatouille, and cod with cabbage and a drizzle of hazelnut oil. Affordable cellar, too. M 150 (lunch), 180 (dinner).

Looking for a restaurant? Refer to the **index.**

 ## La Dinée

85, rue Leblanc - 01 45 54 20 49, fax 01 40 60 74 88
Closed Sat, Sun lunch, 3 wks in Aug. Open until 10:45pm. Priv rm 20. Air cond.
Christophe Chabanel earned his first toque at the tender age of 22. Here in his digs, a pluperfect neighborhood restaurant, he's won toque number two, for his finely honed technique and inventive, modern menu. Among the excellent options on offer are a warm salad of quail and artichokes in a vivid beet jus, and perfectly roasted pike perch garnished with a zesty anchoïade and skewered squid. For dessert, go for the spiced pear tempura in red-wine sauce or the apple-caramel chaud-froid. Another point this year. C 350. M 180 (weekday lunch), 290-450 (weekdays, Sun dinner).

 ## Fellini

58, rue de la Croix-Nivert - 01 45 77 40 77
Closed Sat lunch, Sun, Aug. Open until 10:30pm. Air cond. No pets. No cards.
Giuseppe hails from sunny Napoli, where he learned to cook in a fresh, forthright style. Pull up a seat in his friendly trattoria, and sample a warm salad of baby squid and white beans drizzled with olive oil, or fresh tagliolini with langoustines and tomatoes. His tiramisù is the lightest we've tried. To wash it down, uncork a bottle from the well-stocked Italian cellar. C 260-310. M 130 (weekday lunch).

 ## Le Gastroquet

10, rue Desnouettes - 01 48 28 60 91
Closed Sat, Sun, Aug. Open until 10:30pm.
The *patronne* pampers patrons in the dining room, while her husband, Dany Bulot, cooks up rousing bistro fare in his kitchen. Calf's head, boudin en salade, fresh sausage, and cod marmite are staples on the hearty menu. Moderately priced cellar, with plenty of half-bottles. C 220. M 149 (weekday lunch).

 ## Kim Anh

15, rue de l'Église - 01 45 79 40 96, fax 01 40 59 49 78
Dinner only. Open daily until 11pm. Air cond.
Charming Kim-Anh runs this flower-filled little Vietnamese restaurant while his wife, Caroline, does the cooking in a lilliputian kitchen made for contortionists. Fresh herbs, delectable leaves and shoots, subtle spices enhance her curried shrimp, beef with lemongrass, piquant stuffed crab, and the best egg rolls in town. Steepish prices. C 200. M 220 (dinner).

 ## Restaurant du Marché ❁

59, rue de Dantzig - 01 45 32 26 88, fax 01 48 28 18 31
Closed Sat lunch, Sun. Open until 11pm. Priv rm 20. Terrace dining. Pkg.
A farmer's cartel sends fresh Southwestern produce straight to Christiane Massia's kitchen door. She transforms this bounty into wonderful cassoulet, beef stewed in Madiran wine, and myriad dishes starring plump Landais ducks.

Finish off your feast with a tot of fine Armagnac. C 300. M 190 (weekdays).

 Morot Gaudry

8, rue de la Cavalerie
01 45 67 06 85, fax 01 45 67 55 72
Closed Sun. Open until 10:30pm. Priv rm 24. Terrace dining. Air cond. Pkg.
The thrill is gone. Morot-Gaudry's langoustines with endives, snails with morels and sunchokes, roast lamb with stuffed vegetables, pike perch with tarragon sabayon are all honorable dishes, but they no longer astonish or surprise. A remarkable chocolate cake en chaud-froid with citrus fruits sounded an optimistic note, however. As always, the cellar holds a trove of moderately priced treasures. From the verdant terrace you can glimpse a corner of the Eiffel Tower. C 320. M 230 (lunch, wine incl), 390, 550.

 Le Moulin

70, rue de Vouillé - 01 48 28 81 61
Closed Sat lunch, Sun dinner. Open until 10:30pm.
A quiet, unassuming spot where quality ingredients are handled with care. Roger Buhagiar proposes a fine poached foie gras de canard, roast rack of lamb with fresh vegetables, and a rich double-chocolate dessert. Small list of well-chosen wines; cordial welcome. C 250. M 150 (lunch), 175 (dinner, wine incl).

 L'Os à Moelle

3, rue Vasco-de-Gama - 01 45 57 27 27
Closed Sun, Mon, Jul 22-Aug 22. Open until 11pm. Terrace dining.
Thierry Faucher gives his customers terrific value for their money, with imaginative menus inspired by whatever looks fresh and fine at the market. The 145 F lunch might bring gingerbread-coated foie gras garnished with spinach and beets, veal kidney with celery root purée and bone marrow, cheese, and a chocolate quenelle with saffron sauce. A tour de force, even if portions aren't gigantic. M 145 (lunch), 190 (dinner).

12/20 **L'Ostréade**

11, bd de Vaugirard
01 43 21 87 41, fax 01 43 21 55 09
Open daily until 11pm, in summer 11:30pm. Terrace dining. No cards.
While away an hour before the TGV whisks you out West at this pleasant seafood brasserie. Excellent oysters, ultrafresh fish prepared in clever, uncomplicated ways. C 150-200.

 Le Père Claude

51, av. de La Motte-Picquet
01 47 34 03 05, fax 01 40 56 97 84
Open daily until midnight. Priv rm 50. Air cond.
Claude Perraudin lives like a monk (albeit of the Rabelaisian type), his existence devoted to feeding his faithful patrons. Seven days a week in his jolly brasserie, Father Claude oversees a

gargantuan rotisserie where strings of sausages, plump poultry, beef, and racks of lamb spin slowly on the spit until they're done to a turn. There are oceans of tasty wine to wash it all down. The prices? Blessedly low, of course. C 210-350. M 105-160.

 Le Petit Plat

49, av. Émile-Zola
01 45 78 24 20, fax 01 45 78 23 13
Closed 3 wks in Aug, 10 days at Christmas. Open until 11pm. Terrace dining. Air cond.
A jolly mood pervades this pretty restaurant, owing mostly to the Lampreia brothers' cooking: tomates provençales, cockles and mussels in a tasty broth, succulent veal breast with slow-roasted vegetables are typical of their light, generous fare. The clever wine list was composed by our friend, Henri Gault. C 200. M 130.

 Yves Quintard

99, rue Blomet - 01 42 50 22 27, fax 01 42 55 22 27
Closed Sat lunch, Sun, Aug 6-23. Open until 11:30pm. Air cond.
Yves Quintard wins the votes of city workers who gather here to feast on the attractive set meals. The delicious crépinette sausage that combines pig's trotter and sweetbreads is typical of the chef's skillful blending of noble and rustic ingredients. Warm welcome; rather expensive cellar. C 235. C 130 (weekday lunch), 175, 300.

 Le Relais de Sèvres

Hôtel Sofitel, 8-12, rue Louis-Armand
01 40 60 33 66, fax 01 45 57 04 22
Closed Sat, Sun, hols, Dec 24-Jan 1. Open until 10pm. Priv rm 15. Air cond. Valet pkg.
For its flagship restaurant, the Sofitel chain chose a décor that spells good taste in capital letters: blond woodwork; pale-blue fabric on the walls; champagne-colored napery; Louis XV chairs. Newly appointed young chef Bruno Turbot has now found his balance and his way. His quite attractive dinner menu (220 F) comprises grenouilles in a mountain-celery cream, sole filets with pink artichokes enhanced with coriander or a savory oxtail compote with morel mushrooms, along with a full-fledged cheese tray and a choice of dessert. The same menu, including Champagne, wine and mineral water, goes for 320 F. C 420. M 220 (dinner), 320 (lunch, wine incl).

 Restaurant de La Tour

"Roger Conticini,"
6, rue Desaix - 01 43 06 04 24
Closed Sat lunch, Sun, Aug. Open until 10:30pm.
Roger Conticini (his sons run the triple-toque Table d'Anvers in the ninth arrondissement) is at the helm of this engaging restaurant. The dishes on his single-price menus change often, but all have an earthy, raffish appeal: hot game pâté, a lusty salad of pig's ear and trotter, tuna braised in red wine with risotto, and ginger-snapped duck breast with honey are typical of

the house style. Fine little cellar. Nice going, Roger! C 210. **M** 118 & 138 (weekday lunch), 175 (weekdays, Sat dinner).

 Sawadee

53, av. Émile-Zola
01 45 77 68 90, fax 01 77 57 78
Closed Sun. Open until 10:30pm. Priv rm 80. Terrace dinning. Air cond.
Sawadee is one of the city's best Thais. Spacious, over-decorated, very lively, it offers an immense list of specialties full of unexpected flavors. The salad of pork rinds and fried rice, skewered shellfish, mussels in a fiery sauce, cod with seaweed and wild lemon, duck perfumed with Thai basil, and coconut ice cream all come highly recommended. C 150-200. **M** 75-175.

 Aux Senteurs de Provence ❁

295, rue Lecourbe
01 45 57 11 98, fax 01 45 58 66 84
Closed Sat lunch, Sun, Aug 4-16. Open until 10pm. Terrace dining.
Delicate, freshly fragrant Provençal cuisine. Sun-kissed ingredients lend an authentic savor to the tuna in a tarragon marinade, roast galinette (a Mediterranean fish) à la niçoise, and generous bouillabaisse. The cellar is modest, but the surroundings are neat and cheerful, with cork-covered walls and jaunty nautical prints. C 240-280. **M** 138.

 Pierre Vedel

19, rue Duranton - 01 45 58 43 17, fax 01 45 58 42 65
Closed Sat lunch Oct-Apr, Sun, 1 wk at Christmas. Open until 10:15pm. Priv rm 12.
Be sure to book your table, because Pierre Vedel's warm Parisian bistro is invariably jam-packed. Little wonder the place is popular, given the delectable house foie gras, authentic bourride de lotte à la sétoise (a garlicky monkfish soup), and lush bitter-chocolate charlotte. If you order one of the more modest growers' wines from the interesting list, the bill won't be too bad. C 260-360.

16TH ARRONDISSEMENT

Postal code	75016

12/20 Amazigh

2, rue La Pérouse - 01 47 20 90 38
Closed Sat lunch, Sun. Open until 11pm. No cards.
A Moroccan restaurant with an enticing bill of fare: savory briouates (deep-fried pastries) filled with shellfish, eggplant salad sparked with coriander (zalouk), lamb tagine with fried eggplant, and sumptuous "grand couscous." Also

worthy of interest are the stuffed sardines, lamb's brains in tomato sauce, and cinnamon-scented oranges. Like the setting, the service is pretty posh. C 250. **M** 150.

 La Baie d'Ha Long

164, av. de Versailles - 01 45 24 60 62
Closed Sun, Aug. Open until 10pm. Priv rm 20. Terrace dining. Air cond. No pets.
Roger, the proprietor of this small Vietnamese spot, is more interested in his collection of birds and exotic fish than in food. It's his wife, Nathalie, who toils away in the kitchen producing delicious, exotic dishes from her native Vietnam: spicy soups, brochettes perfumed with fresh herbs, duck grilled with ginger. Generous portions; good desserts. C 180. **M** 105 (weekday lunch).

 Bellini

28, rue Le Sueur - 01 45 00 54 20, fax 01 45 00 11 74
Closed Sat lunch, Sun, 1 wk at Christmas. Open until 10:30pm. Air cond.
Comfy banquettes, mirrors, marble, and chamois-toned walls create a cozy setting for Bellini's somewhat Frenchified Italian fare. Diaphanous slices of prosciutto di Parma lead into such savory dishes as lobster salad with polenta, red mullet with olives, or veal kidney cooked in brawny Barolo wine. The cellar harbors appealing wines from Friulia, Tuscany, and the Veneto. C 250-300. **M** 180.

 Bertie's

Hôtel Baltimore, 1, rue Léo-Delibes
01 44 34 54 34, fax 01 44 34 54 44
Closed 2 wks in Aug. Open until 10:30pm. Priv rm 15. Air cond. Valet pkg.
When Le Bertie's opened, a major London daily ran this tongue-in-cheek headline: "Finally! A good meal in Paris!" The dining room cultivates a clubby British look that Parisians adore. And yes, the menu is English: potted crab, Welsh mussel soup, Scottish lamb with mint sauce, bread-and-butter pudding... The maître d' will astound you with his knowledge of Britain's 400 cheeses; the wine steward will amaze you with his list of prime clarets. And after your meal, you can linger contentedly over a rare whisky or vintage Port. C 280-320. **M** 160 (weekday lunch), 195 (exc Sun), 250 (dinner).

 Bistrot de l'Étoile-Lauriston

19, rue Lauriston - 01 40 67 11 16, fax 01 45 00 99 87
Closed Sat lunch, Sun. Open until midnight. Air cond.
This big, bright bistro continues on its successful career. Chef William Ledeuil handles the neo-bourgeois repertoire with admirable ease, offering rabbit persillé or a vibrant vegetable salad showered with Parmesan to start, followed by steak à la bordelaise or stuffed veal shank simmered in a sparky vinegar sauce. For dessert,

we warmly recommend the apple-rhubarb crumble. C 230.

La Butte Chaillot

110 bis, av. Kléber
01 47 27 88 88, fax 01 47 04 85 70
Open daily until midnight. Priv rm 25. Terrace dining. Air cond. Valet pkg.

Chef and restaurateur Guy Savoy turned an unpromising site (a former bank) into a fashionable restaurant with a star-studded clientele. The keys to his success are a clever contemporary décor, a swift and stylish staff, and—best of all—an ever-changing roster of irresistible dishes: succulent spit-roasted poultry with whipped potatoes, veal breast perfumed with rosemary and olive oil, and lots of luscious desserts. C 240. M 150-210.

Carré Kléber

Hôtel Paris K Palace,
11 bis, rue de Magdebourg
01 47 55 82 08, fax 01 47 55 80 09
Closed Sat lunch, Sun, 3 wks in Aug, 1 wk at Christmas. Priv rm 30. Air cond. Pkg.

Provence, as we know, is furiously à la mode. Christophe Delaunay pays homage to the current fashion with a delicious tart of red mullet and baby mackerel on a bed of tomato fondue and tapenade, and other suitably Southern delights. The very pretty modern dining room opens onto a leafy patio. C 220-270. M 185, 80 (children).

Paul Chène

123, rue Lauriston
01 47 27 63 17, fax 01 47 27 53 18
Closed Sat lunch, Sun, Dec 24-Jan 2. Open until 10:30pm. Priv rm 30. Air cond. Pkg.

Elbow-room is at a premium in Paul Chène's two faded dining rooms, but the owners are unstinting with their hospitality and the kitchen, too, has a generous spirit. You're sure to relish eggs poached in red wine, quality Parma ham, beef tenderloin béarnaise, and profiteroles napped in chocolate. The cellar boasts a varied, judicious selection, yet the house Bordeaux is not to be neglected. C 300-400. M 200, 250.

Conti

72, rue Lauriston
01 47 27 74 67, fax 01 47 27 37 66
Closed Sat, Sun, hols, 1 wk in Jan, Aug. Open until 10:30pm. Air cond.

With Sormani's Jean-Pascal Fayet (see seventeenth arrondissement), Michel Ranvier is a leading French exponent of Italian cooking. Perhaps a shade less creative than Fayet, Ranvier still gives his menu a vigorous zest. Examples? Clams and cockles with fennel in a perfumed broth, a perfect risotto with fresh peas and asparagus, and a fabulous bollito misto with pungent mostarda di Cremona. The Italian cellar is a wonder to behold, and the staff provides silken service. C 360-460. M 198 (lunch).

Le Cuisinier François

19, rue Le Marois - 01 45 27 83 74, fax 01 45 27 83 74
Closed Sun, Mon, Wed dinner, 1 wk in Feb. Open until 10pm.

After stints at La Tour d'Argent, Robuchon, and Boyer in Reims, Thierry Conte did not, as one might expect, open a place with his name in large letters over the door. Instead, he settled for an establishment of modest proportions and a menu that is most moderately priced. Delicious petit-gris snails en sauce and an excellent sole in meat juices are typical of his modern, uncomplicated fare. But desserts are cloying, we find, and the wines too costly. Though Thierry Conte deserves another point for his cuisine. C 250. M 160.

Alain Ducasse

59, av. Raymond-Poincaré
01 47 27 12 27, fax 01 47 27 31 22
Closed Sat, Sun, Jul 4-Aug 4, end Dec-beg Jan. Open until 10pm. Valet pkg.

Who else but Alain Ducasse could replace Joël Robuchon? A megachef takes over from a superstar—it couldn't happen any other way. Alain Ducasse faced a two-fold challenge: to take over from the city's foremost chef and maintain the restaurant's stellar rank, and at the same time preserve his own number one rating on the Riviera. For Ducasse, a *patron* is nothing without his team. Sous-chefs are drilled to follow his principles, his precision, his uncompromising approach to ingredients. Paris gives Ducasse the opportunity to play with a palette of northern flavors: Breton fish, Bresse poultry, prime produce from the Loire or Picardy. Olive oil is not absent from his Parisian kitchen, but it somehow feels right, up here in the north, to embellish a turbot with North Sea shrimp and perhaps a spoonful of salted butter from Brittany. To the magnificent cellar that Robuchon left behind, Ducasse has added selections of his own. Alain Ducasse is well on his way to prove that he is indeed the leading chef of his generation. C 900-1,500. M 480 (lunch), 890.

Duret Mandarin

34, rue Duret - 01 45 00 09 06
Open daily until 11pm. Air cond. Valet pkg.

The Tang family work hard to deliver (with a smile!) such Chinese classics as crispy egg rolls, deep-fried dumplings, and stuffed crab, and interesting options like steamed scallops with black-bean sauce and "special" roast chicken. Terrific Peking duck, with optimally crisp skin (order it when you book your table). C 160-260. M 79, 95.

Fakhr el Dine

30, rue de Longchamp
01 47 27 90 00, fax 01 47 27 11 39
Open daily until 11:30pm. Priv rm 60. No pets. Valet pkg.
See 8th arrondissement. C 290. M 150-360.

Faugeron

52, rue de Longchamp
01 47 04 24 53, fax 01 47 55 62 90
Closed Sat dinner off-seas, Sun, Aug, Dec 23-Jan 3.
Open until 10pm. Priv rm 14. Air cond. No pets.
Valet pkg.
Henri Faugeron hails from the Corrèze countryside, where a man is judged by his work, not his pretensions. This modest, even self-effacing chef doesn't go in for bold experiments, but he knows how to use an uncommon spice, or mustard, or vinegar to give traditional dishes a pungent, modern zest. Faugeron pays tribute to his rustic roots with seasonal variations on cèpes and truffles, with tender veal shank heightened with a piquant touch of Brive's violet mustard, or a beef daube braised à l'ancienne for a full ten hours and served with truffled pasta. A pastoral apple flognarde is a final flourish to be savored along with the last drops of a great Bordeaux, Burgundy, or more modest Chinon or Sancerre, chosen by "World's Best Sommelier", in 1986, Jean-Claude Jambon. C 480. **M** 295 (weekdays), 550 (dinner, wine incl), 650.

Les Filaos

5, rue Guy-de-Maupassant - 01 45 04 94 53
Closed Sun, Aug. Open until 11pm. Priv rm 45.
Spicy savors from Mauritius: try the palate-tingling stuffed crab seasoned with ginger and coriander, or tamarind-flavored codfish beignets, octopus in a saffron marinade, or smoked sausages with fiery rougail. C 220.

Le Flandrin

80, av. Henri-Martin - 01 45 04 35 69
Open daily until 11:30pm. Terrace dining.
This chic brasserie now boasts a much-improved *carte*, thanks to the efforts of young Olivier Denis (trained by mega-chef Alain Passard). We like the shrimp beignets, macaroni and ricotta gratin, crab ravioli, langoustines grilled with wild thyme, and the warming lamb curry. Oysters and other fresh shellfish in season; good service. C 250.

Gastronomie Quach

47, av. Raymond-Poincaré - 01 42 27 98 40
Open daily until 11pm. Priv rm 20. Air cond.
Aquariums decorate the posh dining room where Monsieur Quach serves Cantonese and Vietnamese dishes that now have more good days than bad: prawns grilled with lemongrass, squid with red peppers, and grilled lamb with five spices are more precisely turned out than in the past. And the fine Peking duck keeps the glossy patrons coming back for more. C 230-310. **M** 92 (weekdays, Sat lunch), 109.

La Grande Cascade

Bois de Boulogne, near the racetrack
01 45 27 33 51, fax 01 42 88 99 06
Closed end Dec-mid Jan. Open until 10:30pm. Priv rm 50. Terrace dining. Valet pkg.

The setting of this former pleasure pavillion is exuberantly Belle Époque, and up until recently, the cuisine was discreetly classic. But super-chef Alain Ducasse has commissioned one of his best lieutenants, Jean-Louis Nomicos, to revamp the menu. As a result, the Cascade now shines with exciting tastes: fine potato raviolis; greens with a Parmesan tuile; sea-bass steak with fennel seeds and black pepper served with ground tomatoes in olive oil; and corn-fed chicken stuffed with fresh herbs accompanied by succulent mushrooms gnocchi. Go for the satisfying 285 F menu. C 550-820. **M** 285.

Lac Hong

67, rue Lauriston - 01 47 55 87 17
Closed Sun, Aug. Open until 10:45pm. Air cond. No pets.
Vietnam's cuisine may be the most delicately flavorful in all of Southeast Asia. To test that proposition, just taste Lé Thi Lanh's remarkable salad of grilled scampi and green papaya, ginger-roasted lobster, shrimp-stuffed rice pancakes, steamed smoked duck with fish sauce, or lamb redolent of curry and star anise. Even the Cantonese rice is exquisite: flawlessly cooked and bursting with flavor. C 250. **M** 98 (weekday lunch, Sat).

Jamin

32, rue de Longchamp - 01 45 53 00 07
Closed Sat, Sun, Jul 11-Aug 4. Open until 10:30pm. Air cond. Pkg.
Joël Robuchon's old Jamin has opened its doors again, after a three-year interruption, with Robuchon pupil Benoit Guichard in the kitchen. Prices are considerably lower nowadays, with a 375 F set meal served at lunch and dinner, and an à la carte average of 500 F. The current menu proposes duck and fig terrine, a warm salad of langoustines and cuttlefish spiked with ginger, braised beef with cumin-spiced carrots, and wine-dark stewed rabbit with fresh pasta and cèpes. We'll give the new staff time to learn the ropes before we weigh in with our rating. Stay tuned! C 500. **M** 280 (lunch), 375.

12/20 Chez Ngo

70, rue de Longchamp
01 47 04 53 20, fax 01 47 04 53 20
Open daily until 11:45pm. Priv rm 7. Air cond. No pets. Pkg.
An elegant Chinese table (pretty décor, lovely dishes). Look beyond the menu's classic dishes to the more interesting grilled frogs' legs, delectable steamed fish, curried eel, and zippy salt-and-pepper shrimp showered with herbs. C 250. **M** 97 (lunch), 98 (lunch, wine incl), 168 (wine incl), 398 (for 2 pers).

Nikita

6, rue Faustin Hélié
01 45 04 04 33, fax 01 47 53 92 10
Closed Aug. Open until 12:30am. Air cond. Valet pkg.
The décor of red velvet and gilt mirrors is typical of the city's posher Russian restaurants. What's different about this one, though, is that the prices are not high-hat! Yes, there's a gypsy violinist and a sloe-eyed singer; but for once the shashlik and potato dumplings are creditably prepared, and diners aren't made to feel like cheapskates if they don't order caviar. Take note of the 290 F set meal: it's worthy of a celebration. C 350. M 120 (lunch, wine incl), 290, 490.

 ## Oum el Banine

16 bis, rue Dufrenoy - 01 45 04 91 22
Closed Sat & Sun lunch. Open until 11pm. Air cond.
To enter, knock on the heavy wooden door, just as you would in Morocco. Maria Seguin, a native of Fès, practices authentic Fassi cuisine, whose secrets are handed down from mother to daughter. Five types of couscous are on offer, as well as eight tagines (with olives and pickled lemons, peppers and tomato, zucchini and thyme, etc.). More rarely seen, but typically Moroccan, are brains in a piquant tomato sauce, spiced tripe, and calf's foot with chickpeas. C 275.

 ## Le Pergolèse

40, rue Pergolèse - 01 45 00 21 40, fax 01 45 00 81 31
Closed Sat, Sun, Aug. Open until 10:30pm. Priv rm 32. Valet pkg.
Local stockbrokers are bullish on Le Pergolèse. They've adopted Albert Corre's plush and intimate (indeed, slightly cramped) dining room as their unofficial headquarters. But it may be that Corre is spending too much time at the tables and not enough at the stove, for the cooking has dipped below its previous high. Our carpaccio of salt-cured lamb lacked character, for instance, and an overcooked sea bass was further marred by a dubious sauce. Happily, an unctuous chocolate dessert saved the toque—but only just! C 400-500. M 230, 320.

 ## Le Port Alma

10, av. de New-York - 01 47 23 75 11
Closed Sun, Aug. Open until 10:30pm. Air cond.
Paul Canal isn't one to blow his own horn, but he has few peers when it comes to cooking fish and crustaceans. Count on Canal to pick the best of the day's catch, and prepare his prime specimens with a skilled hand and no superfluous sauces to mask their flavors. Bourride and bouillabaisse are featured on Fridays, or upon reservation. Balanced cellar, with plenty of half-bottles. C 300-500. M 200 (lunch).

 ## Le Pré Catelan

Bois de Boulogne, route de Suresnes
01 44 14 41 14, fax 01 45 24 43 25
Closed Sun dinner, Mon, Feb school hols. Open until 10:30pm. Priv rm 50. Terrace dining. Valet pkg.
The Pré Catelan comes in two versions: summer, with tables set in a leafy garden amid fluttering parasols; and winter, an elegant dining room warmed by a crackling fire. The versatil talent of the chef suits both settings, with dishes that are by turns urbane or rustic. In season, you'll discover an extraordinary "menu truffe et cochon," which demonstrates that with the right perfume—truffles, for example—one can indeed turn a sow's ear into something sublime: in this case a croquant d'oreille with langoustines. Sophisticated spicing marks the black risotto with Thai basil, and lamb's brain salad with its exquisite saffron aspic. Desserts are divine (ah! the hot chocolate-praline pastilla!), and the cellar is well served by a first-rate sommelier. C 650-900. M 280 (weekday lunch), 550, 750.

 ## Prunier Traktir

16, av. Victor-Hugo
01 44 17 35 85, fax 01 44 17 90 10
Closed Sun, Mon lunch, Jul 15-Aug 15. Open until 11pm. Priv rm 10. Air cond. Valet pkg.
The rebirth of Prunier Traktir caused great rejoicing among Paris's pearls-and-tweed set, who regarded the demise of this once-brilliant seafood house as a personal loss. The man behind the revival is Jean-Claude Vrinat of Taillevent. From the moment he opened the doors of the gorgeously restored Art Deco interior, Parisians took the dining room by storm. Handsome rooms are fitted up on the second floor as well, and Prunier is regularly packed with the sleek and famous. In the kitchen, Gabriel Biscay balances Prunier classics (lobster bisque, codfish brandade, marmite dieppoise) with such contemporary items as fish tartare with oysters, red mullet à l'orientale, and langoustines royales au naturel. C 580.

 ## Le Relais d'Auteuil

31, bd Murat - 01 46 51 09 54, fax 01 40 71 05 03
Closed Sat lunch, Sun, 3 wks in Aug. Open until 10:30pm. Air cond. Valet pkg.
Patrick Pignol's imaginative, resolutely modern cuisine is a treat to discover. Uncompromising in his choice of ingredients, he follows the seasons to obtain the very freshest, finest produce. In summer, he'll feature zucchini blossoms and other vegetables at the peak of their flavor; in fall, look for sage-scented braised partridge; winter might bring a mammoth sole in a sauce of lightly salted butter and fiery Szechuan pepper. If only Pignol would keep a tighter rein on his prices...! C 500. M 250 (lunch), 410, 520.

12/20 Le Relais du Bois de Boulogne

Bois de Boulogne, Croix-Catelan, route de Suresnes
01 42 15 00 11, fax 01 42 15 03 52
Closed Sun dinner, Mon. Open until 10:30pm. Terrace dining. Pkg.
This Second Empire hunting pavilion where naughty ladies and gentlemen once engaged in rather outrageous behavior is now the backdrop

for tame family parties and quiet lunches. In summer, nab a table in the garden and enjoy duck carpaccio with balsamic vinegar or fish en papillote. C 200. M 120, 150 (wine incl), 165, 78 (children).

 ### Le Relais du Parc

Hôtel Le Parc, 55-57, av. Raymond-Poincaré
01 44 05 66 10, fax 01 44 05 66 00
Open daily until 10:30pm. Terrace dining. Air cond. Valet pkg.
Le Relais du Parc holds a winning hand. Set in the luxurious Le Parc hotel, it sports a British colonial setting and is now under the supervision of Alain Ducasse (who also has taken over Robuchon next door). Ducasse has kept such Robuchon dishes as the aerial creamy soup in a crustacean gelée, but he has also added Southwestern dishes: cod-stuffed bell peppers; tomatoes stuffed with vegetables; John Dory on a bed of fennel; melon soup in Jurançon wine. Reservations are a must. C 330.

 ### La Salle à Manger

Hôtel Raphaël, 17 av. Kléber
01 44 28 00 17, fax 01 45 54 21
Closed Sat, Sun, hols. Open until 10pm. Priv rm 60. Air cond. Valet pkg.
In an auspicious new departure, the ever-so-swank Hôtel Raphaël has renovated its dining room, and entrusted the kitchen to chef Philip Delahaye. The menu entices with such sophisticated fare as langoustine fricassée flanked by a crisp craquant of apples and pig's trotter, roasted sea bass served en soupière with mild garlic and star anise, or breast of guinea hen with marble-sized potatoes and morsels of smoky sausage set in a pool of green-pea cream. Desserts are equally dainty; indeed, the only quibble we have is that the food occasionally edges awfully close to preciousness. C 450. M 290 (dinner), 295 (lunch).

 ### Le Toit de Passy

94, av. Paul-Doumer
01 45 24 55 37, fax 01 45 20 94 57
Closed Sat lunch, Sun. Open until 10:30pm. Priv rm 25. Terrace dining. Air cond. Pkg.
On a fine day the terrace is unquestionably the place to sit for the unimpeded view of Passy's rooftops. Yet the dining room, accented with plants and partitions, is also an elegant setting for Yannick Jacquot's cuisine. The cellar holds no fewer than 45,000 bottles, so the wine list will take some perusing. C 500 (wine incl). M 195 (weekday lunch), 280-350 (lunch, wine incl), 395-510 (weekdays).

 ### Vivarois

192, av. Victor-Hugo
01 45 04 04 31, fax 01 45 03 09 84
Closed Sat, Sun, Aug. Open until 10pm. Air cond. Valet pkg.
Claude Peyrot imperturbably polishes a concise, unchanging *carte* which he supplements daily with a half-dozen dishes created on the spur of the moment. In the latter category, we

fondly recall a sublime wild-mushroom terrine with foie gras; in the former, we recommend the sweet-pepper bavaroise heightened with an uncommonly fragrant walnut oil. Peyrot's pared-down style leaves little room for error. When a dish is perfectly done, its purity elicits admiration; but the slightest flaw makes simplicity look suspiciously like skimping... Exemplary service in a handsome contemporary dining room. The fine cellar is run by Jean-Claude Vinadier, sommelier extraordinaire. C 650. M 345 (weekday lunch).

 ### Woo Jung

8, bd Delessert · 01 45 20 72 82
Closed Sun, Aug 17-30, Dec 21-Jan 4. Open until 10:30pm. Priv rm 24. Air cond. No pets.
A Korean restaurant filled with Koreans (a good sign) in the chic Passy district. Adventurous diners can opt for a mustardy jellyfish salad, beef tartare with sesame seeds, or pearly-fresh raw sea bream. Every dish is beautifully served. C 250.

 ### Zébra Square

3, pl. Clément-Ader
01 44 14 91 91, fax 01 45 20 46 41
Open daily until 1am. Priv rm 8. Terrace dining. Air cond. No pets. Pkg.
Good food at reasonable prices in an "American-style" setting. Assorted warm vegetables drizzled with Provençal olive oil, crab with sweet-pepper coulis, and sea bream with roasted artichokes and a touch of lemongrass all succeed in revving up the appetite. Brunch is served on weekends. C 250. M 110 (weekday lunch).

17TH ARRONDISSEMENT

Postal code	75017

 ### Albert-Albert

24, rue de Tilsitt · 01 45 72 25 14
Closed Sat lunch, Sun, Aug 10-20. Open until midnight. Priv rm 50. Air cond. Valet pkg.
Albert Nahmias not only has a flair for public relations, he is also a highly professional restaurateur. His handsome premises (salmon-colored walls, blue banquettes, modern paintings...) are in a high-rent district, but he manages to offer a 180 F single-price menu based on very good ingredients: among the choices are Breton oysters, sea bream roasted with fresh thyme, lamb with sweet peppers, a delicious dish of streaky bacon in a sauce spiked with truffle juice, and mango tarte Tatin to finish. All are capably prepared by a young chef trained by

Chapel. Excellent cellar, with wines from 70 F. C 200. M 150 (weekday lunch, wine incl), 180 (weekdays, Sat dinner).

 ## Amphyclès

"Phillipe Groult", 78, av. des Ternes
01 40 68 01 01, fax 01 40 68 91 88
Closed Sat lunch, Sun. Open until 10:30pm. Priv rm 25. Air cond. Valet pkg.
Joël Robuchon imbued his star pupil, Philippe Groult, with a passion for perfection. Superb ingredients, which Groult chooses with discriminating care, are the basis of colorful, flavorful dishes that delight both eye and palate. To wit: a scarlet spider crab stuffed with a blend of its own meat, tourteau crab, and lobster; pearly white John Dory topped with slow-roasted tomatoes and glossy black olives; or golden sweetbreads with dried fruits and nuts and a brilliant green snow-pea fondue. Only the best growers are admitted to the select and expensive wine list. C 550-900. M 720, 820.

 ## Apicius

122, av. de Villiers
01 43 80 19 66, fax 01 44 40 09 57
Closed Sat, Sun, Aug. Open until 10pm. Air cond. Valet pkg.
We know lots of high-class restaurants where the food is perfectly fine—but the ambience is stuffy and dull. At Jean-Pierre Vigato's Apicius, not only is the food simply fabulous, the atmosphere is as warm as can be. The charm begins to work from the moment Madeleine Vigato welcomes you into the lavishly flower-decked dining room. Though Vigato's core repertoire doesn't vary much from one year to the next, he stays sharp by offering a half-dozen different starters and entrées each day (which Madeleine describes at each table in luscious detail). If they're on hand, do try the langoustine tartare seasoned with olive oil, a hint of meat juice, pepper, and a whisper of garlic; or the tiny artichokes flavored with aged Parmesan and white truffles; or (in autumn) the sumptuous duck pie, a performance worthy of Escoffier! C 550-750. M 520 (weekdays).

 ## Augusta

98, rue de Tocqueville
01 47 63 39 97, fax 01 42 27 21 71
Closed Sun, Aug 4-25. Open until 10pm. Air cond.
Scrupulously seasonal, rigorously precise, based on the freshest seafood: Philippe de Saint-Étienne's cuisine is all this and more. The clear, direct flavors of his sweet-and-sour scampi, rockfish soup, fricassée of sole and artichokes, seared sea bass with sea salt, or roast John Dory with a shellfish jus incite us to unashamed gorging! Remarkable wine list; young, eager staff. C 400-600.

12/20 Le Ballon des Ternes

103, av. des Ternes - 01 45 74 17 98
Closed Aug 1-21. Open until 12:30am. Priv rm 40. Terrace dining. Air cond.

Shellfish assortments, tuna carpaccio showered with sesame seeds, veal kidney with mustard sauce, and house-made apple tart are served with top-quality wines at this likeable Belle Époque brasserie. C 250.

 ## Baumann Ternes

64, av. des Ternes - 01 45 74 16 66, fax 01 45 72 44 32
Open daily until midnight. Priv rm 27. Terrace dining. Air cond. Pkg.
A bastion of the Baumann restaurant empire, where you can savor first-class choucroutes and other Alsatian specialties, as well as tasty tartares and grills. Wonderful wines; lively ambience. C 230. M 112 (beer incl), 163.

 ## Billy Gourmand

20, rue de Tocqueville - 01 42 27 03 71
Closed Sat lunch, Sun, hols, 3 wks in Aug. Open until 10pm. Priv rm 14.
Chef Philippe Billy presents his polished, prettily presented cuisine in a spacious dining room decorated with mirrors and plants. On a recent visit we tucked into crab ravioli with mussels and baby broad beans, a tender lamb chop topped with seasoned butter, and a delicate morello cherry cake. The engaging *patronne* oversees a fine cellar of Loire Valley wines. C 280. M 160.

 ## Le Bistrot d'à Côté

10, rue Gustave-Flaubert
01 42 67 05 81, fax 01 47 63 82 75
Open daily until 11:30pm. Terrace dining. Air cond. Valet pkg.
All you want from a bistro: hustle, bustle, and cheeky waiters. Who wouldn't be won over by the simple, savory pleasures of the menu's French provincial specialties? The wines, however, are awfully expensive for this sort of place. C 250-330.

 ## Le Bistrot de l'Étoile-Niel

75, av. Niel - 01 42 27 88 44, fax 01 42 27 32 12
Closed Sun lunch. Open until midnight. Terrace dining. Air cond. Valet pkg.
Here's your typical cheerful neighborhood bistro—except that it's owned and supervised by Guy Savoy. Handily prepared and served with a smile, the tuna carpaccio with shellfish vinaigrette, chicken with pickled lemons, vanilla-chocolate chaud-froid, and house Merlot have won a loyal following. C 230. M 180.

 ## Le Bistrot de l'Étoile-Troyon

13, rue Troyon - 01 42 67 25 95, fax 01 46 22 43 09
Closed Sat, Sun lunch. Open until 11:30pm. Terrace dining. Air cond. Valet pkg.
Guy Savoy can keep a close eye on the firstborn of his bistro annexes, for it stands just across the street from his three-toque restaurant. In the small, convivial dining room you can treat your-

self to such heartwarming bourgeois classics as leek and chicken-liver terrine, roast veal with onion marmalade, coffee parfait, and lush chocolate quenelles. Good growers' wines; democratic prices. C 170. M 160.

 Les Bouchons de François Clerc

22, rue de la Terrasse - 01 42 27 31 51
Open daily until 11pm. Terrace dining. Air cond.
See *5th arrondissement*. M 117 (weekday lunch), 219.

 Caves Pétrissans

30 bis, av. Niel - 01 42 27 52 03, fax 01 40 54 87 56
Closed Sat, Sun, hols, Aug 4-24. Open until 10:30pm. Priv rm 10. Terrace dining.
Four generations of Pétrissans have overseen this wine shop-cum-restaurant, where patrons linger happily over Denis Bischoff's deft cooking. The quality ingredients are simply prepared and generously served; try the terrine maison served with onion marmalade, tête de veau sauce ravigote, and flaky fruit tarts. Fabulous wine list. C 200. M 165.

12/20 Charly de Bab-el-Oued

95, bd Gouvion-Saint-Cyr
01 45 74 34 62, fax 01 45 74 35 36
Closed mid Jul-mid Aug. Open until 11:30pm. Air cond. No pets.
An inviting place to dream of the *Arabian Nights* amid colorful tiles, cedarwood, and palm trees. Feast on excellent couscous, pastillas, and tagines, followed by sweet Eastern pastries made on the premises. Perfect service. C 230-280.

12/20 Les Cigales

127, rue Cardinet - 01 42 27 83 93
Closed Sat, Sun, Aug. Open until 10pm. Pkg.
The décor plays the Provençal card to the hilt (sun-yellow walls, photos of the Riviera...), and so does the bright bill of fare: tomatoes stuffed with creamy goat cheese, grilled sea bream anointed with virgin olive oil, pasta dressed with pistou are all handily turned out. C 190-250. M 135.

 Clos Longchamp

Hôtel Méridien ,81, bd Gouvion-St-Cyr
01 40 68 30 40, fax 01 40 68 30 81
Closed Sat, Sun, Aug 4-24, last wk of Dec. Open until 10:30pm. Priv rm 18. Air cond. Valet pkg.
Jean-Marie Meulien's elegant menu combines the flavors of the Mediterranean with the spices of Southeast Asia. Plump pink shrimp are perfumed with Thai herbs; tender lamb and vegetables are given a spicy tandoori treatment; a thick chop of milk-fed veal is paired with wild mushrooms. A similarly exotic mood inspires the desserts (coconut blancmange). Award-winning sommelier Didier Bureau administers a remarkable cellar. C 450-600. M 250 (weekday lunch), 340, 470.

 L'Écrin d'Or

35, rue Legendre - 01 47 63 83 08
Closed Sat lunch, Mon, Aug. Open until 11pm.
Huge mirrors, moldings, chandeliers, and great swathes of velvet hangings make a precious setting for Gilles Cendres's warm beef salad, scallop fricassée with fresh pasta, and Grand Marnier soufflé. Intelligently chosen wines; friendly welcome. C 260-350. M 95, 115.

 Épicure 108

108, rue Cardinet - 01 47 63 50 91
Closed Sat lunch, Sun, Feb school hols, 2 wks in Aug. Open until 10pm.
A quiet restaurant with a pastel interior (in need, we think, of a brush-up) where chef Tetsu Goya presents hearty Alsatian-style dishes. The 180 F menu brings a salad of quail and foie gras, fish simmered with sauerkraut, and chocolate puffs with pear marmalade. Nice little cellar, with some fine Rieslings. M 180, 250.

 L'Étoile d'Or

Hôtel Concorde La Fayette, 3, pl. du Général-Kœnig
01 40 68 51 28, fax 01 40 68 50 43
Closed Sat, Sun. Open until 10:30pm. Priv rm 40. Air cond. Valet pkg.
Bold harmonies of flavors, split-second timing, and feather-light sauces are the three solid bases of Jean-Claude Lhonneur's alluring repertoire. We know: it isn't easy to find this handsome, wood-paneled dining room, hidden in the labyrinth of the hotel Concorde La Fayette; paying the bill isn't so simple either. But if you make the effort, your reward will be (for example) meltingly savory duck liver in a Banyuls wine jus, smothered sea bass perfumed with truffled oil, or savory stewed ox jowls en ravigote, and a chocolate soufflé that the waiter swears is the best in Paris! C 400-675. M 270.

 Faucher

123, av. de Wagram
01 42 27 61 50, fax 01 46 22 25 72
Closed Sat lunch, Sun. Open until 10pm. Terrace dining. Valet pkg.
Gérard Faucher keeps prices down to keep customers coming. He's crossed a few costly items off of his shopping list, but otherwise his menu is as vivid and modern as ever. He's even managed to preserve some signature dishes, like the millefeuille of thinly sliced raw beef and spinach leaves, and the short ribs with a truffled jus. You'll also find a wickedly tasty combination of foie gras, fried egg, and grilled coppa, and crackling lacquered duck breast. Wines from a revised, less expensive cellar complete the picture. Nicole Faucher greets guests with a smile in the cheerful yellow dining room. C 250. M 385.

 La Gazelle

9, rue Rennequin - 01 42 67 64 18, fax 01 42 67 82 77
Closed Sun. Open until 11:30pm.
The prettiest African restaurant in Paris, La Gazelle boasts a range of intensely tasty dishes

prepared by owner-chef Marie Koffi-Nketsin, who comes from Cameroon: try her shrimp fritters, lemon chicken yassa, and marinated kid baked en papillote with African corn. Crocodile also features on the menu—connoisseurs, take note! Heartwarming ambience. C 180. M 130, 150.

 Chez Georges

273, bd Pereire - 01 45 74 31 00, fax 01 45 74 02 56
Closed Aug 1-21. Open until 11:30pm. Priv rm 30. Terrace dining. Pkg.
Trends may come and go, but the bustling bistro atmosphere and comforting cuisine (ribs of beef with gratin savoyard, cheese ravioli in chive cream, hachis parmentier...) at Chez Georges remain the same. And so do the high prices. C 240-350.

12/20 Goldenberg

69, av. de Wagram
01 42 27 34 79, fax 01 42 27 98 85
Open daily until 11:30pm. Terrace dining.
Patrick Goldenberg creates a typically Yiddish atmosphere of good humor and nostalgia in which to savor Kosher cooking rooted in the traditions of Russia, Hungary, Romania... There's pastrami, corned goose breast, kneidler in chicken broth, veal sausage, and other Central European classics. For dessert, try the poppyseed strudel. C 160-260. M 98 (wine incl).

 Graindorge   🌣

15, rue de l'Arc-de-Triomphe
01 47 54 00 28, fax 01 44 09 84 51
Closed Sat lunch, Sun. Open until 11pm. Priv rm 30. Garage pkg.
When Bernard Broux (long-time chef at Le Trou Gascon) opened a place of his own, he forsook the Southwest in favor of the cuisine of his native Flanders. Broux's menu celebrates hearty Northern savors with creamy beer soup, waterzoï of scallops and shellfish in shrimp fumet, carbonnade of ox jowls laced with gin, and strawberries in a sabayon spiked with raspberry-flavored kriek beer. Good wine list, but beer lovers will be knocked out by the selection of rare brews. The 165 F lunch is a bargain. C 210. M 135, 165 (weekday lunch), 188, 230.

 Guyvonne

14, rue de Thann - 01 42 27 25 43, fax 01 42 27 25 43
Closed Sat, Sun, Aug 4-Sep 1, Dec 23-Jan 1. Open until 10pm. Priv rm 10. Terrace dining. No pets.
Guy Cros's menu balances tradition and modernity, with basil-scented sautéed squid, herbed roast salmon, and veal sweetbreads in a lush cream sauce laced with Port. Fine wine list; peaceful, provincial setting. C 290. M 150, 180.

 Kifune

44, rue Saint-Ferdinand - 01 45 72 11 19
Closed 2 wks in Aug, Dec-Jan. Open until 10pm. No pets. Pkg.

In the best Japanese tradition, large sums are demanded for tiny portions of food. But at Kifune the quality is irreproachable: sparkling fresh sashimi and sushi, shrimp tempura, whiting in soy sauce, ethereal fried chicken. C 300-400. M 135 (weekday lunch, Sat).

 Le Manoir de Paris

6, rue Pierre-Demours
01 45 72 25 25, fax 01 45 74 80 98
Closed Sat lunch, Sun. Open until 10:30pm. Priv rm 60. Air cond. Valet pkg.
Owner Francis Vandenhende and chef Daniel Hébert steer a skillful course between classicism and culinary daring, with nods to Provence (in honor of Vandehende's Niçoise wife). Their pleasingly eclectic menus propose brandade de morue (a purée of codfish and potatoes) swirled inside a sweet red pepper; a traditional bouchée à la reine filled with morsels of kidney, cock's comb, and prawns; coalfish escorted by fried garlic and a delicate white-bean purée studded with chorizo; and fragrant, cumin-spiced rack of lamb. Careful: the desserts are swoon-inducing (just spoon into that coffee mousse...). Rémi Aspect oversees the splendid cellar. C 450. M 195-295 (lunch), 195-350 (dinner).

 Les Marines de Pétrus

27, av. Niel - 01 47 63 04 24, fax 01 44 15 92 20
Open daily until 11pm. Terrace dining. Air cond. No cards.
The nautical décor charms us less than Souad Barrié, the gracious *patronne*, or the menu of tasty seafood: tartare prepared with a trio of fresh fish, empereur (a mild white fish) au curry, or cod with spicy condiments. Meat-eaters can plump for beef tenderloin béarnaise or pig's trotter en crépinette. A buttery brioche feuilleté served with caramel ice cream rounds things off on a satisfyingly rich note. There are two wine lists: one is modest, the other (which you must ask to see) quite grand. C 230-260.

 La Niçoise   🌣

4, rue Pierre-Demours
01 45 74 42 41, fax 01 45 74 80 98
Closed Sat lunch, Sun. Open until 11pm. Priv rm 60. Air cond. Valet pkg.
Sunny Niçois specialties served in a picture-postcard setting that's reminiscent of Nice at holiday time. Prime ingredients are prepared with touching sincerity to yield ricotta ravioli in a creamy pistou sauce, veal sauté with green olives, and sweet polenta with pears. Perfect Provençal cellar. M 90, 125 (wine incl), 165.

 Le Petit Colombier

42, rue des Acacias
01 43 80 28 54, fax 01 44 40 04 29
Closed Sat, Sun lunch, Aug 1-18. Open until 10:45pm. Priv rm 35. Air cond. Pkg.
With loving devotion, Bernard Fournier watches over his "provincial" inn, a family heirloom which he runs with the energy of three men. The reward for his vigilance is a loyal

clientele of contented gourmands who tuck in joyfully to such spirited, full-bodied dishes as hare terrine enriched with foie gras, lobster quenelles, or veal chops tenderly braised en cocotte. Each day also brings a roast—succulent ribs of beef, for example, or poularde truffée aux petits légumes—carved and served at the table. To toast these delights, there is a splendiferous cellar with some 50,000 bottles. C 480. M 200 (weekday lunch), 360 (dinner).

 Paolo Petrini

6, rue du Débarquadère
01 45 74 25 95, fax 01 45 74 12 95
Closed Sat lunch, Sun, 3 wks in Aug. Open until 11pm. Air cond.
Paolo Petrini hails from Pisa, he's a genuine Italian chef (Paris has so few)! His cooking is spare and stylized, yet the full spectrum of Italy's seductive savors are present in his warm, basil-scented salad of squid, clams, and cannellini beans, his delectable risotto ai porcini, grilled beef fillet dressed with balsamic vinegar, pappardelle napped with a rich, winy hare sauce, or tagliarini swathed in melted Fontina. Superb Italian cellar. C 300-350. M 150, 190.

 Petrus

12, pl. du Maréchal-Juin
01 43 80 15 95, fax 01 43 80 06 96
Closed Aug. Open until 11pm. Priv rm 20. Air cond. Valet pkg.
Jacky Louazé is the skipper aboard the good ship Petrus, who deserves another point this year. He handles seafood with discretion and restraint, serving forth a superb carpaccio of sea bream, bass, and salmon, a golden heap of crisp-fried whitebait, gingered tuna cooked as rare as you like, and a sole of pristine freshness. To begin, we always choose a dozen or so glossy Marennes oysters, and to finish, we just as invariably order the chocolate soufflé. Fine selection of white wines. C 400. M 250 (dinner).

 Il Ristorante

22, rue Fourcroy - 01 47 63 34 00
Closed 2 wks in Aug. Open until 10:45pm. Air cond. Pkg.
The Anfuso clan welcomes guests into their Venetian-style dining room to savor Rocco Anfuso's vibrant, high-spirited *cucina*. Outstanding features of a recent feast were sea bass ravioli perfumed with basil, beef fillet paired with peppery arugula, and an authentic tiramisù. Watch out, though: the fine Italian wines can send your bill soaring! C 280. M 165 (lunch).

 Michel Rostang

20, rue Rennequin
01 47 63 40 77, fax 01 47 63 82 75
Closed Sat lunch, Sun, Aug 1-18. Open until 10:30 pm. Priv rm 30. Air cond. Valet pkg.
Why is Michel Rostang down to two toques from four? His creativity isn't in question: his

menu lists hot foie gras infused with mocha and pepper, a fricassée of lamb's sweetbreads and lobster with spiced carrots, and sea bass roasted with pickled lemons, proof that Rostang is still touched by inspiration. But save for a perfectly aged and cooked rib steak in red-wine jus, and a fabulous biscuit au chocolat with a rich, molten center, we were puzzled and disappointed by flavors so evanescent that, had we closed our eyes, we mightn't have known what we were eating. Given Rostang's reputation—and prices—we think diners are entitled to greater gustatory thrills. Marie-Claude Rostang remains a gracious hostess, and Alain Ronzatti still presides over a connoisseur's cellar. C 650. M 298 (weekday lunch), 540, 720.

 Rôtisserie d'Armaillé

6, rue d'Armaillé - 01 42 27 19 20, fax 01 40 55 00 23
Closed Sat lunch, Sun. Open until 11pm, Fri & Sat 11:30pm. Air cond. Pkg.
Jacques Cagna reprises the bistro formula he successfully inaugurated at La Rôtisserie d'en Face (sixth arrondissement). For 218 F you can choose from a wide array of starters and desserts as well as a main course of spit-roasted poultry or meat. Interesting cellar. C 300. M 165 (weekday lunch), 218.

 Guy Savoy

18, rue Troyon
01 43 80 40 61, fax 01 46 22 43 09
Closed Sat lunch, Sun. Open until 10:30pm. Priv rm 35. Air cond. Valet pkg.
Guy Savoy is a real cook, a real artisan—a man who likes simple things. The flower arrangments in a bare Japanese style show his taste for simplicity; his cooking follows the same pattern. Savoy has stripped it of unecessary frills, retaining as much as possible a rustic, yet still elegant, style. He likes strong contrasts and does not hesitate, for instance, to serve as finger-food beets as opposed to cèpes mushrooms. Savoy uses his own products from the terroir to create a vivid and robust cooking with a rural accent, which for us is quite a compliment. A fantastic cellar with a large selection of the best. Wines of all regions—with prices in consequence. C 650-900. M 880.

Sormani

4, rue du Général-Lanrezac
01 43 80 13 91, fax 01 40 55 07 37
Closed Sat, Sun, Aug 4-22. Open until 10:30pm. Priv rm 18. Terrace dining. Air cond. Valet pkg.
Jean-Pascal Fayet's Italian cuisine is emphatically not the textbook version. His menu fairly crackles with such delectable inventions as diaphanous ravioli stuffed with sea urchins in a creamy ricotta sauce; a "pizza" topped with onion purée, lobster, and arugula; tender tagliatelle enriched with bacon and white beans; a sumptuous white-truffle risotto. True, spooning caviar onto leek ravioli may be a mite decadent, but Fayet's taste is more often faultless and his technique is admirably sure. The cellar boasts

fabulous bottles from Piedmont, Sicily, and Tuscany. **C** 350-400 (dinner). **M** 250 (lunch).

 ### La Soupière

154, av. de Wagram - 01 42 27 00 73
Closed Sat lunch, Sun, Aug 11-18. Open until 10:30pm. Terrace dining.
Christian Thuillart pampers his patrons in a pretty *trompe-l'œil* dining room. There's nothing deceptive about Thuillart's classic repertoire, however. A passionate connoisseur of rare and expensive mushrooms, he has built special menus around truffles and morels, served when their season is at its height. **C** 260. **M** 138, 165, 240.

 ### Le Sud Marocain

10, rue Villebois-Mareuil - 01 45 72 39 30
Closed Aug. Open until 10:30pm. Priv rm 10. Air cond.
Here's a find! This tiny restaurant (it holds just 25) run by a *patron* who looks just like Chico Marx serves sensational marinated sardines with ratatouille, a light, fragrantly herbal harira soup, excellent tagines (chicken and olives, lamb with prunes...), and a first-rate couscous royal. **C** 180-215.

 ### La Table de Pierre ✪

116, bd Pereire - 01 43 80 88 68, fax 01 47 66 53 02
Closed Sat lunch, Sun. Open until 11pm. Terrace dining. Air cond.
Pierre Darrieumerlou's table fairly groans beneath the weight of generously served Basco-Béarnais fare. Bring along a healthy appetite and order the codfish-stuffed peppers, confit de canard aux cèpes, or Pyrenees lamb with beans. Warm welcome; jolly atmosphere. Another point. **C** 210.

 ### Taïra

10, rue des Acacias
01 47 66 74 14, fax 01 47 66 74 14
Closed Sat lunch, Sun, 1 wk in Aug. Open until 10pm. Air cond.
Taïra is not a Japanese restaurant, but its chef is Japanese. What does that mean? Since chef/owner Taïra Kurihara's training is western but his roots are oriental, he has his own unique interpretation of bouillabaisse, and his sardines in oil are a summit. Try the aerial spring rolls stuffed with langoustines, the grilled sea-scallops on a potato purée, the John Dory finished with an unusual prawn sauce, the cuttle fish perfumed with basil. One of the the best seafood restaurants of Paris and they are so nice... **C** 300-400. **M** 150, 170, 330 (dinner).

11/20 Timgad

21, rue Brunel - 01 45 74 23 70, fax 01 40 68 76 46
Open daily until 11pm. Priv rm 10. Air cond. No pets. Pkg.
All the fragrant specialties of the Maghreb are on offer in this elegant restaurant, where you can sample hand-rolled couscous, crispy brik pastries, and a wide range of tagines. **C** 270-350.

 ### La Toque

16, rue de Tocqueville
01 42 27 97 75, fax 01 47 63 97 69
Closed Sat, Sun, Jul 20-Aug 20. Open until 10pm. Air cond.
The pretty dining room is tiny and so are the tables at Jacky Joubert's little Toque. Never mind: the good classic cooking is generously apportioned and attractively served. It earns another point. **C** 280. **M** 150, 210.

18TH ARRONDISSEMENT

Postal code	75018

A. Beauvilliers

52, rue Lamarck - 01 42 54 54 42, fax 01 42 62 70 30
Closed Sun, Mon lunch. Open until 10:45pm. Priv rm 34. Terrace dining. Air cond.
If ever a restaurant was designed for celebrations, this is it. Indeed, show-business personalities, celebrities, and politicos regularly scale the Butte Montmartre to toast their triumphs with Beauvilliers's best bubbly. But more care goes into the elegant setting than into the food. A recent visit brought us some decent but unexceptional dishes (chicken en cocotte, red mullet en escabèche, stuffed sweetbreads in aspic...) and one unmitigated disaster. Sea bass in a salt crust, the most expensive item on the menu, arrived horribly overcooked, with greasy fried chayote squash. Adequate desserts; goodish cellar, with a superb selection of Champagnes. **C** 400-500. **M** 185 (weekday lunch), 285 (weekday lunch, Sat), 400 (weekday dinner).

 ### Le Cottage Marcadet

151 bis, rue Marcadet - 01 42 57 71 22
Closed Sun, Aug. Open until 10pm. Air cond. No pets.
This little Cottage has nothing in common with the tourist traps farther up the Butte Montmartre. Here, chef Jean-François Canot pleases his patrons with personalized cooking full of bold, frank flavors. We loved the juniper-spiced calf's foot, the smoked-fish terrine, grilled sea bream dressed with oyster vinaigrette, and duck confit en chartreuse. The 210 F set meal is practically a gift. **C** 350. **M** 120 (lunch), 150, 210 (wine incl).

 ### Langevin

"Au Poulbot Gourmet,"
39, rue Lamarck - 01 46 06 86 00
Closed Sun dinner. Open until 10:15pm.

A glassed-in terrace gives patrons a wide-angle view of this picturesque corner of Montmartre. Jean-Paul Langevin serves forth appetizing versions of traditional country fare: tomatoes stuffed with curried snails, sole with mussels in sauce poulette, and charlotte aux deux chocolats sauce pistache. Tempting cellar. C 260. M 115 (lunch, exc Sun, wine incl), 160.

11/20 Chez Marie-Louise
52, rue Championnet - 01 46 06 86 55
Closed Sun, Mon, hols, Aug. Open until 10pm.
Lobster salad, veal chop grand'mère, lotte with fresh pasta, clafoutis of seasonal fruits—here's honest bistro cooking, unchanged for 35 years, served amid copper saucepans and prints of carousing monks. C 200-240. M 130.

 ### Le Restaurant
32, rue Véron - 01 42 23 06 22, fax 01 42 23 36 16
Closed lunch Sat & Mon, Sun. Open until 11:30pm.
Yves Péladeau worked his way up from busboy to owner-chef of his Restaurant in the trendy Abbesses section of Montmartre. The dining room is as modern, bright, and *à la mode* as the imaginative menu. Give your taste buds a treat with grilled leeks and potatoes with Cantal cheese, gingered pork with soy sauce, and honey-roasted duck spiced with coriander. Small but intelligent wine list (Minervois from Jacques Maris). M 120, 45 (children).

11/20 Le Sagittaire
77, rue Lamarck - 01 42 55 17 40
Closed Sun dinner, Mon. Open until 10:30pm.
In an old-fashioned Belle-Époque dining room adorned with a magnificent carved-wood bar, fill up on the generous all-in menu of homey French favorites. M 100 (lunch, wine incl, exc Sun), 165 (wine incl), 65 (children).

12/20 Wepler
14, pl. de Clichy - 01 45 22 53 24
Open daily until 1am. Air cond. Pkg.
A deluxe brasserie providing reliable food and good service. The shellfish are glossy and ultrafresh; other worthwhile options are the grilled salmon béarnaise, choucroute garnie, and bouillabaisse. C 190. M 92, 105 (weekday lunch), 150 (exc weekday lunch), 80 (children).

19TH ARRONDISSEMENT

Postal code	75019

12/20 Dagorno
190, av. Jean-Jaurès - 01 40 40 09 39
Open daily until 1:15am. Air cond. Valet pkg.
Quite a contrast with the futuristic Cité des Sciences, this opulent brasserie cultivates an old-fashioned image, offering decent, uncomplicated food. You won't be disappointed by the fresh shellfish, calf's head sauce gribiche, or the enormous côte de bœuf sauce bordelaise. C 300. M 157.

12/20 La Pièce de Bœuf
7, av. Corentin-Cariou
01 40 05 95 95, fax 01 40 34 67 78
Closed Sat, Sun, Jul 27-Aug 25. Open until 10:30pm. Air cond.
Well-wrought traditional brasserie fare; despite the name, we find that seafood is the menu's strong suit. The wine list favors Bordeaux and Champagnes. C 250. M 155.

 ### La Verrière d'Éric Fréchon
10, rue du Général-Brunet
01 40 40 03 30, fax 01 40 40 03 30
Closed Sun, Mon, Aug. Open until 11pm. Priv rm 30. Terrace dining. No pets.
There's nothing mysterious about it: when you serve fine food for reasonable prices, gourmets will beat a path to your door, no matter how remote your restaurant! In his neat and tidy little bistro, Éric Fréchon (a former second-in-command to Christian Constant) proposes a dazzling single-price menu for just 190 F. Market-fresh ingredients, balanced flavors, and cutting-edge technique distinguish Fréchon's cream of white bean soup showered with croûtons and shavings of Spanish ham; his langoustine croquants served with a lovely honey-dressed salad of tender lamb's lettuce; or cod stuffed with salt-cod purée and roasted in a spicy herbal crust; or an earthy sausage of pig's trotter enriched with foie gras and presented with whipped potatoes. For dessert, there's a superb mango feuilleté enhanced by lashings of almond cream. Interesting cellar of growers' wines; warm welcome from Sylvie Fréchon. In short, this is one of the year's top tables. M 190.

11/20 Au Rendez-Vous de la Marine
14, quai de la Loire - 01 42 49 33 40
Closed Sun, Mon, 1 wk in Aug. Open until 10pm. Terrace dining.
Sit down to a hearty omelette aux cèpes, confit de canard, or monkfish fillet at this friendly address by the canal. C 130-140.

 ### Chez Vincent
5, rue du Tunnel - 01 42 02 22 45
Closed Sat lunch, Sun. Open until 11pm.
Our friend Henri Gault calls this the "best trattoria in France." Reserve your table well in advance to savor Vincent's beef or salmon carpaccio showered with wonderful vegetables, warm shellfish marinière, deep-fried sardines, squid, and eggplant, or his silky fresh pasta. C 180-200. M 130, 160, 200 (dinner).

20TH ARRONDISSEMENT

Postal code **75020**

 Les Allobroges

71, rue des Grands-Champs
01 43 73 40 00
Closed Sun, Mon, 1 wk at Easter, Aug. Open until 10pm. Pkg.
It's worth the trip out to the twentieth arrondissement to taste Olivier Pateyron's langoustines with ratatouille, braised lamb with garlic confit, and cherry-pistachio dessert. The little 92 F set meal has its charms, and à la carte prices are clement too, inciting one to splurge on lobster and lotte with tarragon or spiced Barbary duck (order both in advance). Only the wine list needs improvement. **C** 250. **M** 92, 164.

12/20 A la Courtille

1, rue des Envierges
01 46 36 51 59, fax 01 46 36 65 56
Open daily until 10:45pm. Terrace dining.
Enjoy a spectacular view of the city from the terrace of this elegant bistro. Even better than the food (which is pretty good: marinated sardines, duck breast with fresh figs, crème brûlée...) is the wine list, compiled by Bernard Pontonnier and Francis Morel. **C** 160-200. **M** 70, 100 (lunch), 140.

11/20 Le Saint-Amour

2, av. Gambetta - 01 47 97 20 15
Closed Aug 15-23. Open until 10pm. Terrace dining.
The owner, an Auvergne native, serves first-rate regional charcuteries and cheeses alongside a few unpretentious hot dishes. Wines by the glass or the carafe. Good-humored ambience, a blessing in this gray, gloomy district. **C** 140-210. **M** 60-75 (exc Sat dinner & Sun, wine incl), 90-120.

PARIS HOTELS

LUXURY

Le Bristol

8th arr. - 112, rue du Faubourg-Saint-Honoré
01 53 43 43 00, fax 01 53 43 43 01
Open year-round. 40 stes 6,500-34,000. 153 rms 2,500-4,500. Bkfst 165-260. Restaurant. Rm ser. Air cond. Conf. Pool. No pets. Valet pkg.
An elegant décor (genuine period furniture, fine pictures), comfortable rooms, lavish suites, and a prestigious clientele make Le Bristol one of the rare authentic luxury hotels in Paris (as well as one of the most expensive). An elegant restaurant (Le Bristol) opens onto a formal French garden, see *Restaurants*. The staff is both cordial and impressively trained.

Castille

1st arr. - 37, rue Cambon
01 44 58 44 58, fax 01 44 58 44 00
Open year-round. 8 stes 3,300-3,700. 99 rms 1,750-2,400. Bkfst 125. Rms for disabled. Restaurant. Rm ser. Air cond. Conf. Valet pkg.
Venetian-style elegance, decked out in brocades, damask, and marble. Next door to Chanel, the Castille provides luxurious amenities and impeccably stylish service. Restaurant: Il Cortile, see *Restaurants*.

Hôtel de Crillon

8th arr. - 10, pl. de la Concorde
01 44 71 15 00, fax 01 44 71 15 02
Open year-round. 43 stes 4,900-29,000. 120 rms 2,550-4,100. Restaurants. Rm ser. Air cond. Conf. Valet pkg.
The Crillon is housed in an honest-to-goodness eighteenth-century palace. Indeed, the accommodations are truly fit for a king, with terraces overlooking the Place de la Concorde, sumptuous public rooms, and an exquisitely trained staff. The guest rooms are beautifully decorated; the suites offer all the splendor one could hope for. Everywhere the eye rests on silk draperies, woodwork ornamented with gold leaf, Aubusson rugs, and polished marble. Relais et Châteaux. Restaurants: Les Ambassadeurs, L'Obélisque and Le Patio, see *Restaurants*.

George V

8th arr. - 31, av. George-V
01 47 23 54 00, fax 01 47 20 22 05
Open year-round. 44 stes 5,700-15,500. 214 rms 1,800-3,900. Bkfst 140-210. Rms for disabled. Restaurant. Rm ser. Air cond. Conf.
The management is making Herculean efforts to instill new life and spirit into this landmark. The bar and the restaurant (Les Princes) have been redecorated, a Grill has been added, and the rooms have been renovated, with as much concern for elegance as for modernity. The pictures, rare ornaments, and lovely furniture in the public rooms radiate the legendary George V charm. *Check for exact date of closing for remodeling.*

Le Grand Hôtel Inter-Continental

9th arr. - 2, rue Scribe
01 40 07 32 32, fax 01 42 66 12 51
Open year-round. 35 stes 3,500-14,000. 479 rms 1,700-2,800. Bkfst 125-160. Rms for disabled. Restaurant. Rm ser. Air cond. Conf. No pets. Valet pkg.
The monumental Second Empire building has recovered all the splendor it displayed when Empress Eugénie inaugurated it in 1862. The huge central lobby, capped by a glittering glass dome, is a wonder to behold. Guest rooms provide everything the international traveler could require in the way of amenities, as well as the most up-to-date business equipment, a health club, and much more. Excellent bar; for the Opéra Restaurant, see *Restaurants*.

Inter-Continental

1st arr. - 3, rue de Castiglione
01 44 77 11 11, fax 01 44 77 14 60
Open year-round. 79 stes 4,200-20,000. 371 rms 2,500-2,700. Bkfst 100-150. Restaurants. Rm ser. Air cond. Conf. Valet pkg.
A three-year renovation program has started at the Inter Continental. The 450 rooms and conference rooms of this monumental Second Empire hotel are being progressively refurbished. The restaurant and patio are also under reconstruction. In the meantime, the hotel remains open and is hosting a series of cultural and culinary events.

Hôtel du Louvre

1st arr. - Pl. André Malraux
01 44 58 38 38, fax 01 44 58 38 01
Open year-round. 4 stes 3,000. 195 rms 1,350-1,950. Bkfst 110. Rms for disabled. Restaurant. Rm ser. Air cond. Valet pkg.
Here is a remarkable example of Second Empire architecture, conveniently situated near Palais-Royal and the Louvre. Tradition and contemporary comforts combine to excellent effect in the posh guest rooms. Business travelers will appreciate the range of services placed.

Hôtel Meurice

1st arr. - 228, rue de Rivoli
01 44 58 10 10, fax 01 44 58 10 15
Open year-round. 35 stes 6,000-15,000. 152 rms 2,250-3,100. Bkfst 150-195. Rms for disabled. Restaurant. Rm ser. Air cond. Conf. Valet pkg.

The Meurice has undergone substantial renovation in the past few years to restore its glamour and prestige. The admirable salons on the main floor were refurbished; the guest rooms and suites (which offer a view of the Tuileries) were equipped with air conditioning and tastefully redecorated; and the pink-marble bathrooms are ultramodern. The Meurice ranks as one of the best grand hotels in Paris. An elegant restaurant, Le Meurice, see *Restaurants*, is lodged in the Salon des Tuileries, overlooking the gardens.

 ## Plaza Athénée

8th arr. - 25, av. Montaigne
01 53 67 66 65, fax 01 53 67 66 66
Open year-round. 40 stes 2,500-13,500. 166 rms 2,500-4,650. Bkfst 160-250. Restaurant. Rm ser. Air cond. Valet pkg.
Discretion, efficiency, and friendly courtesy are the Plaza's trademarks. The accommodations are bright, generous in size, and fitted with every amenity. The rooms overlooking Avenue Montaigne are perfectly soundproofed. At about 11am, guests gather in the Plaza Bar Anglais (where Mata Hari was arrested); and from 4pm to 7pm you'll see them in the gallery (of which Marlene Dietrich was particularly fond). Le Régence restaurant is located across from the patio, where tables are set in the summer among cascades of geraniums and ampelopsis vines, see *Restaurants*.

 ## Prince de Galles

8th arr. - 33, av. George-V
01 47 23 55 11, fax 01 47 20 61 05
Open year-round. 30 stes 3,650-12,000. 138 rms 1,900-2,900. Bkfst 145-175. Restaurant. Rm ser. Air cond. Conf. Valet pkg.
Extensive renovations have restored the brilliance of this renowned hotel, built in the Roaring Twenties. Marble expanses stretch as far as the eye can see, walls sport handsome prints, and guest rooms are outfitted with minibars, safes, and a flock of new facilities. We only wish that the lovely old mosaics had been preserved. As ever, the hotel's open-roofed patio is a delightful place to have lunch on a warm day; the paneled Regency Bar is another pleasant spot, distinguished by excellent service. For Le Jardin des Cygnes, see *Restaurants*.

 ## Raphaël

16th arr. - 17, av. Kléber
01 44 28 00 28, fax 01 45 01 21 50
Open year-round. 25 stes 3,950-24,000. 65 rms 1,850-2,950. Bkfst 120-160. Restaurant. Rm ser. Air cond. Conf. Valet pkg.
Built between the wars, the Raphaël has maintained an atmosphere of rare refinement and elegance, that you only find in a very few hotels throughout the world. Oriental rugs on the marble floors, fine woodwork, old paintings and period furniture make Le Raphaël a very luxurious place to stay, preferred by a wealthy, well-bred clientele. The spacious rooms are rich-

ly furnished in various styles; the wardrobes and bathrooms are immense. A truly extraordinary and splendid new addition is a three-level suite that boasts an eye-popping panoramic view from the terrace (the terrace, by the way, is at the same level as the Arc de Triomphe). The suite is a glittering showcase for the finest in French craftsmanship. Or ask for the duplex suite 515—the bathroom is unbelievable! Top-drawer reception and service, of course. Intimate (and star-studded) English bar. Sumptuous conference facilities. For La Salle à Manger, see *Restaurants*.

 ## Résidence Maxim's de Paris

8th arr. - 42, av. Gabriel
01 45 61 96 33, fax 01 42 89 06 07
Open year-round. 33 stes 2,750-15,000. 4 rms 2,000-2,250. Restaurant. Rm ser. Air cond. Conf. Valet pkg.
Pierre Cardin himself designed the hotel of his dreams, a small but palatial establishment that may well be the world's most luxurious. The landings of each floor are decorated like elegant salons, with beautiful and unusual antique pieces and paintings. Polished stone and sumptuous murals adorn the bathrooms. The suites must be seen to be believed, particularly those on the top floor, which are furnished with pieces designed by Cardin. Obviously, accommodations like these are well beyond the bank balances of most mortals.

 ## Ritz

1st arr. - 15, pl. Vendôme
01 43 16 30 30, fax 01 43 16 36 68
Open year-round. 45 stes 5,500-25,700. 142 rms 2,800-4,300. Bkfst 180-230. Rms for disabled. Restaurant. Rm ser. Conf. Heated pool. Valet pkg.
The world's most famous hotel is poised to enter the 21st century with highest-tech facilities, but without having betrayed the character that won the Ritz its reputation. Even if nowadays you can change the video program or make a phone call without leaving your bed or marble bath (Charles Ritz was the first to provide private bathrooms for his clients), nothing has altered the pleasure of stretching out on a wide brass bed surrounded by fine antiques. Add to that an atmosphere of luxury so enveloping that a new word ("ritzy") had to be coined for it. Impeccable staff. The health club was modeled on a thermal spa of antiquity, and L'Espadon, see *Restaurants*, has its own marvelous garden.

 ## Royal Monceau

8th arr. - 35, av. Hoche
01 42 99 88 00, fax 01 42 99 89 90
Open year-round. 39 stes 3,650-16,000. 180 rms 2,150-3,350. Bkfst 140-190. Rms for disabled. Restaurants. Rm ser. Air cond. Conf. Heated pool. Valet pkg.
Politicians, foreign business people and entertainers appreciate the Royal Monceau's spacious

rooms, magnificent marble bathrooms, and luxurious amenities (excellent room service). Extras include a fashionable piano bar, a prestigious health club, Les Thermes, (with sauna, Jacuzzi, swimming pool, and a massage service), ultramodern conference rooms and a well-equipped "business club." The rooms overlooking the charming flowered patio are the most sought-after by the hotel's habitués. Restaurants: Le Carpaccio and Le Jardin du Royal Monceau, see *Restaurants*.

 Westminster

2nd arr. - 13, rue de la Paix
01 42 61 57 46, fax 01 42 60 30 66
Open year-round. 18 stes 3,600-5,500. 84 rms 1,650-2,450. Bkfst 110-130. Restaurant. Rm ser. Air cond. Conf. Valet pkg.
To celebrate its 150th birthday, the hotel has completed a total renovation. This charming mid-size luxury hotel is advantageously situated between the Opéra and Place Vendôme. The pink-and-beige marble lobby is splendid and luxurious; the bar, Les Chenets, with piano, is more than comfortable. Conference rooms are superbly equipped. As for the guest rooms, they are handsomely decorated with attractive fabrics, chandeliers, and Louis XV–style furnishings and are fitted with minibars, safes, and satellite TV, with marble bathrooms. Restaurant: Le Céladon, see *Restaurants*. Enquire about the guaranteed dollar rates available throughout the year. Call, within the U.S. only, 1-800 203 32 32.

FIRST CLASS

 Ambassador

9th arr. - 16, bd Haussmann
01 44 83 40 40, fax 01 42 46 19 84
Open year-round. 9 stes 2,000-3,800. 289 rms 1,300-1,800. Bkfst 97-122. Restaurant. Rm ser. Air cond. Conf. Valet pkg.
A fine traditional hotel. The guest rooms have been modernized in excellent taste with sumptuous fabrics, thick carpeting, and Art Deco furniture. Nearly all are air conditioned. The lobby and public rooms boast pink-marble columns topped with gilded Corinthian capitals, marble floors, and Aubusson tapestries on the walls. The penthouse suites look out over Sacré-Cœur. Restaurant: Venantius, see *Restaurants*; and a handsome Art Deco bar.

 Astor Madeleine

8th arr. - 11, rue d'Astorg
01 53 05 05 20, fax 01 53 05 05 30
Open year-round. 5 stes 2,950-8,000. 130 rms 1,590-2,650. Bkfst 120-195. Rms for disabled. Restaurant. Rm ser. Air cond. Valet pkg.
The Astor has just completed an ambitious, two-year renovation program directed by ar-

chitect Frédéric Méchiche. The lobby is resplendent with fine woodwork, and the quiet rooms, arranged around a white courtyard, are decorated in English or Empire style, with striped fabrics in shades of lavender, green, or blue. Though not huge, the guest quarters provide plenty of comfort and luxury. Two suites offer terraces with views over the city's rooftops. See *Restaurants* for the restaurant.

 Baltimore

16th arr. - 88 bis, av. Kléber
01 44 34 54 54, fax 01 44 34 54 44
Open year-round. 1 ste 3,500. 104 rms 1,790-2,950. Bkfst 120-195. Restaurant. Half-board 2,040-3,250. Air cond. Conf. Pkg.
Six fully equipped meeting rooms are located on the lower level; the largest and most luxurious is the former vault room of the Banque Nationale de Paris. The bright lobby is quite imposing; the rooms less so, owing to over-decoration. Some are on the small side, too, but amenities abound. Restaurant: Le Bertie's, see *Restaurants*.

 Balzac

8th arr. - 6, rue Balzac
01 44 35 18 00, fax 01 44 35 18 05
Open year-round. 14 stes 3,200-6,000. 56 rms 1,700-2,200. Bkfst 90-150. Restaurant. Rm ser. Air cond. Valet pkg.
A quietly luxurious establishment near the Place de l'Étoile, frequented by celebrities and jet-setters. The huge rooms have been redecorated by Nina Campbell in delicate tones with lovely furniture, beautiful chintzes, and thick carpeting. Most have king-size beds, all have superb modern bathrooms. Unobtrusive yet attentive staff. Let us no forget the arrival of Pierre Gagnaire at the restaurant, see *Restaurants*.

 Caron de Beaumarchais

4th arr. - 12, rue Vieille-du-Temple
01 42 72 34 12, fax 01 42 72 34 63
Open year-round. 19 rms 620-730. Bkfst 48-78. Air cond. Conf.
Here's a find: a hotel overflowing with charm, set in the heart of the Marais. The lobby's eighteenth-century atmosphere is underscored by a Louis XVI fireplace, beamed ceilings, and handsome antiques. The perfectly comfortable rooms are equipped with air conditioning and double glazing for cool quiet in summer.

 Château Frontenac

8th arr. - 54, rue Pierre-Charron
01 53 23 13 13, fax 01 53 23 13 01
Open year-round. 4 stes 1,600-1,700. 102 rms 950-1,450. Bkfst 85. Restaurant. Air cond. Conf.
A reasonably priced hotel (given the location), with various sizes of rooms done in vaguely Louis XV style. Superb marble bathrooms. The soundproofing is effective, but the rooms overlooking the Rue Cérisole are still the quietest. Attentive reception staff; excellent service. Restaurant: Le Pavillon Frontenac.

Clarion Saint-James et Albany

1st arr. - 202, rue de Rivoli
01 44 58 43 21, fax 01 44 58 43 11
Open year-round. 13 stes 1,800-2,500. 198 rms 980-1,500. Bkfst 80. Restaurant. Half-board 200. Rm ser. Conf.
The Clarion Saint James et Albany enjoys an exceptional location across from the Tuileries, and provides studios, two-room apartments, suites, and bilevel suites equipped with kitchenettes. The rooms overlook a courtyard or an inner garden and are perfectly quiet. Modern décor.

 ## Concorde La Fayette

17th arr. - 3, pl. du Général-Kœnig
01 40 68 50 68, fax 01 40 68 50 43
Open year-round. 32 stes 3,000. 938 rms 1,250-1,650. Bkfst 98-122. Restaurants. Rm ser. Conf. No pets. Valet pkg.
The Concorde La Fayette is immense: a huge oval tower that houses the Palais des Congrès, banquet rooms, scores of boutiques, cinemas, and nightclubs. The hotel's rooms meet the chain's usual standards, with all the modern amenities. Panoramic bar, three restaurants, including L'Étoile d'Or, see *Restaurants*. Airport shuttles.

 ## Concorde Saint-Lazare

8th arr. - 108, rue Saint-Lazare
01 40 08 44 44, fax 01 42 93 01 20
Open year-round. 27 stes 2,450-3,500. 273 rms 1,200-1,500. Bkfst 105. Restaurant. Rm ser. Air cond. Conf. Valet pkg.
An enormous hotel, built in 1889 by Gustave Eiffel, with superb rooms and services. The most arresting feature is the lobby, a listed architectural landmark, that soars three storeys up to coffered ceilings aglitter with gilt, marble, and crystal chandeliers. A magnificent billiard room on the main floor is open to the public. Restaurant: Café Terminus, see *Restaurants*.

 ## Édouard VII

2nd arr. - 39, av. de l'Opéra
01 42 61 56 90, fax 01 42 61 47 73
Open year-round. 4 stes 2,000. 65 rms 950-1,400. Bkfst 90. Restaurant. Rm ser. Air cond. Conf.
A luxurious place to stay, with individually styled rooms and beautifully crafted furniture. From the upper storeys there is a wonderful view of the Opéra. Restaurant: Delmonico, see *Restaurants*.

 ## Golden Tulip Saint-Honoré

8th arr. - 218, rue du Faubourg-Saint-Honoré
01 49 53 03 03, fax 01 40 75 02 00
Open year-round. 20 stes 2,400-3,900. 52 rms 1,500-1,800. Bkfst 110. Rms for disabled. Restaurant. Air cond. Pool. Garage pkg.

This comfortable hotel is decorated in modern style using traditional materials (marble, wood, quality fabrics, *trompe-l'œil* paintings). The bright, spacious rooms offer every amenity; all are air conditioned, with splendid marble bathrooms, and kitchenettes. Restaurant: Le Relais Vermeer, see *Restaurants*.

 ## Hilton

15th arr. - 18, av. de Suffren
01 43 38 56 00, fax 01 44 38 56 10
Open year-round. 26 stes 3,700-12,000. 436 rms 1,595-2,365. Bkfst 85-120. Rms for disabled. Restaurants. Rm ser. Air cond. Conf. Valet pkg.
The city's first postwar luxury hotel is still living up to Hilton's high standards. Rooms are airy and spacious, service is courteous and deft, and children—of any age—can share their parents' room at no extra charge. Restaurants, bars, boutiques.

 ## Lancaster

8th arr. - 7, rue de Berri
01 40 76 40 76, fax 01 40 76 40 00
Open year-round. 7 stes 3,000-7,300. 51 rms 1,850-2,650. Bkfst 120-170. Restaurant. Rm ser. Conf. Valet pkg.
Inhale the perfume of the immense bouquet of flowers in the lobby, then admire the general setting—furniture, wall hangings, paintings, ornaments—of this refined and luxurious hotel. The ravishing indoor garden, with its flowers, fountains, and statues (meals are served there on sunny days) lends an unexpected bucolic touch to this hotel, only steps from the Champs-Élysées.

 ## Littré

6th arr. - 9, rue Littré
01 45 44 38 68, fax 01 45 44 88 13
Open year-round. 4 stes 1,350-1,550. 93 rms 695-1,000. Bkfst 70. Rm ser. Conf. No pets. Pkg.
The style and décor of this four-star hotel are stiff and starchy, but the Littré's habitués find the old-fashioned comfort and service entirely satisfactory. In the spacious, recently renovated rooms you'll find high, comfortable beds, ponderous furniture, huge armoires, and big marble bathrooms. English bar.

 ## Lotti

1st arr. - 7, rue de Castiglione
01 42 60 37 34, fax 01 40 15 93 56
Open year-round. 2 stes 4,900-6,500. 129 rms 1,410-3,330. Bkfst 120. Restaurant. Conf. Valet pkg.
An elegant hotel, popular with European aristocracy. Each of the spacious rooms is individually decorated and offers excellent facilities. The restaurant, the lobby, and all the rooms were recently redecorated. The bathrooms are under renovation, and will then feature Jacuzzis. The charming attic rooms are reserved for non-smokers.

Hôtel Lutétia

6th arr. - 45, bd Raspail
01 49 54 46 46, fax 01 49 54 46 00
Open year-round. 30 stes 2,200-12,000. 225 rms 990-1,990. Bkfst 65. Rms for disabled. Restaurants. Air cond. Conf. Valet pkg.
A Left Bank landmark, in the Art Deco style. Marble, gilt, and red velvet grace the stately public areas where well-heeled travelers come and go. Leading off the imposing entrance are the lounge, a bar, a brasserie, a restaurant (Brasserie Lutétia and Le Paris, see *Restaurants*), and conference rooms. The large suites are done up in pink, with understated furniture and elegant bathrooms—the overall look is very 1930s.

 # Marignan

8th arr. - 12, rue Marignan
01 40 76 34 56, fax 01 40 76 34 34
Open year-round. 16 stes 2,650. 57 rms 1,690-1,990. Bkfst 120. Restaurant. Air cond. Valet pkg.
Strategically situated in the heart of the "Golden Triangle," between the Champs-Élysées and Avenue Montaigne, this charming establishment with its listed Art Deco façade and lobby draws a haute-couture crowd. Magnificent rooms done up in marble and expensive fabrics, with every modern comfort; some even boast a little terrace.

 # Hôtel Marriott Paris Champs-Élysées

8th. arr. - 70, av. des Champs-Élysées
01 53 93 55 00, fax 01 53 93 55 01
Open year-round. 18 stes 3,500-12,000. 174 rms 1,700-2,500. Bkfst 135-175. Restaurant. Air cond. Business center. Fitness center. Sauna. Conf. Private pkg.
For its only hotel in France, Marriott has chosen one of the most prestigious addresses in the world. Seventeen of the rooms provide lucky guests with a view of the Champs-Élysées. Rooms are decorated in a classical style with English furniture, and all the modern amenities are provided, including two-line telephones and soundproofed windows and floors. The hotel caters to business travelers and provides a modem in every room, as well as a business center, open from 7am to 10pm. The parking lot is directly beneath the hotel and has direct access to the lobby on the second floor, where a piano bar overlooking the Champs-Elysées is also located.

 # Montalembert

7th arr. - 3, rue de Montalembert
01 45 49 68 68, fax 01 45 49 69 49
Open year-round. 5 stes 2,700-3,700. 51 rms 1,675-2,140. Bkfst 100. Restaurant. Rm ser. Air cond.
Restored to its former splendor, this 1926 hotel sports luxurious materials (marble, ebony, sycamore, leather), designer fabrics and linens. Guests love the huge towels, cozy dressing gowns, and premium toiletries they find in the spectacular blue-gray bathrooms. The eighth-

floor suites afford an enchanting view of the city. The hotel bar is a favorite with writers and publishers.

 # Le Parc

16th arr. - 55-57, av. Raymond-Poincaré
01 44 05 66 66, fax 01 44 05 66 00
Open year-round. 20 stes 3,200-3,500. 100 rms 1,990-2,650. Bkfst 120. Rms for disabled. Restaurants. Air cond. Conf. Valet pkg.
Celebrity decorators were called in to refurbish this elegant hotel. Supremely comfortable, the rooms boast the most refined appointments and every imaginable amenity. The public rooms are accented with beautiful sculpture. A glorious indoor garden is planted with rare specimens. Restaurant: Le Relais du Parc, see *Restaurants*.

 # Pergolèse

16th arr. - 3, rue Pergolèse
01 40 67 96 77, fax 01 45 00 12 11
Open year-round. 40 rms 890-1,590. Bkfst 65-90. Air cond.
The Pergolèse provides a top-class address as well as smiling service and first-rate amenities for what are still (relatively) reasonable prices. Elegant furnishings and vivid, modern, décor by Rena Dumas.

 # Régina

1st arr. - 2, pl. des Pyramides
01 42 60 31 10, fax 01 40 15 95 16
Open year-round. 15 stes 2,700-3,900. 121 rms 1,600-2,200. Bkfst 95-145. Restaurant. Air cond. Conf. Valet pkg.
Opposite the Tuileries is one of the city's most venerable luxury hotels, with immense rooms, precious furniture (Louis XVI, Directoire, Empire) and —a practical addition—double-glazed windows. The grandiose lobby is graced with handsome old clocks that give the time of all the major European cities. Pretty indoor garden; English bar. Restaurant: Le Pluvinel, see *Restaurants*.

 # Royal Saint-Honoré

1st arr. - 221, rue Saint-Honoré
01 42 60 32 79, fax 01 42 60 47 44
Open year-round. 5 stes 2,350. 67 rms 1,250-1,950. Bkfst 90. Restaurant. Rm ser. Conf. No pets.
Closed for over a year, the Royal Saint-Honoré is back with a brighter, fresher look. The attentive staff does its utmost to make your stay enjoyable. All of the rooms are spacious; some boast terraces overlooking the Tuileries. Marble bathrooms, and a new bar.

 # Saint James Paris

16th arr. - 43, av. Bugeaud
01 44 05 81 81, fax 01 44 05 81 82
Open year-round. 24 stes 2,400-3,600. 24 rms 1,550-1,980. Bkfst 95-110. Restaurant. Rm ser. Air cond. Conf. Valet pkg.
A large staff looks after the 48 rooms and suites—a luxury level of attention with prices

fixed accordingly. The huge rooms are decorated in a low-key 1930s style with flowers and plants, and feature bathrooms clad in gray mosaic tile. Don't miss the magnificent library, which also houses the hotel's piano bar. Very luxurious health club with sauna, and a Jacuzzi.

Scribe

9th arr. - 1, rue Scribe
01 44 71 24 24, fax 01 44 71 24 42
Open year-round. 11 stes 1,950-6,400. 206 rms 1,950-2,450. Bkfst 105-125. Rms for disabled. Air cond. Conf. Valet pkg.
Behind the Scribe's Napoléon III façade stands a prime example of the French hotelier's art. All the rooms, suites, and two-level suites are furnished in classic style, and offer huge bathrooms. A multitude of TV channels is on tap, as well as 24-hour room service. Restaurant: Les Muses, see *Restaurants*; and a bar.

Les Suites Saint-Honoré

8th arr. - 13, rue d'Aguesseau
01 44 51 16 35, fax 01 42 66 35 70
Open year-round. 13 stes 3,200-5,400. Bkfst 95. Rm ser. Air cond. Restaurant. Garage pkg.
This is not the only all-suite hotel in Paris, but considering the prices, it is possibly the top of its class. Les Suites Saint-Honoré deliver an incredible product in Paris. Its great location and discreet service and ambience make it the perfect hideaway for celebrities, financiers and families. Each spacious suite has full kitchen facilities and roomy living quarters where you'll feel like a Parisian living in your own apartment. The hotel was entirely rebuilt in 1992 in two styles, modern and classic. All the creature comforts are supplied: TV, video and CD systems, two-line telephones, air conditioning, private parking garage right downstairs, etc. The American-style in-house restaurant, Higgins (see *Restaurants*), is open for lunch only. On your next stay, this is a place to put on the top of your list.

La Trémoille

8th arr. - 14, rue de La Trémoille
01 47 23 34 20, fax 01 40 70 01 08
Open year-round. 14 stes 2,780-5,170. 93 rms 1,400-2,930. Bkfst 100-120. Rms for disabled. Restaurant. Rm ser. Air cond. Conf. Valet pkg.
Cozy comfort, antique furniture, balconies with bright flower-filled window-boxes, and service worthy of a grand hotel. Several suites are quite new and remarkably comfortable; all the rooms have lovely bathrooms and modern amenities. The delightful dining room/salon is warmed by a crackling fire in winter.

Hôtel Vernet

8th arr. - 25, rue Vernet
01 44 31 98 00, fax 01 44 31 85 69
Open year-round. 3 stes 3,500. 54 rms 1,650-2,250. Bkfst 120-150. Restaurant. Rm ser. Air cond. Conf. No pets. Valet pkg.

An admirable hotel, the Vernet combines the best of modern and traditional comforts. The rooms and suites are handsomely decorated with genuine Louis XVI, Directoire, or Empire furniture, and walls are hung with sumptuous fabrics. Jacuzzi in all the bathrooms. Free access to the beautiful Royal Monceau' health club. Restaurant: Les Élysées du Vernet, see *Restaurants*.

Vigny

8th arr. - 9, rue Balzac
01 40 75 04 39, fax 01 40 75 05 81
Open year-round. 12 stes 2,600-5,000. 25 rms 1,900-2,200. Bkfst 90-150. Restaurant. Rm ser. Air cond. No pets. Pkg.
A romantic hotel, the Vigny offers English mahogany furniture, comfortable beds, and fine marble bathrooms: the virtues of another age simplified and brought up to date. The suites provide all-out luxury. Excellent service. Bar.

Warwick

8th arr. - 5, rue de Berri
01 45 63 14 11, fax 01 43 59 00 98
Open year-round. 21 stes 4,200-8,500. 126 rms 1,790-2,650. Bkfst 105-150. Rm ser. Conf. Valet pkg.
Luxurious and modern, just off the Champs-Élysées, this hotel offers bright, spacious, rooms done in pastel colors and chintz. Efficient soundproofing and air conditioning. Newly refurbished lobby. There is an attractive bar with piano music in the evening, with a jazz band on Thursdays. Restaurant: La Couronne, see *Restaurants*.

CLASSIC

Hôtel de l'Arcade

8th arr. - 9, rue de l'Arcade
01 53 30 60 00, fax 01 40 07 03 07
Open year-round. 4 stes 1,100. 37 rms 770-940. Bkfst 55. Rms for disabled. Air cond. Conf.
Here you'll revel in truly spacious, prettily decorated quarters, conveniently sited in the shoppers' mecca between the Madeleine and the major department stores. The perfectly quiet rooms sport pastel fabrics and cherrywood furniture; bathrooms are clad in white marble.

Britannique

1st arr. - 20, av. Victoria
01 42 33 74 59, fax 01 42 33 82 65
Open year-round. 40 rms 645-888. Bkfst 52. No pets.
A warm welcome and good service characterize this family-run hotel. The rooms are decorated with pale walls, dark carpeting and comfortable modern furniture. Rooms on the second and fifth floors have balconies with views of the Châtelet.

Buci Latin

6th arr. - 34, rue de Buci
01 43 29 07 20, fax 01 43 29 67 44
Open year-round. 2 stes 1,590-1,690. 25 rms 900-1,170. Bkfst 55. Rms for disabled. Restaurant. Rm ser. Air cond.
Decorator Alain Perrier turned this small hotel into a showcase of contemporary style. On the ground floor you'll find a pleasant American-style coffee shop.

 Cayré

7th arr. - 4, bd Raspail
01 45 44 38 88, fax 01 45 44 98 13
Open year-round. 118 rms 900-1,200. Bkfst 50-65. Restaurant. Rm ser.
A pink-and-gray marble floor, glass pillars and red-leather furniture lend an air of luxury to the lobby. The modern, thoroughly soundproofed rooms are impersonal but well equipped, with marble bathrooms. Good service, too.

 Colisée

8th arr. - 6, rue du Colisée
01 43 59 95 25, fax 01 45 63 26 54
Open year-round. 45 rms 655-870. Bkfst 45.
Discreetly modern rooms, mostly on the small side (those with numbers ending in an 8 are more spacious), but quite comfortable. Some are soundproofed. The four attic rooms have beamed ceilings and considerable charm. Inviting bar, but no restaurant.

 Commodore

9th arr. - 12, bd Haussmann
01 42 46 72 82, fax 01 47 70 28 81
Open year-round. 11 stes 2,300-3,600. 151 rms 1,250-1,650. Bkfst 110-140. Restaurant. Conf.
A recently renovated establishment located a few steps away from the Drouot auction house. Good-sized rooms, convenient for business travelers.

 Duminy Vendôme

1st arr. - 3, rue du Mont-Thabor
01 42 60 32 80, fax 01 42 96 07 83
Open year-round. 77 rms 525-870. Bkfst 65. Rms for disabled. Rm ser. Conf. Valet pkg.
Duminy Vendôme's rooms have good bathrooms and 1920s–style furnishings. Rooms on the sixth and seventh floors have slightly sloping ceilings, and those with numbers ending in 10 are larger than the rest. A small summer patio is located on the main floor. Charming reception. Some rooms have been renovated.

 Élysa

5th arr. - 6, rue Gay-Lussac
01 43 25 31 74, fax 01 46 34 56 27
Open year-round. 30 rms 450-720. Bkfst 45. Restaurant. Rm ser. Conf. No pets.
In the heart of the Latin Quarter, near the Luxembourg Gardens. The small, inviting rooms are regularly renovated. Gray-marble bathrooms.

 Élysées Maubourg

7th arr. - 35, bd de Latour-Maubourg
01 45 56 10 78, fax 01 47 05 65 08
Open year-round. 30 rms 560-1,000. Bkfst 45. Conf.
The 30 rooms of this hotel are decorated in classic good taste. Adequately sized, they are superbly equipped and comfortable. There is a Finnish sauna in the basement, a bar, and a flower-filled patio.

 Hôtel Étoile Friedland

8th arr. - 177, rue du Faubourg-Saint-Honoré
01 45 63 64 65, fax 01 45 63 88 96
Open year-round. 40 rms 650-1,100. Bkfst 75. Rms for disabled. Rm ser.
The bright yellow lobby is not at all typical of the hotel's décor. Indeed, the rooms are lovely, done up in soft, delicate shades. Excellent soundproofing.

 Frantour-Paris-Suffren

15th arr. - 20, rue Jean-Rey
01 45 78 50 00, fax 01 45 78 91 42
Open year-round. 11 stes 1,990-3,450. 396 rms 890-1,075. Bkfst 80. Rms for disabled. Restaurant. Air cond. Conf. Pkg.
The Frantour Suffren is a large, modern hotel located next to the Seine and the Champ-de-Mars. Though somewhat impersonal, the simple rooms are regularly refurbished and offer excellent equipment. Friendly service. Meals are served in the enclosed garden.

 Grand Hôtel de Champagne

1st arr. - 17, rue Jean-Lantier
01 42 36 60 00, fax 01 45 08 43 33
Open year-round. 3 stes 990-1,230. 40 rms 590-800. Bkfst 55.
A welcoming hotel, with exposed stone walls and ancient beams for atmosphere. The rooms are individually decorated, sometimes in exuberant fashion; some give onto a pretty terrace.

 Holiday Inn

19th arr. - 216, av. Jean-Jaurès
01 44 84 18 18, fax 01 44 84 18 20
Open year-round. 8 stes 1,490. 174 rms 890-1,050. Bkfst 75. Rms for disabled. Restaurant. Rm ser. Air cond. Conf. Garage pkg.
The contemporary architecture and modern comforts of this Holiday Inn are in keeping with the urban environment of La Villette. Many of the perfectly quiet rooms look out onto the Cité de la Musique, an impressive building by noted architect Christian de Portzamparc.

 Holiday Inn République

11th arr. - 10, pl. de la République
01 43 55 44 34, fax 01 47 00 32 34

Open year-round. 7 stes 1,950-2,995. 311 rms 1,395-1,625. Bkfst 105. Rms for disabled. Restaurant. Rm ser. Air cond. Conf.

The architect Davioud, who designed the Châtelet, built this former Modern Palace in 1867. Today it belongs to the largest hotel chain in the world, which completely restored and modernized it. The rooms and suites are functional, pleasant, and well soundproofed; the most attractive ones overlook the flower-filled, covered courtyard.

 ## Holiday Inn Saint-Germain-des-Prés

6th arr. - 92, rue de Vaugirard
01 42 22 00 56, fax 01 42 22 05 39
Open year-round. 22 stes 930-1,030. 112 rms 840-940. Bkfst 75. Rms for disabled. Air cond. Pkg.

This is a quiet, functional establishment. Well-equipped rooms with minibar and satellite TV, some furnished in cruise-liner style. Piano bar filled with plants. American buffet breakfasts, Gregory's Restaurant. Impeccable service.

 ## Libertel Terminus Nord

10th arr. - 12, bd de Denain
01 42 80 20 00, fax 01 42 80 63 89
Open year-round. 4 stes 1,600. 239 rms 600-1,000. Bkfst 80. Rms for disabled. Restaurant. Air cond.

A successful renovation has transformed this hotel into a fine place to stay. The spacious, fully equipped rooms are decorated in a Victorian style; good value for the category.

 ## Madison

6th arr. - 143, bd Saint-Germain
01 40 51 60 00, fax 01 40 51 60 01
Open year-round. 55 rms 760-1,500. Bkfst 70.

A smart, comfortable hotel in the heart of Saint-Germain, decorated with a sprinkling of antique pieces; the bathrooms are done up in pretty Provençal tiles. Quiet, very well equipped rooms.

 ## Méridien Étoile

17th arr. - 81, bd Gouvion-Saint-Cyr
01 40 68 34 34, fax 01 40 68 31 31
Open year-round. 18 stes 3,800-8,000. 1,008 rms 1,350-2,050. Bkfst 85. Restaurants. Rm ser. Air cond. No pets. Valet pkg.

This Méridien is the largest hotel in Western Europe, and one of the busiest in Paris. The rooms are small but prettily furnished. A variety of boutiques, a nightclub, the Hurlingham Polo Bar, and four restaurants liven things up (for the excellent Clos Longchamp, see *Restaurants*), as does the popular cocktail lounge where top jazz musicians play (Club Lionel Hampton).

 ## Méridien Montparnasse

14th arr. - 19, rue du Commandant-Mouchotte
01 44 36 44 36, fax 01 44 36 49 00

Open year-round. 37 stes 3,500-4,500. 916 rms 1,250-1,550. Bkfst 85-115. Rms for disabled. Restaurants. Rm ser. Air cond. Conf. Valet pkg.

Luxurious, soigné, and comfortable—that's the Méridien in a nutshell. Try to reserve one of the newer rooms, which are particularly bright and spacious. Or the Presidential Suite, if your means permit. Certain rooms are for non-smokers only; all afford good views of the city. Fine dining at the Montparnasse 25, see *Restaurants*.

 ## Montana Tuileries

1st arr. - 12, rue Saint-Roch
01 42 60 35 10, fax 01 42 61 12 28
Open year-round. 25 rms 580-1,090. Bkfst 55.

This very chic little hotel doesn't actually overlook the Tuileries, but they are only a stone's throw away. All double rooms, well equipped. Some rooms have balconies.

 ## Napoléon

8th arr. - 40, av. de Friedland
01 47 66 02 02, fax 01 47 66 82 33
Open year-round. 2 stes 3,500-4,500. 100 rms 1,250-1,950. Bkfst 90-110. Restaurant. Rm ser. Air cond. Conf. Valet pkg.

Admirably situated, just renovated from stem to stern, this fine hotel provides top-flight service along with excellent equipment and amenities. The spacious rooms have classic décor, and offer good value in this up-market neighborhood.

 ## Nikko

15th arr. - 61, quai de Grenelle
01 40 58 20 00, fax 01 45 75 42 35
Open year-round. 12 stes 2,500-8,700. 764 rms 1,480-1,980. Bkfst 85-130. Restaurants. Rm ser. Air cond. Conf. Heated pool. Valet pkg.

Thirty-one floors piled up to resemble an immense beehive, housing ultrafunctional rooms whose large porthole windows overlook the Seine and the Pont Mirabeau. You'll also find an inviting bar, restaurants (Les Célébrités, see *Restaurants*), and a brasserie within the complex.

 ## Novotel Les Halles

1st arr. - Pl. Marguerite-de-Navarre
01 42 21 31 31, fax 01 40 26 05 79
Open year-round. 5 stes 1,500. 280 rms 860-955. Bkfst 62. Rms for disabled. Restaurant. Rm ser. Air cond. Conf. Pkg.

This ultramodern building constructed of stone, glass, and zinc is located in the heart of the former market district, near the Pompidou Center and the Forum des Halles. The bright, quiet rooms are impeccably equipped. Loads of services on offer; piano bar until midnight.

 ## Opéra Richepanse

1st arr. - 14, rue de Richepanse
01 42 60 36 00, fax 01 42 60 13 03
Open year-round. 3 stes 1,600-1,900. 35 rms 750-1,400. Bkfst 65-85. Rm ser. Air cond.

The cozy, inviting guest rooms are elaborately decorated in shades of blue, with solid-wood furnishings in Art Deco style. Top-floor suites enjoy a wide-angle view of the Madeleine church. On the basement level is a lovely breakfast room, as well as a little sauna for relaxing steam baths.

 ## Paris K Palace

16th arr. - 11 bis, rue de Magdebourg
01 44 05 75 75, fax 01 44 05 74 74
Open year-round. 15 stes 2,610. 68 rms 1,510-1,910. Bkfst 105. Restaurant. Rm ser. Air cond. Conf. Pool. Garage pkg.
Ricardo Bofill designed this sleek, contemporary structure situated between the Trocadéro and Arc de Triomphe. Guests enjoy bright, spacious quarters with sophisticated designer furniture and equipment. There's a fitness center, sauna, and Jacuzzi, too, as well as a covered pool surrounded by a teak deck. For the Carré Kléber, see *Restaurants*.

 ## La Perle

6th arr. - 14, rue des Canettes
01 43 29 10 10, fax 01 46 34 51 04
Open year-round. 38 rms 850-1,350. Bkfst 70. Rms for disabled. Rm ser. Air cond.
The hotel's courtyard shields guests from the neighborhood's unending hustle and bustle. Inside, you'll find a large marble-clad lobby and nicely fitted rooms with goose-down comforters on the beds.

 ## Résidence Saint-Honoré

8th arr. - 214, rue du Faubourg-Saint-Honoré
01 42 25 26 27, fax 01 45 63 30 67
Open year-round. 8 stes 9700-1,400. 77 rms 770-1,100. Bkfst 50. Air cond. Conf. Pkg.
A smart hotel with elegant rooms and fine furnishings. The public rooms and bar are a shade tastefully done. Dynamic management, uncommonly courteous staff; piano bar. On the lower level, there is an antique store.

 ## Rochester Champs-Élysées

8th arr. - 92, rue de la Boétie
01 43 59 96 15, fax 01 42 56 01 38
Open year-round. 10 stes 1,380. 80 rms 880-1,200. Bkfst 85. Rms for disabled. Air cond. Conf. No pets.
A glitzy hotel that suits the district's flashy clientèle to a T. The rooms are very comfy, with thoughtfully chosen appointments and marble bathrooms. We suggest that you ask to be accommodated in one of the rooms overlooking the indoor garden and fountain. A meeting room is available for business or social occasions.

 ## Sofitel Arc de Triomphe

8th arr. - 14, rue Beaujon or 4, av. Bertie-Albrecht
01 45 63 04 04, fax 01 42 25 36 81

Open year-round. 6 stes 2,300-2,550. 129 rms 1,650-2,150. Bkfst 65-100. Restaurant. Rm ser. Air cond. Conf. Valet pkg.
This solid, austere building dating from 1925 houses a comfortable hotel that is not long on charm. But the facilities (ultramodern equipment for the business clientele) are first-rate, and are constantly being updated. The largish, bright rooms are functionally decorated. Restaurant: Clovis, see *Restaurants*.

 ## Sofitel Champs-Élysées

8th arr. - 8, rue Jean-Goujon
01 40 74 64 64, fax 01 40 74 64 99
Open year-round. 2 stes 1,800. 38 rms 1,500. Bkfst 85-100. Rms for disabled. Restaurant. Rm ser. Air cond. Conf. Valet pkg.
This hotel is quietly luxurious, with rooms that are impeccably decorated and equipped. Lots of thoughtful little extras and a cheerful efficient staff make staying here a pleasure. Delicious breakfasts. Restaurant: Les Saveurs, see *Restaurants*.

 ## Sofitel Forum Rive Gauche

14th arr. - 17, bd Saint-Jacques
01 40 78 79 80, fax 01 40 78 79 04
Open year-round. 14 stes 2,000-2,500. 783 rms 1,000-1,500. Bkfst 95. Rms for disabled. Restaurant. Rm ser. Air cond. Conf. Valet pkg.
The Sofitel Forum Rive Gauche is conveniently close to Orly airport. It offers good-sized rooms (about three-quarters of the hotel have just been redecorated) with comfortable bathrooms, air conditioning, and blackout blinds that allow long-distance travelers to sleep off their jet lag. Over 100 rooms for non-smokers. A new bar, the Nelli's; regional culinary events at the restaurant Le Café Français; and La Table et la Forme, probably the only restaurant in Paris serving meals guaranteed to contain only 1,000 calories, including the wine.

 ## Sofitel Paris Sèvres

15th arr. - 8-12, rue Louis-Armand
01 40 60 30 30, fax 01 45 57 04 22
Open year-round. 14 stes 1,850-2,300. 524 rms 1,450-1,550. Bkfst 95-105. Restaurants. Air cond. Conf. Heated pool. Valet pkg.
The rooms are perfectly functional, very comfortable, with huge bathrooms. A plethora of meeting and conference rooms (with simultaneous translation available in five languages) are connected to a central administration office. Guests enjoy free admittance to the Vitatop gym club on the 23rd floor. Restaurant: Le Relais de Sèvres, see *Restaurants*.

 ## Terrass Hôtel

18th arr. - 12, rue Joseph-de-Maistre
01 46 06 72 85, fax 01 42 52 29 11
Open year-round. 13 stes 1,650. 88 rms 830-1,090. Bkfst 75. Restaurant. Rm ser. Air cond. Conf. Pkg.

Located at the foot of the Butte Montmartre, this fine hotel offers a majestic view of almost all of Paris. Rooms are comfortable and nicely fitted. Up on the seventh floor, the panoramic terrace doubles as a restaurant in summer.

 ## Victoria Palace

6th arr. - 6, rue Blaise-Desgoffe
01 45 44 38 16, fax 01 45 49 23 75
Open year-round. 3 stes 2,500. 80 rms 890-2,000. Air cond. Conf. Garage pkg.
A reliable establishment, with a certain British charm, has been completely refurbished. The rooms are soothing and spacious, with really generous closets and good bathrooms. Bar and restaurant. The welcome is always most courteous.

 ## La Villa Maillot

16th arr. - 143, av. de Malakoff
01 45 01 25 22, fax 01 45 00 60 61
Open year-round. 3 stes 2,300-2,500. 39 rms 1,550-1,770. Bkfst 80-100. Rms for disabled. Restaurant. Rm ser. Air cond. Conf. Valet pkg.
Formerly an embassy, the conversion is sophisticated and modern: an exemplary establishment. The very comfortable rooms (all with queen-size beds, some with camouflaged kitchenettes) have an Art Deco feel. Pink-marble bathrooms; wonderful breakfasts served in an indoor garden.

 ## Yllen

15th arr. - 196, rue de Vaugirard
01 45 67 67 67, fax 01 45 67 74 37
Open year-round. 1 ste 910-995. 39 rms 490-695. Bkfst 45. Rms for disabled.
Yllen's modern, functional rooms have understated décor and are well soundproofed—but they are quite small. Corner rooms (those with numbers ending in 4) on the upper floors are the best. Energetic management, friendly reception.

 ## Waldorf Madeleine

8th arr. - 12, bd Malesherbes
01 42 65 72 06, fax 01 40 07 10 45
Open year-round. 7 stes 1,400. 35 rms 1,100. Bkfst 50. Air cond. Pkg.
This handsome freestone building houses an elegant lobby (notice the Art Deco ceiling) and rooms of exemplary comfort, with double glazing and air conditioning. You can count on a smiling reception.

CHARMING

 ## Abbaye Saint-Germain

6th arr. - 10, rue Cassette
01 45 44 38 11, fax 01 45 48 07 86

Open year-round. 4 stes 1,800-1,900. 42 rms 900-1,500. Bkfst 34. Air cond. No pets.
Set back from the street, this serene eighteenth-century residence located between a courtyard and a garden offers well-kept, conventionally decorated rooms which are not particularly spacious; the most delightful are on the same level as the garden (number 4 even has a terrace). Very quiet; lovely public rooms.

 ## Alba Opéra

9th arr. - 34 ter, rue La Tour-d'Auvergne
01 48 78 80 22, fax 01 42 85 23 13
Open year-round. 6 stes 1,400-1,500. 18 rms 500-700. Bkfst 40.
Georges Bizet, the author of *Carmen*, was born in this street. He would surely have approved the Alba's elegant décor, enhanced with artworks and mirrors. On the top floor an authentic painter's studio has been installed.

 ## Angleterre

6th arr. - 44, rue Jacob
01 42 60 34 72, fax 01 42 60 16 93
Open year-round. 3 stes 1,400. 24 rms 550-1,200. Bkfst 55. No pets.
Hemingway once lived in this former British Embassy, built around a flower-filled patio. The impeccable rooms are fresh and appealing; some are quite spacious, with high beamed ceilings. Large, comfortable beds; luxurious bathrooms. Downstairs, there is a bar and lounge with a piano.

 ## Atala

8th arr. - 10, rue Chateaubriand
01 45 62 01 62, fax 01 42 25 66 38
Open year-round. 1 ste 1,000-1,600. 47 rms 850-1,400. Bkfst 60-120. Air cond. Conf. Pkg.
In a quiet street near the Champs-Élysées, this hotel provides cheerfully decorated rooms that open onto a verdant garden. Balconies and terraces come with rooms on the sixth and eighth floors. Beautiful indoor garden; excellent service.

 ## L'Atelier Montparnasse

6th arr. - 49, rue Vavin
01 46 33 60 00, fax 01 40 51 04 21
Open year-round. 1 ste 950. 16 rms 600-750. Bkfst 45. Restaurant. Rm ser. Garage pkg.
A smart little address done up in modern style, with pretty mosaics in the bathrooms. The rooms themselves are quiet and cozy. Art exhibits are hosted regularly in the hotel's lobby.

 ## De Banville

17th arr. - 166, bd Berthier
01 42 67 70 16, fax 01 44 40 42 77
Open year-round. 39 rms 635-760. Bkfst 50-80. Restaurant. Rm ser. Air cond.
A fine small hotel that dates from the 1930s. There are flowers at the windows (some of which open to panoramic views of Paris) and all man-

ner of pleasing details in the large, bright rooms. Marble or tile bathrooms. Excellent English breakfasts.

 ## Beau Manoir

8th arr. - 6, rue de l'Arcade
01 42 66 03 07, fax 01 42 68 03 00
Open year-round. 3 stes 1,350-1,465. 29 rms 995-1,155. Bkfst 50. Rms for disabled. Rm ser. Air cond. Pkg.
The opulent décor—it features *Grand Siècle* wall hangings—is somehow reminiscent of Versailles. But the Beau Manoir is just steps away from the Madeleine, in the city's fashionable shopping district. Uncommonly delicious breakfasts are served in the hotel's vaulted cellar.

 ## Bersoly's Saint-Germain

7th arr. - 28, rue de Lille
01 42 60 73 79, fax 01 49 27 05 55
Closed Aug 10-20. 16 rms 580-680. Bkfst 50. Garage pkg. No cards.
Writers, artists, and antique dealers frequent this hotel, whose furniture is largely provided by the nearby "golden triangle" of antique shops. Rooms are named for famous artists, and reproductions of their paintings adorn the walls. Breakfast is served in the attractive vaulted basement. Faultless reception.

 ## Bradford Élysées

8th arr. - 10, rue Saint-Philippe-du-Roule
01 45 63 20 20, fax 01 45 63 20 07
Open year-round. 50 rms 650-1,190. Bkfst 65. Air cond. No pets.
A traditional hotel with comfortable, spacious accommodations decorated in understated good taste. Attractive singles; rooms ending with the numbers 6 and 7 are the largest. You can expect a cheerful welcome.

 ## Hôtel de la Bretonnerie

4th arr. - 22, rue Sainte-Croix-de-la-Bretonnerie
01 48 87 77 63, fax 01 42 77 26 78
Closed Jul 28-Aug 24. 3 stes 950. 27 rms 650-780. Bkfst 45. No pets.
A seventeenth-century town house, charmingly decorated. The rooms are made cozy with exposed wood beams and antique furniture (some canopied beds); the large bathrooms are perfectly modern. Look forward to a friendly reception.

 ## Hôtel de Buci

6th arr. - 22, rue de Buci
01 43 26 89 22, fax 01 46 33 80 31
Open year-round. 24 rms 900-1,300. Bkfst 70-110. Rms for disabled. No pets.
Here's a beautiful, spanking-new hotel opposite the Buci street market. The place simply overflows with charm: the cozy rooms are graced with antique furnishings and a wealth of tasteful touches. Excellent breakfasts are served in the hotel's vaulted cellar.

 ## California

8th arr. - 16, rue de Berri
01 43 59 93 00, fax 01 45 61 03 62
Open year-round. 13 stes 3,000-6,000. 160 rms 1,400-2,200. Bkfst 120. Restaurant. Rm ser. Conf. Valet pkg.
What sets this hotel apart from other similar establishments near the Champs-Élysées is a collection of some 3,000 artworks. As you might imagine, that's a lot of paintings per square yard (and alas, not all are in the best of taste). But the bright patio, with its tiled fountain, provides a welcome respite.

 ## Centre Ville Matignon

8th arr. - 3, rue de Ponthieu
01 42 25 73 01, fax 01 42 56 01 39
Open year-round. 4 stes 990-1,500. 19 rms 590-690. Bkfst 55. Restaurant. Rm ser.
A 1930s feel floats about this hotel, perhaps owing to the lobby's mosaics and boxy armchairs. The rooms are small but attractively decorated, and there is a patio for relaxing.

 ## Chateaubriand

8th arr. - 6, rue Chateaubriand
01 40 76 00 50, fax 01 40 76 09 22
Open year-round. 28 rms 1,100-1,400. Bkfst 65. Rms for disabled. Restaurant. Rm ser. Air cond. Garage pkg.
Built in 1991, this luxury hotel tucked away behind the Champs-Élysées boasts a polychrome-marble lobby and a courteous, professional staff. Classically elegant rooms; beautiful bathrooms.

 ## Claridge Bellman

8th arr. - 37, rue François-Ier
01 47 23 54 42, fax 01 47 23 08 84
Open year-round. 40 rms 800-1,350. Bkfst 70. Restaurant. Rm ser. Air cond. No pets.
A small hotel with quietly attractive rooms of reasonable size, each of which boasts a special feature, be it a crystal chandelier, antique furniture, a fine print or painting, or a marble fireplace.

 ## Hôtel Costes

1st arr. - 239, rue Saint-Honoré
01 42 44 50 00, fax 01 42 44 50 01
Open year-round. 29 stes 2,500-3,500. 56 rms 1,500-2,000. Bkfst 95. Rms for disabled. Restaurant. Rm ser. Pool. Fitness center.
An opulent atmosphere prevails at this richly decorated hotel near Place Vendôme, now one of the capital's most sought-after places to stay. Entirely renovated, artistically decorated rooms are both comfortable and blessedly quiet. Duplex suites; gorgeous enclosed courtyard where meals are served in fine weather (see Restaurant Costes in *Restaurants*). There is a fitness center with a pool on the basement level.

Danemark

6th arr. - 21, rue Vavin
01 43 26 93 78, fax 01 46 34 66 06
Open year-round. 15 rms 590-890. Bkfst 55.
This small hotel was carefully renovated in
1930s style. Although the rooms are not very
large, they are elegantly furnished, with pleasant
lighting, mahogany, ash, or oak furniture and
gray-marble bathrooms (number 10 has a Jacuzzi).

 Les Deux Iles

4th arr. - 59, rue Saint-Louis-en-l'Ile
01 43 26 13 35, fax 01 43 29 60 25
Open year-round. 17 rms 700-830. Bkfst 45.
This particularly welcoming hotel, like many
buildings on the Ile-Saint-Louis, is a lovely
seventeenth-century house. You'll sleep close to
the Seine in small, pretty rooms decorated with
bright fabrics and painted furniture.

 Duc de Saint-Simon

7th arr. - 14, rue Saint-Simon
01 44 39 20 20, fax 01 45 48 68 25
*Open year-round. 5 stes 1,800-1,850. 29 rms 1,025-
1,425. Bkfst 70. Air cond. No pets.*
Set back from the street between two gardens,
this quiet, elegant nineteenth-century hotel
provides discreet luxury and comfort, with antiques, fine paintings and objets d'art, good lighting, and enchanting décor. The four rooms have
terraces that overlook the garden. Room 41, in
the annex, boasts an imposing canopied bed.
There is a bar, but no restaurant.

 Ducs d'Anjou

1st arr. - 1, rue Sainte-Opportune
01 42 36 92 24, fax 01 42 36 16 63
Open year-round. 38 rms 480-592. Bkfst 44. Conf.
Located on the delightful small Place Sainte-
Opportune, this ancient building has been restored from top to bottom. The rooms are small
(as are the bathrooms) but quiet; rooms 61 and
62 are larger, and can comfortably accommodate
three people. Those overlooking the courtyard
are a bit gloomy.

 Éber Monceau

17th arr. - 18, rue Léon-Jost
01 46 22 60 70, fax 01 47 63 01 01
*Open year-round. 5 stes 1,050-1,360. 13 rms 500-
660. Bkfst 50. Rm ser. No pets.*
A quiet charming hotel, "adopted," so to
speak, by people in fashion, photography, and
the movies. Rooms are on the small side, and all
have cable TV. A large, two-level suite on the top
floor has a lovely terrace. The lobby impresses
with its Henri II fireplace and Renaissance
beams. Breakfast, which can be served in the
patio in summer, is wonderful. A bar and a small
lounge.

 Grand Hôtel Malher

4th arr. - 5, rue Malher
01 42 72 60 92, fax 01 42 72 25 37

*Open year-round. 1 ste 880-990. 30 rms 470-720.
Bkfst 45. Conf. No pets.*
Now freshly refurbished, this family-owned
hotel in the historic Marais sports a welcoming
country-style décor. After a good night's sleep in
one of the pretty guest rooms, you can go down
to hearty breakfast, served with a smile in a
vaulted seventeenth-century cellar.

 L'Hôtel

6th arr. - 13, rue des Beaux-Arts
01 44 41 99 00, fax 01 43 25 64 81
*Open year-round. 2 stes 2,800-3,600. 25 rms 1,000-
2,500. Bkfst 100. Rm ser. Air cond.*
"L'Hôtel" provides top-notch amenities and
service, of course, but it's the charm of the place
that accounts for its enduring popularity. The
décor resembles no other—whether it's number
16, once occupied by Oscar Wilde, the neo-Egyp-
tian Imperial room, the purple-swathed Car-
dinale room, or number 36, which contains the
Art Deco furniture of music-hall star Mistin-
guett. Bar: Le Bélier.

 **Hôtel
du Jeu de Paume**

4th arr. - 54, rue Saint-Louis-en-l'Ile
01 43 26 14 18, fax 01 40 46 02 76
*Open year-round. 32 rms 895-1,450. Bkfst 80. Rms
for disabled. Rm ser. Conf. Sauna.*
This is a seventeenth-century building with a
splendid wood-and-stone interior, featuring a
glass elevator that ferries guests to bright, quiet
rooms with marble baths. There is a pleasant
little garden, too, and a music room.

 **Left Bank
Saint-Germain**

6th arr. - 9, rue de l'Ancienne Comédie
01 43 54 01 70, fax 01 43 26 17 14
*Open year-round. 32 rms 850-990. Bkfst 30. Rms
for disabled. Air cond.*
Housed in a seventeenth-century building next
to the historic Café Procope, this engaging hotel
offers intimate rooms decorated with Jouy-print
fabrics. Some lodgings afford views of Paris
rooftops and Notre-Dame; all have nicely
equipped little bathrooms.

Lenox

7th arr. - 9, rue de l'Université
01 42 96 10 95, fax 01 42 61 52 83
*Open year-round. 2 stes 1,500. 32 rms 650-1,100.
Bkfst 45.*
These petite but most attractive rooms are
decorated with elegant wallpaper and stylish
furniture; numbers 51, 52, and 53 are the most
enchanting. On the top floor are two split-level
suites with exposed beams and flower-filled balconies. The elegant bar stays open until 2am.

*This **symbol** signifies hotels that offer an exceptional degree of peace and quiet.*

Lenox Montparnasse

14th arr. - 15, rue Delambre
01 43 35 34 50, fax 01 43 20 46 64
Open year-round. 6 stes 980. 46 rms 540-650. Bkfst 45. Rm ser.
In the heart of Montparnasse, a peaceful hotel with a cozy sort of charm. The penthouse suites are awfully attractive—they even have fireplaces. Rooms vary in size, yet are uniformly comfortable and well maintained. Smiling staff; elegant bar (open until 2am).

 Lido

8th arr. - 4, passage de la Madeleine
01 42 66 27 37, fax 01 42 66 61 23
Open year-round. 32 rms 830-980. Bkfst 40. Air cond.
A laudable establishment, situated between the Madeleine and the Place de la Concorde. The lobby is most elegant, with Oriental rugs on the floor and tapestries on the stone walls. The guest rooms, decorated in pink, blue, or cream, have comfortable beds, modern bathrooms, and double-glazed windows. Thoughtful, courteous staff.

 Lutèce

4th arr. - 65, rue Saint-Louis-en-l'Ile
01 43 26 23 52, fax 01 43 29 60 25
Open year-round. 23 rms 70-980. Bkfst 45. Air cond.
A tasteful, small hotel for people who love Paris, this handsome old house has some little twenty rooms (there are two charming mansards on the sixth floor), with whitewashed walls and ceiling beams, decorated with bright, cheerful fabrics. The bathrooms are small but modern and impeccably kept. The lobby features lavish bouquets and a stone fireplace which is often used in winter.

 Luxembourg

6th arr. - 4, rue de Vaugirard
01 43 25 35 90, fax 01 43 26 60 84
Open year-round. 33 rms 700-800. Bkfst 60. Air cond. Conf.
Near the Luxembourg Gardens, in the heart of the Latin Quarter. The pleasant rooms have good equipment but small bathrooms. And there is a beautiful vine-covered patio.

 Majestic

16th arr. - 29, rue Dumont-d'Urville
01 45 00 83 70, fax 01 45 00 29 48
Open year-round. 3 stes 1,520-1,920. 27 rms 920-1,470. Bkfst 60. Air cond.
The big rooms in this exemplary hotel are redecorated by turns, and all boast comfortable beds, fine furniture, and thick carpeting. On the top floor, a lovely penthouse features a small balcony filled with flowers. Old-World atmosphere.

Prices for rooms and suites *are per room, not per person. Half-board prices, however, are per person.*

 Hôtel Mansart

1st arr. - 5, rue des Capucines
01 42 61 50 28, fax 01 49 27 97 44
Open year-round. 6 stes 1,200-1,500. 51 rms 580-950. Rm ser. No pets.
The lobby looks for all the world like an art gallery; the rooms are positively charming, arrayed in elegant furnishings with all the modern comforts and equipment one could wish. If you book well in advance, you can request the "Mansart" room, which overlooks Place Vendôme.

 Hôtel de Notre-Dame

5th arr. - 19, rue Maître-Albert
01 43 26 79 00, fax 01 46 33 50 11
Open year-round. 34 rms 690-750. Bkfst 40. No pets.
Some of the beamed rooms are rather small, but all are comfy and prettily fitted out, with impeccable marble bathrooms. Situated on a quiet street near the river, this hotel is managed by a cheerful staff.

 Nouvel Hôtel

12th arr. - 24, av. du Bel-Air
01 43 43 01 81, fax 01 43 44 64 13
Open year-round. 28 rms 360-530. Bkfst 40.
The rooms of the Nouvel Hôtel are peaceful and attractive, and all were just freshly renovated and redecorated (the prettiest is number 9, on the same level as the garden). Good bathrooms; hospitable reception. Old-fashioned hot chocolate is served at breakfast.

 Panthéon

5th arr. - 19, pl. du Panthéon
01 43 54 32 95, fax 01 43 26 64 65
Open year-round. 34 rms 635-780. Bkfst 45. Air cond. Conf. No pets. Pkg.
Clever use of mirrors makes the entrance, lounge, and bar of this eighteenth-century building seem bigger. The elegant rooms are quite spacious, decorated in Louis XVI or Louis-Philippe style, with pastel wallcoverings. Room 33 has a grand canopied bed. Buffet breakfast; friendly welcome.

 Parc Saint-Séverin

5th arr. - 22, rue de la Parcheminerie
01 43 54 32 17, fax 01 43 54 70 71
Open year-round. 27 rms 500-1,500. Bkfst 50. No pets.
The rooms on the sixth and seventh floors of this 1930s-vintage hotel boast balconies with a view over the church and cloister of Saint-Séverin. All the accommodations are bright and spacious, enhanced with antiques and contemporary art objects.

 Le Pavillon Bastille

12th arr. - 65, rue de Lyon
01 43 43 65 65, fax 01 43 43 96 52
Open year-round. 1 ste 1,200-1,375. 23 rms 650-955. Bkfst 65. Rms for disabled. Rm ser. Air cond.
Across from the Bastille opera house, here are all the comforts of a luxury hotel, with the charm

of a private town house. The bright rooms and lobby are decorated in a bold, high style; the owner welcomes guests with a glass of white wine. Minibar; sumptuous buffet breakfasts.

Pavillon de la Reine

3rd arr. - 28, pl. des Vosges
01 42 77 96 40, fax 01 42 77 63 06
Open year-round. 22 stes 2,300-3,500. 33 rms 1,500-2,100. Bkfst 95-140. Rms for disabled. Rm ser. Air cond. Valet pkg.
Part of the hotel dates from the seventeenth century, while the rest is a clever "reconstitution." The rooms and suites, all with marble bathrooms, are tastefully decorated. The furnishings are an artful blend of authentic antiques and lovely reproductions. Accommodations overlook either the back of the Place des Vosges or a quiet inner patio filled with flowers.

Prince de Conti

6th arr. - 8, rue Guénégaud
01 44 07 30 40, fax 01 44 07 36 34
Open year-round. 3 stes 1,000-1,250. 23 rms 750-990. Bkfst 60. Rms for disabled. Air cond. Conf. No pets.
Probably the handsomest *hôtel de charme* on the Left Bank. Chintzes, stripes, and tartans give the superbly decorated rooms a distinctive British feel. Splendid split-level suites; attentive service.

Regent's Garden Hotel

17th arr. - 6, rue Pierre-Demours
01 45 74 07 30, fax 01 40 55 01 42
Open year-round. 39 rms 640-930. Bkfst 45. Garage pkg.
This handsome Second Empire building, just a stone's throw from the Place de l'Étoile, offers large, nicely proportioned rooms with high, ornate ceilings; some have fireplaces. Comfortable and well kept, the hotel also boasts a gorgeous flower garden.

Relais Christine

6th arr. - 3, rue Christine
01 43 26 71 80, fax 01 43 26 89 38
Open year-round. 15 stes 2,600-3,200. 36 rms 1,630-1,800. Bkfst 95. Rm ser. Air cond. Conf. Valet pkg.
This Renaissance cloister has retained some of the peace of its earlier vocation, but this luxurious hotel also possesses all the comforts of the present age, from double glazing to perfect service. The rooms are decorated with Provençal prints and pink Portuguese marble baths. The best rooms are the two-level suites and the ground-floor room with private terrace, but all are spacious, quiet, and air conditioned. Courteous reception.

Le Relais du Louvre

1st arr. - 19, rue des Prêtres-St-Germain-l'Auxerrois
01 40 41 96 42, fax 01 40 41 96 44

Open year-round. 2 stes 1,280-1,450. 18 rms 600-960. Bkfst 50. Restaurant. Rm ser.
The original façade of this historic building opposite the Tuileries has been preserved, but the interior is fully modernized. The comfortable rooms, elegantly decorated by Constance de Castelbajac, overflow with charm; they all have marble bathrooms, too. Rooms with numbers ending in 1 are slightly smaller than the rest. Wonderfully hospitable reception.

Le Relais Médicis

6th arr. - 23, rue Racine
01 43 26 00 60, fax 01 40 46 83 39
Open year-round. 16 rms 930-1,495. Bkfst incl. Air cond. Conf.
Bright colors adorn the walls of each room: yellow, blue, red... The effect is cheerful and charming, enhanced by ancient beams, pictures, vintage photos. A quiet patio and fountain are conducive to relaxation. The staff visibly cares about guests' comfort and well-being.

Relais Saint-Germain

6th arr. - 9, carrefour de l'Odéon
01 43 29 12 05, fax 01 46 33 45 30
Open year-round. 1 ste 1,950. 21 rms 1,280-1,700. Bkfst 75. Rm ser.
All the accommodations are personalized and decorated in luxurious style, with superb furniture, lovely fabrics, exquisite lighting, and beautiful, perfectly equipped marble bathrooms. The tall, double-glazed windows open onto the lively Carrefour de l'Odéon. You are bound to fall in love with Paris staying at this tiny jewel of an establishment. Exemplary service.

Les Rives de Notre-Dame

5th arr. - 15, quai Saint-Michel
01 43 54 81 16, fax 01 43 26 27 09
Open year-round. 1 ste 2,600. 9 rms 995-1,650. Bkfst 60-85. Rms for disabled. Restaurant. Rm ser. Air cond. Conf.
From the roomy, bright accommodations in this seventeenth-century hotel, you'll enjoy a pretty view of the Seine. The rooms all have fresh, personalized décor in Tuscan or Provençal styles.

Rond Point de Longchamp

16th arr. - 86, rue de Longchamp
01 45 05 13 63, fax 01 47 55 12 80
Open year-round. 1 ste 1,500. 56 rms 510-1,000. Bkfst 65-100. Restaurant. Air cond. Conf.
The sizeable, comfortable rooms are nicely fitted and prettily decorated (gray carpeting, burr-walnut furniture), and have marble bathrooms. A bar, as well as a billiard room.

For a complete guide to our hotel ranking system, see "Symbol Systems", page 8.

Hôtel Saint-Germain

7th arr. - 88, rue du Bac
01 45 48 62 92, fax 01 45 48 26 89
Open year-round. 29 rms 415-730. Bkfst 45. No pets.
In the best Rive Gauche tradition, this posh yet discreet little hostelry charms guests with beamed and vaulted ceilings, elegant décor, and period furnishings. The atmosphere is somehow provincial (in the best sense of the word); rooms offer space and comfort as well as all modern conveniences.

 Saint-Grégoire

6th arr. - 43, rue de l'Abbé-Grégoire
01 45 48 23 23, fax 01 45 48 33 95
Open year-round. 1 ste 1,390. 19 rms 790-990. Bkfst 60.
The cozy lounge is warmed in winter by a fireplace and there's a small garden for fine days. The rooms are painted in subtle shades of yellow and pink, with matching chintz curtains, white damask bedspreads, and some fine antique furniture. Double glazing and modern bathrooms. Expensive.

 Saint-Louis

4th arr. - 75, rue Saint-Louis-en-l'Ile
01 46 34 04 80, fax 01 46 34 02 13
Open year-round. 21 rms 595-795. Bkfst 45.
Elegant simplicity characterizes this appealing hotel, where attention to detail is evident in the gorgeous flower arrangements and polished antiques. Small, perfectly soundproofed rooms offer comfortable beds and thick carpeting underfoot. The modern bathrooms are pretty indeed.

 Saint-Louis Marais

4th arr. - 1, rue Charles-V
01 48 87 87 04, fax 01 48 87 33 26
Open year-round. 16 rms 350-710. Bkfst 40.
Reasonable prices and a delightful reception at this former convent annex in the heart of historic Paris. Each little room is different; all are charming and comfortable. Some rooms have been redecorated.

 Saint-Merry

4th arr. - 78, rue de la Verrerie
01 42 78 14 15, fax 01 40 29 06 82
Open year-round. 1 ste 2,000. 11 rms 400-1,100. Bkfst 50.
A former presbytery, this seventeenth-century building is home to an original collection of Gothic furniture, which the owner has been buying at auctions for many years. The telephone booth near the reception desk is a former confessional! Rooms are mostly small, with bathrooms not much bigger than closets, but the charm of the place is such that you have to book well in advance for the summer.

 Sainte-Beuve

6th arr. - 9, rue Sainte-Beuve
01 45 48 20 07, fax 01 45 48 67 52

Open year-round. 5 stes 1,550-1,700. 18 rms 700-1,300. Bkfst 80. Rm ser.
The Sainte-Beuve is a tasteful, harmonious example of the neo-Palladian style of decoration, promoted in particular by David Hicks. In the guest rooms soft colors, chintzes and the odd antique create a soothing atmosphere. Most attractive marble-and-tile bathrooms; elegant lobby with comfortable sofas arranged around the fireplace.

 Hôtel des Saints-Pères

6th arr. - 65, rue des Saints-Pères
01 45 44 50 00, fax 01 45 44 90 83
Open year-round. 3 stes 1,650. 35 rms 750-1,250. Bkfst 55. No pets.
Situated in two buildings, with all the quiet, elegantly furnished rooms overlooking a garden. Suite 205 is particularly attractive. Downstairs is a pretty breakfast room, and a bar that opens onto the garden.

 San Régis

8th arr. - 12, rue Jean-Goujon
01 44 95 16 16, fax 01 45 61 05 48
Open year-round. 10 stes 3,200-5,500. 34 rms 1,650-2,850. Bkfst 100. Restaurant. Rm ser. Air cond. No pets. Valet pkg.
This jewel of a hotel, much appreciated by celebrities from the worlds of show business and *haute couture*, provides a successful mix of traditional comfort and the latest technology. Beautiful, newly decorated rooms boast splendid period furniture and paintings, sumptuous bathrooms, and lots of space, light, and character. The staff is irreproachable.

 Select Hotel

5th arr. - 1, pl. de la Sorbonne
01 46 34 14 80, fax 01 46 34 51 79
Open year-round. 1 ste 980-1,250. 67 rms 530-890. Bkfst 30. Air cond. Conf.
A glass-roofed atrium with an abundance of plants has been built at the heart of this attractive hotel next door to the Sorbonne. The pleasant, spacious rooms are functionally furnished; some open onto a lively square.

 Solférino

7th arr. - 91, rue de Lille
01 47 05 85 54, fax 01 45 55 51 16
Closed Dec 21-Jan 3. 1 ste 633-756. 32 rms 275-643. Bkfst 37.
Almost opposite the Musée d'Orsay, here are simple rooms done in fresh colors, with bath or shower. There is a cozy little lounge, a sky-lit breakfast room, and pretty ornaments everywhere.

 Université

7th arr. - 22, rue de l'Université
01 42 61 09 39, fax 01 42 60 40 84
Open year-round. 27 rms 600-1,300. Bkfst 45. Air cond. No pets.

Comfortable beds and pink-marble bathrooms in an intelligently renovated seventeenth-century residence, most appealing with its beams, half-timbering, and period furniture. Rooms on the first floor have high ceilings, while the fifth-floor suites boast flower-decked terraces.

 ## Vert Galant

13th arr. - 41, rue Croulebarbe
01 44 08 83 50, fax 01 44 08 83 69
Open year-round. 15 rms 400-500. Bkfst 40. Rms for disabled. Conf. No pets. Garage pkg.
Now for something completely different: this delightful country *auberge* provides adorable rooms (with kitchenette) overlooking an indoor garden where grapes and tomatoes grow! Quiet; good value. Restaurant: Auberge Etchegorry, see *Restaurants*.

 ## Vieux Paris

6th arr. - 9, rue Gît-le-Cœur
01 43 54 41 66, fax 01 43 26 00 15
Open year-round. 7 stes 1,550-1,650. 13 rms 990-1,770. Bkfst 70-80. No pets. Garage pkg.
Here's a hotel that wears its name well, for it was built in the fifteenth century. A recent overhaul turned the Vieux Paris into a luxurious stopover, whose comfort and first-rate amenities fully justify the high rates. Rooms are handsomely furnished and perfectly quiet, with Jacuzzis in every bathroom. Warm reception.

 ## La Villa Saint-Germain

6th arr. - 29, rue Jacob
01 43 26 60 00, fax 01 46 34 63 63
Open year-round. 4 stes 2,000-3,000. 28 rms 900-1,800. Bkfst 80. Rm scr. Air cond.
A laser beam projects room numbers onto the doors; the bathroom sinks are crafted of chrome and sanded glass; orange, violet, green, and red leather furniture stands out vividly against the subdued gray walls: a high-tech environment that attracts a trendy, moneyed clientele. Jazz club on the lower level (La Villa), with name performers.

PRACTICAL

 ## Acacias Saint-Germain

6th arr. - 151 bis, rue de Rennes
01 45 48 97 38, fax 01 45 44 63 57
Open year-round. 4 stes 480-1,130. 37 rms 380-800. Bkfst 40-65.
Some of the small, pleasant rooms of this good hotel have been redecorated. There is a pretty summer garden, too, and the staff is most obliging.

Looking for a hotel? Refer to the index.

 ## Adagio

15th arr. - 257, rue de Vaugirard
01 40 45 11 40, fax 01 40 45 10 10
Open year-round. 3 stes 1,400. 184 rms 590-835. Bkfst 75. Rms for disabled. Restaurant. Rm scr. Air cond. Conf. Garage pkg.
An ultramodern hotel with a bright lobby and comfortable, functional rooms. From the terrace, guests can admire the Eiffel Tower.

 ## Alliance Saint-Germain

6th arr. - 7-11, rue Saint-Benoît
01 42 61 53 53, fax 01 49 27 09 33
Open year-round. 117 rms 895-1,070. Bkfst 75. Rms for disabled. Conf. No pets.
This large, modern hotel, formerly a printing works, is located in the heart of Saint-Germain-des-Prés; its gracious turn-of-the-century façade has been preserved. The spacious rooms are functional and well equipped; each floor is decorated in a different color. A cellar jazz club provides hot and cool live music every night except Sunday, and Monday.

 ## Atlantis Saint-Germain-des-Prés

6th arr. - 4, rue du Vieux-Colombier
01 45 48 31 81, fax 01 45 48 35 16
Open year-round. 34 rms 380-585. Bkfst 30. No pets.
A typical little Left Bank hotel just steps from Saint-Sulpice, with attractive rooms and a flower-filled breakfast room. On the walls hang works by amateur painters for an arty touch.

 ## Bergère Opéra

9th arr. - 34, rue Bergère
01 47 70 34 34, fax 01 47 70 36 36
Open year-round. 134 rms 590-990. Bkfst 60. Rm scr. Air cond. Conf. No pets.
All the quiet rooms (most of which overlook a courtyard garden) have been freshened up and modernized, including the bathrooms.

 ## Best Western Folkestone Opéra

8th arr. - 9, rue Castellane
01 42 65 73 09, fax 01 42 65 64 09
Open year-round. 50 rms 605-800. Bkfst 45. Air cond.
The beamed rooms have Art Deco armchairs and comfortable beds. Rooms on the first floor are air-conditioned. Generous buffet breakfasts; gracious reception.

 ## Hôtel Boileau

16th arr. - 81, rue Boileau
01 42 88 83 74, fax 01 45 27 62 98
Open year-round. 30 rms 360-420. Bkfst 35. Rms for disabled. Conf.
This establishment is warm and bright, with small, simply furnished rooms. A skylight covers the little garden-courtyard.

Brighton

1st arr. - 218, rue de Rivoli
01 47 03 61 61, fax 01 42 60 41 78
Open year-round. 1 ste 1,400. 69 rms 450-920. Bkfst 30. Restaurant. Rm ser. No pets.
A dream setting opposite the Tuileries, near the Louvre, is offered at very reasonable prices. The rooms on the Rue de Rivoli have wonderful views, high molded ceilings, brass beds, and good-sized bathrooms. The little attic rooms are especially good value. Tiny elevator, though, and unsmiling staff.

 Hôtel de Châteaudun

9th arr. - 30, rue de Châteaudun
01 49 70 09 99, fax 01 49 70 06 99
Open year-round. 26 rms 620-760. Bkfst 50. Rm ser. Air cond. Conf.
The chilly reception area and graceless furniture are only part of the picture here. For the comfortable rooms are perfectly soundproofed, and the staff is warm and friendly. Buffet breakfasts.

 Hôtel des Chevaliers

3rd arr. - 30, rue de Turenne
01 42 72 73 47, fax 01 42 72 54 10
Open year-round. 24 rms 590-820. Bkfst 50.
In the heart of the Marais, a small hotel frequented by actors and movie folk. The small rooms are bright and pleasantly furnished, with good bathrooms. Warm reception.

 Claret

12th arr. - 44, bd de Bercy
01 46 28 41 31, fax 01 49 28 09 29
Open year-round. 52 rms 350-650. Bkfst 50. Restaurant. Half-board 450. Rm ser. Air cond. Pkg.
This neat, modernized hotel (formerly a *relais de poste*) offers a family atmosphere and a wine bar in the basement. Each meticulously maintained room is named for a wine region of France. Good value.

 Hôtel du Collège de France

5th arr. - 7, rue Thénard
01 43 26 78 36, fax 01 46 34 58 29
Open year-round. 2 stes 1,030. 29 rms 480-580. Bkfst 33. Rms for disabled. No pets.
The simple rooms of the Hôtel du Collège de France, located on a quiet little street, are tidy and comfortable. Most charming are the attic rooms, with their wooden beams and a view of the towers of Notre-Dame.

 Hôtel du Danube

6th arr. - 58, rue Jacob
01 42 60 34 70, fax 01 42 60 81 18
Open year-round. 6 stes 1,000. 34 rms 450-800. Bkfst 45.
Each room is different, hung with floral wallpaper and furnished with antiques (includ-

ing some canopied beds). And prices are reasonable, considering the neighborhood.

 Ermitage Hôtel

18th arr. - 24, rue Lamarck
01 42 64 79 22, fax 01 42 64 10 33
Open year-round. 12 rms 310-470. Bkfst incl. No pets. Pkg. No cards.
This charming hotel occupies a little white building behind the Basilica of Sacré-Cœur. The personalized décor in each room is punctuated by an antique or *bibelot*. Pretty bathrooms; no TV. There is a garden and a terrace for relaxing, and you can expect a friendly reception.

 Étoile Park Hotel

17th arr. - 10, av. Mac-Mahon
01 42 67 69 63, fax 01 43 80 18 99
Closed Dec 24-Jan 1. 2 stes 610-690. 28 rms 380-710. Bkfst 52. No pets.
Modern and decorated in impersonal good taste, this hotel offers freshly refurbished guest rooms and comfortable, well-designed bathrooms—everything, in a word, but charm.

 Étoile Pereire

17th arr. - 146, bd Pereire
01 42 67 60 00, fax 01 42 67 02 90
Open year-round. 5 stes 1,000. 21 rms 600-760. Bkfst 54. Rms for disabled. Rm ser. No pets.
Attention to detail is a priority at this welcoming hotel, owned by a former pianist. Located at the back of a quiet courtyard, the spacious, pastel rooms are most attractive, with garden views. Both the atmosphere and service are charming and cheerful.

 Familia Hôtel

5th arr. - 11, rue des Écoles
01 43 54 55 27, fax 01 43 29 61 77
Open year-round. 30 rms 380-490. Bkfst 30.
The management of this modest two-star hotel strives to make guests comfortable. Rooms are small but decently equipped; reasonable rates.

Ferrandi

6th arr. - 92, rue du Cherche-Midi
01 42 22 97 40, fax 01 45 44 89 97
Open year-round. 1 ste 980-1,280. 41 rms 480-980. Bkfst 60-70. Air cond. Pkg.
In a quiet street near Montparnasse, with a reception area that matches the charm of the rooms. Some of the guest rooms have four-poster beds, others a fireplace (many could use a fresh coat of paint). All have good bathrooms (with hairdryers) and double glazing. Delightful welcome.

Fleurie

6th arr. - 32-34, rue Grégoire-de-Tours
01 43 29 59 81, fax 01 43 29 68 44
Open year-round. 3 stes 1,200. 26 rms 650-850. Bkfst 50. Air cond. No pets.
From the welcoming dark-green entrance to the period rooms decorated with quality furni-

ture and warm colors, this hotel in the heart of Saint-Germain exudes Left Bank charm. Plants and flower bouquets lend a pleasing, springlike touch.

 ## Forest Hill

19th arr. - 28 ter, av. Corentin-Cariou
01 44 72 15 30, fax 01 44 72 15 80
Open year-round. 13 stes 850-1,250. 246 rms 495-940. Bkfst 40-68. Rms for disabled. Restaurant. Half-board 615-1,060. Rm ser. Air cond. Conf. Garage pkg.
A mammouth concrete structure opposite the Cité des Sciences, the Forest Hill houses functional rooms (with small windows!) that have the virtue of being absolutely quiet.

 ## Hôtel Français

10th arr. - 13, rue du 8-Mai-1945
01 40 35 94 14, fax 01 40 35 55 40
Open year-round. 71 rms 375-460. Bkfst 30. Garage pkg.
You'll appreciate the good value of this convenient hotel, situated opposite the Gare de l'Est. Old-fashioned charm combines with modern comforts (iron and ironing board, hairdryer, and safe in all the rooms).

 ## Galileo

8th arr. - 54, rue Galilée
01 47 20 66 06, fax 01 47 20 67 17
Open year-round. 27 rms 800-950. Bkfst 60. Rms for disabled. Rm ser. Air cond. No pets.
Just steps from the Champs-Élysées, the Galileo offers an elegant lobby and public rooms, an Italian-style garden, and bright guest rooms done in understated good taste, with gray-marble bathrooms. Effective soundproofing and air conditioning.

 ## Grand Hôtel de Besançon

2nd arr. - 56, rue Montorgueil
01 42 36 41 08, fax 01 45 08 08 79
Open year-round. 10 stes 620-650. 10 rms 550-590. Bkfst 40-60. No pets. Garage pkg.
After a full-dress overhaul, the Besançon provides soundproofed rooms furnished with Louis-Philippe–style pieces. Convenient to the Louvre and to the Forum des Halles.

 ## Grand Hôtel des Gobelins

13th arr. - 57, bd Saint-Marcel
01 43 31 79 89, fax 01 45 35 43 56
Open year-round. Rms 320-430. Bkfst 36. No pets.
Situated on the edge of the fifth arrondissement, this hotel offers exceptional value for money. Some of the rooms look out onto the Panthéon. Double-glazed windows; dry cleaning service daily, even on weekends.

Looking for a restaurant? Refer to the **Index.**

 ## Grands Hommes

5th arr. - 17, pl. du Panthéon
01 46 34 19 60, fax 01 43 26 67 32
Open year-round. 2 stes 860-1,220. 30 rms 635-780. Bkfst 45. Conf. No pets.
An eighteenth-century building opposite the Panthéon. The fairly spacious rooms are decorated in ocher and orange tones; room 22 has a canopied brass bed, 60 and 61 boast balconies and pleasant views. The staff is friendly and efficient.

 ## Hameau de Passy

16th arr. - 48, rue de Passy
01 42 88 47 55, fax 01 42 30 83 72
Open year-round. 32 rms 450-530. Bkfst 30-57. Rms for disabled.
Tucked away in a flower-filled cul-de-sac, this exceptionally quiet hotel was recently modernized. Roughcast walls and stained-wood furniture decorate the comfortable rooms (some connecting) that overlook the garden. Bright, tidy bathrooms; smiling service and reception.

 ## Istria

14th arr. - 29, rue Campagne-Première
01 43 20 91 82, fax 01 43 22 48 45
Open year-round. 26 rms 420-590. Bkfst 45.
Elm furniture and pastel colors grace the rooms and bathrooms of this well-kept hotel, where Mayakovski, Man Ray, and Marcel Duchamp once slept. The building is fully modernized.

 ## Le Jardin de Cluny

5th arr. - 9, rue du Sommerard
01 43 54 22 66, fax 01 40 51 03 36
Open year-round. 40 rms 540-800. Bkfst 50. No pets.
A perfectly functional hotel in the heart of the Latin Quarter, with comfortable, cheerful rooms (some are air conditioned) and spotless bathrooms. Professional desk staff.

 ## Les Jardins d'Eiffel

7th arr. - 8, rue Amélie
01 47 05 46 21, fax 01 45 55 28 08
Open year-round. 80 rms 560-960. Bkfst 60. Rms for disabled. Air cond. Conf. Garage pkg.
A handsome old-fashioned hotel that dates from the turn of the century. Attractive, well-equipped rooms: those on the upper floors overlook the Eiffel Tower. Charming reception.

 ## Hôtel du Léman

9th arr. - 20, rue de Trévise
01 42 46 50 66, fax 01 48 24 27 59
Open year-round. 24 rms 390-660. Bkfst 40. Conf.
This charming, out-of-the-ordinary small hotel has been tastefully renovated. Tuscany marble inlays enhance the modern décor in the lobby. The tiny rooms are pleasantly decorated with attractive bedside lamps and original drawings and watercolors. A generous buffet breakfast is served in the vaulted basement. The staff does its utmost to make guests feel at home.

Louvre Saint-Honoré

1st arr. - 141, rue Saint-Honoré
01 42 96 23 23, fax 01 42 96 21 61
Open year-round. 40 rms 496-862. Bkfst 45. Rms for disabled. Rm ser. Air cond.
Convenient to the Louvre, with quiet, functional accommodations. Rooms open onto a patio embellished with wood sculptures and plants.

 ## Jardins du Luxembourg

5th arr. - 5, impasse Royer-Collard
01 40 46 08 88, fax 01 40 46 02 28
Open year-round. 25 rms 850. Bkfst 50. Rms for disabled. Air cond. No pets.
Fresh from a successful year-long renovation, the small rooms sport a cozy Mediterranean look and the tiled bathrooms are immaculate and bright. The basement breakfast room is a mite gloomy, though, and parking is most problematic!

 ## Hôtel Le Laumière

19th arr. - 4, rue Petit
01 42 06 10 77, fax 01 42 06 72 50
Open year-round. 54 rms 265-350. Bkfst 32. Pkg.
This meticulously-kept small hotel is located a few steps away from the Buttes-Chaumont park, in a district where modern hotels are not exactly plentiful. Convenient for the La Villette exhibition center. Rooms are small (those on the courtyard are larger), fully renovated, and moderately priced.

 ## Magellan

17th arr. - 17, rue Jean-Baptiste-Dumas
01 45 72 44 51, fax 01 40 68 90 36
Open year-round. 75 rms 430-630. Bkfst 40-55. Restaurant. Rm ser. No pets. Garage pkg.
The elegant lobby and lounge were just redecorated, but not the rooms (though some of them could use a rehab). It is preferable to choose a room in the quiet annex which gives onto a garden.

 ## Modern Hotel Lyon

12th arr. - 3, rue Parrot
01 43 43 41 52, fax 01 43 43 81 16
Open year-round. 1 ste 750-855. 47 rms 495-580. Bkfst 39. No pets.
The location is most convenient (near the Gare de Lyon), and the building is attractive. Comfortable, unpretentious rooms; skimpy breakfasts.

 ## Hôtel Le Montana

6th arr. - 28, rue Saint-Benoît
01 44 39 71 00, fax 01 44 39 71 29
Open year-round. 1 ste 962. 16 rms 556-762. Bkfst 50. Restaurant. Rm ser.
Streetside rooms are nice and bright, while rooms at the back can be gloomy. All are decorated in a rather stark contemporary style. Hotel guests are offered a free second drink at the bar of the well-known Montana jazz club.

 ## Hôtel des Nations

5th arr. - "Neotel", 54, rue Monge
01 43 26 45 24, fax 01 46 34 00 13
Open year-round. 38 rms 560-630. Bkfst 56.
Across from the Arènes de Lutèce, this hotel is pretty and modern. The comfortable, pleasant rooms are prettily decorated and sport marble baths. Courteous service.

 ## Le Noailles

2nd arr. - 9, rue de la Michodière
01 47 42 92 90, fax 01 49 24 92 71
Open year-round. 58 rms 580-860. Bkfst 45-80. Rm ser. Conf.
Metal, glass, and wood compose this hotel's riveting contemporary architecture. The functional rooms are bright, cheerful, and fully soundproofed. The Noailles features a restful central patio, charming lounges, a bar, and pleasant little library.

 ## Novanox

6th arr. - 155, bd du Montparnasse
01 46 33 63 60, fax 01 43 26 61 72
Open year-round. 27 rms 550-680. Bkfst 50.
The owner of this hotel, opened in 1989, has used an amusing mixture of 1920s, 1930s, and 1950s styles for the décor. On the ground floor, a large, cheerful room serves as lounge, bar, and breakfast room.

 ## Novotel-Bercy

12th arr. - 85, rue de Bercy
01 43 42 30 00, fax 01 43 45 30 60
Open year-round. 1 ste 1,250. 128 rms 690-720. Bkfst 62. Rms for disabled. Restaurant. Rm ser. Air cond. Conf.
This classic chain hotel is located just minutes from the Palais Omnisports and Finance Ministry. Standard rooms and service.

 ## L'Orchidée

14th arr. - 65, rue de l'Ouest
01 43 22 70 50, fax 01 42 79 97 46
Open year-round. 40 rms 450-500. Bkfst 35. Sauna. Jacuzzi. No pets. Garage pkg.
Tucked behind the attractive façade are an inviting lobby furnished with wicker pieces and a small garden-courtyard. Rooms look out over the garden or a square; some have balconies. Impeccable bathrooms.

 ## Opéra Cadet

9th arr. - 24, rue Cadet
01 48 24 05 26, fax 01 42 46 68 09
Open year-round. 3 stes 1,500. 82 rms 710-990. Bkfst 65. Rms for disabled. Air cond. Conf. Garage pkg.
A functional, modern hotel in the heart of the city, offering comfortable accommodations. Double-glazed windows; winter garden.

Orléans Palace Hôtel

14th arr. - 185, bd Brune
01 45 39 68 50, fax 01 45 43 65 64
Open year-round. 92 rms 510-580. Bkfst 55. Restaurant. Conf.
A quiet and comfortable traditional hotel that offers good value. The well-equipped and soundproofed rooms are decorated in contemporary style, and there is a pretty *jardin intérieur.*

 Parc Montsouris

14th arr. - 4, rue du Parc-Montsouris
01 45 89 09 72, fax 01 45 80 92 72
Open year-round. 2 stes 480. 35 rms 310-420. Bkfst 30. Rms for disabled.
This good little hotel features quiet rooms done up in pastel tones and bright, new bathrooms. The lovely Parc Montsouris is just a short walk away.

 Le Parnasse

14th arr. - 79-81, av. du Maine
01 43 20 13 93, fax 01 43 20 95 60
Closed Jul. 79 rms 515-560. Bkfst 42. Rms for disabled. Air cond. Conf.
The Parnasse is lodged in a pretty, white building; it offers large, bright rooms and complete bathrooms. Double glazing ensures peaceful nights. There are views—of the Tour Montparnasse...and the cemetery!

 Hôtel de la Place du Louvre

1st arr. - 21, rue des Prêtres-St-Germain-l'Auxerrois
01 42 33 78 68, fax 01 42 33 09 95
Open year-round. 20 rms 496-812. Bkfst 50.
Lodged in a Renaissance building, this hotel is decorated with paintings and sculptures throughout. The fairly large rooms are all comfortably furnished, with good bathrooms, and there are five charming split-level rooms under the eaves. Breakfast is served in a vaulted cellar.

 Plaza La Fayette

10th arr. - 175, rue La Fayette
01 44 89 89 10, fax 01 40 36 00 30
Open year-round. 48 rms 595-890. Bkfst 50-65. Rms for disabled. Restaurant. Air cond. Pkg.
Here's a fine, brand-new hotel with well-equipped, soundproofed rooms. Breakfast is served on the terrace on warm days. Private bar and restaurant for hotel residents.

 Hôtel du Pré

9th arr. - 10, rue Pierre-Sémard
01 42 81 37 11, fax 01 40 23 98 28
Open year-round. 40 rms 445-575. Bkfst 50. No pets.
Comfortable and close to the Gare du Nord and the Gare de l'Est. Downstairs, guests have the use of a bar, a bright lounge, and a pleasant breakfast room (good breakfasts). The cheerful, spacious guest rooms sport pink, green or white wicker furniture.

 Queen Mary

8th arr. - 9, rue de Greffulhe
01 42 66 40 50, fax 01 42 66 94 92
Open year-round. 1 ste 1,200. 35 rms 725-895. Rms for disabled. Rm ser. Air cond.
On a quiet street in the Haussmann district, this Queen Mary is an adorable, recently refurbished hotel. The cozy little rooms are furnished in the English style, right down to the decanter of Sherry placed on the table.

 Résidence Bassano

16th arr. - 15, rue de Bassano
01 47 23 78 23, fax 01 47 20 41 22
Open year-round. 3 stes 1,600-1,950. 28 rms 750-1,150. Bkfst 65. Restaurant. Rm ser. Air cond.
Housed in a building of Haussmann vintage, the rooms are summarily furnished, yet most are bright and all are thoughtfully designed and equipped. Delightful cocktail bar.

 Résidence des Gobelins

13th arr. - 9, rue des Gobelins
01 47 07 26 90, fax 01 43 31 44 05
Open year-round. 32 rms 320-430. Bkfst 36. No pets.
A delightful small hotel in a quiet street not far from the Latin Quarter and Montparnasse with congenial young owners. Rooms are decorated in blue, green, or orange, a different color for each floor. Some give onto a terrace.

 Résidence Monceau

8th arr. - 85, rue du Rocher
01 45 22 75 11, fax 01 45 22 30 88
Open year-round. 1 ste 865. 50 rms 700. Bkfst 50. Rms for disabled. Restaurant. No pets.
Though it lacks atmosphere, the Résidence Monceau is functional and well kept, and employs a helpful, courteous staff. All the rooms and corridors have just been freshly redecorated.

 Résidence Saint-Lambert

15th arr. - 5, rue Eugène-Gibez
01 48 28 63 14, fax 01 45 33 45 50
Open year-round. 48 rms 380-570. Bkfst 42.
This pleasant, quiet hotel near the exhibition center at Porte de Versailles has tidy, smallish but nicely equipped rooms (double glazing), some overlooking the garden. A laundry and bar are on the premises.

 Résidence Trousseau

11th arr. - 13, rue Trousseau
01 48 05 55 55, fax 01 48 05 83 97
Open year-round. 2 stes 1,350-1,500. 64 rms 300-550. Bkfst 45. Conf. Pkg.
A modern hotel not far from the Bastille. The suites have refurbished with kitchenettes, a practical touch. The quiet rooms are set around an enclosed garden.

Saint-Christophe

5th arr. - 17, rue Lacépède
01 43 31 81 54, fax 01 43 31 12 54
Open year-round. 36 rms 450-600. Bkfst 50. Rms for disabled.
If you like bright pink, you'll love the décor of this quiet, well-maintained hotel. Remarkably warm, courteous reception.

 ## Saint Ferdinand

17th arr. - 36, rue Saint-Ferdinand
01 45 72 66 66, fax 01 45 74 12 92
Open year-round. 42 rms 750-900. Bkfst 50. Air cond.
This small, functional hotel is of recent vintage. The rooms are tiny (the bathrooms even more so), and the décor is fading fast. Obliging staff, however, and good equipment.

 ## Hôtel de Saint-Germain

6th arr. - 50, rue du Four
01 45 48 91 64, fax 01 45 48 46 22
Open year-round. 30 rms 415-695. Bkfst 45-60.
This small hotel with its doll-sized rooms and white-wood furniture has finished its renovation. Many services.

 ## Hôtel de Seine

6th arr. - 52, rue de Seine
01 46 34 22 80, fax 01 46 34 04 74
Open year-round. 30 rms 695-980. No pets.
Just a stone's throw from the Buci open-air market, this establishment provides quiet, well-kept rooms with an old-fashioned feel. Cheerful staff.

 ## Sénateur

6th arr. - 10, rue de Vaugirard
01 43 26 08 83, fax 01 46 34 04 66
Open year-round. 42 rms 720-750. Bkfst 50. Rms for disabled. Conf. No cards.
A comfortable, modern hotel with a huge mural and plenty of greenery brightening up the ground floor. Fine views from the top floor. Attentive service.

 ## Suède

7th arr. - 31, rue Vaneau
01 47 05 00 08, fax 01 47 05 69 27
Open year-round. 1 ste 1,000. 38 rms 400-900. Bkfst 50. Restaurant. No pets.
Decorated in tones of blue in a refined but rather austere Directoire style, the guest rooms are quiet and nicely equipped. Streetside rooms are a trifle gloomy. Though smaller, those overlooking the indoor garden are much more cheerful, and from the sixth floor, they offer a view of the Matignon gardens—and, on occasion, the prime minister's garden parties!

 ## La Tour d'Auvergne

9th arr. - 10, rue de La Tour d'Auvergne
01 48 78 61 60, fax 01 49 95 99 00
Open year-round. 24 rms 450-750. Bkfst 52. Garage pkg.
Modigliani once lived in this hotel. We wonder how he would feel about its current kitsch décor (don't miss the draped headboards). Nonetheless, a competently run, comfortable establishment.

 ## Hôtel Le Tourville

7th arr. - 16, av. de Tourville
01 47 05 62 62, fax 01 47 05 43 90
Open year-round. 2 stes 1,390-1,990. 28 rms 690-1,090. Bkfst 60. Rm ser. Air cond.
A smart, quiet hotel, the Tourville provides cozy and attractive rooms that are much appreciated by a well-bred clientele.

 ## Varenne

7th arr. - 44, rue de Bourgogne
01 45 51 45 55, fax 01 45 51 86 63
Open year-round. 24 rms 530-710. Bkfst 45.
A cheerful reception is assured at this small hotel whose provincial air is underlined by a courtyard filled with flowers and trees (where breakfast and drinks are served on sunny days). The rooms overlooking the street have double windows.

 ## Vieux Marais

4th arr. - 8, rue du Plâtre
01 42 78 47 22, fax 01 42 78 34 32
Closed Aug. 30 rms 410-560. Bkfst 38. No pets.
Bright, spacious accommodations with small but adequate bathrooms, in a friendly, quiet hotel. Rooms on the fourth floor have streetside balconies.

 ## La Villa des Artistes

6th arr. - 9, rue de la Grande-Chaumière
01 43 26 60 86, fax 01 43 54 73 70
Open year-round. 59 rms 660-860. Bkfst 35. Air cond. No pets.
An oasis of calm amid the noise and bustle of Montparnasse. Quiet and comfort are assured in this hotel, built around a garden patio. Good value for this district.

 ## Le Zéphyr

12th arr. - 31 bis, bd Diderot
01 43 46 12 72, fax 01 43 41 68 01
Open year-round. 90 rms 530-720. Bkfst 60. Rms for disabled. Restaurant. Half-board 670-1,000. Air cond. Conf. Garage pkg.
Practically next door to the Gare de Lyon, the Zéphyr is a newly renovated hotel with good equipment. Rooms are bright and neat, the welcome is friendly, and service is reliably prompt. Quality breakfasts.

PARIS FOOD SHOPS

Paris is paradise for food lovers, a mecca for gastro-tourists in search of the rarest, the best, the most luxurious *gourmandises*. The capital's pastry shops, chocolate shops, charcuteries, bakeries, and gourmet grocers overflow with temptations to taste on the spot or to pack up and take back home. Specialties and treats from all over France can be tracked down in Paris, where new taste sensations can be discovered around every *coin de rue*.

• BAKERIES

Daniel Dupuy

9th arr. - 13, rue Cadet - 01 48 24 54 26
Daniel's prize-winning pain de campagne, made of natural leavening agents and stone-ground flour, lives up to its vaunted reputation. Connoisseurs know that bread with this sort of authentic flavor is indeed worth seeking out. The same can be said of Dupuy's specialty, the Rochetour: he keeps the recipe a closely guarded secret.

Philippe Gosselin

1st arr. - 125, rue Saint-Honoré
01 45 08 03 59, fax 01 45 08 90 10
In 1996, Gosselin won the competition for the best baguette in Paris. This marvel of freshness is crusty and flavorful. He supplies them to the Élysée Palace, but ordinary customers are still cordially welcomed.

Au Panetier

2nd arr. - 10, pl. des Petits-Pères - 01 42 60 90 23
Even if you don't want to buy one of the old-fashioned loaves of hazelnut bread, raisin bread, or the house specialty: dense, delicious pain de Saint-Fiacre (all baked in a wood-fired oven), this excellent bakery is worth a visit just for a look at the adorable etched-glass and tile décor.

Au Pétrin d'Antan

18th arr. - 174, rue Ordener - 01 46 27 01 46
Philippe Viron, the inventor of the "Rétrodor" baguette, runs this bakery, where you can be sure to find a baguette made according to traditional methods. When you see the Retrodor sign in other bakeries, a good baguette is guaranteed.

Lionel Poilâne

6th arr. - 8, rue du Cherche-Midi - 01 45 48 42 59
15th arr. - 49, bd de Grenelle - 01 45 79 11 49
Lionel Poilâne is indubitably the best-known baker on the planet; he can be seen hawking his famous sourdough bread in magazines and on television screens throughout the world. And even though his products are sold all over Paris in charcuteries and cheese shops, goodly numbers of Poilâne fans think nothing of crossing town and standing in line to *personally* buy their favorite bread still warm from his ovens. Poilâne's walnut bread is, in a word, scrumptious, and we are also particularly fond of the shortbread cookies (sablés) and the rustic apple turnover (which makes a delicious and inexpensive dessert, accompanied by a bowl of thick crème fraîche).

Max Poilâne

1st arr. - 42, pl. du Marché St-Honoré
01 42 61 10 53
14th arr. - 29, rue de l'Ouest - 01 43 27 24 91
15th arr. - 87, rue Brancion - 01 48 28 45 90
Max Poilâne's bread bears a distinct resemblance to that produced by his brother, Lionel (see above). That's natural enough, since their father taught both of them the secrets of the trade. Max bakes big, hearty loaves with a sourdough tang, delicious rye bread studded with raisins, and buttery white bread that makes a first-class sandwich. For a teatime treat, try the luscious apple tarts. If you can't wait to try these goodies, just take a seat in the bakery's tea room.

Poujauran

7th arr. - 20, rue Jean-Nicot - 01 47 05 80 88
He's a real darling, that Jean-Luc Poujauran! His bakery may be in a ritzy neighborhood, but he hasn't gone high-hat; food writers regularly wax lyrical over his talent, but his head hasn't swelled an inch. And though he bakes a wonderful country loaf with organically grown flour, he's not the type to think he's the greatest thing since sliced bread. Let's just hope he never changes. And let's hope that we will never have to give up his delicious little rolls (or his olive or his poppy seed or his walnut bread), his old-fashioned pound cake (quatre-quarts), his buttery Basque cakes, or the terrific frangipane-stuffed galettes that he bakes for the Epiphany (Three Kings' Day, January 6).

• *CHARCUTERIE & TAKEOUT*

Charcuterie Lyonnaise

9th arr. - 58, rue des Martyrs · 01 48 78 96 45
Lyon's reputed specialties hold pride of place here: try the rosette, jésus, or saucisson de Lyon sausages as well as the superb terrines.

Chédeville Saint-Honoré

1st arr. - 18, pl. du Marché-Saint-Honoré
01 42 61 04 62
The Ritz, Crillon, Plaza Athénéé and other classy hotels buy their traditional French charcuterie here (so does the president of France, incidentally). The quality is excellent, the choice is wide. Recommended are the York ham, the old-fashioned pork knuckle (great picnic food), the elaborate ballottines, and the pigs' trotters stuffed with foie gras.

Coesnon

6th arr. - 30, rue Dauphine
01 43 54 35 80, fax 01 43 26 56 39
Because true practitioners of the charcutier's art are becoming ever harder to find, and because Bernard Marchaudon is one of its most eminent representatives, we recommend that you make a special point of visiting this wonderful pork emporium. Marchaudon's boudin blanc and boudin noir are legendary (his chestnut-studded black pudding has won slews of awards); what's more, his salt-and smoke-cured pork specialties are top-notch—especially when accompanied by the crisp yet tender sauerkraut he pickles himself. So step up to counter with confidence, knowing that you will be competently and courteously served.

Flo Prestige

1st arr. - 42, pl. du Marché-Saint-Honoré
01 42 61 45 46
4th arr. - 10 rue Saint-Antoine · 01 53 01 91 91
7th arr. - 36, av. de La Motte-Picquet
01 45 55 71 25
9th arr. - 64, bd Haussmann, Le Printemps
01 42 82 58 82
12th arr. - 211, av. Daumesnil · 01 43 44 86 36
& 22, av. de la Porte de Vincennes · 01 43 74 54 32
15th arr. - 352, rue Lecourbe · 01 45 54 76 94
16th arr. - 61, av. de la Grande-Armée
01 45 00 12 10
& 102, av. du Président-Kennedy · 01 42 88 38 00
Early or late, every day of the year, you have a sure source of delicious bread, fine wine, yummy desserts—in short, of wonderful meals with Flo Prestige. The selection of foodstuffs is varied and choice, and covers a wide range of prices, from the excellent house sauerkraut to prestigious Petrossian caviar.

Gargantua

1st arr. - 284, rue Saint-Honoré · 01 42 60 52 54

The opulent window displays of this well-known charcuterie could satisfy even the gigantically robust appetite of its Rabelaisian namesake. There are cured meats, foie gras, and terrines, of course, but Gargantua also carries an abundance of prepared dishes, breads, wines, pastries, and ice cream. It's a fine place to go to put together a picnic.

Lewkowicz

4th arr. - 12, rue des Rosiers · 01 48 87 63 17
Since 1928 "Lewko" has been serving up authentic Jewish specialties made from old-country recipes. In his expanded and renovated shop, Lewkowicz *Fils* proposes flavorsome corned beef, pastrami, pressed veal, and Krakow sausage, as well as kosher meats and poultry, and a selection of wines, spirits, and tinned foods.

Pou

17th arr. - 16, av. des Ternes
01 43 80 19 24, fax 01 46 22 66 97
Pou is divine, an excellent charcuterie whose sober décor and rich displays resemble nothing so much as a palace of earthly delights. A look in the window is an irresistible invitation to buy and taste: black and white boudin sausages, duck pâté en croûte, glittering galantines, cervelas sausage studded with pale-green pistachios, and sumptuous pastries too. Since everything really is as good as it looks, making a choice is quite a task. And given the prices, paying isn't so easy, either.

Royal Palais

16th arr. - 29, rue du Docteur-Blanche
01 45 25 67 67
A pretty boutique that offers all sorts of food made with seasonal products. There are wonderful terrines and delicious pastries and jams. Everything is refined and original.

• *CHEESE*

Alléosse

17th arr. - 13, rue Poncelet · 01 46 22 50 45
Father and son Roger and Philippe Alléosse purvey some of the finest cheeses in Paris. With the obsessive zeal of perfectionists, they turn, rinse, brush, and otherwise groom their farmhouse fromages down in the ideally dank depths of their seven maturing cellars. If the shop's astounding stock leaves you at a loss, don't hesitate to seek advice from the staff: they'll introduce you to little-known cheeses from all over France. We understand why so many chefs choose to shop *chez* Alléosse.

Androuet

7th arr. - 83, rue Saint-Dominique · 01 45 50 45 75
8th arr. - 6, rue Arsène-Houssaye
01 42 89 95 00, fax 01 42 89 68 44

This shop, founded in 1909, has two new locations and new owners who carry on the house tradition, offering a wide range of well-chosen, refined cheeses. There is also a restaurant that serves dishes based on the shop's products at rue Arsène-Houssaye. (open noon-2pm & 7:30pm-10:30pm; closed Sat lunch, Sun, hols).

Barthélémy

7th arr. - 51, rue de Grenelle
01 45 48 56 75, fax 01 45 49 25 16
Roland Barthélémy reigns over a treasure trove of cheeses that he selects from farms all over the French countryside, then coddles to perfect ripeness in his cellars. He is also the creator of several marvelous specialties that have the *Who's Who* of French officialdom beating a path to his door (he supplies the Élysée Palace, no less). The Boulamour (fresh cream cheese enriched with crème fraîche, currants, raisins, and Kirsch) was Barthélémy's invention, as was a delicious Camembert laced with Calvados. We also enjoy the amusing Brie Surprise. But not to worry, tradition is never neglected here, witness the rich-tasting Alpine Beaufort, French Vacherin, and other prime mountain cheeses which are a Barthélémy specialty. The luxuriously creamy Fontainebleau is made fresh on the premises. Take one of the appetizing cheese trays sold here as your contribution to a dinner party: your hostess will love it!

Marie-Anne Cantin

7th arr. - 12, rue du Champ-de-Mars - 01 45 50 43 94
The cheeses Marie-Anne Cantin selects and matures herself benefit from unstinting doses of tender loving care. She is an ardent defender of real (read: unpasteurized) cheeses and is one of the few merchants in Paris to sell Saint-Marcellins as they are preferred on their home turf—in their creamy prime, not in their chalky youth. And so it is with the other cheeses she sells, all of which retain the authentic flavors of their rustic origins.

Alain Dubois

17th arr. - 80, rue de Tocqueville - 01 42 27 11 38
& 79, rue de Courcelles - 01 43 80 36 42
Alain Dubois's Gruyère, aged for at least two years in his cellars, is a royal treat. And there's more: Dubois offers farmhouse goat cheeses, unpasteurized Camembert, and authentic Époisses (which he rinses religiously with marc de Bourgogne). The problem is, this expert cheese merchant offers so many enticements (some 150) that we don't know which way to turn. You will not be astonished to learn that Dubois supplies premium cheeses to such noted restaurants as Guy Savoy, Michel Rostang, and more.

La Ferme Saint-Hubert

8th arr. - 21, rue Vignon
01 47 42 79 20, fax 01 47 42 46 97
Cheese seller Henry Voy is so passionate about his vocation that he has no time for anything else. Morning and night you can find him tending to his Beauforts (aged for a minimum of two years), his farmhouse chèvres, Corsican sheep cheeses, or his exclusive Délice de Saint-Hubert. He travels all over France, seeking out the most flavorful specimens. For true aficionados, Voy unearths such rarities as unpasteurized butter churned with spring water, and delicate goat's-milk butter. In the adjoining restaurant you can sample cheese-based dishes (open Mon-Sat noon-3:30pm; Mon-Wed 6:45pm-11pm, Thu-Sat 6:45pm-11:30pm).

Fromagerie Boursault

14th arr. - 71, av. du Général-Leclerc
01 43 27 93 30, fax 01 45 38 59 56
It was here that Pierre Boursault created the triple-creme cheese that bears his name. And it is here, naturally enough, that you will find Boursault at its rich, golden best. Owner Jacques Vernier has made the shop one of the most pleasant in Paris, a showcase for the rare cheeses that he seeks out himself in the French hinterlands. Like incomparable Beauforts aged under his supervision in their native Alpine air; farmhouse goat cheeses (ah, those Picodons!); handcrafted Saint-Nectaire from Auvergne, which has nothing in common with the industrially produced variety; and flawless Camemberts. This is one of the few places on the planet where one may buy Bleu de Termignon, a blue-veined summer cheese from Savoie.

• *CHOCOLATE & CANDY*

Boissier

16th arr. - 184, av. Victor-Hugo - 01 45 04 87 88
Come here for puckery hard candies sold in pretty blue boxes and for delicious caramels.

Christian Constant

6th arr. - 37, rue d'Assas
01 45 48 45 51, fax 01 42 86 97 97
7th arr. - 26, rue du Bac - 01 47 03 30 00
Christian Constant, who chooses the best cocoa beans from the West Indies, Tahiti, Ecuador and elsewhere, is a genius with chocolate. His brilliant innovations include a line of flower-scented chocolates (try the ylang-ylang, vetiver, or the jasmine varieties...), chocolates filled with delicately spiced creams, others spiked with fruit brandies or cordials, still others incorporating nuts and dried fruit (the Conquistador is loaded with hazelnuts, honey, and cinnamon). Constant recommends that we buy his wares in small amounts, for optimum freshness and flavor. Well, given the prices (480 F per kilo), for most people quantity purchases are out of the question!

A l'Étoile d'Or

9th arr. - 30, rue Fontaine - 01 48 74 59 55
Denise Acabo does not make her own chocolate; rather, she is a true connoisseur who selects

the very best handcrafted chocolates made in France, and presents them, in a laudable spirit of impartiality, to her delighted customers (while explaining to interested parties the connection between chocolate and eroticism...). The famed Bernachon chocolates from Lyon are sold in this beautiful turn-of-the-century shop, as well as Dufoux's incomparable palets (in twelve flavors), and Bonnat's chocolate bars. Don't miss Bochard's mandarin de Grenoble: a glazed tangerine with a chocolate mandarin's hat—it's irresistible!

La Fontaine au Chocolat

1st arr. - 101, rue Saint-Honoré - 01 42 33 09 09
& 201, rue Saint-Honoré - 01 42 44 11 66
Pervading Michel Cluizel's shop is a scent of chocolate so intense that your nose will flash an alert to your sweet tooth, and (we guarantee!) have you salivating within seconds. Whether you try one of the five varieties of palets au chocolat or the croquamandes (caramelized almonds coated with extra-dark chocolate), the mendiants studded with nuts and dried fruit, or the bold Noir Infini (99 percent cocoa, perfumed with vanilla and spices), you're in for an unforgettable treat.

Fouquet

8th arr. - 22, rue François-Ier
01 47 23 30 36, fax 01 47 23 30 56
9th arr. - 36, rue Laffitte - 01 47 70 85 00
It's worth going out of your way just to see this shop, which dates from 1824. Everything here is exquisite, from the chocolates to the traditional or more original candies. Also sells fine grocery products.

Jadis et Gourmande

4th arr. - 39, rue des Archives - 01 48 04 08 03
5th arr. - 88, bd de Port-Royal - 01 43 26 17 75
8th arr. - 49 bis, av. Franklin-Roosevelt
01 42 25 06 04, fax 01 53 76 00 71
& 27, rue Boissy-d'Anglas - 01 42 65 23 23
It is delightful indeed to browse around this sugarplum palace, where one is tempted in turn by delicious bonbons, hard candies, caramels, and chocolate in myriad forms (320 F per kilo). The thick slabs of cooking chocolate make one want to rush to the kitchen and whip up a rich devil's food cake! Our favorite confection here is a thick braid of dark chocolate studded with candied orange peel and hazelnuts.

La Maison du Chocolat

6th arr. - 19, rue de Sèvres - 01 45 44 20 40
8th arr. - 52, rue François-Ier
01 47 23 38 25, fax 01 40 70 01 63
& 225, rue du Fg-Saint-Honoré - 01 42 27 39 44
9th arr. - 8, bd de la Madeleine - 01 47 42 86 52
16th arr. - 89, av. Raymond Poincarré
01 40 67 77 83
There's something of the alchemist about Robert Linxe: never satisfied, he is ever experimenting, innovating, transforming mere cocoa beans into something very precious. His

chocolates (480 F per kilo) are among the finest in Paris, maybe even in the world. His renowned buttercream fillings—lemon, caramel, tea, raspberry, and rum—will carry you away to gourmet heaven.

A la Mère de Famille

9th arr. - 35, rue du Fg-Montmartre
01 47 70 83 69
Perhaps the oldest candy shop in Paris (it dates back to 1761), La Mère de Famille is certainly the handsomest, with a façade and interior from the nineteenth century (note the Second Empire-style cashier's booth). The shop's sweet inventory includes luscious jams, candied fruits, and bonbons from all over France. The chocolates are prepared by the current owner, Serge Neveu, and sell for 368 F per kilo. We love the Whiskadines (soft chestnut centers laced with whisky) and the Délices de la Mère with their suave almond and rum-raisin filling.

Richart

7th arr. - 258, bd Saint-Germain
01 45 55 66 00, fax 01 47 53 72 72
8th arr. - 36, av. Wagram - 01 45 74 94 00
The Richart brothers may be the most innovative *chocolatiers* around. Not only are their chocolates perfectly scrumptious (filled with single-malt ganache, for example, or wild-raspberry cream, or nutmeg praline, or prune coulis...) they are presented in imaginative packages unlike any we've seen. Just look at the Secret Pyramid, a clever box that holds fourteen ultrathin chocolates. Richart's flat Easter eggs are pretty unusual, too! And the Petits Richarts, mini-chocolates that weigh just one-sixth of an ounce, are ideal for nibbling with a clear conscience.

• *COFFEE & TEA*

Betjeman & Barton

8th arr. - 23, bd Malesherbes - 01 42 65 86 17
11th arr. - 24, bd des Filles-du-Calvaire
01 40 21 35 52
The name on the sign and the shop's décor are veddy, veddy British, but the firm itself is 100 percent French, directed nowadays by Didier Jumeau-Lafond. An extensive range of premium teas is on offer, comprising over 180 natural and flavored varieties. Indeed, B & B's teas are of such high quality that Harrod's of London (no less) deigns to market them. To help you choose your blend, the staff will offer you a cup of tea—a comforting and highly civilized custom. Excellent jellies and jams and a line of refreshing "fruit waters" intended to be consumed icy-cold in summer, are worth seeking out here. For nibbling with your tea, try the Duchy Originals (sponsored by Prince Charles, don't you know), cookies baked of organic, stone-ground oats and wheat. B & B now produces a line of fine hand-painted china decorated with pretty fruit and flower motifs.

Verlet

1st arr. - 256, rue Saint-Honoré
01 42 60 67 39, fax 01 42 60 05 55

The Verlet family has been roasting and selling coffee beans in their delightful turn-of-the-century shop since 1880. Pierre Verlet imports the finest coffees from Papua, Costa Rica, Colombia, Jamaica, Malabar, Ethiopia, and Brazil, and he also produces several subtle and delicious house blends. He will even create one specially for you, for he is a master at balancing different aromas, different degrees of acidity and bitterness to suit personal taste. If you prefer to sample before you buy, take a seat at one of the little tables and try, perhaps, the Petit Cheval blend, a marvelously balanced and smooth Moka. Verlet also stocks a selection of teas from all over the world and an appetizing array of dried fruits. At lunchtime, crowds pour into the shop for an excellent croque monsieur or a slice of cake and a cup of fragrant coffee.

• ETHNIC FOODS

The General Store

7th arr. - 82, rue de Grenelle - 01 45 48 63 16
16th arr. - 30, rue de Longchamp
01 47 55 41 14

Tacos, tortillas, and all the other traditional fixings for a Tex-Mex feast may be found in this spic-and-span little shop. But the inventory doesn't stop there: You'll find buttermilk-pancake mix, a selection of California wines (not just Paul Masson), familiar American packaged foods (Karo syrup, cream cheese, canned pumpkin, chocolate chips, Hellmann's mayo), and even fresh cranberries at holiday time. If you crave a sweet snack, look for the delectable pecan squares and cookies whipped up fresh every day. As you would expect, English is spoken, and you can count on a warm welcome.

Goldenberg

17th arr. - 69, av. de Wagram - 01 42 27 34 79

Familiar deli fare, made measurably more exotic by the fact that it's served within sight of the Arc de Triomphe. There's herring, there's corned beef, there's gefilte fish (stuffed carp), there's pastrami, and that well-known Yiddish dessert, the brownie.

Marks & Spencer

4th arr. - 88, rue de Rivoli - 01 44 61 08 00
9th arr. - 35, bd Haussmann - 01 47 42 42 91

The food section of this all-British emporium provides ample evidence that English gastronomy is not, as Parisians tend to think, a joking matter. The French are genetically incapable, for example, of producing good bacon. Marks & Spencer's is wonderful: meaty, smoky, with no nasty bits of bone, no inedible rind. The cheese counter carries Stilton, Cheddar, Leicester, and other delicious English dairy products, and the grocery shelves are crowded with all sorts of piquant condiments and chut-

neys. Teas, biscuits, jams, and marmalades are legion, of course, and special refrigerated cases offer fresh sandwiches for a quick lunch on the run. Prices in the Paris branch are considerably higher than on Marks & Sparks' home turf.

Spécialités Antillaises

20th arr. - 14-16, bd de Belleville - 01 43 58 31 30

Here's a one-stop shop for Creole fixings and take-out foods. Among the latter, we recommend the scrumptious stuffed crabs, the crispy accras (salt-cod fritters), the Creole sausage, and a spicy avocado dish called féroce d'avocat. The grocery section offers tropical fruits flown in fresh from the West Indies, as well as a selection of exotic frozen fish (shark, gilthead...), and an intoxicating array of rums and punches.

• FRUITS & VEGETABLES

Le Fruitier d'Auteuil

16th arr. - 5, rue Bastien-Lepage - 01 45 27 51 08

Bernard Rapine, president of the Fruit Retailers' Union, has a personal and professional interest in displaying the best produce he can find. He claims—and we have seen it to be true—that any store posting the union label (the word *fruitier* printed over a basket of fruit) is honorbound to provide top-quality merchandise and service. Rapine's vegetables, incidentally, are just as prime. Some are sold peeled and ready to cook. Even less prep is required for the shop's range of take-out dishes that includes delicious soups, eggplant purée, guacamole, fruit salads, and more.

Palais du Fruit

2nd arr. - 62 & 72, rue Montorgueil - 01 42 33 22 15

Superb fruits and vegetables from all over the globe, beautifully presented. Even when skies are gray in France, in Chile or the Antilles gorgeous produce ripens in the sun, then is picked and packed off to this cheerful store. Wide choice, remarkable quality.

• GOURMET SPECIALTIES

Faguais

8th arr. - 30, rue de la Trémoille - 01 47 20 80 91

Yes, Grandmother would feel quite at home in this charming gourmet shop. A dizzying variety of temptations is set out neatly on the shelves. Old-fashioned jams, oils, honeys, cookies, spices, vinegars, and condiments fairly cry out to be bought. As the shop's pervasive fragrance implies, fresh coffee beans are roasted on the premises daily.

Looking for a gastronomic specialty? Refer to the **index.**

Fauchon

8th arr. - 30, pl. de la Madeleine
01 47 42 60 11, fax 01 47 42 83 75

In 1886, at the age of 30, Auguste Fauchon opened his *épicerie fine* on the Place de la Madeleine, specializing in quality French foodstuffs. The rest is history. After more than a century, Fauchon is the uncontested paragon of what a luxury gourmet emporium should be. The entire staff of 360 employees is committed to the task of tasting, testing, and selling the very finest, the rarest, the most unusual foods in the world. The number of spices alone—110—is enough to make your head spin. And you'll find such delicacies as black-fig or watermelon preserves, lavender or buckwheat honey, Mim tea from India or Kee-yu tea from China, lavish displays of prime vegetables and fruits, and a world-renowned collection of vintage wines and brandies. As for the pastries, well...you try Sébastien Gaudard's creations, which are also featured in Fauchon's on-site restaurants (see Le "30" in *Restaurants*).

La Grande Épicerie de Paris

7th arr. - Le Bon Marché, 38, rue de Sèvres
01 44 39 81 00

A deluxe supermarket filled with a huge array of handsomely presented foodstuffs: a lovely place to browse.

Goumanyat et son Royaume

2nd arr. - 7, rue de la Michodière
01 42 68 09 71, fax 01 45 93 08 10

A magical place where you will find top-quality products. Many of the best chefs shop here. On hand or available through special order are rare spices, delicious chocolates, well-prepared foie gras, wild smoked salmon, excellent caviar, and oils and vinegars with amazing flavors. Professional knives are also sold here.

Hédiard

7th arr. - 126, rue du Bac - 01 45 44 01 98
8th arr. - 21, pl. de la Madeleine
01 43 12 88 88
16th arr. - 70, av. Paul-Doumer - 01 45 04 51 92
17th arr. - 106, bd de Courcelles - 01 47 63 32 14
92200 Neuilly-sur-Seine - 135, rue de Longchamp
01 47 22 90 82

Only the most select foodstuffs are deemed worthy of entry into this shrine of epicureanism, founded in 1854. Distinguished smoked salmon from the best "schools," sophisticated sugars and syrups, pedigreed Ports, vintage wines and brandies, and over 4,500 carefully chosen grocery items attract virtually every cultivated palate in town. Even the ordinary is extraordinary here: mustard spiked with Cognac; vinegar flavored with seaweed; opulent fruits and vegetables, always perfect, that hail from the ends of the earth. Many of the items are as costly as they are exotic, but the wines consistently offer excellent value for the money. Hédiard's flagship store on Place de la Madeleine was remodeled and expanded not long ago. It houses a tasting bar in the wine department. And, not to be outdone by its rival across the *place*, Hédiard, like Fauchon, has a classy restaurant above the store (see *Restaurants*).

Lafayette Gourmet

9th arr. - 48, bd Haussmann or 97, rue de Provence
01 48 74 46 06

A huge space devoted to the pleasures of gastronomy, with fresh foods, rare condiments, teas, coffees, charcuteries, wines... And there are counters for sampling the wares, so that you can stop for a bite after shopping.

Albert Ménès

8th arr. - 41, bd Malesherbes - 01 42 66 95 63

The Albert Menès label marks some of the finest handcrafted products of France. The shop offers around 450 regional products, ranging from fine sardines to rare vinegars. There are also cookies, jam, honey and other sweets from each region. The gift presentation is very attractive.

Escargots

L'Escargot de la Butte

18th arr. - 48, rue Joseph-de-Maistre
01 46 27 38 27

"It's really a shame, but there are no more escargots de Bourgogne left in Burgundy," laments Monsieur Marchal. He imports them, therefore, from the Lot and the Ardèche. But his petits-gris come straight from the Provençal countryside, and arrive still frisky at his little shop located at the foot of the Butte Montmartre. He stuffs them with a deliciously fragrant blend of pure butter, garlic, and parsley and they are a remarkable treat!

Foie Gras

Divay

17th arr. - 4, rue Bayen - 01 43 80 16 97

Priced at 650 F per kilo, Divay sells the least expensive fattened goose liver to be found in the city. What's more, it's delicious. You'll find great traditional charcuterie here, too.

Aux Ducs de Gascogne

1st arr. - 4, rue du Marché-St-Honoré
01 42 60 45 31
4th arr. - 111, rue St-Antoine - 01 42 71 17 72
8th arr. - 112, bd Haussmann - 01 45 22 54 04
15th arr. - 221, rue de la Convention - 01 48 28 32 09
16th arr. - 54, av. Victor-Hugo - 01 45 00 34 78
20th arr. - 41, rue des Gatines - 01 43 66 99 99

This multistore chain specializes in tinned and lightly cooked foie gras, as well as other Southwestern favorites (the thick peasant soup—garbure—sold in jars is excellent indeed). Steep prices, but the quality is dependably high.

L'Esprit du Sud Ouest

7th arr. - 108, rue Saint-Dominique
01 45 55 29 06, fax 01 47 53 90 28
Here you'll find regional products from the southwest of France made without preservatives. On offer: every type of foie gras (preserved, half-cooked, fresh, etc.), salted fish from Cacune in the Tarn, and a most interesting pure-duck dried sausage. To help recreate the ambience of this friendly region of France, the shop also sells rugby shirts from the home team.

Foie Gras Luxe

1st arr. - 26, rue Montmartre
01 42 36 14 73, fax 01 40 26 45 50
This reliable, long-established shop sells raw foie gras year-round, as well as lightly cooked goose and duck livers. More luxury: Iranian caviar and savory cured hams from Parma, San Daniele, and the Ardennes are also for sale.

Honey & Jams

Le Furet-Tanrade

10th arr. - 63, rue de Chabrol
01 47 70 48 34, fax 01 42 46 34 41
Alain Furet is a *chocolatier* first and foremost, but he also makes fabulous jams from recipes developed by Monsieur Tanrade, long the top name in French preserves. Furet took over the Tanrade plant, and now turns out succulent jams (raspberry, strawberry, apricot, blackcurrant...); he also has put the finishing touches on a recipe of his own, for *gelée au chocolat*—a landmark!

La Maison du Miel

9th arr. - 24, rue Vignon - 01 47 42 26 70
Make a beeline to this "House of Honey" to try 28 varieties from all over France, and a few imported honeys, too. There's Corsican honey, luscious pine honey from the Vosges mountains (which comes highly recommended for bronchial irritations), Provençal lavender honey, as well as choice varieties from the Alps and Auvergne, all rigorously tested by a busy hive of honey tasters. In addition, you'll find honey "by-products," such as beeswax, candles, pollen, and royal jelly, as well as a wide range of honey-based cosmetics.

Oils

A l'Olivier

4th arr. - 23, rue de Rivoli - 01 48 04 86 59
Connoisseurs know that this shop is an excellent source for several fine varieties of olive oil, as well as walnut oil, grilled-almond oil, pumpkin-seed oil, and hazelnut oil. The main attraction, however, is an exclusive, top-secret blend of virgin olive oils. We applaud the store policy of selling exceptionally expensive and perishable oils in quarter-liter bottles. Fine vinegars and mustards are presented too—everything you need to mix up a world-class vinaigrette!

Truffles

Maison de la Truffe

8th arr. - 19, pl. de la Madeleine
01 42 65 53 22, fax 01 49 24 96 59
Alongside extraordinary charcuterie, foie gras, smoked salmon, and take-out foods, this luxurious gourmet shop offers truffles (freshly dug or sterilized and bottled) at prices that are emphatically not of the bargain-basement variety. The season for fresh black truffles runs from October to late March; fresh white truffles are imported from Italy from October to December. Owner Guy Monier recently set aside a corner of his shop for tasting: customers may order from a brief menu featuring dishes made with the sublime fungus (truffes en salade, truffes en feuilleté, truffles with fresh pasta, in risotto...). Look too for the range of oils, vinegars, and mustards all perfumed with—you guessed it!

• ICE CREAM & SORBET

Berthillon

4th arr. - 31, rue St-Louis-en-l'Ile - 01 43 54 31 61
Berthillon is the most famous name in French ice cream. The firm's many faithful fans think nothing of waiting in line for *hours* just to treat their taste buds to a cone or dish of chocolate-nougat or glazed-chestnut ice cream. Berthillon's sorbets are our particular weakness: pink grapefruit, fig, wild strawberry... The entire repertoire comes to some 70 flavors, including many seasonal offerings.

Glacier Vilfeu

1st arr. - 3, rue de la Cossonnerie - 01 40 26 36 40
Vilfeu's imaginative productions include surprising and sophisticated novelty flavors—tea, lavender, and foie-gras sorbets—an ice based on Beaujolais nouveau, and ice creams flavored with licorice, cinnamon, and ginger. We also strongly encourage you to sample the sumptuous frozen desserts, notably the molded cream-cheese sorbet served with a vivid raspberry coulis.

Raimo

12th arr. - 59-61, bd de Reuilly - 01 43 43 70 17
Sorbets and ice creams produced according to time-honored methods, with strictly fresh ingredients. Raimo's strong suit is concocting seductive flavor combinations; some of the most successful are piña colada, ginger-honey, and cinnamon-mandarin/orange.

La Tropicale

13th arr. - 180, bd Vincent Auriol
01 42 16 87 27
While you can get a single flavor here, the specialty of the house is flavor combinations, whether they are classic mixes like dates, walnuts, and figs or more unusual ones like litchi, soursop, and cinnamon.

• *MEAT, GAME & FOWL*

Au Bell Viandier

6th arr. - Marché Saint-Germain, 4, rue Lobineau
01 40 46 82 82, fax 01 46 34 06 45
Serge Caillaud is a king among Parisian butchers. Rigorous selection and skillful preparation are the hallmarks of these meats, which hail from the best French producers. There's milk-fed veal and fine beef from the Limousin region, farm-bred pork, poultry from Bresse and Challans (including superb capons for the year-end holidays), and premium game in season. Caillaud's specialties include a truffled roast of beef, veal stuffed with apricots or studded with prunes and pistachios, any of which would garner applause as the centerpiece of a dinner party.

Boucherie Nivernaise

8th arr. - 99, rue du Fbg-Saint-Honoré
01 43 59 11 02, fax 01 42 25 92 32
This wholesale-retail butcher shop is well known in the business. Bernard Bissonet offers his customers meats chosen with scientific care. The excellent price-quality ratio adds to the reputation of this shop.

Le Coq Saint-Honoré

1st arr. - 3, rue Gomboust
01 42 61 52 04, fax 01 42 61 44 64
We might as well make it clear right away: For our money, Le Coq Saint-Honoré is one of Paris's top poulterers. It's no coincidence that among its customers are such culinary notables as Robuchon, Savoy, Senderens, and Dutournier. The refrigerated cases display choice Bresse chickens and guinea hens (fast becoming prohibitively expensive), as well as laudable Loué pullets, Challans ducks, and plump rabbits from the Gâtinais region south of Paris. In season, look for the fine selection of game, including authentic Scottish grouse—a rare and wonderful treat.

• *PASTRY & COOKIES*

Paul Bugat

4th arr. - 5, bd Beaumarchais
01 48 87 89 88, fax 01 48 87 73 70
Paul Bugat is a passionate esthete who orchestrates sweet pastry, chocolate, sugar, and cream into exquisite gâteaux. The specialties of the house are delicious, jewel-like petits-fours, along with the Clichy (chocolate buttercream and mocha cream on an almond-sponge base), and the Almaviva (chocolate-mousse cake). Tea room.

Noël Clément

17th arr. - 120, av. de Villiers - 01 47 63 40 90
Noël Clément is a young *pâtissier* with a bright future ahead. His pastries are nothing short of sublime: the millefeuille is a textbook example of what that often botched sweet should be; his mousses are light and full-flavored. Best of all, Clément keeps the sugar content down in all of his cakes. He bakes excellent bread as well. Prices are eminently reasonable.

Christian Constant

6th arr. - 37, rue d'Assas
01 45 48 45 51, fax 01 45 44 91 93
7th arr. - 26, rue du Bac - 01 47 03 30 00
After a stroll in the Luxembourg Gardens, why not indulge in a treat from Christian Constant's shop on Rue d'Assas? And one needn't feel too guilt-ridden, because these cakes are low in sugar, additive-free, all-natural, and incredibly light. Try a millefeuile, or one of Constant's deep, dark, and exotic chocolate cakes: the Feuille d'Automne, the Figaro, or the poetically named Fleur de Chine. Constant's sorbets and frozen desserts are well worth the money. Tea room.

Dalloyau

2nd arr. - 25, bd des Capucines - 01 47 03 47 00
6th arr. - 2, pl. Edmond-Rostand
01 43 29 31 10
7th arr. - 63, rue de Grenelle - 01 45 49 95 30
8th arr. - 99-101, rue du Fbg-Saint-Honoré
01 42 99 90 00, fax 01 45 63 82 92
15th arr. - 69, rue de la Convention
01 45 77 84 27
Deservedly famous, Dalloyau is a temple of *gourmandise* revered by every discerning sweet tooth in town. Among the most renowned specialties are the memorably good macaroons, the chocolate-and-mocha Opéra cake (created in 1955 and still a bestseller), and the Mogador (chocolate sponge cake and mousse napped with raspberry jam, 21 F). Christmas brings succulent glazed chestnuts and gluttonously rich Yule logs; Easter calls for chocolate hens and bunnies romping among praline eggs and bells in the adorable window displays.

Ladurée

8th arr. - 16, rue Royale - 01 42 60 21 79
8th arr. - 75, av. des Champs-Élysées
01 42 89 11 11
16th arr. - at Franck & Fils, 80, rue de Passy
01 44 14 38 80
Among the wonderful pastries sold here, don't miss the sublime macaroons, which are plump and tender on the inside and crispy on the outside. They come in an array of delicate colors and

flavors and are now made under the direction of Pierre Hermé, formerly of Fauchon.

Lenôtre

8th arr. - 15, bd de Courcelles - 01 45 63 87 63
15th arr. - 61, rue Lecourbe - 01 42 73 20 97
16th arr. - 44, rue d'Auteuil - 01 45 24 52 52
& 49, av. Victor-Hugo - 01 45 02 21 21
& 193, av. de Versailles - 01 45 25 55 88
17th arr. - 121, av. de Wagram - 01 47 63 70 30
92200 Neuilly - 3, rue des Huissiers
01 46 24 98 68
92100 Boulogne - 79 bis, route de la Reine
01 46 05 37 35
  Normandy native Gaston Lenôtre opened his first shop in Paris in 1957. His pastries and elaborate desserts are now internationally recognized as classics: the Schuss, the Plaisir, the Opéra... His most memorable creation may just be the Passion des Iles—passionfruit mousse on a coconut-meringue base sprinkled with shaved chocolate—a tropical fantasy!

Le Moule à Gâteaux

14th arr. - 17, rue Daguerre - 01 43 22 61 25
Also: 5th arr., 14th arr., 15th arr., 16th arr., 17th arr., 20th arr.
  This prospering chain specializes in traditional, homestyle cakes fashioned by young pastry cooks who care about their craft. They use time-tested recipes that we wish we still had the leisure (and know-how) to prepare in our own kitchens. We love the apricot feuilleté covered with a golden short crust; the Mamita, a poem in chocolate and crème fraîche; and the flambéed calvados apple tart. Reasonable prices.

Gérard Mulot

6th arr. - 76, rue de Seine - 01 43 26 85 77
  Mulot is an endlessly inventive personality, never happier than when he is working out a new idea to complete his line of delectable pastries. Recent creations include the Oasis (almond mousse with an apricot wafer) and the Ardèchois (chestnut custard on a whisky-flavored chocolate cookie filled with candied chestnuts and coated with caramel). In a more down-to-earth vein, Mulot also fashions wonderfully flaky, buttery croissants.

Stohrer

2nd arr. - 51, rue Montorgueil - 01 42 33 38 20
  The shop is decorated with rosy, corpulent allegories of Fame painted by Paul Baudry (he also decorated the Paris Opéra) in 1860; these charming murals are pleasant to contemplate while scarfing down a few of Stohrer's butter-rich pastries: the dark-chocolate Criollo, the refreshing Royal Menthe, the Black Forest cake, and flaky croissants all come highly recommended.

• SEAFOOD

Le Bar à Huîtres

3rd arr. - 33, bd Beaumarchais - 01 48 87 98 92
5th arr. - 33, rue St-Jacques
or 82 bis, bd St-Germain - 01 44 07 27 37
14th arr. - 112, bd Montparnasse - 01 43 20 71 01
  At the outdoor oyster bar, you can purchase dozens of succulent oysters, opened for you free of charge by the nimble-fingered écaillers and neatly arranged on disposable trays (no deposit, no return). Just remember to place your order in advance.

Poissonnerie du Dôme

14th arr. - 4, rue Delambre - 01 43 35 23 95
  The lucky residents of Montparnasse can satisfy their urge for seafood at this marvelous fish store, perhaps the best in Paris. Manager Jean-Pierre Lopez admits only "noble" fish (sole, turbot, lotte, sea bass, and the like) to his classy emporium. The merchandise, from French (particularly Breton) and foreign waters, is snapped up by such eminent restaurants as L'Ambroisie and Laurent. Need we mention that these rare and delicate denizens of the deep command regally high prices?

• WINE & SPIRITS

Keep in mind that you can purchase a good bottle of wine for your dinner at many of the city's wine bars.

Les Caves Taillevent

8th arr. - 199, rue du Faubourg-Saint-Honoré
01 45 61 14 09, fax 01 45 61 19 68
  Crack sommeliers—the Vrinat family and their team— select the wines presented by Taillevent. The choice is wide, and the prices are more reasonable than you might expect. Many of the producers represented use biodynamic growing techniques: look for Château Falfas '93 for 56 F, and Nicolas Joly's superb Coulée de Serrant '92 for 190 F.

Legrand Filles et Fils

2nd arr. - 1, rue de la Banque
01 42 60 07 12, fax 01 42 61 25 51
  Even if the wines were not half so interesting as they are, Legrand's wine shop would be worth a visit for its old-fashioned charm and warm atmosphere. Francine Legrand offers a fascinating selection of carefully chosen, inexpensive country wines from up-and-coming growers in the South and the Val de Loire, along with a far-ranging inventory of prestigious Alsaces, Burgundies, and Bordeaux (note the many wines from average vintage years, affordably priced). Also, a few uncommon bottlings: luscious Muscat de Beaumes-de-Venise, Vin de Paille du Jura, and some excellent vintage Ports. Legrand's impressive stock of eaux-de-vie is one of the finest in town.

Nicolas

8th arr. - 31, pl. de Madeleine
01 42 68 00 16, fax 01 47 42 70 26
250 stores in Paris.

Looking better than ever with a spruce gold-and-bordeaux décor, Nicolas's innumerable stores in the Paris area continue to present a wide, diverse, and appealing range of wines for every budget. The chain's monthly promotions are well worth following: featured are (for example) French wines from unfamiliar or underrated appellations—the Ardèche, Corbières, or Savoie—, imports (Spanish, Italian, and even Lebanese bottlings), and the occasional oenological curiosity, all offered at attractive prices. The multilevel flagship store on Place de la Madeleine has a huge inventory of more than 1,000 different wines, including rare, old Bordeaux. Nicolas is also an excellent source of fine distilled spirits (check out the selection of single-malt whiskies). The Avenue Wagram shop stays open until 10pm (tel. 01 42 27 22 07), the Ancienne-Comédie store until 9pm (tel. 01 43 26 61 22). Home delivery service available.

Au Verger de la Madeleine

8th arr. - 4, bd Malesherbes
01 42 65 51 99, fax 01 49 24 05 22

Jean-Pierre Legras's staggering collection encompasses such unique and extravagant bottles as an 1811 Cognac Grande Champagne, a Porto Barros dated 1833 (once the property of the French ambassador to Lisbon), a Trrantez Madeira from 1789, and an 1895 Château Lafite-Rothschild (of which only 10 exist on the current world market). Such treasures are not for everyday drinking, but they make impressive, indeed unforgettable, gifts. Legras also carries various beverage bottles dating from 1900 to the present; they make great birthday presents when you choose one from the year the person was born. All the first growths of Bordeaux (Cheval-Blanc, Pétrus...) are on hand as well, along with superb Burgundies from Montrachet and Meursault, and hard-to-find wines like Château-Grillet and Jasnières. For the faint of wallet, there are inexpensive offerings from the Côtes-d'Auvergne, Saint-Pourçain, and Saumur.

For an in-depth, insider's guide to the City of Light, its restaurants and hotels, shops, nightlife, monuments, and more, consult GaultMillau/Gayot's **Best of Paris.**

PARIS SUBURBS RESTAURANTS & HOTELS

ALFORTVILLE   94140
Paris 10 - Créteil 5 - Maisons-Alfort 1   Val-de-Marne

12/20 Chinagora Restaurant

1, pl. du Confluent-France-Chine
01 45 18 33 09, fax 01 43 53 08 00
Closed Mon. Open until 11pm. No pets. Terrace dining. Garage pkg.
A bit of Beijing in Paris: Chinagora's lengthy menu holds few surprises (except when it comes to dessert—lotus-cream buns, for example), but the dim-sum, beef with saté sauce, and hot-stone grills are decent enough. C 180. M 55-75 (weekdays lunch), 260 (for 2 pers), 320 (for 4 pers), 568 (for 6 pers).

ASNIÈRES   92600
Paris 9 - Argenteuil 6 - Saint-Denis 8   Hauts-de-Seine

Le Van Gogh

2, quai Aulagnier - 01 47 91 05 10, fax 01 47 93 00 93
Closed Sat lunch, Sun, Aug 9-25. Open until 10pm. Terrace dining. Air cond. No pets. Pkg.
The dining room resembles the interior of a luxury liner, with portholes and bay windows framing views of the Seine. The cuisine looks out to sea, with dishes like brill roasted with spices and meat jus, and there are some Southwestern options, too: tender Landes pigeon or civet de canard. C 310-530. M 220 (lunch).

AULNAY-SOUS-BOIS   93600
Paris 16 - Bobigny 8 - Saint-Denis 17   Seine-St-Denis

Auberge des Saints Pères

21, av. de Nonneville
01 48 68 11 06, fax 01 48 66 25 22
Closed Sat lunch, Sun dinner, Mon, 1 wk in Jan, Aug. Open until 9:30pm. Priv rm 12. No pets. Pkg.
Michel Liret turns premium ingredients into rich, classic dishes. Served in an elegant setting, they are accompanied by superb (and expensive) wines. Expect a smiling welcome from Emmanuelle Liret. C 350. M 200, 360, 120 (chilren).

Novotel

N 370, carrefour de l'Europe
01 48 66 22 97, fax 01 48 66 99 39
Open year-round. 139 rms 485-495. Bkfst 56. Rms for disabled. Restaurant. Rm ser. Air cond. Conf. Pool. Pkg.
Near the Villepinte exhibition grounds, this Novotel is set in a garden. The nicely equipped rooms are particularly suited to families.

BLANC-MESNIL (LE)   93150
Paris 18 - Le Bourget 3 - Aulnay-s.-Bois 3   Seine-St-Denis

Bleu Marine

219, av. Descartes - 01 48 65 52 18, fax 01 45 91 07 75
Open year-round. 130 rms 420-480. Bkfst 50. Rms for disabled. Restaurant. Rm ser. Air cond. Pkg.
Comfortable, modern rooms in a well-equipped establishment just five minutes' drive from Le Bourget and Charles-de-Gaulle airports.

Novotel Paris-Le Bourget

2, rue Jean-Perrin
01 48 67 48 88, fax 01 45 91 08 27
Open year-round. 143 rms 400-495. Bkfst 30-55. Rms for disabled. Restaurant. Rm ser. Air cond. Conf. Heated pool. Pkg.
This chain provides reliably comfortable accommodations close to the Air and Space museum.

BOULOGNE-BILLANCOURT   92100
Paris (Porte de St-Cloud) 10 - Versailles 11   Hauts-de-Seine

Acanthe

9, rond-point Rhin-et-Danube
01 46 99 10 40, fax 01 46 99 00 05
Open year-round. 1 ste 1,100. 45 rms 695. Bkfst 65. Rms for disabled. Rm ser. Air cond. Pkg.
Young sporting types will love the contemporary design of this hotel close to the French Open site of Roland-Garros. But no one likes the noise that filters through from the traffic circle.

*Looking for a town or restaurant? A winery? A gastronomic specialty or a celebrated chef? Consult the **alphabetical index** to locate them quickly and easily.*

Adagio

20-22, rue des Abondances
01 48 25 80 80, fax 01 48 25 33 13
Open year-round. 75 rms 695-795. Bkfst 65. Rms for disabled. Restaurant. Rm ser. Air cond. Pkg.
This modern, glass-and-concrete hotel has bright, spacious rooms fitted with every convenience and pleasantly furnished. The basement houses a vast complex of conference rooms. Summer terrace.

 L'Auberge

86, av. Jean-Baptiste-Clément
01 46 05 67 19, fax 01 46 05 23 16
Closed Sat lunch, Sun, Aug. Terrace dining. Air cond. Pkg.
The bright, tidy little dining room of this mellow provincial dwelling draws a public of well-heeled executive types. We share their enthusiasm for Jean-Pierre Roy's varied, deftly crafted menu. The cache of Jura wines in the cellar (which is otherwise strong on Bordeaux) is a relic of the days when the restaurant specialized in food from Franche-Comté. C 350. M 155 & 195 (wine incl).

 La Bretonnière

120, av. Jean-Baptiste-Clément
01 46 05 73 56, fax 01 46 05 73 56
Closed Sat, Sun. Open until 9:45pm.
A former head waiter, René Rossignol switched to cuisine and brought this restaurant back up to standard. In fact, Rossignol cooks as the nightingale sings: naturally and exquisitely. His single-price menu offers excellent value. Interesting cellar. **M** 165.

 Au Comte de Gascogne

89, av. Jean-Baptiste-Clément
01 46 03 47 27, fax 01 46 04 55 70
Closed Sat lunch, Sun, 2nd wk of Aug. Open until 10:30pm. Priv rm 15. Garden dining. Air cond. Valet pkg.
Three palm trees, a fountain, and lots of flowers make the dining room as warm as spring all year round. And Gascon flavors warm the palate, in the half-dozen variations on foie gras, including smoked duck foie gras with cucumber and bacon. But the chef has an oddly clumsy hand with spices. Splendid cellar (with a world-class collection of Armagnacs) but too few half-bottles. C 500. M 260 (weekday lunch).

12/20 La Tonnelle de Bacchus

120, av. Jean-Baptiste-Clément · 01 46 04 43 98
Closed Sat, Sun, Christmas-beg Jan. Open until 10pm. Priv rm 15. Terrace dining.
Here's an adorable vintage bistro with a shady summer terrace, where customers divide their interest among saucisson de Lyon, steamed salmon, and cinnamon-scented apple crumble, all washed down with delicious wines, some of which are served by the glass. C 250-350. **M** 90, 120, 150.

CHARENTON-LE-PONT — 94220
Paris 2 - Saint-Mandé 3 - Alfortville 2 — Val-de-Marne

12/20 Le Grand Bleu

21, av. du Maréchal-de-Lattre-de-Tassigny
01 49 77 65 65
Closed Sun dinner, Mon, Jul 28-Sep 1. Open until 10:30pm.
Here's a pleasant little seafood spot, just steps away from the Vincennes zoo. The 115 F menu brings six oysters, grilled salt-cured salmon with lentils and bacon, and tarte Tatin flambée. Good-humored atmosphere. C 250. M 115 (weekday lunch), 170.

CHAVILLE — 92370
Paris 13 - Versailles 4 - Boulogne 2 — Hauts-de-Seine

 La Tonnelle

29, rue Lamennais
01 47 50 42 77, fax 01 47 50 99 19
Open daily until 10pm. Air cond. Priv rm 60. Terrace dining.
A fine spot for a Sunday lunch: a quiet terrace, a smart décor, well-dressed patrons, and a genial host create a mood conducive to enjoyment. Good food (sometimes a mite too salty) and excellent desserts; extensive cellar. C 200-250. M 155 (weekday lunch), 195, 255, 90 (children).

CHENNEVIÈRES-SUR-MARNE — 94430
Paris 17 - Créteil 5 - Lagny 22 — Val-de-Marne

L'Écu de France

31, rue de Champigny · 01 45 76 00 03
Closed Sun dinner, Mon, 1st wk of Sep. Open until 9:30pm. Priv rm 60. Terrace dining. Garage pkg.
From the pink dining room you have a grand view of the River Marne, which you can savor along with Arnaud Bourguignon's classic and Provençal dishes. For dessert, don't miss the hot-chocolate and pistachio gâteau. The list of fine wines and vintage brandies will encourage you to indulge. C 250.

CHEVILLY-LARUE — 94550
Paris 12 - Créteil 10 - Antony 5 — Val-de-Marne

Chez Fernand ✪

248, av. de Stalingrad · 01 46 86 11 77
Closed Sat, Sun, Aug. Open until 10pm. Pkg.
Fernand Asseline, in his neo-Norman inn by the side of the N7 highway, serves deliciously rich regional meals conclude with prize-winning Camemberts and house-made bread. Good cellar. C 250.

CLAMART   92140
Paris 10 - Versailles 13 - Boulogne-B. 6   Hauts-de-Seine

12/20 La Cosse des Petits Pois

158, av. Victor-Hugo
01 46 38 97 60, fax 01 46 38 08 75
Closed Sat lunch, Sun, Aug 9-19. Open until 10pm. Priv rm 20.
A soothing, provincial mood prevails in this traditional restaurant. The owner cooks and serves his classic dishes with a generous hand. Decent cellar with plenty of Bordeaux. Charming welcome. **M** 145 (wine incl), 195, 260.

CLICHY   92110
Paris 7 - Saint-Germain-en-Laye 17   Hauts-de-Seine

La Romantica

73, bd Jean-Jaurès
01 47 37 29 71, fax 01 47 37 76 32
Closed Sat lunch, Sun. Open until 10:30pm. Terrace dining. Priv rm 25. Valet pkg.
Claudio Puglia is a self-taught cook, but his lack of diplomas is more than compensated by his passion for *la bella cucina.* You'll be dazzled by saffron-tinged spinach risotto, carpaccio like none you've ever tasted (especially those pale French copies), or lotte with raisins, pine nuts, and raspberries. Don't miss the fettuccine tossed with sage and prosciutto, then presented in a hollowed-out Parmesan cheese! In summer, these *delizie* are served on a romantic garden patio. **C** 350. **M** 195, 280 & 350 (dinner).

COURBEVOIE   92400
Paris 11 - Nanterre 6 - Argenteuil 7   Hauts-de-Seine

La Safranée sur Mer

12, pl. des Reflets, La Défense 2
01 47 78 75 50, fax 01 47 76 46 20
Closed Sat, Sun, Aug. Open until 10:30pm. Terrace dining. Air cond. Valet pkg.
With its wood-paneled décor and swift service, this seafood restaurant is a favorite venue for business people with clients to impress. We'd be more impressed with the food if the flavors were more distinctly defined. Good saffron crème brûlée; pleasant summer terrace. **C** 400-450. **M** 200 (dinner, wine incl), 245.

12/20 La Valérianne

32, rue Franklin - 01 47 89 16 80
Closed Sun dinner, Aug 1-15. Open until 10pm.
The lunchtime crowd comes here for fresh, unpretentious food prepared with flair. The single-price menu is most worthwhile. Appealing cellar. **C** 200. **M** 100.

DISNEYLAND PARIS 77   → **Ile-de-France**

ISSY-LES-MOULINEAUX   92130
Paris (Pte de Versailles) 1 - Boulogne-B. 1   Hauts-de-Seine

12/20 Coquibus

16, av. de la République
01 46 38 75 80, fax 01 41 08 95 80
Closed Sat lunch, Sun, 3 wks in Aug. Open until 10:30pm. Priv rm 30. Terrace dining. Garage pkg.
The sign and the winsome dining room evoke Montmartre, oddly enough, but the hearty, homestyle cooking shows a Provençal or Southwestern slant. Small but select cellar. **C** 200. **M** 125, 160.

10/20 Issy Guinguette

113 bis, av. de Verdun
01 46 62 04 27, fax 01 46 38 89 57
Closed Sat lunch, dinner Sun & Mon. Open until 10pm. Terrace dining. Pkg.
A delightful riverside *guinguette* run by wine merchant Yves Legrand. The wines, indeed, are jim-dandy...but what a pity the food lacks flair! **C** 180-200.

Manufacture

20, esplanade de la Manufacture
01 40 93 08 98, fax 01 40 93 57 22
Closed Sat lunch, Sun, 2 wks in Aug. Open until 10:30pm. Terrace dining. Air cond.
Jean-Pierre Vigato, who runs the three-toque Apicius in Paris, has put a new chef in charge of this spacious restaurant converted from a tobacco factory. The single-price menu proposes (for example) headcheese vigorously scented with sage and served with a zesty herb salad, spiced whiting or garlicky bourride (fish stew) followed by goat cheeses and lush desserts—it's all lively, colorful, and reasonably priced. **M** 155-180.

LEVALLOIS-PERRET   92300
Paris (Porte de Champerret) 8 - Neuilly 4   Hauts-de-Seine

Le Petit Poste

39, rue Rivay - 01 47 37 34 46
Closed Sat, Sun, 1 wk at Christmas. Open until 10:30pm. Air cond.
Fifteen tables crowded around the bar—this is the type of bistro Brassens used to write about in his songs. Now it is a favorite with the good people of Levallois, who come to enjoy the cooking of Michel Wante. Excellent single-price menu; alert service. **C** 230. **M** 170.

La Rôtisserie

24, rue Anatole-France
01 47 48 13 82, fax 01 47 48 07 87
Closed Sat lunch, Sun. Open until 10pm. Air cond. Priv rm 100. Valet pkg.
A former hangar converted into a loft-brasserie with Art Deco fittings is the scene for Daniel Ballester's remarkably generous cooking. A 155 F single-price menu offers interesting appetizers followed by spit-roasted meats and

---

Why fizz when
you can sparkle?

Pure exhilaration

poultry, and tasty desserts. The well-chosen wines are a hair too expensive. **M 155.**

MEUDON   **92190**
Paris 12 - Versailles 10 - Boulogne-B. 3   Hauts-de-Seine

 ## Relais des Gardes

42, av. du Général-Gallieni
01 45 34 11 79, fax 01 45 34 44 32
Closed Sat lunch, Sun dinner. Open until 10pm. Terrace dining. Pkg.
A classic repertoire and style reign supreme, yet an occasional—and welcome—creative touch lends extra interest to lobster salad dressed with a subtle vinaigrette, turbot with lemongrass and excellent crisp potatoes, and a rich chocolate tart. Discreet, courteous service. C 300-420. **M 190.**

NANTERRE   **92000**
Paris 13 - Neuilly 5 - St-Germain-en-L. 8   Hauts-de-Seine

12/20 La Rôtisserie

180, av. Georges-Clemenceau
01 46 97 12 11, fax 01 46 97 12 09
Closed Sat lunch, Sun. Open until 10pm. Terrace dining. Valet pkg.
The incongruous Greek exterior leads into a bright, pleasant dining room; there, you can dig into a satisfying 155 F single-price menu of handily prepared bistro classics. **M 155, 80 (children).**

NEUILLY-SUR-SEINE   **92200**
Paris (Porte de Neuilly) 8 - Nanterre 8   Hauts-de-Seine

 ## Le Bistrot d'à Côté

4, rue Boutard
01 47 45 34 55, fax 01 47 45 15 08
Closed 2 wks in Aug. Open until 11pm. Terrace dining. Valet pkg.
See *Paris 17th arrondissement.* **M 109 (weekday lunch), 142, 189.**

12/20 Bistrot Saint-James

2, rue du Général-Henrion-Berthier - 01 46 24 21 06
Closed Sat, Sun. Open until 10pm. Terrace dining.
Genial François Pagnoux treats his patrons to old-time French favorites (blanquette, navarin d'agneau, boudin with apples and potatoes) and expertly grilled meats, washed down by fine Bordeaux wines he selects himself. C 200-250.

12/20 Brasserie des Arts

2, rue des Huissiers - 01 46 24 56 17
Closed Sun, May 1. Open until 10:30pm. No pets.
A simple and unpretentious address often filled with celebrities from this chic suburb. They come for foie gras maison, thyme-scented rack of lamb, shellfish platters, and nougat glacé. C 210-320. **M 109-135 (weekday dinner, Sat).**

12/20 Café de la Jatte

60, bd Vital-Bouhot
01 47 45 04 20, fax 01 47 45 19 32
Open daily until midnight. Air cond. Terrace dining. Valet pkg.
The décor revolves around the giant skeleton of a pterodactyl surrounded by a jungle of plants. The food is OK, but can we really call it cooking? The speedy young waiters zoom around serving salads, raw or steamed fish, and sorbets to tables of tanned people "in advertising." C 240-350. **M 100 (weekday lunch).**

 ### Coco d'Isles

31, rue Madeleine-Michelis
01 46 40 17 21, fax 01 46 40 71 21
Closed Sun, Mon, Aug. Open until 11:45pm. No pets. Pkg.
Wonderful West Indian dishes served in a tropical setting. Every one of the starters is a treat: spiced eggplant and codfish, skate salad, stuffed clams and crab... Follow them with poached or stewed fish or a fiery colombo of chicken or kid. C 250-300. **M 95 & 125 (lunch), 145, 210.**

 ### Les Feuilles Libres

34, rue Perronet - 01 46 24 41 41, fax 01 46 40 77 61
Closed Sat lunch, Aug 5-20. Open until 10:30pm. Terrace dining. Air cond.
Quality ingredients paired in clever ways: that's the kitchen's recipe for success. The local gentry gather here for the delicious likes of rabbit and prunes in aspic, baby mackerel in broth with fresh vegetables, and sea bream with saffron-spiced ratatouille. Guests are courteously welcomed and briskly served in this comfy, country-style dining room. C 250. **M 185.**

Foc Ly

"Chez Mommaton," 79, av. Charles-de-Gaulle
01 46 24 43 36, fax 01 46 24 48 46
Open daily until 11pm. Air cond. Pkg.
No dragons or pagodas in the conservative dining room, no outlandish listings on the menu. Foc Ly serves a classic repertoire of sautéed crab with crispy noodles, rice with shellfish, curried lamb, and ginger ice cream, all skillfully prepared. The salt-and-pepper scampi are exceptional. C 200-280. **M 99 & 109 (weekday lunch), 75 (children).**

12/20 Chez Gérard

10, rue Montrosier - 01 46 24 86 37
Closed Sat lunch, Sun. Open until 11pm. No pets.
Better than the usual bistro chow, Joël Leduc's versions of saffron-stained mussel soup, calf's liver with beans, and crème brûlée are several cuts above standard. C 180.

 ## La Guinguette de Neuilly

Ile de la Jatte, 12, bd Georges Seurat - 01 46 24 25 04
Open daily until 11pm. Garden dining. Air cond. Pkg.

An arty crowd frequents this old barge, fitted out with a handful of tables; Francois Beauvais's cooking suits the scene's holiday mood: try the pork and lentil salad, thyme-scented rack of lamb, and blancmange with fresh fruit. In fine weather, try to nab riverside seats. C 240-370.

10/20 Chez Livio

6, rue de Longchamp - 01 46 24 81 32
Closed Sat & Sun (in Aug), Dec 24, Jan 1. Open until 10:45pm. Priv rm 24. Garden dining. Air cond.
A real Italian trattoria in the heart of Neuilly, manned by the Innocenti clan. The simple bill of fare features ravioli al magro, gnocchi with basil, risotto with wild mushrooms, osso buco, and *tutti quanti*. The roof of the dining room rolls back so that you can dine under a canopy of blue sky or stars. Reservations (sometimes hard to come by) are a must. C 200-250. M 120 (weekdays, wine incl), 75 (children).

12/20 Au New Café Russe

16, rue du Commandant-Pilot - 01 46 24 72 36
Closed Sat lunch, Sun. Open until 11pm.
Something of a surprise in this neighborhood: a Russian restaurant serving good zakuskis, beef Stroganoff, veal cutlet Pojarski, and lush, caloric desserts. Two Fridays per month, Tziganes musicians. C 200-300. M 82 (lunch), 128, 158, 75 (children).

Hôtel du Parc

4, bd du Parc - 01 46 24 32 62, fax 01 46 40 77 31
Open year-round. 67 rms 310-520. Bkfst 38. Rms for disabled. Conf. Pkg.
The rooms in this plain and simple establishment on the Ile de la Jatte have all been carefully renovated. Be sure to choose quarters on the courtyard side (the quay side can be very noisy).

Paris Neuilly

1, av. de Madrid - 01 47 47 14 67, fax 01 47 47 97 42
Open year-round. 6 stes 985-1,090. 74 rms 735-935. Bkfst 70. Rms for disabled. Rm ser. Garage pkg.
The soundproofed rooms are comfortable enough; all are identically decorated in red and beige, and look out over a befrescoed atrium.

12/20 San Valero

209 ter, av. Charles-de-Gaulle
01 46 24 07 87, fax 01 47 47 83 17
Closed Sat lunch, Sun, Dec 24-Jan 1. Open until 10:30pm. No pets.
Come for a fiesta at Valero's Spanish restaurant: the menu offers paella of course, but also more authentic dishes such as quails en escabèche, scallops in a garlicky sauce with dried tuna, and baby lamb marinated in herbs, a specialty of the Rioja region. The Spanish offerings on the wine list are worthy of your attention. C 300. M 150 (weekdays), 190.

12/20 Sébillon

"Paris-Bar," 20, av. Ch.-de-Gaulle
01 46 24 71 31, fax 01 46 24 43 50
Open daily until midnight. Priv rm 30. Air cond.
The chefs come and go, but Sébillon's menu is immutable. Specialties of the house are delicious roast lamb and a giant éclair. Add to that a superb rib of beef and tarte Tatin "à l'ancienne," as well as sparkling fresh seafood. To drink, there's a selection of nice Loire wines at affordable prices. C 250-350. M 179 (wine & coffee incl).

La Truffe Noire

"Jenny Jacquet", 2, pl. Parmentier
01 46 24 94 14, fax 01 46 37 27 02
Closed Sat (exc dinner Jan-Mar), Sun, 3 wks in Aug. Open until 10pm. Air cond. No pets. Terrace dining.
A real stickler when it comes to choosing his ingredients, Jenny Jacquet also has the technique to turn out such first-rate traditional dishes as pike mousseline with beurre blanc, foie gras de canard en terrine, and a textbook pot-au-feu with delicious vegetables. In his provincial-style restaurant near Porte Maillot, he also proposes a different themed menu each month (truffles, mushrooms, shellfish...) which can be partnered by one of the fine growers' wines that Jacquet selects himself. Whatever you order, save room for dessert: the feuillantine au café or truffe au chocolat are the highlight of the meal! C 350. M 195.

ORLY 94310
Paris 16 - Créteil 8   Val-de-Marne

Maxim's

Aérogare d'Orly-Ouest
01 46 86 87 84, fax 01 46 87 05 39
Closed Sat, Sun, hols, Aug, 1 wk at Christmas-New Year's. Open until 10pm. Air cond. Priv rm 25. Pkg.
In the cockpit of Maxim's Orly is Gil Jouanin, whose inspired cooking flies high. To wit, his langoustines and scallops roasted with garlic salt, turbot crusted with black pepper and paprika, and iced pear amandine. The 30,000-bottle cellar holds wines in every price range, from modest to outrageous. C 330. M 195, 46 (children).

Paris-Orly Airport-Hilton

Aérogare Orly-Sud 267
01 45 12 45 12, fax 01 45 12 45 00
Open year-round. 12 stes 1,350-1,650. 345 rms 990-1,350. Bkfst 65-90. Rms for disabled. Restaurant. Rm ser. Air cond. Conf. Heated pool. Tennis. Garage pkg.
Functional, comfortable rooms near the airport (free shuttle) with round-the-clock room service. In addition to excellent facilities for conferences or seminars, there are ten tennis courts, a pool, a fitness center, and a piano bar open from Monday to Thursday.

PANTIN	93500
Paris 3 - Bobigny 4 - Saint-Denis 7	Seine-St-Denis

 Référence Hôtel

22, av. Jean-Lolive
01 48 91 66 00, fax 01 48 44 12 17
Open year-round. 3 stes 1,000-1,450. 120 rms 590-810. Bkfst 50-75. Half-board 890-1,070. Rms for disabled. Restaurant. Rm ser. Air cond. Conf. Pkg.
This hotel has two major assets: fine, recently renovated rooms; and an energetic staff. On the downside: looks (it resembles a blockhouse) and position (near the beltway).

PERREUX (LE)	94170
Paris 15 - Créteil 11 - Vincennes 6	Val-de-Marne

 Les Magnolias

48, av. de Bry - 01 48 72 47 43, fax 01 48 72 22 28
Closed Sat, Sun. Open until 10pm. Air cond.
A brilliant and inviting room is concealed behind Les Magnolias' graceless façade. Gérard Royant presents an appetizing roster that features cool crab aspic made cooler still by a ginger-spiced cucumber granita, veal sweetbreads and kidney in a Sherried sauce, and gingerbread cake with a bright apricot coulis. Expensive wine list. C 350. M 190, 290.

PETIT-CLAMART	92140
Paris 13 - Clamart 5 - Versailles 9	Hauts-de-Seine

12/20 Au Rendez-Vous de Chasse

1, av. du Général-Eisenhower
01 46 31 11 95, fax 01 40 94 11 40
Closed Sun dinner. Open until 11pm. Priv rm 90.
Settle down in the comfortable, spacious dining room and let the courteous staff serve you a pan-roast of wild mushrooms, cod brightened with a basil emulsion, and crêpes Suzette flamed with Grand Marnier. C 320. M 130 & 170 (weekdays), 170 & 230 (Sat, Sun lunch), 210 & 310 (wine incl), 95 (children).

PRÉ-SAINT-GERVAIS (LE)	93310
Paris (Pte de Pantin) 7 - Pantin 3	Seine-St-Denis

 Le Pouilly Reuilly

68, rue André-Joineau - 01 48 45 14 59
Closed Sat, Sun, hols, Aug-Sep 6. Open until 10pm. Priv rm 30. Pkg.
The place may not look like much, but inside you'll find a warm bistro atmosphere and Jean Thibault's generous cooking, inspired by the French countryside and the market's best seasonal produce. The cellar holds a rich (and pricey) cache of premium Burgundy and Bordeaux. C 280.

PUTEAUX	92800
Paris 10 - Saint-Germain-en-Laye 11	Hauts-de-Seine

 Les Communautés

Sofitel-CNIT, Grande Arche de La Défense, in the CNIT, 2, pl. de La Défense
01 46 92 10 10, fax 01 46 92 10 50
Closed Sat, Sun, 2 wks in Aug. Open until 10:30pm. Air cond. Air cond. Priv rm 50. Valet pkg.
Pierre Miécaze offers sunny and sometimes unpredictable exotic cuisine: langoustine ravioli in satay sauce, superb red mullet enhanced with exceptional olive oil, tiramisù. Beautiful cellar with wines from everywhere. Professional service. C 295-400. M 295 (lunch), 170 (dinner).

Sofitel-CNIT

(See restaurant above)
Closed 2 wks in Aug. 6 stes 1,700-3,000. 141 rms 1,500. Bkfst 95-120. Rms for disabled. Restaurant. Rm ser. Air cond. Conf. Valet pkg.
The hotel caters to business travelers, providing huge rooms (some boast a view of the Grande Arche), luxurious bathrooms, and 24-hour room service.

Dauphin

Esplanade de La Défense, 45, rue Jean-Jaurès
01 47 73 71 63, fax 01 46 98 08 82
Open year-round. 30 rms 380-470. Bkfst 40. Rm ser. Tennis. Valet pkg.
The Dauphin stands opposite the Princesse Isabelle, and is run by the same family. Generous buffet breakfasts are set up in the sitting room; rooms are comfortable and pretty, with cable television. Some rooms are reserved for non-smokers. Free shuttle to the RER station.

 Les Deux Arcs

Sofitel Paris-La Défense, 34, cours Michelet,
La Défense 10 - 01 47 76 44 43, fax 01 47 73 72 74
Closed Sat, Sun lunch. Open until 10:30pm. Terrace dining. Air cond. Priv rm 100. Valet pkg.
The elder of the two Sofitel hotels at La Défense is home to a quiet, comfortable restaurant, where wheeler-dealers can talk business in peace while enjoying deft, delicious cuisine. Langoustines are barely seared to juicy perfection; salmon comes lightly cooked (as requested) on one side only; and lamb arrives in a perfumed crust of spices. The fine wine list provides many half-bottles; and the service is just superb. A second toque. C 350. M 290, 345 (weekday lunch).

 Sofitel Paris-La Défense

(See restaurant above)
Open year-round. 1 ste 2,000. 149 rms 1,400. Rms for disabled. Restaurant. Rm ser. Air cond. Conf. Valet pkg.
A creditable chain hotel, warmly decorated with gilt mirrors and pale marble. Rooms are quiet, with lovely pink-marble bathrooms. Top-

notch service; yummy breakfasts. Good facilities for conferences.

 Princesse Isabelle

Esplanade de La Défense, 72, rue Jean-Jaurès
01 47 78 80 06, fax 01 47 75 25 20
Open year-round. 1 ste 950. 30 rms 570-660. Bkfst 50. Air cond. Valet pkg.
The rooms of this hotel near La Défense are prettily decorated, and have bathtubs with Jacuzzi or multijet showers. Some rooms open onto the flowered patio. Note that there's a convenient free chauffeur service to the RER and Pont de Neuilly Métro station.

 Syjac Hôtel

20, quai de Dion-Bouton
01 42 04 03 04, fax 01 45 06 78 69
Open year-round. 2 stes 980-1,500. 29 rms 570-750. Bkfst 60. Rm ser. Air cond. Conf. Pkg.
This modern hotel offers a pleasant alternative to concrete high-rises. Rooms are very pleasing, large and well appointed. There are some nice two-level suites (with fireplace) overlooking the Seine, and a pretty flowered patio.

ROISSY-EN-FRANCE	95700
Paris 26 - Meaux 36 - Senlis 28	Val-d'Oise

 Les Étoiles

Sheraton Paris Airport Hotel, Terminal 2
01 49 19 70 70, fax 01 49 19 71 71
Closed Sat, Sun, hols. Open until 10:30pm. Air cond. No pets. Pkg.
The warm wood-paneled, modern interior of this restaurant will help you forget the hustle and hassle of the airport. Chef Jean-Michel Kirche offers an à la carte menu that provides good value for your money. For each of the three courses, you have a choice of five attractive, well-executed dishes. Some of them were created by the renowned chef of La Chancelière in Montbazon (16/20), including the egg cup surprise, stuffed with morels and foie gras cream, and the sweetbread and lobster sausage with shellfish butter. They are matched in quality by chef Kirche's inventions, such as the escalope of foie gras served with roasted figs, and the brill with mashed potatoes. C 350. M 260.

 Maxim's

Aéroport Charles-de-Gaulle, Terminal 1, Level 11, beyond customs area
01 48 62 92 13, fax 01 48 62 45 96
Closed Sat, Sun, Aug. Open until 10pm. Priv rm 70. Air cond. No pets. Pkg.
Rich rewards await intrepid gastronomes who venture in level 11 of Roissy airport number one. They'll get to savor Alain Bariteau's wonderful stuffed saddle of rabbit, juicy veal tenderloin en pot-au-feu, and wildly rich vanilla and licorice ice creams. Oh yes, and the cellar is magnificent, too. C 200-250. M 120, 180.

 Les Saisons

Sheraton Paris Airport Hotel, Terminal 2
01 49 19 70 70 (R),
01 49 19 70 70 (H), fax 01 49 19 71 71
Open year-round until 11pm. Air cond. No pets. Pkg.
The same chef as Les Étoiles, (see above), serves a brasserie-style menu in a more casual ambience. Dishes include scampi risotto with endives, marinated tuna with salmon tartar, and red mullet and bacon en papillotte. Good wine list at very reasonable prices and excellent service provided by youthful waiters. C 220. M 160 (lunch), 170, 180, 200.

 Sheraton Paris Airport Hotel

(See restaurant above)
Open year-round. 12 stes 2,000-3,500. 240 rms 680-880. Bkfst 90-120. Rms for disabled. Restaurants. Rm ser. Air cond. Conf. Fitness center. Pkg.
This new 4-storey structure conveniently located at the center of the airport offers guests hassle-free "hub" access to their plane, TGV and RER connections. Bold geometric marble, metal and glass architecture and impressive views of the surrounding air and rail traffic are tempered by Andrée Putman's calm, comfortably elegant interiors. Streamlined order and true European flavor prevail in this high-quality establishment, designed with cutting-edge traveler comfort in mind.

 Sofitel

Aéroport Charles-de-Gaulle
01 49 19 29 29, fax 01 48 62 78 49
Open year-round. 8 stes 800-1,700. 344 rms 700-1,400. Bkfst 80. Rms for disabled. Restaurant. Rm ser. Air cond. Conf. Heated pool. Tennis. No pets. Garage pkg.
A comfortable airport hotel that provides round-the-clock room service and a free shuttle to the airport. Entertainment facilities include a disco and piano bar, and there's a coffee shop, too.

ROMAINVILLE	93230
Paris 10 - Livry-Gargan 9	Seine-St-Denis

Chez Henri

72, route de Noisy
01 48 45 26 65, fax 01 48 91 16 74
Closed Sat lunch, Sun, Mon dinner, hols, Aug. Open until 9:30pm. Priv rm 18. Air cond. Pkg.
Chef Henri Bourgin is back on track! We could barely restrain ourselves from begging for seconds (or thirds) of his lobster millefeuille with grenadine-glazed baby onions, his winy civet of oxtail and pig's foot, or lush licorice fondant served with rose-petal jam and a poppyseed brioche. Connoisseur's cellar; convivial atmosphere in a comfortable, flower-filled dining room. C 310-420. M 160.

RUEIL-MALMAISON   92500
Paris 15 - Versailles 11 - Nanterre 13   Hauts-de-Seine

 El Chiquito

126, av. Paul-Doumer
01 47 51 00 53, fax 01 47 49 19 61
Closed Sat, Sun, 2 wks in Aug. Terrace dining. Pkg.
  No, not another Tex-Mex—El Chiquito is a venerable institution where quality seafood is handled with care. Best bets are the grilled scampi, flash-cooked rock lobster and turbot, and hot oysters. The friandise de merlan (whiting) and apple chaud-froid impressed us less. Terrifying prices. C 290-500. M 210 (dinner).

RUNGIS   94150
Paris 13 - Créteil 12 - Évry 19   Val-de-Marne

 Holiday Inn Orly

4, av. Charles-Lindbergh
01 46 87 26 66, fax 01 45 60 91 25
Open year-round. 23 stes 1,025. 168 rms 825-925. Bkfst 70. Rms for disabled. Restaurant. Rm ser. Air cond. Conf. Pkg.
  Comfortable and well-kept rooms near Orly airport (free shuttle). From your window, you'll look down on the Rungis *halles* (the Paris wholesale food market). Shops.

 Pullman Paris-Orly

20, av. Charles-Lindbergh
01 46 87 36 36, fax 01 46 87 08 48
Open year-round. 2 stes 1,400. 188 rms 660-890. Bkfst 63. Rms for disabled. Restaurant. Rm ser. Air cond. Conf. Heated pool. Pkg.
  A reliable, comfortable chain hotel with excellent soundproofing, air conditioning, and such amenities as a non-stop shuttle to and from the airports, a panoramic bar, a restaurant, lounges, shops, and a swimming pool.

SAINT-CLOUD   92210
Paris 12 - Boulogne-B. 3 - Versailles 10   Hauts-de-Seine

10/20 **Quai Ouest**

1200, quai Marcel-Dassault
01 46 02 35 54, fax 01 46 02 33 02
Closed Dec 24 dinner, Jan 1. Open until midnight. Terrace dining. Air cond. Valet pkg.
  Lots of young, perma-tanned faces at this trendy spot, a New York–style eatery with a terrace overlooking the Seine. A squadron of smiling waiters recently delivered decent chicken with baby spinach, good thyme-roasted rack of lamb—and a disastrous tarte Tatin! C 250. M 130, 70 (children).

 Villa Henri IV

43, bd de la République
01 46 02 59 30, fax 01 49 11 11 02
Closed Jul 26-Aug 26. 36 rms 460-510. Bkfst 48. Restaurant. Rm ser. Pkg.
  This charming establishment perched high atop Saint-Cloud features eye-pleasing period furniture. However, the dated striped carpeting and "melancholy gray" marble bathrooms could definitely use an overhaul.

SAINT-DENIS   93200
Paris 10 - Argenteuil 10 - Chantilly 30   Seine-St-Denis

 La Saumonière

1, rue Lanne - 01 48 20 25 56
Closings not available. Open until 10pm. No pets.
  Traditional cooking for robust appetites: lobster bouillabaisse, parsleyed pork croquettes with morels, and old-fashioned crêpes Suzette are all worthy of your notice. It deserves a toque. C 310-510. M 140.

12/20 **La Table Gourmande**

32, rue de la Boulangerie - 01 48 20 25 89
Closed dinner Mon-Wed, Sun, 2nd wk of Feb, last 2 wks of Aug. Open until 9pm.
  You won't go wrong with the perfectly seasoned tuna tartare, savory beef piccata, and baked-to-order apple tart. Small, well-composed cellar, with an attractive choice of half-bottles. C 200-300. M 108.

SAINT-OUEN   93400
Paris 7 - Saint-Denis 4 - Bobigny 10   Seine-St-Denis

 **Le Coq
de la Maison Blanche**

37, bd Jean-Jaurès
01 40 11 01 23, fax 01 40 11 67 68
Closed Sun, Aug 15-18. Open until 10pm. Terrace dining. Air cond. Priv rm 120. Valet pkg.
  Alain François is a genial host, who cultivates a convivial atmosphere in his cheerful, bustling restaurant. Chef André Gamon turns out an immutable list of bistro and bourgeois dishes that satisfy the sauce-lover in us all. In season, savor his tasty asparagus hollandaise; any time of year is right for codfish and vegetables with zesty sauce aïoli. Plenty of fine wines to choose from in the wide-ranging cellar. C 300.

12/20 **Chez Serge**

7, bd Jean-Jaurès - 01 40 11 06 42
Closed Sun. Open until 10:30pm. Air cond. Pkg.
  You won't notice the dreary décor once your waiter plunks down a generous plateful of roast rack of lamb or a huge serving of yummy chocolate cake with custard sauce. Worthwhile wine list. C 150-210.

SURESNES   92150
Paris (Pte Maillot) 11 - Boulogne-B. 6   Hauts-de-Seine

 Les Jardins de Camille

70, av. Franklin-Roosevelt
01 45 06 22 66, fax 01 47 72 42 25
Closed Sun dinner. Open until 11pm. Terrace dining. Priv rm 70. Valet pkg.
  From the terrace, guests can take in a panoramic view of Paris, but the dining room is

inviting, too, with its bright and cheerful look. The single-price menu is rooted in Burgundy: try the snail rissoles with fresh pasta and mushrooms, jambon persillé (the aspic is made with sprightly Aligoté wine), braised lamb, and orange-spiked crêpes Suzette. Splendid cellar, accessibly priced. M 160, 80 (children).

VANVES   92170
Paris 8 - Nanterre 12   Hauts-de-Seine

 Le Pavillon de la Tourelle

10, rue Larmeroux
01 46 42 15 59, fax 01 46 42 06 27
Closed Sun dinner, Mon, Aug. Open until 10pm. Terrace dining. Pkg.
Akio Ikeno, a chef trained by Paul Bocuse, presents a repertoire of delicate dishes like scallops enhanced with truffles or a whiff of vanilla and sole à la japonaise. Try the satisfying 195 F menu: asparagus salad, suckling pig in a mustard sauce, cheeses or desserts. Elegant dining room, with a view of leafy grounds. C 400-560. M 150, 195, 250 (wine incl), 90 (children).

VARENNE-ST-HILAIRE (LA)   94210
Paris 16 - Lagny 22 - Saint-Maur 3   Val-de-Marne

 Brasserie du Regency

96, av. du Bac - 01 48 83 15 15, fax 01 48 89 99 74
Closed Dec 24-26. Open until 1:30am. Air cond. Terrace dining. Pkg.
Michel Croisille's menu is better than ever this year, with ultrafresh ingredients heightened by even more delicate sauces. Among the updated classics on offer, we like the warm oysters, seafood assortment, and luscious soufflé Grand Marnier. C 300. M 140, 40 (children).

 La Bretèche

171, quai de Bonneuil
01 48 83 38 73, fax 01 42 83 63 19
Closed Sun dinner, Mon, Feb school hols. Open until 10pm. Priv rm 16. Terrace dining. Air cond.
Choose a table on the terrace or in the bright, pink-hued dining room to savor Philippe Regnault's nicely wrought lobster croustillant with smoky bacon, lotte with a zingy jus d'épice, and raspberry tartlet in a spun-sugar cage. Extensive cellar; gracious welcome. C 260-330. M 160.

VILLENEUVE-LA-GARENNE   92390
Paris 11 - Saint-Denis 2 - Pontoise 22   Hauts-de-Seine

 Les Chantereines

Avenue du 8-Mai-1945
01 47 99 31 31, fax 01 41 21 31 17
Closed Sat, Sun dinner, Aug 4-24. Open until 10:15pm. Priv rm 30. Terrace dining. Air cond. Pkg.
You'll soon forget the restaurant's unlovely exterior once you're seated in the comfortable dining room, which looks out over the municipal park and pond. Vivid, modern, and precisely wrought, the cooking is often inspired: memorable anchoïade, toothsome tuna grilled with olive oil, and chocolate "childhood dream" for dessert. C 300-380. M 180, 90 (children).

VINCENNES   94300
Paris (Pte de Vincennes) 6 - Montreuil 2   Val-de-Marne

🛏 **Hôtel Saint-Louis**

2 bis, rue Robert-Giraudineau
01 43 74 16 78, fax 01 43 74 16 49
Open year-round. 1 ste 850. 25 rms 410-850. Bkfst 45. Rms for disabled. Conf.
Large rooms, with equally spacious bathrooms, are provided in this pleasant hotel just steps from the château de Vincennes.

Plan to travel?

Look for GaultMillau/Gayot's other Best of guides to Chicago, Florida, Germany, Hawaii, Hong Kong, Italy, London, Los Angeles, New England, New Orleans, New York, Paris, Paris & the Loire Valley, San Francisco, Thailand, Toronto, Washington, D.C., and more to come...

ILE-DE-FRANCE
RESTAURANTS & HOTELS

ANET   28260
Paris 71 - Dreux 16 - Évreux 37 - Chartres 51   Eure-et-Loir

 Dousseine

Route de Sorel - 02 37 41 49 93, fax 02 37 41 90 54
*Open year-round. 20 rms 250-280. Bkfst 35. Rms
for disabled. Conf. Pkg.*
This modern complex on a vast wooded estate
offers simple, well-kept guest quarters with nice
bathrooms. Friendly welcome and service.

ARPAJON   91290
Paris 33 - Étampes 19   Essonne

14   Le Saint-Clément

16, av. Hoche - 01 64 90 21 01, fax 01 60 83 32 67
*Closed dinner Sun & Mon, 3 wks in Aug. Open until
9:30pm. Air cond.*
It's too bad such a wonderful meal had to end
with such ordinary desserts. Guy Courtaux's
classic, interesting, inspired cuisine—with its excellent ingredients and delicate sauces—is the
stuff memories are made of. Precise, nicely
varied wine list with an impressive selection of
Armagnacs. The elegant pastel dining room features an indoor garden extension, and diners
benefit from a warm welcome and top-notch
service. C 300-500. M 220.

AUVERS-SUR-OISE   95430
Paris 42 - Pontoise 7 - Chantilly 29 - Taverny 6   Val d'Oise

12/20   Auberge Ravoux

"Maison de Van Gogh," pl. de la Mairie
01 30 36 60 60, fax 01 30 36 60 61
*Closed dinner Sun, Mon-Wed Jan-Mar 21. Open
until 11pm. Terrace dining. Pkg.*
This historic inn full of turn-of-the-century
charm is where Vincent Van Gogh spent his final
days. Visitors from around the world gather here
to sample tasty home-cooked fare and decent
wines, all affordably priced. C 190. M 140, 175.

12/20   Hostellerie du Nord

6, rue du Général-de-Gaulle
01 30 36 70 74, fax 01 30 36 72 75
*Closed Sun dinner, Mon, Aug 16-Sep 3. Open until
10pm. Terrace dining. Pkg.*
The chef's classic cuisine shows a penchant for
the finest ingredients and careful cooking, but
he'd do well to give his flavors better definition
and add a bit of lemon to his hollandaise sauce.

High-precision wine list, though short on half-
bottle offerings. While the welcome is warm, the
service in the country-style dining room overlooking a mini-garden could be a tad snappier.
C 300-400. M 120 (exc Sun), 190 (Sun).

BARBIZON   77630
Paris 56 - Melun 11 - Fontainebleau 10   Seine-et-Marne

12/20   Auberge Les Alouettes

4, rue Antoine Barye
01 60 66 41 98, fax 01 60 66 20 69
*Closed Sun dinner. Open until 9:30pm. Terrace
dining. HOTEL: 22 rms 180-380. Bkfst 35. Half-
board 345-545. Rm ser. Conf. Tennis. Pkg.*
It's a toss-up as to whether to sit outdoors and
enjoy the surrounding flora and fauna, or in-
doors in the cozy dining room done up with
attractive coffered ceilings. But wherever you
settle, you're sure to enjoy the resolutely traditional fare on hand here, prepared with panache
and served up in generous portions. Smallish,
high-priced cellar. C 300. M 160, 190, 70
(children).

14   Le Bas Bréau

22, rue Grande - 01 60 66 40 05, fax 01 60 69 22 89
*Open daily until 9:30pm. Garden dining. Heated
pool. Tennis. Valet pkg.*
The site is still as enchanting as ever, and the
service commendable indeed. We liked Alain
Tavernier' cuisine we sampled on our last visit:
a delicious béarnaise sauce masked the taste of
the braised John Dory, and rosemary committed
the same offense with the Lozère lamb. And the
craquant au chocolat definitely lacked finesse.
The cheese tray was splendid (don't miss the
Fontainebleau!) and the suprême of bass was as
suprême as can be! Overpriced cellar. C 520-750.
M 350 (weekday lunch, wine incl), 395.

 Le Bas Bréau

(See restaurant above)
*Open year-round. 8 stes 1,700-3,000. 12 rms 900-
1,500. Bkfst 95. Rms for disabled. Half-board 1,200.
Rm ser. Air cond. Conf. Heated pool. Tennis. Valet
pkg.*
The rooms here are beautifully decorated, but
tend to heat up when summer rolls around. The
setting is splendiferous, the service charming,
and the breakfasts sublime: wonderful coffee,
fresh pastries, and homemade jams. Relais et
Châteaux.

Hostellerie Les Pléiades

21, rue Grande - 01 60 66 40 25, fax 01 60 66 41 68
Open daily until 9:30pm. Garden dining. Pkg.
The premises once belonged to the painter Daubigny, and the spacious, nicely decorated dining room, with its cozy hearth and two charming garden extensions, provides a wonderfully relaxing mealtime setting. Owners Yolande and Roger Karampournis' personal touch sets the tone, and chef Jean-Marc Héry's resolutely classical cuisine proves fresh, light, and eminently flavorful. Spot-on cellar. C 300-350. M 145-280, 85 (children).

 ## Hostellerie Les Pléiades ♣♥

(See restaurant above)
Open year-round. 1 ste 620. 24 rms 270-550. Bkfst 45. Half-board 370-490. Rm ser. Conf. No pets. Pkg.
Rooms in the elegant manor house or its extension, La Villa, can be on the smallish side, but all very cozy and prettily decorated and feature nice bathrooms. Charming welcome.

BOUGIVAL	78380
Paris 18 - Versailles 7 - Saint-Germain-en-L. 7	Yvelines

 ## Le Camélia

7, quai Georges-Clemenceau
01 39 18 36 06, fax 01 39 18 00 25
Closed Sun dinner, Mon, 1 wk Feb school hols, 3 wks in Aug, 1 wk at Christmas. Open until 10:30pm. Priv rm 18. Air cond. Pkg.
Once a culinary mecca under chefs Jean Delaveyne and Roland Durand, Le Camélia is now a good-value venue where reasonably priced menus buy the likes of skate terrine à la provençale, caramelized spare ribs with celery-root purée, or more exotic offerings as paella with thai rice, and almond custard. The wine list needs filling out, however, and some of the desserts (that almond custard!) lack verve. C 260.

12/20 Le Cheval Noir

14, quai Georges-Clemenceau
01 39 69 00 96, fax 01 39 18 29 30
Open daily until 10pm. Priv rm 40. Terrace dining. Pkg.
Clever seafood-based cooking draws crowds at this cozy, rustic *auberge*. The single-price menus feature tasty tagliatelle and a fine lobster navarin, but the pastries are served in rather stingy portions (though the cherries in brandy are enjoyable). C 220-300. M 129 & 149 (wine incl), 195, 70 (children).

 ## Forest Hill

10-12, rue Yvan-Tourgueneff
01 39 18 17 16, fax 01 39 18 15 80
Open year-round. 1 ste 1,600-1,700. 171 rms 450-650. Bkfst 40. Restaurant. Half-board 570-770. Rm ser. Conf. Pool. Garage pkg.

A modern hotel complex in a leafy setting on the Seine: Forest Hill offers functional rooms with views of the pool or grounds.

CELLE-SAINT-CLOUD (LA)	78170
Paris 16 - Saint-Cloud 5 - Bougival 2	Yvelines

12/20 Au Petit Chez Soi

Pl. de l'Église - 01 39 69 69 51, fax 01 39 18 30 42
Closed Dec 24-Jan 2. Open until 10pm (11pm in summer). Terrace dining. Pkg.
A polished brasserie with a provincial air, set on a charming little square. Lots of regulars come in for the well-crafted, traditional cooking. Though the chef gives his menu an exotic touch, we find the flavors a shade too pale. Good cellar. M 163.

CERNAY-LA-VILLE	78720
Paris 48 - Rambouillet 11 - Dampierre 4	Yvelines

12/20 Abbaye des Vaux-de-Cernay

Route d'Auffargis - 01 34 85 23 00, fax 01 34 85 20 95
Open daily until 9:30pm. Heated pool. Tennis. No pets. Pkg.
This abbey dates back eight centuries, and is set on a vast estate with its own forests. We'd be hard pressed to find a more enchanting site, despite the debatable shade of blue used to paint the doors and window trim! The cuisine is not as delectable as the setting: scrumptious vinaigrette of asparagus with langoustines, foie gras croquette with gingerbread, rhubarb crumble with sweet orange sauce. Celestial cellar. C 300-390. M 160 (weekday lunch), 255, 300, 395 (wine incl), 395 (weekday dinner), 495 (weekday dinner, wine incl), 120 (children).

 ## Abbaye des Vaux-de-Cernay ♣♥

(See restaurant above)
Open year-round. 3 stes 1,500-3,800. 55 rms 390-1,080. Bkfst 80-150. Half-board 650-890. Conf. Heated pool. Tennis. Pkg.
This twelfth-century abbey is fairly brimming with mysterious, grandiose atmosphere. The Gothic lounge and music room are true splendors with their vaults and columns. Luxurious, spacious rooms, decorated with genuine period furniture.

CHANTILLY	60500
Paris 42 - Compiègne 45 - Pontoise 36 - Senlis 10	Oise

10/20 Capitainerie du Château

Château de Chantilly
03 44 57 15 89, fax 03 44 58 50 11
Lunch only. Closed Tue, Jan-mid Feb. Priv rm 25. No pets. Pkg.
A convenient spot for lunch after touring the château and Musée Condé. The buffet features

fresh and inviting appetizers and decent desserts, served in two very pretty dining rooms. Friendly staff. C 150-200. M 95, 125, 50 (children).

12/20 Le Relais Condé

42, av. du Mal-Joffre - 03 44 57 05 75
Closed Mon. Open until 10pm. Garden dining.
Pascal Maillet presents a traditional repertoire: escargots fricassée with wild mushrooms, loin of lamb with herbs. Charming welcome and service. C 300-330. M 162, 87 (children).

CHAPELLE-EN-SERVAL (LA)	60520
Paris 40 - Chantilly 10 - Beauvais 71	Oise

 ## Mont Royal

On D 118, route de Plailly, Le Château
03 44 54 50 50, fax 03 44 54 50 21
Open year-round. 4 stes 1,500-1,800. 96 rms 990-1,100. Bkfst 90-150. Restaurant. Half-board 1,270-1,380. Rm ser. Air cond. Conf. Heated pool. Tennis. Pkg.
Tucked away in the green Chantilly forest, this eighteenth-century château is just 15 km from Roissy airport. You'll live like a lord or lady of the manor here, amid luxurious amenities (pool, tennis court, fitness center).

CHARTRES	28000
Paris 87 - Orléans 75 - Dreux 35 - Évreux 77	Eure-et-Loir

 ## Le Buisson Ardent

10, rue au Lait - 02 37 34 04 66, fax 02 37 91 15 82
Closed Sun dinner. Open until 9:30pm.
To judge by this restaurant's location in the shadow of the cathedral, one is likely to expect yet another tourist eatery with stratospheric prices. Not at all. The menu features nicely crafted dishes made from fresh market produce. Courteous, lively service; worthwhile cellar. C 250-350. M 98 (lunch, exc Sun), 118 (weekdays, Sat lucnh), 168, 218, 68 (children).

 ## Le Grand Monarque

22, pl. des Épars - 02 37 21 00 72, fax 02 37 36 34 18
Open daily until 10pm. Priv rm 120. Terrace dining. Valet pkg.
On a recent visit, we found dependable and affordable offerings, with set-price menus worth their salt. And like crowns, a toque was restored. The moral of the story is that when we say "off with his head," the head gets a chance to grow back! Very good wine list, specially with Loire and Bordeaux wines. M 158, 215, 280, 80 (children).

 ## Novotel

Av. Marcel-Proust - 02 37 88 13 50, fax 02 37 30 29 56
Open year-round. 78 rms 390-470. Bkfst 52. Rms for disabled. Restaurant. Pool. Pkg.
This modern, functional hotel is located in a leafy setting and provides regularly refurbished rooms. Bar and terrace.

Hôtel de la Poste

3, rue du Général-Kœnig
02 37 21 04 27, fax 02 37 36 42 17
Open year-round. 57 rms 265-320. Bkfst 40. Restaurant. Half-board 265-305. Conf. Garage pkg.
Here's an efficiently modernized hotel close to the cathedral. The soundproofed rooms offer all the comforts one could require, and there is a bar as well as a restaurant on the premises.

 ## La Truie qui File

Pl. de la Poissonnerie
02 37 21 53 90, fax 02 37 36 62 65
Closed Sun dinner, Mon, Aug. Open until 9:30pm. Priv rm 22. Air cond. Terrace dining.
Gilles Chroukroun's bright blue-and-white dining room welcomes local gourmets and food-loving tourists with a menu full of bright, vivid dishes. Mackerel fondant, cod with roasted shallots, tarragon-scented chicken tartlet seasoned with fruity olive oil, and winy stewed ox jowls all combine elegant technique with robust flavors. Less costly fare is served in a newly added room downstairs, so that dining here needn't be a once-in-a-blue-moon treat. Take note of the 100 F set meal: what a bargain! C 300-500. M 180, 280, 360, 70 (children).

La Vieille Maison

5, rue au Lait - 02 37 34 10 67, fax 02 37 91 12 41
Closed Sun dinner, Mon, 1 wk in Jul & in Aug. Open until 9:30pm.
Chef Bruno Letartre, formerly of the Grand Monarque, officiates at this fourteenth-century house featuring rustico-bourgeois décor. Food lovers are sure to enjoy his classic cuisine revisited: duck pâté en croûte, tender farm-raised squab with wild mushrooms, delectable pear and chocolate tart. Somewhat costly cellar. C 380. M 160, 250, 350, 80 (chilren).

And also...

Our selection of places for inexpensive, quick, or late-night meals.
Café Serpente (02 37 21 68 81 - 2, cloître Notre-Dame. Open daily until midnight, 1:30am in summer): Located opposite the cathedral, this simpatico bistro draws quite a crowd any time of day or night, eager to tuck into its nicely done (though predictable) brasserie fare. Small, fairly priced cellar. Friendly, quick service–despite the throngs (150).
Les Épars (02 37 21 23 72 - 11, pl. des Épars. Closed Sun dinner, Mon, Aug. Open until 10pm.): Just opposite the Grand Monarque. Classic cooking, with simple, sincere set-price menus (77-158).

*This **symbol** stands for "Les Lauriers du Terroir", an award given to chefs who prepare traditional or regional recipes.*

CHÂTEAUFORT   78117
Paris 28 - Versailles 10 - Orsay 11   Yvelines

 La Belle Époque

10, pl. de la Mairie
01 39 56 21 66, fax 01 39 56 87 96
Closed Sun dinner, Mon, Aug 16-30. Open until 10pm. Terrace dining. Pkg.
    Alain Rayé made the transition from urban chef to country *cuisinier* with nary a hitch. His village inn overflows with turn-of-the-century charm, and his menu sparkles with full-flavored enticements. He won us over with skewers of langoustines and zingy pickled lemons, Gâtinais rabbit with caramelized eggplant and fabulous olive fritters, and crunchy nougatine au sésame. The cellar holds plenty of finds (like Marc Angeli's white Anjou). C 400. M 215, 360.

CHATOU   78400
Paris 13 - Saint-Germain-en-L. 8 - Le Vésinet 2   Yvelines

11/20   **La Maison Fournaise**

Ile des Impressionnistes
01 30 71 41 91, fax 01 39 52 84 82
Closed Sun dinner in winter. Open until 11pm. Terrace dining. Garage pkg.
    Renoir's famed *Déjeuner des canotiers* features the charming terrace of this establishment on the Seine as its backdrop, and while the fairly eclectic, uncomplicated cuisine proffered here could have a better handle on flavors, it is unfailingly well presented. Gracious welcome. C 180. M 150, 75 (children).

CHESNAY (LE)   78150
Paris 21 - Versailles 5 - Nanterre 14   Yvelines

 L'Étoile de Mer

Pl. du Nouveau-Marché, 17, rue des Deux-Frères
01 39 54 62 70
Closed Sat lunch, Sun dinner, Mon, Aug. Open until 9:30pm. Priv rm 28. Terrace dining. Pkg.
    L'Étoile de Mer's intimate dining room opens onto the town marketplace. The view features a crowded lobster tank, and beyond it, the seafood shop attached to the restaurant. Chef Antoine Vieira transforms the freshest fish and shellfish into appetizing assortments and cooked dishes. You're sure to like his crab soup, octopus à la portuguaise, and mussels marinière. Tiny cellar. C 140-200. M 85 & 110 (lunch).

COIGNIÈRES   78310
Paris 40 - Versailles 18 - Rambouillet 13   Yvelines

 Auberge d'Angèle

296, route Nationale 10
01 34 61 64 39, fax 01 34 61 94 30
Closed Sat lunch, Sun dinner, Mon. Open until 9:30pm. Pkg.
    You'd never expect to find such a charming, half-timbered inn as this one hidden between the highway and the shopping center jungle here. The warm interior, brightened by Delft tiles, overlooks a verdant garden. And the classically spirited cuisine on offer makes the most of excellent ingredients in a pertinent, exacting manner. Precise, well-chosen wine list, high on variety. C 270-390. M 147, 180, 60 (children).

COUILLY-PONT-AUX-DAMES   77860
Paris 45 - Coulommiers 19 - Lagny 12   Seine-et-Marne

14   **Auberge de la Brie**

14, av. Alphonse-Boulingre - 01 64 63 51 80
Closed dinner Sun, Mon, lunch Wed, 3 wks in Aug. Open until 9:15pm. Terrace dining. Air cond. Pkg.
    Not far from Disneyland Paris, this village has become a food-lovers' mecca since young Alain Pavard set up shop in this adorable inn. His strong suits include generous set-price menus and a seasonal menu (game, corn crêpes with pan-roasted foie gras, fricassée of sole with langoustines, French toast brioche with fruit) where his confirmed talents come into the spotlight. C 400. M 150 (lunch), 180, 230.

COULOMMIERS   77120
Paris 63 - Sens 77 - Meaux 28 - Melun 52   Seine-et-Marne

12/20   **Le Clos du Theil**

42, rue du Theil - 01 64 65 11 63, fax 01 64 03 54 66
Closed Mon dinner, Tue, 1 wk in Feb & Aug. Open until 9:30pm. Terrace dining. Air cond.
    What was once the village grocery store is now a bright, comfy restaurant where the kindly owner fills guests' plates to the brim with simple, fresh, flavorful fare and delicious offerings from the grill. Nice little wines are on hand to wash everything down, with some available by the glass or pitcher. C 180-280. M 75 (exc Sun), 150 (wine incl), 200, 60 (children).

CREIL   60100
Paris 61 - Chantilly 7   Oise

13   **La Ferme de Vaux**

Hameau de Vaux, 11 & 19, route de Vaux
03 44 24 76 76, fax 03 44 26 81 50
Closed Sun dinner. Open until 9:45pm. Terrace dining. Pkg.
    This former farmhouse with its inviting stone-walled dining room plays host to Denis Oudart's finesse-filled cuisine. His salad of pan-roasted red mullets brims with wonderful flavor, his veal kidneys are tender and savory (despite their bland jus), and the fresh fruit gratin served with a delicate Champagne sabayon is a scrumptious way to top off your meal. C 240-400. M 150, 200, 60 (children).

Looking for a restaurant? Refer to the Index.

La Ferme de Vaux

(See restaurant above)
Open year-round. 29 rms 295-345. Bkfst 42. Half-board 430. Rm ser. Conf. Pkg.
Comfortable, well-equipped rooms located in the former farm's outbuildings. Charming welcome.

DAMPIERRE-EN-YVELINES	78720
Paris 44 - Versailles 18 - Rambouillet 16	Yvelines

12/20 Auberge Saint-Pierre

1, rue de Chevreuse
01 30 52 53 53, fax 01 30 52 58 57
Closed Sun dinner, Mon. Open until 10:30pm. Terrace dining. Pkg.
Opposite the château, this rambling, half-timbered inn plays host to a dining room replete with prettily laid, flower-bedecked tables. Chefs Ludovic Toutain and Adriano Séquirra's cooking is fairly classic, as the 140 F set-price menu attests. There are no half-bottles on the somewhat imprecise wine list, but it does mention a variety of excellent aged spirits. Friendly service. C 140, 180.

DISNEYLAND PARIS	77206
Access via A4 - Paris 28 - Meaux 28	Seine-et-Marne

Central reservation telephone number:
01 60 30 60 30.

■ **THE HOTELS
& THEIR RESTAURANTS**

 California Grill

Disneyland Hotel - 01 60 45 65 76, fax 01 60 45 65 33
Open daily until 11pm. Priv rm 12. Air cond. No pets. Valet pkg.
The "gastronomic" restaurant of the Disneyland Hotel offers West Coast cuisine with some exotic touches based on quality ingredients. Elegant service, and nary a Disney character in sight! C 250. M 195 & 320 (dinner), 110 (children).

 Cheyenne Hotel

Desperado Road - 01 60 45 62 00, fax 01 60 45 62 33
Open year-round. 1,000 rms 450-750. Bkfst 45. Rms for disabled. Restaurant. No pets. Pkg.
Perhaps the most amusing of all the resort's hotels: fourteen separate structures recall the frontier towns of the Far West. It's not luxurious, but the rooms are tidy and spacious. Adults can enjoy tequila and country music in the saloon-restaurant, while kids have a ball on the playground.

 Davy Crockett Ranch

01 60 45 69 00, fax 01 60 45 69 33

Open year-round. 498 rms 400-815. Restaurant. Heated pool. Tennis. No pets. Pkg.
Bungalows equipped for four to six people dot a huge stretch of forest. Kids love the pony rides, and everyone loves the gorgeous pool and the relaxing, holiday atmosphere.

 Disneyland Hotel

01 60 45 65 00, fax 01 60 45 65 33
Open year-round. 18 stes 3,850-18,000. 478 rms 1,700-3,300. Rms for disabled. Restaurant. Rm ser. Air cond. Conf. Heated pool. No pets. Valet pkg.
This enormous candy-pink Victorian pastiche is the *nec plus ultra* of Disneyland Paris hotels. Sumptuous suites, first-class service; but the "pseudo" setting and formal atmosphere are surely not everyone's cup of tea. The rates are simply staggering. Restaurants: California Grill (above) and Restaurant Inventions (below).

10/20 Hunter's Grill

Sequoia Lodge, near Lake Buena Vista
01 60 45 53 73 (R), fax 01 60 45 51 33
Dinner only. Open daily until 10pm. Air cond. Pkg.
Delicious charcoal-grilled meats, served up swiftly in a jolly ambience. M 145.

 Newport Bay Club

01 60 45 55 00, fax 01 60 45 55 33
Open year-round. 15 stes 1,900-2,200. 1,082 rms 675-950. Rms for disabled. Restaurant. Air cond. Conf. Heated pool. No pets. Pkg.
Were it not so enormous, the Newport Bay Club would be an almost-convincing facsimile of a summer resort in New England. The rooms are decorated with pretty white wicker furniture. Good value for the money.

 New York Hotel

01 60 45 73 00, fax 01 60 45 73 33
Open year-round. 22 stes 3,000-11,000. 536 rms 1,200. Rms for disabled. Restaurants. Rm ser. Air cond. Conf. Heated pool. Tennis. No pets. Pkg.
Manhattan in the 1930s is the theme, complete with skyscrapers, Wall Street, and Rockefeller Center—there's even an ice-skating rink in winter. The Art Deco guest rooms feature mahogany furniture, king-size beds, and impeccably equipped bathrooms. Among the many amenities are a beauty salon, athletic club, conference center, and two restaurants (Parkside Diner, see above, and the Manhattan Club).

11/20 Parkside Diner

New York Hotel - 01 60 45 73 00, fax 01 60 45 73 33
Open daily until 11pm. Air cond. No pets. Garage pkg.
Good, simple American food. The 145 F single-price menu includes options like hamburgers, pasta, poached salmon, grilled steaks, and caloric desserts (cheesecake, banana cream pie). C 150-200. M 95, 145.

Restaurant Inventions

Disneyland Hotel - 01 60 45 65 83, fax 01 60 45 65 33
*Open daily until 11pm. Priv rm 25. Air cond. No
pets. Pool. Valet pkg.*
The lunch buffet is one of the finest and freshest
we've seen. Here's a tip: come to Inventions for
an early midday meal that takes less than an
hour. Then while other folks stand in line at
restaurants and cafeterias inside the park, you
can enjoy the rides! M 195 (lunch), 250 (dinner).

 ## Santa Fe Hotel

Near the Pueblos Indian Village
01 60 45 78 00, fax 01 60 45 78 33
*Open year-round. 1,000 rms 300-615. Rms for dis-
abled. Restaurant. Half-board 455-770. Air cond.
Conf. No pets. Garage pkg.*
Forty-two "pueblos" make up an ersatz Indian
village, dotted with giant cacti. Given the size of
the place, the Santa Fe is inevitably a favorite
with group tours. Game rooms for the children.

 ## Sequoia Lodge

Lake Buena Vista - 01 60 45 51 00, fax 01 60 45 51 33
*Open year-round. 10 stes 1,800. 1,001 rms 795. Rms
for disabled. Restaurant. Air cond. Pool. No pets.
Pkg.*
Bare stone and rough-hewn wood evoke a
Rocky Mountain lodge. The sequoias have yet to
reach their majestic maturity, but guests will find
plenty of entertainment at the hotel's restaurants, shops, piano bar, and exercise room.

11/20 Yacht Club

Newport Bay Club
01 60 45 55 00, fax 01 60 45 55 33
*Closings vary. Open daily until 10pm. Air cond.
Pool. No pets. Pkg.*
New England clam chowder and grilled Maine
lobster are featured in this huge blue dining
room, to which a pleasant terrace was recently
added. C 180. M 150, 195 (dinner), 55 (children).

■ THE PARK

10/20 Auberge de Cendrillon

Fantasyland
01 64 74 24 02, fax 01 64 74 31 93
*Open daily until 4:40pm (10pm in summer). Ter-
race dining. Air cond. No pets. Pkg.*
Cinderella presides over this fairytale inn,
decorated with portraits of handsome princes,
lovely princesses, splendid carriages, and the
rest. Offerings include decent foie gras and good
beef, but the children's menu lacks appeal and
service is interminable. C 213. M 99.

10/20 Blue Lagoon

Adventureland
01 64 74 20 47, fax 01 64 74 38 13
*Closed Wed & Tue off-seas. Open until 10pm. Air
cond. No pets. Pkg.*
Palm trees and a tropical lagoon are the setting
for agreeably spicy dishes served by young
people dressed up in pirate or West Indian cos-

tumes. Nearby are the boats that ferry passengers into the *Pirates of the Caribbean,* one of the
park's most popular attractions. M 99-260.

10/20 The Lucky Nugget Saloon

Frontierland - 01 64 74 24 57
Closings vary with the season.
French cancan dancers prance onto the stage
several times a day at the Lucky Nugget. Too bad
that the chili and chicken wings are so dull! But
then, food is not really the attraction here. C 100.
M 39 & 79 (lunch), 49 & 129 (dinner).

10/20 Plaza Gardens

Main Street
01 64 74 22 76, fax 01 64 74 27 23
*Open daily until 10:30pm. Air cond. Terrace
dining. No pets. Pkg.*
For a quick, hot meal (grilled salmon, chicken)
between trips to Space Mountain and the Temple
of Doom. And the best cup of coffee in the park.
C 140. M 99, 110, 55 (children).

10/20 Silver Spur Steakhouse

Frontierland
01 64 74 24 56, fax 01 64 74 38 13
*Open until 4:30pm (until 10:30pm in summer).
Air cond. No pets. Pkg.*
Hearty appetites meet their match here, with
huge portions of barbecued chicken wings and
prime ribs of beef served in a reconstituted Wild
West saloon. C 195. M 99, 49 (children).

10/20 Walt's An American Restaurant

Main Street
01 64 74 24 08, fax 01 64 74 38 13
*Closed Wed, Thu. Open until 10:30pm. Terrace
dining. Air cond. No pets. Pkg.*
A stairway decorated with photographs of
Walt Disney leads to a series of charming little
dining rooms. The best seats are on the upper
floor, with a view of the parade route. Cheerful
staff. C 140. M 99, 45 (children).

■ FESTIVAL DISNEY

11/20 Buffalo Bill's Wild West Show

01 60 45 71 00, fax 01 60 45 71 51
*Open daily until 9:30pm. Air cond. No pets. Garage
pkg.*
As cowboys and Indians perform daredevil
stunts, diners chow down on chili, spareribs, and
apple crumble in what must be the biggest restaurant in France. M 325 (dinner), 200 (children,
dinner).

> Note that (most) **telephone numbers** in
> France have ten digits, beginning with a
> zero. The initial zero must be omitted if you are
> calling France from abroad. Within France,
> dial the entire ten digits.

12/20 Key West Seafood

01 60 45 70 60, fax 01 60 45 71 33
Open daily until 11pm. Terrace dining. No pets. Pkg.
Overlooking the (artificial) lake is a huge space decked out to resemble an unpretentious Florida fish house. Like most of the other Festival restaurants, this one is managed by the Flo group. The menu features bistro fare, with the accent on seafood. C 150. M 140 & 175 (dinner, wine incl), 49 (children).

11/20 Los Angeles Bar

01 60 45 71 14, fax 01 60 45 70 55
Open daily until midnight. Terrace dining. Air cond. No pets. Pkg.
Also lakeside is this bright, airy, and modern dining room where you can enjoy good pastas, pizzas, and tiramisù. Warm, friendly "American-style" service. C 160. M 48 (children).

12/20 Steakhouse

01 60 45 70 45, fax 01 60 45 70 55
Open daily until midnight. Air cond. Terrace dining. No pets.
Carpaccio, T-bone steaks, and other beef dishes are the specialty at this Chicago-style steakhouse. C 200. M 198 & 260 (dinner, wine incl), 69 (children).

DREUX   28100
Paris 84 - Chartres 35 - Verneuil 34   Eure-et-Loir

Le Beffroi

12, pl. Métézeau - 02 37 50 02 03, fax 02 37 42 07 69
Open year-round. 16 rms 290-320. Bkfst 27-43. No pets.
Tastefully decorated rooms overlooking the sixteenth-century belfry and the Saint-Pierre church, or the neighboring river.

ECRENNES (LES)   77820
Paris 69 - Melun 17 - Montereau 17   Seine-et-Marne

Auberge Briarde

"Jean et Monique Guichard," on A 5, exit Châtillon
01 60 69 47 32, fax 01 60 66 60 11
Closed dinner Sun & Wed, Jan 1-15, Aug. Open until 9:30pm. Priv rm 16. Terrace dining.
In autumn gourmets come from miles around for Jean Guichard's special game menus, full of rousing, earthy flavors. But at any time of year it's a treat to settle down by the fireplace in this comfortably rustic dining room and savor Guichard's well-wrought classic cuisine. Remarkable desserts; admirable cellar. Monique Guichard greets guests warmly, but the staff is still wet behind the ears! C 350. M 135 (weekday lunch), 195, 440.

ENGHIEN-LES-BAINS   95880
Paris 18 - Argenteuil 16 - Chantilly 32   Val-d'Oise

Le Grand Hôtel

85, rue du Général-de-Gaulle
01 39 34 10 00, fax 01 39 34 10 01
Open year-round. 3 stes 920. 44 rms 650-720. Bkfst 80. Restaurant. Half-board 450-950. Conf.
This lakeside luxury hotel boasts a handsome, wood-paneled lobby (and a single glass elevator). Accommodations are quiet and roomy, but the decoration lacks personality.

ÉTAMPES   91150
Paris 49 - Orléans 66 - Melun 47 - Versailles 54   Essonne

12/20 Auberge de Courpain

At Court-Pain
01 64 95 67 04, fax 01 60 80 99 02
Closed Sun dinner & Mon end Nov-beg Apr. Open until 9pm. Priv rm 120. Terrace dining. Pkg.
This former coaching inn is just right for business lunches or dinners with its garden abloom with flowers and finely honed cuisine, which makes the best of top-of-the-mark ingredients (lobster, monkfish with morels, etc.). The wine list alone is worth the trip. C 350-450. M 180, 65 (children).

Auberge de Courpain

(See restaurant above)
Open year-round. 3 stes 450-700. 14 rms 300-350. Bkfst 40-70. Rms for disabled. Restaurant. Half-board 450. Rm ser. Conf. Pkg.
This *auberge*, a little jewel left over from the First Empire, couldn't be more charming what with its picturesque tower, pretty garden, and cobbled courtyard. The rooms are done up in rustic style, which makes the site seem all the more authentic. Unfortunately, the stone-cold welcome and noise from the neighboring road are less than entrancing.

EZY-SUR-EURE   27530
Paris 73 - Evreux 38 - Creux 19   Eure

12/20 Maître Corbeau

15, rue Maurice-Élet
02 37 64 73 29, fax 02 37 64 68 98
Closed Tue dinner, Wed, Jan. Open until 9:15pm. Terrace dining. Pkg.
This restaurant located a short distance from the château d'Anet charms guests with a pretty flower-filled garden and prettily laid tables. But the quality of dishes on Bernard Blandeau's classic menu can be inconsistent: a delicious panaché of terrines, but the ginger-vanilla sole and cranberry-studded breast of duck were both served with too-creamy sauces. Offerings among the three desserts on the sampler plate were disappointingly uneven. Friendly welcome; impressive wine cellar. C 250. M 98 (weekdays), 140, 150 (wine incl), 180, 220, 350 (exc Sun).

FERTÉ-SOUS-JOUARRE (LA)   77260
Paris 64 - Meaux 20 - Melun 63   Seine-et-Marne

 Auberge de Condé

1, av. de Montmirail
01 60 22 00 07, fax 01 60 22 30 60
Closed Mon dinner, Tue. Open until 9:30pm. Terrace dining. No pets. Air cond. Pkg.
Located smack in the center of town, this pretty, flower-bedecked house with its comfortable dining room usually serves traditional cuisine. But why, on a recent visit, was the foie gras too salty, the leeks overcooked, the desserts insipid? Precise cellar with an impressive offering of Champagnes, but a bit more ordinary as other regions go. The welcome is most courteous. C 430-680. M 250 (weekdays, wine incl), 330, 450, 125 (children).

 Château des Bondons

47-49, rue des Bondons
01 60 22 00 98, fax 01 60 22 97 01
Open year-round. 2 stes 500-900. 7 rms 400-550. Bkfst 60. Restaurant. Rm ser. Conf. Pkg.
A mere twenty minutes from Disneyland Paris, this rambling mansion surrounded by vast green grounds offers guests the ultimate in peace and quiet—along with recently renovated rooms.

FLEURINES   60700
Paris 52 - Senlis 7 - Beauvais 57   Oise

12/20 Le Vieux Logis

105, rue de Paris - 03 44 54 10 13, fax 03 44 54 12 47
Closed Sat lunch, Sun dinner, Mon, Aug 1-15. Open until 9:30pm. Priv rm 40. Terrace dining. No pets. Pkg.
The Vieux Logis's pretty terrace complements a comfortable dining room brightened by floral bouquets. But Yann Nivet was having an off-night in the kitchen when last we dined here—bland marinated salmon, runny fruit gratin...we know he can do better! Nicely balanced cellar; service with a smile. C 330. M 140, 180, 250.

FONTAINEBLEAU   77300
Paris 65 - Melun 16 - Nemours 16   Seine-et-Marne

 Le Beauharnais

27, pl. Napoléon-Bonaparte
01 60 74 60 00, fax 01 60 74 60 01
Closed Dec 20-30. Open until 10pm. Priv rm 80. Garden dining. Air cond. Heated pool. Valet pkg.
Rémy Bridon presents inventive, expertly crafted cuisine in a refined yet relaxed setting. We were mighty impressed by his oyster and artichoke millefeuille, lobster and foie gras molded in an aspic spiked with orange juice, turbot "larded" with eggplant strips in a spinach-coriander coulis, and sweetbreads set off by a gingery apple compote. It all adds up to a couple of well-deserved toques. C 380. M 180, 320, 450, 80 (children).

 Hôtel de l'Aigle Noir

(See restaurant above)
Open year-round. 6 stes 1,050-2,000. 51 rms 790-1,050. Bkfst 90. Rms for disabled. Half-board 1,460-2,410. Rm ser. Air cond. Conf. Heated pool. Valet pkg.
Opposite the château's gardens stands a peaceful, elegant hostelry, with luxurious rooms decorated in Louis XVI, Empire, or Restoration style. Amenities include satellite TV, books in English, a gym, and a sauna; active types can ride horses or use the indoor driving range. Courteous service.

12/20 Le Caveau des Ducs

24, rue de Ferrare - 01 64 22 05 05, fax 01 64 22 05 05
Open daily until 10:30pm. Terrace dining. Air cond. Pkg.
In a series of superbly vaulted, seventeenth-century cellar dining rooms located in the center of Fontainebleau, the chef serves forth cuisine geared to classic tastes: chausson of Burgundy snails flavored with mild garlic, duck breast cooked in cider vinegar and served with caramelized apples, and a delicate warm apple tart flambéed in Calvados for dessert. C 280. M 98 (weekdays), 169, 175 (wine incl), 230, 70 (children).

 Napoléon

9, rue Grande - 01 64 22 20 39, fax 01 64 22 20 87
Closed Dec 21-30. 1 ste 790-990. 56 rms 490-700. Bkfst 60. Restaurant. Half-board 620-780. Rm ser. Conf. Garage pkg.
This beautiful hotel in the town center provides good service, excellent bathrooms, and rooms with every comfort. Note that those facing the courtyard are bigger and quieter.

 Victoria

112, rue de France
01 60 74 90 00, fax 01 60 74 90 10
Open year-round. 1 ste 700. 18 rms 250-335. Bkfst 35. Rms for disabled. Restaurant. Half-board 335-410. Rm ser. Garage pkg.
This hotel, currently undergoing a total restoration, features quiet rooms on the gardens. Lots of simple, homey atmosphere (this place is a favorite among anglophone guests on extended stays).

FONTENAY-TRÉSIGNY   77610
Paris 45 - Melun 26 - Coulommiers 23   Seine-et-Marne

 Le Manoir

Route de Coulommiers
01 64 25 91 17, fax 01 64 25 95 49
Closed Tue (exc hols). Open until 9pm. Garden dining. Tennis. Pkg.

The warm atmosphere makes guests feel right at home in this Anglo-Norman manor with its pretty veranda overlooking the grounds. And Denis Come's ultraclassic cuisine takes its cue from the finest ingredients worked in an unfailingly precise, refined, and consistent manner. Wonderfully eclectic wine list, and a tempting selection of spirits. Affable welcome. C 350. M 240 (weekdays, Sat lunch, wine incl), 350, 120 (children).

 ## Le Manoir

(See restaurant above)
Open year-round. 4 stes 990-1,190. 15 rms 790-1,060. Bkfst 70. Rms for disabled. Half-board 790-1,060. Rm ser. Conf. Heated pool. Pkg.
This charming manor house set on calm grounds replete with century-old trees offers guests a variety of spacious, inviting rooms decorated in period or contemporary styles. Charming welcome. Relais et Châteaux.

GARANCIÈRES	78890
Paris 52 - Pontchartrain 11 - Monfort-l'A. 8	Yvelines

 ## La Malvina

4, route du Boissard, La Haute-Perruche
01 34 86 45 76, fax 01 34 86 46 11
Closed Wed dinner, Thu, Jan 2-Feb 2. Open until 9:30pm. Terrace dining.
This little village near the forest seems like something straight out of the past, and the charming inn in its midst, surrounded by gardens full of flowers, features a newly decorated dining room done up with plenty of bright, cheerful atmosphere. There's no better setting for sampling Robert Borré's well-honed traditional cuisine. Borré, who spent many a year manning the stoves on ocean liners, works his repertoire with considerable skill. Nice, reasonably priced cellar. C 250. M 95 (weekday lunch), 160, 250.

GAZERAN	78120
Paris 74 - Rambouillet 4 - Versailles 40	Yvelines

12/20 Villa Marinette

20, av. du Général-de-Gaulle
01 34 83 19 01, fax 01 34 83 19 01
Closed dinner Sun & Tue, Wed, Nov 11-Mar 1. Open until 9pm. Terrace dining. Pkg.
The Villa is a fetching old country house that opens onto a blooming garden. Madame attends to customers, while Monsieur mans the kitchen, producing simple, flavorful dishes based on quality ingredients. M 80 (weekdays, Sat lunch, wine incl), 100, 150, 180 (wine incl), 50 (children).

GOUVIEUX	60270
Paris 43 - Chantilly 9 - Beauvais 43	Oise

 ## Château de la Tour

Chemin de la Chaussée
03 44 57 07 39, fax 03 44 57 31 97

Open year-round. 41 rms 530-930. Bkfst 65. Rms for disabled. Restaurant. Half-board 505. Conf. Heated pool. Pkg.
A certain stateliness pervades this turn-of-the-century dwelling; the accommodations and public rooms are hugely comfortable in a way the French describe as "bourgeois." And there are magnificent grounds to stroll in, as well as a delightful heated pool.

GRESSY	77410
Paris 31 - Meaux 20 - Disneyland Paris 25	Seine-et-Marne

12/20 Le Cellier du Manoir

Chemin des Carosses
01 60 26 68 00, fax 01 60 26 45 46
Open daily until 10pm. Priv rm 100. Terrace dining. Air cond. Heated pool. Valet pkg.
Guests make their way to the restaurant at the Manoir de Gressy hotel by crossing a number of abundantly decorated lounges. But the sensory overload is well worth the trip: no-nonsense rillettes served with very good bread, pan-roasted grouper fillet (not quite firm enough) with spices and melt-in-your-mouth endives, and delicious frozen nougat with candied apricot. Attractive, nicely diversified wine list. C 280-370. M 140, 160, 280.

 ## Le Manoir de Gressy

(See restaurant above)
Open year-round. 2 stes 1,150-1,250. 88 rms 850. Bkfst 70. Rms for disabled. Restaurant. Air cond. Conf. Heated pool. Tennis. Garage pkg.
Le Manoir, built on the site of a seventeenth-century farm, is an extraordinarily modern hotel complex. Guest quarters are tastefully appointed and impeccably equipped, the welcome is consistently friendly...and it's all just a hop, skip and a jump from Roissy–Charles de Gaulle airport!

HÉROUVILLE	95300
Paris 37 - Poissy 27	Val d'Oise

 ## Les Vignes Rouges

5, pl. de l'Église - 01 34 66 54 73, fax 01 34 66 20 88
Closed Sun dinner, Mon, Jan 1-15, 1 wk in May, Aug. Open until 9pm. Terrace dining.
Chef-owner Marcel Desor is uncompromising when it comes to using only the freshest ingredients, and it shows. His traditional menu is prepared with love and care, and served in bright, serene surroundings. You'll find his garden restaurant in the heart of the village, just opposite the church. C 380. M 174 (weekday lunch), 245.

*Looking for a town or restaurant? A winery? A gastronomic specialty or a celebrated chef? Consult the **alphabetical index** to locate them quickly and easily.*

HOUDAN 78550
Paris 62 - Chartres 50 - Rambouillet 29 - Dreux 21   Yvelines

 La Poularde de Houdan

24, av. de la République
01 30 59 60 50, fax 01 30 59 79 71
Closed Tue dinner, Wed, 2 wks in Feb. Open until
10pm. Terrace dining. No pets. Garage pkg.
The institution itself, which stands regally
before a garden, plays host to a spacious, light-
filled dining room done up in slightly austere 50s
style. Chef Sylvain Vandenameele uses picture-
perfect ingredients and treats his great bourgeois
culinary classics with the respect and precision.
The wine list is somewhat limited and lacking in
verve. Efficient welcome. C 300. M 150, 250, 100
(children).

LAMORLAYE 60260
Paris 43 - Chantilly 5 - Beauvais 64   Oise

 Hostellerie du Lys

In Lys-Chantilly, 63, 7e-Avenue
03 44 21 26 19, fax 03 44 21 28 19
Open year-round. 30 rms 250-400. Bkfst 43. Rms
for disabled. Restaurant. Half-board 400-560. Rm
ser. Conf. Pkg.
This opulent country inn, situated in large,
lush grounds, provides comfortable rooms in a
friendly, restful atmosphere. Tennis courts, and
golf course are within easy reach.

MAISONS-LAFFITTE 78600
Paris 21 - Pontoise 18 - St-Germain-en-L. 8   Yvelines

 Le Tastevin

9, av. d'Eglé - 01 39 62 11 67, fax 01 39 62 73 09
Closed Mon dinner, Tue, Aug 16-Sep 9. Open until
10pm. Priv rm 25. Garden dining. Pkg.
Michel Blanchet's patrons are nothing if not
faithful (no, that's not quite true: they are also—
necessarily—rich). They keep piling in to enjoy
the classic yet also contemporay bill of fare:
monkfish with greens lentils, sole and langoustines with pickled vegetables in coriander.
Amélie Blanchet is a gracious hostess, the service
is admirably precise, and the wine list qualifies
as a masterwork. Did we mention that the prices
are incredibly steep? C 380-800. M 230 (weekday
lunch).

 **La Rôtisserie
de la Vieille Fontaine**

8, av. Grétry - 01 39 62 01 78, fax 01 39 62 13 43
Closed Mon, 2 wks in Aug. Open until 10:30pm.
Garden dining.
A cordial welcome and flawless service get
things off to a promising start, and the setting (a
Second Empire villa and garden) is as lovely as
can be. Delicious food, but oddly the dishes
don't always reflect what's announced on the
menu. Never mind. Try the sardine and ricotta
fritters in curry sauce, tender pork shank in a

spicy crust, and mellow chocolate moelleux.
And don't miss the Saint-Estèphe Château de
Bez '90—it's superb! M 172.

MANTES-LA-JOLIE 78200
Paris 60 - Évreux 44 - Rouen 81 - Versailles 44   Yvelines

 La Galiote

18, quai des Cordeliers or 1, rue du Fort
01 34 77 03 02, fax 01 34 77 07 90
Closed dinner Sun & Mon. Open until 10pm. Priv
rm 25. Pkg.
Located opposite the picturesque "Port au
prêtre" which dates from the fifteenth century,
this cold-looking establishment seems barren
and austere at first. But the owner quickly warms
guests' hearts and the cuisine proffered by
Michel Perron, an apostle of the sweet-and-salty
school, does the same for taste buds. The warm
foie gras (which was slightly cool by the time it
reached us) is of the melt-in-your-mouth variety,
and the spiced Challans duck came bathed in a
delicious raspberry jus. Wonderful homemade
caramel ice cream. C 370-420. M 175, 300, 365
(wine incl).

MARLY-LE-ROI 78160
Paris 25 - Versailles 9 - St-Germain-en-L. 4   Yvelines

 Le Village

3, Grande-Rue - 01 39 16 28 14, fax 01 39 58 62 60
Closed Sat lunch, Sun dinner, 3 wks in Aug. Pkg.
The dining room of this exquisite seventeenth-
century house is decorated with charming frescoes, a splendid stage for Éric Poutet's inventive
and polished cooking. Desserts are more adventurous, and the cellar seems a mite overpriced.
You can expect a smiling welcome and swift
service. C 200. M 130 (weekday lunch, wine incl),
250, 80 (children).

MELUN 77000
Paris 55 - Meaux 57 - Sens 66   Seine-et-Marne

 La Melunoise

5, rue du Gâtinais - 01 64 39 68 27
Closed Sat, dinner Sun & Mon, Feb school hols, Aug.
Open until 9:15pm.
Claude and Michel Hinaut's short repertoire
has lost its Nordic accent in favor of traditional
favorites from the Landes and Provence regions.
And we have nary a bone to pick with them on
this front, because their hand remains steady,
their cooking exact, and their flavors as clean and
clear as ever. In addition, a number of their
ingredients are homemade. The cellar is well
stocked with Bordeaux and the décor is warm in
this quaint, flower-bedecked establishment. C
220. M 139, 269, 75 (children).

Please excuse us... (and the chefs). *Menus
are subject to the winds of change, and the
dishes we've described may no longer be
available when you visit.*

MESNULS (LES)	78490
Paris 44 - Versailles 24 - Rambouillet 17	Yvelines

 La Toque Blanche

12, Grande-Rue
01 34 86 05 55, fax 01 34 86 82 18
Closed Sun dinner, Mon, Aug, 1 wk at Christmas.
Open until 10pm. Garden dining. Pkg.
Jean-Pierre Philippe, a sturdy son of Brittany, favors lightened versions of French culinary classics. He imports excellent seafood from his native province but doesn't neglect dishes to please landlubbers: try his sea bream with a brightly flavored fennel garnish or the truffled paupiette of Bresse chicken. Starters and desserts, curiously, are a tone below the rest. C 400-500. M 380.

MONTGRÉSIN	60560
Paris 45 - Chantilly 5 - Beauvais 44	Oise

12/20 **Relais d'Aumale**

37, pl. des Fêtes - 03 44 54 61 31, fax 03 44 54 69 15
Closed Dec 21-28. Open until 10pm. Garden dining. Tennis. Pkg.
When the weather is fine, you can enjoy the sky and trees as your outdoor dining canopy at this restaurant's forest glade location. Good curried lobster ravioli, beef fillet with a meagerly peppered sauce but an out-of-this-world potato galette, and an impeccable chocolate feuillantine. Let the expert maître d' guide you through the extensive offerings in the cellar. C 280-400. M 190 (lunch, exc Sun), 220 (dinne & Sun), 100 (children).

 Relais d'Aumale

(See restaurant above)
Open year-round. 2 stes 700-950. 22 rms 480-620. Bkfst 48. Rms for disabled. Half-board 480-720. Conf. Tennis. Pkg.
The forest primeval surrounds this inviting old hunting lodge boasting sunny, cheerful rooms done up on a modern note. All rooms are exceedingly well equipped.

MONTMORENCY	95160
Paris 18 - Pontoise 20 - Enghien 3	Val-d'Oise

12/20 **Au Cœur de la Forêt**

Av. du Repos-de-Diane - 01 39 64 99 19
Closed Thu, dinner Sun & Mon, 10 days in Feb, Aug 16-Sep 7. Open until 9:30pm. Priv rm 30. Terrace dining. Pkg.
Next time you go walking in the Montmorency forest, ferret around until you find this establishment hidden among the trees. You'll enjoy the family atmosphere and the nicely crafted, seasonal cuisine. Interesting selection of Bordeaux. C 280-400. M 130, 190, 80 (children).

MORET-SUR-LOING	77250
Paris 75 - Fontainebleau 10 - Nemours 17	Seine-et-Marne

12/20 **Auberge de la Palette**

10, av. Jean-Jaurès - 01 60 70 50 72
Closed Tue lunch, Wed, 10 days in Jan, 10 days at Easter, 2 wks mid Aug. Open until 9:15pm. Terrace dining.
Perched on the banks of the Loing River, medieval Moret was a popular site with Impressionist painters. Today, Jean-Louis Binoche's robust cuisine draws hearty appetites to this country setting. They're especially fond of the 175 F set-price menu which features a duo of fresh fish, saddle of hare, magnificent cheese tray, and choice of desserts. Splendid cellar. C 250-300. M 175 (weekday lunch, wine incl), 169, 254, 80 (children).

MORIGNY-CHAMPIGNY	91150
Paris 53 - Étampes 3 - Évry 40	Essonne

 Hostellerie de Villemartin

1, allée des Marronniers
01 64 94 63 54, fax 01 64 94 24 68
Closed Sun (exc hols), Mon, Aug 5-20. 14 rms 310-490. Bkfst 47. Restaurant. Half-board 495. Rm ser. Conf. Pkg.
This turn-of-the-century bourgeois house is set just behind a magnificent fortified farm dating from the sixteenth century. Rooms here are spacious and tastefully decorated for the most part. They all overlook the bucolic splendor of the vast estate surrounding the establishment.

NEMOURS	77140
Paris 79 - Orléans 87 - Fontainebleau 17	Seine-et-Marne

12/20 **L'Écu de France**

3, rue de Paris - 01 64 28 11 54, fax 01 64 45 03 65
Open daily until 10pm. HOTEL: 24 rms 139-259. Bkfst 28. Half-board 220-345. Rm ser. Conf. Pkg.
L'Écu de France is the kind of nice little provincial restaurant that focuses on solid, serious, traditional fare. Maître d' Camille has been watching over his guests for 38 years now! And father and son share behind-the-stove duties day in and day out, in true family spirit. C 250. M 96, 146, 180, 260.

ORSAY	91400
Paris 27 - Versailles 20 - Évry 24	Essonne

 Le Boudin Sauvage

6, rue de Versailles - 01 69 28 42 93
Closed Sat, Sun, Wed dinner, 3 wks in Aug, at Christmas-New Year's. Open until 10:30pm. Terrace dining.
Just ten minutes from the Pont de Sèvres in the concrete suburban wilderness, this pretty nineteenth-century house with its warm, cozy interior and pink-stone terrace bordering a gar-

den is a haven of charm and tranquility. Anne-Marie de Gennes welcome guests and cultivate a friendly atmosphere, while chef Maria Mereira's womanly culinary talents work wonders in the kitchen, starting with *crème de la crème* ingredients. Very impressive choice of Loire wines. C 285-400. M 285 (lunch, wine & coffee incl), 450 (dinner).

OSNY — 95520
Paris 27 - Cergy-Pontoise 1 - Poissy 19 — Val-d'Oise

 Moulin de la Renardière

Rue du Grand-Moulin
01 30 30 21 13, fax 01 34 25 04 98
Closed Sun dinner, Mon. Open until 9:15pm (9:30pm in summer). Priv rm 40. Terrace dining. Pkg.
Jean-Louis Ganier takes justifiable pride in his adorable millhouse, recently embellished with a terrace and bower. On fine days you can sit there by the river and relish Ganier's deft, traditional cooking sparked with touches of whimsy. Well-composed wine list. M 169.

POISSY — 78300
Paris 26 - Pontoise 17 - Mantes-la-Jolie 29 — Yvelines

12/20 Le Bon Vivant

30, av. Émile-Zola - 01 39 65 02 14
Closed Sun dinner, Mon, 1 wk in Feb, Aug. Open until 9:30m. Terrace dining. Pkg.
Generous, classic cooking is the hallmark of Le Bon Vivant's single-price menu. The John Dory with meadow mushrooms and pavé au chocolat in particular rate kudos. Prices are reasonable on the whole. Jolly welcome and service. In summer, ask for a terrace table by the Seine. M 180.

 L'Esturgeon

6, cours du 14-Juillet - 01 39 65 00 04
Closed Thu, Aug. Open until 9:30pm (10pm in summer). Pkg.
A real pro is in the kitchen of this *guinguette* where Impressionists once gathered; he turns out traditional dishes based on top-notch fixings. A lovely view of the Seine may take your mind off the dithery service. C 250-320.

PONTAULT-COMBAULT — 77340
Paris 26 - Melun 29 - Coulommiers 41 — Seine-et-Marne

Saphir Hôtel

Aire des Berchères
01 64 43 45 47, fax 01 64 40 52 43
Open year-round. 20 stes 595-870. 160 rms 400-530. Bkfst 52. Rms for disabled. Restaurant. Half-board 485-870. Rm scr. Air cond. Conf. Heated pool. Tennis. Pkg.
A hotel of recent vintage close to Disneyland. Rooms are airy, pleasant, and well equipped. Facilities include conference rooms, sauna, and a superb indoor swimming pool. Grill.

PONTOISE — 95300
Paris 34 - Beauvais 55 - Rouen 91 - Mantes 39 — Val-d'Oise

12/20 Auberge du Chou

4, route d'Auvers - 01 30 38 03 68
Closed Tue, dinner Sun & Mon. Open until 9:30pm (10:30pm in summer). Terrace dining. No pets. Pkg.
The leafy, flower-decked terrace of this inn on the Oise is lovely indeed. The kitchen does honor to the surroundings with a traditional roster of well-crafted, handsomely presented dishes. Wide-ranging cellar; charming service. C 180-200. M 150, 175, 75 (children).

PORT-MARLY (LE) — 78560
Paris 21 - Versailles 10 - Louveciennes 3 — Yvelines

12/20 Auberge du Relais Breton

27, rue de Paris - 01 39 58 64 33, fax 01 39 58 35 75
Closed Sun dinner, Mon, Aug. Open until 10pm. Garden dining. Pkg.
The décor isn't up to much and the sauces are way too rich and creamy, but among the Auberge's many assets are a genuinely warm welcome and good food served in gargantuan portions. The 229 F set meal brings an appetizer of smoked duck and avocado, sole stuffed with morels, a salad topped with warm chèvre, and vanilla-scented berry gratin—your apéritif, wine, and coffee come at no extra charge! C 250-300. M 159, 229 (wine & coffee incl).

POUILLY-LE-FORT — 77240
Paris 55 - Melun 4 - Meaux 52 — Seine-et-Marne

 Le Pouilly

1, rue de la Fontaine - 01 64 09 56 64
Closed Sun dinner, Mon, Aug 11-31, Dec 23-30. Open until 9:45pm. Terrace dining. Pkg.
This beautifully restored farm is replete with sensory delights: a crackling fire in the monumental hearth, prettily laid tables, an excellent menu, and elaborate but unfailingly light cuisine. The fish dishes rival one another in their ingenious approaches, and the judiciously prepared sauces don't overpower the top-notch ingredients they're paired with. Our favorites: sole beurre marinière, John Dory, and the pan-roasted lamb shoulder and sweetbreads. There's a sumptuous cheese tray, variety of homebaked breads, and post-meal sweets guaranteed to send you straight to seventh heaven. Two toques for chef-in-residence Didier Cadiet. C 400. M 185 (weekdays), 225, 380, 100 (children).

PROVINS — 77160
Paris 85 - Sens 47 - Fontainebleau 53 — Seine-et-Marne

11/20 Le Petit Écu

9, pl. du Châtel - 01 60 67 62 22, fax 01 60 67 77 22

Closed Jan-mid Feb. Open daily until 9:30pm. Terrace dining.

Good things come in small packages! This tiny, simple restaurant is housed in a pretty medieval dwelling. Tuck into curly endive salad with savory bacon bits, confit of duck with sorrel, and a feather-light île flottante. A smiling welcome, and the check is guaranteed to make you smile back! C 120. M 65 & 74 (weekdays), 100 (exc weekdays), 115 (weekdays), 38 (children).

12/20 Quat' Saisons

44, rue du Val - 01 64 08 99 44
Closed Sun dinner, Mon, Jan 10-22. Open until 9pm. Terrace dining.

This restaurant's favorite season has to be spring, given its spacious garden-inspired décor. And the unpretentious but carefully refined cuisine on offer is crafted from the freshest ingredients available. Short list of regional wines. Attentive welcome. C 160. M 96, 32 (children).

12/20 Aux Vieux Remparts

3, rue Couverte - 01 64 08 94 00, fax 01 60 67 77 22
Open daily until 9:30pm. Terrace dining. Garage pkg.

Handsome paneled walls, tiled floors, exposed beams, and white tablecloths prevail in this oasis of quiet in the center of the old town. Apart from the Landes foie gras, other out-of-the-ordinary house specialties include freshwater pike and braised salmon trout. Don't miss the matured Bries, served with nut-studded bread and a nicely seasoned salad. C 370. M 150 (weekdays), 175 5Sat & Sun), 350, 430, 90 (children).

Aux Vieux Remparts

(See restaurant above)
Open year-round. 25 rms 340-650. Bkfst 50-70. Rms for disabled. Restaurant. Half-board 420-765. Rm ser. Pkg.

A more modern building plays host to the hotel, with views on the town's rooftops and ramparts. The rooms are small, but they're cozy, bright, and impeccably kept. Friendly welcome and attentive service.

ROCHEFORT-EN-YVELINES   78730
Paris 50 - Chartres 42 - Étampes 26   Yvelines

L'Escu de Rohan

15, rue Guy-le-Rouge - 01 30 41 31 33
Closed Sun dinner & Mon (exc hols). Open until 9:30pm. Pkg.

It's a pity the checks are so steep, because we'd like nothing better than to settle in more often here after our walks around the charming village. This former coaching inn is done up with a bright, harmonious décor, and Jean Chevrier, the lord of the manor, is a wonderfully attentive host. His new chef, Frédric Cauchye, works the best ingredients with prowess, turning out personalized versions of traditional fare. Nice little cellar. C 350. M 120-390.

ROLLEBOISE   78270
Paris 70 - Versailles 53 - Évreux 37 - Mantes 9   Yvelines

Château de la Corniche

5, route de la Corniche
01 30 93 21 24, fax 01 30 42 27 44
Closed Mon off-seas, Sun (exc Easter), Dec 20-Jan 7. 35 rms 300-750. Bkfst 50-60. Restaurant. Half-board 460-800. Conf. Heated pool. Tennis. Pkg.

This château once belonged to Léopold II. The rooms within are personalized, spacious, and well equipped, and a temple of love and a splendid panoramic view of the Seine await you in the garden.

SAINT-GERMAIN-EN-LAYE   78100
Paris 21 - Chartres 81 - Dreux 70   Yvelines

11/20 Brasserie du Théâtre

Pl. du Château - 01 30 61 28 00, fax 01 39 73 98 73
Closed at Christmas. Open until 1am. Air cond. Terrace dining. Garage pkg.

Conveniently sited opposite the château, this 1930s-vintage brasserie provides solid sustenance at nearly any time of the day, just about every day of the year. C 190-360.

Cazaudehore

1, av. du Président-Kennedy - 01 34 51 93 80 (R)
01 39 73 36 60 (H), fax 01 39 73 73 88
Closed Mon (exc hols). Open until 10pm. Garden dining. Pkg.

On the edge of the forest in a setting of lawns and flowers sits this charming establishment decorated with old prints and English chintzes; for summer dining, there's a huge terrace that looks out over the trees. A few Mediterranean touches now grace Philippe Pactol's menu, but for the most part it remains dedicated to pricey French classics and rich Southwestern dishes, all ably handled. Superb cellar, stylish service. C 450. M 190 & 290 (weekday lunch, wine incl), 360 (Sat, Sun, wine incl), 130.

La Forestière

(See restaurant above)
Open year-round. 5 stes 1,350. 25 rms 750-930. Bkfst 75. Restaurant. Conf. Heated pool. Tennis. Pkg.

Rooms and suites decorated with exquisite refinement, each in an individual style. The forest is close at hand, and is even directly accessible from some of the suites. Guests can count on a warm, attentive welcome. Relais et Châteaux.

11/20 La Feuillantine

10, rue des Louviers - 01 34 51 04 24
Open until 10pm (Sat & Sun 10:30pm). Terrace dining.

You'll be charmingly received into this bright, cozy restaurant (it's a popular spot, so remember to book ahead). Save for a flavorless Barbary duck, we have no complaints about the good salmon crêpe, choucroute garnie with seafood, or cold apple dessert laced with Calvados. Extensively annotated wine list. C 130. M 75 & 85 (weekday lunch), 130.

 ## Le Pavillon Henri IV

21, rue Thiers
01 39 10 15 15, fax 01 39 73 93 73
Open daily until 10:30pm. Terrace dining. Air cond. Pkg.
With its terrific view of just a bit of the Eiffel Tower, this place where the Sun King was born caters to a distinguished clientele which appreciates the first-class ingredients of this very classic cuisine: warm oysters in Champagne sauce, perfectly cooked sea scallops, generous gratin of lobster. The wine cellar could be improved. C 350-450. M 240 (weekday lunch), 265, 320, 400.

 ## Le Pavillon Henri IV

(See restaurant above)
Open year-round. 3 stes 1,900. 42 rms 400-1,300. Bkfst 50-100. Rms for disabled. Restaurant. Half-board 670-870. Rm ser. Conf. Golf. Pkg.
This is where Louis XIV was born, Alexandre Dumas wrote *The Three Musketeers*, and Offenbach composed a number of operettas. We don't find the somber blue-gray furnishings very inspiring, but the 45 rooms and suites are huge and airy. The public rooms are magnificent and there's a splendid view over the extensive grounds.

SAINT-LAMBERT-DES-BOIS	78470
Paris 34 - Rambouillet 22 - Versailles 16	Yvelines

 ## Les Hauts de Port-Royal

2, rue de Vaumurier
01 30 44 10 21, fax 01 30 64 44 10
Closed Sun dinner, Mon, Aug 15-30. Open until 9:30pm. Terrace dining. Pkg.
Located in the middle of the forest, just a stone's throw from the abbey, the charming, restful, ochre-colored dining room here provides the ideal setting for lovers of inventive cuisine. Sweet-and-sour fans will surely appreciated the honey-lacquered suprême of squab and pears with spices, and the tart and tangy Chinon sauce in the lamb dish. The decidedly unfresh red mullets and scalding soufflé were less enticing though, and the welcome, service and timing could be better. C 350. M 150 (exc Sat dinner), 250, 120 (children).

SAINT-LÉGER-EN-YVELINES	78610
Paris 50 - Monfort-l'Amaury 8 - Rambouillet 11	Yvelines

12/20 La Belle Aventure

8, rue de la Croix-Blanche
01 34 86 31 35, fax 01 34 86 36 85
Closed Feb school hols, 3 wks in Aug. Open until 10pm. Priv rm 40. Terrace dining. HOTEL: *2 stes*

500-580. 6 rms 350. Bkfst 70. Rm ser. Conf. Tennis. Garage pkg.
A pretty village and quiet garden surround this charming thatched-roof inn with a spacious, country-style dining room—just right for a romantic getaway! Tomohiro Uido serves forth a short repertoire in the contemporary vein, based on fresh ingredients, an interesting approach, and painstaking preparation. The wine list is imprecise, and not all that appealing. Gracious welcome and friendly, competent service. C 330-440. M 159.

SAINT-SYMPHORIEN-LE-CHÂTEAU	28700
Paris 69 - Rambouillet 23 - Chartres 26	Eure-et-Loir

 ## Château d'Esclimont

02 37 31 15 15, fax 02 37 31 57 91
Open daily until 9:30pm. Terrace dining. Priv rm 200. No pets. Valet pkg.
"It is my pleasure" is the motto that the Duc de La Rochefoucauld had sculpted above the entrance to this ravishing Renaissance château. Our pleasure, as we sit beneath the high ceilings of these comfortable dining rooms, is to savor Éric Douvry's delectable sweetbread salad dressed with truffle vinaigrette, move on to suckling pig cooked three ways, then conclude with spiced mangoes and coconut ice cream. All this deliciousness is served with style, and can be accompanied by superb (and awfully expensive) wines. C 400-480. M 260 (lunch exc Sun, wine incl), 320, 495.

 ## Château d'Esclimont

(See restaurant above)
Open year-round. 6 stes 2,800. 47 rms 600-1,850. Bkfst 85-170. Half-board 730-1,330. Rm ser. Conf. Heated pool. Tennis. Valet pkg.
The 47 rooms and 6 suites of this château are classic, comfortable, and handsomely situated amid 150 acres of enclosed grounds. The site is at the bottom of a valley traversed by a river, near the road that connects Rambouillet and Chartres. Guests can play tennis, swim in the heated pool, and attend wintertime musical evenings. Perfect for a luxurious, romantic weekend, and only 45 minutes from Paris by car. There's even a helipad. Relais et Châteaux, of course.

STE-GEMME-MORONVAL	28500
Paris 72 - Dreux 6 - Chartres 41	Eure-et-Loir

 ## L'Escapade

02 37 43 72 05, fax 02 37 43 86 96
Closed dinner Sun & Mon, Tue, Feb 8-Mar 5, Jul 15-Aug 7. Open until 9:30pm. Air cond. Pkg.
Paul Gomes's seriously good cooking is no mere escapade! Tuck into his sublime marinated, dill-flecked salmon, veal sweetbreads with morels, sautéed lobster with morels, and the raspberry soufflé for dessert. The Figeacs and Bourgueils in the appreciable cellar make mealtime in the Empire-style dining room all the

more splendid. A charming welcome from Lúcia. **C** 300. **M** 135 (weekday lunch), 170.

SAMOREAU
77210
Paris 68 - Melun 16 - Fontainebleau 7   Seine-et-Marne

 La Tour de Samoiselle

2, voie de la Liberté - 01 64 23 93 31
Closed Sun dinner, Mon, Feb school hols, 2 wks in Sep. Open until 9:30pm. Terrace dining. Pkg.
The freshest ingredients, evident skill with an eye for detail, and an imaginative way with fish: these are Patrice Emery's assets in his charming old mansion set in an airy garden not far from the Seine. The dining room plays host to curious tourists, weekend pilgrims from Paris, and foreigners there to visit the château at Fontainebleau. Tuck into a scrumptious saddle of hare salad, melt-in-your-mouth homemade foie gras, turbot sprinkled with almonds, and a berry sabayon for dessert. Wonderful dessert menu, and fromage blanc served by the ladle, just like at your French grandma's house! **C** 280. **M** 142, 198.

SANCY
77580
Paris 57 - Meaux 12 - Melun 52   Seine-et-Marne

 Demeure de la Catounière

1, pl. de l'Église - 01 60 25 71 74, fax 01 60 25 60 55
Closed 2 wks at Christmas. 22 rms 360-400. Bkfst 80. Restaurant. Half-board 540-590. Conf. Pool. Tennis. Pkg.
This seventeenth-century country estate is located in a picturesque village, and offers guests well-equipped rooms with a view on the manicured grounds.

SENLIS
60300
Paris 50 - Compiègne 35 - Soissons 60 - Lille 172   Oise

10/20 La Mitonnée

93, rue du Moulin-Saint-Tron
03 44 53 10 05, fax 03 44 53 13 99
Closed Sun dinner, Mon. Open until 9:30pm. Pkg.
This country inn has something new on the menu: the recipes for the dishes you're about to sample! Tuck into the sweetbread terrine with foie gras, fillet of sole stew, and hazelnut truffier, all served with a healthy dose of charm. **C** 250. **M** 150, 210, 65 (children).

12/20 Le Scaramouche

4, pl. Notre-Dame - 03 44 53 16 87
Closed Wed, 1 wk at Feb school hols, 1 wk in Aug. Open until 9:30pm. Terrace dining. Pkg.
Practically next door to the cathedral, Scaramouche serves honest cooking with its roots in the Picardy *terroir*: goat cheese with Belgian endive, guinea hen à la picarde, fudgy chocolate cake. **C** 260. **M** 145, 190, 320, 60 (children).

THOMERY
77810
Paris 73 - Melun 21 - Fontainebleau 12   Seine-et-Marne

 Le Vieux Logis

5, rue Sadi-Carnot
01 60 96 44 77, fax 01 60 70 01 42
Open daily until 9:30pm. Garden dining. Heated pool. Tennis. Garage pkg.
The success of Le Vieux Logis stems from a team effort that starts with the way guests are greeted and extends through to the way food is cooked. Madame Plouvier rules the roost here with an iron hand in a velvet glove, and the 145 F price of the short set menu is a real *tour de force*, especially in such a refined setting. Indulge in the wonderful fish and precisely prepared garden vegetables. This is one of those restaurants that's well worth the trip from Moret-sur-Loing or Fontainebleau. The desserts are inventive, and the cellar, presided over by Monsieur Plouvier, is a reasonably priced work in progress. **C** 300. **M** 145 (exc Sun), 240.

 Le Vieux Logis

(See restaurant above)
Open year-round. 14 rms 400. Bkfst 50. Half-board 560. Rm ser. No pets. Conf. Heated pool. Tennis. Garage pkg.
This establishment, located in a peaceful little village renowned for its twelfth-century church, offers sunny rooms, bountiful breakfasts, and great prices. If you're tired (or just in love!), you can dine by candlelight right in your room.

TREMBLAY-SUR-MAULDRE (LE)
78490
Paris (Pte de St-Cloud) 42 - Versailles 20   Yvelines

 L'Astrée

Pl. de l'Église - 01 34 87 92 92, fax 01 34 87 86 27
Closed Sun dinner, Mon, Jul 15-Aug 15, 1 wk at Christmas. Open until 9:30pm. Garden dining. Pkg.
Jean-Pierre Bouchereau finally took total restoration of this pretty château—a popular site for weddings, seminars, and weekend getaways—in hand. And now he's happily ensconced behind his stoves, whipping up his celebrated sauces (he's especially gifted for the fish variety). His saffron-laced lobster and sole aumônière features clear, delicate flavors, and his turbot with cabbage and mussels is cooked to perfection. Even though its offerings tend to be costly, the cellar is exceedingly rich–especially in half-bottles. The service could be a tad warmer. **C** 250. **M** 190.

 Château-Hôtel Golf du Tremblay

(See restaurant above)
Closed Jul 15-Aug 15. 30 rms 550-1,300. Bkfst 50. Rm ser. Conf. Tennis. Golf. Pkg.
This Louis XIII château set on 100 acres of land features rooms of varying sizes, some with their own fireplaces, and all with period-style furni-

ture and top-notch equipment. View on the golf course or the French-style gardens.

VERSAILLES 78000
Paris 23 - Mantes 44 - Rambouillet 31 Yvelines

 Bellevue Hôtel

12, av. de Sceaux - 01 39 50 13 41, fax 01 39 02 05 67
Open year-round. 3 stes 450-550. 24 rms 270-450. No pets. Pkg.
The Bellevue's Louis XV/XVI–style rooms are soundproofed and well equipped but a trifle old-fashioned, despite a recent remodeling. Located near the château and conference center.

11/20 Brasserie du Théâtre

15, rue des Réservoirs - 01 39 50 03 21
Open daily until 1am. Terrace dining.
Classic brasserie food (fresh shellfish, pepper steak, cassoulet), served in a supremely Gallic décor of mirrors, glowing woodwork, and leather banquettes. C 160.

 Brasserie La Fontaine

Trianon Palace, 1, bd de la Reine
01 30 84 38 47
Open daily until 10:30pm. Air cond. Valet pkg.
This brasserie annex of the famed Trois Marches (see below) bears the visible stamp of master chef Gérard Vié. He oversees an enticing menu that features marinated mushrooms with an unctuous purée of olives and tuna, roast lobster, and a suave (but stingily served) chocolate-pistachio tart. The superb old-fashioned décor is accented with a series of amusing animal portraits. C 230. M 165, 75 (children).

12/20 La Flotille

Parc du Château - 01 39 51 41 58
Open daily for lunch only until 3pm. Terrace dining. Pkg.
How delightful! A restaurant with a lovely terrace planted in the grounds of the château, just steps away from the boat stand. And a kitchen that acquits itself more than respectably, with assorted Southwestern appetizers, beef tenderloin au poivre, and a yummy cherry cake (all the desserts are tempting). The escargots with oyster mushrooms (served *sans* mushrooms) are skippable. Bare-bones cellar, but the monthly wine specials merit your notice. C 190. M 132 (lunch), 45 (children).

 Home Saint-Louis

28, rue St-Louis - 01 39 50 23 55, fax 01 30 21 62 45
Open year-round. 25 rms 220-320. Bkfst 30.
Quiet, pleasant rooms close to the château.

La Marée de Versailles

22, rue au Pain - 01 30 21 73 73, fax 01 39 50 55 87
Closed Mon dinner, Sun, Dec 23-Jan 1, Aug 4-26. Open until 10:15pm. Air cond. V.
This shipshape little establishment serves sparkling fresh and handily prepared seafood. Don't

miss the generous "all-shellfish" set menu. Skilled, stylish service. C 190. M 260.

11/20 Le Mille et Une Nuits

5, passage Saint-Pierre - 01 30 21 91 05
Closed Mon, Aug. Open until 10:30pm (Sat & Sun 11:30pm). Priv rm 20. Pkg.
White arches and a fountain compose a fantasy setting, where you can indulge in adroitly turned out Moroccan classics. Tiny cellar of Mediterranean wines. C 170-250. M 85 (weekday lunch, Sat).

 Le Potager du Roy

1, rue du Mal-Joffre
01 39 50 35 34, fax 01 30 21 69 30
Closed Sun dinner, Mon. Open until 10:30pm. Priv rm 20. Air cond.
The set meal will pique your appetite, with a soup of mussels and cockles with white beans, a sparky combination of skate and potatoes dressed with capers and lemon, and a smooth guanaja-chocolate dessert (we'd have liked a bit more of that last). Choosing from the *carte* we encountered bitter oysters and a minuscule portion of scallops, as well as some splendid vegetable dishes. Expensive. The cellar spotlights wines from the Loire. C 290-420. M 165.

 Le Quai n°1

1, av. de St-Cloud - 01 39 50 42 26, fax 01 39 51 15 45
Closed Sun dinner, Mon. Open until 11pm. Priv rm 35. Terrace dining. Air cond.
A dependable address for fresh shellfish and decent seafood dishes at reasonable prices. Among the better offerings are a spicy fish soup, a refreshing salad of whelks with mayonnaise, and plaice in a sauce enriched with meat jus. Amusing nautical décor; casual service. One toque for encouragement's sake. C 220. M 120, 160.

 Richaud

16, rue Richaud - 01 39 50 10 42, fax 01 39 53 43 36
Open year-round. 39 rms 220-360. Bkfst 30. Garage pkg.
A classic hotel in the center of Versailles, close to the antique dealers. The rooms were all recently modernized and renovated.

11/20 Rôtisserie Ballester

30 bis, rue des Réservoirs
01 39 50 70 02, fax 01 39 02 24 84
Open daily until 10:30pm. Terrace dining.
Brasserie fare at real brasserie prices (starters for 45 F, main dishes for 65 F and 90 F). Decent cellar. C 170-210. M 138 (exc weekday lunch), 95 (lunch).

 Sofitel

2 bis, av. Paris - 01 39 53 30 31, fax 01 39 53 87 20
Open year-round. 6 stes 1,400. 146 rms 900. Bkfst 80. Rms for disabled. Restaurant. Rm scr. Air cond. Valet pkg.

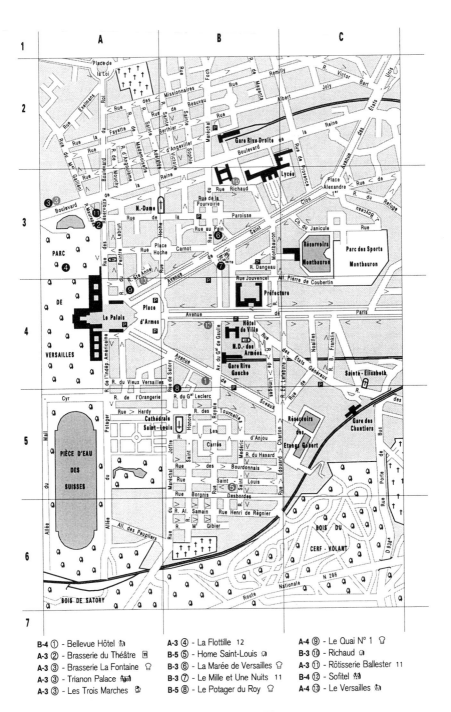

B-4 ① - Bellevue Hôtel 🏨
A-3 ② - Brasserie du Théâtre 🍴
A-3 ③ - Brasserie La Fontaine ♀
A-3 ③ - Trianon Palace 🏨
A-3 ③ - Les Trois Marches 🍴

A-3 ④ - La Flottille 12
B-5 ⑤ - Home Saint-Louis ♀
B-3 ⑥ - La Marée de Versailles ♀
B-3 ⑦ - Le Mille et Une Nuits 11
B-5 ⑧ - Le Potager du Roy ♀

A-4 ⑨ - Le Quai N° 1 ♀
B-3 ⑩ - Richaud ♀
A-3 ⑪ - Rôtisserie Ballester 11
B-4 ⑫ - Sofitel 🏨
A-4 ⑬ - Le Versailles 🏨

This chain hotel is located in immediate proximity to Place d'Armes and the château. Rooms here are spacious and modern, and all of the chain's top-of-the-line services are on offer. Piano bar.

 ## Les Trois Marches

Trianon Palace, 1, bd de la Reine
01 39 50 13 21, fax 01 30 21 01 25
Closed Sun, Mon, Aug. Open until 10pm. Priv rm 20. Terrace dining. Air cond. Valet pkg.

Gérard Vié is as happy as a king in the splendiferous kitchens of the Trianon Palace, where he and his *brigade* benefit from the state of the art equipment. Vié excels in the "sophisticated country" register that recalls his Languedoc roots: cassoulet with Couïza sausages or hearty Lacaune ham. And his updated French classics are models of the genre: morels braised in cream, asparagus with truffles, turbot with fat Tarbais beans, or a magnificent chop of milk-fed Corrèze veal. The brilliant sommelier can uncork a vintage Pauillac or Margaux to complement Vié's creations, and the maître d'hôtel will ensure that every detail of your meal is memorable. A well-earned point. C 700-900. M 270 (weekday lunch), 510, 610.

 ## Trianon Palace

(See restaurant above)
01 30 84 38 00, fax 01 39 49 00 77
Open year-round. 27 stes 2,700-7,500. 67 rms 1,300-1,800. Bkfst 110-140. Restaurant. Rm ser. Air cond. Conf. Heated pool. Tennis. Valet pkg.

Spruced up to the tune of $60 million, the Trianon Palace is a stupendously lavish hotel.

From video-conference equipment to a medically supervised spa, it is the last word in luxury. Restaurants: Les Trois Marches, Brasserie de la Fontaine, see above.

 ## Le Versailles

7, rue Ste-Anne - 01 39 50 64 65, fax 01 39 02 37 85
Open year-round. 3 stes 450-520. 42 rms 450. Bkfst 54. Rms for disabled. Conf. Garage pkg.

Some rooms are located under the rafters, and all are modern, tastefully decorated, and well equipped (satellite TV). This hotel is ideally situated at the entry to the château. Bar, flower-filled terrace where breakfast is served, patio.

VINEUIL-SAINT-FIRMIN   60500
Paris 52 - Chantilly 6 - Beauvais 56   Oise

Golf-Hotel Blue Green

Route d'Apremont, Domaine de Chantilly
03 44 58 47 77, fax 03 44 58 50 11
Open year-round. 2 stes 950-1,350. 107 rms 590-750. Bkfst 75. Rms for disabled. Restaurant. Half-board 565-645. Rm ser. Conf. Tennis. Golf. Garage pkg.

Here in the midst of the Chantilly forest is a long, low hotel with a neoclassic colonnade. Rooms are on the small side and lack air conditioning, but they are attractively decorated. Most open onto views of the hotel's eighteen-hole golf course.

ALSACE

What a lovely garden!

Alsace: where nothing is different from the rest of France...except for what isn't the same! Social Security, real estate laws, the relations between Church and State, and so many other aspects of community life follow rules unique to Alsace. Then there's the dialect, more Germanic than Voltairean. The architecture, too, is definitely different. So are the native costumes. And so is the food...

Despite these differences, Alsatians are more resolutely French than the "inlanders" (as they refer to their countrymen) and have proved to be fervent patriots throughout their turbulent history. For visitors unfamiliar with that history, Alsace will remain an enigma.

So you should know that for seven centuries Alsace belonged to the Holy Roman Empire (which, of course, was really the Germanic Empire). You should also know that despite—or because of—its size, that Empire was not structured like a unified nation or state. Alsace gradually forged stronger and stronger links with the French Crown. In the thirteenth century Philip the Fair, a firm believer in centralized government, claimed Alsace for France. But it was Louis XIV, the Sun King, who in the seventeenth century finally annexed Alsace to France. Gazing down at his conquest from the Saverne Pass he exclaimed: "What a lovely garden!"

A lovely garden indeed, rich with the fruits of prosperity, religious freedom, and unfettered trade. That Alsace prefigured the Europe of the Common Market—now the European Union. Today one of the Union's principal institutions, the European Parliament, is headquartered at Strasbourg, capital of Alsace.

A taste
for celebration

Back to the history: Germany's appetite for expansion on the left bank of the Rhine never abated. Germany snatched Alsace from a defeated France in 1871, controlling the province until the Allied victory of 1918, when Alsace was restored to France. In 1941, attempting to revive the Germanic Empire, Hitler again seized Alsace, which returned to France in 1945. During this time, many Alsatians emigrated rather than become Ger-

man nationals. The presence of Müllers and Schweitzers all over the world attests to these forced exiles. Wounded by battles, victimized by blind ambition, Alsace now symbolizes the desire for peace and harmony felt by people on both sides of the Rhine. For Alsatians love life and they show it! Their *joie de vivre* overflows in village festivals and parades. Led by the local band (in which it is considered an honor to play), decked out in traditional costumes, Alsatians celebrate any and every occasion, from victory in some ancient battle to a patron saint's feast or a successful grape harvest.

Wine and beer lead a peaceful coexistence in Alsace. The best brews in France are produced here and are great favorites with the local population. And since Roman times Alsace has lovingly cultivated the vine, producing divinely fragrant wines (ah! those geranium-scented Gewurztraminers...). You don't have to be a wine buff to be enchanted by the **Route des Vins**, especially in autumn when the grapes glow golden and ripe on the hillsides, tended by genial winegrowers who seem to be another Alsatian specialty. Touring the realm of Riesling and Traminer, you will get to know the locals by sharing their table, an all-important part of life in Alsace. The food is sturdy and filling, suited to a severe climate (but in the restaurant reviews that follow you'll find some lighter alternatives). Typically Alsatian is choucroute garnie: braised sauerkraut piled high with sausages and ham. Modern versions of the dish are garnished with fish, duck, or mushrooms. Traditional, too, are baeckeoffe (marinated meat layered with potatoes and onions and baked for hours), ham en croûte, onion quiche, and wild game—pheasant, hare—from Alsace's extensive forests. And then there's foie gras (which Alsatians claim to have invented), flammekueche (a kind of creamy pizza), and for dessert, kugelhopf, a sweet yeast cake garnished with almonds. Your most unforgettable meal, should the occasion arise, would surely be the one you share with a farm family on the day they slaughter the pig. The farm-reared porker is sacrificed to prepare the hams and sausages that the family will consume throughout the year. The feasting that marks the occasion is worthy of a medieval banquet! And finally, don't neglect to taste (in moderation, of course) the clear fruit brandies for which Alsace is justly famous, distilled from cherries (Kirsch), plums (Mirabelle and Quetsche), and raspberries (Framboise).

There is much to see in this fascinating land, where cultures and languages get along so well together that it is not always easy to sort them out. The *Marseillaise*, that proud French anthem, doesn't come from Marseille, but from Strasbourg where in 1792 it was known as the *Rhine Armies' War Song*. And Gutenberg, inventor of the printing press, lived here in Alsace (you can visit his house in Strasbourg).

An Alsatian itinerary

The Wine Road, Romanesque churches, deep forests, and romantic châteaux—Alsace is all this and more: flower-decked villages and hop fields, a province prized by gastrotourists for its great restaurants and cheerful *winstubs*. But in the end, the puzzle that is Alsace falls together beneath your steps, as you follow your tastes and inclinations. Along the way, you'll cross industrial towns like Strasbourg and Mulhouse, and villages surrounded by small-scale engineering and technological firms.

Starting from the north, at the German border, our itinerary takes us to **Wissembourg** where Stanislaw Leszczynski, the exiled king of Poland, raised his daughter, Marie; in 1725 she wed Louis XV and became Queen of France. She surely knelt to pray in the church of Saint-Pierre-et-Saint-Paul, a Gothic structure capped by a Romanesque tower, with fourteenth-century frescoes; and she certainly strolled along the quays of the River Lauter, admiring the fine Renaissance dwellings.

Saverne, gateway to Alsace as you drive from Paris, boasts a sumptuous eighteenth-century château. After **Haguenau**, with its curious old Wheat and Hops Market and late Gothic church of Saint Nicolas, the magnificent city of **Strasbourg** awaits. The cathedral, built of red and pink granite from the Vosges Mountains, is an undisputed masterpiece of Gothic architecture. Begun in the sixth century, 900 years later it was hailed as the eighth wonder of the Western world: its boldly soaring Gothic spire, in delicate stone filigree, rises to a height of 468 feet. Grandeur marks the Palais Rohan (home to a major art museum); gentle nostalgia haunts the Petite France district, where patrician dwellings line the canals, just like in Venice (minus the gondolas and vaporetti). Along the banks of the Ill visitors stroll through streets and squares touched by history, where famous figures have left their mark: Guten-

berg, Goethe, Frederick of Prussia, Louis Pasteur...

To the south, after following the charming River Bruche, you'll reach **Molsheim**, with its medieval market square and town hall, then **Rosheim**, home of the oldest house in Alsace (twelfth century), and a cathedral that is arguably the most beautiful example of the Alsatian Romanesque style. **Obernai**, at the foot of Mont Sainte-Odile on the Route des Vins, is a picture-postcard vision of Alsace. At **Ottrott**, while meditating on a Bronze Age wall you might want to sample a glass of Pinot Noir, one of the region's rare red wines. A drive through the vineyards leads to **Sélestat**: there, the church of Saint Georges (splendid stained glass) rises above the steep roofs of the town where Charlemagne once lived. Now booklovers come here to marvel at the town's Humanist Library, a treasure trove of rare editions.

An incredible wine fest

By this time, a glass of Tokay, or Riesling, or Muscat, Sylvaner, or Gewurztraminer would go down well... Here's to your health! Each year on September 8, **Ribeauvillé** hosts one of the merriest winefests imaginable: the Riesling flows, washing down mountains of local charcuterie. Due south lies **Riquewihr**, the "pearl" of Alsace's vineyard towns, so called for its superb old homes adorned with carving, corbels, and bay windows. Nearby **Kaysersberg**, birthplace of Nobel Peace Prize–winner Albert Schweitzer is another lovely winegrowing village, with a picturesque fortified bridge, Renaissance houses, and a castle that belonged to Frederick the Great.

In **Colmar** history and poetic beauty await in ancient cloisters, magnificent houses (the Maison des Têtes, the Maison Pfister...), and noble gardens. The genius of medieval art unfolds in the collections of the Musée d'Unterlinden, where Mathias Grünewald's powerfully moving Issenheim altarpiece is displayed. Colmar is pedestrian-friendly: on foot is truly the best way to explore the Petite Venise district, and admire the sculptures of the church of Saint Martin and the Dominican Church (enter to view the sublime *Madonna of the Rosebush*). To the west, the green and peaceful **Munster Valley** lies at the foot of the **Hohneck** peak and the **Schlucht Pass**, which links Alsace to its sister province, Lorraine. Beyond **Guebwiller** and its three remarkable churches, you'll be dazzled by the pink granite abbey church of **Murbach**, nestled in a leafy valley against the backdrop of **Grand Ballon**, the tallest peak of the Vosges. On the back roads of these game-rich mountains, you may well encounter deer, hare, foxes, boars, or grouse; and you may hear the metallic whirr of a sawmill down in a valley.

Alsatians say that while Strasbourg's is the highest and Fribourg's is the biggest, **Thann**'s church of Saint Thiébaut is the most graceful of all. **Mulhouse** is a must-see for car and train buffs, owing to its popular Car Museum (500 vehicles) and French Railway Museum. Mulhouse is also the cradle of local industry: the offset press was invented here—the earliest model was powered by oxen! Now machine tools and locomotives are manufactured here. Nearby are the salt and potassium mines that were once an important source of wealth for the region. Farther south, just beyond **Altkirch** (for some obscure reason Prince Rainier of Monaco holds the title of Count of Altkirch), lies Switzerland. We're already sorry that we couldn't stop in **Lembach** to see the remains of the Maginot Line, in **Rouffach** to admire its medieval church and Renaissance square, or in **Hagenthal**, pride of the river-crossed **Sundgau**.

On your journey through Alsace, you'll surely spy a stork or two. These birds return each spring from Africa to build their nests on the roofs and in the chimneys of Alsatian villages. Symbols of fidelity and perseverance, they are the ideal emblem for Alsace.

RESTAURANTS & HOTELS

COLMAR	68000
Paris 445 - Strasbourg 69 - Nancy 141	Haut-Rhin

12/20 Caveau Hansi ☺

23, rue des Marchands - 03 89 41 37 84
Closed Wed dinner, Thu, Jan. Open until 9:30pm. Terrace dining.
Locals are regulars at this pretty old half-timbered house with its spanking-clean Alsatian interior. Delicious, thoughtfully prepared regional fare; great selection of regional wines and clear brandies; attentive service. C 200-340. M 98, 260.

 Le Colombier

7, rue de Turenne
03 89 23 96 00, fax 03 89 23 97 27
Open year-round. 1 ste 980-1,300. 23 rms 395-950. Bkfst 55. Rms for disabled. Air cond. Conf.
This half-timbered sixteenth-century house is located in the town's Petite Venise section, and features an impressive Renaissance staircase and a fountain in its charming inner courtyard. Pretty rooms with contemporary décor.

 Au Fer Rouge

52, Grand-Rue - 03 89 41 37 24, fax 03 89 23 82 24
Closed Sun dinner & Mon (Oct-Apr), Jan 9-29. Open until 9:45pm. Terrace dining. Pkg.
Patrick Fulgraff's classic cooking puts the spotlight on the regional ingredients he knows so well. Very nice pan-roasted goose liver with a Balsamic vinegar-olive oil vinaigrette; fresh, perfectly done pike perch paired with a remarkable choucroute; roast suckling pig served with pig's trotters en brik. The pear tart, or more original terrine of dried fruits with spice ice cream add delicious finishing touches. Splendid cellar featuring Alsatian wines and Burgundies, but prices are on the high side, and there are no half-bottles. C 400. M 210 (weekday lunch), 295 (weekday lunch, Sat lunch), 360, 480, 110 (children).

COLROY-LA-ROCHE	67420
Paris 402 - Sélestat 30 - St-Dié 30 - Obernai 41	Bas-Rhin

 Les Princes de Salm

03 88 97 61 64, fax 03 88 47 21 73
Closed Jan-Mar. Open daily until 9pm. Terrace dining. Air cond. Heated pool. Tennis. Pkg.
This elder of the two restaurants in the luxurious Chalet de la Cheneaudière is still the star. Its traditional décor is the height of "cozy opulence," with some incredible vantage points on the Vosges forest and countryside. While checks are known to take on princely airs, the abundance of noble ingredients on offer (special foie gras menu) has yet to steal the limelight from Jean-Paul Bossée and his ingenious interpretations of regional themes. The wine list is comprehensive, appealing, and especially lavish when it comes to Alsatian vintages. Attentive welcome. C 480. M 585.

 La Cheneaudière ⚔️

(See restaurant above)
Open year-round. 7 stes 1,330-2,600. 22 rms 500-1,480. Bkfst 90-120. Rms for disabled. Half-board 855-1,225. Conf. Heated pool. Tennis. Pkg.
While people from France's eastern provinces are thought to be reserved, they can also be extremely warm and welcoming, as is the case here. This establishment nestled in greenery has remarkably equipped, superbly decorated rooms. Relais et Châteaux.

ILLHAEUSERN	68150
Paris 553 - Colmar 17 - Sélestat 15	Haut-Rhin

 L'Auberge de l'Ill

Rue de Collonges - 03 89 71 89 00 (R), 03 89 71 87 87 (H),
fax 03 89 71 82 83 (R), 03 89 71 87 88 (H)
Closed Mon dinner (& lunch off-seas), Tue, Feb. Open until 9:15pm. Priv rm 60. Terrace dining. Air cond. Pkg.
The Auberge is like a village within the village, starting at the *place* and extending along the river into the restaurant, garden, and hotel. The dining

rooms are both very sunny; one is decorated in Louis XV-style woods and the other features pretty paintings and a rotunda with a view on the Ill.

Marc Haeberlin's cuisine is: spirited, generous, and less classic than is generally thought, especially where starters and fish dishes are concerned. His experience, exacting choice of ingredients, and flair for combining strong flavors consistently add up to success. His pan-roasted frogs' legs and cabbage ragoût is a dazzling exercise in harmony, as is the superb mix of flavors he achieves with veal kidney and calf's foot done in aged wine vinegar and served with a rich, dense jus. The most exciting combination is the suprême of squab coupled with cabbage and goose liver in an aged Port jus: an incredible medley of flavors. Desserts look every bit as delicious as they taste, with date soufflé and delicate cherry pancakes among the best. A few slip-ups this year: the waiter forgot to give us the dessert menu and the apple pie with honey ice cream was a tidbit oversweet. We wondered if the overwhelming and repeated success of the past wasn't starting to be taken foregranted... The cellar is rich in Alsatian wines and well-stocked in Burgundies and Bordeaux. Nice Alsatian reds for less than 200. C 700. M 510 (weekdays lunch), 620 (lunch Sat & Sun), 730.

 ## Hôtel des Berges

(See restaurant above)
Closed Mon, Tue, Feb. 2 stes 2,100-2,500. 9 rms 1,300-1,750. Bkfst 130. Rms for disabled. Air cond. Pkg.
The hotel's rooms are spacious, sunny, and prettily decorated. All feature blond-wood floors and ceilings and luxurious bathrooms with separate bath and toilet facilities. Scrumptious breakfasts with a selection of cold cuts, cheeses, and a delicious crème brûlée.

LEMBACH	67510
Paris 460 - Strasbourg 56 - Wissenbourg 15	Bas-Rhin

 ## Auberge du Cheval Blanc

4, rue de Wissembourg
03 88 94 41 86, fax 03 88 94 20 74
Closed Mon, Tue, 3 wks in Feb, 3 wks in Jul. Open until 9pm. Air cond. Pkg.
This is the Alsace dreams are made of: flowers everywhere you look, a half-timbered house with a pink stone porch and lovely wood-paneled dining room...and the stoic Fernand Mischler, who has officiated at this *auberge* since 1964. Yet he's always kept his repertoire fresh and exciting: the menu features succulent lamb sweetbreads with goose liver and poppy seeds, suprême of pike perch with schniederspaettle and new onions, and spiced breast of squab. The *symphonie de chocolats* is a real dessert treat. Plentiful cellar. Efficient and attentive service. C 400-600. M 175-410, 120 (children).

 ## Gimbelhof

9 km N on D 3 and Route Forestière
03 88 94 43 58, fax 03 88 94 23 30
Closed Nov 15-Dec 26. 7 rms 83-220. Bkfst 25. Restaurant. Half-board 160-190. Pkg.
The sumptuous forests surrounding this hotel are conducive to lots of long walks. Cozy rooms, gentle prices.

MARLENHEIM	67520
Paris 437 - Strasbourg 20 - Molsheim 12	Bas-Rhin

 ## Le Cerf

30, rue du Général-de-Gaulle
03 88 87 73 73, fax 03 88 87 68 08
Closed Tue, Wed. Open until 9:30pm. Priv rm 30. Terrace dining. Air cond. Pkg.
This bright, clean Alsatian house with a charming, flower-filled courtyard stands twenty kilometers from Strasbourg. And while the décor in the two dining rooms could stand some sprucing up, Michel Husser's classic cooking, based on intelligent reinterpretations of regional fare, makes the whole experience truly worthwhile. His presskopf is a remarkable regional classic; his fricassée of Kochersberg snails with hops in sorrel cream sauce is balanced and flavorful. But the cod with bacon and morels proves too complicated a pastiche of tastes. We recommend the fabulous rhubarb croustillant with strawberry coulis for dessert. And here's some welcome news: almost all dishes are available in mini-portions (at three-fifths the price), which means you don't have to break the bank to indulge! C 250-450. M 250 (lunch exc Sun, wine incl), 295, 395, 85 (children).

 ## Le Cerf

(See restaurant above)
Closed Tue, Wed. 15 rms 300-600. Bkfst 60. Conf. Pkg.
Although the rooms are a little on the dark side, they are well kept. A delight of a breakfast with a wide selection of homemade jams and jellies and kugelhopf. You can park your car in the courtyard of the farmhouse next door.

OBERNAI	67210
Paris 486 - Strasbourg 27 - Sélestat 23	Bas-Rhin

 ## Le Parc

169, route d'Ottrott
03 88 95 50 08, fax 03 88 95 37 29
Closed Sun dinner, Mon, Dec. Open until 9pm. Terrace dining. Air cond. Heated pool. No pets. Pkg.
This comfortable restaurant facing the city park is immensely popular with neighboring Germans and boasts a refined, classic décor: wood paneling warmed with a pink stone fireplace and pretty bouquets. And while energetic and affable owner Marc Wucher has opted for more in the way of tried-and-true and less in the way of innovations, Roland Schaeffer's fine, honest cooking really lets the flavors of his ingredients shine through. Service a bit on the

ceremonious side. C 400. M 190 & 335 (exc Sun), 280 (weekdays, Sat lunch, wine incl), 265 & 290 (Sun), 90 (children).

 ## Le Parc

(See restaurant above)
Closed Dec. 4 stes 1,100-1,500. 46 rms 470-990. Bkfst 65. Rms for disabled. Air cond. Heated pool. Pkg.
This handsome complex of half-timbered buildings houses rooms decorated in rustic or elegant styles with all the latest amenities, including spacious, well-equipped bathrooms.

OSTWALD	67540
Paris 501 - Strasbourg 7	Bas-Rhin

 ## Château de l'Ile

4, quai Heydt - 03 88 66 85 00, fax 03 88 66 85 49
Closed Sun dinner, Mon. Open until 9:30pm. Priv rm 150. Terrace dining. Air cond. Pool. Valet pkg.
This nineteenth-century château in the Strasbourg countryside now plays host to the talents of Megève's celebrated Jean Ferriz (taking over from Bruno Sohn). While resolutely modern in spirit, his cuisine attests to a mastery of regional specialties with a few Mediterranean influences. Comfortable seating in the slightly pompous dining room; some patrons prefer to eat on the pretty terrace overlooking the wooded banks of the Ill. Promising *winstub* annex. C 320-450. M 260 (weekday lunc, wine incl), 230-410, 140 (children).

 ## Château de l'Ile

(See restaurant above)
Open year-round. 4 stes 1,510-3,250. 58 rms 680-1,890. Bkfst 90-130. Rms for disabled. Half-board 430. Rm ser. Air cond. Conf. Pool. Valet pkg.
Like the restaurant, the hotel tends to overplay the "luxury" angle. But no matter: the rooms are gorgeous (decorated with lovely fabrics) and well equipped, and come with perfect bathrooms. Scrumptious breakfasts and all the charm of a country inn—at a conveniently close distance to the city.

ROUFFACH	68250
Paris 458 - Mulhouse 28 - Colmar 15	Haut-Rhin

 ## Les Tommeries

03 89 49 63 53, fax 03 89 78 53 70
Closed mid Jan-mid Mar. Open until 10:15pm. Garden dining. Heated pool. Tennis. Valet pkg.
La vie de château starts as soon as you are seated in the opulent main dining room or on the pretty terrace offering a panoramic view of the Rhine plain, with the Black Forest as a backdrop. You're sure to be further charmed by Didier Lefeuvre's mostly Alsatian cuisine, where low-key originality and precise preparation combine to produce enticingly delicate flavors. Magnificent wine list. Highly professional service. C

420. M 260 & 700 (wine incl), 270-370, 150 (children).

 ## Château d'Isenbourg

(See restaurant above)
Closed mid Jan-mid Mar. 2 stes 1,270-1,780. 38 rms 710-1,430. Bkfst 85-130. Rms for disabled. Half-board 1,070-1,130. Rm ser. Air cond. Conf. Heated pool. Tennis. Valet pkg.
The Château d'Isenbourg (be sure to get a good look at its amazing turret) is located on a vineyard estate, and once served as a residence for the Bishops of Strasbourg. Today it houses a series of plush lounges and rooms (not all equally spacious and comfortable). Relais et Châteaux.

SÉLESTAT	67600
Paris 434 - Strasbourg 47 - Colmar 22 - St-Dié 46	Bas-Rhin

 ## Abbaye La Pommeraie

8, av. Foch - 03 88 92 07 84, fax 03 88 92 08 71
Closed Sun dinner, Mon, mid Jul-beg Aug. Open until 9:30pm. Terrace dining. Valet pkg.
Erected in 1605 along the town's ramparts, this building began as a Cistercian abbey, then went on to house a baron. It now shelters a charming restaurant with a gorgeous garden-terrace on the outside and comfortable, refined surroundings within. Chef Daniel Stein gives the classics he knows so well a personal twist, turning out skillful creations that look as wonderful as they taste. Fine cellar, plentiful in Alsatian wines. C 360. M 290 (wine incl), 450.

 ## Abbaye La Pommeraie

(See restaurant above)
Open year-round. 2 stes 1,800. 12 rms 850-1,500. Bkfst 60-90. Half-board 675-1,150. Rms for disabled. Rm ser. Air cond. Valet pkg.
Spacious, elegant guest rooms prevail on the first floor, and cozy, mansard-roofed rooms with *chalet* flavor take over on the floor above. All rooms are air-conditioned and perfectly equipped. Lovely views of the garden and the old town. Outstanding welcome. Relais et Châteaux.

STRASBOURG	67000
Paris 488 - Colmar 69 - Basel 137 - Lyon 489	Bas-Rhin

12/20 L'Alsace à Table

8, rue des Franc-Bourgeois
03 88 32 50 62, fax 03 88 22 44 11
Closed dinner Dec 24 & Jan 1. Open until midnigh. Air cond.
Loyal locals crowd into this brasserie for regional fare such as seafood, choucroutes, tartares and carpaccios served with a smile in this ever-lively atmosphere. Good selection of wines by the pitcher, especially the Cleebourg Pinot Noir. C 250-400. M 109, 144, 55 (children).

L'Arsenal

11, rue de l'Abreuvoir
03 88 35 03 69, fax 03 88 35 03 69
Closed Sat lunch, Sun, Jul 28-Aug 25. Open until 10pm. Air cond.
The provincial wood décor in this venerable half-timbered house could use a little refreshing, but that's about the only criticism we can make! Thierry Bendler's "nouvelle cuisine alsacienne" takes the best of Alsace's natural bounty and turns it into whimsical, incredibly flavorful beer-based specialties. Some wines available by the pitcher. Friendly welcome. Good buy in the 200 F set meal. C 230. M 135 (weekday lunch), 130-300.

 Beaucour

5, rue des Bouchers
03 88 76 72 00, fax 03 88 76 72 60
Open year-round. 7 stes 950. 42 rms 380-780. Bkfst 65. Rms for disabled. Conf.
A group of eighteenth-century, half-timbered dwellings frame this establishment's splendid courtyard. The charming, individually decorated rooms within have all the latest equipment and boast superb bathrooms with jacuzzis. Perfect welcome.

 Buerehiesel

4, parc de l'Orangerie
03 88 45 56 65, fax 03 88 61 32 00
Closed Tue, Wed, Dec 24-Jan 7, Feb 17-27, Aug 7-20. Open until 9:30pm. Priv rm 65. Air cond. Pkg.
This old Alsatian farmhouse was transported piece by piece from Molsheim and rebuilt here, in the parc de L'Orangerie. And for 25 years now chef Antoine Westermann has been working his magic in its midst, reinterpreting hearty classics with a light, contemporary touch: frogs' legs pan-roasted with chervil and served with Alsatian schniederspaetle for example, or a ginger-roasted duck breast accompanied by the highest-quality vegetables in all Alsace. And the truly exceptional rhubarb tart is a "must" for dessert. We had serious doubts about the continuity of quality last year, but the wise learn from their "mistakes", and Westermann seems to have done just that. Another sign of this: his business luncheon with offerings such as warm-vegetable stew with white bean salad (he just loves veggies!), fresh-water fish stew cooked in Riesling wine, cheese and hazelnut oil millefeuille, and egg custard with orange slices. Wine cellar full of Alsatians at all prices, although most are on the high side. Commendable selection of Bordeaux and Burgundies. Relais et Châteaux. C 460-610. M 290 (weekday lunch), 350 (exc weekday lunch), 660, 120 (children).

 Carlton

15, pl. de la Gare - 03 88 32 62 39, fax 03 88 75 94 82
Open year-round. 60 rms 420-470. Bkfst 50. Rms for disabled. Conf. Garage pkg.
This establishment's comfy-cozy guest rooms clash quite markedly with its futuristic atmos-

phere and architecture. The atrium lobby rises four storeys to a glass roof, and there's even a glass-walled elevator (thrill-seekers, take note). Uninspired bar.

 Le Crocodile

10, rue de l'Outre
03 88 32 13 02, fax 03 88 75 72 01
Closed Sun, Mon, Jul 13-Aug 4, Dec 21-Jan 1. Open until 9:45pm. Priv rm 45. Air cond.
A spacious, flower-filled dining room sets the stage for Émile Jung's precise, light versions of classic cooking. Gorgeous foie gras in Gewurztraminer aspic, fresh, perfectly cooked pike perch, lamb spiked with a hint of red pepper. He seems to have listened to our comments last year; this year we noted more emotion and innovation in this resolutely classic cuisine. The fabulous wine list is sure to spark your enthusiasm, although prices are on the high side: 50 F for a glass of Cahors—5 F more would have bought you a half-bottle of Dubœuf Chiroubles at the Auberge de l'Ill! Fetish eating place for businesspeople and European deputies alike. Relais et Châteaux. C 470. M 295 (weekday lunch), 395 (weekday lunch, wine incl), 395 (weekday dinner, Sat), 640, 120 (children).

Hilton

Av. Herrenschmidt
03 88 37 10 10, fax 03 88 36 83 27
Open year-round. 5 stes 3,500-6,500. 241 rms 890-1,180. Bkfst 90. Rms for disabled. Restaurant. Rm ser. Air cond. Conf. Garage pkg.
Rooms in this hotel, set on a busy avenue, are well-soundproofed and spacious. And what they lack in charm, they make up for by being functional and perfectly appointed. Excellent welcome. Sauna, solarium, piano bar, and shops.

Régent-Contades

8, av. de la Liberté
03 88 15 05 05, fax 03 88 15 05 15
Open year-round. 9 stes 1,500-1,900. 38 rms 790-1,300. Bkfst 87. Rm ser. Air cond. Valet pkg.
This handsome nineteenth-century hotel is set on the banks of the Ill, just a stone's throw from the cathedral and theater. It boasts luxury suites and a health spa, along with comfortable, well-equipped standard rooms, some with balconies looking onto the cathedral.

And also...

Our selection of places for inexpensive, quick, or late-night meals.
La Cuiller à Pot (03 88 16 03 - 18 bis, rue Finkwiller. Open until 11pm.): Suzanne and Dominique will greet you like old friends in this family-run winstub where they offer Alsatian specialities as well as more traditional meat and fish dishes. Charming atmosphere (95-270).
Fink' Stuebel (03 88 25 07 57 - 26, rue Finkwiller. Open until 11pm.): Traditional is the only word for this winstub. Try the dumplings, tourtes and

choucroutes as you dine among the frescoes and polychrome woodwork. Twelve different wines by the glass (100-255).

Aux Mille Pâtes (03 88 35 55 23 - 8, pl. St-Étienne. Open until 11pm.): Feeling dramatic? Here's the place to go in this dining room decorated like a theatre set. Tasty fresh homemade pasta, prepared in original ways: hot spaghetti and salmon tart, tagliatelli with duck fillets, fettucini with calf's liver (120-260).

REGIONAL FOODS

Gastronomically speaking, the eastern provinces of Alsace, Lorraine, and Franche-Comté have one major point in common: a shared and abiding love of pork and charcuterie. Alsace is famous for choucroute—sauerkraut—and for a host of (mostly smoked) pork specialties, as well as for foie gras, pungent Munster cheese, kugelhopf and gingerbread, for its sprightly beers, and aromatic eaux-de-vie. Alsatians, it is said, could "make good brandy from a chair leg!"

• *BEER & BRANDY*

ÉGUISHEIM   68420 – Haut-Rhin

Wolfberger

6, Grand-Rue - 03 89 22 20 20
Ineffably fruity eaux-de-vie distilled from cherries, yellow plums, pears, raspberries, Damson plums, etc. The choice is huge.

SCHILTIGHEIM   67300 – Bas-Rhin

Brasserie Schutzenberger

8, rue de la Patrie - 03 88 33 14 67
Schutzenberger has been brewing beer in Alsace since 1740. Taste the light, mellow lager, the mid-weight amber beer, dark beer, and special beers produced at Christmas and in March. If you only have time to visit one brewery, make it this one.

• *CHARCUTERIE & FOIE GRAS*

COLMAR   68000 – Haut-Rhin

Glasser

18, rue des Boulangers - 03 89 41 23 69

All sorts of expertly smoked pork specialties in the best Alsatian tradition are available at Glasser.

STRASBOURG   67000 – Bas-Rhin

Arso

7, rue de la Mésange - 03 88 32 05 00
Lightly cooked or fully cooked foie gras, smoked charcuterie, and wonderful pâtés (don't miss the hazelnut-studded variety).

Frick Lutz

16, rue des Orfèvres - 03 88 32 60 60
Next to the cathedral is a traditional charcuterie with a full complement of local specialties: presskopf (headcheese), ham en croûte, beer sausage

• *CHEESE*

MULHOUSE   68100 – Haut-Rhin

Au Bouton d'Or

5, pl. de la Réunion - 03 89 45 50 17
Munster, the most famous local cheese, cops top billing here. But all the other cheeses are selected with equal discernment and matured on the premises in this, one of the best cheese shops in Alsace.

• *CHOCOLATE & CANDY*

COLMAR   68000 – Haut-Rhin

Jean

6, pl. de l'École - 03 89 41 24 63
Here's where you'll find the best chocolates in town, filled with superbly rich ganaches. Lots of regional sweets and gingerbread, too.

STRASBOURG   67000 – Bas-Rhin

Au Doux Pays de France

5, rue du Dôme - 03 88 32 74 84
Not far from the cathedral stands the Walter family's sweet shop. Since 1923 they have regaled Strasbourg with chocolates, marzipan, mellow gingerbread, and lots of other dainty indulgences.

• *PASTRY & COOKIES*

Jean-Paul Koffel

14, rue Taufflieb - 03 88 08 93 62
Gingerbread made with pure honey, in all
manner of charming shapes. Around Christmas,
the cakes are delightfully decorated with traditional Alsatian patterns and motifs.

WINE

Here in France's most picturesque
winegrowing region, touring and tasting can be delightfully combined along the
Wine Road of Alsace. From Marlenheim to
Thann, 36 villages welcome visitors with delicious white wines (and a single red, made
from Pinot Noir grapes). The grape varieties
in use are Chasselas and Sylvaner, which
make uncomplicated quaffing wines, Pinot
Blanc, Pinot Gris (also known as Tokay),
noble Riesling, aromatic Muscat d'Alsace,
and spicy, floral Gewurztraminer. Only the
last four may be used in *Grand Cru* wines, the
very best Alsace has to offer. The range of
prices is wide, starting with likable Sylvaners
that sell for not much more than 20 F to
ambrosial Late-Harvested Rieslings and
Gewurztraminers that fetch astronomical
sums.

Gustave Lorentz

35, Grand-Rue - 03 89 73 22 22, 03 89 73 30 49
Open daily 8am-noon & 2pm-5pm.
A full range of varietals for every budget; su-
perb (and expensive) dessert wines and Grands
Crus.

Léon Beyer

2, rue de la Ire-Armée (Tasting: 8, pl. du Château)
03 89 41 41 05, fax 03 89 23 93 63
Open Mon-Fri 8am-noon & 2pm-5pm.
A distinguished firm that dates back to the
Renaissance. Bone-dry Rieslings are the special-
ty of the house: look for Les Écaillers and the
Cuvée Particulière. Some older vintages are
available.

Cave de Pfaffenheim

5, rue du Chai - 03 89 78 08 08, fax 03 89 49 71 65
*Open daily 8am-noon & 2pm-6pm (Sun from
10am; summer until 7pm).* V.
This modern, efficiently run cooperative
winery boasts an enviable collection of medals.
The range of offerings is complete, with red,
white, and effervescent wines represented. The
cream of the crop are the Late-Harvested (Vendanges Tardives) and SGN (Sélection de Grains
Nobles) wines, made from grapes picked one by
one.

Cave Vinicole de Ribeauvillé

2, route de Colmar
03 89 73 61 80, fax 03 89 73 31 21
Open daily 9am-noon & 2pm-6pm.
The oldest wine cooperative in France sells
eight premium Grands Crus. Special mention for
the Altenberg Rieslings, which age beautifully.
But even the more modest bottles proposed here
(Pinot Blanc or Sylvaner) are of reliable quality.

Roger Jung et Fils

23, rue de la Ire-Armée
03 89 47 92 17, fax 03 89 47 87 63
Open daily 9am-noon & 2pm-7pm.
If you have the funds, buy the Jungs' SGN
(Sélection de Grains Nobles: sweet wines made
from individually harvested grapes with high
sugar levels and usually—not always—attacked
by "noble rot."). Otherwise, there are some attractively priced Riesling Grands Crus and
"plain" Rieslings.

BRITTANY

Of Saints, Celts, and Buccaneers

A broad land of low horizons that cul-minates in France's most westerly shores, Brittany rewards the traveler with ex-hilarating landscapes: windswept capes and sheltered fishing ports; strange megaliths and forests primeval; unspoiled islands and smart resorts; fortresses, châteaux, and snug granite cottages which inevitably recall that other—bigger—*Bretagne* across the Channel.

Brittany's ancient Celtic name, *Armorica*, means "country by the sea," and indeed all of its five *départements*—Ille-et-Vilaine, Côtes-d'Armor, Finistère, Morbihan, and Loire-At-lantique—touch the water. The Bretons are justly famed as fearless mariners: fishermen, navigators, explorers (Jacques Cartier, founder of Quebec, sailed from Saint-Malo), and daring *corsaires* like Dugay-Trouin who plagued English shippers. Inland Brittany, known in the Breton tongue as *Argoat* or "the wooded land," is crisscrossed by rivers, dotted with ponds and lakes, and was once thickly covered with forests. Some still survive; the forests of **Paimpont** and **Huelgoat**, for example, are vestiges of the legendary **Broceliande**, the haunt of Galahad, Merlin, Vivien and other Arthurian heroes. But nowadays the interior is a down-to-earth sort of place where farmers raise vegetables and forage crops, dairy cattle, and pigs for the local food-processing industries. Still, travelers who stray away from Brittany's coast will discover such gems as medieval **Josselin**, **Rochefort-en-Terre**, or the stately city of **Vitré**.

Brittany's earliest inhabitants were migrants from the Iberian peninsula, who arrived in successive waves from 4500 to 2000 BC, bringing with them the enigmatic Megalithic civilization. They left behind literally thousands of colossal standing stones or *menhirs*, and massive stone tables called *dolmens*. This Bronze Age legacy is a distinctive feature of Brittany's landscape; the most impressive megalithic ensemble is located in and around Carnac. The meaning of these monuments is still a puzzle, though it is believed that some were solar observatories, while others served a religious purpose. That the megaliths should have a supernatural significance would be in keeping with the Bretons' intense, bred-in-the-bone spirituality, a trait inherited from their Celtic ancestors along with a fondness for legends and lore.

A little Britain

The forebears of today's Bretons arrived around 460 AD, driven out of Great Britain by invading Angles and Saxons. Said to have crossed the Channel in "stone troughs," led by monks and priests, these Celtic colonists flowed into Armorica for two centuries. They revived and Christianized the peninsula, which they renamed Little Britain, later shortened to Brittany. Christianity plunged deep roots into the land: religion plays a vital role in Breton life. Scattered throughout the countryside are countless chapels and *calvaires*—stone carvings that depict the Crucifixion. And Bretons venerate hundreds of saints—many of them not officially canonized. There are patron saints and saints for animals, saints that heal or protect; some are "all occasion" saints, others are invoked to cure specific ailments. Two of the best-loved are Saint Anne and Saint Yves—the latter a native Breton and the most popular of all.

Religious feast days known as *pardons* are an age-old, uniquely Breton custom. The women don starched lace headdresses or *coiffes*, and tie lacy aprons over satin or velvet dresses adorned with ribbons, brocade, and embroidery. Men sport beribboned felt hats and fancy waistcoats. The faithful march in colorful procession, bearing candles, banners, and statues of saints to a chapel or church, where they pray for forgiveness. The *pardon* concludes with a lively *fest noz*, a celebration that goes on well into the night, to the music of *binious* (bagpipes) and *bombardes* (oboes).

Brittany was annexed to France relatively late in the nation's history, in 1532 after the death of Anne de Bretagne. Last Duchess of Brittany and twice Queen of France, Anne had struggled gallantly to keep her domain separate from the Crown. Today, in western Brittany especially, Bretons passionate about their Celtic identity and traditions, keep the language alive through songs, stories, poems—and comic books!

From **Vannes** to **Bénodet**, from **Sainte-Anne-la-Palud** to **Questembert**, sea and land—*Armor* and *Argoat*—come together deliciously in Brittany's cuisine. Sea salt is a regional staple. Salt gatherers called *paludiers* work the salt marshes at **Le Croisic**, raking the crystals into glistening piles. Roadside stands sell the fruits of their labors (including *fleur de sel* sea salt, favored by the best chefs) alongside locally grown vegetables. Brittany's onions and potatoes, cauliflowers, cabbages, and artichokes are a particular source of native pride. And then there is the astonishing variety of fresh fish and shellfish. Each port village has its specialty: **Le Guilvinec** is noted for sardines and tuna, **Erquy** for lobsters; **Saint-Brieuc** bay is famed for scallops and Cancale for oysters. The vineyards around Nantes produce Muscadet and Gros Plant, bracing white wines that perfectly complement this seafood.

Brittany abounds with wonderful places to go, things to do and sites to see. Here we've charted a course from Rennes up to Saint-Malo, then down to Cornouaille (Quimper) and **Morbihan Bay** (Carnac, Vannes) via **Perros-Guirec**, finally fetching up in the port city of Nantes.

Rennes, the capital of Brittany, was rebuilt after a fire destroyed the town in 1720; yet some handsome half-timbered houses survived the blaze, located around the (frankly unimpressive) cathedral and the stately Place de la Mairie. Worth taking in, too, are Rue Le Bastard, Rue d'Estrées, and the Marché des Lices, praised as the prettiest market in France (especially good on Saturdays). Rennes's student population, some 60,000 strong, nurtures a lively night life: Rue Saint-Michel (dubbed *"Rue de la Soif"*, or "Thirsty Street"!), Rue Saint-Georges, and Rue de Montfort overflow with cafés, crêperies, and bistros. In a more cultural vein, the Musée de Bretagne on Quai Émile-Zola offers an instructive overview of Breton history and traditions. It is housed in the same building as the Fine Arts Museum, which displays a superb collection that includes paintings by La Tour and the Pont-Aven School.

Oyster picnic on the beach

Historic **Saint-Malo**, rebuilt to its former likeness after devastating damage in 1944, was home port for explorers and privateers in days of yore. A walk along the ancient ramparts affords splendid sea views; on a rocky island a short way out is the tomb of the beloved French writer and statesman, Chateau-briand. Some 20 km east, the **Pointe du Grouin** exhilarates with panoramic vistas that stretch from the **Cap Fréhel** bird sanctuary to Mont-Saint-Michel bay. **Cancale**, just a few miles south, is the spot for an oyster fest. Vendors sell the shellfish right on

the beach—with a bottle of wine, they make a splendid picnic lunch. Gastronomic thrills of a higher order are in store at the four-toque Restaurant de Bricourt, where Olivier Rœllinger exalts the pure, briny flavors of Breton seafood.

Heading west, travelers should be sure to visit the stretch of Gulf Stream–warmed coast between Perros-Guirec and **Trébeurden** known as the **Côte de Granit Rose**. A high copper content tints the granite pink; wind, rain, and time have sculpted it into extraordinary shapes. Beautiful beaches and coves for sailing lure lots of vacationers in the high season.

A special quality of light, which lends striking clarity to greens and blues, attracts artists to **Cornouaille** on Brittany's southwestern shore. **Quimper**, the region's major city, is perhaps best known for its colorful ceramics, but it also boasts Brittany's most beautiful Gothic cathedral, a first-class art museum (on Place Saint Corentin) and a *vieille ville* brimming with charm. Nearby **Locronan** holds the unofficial title of "prettiest Breton village"; it is surely one of the most popular with tourists! In the high season, crowds figure prominently in **Pont-Aven** as well, where in 1886 Paul Gauguin and his disciples launched a revolutionary style of painting now known as the Pont-Aven School.

Carnac's megaliths loom at the head of **Quiberon Bay**; visitors immune to the spiritual aura of these prehistoric monuments can give themselves over to the pleasures of beachcombing and boating (to **Quiberon**, famous for its spas, or the enchanting island haven of **Belle-Île-en-mer**). Due east, the Golfe du Morbihan, an inland sea scattered with islands and stirred by complex tides, sustains a unique ecosystem of marine life and birds. The ancient, walled city of **Vannes** dominates the gulf, and offers a fine base for exploring the region by boat. This corner of Morbihan is also home to a cluster of exceptional restaurants: Régis Mahé in Vannes, Georges Paineau in Questembert, the Domaine de Rochevilaine in Billiers, and L'-Auberge Bretonne in La Roche-Bernard.

Last stop, the port city of **Nantes**, where the Erdre River meets the Loire. Long the capital of the Dukes of Brittany, Nantes's official allegiance now belongs to the Loire region; but history—and tradition—give the lie to this modern development. François II, the last duke of Brittany, is buried in Nantes's late-Gothic cathedral, his tomb marked by a fine Renaissance sculptural group. François began the construction of the city's most imposing monument, the Château des Ducs, where his daughter, the patriotic Anne de Bretagne, made her home. Today the Château also holds museums devoted to popular and decorative arts. The Musée des Beaux-Arts (behind the cathedral on Rue Clémenceau) is nothing short of superb, with works by La Tour, Watteau, Ingres, Courbet, Sisley, Monet, Kandinsky... Visitors who explore Nantes on foot reap the richest rewards as they wander through the old quarter around the Sainte Croix church, among the handsome town houses of the Ile Feydeau district (the—private—courtyards on Rue Kervégan afford fascinating glimpses of these eighteenth-century homes), and west to the aristocratic Place Royale and Place Graslin. Between those two squares, off Rue Crébillon, rises the graceful, glass-roofed Passage Pommeraye. Wine buffs should remember that a *Route des Vins* through the vineyards of Muscadet begins just outside the Nantes city limits. And indeed, what better way to conclude a tour of this welcoming province than by raising a glass in a toast with a hearty *Breizh o veva*—long live Brittany!

RESTAURANTS & HOTELS

AUDIERNE   29770
Paris 588 - Quimper 35 - Douarnenez 22   Finistère

Le Goyen

1, pl. Jean-Simon
02 98 70 08 88, fax 02 98 70 18 77
Closed Mon off-seas (exc hols), mid Nov-mid Mar. Open until 9pm. Terrace dining.
Will this restaurant, renowned as one of Brittany's best for a number of years, finally get its act together with the arrival of another new chef? The change comes too close to printing time, we haven't had a chance to try the cuisine. We'll keep you posted...

 Le Goyen

(See restaurant above)
Closed mid Nov-mid Mar. 3 stes 760-1,300. 21 rms 430-720. Bkfst 70. Half-board 495-950 (oblig in sea). Conf. Valet pkg.
We trust the recent opening of a second hotel across the port will give Le Goyen a boost. In the meantime, it still offers quality rooms and a consistently cordial welcome. Relais et Châteaux.

Please excuse us... (and the chefs). Menus are subject to the winds of change, and the dishes we've described may no longer be available when you visit.

BAULE (LA)   44500
Paris 463 - Vannes 72 - Saint-Nazaire 17   Loire-Atl.

 Castel Marie-Louise

1, av. d'Andrieu - 02 40 11 48 38, fax 02 40 11 48 35
Closed mid Jan-mid Feb. Open until 10pm. Garden dining. No pets. Pkg.
This opulently decorated seaside villa with its verdant terrace mirrors turn-of-the-century La Baule to a "T." And while chef Éric Mignard's modern, mostly fish repertoire is the model of decorum, the balances and flavors he achieves keep things interesting. Try his marrow bone with truffles and chicken au jus, with its wonderful mixtures of flavors, or his petits-gris (escargots) in pot-au-feu bouillon. Such a wealth of ideas surely merits another toque, even if the wine list prices just keep sliding up and up! Excellent welcome. C 500. M 170 (weekday lunch), 198-440.

 Castel Marie-Louise

(See restaurant above)
Closed mid Jan-mid Feb. 2 stes 1,700-2,250. 29 rms 810-1,900. Bkfst 90-140. Rms for disabled. Half-board 1,140-2,560. Tennis. Pkg.
This wonderful old Belle Époque villa is situated on a quiet expanse of pine-filled property near the water, not far from the grand casino. The rooms are tastefully appointed. Cocktail lounge. Relais et Châteaux.

12/20 La Ferme du Grand Clos

52, av. de Lattre-de-Tassigny - 02 40 60 03 30
Closed Wed off-seas, Mar 3-26, Sep 29-Oct 20. Open until 11pm. Garden dining.
The bill of fare at this cheerful little farmhouse includes crispy buckwheat galettes, traditional crêpes, delicious homestyle dishes, a wide assortment of ice cream desserts, and some nice little wines. Just right for a simple—and thoroughly enjoyable—meal. Delightful welcome. C 100-160.

 Manoir du Parc

3, allée des Albatros
02 40 60 24 52, fax 02 40 60 55 96
Closed Nov-Mar 20. 1 ste 500-700. 17 rms 310-520. Bkfst 50. No pets. Pkg.
The beach is at your doorstep, and squirrels romp in the pine-filled grounds surrounding this fetching nineteenth-century hotel. Rooms are prettily appointed in pastels, and you couldn't ask for better mattresses. Convenient location for those doing seawater therapy a few doors down.

 Royal

Av. Pierre-Loti - 02 40 11 48 48, fax 02 40 11 48 45
Closed Jan. 9 stes 1,500-2,200. 91 rms 800-1,440. Bkfst 90. Rms for disabled. Restaurant. Half-board

1,000-1,640. Rm ser. Conf. Heated pool. Tennis. Valet pkg.
This oceanfront, turn-of-the-century hotel is set on picturesque grounds and features spacious, well-equipped rooms. Some have their own terraces. Connected to the hydrotherapy center.

BELLE-ILE-EN-MER	56360
	Morbihan

 Castel Clara

In Port-Goulphar - 02 97 31 84 21, fax 02 97 31 51 69 Closed mid Nov-mid Feb. Open until 9pm. Garden dining. Heated pool. Tennis. No pets. Valet pkg.
Slowly but surely, chef Christophe Hardouin has been introducing interesting new dishes into the house's standard repertoire: they're based on the best local ingredients, and made all the more flavorful with its velvety sauces. The cellar is small and affordably priced. The restaurant is perched on a cliff, and the bright, comfortable dining room and terrace offer breathtakingly beautiful views. Excellent welcome and service. C 310-460. M 370 (dinner), 175, 250.

 Castel Clara

(See restaurant above)
Closed mid Nov-mid Feb. 10 stes 1,490-2,540. 32 rms 1,095-1,390. Bkfst 120. Rms for disabled. Half-board 675-940 (oblig in seas). Air cond. Conf. Heated pool. Tennis. Garage pkg.
This modern hotel-cum-spa boasts sunny, tastefully appointed rooms and cozy suites with a view over Mitterand's much-loved sea cove. Don't worry about taking half-board (compulsory in high season); the atmosphere is truly congenial and relaxed (as it should be by the seaside), and the meals offer lots of variety. Well-trained staff. Relais et Châteaux.

BÉNODET	29118
Paris 556 - Brest 88 - Quimper 16	Finistère

 Ferme du Letty

2 km SE, in Letty
02 98 57 01 27, fax 02 98 57 25 29
Closed Wed, Thu lunch, mid Oct-end Feb. Open until 9:30pm. Priv rm 30. Garden dining. Pkg.
This quaint blue-shuttered farmhouse with its stone fireplace and Quimper dishes is nestled near the "white sea," a sandy, wildlife-filled lagoon not far from Bénodet. The overall atmosphere is as modest as it is warm and friendly: you'd be tempted to order up crêpes and cider if you didn't know you were in one of Brittany's finest restaurants! Although he's just 33 years old, chef Jean-Marie Guilbault has a level head on his shoulders and his feet firmly planted in the fertile Breton soil. He uses local ingredients harvested from land and sea, pairing them like yin and yang, adding extra interest with a touch of exotic spice. Yet nothing is ever excessive, and he prefers to get straight to the point: local foie gras terrine turns sublime when paired with

oysters; wild curry leaves work their magic on sea scallops; buckwheat beer gives salmon a deliciously flavorful twist. For dessert, there's a strikingly original heart of lettuce compote. Wonderful house breads and a great selection of wines presided over by Jean-Marie's dad, a former Crillon bartender. Unbeatable value, with set menus starting at 98 F. We'd love to see a place like this in every region! C 250-400. M 98-490, 50 (children).

 Kastel-Moor et Ker-Moor

Av. de la Plage - 02 98 57 04 48, fax 02 98 57 17 96 Closed Nov-Mar. 82 rms 300-500. Bkfst 40. Restaurant. Half-board 380-540 (oblig in seas). Conf. Heated pool. Tennis. Pkg.
The Ker-Moor is set back in the greenery, and the Kastel-Moor is right on the beach. They share extremely spacious, well-equipped rooms, great sports facilities, and a pleasant wooded expanse between them. Average breakfasts.

BILLIERS	56190
Paris 458 - Nantes 86 - Vannes 27	Morbihan

 Domaine de Rochevilaine

Pointe de Pen-Lan
02 97 41 61 61, fax 02 97 41 44 85
Open daily until 9:30pm. Garden dining. Heated pool. Pkg.
This restaurant is like an island unto itself! Its site, an elegant waterfront estate, certainly works in its favor, and so does the delicious cuisine on offer. Patrice Caillaut's twenty years of experience serve him well producing perfectly-balanced flavors emphasized with refined, practically grease-free dishes. We savored the Breton lobster as tender as one can imagine, served in tasty clear herb bouillon, as well as the delicate little roasted langoustines with a well-crafted sweet pepper risotto. We pondered over a third toque when we tasted the almond crisp with thyme blossoms, served with Florence-fennel ice cream, a truly inspired combination of flavors, a true work of art. The cellar is improving and is less pricey than in the past. Very efficient, courteous service...even in high season. C 375. M 195-400, 120 (children).

 Domaine de Rochevilaine

(See restaurant above)
Open year-round. 1 ste 995-1,995. 39 rms 495-1,350. Bkfst 70. Rms for disabled. Half-board 425-895. Rm ser. Conf. Heated pool. Pkg.
The spacious, incredibly comfortable rooms here afford guests an ocean view. Impeccable service—you're taken in hand once you cross the threshold; wonderful breakfasts with freshly squeezed juices. Seawater therapy and fitness center.

BREST   29200
Paris 590 - Rennes 244 - Saint-Brieuc 145   Finistère

Le Nouveau Rossini

22, rue du Commandant-Drogou - 02 98 47 90 00
Closed Sun dinner, Mon, 1 wk in mar, mid Aug-mid Sep. Open until 10pm. Terrace dining. Air cond. Garage pkg.
This pretty Breton house features a vast dining room decorated in shades of yellow and beige, and an umbrella-shaded terrace overlooking a garden abloom with flowers. Chef Maurice Mevel's produces a neo-traditional cuisine revealing a festival of flavors and solid *savoir-faire*. We liked the red mullet vinaigrette with artichokes, the red mullet with confit bell peppers and the delicate little baby-lamb chops steamed in tarragon. Fine, reasonably priced cellar (just the place to host a wine-tasting evening!). C 300. M 120 (weekdays, wine incl), 200, 350, 75 (children).

Océania

82, rue de Siam - 02 98 80 66 66, fax 02 98 80 65 50
Open year-round. 1 ste 1,400. 80 rms 460-700. Bkfst 50. Rms for disabled. Restaurant. Air cond. Conf.
A good location for those whose aim is sightseeing. Modern-style hotel just around the corner from the convention center and both the naval and *Beaux Arts* museums. Rooms offer everything needed for comfort. Bar and possibility of eating in hotel.

CANCALE   35260
Paris 360 - Saint-Malo 14 - Dinan 34 - Rennes 72   Ille/Vil.

Restaurant de Bricourt   ۞

"Olivier Rœllinger", 1, rue Du Guesclin
02 99 89 64 76, fax 02 99 89 88 47
Closed Jul-Aug: Tue & Wed (exc dinner); mid Dec-mid Mar. Open until 10pm. Valet pkg.
Hidden up in Cancale's town center behind the church, the stately Rœllinger family manor treats guests to views of a serene Japanese garden and animated duck pond in place of spectacular ocean vistas. But what's outside isn't all that important...because from the second Olivier Rœllinger's cuisine touches your lips, you're sure to set sail on your own sea of dreams. Rœllinger, who dislikes the limelight (he maintains a low profile despite his 1994 "Chef of the Year" title), focuses his energies on giving diners a wonderful world to discover in every dish. When Brittany lost a chemist (his former profession) in Rœllinger, it gained a first-rate chef inspired by every ounce of magic in his region. The tides and seasons determine his offerings: a heavenly medley of sea scallops, clams, and sea urchin in a vinaigrette of herbs from the deep; delicate sea crab with young leeks in an aromatic lemongrass bouillon; incomparable grilled turbot flavored with paprika; spit-roasted salt-marsh lamb; a now-classic John Dory "retour des

Indes," seasoned with no fewer than fourteen spices. Mere words do not do justice to the ethereal tastes we experienced. Could it be that archangel Saint-Michel brushed wings with the Rœllingers? C 450. M 250 (lunch), 120 (children).

Les Rimains   🌲🎋

(See restaurant above)
Closed beg Jan-mid Mar. 6 rms 750-850. Bkfst 90. Pkg.
This six-room establishment is actually more like a private villa than a hotel. The prettily cozy guest quarters spread out along the *chemin des douaniers* (also known as "lovers' walk"!), perched on the cliffs overlooking Cancale harbor. No one can see you except the seagulls and the sea, and housekeeper Annette does everything in her power to make your stay perfect. Exquisite breakfasts. Relais et Châteaux.

CHAMPTOCEAUX   49270
Paris 359 - Angers 67 - Nantes 34   Maine/Loire

Les Jardins de la Forge

1, pl. des Piliers - 02 40 83 56 23, fax 02 40 83 59 80
Closed Sun, Mon dinner, Tue-Wed, Jan 21-Feb 5, Oct 7-22. Open until 9:15pm. Pkg.
Award-winning chef Paul Pauvert is a firm believer in exemplary results, which explains his reluctance to stray from the genuine, classic approach he so favors. He's at his best using traditional preparation methods refined with special effects, and demonstrates a remarkable talent for enhancing natural flavors: he grills or pan-roasts meat to perfection and serves it with delicious, light sauces, and has a wonderfully precise hand with fish. A thoroughly *bourgeois* setting in an old fortress dressed up with fairytale towers. Cellar rich in great Bordeaux and Loire Valley wines, with a nice choice of half-bottles. C 350-400. M 160 (weekdays), 230-400.

HENNEBONT   56700
Paris 482 - Vannes 56 - Concarneau 55   Morbihan

Château de Locguénolé

5 km S on D 781, route de Port-Louis
02 97 76 29 04, fax 02 97 76 39 47
Closed Mon off-seas (exc hols), Jan 2-Feb 5. Open until 9:30pm. Garden dining. Heated pool. Tennis. No pets. Pkg.
Locguénolé will always be one of the most highly regarded Relais and Châteaux listings both for its breathtaking beauty and the top-notch amenities it offers. Fine dining is among them, and Alyette de la Sablière has always regaled her guests with cuisine from France's best chefs. Marc Angelle's cuisine is what we might call "unconventional". Taking a cue from Bricourt's Rœllingers (but bearing in mind that Lorient was once the official headquarters of the Indies Company), Angelle makes discreet use of spices to underscore the flavor of his ingredients:

magnificent sole with braised endives and Indian spices; lamb with five-spice powder from China. But he also makes it clear that we are indeed in Brittany with tempting offerings like oven-roast turbot with bacon-laced baked potatoes, oysters with lemon jelly, tender baby squab done with tripe sausage and cabbage. His gingerbread cooked French-toast style and served with homemade vanilla ice cream is simple but oh-so-good. Summertime lunches are served in the orange grove by the pool. C 400-550. M 190, 260 (Sun lunch), 320, 480.

Château de Locguénolé 🛏♨

(See restaurant above)
Closed Jan 2-Feb 4. 4 stes 1,300-2,200. 24 rms 550-1,480. Bkfst 82-110. Half-board 640-1,202. Rm ser. Conf. Heated pool. Tennis. Pkg.
This resort comprises a nineteenth-century château and much older manor house set on a green, green lawn leading to the romantic banks of the Blavet (where a boat cemetery is visible at low tide). Be sure to take plenty of long walks through its 250-acres of land overflowing with flora and fauna. Rooms come with jacuzzi-equipped bathrooms and genuine character: some are built on two storeys under the eaves, and there's even a spacious, freestanding suite in the orange grove. Special arrangements for boat rides, deep-sea fishing, hydrotherapy spa sessions, etc. Relais et Châteaux.

LORIENT	56100
Paris 491 - Quimper 68 - Rennes 145	Morbihan

 L'Amphitryon

Quartier Keryado, 127, rue du Colonel-Müller
02 97 83 34 04, fax 02 97 37 25 02
Closed Sat lunch & Sun (exc Easter & Mother's day), 2nd wk of Easter school hols, Sep 1-10. Open until 10:30pm. Air cond. No pets. Pkg.
Located as it is in Lorient's northern suburbs (in a business district, no less), uninformed passers-by might well think this small, seemingly ordinary *auberge* was a truck stop. But there's nothing ordinary about what awaits guests inside: from the warm welcome to the cigars at the end of the meal—by way of the petits-fours— and this thanks to chef-owner Jean-Claude Abadie (who hails from the Pyrenees region, but took a Breton wife). His roots explain the foie gras appetizer on the menu, then things take a local turn: tiny, savory snails in a basil jus, green asparagus with crab meat and caviar, scrumptious sea bass in a truffle vinaigrette, and lush desserts like the warm cocoa tart. Ever-smiling Véronique Abadie oversees the diligent, attentive service. Superb selection of wines from every region. Special coffee and brandy menu. This restaurant's name is definitely synonymous with gracious hospitality! C 350. M 125 (lunch), 160 (weekdays), 250-390, 80 (children).

See also: **Hennebont**

MOËLAN-SUR-MER	29116
Paris 514 - Concarneau 26 - Pont-Aven 16	Finistère

 Les Moulins du Duc

02 98 39 60 73, fax 02 98 39 75 56
Closed Dec 1-15, Jan-Feb. Open until 10pm. Priv rm 60. Garden dining. Heated pool. Valet pkg.
A superb sixteenth-century mill set in leafy surroundings near the Belon plays host to this restaurant. The dining room is decorated with beams and warm copper accents; chef Daniel Tauvel is especially talented at interpreting fish dishes and regional fare (try a game dish if the season is right). Limited wine list; somewhat on the expensive side. Charming welcome. C 250-400. M 150, 215, 360, 60 (children).

 Les Moulins du Duc 🛏♨

(See restaurant above)
See restaurants for closings. 5 stes 790-1,100. 22 rms 350-850. Bkfst 50. Rms for disabled. Half-board 475-725. Rm ser. Conf. Heated pool. Valet pkg.
This hamlet hideaway nestled in the woods houses some renovated rooms–and some that could benefit from sprucing up. However, all have good bathrooms. Sauna and nice pool.

NANTES	44000
Paris 392 - Rennes 106 - Angers 87	Loire-Atl.

 Adagio Central Hôtel

4, rue du Couëdic - 02 51 82 10 00, fax 02 51 82 10 10
Open year-round. 6 stes 720-1,500. 156 rms 570-640. Bkfst 58. Rms for disabled. Restaurant. Half-board 500-750. Air cond. Heated pool. Garage pkg.
This recently renovated establishment is situated near the Place Royal. Lively jazz entertainment nightly in the bar.

12/20 **La Cigale**

Pl. Graslin - 02 51 84 94 94, fax 02 51 84 94 95
Open daily until 12:30am. Terrace dining.
When you're in Nantes, stop by to admire the dining room's listed nineteenth-century décor (gorgeous mosaics, ceramics and woodwork). If you stay to eat, try one of the excellent raw seafood platters or generous brasserie-style dishes on the menu. Small but intriguing cellar. Smiling welcome. C 230-300. M 135 (lunch, wine incl), 100 (dinner, wine incl), 150 (dinner), 39 (children).

PLANCOËT	22130
Paris 385 - Dinard 14 - St-Brieuc 47	Côtes-d'Armor

 Chez Crouzil 🕃

Les Quais - 02 96 84 10 24, fax 02 96 84 01 93
Closed Sun dinner & Mon (exc Jul-Aug), 3 wks in Jan. Open until 9:30pm. Garden dining. Air cond. Garage pkg.
Restaurant owners in a state of woe over the recession should take a lesson from Jean-Pierre Crouzil, whose solid, classic dishes—based on

top-notch ingredients and respectful preparation—come with down-to-earth price tags. The cellar offers excellent value, too, with some great Bordeaux on hand. Try his generous, flavorful lobster salad with potatoes and truffles or his fresh, tasty, fried-to-perfection red mullets served in their juices, an exquisitely simple dish that touches on three toques. Gorgeous dark-chocolate soufflé. The bright, pretty dining room is painted pink, and air conditioning has been installed. Rich but reasonable wine list. C 400. M 150 (lunch), 225-500, 100 (children).

 L'Écrin

(See restaurant above)
Closed 2 wks in Jan. 7 rms 400-800. Bkfst 70-90. Half-board 450-650. Rm ser. Conf. No pets. Garage pkg.
Colette Crouzil (Jean-Pierre's wife) runs this luxury establishment with comfortable, roomy guest quarters and wonderful bathrooms. Extraordinary Breton breakfasts. Excellent value.

PONT-AVEN   29930
Paris 522 - Lorient 36 - Quimper 38   Finistère

 Moulin de Rosmadec

02 98 06 00 22, fax 02 98 06 18 00
Closed Sun dinner off-seas, Wed, Feb, Nov 15-30. Open until 9:30pm. Priv rm 25. Garden dining. Pkg.
When this pretty fifteenth-century mill fell victim to a flood a couple of years ago, the owners were quick to rescue its beautiful antique, painting and curio-laden décor. Tourists and regulars come here by the dozens to enjoy brother-team Frédéric and Franck Sébilleau's seafood; some dishes have a distinct—and delicious—Provençal accent this year. Friendly welcome and speedy, efficient service. Well-balanced quality cellar. C 360. M 160, 295, 395.

 Hostellerie de Rosmadec   ♠♥

(See restaurant above)
Closed Feb, Nov 15-30. 4 rms 400-470. Bkfst 42. Pkg.
There are just four charming rooms in this little inn adjacent to the mill. And the setting couldn't be more romantic, pretty riverside garden and all. Super breakfasts.

 La Taupinière

Route de Concarneau, croissant Saint-André
02 98 06 03 12, fax 02 98 06 16 46
Closed Mon dinner & Tue (exc Jul-Aug). Annual closings not available. Open until 9:15pm. Air cond. No pets. Pkg.
A veranda and garden only add to the many charms of this cozy chalet nestled among the pines. The kitchen opens out onto a cheerful, unpretentious dining room where patrons savor tempting seafood cooked simply and precisely by Guy Guilloux: perfect poached oysters and sea scallops in a light chive sauce; exceptional

smoky-flavored grilled lobster. And even if the desserts leave a little something to be desired, the admirable cellar offers a good choice of Bordeaux and half-bottles at fair prices. C 350-450. M 265-465.

QUESTEMBERT   56230
Paris 423 - Redon 33 - Vannes 26 - Rennes 88   Morbihan

 Georges Paineau   ۞

13, rue Saint-Michel
02 97 26 11 12, fax 02 97 26 12 37
Closed Mon & Tue lunch (exc Jul-Sep & hols). Open until 10:30pm. Garden dining. Garage pkg.
While the market in this hard-to-find village is splendid indeed, Georges Paineau's restaurant is definitely the main attraction. The décor is either low or high profile depending on which dining room you're in, and the cellar, although rich in offerings, seems somewhat less than passionate. The food, however, gives new meaning to this latter adjective: it is precise and refined down to the last detail (the way aromas intermingle, the elegant use of counterpoints). This is best illustrated by a single example: artichokes and tiny scallops gently cajoled by coriander then brought to a sublimely flavorful peak with turmeric. A dish like this, where ingredients are combined, cooked, and enhanced to absolute perfection, is the sign of a truly great chef. We only wish everything were so good: the welcome and service seemed a bit on the downside. C 400-600. M 180 (weekdays), 295, 390, 520, 110 (children).

 Le Bretagne et sa Résidence

(See restaurant above)
Closed Sun & Mon (exc Jul-Aug & hols). 3 stes 980-1,400. 9 rms 580-980. Bkfst 90. Rms for disabled. Half-board 750-1,010. Rm ser. Conf. Garage pkg.
The newer rooms and suites within this establishment's ivy-covered walls are colorfully decorated and remarkably spacious and comfortable. The overall décor is slightly incongruous in places. Festive breakfasts. Gift shop with gourmet products and other offerings. Relais et Châteaux.

QUIBERON   56170
Paris 498 - Lorient 52 - Vannes 46 - Auray 28   Morbihan

Le Thalassa

Pointe de Goulvars
02 97 50 20 00, fax 02 97 50 46 32
Closed Jan. Open until 9:45pm. No pets. Pkg.
Angelo Orilieri has set his mostly fish cuisine back on the right track, and this year we enjoyed a variety of light, interesting dishes attesting to precise cooking and harmonious flavors. The menu offers irrefutable proof that food for the calorie-conscious (most of the patrons are in the area on spa stays) doesn't have to be bland and boring. The wine list could use some diversifica-

tion. Efficient service in a dining room with a winter garden and magnificent view of the sea. C 370. M 225-460, 120 (children).

 ## Le Thalassa Sofitel

(See restaurant above)
Closed Jan. 17 stes 1,220-4,000. 116 rms 455-1,610. Bkfst 70. Rms for disabled. Half-board 750-2,500. Rm ser. Conf. Heated pool. Tennis. Pkg.
Most of the pastel-hued rooms in this establishment have been renovated and boast splendid ocean views. Bathrooms a bit on the small side. Direct access to the hydrotherapy spa from the hotel. A buffet is available for quick meals in high season.

RENNES	35000
Paris 348 - Nantes 106 - Le Mans 153	Ille/Vil.

 ## L'Escu de Runfao

11, rue du Chapitre
02 99 79 13 10, fax 02 99 79 43 80
Closed Sat lunch, Sun dinner, 1 wk in Jan, Aug 3-19. Open until 10pm. Terrace dining. Pkg.
In their wonderful sixteenth-century house in the heart of old Rennes, Alain Duhoux proffers high-quality cuisine prepared with the finest regional ingredients, and his efficient, ever-smiling wife Nathalie makes each and every guest feel like a V.I.P. Try the pot-au-feu with tender sea scallops bathed in a flavorful poultry jus, succulent Breton lobster in herb jus, and exquisite tarte Tatin. The first two set-price menus give you a good idea of the chef's talents without breaking the bank, while the 410 F tasting menu is an experience in and of itself! Splendid cellar. C 300-350. M 128 (weekdays), 198-410, 90 (children).

12/20 Le Gourmandin

4, pl. de Bretagne - 02 99 30 42 01
Closed Sat lunch, Sun, 2nd wk of Feb school hols, Aug 1-21. Open until 10pm. Air cond.
This restaurant's repertoire won't bowl you over with its creativity, but the chef has some good ideas nonetheless, and the ingredients he uses are prime. Nice range of attractively priced Loire wines. Friendly, smiling welcome in the dining room or adjoining veranda. C 200. M 80 (weekdays), 110, 155.

 ## Lecoq-Gadby

156, rue Antrain
02 99 38 05 55, fax 02 99 38 53 40
Open year-round. 1 ste 1,100. 11 rms 550-750. Bkfst 60. Rms for disabled. Restaurant. Rm ser. Pkg.
The former owner's daughter took this rather rundown stone building and spruced it up into a really pretty hotel with a pretty garden and terrace. Some rooms have balconies. Extremely comfortable and careful attention paid to your every need.

ROCHE-BERNARD (LA)	56130
Paris 441 - La Baule 31 - St-Nazaire 35	Morbihan

L'Auberge Bretonne

2, pl. Du Guesclin
02 99 90 60 28, fax 02 99 90 85 00
Closed Thu, Fri lunch, Nov 12-Dec 1, Jan 6-24. Open until 9pm. Valet pkg.
Our most recent dining experience here was as sublime—and adventure-packed—as ever: from an escarole-stuffed sea urchin appetizer through to a scoop of daisy (no kidding!) ice cream for dessert, by way of spider-crab charlotte in cockle and bean vinaigrette, superb roast turbot served with succulent marrow and vegetable confit, and equally memorable farm-fresh pork coupled with an interesting tripe sausage parmentier. The great Robuchon himself called Jacques Thorel "a wonderful cook," and his creative talents never cease to amaze us! He's a wizard at coaxing deep, clear flavors out of the finest ingredients, and never misses out on an opportunity to surprise and delight his guests. We'll never forget his godaille du Croisic, a mix of mini-fish only available during a short (March-April) season, served in an invigorating consommé. Then there's the added pleasure of the gigantic cellar housing 38,000 bottles and 1,200 varieties of wine, some from as far away as Lebanon, and New Zealand! Eat, drink, and be merry in the sunny cloister-style dining rooms surrounding the garden. And if rumor (wrongly) has it that Thorel is dark and moody, his wife Solange is all smiles. To avoid embarrassing situations, ask the prices before following the waiters' suggestions on food and wine. C 450. M 210-600, 120 (children).

 ## L'Auberge Bretonne

(See restaurant above)
Closed Nov 12-Dec 1, Jan 6-24. 8 rms 450-1,400. Bkfst 80. Rms for disabled. Half-board 750-1,100 (oblig in seas). Rm ser. Conf. Valet pkg.
The hotel has neat, comfy, soundproofed rooms and serves copious pastry-laden breakfasts with yogurt, compote and fruit juice, all homemade. Relais et Châteaux.

ROSCOFF	29680
Paris 561 - Brest 63 - Morlaix 28 - Landivisiau 27	Finistère

Brittany

Bd Ste-Barbe - 02 98 69 70 78, fax 02 98 61 13 29
Closed Nov-Mar. 2 stes 750-940. 23 rms 390-690. Bkfst 58. Rms for disabled. Restaurant. Half-board 390-610. Pkg.
This elegant manor house offers all the refinement and comfort you could expect in such a setting. You'll be bowled over by the tasteful decoration and the carefully selected furniture in the rooms. And the bathrooms are of the same caliber.

Looking for a town or restaurant? A winery? A gastronomic specialty or a celebrated chef? Consult the alphabetical index to locate them quickly and easily.

Le Temps de Vivre ✪

Pl. Lacaze-Duthiers - 02 98 61 27 28
Closed Sun dinner & Mon (exc Jul-Aug), 2 wks in Feb, 2 wks in Oct. Open until 9:15pm.
This restaurant is aptly named, for while it reminds us to stop and smell the roses, it also implies that good things just get better with time. And we couldn't be more delighted with the cuisine and its perfectly matched, subtle combinations of flavors: wonderful farm-fresh poultry offerings and tip-top seafood, done simply and effectively. Judicious selection of wines rich in half-bottles. Consult the annotated coffee list to choose your end-of-meal cup. C 300-400. M 165-350.

SAINT-MALO	35400
Paris 366 - Rennes 69 - Dinan 34 - St-Brieuc 76	Ille/Vil.

La Korrigane

39, rue Le Pomellec
02 99 81 65 85, fax 02 99 82 23 89
Closed Jan. 12 rms 400-750. Bkfst 55. Garage pkg..
This romantic old mansion boasts a lounge with a piano and white marble fireplace and rooms with period furnishings. A refined, elegant place to stay.

Manoir de la Grassinais

12, rue de la Grassinais
02 99 81 33 00, fax 02 99 81 60 90
Closed Sun dinner & Mon off-seas, mid Dec-mid Jan. Open until 9:30pm. Terrace dining. Pkg.
The outskirts of Saint-Malo's industrial district is the unlikely setting for this pretty old house with its attractive blond-wood dining room where the locals often gather to enjoy Christophe Bouvier's "cuisine with character." Bouvier's regional ingredients are skillfully prepared and presented. Likable little cellar with good selection of Bordeaux, from the most unknown to the famous ones. Smiling welcome, reasonable checks. C 230-270. M 98 (weekdays), 120-190, 60 (children).

SAINTE-ANNE-LA-PALUD	29127
Paris 569 - Quimper 25 - Douarnenez 16	Finistère

Hôtel de la Plage

02 98 92 50 12, fax 02 98 92 56 54
Closed mid Nov-Mar. Open until 9pm. Priv rm 40. Air cond. Heated pool. Tennis. No pets. Pkg.
This very Breton of houses with its splendid seaview, paintings and costumes, produces a cuisine in keeping with its location. Jean-Pierre Gloanec's impeccable ingredients produce such locally-inspired dishes as lobster rye with kig ha farz vegetables, John Dory lipig with baby clams, and smoked bass served with a potato kouignaman. Diversified cellar, rich in Bordeaux. Attentive service in a veranda dining room overlooking the deep blue sea. C 400. M 220- 410, 100 (children).

Hôtel de la Plage

(See restaurant above)
Closed mid Nov-Mar. 4 stes 1,000-1,350. 26 rms 800-1,350. Half-board 750-1,100. Heated pool. Tennis. Pkg.
This hotel's spacious, sun-filled, cozy rooms are done up like elegant guest rooms in a private residence, and boast splendid views of the bay of Douarnenez. Superb collection of Mathurin Méhuest paintings. Delicious breakfasts. Relais et Châteaux.

SORINIÈRES (LES)	44840
Paris 391 - Nantes 9	Loire-Atl.

L'Épicurien

Route des Sables-d'Olonne
02 40 04 40 25, fax 02 40 31 28 45
Open daily until 9pm. Garden dining. Pool. Pkg.
The cavernous dining room, formerly a monks' library, today bids a warm welcome to "consumers" of new chef Tony Riant's tempting cuisine. The combination of his good-quality basic ingredients and solid techniques yield such taste-tinglers as Challand duck breast with slivers of foie gras, red mullet with chervil blanc-manger, and lamb sweetbread crisp with morels, all on a 200 F set-price menu. The cellar boasts some very nice Bordeaux, but could stand more half-bottles. Accommodating staff. C 280-360. M 140-440, 85 (children).

Abbaye de Villeneuve ♠♣

(See restaurant above)
Open year-round. 3 stes 1,095-1,245. 21 rms 390-890. Bkfst 65-75. Half-board 410-925. Rm ser. Conf. Pool. Pkg.
This Cistercian-style abbey dating from the eighteenth century has been turned into a deluxe, impeccably maintained hotel with a magnificent circular pool. The charming rooms are decorated with antique furniture. Breakfasts are wonderful, and the staff is most courteous.

TRÉBEURDEN	22560
Paris 526 - St-Brieuc 77 - Lannion 11	Côtes-d'Armor

Manoir de Lan Kerellec

Allée Centrale - 02 96 15 47 47, fax 02 96 23 66 88
Closed Nov 15-Mar 15. Open until 10pm. Garage pkg.
Patrons are still flocking to this handsome granite edifice by the sea, where chef Reverdy regales them with the freshest, highest quality ingredients imaginable, crafted into the delicious likes of galette of jumbo crab with vinaigrette; golden John Dory in an anise and lime marinière, and warm strawberries topped with mint sherbet. Relaxed, smiling service. C 270-340. M 140 (lunch), 190-370, 85 (children).

Manoir de Lan Kerellec

(See restaurant above)
Closed Nov 15-Mar 15. 3 stes from 2,000. 16 rms 500-1,500. Garage pkg.
This hotel features typically Breton architecture and spacious rooms decorated with remarkable taste. They overlook the sea (especially beautiful here along the pink granite coast). Irreproachable service. Relais et Châteaux.

VANNES	56000
Paris 454 - Lorient 56 - Rennes 106	Morbihan

Régis Mahé

"Le Richemont,"
Pl. de la Gare - 02 97 42 61 41
Closed Sun dinner, Mon, Feb school hols, 2 wks in Nov. Open until 9:30pm. Pkg.
The bright white Gothic-style dining room of this establishment across from the train station is stage to Régis Mahé's sunny, refined cooking: beautifully fresh red mullet fillets poached with aromatic herbs capture the soul of the South of France, accompanied by black olives underscored with chutney-laced fromage blanc. Savory sole meunière and roast potatoes with mozzarella: a generous piece of fish simply cooked on the bone, with light, lemony flavor. Delicious lobster risotto (firm, tasty and perfectly cooked) with garden-fresh peas, mushrooms, and tomatoes. Splendid frozen savarin with Malaga raisins and bitter-orange sauce. The set menu is good value, but it must be ordered by everyone at the table. Small, reasonably priced cellar with a good selection of Loire wines and wines available by the glass (priced from 18 to 42 F). Courteous, efficient service. Air conditioning would be a welcome addition. C 350-500. M 165 (lunch, exc Sun, wine incl), 210 (weekday dinner), 260, 285, 100 (children).

 ## La Marébaudière

4, rue Aristide-Briand
02 97 47 34 29, fax 02 97 54 14 11
Open year-round. 41 rms 290-435. Bkfst 43. Rms for disabled. Conf. Pkg.
This quiet, squeaky-clean hotel is located in the city center, 300 yards from the ramparts. Efficient, friendly service.

See also: **Billiers, Questembert**

REGIONAL FOODS

There are two Brittanies: the inland region traditionally called *Argoat*, and coastal Brittany, or *Armor*. The inland portion long suffered from great poverty, before becoming one of the most productive agricultural regions in France. Pork, poultry, cattle, dairy products, fruit, and vegetables are now produced here in abundance. Large, efficient food-processing industries have put down roots as well. Coastal Brittany's economy is based on tourism and on the sea and its resources. Lured by its wild beauty, spiritual traditions, and fascinating culture, visitors throng to Brittany. And they are charmed to discover the region's fabulous seafood, the delicious crêpes and buckwheat galettes, and typical charcuterie (andouille sausage, ham, pâtés). The taste of Brittany is also found in subtly salted Breton butter, rich shortbread cookies (sablés), unusual salt-butter caramels, and snappy, refreshing hard cider.

• *CHARCUTERIE*

BAYE	29130 – Finistère

Philippe Danielou

180, rue Jean-Marie Carer - 02 98 96 80 13
Andouille sausage made according to a family recipe. Enjoy it either hot or cold.

CESSON-SÉVIGNÉ	35510 – Ille/Vil.

Delaunay

19, rue du Bas-Village - 02 99 50 91 94
The foremost producer of pâté rennais, a typical Breton staple that is traditionally eaten hot or cold, with potatoes and buckwheat crêpes.

GUÉMÉNÉ-SUR-SCORFF	56160 – Morbihan

Rivalan Quidu

5, rue Bellevue - 02 97 51 21 10
Guéméné's famous smoked andouille sausage is one of the oldest types of charcuterie produced in Brittany. This firm makes it in the traditional fashion, and also proposes a delicious country-style pâté breton.

• *CHOCOLATE & CANDY*

LA BAULE	44500 – Loire-Atl.

Confiserie Manuel

2-4, av. du Général-de-Gaulle - 02 40 60 20 66
Traditional French candies—berlingots, nougatines—and the famous niniches (a kind of lollipop) that vacationers adore.

BREST 29200 – Finistère

Histoire de Chocolat

60, rue de Siam - 02 98 44 66 09
Extremely good chocolates, with a high cocoa content. La Recouvrance, an irresistible trio of praline-filled chocolates, is the most popular house specialty.

QUIBERON 56170 – Morbihan

Le Roux

18, rue du Port-Maria - 02 97 50 06 83
This is the place to come for delectable Breton caramels, made with the local lightly salted butter. Unusual chocolates, too, with buckwheat-, beer-, ginger-, or chicory-flavored fillings.

• *CIDER*

COLPO 56390 – Morbihan

Les Cidres Fermiers de la Vallée de la Claie

Kernuel - 02 97 66 82 28
Dark-hued Breton farmhouse cider, as well as other fairly distinctive ciders, all with good fruit flavor.

LA FORÊT-FOUESNANT 29133 – Finistère

François Séhédic

Ty Glas - 02 98 56 96 12
Ciders from this area are the best and most distinctively Breton. An ideal beverage to accompany crêpes and buckwheat crêpes.

PLEUDIHEN-SUR-RANCE 22690 – Côtes-d'Armor

Musée du Cidre

La Ville-Hervy - 02 96 83 20 78
At this interesting little museum you can buy cider with a fruity, rustic flavor.

• *GOURMET SPECIALTIES*

Sardines

CONCARNEAU 29110 – Finistère

Gonidec

2, rue Bisson - 02 98 97 07 09
These delicious, top-quality tinned sardines are available packed in olive oil, peanut oil,

spiked with lemon or with hot pepper. Tasty fish soup, too.

QUIBERON 56170 – Morbihan

La Belle Iloise

ZA "Plein Ouest" - 02 97 50 08 77
These Breton sardines are packed according to traditional methods. Try the white-tuna fillets as well. Sardine museum on the premises.

La Quiberonnaise

30, rue du Port de Pêche - 02 97 50 12 54
Sardines (packed in olive or peanut oil, with tomato sauce or lemon) hold the spotlight here, but the other tinned foods are also worth trying.

Sea Salt

GUÉRANDE 44350 – Loire-Atl.

La Maison des Paludiers

18, rue des Prés Garnier - 02 40 62 21 96
This charming country museum tells the story of salt gatherers. Sea salt is sold in the museum shop.

• *PASTRY & COOKIES*

LANESTER 56600 – Morbihan

La Lorientaise

Le Bel Air - 02 97 76 02 09
Thin, crunchy galettes bretonnes made according to an old-fashioned recipe are featured here.

NANTES 44000 – Loire-Atl.

Michel Hoyet

19, rue Paul Bellamy - 02 40 48 15 20
The galettes (cookies) sold here are light, delicate, and deliciously buttery.

QUIBERON 56170 – Morbihan

Maison Riguidel

38, rue du Port-Maria - 02 97 50 07 41
You won't find better kouing amann (that ultrarich, typically Breton butter cake) than the one made here. Special packaging for transport.

SAINT-JEAN-TROLIMON 29120 – Finistère

Biscuiterie La Bigoudène

Route de Tronoën - 02 98 58 12 21
Near the famous Tronoën *calvaire*, this cottage is a well-known source for tasty galettes bretonnes made with fresh butter, and packed in pretty painted tins.

WINE

From Brittany's southernmost reaches, at the western end of the Loire, comes Muscadet, a bright, bracing white wine made from the Melon de Bourgogne grape. Look for the phrase *sur lie* on the label: it means that the Muscadet has aged for several months on its lees, a process that yields a fuller, fruitier wine with yeasty notes and the hint of a spritz on the tongue.

Gros Plant, made from the Folle Blanche grape, does not pretend to be a world-class wine, but its sharp, crisp tang makes a pleasing counterpoint to oysters and other seafood. Like Muscadets, the finer Gros Plants rest for a few months on their lees; the best examples display a flinty, citrusy character.

BOUAYE   44830 – Loire-Atl.

Michel et Hervé Choblet

11, rue de Nantes - 02 40 65 47 69, fax 02 40 32 64 01
Open Mon-Sat.
  Elegant, concentrated Muscadets from old vines, and fragrant, well-made Gros Plant. Exceptional value.

Domaine des Herbauges

02 40 65 44 92, fax 02 40 32 62 93
Open Mon-Sat 9am-noon & 2pm-6:30pm.
  Elegant, full-bodied Muscadets that get even better with a few years of cellaring.

CORCOU-SUR-LOGNE   44650 – Loire-Atl.

Domaine du Parc

Daheron, Le Parc - 02 40 05 86 11, fax 02 40 05 94 98
Open Mon-Sat 8am-12:30pm & 2pm-6pm.
  Fine Muscadets, Gros Plants, and other regional wines from an independent grower-winemaker.

Champagne
DEUTZ

FONDÉ EN 1838

Plus on est Champagne plus on l'aime.

UN VIGNOBLE SÉLECTIONNÉ.

Quarante hectares dans les meilleurs crus ont été patiemment réunis pour assurer la base qualitative du Champagne Deutz. Viennent s'y ajouter soixante hectares sous contrats appartenant à des vignerons réputés pour l'excellence de leurs vignes.

UNE TECHNIQUE ÉPROUVÉE.

Trois kilomètres de caves exceptionnelles à plus de 20 mètres sous terre et un outil de travail performant garantissent une qualité de vinification au plus haut niveau champenois.

UNE TRADITION, UN STYLE.

Le savoir-faire des hommes, les principes originaux de vinification parcellaire, la composition des cuvées transmise de père en fils depuis cinq générations, une longue maturation dans des conditions idéales donnent au Champagne Deutz sa personnalité et son style inimitable et constant.

UNE CONVICTION...

Deutz doit se maintenir au plus haut niveau de qualité parce que la spécificité traditionnelle des Grandes Marques est la seule garantie de l'image et de la réputation inégalable du Champagne à travers le monde.

Champagne DEUTZ, 51160 AY

L'abus d'alcool est dangereux pour la santé. Consommez avec modération.

A.H.M.I. Hotels & Resorts®

Central Reservation System
Tél : (33) 1 47 55 02 55
Fax : (33) 1 44 05 90 62 - Internet : http://www.ahmi.fr

Golf Hôtel ★ ★ ★

Bussy Saint Georges
Tél. : (33) 1 64 66 30 30
Fax : (33) 1 64 66 04 36

94 - 3-star - rooms, restaurant, bar, meeting and banquet facilities, outdoor swimming pool, 2 private tennis courts and direct access to the 18-hole golf course, 10 minutes from Disneyland®Paris.

 Garden Beach Hotel ★ ★ ★ ★

Juan les Pins
Tél. : (33) 4 92 93 57 57
Fax : (33) 4 92 93 57 56

On the water front, 172 - 4-star - rooms (16 suites), air-conditionned, bar, restaurant, meeting and banquet facilities, fitness. Private beach with bar, restaurant and water sports, casino.

 UGEREL HOTEL Alpexpo GRENOBLE

Grenoble
Tél. : (33) 4 76 33 02 02
Fax : (33) 4 76 33 34 44

100 - 3-star - rooms (2 suites), air-conditionned, bar; restaurant, meeting and banquet facilities. Outdoor swimming pool.

It is our Custom to offer you the Best...

BURGUNDY

"Every bit is edible"

Vous êtes en Bourgogne, ("You are in Burgundy") announces the sign on the A6 Autoroute linking Paris to the South of France, as if to say that you are entering a realm of earthly delights. Indeed, you are; for Burgundy is the heartland of rural France, a deeply civilized region where a spiritual, monastic tradition goes hand in hand with a robust *joie de vivre*, and where wine is the lifeblood of the land.

Burgundy bristles with history. Celts, Gauls, and Romans occupied the area before the advent of the Burgundi in 443 AD, who settled along the banks of the River Saône and gave their name to the region. Embattled throughout the Middle Ages, Burgundy became an independent dukedom in 1015 under Robert Capet, a member of the French royal family. Capetians held the duchy until their line died out in the late fourteenth century. Burgundy then reverted to the Valois branch of the royal family, known for their opulence and love of art. The reign of the Valois Grand Dukes—Philip the Bold, John the Fearless, Philip the Good, and Charles the Bold—straddled a century, producing a golden age during which their capital, Dijon, was transformed into a flourishing, cosmopolitan center of art and culture. Upon the death of Charles the Bold in 1476, the vast territories attached to the cities of Mâcon, Auxerre, and Charolles were annexed by the Crown. The era of power and independence was ended: henceforth, Burgundy belonged to France.

Today Burgundy takes pride in its provincial character. Most Burgundians would agree that the region has acquired that mystical and almost untranslatable status of *France profonde*. Though some industry thrives, compared to the rest of the country Burgundy has a higher proportion of farmers, winegrowers, craftspeople, traders, and small family businesses.

In its Valois heyday, Burgundy extended south to Provence and included most of Belgium, as well as parts of Holland and Switerland. Considerably smaller, modern Burgundy is made up of four *départements*: Yonne, Nièvre, Côte-d'Or, and Saône-et-Loire. **Dijon**, with its fabulous artistic legacy from the days of the Grand Dukes, is the official capital of Burgundy. Yet its influence cannot be said to extend up to the Yonne or Nièvre, which look Parisward for inspiration, while Saône-et-Loire lives under the thrall of Lyon. In truth, Burgundy straddles North and South in a huge swath of largely rural landscapes, a mellow patchwork of vineyards, pastures, rivers, and woods.

All roads lead to Cluny

The French writer Colette, herself Burgundy-born, once said of her homeland that "Burgundy is like a pig: some parts are more memorable than others, but every bit is edible." She was right. Burgundy is enchanting, austere, sensual, and spiritual by turns. The wooded hills and lakes of the romantic **Morvan Forest** exude mysticism and Celtic lore, while the gentle slopes of the **Côte-d'Or** are an intoxicating plunge into some of the world's most illustrious vineyards. Though history tells us that all roads lead to Rome, in the Middle Ages they led to **Cluny**, the site of a Benedictine abbey—long the largest church in Christendom—founded in 910 on the banks of the River Grosne. Between the tenth and fourteenth centuries, the monastic movement fostered an ecclesiastical building boom that endowed Burgundy with some of the crown jewels of Romanesque architecture. The cathedral of Saint-Lazare in **Autun**, the basilica of Sainte-Madeleine in **Vézelay**, and the abbey of Saint-Philibert in **Tournus** are consummate masterpieces; the **Brionnais** and **Mâconnais** districts in southern Burgundy offer humbler but equally moving examples of Romanesque country churches.

The towns of **Sens**, **Auxerre**, **Avallon**, **Saulieu**, **Beaune**, and **Dijon** long served as staging posts on the main southbound road from Paris to Geneva, Lyon, and Marseille. Today, the TGV—France's state-of-the-art bullet train—streaks through the countryside a great deal faster than the stage coaches of yore, bringing visitors to a part of France which has always given top priority to matters culinary. Burgundy's reputation for fine eating is said to date back to Gallo-Roman times. Certainly the Grand Dukes were renowned for their table: Philip the Good is credited with introducing the first menu at a banquet in 1457. So unabashed were the appetites of the Bishop Princes of Sens that they had indentations carved in their dining tables to accommodate their considerable girths! Fine wine and food go naturally together. Thanks to well-tended soil and a cooperative climate, Burgundian produce is renowned for its excellence. Plump snails, Charollais beef, Bresse chicken (the only poultry in France to have its own *appellation contrôlée*), fish from river and lake, wild mushrooms and game, cherries, blackcurrants, and a variety of cheeses (pungent Époisses, legendary Cîteaux, tangy chèvres) make the region a gastronomic galaxy for gourmets and gourmands, a veritable pilgrimage route of fine tables with a prodigious number of multi-toque tables. And while Burgundy's chefs have developed and refined their own personal cooking styles, many remain staunchly loyal to local ingredients and traditions.

"Good wine," said Henry James, "is an inward emotion." Sipping a glass of crisp, green-tinged **Chablis** in the quaint town that gave its name to this famous *cru*, you might well agree. Just a few miles away, in the ancient town of **Tonnerre**, visit the imposing Château de Tanlay. At **Joigny**, not far from Sens with its great Gothic cathedral, chef Jean-Michel Lorain draws discriminating diners at La Côte Saint-Jacques. Further south, Marc Meneau works his magic under the shadow of Sainte-Madeleine in **Saint-Père-sous-Vézelay**, while Bernard Loiseau's Côte d'Or in Saulieu affords an ideal stopover en route to the **Morvan Regional Park**. A tour of the ducal palace and superb museums of **Dijon** (the mustard—and gingerbread—capital of France) could be a prelude to a remarkable repast *chez* Jean-Paul Thibert. A halt at **Autun** to admire the cathedral could be followed by a lingering lunch at the excellent Lameloise in **Chagny**. Not far distant is **Beaune**, the wine-trading center of Burgundy and one of France's prettiest towns; do stop to admire the Hôtel-Dieu, a masterpiece of Burgundian-Flemish architecture (inside is Roger Van der Weyden's awe-inspiring *Last Judgment*).

Keeping in mind a local dictum: "Bordeaux is for the sick, our wines are for the healthy," a slow meander through the vineyards of the **Côte-d'Or** and **Côte de Beaune** (Gevrey-Chambertin, Clos Vougeot, Nuits-Saint-Georges, Pommard, Volnay, Meursault, Montrachet, etc.) could include a purchase of cheese from the monks at the ancient abbey of Cîteaux.

*Note that (most) **telephone numbers** in France have ten digits, beginning with a zero. The initial zero must be omitted if you are calling France from abroad. Within France, dial the entire ten digits.*

RESTAURANTS & HOTELS

ALOXE-CORTON	21420
Paris 320 - Dijon 32 - Beaune 5	Côte-d'Or

Villa Louise

03 80 26 46 70, fax 03 80 26 47 16
Open year-round. 10 rms 500-900. Bkfst 75. Rms for disabled. Conf. Pkg.
Nestled between quiet vineyards and the Corton woods, this charming seventeenth-century house boasts spacious, tastefully decorated rooms and excellent breakfasts. Formerly called the Clarion, it has just been bought out and renamed by the Choice chain. Babysitting and bike rental available.

ARNAY-LE-DUC	21230
Paris 285 - Dijon 57 - Beaune 34	Côte-d'Or

12/20 Chez Camille

1, pl. Edouard-Herriot
03 80 90 01 38, fax 03 80 90 04 64
Open daily until 9:30pm. Priv rm 25. Garage pkg.
The décor is still fresh and the ritual theatrical in this conservatory-style dining room with its lazy cane armchairs, but we found the Burgundy-style cooking a little too dear for what it is. Admirable selection of Burgundy wines. C 250-550. M 78-495.

AUTUN	71400
Paris 389 - Mâcon 10 - Chalon-sur-Saône 53	Saône/Loire

Le Capitole

14, rue Rivault - 03 85 86 58 58, fax 03 85 86 23 07
Open daily until 9:30pm.
This former convent behind the cathedral boasts a pretty pastel dining room and manicured French gardens. The new chef's cuisine is full of savoir-faire, yet remains traditional and unpretentious. We found the Dublin bay prawns with avocado incomparable and the succulent beef was of exceptionally good quality. In fact, we're looking upward toward a second toque. Appealing wine list rich in half-bottles. C 360-460. M 90 (weekday lunch, Sat), 155-375, 80 (children).

Les Ursulines

(See restaurant above)
Open year-round. 6 stes 460-820. 32 rms 350-465. Bkfst 60. Rms for disabled. Half-board 480-657. Rm ser. Conf.
The magnificent, venerable old convent buildings around the garden welcome guests with cheery, well-equipped rooms. Splendid view of the valley and town.

12/20 Le Chalet Bleu

3, rue Jeannin - 03 85 86 27 30, fax 03 85 52 74 56
Closed Mon dinner, Tue. Open until 9:30pm. Priv rm 40.
It's not every day we see such generous, skillfully prepared traditional cuisine at such modest prices. Above all, the ideas here are excellent. The cellar is on the skimpy side, and features mostly Burgundies. Friendly welcome; colorful, pleasingly exotic décor. C 180. M 90 (weekdays, Sat lunch), 135-245, 60 (children).

AUXERRE	89000
Paris 165 - Dijon 148 - Troyes 82	Yonne

 Jean-Luc Barnabet

14, quai de la République
03 86 51 68 88, fax 03 86 52 96 85
Closed Sun dinner, Mon, Dec 23-Jan 11. Open until 9:30pm. Priv rm 50. Garden dining. Pkg.
Jean-Luc Barnabet's children's menu is but one sign of what a thoughtful host he is. This chef is well intentioned and meticulous down to the last detail and we love him for it—but we'd like to see his spontaneous side every now and again! While the inspiration here is mostly regional, Barnabet does make an occasional (delicious!) detour: crayfish in red wine and ginger liqueur; tender confit of pork with onions; hearty lamb stew. If you're lucky, you might run into Alain Delon, a regular at this lovely address. Wines in the cellar have been taste-tested, and Chablis, Burgundies, and some inexpensive Rhônes rule the roost, but this is the nonetheless the perfect place to try the local Yonne wines, which just keep improving these days. C 300. M 200, 270, 345 (wine incl), 95 (children).

 Le Jardin Gourmand

56, bd Vauban - 03 86 51 53 52, fax 03 86 52 33 82
Closed Tue, Wed off-seas, Feb 18-Mar 5, Sep 2-17. Open until 9:30pm. Priv rm 20. Terrace dining. Pkg.
The elegant décor in this manor house is punctuated by paintings and the dining room opens out onto a garden. The service here is seasoned, and it's obvious a lot of thought has gone into the complex, original offerings on the menu. In fact, just about everything is aimed at refinement with an artistic bent, and that's very nice. However, we'd like to see the chef let down his guard, simplify the fare, and differentiate a bit more between flavors. The fricassée of eel and pike we sampled this year was downright bland, the Breton lobster aspic outstanding, and the vegetables consistently exquisite. Admirable cellar stocked with Chablis and other Yonne wines. C 250-350. M 140-270, 80 (children).

 Normandie

41, bd Vauban - 03 86 52 57 80, fax 03 86 51 54 33
Open year-round. 47 rms 240-370. Bkfst 36. Restaurant. Half-board 270. Rm ser. Conf. Valet pkg.
Although the décor in rooms at this handsome nineteenth-century hotel is resolutely old-fashioned, the lounge and bar are more in touch with the times. Sauna and billiard room.

 Parc des Maréchaux

6, av. Foch - 03 86 51 43 77, fax 03 86 51 31 72
Open year-round. 25 rms 295-470. Bkfst 47. Restaurant. Half-board 380. Rm ser. Conf. Garage pkg.
Rooms at this fetching nineteenth-century manor house were totally renovated this year. They're bright and elegant, and some open out onto a pretty park. Lounges and bar.

12/20 La Salamandre

84, rue de Paris - 03 86 52 87 87, fax 03 86 52 05 85
Closed Sun (exc hols), Dec 20-Jan 3. Open until 10pm. Priv rm 25. Air cond.
Serge Colas is often a little lax when it comes to fine-tuning flavor mixes; his sauces are sometimes a little heavier than we like; and we often wish that that certain stroke of magic creativeness would come over him more often. But his selection of good-quality ingredients and his meticulous cooking times make up for the rest on this chiefly seafood menu. Remarkable selection of white wines. C 300. M 98 (weekdays, Sat lunch), 168-278.

AVALLON	89200
Paris 225 - Dijon 101 - Auxerre 52	Yonne

 Hôtel d'Avallon-Vauban

53, rue de Paris - 03 86 34 36 99, fax 03 86 31 66 31
Open year-round. 30 rms 260-490. Rms for disabled. Rm ser. Conf. Pkg.
This well-renovated old post house is located near the heart of the old town and is surrounded by its own little park. The rooms have been brought up to date, and all the ones giving onto the street are soundproof. Good place to taste regional products.

See also: Saulieu, Vézelay

BEAUNE	21200
Paris 312 - Dijon 40 - Chalon-sur-S. 31	Côte-d'Or

Auberge de la Toison d'Or

4, bd Jules-Ferry - 03 80 22 29 62, fax 03 80 24 07 11
Closed Sun dinner, Mon, Dec 24-Jan 6. Open until 9:30pm. Priv rm 160. Air cond. Pkg.
Everyone does his job and does it well at this unpretentious inn. The décor is plain but pleasing, and the carefully prepared cuisine has a pronounced Southwest accent. A breath of fresh air (especially for families looking for a good, affordable meal) in a town where the number of "fancy" establishments seems to have soared. Fairly priced, mostly Beaune cellar. C 185-250. M 88-238, 50 (children).

Le Bénaton

25, rue du Fg-Bretonnière
03 80 22 00 26, fax 03 80 22 51 95
Closed Wed, Thu lunch, 1 wk in Dec. Open until 10pm. Garden dining.
Bruno Monnoir's cuisine is more interesting than it is creative: his talent lies in taking good ideas and turning them into some remarkably crafted dishes (too bad the desserts don't benefit from the same treatment). Excellent bread. Nice wine list, rich in great vintage offerings. Courteous welcome, attentive service, and pretty flowers on the tables. C 240. M 105 (weekdays, Sat lunch), 155-230, 55 (children).

 Central

2, rue Victor-Millot
03 80 24 77 24, fax 03 80 22 30 40
Closed Wed, Nov 21-Dec 20. Open until 9:30pm. HOTEL: 20 rms 340-470. Bkfst 39. Rm ser. Pkg.
The chef in this restaurant, located a stone's throw from the Hospices (and never at a loss for customers!) got so exhausted he suffered a breakdown—which helps explain some of the glitches we've noticed in times past. We're delighted to report that the cuisine is starting to come into its own again. Try the pig's trotters in millefeuille pastry, or the succulent, thinly sliced caramelized duck. Well-chosen offerings in the cellar. C 240-360. M 99 (weekday lunch, exc Sun), 130-200, 60 (children).

 Le Cep

27-29, rue Maufoux
03 80 22 35 48, fax 03 80 22 76 80
Open year-round. 4 stes 1,300-1,600. 49 rms 600-1,200. Bkfst 70. Rms for disabled. Restaurant. Air cond. Conf. Valet pkg.
Arcades grace the courtyard of this luxurious Renaissance mansion located in the heart of Beaune. The individually decorated rooms, some of which have been renovated, couldn't be more charming. Restaurant: see *Bernard Morillon* below.

12/20 La Ciboulette

69, rue de Lorraine
03 80 24 70 72, fax 03 80 22 79 71
Closed Mon dinner, Tue, last 2 wks of Feb, 2 wks of Aug. Open until 10pm.
Located far from the madding (tourist) crowd, this restaurant serves forth simple, fresh cuisine with a smile—in simple, fresh surroundings. The savory calf's foot in vinaigrette, honey-glazed fillet of guinea fowl, and bitter chocolate tart are well worth a try. A number of modestly priced Burgundies are on offer so you don't go thirsty. C 190. M 91-125.

 Climat

Av. Charles-de-Gaulle
03 80 22 74 10, fax 03 80 22 40 45
Open year-round. 2 stes 485. 50 rms 280-340. Bkfst 35. Rms for disabled. Restaurant. Half-board 336-391. Air cond. Conf. Pkg.
This modern hotel offers functional rooms of standard comfort. Located between the interstate and downtown and surrounded by flowers. Wine tasting and sauna available.

 La Closerie

61, route de Pommard
03 80 22 15 07, fax 03 80 24 16 22
Closed Dec 24-Jan 12. 1 ste 750. 46 rms 300-560. Bkfst 42-65. Rms for disabled. Rm ser. Air cond. Conf. Pool. Garage pkg.
The bathrooms were just redone in this good hotel on the southern outskirts of Beaune. All rooms are ground-floor accessible. Quiet.

 L'Écusson

2, rue du Lieutenant-Dupuis, Pl. Malmédy
03 80 24 03 82, fax 03 80 24 74 02
Closed Sun, Wed dinner, 3 wks of Feb. Open until 9:30pm. Priv rm 20. Terrace dining. Pkg.
Modesty is the watchword here; it applies to everything from the décor to the menu. Jean-Pierre Senelet has a talent for combining ingredients in dishes with genuine personal flair: duck foie gras with a mustard glaze served with oxtail fondant; tender morsels of lamb simmered with fresh-from-the-garden herbs; simply scrumptious oatmeal and red-berry ice cream. A marvelous welcome and equally marvelous prices are among the Écusson's other pluses. Ample explanations come with the regional wine list, if desired. C 350. M 148 (lunch), 134-300, 70 (children).

 Henry II

12, faubourg Saint-Nicolas
03 80 22 83 84, fax 03 80 24 15 13
Open year-round. 50 rms 410-720. Bkfst incl. Rms for disabled. Conf. No pets. Garage pkg.
The rooms in this attractive, centrally located Burgundian homestead have all been done up differently (and in good taste). Breakfast is on the house.

 Le Jardin des Remparts

10, rue Hôtel-Dieu
03 80 24 79 41, fax 03 80 24 92 79
Closed Sun, Mon (exc hols), mid Feb-mid Mar. Open until 9:30pm. Priv rm 50. Garden dining. Pkg.
A good stopoff before you visit the *hospice*. You don't find value like this every day. A cuisine that is alert, inspired, and as delightfully eclectic as ever: very nice oysters paired with watercress; flaky cod in savory sardine jus; delectable crème renversée. The 210 F fixed-price menu gives an excellent overview of the talents of chef Roland Chanliaud, and proves to be light and well-executed. The cellar is well-stocked, with really prime choices from the region, such as Gras's Saint-Romain at 150 F and Rapet's 1988 Pernand-Vergelesses at 170 F. C 300. M 135 (weekdays, Sat lunch), 175-290, 90 (children).

Bernard Morillon

31, rue Maufoux - 03 80 24 12 06, fax 03 80 22 66 22
Closed Mon, Tue lunch, Jan 2-22, Aug 10-17. Open until 10pm. Priv rm 55. Terrace dining. Garage pkg.
Like the eye-catching patina on the ceilings of this establishment's lovely old dining room, Bernard Morillon's cuisine may be classic, but it's never boring. This seasoned chef chooses nothing but the finest ingredients for his skillfully interpreted, generously portioned dishes. Extensive, prudently priced wine list. Smiling welcome. C 180-480. M 180-480, 80 (children).

 ## La Poste

1, bd Clemenceau - 03 80 22 08 11, fax 03 80 24 19 71
Closed end Dec. 8 stes 960-1,500. 22 rms 520-870. Bkfst 65. Restaurant. Half-board 150. Rm ser. Air cond. Conf. Garage pkg.
Although the recently renovated rooms in this traditional hotel may be on the small side, they are all very well equipped and overlook either the ramparts of Beaune (front) or the nearby vineyards (back). Friendly service, yummy breakfasts. Room service available.

See also: Bouilland, Chagny

BOUILLAND	21420
Paris 300 - Beaune 27 - Dijon 35	Côte-d'Or

 ## Le Vieux Moulin

On D 2 - 03 80 21 51 16, fax 03 80 21 59 90
Closed Wed & Thu lunch (exc hols), Wed dinner (May-Oct). Open until 9pm (9:30pm in summer). Priv rm 35. Garden dining. Air cond. Heated pool. Pkg.
There's a pleasant river view from the huge bay window in the modern black-and-brown dining room here, and Jean-Pierre Silva's well-honed culinary technique turns out pure, simple dishes, true to their regional roots. While we appreciate this advantage, we'd love to see his imagination soar higher than it currently does: his ultrafresh, pan-browned frogs' legs with peppery onion compote were good, but not great, and we found the mushrooms in the asparagus and fresh morel ragoût savory—but, alas—a bit gritty. We were more taken with his expertly prepared roasted milk-fed veal chop in a nice Beaune mustard sauce, gorgeous cheeses, and interesting fruit soup topped with grape jelly and seasoned with a hint of mint. The impressive cellar holds some of Burgundy's best, but the prices are out of sight. It would be a good idea to stock a less costly bottle or two. In the meantime, try the 260 F Auxey Duresses from Alain Gras. C 450-600. M 130 (exc dinner), 195-480.

 ## Le Vieux Moulin

(See restaurant above)
Closed Jan 2-22. 2 stes 1,200. 24 rms 380-800. Bkfst 80. Rms for disabled. Half-board 570-880. Conf. Heated pool. Pkg.

The mill offers more classic accommodations, while rooms in the annex are modern. King-sized beds ad towel warmers, but the glass shelves in the bathrooms are far too narrow! Mediocre breakfasts.

CHABLIS	89800
Paris 182 - Auxerre 19 - Troyes 75	Yonne

 ## Hostellerie des Clos

"Michel Vignaud," rue Jules-Rathier
03 86 42 10 63, fax 03 86 42 17 11
Closed Wed & Thu off-seas, Dec 23-Jan 10. Open until 9:30pm. Air cond. Valet pkg.
Flowers abound in this establishment's bright dining room with its old stone convent walls. The cuisine shows a penchant for things classic, but it's never plodding or dull. Instead, it's delicate and unfailingly balanced, just like fine Chablis wines (and while we're on the subject, the cellar, full of local offerings, is about as close to complete as you can get). The crayfish and extraordinarily fresh pike perch are both divine dishes. We're pleased to confirm that Vignaud's toques remain firmly in place. C 400. M 175-420, 100 (children).

 ## Hostellerie des Clos

(See restaurant above)
See restaurant for closings. 26 rms 250-530. Bkfst 60. Rms for disabled. Half-board 470-670 (oblig in seas). Conf. Valet pkg.
Located in the town's Clos des Hospices from days of old, this establishment offers bright, modern, tastefully furnished rooms overlooking a flower garden. Very good breakfasts.

CHAGNY	71150
Paris 330 - Beaune 16 - Mâcon 75	Saône/Loire

 ## Lameloise

36, pl. des Armes
03 85 87 08 85, fax 03 85 87 03 57
Closed Wed (exc dinner Jul-Oct), Thu lunch, Dec 18-Jan 24. Open until 9:30pm. Priv rm 24. Air cond.
The first thing you'll notice about this rambling old village house, handed down through three generations of the Lameloise family, is how warm and reassured you feel when you cross its threshold. Although each generation has done its share of renovations, they've all taken care to preserve the beauty of its thick fifteenth-century walls and the white arches and wrought iron gracing the series of small dining rooms, reminiscent of century-old ties between Burgundy and Spain. Jacques Lameloise now wears the chef's hat, and his traditional cuisine upholds the tradition of these walls. It's true we have a fondness for creativity and invention, but who says you can't like both Boulez and Beethoven, both Picasso and Bruegel the Elder, both Gagnaire and Lameloise? Asking for something new at Lameloise would be rather like asking for something new in an antique store... We savored a

delectable squab with cabbage millefeuille and truffles, and an outstanding turbot cooked in clay and served with its caramelized, onion-flecked jus. Something tells us Jacques Lameloise is torn between his own sense of adventure and the more classic tastes of his clientele, but he does manage to add his own (small) personal flare to a sauce here and there and to provide new (and enlightened) interpretations of old classics from time to time. Nicole Lameloise is a radiant hostess, the service is dignified but never stiff, and the divine wines are reasonably priced (on the whole). Then there's that priceless impression you get that all is well with the world—and that's worth the trip in itself! C 350-550. M 370-600.

 Lameloise

(See restaurant above)
Closed Wed (exc Jul-Oct), Dec 18-Jan 23. 17 rms 600-1,500. Bkfst 90. Conf. Pkg.
Several of the rooms in this venerable establishment have been soundproofed to afford guests maximum quiet, and all are fresh, bright, and pretty. White walls showcase the pretty fabrics used to decorate, and a few rooms have rear balconies looking out on the surrounding greenery and the scenic Santenay vineyards. Breakfasts are always a special treat (soft-boiled eggs, mini chèvres, praline-studded brioches, etc.). Relais et Châteaux.

CHAILLY-SUR-ARMANÇON   21320
Paris 280 - Autun 52 - Dijon 47   Côte-d'Or

 L'Armançon

03 80 90 30 30, fax 03 80 90 30 00
Closed Mon, Tue lunch, Dec 19-Jan 11. Open until 9:30pm. Priv rm 30. Heated pool. Tennis. Valet pkg.
The château is Renaissance, and the golf course is technically challenging. Cuisine in the "gastronomic" restaurant (so called to differentiate it from the other, more modest restaurant near the pool) is a mix of high-precision classicism and measured doses of originality. Food here is skillfully prepared, and the set menus are affordably priced. Tuck into the scrumptious nage glacée of duck foie gras laced with peach vinegar, succulent salmon with almonds and red-wine sauce, and warm pink grapefruit tart for dessert. Interesting, regional cellar. Quick, efficient service. C 400. M 180 (weekday lunch), 240-430, 85 (children).

 Château de Chailly 🏌🏻

(See restaurant above)
Closed Dec 17-Jan 25. 8 stes 2,000-3,000. 37 rms 945-1,570. Bkfst 80. Rms for disabled. Conf. Heated pool. Tennis. Golf. Valet pkg.
Pretty rooms in the commons houses and remarkable suites under the eaves of the château: all well equipped and decorated in an understated, refined manner. Be sure to pay a visit to Le Cosmos, a Zen sanctuary set up by the owner in a Renaissance tower.

CHALON-SUR-SAÔNE   71100
Paris 336 - Mâcon 62 - Beaune 29   Saône/Loire

12/20 Le Bourgogne

28, rue de Strasbourg
03 85 48 89 18, fax 03 85 93 39 10
Closed Sat lunch off-seas, Sun dinner, Jul 6-21. Open until 9:30pm. Priv rm 60.
A smiling welcome awaits guests in the comfortable Louis XIII–style dining room. Checks are down to earth and the delightful regional cuisine proffered by Stéphane Reniaume unfailingly respects the flavors of his ingredients through meticulous preparation and expert cooking. Good set-price menu at 105 F, which lets you dip into the reasonably priced, classic cellar full of Burgundies. C 200. M 93-250, 50 (children).

11/20 Café du Verre Galant

8, pl. Saint-Vincent - 03 85 93 09 87
Closed Sun dinner, Mon, 2 wks in Apr, mid Oct-Nov 7. Open until 10pm. Terrace dining.
This little wine bar, located on the marketplace, offers simple regional fare with amusing names such as "la revanche du turfiste" (the revenge of the race-goer), which is in fact braised horse meat cooked in herbs. Short but sweet wine list. C 130-190.

11/20 Restaurant du Marché

7, pl. Saint-Vincent - 03 85 48 62 00
Closed Sun dinner, Mon, mid Aug-beg Sep. Open until 9:30pm. Priv rm 30. Terrace dining. Pkg.
This restaurant is located near the cathedral and the region's best vegetable market. The helpings are generous, and the price is right. The eel mousse with prunes isn't all that relevant, but the langoustines flavored with aniseed are very tasty. Good Burgundy wines. C 180-250. M 85-160, 50 (children).

12/20 Ripert

31, rue Saint-Georges - 03 85 48 89 20
Closed Sun, Mon, 1 wk at Easter, Aug 1-21. Open until 9:15pm.
The pretty little dining room with its tiled floor and waxed furniture is like a breath of country air, and Alain Ripert's three set menus (all reasonably priced) show how wonderful old-fashioned cooking can be. His ingredients come straight from the market, and they're handled in a genuine, forthright manner. The cellar is a bit uninspired, but the prices are right. M 70-150, 40 (children).

 La Rôtisserie

1, rue du Pont - 03 85 48 81 01, fax 03 85 48 15 71
Closed Sun dinner, Wed (Sep-Jun). Open until 9:30pm (10pm in summer). Priv rm 20. Terrace dining. Pkg.
This elegant grill room located a stone's throw from Saint-Vincent cathedral is the workplace of chef Didier Denis, who's an expert at cooking basic, local ingredients, but has recently

dropped his penchant for throwing new ideas on the fire. We can understand his strategy, and it produces some highly worthy dishes, like his truly exceptional foie gras and his very good scallops. The desserts need a fundamental workover, however. We know he's capable of better, and that he can regain his newly lost 14. The appealing little cellar is stocked with mostly Burgundies. C 210-300. M 95-175, 75 (children).

 ### Saint-Georges

32, av. Jean-Jaurès
03 85 48 27 05, fax 03 85 93 23 88
Closed Sat lunch. Open until 9:30pm. Priv rm 120. Air cond. Pkg.
This place is a Chalon institution, so they make no attempt to prove themselves. Yves Choux offers skillfully prepared, up-to-date set-price meals. You can have your choice of simple dishes or rich specialities of the region such as young Bresse hen terrine stuffed with foie gras and winter-cress with olive oil, frog leg ravioli with morel mushrooms, or calf's kidneys cooked in their own grease and in a salt crust. Intelligently selected wine cellar full of interesting Burgundies such as Maranges and Montagny. C 300-475. M 110-400, 70 (children).

 ### Saint-Georges

(See restaurant above)
Open year-round. 1 ste 460-520. 48 rms 280-580. Bkfst 50. Half-board 360-395. Rm ser. Air cond. Conf. Pkg.
This lovely old building has been renovated to make it practical and comfortable. It offers all the amenities necessary to make your stay pleasant: vast rooms full of light and well equipped. Ever-smiling staff always ready to help you.

 ### Saint-Régis

22, bd de la République
03 85 48 07 28, fax 03 85 48 90 88
Open year-round. 3 stes 510-620. 37 rms 360-495. Bkfst 52. Restaurant. Half-board 340-400. Rm ser. Air cond. Conf. Garage pkg.
This regional hotel is located between the train station and the old town. The rooms are spacious, but their overall décor could be a bit more appealing. Pretty stained-glass windows in the lounge.

See also: Chagny, Mercurey

 ### Château André Ziltener

03 80 62 41 62, fax 03 80 62 83 75
Closed Dec 15-Jan 23. 7 stes 1,100-1,800. 3 rms 900-1,000. Bkfst 80. Rms for disabled. Restaurant. Rm ser. Conf. Garage pkg.
This handsome eighteenth-century dwelling set on a venerable estate was built on the ruins of a Cistercian priory. The wonderful rooms each bear the name of a regional wine (the château does double-duty as a hotel and purveyor of fine wines). Come here for the luxury; stay for the wine tastings!

 ### La Fontaine

"Yves Jury" - 03 85 26 26 87
Closed Tue dinner, Wed, Jan 13-Feb 13. Open until 9pm. Priv rm 9. Pkg.
Chef Yves Jury's cuisine is as personalized and atypical as the eccentric, improbable mosaic décor in the dining room of this former cloth mill—and the prices here would gladden even the tightest Scotsman's heart. Try the out-of-this-world wild mushroom and crayfish soup; succulent lobster with rice "pudding," or squab with pig's-trotter stuffing. Intelligent cellar with some nice regional finds. A third toque could well be in this establishment's future. This is the kind of food we love: direct, modest, expressive...and flavorful, to boot! C 350. M 97 (exc Sun), 120-270, 60 (children).

 ### Château de Chaumont

5, rue de la Montagne
03 86 96 61 69, 03 86 96 61 28
Closed Mon lunch. Open until 9:30pm. Priv rm 60. Terrace dining. Pkg.
This magnificently restored château dates from the second half of the eighteenth century. Its splendid dining rooms overlook the bucolic countryside, and the welcome and food here are simply divine: velvety, perfectly seasoned Landes foie gras with figs; original monkfish fricassée with no fewer than fourteen spices; cheeses from Barthélémy in Fontainebleau; and heavenly desserts like melon sherbet with Port, ginger, and candied fruits. Shhh! Let's let this charming place be our little secret! C 350. M 150-350 (wine incl), 90 (children).

 ### Château de Chaumont

(See restaurant above)
Open year-round. 3 stes 600-800. 35 rms 400-600. Bkfst 50-70. Rms for disabled. Half-board 600-800. Rm ser. Conf. Pkg.
A striking mix of old stone, beams, coffered ceilings, oak parquet floors waxed the old-fashioned way, and modern comfort prevails in the tastefully decorated rooms here. Flowers are everywhere, and the atmosphere is good-natured indeed. And while regal tranquility reigns, the prices are unarguably democratic.

CHEVANNES 89240
Paris 174 - Auxerre 9 Yonne

 La Chamaille

In La Barbotière, 4, route de Boiloup
03 86 41 24 80, fax 03 86 41 34 80
Closed Mon, Tue, Jan 13-Feb 8, Dec 22-26. Open until 9:15pm. Pkg.
This charming old house's setting is idyllic: it's nestled in the verdant countryside along a babbling brook. The cuisine, while unsurprising, is nonetheless delicious: grilled red mullets paired with a savory anchovy garnish; choice morsels of lamb with tomato ravioli; a melt-in-your-mouth warm chocolate fondant with custard sauce. Well-stocked wine cellar with the very best regional wines represented. Good selection of wines by the glass. Extremely cordial welcome and service. C 260. M 165-258, 210-330 (wine incl), 70 (children).

CHOREY 21200
Paris 319 - Dijon 40 - Beaune 3 Côte-d'Or

 L'Ermitage Corton

N 74 - 03 80 22 05 28, fax 03 80 24 64 51
Closed Sun dinner, Mon, mid Jan-mid Feb. Open until 9:15pm. Priv rm 35. Garden dining. Garage pkg.
Some things never change. As if the proliferation of pomp and gilded surfaces in the dining room weren't enough, the avalanche of nibbles before the meal and the torrent of desserts at the end are enough to permanently impair a diner's judgment! Even though these tempting tidbits are plentiful, we're sorry to report that most of them are downright bland. What is *not* bland, however, is the salmon millefeuille—a fitting tribute to André Parra's letter-perfect technique—and the memorable panaché de la mer. The grade here remains stable. C 350-600. M 175-765, 60 (children).

 L'Ermitage Corton

(See restaurant above)
Closed mid Jan-mid Feb. 6 stes 1,250-1,800. 4 rms 750-950. Bkfst 95-140. Half-board 1,100-1,500. Rm ser. No cards. Conf. Garage pkg.
Pure Hollywood, smack-dab in the middle of the vineyards! The opulent lodgings here are outfitted with regal bathrooms, the breakfasts are fabulous, and the staff aims to please.

CLUNY 71250
Paris 396 - Mâcon 24 - Tournus 38 Saône/Loire

12/20 **Bourgogne**

Pl. de l'Abbaye - 03 85 59 00 58, fax 03 85 59 03 73
Closed Tue, Wed lunch, mid Nov-mid Mar. Open until 9pm. Terrace dining. Garage pkg.
The nostalgic atmosphere offered by this venerable old dwelling with its antique cupboards and burnished parquet floors is still its main attraction. Its set-price menu at 85 F is a good buy, but the only part of it worth commenting on was the delicious petits-fours at the end. They'll have to make more effort than this to get back their toque. You can peer through the ivy at the nearby abbey while you dine. C 260-490. M 85-160 (lunch), 200-350 (dinner).

 Bourgogne

(See restaurant above)
Closed Tue, mid Nov-mid Mar. 3 stes 930-990. 12 rms 430-520. Bkfst 55-90. Half-board 470-750 (oblig). Rm ser. Conf. Garage pkg.
Located across from the verdant park surrounding the abbey, this charming old hotel offers quiet, comfortable rooms and an impeccably manicured interior garden.

Hôtel Saint-Odilon

In Belle-Croix - 03 85 59 25 00, fax 03 85 59 06 18
Closed Dec 20-Jan 10. 36 rms 280. Bkfst 35. Rms for disabled. Conf. Garage pkg.
This modern hotel located near the abbey and the river offers bright, neat, well-equipped accommodations.

CREUSOT (LE) 71200
Paris 317 - Beaune 47 - Autun 29 Saône/Loire

 Le Moulin Rouge

Route de Moncoy - 03 85 55 14 11, fax 03 85 55 53 37
Closed Fri dinner, Sat lunch, Sun dinner, Dec 20-Jan 6. 32 rms 220-400. Bkfst 45. Restaurant. Half-board 300-400. Conf. Heated pool. Pkg.
This rambling, rustic-style establishment on the town's tranquil outskirts features quiet guest quarters along a vast garden. Its beamed rooms are charmingly decorated with copper accents and pewter and wrought iron sconces.

Le Restaurant

Rue des Abattoirs - 03 85 56 32 33, fax 03 85 77 03 19
Closed Sun dinner, Aug 1-15. Open until 9:30pm. Pkg.
The unique décor brightened up by a few nice paintings serves as stage for this young chef full of enthusiasm. He gets a toque right out from the gate. An intelligent and intelligently priced cuisine prepared by a chef who has a vision. He's a hard worker who takes whatever time is necessary to root through the products available and come up with the best. He's also rather attracted by alternative lifestyles, so he offers organic vegetables and some novel selections of wines like Languedocs and Hermitages. C 140. M 65 (weekdays, Sat lunch), 95-129.

The C (A la carte) restaurant prices given are for a complete three-course meal for one, including a half-bottle of modest wine and service. M (Menu) prices are for a complete fixed-price meal for one, excluding wine (unless otherwise noted).

DIJON 21000
Paris 310 - Reims 283 - Lyon 192 Côte-d'Or

 Les Allées
27, cours du Général-de-Gaulle
03 80 66 57 50, fax 03 80 36 24 81
Closed Sun. 2 stes 400. 33 rms 215-260. Bkfst 35. Conf. Pkg.
All the rooms were just renovated in this comfortable family-run establishment located in a garden setting in the residential part of town, about ten minutes from Dijon's center.

 Jean-Pierre Billoux
13, pl. de la Libération
03 80 38 05 05, fax 03 80 38 16 16
Closed Sun dinner, Mon. Open until 9:30pm. Priv rm 50.
Barring the unexpected Jean-Pierre Billoux has moved from the vaulted cellars of the Hôtel de la Cloche to set up shop in the Pré aux Clercs, a dormant restaurant on Place de la Libération, opposite the town hall. The upstairs drawing room has kept its eighteenth-century style, while the ground floor dining room has been redone in contemporary style. Billoux brought his team and his ambitions with him to this stately architecture, where he found a fresh inspiration for his solid classic and regional repertoire, and where he still offers his undying standards, sweet garlic pigeon terrine and Dublin bay prawn paillasson. His mainstays are still poultry; the guinea fowl with truffle and bean cream sauce is a real work of art. But you will also find surprising combinations such as the crawfish and smoked veal mignon with green salad, or the lobster shish kebab with its bold yet subtle mango butter and a sort of gingerbread pancake (gingerbread being one of Dijon's specialties). Needless to say, the cellar is topped to the hilt with all the great Burgundies, and wine waiter Patrice Gillard is a real expert, so don't hesitate to ask him any questions you might have. C 500-700. M 180 (lunch, wine incl), 230 (weekday dinner, Sat), 300-490.

 Campanile
Parc technologique de la Toison-d'Or, allée Alfred-Nobel
03 80 74 41 00, fax 03 80 70 13 44
Open year-round. 48 rms 278. Bkfst 32. Rms for disabled. Restaurant. Half-board 340-360. Rm ser. Conf. Pkg.
This comfortable chain hotel is right at home in its high-tech commerce park setting. The rooms here are especially well maintained, and pretty floral touches pop up everywhere.

 Central Grill Rôtisserie
3, pl. Grangier - 03 80 30 44 00, fax 03 80 30 77 12
Closed Sun. Open until midnight. Priv rm 45. Terrace dining. Air cond.
Although its name isn't anything out of the ordinary, this centrally located grill room with its spruce new décor is well worth the visit. The cuisine here is based on straightforward interpretations of top-notch ingredients, and prices on the smart little wine list (some goodies available by the pitcher) are a steal. The welcome is friendly, and the service holds steady until midnight. C 210. M 125-155, 65 (children).

13 Le Cézanne
40, rue de l'Amiral-Roussin
03 80 58 91 92, fax 03 80 49 86 80
Closed Sun, Mon lunch, Jan 1-15, Sep 1-15. Open until 10pm. Terrace dining. Air cond.
Chef David Ardoint's talent for coaxing the best from simple, wholesome ingredients won him a toque last year. Too bad that this led to him dropping his menu of the week at 69 F; nonetheless, you still get high quality at a reasonable price. Ardoint's cooking is inventive and full of surprising turns, with offerings such as red mullet salad with citrus fruit vinaigrette, escargots with parsley and chanterelle mushroom cream sauce, roast pigeon with hazelnuts and Banyuls (a sweet wine) vinegar, and turbot cooked in a vanilla "infusion". The chef's brother, Benoît, is there to give you good advice on the reasonably priced wine list, and an all-in-the-family staff diligently attends to patrons in the modern mezzanine dining room. Excellent value. C 180-300. M 99 (exc Sat dinner), 140-250, 80 (children).

Le Chabrot
36, rue Monge - 03 80 30 69 61
Open until 10:30pm. Priv rm 35. Air cond. Garage pkg.
This warm bistro decorated on a wine theme got as high as 14 in our past guides, but the general decline of the quality of the cuisine this year, really from start to finish, leads us to remove it entirely from the ratings. Really too bad, because we know this chef, and we know what heights he is capable of. Suspended for the moment, until we see a change of course. C 200. M 175 (weekday lunch), 100-180, 60 (children).

12/20 Château Bourgogne
22, bd. de la Marne
03 80 72 31 13, fax 03 80 73 61 45
Open daily until 10:30pm. Priv rm 220. Terrace dining. Air cond. Pkg.
It's a real challenge to keep the prices right and the quality high, and this well-intentioned effort is what led us to drop this guide last year. But this year we were pleased to note that quality is back on the marquee with a salmon tartare a step above the average, a more-than-ample fillet with morel mushrooms, and a low-priced list of regional wines. Quick service. C 280-350. M 159-185 (wine incl), 225, 57 (children).

16 Le Chapeau Rouge
5, rue Michelet - 03 80 30 28 10, fax 03 80 33 33 89
Open daily until 9:45pm. Priv rm 120. Air cond. No pets.
Chef Éric Conan's short menu offers diners at this lovely old establishment reassuringly

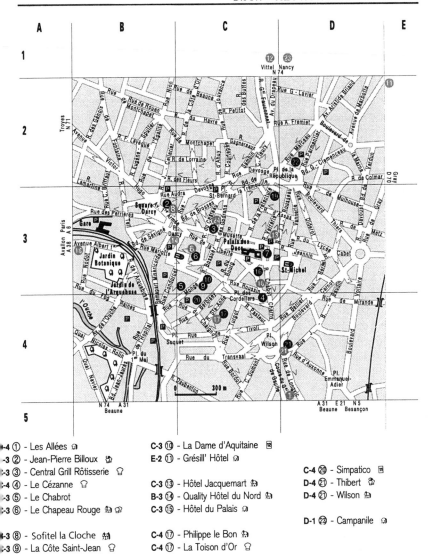

♦-4 ① - Les Allées ☺

♦-3 ② - Jean-Pierre Billoux ☆

♦-3 ③ - Central Grill Rôtisserie ☐

♦-4 ④ - Le Cézanne ☐

♦-3 ⑤ - Le Chabrot

♦-3 ⑥ - Le Chapeau Rouge ☐ ☆

♦-3 ⑧ - Sofitel la Cloche ☐☐

♦-3 ⑨ - La Côte Saint-Jean ☐

C-3 ⑩ - La Dame d'Aquitaine ☐

E-2 ⑪ - Grésill' Hôtel ☺

C-3 ⑬ - Hôtel Jacquemart ☐

B-3 ⑭ - Quality Hôtel du Nord ☐

C-3 ⑮ - Hôtel du Palais ☺

C-4 ⑰ - Philippe le Bon ☐

C-4 ⑰ - La Toison d'Or ☐

C-4 ⑳ - Simpatico ☐

D-4 ㉑ - Thibert ☆

D-4 ㉑ - Wilson ☐

D-1 ㉓ - Campanile ☺

familiar fare treated with just the right touch of derring-do. For instance, his salmon is done in a dill marinade then topped with tangy fresh seaweed cream, and his parsley flan is served with snail fritters and a sesame oil vinaigrette. We loved the farm-fresh poultry: salmis of squab coupled with an interesting mustard-seed matefaim and roast guinea fowl given an under-the-skin coating of parsley, then roasted to perfection. Considering the cuisine's finesse, the prices here are entirely reasonable. And the cellar is honest, too, with a good selection of half-bottles. There's a wonderful twelfth-century

dining room available for groups. C 300-400. M 150-215 (wine incl), 195-400.

🏨 Le Chapeau Rouge
(See restaurant above)

Open year-round. 1 ste 1,600. 30 rms 480-785. Bkfst 67. Half-board 470-585. Rm scr. Air cond. Pkg.

This venerable stone house at the heart of the town's historic district features a pleasant bar and spacious winter-garden lounge. The guest rooms are classic and comfortable; some bathrooms come equipped with with Jacuzzis. Attentive service.

La Côte Saint-Jean

13, rue Monge - 03 80 50 11 77, fax 03 80 50 18 75
Closed Tue, Sat lunch, Jul 18-Aug 9, Dec 25-Jan 17.
Open until 9:30pm.
You may have a hard time spotting this restaurant from the outside, but be sure not to pass it by! Even though the ambitious Bérand brothers go a bit "over the top" from time to time, their cuisine has come to reflect genuine mastery coupled with a healthy dose of creative flair. Their sea scallops and omble aux rattes (salmon trout with yellow potatoes) are almost worth two toques. However the desserts need improving, and patrons need to watch out for extra costs on the set menus. The cellar could use some rounding out, but it's well stocked with growers' Burgundies. C 300. M 100 (weekday lunch), 128 (weekday lunch, wine incl), 155-175.

12/20 La Dame d'Aquitaine

23, pl. Bossuet - 03 80 30 36 23, fax 03 80 49 90 41
Open daily until 10:30pm. Priv rm 50. No pets.
This impressive thirteenth-century crypt—decorated in classic Louis XIII style and opening onto an eighteenth-century courtyard —has to be one of the most inviting settings for dining in all of Dijon. However, regulars tend to ignore the surroundings and look straight at the plates filled with Monique Salera's fresh Southwest cuisine or equally delicious local specialties. Beware however when she lapses into a more inventive domain; it doesn't always work. She'll have to win her toque back by putting a little authenticity and personality into what she does. Let Daniel Salera fill your glass with one of the good wines from his Southwest/Burgundy cellar. C 300. M 155 (weekday lunch, Sat, wine incl), 168, 183, 235, 210 (Sun, wine incl).

 ## Grésill' Hôtel

16, av. Raymond-Poincaré
03 80 71 10 56, fax 03 80 74 34 89
Open year-round. 47 rms 230-290. Bkfst 38. Restaurant. Half-board 260-370. Rm ser. Conf. Garage pkg.
This conveniently located hotel (close to the center of town and the Palais des Congrès et des Sports) may not be high on charm, but it does offer functional, soundproofed rooms and a decent grill-style restaurant.

 ## Hôtel Jacquemart

32, rue de la Verrerie
03 80 73 39 74, fax 03 80 73 20 99
Open year-round. 2 stes 310-390. 60 rms 160-330. Bkfst 34.
This charming seventeenth-century hotel is nestled among the picturesque old town's many antique shops. The rooms have recently been renovated adding a very personal touch and extra comfort. It's difficult to park however; you come here for the charm!

 ## Hôtel du Palais

23, rue du Palais - 03 80 67 16 26, fax 03 80 65 12 16

Open year-round. 15 rms 170-240. Bkfst 25.
This carefully renovated eighteenth-century establishment stands at the heart of Dijon's historic center, right next to the courthouse. Warm family welcome; quiet rooms.

Hôtel Philippe Le Bon

See restaurant La Toison d'Or

 ## Quality Hôtel du Nord

Pl. Darcy - 03 80 30 58 58, fax 03 80 30 61 26
Closed Dec 22-Jan 6. 1 ste 370-750. 26 rms 330-420. Bkfst 49. Restaurant. Half-board 340. Rm ser. Air cond. Conf.
This venerable Burgundian establishment at the heart of town offers country-style guest quarters and a charming welcome. Wine bar.

 ## La Rotonde

14, pl. Darcy - 03 80 30 12 32, fax 03 80 30 04 15
Open daily until 10:30pm. Priv rm 150. Terrace dining. Air cond. Valet pkg.
Since Jean-Pierre Billoux vacated the premises, the spirit of things has changed. The young chef, Dominique Fieux, whose overflowing talent we had already noticed when he was in Poligny, is marching to the beat of a different drummer with combination plates, perfect for a light lunch, as well as set menus full of up-to-date and novel ideas: duck liver poached in milk and paprika, burbot millefeuille in garlic cream sauce, and absolutely tremendous chicken fillets stuffed with morels. Wines with comfortable prices. Terrace dining in an interior garden. Regional dishes and wines for sale in the basement. Life is merry, isn't that the way it was meant to be? C 200. M 185, 240 (wine incl), 75 (children).

 ## Sofitel-La Cloche

(See restaurant above)
Open year-round. 7 stes 890-1,490. 70 rms 510-720. Bkfst 60. Rms for disabled. Rm ser. Conf. Valet pkg.
This deluxe hotel has finally been spiffed up to live up to its own high standards. Sunny, bright colors in completely equipped rooms (some even have their own private wine cellar! Only in Burgundy!), and breakfasts with a different but pleasant slant.

11/20 Simpatico

30, rue Berbisey - 03 80 30 53 33
Closed Sun, lunch Sat & Mon, 1 wk in Feb, 2 wks in Aug. Open until 10pm.
The name fits, the crowd is young, and the atmosphere is lively at this neighborhood Italian eatery, where dishes like tuna or veal carpaccio and agnoletti (fresh pasta) with crayfish offer a refreshing change from basic pizzeria fare. C 190. M 60-80 (lunch), 110-160, 50 (children).

Thibert

10, pl. du Président-Wilson
03 80 67 74 64 (R), 03 80 66 82 50 (H),
fax 03 80 63 87 72 (R), 03 80 36 41 54 (H)
*Closed Sun, Mon lunch, 3 wks in Aug. Open until
9:45pm. Priv rm 20. Air cond. Tennis. Pkg.*
We don't know of many three-toque restaurants offering a remarkable 130 F set menu—in fact, we don't know of any except this one! Wonderfully inspired chef Jean-Paul Thibert is definitely a whiz in the kitchen, but he's also bound and determined to keep his prices down. How does he do it? Well, for starters, he made sure that the recently refurbished dining room would be very attractive, but not sumptuous (that would only add to the check). And he selects the very best ingredients (though not necessarily the most costly), then treats them with an expert hand. His specialties—tender baby cabbages stuffed with snails and served in celery jus, milk-fed veal with parsley purée delicately flavored with walnut oil, original langoustines with green coffee beans—all bespeak admirable talents. Thibert's flavors know exactly when to come into the limelight, and when to stay in the background. His top-notch wine steward dispenses advice on the nicely priced Burgundies in the cellar, and Madame Thibert ensures that the welcome is warm, and the service is flawless. Needless to say, we'll be back for more! C 350-450. M 130 (weekdays), 200-410.

Wilson

(See restaurant above)
*Closed Dec 31. 27 rms 345-480. Bkfst 55. Rms for
disabled. Garage pkg.*
This seventeenth-century coaching inn boasts tastefully decorated, country-style guest quarters. Rooms are all well-soundproofed, and open onto a pretty interior courtyard.

La Toison d'Or

18, rue Ste-Anne - 03 80 30 73 52, fax 03 80 30 95 51
*Closed Sun dinner. Open until 9:30pm. Priv rm
100. Terrace dining. Pkg.*
Excellent value, even for the (young) wines, despite some episodic overheating (undoubtedly due to the hordes of tourists who unexpectedly descend upon this historic site). Daniel Broyer's classic (but never boring) offerings attest to the dedication and virtues of a fine chef. C 280-350. M 160 (weekday lunch, wine incl), 205-260.

Philippe Le Bon

(See restaurant above)
*Open year-round. 29 rms 320-460. Bkfst 45-55. Rms
for disabled. Half-board 320-470. Rm ser. Air cond.
Conf. Pkg.*
This former laboratory converted to a comfortable hotel is located on a quiet street in the historic part of town. Although the décor is a bit heavy-handed the overall effect is appealing, and there's even a garden to enjoy. A good base for exploring old Dijon.

And also...

*Our selection of places for inexpensive,
quick, or late-night meals.*
Bistingo (03 80 30 61 38 - Passage Darcy. Open until 11pm.): The fresh market menu changes daily, and the clientele is mostly business people in-the-know. It's just a pity the layout is so cramped (120).
L'Écailler (03 80 73 42 37 - 6, rue Jean-Jacques Rousseau. Open until 10:30pm.): The 49 F fixed-price meal and the excellent seafood at 100 F make it worthwhile visiting this little café tucked into the government office district. Loire Valley wines (49-150).
Made in Italia (03 80 65 48 00 - 47, rue Jeannin. Open until 10:30pm, 11pm Fri& Sat.): The undisputable charm of the young owner will make you feel at home in this authentic Italian restaurant. Too bad about the gaudy façade...(59-110).
Le Palmier (03 80 73 52 89 - 56, av. du Drapeau. Open until 11pm.): The best couscous in town, even if the décor wouldn't give a whirling dervish cause to whirl (130).

FLAGEY-ÉCHEZEAUX	21640
Paris 324 - Dijon 22 - Beaune 20	Côte-d'Or

Robert Losset

Pl. de l'Église - 03 80 62 88 10
*Closed Sun dinner, Wed, 2 wks in Aug. Open until
8:30pm. Priv rm 18. Air cond.*
Robert Losset's festive dishes make every day seem like a holiday at this authentic village inn: try the marbled medley of artichoke and foie gras, savory pike perch with fennel seed, and scrumptious lemon mousse cake... Perfectly chosen minor Burgundies in the cellar, all priced right. M 100 (lunch, exc Sun), 140-250.

FLEURVILLE	71260
Paris 379 - Mâcon 16 - Tournus 14	Saône/Loire

Château
de Fleurville

03 85 33 12 17, fax 03 85 33 95 34
*Closed Nov-Mar 1. 1 ste 770. 14 rms 420. Bkfst 40.
Rms for disabled. Restaurant. Half-board 645-750
(oblig in seas). Rm ser. Pool. Tennis. Pkg.*
All the rooms in this establishment have been equipped with television sets, and some overlook the surrounding vineyards. There's a château built during the sixteenth and seventeenth centuries on the grounds.

Please excuse us... (and the chefs). *Menus
are subject to the winds of change, and the
dishes we've described may no longer be
available when you visit.*

GEVREY-CHAMBERTIN   21220
Paris 310 - Beaune 26 - Dijon 14   Côte-d'Or

 ## Hôtel Arts et Terroirs

28, route de Dijon
03 80 34 30 76, fax 03 80 34 11 79
*Open year-round. 1 ste 300-580. 20 rms 250-580.
Bkfst 45. Rm ser. Conf. Garage pkg.*
  Not surprising that this hotel with its subdued-color rooms with an oh-so-personal touch offers wine tastings when you think about where its located, right in the heart of the Burgundy wine region. You can use the hotel's bicycles to flit about town, or drop in on the hotel's continuous exhibit of local artists. And what a delight it is to take your breakfast in the garden.

11/20   Le Bonbistrot

Rue du Chambertin
03 80 34 33 20, fax 03 80 34 12 30
Closed Sun dinner, Mon (exc hols), Feb 9-Mar 3, Aug 3-19. Open until 10pm. Priv rm 80. Terrace dining. Pkg.
  This rural café serves up traditional Burgundian fare: warm and satisfying "l'Ami du Chambertin" cheese salad, hearty tripe sausage, and a scrumptious baba au rhum. C 90-120.

 ## Les Grands Crus

Route des Grands-Crus
03 80 34 34 15, fax 03 80 51 89 07
Closed Dec 1-Feb 25. 24 rms 360-440. Bkfst 47. Pkg.
  Happy are the guests here with rooms overlooking some of the world's most famous vineyards. While accommodations are quiet and well maintained, their slightly dated décors could stand refurbishing. Adorable little garden opposite the château.

 ## Les Millésimes

25, rue de l'Église - 03 80 51 84 24, fax 03 80 34 12 73
Closed Tue, Wed lunch, Dec 22-Jan 25. Open until 9:30pm. Priv rm 80. Garden dining. Air cond. Pkg.
  International experts rank the wine list here number one in the world for Burgundy, and among the top fifteen for all regions. Our only regret is that there aren't more half-bottles on hand. The cuisine—rich in lobster, truffles, foie gras, and other deluxe foodstuffs—is on a par with the wine list, and even the simplest dishes are prepared with consummate refinement. Nevertheless, we found the quality slipping this year. The beef fillet was perfect and well worth three toques, but the salmon with caviar cream, escargots polenta and variation on a grapefruit were definitely not in the 16 category. We suggest that he simplify his cooking and put a little more heart into it, because we frankly found it lacking soul. Lap-of-luxury service. C 500-600. M 310-510.

 ## Rôtisserie du Chambertin

Rue du Chambertin
03 80 34 33 20, fax 03 80 34 12 30
Closed Sun dinner, 2 wks in Aug. Open until 9:30pm. Priv rm 110. Air cond. Pkg.
  You'll learn everything you always wanted to know about wine as you make your way through this historic establishment's very own wine and cooperage museum to the dining room! Once you're there, tuck into the celebrated Bresse coq au vin à l'ancienne (a true classic, for a mere 135 F) or the mousseline of carp with gingerbread and celery. A classic regional cuisine with lovely touches of originality. The prestigious cellar is almost entirely stocked with vintage Burgundies, priced accordingly. C 310-350. M 275-410.

La Sommellerie

7, rue Souvert - 03 80 34 31 48, fax 03 80 58 52 20
Closed Sun, Dec 15-Jan 6, 1 wk at Feb school hols, 1st wk in Jul. Open until 9:30pm. Priv rm 24. Air cond.
  The Robuchon-inspired cooking of François Lachaux (who in fact worked for the great Robuchon) is technically perfect: scallops and celery and cockerel with garlic, but perhaps a little too close to that of the master for the moment. The desserts were overly sweet. We visited this restaurant on the fourth day after it opened, so we intend to follow its development. C 280-320. M 97 (weekdays, exc Fri dinner), 148-360, 60 (children).

11/20   Aux Vendanges de Bourgogne

47, rte de Beaune - 03 80 34 30 24, fax 03 80 58 55 44
Closed Sun dinner off-seas, 2 wks in Feb. Open until 9:30pm. Priv rm 14. Terrace dining. Garage pkg.
  The owner-cook was formerly the dining room manager of a Dijon institution, Le Chapeau Rouge. He offers regional bistro fare in this former village bar-hotel: pigs' feet pancake, escargots and chicken fricassée. Wide selection of wines direct from local growers, some of which are offered by the glass, and most interesting of all, at winegrowers' prices. C 120-210. M 69 (weekday lunch), 99.

GILLY-LÈS-CÎTEAUX   21640
Paris 325 - Dijon 23 - Beaune 20   Côte-d'Or

Château de Gilly

Clos Prieur - 03 80 62 89 98, fax 03 80 62 82 34
Closed Jan 26-Mar 7. Open until 9:30pm. Terrace dining. No pets. Tennis. Valet pkg.
  A French landmark well worth visiting in every respect, this former Cistercian monks' retreat nestled in the vineyards has been intelligently restored (gardens included), and the underground passage leading to the restaurant opens onto splendid ribbed vaulting. Chef Jean-Louis Schwendenman produces well-crafted Burgundian classics like eggs en meurette and

coq au vin, and maintains the same precision for his more creative inventions (despite the tourist buses that line up out front). The cellar is a monument to Bacchus himself, and some are even offered by the glass. One more point this year. C 350. M 260 (weekday lunch, wine incl), 195-405.

 ## Château de Gilly

(See restaurant above)
Closed Jan 26-Mar 7. 8 stes 1,580-2,500. 39 rms 660-1,400. Bkfst 85-130. Half-board 1,075-1,815. Rm ser. Air cond. Conf. Tennis. Valet pkg.
This majestic former abbot's residence is set amid French-style gardens, and offers guests spacious, semi-aristocratic, semi-bourgeois quarters with magnificent bathrooms. There's also a huge split-level suite. Breakfasts are out of this world! Relais et Châteaux.

IGÉ	71960
Paris 394 - Mâcon 16 - Lyon 85	Saône/Loire

 ## Château d'Igé

03 85 33 33 99, fax 03 85 33 41 41
Closed Dec-Feb. Open until 9pm. Garden dining. Garage pkg.
This picturesque château was fortified in 1235 by the Counts of Mâcon. Guests marvel at its long history on the floral terrace facing the park—or within the thick walls of the Gothic dining rooms with their opulent Louis XIII décor—while enjoying Laurent Couturier's alert cuisine, based on intelligently interpreted classic themes. We'll let him keep his toque for the moment, because he's full of ideas and vivaciousness, but we found that he neglected lots of details this year. If you aren't up to the medieval heaviness of the setting, you can take your lunch near the dreamy pond. Burgundies feature prominently on the wine list, in particular Mâcons. Smiling welcome. C 300-450. M 155 (weekday lunch), 195-365, 80 (children).

 ## Château d'Igé

(See restaurant above)
Closed Dec-Feb. 6 stes 875-1,100. 7 rms 480-730. Bkfst 65. Half-board 765-1,385. Rm ser. Conf. Garage pkg.
The rooms in this majestic, vine-covered château are both well equipped and beautifully appointed. They overlook a shady, flower-filled park. A handsome vaulted room is available for receptions and seminars. Relais et Châteaux.

JOIGNY	89300
Paris 148 - Auxerre 27 - Montargis 62	Yonne

 ## La Côte Saint-Jacques

14, faubourg de Paris
03 86 62 09 70, fax 03 86 91 49 70
Open daily until 9:45pm. Priv rm 35. Air cond. Heated pool. Tennis. Valet pkg.
The Lorain family has put their heart and soul into turning this old inn on the River Yonne into

the gem of a luxury establishment it is now. Michel has now handed the hearth over to son Jean-Michel, who continues in his father's footsteps, creating the most modern classic cuisine around. The Lorains took a cue from two of their menu's crowning glories—lightly smoked bass with caviar and a cabbage-truffle medley—and came up with a third one: mouth-watering cabbage stuffed with caviar in a smoky sauce. Apart from the occasional feat of daring (cumin-flavored monkfish; veal in coffee sauce) both chefs are resolutely traditional—and that's the way we like them! This visit, we tried the frog's legs with eggplant, sun-dried tomatoes and herb vinaigrette; snails with green asparagus and poached eggs à la bourguignonne; lobster tournedos with Szechuan peppers, chanterelle mushrooms and sweet garlic-flavored peas; and roast duck with fruit, thin cumin tart and herb fritters. We liked the daring rice pudding pyramid à l'Impératrice with gingerbread and caramel ice cream with salty butter. The choice of ingredients and the quality of the craftmanship are perfection itself. Cooking aficionados can take theme-oriented cooking classes in the spacious modern classroom at the end of the elegant underground gallery lined with old Burgundian stone sculptures and linking the restaurant to the River Yonne. The wine list boasts impressive offerings, and is expectedly rich in great Burgundies and local Yonne wines, including one from the restaurant's own vineyard across the river. C 600-900. M 320 (lunch exc Sun, wine incl), 510 (lunch), 720 (wine incl), 180 (children).

 ## La Côte Saint-Jacques

(See restaurant above)
Open year-round. 4 stes 1,380-2,500. 25 rms 500-1,380. Bkfst 110. Rms for disabled. Air cond. Conf. Heated pool. Tennis. Valet pkg.
This lovely group of houses with gardens and balconies overlooking the Yonne River are connected to the restaurant on the other side of the road by an extremely elegant underground passageway embellished with sculptures from old Burgundian churches. The rooms within are extraordinarily comfortable: wonderful mattresses, huge sumptuous bathrooms with separate toilet facilities, etc. The breakfasts are fit for a king (or queen), and you can take them in the lovely glassed-in breakfast room giving onto the river. Relais et Châteaux.

12/20 Godard Père et Fils

17, av. Robert-Petit
03 86 62 16 28, fax 03 86 62 44 33
Closed Sun dinner & Mon off-seas. Open until 9:30pm. Priv rm 40. Terrace dining. Pool. Tennis. Garage pkg.
Claude Godard's little restaurant is a bastion of the traditional French cooking of France's great chefs. He tries to reproduce their recipes without desacralizing them. Most often, it works, although it's sometimes a little on the stiff side. But he's got talent, and he uses good-quality ingredients, so time should do him well.

A fine cellar it is too. C 300. M 140-300, 199 (weekdays, Sat lunch), 360 (exc Sun dinner), 230 (Sat & Sun).

 ## Modern' Hôtel

(See restaurant above)
Closed Sun & Mon off-seas. 1 ste 500-600. 20rms 195-500. Bkfst 45-80. Half-board 375-685. Rm ser. Conf. Pool. Tennis. Valet pkg.
It gets more and more difficult to see the "modernness" of this comfortable hotel. Even though the colors and furniture are completely out of style, the rooms are well-equipped and well-kept. Good breakfast.

 ## Le Rive Gauche

Chemin du Port au Bois
03 86 91 46 66, fax 03 86 91 46 93
Open year-round. 42 rms 250-660. Bkfst 50. Rms for disabled. Restaurant. Half-board 310-535. Rm ser. Air cond. Conf. Tennis. Pkg.
The Lorain family of La Côte Saint-Jacques fame operates this hotel across the Yonne. The standard rooms are very well-maintained, and there's a superb riverside terrace for guests to enjoy.

LADOIX-SERRIGNY	21550
Paris 321 - Dijon 31 - Beaune 6	Côte-d'Or

Les Coquines

N 74, Buisson - 03 80 26 43 58, fax 03 80 26 49 59
Closed Wed dinner, Thu, 2 wks of Feb. Open until 9:30pm. Priv rm 20. Garden dining. Pkg.
This old house in the vineyards at the foot of the Corton slopes is home to a restaurant with a handsome streamlined dining room and a charming garden complete with apple trees. We simply can't maintain the 14 rating, viewing the look-askance attitude of the owner and a cuisine that has fallen more into domain of everyday bistro food than food worthy of a good restaurant. All is not lost however; the cheeses are a downright thrilling experience and perfectly ripe to perfection. We hope the alarm goes off so that this unpretentious place full of charm can win back its rating. C 300. M 145, 215 (exc Sun dinner), 100 (children).

LEVERNOIS	21200
Paris 316 - Dijon 46 - Beaune 4	Côte-d'Or

 ## Jean Crotet

Route de Combertault
03 80 24 73 58, fax 03 80 22 78 00
Closed Nov-Mar: Tue, Wed lunch; 2 wks in Feb; Dec 24-28. Open until 10pm. Priv rm 120. Garden dining. Terrace dining. Air cond. Tennis. Valet pkg.
This is undoubtedly the most prestige establishment in these parts with the dense foliage of its park, the trickling stream and the old-world charm of its Burgundy stone house. Christophe Crotet's cuisine definitely mirrors the refined elegance of his dining room, and that is one of

our hesitations. Both border on being too formal, too meditated, and lacking all spontaneity. Crotet was trained by the best—Bocuse, Troisgros, Girardet—and it shows, but we would prefer a a little more human touch at these outrageous prices. His most amazing dish by far (and this may surprise you) is a succulent roasted Bresse chicken served with creamy whipped potatoes. Be sure to order it (for two) while you're enjoying your pre-meal drink because it's cooked whole. Another of our favorites is the lamb with foie gras and truffles. The wines in the prestigious cellar—even half-bottles—are steeply priced. C 500. M 200-300 (lunch, exc Sun, wine incl), 390-550, 100 (children).

 ## Hostellerie de Levernois

(See restaurant above)
Closed Nov-Mar: Tue; 2 wks in Feb; Dec 24-28. 1 ste 1,500-1,950. 15 rms 950-1,500. Bkfst 95. Rms for disabled. Half-board 1,150-1,500 (oblig in seas). Conf. Tennis. Pkg.
Refined French *art de vivre* abounds at this stately manor. Huge, beautiful rooms. There's a river right on the premises, and the breakfasts are out of this world. Relais et Châteaux.

MÂCON	71000
Paris 395 - Lyon 68 - Bourg-en-Bresse 35	Saône/Loire

 ## Bellevue

416-420 quai Lamartine
03 85 21 04 04, fax 03 85 21 04 02
Open year-round. 1 ste 680-1,100. 24 rms 320-590. Bkfst 55. Restaurant. Half-board 340-500. Rm ser. Conf. Garage pkg.
The real interest of this assortment of old houses-cum-hotel on the banks of the Saône River is its comfortable appointments and highly attentive service. Near the Lamartine public walking path.

12/20 Pierre

7, rue Dufour - 03 85 38 14 23, fax 03 85 39 84 04
Closed Sun dinner & Mon off-seas, Feb school hols. Open until 9:30pm. Terrace dining.
There's always quite a crowd on the terrace or in the country-style dining room of this pleasant establishment, where the owner-chef serves up heaping portions of traditional cuisine. The cooking is often richer in ideas than in technique. The tame wine list is big on Burgundies. Enthusiastic welcome from the owner's pretty wife. C 300. M 100-135 (exc Sat dinner), 170-315.

MARSANNAY-LA-CÔTE	21160
Paris 306 - Dijon 11 - Beaune 32	Côte-d'Or

 ## Les Gourmets

8, rue du Puits-de-Têt
03 80 52 16 32, fax 03 80 52 03 01
Closed Sun dinner, Mon. Open until 9:30pm. Priv rm 40. Garden dining. Pkg.

Don't despair when you come off the highway and find yourself smack in the middle of a business district—the quaint village where this little restaurant-inn is located isn't far off. Once you arrive, you'll be met with ultraconventional décor in the dining room, and you might well expect that the cuisine will follow suit. But you're in for a pleasant surprise: the chef is fond of exotic flavors and shows consummate talent for spicing and seasoning everything he serves. Our favorites: tangy vanilla and pineapple flavored langoustines and artichokes; pan-roasted sea scallops with a zesty pinch of curry; earthy blood sausage served on a bed of warm gingerbread; oxtail and Morteau sausage salad; seven-hour veal done with orange and Parmesan. The desserts are almost worth dying for, and you can wash them down with the sweet wines offerd by the glass. And don't hesitate to give the 150 F set menu a try if you're on a budget. C 400. M 150-400, 85 (children).

MERCUREY	71640
Paris 348 - Mâcon 70 - Chalon 13	Saône/Loire

 Le Val d'Or

Grande-Rue - 03 85 45 13 70, fax 03 85 45 18 45
Closed Mon, Tue lunch, May 26-30, Sep 1-4, Dec 15-Jan 17. Open until 9pm. Air cond. No pets. Pkg.
This venerable provincial establishment with its rustic décor is renowned as a bastion of Burgundian traditions. For some 30 years now, chef-owner Jean-Claude Cogny has been serving forth heaping helpings of his serious fare. And though his repertoire has gradually changed with the times, his expert approach has remained consistent throughout. The good cellar puts the focus on local wines. Friendly welcome. C 350. M 120 (lunch exc Sun, wine incl), 163-345, 85 (children).

MEURSAULT	21190
Paris 320 - Beaune 8 - Chalon-sur-Saône 30	Côte-d'Or

 Les Charmes

10, pl. Murger - 03 80 21 63 53, fax 03 80 21 62 89
Closed Dec-Feb. 14 rms 410-570. Bkfst 45. Rms for disabled. Heated pool. No pets. Garage pkg.
This establishment is located in one of the prettiest villages in "wine country," and the owners saw it fit to name each guest room for one of Burgundy's *crus!* Lots of trees on the surrounding premises.

12/20 **Le Chevreuil**

Pl. de l'Hôtel-de-Ville
03 80 21 23 25, fax 03 80 21 65 51
Closed Wed, Thu lunch, Dec 5-Jan 5. Open until 9pm (10pm in seas). Terrace dining. Pkg.
This establishment was recently refurbished, and now boasts a much warmer dining room and a nice new terrace. The cuisine is mostly inspired by regional classics, with some sunny Southern dishes on the menu every now and again. Ample regional cellar. C 230. **M** 95-195.

 Les Magnolias

8, rue P.-Joigneaux
03 80 21 23 23, fax 03 80 21 29 10
Closed Dec-Mar 15. 1 ste 700-750. 11 rms 380-600. Bkfst 48. No pets. Garage pkg.
This elegant eighteenth-century manor house boasts cozy, individually decorated guest quarters furnished with antiques. Some rooms open out onto the flower-filled courtyard.

NUITS-SAINT-GEORGES	21700
Paris 330 - Beaune 16 - Dijon 22	Côte-d'Or

12/20 **La Côte d'Or**

37, rue Thurot - 03 80 61 06 10, fax 03 80 61 36 24
Closed Wed, Thu lunch. Open until 9pm. Priv rm 30. Terrace dining. Pkg.
This is a no-frill address for those who are visiting the town more for the wine than for the food. Jellied ham marbled with chopped parsley (a speciality of Burgundy), saddle of cod, and strawberry pie make for a simple but perfectly good meal. Good selection of wine, but pricey. C 300. M 100 (lunch, exc Sun), 190-260, 90 (children).

 La Côte d'Or

(See restaurant above)
Closed Wed. 1 ste 600. 6 rms 320-490. Bkfst 50. Rm ser. Pkg.
Good central location. Too bad that the little stream in front of the hotel was covered up to build a parking lot.

 La Gentilhommière

13, vallée de la Serrée
03 80 61 12 06, fax 03 80 61 30 33
Closed Tue, Wed lunch, Dec 15-Jan 15. Open until 9pm (9:30pm Fri & Sat). Priv rm 80. Garden dining. Pool. Tennis. Pkg.
This former hunting lodge decorated in comfortable Louis XIII style provides a charming setting for René-Georges Pianetti's cuisine. His expertise and imagination are readily apparent in the Burgundian fare he serves forth, and in the trendier offerings on the menu as well, but we were once again disappointed by the inconsistency of the quality. The potato and trotter upside down tart is well worth the two toques it shows the result of a perfected style that doesn't take itself overly seriously. But the the scallops and oyster meunière "sandwich" were not up to par. Appealing, mostly regional wine list. Hearty welcome. Poolside buffet in season. C 330-400. M 120-140 (lunch, exc Sun), 195-270.

 La Gentilhommière

(See restaurant above)
Closed Dec 15-Jan 15. 20 rms 390. Bkfst 50. Rms for disabled. Half-board 630 (oblig in seas). Conf. Pool. Tennis. Pkg.
This modern, motel-style building offers comfortable, fairly spacious rooms (all on the ground floor) which open out onto premises complete with a trout stream. Peace and quiet guaranteed!

PONTAUBERT   89200
Paris 229 - Auxerre 55 - Avallon 4   Yonne

 Moulin des Templiers

Vallée du Cousin - 03 86 34 10 80
Closed Oct 31-Mar 15. 14 rms 250-360. Bkfst 35. No pets. Conf. Pkg.
Enjoy breakfast on the terrace of this former mill, set in the middle of the valley. Pleasing guest quarters. Rooms on the small side, but cozy.

PRENOIS   21370
Paris 319 - Dijon 15 - Beaune 51   Côte-d'Or

Auberge de la Charme

03 80 35 32 84
Closed Mon dinner, Tue, Jan 2-17, 1st wk of Aug. Open until 9:45pm. Priv rm 40.
The delicious fare and incredibly reasonable prices make this our idea of everything an inn should be. The modern cuisine is composed of cleverly combined ingredients and clear-cut flavors: pressed duck with foie gras, snail bouillon and croustillant of calf's head, caramelized mango and pineapple cake, etc. David Zuddas always gets it right, and never ceases to amaze us. His 90 F menu is dazzling: scallop cocktail snack in a mouthwatering shellfish juice, good old-fashioned terrine, excellent roast salmon with lentils and Morteau sausage; and his exquisite calf's head bouillon with truffles, intense in flavor and full of aromas, is frankly worth three toques. His wife Catherine makes sure the service is as impeccable as the cooking. The wine cellar has made leaps and bounds in the last year, with an emphasis on good growers' wines from the Burgundy region. C 250. M 90 (weekdays), 110-215, 50 (children).

PULIGNY-MONTRACHET   21190
Paris 327 - Dijon 49 - Beaune 12   Côte-d'Or

Le Montrachet 🙂

Pl. des Marronniers
03 80 21 30 06, fax 03 80 21 39 06
Closed Wed lunch, Dec-Jan 10. Open until 9:30pm. Terrace dining. Pkg.
The wines at this beautiful Burgundy-style house-cum-restaurant are astutely selected and carefully priced (especially the whites), owing to the renowned expertise of the wine steward, and in any case, would you expect otherwise in a town with a name like this? This year we're happy to report that the Burgundy classics we sampled were marvelously done—eggs en meurette, ham braised à la Chablisienne, Gaston Gérard chicken—and chef Michel Bezout also proves great mastery and inventiveness in the seasonal menus he offers. C 410-470. M 195-425, 80 (children).

Le Montrachet
(See restaurant above)
Closed Dec-Jan 10. 2 stes 775-975. 30 rms 450-515. Bkfst 55. Rms for disabled. Half-board 550-575. Conf. Pkg.
After touring the cellar, let the wine steward lead you to this establishment full of bright, cheerful rooms, many of which are done up in pretty country-style décor.

QUARRÉ-LES-TOMBES   89630
Paris 246 - Avallon 19 - Auxerre 72   Yonne

 Auberge de l'Atre

Les Lavaults - 03 86 32 20 79, fax 03 86 32 28 25
Closed Sep 10-Jun 20: Tue dinner & Wed; end Jan-Mar 10; Nov 25-Dec 10. Open until 9:15pm. Priv rm 30. Terrace dining.
This lovingly restored farm house in a forest glade welcomes guests with three cozy little dining rooms decorated with pretty bouquets arranged by Odile, the owner's wife. Chef Francis Salamolard, who knows his local ingredients like the back of his hand, enthusiastically invites diners to discover wild mushrooms, Morvan herbs, and regional wines (very nice cellar). He's a wizard at coaxing marvelous flavors out of the prime produce he chooses. C 300-350. M 145 (weekdays), 210-295, 70 (children).

Auberge des Brizards

03 86 32 20 12, fax 03 86 32 27 40
Open year-round. 4 stes 750. 21 rms 250-750. Restaurant. Half-board 270-510. Conf. Tennis. Pkg.
This old inn nestled in the forest is decorated in charming country style, and the rooms here benefit from added personal touches. Peace and quiet guaranteed; regional restaurant on the premises.

QUEMIGNY-POISOT   21220
Paris 298 - Dijon 22 - Beaune 32   Côte-d'Or

12/20 **L'Orée du Bois**

03 80 49 78 77, fax 03 80 49 78 77
Closed Sun dinner & Mon off-seas, Dec 22-Feb 5. Open until 9pm (9:30pm in summer). Terrace dining. Pkg.
This modest, farm-style inn offers an inviting welcome and exceedingly professional service. The regional fare is wholesome and simple, and the cellar is stocked with growers' wines purchased on-site. This is one fine address for country dining! C 180-280. M 75 (weekdays), 130-170, 55 (children).

REPLONGES   01750
Paris 394 - Bourg-en-Bresse 32 - Mâcon 5   Ain

 La Huchette

On N 79 - 03 85 31 03 55, fax 03 85 31 10 24
Closed Mon, Tue lunch, Nov 15-Dec 15. Open until 9pm. Priv rm 12. Garden dining. Heated pool. Pkg.

The walls in the country dining room, in full Burgundian style yet without the snobbery one might expect, are decorated with frescoes, and young chef Vincent Rivon handles traditional dishes with the ease of an old soldier: chicken liver cake, saddle of lamb "sausages" with thyme butter and Bresse chicken breast with morel mushrooms. Judicious cellar. C 250-425. M 160-230, 60 (children).

 ## La Huchette

(See restaurant above)
Closed Nov 15-Dec 15. 1 ste 1,200. 11 rms 400-600. Bkfst 60-70. Rms for disabled. Half-board 400-500. Rm ser. Conf. Heated pool. Pkg.
This charming, one-storey country house boasts nicely furnished rooms and a pool on the premises.

SAINT-GERVAIS-EN-VALLIÈRE   71350
Paris 328 - Beaune 13 - Chagny 18   Saône/Loire

 ## Moulin de Hauterive

Chaublanc - 03 85 91 55 56, fax 03 85 91 89 65
Closed Mon, Tue lunch (exc Jun-Aug), Jan. Open until 9pm. Priv rm 16. Garden dining. Pool. Tennis. No pets. Pkg.
This admirably restored mill not far from Beaune offers a picture-perfect setting for enjoying a meal or a longer stay. The soothing sound of water lulls patrons on the shady terrace, although we were frustrated over the lack of care put into the fixed-price menus this year, as well as over the general quality. We liked the sauce on the scanty portion of lobster, but frankly larger helpings are definitely called for. Well stocked cellar rich in Burgundies. C 350-450. M 105-160 (lunch), 240-450, 80 (children).

 ## Moulin de Hauterive

(See restaurant above)
Closed Mon (exc summer), Jan. 12 stes 650-850. 10 rms 530-600. Bkfst 70 (oblig in seas). Rm ser. Air cond. Conf. Pool. Tennis. Pkg.
Hauterive has become the headquarters for the "Moulins étape" chain. Member establishments uphold the standards and values of traditional hostelry while paying due respect to modern comforts and amenities. This hotel offers hydrotherapy and a range of facilities for seminars.

SAINT-LAURENT-SUR-SAÔNE   01750
Paris 397 - Bourg-en-Bresse 34 - Mâcon 3   Ain

 ## Le Saint-Laurent   ✿

Rive Gauche, 1, quai Bouchacourt
03 85 39 29 19, fax 03 85 38 29 77
Closed Nov 15-Dec 15. Open until 10pm. Terrace dining. Air cond. Pkg.
Georges Blanc owns this nostalgic bistro by the bridge, overlooking the Saône and the town of Mâcon. Chef Marc Drillien's menu is loaded with clever little dishes: parsleyed oxtail; snail ravioli forestière; blanquette of cod with leeks. He also does Saône fish dishes when the season's

right. There's some good Mâcon-Azay in the cellar, and a charming welcome in store. Splendid terrace. C 210. M 100-200.

ST-PÈRE-SOUS-VÉZELAY   89450
Paris 220 - Auxerre 53 - Vézelay 3   Yonne

 ## L'Espérance

"Marc Meneau",
03 86 20 45, fax 03 86 33 26 15(R),
03 86 33 20 45 (H), fax 03 86 33 26 15
Closed Tue, Wed lunch, Feb. Open until 10pm. Priv rm 80. Air cond. Heated pool. Valet pkg.
After nourishing your soul at the celebrated Vézelay abbey, you owe it to yourself (at least once in your life!) to indulge in the sinfully good sustenance proffered by Marc Meneau. This world-renowned chef extended his domain by opening Le Pré des Marguerites (*see below*), has given the Vézelay *appellation* a new lease on life with his vast vineyards, and runs a hotel complex and boutique. In fact he's so enterprising, you might think he'd traded in his chef's whites for a three-piece suit. Happily though, such is not the case. Marc Meneau is a creative genius at heart, ever in search of challenges and ever eager to reach new culinary heights. Meneau's talents extend beyond a given style (although he does have some "constants," like a penchant for pork) to what we refer to as Meneau "periods" (during our visit he was working on the theme of bitter flavors). Our last meal here was one of the best we've had. We started with a luscious hot-cold cream of lobster soup topped with a very delicate aspic, followed by savory marrow-stuffed baby artichokes in a full-bodied oxtail sauce. Next came a remarkable poached foie gras with white beans (Meneau excels at pairing uppercrust foodstuffs with "peasant" fare), and succulent lamb prepared a number of different ways. While the tab is always less easy to swallow than the splendid food, hostess Françoise Meneau is quick to sweeten the mood with an avalanche of cookies and candy after dessert. C 840-1,350. M 380 (weekday lunch, Sat lunch), 680, 880.

L'Espérance

(See restaurant above)
Open year-round. 6 stes 1,700-2,900. 30 rms 660-1,600. Bkfst 130. Rms for disabled. Half-board 850-980. Rm ser. Air cond. Conf. Heated pool. Tennis. Valet pkg.
Lodgings at the Meneau domain are divided into three distinct parts. There are cozy rooms above the restaurant done in soft, fresh colors; larger, more functional modern rooms with individual terraces at Le Pré des Marguerites; and finally the rooms we like best, at the quiet old mill (charming, intimate, prettily appointed guest quarters, decorated on a country theme). Relais et Châteaux.

Looking for a celebrated chef? Refer to the Index.

12/20 Le Pré des Marguerites

"Marc Meneau" - 03 86 33 33 33, fax 03 86 33 34 73
Open daily until 10pm. Priv rm 400. Air cond.
Heated pool. Tennis. Pkg.

While the annex's modern exterior isn't all that inviting, spring is in the air in the pretty dining room within, where tourists can tuck into 120 F "pilgrim" or 165 F "promenade" set menus featuring a selection of good bourgeois dishes. Conference facilities. M 70 (lunch, exc Sun, wine incl), 120 (dinner, wine incl), 165-230 (wine incl), 70 (children).

SAINT-RÉMY	71100
Paris 341 - Mâcon 56 - Chalon-sur-Saône 3	Saône/Loire

Le Moulin de Martorey

Chalon South exit on A 6,
toward Le Creusot
03 85 48 12 98, fax 03 85 48 73 67
Closed Sun dinner, Mon, Aug 18-27. Open until 9:30pm. Priv rm 22. Garden dining. Air cond. Pkg.

This mill, complete with a flower garden and carp-stocked pond, is a veritable haven of tranquility. The dining room is adorned with stone-tiled floors and a rustic décor, and the tables are beautifully laid. Interestingly enough, master chef Jean-Pierre Gillot learned his craft by making a tour of France's two- to four-toque restaurants. And while his cooking displays intelligence and daring, we wish it were a shade more consistent. The 180 F set menu is an excellent value: you start with fresh, flavorful clotted goat's milk and crab, move on to veal shanks (a tad dry) done in an emulsion of pot-au-feu jus with marrow, accompanied by delicious sautéed potatoes and a mini-plate of vegetables. Dessert is a wonderful guanaja fondant and praline millefeuille in coffee sauce. The à la carte menu's crowning glory is the festival d'escargots where the snails are served three different ways: in a garlic and celery bouillon, with meat jus and roast potatoes, and finally with red wine—a truly memorable dish. Attractive wine list expertly explained by Pierrette Gillot, with a good choice of Côte-Chalonnaise bottles on hand. C 300. M 180 (weekdays, wine incl), 135 (weekdays), 175-400.

SAULIEU	21210
Paris 255 - Dijon 73 - Avallon 39	Côte-d'Or

La Côte d'Or

"Bernard Loiseau",
2, rue de l'Argentine
03 80 90 53 53, fax 03 80 64 08 92
Open daily until 10pm. Priv rm 30. Valet pkg.

Bernard Loiseau has been in this splendid old mansion for twenty years now, and for the past twenty years he's enthusiastically taken on bankers and the media in his efforts to make his restaurant the very best it can be. And by golly, he's succeeded! Loiseau recently replaced an old garage with a vast *salon* built around an impressive fireplace—a lovely setting for enjoying a drink and perusing the menu before moving into one of the dining rooms overlooking the landscaped garden. First-timers will naturally (and rightly) be drawn to Loiseau's best-known dishes like escargots, frog legs in garlic and parsley jus, or the spectacular Bresse chicken with truffle-studded rice, steamed in an enormous clay pot ("oohs" and "ahs" fill the air when the pot is opened in the dining room, revealing this dish's divine aroma). We were keener on some of the newer creations like his lentil and sea urchin soup with carmelized baby onions, hot foie gras with Tarbais beans and duck jus vinaigrette, and crayfish ragoût with peas and chanterelle mushrooms. And Loiseau has no equal when it comes to transforming the most humble ingredients into foodstuffs fit for royalty. He's made an entire "en fête" menu out of potatoes, and caramelizes cauliflower several times over to make an out-of-this-world soup. His cuisine is one of the most modern ones in existence: all his sauces are made from reductions of vegetables, wines and other noble ingredients, and are completely fat-free, but don't worry, it will be feast-day for your tastebuds. Let Hubert Couilloud (who, like fine wines, only gets better with age) or *Meilleur Sommelier de France* Lyonel Leconte guide you through the wine list, replete with splendid Burgundies. C 800. M 390 (weekday lunch), 450, 680 (lunch), 890, 110 (children).

La Côte d'Or

(See restaurant above)
Open year-round. 8 stes 1,400-2,400. 7 rms 700-1,800. Bkfst 120. Conf. Valet pkg.

Bernard Loiseau continues to make improvements on this former coaching inn: it now features five pretty rooms decorated in regional style with exposed beams, tile floors, and warm, natural-colored textiles. The rooms boast balconies overlooking the rooftops and surrounding countryside, and there's a wonderful, large suite under the rafters, complete with a living room and two bathrooms (one with a Jacuzzi). Some smaller, older rooms are also available (less expensive than the remodeled rooms, but minus the prestigious Relais et Châteaux rating). Relais et Châteaux.

La Poste

1, rue Grillot - 03 80 64 05 67, fax 03 80 64 10 82
Closed Nov 15-Mar 15. 45 rms 240-485. Bkfst 45.
Rms for disabled. Restaurant. Half-board 300-450.
Rm ser. Air cond. Conf. Valet pkg.

Ask for a room opening out onto the pretty inner courtyard of this charming seventeenth-century coaching inn. All rooms are well equipped and soundproofed.

SAUVIGNY-LE-BOIS   89200
Paris 228 - Auxerre 54 - Avallon 3   Yonne

 Le Relais Fleuri

Avallon exit on A 6, La Cerce
03 86 34 02 85, fax 03 86 34 09 98
Open daily until 9:45pm. Pool. Tennis. Pkg.
   This place is the essence of peace and quiet, and viewing its location so near the interstate, we're proud that it's stood up to the temptation of becoming a tourist trap. Stéphane Blanchet treats diners to good food at equally good prices in his sunny, quiet dining room. The cuisine here makes a refreshing break with the usual themes: tasty braised hare with an Indian accent; croustillant of snails in a tender garlic bouillon; thinly sliced beef served with marrow; creamy blanquette of fresh cod. Desserts are nicely done too (try the charlotte). C 230. M 112-250 (wine incl), 143-195.

 Le Relais Fleuri

(See restaurant above)
Open year-round. 48 rms 295-400. Bkfst 48. Rms for disabled. Half-board 320-375. Rm ser. Conf. Pool. Tennis. Pkg.
   This country-based complex features ultrafunctional rooms, and the location makes it a convenient overnight stop on the road between Lyon and Paris. Very well equipped for its category.

SENNECEY-LÈS-DIJON   21800
Paris 322 - Dijon 5   Côte-d'Or

 La Flambée

On D 905, route de Dôle-Besançon
03 80 47 35 35, fax 03 80 47 07 08
Open year-round. 1 ste 650-750. 22 rms 315-490. Bkfst 47. Rms for disabled. Restaurant. Half-board 325-450. Rm ser. Air cond. Conf. Pool. Pkg.
   This authentic cottage in an idyllic country setting offers quiet, modern, well-equipped rooms, and every conceivable luxury! Guaranteed to capture your heart.

SENS   89100
Paris 118 - Auxerre 59 - Fontainebleau 53   Yonne

 La Madeleine

1, rue d'Alsace-Lorraine
03 86 65 09 31, fax 03 86 95 37 41
Closed Sun dinner, Mon, 2 wks in Aug. Open until 9:30pm. Garage pkg.
   The young chef here trained at Lasserre, in Paris. This is readily apparent in the skill he demonstrates—and in the delusions of grandeur he possesses. Needless to say, we'd be happier if he dropped the fancy airs and let his craftsmanship and good ideas speak for themselves. A number of dishes work in so many flavors they end up cancelling one another out. Some offerings are well worth two toques; others merit an act of contrition. The cellar, put together by an accomplished wine steward, offers some superb Chablis. C 300. M 175-450.

12/20 Paris et Poste

97, rue de la République
03 86 65 17 43, fax 03 86 64 48 45
Open daily until 10pm. Priv rm 110. Terrace dining.
   "Latecomers get the bones!" or so the saying goes at this well-to-do regional institution. Prices can run on the high side for the less-than-copious portions. This time around we found the classic cuisine more interesting and appealing than on past visits. Good service. C 350-450. M 160-240 (Sun), 99-260, 80 (children).

 Paris et Poste

(See restaurant above)
Open year-round. 8 stes 550. 17 rms 370-500. Bkfst 50. Half-board 450. Conf.
   A pretty provincial hotel dating from the nineteenth century, with handsomely appointed, well-soundproofed rooms. Some rooms open onto the patio. Spacious bathrooms. Breakfasts could be better. Professional service.

SOLOGNY   71960
Paris 416 - Mâcon 14 - Lyon 83   Saône/Loire

 Le Relais du Mâconnais

La Croix-Blanche
03 85 36 60 72, fax 03 85 36 65 47
Closed Sun dinner & Mon (Oct-end Apr), 2 wks in Jan. Open until 9pm. Priv rm 12. Terrace dining. Pkg.
   This big, square house, located in a tiny hamlet on a little-used road, is by far the best address in the Mâcon area. Christian Lannuel has honed his up-to-the-minute cooking style using the classics for bases. The à la carte choice is a work of art, but even the 135 F set-price meal offers good choices like cod with cream cheese and neck of lamb stuffed with kidneys and herbs. Tempting cheese tray. Classic—albeit delicious— desserts. Wise selection of, of course, Burgundies, especially rich in the best of the local Macons and reasonably priced. Try the Thévenet Macon. C 250. M 135-280, 65 (children).

 Le Relais du Mâconnais

(See restaurant above)
Closed Sun & Mon off-seas, 2 wks in Jan. 2 stes 420-500. 8 rms 290-360. Bkfst 36. Half-board 600 (oblig in seas). Conf. Pkg.
   This is a real haven, especially for Mâcon, which is not blessed with good hotels. Friendly reception, attractive rooms, and most of all, quiet.

TONNERRE   89700
Paris 196 - Troyes 57 - Sens 73 - Auxerre 35   Yonne

 L'Abbaye Saint-Michel

Montée de Saint-Michel
03 86 55 05 99, fax 03 86 55 00 10
*Closings not available. 3 stes 1,800-1,900. 11 rms
590-1,600. Bkfst 55-85. Rms for disabled. Half-
board 1,010-1,995. Rm ser. Conf. Tennis. Pkg.*
Both old rooms (a thirteenth-century fresco
awaits guests in the "Chartier" room) and
sumptuous new suites work side by side here,
showcasing the abbey's stone structure (much of
it was destroyed after the Revolution). The surrounding park plays host to a monastic garden,
orchard, and vegetable garden, and the complex
overlooks scenic Tonnerre and the Armançon
Valley.

TORCY   71210
Paris 321 - Mâcon 85 - Le Creusot 4   Saône/Loire

 Le Vieux Saule

03 85 55 09 53, fax 03 85 80 39 99
*Closed Sun dinner, Mon. Open until 9:30pm. Priv
rm 60. Terrace dining. Pkg.*
The décor in this cozy old house has just gotten
a facelift. But Christian Hervé's interesting
cuisine, a skillfully honed combination of traditional themes and bright new ideas, is just as
constant as ever. The salmon tartare is as fresh as
can be, and a mark well above the ordinary.
Game specialties as well. Pertinent wine list,
with a nice selection of regional offerings.
Friendly welcome, with very professional yet
gracious service. C 350. M 100-350, 65 (children).

TOURNUS   71700
Paris 360 - Mâcon 30 - Bourg-en-Bresse 53   Saône/Loire

 Greuze   ✺

1, rue Albert-Thibaudet
03 85 51 13 52, fax 03 85 51 75 42
Open daily until 9:45pm. Priv rm 25. Pkg.
This is an inn with a capital "I," an establishment built in the image of its owner, who is
truly one of a kind. The dining room layout is
conducive to a congenial atmosphere, and everything else is infinitely appealing as well–from the
top-notch service to the wonderful cellar, rich in
southern Burgundies. The menu hardly ever
changes, which is fine by us! Sample the most
memorable sautéed chicken, pâté en croûte, and
grilled turbot you'll ever taste. This is simplicity
at its best: traditional cooking marked by the
finest ingredients and perfect sauces. C 480-650.
M 260-510.

 Hôtel de Greuze

5-6, pl. de l'Abbaye
03 85 51 77 77, fax 03 85 51 77 23
*Open year-round. 2 stes 1,900. 19 rms 590-1,290.
Bkfst 100. Rms for disabled. Rm ser. Air cond. Conf.
Garage pkg.*

The venerable house opposite the abbey has
been turned into a luxury hotel where the cus-
tom-decorated rooms come in a variety of sizes.
Embroidered bed linens, thick carpeting, gorgeous furniture, fireplaces, magnificent
bathrooms... Impeccable service; incredible
breakfasts. Rooms are outfitted with
ultramodern equipment. *See restaurant above.*

 **La Montagne
de Brancion**

Col de Brancion - 03 85 51 12 40, fax 03 85 51 18 64
*Closed beg Nov-mid Mar. Open until 9pm. Pool.
Pkg.*
This is a true haven away from it all with its
refined elegance chocked full of interesting objects collected from all over the region and hidden among the vineyards just three kilometers
outside the charming medieval village of Brancion. The cuisine may be a little less elegant than
the décor, but it is a simple one full of distinctive
flavors. We savored the foie gras with cabbage
and "poaching jus" as well as the delicate
workmanship of the leg of lamb served with its
very distinctive broad bean purée and garlic
cream sauce. The savarin was an utterly moving
experience. The wine list is not far-reaching, but
offers a good selection of local wines such as
Rully, Montagny and others. C 400. M 200-400,
80 (children).

 **La Montagne
de Brancion**

(See restaurant above)
*Closed beg Nov-mid Mar. 20 rms 460-760. Bkfst 70.
Half-board 510-660 (oblig in seas). Rm ser. Conf.
Pool. Pkg.*
One might expect this well-to-do house stuck
on the top of a hill to be more like an eagle's aerie
than the cozy little nest it actually is. Lots to enjoy
here: the panoramic view of the countryside, the
vineyards surrounding you, and the rooms, all
turned toward the sunrise (you're not obliged to
watch it!).

 Le Rempart

2-4, av. Gambetta - 03 85 51 10 56, fax 03 85 51 77 22
Open daily until 9:30pm. Air cond. Valet pkg.
This restaurant, with its twelfth-century
columns, stone walls and straight, high-backed
chairs in the dining room—through to the stiffly
postured service, is slowly losing our favor.
Daniel Rogié's excellent ingredients and skilled
expertise produce a cuisine that is straight as an
arrow, but he seldom lets himself go, which
leads to a distinct lack of emotion, creativity and
outright *joie de vivre*. There's nothing to criticize
about his succulent homemade foie gras or his
incredibly tasty lamb fillet cooked in a potato
crust, but let's be honest. Even the Secretary of
Defense lets down his defenses from time to
time, so we strongly suggest that this chef (and
his staff) do the same. Until then, the two toques
are on the line. Prestigious wine list with a good
selection of half-bottles. C 300-400. M 84-425.

Le Rempart

(See restaurant above)
Open year-round. 6 stes 750-1,100. 31 rms 340-700. Bkfst 50-80. Rms for disabled. Half-board 430-700. Rm ser. Air cond. Conf. Valet pkg.
The spacious, well-equipped rooms here are a bit on the impersonal side. Some overlook the abbey. The bar is warm and comfortable.

 ## Aux Terrasses

18, av. du 23-Janvier
03 85 51 01 74, fax 03 85 51 09 99
Closed Sun dinner, Mon, Jan 6-Feb 3. Open until 9:30pm. Terrace dining. Air cond. Pkg.
This immensely popular, inexpensive restaurant dishes up tasty, uncomplicated fare. Nice choice of regional wines. The décor is heavier than the cooking! C 225-325. M 98 (weekdays, Sat lunch), 120-240.

VAL-DE-MERCY   89580
Paris 184 - Ayxerre 17 - Avallon 44   Yonne

12/20 Auberge du Château

03 86 41 60 00, fax 03 86 41 73 28
Closed Sun dinner, Mon, mid Jan-Feb. Open until 9:30pm. Terrace dining. Pkg.
The décor at this inn (which could well be a château) is extraordinarily tasteful, but chef Marc Ramos has lost his touch (and also his toque!). For the prices he charges, we expect more than marinated salmon, salade gourmande and duck breast. Apart from the growers' Chablis (works in progress), there are some nice, consistently priced Bourgognes on offer. C 300-400. M 95 (weekdays, wine incl), 150-220, 45 (children).

 ## Auberge du Château

(See restaurant above)
Closed Jan 15-Feb 28. 1 ste 550. 4 rms 250-350. Bkfst 45. Half-board 450-560. Rm ser. Conf. Pkg.
The quiet, individually decorated rooms here echo the same impeccable taste as the neighboring restaurant, and the bathrooms are fit for a king (or queen!).

VAL-SUZON   21121
Paris 318 - Dijon 15 - Beaune 51   Côte-d'Or

 ## Hostellerie du Val Suzon

N 71, 1, rue du Fourneau
03 80 35 60 15, fax 03 80 35 61 36
Closed Nov-Mar: Sun dinner, Mon. Open until 10pm. Priv rm 18. Terrace dining. Pool. No pets. Pkg.
This tranquil village inn with its pretty country-style décor and terrace serves as stage for chef Yves Perreau, who continues to regale us after twenty-six years at the stove with his fine-honed interpretations of classic dishes (conscientiously updated as he sees fit). Check out the finds on the interesting and wisely priced

wine list. C 300-350. M 130 (lunch exc Sun, wine incl), 200-420, 85 (children).

 ## Hostellerie du Val Suzon

(See restaurant above)
See restaurant for closings. 3 stes 650-950. 13 rms 320-520. Bkfst 58-78. Half-board 485-520 (oblig in seas). Conf. Pkg.
The pretty, well-equipped rooms in the main building and adjoining chalet are done up in charming, country-inspired décor. (They're due to be renovated shortly.) Nice suite.

VAULT-DE-LUGNY   89200
Paris 231 - Auxerre 57 - Avallon 6   Yonne

 ## Château de Vault-de-Lugny

03 86 34 07 86, fax 03 86 34 16 36
Closed Nov 11-Mar 21. 1 ste 1,700. 11 rms 700-2,200. Rms for disabled. Restaurant. Half-board 560-1,310. Conf. Tennis. Valet pkg.
This noble château is perched on a vast expanse of green, stream-fed property. Inside you'll find remarkable rooms, all done up in the best of taste, and a truly luxurious suite. Quality welcome and service.

VÉZELAY   89450
Paris 221 - Clamecy 23 - Avallon 13 - Auxerre 52   Yonne

11/20 Le Bougainville

26, rue Saint-Étienne
03 86 33 27 57, fax 03 86 33 35 12
Closed Mon off-seas, Tue, Wed lunch, Dec-Jan. Open until 9pm.
A sweet little restaurant serving up such classics as ravigote calf's head and stewed beef jaw, perhaps lacking in divine inspiration, granted, but which will leave you full and satisfied. C 79-180, 98 (wine incl), 40 (children).

 ## Résidence-Hôtel Le Pontot

Pl. du Pontot - 03 86 33 24 40, fax 03 86 33 30 05
Closed Nov 2-Mar 27. 3 stes 800-1,050. 7 rms 350-950. Bkfst 50. Conf.
This fortified medieval building-hotel offers luxurious, well-appointed rooms, and is located right around the corner from the Romanesque-style Madeleine basilica. Breakfast served in the enclosed garden amass with flowers. Bar in hotel.

REGIONAL FOODS

Burgundy takes pride in its gastronomic bounty. Chablis, in the north, is not only the home of justly famous white wines, but of earthy andouillette sausages as well. In the heart of the province, Dijon holds a triple claim to epicurean fame: mustard, gingerbread, and blackcurrant liqueur (crème de cassis, indispensable for an authentic Kir).

To the east, famously good charcuterie is produced on the rugged terrain of the Morvan (the hams are especially flavorful), while southward, in the Mâconnais, Charollais beef cattle graze picturesquely on green hillsides.

From Auxerre to Mâcon, Burgundy boasts a host of capital cheeses made from cow's milk (Époisses, Saint-Florentin, Soumaintrain, Aizy Cendré, Saint-Marcellin) or goat's milk (Montrachet, Claquebitou, Charollais, Bouton de Culotte...). Many are still fashioned according to medieval recipes.

• CHARCUTERIE

ARLEUF   58430 – Nièvre

Maison Dussert

03 86 78 82 00
Since 1904 Dussert has regaled an appreciative public with jambon persillé (ham in parsley aspic), white andouille sausage, and lipsmacking saucisson, a dried sausage that is perfect for a picnic.

CHABLIS   89800 – Yonne

Maison de l'Andouillette Artisanale

3 bis, pl. du Général-de-Gaulle · 03 86 42 12 82
Andouillette sausages are a cult item in Chablis, and this firm has been using the same successful recipe for nearly 120 years. Excellent eating.

DIJON   21000 – Côte-d'Or

Michel Collot

59, rue du Fg-Raines · 03 80 41 34 07
Here's a good address for ham in parsley aspic, ham braised in wine lees, and various types of cured sausages.

• CHEESE

CHALON-SUR-SAÔNE   71100 – Saône/Loire

Crémerie Poure

12, rue Saint-Vincent · 03 85 48 07 79
All the finest cheeses of Burgundy are present and accounted for, including some fabulous chèvres.

DIJON   21000 – Côte-d'Or

Le Chalet Comtois

28, rue Musette · 03 80 30 48 61
A laudable selection of the region's farm cheeses, as well as excellent specimens from all over France.

ÉPOISSES   21460 – Côte-d'Or

Berthaut & Fils

7, pl. du Champ-de-Foire · 03 80 96 44 44
Pungent Époisses owes some of its flavor to the local brandy with which its orange crust is regularly rinsed. Did you know that Époisses was Napoléon's favorite cheese? Now you do!

RIGNY-SUR-ARROUX   71160 – Saône/Loire

Geneviève Richard

Le Tremblay · 03 85 53 07 32
Come here to choose from a vast array of thumpingly good chèvres, produced from the milk of locally raised goats.

• CHOCOLATE & CANDY

AUXERRE   89000 – Yonne

Goussard

3, pl. Charles-Surugue · 03 86 52 04 25
Every single sweet treat is made right here on the premises. Try the luscious chocolate escargots de Bourgogne or the variously flavored chocolate truffles.

BEAUNE   21200 – Côte-d'Or

Bouché

1, pl. Monge · 03 80 22 10 35
Beaune is not just about wine, as you'll see when you taste Bouché's chocolates filled with luscious ganaches, chocolate escargots de Bourgogne, and delectable berry-flavored caramels. An admirable talent is at work here!

CHALON-SUR-SAÔNE   71100 – Saône/Loire

Allex

11, pl. de l'Hôtel-de-Ville - 03 85 48 04 52
The owner selects his own cocoa beans to make the scrumptious chocolates he sells in his shop.

CLAYETTE (LA)   71800 – Saône/Loire

Chocolats Dufoux

30, rue Centrale - 03 85 28 08 10
Bernard Dufoux is a wizard with chocolate. His creations put chocoholics in a trance! The caramelized-almond, blackberry, and mint varieties will bowl you over. He also gives lessons, and students can take away and eat what they've produced.

DIJON   21000 – Côte-d'Or

Au Parrain Généreux

21, rue du Bourg - 03 80 30 38 88
Chocolates filled with original, utterly delectable ganaches: pistachio mousse, gingerbread cream, Burgundy prune, Szechwan pepper, and more! Excellent gingerbread, too.

• *GOURMET SPECIALTIES*

Coffee

CHENÔVE   21300 – Côte-d'Or

Café Campanini

67, route de Beaune - 03 80 58 78 78
Also at 18, rue Musette, 21000 Dijon
Coffee buffs will love the range of premium beans roasted on the premises. Customers include the likes of Paul Bocuse and Bernard Loiseau. Excellent teas also on offer.

Honey & Jams

CHÂTEAU-CHINON   58120 – Nièvre

Les Ruchers du Morvan

Port de l'Homme, Corancy - 03 86 78 02 42
The Ruchers' acacia honey is golden and crystalline. Also on offer: honeys with the delicate flavor of local wild flowers, or of the Morvan forest.

CRAIN   89480 – Yonne

Au Jardin des Fées

Ferme de Misery - 03 86 81 74 27

Old-fashioned jams in a host of irresistible flavors: tomato, pumpkin, sour cherry... Try the raisiné, a traditional Burgundian preserve of grapes and other fruit.

Liqueurs

DIJON   21000 – Côte-d'Or

Cassis Briottet

12, rue Berlier - 03 80 66 18 59
Blackcurrant liqueur (crème de cassis) made with premium berries for a wonderfully true-fruit flavor. Try the liqueur on its own, before you mix it with Bourgogne Aligoté or other white wine to make a Kir.

NUITS-SAINT-GEORGES   21700 – Côte-d'Or

Maison Cartron

25, rue du Dr-Legrand - 03 80 61 09 62
A high-quality crème de cassis made with selected fruit. Also on hand is a range of crème liqueurs made with other types of berries.

Mustard

DIJON   21000 – Côte-d'Or

Maille-Grey-Poupon

32, rue de la Liberté - 03 80 30 44 02
The Dijon mustard mecca. The fiery condiment is sold in jars or decorative antique-style crocks; excellent vinegars also available.

Snails

CHENÔVE   21300 – Côte-d'Or

Hélix S.A.

8, rue du 6-Juillet - 03 80 52 54 23
The helix-shaped shell of the escargot de Bourgogne gives the shop its name. Here the creatures are prepared in the traditional way, with a delicious snail butter.

• *PASTRY & COOKIES*

DIJON   21000 – Côte-d'Or

Mulot et Petitjean

13, pl. Bossuet - 03 80 30 07 10
This is the place for gingerbread. The house recipe dates back to the 1700s, and it produces a fragrant, fine-textured pain d'épice. Lots of decorative and amusing shapes.

SAINT-PEREUSE 58110 – Nièvre

Biscuits Grobost

Coeurty - 03 86 84 44 33
Light, crisp ladyfingers that literally melt in the mouth, baked according to a 1902 recipe.

WINE

• CHABLIS

The wines of Chablis are appreciated by connoisseurs the world over for their richness, underscored by a signature steeliness. The Chardonnay grape is the sole variety in use, from the modest and mostly forgettable Petit-Chablis, through straight Chablis, Chablis Premier Cru, and the superb (and invariably expensive) Grands Crus.

CHABLIS 89800 – Yonne

Coop La Chablisienne

8, bd Pasteur - 03 86 42 89 89, fax 03 86 42 89 90
Open Mon-Sat 8am-noon & 2pm-7pm, Sun 9am-noon & 2pm-6pm.
Well-run cooperative with a full range of local wines.

LIGNORELLES 89800 – Yonne

Alain Pautré

23, rue de Chablis
03 86 47 43 04, fax 03 86 47 56 42
Open daily (exc Sun pm).
Pautré's cellar, just northwest of Chablis, is a welcoming stop for wine buffs and buyers. His wines display considerable charm; even the Petit-Chablis is delightful.

Domaine Thierry Hamelin

1, impasse de la Grappe
03 86 47 52 79, fax 03 86 47 53 41
Open Mon-Sat 9am-noon & 1:30pm-7pm.
Neighbor of the grower cited above, Hamelin is also happy to greet customers passing through the region. Beautifully balanced wines at attractive prices.

*Looking for a town or restaurant? A winery? A gastronomic specialty or a celebrated chef? Consult the **alphabetical index** to locate them quickly and easily.*

SAINT-BRIS-LE-VINEUX 89530 – Yonne

Claude Verret

7, route de Champs
03 86 53 31 81, fax 03 86 53 89 61
Open Mon-Sat 8am-noon & 2pm-7pm.
Fine wines from Sauvignon grapes (not common in Burgundy); crisp Aligoté; tasty red Irancy, redolent of cherries.

• CÔTE DE NUITS

The Côte de Nuits is the northern half of the Côte d'Or, home of some of the world's most prestigious and sought-after wines. Because their names are not household words, wines from **Marsannay-la-Côte** and **Fixin** are often less expensive than bottles of similar quality from better-known villages. Marsannay's reds are structured and tannic; the whites have a pronounced mineral note. Fixin produces red wines with elegant structure and subtle flavors of cherries and cooked plums.

'Twere folly to venture into the part of the Côte de Nuits that lies between **Gevrey** and **Chambolle** without a guide! As a rule, it's best to invest a few dollars more in a Premier Cru (Clos Saint-Jacques, Les Champeaux...) than to be tempted by a straight Gevrey-Chambertin of unknown quality. Morey-Saint-Denis, one of the smaller *appellations* of the Côte de Nuits, is less well known than its illustrious neighbors. Yet it produces some notable Premiers Crus and five prestigious Grands Crus, including Clos de la Roche and Clos de Tart. Chambolle-Musigny's two Grands Crus, Musigny and Bonnes-Mares, are reputed for their finesse; the "Villages" can be uneven—when possible, taste before you buy!

The wines of **Flagey-Échezeaux** and **Vosne-Romanée** are the stuff of connoisseurs' dreams: these towns are home to such exalted Grands Crus as Romanée-Conti, La Tâche, Richebourg, Grands-Échezeaux, and luscious Premiers Crus like Les Suchots, Aux Brûlées, Les Chaumes... **Nuits-Saint-Georges** gave its name to this part of the Côte d'Or, and boasts a number of Premiers Crus of rare breeding.

CHAMBOLLE-MUSIGNY 21220 – Côte-d'Or

Domaine Jacques-Frédéric Mugnier

Château de Chambolle-Musigny
03 80 62 85 39, fax 03 80 62 87 36
Open weekdays by appt only.
This estate includes some of the finest *terroirs* of Chambolle with prime parcels of Bonnes-

Mares and Musigny (Grands Crus). Small quantities, however, and they disappear fast.

COMBLANCHIEN
21700 – Côte-d'Or

René Durand
25, Grande Rue - 03 80 62 94 45, fax 03 80 62 71 22
Open daily (exc Sun pm).
René Durand's mission is to preach the virtues of simple Burgundy and Village wines, here in the sanctuary of the Grand Cru. Very convincing!

FIXIN
21220 – Côte-d'Or

Domaine Berthaut
9, rue Noisot - 03 80 52 45 48, fax 03 80 51 31 05
Open Mon-Sat 8am-7pm, Sun 10am-noon & 2pm-6pm.
For their Fixin Premiers Crus (Les Arvelets, Les Hervelets).

GEVREY-CHAMBERTIN
21220 – Côte-d'Or

Vincent Geantet
3, route de Beaune
03 80 34 32 37, fax 03 80 34 16 23
Open Mon-Fri by appt.
Gevrey from old vines and Charmes-Chambertin that win top ratings year after year.

MARSANNAY-LA-CÔTE
21160 – Côte-d'Or

Domaine Fougeray de Beauclair
44, rue de Mazy - 03 80 52 21 12, fax 03 80 58 73 83
Open daily 9am-8pm.
Concentrated wines for long keeping. Notable Marsannay "Les Grasses Têtes."

MOREY-SAINT-DENIS
21220 – Côte-d'Or

Domaine Pierre Amiot et Fils
27, Grande Rue - 03 80 34 34 28, fax 03 80 58 51 17
Open daily by appt.
Appealing Morey-Village as well as lordly Grands and Premiers Crus (Clos de la Roche, Les Millandes, Les Ruchots...).

NUITS-SAINT-GEORGES
21700 – Côte-d'Or

H. et G. Remoriquet
25, rue de Charmois
03 80 61 08 17, fax 03 80 61 36 63
Open Mon-Sat, Sun by appt.
A winegrower who respects the environment and still turns out an attractive range of wines, including some delectable Nuits-Saint-Georges Premiers Crus.

VOSNE-ROMANÉE
21700 – Côte-d'Or

Armelle et Bernard Rion
8, route nationale
03 80 61 05 31, fax 03 80 61 34 60
Open Mon-Sat 8am-7pm.
When the Rions are not raising truffle dogs (or hunting for truffles) they make admirable wines, from straight Village wines to Grands Crus.

• *CÔTE DE BEAUNE*

The southern portion of the Côte d'Or runs from **Ladoix-Serrigny** to **Santenay**. The first portion, between **Corton** and **Beaune**, admits of several different buying strategies: young wines to lay down can be found at **Pernand-Vergelesses** or at **Beaune** among the village wines. Ready-to-drink bottles at affordable prices come from **Chorey-lès-Beaune** or declassified Côte-de-Beaune-Villages wines grown in the commune of **Ladoix-Serrigny**. The perfumed red wines of **Savigny-lès-Beaune** are also charming in their youth. The mighty, tannic reds and majestic white wines of **Corton** require a large investment of money and time in the cellar: but consider the rewards! Growers don't keep mature bottles of the costliest crus in stock; some shippers sell them, but at exorbitant prices.

When you purchase a bottle of Pommard, you're investing time as well as money: only years in the bottle will soften the wine's powerful tannins to elegance. Silky Volnay seduces even in its youth with bright, raspberry fruit; still, the best Premiers Crus can benefit from as much as two decades in the cellar. The delicious red wines of **Monthélie** are relatively unknown, and thus eminently affordable; they are most charming while young. Between **Auxey-Duresses** and **Montrachet** the Chardonnay grape achieves its apotheosis: Meursault, with its buttery texture and mouth-filling flavors; aristocratic Puligny-Montrachet and rich Chassagne-Montrachet...all rare and expensive. **Saint-Aubin** offers fresh-flavored white wines and fruity reds (including some Premiers Crus) that provide very good value. Though it is best known for white wines, Chassagne-Montrachet produces fine reds as well. Auxey-Duresses does not enjoy the same renown as its neighbors, but the wines meet a high standard of quality. At the southern end of the Côte de Beaune, **Santenay** yields a small quantity of rich, cellar-worthy whites, but is best known for slow-maturing, structured reds that reward your patience. Red wines from **Maranges** also require time to smooth out their robust tannins.

Bouchard Père et Fils

Château de Beaune
03 80 24 80 24, fax 03 80 24 97 56
Open Mon-Fri by appt.
This well-known firm, now in the hands of Henriot (Champagne), boasts a diversified catalog of first-rate wines. Broad range of prices.

Bernard Morey et Fils

3, rue de Morgeot
03 80 21 32 13, fax 03 80 21 39 72
Open Mon-Sat.
Morey's wines invariably place at the top of Gault Millau's tastings. Don't miss the domain's red Chassagne-Montrachets and white Premier Cru Les Embrazées.

Fernand et Catherine Chevrot

03 85 91 10 55, fax 03 85 91 13 24
Open daily (exc Sun pm).
Fernand Chevrot is a tireless booster of the Maranges *appellation.* Interesting whites: Maranges and Hautes-Côtes-de-Beaune.

Dubois d'Orgeval

3, rue Joseph Baud
03 80 24 70 89, fax 03 80 22 45 02
Open Mon-Sat, Sun by appt.
A family-run winery with offerings that run from straight white Burgundy to Côte-de-Beaune, Beaune Premier Cru, Aloxe-Corton, and Pommard.

Jean-Claude Regnaudot

Grande Rue (on the left at the bottom of the village)
03 85 91 15 95
Open daily 8am-8pm.
A perfectionist. Premiers Crus from Santenay and Maranges at unbeatable prices.

Robert et Raymond Jacob

Buisson - 03 80 26 40 42, fax 03 80 26 49 34
Open daily by appt, 8am-7pm.
Recent vintages of Corton-Charlemagne, for laying down.

Domaine Michel Prunier

D 973 - 03 80 21 21 05, fax 03 80 21 64 73
Open Mon-Sat 9am-noon & 2pm-7pm.
Outstanding in recent years: red Auxey-Duresses Premier Cru Clos du Val, and white Auxey-Duresses from old vines.

Domaine Dupont-Fahn

Les Toisières - 03 80 21 26 78, fax 03 80 21 21 22
Open by appt only.
For their Puligny-Montrachet Village and Meursaults from a variety of sites. Half of this wine-making team, Leslie Fahn, is American.

Jean-Michel Maurice

Domaine du Prieuré, 23, route de Beaune
03 80 21 54 27, fax 03 80 21 59 77
Open daily.
From village wines to Premiers Crus, a full range of red and white wines from the commune of Savigny.

• CÔTE CHALONNAISE

Wine buyers in search of good-value Burgundies cannot afford to ignore the Côte Chalonnaise. **Bouzeron** produces a superb Aligoté, much richer and fuller than those found elsewhere. **Rully** offers spicy whites and fruity reds (several Premiers Crus), as well as a worthwhile sparkling wine known as Crémant de Bourgogne. **Mercurey**'s tradition of quality is reflected in big, tannic reds that bear comparison with those of the Côte d'Or. The ambitious growers of **Givry** produce fragrant red wines that won't break the bank, while at **Montagny** you'll discover delicious, nutty-flavored whites to drink right away.

Aubert de Villaine

03 85 91 20 50, fax 03 85 87 04 10
Open Mon-Fri 8am-noon & 2pm-7pm.
Tasty white Rully and red Mercurey, but the star of the show is the golden Aligoté de Bouzeron.

*Looking for a winery? Refer to the **index**.*

BUXY
71390 – Saône/Loire

Cave Coopérative de Buxy

Rue de la Gare - 03 85 92 03 03, fax 03 85 92 08 06
Open by appt only.
Reliable source for Montagny, some aged in oak, some not.

MERCUREY
71640 – Saône/Loire

Domaine Michel Juillot

Grande Rue - 03 85 45 27 27, fax 03 85 45 25 52
Open Mon-Sat 8am-noon & 1:30pm-6pm.
Exceptional red Mercureys from a winemaker with a well-deserved reputation.

• *MACÔNNAIS*

With the exception of prestigious Pouilly-Fuissé, the fruity, refreshing wines of the Mâconnais offer charm and easy, early drinking for not much money. Red Mâcon comes from Gamay grapes (very occasionally blended with some Pinot Noir). The more abundant white Mâcon-Villages and delightful Saint-Véran are pure Chardonnay (Chardonnay, indeed, is the name of a local village).

FUISSÉ
71960 – Saône/Loire

Château de Fuissé

Jean-Jacques Vincent
03 85 35 61 44, fax 03 85 35 67 34
Open Mon-Fri 8am-noon & 2pm-6pm, Sat-Sun & hols by appt.
Wines of uncommon quality. Vincent's Château-Fuissé Vieilles Vignes is justly renowned, but his Saint-Véran and Mâcon-Villages also deserve your attention.

ROCHE-VINEUSE (LA)
71960 – Saône/Loire

Domaine Lacharme

Le Pied-du-Mont - 03 85 36 61 80, fax 03 85 37 77 02
Open daily 8am-7pm.
Hand-picked grapes, traditional winemaking methods, aging in oak barrels result in white Mâcon-Villages of rare character.

GAULT-MILLAU GAYOT

ON THE INTERNET

Welcome to Gayot Publications!

http://www.gayot.com/

What's Cool? Net Search Net Directory Software

Welcome to Gayot's/GaultMillau Travel Guides...

Where you will find knowledgeable information
on the world of dining

RESTAURANTS

THE FOOD PAPER

TASTES

BOOKS

THE GRAPEVINE

CHEF'S STORE

BIG BOOK

LA TIMES

Special Offers! TO ORDER *Guest Book!*

GAULTMILLAU IS PROUD TO FEATURE RESTAURANT, HOTEL AND TRAVEL INFORMATION FROM OUR
BOOKS AND UPDATES ON MANY INTERNET WEB SITES.

WE SUGGEST YOU START SURFING AT:
http://www.gayot.com

WE WELCOME YOUR QUESTIONS AND COMMENTS AT OUR E-MAIL ADDRESS:
gayots@aol.com

CENTRAL FRANCE

AUVERGNE

An austere beauty

❚❚Auvergne produces cabinet ministers, cheeses, and volcanoes," was the ironic observation of Alexandre Vialatte, a prodigious writer and native Auvergnat. For the rest of France, these rugged, wild old mountains—they date back some 600 million years—evoke the image of an isolated citadel in the country's heart, a land turned in on itself and somehow fettered to the past. True, Auvergnats are a tough breed, toughened to hard labor; and yes, they are attached to their past: loyalty to ancestral traditions has allowed them to preserve a culture that otherwise could not have survived. The Auvergnat farmer with muddy boots and backward notions is a cliché, but like most clichés, it contains a grain of truth: Auvergne is indeed a conservative, rural region. The famous men who were born here—from Gregory of Tours to Blaise Pascal, Lafayette, and Teilhard de Chardin—drew strength and inspiration from their land. The Michelin family's industrial empire is also grounded in the solidity and determination of the Auvergnat work ethic.

Auvergnats are passionate defenders of their independence. These mountain people know how to use the terrain as a means to safeguard their freedom, whether against the Romans (beaten back at Gergovia by Vercingetorix, before the Gauls' ultimate defeat at Alésia), the Crown (France failed to annex the Bourbonnais until 1527), or the Nazis (joined in furious battle at Mont Mouchet in 1944).

A unique style of Romanesque architecture took root in Auvergne, and blossomed in Clermont-Ferrand's Notre-Dame-du-Port, the abbey church at **Mozac**, and the twelfth century church of **Saint-Nectaire**. Even tiny villages in Auvergne often possess a treasure, like the church of **Orcival**, with its spare, spiritual statues. The Romanesque long reigned supreme in Auvergne. The Gothic style, which filtered down from its birthplace in Ile-de-France, made only minor inroads and is best represented at the cathedral of Clermont-Ferrand. Throughout Auvergne the vestiges of countless fortified castles repeatedly ravaged and rebuilt over the centuries, perch on their precarious peaks like eagles' aeries. To reinforce the authority of the Crown in Auvergne, Cardinal Richelieu had these citadels systematically destroyed in 1629. The old defensive walls of **Tournoël, Châteaugay, Murols, Arlempdes, Léotoing, Polignac,** and **Billy** bear witness to the region's tumultuous military history.

On these hardscrabble high plains and mountains, life has long been a struggle for subsistence. Farmers had to battle brambles and weeds for a share of stony soil on which only poor crops like buckwheat and barley would grow; they cleared forest for a patch of grass to feed their single cow; they braved floods and bitter storms. "My own grandmother" (says André Gayot), "the eldest of seven children, used to tell me how, when she walked her little brothers and sisters to school on the snowy tracks of Pontgibaut, she would have to ward off hungry wolves who loped out of the forest!"

A taciturn people

Auvergnats are a taciturn race of country people. Their innate reserve is reflected in Auvergne's culture, mentality, and even in the landscape. Opulent dwellings and showy châteaux are rare. The few examples that do exist are found in the cities of the plain: **Clermont-Ferrand, Riom**—and they are usually hidden away at the end of winding, narrow streets, behind ancient ramparts. Others are found on the northern plains of Limagne and the Bourbonnais, where rich soil yields plentiful harvests of wheat, or else in the foothills where almond and peach orchards grow alongside the vineyards of **Saint-Pourçain-sur-Sioule, Corent,** and **Châteaugay.** In fact, there are two Auvergnes: the fertile plains of the north that open out to the progressive influences of Paris (**Moulins, Vichy, Riom,**

Clermont), and the Auvergne of mountains and high plateaus, increasingly abandoned by farmers and given over to grasslands, cattle-grazing, or tourism—skiing in winter, climbing and hiking in summer. In spring the herds of tawny-robed Salers cows are still moved to mountain pastures where they spend the summer in the open air.

These two very different Auvergnes correspond in their way to the linguistic divisions that once prevailed in France: the southern *langue d'Oc* and the northern *langue d'Oïl* which was the language of Gothic art and culture. With Vichy, its major city, the Bourbonnais extends north to just beyond **Moulins** and west to **Montluçon**, a buffer zone, so to speak, between the Paris basin (of which it is geologically a part) and Auvergne (to which it is administratively attached). While Auvergne is mountainous, save for the Limagne plain which is contiguous to the Bourbonnais, the latter's gentle valleys benefit from a milder climate. Life there is less hard and the art of living more gracious.

Because it raises a 250-kilometer barrier to clouds rushing in from the ocean, the Massif Central is literally the water tower of France. Rivers rush out in all directions to irrigate the land. The springs that bubble up to the surface from deep in the earth are charged with beneficial minerals. As far back as antiquity, the Romans established thermal spas in Auvergne. The waters of **Volvic** are filtered by volcanic rock, and are as pure as if they had been distilled. Curists take the waters at **Vichy**, the queen of spas, for digestive problems; at **Châtelguyon**, for the kidneys; at **Le Mont-Dore** and **La Bourboule** for bronchitis; at **Royat** for the heart; at **Bourbon-l'Archambault** for rhumatism... In Auvergne, Nature can soothe nearly any ill!

The young volcanoes—extinct for a mere 5,000 years—that are scattered throughout Auvergne give these springs their vitality (150°F at Vichy!). And they also give the landscape its haunting beauty, softened by the passage of millennia. The spectacular Dômes range and the Monts Dore and their region are protected environments since the creation in 1977 of a vast **Parc Naturel des Volcans**. Lakes sparkle in former craters (**Lac Servière, Lac Pavin, Lac Chauvet, Gour de Tazenat**) or in naturally dammed valleys (**Lac Chambon, Lac d'Aydat**); man-made lakes glitter in the landscape, too (Lac de Bort-les-Orgues and the lake on La Truyère), and provide precious hydroelectric power as well.

In the nineteenth century, Auvergne's mountains were home to a burgeoning population—there were just too many mouths to feed. So each summer, able-bodied young Auvergnats came down from the peaks to work as hired hands on wheat farms

in the plains, while older men tended sheep and sheltered in makeshift huts (called *burons*) high up on the mountain. Nowadays there are cows, not sheep, on the hillsides and they don't need anyone to watch over them: electrified fences do the job! And most of the young men who went down the mountain never came back up: they stayed where they found work, and succeeded by virtue of their peasant tenacity. Not so long ago, the coal merchants of Paris who carried heavy sacks of *charbon* on their backs up flight after flight of stairs—the *bougnats*, as they were derisively called—were all sons of Auvergne. With their savings, many bought a café or a restaurant—and of course a country house back home, where they could retire, once they had made their fortune, and live out their days at the foot of their beloved volcanoes. But among the emigrants from Auvergne there were also scientists and thinkers and prominent political figures, including three recent French presidents: Georges Pompidou, Valéry Giscard d'Estaing, and Jacques Chirac.

A morning at the market

There's no better way to learn to love this French heartland than to spend a morning at one of the local open-air markets, or *foirails*. In the fall, farmers from **Cézallier** or **Aubrac** proudly exhibit their prize Salers cattle: beautifully combed, with their lyre-shaped horns, the beasts are a splendid sight! The men trade and deal in the local dialect, perpetuating an ancestral tradition. The rich milk from these cows lends a special savor to Auvergne's cheeses: fragrant Saint-Nectaire, robust Cantal, pungent Bleu d'Auvergne, and buttery, blue-veined Fourme d'Ambert.

The famous knives of **Thiers** are back in fashion, giving the cutlery industry a boost, but the lace that made the town of **Le Puy** a byword with elegant ladies—and employed some 100,000 lacemakers—has practically disappeared with the advent of machine-made lace. The superb rag paper once made by hand at **Ambert** has met a similar fate. But the rubber industry established in the nineteenth century by the Michelin brothers still fuels the local economy, providing jobs for farmers who work their fields half-time, after leaving the factory. Michelin made Clermont-Ferrand the tire capital of France. Close to transportation—an excellent highway links Clermont to Paris—new industries have taken root: pharmaceuticals, glassworks, and mills producing special types of steel.

This is the new face of Auvergne, open to progress but deeply attached to its traditions and its rustic cuisine. Potée auvergnate, which combines pork, smoky bacon, cabbage, and other vegetables in an aromatic broth, satisfies the most voracious appetite. In **Aurillac**, be sure to sample the tripoux d'-Auvergne (stuffed mutton tripe—much tastier than it sounds...) accompanied by aligot, a savory blend of mashed potatoes and Tomme cheese. For dessert, there will be clafoutis (a fruit-studded batter cake) or delicious candied fruits, a Clermont specialty, which are perfectly partnered with Corent, a rare, delicate rosé wine. Liqueur lovers will want to try the verbena elixir called Verveine du Velay.

Set in grandiose landscapes, Auvergne's austere cities built (like the Clermont cathedral) of black basalt, express the local belief that ostentation is an unpardonable sin, prodigality a vice. For the richest Auvergnat on earth, driving a Rolls through the streets of hard-working Clermont would be the acme of bad taste. This story sums up the Auvergnat's attitude: upon landing at JFK airport in New York, François Michelin was informed that he could not bring fresh fruit into the United States, and that he would have to discard the apples he had packed into his carry-on bag. With perfect aplomb, he sat down, peeled his apples, and ate them. Waste not, want not: hard work and thrift are the keystones of the Auvergnat's character—and the keys to his success!

BERRY

At the heart of the matter

The center, the middle, or—more poetically—the heart of France: that special spot belongs to Berry. This site at the country's center of gravity confers a certain balance. Berry can claim kinship with the all the larger regions that surround it: like Touraine and Anjou, Berry boasts romantic châteaux; like Auvergne and the Bourbonnais, Berry's landscapes are alive with springs and rivers, and are dotted with Romanesque churches; Burgundy's wines and ancient abbeys find an echo in Berry's delicious Sancerre and Menetou-Salon, and in the noble monastery of **Noirlac**; the wheatfields and Gothic cathedrals of Ile-de-France are mirrored in Berry's prosperous farms and the cathedral of Bourges, one of the most impressive in France. It's logical, perhaps, that those larger regions drain off the flow of tourists, many of whom are not even aware that Berry exists! All the more reason then, for the curious traveler to take the time to savor Berry's quiet but very real beauty.

The Berry region covers two *départements*, Cher and Indre. The northern portion is occupied by **Sologne**'s endless forests, stippled with ponds and teeming with game. The center, known as Champagne Berrichonne, is agricultural, while the slopes of eastern Berry (the Sancerrois) are covered by vineyards. To the west, the marshy **Brenne** is home to flocks of waterfowl. Two hours from Paris by car or train, Berry is an ideal destination for ecology-minded travelers; but art and history buffs will find plenty to occupy them, too.

This rich, temperate region was naturally a coveted prize for conquerors. To win it (along with Aquitaine, of which Berry was once a part), England's Plantagenet kings (a line born of the French Count of Anjou and the daughter of William the Conqueror) warred against the French Crown. It was from Bourges that Charles VII, spurred by Joan of Arc, set out to win back his kingdom from the English. The Scots, too, rallied to the French cause according to the terms of the "Auld Alliance," a defensive pact against the English which, the Scots maintain, still holds good today! In any case, to thank Scotland for its aid, John Stuart of Darnley was made Seigneur d'Aubigny. In beautifully preserved **Aubigny-sur-Nère**, also known as the Stuarts' town, bagpipe-playing Scots decked out in kilts parade down the main street each July 14. On the outskirts of Aubigny, at the château de la Verrerie, the hospitable Comte de Vogüé has fitted out princely accommodations where a few privileged paying guests can spend the night or a few idyllic days.

To reconquer his realm Charles VII required considerable forces, and to obtain them he needed considerable funds. The man to supply them was financier Jacques Cœur, the hugely rich merchant prince whose commerce with the East (he had his own Mediterranean fleet) allowed him to build up the royal war chest. Jacques Cœur also built himself a superb palace, one of the architectural glories of **Bourges**. The town's other glory, of course, is the magnificent cathedral of Saint-Étienne, completed in the thirteenth century and recently registered as a world landmark by UNESCO.

If you are driving to Bourges from Paris, why not follow the **Route Jacques Cœur**? It begins at **La Bussière** with the lakebound château des Pêcheurs, then continues south through Aubigny-sur-Nère and Bourges to the Cistercian abbaye de **Noirlac** (where a music festival is held in July and August) and the exuberant Renaissance castle of **Meillant**. Last of the seventeen stops on the Route Jacques Cœur is the triple-towered medieval fortress of **Culan**, not far from the Auvergne border.

Sancerre occupies a rocky spur on the banks of the Loire. The town's ancient vineyards (mentioned by Pliny the Elder, a Roman naturalist writing around the time of Christ) are best known for a crisp, flinty white wine produced from the Sauvignon grape. Sauvignon is also planted at nearby **Menetou-Salon**,

Quincy, **Reuilly**, and **Châteaumeillant**, along with Pinot Noir, Pinot Gris, and Gamay. Appreciated in their day by kings and royal courts, the wines of Berry nearly disappeared in the nineteenth century, attacked by the phylloxera root louse. The region's vineyards are coming back in strength today. These fruity wines make perfect partners for the famous Crottin, a tangy chèvre made in **Chavignol**, not far from Sancerre.

A final note for lovers of mystery: Berry has long been suspected—and still is, today—of siring witches and sorcerers. It seems that this quietly lovely land is particularly fertile terrain for superstition (or overactive imaginations). Whether to thwart the witches' power, or simply to celebrate their legend, the inhabitants of **Bué**, once a hotbed of witchcraft, masquerade as wizards and witches during an annual festival. Nowadays, it's more frolicsome than fearsome. If black magic fascinates you, don't miss the Musée de la Sorcellerie in **Concressault**, where you can explore the weird world of witchcraft. You'll leave all the gladder knowing that the natural magic of Berry's gentle beauty awaits you outside!

LIMOUSIN

Art treasures from an unyielding land

The last low hills of the Massif Central come to a rolling halt in the Limousin. It's something of a puzzle, really, to pinpoint exactly where one region ends and the other begins. The Limousin's connection to Auvergne is evident at Guéret, Ussel, or Aubusson, but links with Quercy are equally apparent at Collonges-la-Rouge, one of France's most beautiful villages, constructed entirely of red sandstone, and lively **Brive-la-Gaillarde** would look quite as much at home in Périgord as in the Limousin.

What the Limousin's three *départements*—Haute-Vienne, Creuse, and Corrèze—have in common are vast, deserted stretches of poor, rocky soil (like the barren **plateau de Millevaches** threaded with springs and streams), with precious little farmland. The land's unyielding character explains the many small holdings scattered wherever patches of arable soil make it possible to cultivate such undemanding crops as rye or potatoes.

The population has a certain unity, too, although we have to rewind the reel of time back through thousands of years. The Lemovices, who gave the Limousin its name, descended from even more ancient tribes of Iberians, Ligurians, and Celts. Rome conquered, then colonized the region, but when the Empire imploded the Limousin fell prey to the slings and arrows and hatchets and swords of marauding barbarians. The Merovingian kings introduced order and the monastic movement to the Limousin. Eleanor of Aquitaine's marriage to Henry Plantagenet in 1152 put the Limousin in the hands of the English, but during the Hundred Years' War the inhabitants rebelled against the oppression of the Black Prince. During this period of British occupation, Richard the Lionheart met his death in the Limousin, mortally wounded by an archer of his own camp who couldn't shoot straight. Though Richard's death was accidental, the hapless archer was flayed alive. Traces of these turbulent times can still be seen at the fortress of **Curemonte** and at

Uzerche on the Vézère River, a village of ancient gables and turrets.

Christianity was embraced with fervor in the Limousin, which gave the Catholic Church three popes. Many pious hermits took refuge in the region's deep forests, and the influence of abbeys like Saint-Martial in **Limoges** touched all Christendom. The Limousin's many Romanesque churches display a distinctively sober style, due in part to the hardness of the local granite, which resists the sculptor's chisel. Examples are the twelfth-century collegiate church of Saint-Pierre at **Le Dorat** in Haute-Vienne, **Tulle's** superb medieval cloister, and the church of Saint-Martin in **Ussel**.

Enamels, tapestries, and china

This spirituality, expressed in *langue d'Oc* (the dominant tongue in southern France) also fostered the development of a poetic literature popularized by the troubadours, who sang their songs of love in a variant of *langue d'Oc* called *limousine*.

Enamels were another art form that flourished in the Limousin. Medieval silversmiths discovered that by blending sand with metallic oxydes they could obtain brilliantly colored ornaments with a hard, glossy surface. Inspired by their Christian faith, master enamelists like Limosin and Penicaud created magnificent reliquaries to hold the remains of saints or holy hermits, such as the twelfth-century reliquary of Saint Stephen in the church of **Gimel-les-Cascades**. The **Guéret** museum preserves a remarkable collection of medieval reliquaries. These marvels of craftsmanship were admired throughout the Christian world, and by the fourteenth century **Limoges** was the capital of fine enamelwork.

In **Felletin** and **Aubusson** still other artists expressed their talents in the tapestries for which the picturesque town of Aubusson, especially, has been famous since the Renaissance. Workshops in both towns still function today, producing tapestries designed by modern artists.

The discovery in 1765 of kaolin deposits near **Saint-Yrieix-la-Perche** allowed Limoges to rival China in creating beautiful yet strong, translucent porcelain. Madame de Pompadour, mistress of King Louis XV, was enthralled by the prospect of such luxury and lavished her encouragements on the fledgling industry. Supported and organized by Turgot, the king's administrator, the porcelain makers of Limoges made their city the world's china capital. Long the hallmark of an elegant table, bone china from Limoges is threatened by copies and imitations made with cheap labor. The number of china factories has dropped sharply in recent decades, and not even consolidations have managed to revitalize this industry in crisis.

It is astonishing that a land so hard and austere, removed from the major routes of commerce and exchange (but not from the path of war: the Black Prince torched Limoges for rebelling against his tyrannical rule), should have contributed so much to the world of art—enamels, stained glass, poetry, and porcelain—and to the history of religion, producing three popes and several saints, among them the great Saint Martial.

The sparsely populated Limousin has remained an agricultural region, dominated by tawny Limousin cattle which have been bred to produce excellent beef. And although vineyards never took root here, the Limousin's vast forests of oak supply wine growers all over the world with splendid barrels for aging fine Bordeaux, Napa Chardonnay, and Cabernet from Australia's Alexander Valley.

RESTAURANTS & HOTELS

AUVERGNE

BORT-L'ÉTANG
63190
Paris 447 - Clermont-Ferrand 30 - Vichy 48   Puy-de-Dôme

 Château de Codignat 🌲🍷
8 km SE on D 223 & D 115 E,
04 73 68 43 03, fax 04 73 68 93 54
Closed Nov 3-Mar 20. 4 stes 1,300-2,000. 15 rms 650-1,300. Bkfst 75. Rms for disabled. Restaurant. Half-board 720-1,400. Rm ser. Air cond. Conf. Heated pool. Tennis. Pkg.
This fifteenth-century château, set in a huge estate, still has its wrought iron, armor, and parapets. There are four luxurious suites, as well as spacious rooms, all decorated in the rather heavy Haute Époque style. Some bathrooms are equipped with Jacuzzis. Balneotherapy center. Relais et Châteaux.

BOURBON-LANCY
71140
Paris 308 - Autun 62 - Moulins 36 - Nevers 72   Saône/Loire

 Raymond
Allée Sornat, route de Moulins
03 85 89 17 39, fax 03 85 89 29 47
Closed Sun dinner off-seas, Mon lunch, 2 wks in Jan. Open until 9:30pm. Priv rm 30. Garden dining. No pets. Pkg.
Set in a pretty park, this peaceful restaurant resembles a nineteenth-century Norman castle. In this bucolic ambience, Gérard Raymond offers a cuisine that is perfumed with herbs and spices from his garden: chicken compote with creamed spices and dried tomatoes, roast langoustines flavored with angelica and lemon, spiced French toast with honey ice cream. The cellar is small but interesting, with a good selection of growers' Burgundies. C 350-450. M 150 (weekdays), 180 (Sat & Sun), 240-400.

 Manoir de Sornat 🌲🍷
(See restaurant above)
Closed Sun off-seas, 2 wks in Jan. 13 rms 350-700. Bkfst 60-120. Half-board 450-700 (oblig in seas). Conf. Pkg.
Total quiet welcomes you in this hotel with beautiful, spacious rooms that offer good value for your money. Some have gorgeous sculpted-wood fireplaces. You will think that you have awakened in a fairytale castle.

The prices in this guide reflect what establishments were charging at press time.

CHAISE-DIEU (LA)
43160
Paris 470 - Brioude 40 - Ambert 33   Haute-Loire

11/20 **Hostellerie du Lion d'Or**
04 71 00 01 58, fax 04 71 00 08 84
Closed Nov-Apr: Sun dinner, Mon, 3 wks in Jan. Open until 10pm. HOTEL: 11 rms 190-450. Bkfst 38. Rm ser. Half-board 325. Pkg.
A city-center restaurant with a restful salmon-pink and wine-red décor. The smiling *patronne* will guide you through her husband's menu, which takes agreeable detours from traditional cuisine and shows a great deal of character. Small, well-diversified wine list. C 330. M 99, 157, 199, 320.

CHÂTELGUYON
63140
Paris 375 - Clermont-Ferrand 21 - Vichy 47   Puy-de-Dôme

 Splendid Hotel 🌲🍷
5-7, rue d'Angleterre
04 73 86 04 80, fax 04 73 86 17 56
Closed Oct 15-Apr 15. 1 ste 860-1,260. 79 rms 480-950. Bkfst 60. Restaurant. Half-board 500-1,420. Rm ser. Conf. Pool. Pkg.
A formal hotel set amid a park and flower gardens. Facilities include a spa, fitness center, sauna, and nightclub. Original program of activities: hot-air ballooning, helicopter rides, anti-stress package, etc.

CLERMONT-FERRAND
63000
Paris 389 - Lyon 183 - Moulins 96   Puy-de-Dôme

 Jean-Yves Bath 🎄
Pl. du Marché-Saint-Pierre
04 73 31 23 23, fax 04 73 31 08 33
Closed Sun, Mon, hols, Feb 10-28, Aug 24-Sep 8. Open until 10pm. Priv rm 30. Terrace dining. Air cond. Pkg.
The standout here is the Cantal rissoles and ravioli, perfumed with herbs and enhanced with an elegant meat jus—it approaches three-toque status. The fried pike perch with veal marrow is another example of the accomplished cuisine of Jean-Yves Bath, who likes to discuss his love for local foodstuffs and his inspirations with his customers. Modern-style service and décor. The cellar, very well chosen and rich in top-quality vintages, lives up to the high standards of the cuisine. Unfortunately, so do the prices. C 300-400. M 260, 350.

12/20 Le Brezou

51, rue Saint-Dominique
04 73 93 56 71, fax 04 73 38 35 30
Closings not available. Open until 9:30pm. Terrace dining. Garage pkg. No cards.
The prices here will put you in a good mood, as will the warm ambience of the recently restored restaurant whose homestyle cooking always attracts a crowd. Game is a specialty. The small wine list has some interesting regional offerings. Friendly welcome. C 180-230. M 75, 100, 140.

 ## Gallieni

51, rue Bonnabaud
04 73 93 59 69, fax 04 73 34 89 29
Open year-round. 80 rms 215-340. Bkfst 35-38. Restaurant. Half-board 335. Rm ser. Conf. Pkg.
Near the town center, a functional, unpretentious hotel whose rooms have been completely renovated. Some look out on the cathedral and others on the mountains.

DURTOL	63830
Paris 428 - Clermoont-Ferrand 4	Puy-de-Dôme

 ## Bernard Andrieux

Av. du Puy-de-Dôme
04 73 37 00 26, fax 04 73 36 95 25
Closed Sun dinner, Mon, Feb school hols, 1st wk of May, Jul 15-Aug 10. Open until 9:30pm. Priv rm 20. Air cond. No pets. Pkg.
Located in an uninteresting suburb, this handsome stone house offers an oasis of elegance. Prettily decorated outside, the restaurant has pleasant lighting, Empire furnishings, and pastel tablecloths. The service is efficient and dignified. The classic cuisine is based on good but rich ingredients, so don't overindulge. The fine scallops à la Nantaise are served with leeks. The excellent wild duck with spices is perfectly cooked and served with a dense jus. The cheeses are gorgeous, and the desserts come close to earning three toques. Not the place to go if you're on a budget. The wine cellar is superb, with a complete range and a good selection of half-bottles. C 400-540. M 185-400 (exc Sat lunch, wine incl), 100 (children).

LAGUIOLE	12210
Paris 552 - Aurillac 82 - Rodez 56 - Espalion 24	Aveyron

 ## Michel Bras ☺

Route de l'Aubrac
05 65 44 32 24, fax 05 65 48 47 02
Closed Mon & Tue lunch (exc Jul-Aug), beg Nov-end Mar. Open until 9:30pm. Air cond. No pets. Valet pkg.
The restaurant looks like an observatory, perched up high and built of rough-hewn wood, stone, and glass. That's the way Michel Bras wanted it, the better to commune with nature. His passion for nature is also seen on the menu. Bras rarely comes out of the kitchen, where he produces his illustrious tart of baby vegetables,

homemade country bread, crisp-cooked peas with rabbit in olive oil, baby cabbage with pork shoulder, chicken stew, and so on. Just reading the menu, with its poetic names, makes your mouth water. For dessert there are all the varieties of cane sugar from the Ile Maurice, and fluffy ice cream with hazelnuts. The wines are offered at incredibly low prices. With the 205 F set menu and a bottle of Marcillac, for example, at 120 F, you can get to know the true Michel Bras just as well as you can from the pricier à la carte offerings. The service provided by Ginette Bras and her staff dressed in shepherd's smocks is as amiable as ever, as is the excellent sommelier, Serge Calderon. C 460-760. M 205 (weekdays), 410-630, 100 (children).

 ## Michel Bras

(See restaurant above)
Closed Mon & Tue am (exc Jul-Aug), beg Nov-end Mar. 15 rms 950-1,700. Bkfst 90. Rms for disabled. Air cond. No pets. Valet pkg.
All the rooms offer spectacular views of the rugged countryside. Rooms have white walls and wool rugs and are even more appealing on snowy or windy days. Fantastic breakfasts. Relais et Châteaux.

MONTROND-LES-BAINS	42210
Paris 441 - St-Étienne 28 - Lyon 68 - Montbrison 14	Loire

 ## Hostellerie La Poularde

2, rue de Saint-Étienne
04 77 54 40 06, fax 04 77 54 53 14
Closed Mon & Tue lunch, Jan 2-17. Open until 10:30pm. Priv rm 40. Air cond. Valet pkg.
Wood paneling and real silver set the tone in the exquisite dining room of this restaurant, a guardian of French culinary traditions that valued the quality of ingredients more than pretentious *appellations*. Gilles Étéocle has understood that there is still a place for such cooking, even amid the tough competition in the area from chefs like Troisgros. He continues to please his customers with good duck foie gras, poached and roasted rabbit, remarkable cheeses, and a superb cellar supervised by talented sommelier Eric Beaumard, who also tends the recently added wine shop. C 410-610. M 220-380 (exc Sat dinner & Sun lunch), 290-570.

 ## Hostellerie La Poularde

(See restaurant above)
Closed Mon, Jan 1-17. 3 stes 700-850. 11 rms 550-650. Bkfst 80-100. Air cond. Conf. Valet pkg.
Handsome, well-equipped rooms, three modern duplex suites overlooking a pretty courtyard, and the renovated reception area, lobby, and bar all add up to top-level comfort. Relais et Châteaux.

*Some establishments change their **closing times** without warning. It is always wise to check in advance.*

ROANNE — 42300
Paris 390 - Lyon 88 - St-Étienne 77 - Mâcon 97 — Loire

 Troisgros

Pl. de la Gare
04 77 71 66 97, fax 04 77 70 39 77
Closed Tue dinner, Wed, Feb school hols, 1st 2 wks of Aug. Open until 9:30pm. Priv rm 25. Air cond. Valet pkg.
The true miracle of this restaurant is the consistency of the exceptional cuisine, the perfect technique that never turns into conventional classicism. Oysters with shallots is not an original dish, but Michel Troisgros invents a bewitching turnip sauce for them. The breading on the frogs' legs is perfumed with ginger, and they are fried "Japanese–style" with a superb mustard-flavored cream. The excellent squab en cocotte comes with a subtle sauce. The veal sweetbread escalope is simply magnificent. Wonderful cheese platter, with local goat cheeses, served with walnut-and-pistachio bread. Even the dessert cart is stunning, presented along with fruits, compotes, and the fabulous pastries. The wine list is an anthology tended by no fewer than four sommeliers, but it includes affordable bottles: 90 F for a 1993 Côte Roannaise, and 140 F for a pitcher of 1988 Burgundy. Many wines served by the glass. C 700. M 300 (weekday lunch), 600-730, 140 (children).

 Troisgros

(See restaurant above)
See restaurant for closings. 4 stes 1,600-1,850. 15 rms 700-1,400. Bkfst 120. Rms for disabled. Rm ser. Air cond. Valet pkg.
The pleasant air conditioned rooms are tastefully decorated in contemporary style. Little details like separate dressing rooms and innumerable towels add to the charm. Exceptional breakfasts—you'll never find better. Relais et Châteaux.

SAINT-BONNET-LE-FROID — 43290
Paris 558 - St-Étienne 59 - Tournon 53 — Haute-Loire

 Auberge des Cimes 🔷

04 71 59 93 72, fax 04 71 59 93 40
Closed Sun dinner, Mon (exc Jul-Aug), Nov 15-Easter. Open until 9:30pm. Priv rm 18. Air cond. Garage pkg.
Régis Marcon has recently added an annex, Le Clos des Cimes, with drawing and cooking studios, exhibition space, and a boutique selling regional foods and crafts, all of which livens up an area with a short season. But his true strength is, of course, cooking, which he does with fine technique and an acute sensitivity to the flavors of his native region. He grew up at this inn before training in some of the top restaurants, and you can taste his origins in his cuisine. His Margaridou brochette, made of morels, veal sweetbreads, ham, and lightly breaded Swiss chard, must be tasted. It is a traditional Auvergne recipe that has been updated and

makes a fine showcase for his talents. And then there's the lamb en croûte, served with vegetables and cured pork, seasoned with a mix of spices—a fabulous dish that merits a detour in itself. Succulent, ingenious desserts. Very good homemade bread. Relaxed but efficient service. Well-chosen cellar, with many half-bottles. C 360. M 150 (weekdays), 210 (Sat & Sun), 320-490, 70 (children).

 Auberge des Cimes ▲🔔

(See restaurant above)
See restaurant for closings. 17 rms 400-700. Bkfst 70. Rms for disabled. Half-board 500-800. Conf. Garage pkg.
The simple yet cozy village inn on the slopes just above a second hotel that overlooks the valley, offers large, bright rooms in keeping with the rustic surroundings.

SANSSAT — 03150
Paris 405 - Moulins 43 - Vichy 24 — Allier

 Château de Theillat ▲🔔

04 70 99 86 70, fax 04 70 99 86 33
Open year-round. 18 rms 650-1,230. Bkfst 70. Rms for disabled. Restaurant. Half-board 650. Rm ser. Conf. Pool. Garage pkg.
Set in an immense park, a beautiful eighteenth-century château that offers luxury and tranquility. The rooms are spacious and their decoration befits a château. Lovely swimming pool.

VÉZAC — 15130
Paris 546 - Clermont-Ferrand 160 - Aurillac 7 — Cantal

 Hostellerie du Château de Salles

04 71 62 41 41, fax 04 71 62 44 14
Closed Feb. Open until 10pm. Garden dining. Pool. Pkg.
If your visits to the numerous castles in the Cère Valley have whetted your appetite, trust Thierry Guillot and his cuisine. We were impressed by his scampi with vegetable spaghetti, Szechuan-pepper monkfish, and duck breast with apples and Calvados sauce. But let's be honest: his sauces could be lighter. And it's nice to have prettily decorated preparations, but we sometimes found it a bit over the top. The 120 F set-price menu is a good value. C 250. M 120, 190, 260, 340.

Hostellerie du Château de Salles ▲🔔

Closed beg Jan-beg Feb. 8 stes 700-1,100. 6 rms 400-600. Bkfst 50. Half-board 170. Pool. Tennis. Golf. Pkg.
The location? Just ask Depardieu: some scenes from his last movie were shot here in this fifteenth-century watchtower castle. The view of the Auvergne mountains is magnificent. The hotel has been restored from top to bottom, and

all the rooms are very comfortable and stylish, with brand new amenities and bathrooms.

VICHY	03200
Paris 348 - Clermont-Ferrand 59 - Lyon 160	Allier

 L'Alambic

8, rue Nicolas-Larbaud - 04 70 59 12 71
Closed Mon, Tue lunch, 2 wks end Feb-beg Mar, 3 wks end Aug-beg Sep. Open until 10pm.
We applaud Jean-Jacques Barbot, who has announced that even in these difficult times, he will not raise his prices. This is even more laudable in light of the fact that he uses the best-quality ingredients and can only serve eighteen people at a time in the tiny dining room. You must try the flavorsome Bourbonnais chicken that local farmers have started breeding again: the suprême stuffed with cock's comb and morels is a steal at only 95 F. We also appreciated the plethora of half-bottles on the magnificent new wine list decorated with watercolors. C 250-400. M 160, 280, 90 (children).

 Les Célestins

111, bd des États-Unis
04 70 30 82 00, fax 04 70 30 82 01
Open year-round. 11 stes 1,580-2,280. 120 rms 650-1,400. Bkfst 85. Rms for disabled. Restaurant. Half-board 850-3,240. Air cond. Conf. Heated pool. Valet pkg.
On the edge of the Napoléon III park, a contemporary hotel that is quietly elegant and perfectly equipped. A hanging garden links it to the fitness center and spa. There are tennis courts at the Sporting Club, and a nearby sailing club.

 La Véranda

3, pl. Joseph-Aletti
04 70 31 78 77, fax 04 70 98 13 82
Annual closings not avalaible. Open until 10pm. Priv rm 250. Terrace dining. Air cond. Heated pool. Valet pkg.
In the heart of town, this majestic turn-of-the-century establishment was recently renovated and boasts an enormous, high-ceilinged restaurant. The cuisine is not without personality, even though it is occasionally too complicated. Dishes are carefully prepared from top-quality ingredients and are attractively presented. Well-chosen cellar. Very professional welcome. C 300-470. M 135 (exc Sun lunch), 180, 230, 80 (children).

 Aletti Palace Hotel

(See restaurant above)
Annual closings not available. 7 stes 950-1,100. 126 rms 500-760. Bkfst 70. Rms for disabled. Half-board 500-760. Rm ser. Air cond. Conf. Heated pool. Valet pkg.
Facing the casino and the Parc des Sources, a pleasant Rococo hotel, entirely renovated, with huge rooms that are deliciously decorated and perfectly equipped, with large marble bathrooms.

AUBIGNY-SUR-NÈRE	18700
Paris 180 - Orléans 74 - Bourges 46	Cher

 Château de la Verrerie

In Oizon - 02 48 58 06 91, fax 02 48 58 21 25
Closed Dec 15-Jan 15. 1 ste 1,300. 11 rms 680-1,100. Bkfst 60-80. Restaurant. Half-board 660-880. Conf. Tennis. Garage pkg.
Set in the Berry forest, a sixteenth-century château that is the permanent residence of the Count and Countess de Vogüé, who will welcome you to their elegant and tranquil bed and breakfast with a view of a park and a lake.

BOURGES	18000
Paris 226 - Nevers 68 - Dijon 245 - Châteauroux 65	Cher

 L'Abbaye Saint-Ambroix

Bd de la République
02 48 70 70 00, fax 02 48 70 21 22
Closed Sat lunch. Open until 10pm. Priv rm 60. Air cond. Pkg.
It's a rare treat to dine under the magnificent vaulted ceiling of a sixteenth-century chapel. The dining room is comfortable and elegant, and the cuisine of the young chef, Christophe Langrée, is harmonious and attractively presented. He makes clever use of country produce and knows how to present noble ingredients in a simple, elegant way. Complete cellar. Professional service. C 390. M 240 (weekday lunch, wine incl), 220 (exc weekday lunch), 149-320, 100 (children).

Hôtel de Bourbon

(See restaurant above)
Open year-round. 2 stes 810-890. 57 rms 420-650. Bkfst 65. Rms for disabled. Half-board 485. Rm ser. Conf. Pkg.
Near the Hôtel Jacques-Cœur and the Saint-Étienne cathedral, a hotel in a former abbey. The rooms are impersonal, though well designed and equipped. Some are air conditioned. Excellent reception.

Philippe Larmat

62 bis, bd Gambetta
02 48 70 79 00, fax 02 48 69 88 87
Closed Sun dinner, Mon (exc hols), last week of Feb, Aug 25-Sep 5. Open until 9:30pm. Garden dining. Air cond.
Philippe Larmat learned the art of cooking from Jean Bardet, who says of him, "He is a true chef." In spite of his discretion and natural reserve, he insists on precision and rigor in the kitchen. If his staff becomes overwhelmed, he

will turn away customers—to the great dismay of local gourmets—rather than compromise his standards. Only 35 people at a time can sample his harmonious cuisine, prepared with great finesse along classic lines: scallop and herb salad, bass with a purée of black olives, and a rustic yet elegant tête de veau. The pleasure begins with the 95 F menu and continues with the amazing 140 F menu. The service is attentive, and the smiling young sommelier presides over a dazzling yet affordable cellar. C 300. M 95 (weekdays, Sat lunch), 140-230, 60 (children).

LIMOUSIN

LIMOGES   87000
Paris 374 - Poitiers 118 - Angoulême 103   Haute-Vienne

 L'Amphitryon

26, rue de la Boucherie
05 55 33 36 39, fax 05 55 32 98 50
Closed Sun, Mon lunch, 1 week in Mar, Aug 3-18. Open until 10:30pm. Priv rm 24. Terrace dining.
Pascal Robert is a perfectionist and knows how to harmonize the tones, aromas, and flavors in his cooking. The dining room has an updated rustic décor, and each place setting is different. The careful presentation of each dish is an added plus. Located in the heart of what was once the butchers' quarter, L'Amphitryon offers inventive, modern food. C 210. M 98 (weekday lunch, Sat), 140 (weekday lunch, Sat, wine incl), 130-290, 60 (children).

 Le Richelieu

40, av. Baudin - 05 55 34 22 82, fax 05 55 32 48 73
Open year-round. 32 rms 305-495. Bkfst 48. Restaurant. Half-board 375-430. Rm ser. Conf. Garage pkg.
This pink-and-green-decorated hotel offers extremely helpful service and serious comfort. The building is new and well-adapted to its function. You'll get good value for your money.

NIEUL   87510
Paris 409 - Limoges 9 - Saverne 38   Haute-Vienne

 La Chapelle Saint-Martin

In Saint-Martin-du-Fault
05 55 75 80 17, fax 05 55 75 89 50
Closed Mon, Jan. Open until 10pm. Priv rm 60. Terrace dining. Heated pool. Tennis. No pets. Garage pkg.
In a luxurious nineteenth-century décor, facing the park with its hundred-year-old sequoias, you will discover elegant, flavorful cuisine prepared by Christophe Blanc. Tempt yourself with the cold asparagus chartreuse and hen's breast, the sole with shellfish sauce, or the veal

sweetbread Pithiviers with cèpes. He may not let his imagination go totally wild, but the presentation and service are absolutely impeccable. A fine wine list that includes some very affordable bottles, like the delicious 1992 Vouvray. C 300-400. M 200 (lunch, wine incl), 280-390.

 La Chapelle Saint-Martin

(See restaurant above)
Closed Jan. 3 stes 1,350-1,500. 9 rms 500-1,100. Bkfst 78-85. Rms for disabled. Half-board 650-950. Rm ser. Conf. Heated pool. Tennis. Garage pkg.
An all-white house in a tranquil park with huge rooms and suites that are comfortably furnished and decorated with refinement. Relais et Châteaux.

ROCHE-L'ABEILLE (LA)   87800
Paris 412 - Limoges 31 - Brive 72   Haute-Vienne

 Au Moulin de la Gorce

2 km S on D 17 - 05 55 00 70 66, fax 05 55 00 76 57
Closed Sun dinner & Mon off-seas, Jan. Open until 9pm. Priv rm 30. Terrace dining. Pkg.
A charming old mill, with a stream and waterfall, situated on the edge of a pond in the countryside. The setting suits the classic cuisine of Jean Bertranet, an old hand who enjoys recounting how he learned his métier at the Élysée Palace when Vincent Auriol was president, from 1947 to 1950. He has also been a pastrymaker, and his tarts, fondants, and cookies are as delectable as his tuna tournedos, veal sweetbread lasagna, and pigeon suprême. The fine wine list is well balanced and will satisfy connoisseurs as well as more modest wine lovers. Good selection of half-bottles. C 350-500. M 250, 380, 480.

 Au Moulin de la Gorce

(See restaurant above)
See restaurant for closings. 1 ste 1,300. 9 rms 350-900. Bkfst 75. Half-board 850-900 (oblig). Pkg.
The Bertranet family has done a fine job of recovering from the floods of 1994. The hotel is now more comfortable than ever. Relais et Châteaux.

VARETZ   19240
Paris 484 - Tulle 29 - Brive-la-Gaillarde 10   Corrèze

Domaine de Castel Novel

05 55 85 00 01, fax 05 55 85 09 03
Closed mid Oct-beg May. Open until 9:15pm. Terrace dining. Heated pool. Tennis. Valet pkg.
This fabulous fairytale manor house has finally found a Prince Charming for its kitchen. The young Breton draws on his roots with numerous seafood-based dishes, such as wine-based

lobster stew and melt-in-your-mouth crab with artichokes, but is quickly learning to dip into the infinite food resources the region has to offer, incorporating truffles, foie gras and farm-raised veal with chanterelle mushrooms. He's even managed to come up with a dish that joins the two diverse influences: chitterling and cabbage chartreuse in sweet and sour sauce. Extremely attentive service in an old-fashioned dining room or in the summer, on the terrace. Wine list overflowing with the very best years in Bordeaux. C 470-550 (and up). M 240-390, 200 (weekday lunch), 85 (children).

 ## Domaine de Castel Novel

(See restaurant above)

Closed mid Oct-beg May. 5 stes 1,420-1,595. 32 rms 595-1,225. Bkfst 80. Half-board 710-1,815. Rm ser. Air cond. Conf. Heated pool. Tennis. Valet pkg.

Albert Parveaux doesn't stint on the maintenance of this château where Henri de Jouvenel once lived with his wife, none other than the writer Colette. The romantic rooms are all decorated differently. Handsome park and a welcome that befits the setting. Relais et Châteaux.

REGIONAL FOODS

South of the Loire River extends an ancient land of volcanoes, mountains gentled by time, cool valleys... Winters are hard here, but the summers are splendid: there's no better place to get close to nature and renew your spirit. The outdoor life breeds hearty appetites, but the farms and fields of Central France supply all manner of earthy, authentic satisfactions.

• *CHARCUTERIE*

LAGUIOLE   12210 – Aveyron

Conquet

05 65 44 31 93
Lacalm - 05 65 44 33 05
Two shops, one in Laguiole and the other in Lacalm, feature the firm's excellent hams and dried sausages, cured in the bracing mountain air of Aubrac.

PARLAN   15290 – Cantal

Salaisons Laborie

04 71 46 19 46
Hams, cooking sausages, and dried country sausage of superb quality.

PIERREFORT   15230 – Cantal

Dutrevis

14, pl. de la Fontaine - 04 71 23 33 04
Fresh and dry-cured sausages that contain nice, meaty bits of pork. For an authentic taste of the French countryside.

Joffrois

10, av. Georges-Pompidou - 04 71 23 31 80
Hams and sausages brimming with rich flavor, as well as superb dried Aubrac beef, sliced paper-thin and sold vaccum-packed.

• *CHEESE*

LAGUIOLE   12210 – Aveyron

Jeune Montagne

Route de Saint-Flour - 05 65 44 35 54
If you're in the area, do visit this dairy cooperative which sells tender, smooth-textured Laguiole AOC cheese at an unbeatable price.

MURAT   15300 – Cantal

Produits d'Auvergne

3, rue Justin-Vigier - 04 71 20 11 26
A first-rate range of perfectly matured Auvergne cheeses.

PIERREFORT   15230 – Cantal

Condutier

Cezens - 04 71 73 30 37
This small dairy offers terrific handmade cheeses, all expertly matured: Cantal, Fourme d'Ambert, Bleu d'Auvergne.

ST-GERMAIN-LEMBRON   63340 – Puy-de-Dôme

La Ferme Auvergnate

4, rue Neuve - 04 73 96 41 11
A fine selection of regional cheeses, matured with care.

SANCERRE   18300 – Cher

Fromagerie Dubois-Boulay

Chavignol - 02 48 54 15 69
Goat cheeses: the famous Crottins de Chavignol are a special treat when accompanied by the region's flinty white wine.

• *CHOCOLATE & CANDY*

AIGUEPERSE   63260 – Puy-de-Dôme

Jacques Vernet

154, Grande-Rue - 04 73 63 61 85
Don't miss these pralines: flavorful almonds coated in crunchy caramel—yum!

AURILLAC   15000 – Cantal

Favre

11, rue des Carmes - 04 71 48 06 50
The big noise here is the Folidou, a caramel made with crème fraîche that melts in the mouth! Try the other specialties of the house as well, you won't be disappointed.

BOURGES
18000 – Cher

La Maison des Forestines

3, pl. Cujas - 02 48 24 00 24
Forestines are a traditional French treat, stuffed with rich praline cream. You should also sample the very good nougatines and amandines on sale here.

BRIVE-LA-GAILLARDE
19100 – Corrèze

La Noix Gaillarde

Rue Georges-Claude - 05 55 86 03 85
You surely won't want to miss these meaty walnut halves coated with dark chocolate—simply scrumptious.

CLERMONT-FERRAND
63000 – Puy-de-Dôme

Noël Cruzilles-Aubert

Saint-Jean, 226, av. Jean-Mermoz - 04 73 91 24 46
On the outskirts of Clermont is this small firm that produces luscious fruit jellies (pâtes de fruits), tender candied fruits, glazed orange peel, and very good jams.

Vieillard

31, rue Pascal - 04 73 91 31 35
A reliable source for delicious chocolates and flavorful fruit jellies. The house specialties, well worth sampling, are coffee Briquettes and liqueur-filled fruit jellies (pâtes de fruits).

• *GOURMET SPECIALTIES*

Honey & Jams

CHEZELLES
36500 – Indre

Domaine Apicole de Chezelles

02 54 36 66 01

Thirteen varieties of honey are on offer, including a delicious golden honey from Berry. And make a point of tasting the yummy caramels, lollipops, and gingerbread also available here.

SAINT-MARTIN-VALMEROUX
15140 – Cantal

Nutrel

04 71 69 05 07
Mountain fruits and berries make these jams just irresistible: wild strawberries, blackberries, blueberries...

Walnut Oil

CHARROUX
03140 – Allier

Ets. Maenner

Rue de la Poulaillerie - 04 70 56 87 61
Stone-ground walnuts yield a mild, fruity oil that is a lovely seasoning for slightly bitter greens.

• *PASTRY & COOKIES*

LAGUIOLE
12210 – Aveyron

Maison Roux

12, rue Bardière - 05 65 44 33 30
Fouace de Laguiole is a famed local specialty, a delicately flavored brioche-type cake that is divine for breakfast or tea.

TRIZAC
15400 – Cantal

Biscuiterie Christian Raynal

04 71 78 60 55
The Carrés de Trizac are thin, crisp, very delicate cookies that are celebrated throughout the region. The secret ingredient is butter from cows grazed in mountain pastures.

WINE

AUVERGNE & THE BOURBONNAIS

CENTRAL FRANCE & BERRY

Auvergne's winemaking tradition was nearly wiped out by the twin onslaughts of phylloxera and urban sprawl. Still, some hardy growers survived, and they produce sturdy, pleasing wines that are a delight to discover, especially in company with the region's charcuterie and cheese. The Côtes d'Auvergne is home to a handful of minuscule crus planted mostly with Gamay, along with some Pinot Noir and Chardonnay. The wines are rarely encountered outside of their home turf, so be sure to seek out spicy red Châteaugay and Chanturgue, and refreshing Corent, the local rosé. To the north, in the Bourbonnais, Saint-Pourçain vineyards of Gamay and Pinot Noir produce lively reds and rosés for early drinking, while Chardonnay and Tressalier grapes yield interesting white wines.

At the eastern end of the Loire Valley, the vineyards of Central France are best known for crisp, keen, bone-dry white wines made from Sauvignon Blanc grapes. Wines from the steep slopes of **Sancerre** are the most familiar—and the priciest. Devotees of that fresh, aromatic style should sample the region's other, less-expensive Sauvignon Blancs from **Menetou-Salon, Quincy,** and **Reuilly. Pouilly-Fumé** wines, made exclusively of Sauvignon Blanc grapes, are richer and longer-lived than Sancerres, and at least as expensive. Some fruity, vivacious rosés are made in the region, either from Pinot Noir or Pinot Gris grapes (Reuilly and Menetou are notable). Pinot Noir and Gamay produce the local reds, which tend to be light and delicate. For the money, a Menetou is usually better value than red Sancerre. Other reds worthy of interest hail from **Châteaumeillant** and **Valençay.**

ROMAGNAT 63540 – Puy-de-Dôme

Michel Bellard

04 73 62 66 69, fax 04 73 62 09 22
Open Mon-Sat. V.
Once you find the village, it's easy to locate Bellard's winery, for the cellars occupy one whole side of a main street. Bellard offers wines from all of the Côtes d'Auvergne sites. Very good Chanturgue.

ST-POURÇAIN-SUR-SIOULE 03500 – Allier

Union des Vignerons de Saint-Pourçain

Rue de la Ronde - 04 70 45 42 82, fax 04 70 45 99 34
Open daily 8am-12:30pm & 1:30pm-6:30pm.
The very model of a dynamic wine coop, with modern equipment and a reputation for making clean, pleasing wines. The Gamay or Gamay-Pinot Noir reds show plenty of youthful fruit; the Blanc Réserve Spéciale (Tressalier-Chardonnay) is well worth trying.

AIX-D'ANGILLON (LES) 18220 – Cher

Henri Pellé

Morogues - 02 48 64 42 48, fax 02 48 64 36 88
Open Mon-Sat.
Expressive white Menetous from vineyards that adjoin Sancerre; smoky, berry-flavored red Menetou. There are four *gîtes ruraux* (furnished rentals) on the property.

BUÉ 18300 – Cher

Jean-Max Roger

8, rue de la Cure - 02 48 54 32 20, fax 02 48 54 10 29
Open daily 9am-7pm.
Well-crafted Sancerres. The Vieilles Vignes selection shines for its concentration. Some barrel-aged red Sancerre is also available.

CHÂTEAUMEILLANT
18370 – Cher

Maurice Lanoix

Domaine du Feuillat
02 48 61 33 89, fax 02 48 61 43 43
Open daily.
Châteaumeillant is a tiny area between La Châtre and Montluçon. The wines have improved notably in the past few years, and those of Maurice Lanoix are among the best. Taste his thirst-quenching Gamay-Pinot blend, and the Gamay aged in oak with lovely cherry nuances.

PREUILLY
18120 – Cher

Jean-Michel Sorbe

9, route de Boisgisson
02 48 51 30 17, fax 02 48 51 35 47
By appt only.
Reuilly in red, white, and rosé, and white Quincy (there isn't any other kind!) are produced at this winery not far from Bourges. Sorbe prefers a ripe, rich style of Quincy that is a revela-

tion to those who have only tasted the more usual flinty version.

SAINT-ANDELAIN
58150 – Nièvre

Serge Dagueneau et Filles

Les Berthiers - 03 86 39 11 18, fax 03 86 39 05 32
Open Mon-Sat 8am-noon & 2pm-7pm (Sun by appt).
A family dedicated to producing Pouilly-Fumés that reflect the *terroir* as well as the essential character of the Sauvignon Blanc grape.

SANCERRE
18300 – Cher

Domaine Henri Bourgeois

Chavignol - 02 48 54 21 67, fax 02 48 54 14 24
Open daily 9am-noon & 3pm-7pm.
Still family-owned, this is one of the major firms in Sancerre. The cuvée called La Bourgeoise, from vines over 50 years old, will astound you with its complex flavors. Very good straight Sancerre, too, and some Pouilly-Fumé.

club france

The official benefit card of the
French Government Tourist Office

unlock all the wonders of france

Join Club France and get more for your money both abroad and at home. The Club France Card unlocks the door to French culture, cuisine, adventure and history by offering you unique benefits like a 3-day Paris museum pass, a complimentary Michelin guide, a subscription to the quarterly newsletter "France Insider's News/Club France" and much more. Your annual membership fee enables you to travel throughout France in true VIP style. Upgrades and special treatment await you at more than 500 hotels, inns and chateaux. Personal touches like priority reservations and a complimentary drink welcome you at over 100 superb restaurants. You'll also receive bonus frequent flyer miles, car rental upgrades and discounts as well as saving money on specialty tours and language and cooking courses. Take advantage of this extraordinary opportunity to experience the delights of France—it's in your hands.

Annual dues are $65 for single membership, $35 each additional. Mail to: Club France, c/o French Government Tourist Office, 444 Madison Ave. NY, NY 10022. For a free brochure, call 1-800-888-5060 ext. GY7 or visit our website: http://www.fgtousa.org/clubfrance

CLUBFRANCE

350130   12/31/97
John D. Smith

The Good Life.

Forbes *FYI*

"Forbes FYI is the magazine that GQ and Esquire want to be."

CHAMPAGNE

A lesson in optimism, or why the angel smiles

La Champagne and *le Champagne*: a single letter distinguishes the province and its product, the nurturing land and its ebullient offspring. It was in the late 1600s, at the abbey of **Hautvillers** (a charming spot you can still visit today) that a Benedictine monk named Dom Pierre Pérignon invented the sparkling wine known as Champagne, using grape juice from vineyards that Celtic Gauls may have planted before the birth of Christ. If we had to choose just one product to symbolize France—and the lively effervescence of French wit—it would surely be *le* Champagne. And if a single region were to sum up the history and traditions of this complex country, no part of France could do it better than *la* Champagne.

The Roman legions that marched into Gaul around 50 BC brought with them the building blocks of a highly advanced civilization. They introduced their architecture, agricultural methods, even their taste for thermal spas. More than other regions of Gaul, Champagne prospered under the *pax romana*. Inevitably, the province's wealth excited envy among its neighbors. Wave after wave of Germanic invaders had to be repelled: Vandals, Alamans, Huns... The latter, under the terrible Attila, were beaten back in 451 at the Battle of Châlons (today's Châlons-sur-Marne).

Champagne was the scene of crucial events in French history. Here Clovis, king of the Franks, was baptized in Reims by Bishop Remi (later Saint Remi) in 496. Clovis's conversion to Christianity was a political act of supreme importance: it marked the birth of the French state. Across the ages, 25 French kings and emperors were anointed at Reims. Over centuries and at the cost much bloodshed, France gradually came under control of a single, central authority. That process of nation-building began 1500 years ago, with the baptism of the Frankish king.

The sublime cathedral of **Reims** is illuminated by the pure and radiant expression of its famous *Smiling Angel*, a masterpiece of French Gothic sculpture. The vertiginous spires, glowing stained glass, and lacy stonework of Champagne's cathedrals (Soissons, Laon, Troyes, and Châlons-sur-Marne in addition to Reims) are testaments not only to an enduring Christian faith, but also to a common will to assert France's unique place in the world, through its art, its technical mastery, its political, military, and financial might—in other words, all the elements required to build a modern state. This resolve, initiated by kings and bishops, relayed to the common people by their priests, flowed through the land, giving rise to churches, abbeys, and monasteries: signs of the spiritual continuity and political cohesion that ultimately extended to all of France. Painfully, painstakingly, the French nation was constructed on this alliance of Catholic spirituality and monarchical policy, mocked by free-thinkers as the union of the "saber and the censer," the Army and the Church. The alliance ignited the fratricidal Wars of Religion and provoked the cruel persecutions of religious dissenters from Cathars and Templars to Huguenots and Camisards. These conflicts of belief ripped apart the nation's social and economic fabric; they fueled violent anti-clerical reactions as well, especially during the Revolution. Now that its national unity is unquestioned, the alliance is no longer necessary to France's survival. The twentieth century saw the official separation of Church and State, the end of the tumultuous marriage that began with Clovis and endured for fifteen centuries.

Breaking the Soissons Vase

Reflections like these come to mind as we contemplate the gallery of kings on the façade of Notre-Dame de Reims or as we wander in the nearby basilica of Saint-Remi; as we admire the spectacular stained glass of **Troyes**'s cathedral or the intricate rood screen in the church of Sainte-Madeleine; as we visit **Châlons-sur-Marne**'s cathedral and the basilica of Notre-Dame-de-l'Épine. Along the way, we also spot headless statues of saints: victims of rebels lashing out blindly against the symbols of Church authority.

Clovis's first capital was **Soissons**, northwest of Reims. In their very first history book, every French child learns the story of the Soissons Vase. Clovis, one day, ordered a soldier to give him a vase taken as booty from a church. The soldier broke the vase rather than return it. A year later, spying the disobedient soldier, Clovis split open his head saying: "There! I've done to you what you did to the Soissons Vase." Nothing more is known of that vessel, but visitors to Soissons can view the ancient abbey of Saint-Jean-des-Vignes and an imposing Gothic cathedral (look inside for Rubens's *Adoration of the Shepherds*).

Laon, a fortress town moored on an isolated hill that dominates a billowing ocean of wheat fields, claims one of France's earliest Gothic cathedrals. This many-towered sanctuary is the jewel of Laon's beautifully preserved upper town, a rare ensemble of intact medieval streets and structures. Throughout the Middle Ages and beyond, Champagne showed uncommonly strong spiritual aspirations, and the monastic movement flourished. One of the most celebrated abbeys (of which only a small part survives) is the Cistercian monastery of **Clairvaux**, founded by the abbot Bernard—the future Saint Bernard—in 1115. As one travels through this deeply religious region, it is easier to understand the pivotal role that France, "eldest daughter of the church," with its saints, popes, and crusaders, has played in the history of Catholicism.

Like the rest of France, Champagne suffered abominably during the Hundred Years' War. At Troyes, in 1420, Queen Isabelle disinherited the Dauphin and handed over the French Crown to England's Henry V. From the North, Henry marched triumphant into Champagne. But it was also from Champagne that the reconquest began nine years later, when Joan of Arc had the Dauphin crowned at Reims. Pillaged, burned, ravaged: despite the mayhem, Champagne's rich resources were never totally exhausted. Since the tenth century, the region had been wisely administered and enriched by the Counts of Champagne—counts in name, but closer to sovereigns in power.

They shrewdly took advantage of the flow of trade between Flanders and Italy and organized fairs in Troyes, Provins, and **Bar-sur-Aube**. Merchants from the north and south, and buyers from just about everywhere thronged to these fairs for spices, fabrics, furs, wines, and foodstuffs. Lombard bankers facilitated the exchange of currencies among foreigners at these ancestors of the Common Market.

A red rose for the King of England

Troyes's more recent claim to fame is as France's hosiery capital, but competition from cheaper imported wares is taking a toll on that industry. The city has found a new commercial niche with factory outlets: the low prices draw consumers to Troyes just as the medieval trade fairs did! Art lovers will find in Troyes a restored historic center chockablock with half-timbered houses, the ancient churches we noted above, and a surprising modern art museum with pictures by Derain, Vlaminck, and Van Dongen.

Provins, too, closer to Paris (see *Ile-de-France*), preserves a fabulous heritage from its medieval heyday, not least of which is a very special rose garden. Thibault IV, crusader and Count of Champagne, introduced roses to France from the Middle East. Legend has it that a member of England's House of Lancaster, who was *seigneur* of the town, chose a red rose from Provins as his emblem. In the famous War of the Roses, it opposed the white rose of York.

The Seine, the Marne, the Aube, and the Meuse spring to life in the Langres plateau which dominates southeastern Champagne. The walled town of **Langres**, poised on a rocky promontory and curiously untouched by time, has changed little since the days of Diderot, the eminent philosopher born there in 1713.

At the opposite end of the province, Champagne is bordered by the densely wooded **Ardennes**, whose somber dwellings contrast with the whiteness of lower Champagne's limestone. The climate is harsher here and the terrain more rugged. As it rushes toward Belgium and the North sea, the River Meuse has carved fantastic landscapes out of the rock. This scenic and little-traveled area is ideal for a relaxing holiday in the open air. The Meuse nearly encircles the town of **Revin** before crossing **Sedan** and **Charleville-Mézières**—birthplace of the visionary poet, Arthur Rimbaud—before flowing out of France at **Givet**.

In 1814 Champagne was the scene of Napoléon's final battles, at **Montmirail**, **Brienne**, and **Nogent-sur-Seine**, and the defeat that precipitated his abdication at Fontainebleau. In 1871 his nephew, Emperor Napoléon III, was routed by the Prussians at Sedan in the Ardennes. Champagne witnessed two turning points of the Great War, at the battles of the Marne: the first, in 1914, saw France spring resolutely into action; the second, in 1918 marked the Allies' ultimate victory. Germany invaded France through the Ardennes in 1940, and it was across Champagne that the Allies pushed the Nazis back in 1944. Echoes of all the conflicts and crises that France has endured still resound in Champagne. While that history is reason enough to make a pilgrimage to this province, there are other reasons, too. Like Champagne, for instance.

The **Route du Champagne** lies within a triangle formed by Reims, Châlons, and Épernay and rambles through the vineyards of the Montagne de Reims, the Côte des Blancs, and the Marne Valley. Champagne buffs (and who isn't?) can stop for a tour of Moët & Chandon's impressive cellars, or those of Mercier in Épernay. At Pommery's remarkable cellars in Reims you'll see a gigantic 75,000-liter cask carved by the Art Nouveau master, Gallé, and underground galleries adorned with statues. A constant, cool temperature, perfect for holding Champagne, prevails in these *crayères* (from *craie*, or chalky limestone), dug far back in Gallo-Roman times. Equally spectacular are Taittinger's and Ruinart's cellars. (See visitors' information at the end of the chapter). Champagne is the sparkling expression of an elegant way of life, which is also mirrored in the local cuisine (ah! those creamy Champagne sauces). Soft, bloomy Chaource cheese hails from Champagne, as does the triple-crème cheese called Pierre-Robert. And it is said that the king's soldiers lost a battle at Troyes for having indulged too freely in that city's celebrated andouillette sausages—instead of fighting, with full bellies they fell into a satisfied sleep!

Since an excellent *autoroute* puts Paris within two hours of Reims, it is a simple matter to savor those specialties and more on their home turf. As you sit, for example, at the splendiferous Château des Crayères in Reims, and sip a *flûte* of "Comtes de Champagne," "Dom Pérignon," or "Dom Ruinart" (a colleague of Dom Pérignon's) or Gosset (mayor of Aÿ in 1584), or Roederer, (that the czars of Russia liked so much) or Mumm, you can also drink in the rich history of Champagne, and understand why such firms as Taittinger, Moët & Chandon, Ruinart, Gosset, Roederer, or Mumm pay homage to the men who built the region's wealth and glory, by naming the finest Champagnes in their honor.

A tour of Champagne is a lesson in optimism. In spite of the ordeals the region has survived, it retains its gentle aspect and patiently rebuilds its resources. An example: barely 50 years ago la **Champagne Pouilleuse**, an arid, chalky district in the center of the province, seemed doomed to permanent poverty. Today that "flea-ridden" land is one of France's richest grain-bearing regions, thanks to improved farming technology. It's just one more reason never to give up hope. And that, perhaps, is why, on Reims cathedral, the Angel smiles for all eternity.

RESTAURANTS & HOTELS

CHAMPILLON 51160
Paris 156 - Épernay 5 Marne

Royal Champagne

RN 2051 - 03 26 52 87 11, fax 03 26 52 89 69
Open daily until 10pm. Priv rm 50. Tennis. Garage pkg.
This establishment offers the prettiest view in the region of Épernay and the surrounding vineyards, along with every amenity its well-heeled clientele could desire! A courteous welcome and plenty of warm atmosphere await guests who come to enjoy Christophe Blot's extraordinarily regular, precise cuisine. His rigorously selected ingredients tend toward the classic, and he combines them in amazing fresh flavor combinations that must be tasted to be believed! Sparkling wine list; tempting nibbles before and after the meal. Smiling, efficient service. C 460. M 195 (lunch, exc Sun), 275-350, 110 (children).

Royal Champagne

(See restaurant above)
Open year-round. 3 stes 1,200-1,800. 27 rms 780-1,350. Bkfst 85. Half-board 865-1,030 (oblig in seas). Rm ser. Conf. Tennis. Pkg.
This remarkable house perched above Épernay offers a splendid view of the hillside vineyards. The large, comfortable guest quarters have their own quiet terraces. Ideal for conferences. Relais et Châteaux.

COURCELLES-SUR-VESLES 02220
Paris 128 - Soissons 23 - Reims 56 Aisne

Château de Courcelles

03 23 74 13 53, fax 03 23 4 06 41
Open daily until 9:30pm. Priv rm 25. Terrace dining. Heated pool. Tennis. Valet pkg.
This seventeenth-century château's dining room, with its monumental sculpted stone fireplace, refined décor, and adjacent terrace, is a favorite location for business lunches and dinners. But lovers of fine food are also sensitive to the charms of chef Pascal Mottet's cuisine, marked by resolute classicism interpreted with impeccable skill. Costly but well-composed wine list, with a nice selection of Bordeaux and a remarkable choice of Champagnes. Wonderful welcome. C 350-400. M 200 (weekday lunch, wine incl), 230, 360, 90 (children).

Château de Courcelles

(See restaurant above)
Open year-round. 2 stes 1,300-1,500. 12 rms 700-1,200. Bkfst 85. Rms for disabled. Half-board 735-1,885. Conf. Heated pool. Tennis. Valet pkg.
The tastefully appointed rooms in this striking château set amid French gardens are all comfortable and exceedingly well-equipped. Delicious breakfasts and exquisite service. Numerous leisure-time activities: day trips, fishing, swimming pool and sauna. An array of conference facilities are available. Relais et Châteaux.

FÈRE-EN-TARDENOIS	02130
Paris 110 - Soissons 26 - Reims 46 - Laon 54	Aisne

Château de Fère

3 km N on N 967, route de Fismes
03 23 82 21 13, fax 03 23 82 37 81
Closed beg Jan-beg Feb. Open until 9pm (10pm in summer). Terrace dining. Heated pool. Tennis. Pkg.
This historic hotel, nestled among the feudal and Renaissance ruins, is the essence of a prestige hotel, down to the most minute detail. The new chef, Dominique Quay, arrived too close to press time for us to sample his food, but we can tell you that the wine list is exceptional.

 ## Château de Fère

(See restaurant above)
Closed beg Jan-beg Feb. 6 stes 1,150-1,950. 19 rms 850-1,200. Bkfst 90. Rm ser. Conf. Heated pool. Tennis. Pkg.
This luxurious establishment set on scenic country grounds offers a range of spacious, prettily decorated rooms and suites. Some are furnished with antiques, and all are superbly equipped, with Jacuzzis in the bathrooms. Competent welcome and service.

REIMS	51100
Paris 145 - Lille 212 - Metz 187 - Verdun 118	Marne

 ## Boyer

"Les Crayères", 64, bd Henri-Vasnier
03 26 82 80 80, fax 03 26 82 65 52
Closed Mon, Tue lunch, Dec 23-Jan 12. Open until 10:30pm. Priv rm 50. Air cond. Valet pkg.
Grounded in the classics, distinguished by remarkable sauces, Gérard Boyer's cuisine possesses a singular grace, a particular personality. Boyer has a way of drawing all manner of novel nuances from his ingredients and many of his dishes are unique. This majestic Louis XV–style mansion shines like a contemporary Versailles over which Gérard Boyer presides as master of ceremony. Refinement spreads to the details but with discretion. Boyer, the aristocrat of light classicism, combines rich ingredients in an inimitable and "filtered" manner, thus eliminating over-richness, and leaving only the essence of it. His artichoke cappucino with truffles and his simple smoked-on-the-spot salmon with caviar cream are as wonderful as his veal. The wine

cellar is beyond description. C 520-660. M 870 (wine & Champagne & coffee incl).

 ## Boyer

(See restaurant above)
Closed Dec 23-Jan 12. 3 stes 1,890-2,400. 16 rms 990-1,890. Bkfst 110. Rms for disabled. Air cond. Conf. Valet pkg.
This magnificent turn-of-the-century mansion is situated on a vast estate in the middle of the city. The spacious, comfortable rooms here open out onto the surrounding greenery, and the service is competent without being obsequious. Relais et Châteaux.

12/20 Le Drouet

96, pl. Drouet-d'Erlon - 03 26 88 56 39
Open daily until 10:30pm (11:30pm Fri & Sat). Priv rm 80. Terrace dining. Air cond. Pkg.
The Maillot family serves up nicely done bistro fare here, at equally nice prices. Enjoy a main course with a glass of wine in the bar, or try the 130 F restaurant menu, served with a pitcher of wine. Pretty shaded terrace. C 170-220. M 95 (exc Sun), 130, 190, 62 (children).

 ## Grand Hôtel des Templiers

22, rue des Templiers
03 26 88 55 08, fax 03 26 47 80 60
Open year-round. 2 stes 1,800. 15 rms 950-1,400. Bkfst 85. Rms for disabled. Restaurant. Air cond. Conf. Heated pool. Valet pkg.
Located near the cathedral, this magnificent nineteenth-century house boasts neo-Gothic décor, a monumental wooden staircase, stained glass windows and handsome lounges with dark wood paneling. Luxurious rooms with period furniture. Swimming pool with balneotherapy, Turkish bath, sauna and tanning bed. First-class service and reception.

SAINTE-PREUVE	02350
Paris 169 - Laon 28 - Reims 52	Aisne

 ## Château de Barive

03 23 22 15 15, fax 03 23 22 08 39
Closed mid Dec-mid Jan. Open until 9:30pm. Priv rm 22. Terrace dining. Heated pool. Tennis. Pkg.
Tables in the dining room are grouped around the fireplace for cold-weather dining, and a charming garden and terrace play host to guests when the weather gets warm. Chef Jos Bergman regales diners in this charming setting with his short but sweet à la carte menu, and a series of nicely done set meals as well. Another point for the total mastery he displays: a wonderful combination of flavors and textures in the beef carpaccio with Parmesan, succulent, perfectly cooked sea scallops served with wild mushrooms seasoned with herbs from the chef's garden, and tender, juicy lamb. Try the delicious sablé with caramelized fruit for dessert. The well-balanced wine list is short on half-bottles, but does feature affordable offerings for each

region, and is (surprisingly?) rich in Champagnes. C 320. M 160-330, 80 (children).

 ### Château de Barive 🚹🏮

(See restaurant above)
Closed mid Dec-mid Jan. 3 stes 780-880. 11 rms 380-650. Bkfst 60. Half-board 460-660. Conf. Heated pool. Tennis. No pets. Pkg.
This former hunting lodge is located on the grounds of an eighteenth-century château (complete with Baroque gardens). Rooms are luxuriously equipped and prettily appointed with antiques. Horseback riding.

VINAY	51200
Paris 138 - Châlons-sur-Marne 41 - Épernay 7	Marne

 ### La Briqueterie

4, route de Sézanne
03 26 59 99 99, fax 03 26 59 92 10
Closed Dec 21-26. Open until 9:30pm. Priv rm 80. Heated pool. Valet pkg.
This half-timber house with its cozy décor bespeckled with handmade rustic objects is a favorite haunt of local business executives. New chef Christophe Bernard's cuisine is a well-crafted mixture of regional influences and up-to-date home cooking. Shock value is not on the agenda, and that sometimes makes for a lack of personality. We relished the red mullet and potatoes served on a delicate jus, although it was almost too discreetly seasoned, and the chocolate sponge cake was excellent. A connoisseur's cellar, stacked full of Champagnes and Rhône Valley wines alike, but not forgetting the more unknown regions. A wide choice of after-dinner drinks, and a selection of cigars. C 350. M 135 & 215 (lunch), 250 (weekday dinner, Sun), 350, 410, 115 (children).

 ### La Briqueterie 🚹🏮

(See restaurant above)
Closed Dec 21-26. 2 stes 1,150. 40 rms 620-870. Bkfst 75. Rms for disabled. Rm scr. Conf. Heated pool. Valet pkg.
This charming, refined hotel nestled amid the vineyards offers spacious, elegantly appointed guest quarters with marble bathrooms. Guests enjoy taking leisurely strolls through the surrounding flower-filled grounds.

REGIONAL FOODS

Champagne's native flavors are soft, and round: think of ivory-skinned Chaource or buttery Pierre-Robert cheeses, silken boudin blanc sausage, and such typical sweets as pink-tinged biscuits de Reims or croquignoles (tiny meringues). And naturally, there's Champagne itself, the sparkling, elegant soul of the region's chalk-rich soil.

• CHARCUTERIE

HAYBES	08170 – Ardennes

Maison Maurice Roffidal

25, Grand-Rue - 03 24 41 12 97
An excellent source for dried, unsmoked jambon des Ardennes, the region's wonderful country ham.

RETHEL	08300 – Ardennes

Yves Duhem

9, rue Colbert - 03 24 38 46 19
Among the vast range of Ardennais charcuterie, you'll find a flavorful boudin blanc, which is the specialty of the house.

Charcuterie Demoizet

1, rue Taine - 03 24 38 42 05
For boudin blanc (a white-meat sausage) fit for a king, with or without truffles.

• CHEESE

REIMS	51100 – Marne

La Cave aux Fromages

16, pl. du Forum - 03 26 47 83 05
For generations, the same family has overseen this shop, where you can sample excellent Chaource, Langres, and Pierre-Robert, as well as other appetizing cheeses.

• CHOCOLATE & CANDY

REIMS	51100 – Marne

Deléans

20, rue Cérès - 03 26 47 56 35
Since 1810 the gourmets of Reims have indulged their sweet tooth here, with a vast array of candies and assorted chocolates. The pride of the house is the chocolate-coated cherry in brandy called the Nelusko.

• *GOURMET SPECIALTIES*

REIMS   51100 – Marne

Charbonneaux-Brabant

5, rue de Valmy - 03 26 49 58 70
  Mustard spiked with Champagne (in smooth
or grainy versions) and Champagne vinegar that
is cask-aged for at least four years are two
remarkable condiments, well worth seeking out.

• *PASTRY & COOKIES*

REIMS   51100 – Marne

Fossier

44, bd Jamin - 03 26 07 27 56
  The city's famous pink lady fingers (often
dipped in sweet or demi-sec Champagne) are
featured here. In fact, they're far better with
custards or puddings than with bubbly! Also on
hand is the local version of gingerbread, made
with rye flour.

WINE

T he vineyards of Champagne are the
  most northerly in France. The cool,
damp climate, coupled with Champagne's
chalky soil and subsoil, yields slow-ripening
grapes that achieve a high level of acidity,
which accounts for Champagne's bright
vivacity.
  To make Champagne, three grape varieties,
two red and one white, are combined in varying proportions: black-skinned Pinot Noir
gives the wine power and aging potential;
Pinot Meunier provides long-lasting fruitiness; and white Chardonnay supplies round-
ness and elegance. Hence a Blanc de Blancs
Champagne is one vinified exclusively from
Chardonnay grapes, while Blanc de Noirs is
made from the Pinots, either alone or in combination.
  The *méthode champenoise*, the fermentation
process employed for making Champagne
(or indeed, any first-class sparkling wine)
began to develop in the late seventeenth century. Dom Pérignon, a Benedictine monk, had
the brilliant notion of blending wines from
different vineyards and villages to obtain a
wine of consistent quality. He is also credited
with introducing corks and glass bottles thick
enough to withstand the pressure of sparkling wine.

Those precious bubbles are produced
during a second fermentation (*prise de mousse*)
which occurs in the bottle, as the wine rests in
Champagne's cool, deep cellars. And while
the bubbles form, the wine also acquires the
distinctive flavors and bouquet that only real
Champagne can deliver.
  After the second fermentation, non-vintage
Champagne ages for about eighteen months.
In contrast, vintage Champagne remains in
contact with its flavor-giving sediments for at
least three years—hence its significantly
higher price.
  Among the addresses listed below, we've
included major Champagne houses, which
purchase grapes from growers and blend
them to produce Champagnes in their signature style, and independent producers from
all five of Champagne's growing districts
(Montagne de Reims, Côte des Blancs, Vallée
de la Marne, Côte de Sézanne, and Aube) who
cultivate and vinify their own grapes.

• *MAJOR CHAMPAGNE HOUSES*

AŸ   51160 – Marne

Bollinger

20, bd Maréchal de Lattre De Tassigny
03 26 53 33 66, fax 03 26 54 85 59
*Open 8:15am-noon & 1:45pm-6pm. Closed Sat, Sun
& hols.*

Gosset

69, rue Jules Blondeau
03 26 56 99 56, fax 03 26 51 55 88
*Open Mon-Fri 8am-11am & 2pm-4:30pm. Closed
Fri pm, Sat, Sun.*

ÉPERNAY   51200 – Marne

Moët et Chandon

03 26 51 20 20, fax 03 26 51 20 21
*Open daily Apr-Nov 15: 9:30am-11:30am & 2pm-
5pm. Closed Nov 16-Mar: Sat, Sun & hols.*

REIMS   51100 – Marne

Krug

03 26 84 44 20, fax 03 26 84 44 49
*Open Mon-Fri 9am-noon & 1:30pm-5:30pm.
Closed Sat, Sun & hols.*

Some establishments change their **closing
times** without warning. It is always wise to
check in advance.

Mumm

34, rue du Champ-de-Mars
03 26 49 59 70, fax 03 26 49 59 01
Open daily 9am-11am & 2pm-5pm. Closed Nov-Feb: Sat am, Sun & hols.

Roederer

21, bd Lundy - 03 26 40 42 11, fax 03 26 87 49
Open Mon-Fri 9am-11am & 2pm-5pm. Closed Sat, Sun, hols.

Ruinart

4, rue des Crayères
03 26 77 51 51, fax 03 26 82 88 43
Open Mon-Fri 9am-noon & 2pm-5pm. Closed Sat, Sun, hols.

Taittinger

9, pl. St-Nicaise - 03 26 85 45 35, fax 03 26 85 44 39
Open Mar-Nov: Mon-Fri 9:30am-noon & 2pm-4:30pm; Sat, Sun & hols: 9am-11am & 2pm-5pm. Closed Dec-Feb: Sat, Sun & hols.

Veuve Clicquot-Ponsardin

1, pl. des Droits de l'Homme
03 26 89 54 41, fax 03 26 40 60 17
Open Mon-Sat 10am-12:30pm & 1:30pm-6pm. Closed Mar-Oct: Sun; Nov-Feb: Sat & Sun.

• *INDEPENDENT PRODUCERS*

AVIZE 51190 – Marne

Champagne de Saint-Gall

7, rue Pasteur - 03 26 57 94 22, fax 03 26 57 57 98
Open Mon-Fri 8am-11am & 2pm-4:30pm.
This cooperative handles 40 percent of the Côte des Blancs' production, and offers a wide range of Champagnes under the Saint-Gall label. One of our favorites here is the golden Blanc de Blancs Extra Brut, for expressive bouquet and rich flavors.

CHARLY-SUR-MARNE 02310 – Aisne

Champagne Baron-Fuenté

21, av. Fernand-Drouet
03 23 82 01 97, fax 03 23 82 12 00
Open Mon-Sat 9am-noon & 2pm-6pm.
Excellent value at this family firm in the Vallée de la Marne district, where Pinot Meunier is the major grape variety. The Brut Tradition is a fine, simple non-vintage Champagne, perfect for an apéritif.

Looking for a winery? Refer to the index.

COURTERON 10250 – Aube

Jean-Pierre Fleury

43, Grande Rue - 03 25 38 20 28, fax 03 25 38 24 65
Open Mon-Fri 9am-noon & 2pm-6pm.
Elected "Winegrower of the Year" for Champagne in 1993 by the Gault Millau jury, Jean-Pierre Fleury cultivates organically raised vines in the Aube district, at the southern limit of Champagne. A splendid range of special cuvées, and a superb non-vintage Fleur de l'Europe Champagne.

CRAMANT 51530 – Marne

Champagne Bonnaire

120, rue d'Épernay
03 26 57 50 85, fax 03 26 57 59 17
Open Mon-Fri 9am-noon & 2pm-5pm. Closed Sat pm, Sun.
The Bonnaire family, winegrowers for three generations, cultivate Chardonnay grapes on the Côte des Blancs for their vintage Brut Blanc de Blancs. The non-vintage Brut Tradition is a blend of red and white grapes, containing a third each of Pinot Noir, Pinot Meunier, and Chardonnay.

MONTIGNY-SOUS-CHÂTILLON 51700 – Marne

Charlier et Fils

4, rue des Pervenches
03 26 58 35 18, fax 03 26 58 02 31
Open daily 8am-noon & 2pm-6pm (exc Sun pm).
A reliable producer who welcomes visitors with heartwarming cordiality (note that there are some furnished rentals on the property). Consistent, affordably priced Champagnes.

VERZENAY 51360 – Marne

Champagne De Carlini

13, rue de Mailly
03 26 49 43 91, fax 03 26 49 46 46
Open daily 8am-8pm.
Powerful and aromatic Champagnes made from 90 percent Pinot Noir grapes, with a bit of Chardonnay. De Carlini also produces a bone-dry Extra Brut with absolutely no added sugar.

Jean-Claude Mouzon

4, rue des Perthois or 40, rue Thiers
(opposite the post office)
03 26 49 48 11, fax 03 26 49 45 45
Open daily 9am-6pm.
Jean-Claude Mouzon likes the life of an independent producer: growing his own grapes on the Montagne de Reims (where Pinot Noir predominates) and turning them into elegant Champagnes. We especially admire his Cuvée Spéciale La Montgolfière and delicately floral non-vintage Brut.

• *CHAMPAGNE CELLARS*

Many of the major Champagne firms offer interesting tours of their cellars, where millions of bottles of precious bubbly mature in ideal conditions. It's fun—and refreshingly cool in summer—to explore these underground galleries, carved from Champagne's chalky subsoil. Some are former limestone quarries that date back to Gallo-Roman times.

AŸ	51160 – Marne

Bollinger

20, bd Maréchal de Lattre De Tassigny
03 26 53 33 66, fax 03 26 54 85 59
Open by appt only. Free.

Deutz

16, rue Jeanson - 03 26 55 15 11, fax 03 26 54 01 21
*Open by appt only: Mon-Fri 8:30am-11:30am &
1:30pm-6pm. Closed Sat & Sun; Fri pm (in summer). Fee.*

Gosset

69, rue Jules Blondeau
03 26 56 99 56, fax 03 26 51 55 88
*Open by appt only: Mon-Fri 8am-11pm & 2pm-
4:30pm. Closed Fri pm, Sat & Sun. Free.*

ÉPERNAY	51200 – Marne

De Castellane

57, rue de Verdun
03 26 51 19 11, fax 03 26 51 19 12
*Open daily Apr 15-Oct 10am-noon & 2pm-6pm.
Fee 20.*

Mercier

68, av. de Champagne
03 26 51 22 22, 03 26 51 22 23
*Open Mon-Sat 9:30am-11:30am & 2:30pm-
4:30pm; Sun & hols until 5pm. Closed Dec-Feb: Tue
& Wed. Fee 20 F.*

Moët et Chandon

20, av. de Champagne
03 26 51 20 20, fax 03 26 51 20 21
*Open daily Apr-Nov 15: 9:30am-11:30am & 2pm-
4:30pm. Closed Nov 16-Mar: Sat, Sun & hols. Fee
20 F.*

Pol Roger

1, rue Henri Lelarge
03 26 59 58 00, fax 03 26 59 25 70
Open by appt only. Closed Sat, Sun & hols. Free.

REIMS	51100 – Marne

Henriot

1, pl. des Droits de l'Homme
03 26 89 53 00, fax 03 26 53 10
Open by appt only. Closed Sat, Sun & hols. Free.

Krug

5, rue Coquebert - 03 26 84 44 20, fax 03 26 84 44 49
*Open by appt only Mon-Fri: 10am-noon & 3pm-
5pm. Closed Sat, Sun & hols. Free.*

Mumm

34, rue du Champ-de-Mars
03 26 49 59 70, fax 03 26 49 59 01
*Open daily 9am-11am & 2pm-5pm. Closed Nov-
Feb: Sat am, Sun & hols. Fee 20 F.*

Pommery

5, pl. du Général Gouraud
03 26 61 62 55, fax 03 26 61 63 98
*Open daily Apr-Oct 11am-5pm; winter by appt only.
Closed Dec 22-Jan 3. Fee 30 F.*

Roederer

21, bd Lundy - 03 26 40 42 11, fax 03 26 86 87 49
Open by appt only. Free.

Ruinart

4, rue des Crayères
03 26 85 40 29, fax 03 26 82 88 43
Open by appt only. Free.

Taittinger

9, pl. St-Nicaise - 03 26 85 45 35, fax 03 26 85 44 39
*Open Mar-Nov: Mon-Fri 9:30am-noon & 2pm-
4:30pm; Sat, Sun & hols: 9am-11am & 2pm-5pm.
Closed Dec-Feb: Sat, Sun & hols. Fee 20 F.*

Veuve Clicquot-Ponsardin

1, pl. des Droits de l'Homme
03 26 89 54 41, fax 03 26 40 60 17
*Open by appt only: Mon-Sat 10am-6pm. Closed Sun.
Free.*

TOURS-SUR-MARNE	51150 – Marne

Laurent-Perrier

32, av. de Champagne
03 26 58 91 22, fax 03 26 58 95 10
*Open by appt only: Mon-Fri 9am-11am & 2pm-
4pm. Closed Sat, Sun & hols. Free.*

FRANCHE-COMTÉ

A secret shared

The Jura or Franche-Comté: call it what you will, these rugged, river-crossed mountains bordered by Switzerland to the east and Burgundy to the west, are one of France's best-kept secrets. Had Steven Spielberg given the matter some thought, he could have—maybe should have—shot *Jurassic Park* in Franche-Comté. For it was here, some 260 million years ago, that the geological upheavals that wracked our planet for 45 million years reached the most violent pitch. In Spielberg's defense, we have to admit that the Jura's palm-shaded ocean where dinosaurs once splashed is long (long!) gone.

Independent, introspective, Franche-Comté tends to keep out of the limelight. A past sown with bloody battles, devastation, pillaging, struggles pitting the Holy Roman Empire against Burgundy's dukes, France against England, and the people against marauding mercenaries has bred a healthy distrust of those in power. With considerable difficulty, Louis XIV annexed Franche-Comté to the Crown in 1678. And the province has remained fiercely French: in 1870 the besieged town of **Belfort** resisted the Prussian army for 103 days. The colossal statue of the *Lion of Belfort* that stands in this French version of the Alamo honors the courage of Colonel Denfert-Rochereau and his men in the face of 40,000 enemy soldiers. In recognition of their heroism, Germany allowed Belfort to remain French, and did not annex it along with Alsace and Lorraine. Today, Belfort is home to the *TGV*, the fastest train on rails; and Peugeot manufactures its automobiles at nearby **Sochaux**.

Enveloped in immense forests (the name Jura may come from a Latin word meaning "wood") Franche-Comté's small towns and villages are tucked into valleys or perched on mountain tops for protection. On the heights, farmhouses shelter beneath oversized roofs (the better to collect sweet rainwater) and behind thick walls that keep out the cold—and strangers.

Wealth from wood and water

Wood and water are the twin sources of Franche-Comté's wealth. As early as the fifth century, Christian monks cleared and exploited the region's forests, a precious capital which the Crown and later the state carefully preserved. Water runs, rushes, streams, springs, and spreads out into splendid green-tinged lakes (some 70 in all) like Lac Saint-Point in **Malbuisson**. Broad rivers—the Loue, the Doubs, the Ain—cross the Jura range, transporting the timber which has always been the region's principal resource. From time immemorial the Franche-Comtois have built their houses, churches, and furniture of wood, have carved it into toys for their children, and fashioned it into violins and oboes. Local timber furnished railroad ties, reinforcements for mine shafts, and telephone poles, too. Still, Franche-Comté is not solely a land of hard-bitten lumberjacks and sinewy sawyers. A centuries-old watchmaking tradition is perpetuated by generations of meticulous craftsmen (they even export to Switzerland!). For an example of their skill, just look at the fabulous astronomical clock on the cathedral of **Besançon**, long the capital of France's clockmaking industry. The city occupies a spectacular site in a bend of the River Doubs, where the military engineer Vauban erected one of his finest citadels. Birthplace of Victor Hugo and the Lumière brothers, Besançon can also claim one of the country's most remarkable art museums.

An visionary's city

South of Besançon, in the bucolic Loue Valley, **Arc-et-Senans** presents the intriguing Royal Saltworks designed in 1773 by the visionary architect Claude-Nicolas Ledoux as the centerpiece of a rationally planned "ideal city." The forceful neo-Palladian structures give a tantalizing hint of what Ledoux's monumental ensemble might have been. The saltworks, unfortunately, proved to be unprofitable and was abandoned in the nineteenth century. To the west, the busy provincial city of **Dole** is worth a visit: the birthplace of Louis Pasteur possesses an old town of considerable charm, reflected in the waters of the Canal du Rhône au Rhin.

In Franche-Comté *le bon pays* is so called because the climate is less rigorous than on the plateaus or mountain tops. On hillsides from **Arbois** to **Lons-le-Saunier** vineyards spread over rocky valleys called *reculées* in the local parlance. Arbois produces delectable rosé wines; there and at **Château-Chalon** connoisseurs seek out the Jura's remarkable *vin jaune*, a wine with a distinctive Sherry-like bouquet, vinified from the rare Savagnin grape.

When you take time out from your touring to enjoy the local cuisine, you'll dine on fine country cooking that features flavorsome farm-bred poultry, freshwater fish from the region's rivers and lakes, smoked Morteau sausages, and Comté cheese from the Jura. **Poligny** prides itself on being the foremost center for this firm mountain cheese with a subtle, nutty savor. Produced from the milk of the Montbéliard cows who graze in legions over the plateaus, Comté has been made here since medieval times in dairy cooperatives called *fruitières*.

Hearty food matches the robust appetites that travelers invariably work up in Franche-Comté, skiing or hiking at rustic resorts like **Les Rousses**, taking in the soul-stirring scenery of jagged peaks or the glittering waterfall of the **Saut-du-Doubs**, not far from **Villers-le-Lac**. Anglers, white-water rafters, hang-gliding enthusiasts will also find happiness here. As you can see, there are reasons aplenty to come and discover the Jura—even if it means that Franche-Comté won't be a secret anymore!

RESTAURANTS & HOTELS

ARBOIS   39600
Paris 393 - Lons-le-Saunier 39 - Pontarlier 56   Jura

 ## Jean-Paul Jeunet

9, rue de l'Hôtel-de-Ville
03 84 66 05 67, fax 03 84 66 24 20
Closed Tue & Wed lunch (exc Sep & school hols), Dec-Jan. Open until 9:30pm. Priv rm 40. Pkg.

This imposing establishment was originally a convent and then a coaching inn. And in its theatrically decorated dining room, Jean-Paul Jeunet serves forth cuisine of the elaborate variety—with the pluses and minuses that implies. Feeling does surface in what he cooks, but it can get diluted when invention takes precedence over substance, especially in some of his heartier offerings. Happily, such is not the case for the cabbage and truffle millefeuille in a tight, aromatic jus enriched with sunchoke emulsion, and served with mushroom-spiced potato chips: a sophisticated, yet well-constructed dish. On the other hand, the sautéed frogs' legs with garlic confit were fairly bland, as was the chick-

en, despite its superb yellow wine sauce. The cellar holds an extraordinary selection of Jura wines: try the '92 "Les Docteurs" Arbois Poulsard from Lucien Aviet at 200 F a bottle. Good choice of half-bottles. The service, although competent, can be on the slow side. C 400-475. M 190-500, 85 (children).

 ## Jean-Paul Jeunet

(See restaurant above)
Closed Tue & Wed (exc Sep & school hols), Dec-Jan. 1 ste 500-550. 17 rms 320-550. Bkfst 62. Pkg.

The rooms here are nicely renovated and comfortable, done up in light wood and patterned textiles. Breakfasts feature wonderful country bread and delicious homemade preserves.

BESANÇON   25000
Paris 390 - Nancy 199 - Belfort 90 - Dijon 91   Doubs

 ## Le Mungo Park

11, rue Jean-Petit
03 81 81 28 01, fax 03 81 83 36 97
Closed Sun lunch, Mon, 1 wk in Feb, 2 wks in Aug. Open until 9:30pm. Terrace dining.

Situated on the scenic banks of the Doubs, this former café, named for a Scottish explorer, has become the best restaurant in the city. Assisted by Benoît Rotschi, Jocelyn-Lotz Choquart's deft technique turns out elaborate cuisine without the usual mannerisms: savory morel galette topped by a poached egg, superb ravioli with artichokes cooked in chicken bouillon, a nice selection of cheeses, and excellent rhubarb and almond custard tart. The limited wine list is long on charm. A most memorable dining experience... C 450. M 140 & 260 (lunch), 195 & 235 (weekday lunch, wine incl), 490.

Relais Castan

6, sq. Castan - 03 81 65 02 00, fax 03 81 83 01 02
Open year-round. 1 ste 980. 7 rms 550-880. Bkfst 50. Rms for disabled. Rms for disabled. Pkg.

This mansion seated at the foot of the citadel, very conventional from the outside, is much less so on the inside. The almost comical décor of some of the bathrooms is much more in keeping with the Roman style of the square it gives on to than with the style of the house. Studied charm is not lacking, and sometimes you'll be overwhelmed by just how well thought-out it is. Best hotel in town.

COURLANS   39570
Paris 403 - Lons-le-Saunier 4   Jura

 ## Auberge de Chavannes   ✪

03 84 47 05 52, fax 03 84 43 26 53
Closed Sun dinner, Mon, Feb 3-Mar 4, Jun 23-Jul 1. Open until 9pm. Garden dining. Air cond. Pkg.

The pink décor and the menu here aren't any too original; in fact, they border on conventional. But all ingredients are selected with the same eagle eye for quality and prepared with such exactitude that your taste buds will never be bored: melt-in-your-mouth duck terrine, perfectly cooked squab, and feather-light cornmeal crêpettes with bacon. The cellar is high in Bordeaux and well stocked in southern Juras. C 350-450. M 165-350.

FOUGEROLLES 70220
Paris 363 - Épinal 43 - Vesoul 38   Haute-Saône

 ## Au Père Rota
8, Grande-Rue - 03 84 49 12 11, fax 03 84 49 14 51
Closed Sun dinner & Mon (exc hols), Jan 2-23. Open until 9pm. Air cond. Pkg.
The remarkable cellar here—coupled with the kind of service we rarely find anymore and Jean-Pierre Kuentz's meticulous cooking—make this place a favorite of ours. Kuentz makes no bones about calling a spade a spade, and the result is regional (as opposed to archeological!) fare with a genuine regard for ingredients. Try the warm Fougerolles gandeuillou (a type of smoked andouille with potatoes), perch done in a Franche-Comté pochouse (stew), and crêpes stuffed with small Fougerolles cherries and Kirsch-flavored ice cream. C 320. M 155-240 (weekdays, Sat lunch), 210 (Sun), 310, 85 (children).

NANTILLY 70100
Paris 356 - Besançon 45 - Dijon 46   Haute-Saône

12/20 ## Restaurant du Parc
03 84 67 78 00, fax 03 84 67 78 01
Closed Nov 15-Feb. Open until 10pm. Terrace dining. Pool. Garage pkg.
The wild eighteenth-century country-style décor might amuse you. Too bad the chef prepares his high-quality ingredients in a rather affected manner; if he were a little more modest, he would produce an excellent cuisine...sand it might be more affordable too. C 210-350. M 180-300.

 ## Château de Nantilly
(See restaurant above)
Closed Nov 15-Feb. 11 stes 900-1,400. 41 rms 300-800. Bkfst 50. Rms for disabled. Half-board 510-910. Conf. Heated pool. Tennis. Garage pkg.
The vast, tree-filled park here has a river running through it, and the rooms in its fashionably decorated pavillion are as spacious as can be. The fitness club is top-notch, and the new owners are making big efforts to keep things lively. This is the ideal spot for a get-in-shape weekend (biking, swimming, etc.). However, there's an extra charge if you bring a four-legged friend along.

> *Some establishments change their closing times without warning. It is always wise to check in advance.*

POLIGNY 39800
Paris 404 - Besançon 58 - Lons-le-Saunier 28   Jura

12/20 ## Hostellerie des Monts de Vaux
5 km E on N 5 - 03 84 37 12 50, fax 03 84 37 09 07
Closed Tue (exc dinner in seas), Wed lunch off-seas, end Oct-end Dec. Open until 9:15pm. Terrace dining. Tennis. Garage pkg.
This old-style coaching inn boasts a comfortable dining room that opens onto a tree-filled garden. The kitchen shows a penchant for morels, yellow wine, and beurre blanc, and dishes are prepared with the utmost care. Good selection of Jura wines. C 400. M 180 (lunch), 400.

Hostellerie des Monts de Vaux
(See restaurant above)
Closed Tue (exc Jul-Aug), end Oct-end Dec. 3 stes 1,050-1,200. 7 rms 770-900. Bkfst 70. Half-board 650-800 (oblig in seas). Tennis. Valet pkg.
Situated on the edge of the magnificent Vaux blind valley, this seventeenth-century coaching inn boasts pretty rooms furnished on an old-fashioned note, overlooking the park and the forest. Good breakfasts. Relais et Châteaux.

REGIONAL FOODS

In rustic Franche-Comté, gourmets will discover earthy mountain cheeses: don't leave without tasting a nutty-flavored wheel of Comté, lush and golden Vacherin, and Morbier, with its distinctive line of ash in the middle. There are sausages, too, such as the smoky jésus de Morteau.

• CHARCUTERIE

MONTBENOIT 25650 – Doubs

Au Bon Fumé
Chez Rose-Marie Faivre - 03 81 38 10 14
Marvelous Morteau sausages made from grain-fed porkers, then smoked over juniper and fir wood. The lady responsible for these delicacies is a devoted marathon runner, who has participated in races in London, Berlin, and New York!

• *CHEESE*

BESANÇON   25000 – Doubs

La Ferme Comtoise

12, rue Battant - 03 81 81 38 78
Farmhouse cheeses chosen from small, quality producers and matured on the premises. Try the Comté, Vacherin Mont d'Or, and Bleu de Gex.

• *CHOCOLATE & CANDY*

BESANÇON   25000 – Doubs

Chocolaterie Belin

23, rue de la République - 03 81 82 18 69
The shop is an Art Deco gem, and the chocolates are presented as if they were precious jewels! They are indeed the best in the region.

WINE

Travelers in the region should make a point of sampling the Jura's rare *vin de paille* (sweet wine made from grapes dried on straw—*paille*—mats) and long-lived *vins jaunes*, from Savagnin grapes, whith a flavor reminiscent of dry Sherry. Whites from Chardonnay grapes (or from a blend of Chardonnay and Savagnin), red wines made with Pinot Noir and/or the local Poulsard and Trousseau varieties, rosés, and some sparkling wines complete the picture. The *appellation contrôlée* Arbois covers reliable white, red, and rosé wines.

ARBOIS   39600 – Jura

Domaine Rolet Père et Fils

Montigny
03 84 66 00 05, fax 03 84 37 47 41
Open daily 9am-noon & 2pm-7pm.
Irreproachable quality; the Rolet winery is a worthy ambassador for the Jura region. Excellent Arbois Tradition made from three red grape varieties.

GEVINGEY   39570 – Jura

Richard Delay

Rue du Château - 03 84 47 47 78, fax 03 84 43 26 75
Open Mon-Sat 10am-7pm.
In a beautiful cellar tasting room, the owner offers samples of his fine Pinot Noir and typically flavored white Jura wines.

MENETRU-LE-VIGNOBLE   39210 – Jura

Domaine Victor Credoz

03 84 85 26 98, fax 03 84 44 62 41
Open daily 8am-8pm.
Excellent white Côtes du Jura, with a pronounced flavor of walnuts and honey; also a full range of red, white, and rosé wines.

The Newsletter All About Romantic Travel

If you have ever dreamed of another
life in Provence, another home in Tuscany
or a secret retreat in the Caribbean. . .
then Les Romantiques, a selection of the
most romantic hideaways, is just for you.
Send your subscription form today,
and Bon Voyage!

♡ Yes! Please start my subscription to Les Romantiques
immediately at the special rate of $20.

♡ Enclosed is a check payable to MCM.

♡ Charge to credit card _____

      Card number_____

      Exp. Date _____

      Signature _____

Name _____

Address _____

City _____State _____Zip _____

Please mail to MCM • 211 East 43rd Street
Suite 1404 • New York • NY 10017
Tel. 212-986-1972 • Fax. 212-599-1755
Email EMROM@ICHANGE.COM
Web Address: LESROMANTIQUES.COM

LANGUEDOC-ROUSSILLON & MIDI-PYRÉNÉES

In the footsteps of troubadours

Languedoc, *langue d'Oc*: one word designates this land and its language. The roots of Languedoc's culture plunge deep into a landscape of plains and limestone hills that stretches out beside the Mediterranean, cupped by the Massif Central to the north and the Pyrenees to the east. Langue d'Oc blended Latin with the language spoken by the Gauls ("oc," from the Latin *hoc*, means "yes"; could it be the ancestor of today's universal "O.K."?). In Paris, by contrast, "yes" was *oïl*, hence the name of the rival tongue, *langue d'Oïl*. These two distinctive forms of French were spoken in two halves of the country, divided by a line that roughly corresponds to the limit beyond which olive trees no longer thrive. To the north of that invisible border, no one said *Oc*, and no one cooked with olive oil. Not until the late twentieth century did dieticians confirm the virtues of olive oil: now, of course, cooks the world over are swearing allegiance to Provençal—and more broadly, to Mediterranean—cuisine. What we eat, incidentally, is by no means an accident. Food reflects the evolution of a culture as much as migrations, conquests, and language do. The Romans brought grapevines and olive trees with them into Gaul, and grafted them onto the conquered territory.

The mark of the Romans

It may well be here, in this rugged, vivid region between the Rhône and the Pyrenees that the Romans' influence in France left its most enduring mark. For the Romans who arrived in the wake of Ligurians, Greeks, and Celts, this land was the most attractive of the transalpine provinces. They called it Gallia Narbonensis, and developed it with a will. They built roads: the Via Domitia to link the Iberian peninsula with Rome, and the Via Agrippa to travel north. They equipped the province with structures that we can still admire 2,000 years after the fact: the triple-tiered aqueduct at **Pont-du-Gard**, for example, and the arena and temple at **Nimes**, not to mention the bridges, theaters, and other Roman

monuments of Vaison-la-Romaine, Orange, and Arles, cities which today are part of Provence, on the other side of the Rhône.

With Rome's decline, other would-be conquerors came to stake their claim in Languedoc, the Vandals, Visigoths, Saracens, and Spaniards among them. After a long spell as a fief of the powerful counts of Toulouse, Languedoc became French in the thirteenth century. Roussillon was not definitively annexed to France until the reign of Louis XIV. Languedoc lies open to the most diverse influences. Not only opposing armies, but also conflicting ideas clashed here, sometimes violently. The universities of **Toulouse** and of **Montpellier**, founded in the thirteenth century, were (and remain) brilliant intellectual centers. Montpellier's medical school, in particular, has been renowned since well before Rabelais studied there in the Renaissance. Here the troubadours sang of courtly love in *langue d'Oc*. Today visitors can get a feel for Montpellier's rich history by exploring the old town, where medieval vestiges stand side by side with Baroque buildings and splendid eighteenth-century town houses. Place de la Comédie is the premier scene of Montpellier's vibrant social life. Just a few steps away, on Boulevard Sarail, is the Musée Fabre, one of the finest art museums in France.

The massacre of the "perfect ones"

The spiritual movement known as Catharism swept through the south of France in the twelfth and thirteenth centuries. The Cathars' doctrine of absolute purity was a violent rejection of the opulence and worldliness of the Church. Accusing him of heresy, Pope Innocent III excommunicated the Count of Toulouse and in 1208 preached the Albigensian crusade against the Catharist sect, centred in the city of **Albi**. It took more than twenty years to defeat the Cathars, the "perfect ones," as they were known, though the city of **Béziers** was burned and its population massacred (even the unfortunates who sought refuge in the Romanesque church of the Madeleine, which still stands today). Carcassonne fell too, despite its awesome fortifications. The town's ramparts survived, however, and we can see them now much as they appeared to Simon de Montfort, the ferocious commander of the papal army (he is buried within the ramparts, in the splendid church of Saint-Nazaire). Abetted by terror, torture, and burnings at the stake, the Inquisition finally brought down the Albigensians. Albi's Southern Gothic cathedral of Sainte-Cécile was built to glorify the triumph of the established Church. Although the Cathars were exterminated, Languedoc's passionate idealism never abated.

That idealism may explain the region's ardent response to Protestantism, especially in the Cévennes mountains around **Anduze** (a charming old town with many fine seventeenth-century houses). With countless converts, the reformed religion became a major force of dissent in southern France. Ill-inspired and—especially—ill-informed about the Protestants' true strength, Louis XIV sought to stamp them out. The merciless repression led by the King's Dragoons sparked bitter resistance: peasants in shirtsleeves called *camisards* (from *camisa*, a *chemise* or shirt), armed with pitchforks and scythes, battled the royal troops led by the Maréchal de Villars. The memory of that struggle still endures in the Cévennes. Anduze is home to the largest Reformed church in France, and Protestants are still numerous in Nîmes, Uzès, and the old mining town of Alès.

Languedoc's flat, marshy, and increasingly built-up coast (lots of camp grounds and crowded beach resorts), is less alluring than the Cévennes, the rugged Causses, and the vine-clad Corbières hills crowned with feudal fortresses (like the château de **Peyrepertuse**). Red and ocher villages punctuate grandiose natural sites: the vividly tinted **Gorges du Tarn**, the **Corniche des Cévennes** with its hairpin turns, the **Cirque de Mourèze** in the gorgeous **Hérault Valley**...

A wine lake for Europe

The vineyards that once carpeted the coastal plain—and contributed copiously to Europe's "wine lake"—are yielding ground to vegetable fields and fruit orchards. Wine growers on higher ground, where better grapes grow, are determinded to improve quality. Nowadays they plant Syrah and Cabernet vines and severely limit yields. Travelers should make a point of sampling some of the newer *appellations contrôlées* from the Coteaux du Languedoc and Corbières.

Rich dessert wines—Rivesaltes, Banyuls, Maury—are a specialty of the Roussillon region, west of Languedoc. Here, too, a mild climate and brilliant sunshine produce spectacular fruits and vegetables: Roussillon's juice-gorged apricots and peaches are the epitome of lusciousness!

The **Côte Vermeille** runs from **Perpignan** to Spain; this is Catalan country. Attracted by the coast's intense and beautiful light, Picasso, Matisse, and Derain all came to paint in the improbably scenic fishing village of **Collioure**, which also has the distinction of being the anchovy capital of France. By a curious coincidence, local fishermen use *lamparos*—intense (and beautiful?) lights—to draw the anchovies to their boats... Here, as in Barcelona, the natives speak Catalan (a close cousin to *langue d'Oc*), and they dance the *sardane*. Sheep and goats graze on the herb-rich scrub that covers Roussillon's hill country, producing fragrant chèvres and ewes'-milk cheeses. Hams and all manner of rustic air-dried sausages are also prepared according to ancestral methods.

The region's visceral attachment to its past—and the past, here, goes back at least 450,000 years, date of the human remains unearthed at **Tautavel** in the Corbières hills—does not exclude a commitment to the future. **Toulouse**, the famous *Ville Rose* at began life as a Roman camp, and which boasts a wealth of medieval, Renaissance, and eighteenth-century monuments, is also the capital of France's cutting-edge aerospace industry.

RESTAURANTS & HOTELS

LANGUEDOC-ROUSSILLON

AGDE   34300
Paris 818 - Montpellier 57 - Sète 23   Hérault

 La Tamarissière   ❧

4 km SW on D 32 E, at La Tamarissière
04 67 94 20 87, fax 04 67 21 38 40
Closed mid Mar-mid Jun & mid Sep-Dec: Sun dinner, Mon; mid Jun-mid Sep: Mon lunch; Jan-mid Mar. Open until 10:30pm. Priv rm 60. Garden dining. Pool. Pkg.
A pre-war mood floats about this charming, riverside restaurant set in an unspoiled spot on the Languedoc coast. The menu, though, is resolutely modern: try the scallops with firm little ratte potatoes in a tasty meat jus, sea bass in a jus sparked with quinine, and the pluperfect mango tart Tatin. Superb regional wines and Bordeaux dominate a cellar regrettably short on half-bottles. C 400-550. M 149-350.

 La Tamarissière

(See restaurant above)
Closed Jan-mid Mar. 27 rms 310-600. Bkfst 65. Half-board 410-570. Conf. Pool. Pkg.
The décor is refreshing and stylish, although the rooms are on the small side. The surrounding rose garden and pine forest are pure delight, and the Hérault canal passes in front of the hotel. Excellent breakfasts and service.

BAGNOLS-SUR-CÈZE   30200
Paris 667 - Pont-Saint-Esprit 11 - Avignon 33   Gard

 Les Jardins de Montcaud

Hameau de Combe-Sabran
04 66 89 60 60, fax 04 66 89 45 04
Closed Jan 2-mid Mar. Open until 9:30pm. Priv rm 50. Terrace dining. Air cond. Heated pool. Tennis. Pkg.
This handsome farmhouse with summery décor and an inviting patio stands at the entrance to the lovely, leafy grounds of a château. René Graf, the new man at the stove, is getting off to a slow start, but the ultra-freshness of his ingredients leads to a successful result nonetheless. He has wisely kept the seaweed-smoked oysters—a model of finesse—from the former menu, and his addition of a gazpacho-style vegetable soup served with thyme sherbet is a

pure delight. The desserts are conventional without any real touch of creativity. The appealing wine list focuses on Côtes-du-Rhônes at very interesting prices. Charming patio and garden. C 290-350. M 175 (lunch exc Sun), 240-410, 95 (children).

 Château de Montcaud   ♠♣

(See restaurant above)
Closed Jan 2-mid Mar. 7 stes 1,500-2,900. 25 rms 790-1,550. Bkfst 100. Rms for disabled. Half-board 795-1,750. Rm ser. Air cond. Conf. Heated pool. Tennis. Pkg.
In a stunning site between Avignon and the Cévennes Mountains, this fully restored nineteenth-century château and adjoining farmhouse offer cozy, tastefully decorated rooms. One of the best breakfast buffets in all Provence, and you can take it on the lovely terrace. Such welcome amenities as a sauna, steam bath, and parcourse. Charming reception. Bistro fare under the chestnut trees with a jazz brunch on Sundays. Relais et Châteaux.

CARCASSONNE   11000
Paris 905 - Perpignan 107 - Toulouse 92 - Albi 107   Aude

La Barbacane

Pl. de l'Église (La Cité)
04 68 25 03 34, fax 04 68 71 50 15
Closed Sun dinner & Mon off-seas, beg Jan-mid Feb. Open until 10:30pm. Air cond. Terrace dining. Valet pkg.
You will wax poetic after feasting in La Barbacane's huge dining room, a neo-Gothic affair bedecked with fleurs-de-lys and coats of arms. New chef Christophe Turquier is so newly arrived that we didn't have time to sample his ware, but the menu he sent us sounds promising. Many dishes throw a bit of fantasy into traditional preparations, such as the soupe maraîchère cooked "like a garbure" (a garbure is a thick meat or vegetable soup) and served with pork-rind sausage, confit duck and pan-fried foie gras. Others, like the loin of milk-fed mutton roasted in a brown sugar/sweet red pepper glaze and served with a braised shoulder enhanced with Espelette hot peppers, present interesting constrasts of flavor. Pastry chef Régis Chanel also demonstrates a penchant for contrast with his chocolate and hazelnut *délice*, Earl Grey tea mousse and whisky ice cream dessert. The cellar holds a fascinating cache of Corbières wines (they are ideal foils for the food). C 450. M 180 (lunch), 280, 420.

*Looking for a restaurant? Refer to the **index.***

Hôtel de la Cité

(See restaurant above)
Closed beg Jan-mid Feb. 3 stes 1,600-1,950. 23 rms 750-1,580. Bkfst 100-120. Rm ser. Air cond. Pool. Valet pkg.
Extensive restoration accounts for the elegant comfort of the rooms and suites in this gorgeous, thoughtfully equipped little luxury hotel. The grand lounge and library are utterly oustanding. Uncommonly attentive service.
Check for exact date of closing for remodeling.

 Domaine d'Auriac

4 km SW, route de St-Hilaire, in Auriac
04 68 25 72 22, fax 04 68 47 35 54
Closed Oct: Sun dinner, Mon lunch; Nov-Easter: Sun dinner, Mon; Feb 17-Mar 3, Nov 17-Dec 8. Open until 9:15pm. Priv rm 120. Garden dining. Air cond. Conf. Pool. Tennis. Garage pkg.
This moss-covered manor set in twenty acres of lawns and trees is the distinguished setting for generous, classic cooking with a pleasing regional slant. The local Lauragais pigeon is definitely worth your notice, and the upside-down apple tart, which boasts ethereal pastry, comes with a scoop of sinfully rich vanilla ice cream. This charming picture is rounded out by local cheeses, house-made breads, and an eclectic but generally pricey cellar (there are some excellent wines, such as the La Voulte Gasparets '93 Corbières, for only 90 F, but where oh where are the half-bottles?). Expect perfect hospitality, in the best French tradition. C 360. M 260 (wine incl), 180-360, 120 (children).

 Domaine d'Auriac

(See restaurant above)
Closed Oct: Sun; Nov-Easter: Sun, Mon; Feb 17-Mar 3, Nov 17-Dec 8. 27 rms 400-1,500. Half-board 720-1,170. Rm ser. Air cond. Conf. Pool. Tennis. Garage pkg.
This former manor house, covered with vines and stuck smack in the middle of a park full of 300-year old trees, boasts rooms very tastefully decorated with Jouy fabrics and antique furniture. The grey-marble bathrooms offer every modern convenience, and the toilets are separate. Hearty but refined breakfast including eggs and cereal, and served with a newspaper and fresh flowers every morning. Charming reception. Relais et Châteaux.

CASTILLON-DU-GARD   30210
Paris 690 - Nîmes 25 - Avignon 27 - Pont-du-Gard 4   Gard

 Le Vieux Castillon ✪

Rue Turion-Sabatier
04 66 37 61 61, fax 04 66 37 28 17
Closed beg Jan-beg Mar. Open until 9pm. Terrace dining. Air cond. Pool.
After the costly restoration of these Huguenot village dwellings, diners now enjoy a marvelous setting in which to sample chef Gilles Bauteuil's Southern-inspired cuisine, elegant yet chock-full of personality. The brightest jewel of his menu is

surely the Alpilles mountain milk-fed lamb, either "frosted" with garlic cream and wedded with thyme-bespeckled baby vegetables, or stuffed with its own sweetbreads and wedded with a delicate little artichoke barigoule. In a still Southern tone, try the bass roasted in olive oil, the escargot pancakes, or the red mullet and tapenade open-faced "sandwich". All this together demands a second toque. Very respectable selection of Rhône Valley wines. New highly dynamic management. C 450. M 250-510, 100 (children).

 Le Vieux Castillon ✪

(See restaurant above)
Closed beg Jan-beg Mar. 2 stes 1,590. 33 rms 750-1,390. Bkfst 90. Half-board 1,270-2,110. Air cond. Conf. Pool. Pkg.
Comfortable, charmingly furnished rooms, with a view of either the Rhône Valley, flower-packed patios, or terraces giving on to the garden, in a labyrinthine building with walls three-feet thick. The new manager has devised a complex system of lighting that shows off this stunning medieval architecture to a maximum. Most rooms have spanking new bathrooms that are really gorgeous. Fitness center with sauna and Turkish bath. Musical evenings from April to October. Relais et Châteaux.

CÉRET   66400
Paris 945 - Perpignan 30 - Port-Vendres 36   Pyrénées-O.

Les Feuillants ✪

1, bd La Fayette
04 68 87 37 88, fax 04 68 87 44 68
Closed Sun dinner, Mon. Open until 10pm. Priv rm 30. Terrace dining. Air cond.
Didier Banyols, always vivid, expressive, and sincere, has of late acquired a certain subtle grace in his cooking—call it inspiration. It transforms a simple dish like baby squid sautéed in chili-infused oil; it imbues the diaphanous pork and snail ravioli that float in a sapid chicken bouillon; it harmonizes the duo of sweetbreads and foie gras in a Banyuls-laced jus. As always, desserts are pure delight: the pear croustillant mellowed with honey and herbed with thyme is unforgettable. With each course of the "regional" set meal comes a Roussillon wine chosen by Marie-Louise Banyols. The scene of these sun-kissed Catalan feasts is a ravishing Belle Époque villa nestled amid Céret's tall plane trees. If you can't tear yourself away, try to book one of the three delightful rooms upstairs, furnished with rare burled-elm pieces. C 350-450. M 250-420.

 La Terrasse au Soleil

1.5 km on route de Fontfrède
04 68 87 01 94, fax 04 68 87 39 24
Closed Nov-Feb. 2 stes 1,100-1,200. 14 rms 595-795. Bkfst 80. Restaurant. Half-board 497-677 (oblig in seas). Air cond. Conf. Heated pool. Garage pkg.
Three modern villas with large sunny rooms decorated in pretty Southern style. Nice view

over the Canigou, and all rooms have a terrace or small garden and are air conditioned.

COLLIOURE	66190
Paris 955 - Perpignan 27 - Céret 32	Pyrénées-O.

12/20 La Balette

Route de Port-Vendres
04 68 82 05 07, fax 04 68 82 38 08
Closed Nov 14-Dec 20. Open until 9:30pm (10:30pm in summer). Garden dining. Air cond. HOTEL: 5 stes 1,095-1,695. 19 rms 465. Bkfst 78. Half-board 601-1,088 (oblig in seas). Rm ser. Air cond. Conf. Pool. Garage pkg.
The pink stucco dining room looks out onto a little creek and the port, a charming view indeed. Chef Christian Peyre's regionally-inspired cuisine has lost some of the spark it had in the past. Our quail-breast puff pastry was on the dry side and the desserts are just ordinary. Appealing wine list, starring the best local vintages. Slow service. C 200-400. M 175-365.

 ## Casa Païral

Impasse des Palmiers
04 68 82 05 81, fax 04 68 82 52 10
Closed Nov 2-Apr 1. 2 stes 750-890. 26 rms 340-710. Bkfst 55. Rms for disabled. Pool. Pkg.
A delightful Catalan residence in the town center with large, quiet, attractively furnished rooms. Lush garden surroundings. Charming welcome and efficient service.

LIGNAN-SUR-ORB	34490
Paris 853 - Montpelliers 79 - Béziers 9	Hérault

 ## Château de Lignan

"L'Orangeraie" - 04 67 37 91 47, fax 04 67 37 99 25
Closed may be Sun dinner & Mon lunch off-seas, check. Open until 10pm (10:30pm in summer). Priv rm 80. Air cond. Pool. Garage pkg.
Chef Pascal Alonso, formerly right hand man of Michel Guérard, officiates in the kitchen of this elegant château. He's young, but he knows how to choose quality ingredients and he prepares them expertly with an innovative touch. We were bowled over by a red-mullet and asparagus terrine perfumed with anise, delicious Catalan-style braised squid, beef tender-

loin in a vigorous sauce laced with Saint-Chinian wine, and a subtly spicy fruit soup. The cellar, naturally enough, highlights bottles from Languedoc-Roussillon. A competent young staff handles the service. C 300-420. M 170 (wine incl, weekday lunch), 150-340, 85 (children).

 ## Château de Lignan

(See restaurant above)
Open year-round. 2 stes 540-650. 47 rms 340-600. Bkfst 65-100. Rms for disabled. Half-board 450-550 (oblig). Rm ser. Air cond. Pool. Garage pkg.
The Orb River runs through the extensive grounds of this eighteenth-century château. The fully renovated accommodations are as comfortable as they are tastefully appointed.

MADIÈRES	34190
Paris 775 - Montpelliers 25 - Ganges 20	Hérault

 ## Château de Madières

By Ganges - 04 67 73 84 03, fax 04 67 73 55 71
Closed Nov-Mar. Open until 9:30pm. Terrace dining. Heated pool. Pkg.
One of the two dining rooms has a vaulted ceiling and a splendid view of the Vis River gorges and the tiny village. Françoise Bucy and Guy Bonafous cook up traditional fare that highlights the region's best foodstuffs: tender and tasty duck foie gras, delicious lamb chops grilled with herbs, and a baba liberally spiked with rum. Cellar not rich in different regions, but there is a good selection of Faugères and Saint-Chinians. Warm welcome, fine service. C 350. M 195-380.

 ## Château de Madières

(See restaurant above)
Closed Nov-Mar. 4 stes 925-1,330. 8 rms 585-1,150. Bkfst 80. Half-board 600-895 (oblig in seas). Heated pool. Pkg.
An island of charm, protected by the thick walls of a high-perched medieval fortress. Personalized guest rooms are arranged around a central patio-courtyard; adding to the enchantment are a garden and a lovely terrace. Lovely reception, peaceful drawing rooms and a superb Renaissance fireplace in the library.

MOLITG-LES-BAINS   66500
Paris 978 - Prades 7 - Perpignan 50   Pyrénées-O.

Château de Riell

On D 116 - 04 68 05 04 40, fax 04 68 05 04 37
*Closed Nov 3-Mar 29. Open until 10pm. Terrace
dining. Air cond. Heated pool. Tennis. No pets.
Valet pkg.*
Lionel Migliori, trained by Michel Guérard,
puts a high-tone spin on regional ingredients
(after all, this *is* a château) and comes up with a
puff-pastry tart filled with tiny squid and wild
mushrooms, langoustine lasagne, and honey-
glazed pigeon ballottine with cumin-spiced carrot beignets. Simple it isn't, but this highfalutin
fare has a charm all its own. In a more rustic
setting out by the pool, an attractive 195 F set
meal is served. Splendid cellar, with a goodly
number of local wines. **C** 380-420. **M** 195 (wine
incl), 250 (weekdays, Sat lunch), 330-430, 150
(children).

Château de Riell 🌲🍷

(See restaurant above)
*Closed Nov 2-Mar 29. 3 stes 1,700. 19 rms 1,000-
1,300. Bkfst 90. Half-board 885-1,720. Conf.
Heated pool. Tennis. Valet pkg.*
In a marvelous wooded setting that towers
above the thermal spa, this fantastic nineteenth-
century version of a medieval castle contains
charming, romantic rooms that contrast markedly with the heavy-handed exterior. Exceptional
amenities including spa facilities and two swimming pools. Relais et Châteaux.

MONTPELLIER   34000
Paris 760 - Marseille 164 - Nîmes 51   Hérault

Alliance Métropole

3, rue du Clos-René
04 67 58 11 22, fax 04 67 92 13 02
*Open year-round. 7 stes 700-950. 74 rms 450-600.
Bkfst 75. Restaurant. Half-board 440. Rm scr.
Conf. Pkg.*
Thoroughly modernized, this hotel near the
pedestrian precinct has retained a certain old
world charm. Perfectly appointed rooms with
ultramodern comfort and ravishing marble
bathrooms; quiet, pleasant inner garden. Amusing elevator converted into a telephone booth.
Highly attentive service, and always with a
smile.

Demeure des Brousses 🌲🍷

Route de Vauguières
04 67 65 77 66, fax 04 67 22 22 17
*Open year-round. 17 rms 380-580. Bkfst 50. Res-
taurant. Half-board 590-790. Rm scr. Conf. Pool.
Pkg.*
You wouldn't expect to stumble upon this
lovely eighteenth-century farmhouse, set in an
oasis of exotic trees and vines, right on the edge
of town. It's just been all spiffed up: a pool was

added, the *orangerie* was converted into a dining
room, and all the bathrooms have been refurbished without damaging the style of the comfortable Louis XVIII, Directoire and Second
Empire bedrooms. Sumptuous breakfasts with
fruit straight from the orchard and taken under
the 200-year old cedar tree.

12/20 Isadora

6, rue du Petit-Scel
04 67 66 25 23, fax 04 67 66 25 23
*Closed Sat lunch, Sun, Mon lunch in seas. Open until
10pm. Priv rm 40. Terrace dining. Air cond.*
For a romantic dinner in Montpellier, you
could hardly do better than Isadora, a cozy,
vaulted dining room in a pretty part of town.
Gilbert Saugo's fresh and appealing menu
presents a delectable salad of quail, snow peas,
and foie gras, and tender squab served with
buttery braised cabbage. On the wine list, look
for Terre Ardente, a lusty Fitou priced under
100 F. Obliging service. **C** 220-350. **M** 80 (weekday lunch), 120-250.

Le Jardin des Sens ✪

11, av. Saint-Lazare
04 67 79 63 38, fax 04 67 72 13 05
*Closed Sun. Open until 10pm. Priv rm 45. Garden
dining. Air cond. Valet pkg.*
At first, the food lovers of Montpellier didn't
know how to react to Jacques and Laurent Pour-
cel's cuisine, with its surprising combinations of
tastes, contrasting textures, and "evolved"
sauces. They found the austere, stripped-down
décor a bit off-putting, too. But today, the Pour-
cel twins number among the foremost chefs of
the Midi. More homegrown ingredients have
given the menu a stronger local accent of late, but
the Pourcels' inspiration remains eclectic. From
the enticing tidbits set out to welcome you
(oysters in aspic, lemony clams in olive oil and
parsley, crushed sardines with eggplant
mousse), through a procession of dishes as vivid
as they are delicious (tiny baudroies from local
waters, breaded and roasted and set atop a
tomato-onion tartlet napped with fragrant
thyme jus; rack of Pyrenees lamb roasted with its
sweetbreads and served with a galette of
chanterelles and a curried carrot fricassée), to
fabulous desserts redolent of heady spices, each
offering is a feast that enchants all the senses. The
cellar—a jewel—is overseen by Olivier Château.
C 480. **M** 200 (weekday lunch), 330-520.

NARBONNE   11100
Paris 850 - Perpignan 62 - Carcassone 56   Aude

La Table Saint-Crescent ✪

Domaine Saint-Crescent-le-Vieil
04 68 41 37 37, fax 04 68 41 01 22
*Closed Sun dinner. Open until 10pm. Terrace
dining. Garage pkg.*
Claude Giraud is the bard, the defender of
Languedoc cooking, and even though he hops

around a lot, he's worth following! This time he's scrounged up an eighth-century chapel, which was later a leper colony, and then a wine warehouse, which he's now converted into a dining room full of light and charm with its vaulted ceilings and its thick stone walls (talk about a history...). And the change of *lieu* seems to have inspired him even more than in the past: he draws on the best of the Corbières region and of the nearby Mediterranean to transcend the regional repertory. Two smashing successes: the pig trotter andouillette sausage with home-grown puréed chickpeas and the confit lamb "sausage" with spring vegetables. But if we really get down to the brass tacks, the most surprising thing is the price. Radiant smile from Sabine Giraud. C 200. M 100 (weekdays, wine incl), 148-248.

NÎMES
Paris 712 - Lyon 249 - Montpellier 52   30000   Gard

12/20 L'Enclos de la Fontaine
Quai de la Fontaine
04 66 21 90 30, fax 04 66 67 70 25
Open daily until 10pm. Priv rm 110. Garden dining. Air cond. Heated pool. Valet pkg.
This patrician town house filled with fine antiques is an elegant setting for Jean-Michel Nigon's carefully wrought Southern specialties. Sample his foie gras terrine served with chestnut bread, whole grilled sea bass served with a fennel gratin, and strawberry soup spiced with star anise. Well thoughtout wine list with relatively reasonable prices; stylish service. The place to see and be seen in Nîmes. C 335-440. M 165-330, 80 (children).

 ### Impérator Concorde
(See restaurant above)
Open year-round. 3 stes 1,100-1,300. 59 rms 530-1,000. Bkfst 65. Half-board 710-1,180. Rm ser. Air cond. Conf. Heated pool. Valet pkg.
Undoubtedly the best hotel in town, and a full-dress renovation has recently freshened it up. This handsome old hotel, set between the Maison Carrée and the Jardins de la Fontaine, boasts huge pleasant rooms with attractive furniture and all dressed up in Provence-style fabrics. Well-equipped bathrooms.

 ### New Hotel La Baume
21, rue Nationale
04 66 76 28 42, fax 04 66 76 28 45
Open year-round. 33 rms 300-350. Bkfst 40. Rms for disabled. Restaurant. Rm ser. Air cond. Conf.
A charming hotel set in the heart of old Nîmes in a seventeenth-century dwelling (notice the monumental staircase, listed on the national historical register). All the rooms, large or small, boast modern comforts and are brightened up with painted beams. Very friendly welcome and a general feeling of well-being. There's a bar, and a parking garage 300 yards away.

PERPIGNAN
Paris 908 - Toulouse 208 - Foix 137   66000   Pyrénées-O.

 ### La Passerelle
1, cours Palmarole - 04 68 51 30 65
Closed Sun, Mon, Dec 20-Jan 4. Open until 9:45pm. Priv rm 25. Air cond.
The fish here is the freshest in town—too bad it's usually overcooked! You can get around the problem by ordering the ultrafresh fish tartare or rich skate rillettes, then finish up with a good chocolate fondant. Cellar rich in local wines. The welcome is warm and friendly, whether you choose the mahogany-paneled dining room or its bigger, brighter neighbor. C 180.

12/20 Villa Duflot
109, av. Victor-d'Albiez
04 68 56 67 67, fax 04 68 56 54 05
Open daily until 11pm. Terrace dining. Air cond. Pool. Garage pkg.
Stop here for a quiet, poolside lunch close to the *autoroute* (you won't have to mess with downtown traffic). The well-crafted cooking, with offerings as diverse as hot liver lasagna and cod with garlic cream, is accompanied by well-chosen local wines, all at reasonable prices. Professional, gracious service. Always running over at lunchtime. C 200-350. M 200 (Sat, Sun, wine incl), 80 (children).

 ### Villa Duflot
(See restaurant above)
Open year-round. 1 ste 950. 24 rms 540-740. Bkfst 55-95. Rms for disabled. Half-board 505-605. Rm ser. Air cond. Conf. Pool. Garage pkg.
The rooms are huge and well designed, with top-flight equipment, pretty furniture and beautiful bathrooms. Broad, green grounds keep the Villa hidden from the nearby superhighway and shopping centers. A really special breakfast including fresh fruit, locally-made jams and homemade pastries to start the day off right .

PONT-DU-GARD
Paris 690 - Avignon 25 - Nîmes 23 - Alès 47   30210   Gard

La Bégude Saint-Pierre
D 981, Les Coudoulières
04 66 63 63 63, fax 04 66 22 73 73
Closed Sun dinner, Mon, Nov-Feb. Open until 9:30pm (10:30pm in summer). Garden dining. Air cond. Pool. Garage pkg.
Bruno Griffoul fell under the spell of this seventeenth-century coaching inn the moment he saw it. So he transferred all his pots, pans, and other kitchen impedimenta from the Auberge Saint-Maximin to this spot, right next to the famous Roman bridge. His classic repertoire, inspired by the fruits of local farms and fields, produces the likes of artichoke barigoule with red mullet, Florence fennel compote with sea perch, sage and marjoram with a saddle of

young rabbit, and milk-fed leg of lamb stuffed with fresh thyme. A cuisine that is a pretty sight to the eye, is full of aromas, and is pregnant with taste. Good selection of set-price meals. Complemented by a judicious list of wines principally from the Rhône Valley and Provence. Charming welcome and service. C 250-300. M 150-360.

 La Bégude Saint-Pierre

(See restaurant above)
Closed Sun & Mon off-seas. 3 stes 1,000-1,300. 30 rms 415-800. Bkfst 60. Rms for disabled. Half-board 210-360. Rm ser. Air cond. Conf. Pool. Garage pkg.
A fine old seventeenth-century residence-cum-inn surrounded by quiet gardens and conveniently located just 800 yards from the Pont du Gard. The comfortable rooms are attractively done up; the quietest are at the back of the hotel. New helicopter landing pad and glider runway.

SAINT-CYPRIEN	66750
Paris 948 - Perpignan 20 - Collioure 18	Pyrénées-O.

 L'Almandin

Les Capellans, bd de l'Almandin
04 68 21 01 02, fax 04 68 21 06 28
Closed Sun dinner & Mon (off-seas), hols, Jan-Feb. Open until 9:30pm. Garden dining. Air cond. Garage pkg.
Jean-Paul Hartmann, transplanted from his native Alsace to *le pays catalan*, tacks back and forth between classic and regional cuisine. We like his snail-stuffed cannelloni with a gentle garlic sauce, fricassée of scampi, squid, and mild chilis, and bouillabaisse enriched with saffron-stained potatoes. For dessert, try the pineapple fritters with warm raspberries. L'Almandin's bay windows frame a lovely view over the lagoon, even prettier when seen from the terrace. High-class service. Very interesting selection of wines, both in terms of regional Collioures and Roussillons, but also in terms of the reasonably priced grands crus Bordeaux. C 310. M 160-380, 80 (children).

 L'Ile de la Lagune

(See restaurant above)
Closed restaurant above for closings. 4 stes 800-1,250. 18 rms 500-900. Bkfst 65. Rms for disabled. Half-board 520-850. Rm ser. Air cond. Conf. Pool. Tennis. Garage pkg.
The architecture of this beautifully designed hotel is Hispano-Mauresque, with large terraces overlooking the lagoon. Guest rooms are fresh and pretty, with small but attractive bathrooms. Private beach. Shuttle boat to the port.

SIGEAN	11130
Paris 888 - Carcassonne 74 - Narbonne 28	Aude

 Château de Villeflase

Le Lac - 04 68 48 54 29, fax 04 68 48 34 37

Open year-round. 15 stes 500-1,800. 10 rms 350-500. Bkfst 60. Rms for disabled. Restaurant. Half-board 375-1,200. Rm ser. Conf. Heated pool. Tennis. Pkg.
This manor house surrounded by vineyards offers luxurious rooms and suites with fine furniture, embroidered linens, and other opulent touches. From the upper floor, guests can admire lovely views of the countryside. The fitness center and huge swimming pool will help you work off the sumptuous breakfasts.

VIALAS	48220
Paris 650 - Mende 77 - Florac 40 - Génolhac 9	Lozère

 Chantoiseau ۞

Route-du-Haut - 04 66 41 00 02, fax 04 66 41 04 34
Closed end Oct-beg Apr. Open until 8:30pm. Priv rm 25. Pool. Pkg.
This ancient wood-and-stone post house clinging to Mont Lozère offers no opulent trappings, just the wild beauty of the Cévennes Mountains, where wolves still howled not so long ago. Patrick Pagès, poet and chef, draws incomparable notes and nuances from the bounty of this rugged land. His repertoire reflects a commitment to the region's unique flavors. Consider the possibilities: green asparagus brandade with wild trout tartare; kid in a delicate Muscat aspic flanked by local lentils; crayfish fricassée made with real mountain cream and abetted by a truffled risotto. You can order the frugal 130 F menu, or splurge on a ten-course meal that brings ten different wines (at 760 F, it's one of the most popular). As a finale to this gastronomic adventure, take a tour of the cellar, where 12,000 different wines await your pleasure. C 350-450. M 130-760, 60 (children).

 Chantoiseau

(See restaurant above)
Closed end Oct-beg Apr. 15 rms 400-500. Bkfst 50. Half-board 420-450. Conf. Pool. No pets. Pkg.
Unpretentious but appealing, for people whose idea of luxury is a pristine setting with splendid mountain views. There are some amenities, though, like a nice little pool, wonderful breakfasts, and attentive service.

ALBI	81000
Paris 709 - Toulouse 75 - Rodez 79	Tarn

 La Réserve

Route de Cordes - 05 63 60 80 80, fax 05 63 47 63 60
Closed Nov-Apr. Open until 10pm. Terrace dining. Air cond. Heated pool. Tennis. Garage pkg.

Abandon your reserve and tuck recklessly into Sylvain Martin's turbot with mushroom ravioli and heady chocolate *symphonie*—they're delicious! A close look at the wine list will reveal some accessibly priced Bordeaux. Forthright welcome; smooth service. C 280-380. M 95-125 (lunch), 160-300, 60 (children).

 ### La Réserve

(See restaurant above)
Closed Nov-Apr. 4 stes 1,100-1,300. 20 rms 490-980. Bkfst 70. Half-board 650-950. Rm ser. Air cond. Conf. Heated pool. Tennis. Garage pkg.
A hacienda, of sorts, on the banks of the Tarn, set down in tranquil grounds. The rooms, with river views, are all different, but equally pretty; those above the pool aren't always absolutely quiet. Good breakfasts; superior service. Relais et Châteaux.

BELCASTEL	12390
Paris 625 - Rodez 27 - Rignac 11	Aveyron

 ### Le Vieux Pont

05 65 64 52 29, fax 05 65 64 44 32
Closed Sun dinner, Mon (exc lunch in summer), Jan-Mar 15. Open until 9pm. Air cond. Pkg.
The spot looks too scenic to be true: a hidden valley, a village clinging to a cliff, a rushing river with an ancient hotel and restaurant on either bank. The village is in fact listed as one of the most beautiful in France. This enchanted countryside is the domain of the Fagegaltier sisters, Nicole and Michèle. You, too, will fall under Nicole's (she learned under none other than Michel Bras) spell when you taste her menu of traditional local dishes, which here attain a rare lightness, without losing their deep, resonant flavors: pascade (a crêpe) stuffed with escargots, plump pasta dumplings filled with lamb's tripe, pompe à l'huile (an age-old holiday cake made with olive oil and orangeflower water), and fresh farm cheese. Excellent fixed-price meal at 135 F. All these good things are served in a jovial atmosphere, with wines from an enticing regional cellar. You might want to try the local Marcillac at 70 F or one of the more expensive Daumas-Gassacs. C 300. M 135-330.

 ### Le Vieux Pont

(See restaurant above)
Closed Sun, Mon, Jan-Mar 15; 7 rms 360-450. Bkfst 45. Rms for disabled. Half-board 400-450. Pkg.
After dinner, just trot over the arched medieval bridge to the charming little hotel. It may be in a centuries-old barn (in the past), but the inside is as modern and clean as you could hope for. The rooms give on to the river with its ducks and view of the breathtaking medieval village and fortress on the hillside opposite.

FOUILLADE (LA)	12270
Paris 635 - Rodez 75 - Villefranche-de-Rouergue 20	Aveyron

Longcol

05 65 29 63 36, fax 05 65 29 64 28
Closed Tue lunch off-seas, Nov 15-Easter. Open until 9:30pm. Terrace dining. Heated pool. Tennis. Pkg.
Oriental fabrics lend an exotic touch to Longcol's dining room, which leads out to a terrace with a riveting view of the Aveyron River. Confusion was in the air last time we were there. A new chef, Bernard Borderies (who had two toques when he was near Toulouse and in Fontainebleau), had just come on the scene; he was gone before summer even came 'round. No judgment for the time being. C 300. M 145 (lunch), 195, 95 (children).

 ## Hôtel Longcol

(See restaurant above)
Closed Nov 15-Easter. 1 ste 900-995. 17 rms 550-850. Bkfst 70. Rms for disabled. Half-board 540-685. Rm ser. Conf. Heated pool. Tennis. Pkg.
Restored from the remains of a twelfth- and thirteenth-century farm, this delightful hotel on the Aveyron River is set in 60 acres of wooded grounds surrounded by hills (fishing on the premises). The rooms are decorated in impeccable taste, with superb furniture and carpets. Spectacular swimming pool that seemingly reaches out to the cliffside. The owner doubles as an antique dealer, so you can view his collections of Oriental art. Relais et Châteaux.

SAINT-FÉLIX-LAURAGAIS	31540
Paris 755 - Carcassone 54 - Toulouse 45	H.-Garonne

 ## Auberge du Poids Public

05 61 83 00 20, fax 05 61 83 86 21
Closed Sun dinner off-seas, Jan. Open until 9:30pm. Terrace dining. HOTEL: 13 rms 260-310. Bkfst 45. Half-board 285-310. Rm ser. Conf. Pkg.
Claude Taffarello is a chef in tune with his roots. He has an innate feel for the finest local foodstuffs, which he handles with intelligence and respect. The cassoulet "Saint-Félicien," a traditional family recipe, is alone worth the trip to this sleepy country town, and his versions of foie gras and Pyrenees lamb are second to none. Vegetarians (or travelers stuffed with too much foie gras) will love his splendid all-vegetable menu. Whatever you choose, don't miss the millas, a white-corn porridge that is cooled, sliced, and fried, to be savored with warm foie gras or as a dessert with orange butter. Neighboring growers are well represented in the attractive cellar. C 290-480. M 135-310, 90 (children).

SAUVETERRE-DE-COMMINGES   31510
Paris 805 - Toulouse 105   H.-Garonne

12/20 Hostellerie des Sept Molles

3 km S on D 9, in Gesset
05 61 88 30 87, fax 05 61 88 36 42
Closed Tue off-seas, Nov-mid Dec, Jan-end Mar. Open until 9:30pm. Terrace dining. Pool. Tennis. Pkg.
Up here at nearly 1,500 feet above sea level, the Pyrenees are not far distant. This cozy inn provides a dining room warmed by a fire in winter, and a pretty flowered terrace for sunny days. Simplicity reigns here, sometimes to the point of laxity. It's a shame, really, because there's real heart put into the salmon and oyster tartare and the grilled duck breast with rock salt, but they both need a touch more care if the chef wants to win back his toque. Brief and overpriced wine list. C 300. M 190-295.

 Hostellerie des Sept Molles

(See restaurant above)
See restaurant above for closings. 3 stes from 920. 16 rms 420-780. Bkfst 75. Half-board 500-705. Air cond. Conf. Pool. Tennis. Pkg.
The seven ancient millstones for which the inn is named dot the garden. A huge white house nestled in between the hills and surrounded by trees and flowers. The romantic rooms are large and bright, the furniture is lovely, and the breakfasts are generous. Charming welcome. Relais et Châteaux.

TOULOUSE   31000
Paris 681 - Marseille 400 - Bordeaux 249   H.-Garonne

 Hôtel des Beaux-Arts

1, pl. du Pont-Neuf
05 61 23 40 50, fax 05 61 22 02 27
Open year-round. 1 ste 900. 18 rms 450-800. Bkfst 65-75. Half-board 690-1,040. Air cond. Conf. Valet pkg.
A friendly hotel in an eighteenth-century building in the historic center of Toulouse (close to the Musée des Augustins), with well-equipped, soundproofed rooms that have just been fully renovated. Lovely spaces and beautiful waxed wood floors. Fine views of the Garonne, and some rooms even have roof terraces. Room service from Brasserie Flo (Brasserie des Beaux Arts) next door.

12/20 Brasserie des Beaux-Arts

"Flo", 1, quai de la Daurade
05 61 21 12 12, fax 05 61 21 14 80
Open daily until 1am. Terrace dining. Air cond.
Come here for the Art Nouveau décor, bustling waiters, sparkling shellfish platters, and deftly turned brasserie fare. Crowds of customers create a rather jolly brouhaha, which the good and inexpensive wines do their part to maintain! C 190. M 103-149 (wine incl).

12/20 Le Capoul

13, pl. du Président-Wilson
05 61 21 08 27, fax 05 61 21 96 70
Closed Dec 24-Jan 1. Open until 11:30pm. Terrace dining. Air cond.
This elegantly mirrored and paneled brasserie stays open late, seven days a week. The traditional menu proposes pot-au-feu salad, steak with blue cheese and sautéed potatoes, and other traditional bistro favorites, delivered by an energetic staff. Good selection of wines. C 240. M 150 (Sun).

 L'Edelweiss

19, rue de Castellane
05 61 62 34 70, fax 05 61 62 34 70
Closed Sun, Mon, Aug. Open until 10:30pm. Priv rm 50. Air cond.
Jacky Auriau has taken over the former Darroze restaurant, a posh and comfortable space where patrons can savor his son Laurent Auriau's toque-worthy cuisine. Simplicity and fine ingredients are the key to such successful entries as a salad of scallops and red mullet with asparagus tips or seafood lasagne sparked with a puckery touch of verjuice, as well as really good cassoulet made with Tarbes beans. Small principally Southwest wine selection. C 200-300. M 88, 97, 128, 138, 158, 100 (children).

 Holiday Inn Crowne Plaza

7, pl. du Capitole
05 61 61 19 19, fax 05 61 23 79 96
Open year-round. 2 stes 1,700-2,000. 160 rms 800-1,000. Rms for disabled. Restaurant. Half-board 130-350. Rm ser. Conf. Valet pkg.
This beautiful building on Place du Capitole offers spacious, sophisticated rooms. Some are reserved for non-smokers and some are designed for the disabled. Excellent reception, New Orleans–style bar, many lounges. The health club features a sauna and Jacuzzi. Impeccable welcome.

 Les Jardins de l'Opéra

1, pl. du Capitole
05 61 23 07 76 (R), 05 61 21 82 66 (H),
fax 05 61 23 63 00 (R), fax 05 61 23 41 04 (H)
Closed Sun, hols, 1st week in Jan, Aug 3-26. Open until 10pm. Terrace dining. Air cond. Heated pool.
The calculated theatricality of the dining room's glass ceilings, sensuous lighting, elegant tables, and sumptuous flowers is more "Opéra" than "Jardin." Staged in a Tuscan-style courtyard, the setting is both larger and more convincing than title. One forgets that Place du Capitole, with its traffic and noise, is but a few yards away. Here the only sounds are of quiet conversation and the splash of the fountain under the veranda. Dominique Toulousy revisits the Midi's *terroir*

with polished interpretations of cassoulet (his is made with fresh fava beans), as well as pinkly roasted lamb with croquettes of Lautrec garlic, flavorsome Lauragais squab, and fat figs lusciously roasted in sweet Banyuls wine. The desserts are a real grand finale, and Maryse Toulousy is a true prima donna in her role as hostess! A brilliantly stocked cellar provides fine vintage Bordeaux and lusty Madirans. C 500. M 200 (lunch, wine incl), 295-495.

 ## Grand Hôtel de l'Opéra

(See restaurant above)
Open year-round. 9 stes 1,350-1,500. 40 rms 700-1,300. Rm ser. Air cond. Heated pool. Valet pkg.
Entering here from the turbulent Place du Capitole is like traversing a time warp. Back to another age of grace and beauty: this former convent has been remodeled with a sure hand, in elegant taste. In addition to its Florentine charm and old-Provençal art of living, there is modern comfort (saunas, Jacuzzis, air conditioning). Guest rooms are extremely restful and comfortable, though the décor is sometimes a little sad. Some have balconies overlooking the city's red-tiled roofs. Lovely lounges with an atmosphere of pure elegance. Fitness center. Excellent reception. Indian restaurant in hotel.

 ## Le Pastel ☺

237, route de Saint-Simon
05 61 40 59 01, fax 05 61 44 29 22
Closed Sat lunch, Sun, Aug 2-27. Open until 10:30pm. Priv rm 20. Terrace dining. Pkg.
Le Pastel is not easy to find, but you'll be glad you did when you settle into one of the two yellow-tinted dining rooms to sample Gérard Garrigues's cooking. He has excellent credentials (thirteen years with Alain Dutournier) and for food of this quality, his prices can't be beat. A jovial almost family-style atmosphere for a cuisine clean-to-the-taste and full of the flavors of its region (Garrigues even makes his own pork products). We're partial to the chilled-turnip upside down tart with foie gras, pig's head with oysters, truffle-speckled stuffed cabbage en crépinette with ratte potatoes in jus, and milk-fed lamb *envie* (desire). Old-fashioned desserts such as pumpkin pie, all to be washed down with one of the regional wines on the superb wine list. There's a fine 175 F set lunch, too, generously served as is the custom in Toulouse, a city of trenchermen. In this land-of-plenty establishment, their greatest pleasure is yours. C 320. M 140-175 (weekday lunch), 380 (weekday dinner, wine incl), 320 (weekdays).

 ## Au Pois Gourmand

3, rue Émile-Heybrard · 05 61 31 95 95
Closed Sat lunch, Sun, 3 wks in Aug. Open until 10pm. Terrace dining. Air cond. Pkg.
Guests are charmingly ushered into the bright dining room (or, in summer, to the outdoor gallery) where they can admire a view of the Garonne river while sampling self-taught Claude Plazzotta's ever-better cooking in the

highly attractive décor of this big old red-brick, colonial-style house. His creativity flows when he feels inspired, when a product inspires him: the so-evident *joie de vivre* of his pan-fried wild asparagus with hot foie gras and fresh morels, his bass steak with vanilla and lime, and his ultralight puff pastry with orange cream bring him to two-toque level. Extra-good selection of wines from the region. Set amidst a park full of flowers. C 300. M 120 (weekday lunch), 180-380.

 ## Michel Sarran ☺

21, bd Armand-Duportal
05 61 12 32 32, fax 05 61 12 32 32
Closed Sat lunch, Sun, last week of Jul. Open until 9:30pm. Priv rm 30. Terrace dining. Air cond. Valet pkg.
Michel Sarran's last post was at the Mas du Langoustier on the island of Porquerolles, where he won himself three toques. He bids fair to do just as well here, in this lovely nineteenth-century house, decorated with pretty Provençal fabrics and vibrantly colorful artwork. Sarran has retained his light, refined style along with a penchant for Mediterranean flavors, but he's adopted Southwestern ingredients and recipes as well, for an eclectic, exciting repertoire. You'll discover the Mediterranean in dishes like the red mullet pancake with chorizo sausage and tapenade or the excellent John Dory and artichoke fricassée. The Southwest will come to mind in his personalized interpretations of dishes such as Basque country ham crisp and ham hock with onions and piperade, or lamb fillet served with potato blinis with brains, baby carrots and Tarbes beans in jus. Another point this year. An expert maître d' helps guests navigate the well-designed wine list and directs the attentive staff. C 350. M 200 (wine incl), 320.

 ## Sofitel-Centre

84, allée Jean-Jaurès
05 61 10 23 10, fax 05 61 10 23 20
Open year-round. 14 stes 1,200-1,550. 105 rms 840-900. Bkfst 80. Rms for disabled. Restaurant. Rm ser. Air cond. Conf. Valet pkg.
This town-center hotel not far from the train station and convention center offers all the comforts and services for which the chain is known. Piano bar Monday through Friday. Excellent service.

 ## Ubu Club

16, rue St-Rome · 05 61 23 97 80, fax 05 61 23 14 56
Closed Sun. Open until 2am. Air cond. No pets. Garage pkg.
Under the vaulted ceilings of this comfortable, English-style club dressed up like a 1930s speakeasy (you have to cross the dance floor to reach the dining room), the city's late-night set feeds on Honoré Guillem's accomplished cooking based on good-quality ingredients: harmonious rock-lobster salad, roast kid napped with a flavorful jus, and flaky, apple-filled pastis gascon. Temperamental service. Some good finds in the cellar. C 250-450. M 150 (dinner).

REGIONAL FOODS

This vast region extends from the foothills of the Massif Central to the Mediterranean and the Spanish border. Naturally, the landscapes vary enormously, with wild, arid mountains, vine-bearing plains, luxuriant orchards, the sandy beaches of Languedoc, and the rocky shores of Roussillon. Local cuisines and ingredients vary too, but all over the Midi the sun's nurturing rays ripen vegetables and fruits to succulent sweetness, and brighten the natives' cheerful humor.

• *CHARCUTERIE*

FOURQUES   66300 – Pyrénées-O.

Roger Paré

Pl. de la Mairie - 04 68 38 80 53
This producer is rightfully proud of the firm's thin, air-dried Catalan sausage known as fouets ("whips"). Try all three varieties: plain, flavored with anise, or spiked with hot chilies.

LANGOGNE   48300 – Lozère

Rabaste

18, bd du Général-de-Gaulle - 04 66 69 05 36
For a taste of down-home country sausage (dried or uncooked), andouillettes, and air-dried hams, give this address a try.

• *CHEESE*

ROQUEFORT-SUR-SOULZON   12250 – Aveyron

Gabriel Coulet

3, av. de Lauras - 05 65 59 96 60
Taste tangy Roquefort cheese on its home turf: Coulet's version is excellent, made in traditional fashion from the milk of ewes that graze on the region's rugged terrain.

• *CHOCOLATE & CANDY*

ALBI   81000 – Tarn

Belin

4, rue du Docteur-Camboulives - 05 63 54 18 46

Good chocolates, in sweet and bittersweet varieties, with classic or unusual fillings.

LIMOUX   11300 – Aude

P. Labadie

37, av. Fabre-d'Églantine - 04 68 31 08 75
The honey and almond flavors come through deliciously in this firm's good, chewy nougat.

MONTAUBAN   82000 – Tarn/Gar.

Blandino

15, pl. de la Cathédrale - 05 63 63 06 08
Blandino's chocolate truffles, filled with tea-, prune-, and Armagnac-flavored ganaches, are known throughout the region for their quality. The rest of the range is definitely worth tasting, too.

PERPIGNAN   66000 – Pyrénées-O.

Begrem

13, av. du Général-de-Gaulle - 04 68 34 89 69
Touron catalan, an almond-based local specialty, is particularly delicious here, but the other regional sweets also deserve your attention.

PRÉVENCHÈRES   48800 – Lozère

La Chocolatière

04 66 46 01 93
Here in a tiny mountain village, Jean-Claude Briet produces fabulous chocolates filled with irresistible ganaches in an amazing range of flavors. Well worth a detour!

• *GOURMET SPECIALTIES*

Anchovies

COLLIOURE   66190 – Pyrénées-O.

In Collioure, the anchovy capital, two of the best sources are:

Desclaux
Carrefour du Christ - 04 68 82 05 25

Roque
40, rue de la Démocratie - 04 68 82 04 99

For the most authentic flavor, plump, salt-cured anchovies have no peer, but oil-cured anchovies are also available if you prefer.

Cassoulet & Confit

CASTELNAUDARY 11400 – Aude

Escourou

30, rue de Dunkerque - 04 68 23 16 88
No, a tinned cassoulet is never as good as the fresh-baked article, but you'd be surprised at just how good it can be. Escourou's version enriched with goose confit is a lusty, warming treat. Look, too, for the fine duck confit and the tasty combo of simmered lentils and duck wings.

ST-FELIX-LAURAGAIS 31540 – H.-Garonne

Baron de Roquette Buisson

Ferme de Bordeneuve - 05 61 83 02 23
Delectable terrines, confits, and other savory take-home treats from a pigeon-farmer who prepares his own home-raised birds.

**VILLEFRANCHE-
DE-LAURAGAIS** 31290 – H.-Garonne

Conserverie du Lauragais

RN 113, Montgaillard - 05 61 81 64 84
Authentically flavorful cassoulet, confit, foie gras, pâtés, and rillettes prepared and preserved by a talented producer.

Honey & Jams

ESCARO 66360 – Pyrénées-O.

Flor de Xicoia

04 68 97 07 00

An amazing collection of jams made with Pyrenees fruits, flowers, and vegetables: where else can you find dandelion jam or thyme jelly or onion marmalade?

SOURNIA 66730 – Pyrénées-O.

Ateliers du Val Sournia

Hameau du Puigt - 04 68 97 73 09
For wholesome jams made from organically grown fruit, this is the place to stop.

Olive Oil

BIZE MINERVOIS 11120 – Aude

Coopérative de l'Oulibo

04 68 46 10 37
Fruity, powerfully aromatic yet delicate olive oil, plus excellent tapenade, and black or green olives.

COLLORGUES 30190 – Gard

Ets. Soulas

Route de la Masade - 04 66 81 21 13
Assertively flavored olive oil, fruity and powerful.

• PASTRY & COOKIES

ARLES-SUR-TECH 66150 – Pyrénées-O.

Jean Touron

6, placette d'Availl - 04 68 39 10 47
Almond-based sweets and cookies: don't miss the Rousquilles, which simply melt in the mouth!

WINE

Languedoc-Roussillon is not only the largest wine-growing region in France: it's one of the biggest in the world! It stretches in a broad arc between the Mediterranean and the foothills of the Massif Central, from the Camargue, on the right bank of the Rhône, to the Spanish border. Vineyards have flourished in the Midi since the second century BC. Yet not so long ago, the Midi was notorious for high-yielding vineyards that pumped out floods of undistinguished wine. But in recent years, in France as elsewhere, wine drinkers have become more discerning. The demand for cheap, plentiful plonk simply dried up. Vintners in Languedoc and throughout the South had either to evolve with the times or trade in their tractors. In order to survive, a significant number resolved to go the "quality" route, and stop producing watery *Vin de Table*. So they pulled up the vines they had planted on the plains (the fertile soil is great for fruit and vegetables, but terrible for wine), and literally took to the hills.

Languedoc-Roussillon's rugged, chalky slopes are now planted with the better local grape varieties (Carignan, Mourvèdre, Grenache, Cinsault, Muscat, Clairette...), as well as recently introduced premium vines (Syrah, Cabernet Sauvignon, Chardonnay, Viognier...) which add structure, style, and aromatic complexity to the native varieties.

The results are quite spectacular. Today the Midi boasts a growing number of AOC districts and reputed *terroirs*, where growers proudly sign the labels of their estate-bottled wines. There are lots of exciting discoveries to be made between the Costières de Nîmes and the coast of Collioure. And save for a handful of world-famous names—Mas de Daumas-Gassac in the Coteaux du Languedoc, or certain lush, vintage Banyuls—these vigorous, explosively fragrant wines sell for incredibly low prices.

Roussillon, in the eastern Pyrenees, is Catalan country, where grapes have ripened for centuries under a scorching sun. There are some fine red wines made here, as well as powerful rosés. Good whites are rare. But Roussillon's real treasures, for the wine buff at least, are its Vins Doux Naturels, fortified wines made mostly with Grenache and varying proportions of other grapes, to which distilled spirits are added to stop the fermentation process. The wine thus retains much of its natural sweetness. Rivesaltes, Banyuls, and Maury are bound to be a revelation to those who think that dessert wines are just for old ladies!

• COSTIÈRES DE NÎMES

Though geographically in Languedoc, the Costières de Nîmes area chose to ally itself with the Rhône Valley Vintners Association. The red wines especially have made enormous progress in recent years.

CAISSARGUES 30132 – Gard

Château de Belle-Coste

Bernard du Tremblay
04 66 20 26 48, fax 04 66 20 16 90
Open Mon-Sat 9am-noon & 2pm-6pm.
Visitors are warmly welcomed at this aristocratic estate, where some of the best Costières de Nîmes is produced. Taste the special Cuvée Saint-Marc, which comes in red (Grenache, Syrah, Mourvèdre) and white (Viognier and Roussane).

ORANGE 84100 – Vaucluse

Château de Nagès

Domaine Michel Bernard, route de Sosignan
04 90 34 35 17, fax 04 90 34 87 30
Open Mon-Thu 8am-noon & 2pm-6pm (Fri until 5pm).
The Réserve du Château from Château de Nagès (70 percent Syrah, 30 percent Grenache) is a fine reflection of this rugged *terroir*, with a distinctive aroma of truffles.

• FRONTIGNAN

The Frontignan AOC, an area between Montpellier and Sète produces Vins Doux Naturels (VDNs) made mostly from Muscat grapes. The best display luscious flavors of fruit and honey, and make fine apéritifs or partners to blue-veined cheeses.

*Some establishments change their **closing times** without warning. It is always wise to check in advance.*

223

FRONTIGNAN
34110 – Hérault

Frontignan Coopérative SCA

14, av. du Muscat
04 67 48 12 26, fax 04 67 43 07 17
Open by appt.
This coop produces an admirable range of Muscats at very attractive prices. Taste the aromatic, nicely balanced Cuvée Grande Première, elegant Cuvée du Président, and richly flavored Hors d'Age.

• *COTEAUX DU LANGUEDOC*

ANIANE
34150 – Hérault

Mas de Daumas-Gassac

04 67 57 71 28, fax 04 67 51 41 03
Open Mon-Sat 9am-6:45pm.
A book has been written about this groundbreaking estate: *Birth of a Grand Cru*. Daumas-Gassac's red Vin de Pays is anything but a modest tipple: certain older vintages can fetch up to 300 F. Prices for vintner Aimé Guibert's other wines, however, start as low as 20 F a bottle.

NARBONNE
11100 – Aude

Château Notre-Dame-de-Quatourze

Georges Ortola - 04 68 41 58 92, fax 04 68 42 41 88
Open daily 8am-7pm.
The *terroir* of Quatourze is perhaps the oldest wine-producing region in France, and is now recognized as one of the most promising in the Coteaux du Languedoc. Georges Ortola prunes his Mourvèdre and Syrah vines hard, for low yields and high quality. His red Notre-Dame-de-Quatourze wines are all aged in wood.

VALFLAUNES
34270 – Hérault

Mas Bruguière

La Plaine - 04 67 55 20 97
Open daily 5pm-8pm.
Guilhem Bruguière's spicy, tannic red wines are based predominantly on Syrah. Ask to taste the barrel-aged Pic Saint-Loup. Note that there is a furnished rental (*gîte*) on the property.

VENDRES
34350 – Hérault

Domaine Le Nouveau Monde

Jacques et Any Gauch
04 67 37 33 68, fax 04 67 37 58 15
Open daily 9am-1pm & 4pm-8pm.
The estate is surrounded by water, but it produces earthy, robust wines: Coteaux du Languedoc AOC and a noteworthy barrel-fermented Chardonnay. There is a furnished rental (*gîte*) on the property.

• *FAUGÈRES SAINT-CHINIAN & MINERVOIS*

CABREROLLES
34480 – Hérault

Domaine Léon Barral

Didier Barral, Lenthéric
04 67 90 29 13, fax 04 67 90 13 37
Open daily 9am-noon & 4pm-7pm (exc Sun).
Faugères is a young AOC that deserves to be better known. Taste Didier Barral's special cuvées: big, rich wines. He also offers delicious "plain" Faugères that sells for half the price.

CAUNES-MINERVOIS
11160 – Aude

Château Villerambert-Julien

04 68 78 00 01, fax 04 68 78 05 34
Open daily 8:30am-11:30am & 1:30pm-6:30pm.
This is a venerable Minervois estate, in the Julien family since 1850. The vines push their roots into a subsoil of red and pink marble. Blocks of the stuff were used to build the Trianon at Versailles and the Grand Staircase of the Paris Opéra. Hence the names of two of the domaine's remarkably powerful, long-lived wines: Opéra and Trianon.

CAUSSES-ET-VEYRAN
34490 – Hérault

Château Maurel-Fonsalade

04 67 89 57 90, fax 04 67 89 72 04
Open by appt.
Recent vintages of the Maurel family's Saint-Chinian Fonsalade have garnered excellent marks from Gault Millau's testers. Syrah predominates in these brawny wines, blended with Grenache and Cinsault.

LIVINIÈRE (LA)
34210 – Hérault

Jacques Maris

Chemin de Parignoles
04 68 91 42 63, fax 04 68 91 62 15
Open daily 8am-noon & 2pm-8pm (exc Sun pm).
This is one of the best Minervois estates: it occupies a site that will soon be given "Village" status. The red wines are deep-colored and spicy—well worth your attention. Rosés and white wines available, too.

• *FITOU & CORBIÈRES*

BOUTENAC   11200 – Aude

Château La Voulte Gasparets
Patrick Reverdy - 04 68 27 07 86, fax 04 68 27 41 33
Open daily 8am-noon & 2pm-7pm.
From one of the best *terroirs* in the Corbières district come firm-structured red wines with an herbal bouquet. Three different cuvées are offered: "plain" Corbières from vines less than twenty years old; the Reservée from vines under 45 F; and the Cuvée Romain Pauc, a super-selection aged in wood (the '93 vintage sells for around 60 F).

DURBAN-CORBIÈRES   11360 – Aude

Château Haut Gléon
Duhamel - 04 68 48 85 95, fax 04 68 48 46 20
Open daily 9am-7pm.
Léon-Claude Duhamel used to be the owner of K-Way, the windbreaker manufacturer. He sold the firm in 1990 to realize his dream of becoming a wine grower. Mission accomplished: his red Corbières is a model of finesse. Six guest rooms occupy the former harvesters' quarters.

TALAIRAN   11220 – Aude

Jean-Pierre et Annie Mazard
04 68 44 02 22, fax 04 68 44 08 47
Open by appt.
The Mazards are as proud of their environment (the Montagne d'Alaric is the second largest orchid reserve in Europe, with over 70 varieties) as they are of their wines. Their vineyards occupy the magnificent, high-perched *terroir* of Saint-Victor, where every peak is crowned with a Cathar castle. Furnished rentals (*gîtes*) are available at the property.

TUCHAN   11350 – Aude

Château de Nouvelles
Robert Daurat-Fort
04 68 45 40 03, fax 04 68 45 49 21
Open Mon-Sat 8am-11:45am & 2pm-5:30pm.
Mature vines situated on magnificent hillsides and his own incomparable experience have made Robert Daurat-Fort the king of Fitou. His powerful, full-bodied, concentrated red wines are for long keeping.

• *CÔTES DU ROUSSILLON & RIVESALTES*

ALÉNYA   66200 – Pyrénées-O.

Domaine du Mas Bazan
Paul et Annie Favier
04 68 22 98 26, fax 04 68 22 97 37
Open daily 8am-noon & 3pm-7pm.
The village is not easy to find, but once you're there, you'll have no trouble locating the vineyards that lead up to Mas Bazan (where, incidentally, a few inviting guest rooms are available). Taste the Faviers' honeyed white Vin de Pays Catalan made from Chardonnay, Roussane, and white Grenache, and the balanced, wonderfully fruity red Côtes du Roussillon.

PERPIGNAN   66000 – Pyrénées-O.

Domaine Sarda-Malet
Mas Saint-Michel, 12, chemin Sainte-Barbe
04 68 56 72 38, fax 04 68 56 47 60
Open Mon-Fri 8am-noon & 2pm-6pm.
Suzy Sarda-Malet is a tireless booster of her region's wines, and she herself produces some of the best. At the Domaine she will have you taste from a full range of white and red Côtes du Roussillon (there are several fine special cuvées), as well as a luscious 20-year-old Rivesaltes, an ideal partner for chocolate desserts.

RIVESALTES   66600 – Pyrénées-O.

Denis Sarda
Domaine du Mas Kilo
04 68 38 92 01, fax 04 68 38 92 01
Open Mon-Fri 9am-noon & 2pm-6pm.
The Rivesaltes '93 is a thing of beauty, rich and complex, with dried-fruit and nut flavors. The red Côtes du Roussillon from the same vintage comes from old vines (Syrah, Mourvèdre, Carignan) and spent six months in wood: very supple and harmonious.

• *BANYULS & COLLIOURE*

BANYULS-SUR-MER   66650 – Pyrénées-O.

Cellier des Templiers
Route du Mas Reig
04 68 88 31 59, fax 04 68 88 53 56
Open Apr-Oct: daily 9am-7pm; Nov-Mar: Mon-Sat 9:30am-12:30pm & 2pm-6pm.
This coop produces some of the best Banyuls to be found. Sample the gloriously aromatic Cuvée Amiral Vilarem or the Rimatge (the

Catalan word for "vintage"), made like a vintage Port. And like Port, these wines are ideal with strong cheeses or with chocolate desserts.

Domaine Vial Magnères

Bernard Sapéras, 14, rue Emile-Herriot
04 68 88 31 04, fax 04 68 55 01 06
Open daily 10am-12:30pm & 3pm-7pm.
   Visit this vintner to sample his unusual tawny Banyuls made from white-wine grapes. He also makes a powerful, fruity red Collioure.

Looking for a winery? Refer to the **index**.

• *MAURY*

MAURY   66460 – Pyrénées-O.

Mas Amiel

04 68 29 01 02, fax 04 68 29 17 82
Open daily 8am-7:30pm (weekend by appt; off-seas 8am-6pm).
   Maury is an excellent dessert wine, and this is the place to taste it. The Vintage and Vintage Reserve wines especially are notable for their balance and length—not to be missed!

THE LOIRE VALLEY

France's
valley of kings

Mention the Loire Valley and you con-
jure up visions of fairytale castles set
against a backdrop of green fields and rows
of poplars, hillside vineyards, and the swift-
flowing Loire. The river, France's longest,
gives the region its name; the Loire's waters
nourish this land, the "garden of France," a
gentle, rolling landscape that seems to
breathe peace and prosperity. The magnificent châteaux that suddenly appear on the
horizon take one's breath away: these man-
made wonders are surely as dramatic as any
natural landscape could be. Built of *pierre de
Loire*, the porous local limestone, each of the
region's 300-odd châteaux played a role in
French history, serving first as fortresses, later
as elegant residences for aristocrats and royalty, and then as barracks or even quarries after
the Revolution. Now the major châteaux have
been restored and transformed into
museums, drawing hundreds of thousands of
visitors each year from all over the world.

But the châteaux are not the whole story of
the Loire Valley. This is the heartland of
France, renowned for its tender light,
moderate climate, and bounteous farmlands.
The Renaissance poet Joachim du Bellay
wrote of his longing for *"la douceur angevine"*
of his native Anjou, and of how he preferred
the modest house built there by his
grandparents to all the palaces of Rome.
Covered by the sea when the world was still
young, the Loire Valley still shows its marine
heritage in the rolling hills, fertile soil, and
network of rivers left behind by the salty
waters. This former sea bed is bordered by the
Massif Central plateau to the south,
Burgundy's Morvan range to the east, the
green, green grass of Normandy and plains of
Ile-de-France to the north, sea-battered Brittany to the west, and rural Poitou to the south.
Within these boundaries, the pastoral
landscapes of the Loire Valley display subtle
but distinctive differences. The Orléanais
boasts forests and fertile fields, streams and
moors, and is famous for its roses: they not
only enhance the beauty of the area, but also
supply an export crop. From Orléans the
Loire flows southwest to Touraine, with its
vineyards, orchards, market and flower gardens. The Loire then meanders to Anjou, in
whose most westerly reaches—known as
Black Anjou—the countryside begins to
resemble the wilder scenery of Brittany.
White Anjou, however, remains firmly attached to the Loire Valley's pastoral tradition,
with vineyards and gardens covering gentle
slopes.

Turmoil,
and a golden age

While the Loire Valley today may seem to
be a haven of tranquility, this has not always
been the case. Controlled by the Romans for
the first two centuries AD, the Loire Valley
fell prey to invasions by Huns, Franks,
Visigoths, Vikings, and Saracens over the following centuries. Peace did not reign after the
suppression of the barbarians, though, as the
lords of Orléans, Blois, Touraine, Anjou, and
the Maine continued to battle each other for
control of the territory. In the mid-twelfth
century Henri, Count of Anjou, seemed to
have gained the upper hand when he was
crowned Henry II of England and married
Eleanor of Aquitaine, whose dowry brought
him lands that reached as far as the southwest
corner of France. His dominion did not en-
dure, however, and the Loire Valley reverted
to French control early in the thirteenth century. Still, the English did not relinquish the
idea of owning the rich lands of France. They
returned with a vengeance during the
Hundred Years' War (1337-1453), inspiring
Joan of Arc to take up arms to defend her king,
Charles VII. The "Maid of Orleans" liberated
that city, the last French fortress, in 1429. She
was burned at the stake by the English in
1431, becoming a martyr who is venerated by
French nationalists (and royalists) to this day.

The importation of the Italian Renaissance
to France in the sixteenth century, in the relative peace after the Hundred Years' War,
changed the face of the Loire Valley. Gloomy
fortresses metamorphosed into graceful,
light-filled castles that displayed their
owners' wealth and power to best advantage.
Kings Charles VIII, Louis XII, and François I
brought the artistic ideals of the Italian
Renaissance to the Loire Valley. To them we
owe the renovation and construction of the

great châteaux at Blois, Amboise, and Chambord. François I invited Leonardo da Vinci and Benvenuto Cellini from Italy to embellish his residences. Queen Catherine de Médicis, the Florentine wife of Henri II, continued the tradition of patronizing Italian artists.

The Renaissance was the golden age of the Loire Valley. When its importance as a royal seat diminished, the region reverted to its agricultural vocation. The gastronomic bounty produced by this rich land is nearly as celebrated as the châteaux. The Loire River yields shad, trout, pikeperch, eels, and (for a brief season each year) salmon. In the Orléanais and Touraine, the abundance of asparagus, leeks, strawberries, melons, pumpkins, apples, and more prove that this is indeed the garden of France. The Loire Valley is also wine country: Anjou boasts long-lived white dessert wines, aromatic reds, and tender rosés; from Touraine come tannic Chinons and Bourgueil, the best of which will improve with age. The ideal accompaniments to these wines are the region's excellent chèvres, from **Selles-sur-Cher** or **Sainte-Maure**, or the potted pork known as rillettes, a specialty of **Le Mans**.

Exploring the châteaux

Originally a feudal castle, the château de **Blois**, located in the center of the town of the same name, became a royal residence in 1498 when Louis XII ascended the throne (he's the man on horseback above the château's entrance). Louis added a brick-and-stone wing to the château. The next tenant, François I, built yet another wing in the Renaissance style with an Italianate façade and a fantastic open octagonal staircase. The classical sobriety of the Gaston d'Orléans wing, added in 1635, contrasts with the exuberance of the Renaissance portions.

The ubiquitous François I also pops up at **Chambord**, the most colossal of the Loire châteaux, with no fewer than 440 rooms. Originally a humble hunting lodge, François had Chambord enlarged to its present extravagant state in the early sixteenth century. The Italianate structure may have been influenced by Leonardo da Vinci, who had been a guest at Francois's court. Many perceive his genius in Chambord's celebrated double-helix staircase, which allows one person to mount and another to descend without running into each other. On Chambord's broad rooftop terraces, visitors may wander amid pinnacles, turrets, and fantasy sculptures, then pause to admire the view of the immense park that surrounds the château. Once the hunting grounds of royalty, the land is now a national wildlife reserve. Nearby, at the

elegant seventeenth-century château of **Cheverny**, the hunt is still a vital tradition. After viewing the castle's richly furnished interior, one can stroll around the grounds and visit the beautiful hounds in their kennel.

Set high on a cliff, the château at **Chaumont-sur-Loire** is slightly older than Chambord but has a similar massive construction, with fat turret-tipped towers. Catherine de Médicis brought her Italian astrologer, Cosimo Ruggieri, to live at Chaumont. He beguiled his patroness by making the faces of the king and their sons appear in the moonlight, along with the number of years they had left to live (a precursor, perhaps, of today's *son et lumière* shows?).

Though the town of **Chenonceaux** is often thronged with tourists, its château is still very much worth visiting for its intrinsic beauty, interesting history, and the rare works of art it holds. Built plumb over the waters of the Cher River, Chenonceau stands on the foundations of a former mill. François I acquired the castle in 1535 as payment for debts owed the Crown. Henri II made a gift of Chenonceau to his beautiful and ambitious mistress, Diane de Poitiers, but upon his death in 1559, his widow Catherine de Médicis ousted her rival, packing her off to the less majestic château at Chaumont. Catherine had a two-storey gallery built on the bridge that links the castle to the opposite bank of the Cher. The gallery served as a hospital during World War I, and during World War II provided a precious escape route, for it spanned the line of demarcation between France's Free Zone and Occupied France.

Reflected in the tranquil waters of the Indre, **Azay-le-Rideau** is a romantic château that time has barely touched. The early Renaissance architecture shows Italian influences, and the military features—turrets, battlements, and such—serve a purely decorative purpose. Inside, period furnishings and Flemish tapestries embellish the rooms.

The château of **Amboise** is an impressive sight: set at a lordly height above the town, it affords an exceptional view of the river and the Loire Valley. François I established a brilliant court here, graced by poets and artists: Clément Marot, Pierre de Ronsard, and, Leonardo da Vinci. Just outside of Amboise, and well worth visiting, is **Clos-Lucé**, where Leonardo spent the last years of his life. Visitors can admire models of his plans for a helicopter and other amazing inventions, but the real interest is in seeing the place where the great man lived and worked. The kitchen, where he liked to sit, is especially moving.

This is just a taste of the riches of France's "valley of kings." Those interested in the region's earlier history should visit the troglodyte village of **Trôo**, which features cave dwellings dug out of limestone, grottos, a "talking well" (it has a startling echo), and Romanesque church. The château at Le Grand-Pressigny, a major prehistoric site, houses a museum with a fine collection of artifacts.

Apocalypse now... and forever

The cities of the Loire Valley hold their own share of treasures. Flower-filled **Angers**, situated on the Maine River in the western Loire Valley, is dominated by a powerful medieval fortress with seventeen striped towers. The castle houses the *Apocalypse Tapestries*, a fourteenth-century masterpiece depicting 70 scenes from the Book of Revelation. Light filters into Angers's Gothic cathedral of Saint-Maurice through magnificent stained-glass windows; those in the choir are especially fine (notice the Saint Christopher with the head of a dog).

Due east, in the heart of the Loire Valley, is **Tours**, a university town that makes a good base for both château and wine tours. Though Tours suffered bomb damage in World War II, many of its Renaissance town houses (the Hôtel Gouin is a fine example) and ancient half-timbered dwellings on Place Plumereau were spared. The cathedral of Saint-Gatien (named for Tours's first bishop) is a compendium of Gothic styles, with Renaissance towers for good measure. The glorious stained-glass windows date from the thirteenth to the fifteenth century. By all means make time to visit the Musée des Beaux-Arts in the former archbishops' palace, and admire a collection that includes works by Mantegna, Rubens, and Rembrandt in a precious setting.

Following the Loire River north and east takes the visitor to **Orléans**, a city whose main claim to fame is its association with Joan of Arc, who saved it from the English in 1429. Orléans sustained heavy bomb damage during World War II, but was meticulously reconstructed. The eclectic cathedral of Sainte-Croix (called "the ugliest in France" by one of Marcel Proust's characters), was built, destroyed, and rebuilt repeatedly over 600 years. Inside is a chapel dedicated to Joan. Those interested in the life of the warrior shepherdess will also want to visit the Maison de Jeanne d'Arc and the Centre de Jeanne d'Arc, which exhibit documents and memorabilia. Not surprisingly, Orléans hosts a Joan of Arc festival every year on May 7-8. The city's Musée des Beaux-Arts displays a *Saint Thomas* by Velázquez, and exceptional French portraits from the seventeenth and eighteenth centuries.

Completing the circle of the region's major cities is **Le Mans** in the north, between Nor-

mandy and Touraine. Its name is synonymous with car racing: the famous *24 Heures* takes place in June, at the Circuit just south of the town. Racing buffs should not miss the Musée de l'Automobile, also at the site. Le Mans's historic center, just west of the cathedral of Saint-Julien inside the ancient Gallo-Roman wall, holds a wealth of fine medieval and Renaissance houses. The cathedral itself is an architectural marvel, combining Romanesque and Gothic elements with splendid stained glass.

RESTAURANTS & HOTELS

AMBOISE	37400
Paris 206 - Vendôme 50 - Blois 35 - Tours 25	Indre/Loire

12/20 Le Blason

11, pl. de Richelieu
02 47 23 22 41, fax 02 47 57 56 18
Closed Tue, Sat lunch, Jan. Open until 9:30pm (10pm in summer). Terrace dining. Air cond. HOTEL: 28 rms 270-295. Bkfst 30. Half-board 245-365. Rms for disabled. Conf. Pkg.

The menu has some surprises in store, most of them good: like the roast chicken wings, honeyed foie gras croustillant, garlic-roasted kid with ginger confit, and tea-flower mousse with prune custard sauce that figure on the 155 F set meal. Pretty surroundings; clement prices. M 75-225, 49 (children).

🏰 Château de Pray

2 km on D 751 - 02 47 57 23 67, fax 02 47 57 32 50
Closed Jan 2-Feb 3. Open until 9:30pm. Priv rm 20. Terrace dining. No pets. Garage pkg.

Here's an enchanting Loire Valley hostelry, perfect for a romantic getaway. Chef Bruno Delagneau (who trained with Gagnaire and Boyer) is new on the scene, but he impressed us with an inventive repertoire based on premium ingredients. So long as he pays as much attention to substance as to style (watch those cooking times!), all will be well. Try the langoustine tempura with seaweed, sea bream with red cabbage, or morsels of tender spiced suckling pig. Superb desserts, and an interesting cellar to boot, with a memorable collection of Vouvrays. C 230. M 145, 160 (lunch, wine & coffee incl), 295, 70 (children).

Château de Pray

(See restaurant above)
Closed Jan 2-Feb 3. 2 stes 820-890 (4 pers). 17 rms 470-750. Bkfst 50. Half-board 550-640. Conf. Garage pkg.

Just on the edge of the royal town of Amboise sits this thirteenth-century château, flanked by two towers and surrounded by manicured grounds. The rooms are a bit austere, but they are accented with carved pieces of solid-wood furniture.

 ## Le Choiseul

36, quai Charles-Guinot
02 47 30 45 45, fax 02 47 30 46 10
Closed Dec-Jan 20. Open until 9pm. Terrace dining. Air cond. Heated pool. Garage pkg.
The main dining room is certainly handsome, but we prefer a table facing the Italian-style terraced garden (the room is smaller but has more charm). Pascal Bouvier puts an elegant spin on Touraine's prime ingredients, in dishes like foie gras with a caramelized balsamic-vinegar sauce, lake char in mushroom fumet with an unusual garnish of spelt and barley, or roast rack of lamb in a creamy bacon-flecked sauce with a fricassée of snow peas. For dessert, luscious babas au rhum come with tea-soaked prunes and a scoop of licorice ice cream. Connoisseur's cellar. C 270-380. M 220 (weekday lunch, wine incl), 250-440.

 ## Le Choiseul

(See restaurant above)
Closed Dec-mid Jan. 4 stes 1,400-1,700. 28 rms 600-1,300. Bkfst 85-130. Rms for disabled. Half-board 770-1,245. Conf. Heated pool. Garage pkg.
The hotel offers 32 well-kept, variously furnished rooms, some of which have private terraces. There is a pool in the small, very pretty garden. Relais et Châteaux.

 ## Le Lion d'Or

17, quai Charles-Guinot
02 47 57 00 23, fax 02 47 23 22 49
Closed Sun & Mon off-seas, Jan 5-Feb 10. 1 ste 394. 22 rms 185-316. Bkfst 37-49. Restaurant. Half-board 285. Garage pkg.
At the foot of the Renaissance château of Amboise stands this aging but well-equipped little hotel. The lobby and bar were renovated, and the rooms are scheduled for a facelift, too.

 ## Le Manoir Saint-Thomas

Pl. Richelieu
02 47 57 22 52, fax 02 47 30 44 71
Closed Mon. Open until 9:30pm. Priv rm 65. Terrace dining. Pkg.
The stately décor of beamed ceilings, stained glass, antique chests, and rich table settings is as heady as the sensational cellar of Chinons and Vouvrays. Classic dishes—foie gras with wild mushrooms, pikeperch in sorrel sauce, orange craquelin—are delivered by a staff decked out in seventeenth-century costumes. Another point. C 300-350. M 175 (exc Sat dinner, Sun), 220, 300.

 ## Novotel

17, rue des Sablonnières
02 47 57 42 07, fax 02 47 30 40 76

Open year-round. 121 rms 420-570. Bkfst 50. Rms for disabled. Restaurant. Rm ser. Conf. Heated pool. Tennis. Garage pkg.
This chain hotel is built in typical regional style, with a slate roof and dormer windows. The quiet, comfortable rooms afford outstanding views of the Loire and the château. Bar.

ANGERS	49000
Paris 305 - Rennes 126 - Tours 106	Maine/Loire

 ## Continental Hôtel

12-14, rue Louis-de-Romain
02 41 86 94 94, fax 02 41 86 96 60
Closed Sun 12:30pm-5:30pm. 25 rms 195-310. Bkfst 32-55. Rms for disabled. Rm ser.
A modern and comfortable hotel near the cathedral, with clean, smallish rooms (some are not absolutely quiet). But guests can count on a friendly reception, smiling service, and very reasonable rates.

 ## Hôtel de France

8, pl. de la Gare - 02 41 88 49 42, fax 02 41 86 76 70
Open year-round. 3 stes 550. 53 rms 330-480. Bkfst 20-50. Rms for disabled. Restaurant. Rm ser. Air cond. Conf. Garage pkg.
Double windows conceal the fact that the hotel is situated just opposite the train station. The rooms are nicely equipped, there's a brasserie on the premises, and jazz evenings are scheduled regularly. Expect a warm reception.

 ## Le Mail

8, rue des Ursules - 02 41 88 56 22, fax 02 41 86 91 20
Open year-round. 27 rms 230-260. Conf. Pkg.
A hotel with character on a quiet street in the center of Angers, with small but prettily decorated rooms. Good amenities; charming welcome. And you can look forward to a lovely breakfast.

 ## Pavillon Paul Le Quéré

3, bd Foch - 02 41 20 00 20, fax 02 41 20 06 20
Closed Sun dinner. Open until 9:45pm. Priv rm 55. Air cond. Pkg.
What a pleasure it is to enter this elegant town house, an ideal setting for Paul Le Quéré's limpid, luminous cuisine. His expert technique shows to advantage in the 220 F set menu, which brings grilled scallops dressed with a sparky orange vinaigrette, veal shank braised with walnuts in sweet Layon wine, escorted by potatoes dauphinois and chestnut confit, a trio of farm cheeses, and rum-spiked banana-pineapple gratin dolloped with lime sorbet. The cellar is awash in fabulous Loire wines (with an emphasis on Anjous); a knowledgeable sommelier is on hand to help you choose. C 280-420. M 220 (wine incl), 150, 450, 100 (children).

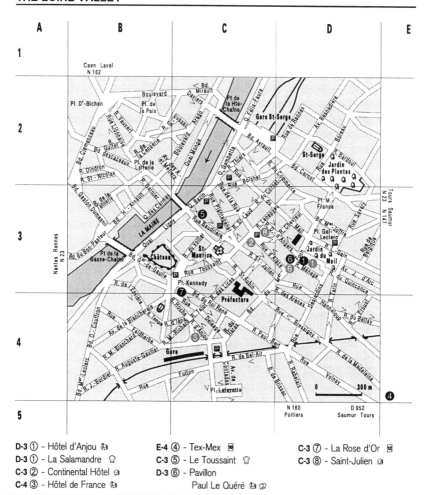

D-3 ① - Hôtel d'Anjou 🏠
D-3 ① - La Salamandre 🍴
C-3 ② - Continental Hôtel 🏠
C-4 ③ - Hôtel de France 🏠

E-4 ④ - Tex-Mex 🍴
C-3 ⑤ - Le Toussaint 🍴
D-3 ⑥ - Pavillon
    Paul Le Quéré 🏠🍴

C-3 ⑦ - La Rose d'Or 🍴
C-3 ⑧ - Saint-Julien 🏠

Pavillon Paul Le Quéré

(See restaurant above)
Open year-round. 3 stes 1,200. 7 rms 450-750. Half-board 505-880. Bkfst 60. Rm ser. Conf. Pkg.
This handsome town house, vintage 1862, was renovated under the supervision of the Beaux-Arts commission. Nicely proportioned rooms, charmingly furnished with every imaginable convenience. Excellent breakfasts.

12/20 La Rose d'Or

21, rue Delaâge - 02 41 88 38 38
Closed Jul 28-Aug 18. Open until 9pm. Air cond. No pets.
Don't be put off by the look of the place (the street, the façade, the décor—ah! the décor—the dishes, and the rest), for you would miss out on some fine, fresh, uncomplicated cooking. The sauces, especially, are nicely done. Friendly prices. M 110, 180, 65 (children).

Saint-Julien

9, pl. du Ralliement
02 41 88 41 62, fax 02 41 20 95 19
Open year-round. 34 rms 160-300. Bkfst 32-50.
You'll find this modern hotel not far from the château (opposite the theater, to be precise). Rooms are on the small side.

La Salamandre

1, bd du Mal-Foch - 02 41 88 99 55 (R),
02 41 88 24 82 (H), fax 02 41 87 22 21
Closed Sun. Open until 9:45pm. Priv rm 20. No pets. Pkg.
Sculpted woodwork and stained-glass windows impart a certain neo-Renaissance gran-

deur to La Salamandre's dining room. Daniel Louboutin gives a clever, personal touch to traditional recipes; his desserts are particularly tempting, and game is featured in season. The cellar holds an excellent selection of local wines. C 280-380. M 130 (lunch), 170, 210.

 Hôtel d'Anjou

(See restaurant above)
Open year-round. 3 stes. 53 rms 380-650. Half-board 420-550. Bkfst 62. Rm ser. Conf. Valet pkg.
Fine, spacious rooms may be had at this venerable, flawlessly renovated hotel.

10/20 Tex-Mex

9, rue de Château-Gontier - 02 41 87 96 00
Closed lunch, Aug. Open until 11pm (midnight upon reservation). Terrace dining.
The chef, who actually did learn to cook in the U. S. of A., makes laudable efforts to serve authentic Tex-Mex fare here in the French heartland. Chili, enchiladas, onion rings, gambas and the like, all washed down with Mexican beer or French wine. C 150-220. M 72, 140, 43 (children).

 Le Toussaint

"Michel Bignon", 7-9, place du Pdt-Kennedy
02 41 87 46 20, fax 02 41 87 96 64
Closed Sun dinner, Mon, Feb school hols. Open until 9:30pm (10pm in summer). Priv rm 20. Air cond.
Given its location and view of the château, this place could survive nicely on the tourist trade, even if it took no trouble with its food and service. But as it happens, the chef is not content merely to go through the motions: he takes pride in his savory shad spread (rillettes), pan-roasted andouillette sausage, and roasted pear in a zippy pepper infusion. The cellar boasts a good selection of Bordeaux and regional wines. C 200-360. M 100 (exc Sat dinner), 130-250, 65 (children).

And also...

Our selection of place for inexpensive, quick, or late-night meals.
Le Petit Mâchon (02 41 86 01 13 - 43, rue Bressigny. Closed Sat lunch, Sun, hols. Open until 9:45pm.): A former butcher's shop transformed into a bistro. Good country-style cooking at low prices (100, 69 weekdays).

ARNAGE   72230
Paris 207 - Le Mans 10   Sarthe

 Auberge des Matfeux

500m beyond the village, via D 147, N 23
02 43 21 10 71, fax 02 43 21 25 23
Closed Mon, Sun dinner, hols, Feb school hols, Jul 21-Aug 11. Open until 9pm. Priv rm 45. Pkg.
The Le Mans auto race seems worlds away from this grand old country restaurant, where Alain and Xavier Souffront take the time to select choice Loué chickens, flavorsome Pauillac lamb,

and milk-fed veal; to install special ovens so that the Auberge can bake its own bread; to grow rare herbs, fresh vegetables, tender lettuces. This commitment to quality ingredients has everything to do with the pristine flavors of their updated classic cuisine. The cellar, too, is splendid, with bargain bottles (marked in red) from every region. C 300-430. M 115, 348, 55 (children).

AZAY-LE-RIDEAU   37190
Paris 254 - Tours 26 - Châtellerault 60   Indre/Loire

 L'Aigle d'Or

10, rue Adélaïde-Riché
02 47 45 24 58, fax 02 47 45 90 18
Closed Sun dinner, Tue off-seas, Wed, Feb school hols, Dec 10-25. Open until 9pm. Priv rm 40. Air cond. Terrace dining.
In a posh, pastel setting Jean-Luc Fèvre presents polished, classic cuisine made with ultrafresh ingredients. While Loire wines dominate the cellar, there's an interesting array of Bordeaux and Burgundies, too. C 250. M 92 (weekday lunch), 143-270, 50 (children).

12/20 Le Grand Monarque

3, pl. de la République
02 47 45 40 08, fax 02 47 45 46 25
Closed Mon lunch off-seas, Thu, Jan, Dec 15-31. Open until 9:30pm. Priv rm 40. Terrace dining. Pkg.
From the look of the place, one would expect to find plates heaped high with generous portions... Well, appearances can be deceiving! Your best bet is the ably prepared 155 F menu: foie gras terrine, fillet of cod with garlicky potatoes, cheeses, and candied citrus fruits in aspic. Tasty Touraine wines fill the cellar. C 260. M 90 (lunch), 155, 275, 60 (children).

 Le Grand Monarque

(See restaurant above)
Closed Jan, Dec 15-31. 1 ste 600-900. 25 rms 250-620. Half-board 360-480. Bkfst 45. Conf. Pkg.
This welcoming eighteenth-century inn offers mostly pleasant, well-kept rooms. Some are soundproofed, the majority have satellite TV.

BEAUMONT-EN-VÉRON   37420
Paris 282 - Tours 51 - Chinon 6   Indre/Loire

Château de Danzay

02 47 58 46 86, fax 02 47 58 84 35
Closed Nov 2-Mar 25. 2 stes 1,400-1,500. 8 rms 650-1,400. Bkfst 80. Restaurant. Half-board 695-1,120 (oblig in seas). Pool. Garage pkg.
This lovely fifteenth-century manor has been completely restored. Huge rooms are decorated in medieval style (solid-wood furniture, mullioned windows, canopied beds), and everywhere there reigns a warm atmosphere.

BÉZARDS (LES) 45290
Paris 136 - Orléans 69 - Gien 16 Loiret

 Auberge des Templiers

N 7 - 02 38 31 80 01, fax 02 38 31 84 51
Closed Feb. Open until 9:45pm. Priv rm 60. Terrace dining. Heated pool. Tennis. Golf. Valet pkg.

Sologne, a lovely land of mists and forest pools, is also the setting for this restaurant. An elegant French provincial ambience emanates from the oaken beams overhead, the antiques and tapestries, the tables set with candelabra and beautiful china. Owner Philippe Dépée keeps this jewel perfectly burnished, while his chef, François Rodolphe, produces the luxurious dishes that are the Templiers' hallmark. Autumn is the time to savor Rodolphe's remarkable game repertoire: terrine de gibier à l'ancienne, spit-roasted partridge swaddled in vine leaves, spiced wild duck, and venison with sauce poivrade all display rich, haunting flavors that hark back to another time. More delicate appetites can choose a saffron-tinged vegetable bouillon afloat with tiny shellfish, quick-seared scallops with barley risotto, or truffled chicken braised in a "crust" of the local blue clay—as savory as it is spectacular! The cellar's 700 wines range in price from 95 F (for a Coteaux-du-Giennois) to 14,000 F for a Romanée-Conti '29: the choice is yours! C 500-750. M 290 (lunch), 390-690, 120 (children).

 Auberge des Templiers

(See restaurant above)
Closed Feb. 8 stes 1,500-3,500. 22 rms 600-1,380. Bkfst 90. Half-board 750-1,650. Rm ser. Conf. Heated pool. Tennis. Golf. Valet pkg.

The taste and attention to detail lavished on these lodgings—an opulent bungalow on the edge of the park, and a clutch of Sologne-style cottages—know no limits, nor hardly an equal anywhere. One is transported with delight by the ambience and amenities, including the regal breakfasts. Relais et Châteaux.

BLÉRÉ 37150
Paris 230 - Blois 45 - Tours 27 - Loches 25 Indre/Loire

 Le Cheval Blanc

Pl. de l'Église - 02 47 30 30 14, fax 02 47 23 52 80
Closed Sun dinner & Mon (exc Jul-Aug), Jan 2-Feb 12. Open until 9:15pm. Terrace dining. Pool.

Michel Blériot regales his patrons (lots of tourists among them) with generous, accessibly priced cuisine. You'll make a satisfying meal of his langoustines and baby vegetables swathed in beurre blanc, beef tournedos in a snappy Szechuan-pepper sauce, and peaches in apricot coulis with pistachio ice cream. Interesting cellar; plush surroundings. C 250. M 99 (week-days), 200, 275, 60 (children).

BLOIS 41000
Paris 180 - Tours 60 - Orléans 56 - Le Mans 109 Loir/Cher

 L'Espérance

189, quai Ulysse-Besnard
02 54 78 09 01, fax 02 54 56 17 86
Closed Sun dinner, Mon, Feb school hols, Aug 7-28. Open until 9:30pm. Air cond. No pets. Pkg.

Admire the view of the Loire River as you savor a clever combination of scallops with lamb's lettuce, an elegant blanquette de sole, or leek-stuffed skate surrounded by slices of grilled andouillette sausage. The cheese tray left us longing for more, but the wine list is extensively annotated and presented with flair. C 250. M 130, 175, 245, 345, 60 (children).

 Holiday Inn Garden Court

26, av. Maunoury - 02 54 55 44 88, fax 02 54 74 57 97
Open year-round. 78 rms 390-430. Bkfst 30-48. Rms for disabled. Restaurant. Half-board 383-401. Rm ser. Conf. Garage pkg.

High up overlooking the town of Blois, the freshly renovated Holiday Inn offers functional rooms done up in contemporary style. For entertainment, there's a piano bar where theme evenings are held. Guests can also make use of fitness and hydrotherapy facilities located nearby.

 L'Orangerie du Château

1, av. Jean-Laigret - 02 54 78 05 36, fax 02 54 78 22 78
Closed Sun dinner, Wed (exc hols), Feb 17-Mar 7, Aug 20-27. Open until 9:30pm. Priv rm 50. Terrace dining.

Eager to show their good will, newcomers Karine and Jean-Marc Molveaux tend to go over the top: an avalanche of extra vegetables threatens a delicious pikeperch with pan-roasted mushrooms; terrine de foie gras with fig purée suffers from a fussy presentation. But an apple gratin with frangipane cream proves that the chef knows what he's about. Expect a pleasant welcome in this fine fifteenth-century dwelling just opposite the château. C 310. M 130 (week-day, Sat lunch), 205, 330, 70 (children).

 Au Rendez-Vous des Pêcheurs

27, rue de Foix - 02 54 74 67 48, fax 02 54 74 47 67
Closed Mon lunch, Sun, Feb 17-24, Aug 3-25. Open until 10pm. Priv rm 35. Air cond.

Éric Reithler cultivates an inventive yet fresh and uncluttered culinary style. Seafood inspires him: try his langoustines en vinaigrette with bits of bacon and red beans, or sea-sweet scallops counterpointed by slightly bitter Belgian endive, the whole bound together by an earthy lentil jus. For dessert, there's a wonderful apple-walnut shortbread swirled with spiced caramel. Watch out, though: à la carte prices are steep at this fashionable bistro. C 250-350. M 145, 90 (children).

Le Savoie

6-8, rue Ducoux - 02 54 74 32 21, fax 02 54 74 29 58
Open year-round. 26 rms 180-280. Bkfst 30. No pets.
Here's a commendable little hotel situated between the train station and the château. Rooms on the first floor have been refurbished. Cheerful personnel.

BRACIEUX	41700
Paris 198 - Blois 19 - Romorantin-Lanthenay 32	Loir/Cher

Hôtel de la Bonnheure

02 54 46 41 57, fax 02 54 46 05 90
Closed Jan-beg Feb. 2 stes 600-800. 12 rms 250-320. Bkfst 38. Rms for disabled. Rm ser. Pkg.
A comfortable, modern hotel near the forest, enhanced by lawns and flower beds.

Bernard Robin

"Le Relais de Bracieux,"
1, av. de Chambord
02 54 46 41 22, fax 02 54 46 03 69
Closed Tue dinner & Wed exc Jul-Aug, Dec 20-Jan 20. Open until 9pm. Terrace dining. Air cond. No pets. Pkg.
True, times are hard in the restaurant business nowadays, even out here in château land. So we must forgive the absence of a sommelier (too bad, for Bernard Robin's cellar is one of the Loire Valley's finest), and overlook the fact that Robin's repertoire may be falling into a routine. Better days will surely come. In the meantime, Robin remains a remarkable craftsman, as adept at exalting humble sardines (with fresh tomato concassée and whipped potatoes) or frogs' legs (breaded then sautéed and served with an exquisite parsley jus) or stewed rabbit (with a whiff of rosemary and a potato pâté on the side), as he is of enhancing such costly ingredients as foie gras (presented in three guises: poached with Port aspic, braised in Chinon wine, grilled with Guérande sea salt and spices). If it's game you crave, by all means book a table here in autumn, when Robin's menu highlights the bounty of Sologne's deep forests. The 180 F menu is a very good value. Relais et Châteaux. C 450-600. M 230 (weekdays), 300- 545.

BRIOLLAY	49125
Paris 285 - Angers 14 - Château-Gontier 41	Maine/Loire

Château de Noirieux

26, route du Moulin
02 41 42 50 05, fax 02 41 37 91 00
Closed Sun dinner & Mon off-seas, Feb 6-Mar 15, Nov 23-Dec 4. Open until 9:30pm. Priv rm 100. Terrace dining. Heated pool. Tennis. Valet pkg.
The famous *douceur angevine* is everywhere in evidence at this opulent château, but it hasn't (thank goodness!) sapped the energy of chef

Gérard Côme, whose delicate, delicious cuisine is sheer delight. In the bright dining room or on the tranquil terrace, guests savor scallops bathed in a meat-based jus with a crisp crab and lobster galette, rabbit with fava beans in a lush tarragon cream sauce, then finish on a high note with Côme's splendid "apple variations." Fabulous cellar; distinguished service. C 320-450. M 195 (weekday lunch), 245 (exc weekday lunch), 300, 460, 120 (children).

Château de Noirieux

(See restaurant above)
Closed Feb 6-Mar 15, Nov 23-Dec 4. 19 rms 650-1,350. Bkfst 85-135. Rms for disabled. Half-board 620-1,550. Rm ser. Conf. Heated pool. Tennis. Pkg.
Set in lovely grounds graced with ancient chestnut trees, the eighteenth-century château and fifteenth-century manor provide nineteen individually decorated, fully equipped guest rooms. Pretty bathrooms; excellent breakfasts. Delightful welcome. Relais et Châteaux.

CANDÉ-SUR-BEUVRON	41120
Paris 194 - Blois 15 - Amboise 29	Indre/Loire

La Caillère

36, route des Montils
02 54 44 03 08, fax 02 54 44 00 95
Closed Wed, Jan-Feb. Open until 9pm (9:30pm in summer). Terrace dining. Pkg.
A quiet, leafy haven in the heart of Touraine, La Caillère stands atop a knoll overlooking the Beuvron River. Jacky Guindon possesses sure technique and a knack for bringing the best out of quality ingredients: crisp-crusted skate on a bed of lentils studded with bits of seared foie gras, rack of lamb with julienne vegetables and an aromatic jus, flaky cornucopias filled with coconut ice cream are typically delicate dishes. Fascinating, affordable cellar. C 300. M 92 (weekdays), 178 (wine incl), 60 (children).

CHAPELLE-ST-MESMIN (LA)	45380
Paris 130 - Orléans 6	Loiret

Orléans Parc Hôtel

55, route d'Orléans
02 38 43 26 26, fax 02 38 72 00 99
Open year-round. 2 stes 580. 32 rms 300-450. Bkfst 40. Rms for disabled. Restaurant. Conf. Garage pkg.
The singular charm of this hotel (the centerpiece of a vast estate) lies in its location on the banks of the Loire, and in its elegant interior decoration. The personalized rooms, done up in royal blue and old rose, are designed to include a little *salon*. The equipment is flawless, the bathrooms large and handsome. Absolute quiet guaranteed, just five minutes from central Orléans.

Some establishments change their closing times without warning. It is always wise to check in advance.

CHAUMONT-SUR-THARONNE — 41600
Paris 152 - Orléans 36 - Romorantin 33 - Blois 52 — Loir/Cher

La Croix Blanche de Sologne

5, pl. de l'Église - 02 54 88 55 12, fax 02 54 88 60 40
Open daily until 9:30pm. Priv rm 40. Terrace dining. Pkg. HOTEL: 3 stes 580-780. 13 rms 250-580. Half-board 420-520 (oblig in seas). Bkfst 45. Rms for disabled. Rm ser. Conf. Tennis. Pkg.
Sologne meets Périgord in this posh little eating house. Françoise Richard coddles her patrons with rich foie gras specialties, sweetbreads with cranberries, and tarte solognote. C 300-360. M 118 (weekday lunch), 145 (weekdays), 169 (weekdays, Sat dinner), 250, 350.

CHÊNEHUTTE-LES-TUFFEAUX — 49350
Paris 287 - Angers 37 - Saumur 14 — Maine/Loire

Le Prieuré ✪

D 751 - 02 41 67 90 14, fax 02 41 67 92 24
Closed Jan 20-Mar 7. Open until 9:30pm. Priv rm 40. Terrace dining. Heated pool. Tennis. Garage pkg.
Jean-Louis Lumineau presents a balanced, classic repertoire that spotlights fish and regional ingredients. Settle down in the dining room of this former convent overlooking the Loire, and tuck into the fine 230 F prix-fixe meal: it brings a fondant of rabbit and langoustines infused with tarragon, pikeperch with bacon and cabbage in a brawny Chinon sauce, cheese, and a creamy crémet with fresh berries for dessert. Admirable cellar, with a wide range of local wines, including a Chinon from Olga Raffault for 85 F the half-bottle. C 330-450. M 160 (weekday lunch), 230, 400, 220-250 (weekday lunch, wine incl), 525 (wine incl).

Le Prieuré

(See restaurant above)
Closed Jan 20-Mar 7. 2 stes 1,250-1,750. 33 rms 550-1,350. Bkfst 85. Half-board 695-1,170. Rm ser. Conf. Heated pool. Tennis. Garage pkg.
A basket of fresh fruit awaits guests in each enormous room of this medieval priory nestled in over 50 acres of verdant grounds above the Loire. Wine-tasting courses offered. Elegant breakfasts. Relais et Châteaux.

CHENONCEAUX — 37150
Paris 213 - Tours 35 - Amboise 11 — Indre/Loire

12/20 Le Bon Laboureur et Château

6, rue du Docteur-Bretonneau
02 47 23 90 02, fax 02 47 23 82 01
Closed Nov 15-Dec 15. Open until 9:30pm. Priv rm 30. Terrace dining. Oool. Valet pkg.
A million tourists wander through Chenonceaux every year, so the Jeudi family hardly

needs to make an effort to attract customers. And yet they take pride in presenting a polished repertoire of traditional dishes that includes duck-giblet salad, chicken breast in a delicate chervil sauce, and licorice parfait. C 280-400. M 150, 280, 90 (children).

Le Bon Laboureur et Château

(See restaurant above)
Closed Nov 15-Dec 15. 4 stes 800-1,000. 30 rms 300-650. Bkfst 45. Rms for disabled. Half-board 500-700. Rm ser. Conf. Pool. Valet pkg.
Here's a vine-covered *auberge* with pleasant rooms that overlook a flower-filled courtyard. Cocktail bar; herb garden; mountain bike rental.

CHEVERNY — 41700
Paris 194 - Blois 15 - Romorantin-Lanthenay 30 — Loir/Cher

Château du Breuil

D 52, route de Fougères-sur-Bièvre
02 54 44 20 20, fax 02 54 44 30 40
Closed Sun, Mon lunch off-seas, Jan 2-Feb 15. Open until 9:30pm. Terrace dining. No pets. Pkg.
A young chef, Patrick Léonce, has taken over the kitchens of this charming château not far from its noble peers, Chaumont, Chambord, and Cheverny. A nice place to stop, with a dining room beautifully fitted out with period furniture. As for the food, it's classic but with modern touches—sometimes we wish Léonce would keep things more simple! Good wine list, reasonably priced, and obliging service. C 380-450. M 195, 250, 120 (children).

Château du Breuil

(See restaurant above)
Closed Sun, Mon off-seas, Jan 2-Feb 15. 2 stes 1,200-1,500. 16 rms 530-890. Half-board 1,100-1,340 (oblig in seas). Bkfst 65. Conf. Pkg.
The château stands proudly in its wooded grounds, a typical Solognot edifice with fifteenth- and eighteenth-century portions, tastefully appointed and furnished. The rooms all have different, personalized décor as well as modern bathrooms and fixtures.

CHINON — 37500
Paris 282 - Tours 47 - Poitiers 95 - Angers 80 — Indre/Loire

Hostellerie Gargantua

73, rue Haute-St-Maurice - 02 47 93 04 71
Closed Wed & Thu lunch off-seas, Feb. Open until 10pm. Terrace dining. HOTEL: 8 rms 240-500. Half-board 550-850 (for 2 pers, oblig in seas). Conf. No pets. Pkg.
We give our vote of confidence to the omelette Gargamelle, cod bathed in meat juices, and duck pot-au-feu, served here in a medieval dwelling where Rabelais's father once resided. C 200. M 98, 130.

Au Plaisir Gourmand ✪

2, rue Parmentier - 02 47 93 20 48, fax 02 47 93 05 66
Closed Sun dinner, Mon, Feb. Open until 9:15pm.
Garden dining. Air cond.
Jean-Claude Rigollet is no publicity hound, and his restaurant built of tufa stone at the foot of the château de Chinon will never attract those who go out to see and be seen. Just as well. His faithful customers and tourists in the know can better appreciate the elegant surroundings and fine set meals. The 175 F menu is a paragon: it brings duck sausage in a truffled jus, pike mousseline, tangy goat cheese, and iced candied-chestnut parfait. Superb choice of Loire wines at reasonable prices; smiling welcome. C 290-380. M 175, 245.

CHISSAY-EN-TOURAINE	41400
Paris 223 - Blois 42 - Montrichard 4	Loir/Cher

La Table du Roy

02 54 32 32 01, fax 02 54 32 43 80
Open until 9:30pm. Terrace dining. Heated pool.
No pets. Valet pkg.
The vaulted Gothic dining room and massive Renaissance furniture make an elegant setting for Olivier Géraud's classic, but increasingly personalized cooking (lots of good ideas on the menu the day we swung by). Courteous welcome; competent service. But why on earth do they offer only shippers' wines here in the heart of Touraine wine country? C 350-450. M 185, 220, 295, 75 (children).

Château de Chissay ♣♠

(See restaurant above)
Closed Nov 15-Mar 15. 6 stes 920-1,600. 25 rms 390-1,000. Bkfst 60. Half-board 675-1,180. Rms for disabled. Rm ser. Conf. Heated pool. Valet pkg.
A château erected in the twelfth and fifteenth centuries (Charles VII, Louis XI, and de Gaulle stayed here), set among wooded grounds and gardens. The luxuriously decorated rooms have eighteenth-century furniture and mosaic-tile bathrooms (but no televisions). The lounges and gardens are simply magnificent, and the welcome and service are very attentive.

COMBREUX	45530
Paris 125 - Orléans 35 - Montargis 36 - Gien 49	Loiret

Domaine de Chicamour

5 km SE on N 60 - 02 38 55 85 42, fax 02 38 55 80 43
Closed Nov 15-Mar 15. Open until 9pm. Priv rm 70. Terrace dining. No pets. Tennis. Pkg.
The kitchen has made a remarkable comeback, with fresh, contemporary takes on traditional dishes that are as lovely to look at as they are to eat. A seasonal cellar (springtime brings Loire wines to the fore) only adds to the pleasure. In fine weather, book a table on the terrace behind the château. C 280-400. M 100, 170, 230, 250 (wine incl), 350 (wine incl), 75 (children).

Domaine de Chicamour ♣♠

(See restaurant above)
Closed Nov 15-Mar 15. 12 rms 340-385. Bkfst 50. Half-board 420. Conf. Tennis. Pkg.
A peaceful stopover indeed is this Directoire château hidden in the forest of Orléans. Fresh, bright rooms open onto leafy grounds, with a riding club on the premises.

COURTENAY	45320
Paris 120 - Sens 26 - Montargis 25 - Orléans 96	Loiret

Auberge La Clé des Champs

Les Quatre-Croix
02 38 97 42 68, fax 02 38 97 38 10
Closed Tue dinner, Wed, last 3 wks of Jan, last 2 wks of Oct. Open until 9pm. Pkg.
This elegant country restaurant, housed in a seventeenth-century farmhouse, is all the more attractive that Marc Delion's skillful cooking. His menu features classics as well as some inventive dishes, like veal sweetbreads scented with a whiff of vanilla or rabbit ballottine with escargots. Excellent but expensive cellar. C 300-460. M 120, 280 (wine incl), 450.

Auberge La Clé des Champs ♣♠

(See restaurant above)
Closed Tue, Wed, last 3 wks of Jan, last 2 wks of Oct. 1 ste 720-950. 6 rms 395-550. Bkfst 55. Pkg.
A seventeenth-century farmhouse has been converted into a luxury inn, with just a handful of rooms decorated in a chic, rustic style. Perfect for a romantic country weekend. Expensive? Of course, but can you put a price tag on true pleasure ?

FERTÉ-SAINT-AUBIN (LA)	45240
Paris 152 - Blois 54 - Salbris 35 - Orléans 21	Loiret

12/20 Auberge de l'Écu de France

6, rue du Général-Leclerc - 02 38 64 69 22
Closed Tue dinner, Wed, 2 wks in Mar, 2 wks in Oct-Nov. Open until 9:30pm. Terrace dining. Pkg.
You'll find this handsome, half-timbered *auberge* in the center of La Ferté-Saint-Aubin, an old town of considerable character. The traditional (but not fusty) cooking is attractively presented, and the smallish cellar focuses on the wines of Touraine. C 250. M 78 (weekdays), 130, 220, 50 (children).

Ferme de la Lande

Route de Marcilly-en-Villette
02 38 76 64 37, fax 02 38 64 68 87
Closed Sun dinner, Mon, Feb school hols, Aug 18-Sep 1. Open until 9:15pm. Terrace dining. Pkg.
Set down in a bucolic landscape of ferns and pines, this seventeenth-century Sologne

farmhouse is a picturesque spot for a fine meal. From the list of regional dishes you could choose tangy céleri rémoulade with smoked chicken breast or duck breast done with cider and honey (the latter came with a disappointing garnish). There's a cool covered terrace for summer dining. Attractive cellar; hospitable welcome. C 250. M 138, 153 (weekdays & Sat lunch, wine incl), 168 (Sat dinner, Sun lunch), 184, 224 (Sat dinner, Sun lunch), 80 (children).

FONTEVRAUD-L'ABBAYE	49590
Paris 306 - Chinon 23 - Saumur 16	Maine/Loire

11/20 Hôtellerie du Prieuré Saint-Lazare

Abbaye Royale de Fontevraud
02 41 51 73 16, fax 02 41 51 75 50
Closed Jan 2-Feb 28, Dec 21-26. Open until 9:30pm. Priv rm 45. Terrace dining. No pets.
After a tour of Fontevraud's magnificent abbey church, you can set yourself up to a simple, solid meal at this unpretentious restaurant. Try the smoked-haddock carpaccio and rabbit with a fragrant thyme jus. M 98 (exc Sun), 160, 235, 75 (children).

 ### Hôtellerie du Prieuré Saint-Lazare

(See restaurant above)
Closed Jan 2-Feb 25, Dec 21-26. 52 rms 290-470. Bkfst 55. Half-board 375. Conf. No pets.
The orchards, the abbey, and an austere décor magnify the impression of serenity that reigns in this hostelry's small but comfortable rooms.

 ### La Licorne

Allée Ste-Catherine
02 41 51 72 49, fax 02 41 51 70 40
Closed Sun dinner & Mon off-seas. Annual closings not available. Open until 9pm. Pkg.
Michel Lecomte does best when he sticks to the classics (his forays into creative cooking usually leave us cold). Still, his precise technique succeeds in coaxing out the flavors of choice regional ingredients. The cellar holds a full complement of Loire wines, in every price range. The lovely eighteenth-century dining room is far warmer than the welcome, but the serving staff is friendly. C 280. M 110 (weekday lunch), 168, 228.

GIEN	45500
Paris 154 - Orléans 64 - Bourges 76 - Cosne 41	Loiret

 ### Le Rivage

1, quai de Nice - 02 38 37 79 00, fax 02 38 38 10 21
Closed beg Feb-beg Mar. Open until 9:30pm. Air cond. Pkg.
Almost too pretty to eat: the chef takes such pains over the plates he sends out that we hesitate to spoil the effect! So take a moment to admire, but then dig in... It would be a pity to miss out on the fine, full flavors of crab and

avocado tian with tomato coulis, or hake vividly spiced with paprika and saffron, or calf's liver mellowed with balsamic vinegar. Owner Christian Gaillard oversees the impeccable service; the cellar holds riches from Burgundy and Touraine. C 345. M 140, 390, 100 (children).

 ### Le Rivage

(See restaurant above)
Closed beg Feb-beg Mar. 3 stes 700. 16 rms 305-520. Bkfst 47. Air cond. Conf. Garage pkg.
On the quay by the old Anne de Beaujeu bridge. Some of the rooms are simple and well furnished, others definitely more luxurious. Very nice bathrooms, too. First-rate breakfasts; cordial reception.

GRAND-PRESSIGNY (LE)	37350
Paris 293 - Tours 58 - Châtellerault 29	Indre/Loire

 ### L'Espérance

Pl. du Carroir-des-Robins - 02 47 94 90 12
Closed Mon, Jan. Open until 9:30pm. Pkg.
Market-fresh ingredients and vegetables from his own garden are the keystones of chef Bernard Torset's menu. He updates dishes typical of Touraine with lightened sauces and a vigorous, modern touch. Try his locally produced foie gras, matelote (a winy stew) of local eels, or spiced Touraine squab. The dining room is as rosy as life becomes after a few glasses of Loire Valley wine from the well-stocked cellar. The friendly *patronne* gives excellent advice about things to see and do in the area. C 250-300. M 110 (exc Sun), 160, 200, 50 (children).

LAVAL	53000
Paris 291 - Tours 140 - Angers 73	Mayenne

Le Bistro de Paris

67, rue du Val-de-Mayenne
02 43 56 98 29, fax 02 43 56 52 85
Closed Sat lunch, Sun, Aug 15-31. Open until 10:15pm. Priv rm 25. No pets.
Envied by other restaurateurs in the region, award-winning chef Guy Lemercier creates terrific meals at unbeatable prices. His chic little establishment on the banks of the Mayenne, presided over by his smiling wife, is always booked solid. No wonder the competition wishes he would take it elsewhere! Just look at what 135 F can buy: a warm pikeperch gâteau (a *very* high-class fishcake) with shellfish coulis, duck confit with eggplant gratin, and crisp langue de chat cookies with citrus compote. From the *carte*, we recommend the calf's head given a snappy spin with hot spices, the Munster shortbread, and Kirsch-spiked raspberry gratin. The cellar is choice, and just as democratically priced as the food. But remember: reserve your table in advance! C 260-300. M 135-245 (weekdays), 85 (children).

Les Blés d'Or

83, rue Victor-Boissel
02 43 53 14 10, fax 02 43 49 02 84
Closed Sun dinner, Mon. Open until 10pm. Priv rm 15. Pkg.

Gilles Arzur is the new man in the kitchen here. His style is more forthright than that of his predecessor, but the results are appetizing and full of frank flavors. Among the offerings you'll find lotte and tomatoes in a light curry sauce, pan-roasted saddle of rabbit vigorously perfumed with rosemary, and ginger-spiced duck confit. Pleasant desserts; fabulous Loire wines (as well as a selection of modestly priced bottles) overseen by owner Pierre Portier, an award-winning sommelier. M 95-120 (lunch, exc Sun), 165, 55 (children).

 ### La Gerbe de Blé

(See restaurant above)
Open year-round. 2 stes 500-550. 6 rms 340-440. Bkfst 60-80. Half-board 460-520. Rm ser. Conf. No pets.

The spacious, nicely decorated rooms are well equipped and now have double windows. Friendly owners.

LUYNES	37230
Paris 257 - Amboise 50 - Tours 17 km	Indre/Loire

 ### Domaine de Beauvois

2 km NW on D 49 - 02 47 55 50 11, fax 02 47 55 59 62
Closed Jan 15-Mar 15. Open until 9:30pm. Priv rm 125. Terrace dining. Heated pool. Tennis. Garage pkg.

This country manor set in vast wooded grounds ranks among the most luxurious establishments in Touraine. Stéphane Pineau cooks in a classic style, making intelligent use of the region's rich resources. Taste his beignets of tiny snails with a bold sauce of violet mustard, pikeperch with a pilaf of winter wheat, or lamb croustillant with sweet-pepper coulis, then polish off a lovely apple soufflé with Calvados granita. Fine wine list at reasonable prices, with many *grands crus* available by the glass. Irreproachable service. C 300-400. M 200-260 (lunch, exc Sun), 270, 370, 100 (children).

 ### Domaine de Beauvois

(See restaurant above)
Closed Jan 15-Mar 15. 2 stes 1,170-1,550. 36 rms 950-1,450. Conf. Heated pool. Tennis. Pkg.

Ideally situated for a holiday touring the Loire Valley's châteaux, this fine hotel has huge, delightfully furnished rooms with marble bathrooms. Fishing, riding, and other sporting activities are arranged, and visits to local wine growers are organized after the autumn harvest. Relais et Châteaux.

MANS (LE)	72000
Paris 216 - Tours 81 - Angers 88	Sarthe

 ### Patrick Bonneville

14, rue Bourg-Belé
02 43 23 75 00, fax 02 43 23 93 10
Closed Wed, dinner Tue & Sun, Jul 14-Aug 15. Open until 9:30pm. Priv rm 30. Garage pkg.

Patrick and Chantal Bonneville's restaurant is set in a quiet (not to say lifeless) neighborhood, but the dining room is welcoming, with its sunny yellow and blue walls and romantic mural. As for the cooking, it's fresh and carefully crafted. Good bets are the creamy watercress soup dotted with morsels of sweetbreads, and the thyme-roasted leg of lamb. Wide-ranging cellar. C 290. M 135, 315.

 ### Chantecler

50, rue de la Pelouse
02 43 24 58 53, fax 02 43 77 16 28
Open year-round. 3 stes 470-530. 32 rms 310-365. Bkfst 47. Garage pkg.

Centrally located near the station, this recently redecorated hotel is thoroughly soundproofed. Zealous service; bar and restaurant: La Feuillantine, see below.

 ### La Ciboulette

14, rue de la Vieille-Porte
02 43 24 65 67, fax 02 43 87 51 18
Closed Sat lunch, Sun, 3 wks in Aug. Open until 10pm. Air cond.

Near Place de l'Éperon, the Ciboulette's bistrostyle dining room is a late-night favorite. Jack Desmats's menus provide plenty of fresh, contemporary offerings, like langoustines wrapped in pillowy crêpes with roasted bananas, cod seasoned with a touch of vanilla, and a crispy ginger croustillant for dessert. C 158. M 120 (weekdays).

 ### La Closerie

4 km route de Laval
02 43 28 28 44, fax 02 43 28 54 58
Closed Oct 15-Apr 10: Sun. 29 rms 320-530. Bkfst 47. Rms for disabled. Restaurant. Half-board 390-630. Rm ser. Air cond. Conf. Pool. Pkg.

The outside doesn't look like much, but inside this hotel are (mostly) pretty, well-tended rooms. Out back are a flower garden, terrace, and pool.

 ### La Feuillantine

Hôtel Chantecler, 19 bis, rue Foisy
02 43 28 00 38, fax 02 43 23 22 31
Closed Aug 10-18. Open until 10pm. Priv rm 50.

Chef Jean-Claude Adam knows his way around a kitchen. All of his dishes show a veteran's skill and a winning personal touch, too. Worth ordering are the escalope of sweetbreads and foie gras, turbot with shallot compote in a pool of crab coulis, and roasted fig with vanilla-scented caramel. Huge mirrors,

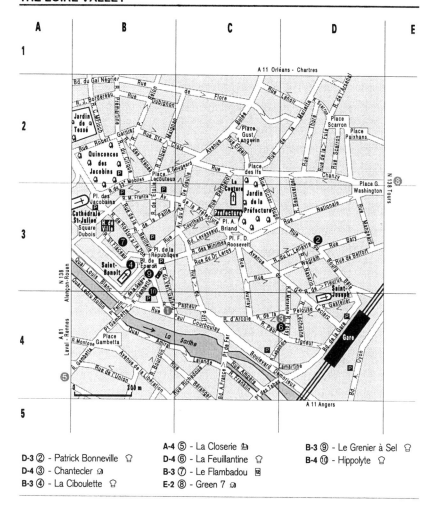

A 11 Orléans - Chartres

A 11 Angers

A-4 ⑤ - La Closerie 🏛
D-4 ⑥ - La Feuillantine ♀
B-3 ⑦ - Le Flambadou 📺
E-2 ⑧ - Green 7 ♨

D-3 ② - Patrick Bonneville ♀
D-4 ③ - Chantecler ♨
B-3 ④ - La Ciboulette ♀

B-3 ⑨ - Le Grenier à Sel ♀
B-4 ⑩ - Hippolyte ♀

mosaics, and potted plants give the dining room a 1930s feel. C 225-420. M 75-95 (weekdays), 115-300 (weekdays, wine incl), 140 (weekdays).

12/20 Le Flambadou

14 bis, rue Saint-Flaceau - 02 43 24 88 38
Closed Sun, Easter school hols, wk of Aug 15. Open until 10:30pm. Priv rm 30. Terrace dining.
Here's a Southwestern enclave in the middle of Le Mans: fresh foie gras with caramelized apples, duck confit with sautéed potatoes, and iced nougat with apricot sauce are washed down with a good Bordeaux from the cellar. C 200.

 Green 7

Route de Tours, 447, av. Georges-Durand
02 43 85 05 73, fax 02 43 86 62 78

Closed Aug. 50 rms 270-330. Rms for disabled. Restaurant. Rm ser. Conf. Pkg.
A former hunting lodge, this American-style, modernized hotel is near the track of Le Mans's famous 24-hour auto race. Well-equipped rooms painted in bold colors. English breakfasts.

 Le Grenier à Sel

26, pl. de l'Éperon
02 43 23 26 30, fax 02 43 77 00 80
Closed Sun dinner, Mon, Aug 1-15. Open until 10pm. Air cond.
Once a salt storehouse, now a handsome restaurant: Le Grenier à Sel draws an elegant crowd to its flower-filled dining room hung with contemporary paintings. Bruno Godefroy's menu shows a marked preference for fish and seafood: sample his lobster fricassée with fresh tagliatelle.

Fine wine list. **C** 190-260. **M** 130, 250, 80 (children).

 Hippolyte

12, rue Hippolyte-Lecornué
02 43 87 51 00, fax 02 43 87 51 01
Open daily until 11:30pm. Air cond.
Local competitors have envy in their hearts whenever they walk by Hippolyte's fully booked dining rooms. Franck Morillon's menu of seafood platters, grilled meats, and other brasserie dishes has a lot of fans. So does the gloriously befrescoed 1900s–style décor. Friendly welcome; professional service. **C** 180-250. **M** 79, 102, 51 (children).

MARÇAY   37500
Paris 289 - Tours 57 - Chinon 10   Indre/Loire

12/20   Château de Marçay

02 47 93 03 47, fax 02 47 93 45 33
Closed Sun dinner off-seas, Mon (exc hols), Jan 31-Mar 15. Open until 9:30pm. Terrace dining. Heated pool. Tennis. Garage pkg.
The setting is as majestic as ever, but the kitchen has lost its Midas touch. A recent meal brought pheasant consommé prepared "à ma façon" (we suggest the chef adopt someone else's...), a toque-worthy chicken pot-au-feu à la tourangelle, and a decent (just decent) goat-cheese galette. Gorgeous cellar, but not enough half-bottles. **C** 380-450. **M** 150 (weekday lunch), 270, 385, 100 (children).

 Château de Marçay

(See restaurant above)
Closed Jan 31-Mar 15. 4 stes 1,420-1,660. 34 rms 495-1,490. Bkfst 90-130. Half-board 685-1,185. Rm ser. Conf. Heated pool. Garage pkg.
Huge, bright rooms with elegant tapestry hangings adjoin spacious bathrooms, some with Jacuzzi. In these peaceful, pampering surroundings, your every need is efficiently attended to. Relais et Châteaux.

MOLINEUF   41190
Paris 189 - Blois 10   Indre/Loire

 La Poste

"Thierry Poidras", 11, av. de Blois
02 54 70 03 25, fax 02 54 70 12 46
Closed Sun dinner, Wed, Feb. Open until 9:30pm. Priv rm 30. Air cond. Pkg.
Follow the gourmets into this blue-and-yellow dining room, adorned with a mural depicting the game-rich Sologne region. Thierry Poidras puts a fresh spin on traditional cuisine. The 90 F set menu is a real bargain: chicken-liver terrine, a juicy beef steak seasoned with fleur de sel, roasted chèvre on a bed of greens, the pastry *du jour,* and petits fours. The cellar is eclectic, and like the food, is clemently priced. **C** 230-300. **M** 90 (exc Sun), 140, 220, 50 (children).

MONTBAZON   37250
Paris 247 - Chinon 41 - Tours 12 - Loches 32   Indre/Loire

 La Chancelière

1, pl. des Marronniers
02 47 26 00 67, fax 02 47 73 14 82
Closed Sun dinner & Mon (exc hols), Aug 25-31. Open until 9:30pm. Air cond. Pkg.
In this snug and refined establishment, Michel Gangneux has simplified his flamboyant cuisine. The result is satisfying and attracts many locals. Like us, they enjoy the red mullet served osso buco style, warm oysters in Champagne sauce, or sweetbreads sparked with citrus vinegar. Magnificent Loire wines, with a wide choice of half-bottles. Le Jeu de Carte, a bistro annex, offers excellent menus at attractive prices in an elegant, postmodern garden décor. **C** 330-350.

 Château d'Artigny

Route d'Azay-le-Rideau
02 47 26 24 24, fax 02 47 65 92 79
Closed Nov 29-Jan 11. Open until 9:30pm. Priv rm 120. Terrace dining. Heated pool. Tennis. Pkg.
We may as well tell you: this "eighteenth-century" château seemingly steeped in history is in fact a bit of megalomania built in 1919 by perfumer René Coty. Revived at huge expense, the interior is a spectacular—if not always harmonious—jumble of antiques, tapestries, and all the other trappings of Château Life. The menu, predictably, strikes rich, full chords but it avoids the heaviness that often marks this genre. Chef Francis Maignaut's elegant offerings include a light and pretty parsleyed fish terrine, truffled Touraine chicken with asparagus risotto, and a flawless strawberry millefeuille. The cellar is one of the finest in France (the wine list is 70 pages long!). Distinguished welcome and service. **C** 400. **M** 250 (weekday lunch, wine incl), 285 (weekday dinner, wine incl), 280-440, 100 (children).

 Château d'Artigny

(See restaurant above)
Closed Nov 29-Jan 11. 2 stes 2,300-2,860. 44 rms 650-1,640. Bkfst 90-130. Half-board 780-1,260. Rm ser. Air cond. Conf. Heated pool. Tennis. Pkg.
An immense terrace overlooking the River Indre, vast landscaped grounds, and formal French gardens unrolling to the horizon: such is the magnificent setting for the Château d'Artigny's luxuriously appointed, over-decorated rooms and suites. Exercise room; golf; musical weekends. Relais et Châteaux.

 Domaine de la Tortinière

2 km N on N 10 & D 287,
Les Gués-de-Veigné
02 47 34 35 00, fax 02 47 65 95 70
Closed Dec 20-Feb 28. Open until 9:15pm. Priv rm 100. Terrace dining. Pool. Tennis. No pets. Pkg.

It looks like a Renaissance château (most tourists take it for one), but in fact this imposing structure dates only from the Second Empire. Édouard Wehrlin's proficient cooking is of a classic cast, although some dishes draw inspiration from the local *terroir*, like the beef tenderloin with Chinon marmalade. Fine selection of Loire wines. C 300-400. M 215 (lunch, wine incl), 285, 360.

Domaine de la Tortinière

(See restaurant above)
Closed Dec 20-Feb 28. 7 stes 1,010-1,500. 14 rms 470-890. Bkfst 70. Rms for disabled. Half-board 570-890 (oblig in seas). Heated pool. Tennis. Conf. No pets. Pkg.
Set down in wooded grounds, here is a luxurious stopover with impeccably equipped and decorated rooms (the ones in the separate pavilions were recently renovated), a heated pool, and tennis courts. Some rooms are equipped with Jacuzzis; all have good bathrooms.

MONTLOUIS-SUR-LOIRE 37270
Paris 241 - Tours 12 - Amboise 15 Indre/Loire

Château de la Bourdaisière

25, rue de la Bourdaisière
02 47 45 16 31, fax 02 47 45 09 11
Open year-round. 2 stes 750-1,100. 12 rms 550-1,100. Bkfst 50. Rms for disabled. Pool. Tennis. Pkg.
Philippe-Maurice and Louis-Albert de Broglie give château buffs a princely welcome to this Renaissance castle in the Cher Valley. Rooms are large and bright, with lots of charm. Swimming pool and tennis court on the grounds. The cellars have just been opened to the public this year, and the lovely greenhouse has been freshly refurbished.

MONTRICHARD 41400
Paris 204 - Tours 44 - Blois 32 - Loches 31 Loir/Cher

Château de la Menaudière

Route d'Amboise
02 54 71 23 45, fax 02 54 71 34 58
Closed Sun dinner & Mon off-seas, Nov 30-Mar 1. Open until 9pm (10pm in summer). Terrace dining. Pool. Tennis. Pkg.
Our waiters looked a bit awkward in their formal clothes (why do they always remind us of penguins?) but the service dispensed in this Renaissance château is never anything but obliging and amiable. The menu is never anything but sedate—warm salad of sea scallops and mushrooms, fillet of turbot with truffle sabayon, stuffed saddle of rabbit—yet every dish is admirably crafted. Don't be intimidated by the setting: go ahead and order the least expensive set meals! That's what they're there for... C 270. M

90 (lunch), 150 (wine incl), 190-300, 60 (children, free until 6).

Château de la Menaudière

(See restaurant above)
Closed Sun dinner & Mon off-seas, Nov 30-Mar 1. 25 rms 360-650. Bkfst 58. Half-board 475-540. Air cond. Conf. Pool. Tennis. Pkg.
This handsome old château proposes classically decorated, well-kept, comfortable rooms with views of the surrounding countryside or a pretty inner courtyard with a fountain. Warm welcome; attentive service.

La Tête Noire

24, rue de Tours - 02 54 32 05 55, fax 02 54 32 78 37
Closed Jan. 36 rms 200-330. Bkfst 36. Restaurant. Half-board 285-345. Pkg.
A respectable level of comfort can be found at this rustic hotel in château country.

NOIZAY 37210
Paris 236 - Amboise 9 Indre/Loire

Château de Noizay

Route de Chançay
02 47 52 11 01, fax 02 47 52 04 64
Closed Jan 2-Mar 14. Open until 9:45pm. Priv rm 21. Terrace dining. Pool. Tennis. No pets. Pkg.
In the château's serenely elegant dining room, chef Didier Frébout presents a menu of such carefully wrought classics as a salad of lightly smoked pigeon and bits of pork belly, pikeperch in a sauce of Chinon wine, and rack of lamb with a delicate white-bean velouté. Desserts are no great shakes, but the cellar harbors a superb selection of Loire wines. C 350. M 150 (lunch), 225 (weekday lunch, wine incl), 240-360, 60 (children).

Château de Noizay

(See restaurant above)
Closed Jan 2-Mar 14. 14 rms 650-1,300. Bkfst 80-120. Half-board 755-1,080. Rm scr. Conf. Pool. Tennis. Pkg.
This sixteenth-century château offers very comfortable, prettily decorated rooms (number five has a canopied bed) that open onto a formal French garden. Professional reception, elegant ambience. Good breakfasts with homemade pastries. Relais et Châteaux.

NOYERS-SUR-CHER 41140
Paris 220 - Romorantin-Lanthenay 32 - Valençay 22 Loir/Cher

Le Clos du Cher

Route de St-Aignan
02 54 75 00 03, fax 02 54 75 03 79
Closed Wed off-seas, Jan 6-Feb 5, Nov 12-19. 10 rms 390-550. Bkfst 60. Rms for disabled. Restaurant. Half-board 395-460. No pets. Pkg.
At the heart of the château circuit, this posh hostelry occupies a vast, wooded estate. The

comfortable rooms are decorated in an understated style. Attractive packages for cycling holidays are offered.

ONZAIN	41150
Paris 198 - Blois 19 - Amboise 21	Indre/Loire

 ## Domaine des Hauts de Loire

Route d'Herbault - 02 54 20 72 57, fax 02 54 20 77 32
Closed Mon & Tue lunch off-seas, Dec-Jan. Open until 9:30pm. Priv rm 60. Terrace dining. Heated pool. Tennis. No pets. Valet pkg.
Oak paneling, antiques, and subtle color schemes compose a setting of restrained elegance in this vine-covered former hunting pavilion. Restrained is not the word we'd use to describe the prices, however. Diners who wish to indulge in Rémy Giraud's appealing cuisine (which has taken on an exotic, Mediterranean flavor) will need to line their wallets first! Irreproachable staff; short but diversified wine list. C 350-400. M 290-360, 300 (lunch, exc Sun, wine incl), 150 (children).

 ## Domaine des Hauts de Loire

(See restaurant above)
Closed Feb-Mar, Nov-Jan. 8 stes 1,600-2,200. 27 rms 550-1,400. Bkfst 85. Rms for disabled. Half-board 1,100-1,200. Rm ser. Heated pool. Tennis. No pets. Valet pkg.
The immense rooms, suites, and bathrooms of this enchanting estate have been decorated in impeccable taste. The best suites are in the Sologne-style annex. To relax, guests may fish in the lake, swim in the heated pool, or go for a ride in a hot-air balloon. Relais et Châteaux.

ORLÉANS	45000
Paris 116 - Chartres 72 - Tours 113 - Blois 56	Loiret

 ## Les Antiquaires

2-4, rue au Lin - 02 38 53 52 35, fax 02 38 62 06 95
Closed Sun, Mon, Apr 13-21, Aug 3-26, Dec 24-Jan 2. Open until 10pm. Priv rm 15.
France's provincial bourgeoisie loves to eat well. Their favorite restaurant in Orléans is Michel Pipet's refined establishment near the Pont Royal. You'll discover the sure-handed skill of a veteran chef whose cooking simply never misfires. Try his elegantly balanced warm salad of sweetbreads and foie gras, an exceptional duo of John Dory and mussels with Belgian endive (the latter's faint bitterness points up the sweet shellfish), and a thin apple-caramel tart with cinnamon ice cream. Remember to book ahead at this, the best table in Orléans. Magnificent cellar. C 300. M 115 (weekday lunch), 200 (wine & coffee incl), 300.

 ## L'Archange

66, rue du Faubourg-Madeleine
02 38 88 64 20, fax 02 38 43 08 81
Closed Sun dinner, Mon (exc Jul-Aug), Tue dinner, Feb school hols, Aug 3-28. Open until 10pm. Priv rm 20. Terrace dining.
It's not for the atmosphere that we come here (the faded sea-green décor doesn't raise the spirits), but for the "nougat" of beef and foie gras, spiced sea bass in a meat-based jus, and apple-raspberry crumble. The wine list offers a diverse choice of shippers' wines. Efficient service. C 220. M 90 (exc Sun), 138, 235, 60 (children).

 ## Eugène

24, rue Ste-Anne - 02 38 53 82 64, fax 02 38 54 31 89
Closed lunch Sat & Mon, Sun, Aug. Open until 10pm. Air cond.
Ludovic keeps the crowds coming to his retrostyle bistro with an affordable menu that offers the enticing likes of asparagus and foie gras salad, red mullet with vegetables à la grecque, and minted berry gazpacho. Limited cellar of inexpensive wines. And the welcome, like the service, is faultless. C 230. M 125, 180.

Le Florian

70, bd Alex-Martin
02 38 53 08 15, fax 02 38 53 08 49
Closed Sun, Aug 4-25. Open until 10pm. Terrace dining.
A lively brasserie décor, a pretty garden, and Bernard Viron's good cooking bring us back time and again to Le Florian. You're sure to savor the curried leek and mussel tart, tiny red mullet cooked with puckery pickled lemons, and peach soup perfumed with fresh mint. The wine list is a perfect match for the food. C 260. M 120 (weekdays, Sat lunch), 150, 200 (exc Sun).

12/20 La Loire

6, rue Jean-Hupeau - 02 38 62 76 48
Closed Sat lunch, Sun, Aug 1-17. Open until 9:30pm.
The owner's warm welcome puts patrons at ease in this cool, uncluttered blue dining room. The menu highlights seafood, prepared in a variety of clever ways, but sauces are clearly not the chef's strong suit. Limited cellar. C 195. M 105-260, 60 (children).

 ## Novotel-La Source

11 km S on N 20, La Source,
2, rue Honoré-de-Balzac
02 38 63 04 28, fax 02 38 69 24 04
Open year-round. 119 rms 410-470. Bkfst 49. Rms for disabled. Restaurant. Rm ser. Air cond. Conf. Pool. Tennis. Pkg.
Modern, well-maintained, and comfortable, this chain hotel has sporting facilities and a children's playground. Set in wooded grounds, with a poolside bar.

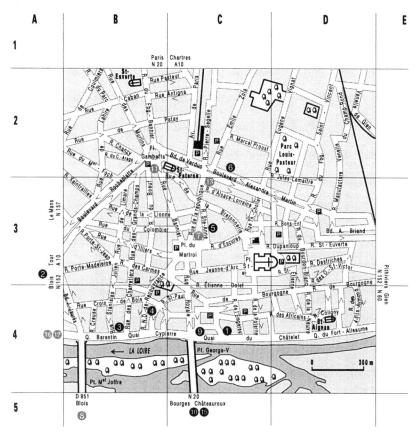

A   B   C   D   E

C-4 ① - Les Antiquaires   **C-2** ⑥ - Le Florian   **B-2** ⑪ - Saint-Aignan
A-3 ② - L'Archange   **C-3** ⑦ - Hôtel d'Orléans   **A-4** ⑫ - Sanotel
   C-3 ⑬ - Terminus
   C-4 ⑨ - La Loire   **B-5** ⑭ - Novotel-La Source
C-3 ⑤ - Eugène   **C-5** ⑩ - Le Restaurant des Plantes   **C-5** ⑮ - La Poutrière

---

🏠 Hôtel d'Orléans

6, rue Adolphe-Crespin
02 38 53 35 34, fax 02 38 53 68 20
Open year-round. 18 rms 260-380. Bkfst 38. Pkg.
The modern rooms of this centrally situated hotel lack charm, but they are well equipped and practical.

👨‍🍳 Le Restaurant des Plantes

44, rue Tudelle - 02 38 56 65 55, fax 02 38 51 33 27
Closed Sat lunch, Sun, Mon dinner, May 1-9, 3 wks in Aug, 1 wk at Christmas. Open until 9:30pm.
This cozy dining room has the look of a family house, and the cooking is homestyle, too, with some bright touches. Try the fricassée d'escargots perked up with a fresh tomato fondue, savory goujonnettes of cod and red mullet in balsamic vinegar sauce, and wreath of roasted apple slices topped with cinnamon ice cream. Fine regional wines. C 250-320. M 98 (weekdays), 138, 220.

👨‍🍳 La Poutrière

8, rue de la Brèche
02 38 66 51 71, fax 02 38 51 19 38
Closed Sun dinner, Mon, Dec 24-Jan 10. Open until 10pm. Air cond. Terrace dining. Pool. Pkg.
Imposing beams, country furniture, and pretty *bibelots* make a charming setting for Simon Le Bras's good classic cooking. On fine days, the tables set out by the pool are awfully inviting! Nice wine list with a good choice of Burgundies

and Bordeaux; cheerful welcome and stylish service. C 280. M 120 (lunch, exc Sun), 240, 350.

 ## Saint-Aignan

3, pl. Gambetta - 02 38 53 15 35, fax 02 38 77 02 36
Open year-round. 27 rms 200-325. Bkfst 35. Conf. Garage pkg.
Under new management, this hotel has been fully renovated. Pleasant and inexpensive. A warm welcome. Simple meals are served in the evening.

 ## Sanotel

16, quai Saint-Laurent
02 38 54 47 65, fax 02 38 62 05 91
Open year-round. 50 rms 296-370. Rms for disabled. Air cond. Conf. Garage pkg.
Behind the eighteenth-century façade is a modern hotel with quiet, perfectly adequate rooms. Located on the western edge of town, on the banks of the Loire.

Terminus

40, rue de la République
02 38 53 24 64, fax 02 38 53 24 18
Closed Dec 22-Jan 3. 47 rms 310-370. Bkfst 40. Conf.
Opposite the train station (as the name implies), this hotel's drab exterior conceals a truly comfortable place to stay. Rooms are not large, but are elegantly furnished.

PETIT-PRESSIGNY (LE)	37350
Paris 305 - Tours 64 - Loches 35	Indre/Loire

 ## La Promenade

02 47 94 93 52, fax 02 47 91 06 03
Closed Sun dinner, Mon, Jan 6-28, Sep 22-Oct 7. Open until 9:30pm. Air cond.
Jacky Dallais has few peers when it comes to serving up bold, generous cooking at top-value prices. Consider this: 195 F buys creamy scrambled eggs with morels, followed by sole stuffed with chive butter, roast local chicken with salsify, cheese (with homemade bread), and a dessert. The *carte* lists a host of irresistible offerings, like Dallais's famous bacon-flecked carrot bouillon with fava beans and wild thyme, a huge chop of farm-bred pork, and a cocoa feuilleté lavished with molten spiced chocolate. Come here with an appetite, but leave your watch at home: the kitchen and the staff like to take their time. C 375. M 120 (weekdays, Sat lunch, wine incl), 195, 360.

ROCHECORBON	37210
Paris 232 - Tours 5	Indre/Loire

 ## Les Hautes Roches

86, quai de la Loire
02 47 52 88 88, fax 02 47 52 81 30
Closed Sun dinner & Mon off-seas, mid Jan-mid Mar. Open until 9:30pm. Priv rm 25. Terrace dining. Heated pool. Pkg.

Here's an uncommon—and uncommonly charming—restaurant built into the tufa cliffs above the Loire. The view from the riverside terrace will take your breath away! Chef Didier Édon's deft cooking sometimes tips over into excess, but that shouldn't mar your enjoyment of his squab with glazed citrus peel or mocha tart with a buttery short crust. Superb wine list. Service is straightforward and smiling. C 360. M 150 (weekday lunch), 270, 355, 100 (children).

 ## Les Hautes Roches

(See restaurant above)
Closed mid Jan-mid Mar. 3 stes 1,350. 12 rms 600-1,250. Bkfst 85. Rms for disabled. Half-board 735-1,110. Rm ser. Heated pool. Conf. Pkg.
The stupendous size of these twelve rooms and three suites easily absorbs the opulent décor: refined appointments provide an exquisite contrast to the walls of bare, pale stone. The Loire flows below, with vineyards all around, and the spire of Tours cathedral keeps watch from a distance. Relais et Châteaux.

12/20 L'Oubliette

34, rue des Clouets - 02 47 52 50 49
Closed Sun dinner, Mon, 1 wk in Jan, 2 wks in Feb, 1 wk in Aug, 1 wk in Nov. Open until 9:30pm. Terrace dining. Pkg.
Our enthusiasm for menu at this rock-walled restaurant has waned a bit, but the site remains most attractive. The new chef is still getting his bearings, so we won't be too severe in our criticism of the bland (was it really truffled?) sauce that escorted our magret de canard. On balance, the food is simple, honest, and based on good ingredients. Decent little cellar. C 280. M 104 (weekdays, Sat lunch), 165, 298.

ROMORANTIN-LANTHENAY	41200
Paris 183 - Tours 92 - Bourges 65 - Blois 41	Loir/Cher

Grand Hôtel du Lion d'Or

69, rue Georges-Clemenceau
02 54 94 15 15, fax 02 54 88 24 87
Closed Feb 17-Mar 20. Open until 9:30pm. Priv rm 45. Terrace dining. Air cond. Valet pkg.
Didier and Marie-Christine Clément spend their free hours exploring the countryside, coming up with new sources for rare vegetables, herbs, and authentic wild game. Both are experts on exotic spices, and Marie-Christine seeks out forgotten recipes in her library of antique cookery books. The cuisine that evolves from this passionate quest is inventive, cerebral—and very expensive. The 410 F menu is inventive, with fresh tuna set off by gooseberry chutney, oysters cooked in Muscat wine and poised in a ryebread croûte, Loire salmon with purslane and anchovies, and iced figs with date confit. But (because this is "just" the cheaper set meal?) the execution fell short somehow, was less exciting than we remembered... Didier Clément is uncompromising on the quality of his ingredients; at these prices, patrons—whatever they spend—

are bound to be uncompromising, too. **C** 660-1,000. **M** 410, 600.

Grand Hôtel du Lion d'Or

(See restaurant above)
Closed Feb 17-Mar 20. 3 stes 1,200-2,100. 13 rms 600-1,800. Bkfst 100. Rms for disabled. Rm ser. Air cond. Conf. Valet pkg.
What was formerly a dilapidated post house is now an inn with luxurious rooms and suites overlooking a Renaissance fountain. Elegant public rooms (a pianist plays on Friday evenings in the delightful lounge by the garden). Relais et Châteaux.

ROSIERS-SUR-LOIRE (LES)	49350
Paris 279 - Angers 29 - Saumur 16	Maine/Loire

Auberge Jeanne de Laval

54, rue Nationale - 02 41 51 80 17, fax 02 41 38 04 18
Closed Mon off-seas, 2 wks in winter. Open until 10pm. Terrace dining. No pets. Pkg.
Michel Augereau's sauce au beurre blanc is truly one of a kind, a culinary secret handed down from his father. Michel also picked up a few tips from Joël Robuchon, and these old and new influences combine to produce beautifully crafted classic cuisine. You must taste Michel's poached foie gras glazed with Saumur wine aspic, Loire River pikeperch with that famous beurre blanc, pigeon ballottine perfumed with truffles, and crayfish cooked in Chardonnay. Game is featured in hunting season, and the cellar is a treasure house of venerable Loire vintages. Charming welcome. **C** 330-450. **M** 170, 300, 400.

 Ducs d'Anjou

(See restaurant above)
Closed 2 wks in winter. 10 rms 350-550. Bkfst 50. Rms for disabled. Half-board 540-620 (oblig in seas). Rm ser. Pkg.
Here you'll find a handful of large, freshly renovated, thoughtfully appointed rooms that look onto a garden and the village church. Marvelous breakfasts; good soundproofing; excellent service.

SAINT-OUEN-LES-VIGNES	37530
Paris 206 - Tours 39 - Amboise 11	Indre/Loire

L'Aubinière

Rue J.-Gauthier - 02 47 30 15 29, fax 02 47 30 02 44
Closed Tue dinner & Wed (exc Jul-Aug), Sun dinner Nov-Easter, Feb 15-Mar 15. Open until 9:45pm. Priv rm 18. Terrace dining. Garage pkg.
The village is tucked away in a verdant valley, but food-loving locals quickly discovered L'Aubinière. Jacques Arrayet's precise, full-flavored cooking wins more fans every day, with the likes of slow-roasted tomatoes dressed with

oxtail vinaigrette, sea bass with zucchini in a saffron-tinged shellfish fumet, and poached cherries with red-wine coulis and verbena ice cream. In fine weather, book a table on the bucolic terrace. Cordial service. **C** 320. **M** 98-160 (weekday lunch), 190, 340, 95 (children).

SAINT-PATRICE	37130
Paris 273 - Chinon 26 - Tours 33 - Langeais 9	Indre/Loire

 Château de Rochecotte

02 47 96 16 16, fax 02 47 96 90 59
Closed Feb. Open until 9:30pm. Priv rm 90. Heated pool. Pkg.
In this ravishingly beautiful Renaissance château, you can choose a table on the flower-decked Italianate terrace or in the elegant contemporary dining room: both are seductive settings for Emmanuelle Pasquier's flawless, full-flavored cooking. Taste the perfection of her basil-scented shrimp risotto, then go on to a superb turbot with asparagus and morels, or beef tenderloin spiced with pink peppercorns. Franck Joly signs the haute-couture desserts, while Christelle Pasquier guides guests through the connoisseur's cellar. Stylish, smiling service. **C** 350. **M** 195, 285, 80 (children).

 Château de Rochecotte

(See restaurant above)
Closed Feb. 3 stes 580-1,250. 27 rms 580-1250. Bkfst 60-90. Rms for disabled. Half-board 580-1,280. Rm ser. Conf. Heated pool. Pkg.
Talleyrand gave this breathtaking château to the Duchesse de Dino, his last love. French formal gardens and Italianate terraces form an exquisite setting for the hotel's magnificent contemporary rooms. The atmosphere is relaxed, the Pasquier family's welcome heartfelt. Gorgeous swimming pool.

SAINT-SYLVAIN-D'ANJOU	49480
Paris 283 - Angers 17 - La Flèche 41	Maine/Loire

 Auberge d'Éventard 🙂

N 23, route de Paris
02 41 43 74 25, fax 02 41 34 89 20
Closed Sun dinner, Mon. Open until 10pm. Priv rm 20. Terrace dining. Air cond. No pets. Pkg.
The superhighway has siphoned off the traffic that used to thunder by this pretty inn on the side of the *route nationale*. Though close to Angers, the Auberge has a decidedly country feel. So does the menu, reflecting Jean-Pierre Maussion's commitment to the authentic flavors of market-fresh, local ingredients. Choose from zesty andouillette sausage with shallots, osso buco of farm-raised chicken with fresh tomatoes, Anjou squab in a honeyed sauce, pikeperch with citrus fruit in a suave sauce based on Savennières wine... The admirable cellar of Loire wines includes magnificent finds straight from the

growers. **C** 300-500. **M** 155 (weekday lunch), 210-355, 100 (children).

SAUMUR 49400
Paris 300 - Angers 53 - Tours 65 - Nantes 127 Maine/Loire

 ## Anne d'Anjou

32-33, quai Mayaud
02 41 67 30 30, fax 02 41 67 51 00
Closed Dec 23-Jan 4. 50 rms 285-575. Bkfst 48. Rms for disabled. Restaurant. Half-board 400-450. Rm ser. Conf. No pets. Garage pkg.
At the foot of Saumur's château and overlooking the Loire, this wonderful eighteenth-century hotel is in part a registered landmark (the façade and grand staircase). Recently remodeled, the rooms are pleasant and well equipped (the spectacular number 102 was designed by Napoléon's architects).

12/20 Les Chandelles

71, rue Saint-Nicolas
02 41 67 20 40, fax 02 41 50 64 21
Closed Wed & Thu lunch off-seas, Feb 1-20. Open until 10pm. Priv rm 30. Terrace dining.
The freshly refurbished dining room makes Les Chandelles more welcoming than ever, adding to the enjoyment of the kitchen's updated classic cuisine. The cellar, naturally enough, majors in Loire Valley wines. **C** 270. **M** 98, 110.

11/20 Le Clos des Bénédictins

2 km SW on D 751, in St-Hilaire-St-Florent
02 41 67 28 48, fax 02 41 67 13 71
Closed mid Nov-Feb. Open until 9:15pm. Priv rm 20. Terrace dining. Pool. No pets. Pkg.
Though rustic in tone, the setting is polished to a high sheen, and there is a very pretty view of the Thouet Valley. What a shame that the cooking is so uneven! But the cellar is a dream, with wines from the best local growers. **C** 280. **M** 120 (weekday lunch, Sat), 159, 189, 75 (children).

 ## Le Clos des Bénédictins

(See restaurant above)
Closed mid Nov-Feb. 3 stes 600-800. 2 rms 300-500. Bkfst 55. Rms for disabled. Half-board 380-550 (oblig in seas). Rm ser. Conf. Pool. Pkg.
This quiet hotel affords a lovely view of Saumur and the Loire. The welcoming rooms are modern, well-equipped, spacious, and considerably more comfortable than in the past.

12/20 Les Délices du Château

Les Feuquières
02 41 67 65 60, fax 02 41 67 74 60
Closed Sun dinner, Dec. Open until 10:30pm. Priv rm 45. Terrace dining. Pkg.
Foremost among the *délices* of this particular château are appetizing, lively dishes like duck livers and pears under a fluffy potato blanket, squab stuffed with foie gras, and chocolate-raspberry millefeuille. Fine cellar; devoted ser-

vice. **C** 330. **M** 130 (lunch, exc Sun), 200 (wine incl), 175, 285.

 ## Loire Hôtel

Rue du Vieux-Pont
02 41 67 22 42, fax 02 41 67 88 80
Open year-round. 1 ste 530-670. 43 rms 270-560. Bkfst 48. Rms for disabled. Restaurant. Half-board 380-535. Rm ser. Air cond. Conf. Pkg.
Precisely opposite the château, on the île d'-Offard, the Loire Hôtel offers charming views of wild ducks on the river and large, blessedly peaceful rooms decorated in a fresh, dainty style.

 ## Les Ménestrels

11, rue Raspail - 02 41 67 71 10, fax 02 41 67 89 64
Closed Sun (exc lunch in seas). Open until 9:30pm. Priv rm 45. Terrace dining. Pkg.
The dining room's stone walls and beamed ceiling set a mood of rustic refinement, a mood mirrored in Lucien Vion's menu. He pairs costly and countrified ingredients in (mostly successful) dishes brimming with personality. The wine list presents an appealing selection of Loire Valley vintages. **C** 230-380. **M** 120 (weekday lunch) 160, 340, 65 (children).

TAVERS 45190
Paris 150 - Blois 31 - Orléans 25 Loiret

12/20 La Tonnellerie

12, rue des Eaux-Bleues
02 38 44 68 15, fax 02 38 44 10 01
Closed Jan-Feb. Open until 10pm. Terrace dining. Pool.
Tourists adore this pretty establishment with its soothing décor and summer terrace. The cooking has its ups and downs, though: on the downside, carelessly peeled asparagus tips and lobster presented in clumsy slices on salad greens "cooked" by a long soak in their vinaigrette. These lapses were (nearly) redeemed by a ginger-spiced pikeperch, very good blue-cheese feuilleté, and a wonderful banana Tatin with orange-flavored caramel. The service lacks polish. **C** 200. **M** 95 (lunch, exc Sun), 125, 230, 65 (children).

La Tonnellerie

(See restaurant above)
Closed Jan-Feb. 3 stes 840-1,825. 17 rms 350-1,095. Bkfst 55. Rm ser. Half-board 505-730 (oblig in seas). Conf. Pool.
Bright, fully renovated rooms and suites decorated with quiet good taste. Lovely swimming pool; hiking excursions and river cruises arranged.

*This **symbol** stands for "Les Lauriers du Terroir", an award given to chefs who prepare traditional or regional recipes.*

TOURS 37000
Paris 234 - Angers 105 - Orléans 113 Indre/Loire

 L'Alliance

292, av. de Grammont
02 47 28 00 80, fax 02 47 27 77 61
Open year-round. 5 stes 600-1,200. 119 rms 380-450. Bkfst 50. Restaurant. Rm ser. Conf. Pool. Tennis. Pkg.
A large hotel (vintage 1970) with a formal French garden built close (too close, we say) to the A-10 highway. The lobby is oddly ostentatious, the rooms are decorated in period style.

 Jean Bardet ✪

57, rue Groison
02 47 41 41 11, fax 02 47 51 68 72
Closed Apr-Oct: Mon lunch; Nov-Mar: Sun dinner, Mon. Open until 10pm. Priv rm 40. Pool. Valet pkg.
Jean Bardet is a real gardener, and he grows his own vegetables and herbs. He can coax delectable nuances from his better-than-prime ingredients, and we admire his fine-tuned taste and fine-honed technique. Bardet is an alchemist when it comes to sauces, like the jus that embellish his eels in aged wine vinegar or foie gras de canard au Maury; an artist who creates compositions of rare beauty, like the lobster civet perfumed with ginger, Vouvray wine, and a hint of lime. Oh, and his cellar! It's immense, with a wealth of rare bottles from all over France and some affordable Loire wines, too. C 600-900. M 420 (exc Sat dinner, wine incl), 300 (weekdays, Sat lunch, wine incl), 450 (Sun lunch, wine incl), 380-750, 150 (children).

 Jean Bardet ♣♥

(See restaurant above)
Open year-round. 5 stes 500-1,900. 16 rms 500-1,900. Bkfst 120. Rm ser. Air cond. Pool. Valet pkg.
This early-nineteenth-century villa, remodeled during the Second Empire, is surrounded by romantic, stream-fed grounds. The Bardets have taken infinite pains to restore and enlarge the premises—a beautifully refurbished greenhouse with a befrescoed ceiling is their most recent accomplishment. Just over the reception area and gift shop, several new suites and English-style guest rooms have been added. Several boast balconies and sumptuous marble baths (the latter hold all the accessories and complimentary toiletries one could wish). Fabulous breakfasts. Relais et Châteaux.

 Barrier

101, av. Tranchée
02 47 54 20 39, fax 02 47 41 80 95
Closed Sun dinner. Open until 9:30pm. Priv rm 30. Air cond. Garage kg.
Charles Barrier has sold his restaurant, but he lingers on like a persistent ghost. For the next year, he has veto rights over everything that goes on in his former establishment. The new chef, for example, is not allowed to take any of Barrier's signature dishes off the menu; so far, only two

new offerings have been added. We'll come back to rate the restaurant after Barrier is definitely out of the picture. Stay tuned! M 150 (weekdays), 230-560.

 Hôtel Harmonie ♣♥

15, rue Frédéric-Joliot-Curie
02 47 66 01 48, fax 02 47 61 66 38
Closed Dec mid-mid Jan. 6 stes 550-950. 48 rms 400-500. Bkfst 55. Rms for disabled. Conf. Pkg.
Music fills the air (even in the elevator!) at this pleasant hotel, located on a quiet street not far from the railway station. The modern rooms are beautifully appointed in a bright, Art Deco spirit. English bar.

 Holiday Inn

15, rue Édouard-Vaillant
02 47 31 12 12, fax 02 47 38 53 35
Open year-round. 2 stes 980. 103 rms 440-515. Bkfst 60. Rms for disabled. Restaurant. Half-board 410. Rm ser. Conf. Air cond. Pkg.
This futuristic, mirror-clad Holiday Inn provides air conditioned, soundproofed rooms furnished with wicker pieces.

 Mirabeau

89 bis, bd Heurteloup
02 47 05 24 60, fax 02 47 05 31 09
Open year-round. 25 rms 250-310. Bkfst 39. Garage pkg.
Conveniently close to the train station, the Mirabeau occupies a stately town house, whose attractive rooms are decorated with antique furniture. A terrace looks out on the pleasant garden.

 La Roche Le Roy

55, route de Saint-Avertin
02 47 27 22 00, fax 02 47 28 08 39
Closed Sat lunch, Sun dinner, Mon, Feb school hols, 3 wks in Aug. Open until 9:30pm. Priv rm 40. Terrace dining. Pkg.
Touraine's food lovers flock to this lovely Renaissance manor, so you must reserve in advance for a chance to sample Alain Couturier's polished, seasonal cuisine. The menu includes a lush combination of scallops and lobster in a butter sauce hinting of vanilla, John Dory with chanterelles enhanced by a meaty jus, roast breast of squab with bacon-flecked potatoes, and a delectable bitter-chocolate and raspberry tart. Distinguished cellar; service charmingly directed by Marilyn Couturier. C 300-400. M 160 (lunch), 200, 350.

 Rôtisserie Tourangelle

23, rue du Commerce
02 47 05 71 21, fax 02 47 61 60 76
Closed Sun dinner, Mon. Open until 10pm. Priv rm 60. Terrace dining. Pkg.
This airy eating house next to the town's archaeological museum is understandably popular: diners are warmly welcomed and nice-

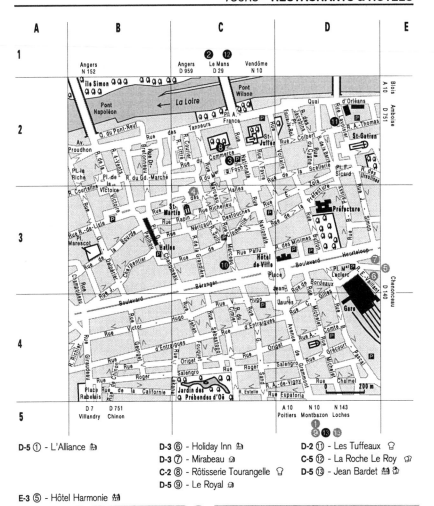

D-5 ① - L'Alliance 🏨

E-3 ⑤ - Hôtel Harmonie 🏨

D-3 ⑥ - Holiday Inn 🏨
D-3 ⑦ - Mirabeau 🍴
C-2 ⑧ - Rôtisserie Tourangelle ♀
D-5 ⑨ - Le Royal 🍴

D-2 ⑪ - Les Tuffeaux ♀
C-5 ⑫ - La Roche Le Roy ♀
D-5 ⑬ - Jean Bardet 🏨🍴

ly fed. True, there are occasional lapses, but on the whole there's nothing at all wrong with sea scallops in a delicate jus, tiny red mullets spiced with cardamom (we could have done without the pistachio garnish), and tender crêpes in a bright orange-flavored jus. Lots of fine Chinons in the cellar. An extra point this year. **C** 230. **M** 95 (weekdays, Sat lunch), 145, 195.

🏠 Le Royal-Clarine

65, av. de Grammont
02 47 64 71 78, fax 02 47 05 84 62
Open year-round. 50 rms 295-350. Bkfst 39. Rms for disabled. Conf. Garage pkg.
A hideous modern building conceals beautiful, well-equipped rooms, most with period furnishings. Private garage. Professional reception.

🏠 Les Tuffeaux

19, rue Lavoisier - 02 47 47 19 89
Closed Sun, Mon lunch. Open until 9:30pm. Air cond.
We needled chef Gildas Marsollier last year for what looked like lethargy in the kitchen. Well, he's back on track again, we're pleased to say, cooking up the creative likes of pigeon on a bed of Belgian endive with a suave walnut sauce, veal kidney with a radish gratin, and a lush pear

stuffed with caramelized nuts. Perfectly decent cellar. C 230. M 110 (weekdays, Sat lunch), 130 (weekdays, Sat lunch, wine incl), 150 (wine incl), 200, 50 (children).

And also...

Our selection of places for inexpensive, quick, or late-night meals.
Le Singe Vert (02 47 20 02 76 - 65, rue Marceau. Closed Sun off-seas. Open until 12:30am.): Traditional Touraine specialties are featured at this old-fashioned bistro, run by a likable chap who's fond of accordion music (*musette* evenings are held here twice a month) (68-260).
Zafferano (02 47 38 90 77 - 47, rue du Grand-Marché. Closed Sun, Mon, at Christams. Open until 10:30pm.): Genuine Italian food and wine in Tours's historic center (95-150).

VENDÔME	41100
Paris 170 - Tours 55 - Orléans 75 - Blois 32	Loir/Cher

🍽️ La Cloche Rouge

15, fg Chartrain - 02 54 77 02 88, fax 02 54 73 90 71
Closed Nov-Jan: Fri & Sun dinner. Open until 9:30pm. Priv rm 30. Pkg. HOTEL: "Le Vendôme," 35 rms 210-435. Bkfst 45. Half-board 260-380. Conf.
After visiting Vendôme's charming old town (don't miss the truly splendid church), relax in this posh, peach-toned dining room with the good-value 130 F menu: it brings warm pike terrine, steak with bone marrow à la bordelaise, a selection of cheeses, and a fine fruit tart. The local wines are affordably priced, too. C 225. M 75, 130, 190, 55 (children).

REGIONAL FOODS

Best known for its collection of royal and aristocratic châteaux, the Loire Valley also deserves its reputation as the Garden of France. So as you tour the châteaux, do take time to pause to take in the region's many and varied gastronomic glories: charcuterie (rillettes, rillons, terrines...), cheeses, distinctive candies and cookies, and wines (see Wine, below).

• BAKERIES

ANGERS	49100 – Maine/Loire

La Maison du Pain

4, pl. de la Visitation - 02 41 87 53 11

Breads based on a natural sourdough sponge. Don't miss the delicious whole-grain bread (pain aux céréales) and the splendid round country loaves. Good brioches and buns, too.

BLOIS	41100 – Loir/Cher

Jean-Paul Marchau

147, bis av. du Maréchal Maunoury - 02 54 78 27 78
Very good bread and delicious, buttery buns and brioches.

Jacky Sailly

7, rue du Commerce - 02 54 78 07 41
Jacky Sailly, who trained with the famed Parisian baker Jean-Luc Poujauran, creates chewy, full-flavored loaves that bear comparison with those of the master. Exceptional whole-grain bread.

CONTRES	41700 – Loir/Cher

Dubois-Coquin

6, rue Bracieux - 02 54 79 53 90
Remarkable sourdough breads, with special mention for the whole-grain loaf (pain aux céréales) and the pain bûcheron. Do try the tasty potato galette, too.

• CHARCUTERIE

AMBOISE	37400 – Indre/Loire

Michel Budts

26, pl. du Général-Leclerc - 02 47 57 23 71
Top-notch rillettes (minced pork spread), made with quality meat and expert seasoning.

ANGERS	49100 – Maine/Loire

Noël Amiot

13, rue Saint-Lazare - 02 41 73 89 83
Stop by this charcuteries for rich, delectable rillettes and excellent pâté en croûte.

CHÂTILLON-SUR-LOIRE	45360 – Loiret

Coilbeau

23, Grande-Rue - 02 38 31 45 52
Excellent charcuteries of all types, but andouillettes (AAAAA) are the house specialty.

CONNERE	72160 – Sarthe

Jean-Louis Guéret

27, rue de Paris - 02 43 89 01 05
This expert charcutier has won prizes for his rillettes (minced pork spread), but he also serves up delicious chunks of belly bacon (rillons), juicy

roast pork, and an authentic andouille (chitterling sausage).

CONTRES 41700 – Loir/Cher

Gilles Gasnier

1, rue Julien Nadau - 02 54 79 51 60
Come here for tender, tasty rillettes and rillons, as well as full-flavored andouillettes (tripe sausages).

JARGEAU 45150 – Loiret

Charcuterie Martroy

14, pl. du Martroy - 02 38 59 71 48
Come here for the andouillette de Jargeau, tasty rillons (chunks of pork belly, a local specialty), and other appetizing charcuteries.

LOCHES 37600 – Indre/Loire

Gendrot

5, pl. du Blé - 02 47 59 00 67
Rillettes (minced pork spread) that boast outstanding texture and flavor.

TOURS 37000 – Indre/Loire

Yves Lebeau

34, rue des Halles - 02 47 05 66 97
Lebeau's rillettes are not minced too fine: their chunky texture is wonderfully appetizing! A very good charcuterie.

VILLEBAROU 41000 – Loir/Cher

Gillet

8, rue de la Poste - 02 54 78 25 13
Gillet's boudins blancs (white sausage made with veal or chicken and pork) are sold in Paris at Fauchon—now, that's a recommendation! The rest of his specialties are of equally high quality.

VOUVRAY 37210 – Indre/Loire

Hardouin

L'Étang Vignon - 02 47 40 40 40
The Hardouin brothers work hard to maintain their excellent reputation for rillettes, rillons, and andouillettes.

• *CHEESE*

CHEMILLE 49120 – Maine/Loire

Cabri d'Anjou

La Chaponnière - 02 41 30 60 15

The Socteleaus raise their own goats, and from the milk produce excellent fresh and matured cheeses: particularly recommended are the Chabis, Bûchettes, Crottins, and Sainte-Maures. Visitors may tour the dairy, if they like.

PONTLEVOY 41400 – Loir/Cher

Jean-Pierre et Martine Moreau

Ferme de Bellevue,
80, route de Montrichard - 02 54 32 50 39
All the best goat cheeses made in the region are on hand: Selles-sur-Cher, Sainte-Maure, Valençay, crottins...

ROMILLY-DU-PERCHE 41270 – Loire/Cher

Ferme de la Bretonnerie

02 54 80 65 14
The Pelletier family always extend a warm welcome to visitors who come to admire their goat farm and sample their fine chèvres. Among our favorites are the Petit Perche, the Pyramide, and the Crottin.

STE-MAURE-DE-TOURAINE 37800 – Indre/Loire

La Haute Piltière

N 10 - 02 47 65 65 03
You can tour the premises and sample the wares at this dairy, where prime Sainte-Maure goat cheeses are produced.

SANCERRE 18300 – Cher

Fromagerie Dubois-Boulay

Chavignol - 02 48 54 15 69
We can't decide which we like better, the creamy fresh goat cheeses sold here, or the more pungent, matured variety. Both are absolutely delicious!

SELLES-SUR-CHER 41130 – Loir/Cher

La Fromagerie

2, rue Docteur Massacré - 02 54 88 57 60
All the local chèvres are available here, in fresh or matured versions.

VILLANDRY 37510 – Indre/Loire

Béatrice de Montferrier

Domaine de la Giraudière - 02 47 50 08 60
Goat cheeses sold fresh, direct from the producer, or as ingredients in tasty prepared dishes.

• *CHOCOLATE & CANDY*

ANGERS
49100 – Maine/Loire

La Petite Marquise
22, rue des Lices - 02 41 87 43 01
Quernons d'Ardoise (nougatine coated with slate-blue chocolate) have become something of a specialty in Angers. Unusual and quite delicious.

Le Trianon
7, rue Lenepveu - 02 41 47 44 39
Elegant, unusual chocolates: try the Bouchon d'Anjou, the Plantagenêt, the Panaché d'Anjou...or opt for a rich and yummy gâteau.

BOURGES
18000 – Cher

La Maison des Forestines
3, pl. Cujas - 02 48 24 00 24
Candy fanciers come here for the justly famous Forestines de Bourges (crunchy pralines), but the other house specialties are worth tasting, too.

CHOLET
49300 – Maine/Loire

Serge Boisliveau
48, pl. Rouge - 02 41 62 20 31
Here you'll find a wonderful collection of chocolates: do sample the Cholon de Cholet, the Galet d'Or, and the Crottin de la Jument Verte (the latter would definitely lose something in the translation...).

LANGEAIS
37130 – Indre/Loire

Maison Rabelais
4, pl. Pierre-de-Brosse - 02 47 96 82 20
This chocolate maven is famed for his delectable Muscadins and Noisetons.

MANS (LE)
72000 – Sarthe

Chocolaterie Béline
5, pl. Saint-Nicolas - 02 43 28 00 43
The specialties here are (aptly enough) called Buggatises, Pavés du Vieux Mans, or Mancelles. But all of the goodies here are worth tasting, with special mention for the chocolate "rillettes."

MONTARGIS
45200 – Loiret

Au Duc de Praslin
Pl. Mirabeau - 02 38 98 63 55
Almond and hazelnut candies, including the famous pralines that are a Montargis specialty, are sold in this pretty sweet shop.

ORLÉANS
45000 – Loiret

Chocolaterie Royale
51, rue Royale - 02 38 53 93 43
No fewer than 90 varieties of chocolates, pralines, candied fruits, sugar-coated almonds, and scores of other treats: a truly royal array!

TOURS
37000 – Indre/Loire

La Chocolatière
6, rue de la Scellerie - 02 47 05 66 75
The star attractions here are ganache- and praline-filled chocolates, but the plump and tender stuffed prunes (a local specialty) are well worth tasting.

• *FRUITS & VEGETABLES*

BLOIS
41000 – Loir/Cher

Sastre
5, rue des Trois Clefs - 02 54 74 35 09
This is the best place in town for fresh fruit and vegetables: the selection is truly superb.

CONTRES
41700 – Loir/Cher

Gillet
5, av. des Platanes - 02 54 79 53 05
Top-quality fruits and vegetables in tins and jars; look for the outstanding Sologne.

LONGUÉ
49160 – Maine/Loire

Alain Guitton
Petit Chantenay - 02 41 52 16 11
Seasonal fruits and vegetables from a reliable producer.

SAINT-SYLVAIN-D'ANJOU
49480 – Maine/Loire

Gilbert Manseau
Vergers de Séné - 02 41 43 71 57
Ripe, fresh fruit sold direct by the grower.

We're always happy to hear about **your discoveries** and receive **your comments** on ours. Please feel free to write to us stating clearly what you liked or disliked. Be concise but convincing, and take the time to argue your point.

• *GOURMET SPECIALTIES*

Boar

AUTRECHE   37110 – Indre/Loire

Élevage de Sangliers Grand Veneur
Domaine de Beaumarchais - 02 47 56 22 30
  Take a tour of the farm, then browse in the shop for gourmet treats based on boar meat.

Buffalo

CHAUVIGNY-DU-PERCHE   41270 – Loir/CHer

Ferme de la Sirotière
J. et M.-C. Dufournier - 02 54 80 65 46
  A buffalo farm in the Loire Valley? Well, why not? Visitors may tour the "ranch," then stop for a bite of bison-based lunch, or purchase jars of buffalo terrine, rillettes, or civet (a winy stew) in the little shop on the premises.

Escargots

ST-ANTOINE-DU-ROCHER   37360 – Indre/Loire

Ferme du Plessis
02 47 56 62 74
  The little gastropods are raised, prepared, and served right on the premises.

Fish

CHAMPTOCEAUX   49270 – Maine/Loire

Le Fumoir
La Marionnière - 02 40 83 50 76
  Alain Deltombe harbors an irrepressible passion for fish. Depending on the season, he smokes locally caught Loire River salmon and eels, as well as farmed salmon from Norway, Scotland, and Ireland. When he's in the mood, he even cooks for visitors: Deltombe's **table d'hôte** is famed for its fine food and friendly ambience.

SAINT-DIÉ-SUR-LOIRE   41500 – Loir/Cher

La Bourriche aux Appétits
Chemin Creux de l'Ecuelle - 02 54 81 65 25
  Gilles Quesneau turns Loire River fish into delectable prepared dishes that you may pur-chase on the premises: we're fond of his cocktail spreads made from pikeperch, or crayfish, or salmon, as well as his crayfish terrine, eel stewed in wine, fish choucroute, and chicken confit with crayfish.

Foie Gras

LION D'ANGERS (LE)   49220 – Maine/Loire

Les Treilles Gourmandes
Route de Candé - 02 41 95 82 82
  Swing in here to stock up on fine foie gras and very good tinned specialties based on duck and pigeon.

Jams

CHAUVIGNY-DU-PERCHE   41270 – Loir/Cher

Les Diorières
02 54 80 35 80
  Franck Johanny sells traditional jams made the old-fashioned way, as well as a range of unusual flavors: caramel, cider, and wine among them. You'll also want to try the Joudry, a wonderfully mellow orange cake.

CHENU   72500 – Sarthe

La Ferme de la Métairie
La Métairie - 02 43 46 01 01
  The fruit that goes into these full-flavored jams and preserves (34 varieties) is guaranteed organically grown.

CHINON   37500 – Indre/Loire

Claude Fleurisson
18, quai Jeanne d'Arc - 02 47 93 99 82
  Irresistible wine jellies, made mostly with local vintages. They are wonderful on bread or in cooking, or as an unusual condiment for rillettes and other charcuteries.

SANCERRE   18300 – Cher

Maison Joseph Mellot
Route Ménétréol, Le Pavé - 02 48 54 21 50
  This well-known winery also proposes an extraordinary range of wine-based jams.

*Looking for a town or restaurant? A winery? A gastronomic specialty or a celebrated chef? Consult the **alphabetical index** to locate them quickly and easily.*

Pigeon

Mireille et Pierre David

Maumusson - 05 49 96 89 12
  Delicious home-prepared specialties (rillettes, terrine, confits...) based on farm-raised pigeon and squab.

Venison

Ferme de la Roussetière

J.-P. Odeau - 02 54 72 04 68
  After a tour of the farm, you can stop at the little boutique to purchase rillettes, terrines, or other prepared dishes featuring farm-raised venison.

Vinegar

Martin-Poulet

236, fbg Bannier - 02 38 88 78 49
  For hundreds of years, Orléans has been known for its premium vinegars. Here you'll find a wide selection of barrel-aged vinegars made from fine wines: Chinon, Bourgueil, Bordeaux, and Muscadet.

Walnut Oil

Huilerie du Berry

42, rue de Tours - 02 54 75 09 09
  Delicately flavored walnut oil for your vinaigrettes, as well as extra-fresh pinenuts and pistachios.

• *PASTRY & COOKIES*

Pâtisserie Bigot

Pl. du Château - 02 47 57 04 46
  By all means stop here to taste the raspberry Pavé Royal, but don't overlook the creamy almond paste and fine hand-dipped chocolates.

Au Goût des Saveurs

74, rue du Commerce - 02 54 78 20 73
  Éric Saguez is an award-winning chocolatier, whose cakes and candies are well worth a detour. You'll love his ethereal mousses and desserts.

Olivier Couléon

16, rue Montrésor - 02 47 43 40 25
  Incomparable macarons (almond cookies) made according to a recipe handed down by the monks in the neighboring monastery.

Au Petit Chasseur

3, rue Tlemcen - 02 38 67 01 62
  Jean-Claude Bouclet proposes a range of yummy candies and several creative specialties, such as his Giennois, Tronc Solognot, and Succès.

Les Musardises

38, rue de la République - 02 38 53 30 98
  Sweets with a sophisticated touch: we're partial to the raspberry Val de Loire, the Manjari (chocolate and hazelnut), and Plaisir (chocolate and pear). Fine hand-dipped chocolates, too.

Biscuiterie Artisanale

Michel Paupardin,
La Petite Billardière - 02 38 96 22 59
  Premium ingredients and traditional recipes produce scrumptious Croq'noisettes (hazelnut cookies), shortbread cookies, pound cakes Gingerbread.

Aux Délices de Sologne

Jean-Claude Léchaudé
84, rue Georges Clémenceau - 02 54 96 05 10
  Come here to taste the legendary Tarte Tatin on its home turf, but don't neglect the other exquisite sweets (the chocolate cakes are divine).

Poirault

31, rue Nationale - 02 47 66 99 99
  We stop here for the lovely Tarte Tatin and Pithiviers (puff pastry stuffed with almond

cream), as well as for such treats as Nougat de Tours, stuffed prunes (a local specialty), barley sugar, and yummy chocolates.

VENDÔME   41100 – Loir/Cher

Pierre Bouard

9, pl. Saint-Martin - 02 54 77 32 78
Here's an inventive and highly skilled candy man, who creates all manner of delectable pastries and petits fours.

VILLENY   41220 – Loir/Cher

Lionel Girard

02 54 98 34 07
Appetizing pastries and irresistible candies to bring back home: look for the almond-flavored Malice du Loup, a specialty of the house.

OFF THE BEATEN TRACK

• *MUSEUMS*

After you tour the châteaux, the churches, and the rest of the region's most famous sites, why not take time to explore some out-of-the-way museums that present the local crafts and customs? You'll discover a fascinating side of the Loire Valley and its age-old traditions.

BOURGUEIL   37140 – Indre/Loire

Musée de la Cave et du Vin

02 47 97 72 01
Learn about the traditions and lore of wine-making as you wander through cool cellars carved out of limestone.

BOYNES   45300 – Loiret

Musée du Safran

21, route de Pithiviers - 02 38 33 13 05
Once upon a time the Loiret region was one of the world's major centers for processing saffron. That tradition is beginning to flower again, as you'll discover when you visit this charming museum.

CHECY   45430 – Loiret

Musée de la Tonnelerie

8, pl. du Cloître - 02 38 86 93 93
If you're in the area, stop in and visit this cooperage museum, where an array of antique barrels and tools is on display.

CHINON   37500 – Indre/Loire

Musée Animé du Vin et de la Tonnelerie

12, rue Voltaire - 02 47 93 25 63
The exhibits in this wine and cooperage museum are animated by mechanical figures. Wine-tastings are offered here, too.

CHOLET   49300 – Maine/Loire

Musée du Textile

Route de Beaupréau - 02 41 75 25 40
Cholet, for the French, is synonymous with handkerchiefs. Here in the local textile museum, the town's industrial traditions are presented in a series of exhibits and demonstrations. Samples may be purchased in the gift shop.

MORMANT-SUR-VERNISSON   45700 – Loiret

Écomusée de l'Apiculture

N 7 - 02 38 89 39 95
Everything you ever wanted to know about bees and honey can be learned at this little museum. All manner of honey and beeswax products are presented for sale.

RAIRIES (LES)   49430 – Maine/Loire

La Maison de la Terre Cuite

Route de Fougeré - 02 41 76 33 12
Fashioning and firing clay are age-old activities hereabouts. These traditional crafts are amply documented in the local museum, where terracotta tiles and other objects are on display. In the town, visitors are invited to explore the clay quarry and brickyard.

RIVARENNES   371906 – Indre/Loire

Musée de la Poire Tapée

7, chemin Buronnière - 02 47 95 47 78
Now here's a find: a museum devoted to the local tradition of preserving pears by drying and flattening them with a curious wooden instrument. Don't miss it!

STE-MAURE-DE-TOURAINE 37800 – Indre/Loire

Musée de la Ville de Sainte-Maure

Pl. du Château - 02 47 65 66 20
Local crafts, folk art, and traditions are presented here, with an emphasis on raising goats and making the goat cheese for which Sainte-Maure is famous. Cheese is also offered for sale.

SAUMUR 49400 – Maine/Loire

Musée du Champignon

Route de Gennes,
Saint Hilaire-Saint Florent - 02 41 50 31 55
See how mushrooms sprout and grow along miles of underground tunnels: there are white mushrooms (champignons de Paris), oyster mushrooms, shiitakes, and more. A well-documented exhibit presents some 200 varieties of mushrooms.

VOUVRAY 37210 – Indre/Loire

Espace de la Vigne et du Vin

30, rue Victor-Hérault - 02 47 52 66 04
After examining an array of tolls and implements used to cultivate grapes and make wine, you can sample some of the local production.

• FAIENCE & PORCELAIN

FOECY 18500 – Cher

Philippe Deshoulières

39, rue Grandjean - 02 48 51 04 60
Smart shoppers visit this factory outlet for lovely tableware (china, crystal, silver...) at extremely attractive prices.

GIEN 45500 – Loiret

Faïencerie de Gien

78, pl. de la Victoire - 02 38 67 00 05
This charming museum, which dates from the turn of the century, houses a unique collection of Gien's world-famous blue faïence. There is a shop on the premises.

• ROSES

DOUE-LA-FONTAINE 49700 –Maine/Loire

La Rose en Fête

02 41 59 20 49

Roses are grown in abundance in this small town near Saumur. Early in July, a huge rose show is staged in the town's Gallo-Roman arena. Cave dwellings are another local curiosity worth visiting.

PITHIVIERS-LE-VIEIL 45300 – Loiret

Les Roses Anciennes d'André Eve

Morailles - 02 38 30 01 30
One of the most famous nurseries in France for old-fashioned roses. Tours may be arranged by appointment.

WINE

Château-hopping in the Loire Valley can be most pleasantly combined with visits to the region's wineries. Touraine and Anjou-Saumur are the major districts we cover here; they lie along the central portion of the Loire River, from Cheverny in the heart of château country, westward to Savennières in the environs of Angers.

A large palette of grape varieties is cultivated in the region, reflecting the diversity of terrains (clay, sand, limestone, gravel—you name it). Cabernet Franc for red wines, and Chenin Blanc for whites, are the Loire Valley's two most distinctive varieties, but Gamay, Cabernet Sauvignon, Pinot Noir, Pineau d'Aunis, and Cot are also employed for red wines, Sauvignon Blanc, Chardonnay, and Romorantin for whites, with Grolleau for good measure in rosés. Consequently, the Loire Valley produces just about every type of wine you could think of (yes, even sparkling red). Chenin Blanc alone can be vinified as a dry, off-dry, sparkling, or mellow dessert wine—it all depends on the weather.

Touraine has borne vines since Roman times, and in the Renaissance the comic genius, François Rabelais, lavished praise on the wines of his native region. Touraine's top red wines—Chinon, Bourgueil, and Saint-Nicolas-de-Bourgueil—share the characteristic violet and raspberry aromas of the Cabernet Franc grape, which each wine expresses differently, in response to specific soil and growing conditions. In Vouvray and Montlouis, Chenin Blanc grapes attain a nearly ideal balance of lusciousness and acidity when long, hot summers concentrate their sweetness. In cooler years, the same variety produces dry (indeed, rather sharp) or sparkling wines.

But it is in **Anjou** that the Chenin Blanc reaches its apotheosis, with the richly perfumed (and nearly immortal) late-harvested wines of Bonnezeaux, Coteaux du Layon, and Quarts-de-Chaume. At Savennières, the Chenin Blanc grape produces one of the world's greatest dry white wines. Lots of rosé is still produced in Anjou, though it is gradually falling from favor with the wine-drinking public. In Anjou and Saumur, reds based on (mostly) Cabernet Franc and (some) Cabernet Sauvignon have appetizing, fruity bouquets. Saumur-Champigny yields some of the area's most delicious red wines, which improve with a few years in the cellar.

• *TOURAINE*

BEAUMONT-EN-VÉRON   37420 – Indre/Loire

Domaine du Colombier

16, rue du Colombier
02 47 58 43 07, fax 02 47 58 93 99
Open Mon-Sat 8:30am-7pm.
At this estate just six kilometers outside of Chinon, taste the Assemblage Domaine (estate blend), ready to drink now and until the year 2000 (peony nose, raspberry finish—a delightful Chinon) and the cuvée made from older vines, a wine for long keeping. New this year: some white Chinon, from Chenin Blanc vines planted a few years back.

BOURGUEIL   37140 – Indre/Loire

Yannick Amirault

La Coudraye, route du Moulin-Bleu
02 47 97 78 07, fax 02 47 97 94 78
Open daily (exc Sun).
Bourgueil and Saint-Nicolas-de-Bourgueil, both born of the Cabernet Franc grape, have seductive berry bouquets and good tannic structure. Vines grown in sandy soil produce wines for early drinking, while those from the higher slopes yield wine for longer keeping. Amirault's cuvée Les Graviers of Saint-Nicolas-de-Bourgueil is worthy of note, as is his Bourgueil from old vines, with a distinctive cherry nose.

CHENONCEAUX   37150 – Indre/Loire

Château de Chenonceau

Domaine de Chenonceau
02 47 23 90 07, fax 02 47 23 89 91
Open daily 11am-6pm.
It is said that Chenin vines were first planted here in the fifteenth century. Today, the château benefits from the most modern equipment. Try the dry white Touraine called Les Dômes de Chenonceau—rich and robust, it's quite a mouthful!

COUR-CHEVERNY   41700 – Loir/Cher

Domaine des Huards

Marcel Gendrier, Les Huards
02 54 79 97 90, fax 02 54 79 26 82
Open Mon-Sat 8am-12:30pm & 2pm-7pm (Sun by appt).
Cheverny, in the heart of château country, produces crisp, fruity wines in every color. This estate's white Cheverny AOC, a blend of Sauvignon and Chardonnay, is firm with a long finish; there's a nice, spicy red Cheverny, too. Don't miss the aromatic white Cour-Cheverny AOC made from the local Romorantin grape.

CRAVANT-LES-COTEAUX   37500 – Indre/Loire

Pierre Sourdais

Le Moulin à Tan - 02 47 93 31 13, fax 02 47 98 30 48
Open daily by appt.
The best Chinons, from vines grown on chalky plateaus, have surprising depth and can age for decades. When mature, Chinons have an incomparable bouquet of violets, blackcurrants, and a hint of spice. This estate offers Chinons for early drinking and others for long keeping (like the Réserve Stanislas Vieilles Vignes '93: a monster!). There are three furnished rentals (*gîtes*) on the property.

MONTLOUIS-SUR-LOIRE   37270 – Indre/Loire

Domaine de la Taille aux Loups

Husseau, 3, rue du Serpent-Volant
02 47 39 50 80, fax 02 47 38 45 60
Open daily 9am-7pm.
Less well known than Vouvray, Montlouis, on the opposite bank of the Loire, also produces a complete range of wines from the Chenin Blanc grape. Slightly sparkling Montlouis Pétillant, made in years when the weather is uncooperative, is a lovely apéritif. This estate produces excellent dry Montlouis and in warm, sunny years, glorious dessert wines (the fat, full '90 vintage is a treasure).

MAREUIL-SUR-CHER   41110 – Loir/Cher

Clos Roche Blanche

Catherine Roussel, Didier Barrouillet
02 54 75 17 03, fax 02 54 75 17 02
Open by appt only.
Organically grown vines. Very tasty Touraine Gamay, and a special cuvée of red Touraine that blends Gamay, Cabernet Franc, and Cot (a local grape).

The prices in this guide reflect what establishments were charging at press time.

ST-NICOLAS-DE-BOURGUEIL 37140 – Indre/Loire

André Delagouttière

Domaine des Bergeonnières
02 47 97 75 87, fax 02 47 97 48 47
Open daily (exc Sun pm).
A new tasting cellar is an inviting spot in which to sample the estate's red and rosé wines. The Saint-Nicolas-de-Bourgueil Cuvée Vieilles Vignes (made from older vines) is our favorite.

SOINGS-EN-SOLOGNE 41230 – Loir/Cher

Domaine de la Charmoise

Henry Marionnet - 02 54 98 70 73, fax 02 54 98 75 66
Open Mon-Fri 9am-noon & 1:30pm-5:30pm.
This well-known (and justly reputed) estate offers a complete range of Touraine AOC wines in red, white, and rosé. Do sample the fruity, floral Sauvignon de Touraine.

VOUVRAY 37210 – Indre/Loire

Noël Pinguet-Huet

Le Haut Lieu - 02 47 52 78 87, fax 02 47 52 66 51
Open daily 8:30am-noon & 2pm-6pm (exc Sun).
Top-quality Vouvrays in every style, from dry to sparkling to honey-sweet. Huet's deep, deep cellars harbor a stock of older vintages that collectors won't want to miss.

• *ANJOU-SAUMUR*

BLAISON-GOHIER 49320 – Maine/Loire

Château-de-Bois-Brinçon

Xavier Cailleau - 02 41 57 19 62, fax 02 41 57 10 46
Open Mon-Sat 8am-7pm (Sun by appt).
This ancient estate (it dates back to the thirteenth century) presents a lovely red Anjou from very old Cabernet Franc and Cabernet Sauvignon vines, and a gorgeously honeyed Coteaux du Layon Grains Nobles. Making late-harvested wines is an arduous, labor-intensive process: the grower must wait for the grapes to be attacked by noble rot (and not just the "vulgar" sort!), then the fruit is hand-picked, bunch by bunch (sometimes grape by grape). Low yields are the rule. So don't be surprised by the 100 F–plus price tags—a fine Coteaux du Layon is well worth the money.

PUY-NOTRE-DAME (LE) 49260 – Maine/Loire

La Paleine

9, rue de la Paleine - 02 41 52 21 24, fax 02 41 52 21 66
Open Mon-Sat 8am-7pm.
Joël Levi proposes a full range of Saumur wines: red, white, rosé, and sparkling. His pure Chenin Blanc white Saumur is rich and nutty; the sparkling Saumur Brut has plenty of character.

ST-LAMBERT-DU-LATTAY 49750 – Maine/Loire

Vincent Ogereau

44, rue de la Belle Angevine
02 41 78 30 53, fax 02 41 78 43 55
Open daily 9am-noon & 2pm-7pm (exc Sun).
Vincent and Catherine Ogereau do their utmost to produce personalized wines that express the essence of their superb vineyards. Among the offerings are a deliciously fruity red Anjou-Villages, a "plain" red Anjou for early drinking, and an elegant, silky sweet Coteaux du Layon Saint-Lambert.

ST-MELAINE-SUR-AUBANCE 49320 – Maine/Loire

Domaine de Haute Perche

Christian Papin, 9, chemin de la Godelière
02 41 57 75 65, fax 02 41 45 92 51
Open daily (exc Sun).
Papin's dry white Anjous get better with every vintage, but we also are partial to his sweet Coteaux de l'Aubance (the '94 displays an ideal balance of acidity, alcohol, and sugar).

SAVENNIÈRES 49170 – Maine/Loire

Nicolas Joly

Château de la Roche aux Moines
02 41 72 22 32, fax 02 41 72 28 68
Open daily (exc Sun & hols).
The best dry wine from Chenin Blanc grapes is made at Savennières: their bouquet is as richly aromatic as a sweet wine's but on the palate they are nutty with mineral notes and lively acidity. Nicolas Joly produces stupendous wines from Savennières's two great vineyards: Coulée-de-Serrant and Roche-aux-Moines.

SOUZAY-CHAMPIGNY 49400 – Maine/Loire

Chevallier

3, rue J.-Brevet - 02 41 51 14 04, fax 02 41 50 58 24
Open Mon-Sat 9am-noon & 2pm-6pm.
Hand-picked, hand-sorted grapes are vinified here into superb Saumur-Champigny, with deep color, firm tannins, and admirable richness. The Viei lles Vignes cuvée is destined for long keeping.

THOUARCÉ 49380 – Maine/Loire

Château de Fesles

02 41 54 14 32, fax 02 41 54 06 10
Open Mon-Sat 10am-noon & 2pm-6pm (& Sun in Jul-Aug-Sep).
Gaston Lenôtre, *pâtissier extraordinaire*, owns this venerable château. He's justly proud of his Bonnezeaux: the '88, '89, and '90 vintages of this succulent dessert wine are truly fabulous. Also available: sweet Coteaux du Layon and a dry Chardonnay Vin de Pays.

LORRAINE

Unsung
but unforgettable

Lorraine is the quiet type. A tranquil, industrious province, Lorraine doesn't clamor for attention the way its neighbors—turbulent Alsace, exuberant Burgundy—are inclined to do.

The *pax romana* brought prosperity to Lorraine's early Celtic population, for the Romans built towns and good roads. The Franks brought Christianity and the first abbeys and churches, some of which survive to this day. The episcopal cities of Metz, Toul, and Verdun, important crossroads in Carolingian Europe, evolved into the powerful Triple See. But over the centuries, the dukes of Lorraine were hard pressed to defend their territory from the dukes of Burgundy, the Holy Roman Empire, and the kings of France. By a quirk of European history, the exiled Polish king Stanislaw Leszczynski (who also happened to be the father-in-law of Louis XV) traded his claim to Tuscany to rule Lorraine in 1738. Under his vigorous influence, the province was industrialized (iron works, crystal and ceramics factories) and gloried in an artistic golden age. When Stanislaw died in 1766, Lorraine became subject to the French Crown until Germany snatched it away, along with Alsace, in 1870. And like Alsace, Lorraine returned to French sovereignty in 1919 after World War I. Hitler in turn annexed the province in 1940, but Lorraine, with Alsace, was restored to France by the Allied victory.

This rapid overview of Lorraine's history helps us discover and understand a province often neglected—underestimated!—by travelers to France. Religious tolerance is an age-old tradition here; so much so that in the Reform era Luther's message was favorably received. The arts flourished in Lorraine's liberal climate, architecture in particular. Romanesque and Gothic churches spring up in odd places: a magnificent basilica in tiny **Saint Nicolas-de-Port**, or a Rhenish-style cathedral in **Saint-Dié**. Metz claims Saint-Pierre-aux-Nonnains, the oldest (fourth century) church in France, and the towering cathedral of Saint-Étienne, with its inspiring, jewel-like stained glass (notice the *King David Window* by Chagall). Amid the ancient dwellings of **Bar-le-Duc** stands the Gothic church of Saint-Étienne, known for its macabre statue

of the *Décharné* (skeleton) by sculptor Ligier Richier.

A land of patriots from Joan of Arc to de Gaulle

Ever-embattled Lorraine naturally bristles with military architecture. The medieval fortress at **Bitche** in the Moselle, and the citadel at **Montmédy**, north of Verdun, begun by Charles V in the 1400s, were both transformed in the seventeenth century by Vauban, a brilliant engineer and marshal of France also responsible for the fortified gates at **Phalsbourg** and **Longwy**. In this century the **Maginot line** was conceived to prevent German armies from penetrating France, with an incredible—and, as it happened, utterly useless—system of underground fortifications at **Bitche** (Simserhof Fort), **Longuyon** (Fort Fermont), and **Veckring** (Fort Hackenberg). This architectural inventory would be incomplete without a word for the magnificent châteaux and opulent dwellings at **Haroué, Fléville**, and **Commercy**, and for **Lunéville**, which Voltaire called "the Versailles of Lorraine." Place Stanislas in **Nancy** is an exquisite eighteenth-century ensemble; the city also possesses fine Renaissance and Baroque mansions, and Art Nouveau town houses designed by the artists of the École de Nancy.

Though Lorraine is hospitable, open to new ideas and commerce, it is also fiercely patriotic. Joan of Arc, who spurred King Charles VII to expel the English from France, was born at **Domrémy-la-Pucelle**. The Cross of Lorraine, borrowed from medieval crusaders, rallied the French who, with de Gaulle, resisted the Nazi occupation. And **Verdun** crystallized France's defiance of Germany in the Great War, though it cost 600,000 men dead or wounded. Lorrainers honor the memory of these sacrifices at the World Center for Peace in Verdun, at the battlefields of **Vaux** and **Douaumont**, at the German cemetery of **Andilly**, the American cemetery at **Dinozé**, the Pershing memorial on **Montsec**. With its 10,489 graves **Saint-Avold** is the largest American cemetery in Europe.

For all its battle scars, Lorraine is the most densely wooded area in France, and it sparkles with rivers and fish-filled lakes. Water's purifying virtues have been celebrated here since Celtic and Roman times. Locals even brag that the custom of "taking the waters" began in Lorraine. However that may be, curists flock to the spa-resorts of **Vittel**, **Contrexéville**, **Plombières**, and **Bains-les-Bains** to gulp lungfuls of mountain air and drink from crystalline springs.

Lorraine's iron-ore deposits were the basis of its once-mighty steel industry. In its heyday the foundry at **Pompey** produced the 7,300 metric tons of steel that built the Eiffel Tower! Lorraine's industrial base also covers timber from the Vosges, paper mills, breweries, and tires. Though it is no longer an industrial powerhouse, Lorraine's location in the heart of Europe has attracted high-tech manufacturers from America, Sweden, and Japan. Next to iron, crystal is Lorraine's most famous export. Crystal and fine glass have been produced in the towns of **Baccarat** and **Saint Louis** since the third century. At their apogee in the eighteenth century, Lorraine's *cristalliers* (who had learned the secrets of their Italian and Bohemian rivals) supplied all the royal and imperial courts of the world. Today Baccarat produces 40 percent of French crystal; the town's Crystal Museum is a must-see. The glassworks of **Saint-Louis-lès-Bitche**, the oldest in Lorraine, offers guided tours. In Nancy, Daum's art glass can be seen at the Fine Arts museum as well in the firm's workshops on Rue des Cristalleries.

A tradition of art and craftsmanship

Lorraine's inhabitants are taciturn, known for their reserve (an effect of the inclement climate, perhaps?), yet the province has a deep-rooted tradition of fostering the arts. The painter Georges de La Tour, master of chiaroscuro, is perhaps the region's most renowned artist (see his paintings in the art museum of Épinal), along with Claude Gellée, better known as Claude Le Lorrain, and the sculptor Ligier Richier whose affecting works grace churches in **Saint-Mihiel**, **Bar-le-Duc**, and **Briey**. Connoisseurs and collectors of Art Nouveau should know that the movement was born in Nancy, with Émile Gallé. Rallying other brilliant artists and craftsmen, he launched the École de Nancy, which included the Daum brothers, Louis Majorelle, Jacques Grubert, the sculptor Victor Prouvé, and cabinetmakers Eugène and Auguste Vallin. Lorraine's ceramics industry, based in **Lunéville**, **Longwy**, and **Sarreguemines** was strongly influenced by the

sinuous forms and floral motifs of Art Nouveau.

Beyond quiche lorraine

It is said that the great Stanislaw Leszczynski, Count of Lorraine, was so fond of the table that he employed a staff of 30 just to prepare and serve his meals. He is credited with inventing the baba au rhum, and introduced Commercy's buttery madeleines into royal circles. Today Lorraine's restaurateurs regale guests with local specialties that go beyond the well-known quiche lorraine to include matelotes made with fish from river and lake, trout pâté, and potée lorraine brimming with hearty cuts of smoked pork. The cheese course might include a nutty Brie made with milk from Lorraine's dairy herds; and dessert will surely include a tart garnished with the region's bounty of cherries, damsons, blueberries, or mirabelles (which are also distilled into the clear fruit brandies that bring meals in these parts to a close).

Unsung Lorraine, as you can see, has many surprises in store. Here's one more: while it wasn't a Lorrainer who discovered America, it was a native of Saint-Dié who printed the first work that called the New World by that name: America. The rest, as they say, is history.

RESTAURANTS & HOTELS

FLAVIGNY-SUR-MOSELLE   54630
Paris 321 - Nancy 16 - Lunéville 36   Meurthe/M.

 Le Prieuré

3, rue du Prieuré - 03 83 26 70 45, fax 03 83 26 75 51
Closed Sun dinner, Wed, Aug 25-Sep 10. Open until 9:45pm. Priv rm 50. Garden dining. No pets. Valet pkg.
    The façade may be modest, but the four dining rooms inside—decorated with exposed beams, fireplaces, tile floors, beautiful furniture, and pewter accents—exude charm and comfort. And the picturesque garden behind the house is as pretty as they come. It's no wonder then that a host of regional regulars gather here to enjoy the restful atmosphere and chef Joël Roy's seafood cuisine, frequently inspired by Mediterranean recipes. The cellar is well-stocked with Bordeaux and Burgundies. A friendly welcome awaits guests from the owner's wife. C 350-510. M 200 (weekday lunch), 300 (weekday lunch, wine incl), 420.

Le Prieuré

(See restaurant above)
See restaurant for closings. 4 rms 600. Bkfst 55. No pets. Valet pkg.
This little yellow house features spacious rooms deliciously done up in modern style and a pastel palette. All have luxurious bathrooms, are perfectly equipped, and open out onto a quiet garden. Wonderful breakfasts.

GÉRARDMER   88400
Paris 421 - Colmar 52 - Épinal 40 - Saint-Dié 30   Vosges

 Les Bas Rupts et Chalet Fleuri

3 km on D 486 - 03 29 63 09 25, fax 03 29 63 00 40
Open daily until 9:30pm. Garden dining. Heated pool. Tennis. Pkg.
In his pretty, flower-bedecked chalet, Michel Philippe offers expertly cooked traditional fare made from the best ingredients money can buy—and which can be sampled in half-portions at half the price! The confit of rabbit with Puy lentils was incredibly tender, but there was a tad too much garlic in the sorrel-infused snails. Delicious roasted sea scallops served with nicely seasoned greens. Excellent tripe (although the flavor of the Riesling should be more pronounced). Wonderful Munsters. Delicious chocolate cake served with tangy mango sherbet. The impressive cellar features the best of Alsace at unbeatable prices, and a number of half-bottle offerings. Marvellous 160 F set-price menu and perfect reception. This is the best—not to mention the prettiest!—restaurant in the upper Vosges. C 250-320. M 160 (exc Sat dinner & Sun lunch), 200, 250, 320, 400, 100 (children).

 Les Bas Rupts et Chalet Fleuri

(See restaurant above)
Open year-round. 1 stes 900. 30 rms 380-800. Bkfst 80. Half-board 550-750 (oblig in seas). Rm ser. Conf. Heated pool. Tennis. Pkg.
Two flower-covered chalets connected by a covered passageway. Perfectly delightful rooms decorated in the height of taste and giving onto either the swimming pool or the restaurant. Magnificent breakfast buffet. Quiet, swear on your mother's back.

METZ   57000
Paris 313 - Nancy 59 - Strasbourg 157   Moselle

12/20 Le Bistrot des Sommeliers

10, rue Pasteur - 03 87 63 40 20, fax 03 87 63 54 46
Closed Sun. Open until midnight. Terrace dining. Air cond.
Wine-inspired decoration in this recently opened wine bar: choice bottles on display as well as informative books on wine. Wide choice of wine either by the bottle or by the glass. Excellent cod with herb butter, country-style beef jaw stew with homemade pasta. Hip décor, fresh and modern in its approach; the future looks good. C 120-165.

 La Dinanderie

2, rue de Paris - 03 87 30 14 40, fax 03 87 32 44 23
Closed Sun, Mon, 3 wks in Aug. Open until 10:30pm. Air cond. Pkg.
Claude Piergiorgi's strength lies in the high regard he holds for his ingredients. In their slightly eccentric house close to the banks of the Moselle his charming wife oversees the plush dining room, where the dishes her husband takes such joy in preparing are expediently served. From the wonderful warm langoustines through to the classic but very tasty pear aumônière—by way of a remarkable roasted salmon with bacon and turnip cream sauce—this place is a "must." Nice wine list. C 320-420. M 160, 240.

 Le Royal Bleu Marine

23, av. Foch - 03 87 66 81 11, fax 03 87 56 13 16
Open year-round. 6 stes 900. 61 rms 350-480. Restaurant. Rm ser. Conf. Pkg.
Located just five minutes from the train station, this attractive, comfortable turn-of-the-century establishment offers rooms done up in old-fashioned and contemporary styles. Twenty of the rooms have just been renovated. Sauna and fitness facilities on the premises.

MONTHAIRONS (LES)   55320
Paris 277 - Bar-le-Duc 51 - Verdun 19   Meuse

 Château des Monthairons

03 29 87 78 55, fax 03 29 87 73 49
Closed Sun dinner off-seas, Mon & Tue lunch, Jan 2-Feb 10. Open until 10pm. Garden dining. Garage pkg.
This elegant château, which was rebuilt during the last century along the lines of Azay-le-Rideau, is home to a restaurant with a tastefully decorated dining room opening out onto a wonderful park bordering the Meuse. Despite occasional misfires, Benoît Thouvenin displays great prowess in his use of regional ingredients and vegetables and herbs from his own garden. The resulting dishes display great character. Admirable wine list, and an excellent welcome from the ladies of the manor. Smokers beware: there's a distinct preference that such activities be carried out in the drawing room. C 350-400. M 120 (weekday lunch, Sat), 165 (exc Sat dinner & Sun lunch), 250-395.

 Château des Monthairons

(See restaurant above)
Closed Sun off-seas, Mon, Jan 2-Feb 10. 6 stes 900-1,200. 14 rms 400-890. Bkfst 60. Rms for disabled.

Half-board 450-650 (oblig in seas). Conf. Garage pkg.
The roomy guest quarters here are a bit on the austere side but exceedingly well equipped, and offer a wonderful view of the park (horseback riding, hunting) and the Meuse (private beach, canoeing, private fishing). Very nice bathrooms.

NANCY	54000
Paris 307 - Metz 57 - Épinal 69 - Dijon 201	Meurthe/M.

12/20 Comptoir du Petit Gastrolâtre

1, pl. de Vaudémont
03 83 35 51 94, fax 03 83 32 96 79
Closed Sun, Mon, 1 wk in May, Aug 15-30, 1 wk at Chritmas. Open until 10:30pm. Terrace dining. Pkg.
This is the best address ever for lively late-night dining in Nancy. The bistro atmosphere is charming, the cellar is well put together (though a tad limited), and the hearty cooking makes the most of tradition. We tasted a tantalizing charlotte à la mirabelle, but alas, our perch came with burned garlic. Just a hint more precision, and it will be time for a toque. C 250. M 85 (lunch), 175, 190.

 ## Le Stanislas

2, pl. Stanislas - 03 83 35 03 01, fax 03 83 32 86 04
Open daily until 10pm. Priv rm 72. Terrace dining. Valet pkg.
This mansion, built in 1755 on the famous Place Stanislas, is home to a restaurant fairly swimming in elegant, Louis XV décor. It comes as no surprise then that this is one of the most sumptuous places to dine in Nancy, nor that Michel Douville's repertoire can't stray too far from the set tone. Still, his very genuine talents shine through in great classics and tempting regional dishes alike. Elaborate cellar full of Bordeaux. Highly competent welcome and service. C 400. M 235 (weekday lunch, Sat, wine incl), 180 (weekday lunch, Sat), 240, 290, 80 (children).

 ## Grand Hôtel de la Reine

(See restaurant above)
Open year-round. 8 stes 1,200-2,000. 40 rms 600-840. Bkfst 50-80. Rms for disabled. Half-board 560-620. Conf. Valet pkg.
Emmanuel Héré, architect to Stanislas I, designed the magnificent staircase in this house. The very pretty Louis XV–style rooms are bright and well equipped, and some overlook the place. A full range of services (secretarial, babysitting, etc.) is available to guests.

RÉHAINVILLER	54300
Paris 343 - Lunéville 5 - Nancy 38	Meurthe/M.

 ## Château d'Adoménil

03 83 74 04 81, fax 03 83 74 21 78
Closed Nov-Apr 15: Sun dinner, Mon, Tue lunch; Apr 16-Oct: lunch Mon & Tue. Open until 9:30pm. Priv rm 35. Terrace dining. Air cond. Pkg.
There's lots of space between the tables in the pretty dining rooms at this idyllic château, set amid the greenery. And the atmosphere is just right for tucking into Michel Million's refined cuisine, which offers some subtle, strikingly original flavor combinations—red mullets with eggplant, lobster spiked with vanilla, fillet of John Dory with rhubarb (wonderful!)— alongside his great classics. For dessert, try the tempting assiette Lorraine, which plays on mirabelle plums (the region's all-star fruit) in a variety of forms. Large cellar somewhat lacking discrimination but with a nice selection of half-bottles. C 480. M 245 (weekdays, Sat lunch), 355-460, 100 (children).

 ## Château d'Adoménil

(See restaurant above)
Closed Sun & Mon off-seas. 1 ste 1,200. 10 rms 620-1,050. Bkfst 70. Half-board 925-1,475 (oblig). Conf. Pool. Pkg.
Apart from the helicopter pad, there's not much to brag about at this château: there's nary a golf course on the vast (and we do mean vast!) estate, nor a tennis court...but they've just added a heated swimming pool. A restful break with routine for sure—in a series of spacious, tastefully appointed rooms. More distinction than luxury. Relais et Châteaux.

STIRING-WENDEL	57350
Paris 391 - Metz 59 - Forbach 4	Moselle

La Bonne Auberge

15, rue Nationale - 03 87 87 52 78, fax 03 87 87 18 19
Closed Sat lunch, Sun dinner & Mon (exc hols). Open until 10:15pm. Priv rm 14. Terrace dining. Air cond. Garage pkg.
This restaurant is an old-style *auberge* in name only given that the owner Egloff sisters have opted for light, modern surroundings (complemented by a nice patio) over quaint exposed beams and fireplaces. Chef Lydia has developed a cooking style of her own, sidestepping local stereotypes. Mirabelle plums, yes, but in a chutney that goes with the stuffed rabbit. A little beer, but used in a clever, sweet dessert sauce. A Jerusalem artichoke here and there, but in a spicy crust—a marvelous match for goose liver. Hostess Isabelle presides over the efficient staff and well-chosen, well-balanced cellar. The set-price menus are obviously given special consideration, and cost the same as they did last year. C 400-450. M 170 & 240 (weekday lunch), 265 (exc weekday lunch), 410, 95 (children).

🍴 Le Dauphin

Route de Villey-St-Étienne
03 83 43 13 46, fax 03 83 64 37 01
*Closed Sun dinner, Mon. Open until 10:30pm. Priv
40. Garden dining. Pkg.*
At a time when so many three-toque establishments feel compelled to take on *Grand Siècle* airs, this restaurant's somewhat austere environment and décor (it is set in an industrial park in what used to be an American officers' mess) and efficient, low-profile service are refreshing indeed. It's a pity some people think fine cuisine is best sampled in flashy surroundings, because they're missing out on a memorable gastronomic experience here, especially since Christophe Vohmann's 189 F menu is an unbeatable value. The morels that come with the monkfish are alone worth the trip: their intense flavor is sure to send gourmets straight to seventh heaven! The incredibly tender milk-fed veal is flecked with grated truffle, resounding proof that a little bit of strong flavor goes a long way. For dessert, be sure to indulge in the crispfritters filled with a rich, lime-flavored cream. This is cooking with a style all its own, and the ingredients used are the finest money can buy. Connoisseur's cellar, with a good choice of half-bottles. C 400-500. M 189-360, 80 (children).

VERDUN 55100
Paris 265 - Metz 78 - Châlons-sur-Marne 88   Meuse

⛪ Le Coq Hardi

8, av. de la Victoire
03 29 86 36 36, fax 03 29 86 09 21
Open year-round. 3 stes 700-1,200. 32 rms 360-750. Bkfst 70. Rms for disabled. Restaurant. Half-board 550. Conf. Garage pkg.
This large half-timbered house, typical of the local architectural style, features regularly renovated rooms and gleaming bathrooms.

REGIONAL FOODS

Lorraine boasts a wide array of charcuterie: sausages, boudins, andouillettes, and some very worthy pastries, such as babas au rhum, macarons de Nancy, and madeleines de Commercy.

• CHOCOLATE & CANDY

NANCY 54000 – Meurthe/M.

Lalonde

59, rue Saint-Dizier - 03 83 35 31 57
Founded in 1850, Lalonde continues to delight Nancy's gourmets with divine chocolates and such evocative sweets as Craquelines, Duchesses de Lorraine, and many more.

• GOURMET SPECIALTIES

Brandies

BULLIGNY 54113 – Meurthe/M.

Maison Becker

54, rue Saint-Vincent - 03 83 62 50 08
Becker's Mirabelle de Lorraine, a clear brandy made with the region's tiny yellow plums, is a model of its kind. Aged for six years in oak casks it explodes with fruit flavors and aromas.

Jams

BAR-LE-DUC 55000 – Meuse

Confitures Dutriez

35, rue de l'Étoile - 03 29 79 06 81
A goose quill is used to deseed the red currants used in this vivid, sweet-tart jam, one of the most famous preserves in the world. A treat to be sampled at least once in a lifetime.

• PASTRY & COOKIES

COMMERCY 55200 – Meuse

A La Cloche Lorraine

8, pl. du Général-de-Gaulle - 03 29 91 02 53
Proustians will want to make a pilgrimage to Commercy, to taste the tiny tea cake that their idol described in *A la recherche du temps perdu* as "a little shell-shaped butter cake, so richly sensual beneath its severe, pleated surface."

NANCY 54000 – Meurthe/M.

Maison des Sœurs Macarons

21, rue Gambetta - 03 83 32 24 25

The house recipe for macarons (tender, puffy almond cookies) dates from the Revolution and still boasts innumerable enthusiastic fans.

WINE

Worth seeking out in this frontier region are the refreshing white or "gris" Vins de Pays de la Meuse, and lively, aromatic white wines of the Côtes de Toul (vinified from Pinot Auxerrois grapes). A "gris" or slightly pink version is also produced, from Gamay grapes. In red, some Pinot Noir is available too.

BRULEY   54200 – Meurthe/M.

Domaine Laroppe

253, rue de la République
03 83 43 11 04, fax 03 83 43 36 92
Open Mon-Sat 8am-6pm (Sun 3pm-7pm).
 A range of well-made, inexpensive wines with regional character.

MONT-LE-VIGNOBLE   54113 – Meurthe/M.

Vignerons du Toulois

43, pl. de la Mairie - 03 83 62 59 93
Open Tue-Sun 2pm-6pm.
 An energetic team of devoted wine makers; reliably tasty wines.

THE LYONNAIS

Bring
on the Beaujolais!

The Lyonnais, naturally enough, fans out from the sprawling, riverrun city of Lyon. To the north, it begins just beyond Mâcon, where the steep, hillside vineyards of Saint-Véran and Pouilly-Fuissé give way to **Beaujolais** country. As Gabriel Chevalier, author of the rollicking classic *Clochemerle*, wrote "The more of it (Beaujolais) you drink, the more delightful you find your wife, the more loyal your friends, the rosier your future, and the more bearable mankind." Though they lie outside its modern-day borders, the **Bresse** and **Dombes** regions, east of the Saône, are historically attached to Burgundy. Bresse owes its fame to the succulent blue-footed chickens, fattened on milk and corn, which eighteenth-century gastronome Brillat-Savarin hailed as "the Queen of poultry, and the poultry of Kings." Other reasons to make a detour into Bresse are the fortified medieval village of **Pérouges**, with its cobblestones and half-timbered dwellings, and the elegant town of **Bourg-en-Bresse**, site of the Flamboyant Gothic church and monastery of Brou. Besides, Georges Blanc's four-toque establishment is just a few kilometers distant, at **Vonnas**. Nature-lovers, meanwhile, flock to **La Dombes**, a marshy land of a thousand lakes and ponds, to observe the habits of waterfowl and other migrators at the bird sanctuary of **Villars-les-Dombes**. The gourmets among them then alight at **Mionnay** for a fine meal at the Restaurant Alain Chapel.

Lyon:
a gastronomic capital

At the confluence of the Saône and Rhône rivers lies **Lyon**, France's second largest city. Called *Lugdunum* by the Romans who founded it in 43 BC on the Fourvière Hill, Lyon was once the capital of Gaul. Successive Barbarian invasions sent the city into a long decline, but Lyon ultimately arose from its ashes. In the fifteenth century, refugees from Italy's civil wars introduced the silk industry to the city. Florentine merchant bankers followed in their wake, making Renaissance Lyon a major commercial and artistic center, more prosperous and populous than Paris. The silk weavers are long gone, but the Musée

des Tissus (fabric museum), on Rue de la Charité, displays fabulous samples of their art. From the top of the Fourvière hill, one can take in the city at a glance: the panorama reaches as far as the beautiful Tête d'Or park. After a look at the Roman ruins, a visitor might descend into old Lyon to explore the Saint-Jean and Saint-Paul districts, and wander through the narrow, winding passages called *traboules*, a Lyon trademark. Embraced by the Rhône and the Saône, the Presqu'île ("Peninsula") is home to the city's museums, antique dealers (between Place Bellecour and Place Carnot), and a host of restaurants.

Lyon takes pride in its culinary traditions. Its claim to be the gastronomic capital of France may be overstated, but in Lyon food is certainly a serious matter! Although Lyon harbors its share of legendary restaurants, from Bocuse to Léon de Lyon, La Tour Rose, and the Mère Brazier, the best place to savor the hearty local fare is in a *bouchon* like La Meunière on Rue Neuve. Why look for complications when simple things—rosette sausage, tender fish quenelles, garlicky herbed cream cheese, jugs of fruity Beaujolais—are so delicious? *Bon appétit!*

RESTAURANTS & HOTELS

BAGNOLS　　　　　　　　　　　　　　　　69620
Paris 450 - Lyon 33 - Villefranche 12　　　　　Rhône

 ## Château
de Bagnols

04 74 71 40 00, fax 04 74 71 40 49
Closed end Oct-mid Dec, Jan 2-mid Mar. Open until 9:30pm. Priv rm 20. Terrace dining. No pets. Garage pkg.
This château dates from the thirteenth century, and belonged to Charles VIII's advisor Geoffroy de Balzac, who made it one of the most picturesque châteaux in France. Luxury prevails in the carved Gothic fireplace, music room, etc., and in the plate as well. Chef Philippe Lechat

won't disappoint with you his vegetable terrine with pea-purée sauce, green-asparagus with vinaigrette and crab cake, Bresse chicken in lightly browned crust, and pot-roasted squab, all to be washed down with one of the first-rate Beaujolais from the region. The formula for success seems to have announced its arrival: his Sunday all-you-can-eat *table d'hôte* lets a hundred or so people feast in the large dining room of the château; needless to say, people love it. C 450. M 195, 280-440, 110 (children).

 ## Château de Bagnols

(See restaurant above)
Closed end Oct-mid Dec, Jan 2-mid Mar. 4 stes 4,000-5,000. 17 rms 2,200-5,000. Bkfst 120. Rms for disabled. Rm ser. Air cond. Conf. No pets. Garage pkg.
This is truly one of the Beaujolais's (and France's) jewels: no expense has been spared on its "historically correct" restoration, and its eye-dazzling sixteenth- and seventeenth-century frescoes and majestic guards' hall might well make you think you're in a museum! However, individually decorated guest quarters with canopied beds and elegant bathrooms await you when you're finished touring.

COLLONGES-AU-MONT-D'OR	**69660**
Paris 457 - Lyon 18 - Villefranche-sur-Saône 24	Rhône

 ## Paul Bocuse

50, quai de la Plage
04 72 42 90 90, fax 04 72 27 85 87
Open daily until 10pm. Air cond.
No matter what anyone says, because progress has its place in the culinary arts field and the number of good restaurants increases from year to year, this establishment has become one of the best among many. But how can we treat it like its peers? After all, we can't help but be influenced by its fascinating past, let alone the formidable media image of "Monsieur Paul." However, if we concentrate on cooking and ignore the ongoing battle between admirers and detractors, what surfaces is that Paul Bocuse is more a sanctuary for tradition than a launch pad for cutting-edge gastronomy. Scores of pilgrims are eager to sample sweet nostalgia in the establishment's posh, bourgeois dining room (replete with chandeliers, paintings, curios, and copper): fillet of sole with noodles; sea bass en croûte; squab in puff pastry with cabbage; volaille en vessie, and a host of other timeless dishes lovingly crafted by Bocuses's team of chefs. It behooves us to overlook the minor glitches in sauces and cooking we experienced, for they do not stay etched in diners' memories. The contagious good humor (another Bocuse specialty), upbeat interpretations of traditional fare, and wonderful staff at this baroque temple-on-the-Saône do. C 430-680. M 410 (weekdays lunch), 510 (dinner), 610, 710, 740.

Looking for a restaurant? Refer to the **index.**

LYON	**69000**
Paris 462 - Grenoble 106 - Valence 100	Rhône

Lyon's restaurants and hotels are classified by *arrondissement.*

1ST ARRONDISSEMENT

12/20 La Gousse d'Ail

20, rue du Sergent-Blandan - 04 78 30 40 44
Closed Jul 31-Aug 24. Open until 10:30pm. No pets. No cards.
Parking in the Terreaux district may not be easy, but this pleasant, beam-filled bistro is definitely worth the trouble for its genuine, imaginative fare. Nice little cellar. A friendly welcome—and friendly prices—await you. C 180-220. M 90, 110, 160.

Léon de Lyon

1, rue Pléney
04 78 28 11 33, fax 04 78 39 89 05
Closed Sun, Aug 10-18. Open until 10pm. Priv rm 18. Air cond. Valet pkg.
Following in the footsteps of his father, whose name stretches along the restaurant's stained-glass façade, Jean-Paul Lacombe continues to celebrate the great culinary traditions Lyon is famous for. After all, no one should ever forget that this vital cuisine turns the humblest ingredients into noble dishes, and makes conservative cooking seem cheerful and refreshingly unstuffy. Time-honored regional favorites like suckling pig terrine, savory veal served "from head to hoof," or even Bresse chicken are still young at heart here, and the less-than-local dishes are authentically interpreted: pan-roasted crayfish with thyme; lamb with garlic custard. This cuisine targets flavors and hits them on the mark, without a lot of fuss. The 280 F lunch menu is a real gem. Efficient service, and a full and focused cellar. Outstanding welcome from Fabienne Lacombe. Relais et Châteaux. C 450-600. M 280 (lunch), 490-650, 90 (children).

La Mère Brazier

12, rue Royale - 04 78 28 15 49, fax 04 78 28 63 63
Closed Sat lunch, Sun, Aug. Open until 10pm. Priv rm 16. Air cond. Pkg.
The hearty welcome Jacotte Brazier extends to her patrons is celebrated throughout Lyon, and her culinary talents have turned this Croix Rousse restaurant into a pilgrimage site for lovers of Lyonnais cuisine. They come here to delight in artichoke hearts stuffed with foie gras (which were not on the mark this year), Bresse chicken en demi-deuil, quenelles, and scrumptious chabraninoff (apples soaked in rum served with vanilla ice cream), all of which have been on the menu for time immemorial. One point less however; nostalgia is not enough to keep the flame lit eternally. Wash your meal down with the wonderful Beaujolais and Rhônes

on offer. And brace yourself for a hefty check. **C** 300-400. **M** 170 (lunch), 290-370.

And also...

Our selection of places for inexpensive, quick, or late-night meals.
Hugon (04 78 28 10 94 - "Le Bouchon Lyonnais," 12, rue Pizay. Open until 10pm.): Arlette Hugon rustles up salads, blanquette, chicken in vinegar, and the best chocolate cake there is in the back room of this homey spot (120-150).
Le Petit Léon (04 72 00 08 10 - 3, rue Pléney. Open lunch only until 2pm): This small bistro next to Léon de Lyon serves up Lyonnais cuisine and family-style fare (95).

2ND ARRONDISSEMENT

 Assiette et Marée

49, rue de la Bourse
04 78 37 36 58, fax 04 78 37 98 52
Closed Sun. Open until 11pm. Terrace dining. Air cond. Pkg.
The blackboard lists five appetizers and five main courses—mostly fish—and five desserts, the white wines on hand rarely cost more than 89 F, and there's bouillabaisse on offer every night. Good for the money. Unfailingly professional welcome and service. **C** 150-200. **M** 100 (lunch only).

12/20 **Brasserie Georges**

30, cours de Verdun
04 72 56 54 54, fax 04 78 42 51 65
Closed May 1. Open until 11:15pm (0:15am Fri & Sat). Priv rm 120. Terrace dining. Air cond. Pkg.
The specialties here (choucroute Saint-Georges among them) and the amazing frescoes on the ceiling have contributed to this establishment's glowing reputation. The new chef continues in the same tradition as always with hearty brasserie fare. An orchestra serenades diners on Saturday nights. **C** 139. **M** 138 (Sun lunch), 85-125 (exc Sun lunch), 49 (children).

 Carlton

4, rue Jussieu - 04 78 42 56 51, fax 04 78 42 10 71
Open year-round. 4 stes 405-725. 79 rms 405-770. Bkfst 59. Rm ser. Air cond. Conf.
This distinguished, centrally located hotel offers comfortable, quiet rooms with air conditioning. Its Arts Déco interior was recently spruced up, and the bar's atmosphere and decoration take their cue from the opera. Highly efficient service.

 Caro de Lyon

25, rue du Bât-d'Argent
04 78 39 58 58, fax 04 72 07 98 96
Closed Sun. Open until midnight. Priv rm 40. Garden dining. Air cond.
This bright, spacious establishment located between the opera house and the chamber of commerce is decked out with a green-columned arcade, glass roof, and mezzanine. Take a seat at one of the 60s style tables and tuck into a pillow of pasta stuffed with savory crab and served with shellfish sauce; a salad of mixed greens; yummy chicken with marinated onions; a nice mushroom, ham, and mozzarella pizza; and classic pineapple and lemon sherbets. Zesty Italian cellar. Prices are more than reasonable. **C** 150-200. **M** 120, 60 (children).

12/20 **Le Cintra**

43, rue de la Bourse
04 78 42 54 08, fax 04 72 41 83 42
Closed Sun. Open until 2am. Priv rm 60. Terrace dining. Air ocnd. No pets. Garage pkg.
This pleasant brasserie has a discreetly British look about it, and is a popular spot for business lunches and after-theater suppers. The classic bistro-style cooking is skillfully prepared, with pot-roasted veal kidney, vanilla-spiced roast burbot and beef fillet with its marrow. Cheeselovers should try the local cheese, Saint-Marcellin, from the highly reputable Mère Richard. Diligent service. A brasserie of this caliber could afford itself a better-stocked cellar. **C** 250. **M** 130 (wine incl), 80 (children).

 Fleur de Sel

7, rue Adélaïde-Perrin
04 78 37 40 37, fax 04 78 37 26 37
Closed Sat, Sun, Aug. Open until 9:30pm. Pkg.
Even the short weekday lunch menu attests to expertly trained (none other than Senderens in Paris) Cyril Nitar's culinary prowess. Excellent ingredients, full flavors, large portions, well-controlled prices and professional service: now you understand why it's always full, so you'd better think to reserve ahead of time. We were particularly impressed by the calf's sweetbreads flavored with mustard and basil oil and the venison with cocoa and wild mushrooms. We'd like to make one suggestion: order your desserts at the beginning of the meal to avoid a long wait at the end. Appealing wine list with a small but nice selection of half-bottles. A smiling welcome and friendly service await guests in the tastefully decorated dining room. **C** 200-300. **M** 128 (weekday lunch), 220-280, 98 (children).

 Grand Hôtel Concorde

11, rue Grôlée - 04 72 40 45 45, fax 04 78 37 52 55
Open year-round. 3 stes 1,700-2,250. 140 rms 650-980. Bkfst 69. Restaurant. Rm ser. Conf. Valet pkg.
This turn-of-the-century hotel on the banks of the Rhône has been redecorated from stem to stern. Traditional notions of service prevail, and its pretty and spacious rooms are remarkably well-soundproofed. Lively bar. Ten rooms available for meetings and seminars.

Please excuse us... (and the chefs). *Menus are subject to the winds of change, and the dishes we've described may no longer be available when you visit.*

Grand Hôtel des Beaux-Arts

73, rue du Président-Herriot
04 78 38 09 50, fax 04 78 42 19 19
Open year-round. 4 stes 695-760. 71 rms 395-630. Bkfst 58. Air cond. Conf.
This establishment is full of 1930s charm and style, and offers refined accommodations just a stone's throw from Place des Jacobins. Well soundproofed, highly functional rooms. Service with a smile.

12/20 Chez Jean-François

2, pl. des Célestins - 04 78 42 08 26
Closed Sun, hols, Jul 20-Aug 20. Open until 10pm (later upon reserv). Air cond.
Paintings and bouquets of flowers fill the charming pink dining room here. The culinary repertoire is as classic as it is conscientiously prepared, well cooked, and prettily presented. While the welcome is friendly, the young staff's inexperience shows. C 250. M 90-160.

 Les Trois Dômes

20, quai du Docteur-Gailleton
04 72 41 20 20, fax 04 72 40 05 50
Closed Aug. Open until 10:15pm. Priv rm 300. Air cond. Valet pkg.
It's a shame more guests at the Sofitel don't take advantage of the attractive dining room located on the hotel's eighth floor. The view of Lyon is wonderful from there, but we guess they're in too much of a hurry to taste the fare they've heard so much about down below—which is a shame, because Alain Desvilles' cuisine is among the best in the city. His ingredients couldn't be fresher, his preparation is unerring, and he has a wonderful sense of style. We liked the Bresse chicken aspic, John Dory, red mullets, and squid done in an aniseed-flavored bouillon, and the beef tenderloin in a Banyuls glaze. The distinguished wine list features a few selections at friendly prices, and the service is beyond reproach. C 360. M 180-260.

 Sofitel-Bellecour

(See restaurant above)
Open year-round. 29 stes 1,200-1,300. 137 rms 870-970. Bkfst 80. Rms for disabled. Restaurant. Rm ser. Air cond. Conf. Valet pkg.
This well-maintained hotel is one of Lyon's mainstays. It plays host to any number of political and social events, and is conveniently located in the center of town. Good quality for the price and truly exceptional breakfast buffet. Bill Clinton stayed here during the Lyon G7 meetings.

12/20 Le Vivarais

1, pl. du Docteur-Gailleton - 04 78 37 85 15
Closed Sun, Aug. Open until 10:15pm. Air cond. Garage pkg.
Paintings grace the paneled walls in this old-fashioned bistro, which plays host to a steady stream of *bouchon* cuisine fans. Robert Duffaud takes to the stoves to turn out dishes like tender rabbit salad, and savory fillet of John Dory with tomatoes. The first set menu (Vivarais terrine, braised sea bream, house dessert) is wonderful washed down with the tasty regional wines on offer. C 200. M 115-140.

And also...

Our selection of places for inexpensive, quick, or late-night meals.
Brasserie Francotte (04 78 37 38 64 - 8, pl. des Célestins. Open until midnight.): The new owners have given this restaurant back its old name. Good set-price meals as well as "formulas" like the 78 F one with cod, French fries and beer. Open until late (70-140).
Le Pasteur (04 78 37 01 04 - 83, quai Perrache. Open until 10pm.): This *bouchon* is home to Friday-night Guignol puppet shows, typical Lyonnais cuisine, and Gigondas wines. Louis Chabanel has been cooking here for 25 years now. God bless—and keep—him! (140).

3RD ARRONDISSEMENT

 L'Alexandrin

83, rue Moncey - 04 72 61 15 69, fax 04 78 62 75 57
Closed Sun, Mon, 1 wk in May, 3 wks in Aug, 1 wk in Nov, end Dec-beg Jan. Open until 9:30pm. Terrace dining. Air cond. Pkg.
Lyonnais "in the know" swear by L'Alexandrin, and we're proud to say we were among the first to discover this wonderful restaurant. Alain Alexanian favors atypical cuisine and is unfailingly true to his own unique style. He's an expert at pairing up ingredients and flavors: succulent chicken broth delicately flavored with chestnuts; smoked Dombes carp roe served in a salad; sublime roast squab done with dandelion flower honey, and the list goes on. Véronique, the *sommelière*, is especially fond of Saint-Josephs, Hermitages, and Condrieus, and consistently chooses the best. Prices, even à la carte, are relatively gentle. C 250-300. M 160-210, 95 (children).

 Bistrot d'en Face

220, rue Du Guesclin
04 72 61 96 16, fax 04 78 60 59 97
Closed Sun, Aug 3-24. Open until 9:30pm. Terrace dining. No pets.
The single set menu changes daily and is always chock-a-block with great ideas, enabling diners to sample delightful homestyle cooking at down-to-earth prices. The chef worked for Jean-Paul Lacombe (at Léon de Lyon) for five years, and he was obviously a good student. His full professionalism comes through even in the 110 F prix-fixe menu, a real jewel of a value: skate-fin terrine à la provençale, poached chicken with mushroom cream sauce, and praline tart. This popular spot is located near the Halles part of town and the new Law center. Fine wine selection. Wonderful welcome. M 108-110.

And also...

Our selection of places for inexpensive, quick, or late-night meals.

Merle (04 78 62 30 29 - Halles de la Part-Dieu, 102, cours Lafayette. Open until 10:30pm.): This is arguably the best seafood specialist in Les Halles. The food is fresh, and the surroundings are comfortable. Relax and tuck into your choice of oysters, shellfish, moules marinière, or snails (180-220).

Le Val d'Isère (04 78 71 09 39 - 64, rue de Bonnel. Open lunch only until 2pm.): The chef at this *bouchon* near Les Halles feeds the likes of Bocuse, Orsi, and other culinary legends after they do their crack-of-dawn marketing—so it's easy to understand why the early-morning snacks, terrines, mushroom-studded scrambled eggs, and the rest are always tip-top (110-160).

4TH ARRONDISSEMENT

 ## Les Eaux Vives

85, quai Joseph-Gillet
04 72 10 44 44, fax 04 78 39 99 20
Open daily until 10pm. Priv rm 30. Air cond. Pool. Tennis. Valet pkg.

Young Frédéric Cotte has taken over the kitchens at Eaux Vives under teaching chef Stéphane Gaboriau's expert guidance, and we're still just as fond of the solid, nicely articulated fare at this restaurant on the banks of the Saône. The inspiration behind the cuisine is more Mediterranean than Lyonnais, and everyone who samples it is eager to return. The bay windows in the dining room overlook a spectacular pool. Service styled after the *grands restaurants*, yet cordial and unpretentious. The toque is on solid ground. C 320-420. M 160, 300.

 ## Hôtel Métropole Concorde 🌲

(See restaurant above)
Open year-round. 2 stes 890-1,700. 116 rms 590-750. Bkfst 70. Rms for disabled. Rm ser. Air cond. Conf. Pool. Tennis. Valet pkg.

This large four-star hotel boasts an extensive sports complex with fifteen tennis courts and a pool, located along the banks of the Saône. Not far from downtown, and there's a fairly non-stop hotel shuttle bus. Keen prices considering all you get!

12/20 Le Petit Gadin

17, rue d'Austerlitz - 04 78 39 72 85
Closed Sat lunch, Sun, wk of Aug 15, 1 wk end Dec-beg Jan. Open until 10pm. Terrace dining.

This simply decorated restaurant with a terrace offers updated classics at moderate prices. The unpretentious fare is interpreted with a fresh, right-on-the-mark approach. Some wines available by the pitcher. Hangout for young music lovers, which makes it lively (i.e. noisy) at

times. Friendly welcome and service. C 160-220. M 115 (dinner), 66-105 (weekday lunch).

And also...

Our selection of places for inexpensive, quick, or late-night meals.

Le Tailleviande (04 78 28 48 82 - 3, pl. des Tapis. Open until 10pm.): Meat lovers are in seventh heaven at the hands of former butcher Yves Daguin, who regales them with his prime cuts, liver, kidneys, etc., and tartares. Saint-Josephs and Beaujolais are the perfect thirst-quenchers (95-250).

5TH ARRONDISSEMENT

 ## Cour des Loges

6, rue du Bœuf - 04 78 42 75 75, fax 04 72 40 93 61
Open year-round. 10 stes 2,000-3,000. 53 rms 880-1,800. Bkfst 110. Rms for disabled. Restaurant. Rm ser. Air cond. Conf. Heated pool. Pkg.

The design-bedecked rooms in this establishment—built around a Florentine-style courtyard complete with arcades, terraces, and hanging gardens—may be on the dark side, but they're extraordinarily well-equipped (satellite TV, VCR, etc.). Hot baths, fitness center, wine bar, and tapas bar.

12/20 Les Lyonnais

1, rue Tramassac - 04 78 37 64 82, fax 04 72 56 06 48
Open daily until 11:30pm.

Portraits of Lyon luminaries line the walls of this popular old town bistro, where satisfying local cuisine is proffered by Jean-Louis Manoa du Mercière. M 99.

La Maison de la Tour

See restaurant La Tour Rose

 ## Les Terrasses de Lyon

25, montée Saint-Barthélemy
04 72 56 56 56, fax 04 72 40 90 56
Open daily until 9:45pm. Priv rm 17. Air cond. Terrace dining. Pool. Valet pkg.

When Orsi-trained Stéphane Gaborieau recently took over from Fabrice Bugaud here, he had some big shoes to fill. We're happy to report that he has more than risen to the occasion. This scrupulous chef is currently turning out some truly admirable fare: succulent lobster, truffle, and salsify mosaïque, tender veal teamed with green asparagus, and a flavorful fricassée of mushrooms with sorrel jus. The 170 F set menu at lunchtime is an excellent value. This splendid former convent perched on the Fourvière hill offers breathtaking views of Lyon from its terraces and gardens, and the welcome and service are exceedingly professional. This is an expert's cellar, and you'll get all the explanations you could possibly need from sommelier Hervé Luzi, who is of an almost unselfconscious eloquence.. **C** 450. **M** 170 (weekday lunch, Sat), 290, 320, 400.

 ## Villa Florentine

(See restaurant above)
Open year-round. 3 stes 1,600-1,900. 16 rms 1,300-1,900. Bkfst 90. Rms for disabled. Rm ser. Air cond. Conf. Heated pool. Valet pkg.
This ancient architectural marvel atop "praying hill" is Lyon's crowning glory. The sunny, posh rooms all overlook the city below, and the whole establishment enjoys privileged "national historic monument" status. Swimming pool (practically) jutting out of the hillside and overlooking the old city. Relais et Châteaux.

 ## La Tour Rose

22, rue du Bœuf - 04 78 37 25 90, fax 04 78 42 26 02
Closed Sun. Open until 10:30pm. Garden dining. Air cond. Valet pkg.
Dining in Philippe Chavent's magnificent restaurant is a memorable experience. Try the fabulous oyster cream with caviar, excellent pan-roasted red mullet with lentils, and anything from the tempting dessert cart. We were less enthralled by the saffron-laced mashed potatoes whipped with olive oil and the cherry soup. Superb wines, with a good selection of Burgundies. Efficient though somewhat chilly and unsmiling service. **C** 600-700. **M** 295-595 (weekdays, Sat lunch), 500.

 ## La Maison de la Tour

(See restaurant above)
Open year-round. 6 stes 1,650-2,800. 6 rms 950-1,400. Bkfst 95. Rms for disabled. Rm ser. Air cond. Conf. Valet pkg.
Located in the heart of the old town, this hotel's attractive guest quarters are decorated with silks from individual Lyon mills. While the rooms are not as functional as they could be, they're very well equipped and have oodles of personality.

Villa Florentine

See restaurant Les Terrasses de Lyon

6TH ARRONDISSEMENT

 ## Le Gourmet de Sèze

129, rue de Sèze
04 78 24 23 42, fax 04 78 24 66 81
Closed Sat lunch, Sun, Feb school hols, 3 wks in Aug. Open until 9:30pm. Air cond.
While the dining room here may be short on style, it's long on taste, as you'll see when you tuck into Bernard Mariller's ultrafresh cuisine. He may put the bridle on his prices, but not on his imagination, which goes from lamb's trotters with artichoke barigoule to roast bass with verjuice sauce and roast squab stuffed with foie gras-laced cabbage butter. Good selection of set-price meals. Cleverly chosen wine list. Slightly distant welcome; efficient service. **C** 260. **M** 125 (weekdays), 250-470, 60 (children).

 ## Lutétia

112-114, bd des Belges
04 78 24 44 68, fax 04 78 24 82 36
Open year-round. 55 rms 385-495. Bkfst 45. Rm ser. Air cond.
This hotel located between the parc de la Tête d'Or rose gardens and the Brotteaux plaza is done up in Art Nouveau style. While the lobby may seem a bit dark, the rooms do get enough sunlight. One floor reserved for non-smokers.

 ## Pierre Orsi

3, pl. Kléber - 04 78 89 57 68, fax 04 72 44 93 34
Closed Sun (exc hols); Aug: Sat, Sun. Open until 10pm. Priv rm 50. Terrace dining. Air cond.
This is one of Lyon's very best bets! The restaurant itself—located at the heart of the Brotteaux district—is a showcase, and the service couldn't be more perfect. Chef Pierre Orsi has a razor-sharp instinct for ingredients and cooking times, and his foie gras and house-smoked salmon are truly beyond compare. Be sure to taste the succulent pan-roasted veal sweetbreads done in Sherry, the crunchy vegetable chartreuse (a veritable monument), and the gorgeous, ultraclassic desserts. The ample wine list is rich in Bordeaux and Burgundies from top-notch sources. And believe us, the 200 F summer lunch in the rose garden may just be the bargain of the century! **C** 500. **M** 200 (weekday lunch), 320 (weekday dinner), 400, 500, 600, 150 (children).

12/20 Le Rive Gauche

31, cours Franklin-D.-Roosevelt
04 78 89 51 21, fax 04 78 94 38 37
Closed Sat dinner & Sun off-seas. Open until 11:15pm. Terrace dining. Air cond.
Neighborhood food lovers flock to this cozy bistro with antique engravings on the walls, where the new chef serves forth Lyonnais classics and more "earthy" regional delights at the same reasonable prices, accompanied by nice wines by the pitcher. **C** 150-200. **M** 79 (weekday lunch), 99 (exc Sun), 149 (exc Sun dinner).

And also...

Our selection of places for inexpensive, quick, or late-night meals.
Le Théodore (04 78 24 08 52 - 34, cours Franklin-D.-Roosevelt. Open until 11pm.): This super-friendly spot is among Lyon's most popular eateries, and its seventeenth-century décor makes it one of the most elegant spots in all Lyon. Tuck into daily specials including creamed chicken and breaded veal cutlet. The wine list is longer than the menu (128-200).

7TH ARRONDISSEMENT

 ## Thierry Gache

37, rue de la Thibaudière
04 78 72 81 77, fax 04 78 72 01 75
Closed Sun. Open until 10:30pm. Air cond.

You'd think that winding our way through the dismal part of town where this establishment is located would earn us at least one smile from the (efficient, albeit distant) staff. Oh well, it's still better than last year. The dining room is attractive here—as is the food—and that's what *really* matters. The generous 125 F set-price menu offers diners a golden opportunity to sample Thierry Gache's inventive, intelligently handled cuisine. The cellar houses a good variety of wines at reasonable prices with excellent selection of Saône and Rhône wines. C 275-375. M 99 (lunch, wine incl), 125-395, 60 (children).

And also...

Our selection of places for inexpensive, quick, or late-night meals.
Carnegie Hall (04 78 58 85 79 - 253, rue Marcel-Mérieux. Open until 12:30am.): This popular eatery owned by a former butcher serves up the juiciest, choicest cuts of meat imaginable. Formidable service. (150-200).

9TH ARRONDISSEMENT

 ## Auberge de l'Ile

Ile Barbe, pl. Notre-Dame
04 78 83 99 49, fax 04 78 47 80 46
Closed Sun dinner, Mon, 2 wks in Aug. Open until 10pm. Priv rm 40. Garage pkg.
This restaurant, located at the heart of the île Barbe on the Saône River, has made progress on all fronts since our last visit. Its smiling hostess oversees a friendly, efficient staff which helps account for the relaxed atmosphere that prevails in the pretty old dining room (the building itself is a *bona fide* historical monument). And now that chef Jean-Christophe Ansanay-Alex has taken over from his father, he seems even more adept at taking the finest ingredients and fine-tuning them into interesting, light, tremendously flavorful dishes. What may appear to be simple also proves to be rich in flavor and never, but never, commonplace: not the scrambled eggs with sea urchins, not the saddle of salmon with mixed vegetables in caviar butter, and certainly not the enticing desserts, such as the prune soufflé with Earl Grey tea cream sauce. If you're a big eater, you'll be satisfied with the hefty Charlemagne prix-fixe menu. Impressive cellar. C 320. M 140 (weekdays lunch), 180-365, 100 (children).

MIONNAY   01390
Paris 461 - Lyon 27 - Bourg-en-Bresse 42   Ain

 ## Alain Chapel

N 83 - 04 78 91 82 02
04 78 91 82 37
Closed Mon & Tue lunch (exc hols), Jan. Open until 9:30pm. Priv rm 40. Garden dining. Terrace dining. Garage pkg.

The faith of Chapel's team—coached by maître d' Hervé Duronzier and rallied 'round Alain's widow, Suzanne—has moved mountains, and Philippe Jousse, the master's true disciple, is still behind the stoves kindling the Chapel flame. But while this charming Dombes-based inn could have gone the route of a soulless, stone-cold Chapel memorial monument, it has done just the opposite. Jousse "does" Chapel, but also (to our delight!) "does" Jousse now, and warm, personal touches like gorgeous bouquets of orchids in blue enamel pitchers (not to mention the extraordinary comfort of the *grand salon*) abound. Savor the deep, ample flavors of Jousse's cooking: mouthwatering braised lamb with chestnuts; veal shank minestrone; savory spiced duck; meaty, truffle-studded lobster and squab salad; and a honey-glazed fromage blanc that's out of this world. Choosing a wine is rather like a five-year-old walking through Hamley's toy store at Christmas; in other words, it's exciting and so rich in choices that you may have a hard time choosing! Try the Château Rayas if you like white, or one of Jayer's sublime Burgundies. C 550-1,000. M 330 (weekday lunch), 595, 695, 795, 120 (children).

 ## Alain Chapel

(See restaurant above)
Closed Mon, Jan. 13 rms 600-800. Bkfst 57-89. Conf. Garage pkg.
There's video surveillance in the parking garage, and the breakfasts are fit for a king (or queen). The garden is a haven of peace—and helps guests ignore the steady hum of traffic on the nearby highway. Relais et Châteaux.

PÉROUGES   01800
Paris 454 - Bourg 37 - Lyon 36 - St-André-de-Corcy 20   Ain

12/20 Hostellerie du Vieux Pérouges

Pl. du Tilleul - 04 74 61 00 88, fax 04 74 34 77 90
Open daily until 9:15pm. Garage pkg.
The dining room in this eye-catching fourteenth-century inn was built around a huge fireplace and acts as a sort of "mini-museum" for a range of period furniture and pewter and copper objects. Classic, resolutely regional cuisine. C 280-360. M 190-420, 280 (exc Sun dinner).

Hostellerie du Vieux Pérouges

(See restaurant above)
Open year-round. 3 stes 1,050. 25 rms 450-1,000. Bkfst 60-85. Rms for disabled. Conf. Garage pkg.
Modern comfort and spacious, prettily appointed rooms prevail in this comely peaceful establishment. Guests can enjoy breakfast—and a breathtaking view of the medieval city below—on the covered terrace atop the tower.

The prices in this guide reflect what establishments were charging at press time.

ROANNE 42
→ **CENTRAL FRANCE** *(Auvergne)*

TARARE   69170
Paris 467 - Lyon 65 - Feurs 35 - Villefranche 32   Rhône

 Jean Brouilly
3 ter, rue de Paris
04 74 63 24 56, fax 04 74 05 05 48
Closed Sun (exc hols lunch), Mon, Feb school hols, 2 wks in Aug. Open until 9:30pm. Priv rm 15. Terrace dining. Air cond. Pkg.
The bright, contemporary veranda dining room in Jean Brouilly's stately manor makes for less stuffy, more comfortable surroundings, and Josette Brouilly is absolutely the perfect hostess (to regulars and tourists alike!). This may not be the cuisine of a young chef overflowing with new ideas, but we never get bored, because his enthusiasm for good ingredients, his skillful and accurate preparation, and his bursts of ir-reverence for traditional flavor combinations produce always-excellent results. Are you ready: melon soup with berries and Sherry-flavored jus; Oléron oysters in not-so-hot pepper compote; red mullet stuffed with garden herbs; and sea bream in lemon brine. Good homemade bread. And all this is offered at prices so reasonable we'd be hard-pressed to criticize them. The friendly cellar with prices to match offers a discerning selection of Beaujolais. This restaurant really pulled at our heartstrings, and that's why we've given back the third toque. C 320-400. M 160, 230, 300, 370, 60 (children).

VONNAS   01540
Paris 407 - Bourg-en-Bresse 27 - Mâcon 16   Ain

 Georges Blanc
04 74 50 90 90,
fax 04 74 50 08 80
Closed Mon (exc hols), Tue (exc hols & dinner Jun 15-Sep 15), Jan 2-Feb 10. Open until 9:30pm. Air cond. Heated pool. Tennis. Valet pkg.
Okay, it's true. His name *is* omnipresent: it crops up all around the town square, on the hotel-restaurant itself, on the Ancienne Auberge (a charming little bistro-museum devoted to generations of *mères Blanc*) on the boutique prof-fering everything from Georges Blanc dishes to Georges Blanc sausage. As if this weren't enough, Vonnas owes a carriage museum, foun-tains and gardens, and the total overhaul of the nearby Château d'Épeyssoles to this native son and active town council member. Needless to say, a fair share of Frenchmen are envious of Georges Blanc, who has glided through the recession the way Veyle River water slides off a duck's back. His spacious dining room with its exposed beams, fireplace, burnished furniture and magnificent Aubusson tapestry consistently seats 100 guests for lunch and 100 for dinner. Yet Georges Blanc is not only a good businessman, he's also a world-renowned chef who isn't con-tent to rest on his laurels. He's a wizard at time-

honored favorites like his wonderful blanquette of frogs' legs done in a savory blend of spices and garlic powder, and tempting hors d'œuvre: mini-portions of parmentier de sot-l'y-laisse (poultry "oysters") and pig's trotters so good you want to make a meal of them! He's also a master at pairing up flavors without resorting to a lot of unnecessary hoopla: asparagus and truf-fles; foie gras and artichokes; lobster and en-dives; sea scallops and wild boletus mushrooms; tender squab and vegetables in a pot-au-feu. Concise, streamlined fare, cooked to within a millisecond—all the more reason to come to Vonnas with your eyes closed and your wallet open. Jacqueline Blanc welcomes guests with a warm smile, and the ever-loyal Marcel Périnet presides over a remarkable cellar. C 700. M 470-850, 150 (children).

Georges Blanc
(See restaurant above)
Closed Jan 2-Feb 10. 9 stes 1,900-3,000. 21 rms 850-1,600. Bkfst 105. Air cond. Conf. Heated pool. Tennis. Valet pkg.
When Georges Blanc renovates, he starts from scratch. As a result, the spacious guest quarters here now offer every conceivable comfort, the bathtubs are all equipped with Jacuzzis, and rooms are decorated in sunny new colors reminiscent of the South of France. Some rooms have balconies overlooking the romantic River Veyle, and the La Cour aux Fleurs extension mirrors the original hotel's style. A garden abloom with flowers, heated pool, tennis courts, helipad, gift shop, etc., complete the complex. Relais et Châteaux.

REGIONAL FOODS

Lyon and its environs produce a multi-farious range of savory charcuterie, and Bresse, to the east, raises prize-winning pul-lets, pigeons, and capons. Hunting for these and other regional specialties is a terrific way to explore the highways and—especially—the byways of the Lyonnais.

• *CHARCUTERIE*

LYON   69000 – Rhône

Bobosse
3rd arr. - 66, rue de Bonnel - 04 78 62 66 10
If you like Lyonnais food, you'll love Bobosse! The charcuterie is no longer crafted on the small scale of yore, but the offerings are still absolutely delicious.

Au Chapon Fin

3rd arr. - 25, av. du Maréchal-de-Saxe
04 72 73 02 04
What we like best here are the saucissons de
Lyon, plain or pistachio-studded cervelas
sausage, aromatic terrines, and fabulous house
foie gras.

Chorliet-Bellet

2nd arr. - 12, rue du Plat - 04 78 37 31 95
The entire range of traditional Lyonnais charcuterie is set out for your delectation: real saucisson de Lyon, cervelas, smoked jésus sausages,
etc.

VONNAS   01540 – Ain

La Boutique Gourmande

Pl. du Marché - 04 74 50 10 79
Take away a taste of Georges Blanc's famous
charcuterie specialties (they're the same as the
items that appear on his menu): Bresse chicken-
liver terrine, duck pâté, and more.

• CHEESE

LYON   69003 – Rhône

Fromages Maréchal

3rd arr. - Halle de Lyon, 102, cours Lafayette
04 78 62 36 77
In Lyon, this is *the* place for farm cheeses, most
of them made from unpasteurized milk. Some
100 varieties are usually available. High marks
for the Comté aged for two full years: an exceptional cheese. Small-batch jams are also sold
here.

• CHOCOLATE & CANDY

LYON   69006 – Rhône

Bernachon

6th arr. - 42, cours Franklin-D.-Roosevelt
04 78 24 37 98
A great chocolatier, one of the world's best,
who uses fifteen different types of cocoa beans
in his creations. Bernachon's Palets d'Or (chocolates filled with rich ganache and daubed with
gold leaf) are deservedly famous, but don't
neglect his fruit jellies and other sweet treats.

• GOURMET SPECIALTIES

Oils

POLLIONNAY   69290 – Rhône

Noiseraies du Lyonnais

La Garnière - 04 78 48 13 97
Direct from a hazelnut orchard, exquisitely
delicate hazelnut oil that will make your salads
very special.

WINE

Beaujolais country begins just beyond
Mâcon. Covered with Gamay vines, this
land is home to the ten crus that form the
aristocracy of the *appellation*, from **Saint-
Amour** in the north to **Brouilly** in the south.
Surrounding the crus is the longer, broader
region of the Beaujolais-Villages and plain
Beaujolais *appellations*. **Morgon, Moulin-à-
Vent**, and **Côte de Brouilly** have the staying
power for long keeping, while **Fleurie,
Chiroubles**, and **Brouilly** are perfect in their
fragrant youth. Rustic **Régnié, Chénas**, delicate **Saint-Amour**, and sturdier **Juliénas**
from a first-rate vintage can last up to ten
years.

FLEURIE   69820 – Rhône

Guy Depardon

Domaine du Point du Jour
04 74 04 10 52, fax 04 74 69 82 87
Open daily 8am-9pm (exc Sun pm).
One of the best Fleuries in the village, and
memorable Morgons as well.

JULIÉNAS   69840 – Rhône

Domaine de la Bottière

Jacques Perrachon
03 85 36 75 42, fax 03 85 33 86 36
Open Mon-Sat, Sun by appt.
Generous wines, all models of their kind:
Juliénas, Morgon, Moulin-à-Vent.

NORMANDY

An affair
of the heart

Normandy is an affair of the heart. To visit this land of apple orchards and loamy pastures, of windswept cliffs and wave-dashed beaches, is to fall in love with its generous charms. This is one of France's largest regions. Its five *départements*—Calvados, Eure, Manche, Orne, and Seine-Maritime—are divided into **Upper** and **Lower Normandy**. Within easy reach of the French capital, Normandy is often called the "lungs of Paris"; and it lies but a short sail across the Channel from Britain. Normandy's 375 miles of coastline have been crossed by countless invaders, both incoming and outgoing, throughout its long history.

Like other parts of France, Normandy saw the passage of Celts, Romans, and Franks before 820 AD, when the first wave of Vikings from Denmark glided up the River Seine in their flat boats. They went on to rape, pillage, and generally devastate the region to which they later gave their name: Normandy, land of the Norsemen. By the tenth century, these uncouth invaders had settled down. In 911, the Norman leader, Rollo, made peace with the Frankish king, and was officially recognized as Duke of Normandy, converting to Christianity as part of the bargain. Thus began a period of prosperity carried forward by a line of dukes who combined ability as statesmen and warriors. In 1066, Rollo's descendant, Duke William (The Conqueror), defeated his English rival, Harold, at the Battle of Hastings and became King of England, shuttling between his two capitals at London and Caen. For the next four centuries, Normandy played as great a role in English as in French history.

Under civilized rule, the medieval Church flourished. Benedictine and Cistercian monks set about building abbeys and churches and perfecting the Norman Romanesque style. In 1154, Henry, Duke of Normandy, became king of England. His marriage to land-rich Eleanor of Aquitaine gave the English Crown control over almost half of France. It was just a matter of time before the Hundred Years' War—which lasted from 1337 to 1453 and was fought largely on Norman soil—erupted between France and England. Eventually, and with heroic help from Joan of Arc, the English were sent packing and France reasserted its control over Normandy.

From that period on, Normandy prospered. As urban centers flourished so, too, did the bourgeoisie. Textile manufacture and the cotton industry put the river-port town of Rouen on the map and Norman sailors set to sea for broader horizons, exploring Canada and other parts of North America.

A paradise
for Impressionists

In 1824 a new invasion of Normandy began, instigated by the Duchesse de Berry. She launched the fashion for sea-bathing at Dieppe, where she was carried into the water, fully garbed, in a sedan chair. The craze picked up steam thanks to the new Paris-Dieppe railway which rumbled into Normandy in 1848. This time it was from Paris's Gare Saint-Lazare that inland invaders sped to the new resort towns which bloomed along the Normandy coast. Dieppe, Deauville, Trouville, Cabourg, Étretat, and Le Tréport boomed during the Second Empire, reaching their peak in the Belle Époque. Simply everyone in society flocked to the luxurious hotels, casinos, and race courses (horse breeding remains an integral part of Norman life), to see and be seen. Rich Americans like William Vanderbilt erected huge estates at Deauville and Trouville. The British congregated in Dieppe—the first place Oscar Wilde went after leaving his English jail. Famous artists such as Boudin, Monet, Corot, Courbet, Sisley, Pissarro, and Cézanne turned Normandy into a vast outdoor studio. Writers, too, came in droves. Marcel Proust boasted that he could "leave Paris from the Gare Saint-Lazare at lunchtime and be in Cabourg in time to change for dinner." And Guy de Maupassant, a native son, set many of his most memorable tales in Belle Époque Normandy.

World War I spared Normandy. World War II devastated it. The Allied Normandy landings or **Operation Overlord** took place on June 6, 1944 on the beaches of Calvados and the Manche. Once more invaders swarmed over Normandy. Today, those stretches of shoreline still carry their wartime names:

Omaha, Utah, Gold, Juno, and Sword. Above the beach at Omaha, rows and rows of crosses honoring the American dead are a poignant reminder of battles fought within living memory.

By September 1, 1944, Normandy was liberated, but at a terrible price. Towns and cities, industrial sites, bridges and communication systems, countless works of art and architectural gems were totally or partially destroyed. The long, slow task of rebuilding began. Tourism has been a driving economic force in post-war years; ironically, while that sea-bound jewel of medieval architecture, the **Mont-Saint-Michel**, attracts 850,000 visitors a year, some 2.5 million people come to see the **Landing Beaches** and the **Battle of Normandy** sites, proving that events which ravage a region can in time contribute to restoring its fortunes.

Normandy is eminently accessible by road or train; it boasts monuments and places of interest to suit every palate. History buffs can stroll in the steps of William the Conqueror at **Caen** (Lower Normandy's capital city), visiting his castle and twin abbeys—the Abbaye aux Hommes, the finer of the two, and the Abbaye aux Dames—commissioned by King William and his consort, Queen Matilda. Another town closely associated with William is **Bayeux**, miraculously spared destruction in 1944, and home to the justly famous Bayeux tapestry, one of the world's earliest and most engaging historical "comic strips." Said to date from about 1077, the embroidered linen scroll shows 58 scenes of William's conquest of England.

Characterful **Rouen**, capital of Upper Normandy, lies on the Seine between Paris and the sea. Not everyone will appreciate the tourist train—now a questionable feature of many French cities—which trundles through the heavily restored medieval streets in the pedestrian zone of old Rouen. Little is left of the bohemian quarter, that "district of theaters, bars, and brothels" described by one the city's most famous native sons, Gustave Flaubert, in his great work, *Madame Bovary*. But in the Place du Vieux-Marché, look for the spot where Joan of Arc was burned at the stake. The train disgorges its passengers at the foot of Rouen's cathedral, so often painted by Claude Monet.

Monet ended his life in Normandy, at his house in **Giverny** upriver from Rouen, in 1890. The house and garden have been meticulously restored and attract busloads of visitors in the spring when the garden is at its best. Despite the crowds, Giverny always breathes a magical tranquility and seems happily haunted by the grand old man of Impressionism.

Seaside glamour

Not far from Rouen the impressive remains of a medieval fortress, **Château Gaillard**, perches on a rocky outcrop strategically overlooking the Seine. Built in 1196 by Richard the Lionheart, King of England and Duke of Normandy, the castle's hulking ruins offer one of France's most famous views over the Seine at **Les Andelys**. Another striking view, over the estuary of the Seine, is that from the new *Pont de Normandie* linking directly Le Havre to Honfleur. Downstream from Rouen is Normandy's second great medieval ruin, the tenth-century abbey of **Jumièges**, once a powerful Benedictine seat, now stripped by time and conquest to its architectural bare bones—a romantic, melancholy site.

On the **Alabaster Coast** between Dieppe and Le Havre, **Étretat** has remained remarkably unspoiled with its swimming beach, busy promenade, and plunging, limestone cliffs. Sadly, much of its former enchantment has worn off **Honfleur**, a charming port town at the mouth of the Seine. Beware of the overpriced cafés, gewgaw boutiques, and crush of vacationers. Similar dangers lurk at mystical Mont-Saint-Michel. Wait until nightfall when the crowds disappear and you won't fail to be moved by the spiritual mystery of this sea-swept, anchored stone vessel of medieval piety.

The "Belle Époque" of **Deauville**, **Trouville**, and **Cabourg** has passed, but these resort towns retain a definite whiff of glamour which mingles with the crisp scent of sea air sweeping across beaches dotted with gaily striped deckchairs and umbrellas. Venerable establishments like the Deauville and Trouville Casinos, the Normandy Hotel at Deauville or the Grand at Cabourg maintain a dowager-like dignity. Designer boutiques (Gucci, Cartier, Hermès), sumptuous villas, a popular racetrack, and some enticing restaurants and night spots testify to a smart and very *mondain* presence from Paris and abroad. The annual American Film Festival at Deauville also brings today's glitterati to Norman shores.

"White gold" and briny seafood

Normandy in a nutshell? Well, it's not very hilly; it get lots of rain; and the sea is never very far away. But that definition gives short shrift to Normandy's myriad charms. South of the **Pays d'Auge** (Calvados country) lies **La Suisse Normande**. This "Norman Switzerland" may lack Alpine peaks but its bluffs, woods, and river valleys lend drama to an otherwise pastoral landscape. The **Cotentin** peninsula, which juts out into the Channel, is wild and weatherbeaten, with craggy cliffs, vast beaches, and marshland. The southern Cotentin around the cathedral town of **Coutances** is a bucolic vision of small fields bordered by raised hedges so characteristic of Lower Normandy.

An astounding 90 percent of Normandy is farmland, and milk is the region's white gold. A Norman cow produces five tons of milk a year and Normandy produces ten percent of all France's dairy products. No wonder that cream, butter, and cheese are the keystones of Norman cooking! To taste authentic examples of Normandy's cheese "trinity"— Camembert, Livarot, and Pont-l'Évêque— just follow the sign-posted **Route du Fromage** that meanders through the Pays d'-Auge, a brilliant emerald canvas dotted with brown-and-white cows grazing amid apple orchards. Along the way, you can explore scenic villages such as **Beuvron-en-Auge** or **Saint-Pierre-sur-Dives**, with its informative Cheese Museum, which tells you everything you ever wanted to know about Camembert (invented by Marie Harel in 1785).

Cider and the apple brandy known as Calvados are also Norman specialties. Calvados is made from local cider twice distilled and slowly aged in oak casks. The best comes from small, independent producers in the Pays d'-Auge. Along the **Route du Cidre** you will stumble upon cider farms advertising their wares. Sample with caution: "Calva," as the natives call it, is strong stuff!

What better place than Normandy to indulge a taste for seafood? From beds at **Saint-Vaast-la-Hougue** or **Isigny-sur-Mer** come plump, meaty oysters; sweet-tasting scallops hail from Dieppe, as do mussels, clams, shrimps, crabs, and tiny lobsters. Sole is also a great specialty, often served à la normande (Norman-style usually implies an addition of cream and perhaps a touch of cider or Calvados). But carnivores need not feel neglected: the Norman table offers lamb from the salt marshes near Mont-Saint-Michel, duck in many guises, tripes à la mode de Caen, and andouille de Vire, a gutsy chitterling sausage for robust appetites. Not for nothing does a local dictum say: *Qui a fait Normand, a fait gourmand,* loosely translated as "Every Norman loves his food"! By now, you are probably ready to judge for yourselves.

RESTAURANTS & HOTELS

ALENÇON   61000
Paris 195 - Rouen 145 - Le Mans 49 - Chartres 116   Orne

12/20 Au Jardin Gourmand
14, rue de Sarthe - 02 33 32 22 56
Closed Sun dinner, Mon. Open until 9:30pm. Priv rm 16.
A Chinese influence shows in the amazing, colorful décor of this restaurant in the old town, but the young owner's skillful, creative cuisine has its roots in Normandy. Interesting selection of Loire wines. C 220-280. M 70 (wine incl), 95-235, 50 (children).

Au Petit Vatel
72, pl. du Commandant-Desmeulles
02 33 26 23 78, fax 02 33 82 64 57
Closed Sun dinner, Wed, Feb school hols, end Jul-mid Aug. Open until 9:30pm. Priv rm 50.
The fabulous homemade ice creams and sherbets are a big hit with the locals and tourists who flock to this restaurant. They are a fine conclusion to the rich and generous traditional dishes deftly prepared with quality seasonal ingredients by Michel Lerat. The wine list is short but well diversified. Friendly welcome in the spacious and comfortable beige dining room. C 250. M 118-238, 58 (children).

ANDELYS (LES)   27700
Paris 92 - Beauvais 63 - Rouen 39 - Évreux 36   Eure

La Chaîne d'Or
27, rue Grande - 02 32 54 00 31, fax 02 32 54 05 68
Closed Sun dinner, Mon, Jan. Open until 9:30pm. Priv rm 30. Pkg.
In her superb Norman inn on the banks of the Seine, Monique Foucault has put a culinary whiz kid in the kitchen. Francis Chevalliez knows how to bring out the flavors of regional foodstuffs: coddled egg croustillant with asparagus and oysters in Champagne sauce, pan-fried veal sweetbreads and vegetables with truffles, and a warm chocolate dessert with jasmine syrup. Nice cellar with a variety of offerings, and a fine first set menu. Warm welcome. C 300-400. M 140, 230, 298.

La Chaîne d'Or
(See restaurant above)
Closed Sun pm, Mon, Jan. 2 stes 710-740. 8 rms 410-550. Bkfst 68. Pkg.
Pleasant, pretty, nicely decorated and irreproachably clean rooms. All are well equipped, and some have views of the river.

AUDRIEU   14250
Paris 270 - Caen 17 - Bayeux 13 - Deauville 60   Calvados

 Château d'Audrieu

On D 158 - 02 31 80 21 52, fax 02 31 80 24 73
Closed Mon & Tue lunch off-seas, Dec 23-Jan. Open until 9:30pm. Heated pool. No pets. Valet pkg.
In this showpiece of Norman farmland and gardens, in this majestic group of buildings, Alain Cornet somehow manages to maintain a country flavor in his cuisine of very high standing. Sometimes he literally makes excursions into the Norman cookery repertory with dishes like his sea trout and brown jus with juniper berries or his tête de veau simmered with Vire chitterlings. His market-of-the-day specials are also quite appetizing. Very attentive service, excellent cellar rich in Burgundies and Bordeaux. Choice of three dining rooms with light-colored wood paneling and a refined décor. C 400. M 180 (weekdays lunch), 250-430, 90 (children).

 **Château d'Audrieu**

(See restaurant above)
Closed Dec 23-Jan. 5 stes 2,000. 25 rms 700-1,700. Bkfst 100. Half-board 770-1,200. Rm ser. Conf. Heated pool. Tennis. Valet pkg.
This superb eighteenth-century château in a large park with hundred-year-old trees is a listed monument. Rooms are huge, comfortable, elegant, and charming. Wonderful bathrooms. Charming welcome, attentive service. Relais et Châteaux.

BAGNOLES-DE-L'ORNE   61140
Paris 234 - Alençon 48 - Caen 86   Orne

 Le Manoir du Lys   ⚙

Route de Juvigny - 02 33 37 80 69, fax 02 33 30 05 80
Closed Sun dinner & Mon off-seas, Jan 5-Feb 13. Open until 9pm (10:15pm in summer). Garden dining. Pool. Tennis. Garage pkg.
Paul and Marie-France Quinton restored this old manor house overlooking a golf course and on the edge of the forest, turning it into a peaceful, pleasant spot. The spacious, comfortable dining room opens out onto the apple orchard, where meals are served in summer. The cuisine of the couple's son, Franck, still needs an extra injection of imagination, but the quality ingredients and his know-how translate into fine traditional and regional dishes. C 250-300. M 130-265, 90 (children).

 Le Manoir du Lys

(See restaurant above)
See restaurant for closings. 23 rms 300-780. Bkfst 57. Rms for disabled. Half-board 360-540 (2 pers). Conf. Pool. Tennis. Garage pkg.
Not everyone will like the décor of the rooms, but they are bright, cozy, and peaceful. Near a golf course and forest. Meeting rooms.

BARNEVILLE-CARTERET   50270
Paris 364 - Coutances 48 - Cherbourg 37   Manche

 La Marine

11, rue de Paris - 02 33 53 83 31, fax 02 33 53 39 60
Closed Feb 15-Mar & Oct: Sun dinner & Mon; beg Nov-Feb 15. Open until 9:30pm. Terrace dining. Pkg.
You can reach out and touch the boats from the tables at Laurent Cesne's restaurant, and he can practically reach out and scoop up the fish from the bay. His father, Emmanuel, oversees the service, provided by a crew of nimble deckhands. Lovely roasted langoustines with green-pea cream. Original flounder with Camembert cream sauce. Tasty cod brandade. The craquant de tripes is rich, flavorful, and well executed. The chèvre tart is not very convincing, but the dark chocolate tart is. Excellent wine list with hefty prices, except for those from the Loire Valley. C 135-190. M 135 (weekdays, Sat lunch, Sun dinner), 198-400, 65 (children).

 La Marine

(See restaurant above)
See restaurant for closings. 2 stes 620-790. 29 rms 290-550. Bkfst 50. Half-board 398-480. Conf. Pkg.
On the water, facing a peninsula, with small, sober, comfortable rooms facing on the open sea. Madame Cesne provides a warm welcome. Good breakfasts. The perfect getaway for an amorous escapade.

BAVENT   14860
Paris 232 - Caen 15 - Cabourg 10   Calvados

 Hostellerie du Moulin du Pré

Route de Gonneville-en-Auge
02 31 78 83 68, fax 02 31 78 21 05
Closed Sun dinner & Mon (exc hols & Jul-Aug), Mar 4-17, Sep 29-Oct 29. Open until 9pm. Pkg.
On the weekends, this country restaurant attracts both Parisians and local people who enjoy the view and the cuisine of Jocelyne Holtz: avocado bavarois with poached oysters, scampi flan with shellfish sauce, lamb sweetbreads with morels, and a red-berry soup. Good cellar; cheerful, competent service. C 225-260. M 255-295.

BAYEUX   14400
Paris 270 - Cherbourg 92 - Caen 30 - St-Lô 36   Calvados

 Château de Bellefontaine

49, rue de Bellefontaine
02 31 22 00 10, fax 02 31 22 19 09
Closed Jan 15-Feb 15. 3 stes 650. 12 rms 380-450. Bkfst 50-70. Rms for disabled. Tennis. Garage pkg.
A small eighteenth-century château near the cathedral, set in the middle of a park with a pond. Truly spacious rooms, decorated with good taste.

Churchill Hotel

14-16, rue Saint-Jean
02 31 21 31 80, fax 02 31 21 41 66
Closed Nov 15-Mar 15. 1 ste 520-680. 31 rms 300-460. Bkfst 42. Rms for disabled. Restaurant. Half-board 360-380. No pets. Pkg.
This well-kept hotel on a pedestrian street in the heart of town was recently soundproofed. The pleasant, medium-sized rooms are individually decorated and well equipped. Warm welcome. Pleasant breakfast room on porch.

12/20 Le Lion d'Or

71, rue St-Jean - 02 31 92 06 90, fax 02 31 22 15 64
Closed Dec 20-Jan 20. Open until 9:30pm. Priv rm 30. No pets. Garage pkg.
You know you're in Normandy in this restaurant's charming dining room. Patrick Mouilleau is attached to the tradition of the region, but his cooking could use some lightening up. Vire chitterlings with a mixture of sorrel and spinach, cream plus a pancake, well, it's just too much. Well-diversified wine list and very warm welcome by the proprietress. C 280. M 100 (lunch, exc Sun), 150 (dinner, exc Sun), 180, 210, 260, 320, 80 (children).

 # Le Lion d'Or

(See restaurant above)
Closed Dec 20-Jan 20. 2 stes 600-1,000. 24 rms 350-480. Half-board 345-435. Rm scr. Conf. Garage pkg.
In a peaceful neighborhood in the heart of town, a former post house on a cobbled courtyard. Regularly renovated.

BÉNOUVILLE 14970
Paris 242 - Caen 10 Calvados

12/20 Manoir de Hastings

18, av. de la Côte-de-Nacre
02 31 44 62 43, fax 02 31 44 76 18
Closed Sun dinner & Mon (exc Jul-Aug), Nov 15-Dec 5. Open until 9:30pm. Priv rm 70. Garden dining. Pkg.
This restaurant in a seventeenth-century abbey located near the famous Pegasus Bridge continues to serve sincere cuisine that takes inspiration from the region. The sole and red mullet with rosemary was marred by overcooking, but the crab and smoked salmon baluchon was irreproachably fresh, and the apple "symphony" ended the meal with the perfect regional note. Varied wine list and reasonable prices. C 270. M 120 (weekday lunch), 170-360, 390 (Champagne for 2 incl).

 # La Pommeraie

(See restaurant above)
Closed Nov 15-Dec 5. 15 rms 300-800. Bkfst 50. Rms for disabled. Half-board 450-475. Rm scr. Conf. Pkg.
Facing the restaurant, a hotel surrounded by flowers, with pleasant, extremely cozy rooms. Rustic charm in a seventeenth-century priory.

BEUVRON-EN-AUGE 14430
Paris 224 - Pont-l'Évêque 32 - Caen 30 Calvados

 # Le Pavé d'Auge

Pl. du Village - 02 31 79 26 71, fax 02 31 39 04 45
Closed Mon, Tue off-seas, Dec-Jan 15. Open until 9pm.
Beuvron is one of the most beautiful villages in France, and its former covered market, with its stone floor and wooden beams, has been turned into a comfortable, charming restaurant, a place to linger and enjoy the savory cuisine of Jérôme Bansard, a chef who knows how to bring out the best in regional products and recipes while showing his own personality. Good choice of half-bottles on the wine list. C 280. M 133 (exc Sat dinner, Sun lunch), 178-225.

BEUZEVILLE 27210
Paris 190 - Evreux 80 - Honfleur 15 Eure

12/20 Le Cochon d'Or

"Le Petit Castel", pl. du Général-de-Gaulle
02 32 57 70 46, fax 02 32 42 25 70
Closed Sun dinner & Mon off-seas, Dec 15-Jan 15. Open until 9pm. No pets. Pkg.
In the heart of town, a pleasant, traditional inn with a cozy décor and exposed beams. The staff is amiable and devoted, but the food lacks imagination and the service goes overboard. A little work will be necessary to get back the toque they have lost. The small wine list is well diversified and affordably priced. C 218. M 81 (weekdays), 114 (exc Sun lunch), 162-240.

BÉZANCOURT 76220
Paris 95 - Gournay-en-Bray 10 Seine-Mar.

 # Château du Landel

02 35 90 16 01, fax 02 35 90 62 47
Closed Sun, Nov 15-Mar 15. 2 stes 460-750. 17 rms 750. Bkfst 55. Restaurant. Half-board 460-590 (oblig in seas). Rm scr. Conf. Heated pool. Tennis. Pkg.
In a peaceful, flower-filled park, an elegant eighteenth-century post house with huge rooms individually decorated in a cozy, attractive style. The handsome public rooms were refurbished last year. Billiards.

BONSECOURS 76240
Paris 138 - Rouen 2 Seine-Mar.

Auberge de la Butte

69, route de Paris - 02 35 80 43 11, fax 02 35 80 69 74
Closed Sun, Mon, Aug 1-24, Christmas school hols. Open until 10pm. Priv rm 50. No pets.
This seventeenth-century post house has been turned into a magnificent Norman inn, thanks to the enthusiasm and talent of Pierre Hervé, who helped to build it with his own two hands. He then decorated it with art objects and antique earthenware in the traditional Rouen style. His

passion for authenticity also shows in his solid, classic dishes, which occasionally display modern touches, some of which work (sweet and sour combinations), and some of which are hit or miss (use of spices). The sweetbreads' barberry sauce is certainly worth the two toques, but the other sauces are drenching in butter. Classic, well-thoughtout selection of wine. Pleasant welcome by Nicole Hervé. C 350-500. M 200 (weekday lunch, wine incl), 250-340.

BREUIL-EN-AUGE   14130
Paris 204 - Caen 55 - Lisieu 9   Calvados

 Le Dauphin   ۞

02 31 65 08 11, fax 02 31 65 12 08
Closed Sun dinner, Mon. Open until 9pm. Priv rm 12. No pets.
A beautiful, peaceful Norman inn full of flowers, where Régis Lecomte proves that regional cooking does not rule out originality. Try the duck foie gras with apples, the barbecued oysters with lardons, the chicken roasted with apples under the skin, and warm bitterchocolate soufflé with vanilla and Bourbon cream. Fine cellar. Charming welcome, and friendly, efficient service. C 320-380. M 175-225 (exc Sat dinner).

CABOURG   14390
Paris 225 - Caen 24 - Deauville 19   Calvados

12/20   Le Balbec

Promenade Marcel-Proust
02 31 91 01 79, fax 02 31 24 03 20
Closed Tue & Wed off-seas. Open until 10pm. Priv rm 300. Terrace dining. Beach. Valet pkg.
Diners come here as much for the place's literary associations with Proust and the view of the sea as for the capable cuisine: beef terrine with cèpes and hazelnut vinaigrette, squab with red currants and balsamic vinegar, and fig soup with honey and peach sorbet. C 280. M 155, 195-240 (exc Sun lunch), 210 (Sun lunch), 75 (children).

 Grand Hôtel

(See restaurant above)
Open year-round. 2 stes 1,500-2,500. 68 rms 480-1,220. Bkfst 75. Conf. Beach. Valet pkg.
This enormous hotel hovering over the beach has been completely renovated. Ask to see room 147, where Marcel Proust roosted once a year from 1907 until World War I.

 Le Cottage   ♠♥

24, av. du Général-Leclerc
02 31 91 65 61, fax 02 31 28 78 82
Open year-round. 14 rms 240-390. Bkfst 38. Halfboard 275-310. Pkg.
A sauna, a solarium, and a billiard room were recently added to this little Norman hotel with simple, well-equipped rooms and a homey atmosphere.

CAEN   14000
Paris 222 - Rouen 124 - Évreux 121   Calvados

 La Bourride   ۞

15-17, rue du Vaugueux
02 31 93 50 76, fax 02 31 93 29 63
Closed Sun dinner, Mon, Jan 5-27, Aug 18-Sep 2. Open until 10pm. Priv rm 20.
Old Caen suffered a great deal during World War II. Only this small part remains, and it is full of fast food stands and pizzerias, making Michel Bruneau's handsome Norman house stand out even more. Inside, you'll find a huge fireplace and polished wood stairways. He is an enthusiastic cook who loves his region and its foods, but with an imagination like his, you can be sure you'll also enjoy his inspirations of the moment, consisting of lovely and surprising mixtures of herbs and spices mixed with the fruit of the sea and the land. The oyster tartare with root vegetables and cumin and served with an apple cider and soya oil vinaigrette was out of this world, as were the chitterling pancake with watercress and roasted corn; the pleasantly surprising seafood-stuffed gingerbread served with sea urchin bisque; the tomato stuffed with baby escargots and flavored with licorice and vanilla; and the ham hock stewed for four hours in apple cider and served with tapioca juice. And you can finish it all off right with eggs filled with hot bittersweet and sweet chocolate, ageless calvados (a must!) or Père Jules apple cider. The wine list is long and pricey, with fine bottles from the Loire Valley. C 360. M 250 (lunch, wine incl), 345-495, 100 (children)

 Le Carlotta

16, quai Vendeuvre
02 31 86 68 99, fax 02 31 38 92 31
Closed Aug 8-20. Open until 11pm (midnight Fri & Sat). Terrace dining. Air cond. Pkg.
A typical brasserie in both its décor and cuisine. On the menu you'll find good, well-prepared fish: galette of cod brandade, roast fresh cod with rosemary cream, and monkfish brochette. There are also such traditional dishes as tête de veau gribiche, duck confit parmentier, and steak tartare. Nice little cellar and a lively ambiance. C 200-260. M 92-148, 110 (wine incl), 40 (children).

 Les Cordeliers   ♠♥

4, rue des Cordeliers
02 31 86 37 15, fax 02 31 39 56 51
Open year-round. 21 rms 130-350. Bkfst 30. Restaurant. Conf. Pkg.
In one of the few quarters spared by the war, a quiet hotel with stone walls. The décor of the rooms sometimes gets a little psychedelic.

 Le Dauphin   ۞

29, rue Gémare - 02 31 86 22 26, fax 02 31 86 35 14
Closed Sat lunch, Feb 15-Mar 2, Jul 15-Aug 10 (restaurant only). Open until 9:30pm. Priv rm 40.

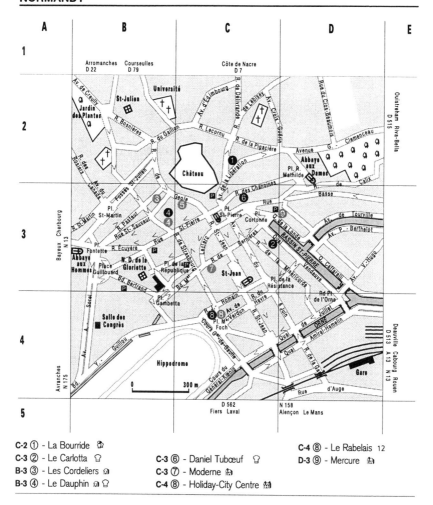

C-2 ① - La Bourride 🐟
C-3 ② - Le Carlotta ♀
B-3 ③ - Les Cordeliers ♨
B-3 ④ - Le Dauphin ♨ ♀

C-3 ⑥ - Daniel Tubœuf ♀
C-3 ⑦ - Moderne 🛏
C-4 ⑧ - Holiday-City Centre 🛏

C-4 ⑧ - Le Rabelais 12
D-3 ⑨ - Mercure 🛏

HOTEL: 22 rms 230-610. Bkfst 50. Half-board 360-470. Rm ser. Conf. Pkg.

Robert Chabredier doesn't miss out on a single regional ingredient. His menu is an ode to Normandy: seafood ravioli, rack of lamb, apple and rhubarb tart. The service is inspired and the welcome courteous. Intelligently chosen wine list. This solid establishment faces William the Conqueror's château. **C** 300. **M** 100-310, 65 (children).

🛏 Mercure

1, rue de Courtonne
02 31 47 24 24, fax 02 31 47 43 88
Open year-round. 4 stes 750-850. 110 rms 460-550. Bkfst 50. Rms for disabled. Restaurant. Rm ser. Air cond. Conf. Garage pkg.

This modern hotel faces the pleasure port and has large, comfortably equipped rooms. It is practical and centrally located, but the rooms are rather dark and not too well soundproofed.

🛏 Moderne

116, bd du Maréchal-Leclerc
02 31 86 04 23, fax 02 31 85 37 93
Open year-round. 40 rms 320-630. Bkfst 47. Rms for disabled. Garage pkg.

Near the château, a modern establishment with the feel of an English pub. The rooms have been renovated in a more personalized style. The breakfast room has view of the town. Sauna.

The **prices** in this guide reflect what establishments were charging at press time.

12/20 Le Rabelais

Pl. Foch - 02 31 27 57 57, fax 02 31 27 57 58
Closed Sat lunch. Open until 10pm. No pets.
This hotel restaurant still manages to make
innovations, but they have a long way to go if
they want to win back the toque they lost three
years ago. It will take more than the very disappointing escargot turnover and chitterlings in
Pommeau or the slice of turbot with shallot
"pulp" to get it back. The prices remain
reasonable, with a set menu at 90 F and a business menu. C 250. M 90 (weekday lunch), 125-
235, 50 (children).

Holiday Inn-City Centre

(See restaurant above)
*Open year-round. 92 rms 350-580. Bkfst 55. Rms
for disabled. Rm scr. Conf.*
Most of the rooms in this 1950s–vintage hotel
have a view of the racecourse. Everything has
been impeccably renovated. Cocktail bar. Breakfast needs improvement.

 ## Daniel Tubœuf

8, rue Buquet - 02 31 43 64 48
*Closed Sun, Mon, Aug 1-22. Open until 9:45pm.
Air cond.*
Healthy servings are not what's missing in
Daniel Tubœuf's regional cooking, and the term
"light" has not yet reached these parts (the
sauces are particularly heavy). His tripe cake
served with thin slivers of potatoes in an apple-
flavored sauce is a clever idea and quite tasty; the
just-cooked bass served with a surprising pepper sauce really works; so does the beef fillet
served with a thick wine sauce and a "woven"
potato cake. The wine cellar has a glaring lack of
Loire Valley wines. We're obliged to drop a
point. M 105-140 (weekday dinner), 129 (lunch),
175 (Sat dinner), 205.

And also...

*Our selection of places for inexpensive,
quick, or late-night meals.*
L'Assiette (02 31 85 29 16 - 2, pl. Fontelle. Open
until 10pm.): Between the Palais de Justice and
the Hôtel de Ville, market cuisine with different
menus for the products of the sea and the land.
Do try the desserts (59-200).
La Muscade (02 31 85 61 84 - 21, pl. St-Martin.
Open until 10:30pm.): Skillfully-prepared fish
and meat grilled over a wood fire, which adds
even more warmth to this already-warm atmosphere. Reasonable prices (150-250).
Le Panier à Salades (02 31 34 22 22 - 24, rue
Pierre-Girard. Open until 11pm.): Good meat
dishes, a huge choice of salads, and good desserts in an old-fashioned atmosphere (100).
Le Saïgon (02 31 86 13 48 - 13 rue du Tout-de-
Terre. Open until 9pm, 9:30pm Fri & Sat.): Good
quality Vietnamese food at very reasonable
prices. Too bad they don't freshen the place up a
bit (110-180).

CANAPVILLE 14800
Paris 205 - Caen 53 - Deauville 6 Calvados

 ## Jarrasse

N 177 - 02 31 65 21 80, fax 02 31 65 03 75
*Closed Tue & Wed (exc Aug), Feb school hols, Dec.
Open until 9pm. Garden dining. Pkg.*
A tidy, thatch-roofed inn with an adorable garden where you can appreciate the talent of
François Jarrasse. The foie gras and smoked salmon are homemade, and the farm chicken with
morels and the fried bass are exquisitely simple.
The crêpes soufflées and the nougat ice cream
are pleasing desserts. The Cuvée LM Muscadet
at 105 F and the Seigneurs de Cahors at 80 F are
good choices. C 250-300. M 160 (wine incl), 200.

CAUDEBEC-EN-CAUX 76490
Paris 175 - Rouen 36 - Pont-Audemer 28 Seine-Mar.

 ## Manoir de Rétival

2, rue St-Clair - 02 35 96 11 22, fax 02 35 96 29 22
*Closing not available. Open until 9:30pm. Priv rm
40. Terrace dining. No pets. Pkg.*
In his handsome Norman manor house, Jean-
Luc Tartarin offers meals that are both hearty
and rigorously prepared, and highly eclectic in
the choice of ingredients and flavor combinations. The poached foie gras is complemented by
a soup of clams and line-caught whiting with
cumin. Smoked bacon accompanies the rabbit
kidneys with mussels, enriched by a cream of
Tarbais beans with Chinese pepper. Nothing
here is bland; everything is vibrantly spiced. The
cellar matches the quality of the food, with most
bottles coming from top producers, and there is
a good selection of half-bottles. C 400-550. M
195-495, 95 (children).

COLOMBIERS-SUR-SEULLES 14480
Paris 266 - Caen 20 - Bayeux 16 Calvados

 ## Château du Baffy

02 31 08 04 57, fax 02 31 08 08 29
*Closed Sun off-seas, Mon, Jan. 35 rms 320-560. Rms
for disabled. Restaurant. Half-board 250-380.
Conf. Tennis. Pkg.*
This eighteenth-century château set in a
wooded park provides plenty of space and quiet.
The spacious, old-fashioned rooms have high
ceilings. The Normandy landing beaches are five
minutes away.

COMMES 14520
Paris 284 - Caen 40 - Bayeux 9 Calvados

 ## La Chenevière

Les Escures - 02 31 21 47 96, fax 02 31 21 47 98
*Closed Nov 15-Mar 1. 3 stes 1,100-1,500. 16 rms
700-1,100. Bkfst 80. Rms for disabled. Restaurant.
Half-board 650-1,050. Rm scr. Conf. Garage pkg.*
A charming manor house set in a park with
hundred-year-old trees. The rooms are huge,

tastefully decorated in soft colors, well soundproofed and maintained, and have superb bathrooms. Good, generous breakfasts.

CONDÉ-SUR-NOIREAU — 14110
Paris 280 - Caen 46 - Bayeux 60 — Calvados

 Le Cerf ♦

18, rue de Chêne - 02 31 69 40 55, fax 02 31 69 78 29 *Closed Fri (Oct 20-Mar 15), Sun dinner, 1 wk in Nov. Open until 9:15pm. Pkg.*
Patrice and Catherine Malgrey are planning to make their charming restaurant with its ivy-covered façade and Norman country décor even more comfortable. The region's best ingredients go into Patrice's delicate, attractive cuisine: salmon with cider butter, beef ficelle with Camembert cream sauce. Wide variety of wines. Smiling welcome, and prices that will make you smile. C 200-280. M 67 (weekdays), 95-170, 47 (children).

CONDEAU — 61110
Paris 15 - Le Mans 75 - Chartres 40 — Orne

 Moulin de Villeray ♠♣

02 33 73 30 22, fax 02 33 73 38 28
Closed Jan 25-end Feb. 2 stes 950-1,200. 16 rms 450-1,050. Bkfst 68. Rms for disabled. Restaurant. Half-board 773 (oblig in seas). Rm ser. Conf. Pool. Pkg.
An old mill on the banks of the Huisne amid the green countryside. Inside, a stone fireplace in the former wheel room with rough-hewn Norman beams. Large, peaceful rooms, and a new swimming pool in the park.

CONTEVILLE — 27210
Paris 190 - Deauville 28 - Le Havre 42 — Eure

 Auberge du Vieux Logis

02 32 57 60 16, fax 02 32 57 45 84
Closed Tue dinner, Wed, Jan 20-Feb 20. Open until 9:30pm. Priv rm 30. Pkg.
A peaceful inn with gleaming furnishings and copperware. Guillaume Louet, who has worked under the likes of Robuchon, has taken over his father's kitchen and with a bang. He adds new life to the classic cuisine of his father with dishes like fresh cod steak with andouille sausage (chitterling) and potato pie, veal sweetbread and lobster with shellfish sauce, and chocolate and morello cherry puff pastry. Service and welcome are perfect in the traditional Louet family style. His *Menu du Terroir* full of regional dishes and ingredients is well worth trying, and the prices are palatable. C 250-380. M 145-330.

COURSEULLES-SUR-MER — 14470
Paris 260 - Caen 18 - Arromanches 13 — Calvados

 La Crémaillère et Le Gytan ♠♣

Bd de la Plage - 02 31 37 46 73, fax 02 31 37 19 31 *Open year-round. 16 stes 300-750. 42 rms 195-435. Bkfst 45. Rms for disabled. Restaurant. Half-board 295-435. Rm ser. Conf. Pkg.*
Located near the beaches, with bright, pleasant rooms that were recently renovated. Some have a view of the sea, and those in the annex look out on the garden. Hotel constantly be improved. Excellent facilities: tanning bed, sauna and Jacuzzi. Four new apartments last year.

COURTILS — 50220
Paris 307 - Rennes 61 - Fougères 37 — Manche

 Le Manoir de la Roche-Torin ♠♣

Route du Mont-St-Michel
02 33 70 96 55, fax 02 33 48 35 20
Open year-round. 1 ste 850. 12 rms 440-850. Bkfst 58. Restaurant. Half-board 440-680 (oblig in seas). Rm ser. Conf. Pkg.
A nineteenth-century edifice set in a large park near the shores of Mont-Saint-Michel bay. Well-appointed rooms, one of which has a whirlpool bath.

CRÉPON — 14480
Paris 269 - Caen 25 - Bayeux 12 — Calvados

 Ferme de la Rançonnière

Route d'Arromanches
02 31 22 21 73, fax 02 31 22 98 39
Closed Feb. 34 rms 295-480. Bkfst 45. Rms for disabled. Restaurant. Half-board 300-400 (oblig in seas). Conf. Pkg.
This 500-year-old farm has been entirely restored and has beautiful, individually decorated rooms that are adequately equipped.

DEAUVILLE — 14800
Paris 210 - Le Havre 40 - Caen 43 — Calvados

Le Ciro's

Bd de la Mer - 02 31 88 18 10, fax 02 31 98 66 71 *Open daily until 9:30pm (10:30pm in summer). Terrace dining. Pkg.*
Near the beach, but without a view of the sea, this restaurant with a split-level dining room attracts a well-off clientele of a certain age who come to see and be seen. They fortify themselves with good marinated salmon, perfectly grilled sole, and a light-as-a-feather strawberry charlotte. The cellar holds some prestigious bottles, but there are still some decent wines priced between 120 F and 200 F. C 330-470. M 190-320, 85 (children).

12/20 Côté Royal

Hôtel Royal, bd Eugène Cornuché
02 31 98 66 33, fax 02 31 98 66 34
Closed Mon-Fri off-seas, mid Nov-mid Mar. Open until 10:30pm. Heated pool. Valet pkg.
L'Étrier, the Royal hotel's main restaurant, is no longer open at noon, so they serve a lighter but good lunch in this large, pleasantly renovated drawing room. Don't look for surprises on the wine list, but you'll find what you need to eat with the various seafood dishes, excellent tarama, tender veal cooked in breadcrumbs and appetizing pastries. C 215-220.

12/20 L'Étrier

Hôtel Royal, bd Eugène-Cornuché
02 31 98 66 33, fax 02 31 98 66 34
Open dinner only. Closed mid Nov-beg Mar. Open until 10pm (10:30pm Fri & Sat). Priv rm 200. Terrace dining. Heated pool. Valet pkg.
A pleasant restaurant that looks like a pink candy box, abundantly decorated with flowers. The menu is appetizing, even tantelizing, but the craftsmanship doesn't live up to its promises. The clams and crab marinated in olive oil and the grilled Dublin prawns with eggplant caviar lasagna were good ideas, but not so good on the tongue; the burbot osso-buco was well prepared, but the chop suey vegetables simply didn't go with it. A point just has to go. Fine cellar. C 500. M 220-390.

Royal

(See restaurant above)
Closed mid Nov-beg Mar. 24 stes 1,600-10,000. 249 rms 1,250-2,200. Bkfst 120-150. Rms for disabled. Rm ser. Conf. Heated pool. Valet pkg.
Near the casino, this luxurious hotel faces the sea. The rooms are spacious, classically comfortable, and have superb views. Several meeting rooms. A second restaurant, Le Royal, holds theme parties.

Hélios Hôtel

10, rue Fossorier - 02 31 14 46 46, fax 02 31 88 53 87
Open year-round. 1 ste 700-900. 44 rms 290-460. Bkfst 46. Rms for disabled. Heated pool. No pets.
Between the beach, the casino, and the racetrack, a decent modern hotel with a Norman-style façade. Some rooms have mezzanines for families.

Le Kraal

Pl. du Marché - 02 31 88 30 58, fax 02 31 88 47 77
Open daily until 11pm. Terrace dining. No cards. Pkg.
The Norman and Parisian regulars take their places on the third floor, the most pleasant of the dining rooms in this handsome restaurant. Jean Chauvin has been cooking here for 26 years, and in the past, he knew how to bring out the best in seafood, but this year he's slipping (is he just too tired?). We get the feeling he's trying to get a maximum of money for a minimum of effort. A fourteen is no longer deserved. Friendly welcome. C 300-380. M 160, 320.

La Potinière

38, rue Jean-Mermoz
02 31 98 66 22, fax 02 31 98 66 23
Closed Mon lunch. Open until 10:30pm. Priv rm 45. No pets. Heated pool. Valet pkg.
The handsome façade of this large, lovely building hides a dining room on three levels decorated in light tones, with antique furniture. You'd think it hard to find an affordable wine that could live up to the quality you find on your plate, but that's not the case. For 190 F you can drink an excellent Château Moulin Riche Saint-Julien with your superb crab puff pastry in sesame oil or your roast sea bass served in tandoori concentrate. The same wine also goes well with the 250 F fixed-price menu centered around pan-fried duck breast fillet cooked in sesame seeds and served with a spicy sauce. Fine cellar. Professional, fairly rapid service. C 400. M 250-420.

Hôtel Normandy

(See restaurant above)
Open year-round. 26 stes 2,300-7,500. 281 rms 1,000-2,200. Bkfst 96-130. Rms for disabled. Rm ser. Conf. Heated pool. Tennis. Valet pkg.
Facing the sea, a Norman cottage grown into a palace, with charming rooms renovated on a regular basis. Regular hangout for the weekend Paris-Deauville crowd. Fitness center and room service. Breakfast room near the swimming pool.

Le Spinnaker

52, rue Mirabeau - 02 31 88 24 40, fax 02 31 88 43 58
Closed Wed (exc Aug), Tue (exc summer), Jan. Open until 9:30pm. Priv rm 25. Garage pkg.
Pascal Angenard's success lies in hard work with good, dependable results. We like the classic, unpretentious cuisine of this excellent saucemaker, who brings out the best in quality ingredients, and does it with great precision. Pretty, homy dining room. The 160 F "Market Special" menu is a delight. Yummy desserts, good cellar. Professional, amiable service in a comfortable décor. C 350-420. M 220 (wine incl), 160-320.

Yacht Club

2, rue Brency - 02 31 87 30 00, fax 02 31 87 05 80
Closed Jan-Feb. 1 ste 900-1,300. 52rms 450-750. Bkfst 50. Rms for disabled. Conf. Pkg.
Very British-looking clubhouse-style residences near the yachting marina, located between the open-air market and the quay. Surrounded by a calm garden. The décor of the rooms is not at all what you expect: Provence-style!

DIEPPE	76200
Paris 185 - Rouen 58 - Le Havre 103	Seine-Mar.

Aguado

30, bd de Verdun - 02 35 84 27 00, fax 02 35 06 17 61
Open year-round. 56 rms 230-435. Bkfst 45-60.

Near the port and the city center, with comfortable rooms overlooking the ocean. Pleasant welcome.

11/20 Comptoir Deep

Pl. Camille-Saint-Saëns
02 35 06 09 11, fax 02 35 06 22 08
Closed Mon, Jan. Open until 10pm. Priv rm 35.
You've never lunched in the middle of an antique store? Here's your chance, and charm is not what's missing! In addition, you'll have a view of the lovely garden. You'll savor fresh-as-can-be dishes such as scallops in sea urchin butter and Deep fish stew, cooked to perfection. It's surprising the desserts aren't better since the restaurant turns into a tea room in the afternoon. C 100-230. M 78 (lunch), 98 (dinner), 145.

Hôtel de l'Europe

63, bd de Verdun - 02 32 90 19 19, fax 02 32 90 19 00
Open year-round. 60 rms 270-340. Bkfst 35. Conf.
Facing the sea, a modern hotel with a huge lobby and picture windows. Spacious, pleasant rooms. Everything here smells new. Good location and good quality for the price.

La Présidence

1, bd de Verdun - 02 35 84 31 31, fax 02 35 84 86 70
Open year-round. 1 ste 755. 88 rms 300-560. Bkfst 47-55. Rms for disabled. Restaurant. Half-board 600. Rm ser. Conf. Garage pkg.
Modern, well-equipped rooms, some of which have views of the sea. Numerous leisure and fitness activities. English bar, golf package, seawater therapy.

11/20 Restaurant du Port

99, quai Henri-IV - 02 35 84 36 64
Closed Thu off-seas, Jan 5-31. Open until 10:30pm. Terrace dining. Pkg.
Fresh seafood on a lovely terrace overlooking the marina. Service with an extra-big smile. C 85. M 85-185, 45 (children).

Le Saint-Jacques

12, rue de l'Oranger - 02 35 84 52 04
Closed 10 days at Christmas. Open until 9pm. Pkg.
We have only compliments for the fine seafood-based cuisine of Benoist Carteret, who charmed us with fresh ingredients, precise cooking times, delicate sauces, and who has just bought the restaurant after eleven years in the kitchen. Try the good-value 115 F fixed-price menu: rockfish soup, Dieppe fish stew, Normandy cheeses and hot Normandy-style apple pie; the rest of the menu is quite affordable as well. Well-chosen cellar. Amiable welcome and friendly, competent service in the pretty dining room furnished with antiques and paintings. M 65 (lunch), 115-205, 45 (children).

10/20 Windsor

18, bd de Verdun - 02 35 84 15 23, fax 02 35 84 74 52

Open daily until 9:30pm (11pm Fri & Sat).
HOTEL: *48 rms 139-340. Bkfst 37. Half-board 250-440. Rm ser. Conf. Air cond. Garage pkg.*
This large old house facing the sea was already a hot spot with seawater therapy lovers in Napoleon's time, so things have not changed all that much... The rooms with a seaview are best, but otherwise you'll have a view of the medieval château or the cliffs. Pleasant reception. C 300-450. M 79 (weekday lunch, Sat), 50 (children).

DIVES-SUR-MER	14160
Paris 228 - Caen 22 - Cabourg 3	Calvados

Chez le Bougnat

27, rue Gaston-Manneville - 02 31 91 06 13
Closed Fri, Sat dinner. Open until 10pm. No cards.
The setting leaves something to be desired, but who cares? When you open the door, you find yourself in what looks like a Paris métro station with its white-and-green-tiled walls, vintage posters, and banquettes. Owner and ex-butcher Fred certainly knows his way around meats and charcuterie, and he makes his own terrines. The fresh fish and mussels are also worth tasting. A little bar in the same style is being created. M 79, 50 (children).

DOUAINS	27120
Paris 86 - Evreux 23 - Rouen 57	Eure

Le Grand Siècle

02 32 52 40 50, fax 02 32 52 69 65
Open daily until 9:30pm. Priv rm 350. Terrace dining. Heated pool. Tennis. Pkg.
A typical seventeenth-century château, complete with park and moat. The elegant dining room has exposed beams and is warmed by a large fireplace. Chef Christian Langlais enjoys unearthing forgotten recipes (found on the interesting "Grand Siècle" menu), but he also makes a flavorful, precise, and more personal cuisine. Fine wine cellar. Friendly, competent service. C 300-400. M 190 (lunch), 220 (lunch, wine incl), 120-360, 90 (children).

Château de Brécourt ♣♥

(See restaurant above)
Open year-round. 5 stes 1,150-1,500. 25 rms 410-1,040. Bkfst 73. Half-board 630-990. Rm ser. Conf. Heated pool. Tennis. Pkg.
A splendid Louis XIII château in a large, wooded park. The rooms are all different, and some of them are huge. They are all cozy and prettily decorated. Wonderful covered swimming pool with Jacuzzi. Weekend packages.

DUCEY	50220
Paris 330 - Avranches 10 - Fougères 37	Manche

Auberge de la Sélune ♣♥

2, rue de Saint-Germain
02 33 48 53 62, fax 02 33 48 90 30

Closed Oct-mid Jan: Mon, Jan 15-Feb 15. 20 rms 220-300. Bkfst 42. Restaurant. Half-board 305-315 (oblig in seas). Garage pkg.
Away from the road on the river bank, a charming, restful inn. New carpets and fabric wall coverings in the bright, carefully decorated rooms.

ÉVREUX	27000
Paris 100 - Rouen 51 - Mantes 44 - Dreux 44	Eure

 Hôtel de France

29, rue Saint-Thomas
02 32 39 09 25, fax 02 32 38 38 56
Closed Sun dinner, Mon. Open until 10pm. Priv rm 25. HOTEL: 1 ste 440. 15 rms 255-340. Bkfst 35. Half-board 290-350. Rm ser. Conf. Garage pkg.
A popular spot for business lunches, this pleasant restaurant has an elegant Norman dining room that looks out on a riverside garden. Mario Mathoux's variety of set menus allows customers to sample discreetly inventive, interesting cuisine that respects the flavors of quality local ingredients without emptying their wallets. The charming owner, Bernard Meyruey, comments on the highly intelligent wine list. M 148-195.

FALAISE	14700
Paris 272 - Caen 34 - Argentan 23 - Vire 57	Calvados

 L'Attache

"Alain Hastain," N 158, 1 km toward Caen,
Rond-point de l'Attache
02 31 90 05 38, fax 02 31 90 57 19
Closed Wed off-seas, last wk of Oct. Open until 9:30pm. Priv rm 40. No pets.
Chef Hastain, a follower of Michel Bras, has a passion for herbs and plants, so don't be surprised at the lovely langoustine terrine accompanied by wild herbs. Yes, they are edible. The combination of hazelnut milk with perfectly cooked monkfish, and the irreproachable marquise au chocolat don't lead us to award a second toque quite yet, but things are looking in the right direction. Reasonable prices and pleasant surroundings. C 320. M 90-310.

FÉCAMP	76400
Paris 215 - Rouen 71 - Le Havre 40	Seine-Mar.

 Hôtel de la Plage

87, rue de la Plage
02 35 29 76 51, fax 02 35 28 68 30
Open year-round. 22 rms 200-340. Bkfst 32.
A small, cozy hotel that has been entirely renovated, located just ten yards from the sea and the city center. Good value for the price.

12/20 Le Viking

63, bd Albert-Ier - 02 35 29 22 92, fax 02 35 29 45 24
Closed Sun dinner & Mon (exc Apr-Sep). Open until 9:30pm (10pm in summer). Priv rm 120.

With its modern armor of slate and glass, this comfortable "Viking" looks out on the magnificent cliffs and the sea, best viewed from the upstairs dining room. The cuisine is intelligent and serious, with an emphasis on seafood and local ingredients. C 230-350. M 98 (exc Sun), 128-260, 68 (children).

FLEURY-SUR-ORNE	14000
Paris 247 - Caen 5	Calvados

L'Ile Enchantée

1, rue St-André - 02 31 52 15 52, fax 02 31 72 67 17
Closed Sun dinner & Mon (exc hols), Feb school hols, Aug 3-12. Open until 9:30pm. Priv rm 15. Pkg.
The banks of the Orne are the perfect setting for the cuisine of Alain Jamet. While we don't recommend the langoustine and lobster jardinière with foie gras because of its lackluster seasoning, we are enthusiastic about the bass fillet stuffed with salmon, whose seafood sauce perfectly rounded out the flavors of the sea. The caramelized apple croustillant has become a classic here. Reasonable prices. C 270. M 98 (exc Sun), 135-220, 55 (children).

FOURGES	27630
Paris 72 - Les Andelys 33 - Evreux 56 - Vernon 14	Eure

12/20 Le Moulin de Fourges

02 32 52 12 12, fax 02 32 52 92 56
Closed Sun dinner & Mon (exc in summer). Open until 10:15pm. Priv rm 20. Terrace dining. Pkg.
While the owners pamper customers in the rustic dining rooms of this adorable eighteenth-century mill, the young chef cooks up generous, tasty dishes. Interesting selection of regional wines. C 200-300. M 95 (weekdays), 150-290.

FRICHEMESNIL	76690
Paris 165 - Rouen 29 - Dieppe 47	Seine-Mar.

Au Souper Fin

Pl. de l'Église - 02 35 33 33 88, fax 02 35 33 50 42
Closed Wed dinner, Thu, Aug 18-Sep 4. Open until 9pm. Priv rm 10. Terrace dining.
Éric Buisset knows how to keep us coming back. He recently purchased the house next to his restaurant, which he has converted into a lounge and two pretty guest rooms. An excellent idea, since as soon as you are welcomed by his smiling wife, Véronique, you will want to prolong your stay, especially after you taste his lobster and langoustine waterzoï, the turbot with truffle juice, and the warm apple tart with honey ice cream. Everything is served with diligence and accompanied by well-chosen wines at fair prices. C 320. M 165, 230.

The C (A la carte) restaurant prices given are for a complete three-course meal for one, including a half-bottle of modest wine and service. M (Menu) prices are for a complete fixed-price meal for one, excluding wine (unless otherwise noted).

GIVERNY	27620
Paris 79 - Evreux 34 - Rouen 65	Eure

12/20 Les Jardins de Giverny

Chemin du Roy - 02 32 21 60 80, fax 02 32 51 93 77
*Closed Sun dinner, Mon, Feb. Open until 9pm.
Terrace dining. Pkg.*
A stone's throw from Claude Monet's house, this fine Norman dwelling sits in a dreamy estate filled with roses and rare trees. The kitchen has its ups and downs, but on his good days the chef delivers appetizing, seasonal cuisine. The cellar harbors a great choice of white wines from the Loire Valley. C 250. M 130, 250.

GRANVILLE	50400
Paris 350 - Cherbourg 104 - Coutances 29	Manche

12/20 La Citadelle

10, rue Cambernon - 02 33 50 34 10
Closed Sun dinner & Mon off-seas, 2 wks in Jan, 2 wks in Feb. Open until 9:30pm (10:30pm in summer). Terrace dining.
In the old part of town, a restaurant with an amusing décor of stone walls and pastel wood paneling, brightened by modern paintings and green plants. This relaxed atmosphere is the setting for classic, forthright cuisine prepared without fuss. A nice little wine list that is well diversified. C 250-300. M 100 (exc Sat dinner & Sun), 145-250, 70 (children).

11/20 La Potinière

19, rue Georges-Clemenceau
02 33 50 17 31, fax 02 33 50 89 22
Closed Sun dinner, Mon, Nov-Feb. Open until 9:30pm (10pm in summer).
One of the few places where you can eat well in Granville. Uncomplicated but good food. C 260-390. M 98-176, 55 (children).

Hôtel des Bains

(See restaurant above)
Closed Sun pm, Mon, Nov-Feb. 1 ste 280-780. 46 rms 230-550. Bkfst 40. Half-board 395-795. Conf.
Facing the casino and the sea, an Anglo-Norman hotel built in the early nineteenth century. Charming, spacious rooms that are a bit outmoded. The lobby is enormous, but the bathrooms are extremely cramped.

HAVRE (LE)	76600
Paris 204 - Amiens 179 - Rouen 86	Seine-Mar.

Bordeaux

147, rue Louis-Brindeau
02 35 22 69 44, fax 02 35 42 09 27
Open year-round. 31 rms 385-530. Bkfst 47. Conf. Beach. Pkg.
Right in the center of town, facing the harbor, this hotel offers spacious rooms at decent prices.

Hôtel Foch

4, rue de Caligny - 02 35 42 50 69, fax 02 35 43 40 17
Open year-round. 33 rms 300-335. Bkfst 38. Pkg.
Very simple but well equipped and near the center of town.

Le Marly

121, rue de Paris - 02 35 41 72 48, fax 02 35 21 50 45
Open year-round. 37 rms 340-420. Bkfst 42. Conf. Pkg.
Well-located in the center of town; practical and well equipped. Good value.

13 L'Odyssée

41, rue Général-Faidherbe
02 35 21 32 42, fax 02 35 21 32 42
Closed Sat lunch, Sun dinner, Mon, Feb 1-15, 2 wks beg Aug. Open until 9:30pm. Terrace dining.
Don't let the plainness of the décor fool you, because the cooking is studied refinement itself. Fish-oriented, which is appropriate since it is located near the fish market. Carefully prepared and carefully presented, letting you savor the likes of a fish terrine served on a bed of hot-peppered avocado cream with slices of house-smoked salmon—an interesting mixture of flavors—or the excellent turbot steak studded with poppy seeds, grilled on one side only and served with a lovely little cream sauce. Delicious "packet" of season's fruits. Good wine list with a well-balanced selection of half-bottles. C 350. M 125 (weekdays), 155, 195 (Sat & Sun).

13 Petit Bedon

37-39 rue Louis-Brindeau
02 35 41 36 81, fax 02 35 21 09 24
Closed Sat lunch, Sun, Feb school hols, 3 wks in Aug. Open until 9:30pm. Air cond. Pkg.
The irreproachable quality of Guy Poyer's traditional cuisine, tinted with occasional hints of imagination, produces inventive dishes such as hot brioche with marrow, burbot piccata with cuttlefish-ink-flavored rice verjuice, and thinly sliced rump steak wrapped in a crêpe coated with an emulsion of foie gras. The décor rather lacks imagination, but Poyer makes up for it with his delicious market specials and an inviting wine cellar that is well-balanced yet full of unusual finds. C 210. M 155-330.

12/20 La Petite Auberge

32, rue de Sainte-Adresse
02 35 46 27 32, fax 02 35 48 26 15
Closed Sun dinner & Mon (exc hols), 1 wk at Feb school hols, Aug 4-25. Open until 9:30pm. Priv rm 26. Air cond.
In this half-timbered house with its pink-and-gray décor, everyone is gracious and well-meaning, but nice is just not enough. The set-price meals, as well as the freshness of such creations as the tomato and basil Bavarian cream and the professionalism in the preparation of the salmon fillet with chive cream sauce serve as saving grace for the general lack of quality. Well-rounded wine list. Efficient service. C 230. M 118

(weekdays, Sat lunch), 130 (Sat dinner, Sun), 155-205.

12/20 Le Saint-Pierre

24, rue d'Ingouville - 02 35 42 64 32
Closed Sat lunch, Sun, mid Jul-mid Aug. Open until 9:30pm. Air cond.
The small, simple dining room has a rustic décor, but the generous seafood-based cuisine is not without imagination. The owner is very careful about cooking times and presentation. A likable little wine list. C 240-300. M 78 (weekdays), 105-138.

12/20 Le Trois Mâts

Chaussée d'Angoulême
02 35 19 50 50, fax 02 35 19 50 99
Open daily until 10:30pm. Terrace dining. Air cond. Garage pkg.
At the foot of the World Trade Center, the perfect stopping place for businesspeople. There is a wide selection of set menus, as well as seafood and *terroir* platters for quick meals. Efficient service. Limited wine list. C 200. M 99-159, 49 (children).

Mercure

(See restaurant above)
Open year-round. 96 rms 496-645. Bkfst 55. Rms for disabled. Restaurant. Rm scr. Conf. Garage pkg.
Facing the handsome Commerce docks, a hotel with spacious rooms that are pleasant and functional, although the windows are too small and the soundproofing is inadequate. Modern seminar facilities.

And also...

Our selection of places for inexpensive, quick, or late-night meals.
Le Bistrot des Halles (02 35 22 50 52 - 7, pl. des Halles-Centrales. Open until 11pm.): A wine bar with homestyle food like beef marrow on toast and chocolate tart (72-160).
Le Grignot (02 35 43 62 07 - 53, rue Racine. Open until midnight.): A lively, old-fashioned bistro with good *plats du jour* and a choice of crêpes (150).
Le Petit Bouchon (02 35 43 22 43 - 42-44, rue Louis-Philippe. Open until midnight.): Fresh ingredients, excellent meats, generous servings, and charming service (69-180).

HONFLEUR	14600
Paris 192 - Le Havre 25 - Caen 60 - Lisieux 34	Calvados

L'Absinthe

10, quai de la Quarantaine - 02 31 89 39 00 (R), 02 31 89 23 23 (H), fax 02 31 89 53 60
Closed mid Nov-end Nov. Open until 9:30pm. Terrace dining. Garage pkg.
Facing the port, one of the most popular restaurants in Honfleur. Under the exposed beams in the dining room hung with paintings, the ever-smiling but highly profressional owner,

Antoine Ceffrey, has just changed chefs, but the party-atmosphere has not changed one iota. Nor has the sophistication of the food with offerings such as rock lobster piperade with hot-pepper cream sauce, pan-fried red mullet fillets with calamari "pulp", and roast pigeon with confit artichokes. Subtle but sophisticated wine list offering wide selection. C 350-400. M 165-330.

L'Absinthe

(See restaurant above)
Closed mid Nov-end Nov. 1 ste 1,200. 6 rms 500-700. Bkfst 55. Rms for disabled. Conf. Pkg.
In the heart of the old town, a sixteenth-century Norman-style presbytery converted into a charming hotel with bright, pleasant, well-equipped (satellite TV) rooms, and nice bathrooms with whirlpool baths. Cozy salon with fireplace.

L'Assiette Gourmande

2, quai des Passagers
02 31 89 24 88, fax 02 31 89 90 17
Closed Mon off-seas. Open until 10pm. Air cond. Pkg.
In this handsome dining room in an imposing building on the quay, the welcome extended by Madame Bonnefoy and the cuisine of her husband Gérard complement each other perfectly. The proof is that their restaurant is always full. The dishes enhance the flavors of quality ingredients: excellent salmon tartare with caviar cream, langoustine risotto with parsley sauce, very good veal sweetbreads, and remarkable vanilla crème brûlée. Interesting wines starting at 200 F. Excellent service. C 480-550. M 160-410.

Castel Albertine

19, cours A.-Manuel
02 31 98 85 56, fax 02 31 98 83 18
Open year-round. 1 ste 600-800. 25 rms 350-600. Bkfst 50. Rms for disabled. Conf. Pkg.
This manor house, practically untouched since its construction, is tucked into the back of an embellished park. Carefully decorated in keeping with the architectural style and very comfortable. Huge foyer, breakfast in your room or in an exquisite drawing room. Finnish sauna and multi-head showers.

L'Écrin

19, rue Eugène-Boudin
02 31 14 43 45, fax 02 31 89 24 41
Open year-round. 1 ste 400-1,000. 21 rms 400-950. Bkfst 50-85. Rms for disabled. Conf. No pets. Garage pkg.
On a little cobbled street in the center of town, a picturesque old Norman manor house. With its statues, painting, piano, and tropical plants, the lobby resembles a museum. Louis XV–style rooms with four-poster beds and period furniture.

*Looking for a restaurant? Refer to the **index**.*

La Ferme Saint-Siméon

Rue Adolphe-Marais
02 31 89 23 61, fax 02 31 89 48 48
Open daily until 9:30pm. Priv rm 85. Garden dining. Heated pool. Pkg.
Perhaps we should have listened to the local gourmets, because we were sorely disappointed with our last visit here. The patrons are mostly moneyed Parisians who don't pay much attention to the bill. They'd rather look at the superb rustic décor of the dining room with its handsome furnishings and view of the estuary. But this is no excuse for the decline in Denis Le Cadre's cuisine, which continues despite our comments last year. It's true that the foie gras was tasty, but the polenta accompanying it was disastrously greasy, and the perfectly cooked pigeon would have been superb if it hadn't been drowning in a heavy sauce which competed heavily with the delicate watercress cream. And what can we say about a sea bream that is simply not fresh, an invisible sommelier, and a clueless staff? Something must be done, quick! One less toque. C 500-750. M 240 (weekday lunch), 420-590.

 La Ferme Saint-Siméon

(See restaurant above)
Open year-round. 4 stes 4,400-5,100. 25 rms 790-2,690. Bkfst 95-175. Rms for disabled. Half-board 1,095-3,250. Rm ser. Conf. Pool. Tennis. Pkg.
A lot of care goes into the upkeep of these costly rooms, which are renovated every year. The hydrotherapy complex is impressive, and the Norman house itself is gorgeous. Exquisite furnishings. Relais et Châteaux.

 Hostellerie Lechat

Pl. Ste-Catherine - 02 31 14 49 49, fax 02 31 89 28 61
Closed Jan. 1 ste 850. 22 rms 360-550. Bkfst 48. Restaurant. Half-board 345-445 (oblig in seas).
A charming traditional, provincial stop after a visit to the Pont de Normandie. Rustic rooms, most with a view of the church of Sainte-Catherine.

 La Lieutenance

12, pl. Sainte-Catherine
02 31 89 07 52, fax 02 31 89 07 52
Closed Sun off-seas, Nov 12-Dec 17. Priv rm 15. Terrace dining.
A pleasant terrace and an impeccable dining room just off the pedestrian square in the old town, which was built for Norman sailors in the fifteenth century. Let yourself be tempted by the oysters gratinées, the duck with Pommeau, and the pear feuilleté with caramel sauce. The wine list offers a wide selection of Calvados and fruit eau-de-vie. C 230. M 98 (exc Sat dinner & Sun lunch), 120 (weekdays, Sat lunch).

 Le Manoir du Butin

Phare du Butin - 02 31 81 63 00, fax 02 31 89 59 23
Open daily until 9:30pm. Priv rm 35. Terrace dining. Pkg.
It may have a new name, but it's still the annex of the Ferme Saint-Siméon. This lovely eighteenth-century manor house overlooking the sea offers a very bold, bistro-like, regional cuisine: perfectly cooked scallops in a subtle mussel juice with a touch of cream; beautifully seasoned salad with a top-choicee lobster from Brittany, but the lobster was served a tad cold and overcooked; worthy coalfish tournedos with ham; and well-prepared iced nougat with apples. Wine far too expensive and list lacks that personal touch. C 225-240. M 128-285.

 Le Manoir du Butin

(See restaurant above)
Open year-round. 9 rms 640-1,970. Bkfst 65. Half-board 565-1,230. Rm ser. Conf. Heated pool. Pkg.
Nine rooms recently opened in this lovely half-timber house located in a park full of ancient trees. Rooms give either onto the sea or onto the garden. Plush carpet, fabric-covered walls and marble bathrooms, but nonetheless some disappointments: the bathrooms are not always finished properly and the service is still trying to get in gear. Lovely breakfast offering fresh-fruit salad and yogurt. Since the place is still being "run in", you wonder how they can justify prices that send a chill down your spine.

12/20 Au P'tit Mareyeur

4, rue Haute - 02 31 98 84 23, fax 02 31 89 99 32
Closed Mon dinner, Tue, 2 wks Jan, Nov. Open until 9:30pm.
The owner-chef of this appealing restaurant refuses to cater to the tastes of tourists. He offers an interesting seafood and regional menu that is carefully crafted: shellfish gratinée with garlic, tripe in a spicy crust. Intelligent wine list. M 120.

 La Terrasse de l'Assiette

8, pl. Sainte-Catherine
02 31 89 31 33, fax 02 31 89 90 17
Closed Sun dinner, Tue, Dec. Open until 10pm. Terrace dining.
Undoubtedbly the best deal in town, this little bistro is in fact an annex of the Assiette Gourmande. Truly remarkable menu and fixed-price meals with taste-tinglers like the large confit tomato stuffed with cockles and mussels, the pan-fried saddle of cod studded with anchovies and Niçois tian, or the young rabbit, potato and turnip stew with new carrots. The clever desserts practically compete with those of the main restaurant! A toque well-merited. M 129.

HOULBEC-COCHEREL	27120
Paris 93 - Rouen 59 - Évreux 25	Eure

11/20 La Ferme de Cocherel

Route de la Vallée d'Eure
02 32 36 68 27, fax 02 32 26 28 18
Closed Tue & Wed (exc hols), 3 wks in Jan, 1 wk in Sep. Open until 9:15pm. Garage pkg.
After a walk in the peaceful countryside, stop in at this Norman farm with its pleasant, comfortable rustic décor, large fireplace, and rotunda

facing the garden. The carefully-crafted cuisine uses ingredients in a way that is more prestigious than imaginative. New dishes: oxtail crisp with candied turnips, lobster stew, and veal chop with morel mushrooms. Watch out for the prices. Nice selection of Bordeaux. C 350-400. M 195 (exc hols).

INGOUVILLE	76460
Paris 215 - Rouen 64 - Fécamp 30	Seine-Mar.

Les Hêtres

Rue des Fleurs - 02 35 57 09 30, fax 02 35 57 09 31
Closed Mon dinner & Tue off-seas, end Jan-beg Feb. Open until 10pm. Priv rm 15. Terrace dining. Pkg.
Set amid a riot of flowers in the garden is this half-timbered house with a thatched roof. In the dining room, a huge fireplace and a refined, warm décor. Éric Liberge is the attentive host, and Bertrand Warin is attracting new customers every day with his imaginative cuisine. Try the delicious tartelette of very fresh mackerel fillets, Brittany langoustine with Chinese cabbage, and quail brochettes with Swiss chard and a Parmesan galette. Good-value set meals. Well-balanced cellar with some exceptional bottles and many affordable ones. There are now four hotel rooms as well. C 370-450. M 160-350.

Les Hêtres

(See restaurant above)
See restaurant for closings. 4 rms 520-690. Bkfst 70. Rms for disabled. Conf. Garage pkg.
This absolutely charming half-timber house serves as both restaurant and hotel. Heartfelt welcome by Eric Liberge and his highly efficient staff. Large garden, adjoining Norman thatch cottage, and tastefully furnished rooms.

JUMIÈGES	76480
Paris 158 - Rouen 42 - Caudebec-en-Caux 15	Seine-Mar.

Auberge des Ruines

Pl. de la Mairie - 02 35 37 24 05
Closed Nov 1-Mar 15: Sun dinner & Mon, Feb school hols, Christmas school hols. Open until 9:30pm. Terrace dining. Pkg.
The magnificent ruins are those of a medieval abbey, with a charming terrace protected by an arbor. The décor of the inn, with its half-timbering and copperware, bears witness to its Norman origins. Loïc Henry, the young owner-chef, prepares delicious market cuisine that shows plenty of imagination and is inspired by rustic ingredients. The wine cellar is well put together, but awfully difficult to read. Friendly welcome by Agnès Henry. C 300. M 94 (weekdays, Sat lunch), 167-240, 70 (children).

LISIEUX	14100
Paris 215 - Évreux 72 - Caen 49 - Deauville 28	Calvados

12/20 Aux Acacias

13, rue de la Résistance - 02 31 62 10 95

Closed Sun dinner & Mon (exc hols), Feb school hols. Open until 9:30pm.
An attractive, spic-and-span house right in the heart of town and full of flowers. Traditional cooking with a spark of inventiveness. We liked the rock lobster ravioli with lobster sauce, the crispy pigs' feet, and the fricassée of rabbit cooked in white wine and wrapped and served as a flat sausage. C 250. M 90 (weekdays, Sat lunch), 130-280.

Azur

15 rue du Char - 02 31 62 09 14, fax 02 31 62 16 06
Open year-round. 15 rms 350-650. Bkfst 40. No pets. Garage pkg.
This centrally located little hotel has all the conveniences of a city just right around the corner. A modern hotel with a pretty fireplace and offering sunny, cheerful rooms.

LOUVIGNY	14111
Paris 249 - Caen 5	Calvados

Auberge de l'Hermitage

11, La Haule - 02 31 73 38 66, fax 02 31 74 27 30
Closed Sun dinner, Mon, Feb 17-28, Aug 25-Sep 14. Open until 9pm. Terrace dining. Air cond. Pkg.
This is how Normandy should be. From the terrace of this typical house, you can watch the peaceful Orne River flow by, and the bright, flower-adorned dining room boasts a large fireplace. Michel Grandsire's tasty cuisine makes skillful use of local ingredients, in both à la carte and inexpensive set menu offerings. Charming welcome. C 230. M 98 (exc Sun), 160-230.

MARTIN-ÉGLISE	76370
Paris 202 - Rouen 58 - Dieppe 7	Seine-Mar.

Auberge du Clos Normand

22, rue Henri-IV - 02 35 04 40 34, fax 02 35 04 48 49
Closed Mon dinner, Tue, mid Nov-mid Dec. Open until 9pm. Garden dining. No pets. Pkg.
On the banks of the river, facing the forest, this beautiful old village house surrounded by a flower garden has a charming, rustic décor and a collection of antique copperware. Régis Hauchecorne's limited repertory is ever-so-classic, but his generous and attractively presented cuisine charms with its precision and honest flavors. The choice of wines is a bit confused. Friendly welcome. C 300. M 160, 260.

MONT-SAINT-MICHEL (LE)	50170
Paris 323 - Rennes 66 - St-Malo 52	Manche

La Mère Poulard

02 33 60 14 01, fax 02 33 48 52 31
Open daily until 10:30pm. Priv rm 150. Garage pkg.

It may be the best omelette in the world, and it may well be the most expensive one at 150 F a shot (granted, they throw in a little smoked salmon on the side). The new chef admirably prepares other regional dishes as well, but he fails to add that special touch needed to merit the fourteen points of before. If you don't like touristy places, you should definitely go someplace else. The small cellar is reasonably priced. Smiling welcome from Édith Rébillon in the huge stone-walled dining room with a warm ambience. C 360-510. M 150-450, 60 (children).

 La Mère Poulard

(See restaurant above)
Open year-round. 27 rms 300-900. Bkfst 60. Pkg.
No wonder the paintings, carpeting, mattresses, bed springs and toilets are tired; you'd be tired too if you'd welcomed so many hoards of tourists. Some have a view of the bay. Panoramic piano bar, boutique. Meeting rooms. Friendly, competent welcome.

11/20 Auberge Saint-Pierre

Grande-Rue - 02 33 60 14 03, fax 02 33 48 59 82
Closed Dec 15-Feb 10. Open until 10pm. Garden dining.
A listed building with a rustic décor and ambience. The pleasing cuisine is simple and honest: grilled Brittany lobster, fresh seafood, roast leg of lamb, millefeuille laced with liqueur. C 135-260. M 98-290, 48 (children).

 Auberge Saint-Pierre

(See restaurant above)
Closed Dec 15-Feb 10. 21 rms 290-620. Bkfst 50. Half-board 330-440. Conf.
Under the ramparts in the fabulous city, a superb fifteenth-century hotel with pretty, well-equipped rooms.

 Les Terrasses Poulard

Rue Principale - 02 33 60 14 09, fax 02 33 60 37 31
Open year-round. 29 rms 200-800. Bkfst 40. Restaurant. Conf. Pkg.
This hotel fits admirably into its historic setting, a few giant steps away from the restaurant. The elegant, cheerful rooms are on the small side, but afford views of the sea or the town. Excellent service.

OUILLY-DU-HOULEY	14590
Paris 179 - Caen 59 - Lisieux 8	Calvados

 Auberge de la Paquine

02 31 63 63 80
Closed Tue dinner, Wed. Open until 9pm. Garden dining. No pets. Pkg.
This restaurant could provide the illustration for a postcard, with its typically Norman half-timbering and its location in a field next to a stream. The cuisine based on regional produce is also picture-perfect: scallops, veal filet mignon with walnut sauce, and an irreproachable apple

tart. The food is as soothing as the setting. C 350. M 160-345.

OUISTREHAM	14150
Paris 251 - Caen 14 - Cabourg 19 - Bayeux 35	Calvados

 Thermes Marins

Complexe Riva-Bella-Normandie,
plage de Riva-Bella, av. du Commandant-Kieffer
02 31 96 40 40, fax 02 31 96 45 45
Closed 2 wks in Jan. Open until 10pm. Heated pool. No pets. Pkg.
It's not easy to cook without butter or cream, but Gilles Defives rises to the challenge with interesting, tasty low-fat cuisine made of quality seasonal produce, inspired by the teachings of Michel Guérard. There is a small menu of classic dishes. The wine list is a bit strange, but the list of mineral waters is superb! Cheerful welcome and service in the bright but rather boring dining room, which looks out on the sea. C 200. M 110-235, 60 (children).

 Thermes Marins

(See restaurant above)
Closed 2 wks in Jan. 5 stes 700-1,100. 46 rms 450-600. Bkfst 50. Rms for disabled. Half-board 445-590. Rm ser. Conf. Heated pool. Pkg.
This thermal establishment on the beach has huge, bright, pleasant rooms, most of which look out to sea. Great bathrooms. Beauty and seawater treatments available.

PONT-AUDEMER	27500
Paris 168 - Rouen 52 - Honfleur 24 - Évreux 68	Eure

12/20 Auberge du Vieux Puits ۞

6, rue Notre-Dame-du-Pré
02 32 41 01 48, fax 02 32 42 37 28
Closed Mon dinner & Tue (exc in summer), Dec 20-Jan 28. Open until 9pm. Priv rm 18. Pkg.
A romantic seventeenth-century inn with a charming Norman décor and a garden situated between the canals of the old town. In spite of sometimes timid flavorings, the traditional cuisine showcases the chef's technical flair. C 220-320. M 200 (lunch, exc Sun), 310.

 Auberge du Vieux Puits

(See restaurant above)
Closed Mon pm & Tue (exc in summer), Dec 20-Jan 28. 12 rms 280-430. Bkfst 45. Rms for disabled. No pets. Pkg.
A superb collection of seventeenth-century half-timbered buildings set around a vast courtyard houses some simple, rustic but charming rooms and a few larger, well equipped ones with antique furnishings. Friendly welcome; good breakfasts.

Belle Isle-sur-Risle ♣♥

1.5 km on N 175, 112, route de Rouen
02 32 56 96 22, fax 02 32 42 88 96
Open year-round. 4 stes 980-1,300. 16 rms 585-
1,250. Bkfst 75. Restaurant. Half-board 700-1,100
(oblig in seas). Rm ser. Conf. Heated pool. Tennis.
Garage pkg.
A handsome nineteenth-century hotel set on a
little island in a shady, flower-filled park. The
lobby is very elegant, as are the spacious rooms
with period furnishings.

12/20 Les Cloches
de Corneville ✿

Route de Rouen, 4 km SE on N 175
02 32 57 01 04, fax 02 32 57 10 96
Closed Mon lunch, Nov-end Mar. Open until 10pm.
Terrace dining. Garage pkg.
In tune with the famous operetta, this picturesque inn houses a set of bells above the
bistro-style dining room. The cuisine wavers at
times, but for the most part, you will find simple,
honest dishes. C 320. M 120 (weekdays, Sat
lunch), 165-260, 60 (children).

PONT-L'ÉVÊQUE 14130
Paris 190 - Deauville 11 - Lisieux 17 - Rouen 79   Calvados

11/20 Auberge de la Touques

Pl. de l'Église - 02 31 64 01 69
Closed Mon dinner, Tue, Jan 2-24, Dec 3-26. Open
until 9:30pm. Terrace dining. Pkg.
You'll always have a hearty welcome at this
thoroughly Norman house (it's almost
gingerbread-like!). The cooking is not always up
to par with the surroundings, however. The chef
can't seem to decide whether to produce a true
Norman cuisine or a tourist trap-type cuisine. C
290. M 105-170, 50 (children).

PONTORSON 50170
Paris 326 - Dinan 45 - Rennes 57 - Avranches 22   Manche

12/20 Le Bretagne

59, rue Couesnon - 02 33 60 10 55, fax 02 33 58 20 54
Closed Sun dinner & Mon off-seas, Jan 15-Feb 15.
Open until 9:30pm. Priv rm 100. Terrace dining.
Pkg.
Tourists on the way to Mont-Saint-Michel join
the locals in this charming paneled dining room.
Jérôme Carnet, the owners' son, has left, and his
mother's cooking has reverted to a regional one
drenched in grease. Good quality ingredients,
carefully prepared desserts, wide selection of
wine. One less point. C 250-360. M 85-260 (exc
Sun dinner), 45 (children, exc Sun dinner).

PORT-EN-BESSIN-HUPPAIN 14520
Paris 280 - Bayeux 9 - Caen 37 - Cherbourg 91   Calvados

12/20 Le Bistrot d'à Côté

12, rue Letournier
02 31 51 79 12, fax 02 31 51 79 33
Closed Dec 23-Feb 10. Open until 10pm.

This bistro with a simple, fresh décor is located
near the fishing port and offers deftly prepared
seafood dishes. Perfect cooking times, large portions, but most of all, the fine sauces almost led
us to give him a toque. Absolutely splendid
seafood platters. Good enough cellar, with some
wines served by the pitcher. Friendly welcome.
C 180. M 95 (wine incl), 125, 149, 185.

PORT-VILLEZ 78270
Paris 78 - Versailles 63 - Evreux 34   Yvelines

 La Gueulardière

At Le Village - 01 34 76 22 12
Closed Sun dinner & Mon (exc hols). Open until
9:30pm. Priv rm 15. Garden dining. Air cond. Pool.
Garage pkg.
A pleasant, ivy-covered inn with a warm
country décor, a collection of copperware, and
bouquets of flowers is just across from Monet's
house and gardens at Giverny. There is also a
winter garden and a terrace. Diners can expect to
be greeted with a smile before tasting the personalized classic cuisine prepared with a sure
hand by Claude Marguerite. Diverse, well-
chosen cellar. C 350-400. M 150 (exc Sun).

ROUEN 76000
Paris 139 - Caen 124 - Le Havre 40   Seine-Mar.

Le Beffroy

15, rue du Beffroy
02 35 71 55 27, fax 02 35 89 66 12
Closed Sun, Tue dinner. Open until 9pm.
This charming restaurant is the picture of Normandy: half-timbering, a huge fireplace, and
bouquets of fresh flowers. Odile Engel claims
that her cuisine is made in her own image:
"simple, unpretentious, friendly, and
generous." You will be seduced by the croustillant of brill with coriander, the duck à la Rouen-
naise, and the tarte Tatin. The cellar is rich in
Alsatian and Sancerre wines, but the prices are
high. C 280. M 100-275.

10/20 Brasserie
des Deux Rives

Railway station, 1st floor
02 35 71 48 66, fax 02 35 15 14 43
Closed Sat, Aug. Open until 10:30pm. Priv rm 30.
A practical eating spot located right in the train
station. A good set menu at 120 F includes an
apéritif, wine, and coffee, in addition to a salad
with shavings of foie gras, cod with smoked
salmon butter, and an apple tart with Calvados.
Calm, cozy ambience. C 140-200. M 120 (lunch,
wine incl), 49 (children).

11/20 Le Catelier

134 bis, av. Martyrs-de-la-Résistance
02 35 72 59 90, fax 02 35 73 96 64
Closed Sun, Aug 1-15. Open until 9pm. Priv rm 18.
Terrace dining. Pkg.
Near the Jardin des Plantes, this peaceful
dining room with a conventional décor is

D-3 ① - Le Beffroy ☐

D-2 ② - Brasserie des Deux Rives ☐

D-4 ③ - Hôtel de la Cathédrale ☐

C-4 ④ - Hôtel Frantour-Vieux
Marché ☐

C-2 ⑤ - Hôtel de Dieppe ☐

C-2 ⑤ - Les Quatre Saisons ☐

D-4 ⑥ - Dufour ☐

C-3 ⑦ - L'Ecaille ☐

D-4 ⑧ - L'Episode ☐

D-4 ⑨ - Gill ☐

D-3 ⑩ - Au Jardin de Chine ☐

D-3 ⑪ - Les P'tits Parapluies ☐

D-4 ⑫ - Le Réverbère ☐

D-3 ⑬ - Versan ☐

D-7 ⑭ - Le Catelier 11

D-4 ⑮ - Mercure Centre ☐

C-4 ⑯ - Les Nymphéas ☐

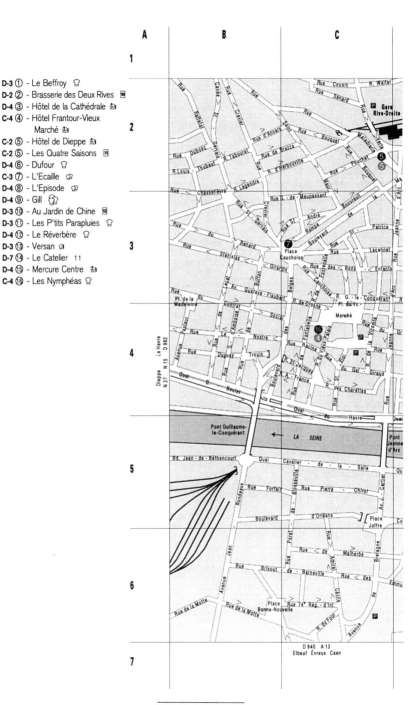

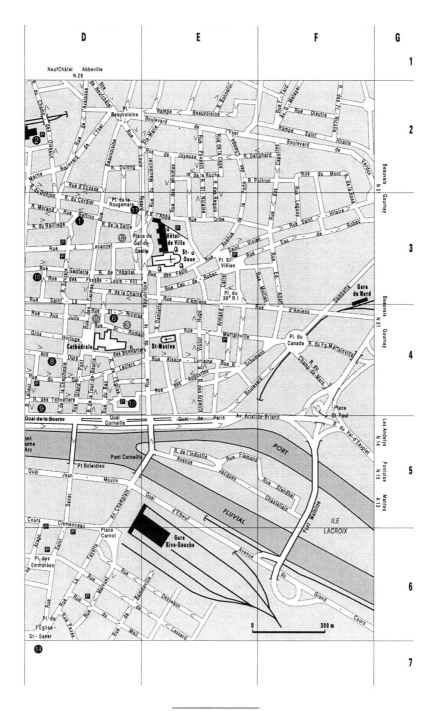

favored by businesspeople, who enjoy the nostalgic cuisine. As the restaurant's business card says, "A woman's cooking and a high-quality cellar." We might add that "there is a certain love for the fruit of the land displayed in the selection of ingredients, an intimate décor, and a warm welcome." C 300. M 98-225, 195 (wine incl).

 ## Hôtel de la Cathédrale

12, rue Saint-Romain
02 35 71 57 95, fax 02 35 70 15 54
Open year-round. 24 rms 260-375. Bkfst 37.
A half-timbered house typical of old Rouen, situated in a pedestrian street. The entrance, with its outdated tiles, is reached through a flower-filled cobblestoned courtyard. Rooms are furnished with antiques.

 ## Dufour

67 bis, rue Saint-Nicolas
02 35 71 90 62, fax 02 35 89 70 94
Closed Sun dinner, Mon. Open until 9:30pm. Priv rm 30.
A charming and pretty fifteenth-century Norman house, with its stone walls, exposed beams, and model ships. The father and son team remain true to their origins, serving Auge Valley chicken (cooked in apple cider), Normandy sole and Calvados soufflé in this so-appropriate décor. It's true that for less than 400 F, including some fine Bordeaux wines from good years, you can even eat à la carte, so we'll let them keep their toque for the time being, but don't look for any innovation. Tradition reigns here, seemingly forever. C 280. M 80 (weekdays & Sat lunch, wine incl), 120-230.

 ## L'Écaille

26, rampe Cauchoise
02 35 70 95 52, fax 02 35 70 83 49
Closed Sun dinner, Mon, 2 wks in Aug. Open until 9:30pm. Priv rm 30. Terrace dining. Air cond.
The green-and-blue dining room is charming, as is the welcome. You will find the same charm in the cuisine, which shows off Marc Tellier's knack for sauces. He uses this skill circumspectly to reveal the flavors of the fresh, high-quality seafood: red mullet with sweet red peppers and anchovy vinegar, John Dory and clams with parsley purée and light butter, chocolate and raspberry soufflé perfumed with coriander. Diverse and well-presented wine list. Appealing set menu at 145 F. C 380. M 145 (weekdays, Sat dinner), 175 (Sat dinner, Sun), 255-480.

 ## L'Épisode

37, rue aux Ours - 02 35 89 01 91, fax 02 35 07 06 21
Closed Wed, Sun, 2 wks in Aug. Open until 9:30pm.
A narrow restaurant in a narrow street near the cathedral. Patrick Picard's original cuisine has a modern spin. Some of the combinations may shock the Rouen crowd so fond of their traditional duck dishes, but apart from the vanilla oil which wasn't quite tasty enough for the roast scampi, we found only pleasant surprises. We liked the taste combinations of the escargots with

the chanterelle mushrooms, wild spinach leaves and oatmeal pancake; the John Dory with shallots, fennel seeds and green-tomato marmelade; and the utter simplicity of the slowly, perfectly cooked coalfish served with roughly-mashed potatoes seasoned with olive oil. And what purely delightful desserts. We devoured the dried hazelnut dacquoise served with a bitter-chocolate mousse and a ginger-flavored pear marmelade. C 280. M 110 (lunch), 170-235.

 ## Gill

9, quai de la Bourse
02 35 71 16 14, fax 02 35 71 96 91
Closed Mon, Oct-May: Sun dinner. Open until 9:45pm. Priv rm 20. Air cond.
Perfectly in tune with the times, drawing on both the modern and the traditional, freely from either Normandy or Provence, the cuisine of Gilles Tournadre is a sure value. It is well-crafted yet light. We savored the subtle artichoke terrine and mesclun mixed salad with thinly sliced truffles as well as the Rouen-style pigeon, as succulent as they come. The business set menu at 199 F simply can't be beat; it draws on dishes from the regular menu, and even includes a daily fish special between the starter and the meat dish. You might want to try one of Lucien Crochet's Sancerre wines, Mr. Crochet being none other than Sylvie Tournadre's father! Irreproachable welcome and service in the calm, slightly stiff atmosphere of the comfortable 1930s–style dining room. C 450. M 199 (weekdays, Sat lunch), 290-390, 120 (children).

 ## Hôtel Frantour Vieux Marché

33, rue du Vieux-Palais
02 35 71 00 88, fax 02 35 70 75 94
Open year-round. 48 rms 435-495. Bkfst 50. Rms for disabled. Restaurant. Half-board 522. Valet pkg.
Right in the heart of the Rouen's historic downtown. Hotel completely renovated in 1995, offering modern, functional rooms. Restrained décor.

12/20 Au Jardin de Chine

36, rue Percière - 02 35 89 72 07
Closed Aug. Open until 10pm. Priv rm 60. No pets.
Don't let the slightly faded décor put you off: the long menu is in better shape and includes pork spareribs, spicy chicken, and deep-fried bananas. Modest cellar. C 160. M 95 (exc Sun), 68 (lunch).

 ## Mercure Centre

7, rue de la Croix-de-Fer
02 35 52 69 52, fax 02 35 89 41 46
Open year-round. 4 stes 850-950. 121 rms 450-550. Bkfst 60. Conf. Air cond. Pkg.
An ideal base for a walking tour of town. There is an underground garage, and the rooms are very well equipped by chain standards; some have views of the cathedral's gables.

Les Nymphéas

7-9, rue de la Pie - 02 35 89 26 69, fax 02 35 70 98 81
*Closed Sun dinner, Mon, Aug 25-Sep 7. Open until
10pm. Priv rm 40. Terrace dining. Pkg.*
An old Rouen house with exposed beams and
an elegant contemporary décor, located near the
old marketplace. The serious, traditional cuisine
is prepared by Pierre Kukurudz. The best deal is
still the set menu at 165 F; the regular menu fare
we tried—pan-fried scallop salad, pike perch
fillet with two sauces and veal kidneys with
full-grain mustard—were strictly disappointing.
Pretty courtyard garden for summer dining.
Amiable welcome, diligent service. C 350. M
165-400, 120 (children).

 Les P'tits Parapluies

46, rue du Bourg-l'Abbé
02 35 88 55 26, fax 02 35 70 24 31
*Closed Oct-beg Jul: Sun dinner, Mon; beg Jul-Sep:
Sun, Mon, Open until 10pm.*
The new decoration has gotten rid of the turn-
of-the-century spirit that reigned here before,
and something seems to have died in the chef
when he did so. His oyster rolls and caviar salmon, mushroom-stuffed turbot, and apple pastilla with milk jam are good, but lack life. Maybe
we'll wake him up by taking away a point. The
wine list is eclectic, with a good selection of
Bordeaux, but short on wines from lesser-known
regions. Warm welcome from the *patronne*. C
350-450. M 180 (lunch, wine incl), 190, 240.

11/20 Le Quatre Saisons

Pl. Bernard-Tissot - 02 35 71 96 00, fax 02 35 89 65 21
Open daily until 10pm. Priv rm 40. Pkg.
The traditional place to go for canard au sang,
a Rouen specialty. The ambience is that of a lively
brasserie. You can also sample salmon with sorrel, veal sweetbreads with lemon, and pear
croustillant with spices. Fast service, reasonable
cellar. C 250. M 138, 198.

 Hôtel de Dieppe

(See restaurant above)
*Open year-round. 41 rms 390-595. Bkfst 45. Half-
board 360-500. Rm ser. Air cond. Conf. Pkg.*
A new seminar/banquet room just opened in
this city-center hotel facing the train station.
Pleasant, modern rooms.

 Le Réverbère

5, pl. de la République
02 35 07 03 14, fax 02 35 89 77 93
*Closed Sun dinner off-seas, Aug 5-20. Open until
10:30pm. Priv rm 16.*
Ignore the unattractive façade of this 1950s–
style building and take a seat among the regulars
in the pleasant, modern dining room done up in
beige and blue, with smoked-glass mirrors. The
traditional cuisine has been updated by José
Rato and is light and accomplished. An eclectic
wine list, with some Bordeaux served by the
glass. Amiable welcome and efficient, attentive
service. Gentle prices. C 150-300. M 165-310.

 Versan

3, rue Jean-Lecanuet
02 35 70 22 00, fax 02 35 70 22 60
*Open year-round. 34 rms 310-355. Bkfst 39. Rms
for disabled. Rm ser. No pets. Pkg.*
Simple but well-equipped hotel located near
the cathedral. Quiet, pleasant rooms.

And also...

*Our selection of places for inexpensive,
quick, or late-night meals.*
Pascaline (02 35 87 67 44 - 5, rue de la Poterne.
Open until 11:30pm.): Just around the corner
from the old marketplace and the cathedral, a
semi-chic, semi-down-and-out bistro where you
can eat at the counter. Charming waitresses (57-
122).
Le P'tit Bec (02 35 07 63 33 - 182, rue Eau de
Robec. Open until 3pm.): Tucked into the heart
of the antique district in a pedestrian street, this
hugely successful little restaurant offers good
downhome cooking (80-100).
Le Veau d'Or (02 35 72 76 60 - 3, rue Desseaux.
Open until 3pm.): Once the meeting-place for
butchers and abattoir workers, now a good bet
for excellent meats and traditional fare (220).

SAINT-ANDRÉ-D'HÉBERTOT   14130
Paris 205 - Caen 53 - Honfleur 18   Calvados

 Auberge du Prieuré

02 31 64 03 03, fax 02 31 64 16 66
*Closed Wed. Open until 9:30pm. Garden dining.
Heated pool. Garage pkg.*
This former priory surrounded by trees is
purely Norman. The cuisine is no less so, with its
chitterlings in chive cream; a fish stew with
lobster, turbot, and scallops; and warm cherries
with vanilla ice cream. As the wine list is very
pricey, try the excellent local cider instead. C
300-400. M 145, 180 (lunch).

☐ Auberge du Prieuré

(See restaurant above)
*Closed Wed off-seas. 3 stes 620-980. 10 rms 310-780.
Bkfst 42. Rms for disabled. Half-board 670-1,340.
Conf. Heated pool. Garage pkg.*
Cozy rooms with a view of the garden in a
lovely house in the countryside. Excellent wel-
come.

SAINT-ARNOULT   14800
Paris 214 - Caen 42 - Deauville 3   Calvados

☐ Campanile

Route de l'Hippodrome
02 31 87 54 54, fax 02 31 87 09 42
*Open year-round. 58 rms 278-305. Bkfst 32. Rms
for disabled. Restaurant. Half-board 394-411.
Conf. Pkg.*
A hotel with verdant surroundings and a little
park where children can play. Functional rooms
and professional service.

12/20 La Pommeraie

Mont Canisy - 02 31 14 24 00, fax 02 31 14 24 01
*Closed mid Nov-Dec 25, beg Feb-mid Mar. Open
until 10:30pm. Terrace dining. Pool. Tennis. Pkg.*
The luxurious dining room of this hotel has not
changed one iota, but the chef has. He needs to
sharpen his knives a little more; we wouldn't
want to judge too quickly... C 300-450. M 195, 55
(children).

 ## Hôtel du Golf

(See restaurant above)
*Closed mid Nov-Dec 25, beg Feb-mid Mar. 10 stes
1,300-2,200. 168 rms 710-1,500. Bkfst 90-120.
Half-board 195-245. Rm ser. Conf. Heated pool.
Tennis. Pkg.*
Golfers and their families will find their happiness in this hotel. The fitness center and the many
sporting activities will fulfill all their desires. The
comfortable rooms overlook a park dotted with
apple trees.

SAINT-AUBIN-LE-VERTUEUX 27300
Paris 155 - Évreux 54 - Lisieux 38 Eure

 ## Hostellerie du Moulin Fouret

02 32 43 19 95, fax 02 32 45 55 50
*Closed Sun dinner & Mon off-seas. Open until
9:30pm. Priv rm 20. Terrace dining. Pkg.*
A charming old mill with a terrace overlooking
the park and the river, and a warm, country-
style dining room. The traditional regional
cuisine is attractively presented but is sometimes
a bit too rich. Well-balanced cellar. Affable welcome and efficient service. C 350. M 100-285.

SAINT-GERMAIN-DES-VAUX 50440
Paris 389 - Cherbourg 29 - Nez de Jobourg 8 Manche

 ## Le Moulin à Vent

02 33 52 75 20, fax 02 33 52 22 57
*Closed Sun dinner & Mon (exc hols). Check for
annual closings. Open until 9pm. Pkg.*
You might think you're in Ireland before you
even arrive at this mill, isolated on a cliff next to
the restaurant. In the appealing pink, dark red,
and wood décor of the dining room, the serene
patronne will advise you on what to eat: excellent
smoked ham from Vire, bass (well cooked), or
tuna tartare with raw spinach. It's too bad that
such a wonderful place attracts so few people. C
220-300. M 95 (exc Sun dinner, hols), 40
(children, exc hols).

SAINT-JOUIN-BRUNEVAL 76280
Paris 239 - Rouen 93 - Étretat 11 Seine-Mar.

12/20 Le Belvédère

Falaise d'Antifer - 02 35 20 13 76, fax 02 35 30 74 60
*Closed Sun dinner, Mon, mid Dec-mid Jan. Open
until 9:30pm. Garage pkg.*
Good food with an emphasis on the sea
(shellfish, bass fillet à la Dieppoise with rice and

seaweed). The comfortable, wood-paneled
dining room has uninterrupted views of the
cliffs. C 200-380. M 75, 135, 172.

ST-MARTIN-AUX-CHARTRAINS 14130
Paris 120 - Caen 54 - Deauville 9 Calvados

 ## Manoir de Roncheville

02 31 65 14 14, fax 02 31 65 20 44
*Closed Nov 15-Mar 31. Open until 10pm. Priv rm
20. Terrace dining. Pkg.*
On the banks of a river, in a park that is home
to geese and rabbits, this rambling manor house
with handsome sculpted-wood fireplaces and
sumptuous grisaille tapestries has charm to
spare. Patrick Brignon's cuisine is still somewhat
lacking in imagination, but this year a touch of
flavorful fantasy peaked its head. So-so desserts.
Small wine list but rich in Bordeaux. Amiable
welcome (most of the time). C 350. M 170-210, 80
(children).

SAINT-MARTIN-DE-MIEUX 14700
Paris 276 - Caen 38 - Argentan 25 Calvados

 ## Château du Tertre

02 31 90 01 04, fax 02 31 90 33 16
*Closed Sun dinner, Mon, Jan 5-Feb 13. Open until
9:30pm. Priv rm 18. Pkg.*
Don't be intimidated by the elegant dining
room with its gorgeous gray-blue-painted
eighteenth-century paneling. You can play at
being lord of the manor without spending like
one, thanks to the 160 F lunch menu (195 F with
wine and Pommeau). Great chefs seem to be
attracted to this site, and new chef Laurent
Picharles, only twenty-eight years old, is a real
revelation. His style is so meticulous and full of
studied elegance that one could almost put him
in the ranks of such as Robuchon. He is gradually
trying to integrate Normandy ingredients into
his repertory giving highly pleasing results such
as crab b'steeya and new cabbage served with
chicken livers slowly cooked in their own fat;
roast John Dory with chitterlings and country-
style charlotte; and tender farm-raised pigeon
with Carrouges-cheese (the local cheese) gnocchi. The pan-fried cherries with licorice are absolutely wonderful. Excellent wine list and a
"calvathèque" in the basement that you can visit.
C 300-450. M 160-195 (wine incl), 250-410.

 ## Château du Tertre

(See restaurant above)
*Open year-round. 2 stes 980-1,100. 9 rms 490-880.
Bkfst 55-80. Half-board 680-800. Conf. Pkg.*
The rooms are named after a long list of famous
writers who frequented this site: Marcel Proust,
Gustave Flaubert, and Guy de Maupassant,
among others. Cozy, attractive rooms, each one
unique, in a smashing little pink-brick castle surrounded by woods, grassy meadows, a
vegetable garden, a duck pond, roses and

daisies, and a croquet lawn. The French art of living with a little English upper middle class thrown in!

SAINT-VAAST-LA-HOUGUE   50550
Paris 350 - Cherbourg 31 - Barfleur 13   Manche

12/20   Le Chasse-Marée

8, pl. Général-de-Gaulle -02 33 23 14 08
Closed Tue off-seas, 3 wks in Jan, 2 wks in Nov. Open until 9:30pm. Terrace dining. No pets.
The freshness of the fish is what makes this little bistro on the port a good address. The owner is a former fishmonger, so he knows his business. His pan-fried shellfish, roast salmon with bacon, and skate jaws with butter are all simple, but good enough to have gained him a strong following in these parts. Too bad his wine list is so short on white wines. C 150-250. M 75 (exc Sat dinner & Sun lunch), 98, 135.

Fuchsias

18, rue du Maréchal-Foch
02 33 54 42 26, fax 02 33 43 46 79
Closed Sep 15-May 15: Mon; Nov-Mar: Tue lunch; Jan 8-Feb 20. Open until 9:15pm (10pm in summer). Priv rm 28. Air cond. Terrace dining. Pkg.
A thatched-roof porch, a courtyard dripping with fuchsias, and a pleasant veranda add up to a charming scene. The nearby sea inspires Jean-Pierre Letellier, who also makes good use of farm-fresh produce. Warm oysters with garlic butter, and homemade duck foie gras terrine compete with each other as great first courses, while the traditional skate with cider and the classic noisettes of local veal are fine main dishes. C 230. M 79 (weekdays), 60 (children).

Hôtel de France   🌲🍴

(See restaurant above)
Closed Sep 15-May 15: Mon; Jan 8-Feb 20. 1 ste 495. 33 rms 152-425. Bkfst 43. Half-board 226-355 (oblig in seas). Conf.
Cute rooms in the middle of an extraordinary garden. In addition to the fuchsias, there are eucalyptus and banana trees. Chamber music concerts are held during the last ten days of August.

TOUQUES   14800
Paris 209 - Caen 43 - Deauville 3   Calvados

L'Amirauté

02 31 81 82 83, fax 02 31 81 82 93
Open year-round. 6 stes 1,300. 114 rms 725-825. Bkfst 60. Rms for disabled. Restaurant. Rm ser. Conf. Air cond. Pool. Tennis. Golf. Pkg.
This modern hotel is the perfect place for conferences. Sports lovers will feel at home in the sports complex next door and with the numerous fitness machines. Large but rather anonymous rooms.

12/20   Aux Landiers

90, rue Louvel-et-Brières
02 31 88 00 39, fax 02 31 88 00 39
Closed Wed, Thu lunch, Feb. Open until 9:30pm. Priv rm 24. Terrace dining. Pkg.
The owner's resolutely traditional cuisine concentrates on regional ingredients, with sauces that are sometimes too creamy for the otherwise tasty and well-balanced dishes. Diversified wine list. Amiable welcome and friendly service in a warm Norman décor. C 450-540. M 98 (weekday lunch, Sat), 140-295, 60 (children).

TOURVILLE-LA-RIVIÈRE   76410
Paris 124 - Rouen 16 - Evreux 45   Seine-Mar.

Le Tourville

A 13, exit 21, 12, rue Danielle-Casanova
02 35 77 58 79
Closed Mon, dinner Tue-Thu & Sun, 2 wks in spring, Aug. Open until 10pm. Priv rm 30. Terrace dining. Garage pkg.
In an elegant house situated in a pretty park, Michel Florin proves the adage that the best soups are made in old pots. At the age of 75, he still manages to generate enthusiasm with his flavorful cuisine. Try the poultry liver terrine, the scallops, the skate with mustard cream, and the Grand Marnier soufflé. Fine wine list, intelligently explained by Madeleine Florin. C 300-500.

TROUVILLE-SUR-MER   14360
Paris 206 - Le Havre 76 - Caen 43 - Lisieux 29   Calvados

12/20   Bistrot les Quatre Chats

8, rue d'Orléans - 02 31 88 94 94, fax 02 31 88 24 41
Closed Wed & Thu off-seas, Jan. Open until 9:30pm (10:30pm Fri & Sat).
More Parisian than Norman! The place to be for the pseudo-intellectual jet set. When they're not there, it's a nice place. Bistro cooking with new slants such as rabbit in jelly and leg of lamb stuffed with spinach, almonds and grapes. Quite drinkable little list of wines displayed on a chalkboard. C 150-200.

Les Roches Noires

16, bd Louis-Breguet - 02 31 88 12 19
Closed exc school hols Easter-beg Jul & Sep-mid Nov: Tue dinner, Wed; Jul-Aug: Wed; mid Nov-Easter: Mon dinner, Tue, Wed; 2 wks at Feb school hols. Open until 10pm. Terrace dining. Pkg.
A restaurant near the beach with a lovely terrace that looks out to sea. The self-taught chef, ex-Parisian Denise Leconte-Ducroux, has not turned her back to the Channel; she serves fried langoustines, cockles (completely sand-free!) with thyme, and steamed sea bream. Some nice wines at reasonable prices: a Domaine Mardon Quincy at 104 F and an Épineuil from La Chablisienne at 105 F. C 200-250.

12/20 Les Vapeurs
160, bd Fernand-Moureaux
02 31 88 15 24, fax 02 31 88 20 58
Open daily until 1am. Priv rm 40. Terrace dining.
For nearly 70 years, this restaurant frequented by le Tout-Paris has been offering good brasserie cuisine, with an emphasis on seafood: fresh anchovies, smoked-haddock salad, warm shrimp, whiting, and fish choucroute in Champagne. Diners eat it all up in the bright dining room or on the terrace, where they are served by tireless waiters. Good selection of wine. C 180-400.

VASOUY	14600
Paris 200 - Caen 63 - Honfleur 2	Calvados

La Chaumière
Route du Littoral - 02 31 81 63 20, fax 02 31 89 59 23
Closed Tue & Wed lunch off-seas. Open until 9:30pm. Terrace dining. Pkg.
Another annex of the Ferme Saint-Siméon, located in a picturesque converted sheepfold overlooking the estuary of the Seine and the sea. The *carte* created by Denis Le Cadre is very capably interpreted by Claude Le Tohic, who prepares dishes that are more classic than those offered in the main restaurant, but are still very attractive: mussels with saffron pistils, pigeon in a cabbage papillote, and bacon with foie gras. C 350. M 190-380.

La Chaumière
(See restaurant above)
Open year-round. 1 ste 2,400. 8 rms 990-1,350. Bkfst 85. Half-board 945-1,650. Rm ser. Pkg.
Located in a peaceful pasture, a converted half-timbered sheepfold with cozy, pretty rooms decorated in country style. There is a charming salon with a fireplace. Friendly welcome. Relais et Châteaux.

VERNON	27200
Paris 82 - Évreux 31 - Rouen 63 - Mantes-la-Jolie 25	Eure

12/20 Les Fleurs
71, rue Carnot
02 32 51 16 80, fax 02 32 21 30 51
Closed Sun dinner, Mon, Feb school hols, Aug 1-15. Open until 9:30pm. No pets.
Flowers brighten the walls, the upholstery, and fill vases, too, in the pretty and cheerful dining room. The owner-chef offers an interesting menu of such deftly turned out classics as escargots à la normande, truffled lamb fillet, and parfait au chocolat. C 210-340. M 120-240.

Normandy
1, av. Pierre-Mendès-France
02 32 51 97 97, fax 02 32 21 01 66
Open year-round. 3 stes 490-655. 44 rms 350-390. Bkfst 40. Rm for disabled. Air cond. Garage pkg.
Located in the town center, this hotel is modern and convenient. The rooms of this hotel at the back are the quietest; all are comfortable, but the '70s–style décor is not to everyone's taste.

VEULES-LES-ROSES	76980
Paris 200 - Dieppe 24 - Rouen 57	Seine-Mar.

Les Galets
3, rue Victor-Hugo
02 35 97 61 33, fax 02 35 57 06 23
Closed Tue dinner & Wed. Open until 8:30pm (10pm in summer). Priv rm 15. Air cond. Pkg.
Gilbert Plaisance's restaurant near the beach is in top form. He concentrates on seafood and knows how to treat it properly, but offers other choices as well. Try the excellent scallop tartare, scallop fricassée with olive oil and truffles, rabbit with foie gras, and the large, delicious dessert assortments. An attentive maître d'hôtel provides a nice welcome. Food still too pricey apart from the 150 F set-price menu. The prices on the admirable wine list will drive up your bill as well. C 400. M 150-400, 87 (children).

YERVILLE	76760
Paris 170 - Rouen 35 - Yvetot 8 - Tôtes 11	Seine-Mar.

11/20 Hostellerie des Voyageurs
Rue J.-Ferny - 02 35 96 82 55, fax 02 35 86 16 86
Closed Sun dinner & Mon (exc hols). Open until 9pm. Garage pkg.
A half-timbered house with a cozy, rustic dining room where a pleasing, innovative (especially in the preparation of fish) cuisine is served. Try the fish-sausage salad with lentil sauce, the monkfish gratin with saffron zabaglione, and the white chocolate dessert with citrus fruits. If the chef continues in the same meticulous fashion, the results should be very interesting. C 220. M 80, 92 (weekdays, Sat lunch), 108-188, 55 (children).

YVETOT	76190
Paris 175 - Fécamp 34 - Le Havre 51	Seine-Mar.

12/20 Auberge du Val-au-Cesne
4 km SE on D 5, Val-au-Cesne
02 35 56 63 06, fax 02 35 56 92 78
Open daily until 9pm. Terrace dining. Pkg.
The décor and ambience of the small dining rooms in this pretty half-timbered house make you feel that you have stepped back into the nineteenth century. The kitchen has lost its touch however. The sauces have no character, the calf's head and ruffle was water-logged, and the young squab was over-seasoned. C 260-350. M 150.

Please excuse us... (and the chefs). *Menus are subject to the winds of change, and the dishes we've described may no longer be available when you visit.*

Auberge du Val-au-Cesne

(See restaurant above)
Open year-round. 5 rms 400. Bkfst 50. Rms for disabled. Half-board 400. Conf. Pkg.
Set in a tranquil green valley, a Norman cottage with outbuildings that house a few simple, pretty rooms.

REGIONAL FOODS

Half-timbered farmhouses set in lush meadows dotted with apple trees and contented cows: it sounds like a come-on cribbed from a tourist brochure! But as anyone who has traveled in Normandy will tell you, the scene we describe is absolutely true-to-life! From those farms comes the rich milk for Normandy's world-class cheeses (Camembert, Neufchatel, Livarot, Pont-l'Évêque), the pork for rustic charcuteries (andouilles de Vire, andouillettes, and boudin noir), and the apples that are fermented into sparkling cider or distilled into Calvados, the spirit of Normandy.

• *CHARCUTERIE*

CAEN   14000 – Calvados

Poupinet
8, rue Saint-Jean · 02 31 86 07 25
Exceptional andouillette (chitterling sausage) and fine smoked hams share shelf space here with beautifully crafted country pâtés.

ROUEN   76000 – Seine-Mar.

Maison Hardy
22, pl. du Vieux-Marché · 02 35 71 81 55
Come here to taste superb charcuterie with typical Norman flavor: fine andouille de Vire sausage, tripes à la mode de Caen (slow-simmered for twelve hours), and boudin noir.

SAINT-DENIS-LE-GAST   50450 – Manche

Andouillerie de la Vallée de la Sienne
Pont de la Balcine · 02 33 61 44 20
Smoked andouille sausage made according to a traditional recipe. Tasty smoked hams, too.

VIRE   14500 – Calvados

Charles Amand
5, rue André-Halbout · 02 31 67 01 79
This authentic andouille de Vire (cooked pork chitterling sausage) is smoked over apple and beech wood. For years, it was the only andouille served at the French President's table. Also available: excellent hams.

• *CHEESE*

CAMEMBERT   61120 – Orne

Ferme de la Héronnière
02 33 39 08 08
Come here to purchase a wonderful farmhouse Camembert, worthy of its place of origin. And don't miss the statue of Marie Harel, the woman who invented Camembert—it was donated by the people of Ohio, U.S.A.

DIEPPE   76200 – Seine-Mar.

L'Épicerie Olivier
16, rue Saint-Jacques · 02 35 84 22 55
A splendid selection of mostly Norman cheeses, matured by the owner in a cool, natural cellar.

LESSAY   50430 – Manche

Laiterie du Val d'Ay
1, rue de Planquettes · 02 33 46 41 33
These Camemberts are made according to traditional methods, from unpasteurized milk. The result is a tender, mellow cheese with an appealing, earthy aroma.

ST-BENOÎT-D'HÉBERTOT   14130 – Calvados

Henri Pennec
Nationale 175 · 02 31 64 25 38
No wimpy cheeses here, just fine, full-flavored specimens, many with amusing names (Vierge Folle, Coup-de-Pied-au-Cul...). The selection is vast.

• *CHOCOLATE & CANDY*

CAEN   14000 – Calvados

Hotot
13, rue Saint-Pierre · 02 31 86 31 90
Among the tempting chocolates, we like the Cancan de Caen; the candy selection features

local sweets like the chewy Chique Caennaise and apple-sugar bonbons.

DEAUVILLE   14800 – Calvados

Pâtisserie Hug Sergent

20, pl. de Morny - 02 31 88 20 79
The Tout-Deauville crowds into this shop, not only for the pastries but (especially!) for the rich caramels made with Norman butter, for bright fruit jellies, and other delectable sweets.

ROUEN   76000 – Seine-Mar.

Roger Granger

29, rue du Général-Leclerc - 02 35 70 10 64
Some 60 types of chocolates on hand. We particularly recommend the Figaros, the Cent Clochers, and the Rothomagus.

• *GOURMET SPECIALTIES*

Cider & Calvados

DOMFRONT   61700 – Orne

Les Chais du Verger Normand

Rue du Mont-Saint-Michel - 02 33 38 53 96
Cider and poiré (a delightful sparkling pear-based beverage) made with fruit from Norman orchards, and aged Calvados can be purchased here.

FRESNAIE FAYEL (LA)   61230 – Orne

Vergers de la Morinière

02 33 35 51 13
Come to this charming farmhouse to buy home-fermented cider, with a sparkly tingle and a true-fruit taste.

LISIEUX   14100 – Calvados

Maison Marlet

Le Friche Menuet, Saint-Germain-de-Livet
02 31 31 18 24
Vallée-d'Auge cider, expertly fermented and bottled.

VILLERS-BOCAGE   14310 – Calvados

Le Clos d'Orval

Amayé-sur-Seulles - 02 31 77 02 87
Here's the place to buy exceptional Calvados, as well as Pommeau (apple juice laced with Calvados). Well worth a stop!

Foie Gras

GAPRÉE   61390 – Orne

Les Foies Gras de la Lipomerie

La Lipomerie - 02 33 27 62 54
Foie gras from Norman ducks, good enough to compete with the best that the Southwest and Alsace have to offer.

Jams

ST-HILAIRE DU HARCOUËT   50600 – Manche

Maison Gueprate

ZA de Virey - 02 33 49 21 95
Classic and unusual jams, including a terrific blackberry variety sweetened with red-currant juice. Also: fruit sauces to embellish ice creams and desserts.

ST-PIERRE-SUR-DIVES   14170 – Calvados

Au Frisson Normand

Garnetot - Ferme de la Houssaye - 02 31 20 70 07
Not for everyone, perhaps, but its fans swear by this lush confiture de lait (milk jam, made with extra-rich milk), which regularly wins prizes at food fairs.

THE NORTH

Battlefields, giants, and windmills: travels in the North Country

The North is known as *le plat pays*, the flat land. Hills hereabout are the merest ripples, rarely rising more than a hundred yards. **Mont Cassel** dominates the vast Flanders plain although its altitude is just 580 feet. In the North, what appear from a distance to be mountains turn out to be huge heaps of black slag, a legacy of the coal-mining industry that long fueled the region's economy. The low horizons, the piles of dross: these images recall the setting of *Germinal*, Zola's gripping portrayal of life in Northern coal mines at the end of the last century. But that is only the topmost layer of the North's rich and turbulent history.

All the way north, where France ends and Belgium begins, the very name of Flanders resonates with associations that date back much further than the sooty saga of coal miners and modern industrialization. It isn't easy to find one's way through the labyrinth of the North's prodigious past.

How can we solve the multiple trails of Celts, Romans, Normans, Burgundians, Hungarians, Vandals, Britons, Germans, Austrians, and Spaniards, all of whom marched into the North as conquerors, leaving destruction (and occasionally something of their art or culture) in their wake? These broad, open plains where no natural obstacles slow an army down, provided ideal battlefields for all-out war.

Because of its geographic position, the North was often the battleground where France and England played out their eternal conflicts. Often enough, France got the worst of it. At **Crécy** in 1346 the archers and newfangled artillery of England's King Edward III massacred the French cavalry. After a hard-fought battle in 1347, England captured Calais. Rodin's powerful sculpture, *The Burghers of Calais*, commemorates the moment when six leading citizens offered their lives and the keys to their city in exchange for a promise that it would not be destroyed. In 1415 Henry V decimated the French nobility at **Azincourt**. Joan of Arc was taken prisoner at Compiègne in 1430. At Guîne the opulence of the summit conference (as it would be

called today) where François I met Henry VIII at the Field of the Cloth of Gold in 1520, prompted England to join forces with Emperor Charles V against France. France met in battle here with the Spanish and the Austrians as well. Religious quarrels, in this region where the Reformation made significant inroads (Calvin was born in **Noyon**), provided yet another pretext for massacres. Much bloodshed also preceded the Treaty of Utrecht, signed under Louis XIV, which made the North a permanent part of France. The two World Wars took a terrible toll here, too, as the immense Allied cemeteries movingly attest (the American Memorial at **Bellicourt**, the Canadian Memorial at **Vimy**).

This thumbnail historical sketch should help to clear up the mystery behind the mix of Spanish, Flemish, German, and French place names in the North, and to explain the palette of architectural styles that ranges from German and English Gothic to Renaissance and Baroque. The classic Flemish style marks many of the North's town halls, and their bell towers that symbolize the cities' proud independence.

Flanders' seashore is known as the **Opal Coast** for the milky, shimmering light that bathes its white sands. Further inland, fertile fields reclaimed from the sea yield splendid harvests of grain, hence the prosperous look of the North's rambling, red-roofed farmhouses. Some are flanked by windmills, which used to number in the hundreds on these flat, windswept plains.

A tour of the heart of Flanders and Artois will take you from the harbors of **Dunkerque** and **Boulogne**, Europe's foremost fishing port, to the historic towns of **Arras** (famed for its tapestries), **Cambrai, Douai** (the coal capital, with its musical bell tower), and finally to **Lille**, a vital metropolis with ambitions to become a major player in the European marketplace. The textile and steel mills that made Lille's fortune have been replaced by high-tech chemical, electronic, and computer industries. A commercial crossroads for centuries, Lille also claims a remarkable cultural and artistic heritage, visible in the refurbished seventeenth- and eighteenth-century town houses that grace Old Lille, the Vieille Bourse—a jewel of Flemish architecture, also expertly restored—and the Hospice Comtesse. To the regret of art lovers, Lille's world-class museum remains closed for renovations.

Unlike the climate, the people of the North are warm and convivial. Carnival goes on all year, and each town trots out its "giant" for every festival or feast day. These huge figures crafted of wicker and papier-mâché are often inspired by legendary characters, such as Gargantua, the mascot of **Bailleul**, **Cassel**'s Reuze-Papa and Reuze-Maman, **Steenvorde**'s Jean the Lumberjack, **Hazebrouck**'s Tisje-Tasje family, or Douai's Gayent, perhaps the most famous of them all. Hidden under the giants' costumes are human "helpers" who make the figures frolic and dance. The kermesses or fairs where the giants appear are liberally lubricated with local beers—Trois Monts or Hommelpap, produced in boutique breweries. You can sample them, along with hearty snacks served on traditional wooden boards, in what locals call an *estaminet*: an old-fashioned bistro often warmed by a pot-bellied stove and decorated with vintage musical instruments.

Flemish cooking reflects Northerners' warm-hearted nature, with comforting stews like carbonnade (beef braised in beer), potjevfleisch (a hearty meat terrine with herbed aspic), wine-stewed rabbit with prunes, and eel in a green herb sauce laced with wine. Northern cheeses—Vieux-Lille, beer-washed Maroilles, and peppery Boulette d'Avesnes—are famed for their pungent flavors (and strong aromas!).

Picardy: a far-flung suburb of Paris

It's hardly an exaggeration to say that high-speed transport has turned **Picardy**, the area north of Ile-de-France that extends from Champagne to the sea, into a far-flung suburb of Paris. Plateaus and verdant valleys form landscapes more varied than those farther north. The limestone that underpins the terrain bares its white teeth to bite into the sea, but inland it burrows under a mantle of fertile soil that nourishes grain and vegetable crops. In Picardy low-slung farmhouses shelter under strong slate roofs.

Agriculture, not industry, is Picardy's traditional source of wealth. Yet today **Amiens** produces tires, chemicals, and electronics, while its unique *hortillonnages*—market gardens set along a maze of canals—totter on the verge of extinction; a shame, for they have been cultivated here since medieval times.

From spring to fall, boats ferry visitors through the gardens, to admire row upon row of lovingly tended peas, artichokes, leeks, beans... Birds, too, love the *hortillonnages* (the canals are aswarm with fish).

The capital of Picardy, Amiens was savagely bombed in World War II, and the town was rebuilt in a rather graceless style. Yet Amiens's Gothic cathedral stands as proud as ever, the largest church in France. Inside, be sure to examine the early Renaissance choir stalls, carved with thousands of curious, often droll and lifelike figures.

On the edge of one of the most beautiful forests in France, **Compiègne** (just 50 miles from Paris) claims a long and illustrious history: for 900 years it was a favorite residence of French royalty. The eighteenth-century château de Compiègne, designed by Gabriel and restored by Napoléon, was the scene of sumptuous festivities arranged by Emperor Napoléon III, who received all the crowned heads of Europe in opulently decorated apartments. This frivolous era is commemorated in the château's Second Empire museum.

History inhabits every mile of the roads that lead from Paris to Belgium and northern Europe, and out to the chalky cliffs that face the sea and England beyond. For centuries that island kingdom has sought to emerge from its insularity, while at the same time proudly protecting it. After William the Conqueror, no invader—not Napoléon, not Hitler—sailed from Calais or Boulogne to land triumphant in Dover.

Now, at the end of the twentieth century, France and England, those eternal *frères ennemis*, have combined their talents to create a miracle of engineering that the entire world applauds. As the **Eurostar** train speeds through the Channel Tunnel that links the Continent to Britain, it obliterates the last traces of an age-old rivalry.

RESTAURANTS & HOTELS

BÉTHUNE	62400
Paris 213 - Arras 33 - Dunkerque 67	P./Calais

 Marc Meurin

15, pl. de la République
03 21 68 88 88, fax 03 21 56 37 15
Closed Sun dinner, Mon (exc hols), 2 wks in Aug.
Open until 10pm. Terrace dining. Air cond. Pkg.
"I had the best meal I tasted in the region here this year," states one of our readers, who like

many fine-food lovers in France's Nord and in Belgium regularly come to Béthune for the culinary pleasures offered up by this charming white house, with its entirely renovated dining rooms. Marc Meurin's unaffectedly elegant cuisine takes its discreet flavor cues from herbs and spices and consistently seeks out impressive new harmonies. We savored his distinctive iced bass "leaves" with marjoram, the round slices of breaded chitterling sausage (andouillette) with red cabbage, and the turbot with charcoaled onion and veal jus. Incredible fixed-price meals, wide variety of beautifully presented desserts, and nice friendly-priced cellar, well-stocked with Bordeaux and Burgundies. A friendly welcome, attentive service, and genuinely restful atmosphere. C 400-500. M 150 (exc Sat & Sun), 210-330, 80 (children).

 Vieux Beffroy

48, Grand-Place - 03 21 68 15 00, fax 03 21 56 66 32
Open year-round. 65 rms 150-500. Bkfst 30. Restaurant. Half-board 250-400. Rm ser. Conf. Pkg.
A big old house in front of the old belfry offering simple but comfortable rooms. Live music in the evenings with a Brazilian guitarist and jazz concerts on Saturday.

CALAIS   62100
Paris 305 - Amiens 155 - Dunkerque 39   P./Calais

 Aquar'Aile

Plage de Calais, 255, rue Jean-Moulin
03 21 34 00 00, fax 03 21 34 15 00
Closed Sun dinner. Open until 11pm. Air cond. Pkg.
The panoramic bay windows afford diners a splendid view of the passing boats, and the décor takes its cue from the sea. The service here is impeccable, and Olivier Taildeman is one of the most talented chefs around. Don't miss his smoked fish sampler platter, tasty halibut steak in Chardonnay sauce, and strawberry croustillant with raspberry coulis. Don't hesitate to ask Tino Bellacappa for "cellarly" advice. C 250. M 98, 160, 230, 60 (children).

12/20 Le Channel

3, bd de la Résistance
03 21 34 42 30, fax 03 21 97 13 14
Closed Sun dinner, Mon dinner, Tue, end Jul-beg Aug, end Dec-beg Jan. Open until 9:30pm. Priv rm 30. Air cond. Pkg.
Tuck into succulent seafood, offerings from the grill, or confits—as well as a few more ambitious classic dishes—in the restful atmosphere and comfortable Louis XIII décor of the spacious dining room here, with a view of the passing boats in the nearby harbor. C 280. M 95 (exc Sun), 150, 220, 280.

12/20 George V

36, rue Royale - 03 21 97 68 00, fax 03 21 97 34 73
Closed Sat lunch, dinner Sun & hols, Dec 23-Jan 4. Open until 10pm. Priv rm 50. Air cond. HOTEL:

42 rms 310-460. Bkfst 42. Rms for disabled. Half-board 305-400. Rm ser. Air cond. Conf. Garage pkg.
There's the Petit George, where diners take their pick from affordably priced set menus featuring treats from the grill. Then there's the Grand George which was redecorated last year in classic style, and boasts a repertoire for guests with a yen for meticulously prepared gastronomic fare. Lovely selection of wines. C 100-250. M 275 (wine incl), 90-150.

 Holiday Inn Garden Court

Bd des Alliés - 03 21 34 69 69, fax 03 21 97 09 15
Open year-round. 62 rms 550-580. Bkfst 85. Rms for disabled. Restaurant. Conf. Pkg.
This portside establishment welcomes a steady flow of tourists from across the Channel, which perhaps explains the English-style equipment (trouser presses, electric kettles) in the comfortable, modern rooms. Efficient, smiling welcome and service.

ÉLINCOURT-STE-MARGUERITE   60157
Paris 94 - Beauvais 74 - Compiègne 17   Oise

 Château de Bellinglise

Route de Lassigny
03 44 96 00 33, fax 03 44 96 03 00
Open year-round. 2 stes 1,440-1,630. 35 rms 820-1,490. Bkfst 74-95. Restaurant. Half-board 615-1,790. Rm ser. Conf. Tennis. Garage pkg.
This immense Louis XIII-era castle on a 600-acre estate has been remarkably preserved and restored; guests stay in huge newly renovated rooms that are impeccably furnished and equipped. Pond, tennis, horseback-riding, balloon rides, skeet shooting, and archery are just some of the activities in store. Fitness center.

LAMBERSART   59130
Paris 222 - Lille 2   Nord

 La Laiterie

138, av. de l'Hippodrome
03 20 92 79 73, fax 03 20 22 16 19
Closed Sun dinner, 1 wk in Feb, wk of Aug 15. Open until 10pm. Priv rm 40. Garden dining. Valet pkg.
Ludovic Vantours's marvelously appealing cuisine—technically at ease with itself and demonstrating an intelligent use of regional ingredients and a precise analysis of flavor combinations—just gets better every year. What could be more charming than his regional menu in all its simplicity and perfection for only 155 F? Pleasant variations on a seafood theme: red mullet fillets with spinach and tomatoes in Bandol wine, spirals of sole with bourbon grain, hazelnuts and dandelion greens, and lovely local poultry. The relaxed but refined atmosphere is good for the digestion. A cellar abound with bottles, but don't count on unexpected finds. C 420. M 155, 270, 370 (wine incl).

LILLE 59000
Paris 219 - Dunkerque 80 - Arras 51 Nord

Alliance
See restaurant Le Jardin du Cloître

12/20 Le Bistrot de Pierrot
6, pl. de Béthune - 03 20 57 14 09, fax 03 20 30 93 13
Closed Sun. Open until 10:30pm. Terrace dining. Air cond.
Diners pack this good old-fashioned bistro "elbow to elbow" to tuck into generous portions of flavorful, earthy fare. A few Flemish specialties. Judicious cellar. C 180-300.

 Carlton
3, rue de Paris - 03 20 13 33 13, fax 03 20 51 48 17
Open year-round. 7 stes 1,020-2,400. 52 rms 800-1,020. Bkfst 75. Rms for disabled. Restaurant. Rm ser. Air cond. Conf. Valet pkg.
This corner building across from the opera house offers large, comfortable guest quarters with beautifully renovated bathrooms. Breakfasts could be more exciting, but the welcome is unfailingly warm and friendly.

 L'Huîtrière
3, rue des Chats-Bossus
03 20 55 43 41, fax 03 20 55 23 10
Closed dinner Sun & hols, Jul 22-Aug 25. Open until 9:30pm. Priv rm 60. Terrace dining. Air cond.
The front of this establishment boasts a famous fishmonger's shop done up in pretty mosaics; the dining room behind it is warm and elegant, the service flawless, the cellar remarkable, and the cuisine—well, it's simply beyond compare (crafted from the front room's finest ingredients, *naturellement*): sorrel-flavored eel flan; juicy monkfish cooked in Monts beer. Be sure to leave room for locally-inspired desserts like cramique (raisin brioche) French toast and gingerbread ice cream. Interesting theme menus based on a single ingredient (mushrooms, endives, etc.) and a new 260 F set lunch menu. C 500-550. M 260 (weekday lunch), 450, 550.

10/20 Le Jardin du Cloître
17, quai du Wault - 03 20 30 62 62, fax 03 20 42 94 25
Closed Sun dinner & Mon in summer. Open until 10:30pm. Pkg.
This former cloister was painstakingly restored and turned into an elegant restaurant. Unfortunately the cuisine fails to measure up to the surroundings: the gratiné of sea scallops with Sancerre sauce we tasted was thoroughly uninspired. C 260. M 110 (weekdays), 160.

 Alliance
(See restaurant above)
Open year-round. 8 stes 900-1,500. 75 rms 640-750. Bkfst 70. Rms for disabled. Half-board 500-600. Rm ser. Conf. Pkg.
The prestigious seventeenth-century Minimes convent with its vaulted-ceiling gallery has been turned into this luxury hotel with superb rooms and ultra-modern comforts. Seminar facilities. Attentive, make-you-feel-at-home service.

 Le Varbet
2, rue de Pas - 03 20 54 81 40, fax 03 20 57 55 18
Closed Sun, Mon, hols, wk of Jul 14, wk of Aug 15, end Dec-beg Jan. Open until 9:30pm. Priv rm 30.
One of our readers told us that he tasted the best blinis he'd ever had in his life here! They're made to order (of course), and served with superbly fresh salmon roe. But Gilles Vartanian has some other nifty culinary tricks up his sleeve as well, and adapts his savory contemporary cuisine to fit the seasons. The wine list goes heavy on Bordeaux, and boasts some growers' treasures. Friendly welcome; inviting wood-and-fabric décor. C 350-400. M 165, 250, 400 (dinner).

And also...
Our selection of places for inexpensive, quick, or late-night meals.
Brasserie de la Cloche (03 20 55 35 34 - 13, pl. du Théâtre. Open until 11pm.): This wine bar features regional dishes and cheery service (130-180).
Le Caveau de Bacchus (03 20 57 35 00 - 196, bd Victor-Hugo. Open until 9:30pm.): The lofty of Lille don't hesitate to drop down to this underground wine bar-cellar to nip some refined wine and nibble some not-so-refined food. Charming service (200).
Christian Leclercq (03 20 74 17 05 - 9, rue Lepelletier. Open until 11pm.): A *maître-fromager* offers a variety of cheese-based dishes (try the hot cheese "tour of France"!) in three tiny dining rooms (130-210).

MARCQ-EN-BARŒUL 59700
Paris 226 - Lille 15 - Roubaix 8 Nord

Le Septentrion
Parc du Château du Vert-Bois, in Bondues
03 20 46 26 98, fax 03 20 46 38 33
Closed Sun dinner Sun, Mon, Feb school hols, 1st 3 wks of Aug. Open until 9:30pm. Garden dining. Valet pkg.
The shady terrace affords guests a splendid view of the château du Vert-Bois's grounds, as do the two dining rooms (one modern, the other classic) inside. Gilbert Lelaurain has been working his culinary wonders here for more than twenty years now, displaying the same enthusiasm and talent all along the way. He's recently added some sunny, more imaginative creations to his repertoire. His mussel soup, Jenlain-style (Jenlain is a local artisanal brown beer) guinea fowl "ham," roast with Maroilles cheese, and chicory-flavored crème brûlée compose an incredibly tasty song of praise to Flemish cooking. On sunny days, take a seat under the tree-filled terrace in the château's lovely park. Excellent cellar. C 300. M 180, 290, 60 (children).

Sofitel

Av. de la Marne - 03 20 72 17 30, fax 03 20 89 92 34
*Open year-round. 1 stc 1,300. 124 rms 450-750.
Bkfst 35-75. Rms for disabled. Restaurant. Half-
board 355-655. Rm scr. Air cond. Conf. Valet pkg.*
This mammoth hotel complex is just a few
minutes from Lille by highway. Guest quarters
here are impeccably equipped, and large meeting rooms, a fitness center, piano bar and garden
are at guests' disposal. Laundry-ironing service.

MONTREUIL-SUR-MER	62170
Paris 204 - Boulogne 37 - Lille 114	P./Calais

 **Château
de Montreuil** ♻

4, chaussée des Capucins
03 21 81 53 04, fax 03 21 81 36 43
*Closed Mon off-seas (exc hols), Thu lunch, mid Dec-
beg Feb. Open until 9:30pm. Priv rm 65. Garden
dining. Garage pkg.*
This rambling bourgeois homestead from the
30s set on sumptuous grounds served as headquarters for the Germans during World War II.
Today, it draws a predominantly British clientele eager to sample the delicacies served forth
by owner (and fellow Brit) Lindsay Germain and
her hubby chef Christian, who did a stint with
the Roux brothers in England. That being said,
the cooking here is definitely French: at once
simple and refined, lively and flavorful—made
from excellent ingredients, with lovely hints of
its region in dishes like the roast cod and mussels
cooked in white beer or the veal chop and
Romaine lettuce à la flamande. The cellar is a
harmonious mix of mainly Burgundies and Bordeaux, all courteously served in grand style in
delicate pastel surroundings. C 300. M 280 (wine
incl), 200 & 230 (lunch), 300, 400, 130 (children).

 **Château
de Montreuil** ⚔♦

(See restaurant above)
*Closed Mon off-seas, mid Dec-beg Feb. 1 stc 980. 13
rms 750-900. Bkfst 70-90. Rms for disabled. Half-
board 900-1,200. Rm scr. No pets. Garage pkg.*
The spacious, bright, comfortable guest
quarters here have well-equipped bathrooms
and overlook an English-style garden. Attentive
welcome. Very quiet and relaxing. Relais et
Châteaux.

RETHONDES	60153
Paris 92 - Beauvais 77 - Compiègne 17	Oise

 Alain Blot

"Auberge du Pont", 21, rue du Maréchal-Foch
03 44 85 60 24, fax 03 44 85 92 35
*Closed Sat lunch, Sun dinner, Mon, hols. Open until
9:15pm. Priv rm 25. Pkg.*
The restful pale-pink dining room with white
beams overlooks a peaceful garden with century-old trees. Alain Blot's Picardy cooking
echoes this gentleness with market-fresh

ingredients that change with the seasons: frog's
legs cooked in sweet garlic, fresh salmon cooked
with its skin and served with vegetable straws,
and rabbit fillet on a roasted hazelnut sauce. The
200 F set-price menu is really set (it doesn't offer
any choice), but it is well composed. A bucolic
atmosphere set in the heart of the Compiègne
forest. C 400. M 140 (weekday lunch), 200 (weekdays), 270-350, 80 (children).

ROYE	80700
Paris 105 - Amiens 41 - Compiègne 38	Somme

 La Flamiche

20, pl. de l'Hôtel-de-Ville
03 22 87 00 56, fax 03 22 78 46 77
*Closed Sun dinner, Mon, Jul 5-15, Dec 20-Jan 13.
Open until 9:30pm. Priv rm 40. Air cond. Pkg.*
This fine restaurant equidistant from Calais,
Lille, and Paris has become a favorite among
Brits and Belgians, and we hope Parisians will
soon follow suit! You couldn't ask for a more
attentive host than Gérard Borck, nor a more
dedicated and talented chef than Marie-Christine Klopp. Both display a deep passion for the
fine art of entertaining and the most wonderful
(and sometimes the rarest) local ingredients
money can buy: perch or pike fished from the
Somme; wild duck and eels from the marshes;
herbs and vegetables from the lower Somme
Valley. But the tributes here extend beyond
Picardy: the lobster comes from Brittany and the
poultry from Bresse; the milk-fed veal from
Corrèze and the lamb from the Pyrenees. Marie-
Christine Klopp brings the right touch of derring-do and originality to everything she cooks:
she bravely pairs hot duck foie gras with rhubarb
or Jerusalem artichokes; monkfish with a fondant of ginger-flecked carrots; veal sweetbreads
with caraway seeds; and pig's ears and
cauliflower are deep-fried in tempura batter.
And the results are out of this world! Time seems
to stand still in the warm, dining room decorated
with antique furniture, charming ducks, and
pretty bouquets. Wonderful wine, coffee, and
cigar lists. C 400-600. M 135 (weekdays, Sat
lunch), 360 (Sun lunch), 350 & 695 (wine incl), 195
(exc Sun), 260 (exc Sun), 480, 100 (children).

 Hôtel Central

36, rue d'Amiens - 03 22 87 11 05, fax 03 22 87 42 74
*Closed Sun, Mon, last 3 wks of Aug, end Dec-beg Jan.
8 rms 230-320. Bkfst 30. Restaurant. No pets.*
This well-kept establishment offers a pleasant
welcome and small-but-functional rooms. Just
right for an overnight stay.

TILQUES	62500
Paris 247 - Arras 75 - St-Omer 6 km	P./Calais

 Château Tilques

03 21 93 28 99, fax 03 21 38 34 23
*Open year-round. 2 stcs 850. 51 rms 395-690. Bkfst
50. Rms for disabled. Restaurant. Conf. Tennis. No
pets. Pkg.*

This charming nineteenth-century château offers recently redecorated, comfortable, well-equipped rooms. The overall setting is elegant, and lends itself to seminars and receptions.

TOUQUET-PARIS-PLAGE (LE)	62520
Paris 222 - Abbeville 61 - Lille 132	P./Calais

 ### Flavio Club de la Forêt

1, av. du Verger - 03 21 05 10 22, fax 03 21 05 91 55
Closed Mon (exc Jul-Aug & hols), Jan 10-Feb 10. Open until 10pm. Terrace dining. Pkg.
The least we can say about this place is that it's elegant. And Guy Delmotte's cuisine—based on top-notch ingredients and outstanding flavors—goes hand in hand with the setting: roasted langoustines, salmon done with bread and beer, Sauternes-soaked fruit sabayon—not to mention lobster, one of the specialties of the house! We're just sorry the check brought us out of this dream world back to cold, hard reality. C 550-650. M 200 (weekday lunch, wine incl), 360, 650.

 ### Grand Hôtel

4, bd de la Canche
03 21 06 88 88, fax 03 21 06 87 87
Open year-round. 20 stes 800-3,150. 135 rms 550-850. Bkfst 70-90. Rms for disabled. Restaurant. Half-board 740. Rm scr. Heated pool. Valet pkg.
This quiet palace set on manicured green grounds with a view of Canche Bay is luxuriously appointed with marble, Persian rugs, and enormous crystal chandeliers. The commodious guest rooms are furnished *à l'anglaise*, and are remarkably well equipped. Fine breakfasts.

REGIONAL FOODS

The flavors of northern France are vigorous and robust, with a distinctive Flemish cast. The North's charcuterie displays a rustic character which rouses modern palates used to soft, bland, overprocessed food: make a point of savoring such memorable specialties as jambon des Ardennes and juniper-scented game pâtés made with venison, boar, or hare. Northern cheeses are pungent, too, and may take some getting used to—Maroilles, Vieux-Lille, Boulette de Cambrai or d'Avesnes are not for timid palates! Instead of wine, partner them with a glass of local beer or (why not?) a tot of aromatic Northern gin.

Some establishments change their closing times without warning. It is always wise to check in advance.

• CHARCUTERIE

LILLE	59800 – Nord

Cnockaert

37, rue de la Grande-Chaussée - 03 20 55 18 82
Most of the appetizing items sold here are produced on the premises. For a taste of the true North, sample the house specialty, potjevfleisch, a terrine made with a trio of meats.

• CHEESE

AMIENS	80000 – Somme

Fromathèque Picarde

9, rue de Noyon - 03 22 91 84 63
The region's distinctive cheeses are all on array in this tempting shop. Many come direct from local monasteries, where cheesemaking is still an artisanal activity.

BOULOGNE-SUR-HELPE	59440 – Nord

Ferme du Château Courbet

03 27 61 18 75
Farmhouse Maroilles, Boulettes, and other specialties based on the North's robust cheeses.

BOULOGNE-SUR-MER	62200 – P./Calais

Philippe Olivier

43, rue Adolphe-Thiers - 03 21 31 94 74
The full range of sturdy Northern cheeses (farmhouse Maroilles, Vieux Gris...) is on hand, matured on the premises by the owners, since 1907.

MAROILLES	59550 – Nord

Ferme du Verger Pilote

03 27 84 71 10
Visitors are welcome at this oderiferous dairy, where Maroilles, Boulettes, and other cheeses are produced.

• CHOCOLATE & CANDY

BERCK-PLAGE	62600 – P./Calais

Le Succès Berckois

56, rue Carnot - 03 21 09 61 30
Berlingots, another familiar French bonbon, are the specialty of this family-run firm. There are 17 varieties to choose from, including the traditional peppermint flavor.

CAMBRAI 59400 – Nord

Afchain

ZI Cantimpré - 03 27 81 25 49
Since 1830 this firm has produced the celebrated mint candies known as Bêtises de Cambrai. A traditional French favorite.

LILLE 59800 – Nord

Dominique Benoit

77, rue de la Monnaie - 03 20 31 69 03
First-rate chocolates, all hand-dipped on the premises.

Meert

27, rue Esquermoise - 03 20 57 07 44
The house-made chocolates are yummy, but don't neglect the delectable caramels for which Meert is famous.

TOUQUET-PARIS-PLAGE (LE) 62520 – P./Calais

Au Chat Bleu

47 bis, rue Saint-Jean - 03 21 05 03 86
Delicious chocolates and a house exclusivity, called Le Chat Bleu (for the first owners' Bluepoint Persian cat.

• *GOURMET SPECIALTIES*

Beer

BENIFONTAINE 62410 – P./Calais

Brasserie Castelain

13, rue Pasteur - 03 21 40 38 38

The beer to try here is the bière du "Ch'ti," offered in pale, amber, or dark versions. Or sample the organically brewed beer called Jade.

HORDAIN 59111 – Nord

Brasserie la Choulette

16, rue des Écoles - 03 27 35 72 44
These craft beers are brewed in small batches and have a wonderful "handmade" flavor. We especially like La Choulette (pale, amber, or raspberry-flavored) and the beer from the Abbaye de Vaucelles.

JENLAIN 59144 – Nord

Brasserie Duick

Route Nationale - 03 27 49 70 03
Amber brews are the top draw at this noted brasserie, but beer buffs will also want to try La Sébourg, a powerful pale beer.

• *PASTRY & COOKIES*

AMIENS 80000 – Somme

Aux Délices de France

130, rue Laurendeau - 03 22 89 42 11
All the sweet indulgences are made on the spot: try the tempting chocolates, macarons, and crisp little cookies.

LILLE 59800 – Nord

Yanka

75, rue Nationale - 03 20 54 73 06
Loads of unusual local specialties can be discovered here. For the gastro-tourist with a sweet tooth, this is heaven!

POITOU, VENDÉE & CHARENTES

A pilgrimage through western France

Poitou is one of France's oldest provinces. Out of it were carved the *départements* of Vendée, Deux-Sèvres, the two Charentes, and Vienne. The entire history of medieval and modern France can be deciphered in the region's landscape and monuments. Inhabited from the earliest times, and covered—like all of western France—with megaliths and Bronze Age sites, Poitou entered history as the land of the Pictones, hence its name. In Roman times Poitou was a division—a *civitas*—of the province of Aquitaine. As ancient remains demonstrate beyond a doubt, Poitou was deeply, enduringly Romanized. The conquerors' influence was centered in the *oppidum*, or town, of Limonum, which from the ninth century became known as Poitiers. In the latter days of the Empire, Limonum grew into a major transport and administrative center—the imperial legate resided there. Archaeological digs in and around Poitiers continue to reveal Gallo-Roman structures. The remains of a third-century rampart are still visible in several districts of Poitiers, and the city's cultural center displays Gallo-Roman inscriptions, furniture, and a magnificent statue of Minerva. A few miles north, at **Vandeuvre-du-Poitou** is the Gallo-Roman archaeological site of Les Tours Mirandes, the largest in western France.

Poitou was the scene of three epic battles that proved decisive for the course of French history. At **Vouillé** in 506 the Frankish ruler Clovis chased the Visigoths out of France and consolidated his kingship. In 732 Charles Martel, grandfather of Charlemagne, beat back the Moorish invasion of Europe at Poitiers. And in 1356 Poitiers witnessed one of France's worst defeats in the Hundred Years' War, when King John the Good was taken prisoner by the English. Christianity rapidly took root in Poitou, and flourished with rare vigor. In the fourth century the bishop of Poitiers (later Saint Hilary the Great), and his disciple, the future Saint Martin of Tours, founded the influential abbeys of **Noirmoutier** and **Ligugé**.

Poitou's golden age spanned the tenth to the twelfth centuries. The Guilhem family, counts of Poitiers, rose to the rank of dukes of Aquitaine in 928 and retained the title for 200 years. These opulent *seigneurs* had themselves crowned in royal style at the abbey of Saint-Martial in Limoges. Under their rule, **Poitiers** acquired its great Romanesque sanctuaries: from atop the city's hill, Notre-Dame-la-Grande, Saint-Jean-de-Montierneuf, Saint-Porchaire, Sainte-Radegonde, and Saint-Hilaire-le-Grand dominate the surrounding plains. Throughout Poitou, the Guilhem era saw the construction of important Romanesque monuments, the tangible sign of an intense spiritual revival, marked by the erection of the abbey of **Fontevraud** (just over the Poitou border, in Anjou), and by the endless procession of pilgrims to Santiago de Compostela, in Spain. Abbots, feudal lords, and city fathers fostered a boom in church construction. Many of those churches still stand today, their eloquent carvings and frescoes intact. At **Chauvigny**, a craggy promontory supports the imposing remains of several feudal fortresses, while in the lower town, the church of Saint-Pierre displays fascinating carved capitals. A few miles away, the church of **Saint-Pierre-les-Églises** preserves the oldest wall paintings in Poitou. In the church at **Saint-Savin**, once part of a Carolingian abbey, visitors gaze in wonder at the most remarkable cycle of Romanesque frescoes in Europe: scenes from the Apocalypse decorate the porch; the Passion and the Resurrection are depicted on the western wall. The nave's grandiose fresco made it possible for illiterate medieval Christians to learn the major of episodes of Bible history, from the Creation to Abraham: Adam and Eve, the Crossing of the Red Sea, the Tower of Babel... Local peasants could even see a reflection of their own lives, in the tools and gestures of Noah pruning his vines.

At the same time, the province sprouted with fortresses and châteaux at **Loudun, Châtellerault, Lusignan, Vivonne, Montmorillon**... The dean of them all was founded at Chauvigny around 1025, by the Poitiers-Bourges road that crossed the Vienne River at the very foot of the fortress.

In 1137 the Guilhem dynasty ran out of male heirs, and Eleanor of Aquitaine presented the duchy as part of her dowry when she wed King Louis VII of France. When he repudiated her, and Eleanor married England's Henry

Plantagenet, she took the duchy with her. Energetic, elegant, celebrated by troubadours who compared her to the "eagle, queen of the air," Eleanor brought a final burst of brilliance to her house, but with her Poitou lost its independence.

Thereafter, Poitou opened up to different cultural and artistic influences. The new Gothic architecture, imported from Ile-de-France and Anjou, coexisted with the Romanesque in Poitiers's churches of Saint-Jean-de-Montierneuf and Sainte-Radegonde, but the Gothic style triumphed in Poitiers's cathedral of Saint-Pierre. The 1200s saw the launch of major sculpture workshops in Poitou. The wooden stalls of Poitiers's cathedral, executed under Bishop Jean de Melun between 1235 and 1257, and the sculptures currently exhibited in the chapter room of the abbey of **Charroux** (52 km south of Poitiers) are undisputed masterpieces. Military architecture evolved as well: the squat, square donjons of the Romanesque period gave way to cylindrical towers, like those at **Montreuil-Bonnin**, typical of the style that prevailed from the time of King Philippe-Auguste.

As the front line of Aquitaine, Poitou played an essential role during the Hundred Years' War. After John the Good's defeat in 1356, England's Edward III used the province as a base for threatening the Paris region. After a welcome spell of peace under the rule of King Charles V's brother, art patron Jean de Berry, the Dauphin (future Charles VI) made Poitou and Berry the base for his reconquest of France. He founded the University of Poitiers in 1431 as a counterweight to the Sorbonne. The university gave Poitiers international stature; the printing and the book trades flourished so vigorously that Poitiers rivaled Paris. Along with the musical works of composer Clément Jannequin (1485-1558), the greatest artistic legacy of the the Renaissance in Poitou is a collection of sumptuous town houses, notably the Fumé, Berthelot, and Beaucé houses in Poitiers.

In 1537 the first persecutions of Protestants began in Poitiers. The Wars of Religion engulfed Poitou in earnest from 1562 on. The destruction they wrought is still visible today at the abbey of Charroux or the churches of Sainte-Radegonde and Saint-Hilaire. Militant Protestantism in the region dates from this era, particularly in the western reaches of the province, where Louis XIII and Richelieu led a ruthless siege against Protestant troops at La Rochelle in 1628. The Edict of Nantes guaranteed religious freedom for Protestants; its revocation by Louis XIV in 1685 meant forced exile for 7,000 Huguenots.

Vendée: the green Venice

What was called **Lower Poitou** before the Revolution now makes up the *département* of Vendée, composed of the two very different zones that are inland and coastal Vendée. **Inland Vendée** is a land of hills and low mountains that prolongs the Armorican massif, before it plunges into the wetlands of the **Marais Poitevin**, west of Niort. The Marais is a unique and magical landscape made up of polders—swamps reclaimed from the sea. The effort began far back in the eleventh century, when the abbey of **Maillezais** was founded on an outcrop of limestone, for the express purpose of draining the land and making it arable (the ruins of the Romanesque abbey church can be visited today). Known as the **Venise verte** or "green Venice," the Marais Poitevin is crisscrossed by a maze of canals, which visitors can explore in flat-bottomed boats that leave from **Coulon**, on the River Sèvre. The drier, eastern portions of the Marais Poitevin support livestock, especially beef cattle. Industrialized towns are few in Vendée: **Cholet**, famous for its printed handkerchiefs, **Fontenay-le-Comte** (also home to the Musée Vendéen), and the meat-packing center of **Parthenay** all share the discreet charm of sleepy provincial towns.

Coastal Vendée bears little resemblance to the interior. Its long stretch of shore is punctuated with port towns that once enjoyed considerable renown, Les Sables-d'-Olonne, for example. Nowadays, the oyster and mussel beds of the **Bourgneuf** and **Aiguillon** bays, seashells collected for sale, and sea salt gathered from glittering salt marshes are the area's chief resources. Away from the coast, beyond the wooded dunes that protect immense white beaches, vegetable growers cultivate delicious carrots, lettuces, garlic, beans, and potatoes on small truck farms. This prime produce rarely leaves the region, but along with ducks from **Challans**, butter from Charentes, and glistening fresh shrimp, oysters, soles, and brill from local waters, it makes the markets of Vendée a food lover's dream. The booming tourism industry has changed the face of coastal Vendée in the past twenty years. Over 180 miles of beaches and a sunny climate with dry summers attract holiday-makers from all over Europe to **Saint-Jean-de-Mont**, **Les Sables-d'Olonne** (in addition to huge beaches, there is a fine contemporary art museum there), and to the pleasure islands of **Yeu** and **Noirmoutier**.

In France's collective memory Vendée is forever linked to the popular uprising of 1793, when the levying of 300,000 troops by the young *république française* unleashed a revolt in the western provinces, which were still loyal to the ideal of a Catholic monarchy. There followed what Napoléon called a "war of Giants" that opposed the *la grande armée catholique et royale* and the republican army, a war that dragged on until 1815. As one travels through this landscape, which has changed but little since the eighteenth century, it is easy to imagine the pitched battles fought at Cholet and Chantonnay, or the countless ambushes laid by Vendéens in the wooded hills of the *bocage*. On summer nights at the castle of Le Puy-du-Fou a brilliant sound-and-light show recreates the saga of the Vendée wars.

Charentes: a most fertile district

"I do not wish to hear our Touraine anointed 'Garden of France,' for it is in no wise comparable to this; or, if Touraine is a garden, then this is paradise on earth!" The Charente Valley and its verdant countryside elicited that compliment from historian Estienne Pasquier in 1585. A century later, Albert Jouvin, the royal treasurer and a famous traveler besides, saw in the provinces around the cities of La Rochelle and Saintes "one of the most fertile districts of the realm, rich in wine, wheat, ship timber, fish, salt, cattle, meadows, and good seaports." South of Vendée, these western reaches of the old province of Poitou (home of Cognac and of the late President François Mitterrand), beguiles the visitor with bucolic visions of deep-plowed fields and vineyards, and with maritime scenes as colorful as any Mediterranean seascape.

Coastal Charentes opens onto the Gironde River estuary to the southwest. To the west lies a sea of narrows and channels protected by two island versions of the local countryside: the enchanting Ile de Ré and Ile d'Oléron. It adds up to more than 320 miles of coastline, where the admirably preserved ports of La Rochelle and seventeenth-century Rochefort testify to the grandeur of Charentes's naval past (Rochefort's Corderie Royale, a former ropewalk, is a remarkable sight). Royan, a popular resort town entirely rebuilt after the war, lures visitors to the tip of Charentes's coast with its broad beaches and casino.

Limestone cliffs eaten away by the waves, ancient valleys filled up by silt from river and sea, sand dunes pinned down by plantations of pines: Charentes's shoreline offers the intriguing spectacle of a titanic battle between ocean and earth. Centuries of effort have gone into mastering the sea, by medieval monks and modern engineers: their legacy is a maze of canals and ditches, dikes and locks, and a checkerboard of salt pans and oyster beds. The wetlands around La Rochelle prove that reclamation can be a success; but the barren marshes near Rochefort and Brouage (birthplace of Samuel de Champlain, founder of Quebec), a former port that is now miles from the sea, show that even the most valiant efforts can fail.

Farther inland the Charente River, an important commercial artery since the Late Empire, connects the ancient cities of Saintes (the site of major Roman and Romanesque monuments) and high-perched Angoulême. To the north of the river, limestone plains unfurl their fertile fields, cultivated for many centuries. In the 1700s, the vineyards which had flourished here since the Middle Ages gradually encroached on wheat-bearing land, owing to the high prices paid at export for the region's celebrated brandy. In Cognac and Jarnac visitors can tour the cellars of such prestigious distillers as Hennessy, Otard, and Martell, Hine, and Courvoisier. The very air in these towns is intoxicating! The slopes of the "Champagne" (the word comes from the Latin for "chalk") districts—Cognac, Segonzac—yield the highest quality brandy. The outlying "Bois" or wooded areas still bear the scars of huge swathes of forest felled in the seventeenth and eighteenth centuries, to provide firewood for Cognac's stills and timber for the shipyards at La Rochelle.

A quiet, provincial backwater for some 200 years Poitou-Charentes, as the region is now officially known, only recently began to exploit its resources in a dynamic, forward-looking way. This traditionally rural area now actively seeks to attract high-tech research and industry. The *Futuroscope* theme park at Jauny-Clan, just north of Poitiers, symbolizes the region's new vocation. Hailed as a "showcase of the future," the park draws more than a million visitors each year. What's more, it is now home not only to French, but also to American and Japanese advanced technology firms, which have adopted Poitou as their European base.

Linked to Paris by the TGV bullet train, Poitou, Vendée, and Charentes are emerging—with a vengeance!—from their long torpor. They are only too eager to welcome visitors, and show off their ancient history and rich artistic heritage. The time is ripe to discover the still-secret treasures of western France.

RESTAURANTS & HOTELS

ANGOULÊME 16000
Paris 450 - Bordeaux 116 - Limoges 103 — Charente

 Européen Hôtel

1, pl. Gérard Pérot
05 45 92 06 42, fax 05 45 94 88 29
Closed Dec 23-31. 32 rms 320-480. Bkfst 45. Rms for disabled. Conf.
Behind the pastel façade you'll find spacious, modern, thoroughly equipped rooms (some even have a touch of style). Pleasant reception. Meals are served in the rooms on request.

 La Ruelle

6, rue des Trois-Notre-Dame - 05 45 95 15 19
Closed Sat lunch, Sun, Jan 1-5, Feb 17-23, Apr 14-20, Aug 4-18. Open until 10pm.
Véronique Dauphin and her husband restored this fine old house (notice the great timbers, imposing fireplace, rough-hewn stone walls) and turned it into Angoulême's top restaurant. Véronique's signature dishes are chaudrée charentaise en lasagnes (the local version of chowder, with fresh pasta) and assiette gourmande d'agneau, which brings a boneless lamb chop, leg of lamb en brochette, lamb kidney, and shoulder of lamb wrapped up in a crêpe with a hint of lemon. The solid, balanced cellar holds no half-bottles but there's a score of wines priced under 100 F. C 250-350. M 160 (lunch, wine incl), 150-250.

COGNAC 16100
Paris 481 - Angoulême 42 - Saintes 26 — Charente

 Domaine du Breuil 🏨🎋

104, rue Robert-Daugas
Open year-round. 22 rms 280-450. Bkfst 40. Rm scr. Conf. Pkg.
This superb eighteenth-century dwelling with its pretty rooms and vast bathrooms is set in the midst of an immense, quiet park. Rooms entirely renovated in subtle modern style. Buffet breakfast.

 Le Nautile

2, rue du Port - 05 45 82 68 56
Closed Mon lunch, Sun. Open until 9:30pm. Priv rm 10.
Light, refined seafood dishes are served here in a handsome rustic décor highlighted by elegantly set tables and beamed. We're partial to the chef's glistening fresh shellfish platters and seafood pot-au-feu enhanced with a lemony butter sauce. Mouthwatering selection of prix-fixe menus. Skimpy wine list; warm welcome. C 260-280. M 60 (lunch), 95-175, 40 (children).

CURZAY-SUR-VONNE 86600
Paris 364 - Poitiers 28 - Lusignan 9 — Vienne

 Château de Curzay

05 49 36 17 00, fax 05 49 53 57 69
Open until 9:30pm. Terrace dining. Pool. Valet pkg.
This stately castle affords smashing drawing rooms and two dining rooms, one wainscotted and doting a marvelous wood-sculpted fireplace that is a monument in and of itself. Chef Yves Labrousse proffers a well-crafted classic cuisine: tasty sweetbread and langoustine salad, irreproachable steamed bass with seaweed, choice cheese platter, and a skillfully prepared chocolate soufflé. The cellar is gradually being expanded, and offers mainly Loire Valley wines as well as a goodly number of half-bottles. C 320. M 220-330, 260 (weekdays, wine incl).

Château de Curzay

(See restaurant above)
Open year-round. 2 stes 1,550. 18 rms 750-1,350. Bkfst 70. Rms for disabled. Conf. Pool. Valet pkg.
Lost in the countryside, this elegant eighteenth-century château stands in a magnificent park with a formal French garden. Each huge, tastefully decorated room and suite has a distinctive personality. Relais et Châteaux.

MOSNAC 17 → Pons

NIEUIL 16270
Paris 430 - Limoges 65 - Ruffec 36 — Charente

 Château de Nieuil ⚙

Route de Fontafie - 05 45 71 36 38, fax 05 45 71 46 45
Closed Sun dinner, Mon (exc Jul-Aug), Nov 3-Apr 26. Open until 9pm. Garden dining. Air cond. Pool. Tennis. Pkg.
A Venetian-style interior, brightened by mirrors and stained glass, is a lovely stage for the personalized regional cooking of Luce Bodinaud and Pascal Pressac. We loved the perfectly timed cooking and delicate flavors of the seafood panaché with Marennes oysters in a subtle creamy sauce. Desserts are to die for, and the ultrafresh vegetables and herbs come straight from the kitchen garden. Host Jean-Michel Bodinaud has assembled a terrific collection of Cognacs to put diners in a mellow post-prandial mood, and the selection of Bordeaux is remarkable, but reasonably priced bottles are listed as well. From December 15 to April 15, La Grange aux Oies, opposite the château, offers country cooking at friendly prices, with a prix-fixe menu at 190 F. C 350-460. M 190 (lunch exc Sun), 250-330.

 Château de Nieuil 🏨🎋

(See restaurant above)
Closed Nov 3-Apr 26. 3 stes 1,400-2,200. 11 rms 700-1,400. Bkfst 75. Rms for disabled. Half-board 1,510-2,040 (2 pers). Conf. Pool. Tennis. Pkg.

The Bodinauds' avocation is collecting antiques. It shows, in the regal décor and sybaritic comforts of this Renaissance hunting lodge, which features immense guest rooms and grandiose bathrooms. Each room is distinctively decorated and opens onto a garden à la française. Stroll around the vast grounds, fish in the private pond, or take a ride in a horse-drawn carriage. Sumptuous breakfasts. Relais et Châteaux.

PONS	17800
Paris 495 - Bordeaux 96 - Cognac 23	Charente-M.

■ **In Mosnac 17240** *11 km S on N 173, D 134*

 Le Moulin de Marcouze

05 46 70 46 16, fax 05 46 70 48 14
Closed Feb, 10 days in Nov. Open until 9:30pm. Priv rm 18. Air cond. Pool. Pkg.
  This hotel-restaurant, built around an old mill and owned by Dominique Bouchet, the new chef at Les Ambassadeurs in Paris, caters to those who like to relax in a leafy setting and watch the river flow—the Seugne runs right past the dining room. Fine restaurants are not so thick on the ground around here that we can turn up our nose at Le Moulin, so don't hesitate to try David Vincent's cuisine: scallop dumplings with lobster sauce, roast bar with artichokes, glazed peach on a Champagne granité. Homemade bread and delicacies. Some wines are served by the glass, and the Cognac selection is sublime. C 300-350. M 160, 200 (weekdays lunch), 250, 420.

 Le Moulin de Marcouze

(See restaurant above)
Closed Feb, 10 days in Nov. 1 ste 1,100. 9 rms 525-700. Bkfst 75. Rms for disabled. Half-board 710-760. Air cond. Conf. Pool. Pkg.
  Dominique's wife and daugher, Marie-Hélène and Gaëlle, welcome you more like friends than customers in this haven of peace lost in the countryside. Whether you choose to look out over the river or the lawn, you will enjoy these very large and very comfortable rooms with terra-cotta floors.

OLÉRON (ILE D')	17000
Paris 500 - Marennes 10	Charente-M.

■ **In La Rémigeasse 17550** *10 km from Oléron bridge*

 Amiral

05 46 75 37 89, fax 05 46 75 49 15
Closed end Sep-end Apr. Call off-seas. Open until 9:15pm. Heated pool. Tennis. Garage pkg.
  Captained by Joël Lebeabin, the Amiral is steering a bold course with an exciting, mostly seafood menu based on superb regional ingredients: taste the excellent hot oysters spiked with Pineau and paired with green apples, a vivid shellfish and vegetable medley accented

with sea-salted butter, and finish up with Caribbean chocolate cake. Splendid cellar, with notable Bordeaux; really perfect welcome and service in a dining room with a view of the waves. C 400. M 170-180 (lunch), 270-380.

 Le Grand Large

(See restaurant above)
Closed end Sep-end Apr. 5 stes 1,540-1,880. 21 rms 680-1,740. Bkfst 95. Half-board 1,590-2,700 (2 per, oblig in seas). Heated pool. Tennis. Garage pkg.
  The hotel's modern, ivy-clad buildings are set in five acres of well-groomed grounds. Rooms are perfectly comfortable, and the nicest look out over the sea. Relais et Châteaux.

RÉ (ILE DE)	17000
Via bridge	Charente-M.

■ **In La Flotte-en-Ré 17630**

 Le Richelieu

44, av. de la Plage - 05 46 09 60 70, fax 05 46 09 50 59
Closed Jan 5-Feb 10. Open until 10pm. Priv rm 300. Garden dining. Air cond. Heated pool. Tennis.
  This hotel has just undergone major renovation for conversion into a seawater therapy center, so the prices are at high tide (lobster is billed at 650 F a kilo!). Frankly, we'd prefer a simpler fare with sauces lighter on the cream, a cuisine with a more personal touch. Some originality nonetheless: smoked oyster and scampi timbale, burbot studded with smoked ham and garnished with leek fondue, but for the most part dishes we've seen too many times before (aiguillettes, cassolettes and of course croustillant). The cellar? Exceptional—and so are the prices (you might want to save the day's budget with the island's cooperative wine for 100 F)! C 390. M 300-400, 150 (children).

 Le Richelieu 🌲🎐

(See restaurant above)
Closed Jan 5-Feb 10. 5 stes 1,000-2,000. 38 rms 500-1,500. Bkfst 100-150. Rms for disabled. Rm ser. Air cond. Conf. Heated pool. Tennis. Garage pkg.
  This is the island's most luxurious hotel, located in a charming coastal village. The sunny bay-windowed rooms are comfy (but not everyone likes dusty rose) and have large balconies looking out to sea. You might prefer the greener setting of the houses near the Riviera-style swimming pool. The little seawater cure center is well equipped and charming, but the prices are reflective of the amenities offered.

ROCHELLE (LA)	17000
Paris 475 - Bordeaux 188	Charente-M.

 Richard Coutanceau ⬦

Plage de la Concurrence
05 46 41 48 19, fax 05 46 41 99 45
Closed Sun. Open until 9:30pm. Air cond. Pkg.

Richard Coutanceau snaps up the choicest fish and shellfish at the market each day, then prepares his briny booty with precision and simplicity. We were enchanted by his exquisite langoustine tartare with oyster jelly, his escargot cassolette which proves that he's not forgotten the products of the region, and his first-rate bream baked in its fresh-herb jus with confit lemons. This dish alone brings back his third toque, which is strengthened even further by remarkably refined desserts such as the incredibly delicate rhubarb sablé. The dining room is a model of discreet elegance and you can look through the bay windows and watch the sun set over the sea. C 400-450. M 210-410,110 (children).

12/20 La Toque Blanche

39, rue Saint-Jean-du-Pérot
05 46 41 60 55, fax 05 46 50 51 08
Closed Sat lunch. Open until 10pm.
Seafood dominates Franck Loizeau's menu, but there are a few offerings suitable for carnivores (try the veal kidney braised in Pineau des Charentes—almost worth a toque). Delicious mouclade charentaise; unexciting chocolate cake with mint sauce. Short wine list. C 250-380. M 100, 148, 295.

 33 Rue Thiers

33, rue Thiers - 05 46 41 62 23, fax 05 46 41 10 76
Closed Feb. 1 ste 420-480. 6 rms 350-450. Bkfst 40-45. Conf. No cards. Garage pkg.
It isn't easy to find this eighteenth-century dwelling with its newly painted façade (here's a hint: look near the flower market). To reach the pretty rooms, you must climb flights of ancient wooden stairs. Not all rooms have TV, but there is a library and an enclosed garden as well.

SABLES-D'OLONNE (LES)	85100
Paris 450 - Nantes 90 - La Roche-sur-Yon 35	Vendée

 Beau Rivage

40, promenade Georges-Clemenceau
02 51 32 03 01, fax 02 51 32 46 46
Closed Sun dinner & Mon off-seas (exc hols), Jan. Open until 9:30pm. Air cond.
The restaurant's terrace looks onto the beach, but don't dream of drifting in here in a bathing costume. Understated elegance is the Beau Rivage style. Fish and shellfish star in Joseph Drapeau's classic, accomplished repertoire, although his menu extends to Challans duck, Limousin beef, and even a truffle-stuffed pig's trotter. But his talents shine brightest in seafood dishes like cuttlefish ragoût with ratatouille and a dash of lobster jus, or sublimely simple pan-roasted langoustines accented with fruity olive oil. Everything is top-quality, and the prices reflect that. Luckily, the excellent cellar posts reasonable tariffs. C 400. M 190 (weekdays, Sat lunch), 260 (wine incl), 350-480,120 (children).

12/20 Le Navarin

18, pl. Navarin - 02 51 21 11 61
Closed Sun dinner & Mon (exc Jul-Aug), 1 wk in Nov. Open until 9:30pm. Terrace dining. Air cond.
The waves that break just opposite this venerable brasserie do much to inspire Yves Privat's seafood menu. Though his ingredients are prime, they don't always show to advantage—overcooking and raggedy sauces are to blame. Interesting cellar of Vendée wines; kind, competent service. C 200-300. M 102-295.

 Les Roches Noires

12, promenade Georges-Clemenceau
02 51 32 01 71, fax 02 51 21 61 00
Open year-round. 37 rms 320-660. Bkfst 40.
The sunny, pleasant rooms look out to sea. Well-equipped bathrooms and friendly service. Breakfast is served in a panoramic dining room until noon.

SAINTES	17100
Paris 465 - Bordeaux 118 - Royan 37	Charente-M.

 Relais du Bois Saint-Georges

1.5 km W on D 137, Cours Genêt-rue de Royan
05 46 93 50 99, fax 05 46 93 34 93
Open daily until 9:45pm. Garden dining. Heated pool. Tennis. Garage pkg.
Philippe Gault has the good fortune to work with absolutely first-class ingredients: Marennes oysters, local escargots (cagouilles), fish and other seafood from La Cotinière. He handles these riches with uncommon tact, enhancing and balancing their flavors with precise cooking and sauces that are always *à propos*. His handiwork is delivered by a charming and efficient young staff in a setting of consummate beauty. Such luxury has a price, of course, but it's one that many regulars don't mind paying. An excellent address, in a region where such places are thin on the ground. C 240-290. M 190-490 (wine incl).

 Relais du Bois Saint-Georges

(See restaurant above)
Open year-round. 3 stes 850-1,500. 27 rms 380-980. Bkfst 74. Rms for disabled. Rm ser. Conf. Heated pool. Tennis. Garage pkg.
Tucked away in a vast estate on the edge of Saintes, the Relais is scented by the sweet smell of century-old magnolia trees. The setting is peaceful, the hotel elegantly decorated, and the spacious rooms fetchingly finished with modern touches (dreamy bathrooms, loggias and solarium). Guests enjoy a heated, covered pool and gracious hospitality. Generous breakfasts

319

VIGERIE (LA)   16290
Paris 454 - Angoulême 8   Charente

Le Moulin Gourmand

05 45 90 83 00, fax 05 45 96 91 14
*Closed Mon lunch, Oct 15-Apr 15. Open until
9:30pm. Garden dining. Pool. Pkg.*
Now that Nathalie and Bruno Nicollet have
taken over management of this old mill lost in
the middle of its park, the décor is moving in a
more tasteful direction (perhaps they'll soon get
around to redoing the faded walls!). Bruno's
polished repertoire resounds with full, rich
flavors: foie gras de canard au vieux cognac,
monkfish stewed in red Pineau wine, an apple
tart glazed with acacia-honey caramel, and
chocolate pavé swirled with chestnut cream
sauce are typical of his style. The fixed-price
menus offer good quality for the money. The
cellar is stocked lightly, but you can savor a
regional Haut-Poitou for less than 100 F. C 250.
M 98-195, 55 (children).

Hostellerie du Maine Brun

(See restaurant above)
*Closed Oct 15-Apr 15. 2 stes 900-1,300. 16 rms
325-750. Bkfst 65. Half-board 470-695. Rm ser.
Conf. Pool. Pkg.*
Picture it: an antique-filled mill set in a pretty
park where deer and ducks roam free. The Louis
XVI- and Empire-style rooms are large and comfortable, and offer added improvements every
time we go. Breakfasts on the terrace or balcony
so good that they make you want to get up in the
morning so as not to miss them.

REGIONAL FOODS

Here in France's bucolic western
reaches, the pace of life is measured
and calm. In between visits to abbeys and
Romanesque chapels, travelers will discover
countless farms where they can stop and purchase produce fresh from the field, as well as
wonderful honey and delicious little goat
cheeses with such charming names as
Sableau, Trois Cornes, Lusignan, Frimaillou...
Throughout Charentes, roadside signs adver-
tise Pineau des Charentes (a sweet apéritif
wine), and of course, Cognac, which may be
bought direct from small producers. Foie gras
and confit are also a staple in this region (after
all, Périgord is just over the river). And all up
and down the long coastline, oyster and mussel growers hawk their production from little
stands, where one can stop for a briny, ocean-
fresh snack of shellfish and a glass of local
wine.

• CHARCUTERIE & FOIE GRAS

BLANZAC PORCHERESSE   16250 – Charente

Ferme Auberge Laurent

Les Grands Aulnais, Cressac - 05 45 64 02 97
Ducks are big business in this part of the
country. Come to this welcoming farm-cum-inn
for home-prepared tinned foie gras, confit, rillettes, pâtés, and more.

CHALAIS   16210 – Charente

Chaume Frères

2, av. de la Gare - 05 45 98 12 62
Ready to heat and eat: duck, goose, and turkey
confit, foie gras, and such traditional entrées as
veal à l'ancienne and bœuf bourguignon.

ÉTAULES   17750 – Charente-M.

Charcuterie Étaulaise

42, rue Charles-Hervé - 05 46 36 42 73
All the appetizing offerings are made on the
premises. Most popular are the sausages cooked
in white wine, grillons charentaises (chunks of
belly bacon), and cracklings. Come Christmas,
the crépinettes (sausage patties) laced with
Cognac are in great demand.

POITIERS   86000 – Vienne

Francis Cousin

13, rue Magenta - 05 49 41 06 49
Come here for quality hams, sausages, and
sausages braised in white wine, as well as tasty
terrines and pâtés.

ROCHELLE (LA)   17000 – Charente-M.

Christian Lacaud

27, rue du Temple - 05 46 41 19 16
This attractive shop purveys charcuterie made
from locally raised pork: excellent hams, grillons, and pâtés.

• CHEESE

CLAIX   16440 – Charente

Laiterie Lescure

Bougon - 05 45 66 30 02
In addition to superb butter that proudly
wears the label AOC Charentes-Poitou (taste the

exquisite Lescure salé, a nutty-flavored butter salted with Marennes sea salt), you'll find a wonderful goat cheese called Le Bougon, made with unpasteurized milk, and tourteau fromagé, a black-topped cake with a mild cheese flavor.

NIORT	79000 – Deux-Sèvres

Fromagerie Sainte Marthe

19, rue Saint-Jean - 05 49 24 06 97
Stop by this shop for excellent regional chèvres. Sample the Taupinière Charentaise, the Frimaillou, Chèvre-sur-Feuille, and Chabi de Pougne. Other classic French cheeses are also on offer.

POUZAUGES	85700 – Vendée

Ferme Bremaud

Le Côteau, L'Aufraire - 02 51 91 83 67
The family's herd of goats gives the milk for all manner of chèvre specialties: creamy fresh cheese, half-dry, or pungent, rock-hard varieties.

ROCHELLE (LA)	17000 – Charente-M.

La Ferme Saint-Yon

46, rue Saint-Yon - 05 46 01 01 28
Your best bets here are the locally produced chèvres, but there are also fine cheeses that hail from all over France.

• *CHOCOLATE & CANDY*

ANGOULÊME	16000 – Charente

Éric Geslin

1, pl. Francis-Louvel - 05 45 95 00 73
A terrific range of chocolates. Note the house specialty, called Marguerite d'Angoulême, a chocolate laced with Pineau and Cognac.

CHOLET	49300 – Maine/Loire

Serge Boisliveau

48, pl. Rouge - 02 41 62 20 31
Lots of irresistible sweets based on nougatine and chocolate. The Cholon de Cholet, Galets d'or, and Crottins are our favorites.

NIORT	79000 – Deux-Sèvres

Angeli Cado

6 bis, rue Sainte-Marthe - 05 49 24 10 23
Among the many sweet treats on offer, angelica (a local specialty) is presented in myriad forms: chocolate coated, glazed, candied, as jam, or a flavoring for liqueur.

Confiserie Chantilly

13, rue Sainte-Marthe - 05 49 28 35 52
These yummy chocolates are filled with an original range of ganaches, notably one flavored with candied angelica. The herb is also sold in its natural state, to munch on or for use in pastry-making.

POITIERS	86000 – Vienne

Fink

42, rue Gambetta - 05 49 41 01 51
Good chocolates with interesting fillings, and an array of tasty confections that includes macarons, nougatines, and amandines.

Robert Bayard

8, rue Carnot - 05 49 41 22 49
The man who dips these chocolates is a prize-winning chocolatier—and it shows.

• *GOURMET SPECIALTIES*

OLONNE-SUR-MER	85340 – Vendée

Olvac

Rue Clément, ZI Les Fruchardières
02 51 21 45 36
Mogettes, as the local white beans are called, are processed here and sold on their own, or alongside the firm's delicious duck confit, duck-gizzard confit, pork knuckle, and more.

Cognac & Pineau des Charentes

AMBLEVILLE	16300 – Charente

Ets. Ragnaud-Sabourin

Domaine de la Voûte - 05 45 80 54 61
Wonderful Cognacs! Special mention goes to the two "family reserve" brandies (Fontvieille and Florilège) that are several dozen years old. Connoisseurs will want to try the Héritage Ragnaud Cognac for its spicy nuances, as well as the Héritage Briand, and the 100-year-old Paradis Cognac.

BARBEZIEUX-ST-HILAIRE	16300 – Charente

Logis de la Montagne

Challignac - 02 47 78 52 71
This address offers a superb XO Cognac and a top-quality Napoléon, as well as a creditable collection of white and rosé Pineau des Charentes. These sweet vins de liqueur are obtained by blending grape must with Cognac.

Château de Beaulon

05 46 49 96 13
First-rate Cognacs are proposed for sale in this dreamy château (don't miss the Napoléon and XO brandies). The Pineaus produced here are among the very best in the region.

Maison Geffard

05 45 83 02 74
Here you'll find Cognacs of various ages, as well as very good Pineau des Charentes. The white version (ten years of bottle age) is remarkable.

WINE

The Fiefs Vendéens, a winegrowing area centered around **Les Sables-d'Olonne** and **Fontenay-le-Comte**, attained VDQS status (*Vins Délimités de Qualité Supérieure*) only a dozen years ago. Yet the region has a venerable winemaking tradition that originated in the Middle Ages; later, in the seventeenth century, Cardinal Richelieu pronounced himself well pleased with the white wines of the Fiefs Vendéens. Today, the local rosés are more popular, and some tasty reds are produced as well. A wide array of varietals is cultivated: Gamay, Cabernet Franc, Cabernet Sauvignon, Grolleau, Pineau d'Aunis, and Côt for red and rosé wines, Chenin Blanc, Colombard, Melon de Bourgogne, Sauvignon, and Folle Blanche for whites. All of the Fiefs Vendéens show best, naturally enough, when savored alongside local gastronomic specialties (goat cheeses, oysters, ham, poultry...). They are not made for keeping, and should be enjoyed while still fresh and young.

Haut-Poitou is a VDQS dominated by the successful cooperative located at **Neuville-du-Poitou**. Brilliantly marketed, bottles of Haut-Poitou appear in wineshops as far afield as Japan and the U.S. Nonetheless, these are unpretentious wines meant for casual drinking. The Vins de Pays Charentais are very simple, mostly white wines made to be quaffed along with a platter of local oysters.

Domaine de La Thibauderie

Yves & Jean-Pierre Boutin, 2, rue de la Thibauderie
05 49 51 56 58, fax 05 49 51 63 04
Open daily.
These independent Haut-Poitou producers grow curious and little-known varietals on their estate. Try the Sauvignon Cabernet, a wine somehow reminiscent of a Chinon, made with a blend of Sauvignon, Gamay, Pinot/Gamay, and Cabernet Franc grapes.

Cave Coopérative du Haut-Poitou

32, rue Plault - 05 49 51 21 65, fax 05 49 51 16 07
Open Mon-Sat 8:30am-noon & 1:30pm-6pm.
Under the leadership of oenologist Pascale Bonneau, the coop's white wines have made a huge leap forward. Taste the different cuvées of Fié (as Sauvignon Blanc is called locally) or the spicy Cuvée Héritage, a red wine blended of Cabernet Sauvignon and Cabernet Franc grapes.

Domaine La Petite Groie

Xavier Coirier, 15, rue des Gélinières
02 51 69 40 98, fax 02 51 69 74 15
Open Fri pm-Sat.
Xavier Coirier's holdings are on the exceptionally sunny hillsides of Pissotte. He produces lively and appealing white Fiefs Vendéens composed of 50 percent Chenin Blanc, 30 percent Melon (the grape used to make Muscadet), and 20 percent Chardonnay. Also: light, likable reds and rosés.

Domaine de la Chauvillière

The Hauselmann Family, Sablonceaux
05 46 94 44 40, fax 05 46 94 44 63
Open daily.
The Hauselmanns invented Blanc Marine, a white Vin de Pays Charentais made with Ugni Blanc grapes (normally used for Cognac), that goes perfectly with Marennes oysters and other seafood. Taste the Chardonnays, too, especially the Cuvée Spéciale, which undergoes a double fermentation.

Domaine de La Chaignée

Roger Mercier - 02 51 00 65 14, fax 02 51 00 67 60
Open Mon-Sat 8am-noon & 1:30pm-6:30pm.
Light rosés and fuller, aromatic reds, the latter based on Cabernet and Pinot Noir.

PROVENCE
& THE RIVIERA

Welcome to the land of sunshine

Provence! Land of sunshine! Advertisements tout the wines of the Sun, the freeway of the Sun, the fabrics of the Sun... The city of Nice brags of 299 sunny days a year. "Oh, those who don't believe in the sun here are real infidels," wrote Vincent Van Gogh, whose discovery of Provençal light changed his life and the history of painting. The bright, hot Mediterranean summers make aromatic herbs more pungent, give wines a higher degree of alcohol, and draw vacationers from all over the world.

Outsiders have been traveling to Provence since Greek merchants began to set up trading posts around 600 BC, buying metals from tribes settled there in Paleolithic times. Prehistoric sites and caverns remain near Nice and Monaco, Greek vestiges survive at Antibes and in the Hellenes' most powerful center, Marseille. A Greek ship lifted from this city's harbor by Jacques Cousteau's team stands proud in the History Museum on Rue Neuve Saint-Martin. The Roman chronicler Tacitus once described Marseille as "a happy mixture of Greek urbanity combined with Gallic temperance." This spirit produced Marseille's most famous culinary specialty, the fish soup sunny with saffron, called bouillabaisse.

Next to come were Celtic tribes from the north, fierce headhunters whose capital city stood near Aix-en-Provence. They were conquered in the second century BC by the Romans, who left their mark on everything in Provence for centuries after: the language, the legal system, agricultural methods and tools, architecture. Orange, Saint-Rémy-de-Provence, Arles, and Fréjus still have impressive and beautifully preserved Roman monuments, and Arles's new archaeological museum is one of the most fascinating in Europe.

In medieval times, the picturesque perched villages of Provence came into being, houses clustered high up around a church and fortified castle: Gordes, Oppède, and Peter Mayle's Lacoste in the Luberon, Moustiers-Sainte-Marie and Biot on the Riviera among them. Les Baux-de-Provence remains one of the most striking of these vertiginous villages, especially at sunset when one can almost hear the voices of former lords throwing captives off the castle's battlements, or the songs of troubadours courting Alix of the golden hair. In the fourteenth century, Avignon became one of Europe's major cities when a series of seven popes chose to live there instead of in Rome, building the majestic Papal Palace where theater festivals are held now every summer. From this time, too, dates the famous Pont d'Avignon, of which only a graceful fragment remains—enough to dance on still, however... Fifteenth-century Provence was dominated by the powerful personality of Good King René; a poet and musician of talent, patron of the arts and an innovative gardener, René lost almost every battle he ever fought. Shortly after his death, Provence became the property of the French Crown.

The seventeenth and eighteenth centuries were prosperous in Provence: the cities filled up with fountains and elegant town houses with wrought-iron balconies. Aix-en-Provence provides one of the most exquisite examples: its summer opera festival is held in the former archbishop's palace. The Riviera mountain town of Grasse was also rebuilt in the eighteenth century, though it was already famous for its flowers and perfumes. In that era too, Tarascon, Avignon, and Orange began manufacturing Indian-inspired fabrics with great success. The Souleïado company in Tarascon and the Olivades in nearby Saint-Étienne-du-Grès are the two leading examples that remain today.

The birth of the Riviera

Nineteenth-century poets and painters celebrated the romantic charms of the Provençal countryside. In 1834, an English Lord Chancellor set out to take his consumptive daughter to Italy, but was turned back at the border because of a cholera epidemic. He chose to stop in a tiny fishing village called Cannes. His friends followed, and thus was founded the French Riviera as it came to be known by cosmopolitans, whose contemporary counterparts still spend part of every year there. Monaco made its fortune by opening a casino when the railroad was built in the 1850s. Nice, a long-established city, belonged to the house of Savoy until 1860, when a treaty ceded the town to France. Its Italian connections shine through in Niçois cuisine: here pesto is pistou, and is usually stirred into a vegetable soup rather than pasta. In the last hundred years, southern light has drawn wave after wave of painters: Van Gogh, Gauguin, Renoir, later Matisse, Dufy, Picasso, Chagall... Cézanne, of course, was a born Provençal, and devoted his life to celebrating "Nature's infinite diversity" in his native region.

Provence takes its name from the Romans' affectionate nickname for the region, *nostra provincia*, "another Italy," as Pliny called it. In Roman times Provence extended all the way to Spain! The western boundary is for most people marked by the Rhône River—but Arles, on the far side, somehow always finds itself included in Provence. Frédéric Mistral, a nineteenth-century Nobel Prize–winning poet who championed the area's regional culture, established his Provençal museum in **Arles**. It still has one of the best collections of local antiques, though for antique shopping, the weekend and holiday fairs at **Isle-sur-la-Sorgue**, east of Avignon, have achieved great renown.

The **Camargue**, just south of Arles, offers yet another landscape, another world, another cuisine. This is the delta land of the Rhône, a magic blend of fresh and salt water similar to the lower Mississippi. There is nothing else like it anywhere in Europe. Here houses made of mud and straw are surrounded by expansive rice paddies. Here rare birds migrate, shellfish abound, and cowboys called *gardians* herd small, tough bulls around groves of wild tamarisk. These bulls are not killed in the local arenas, where they return to fight many times to the public's enthusiastic applause. But they do sometimes end up as bull stew, with black olives in a heavy, dark sauce.

The northern limit of Provence corresponds roughly to the realm of the olive tree in the west, this symbol of eternity which has nourished the people of Provence since the Greeks showed them how to graft it productively. In the east, however, the Alpes de Haute Provence's high, wild valleys are no longer Mediterranean but mountain country, with good ski resorts. Here, too, nestles the hill town of **Moustiers-Sainte-Marie**, a producer of colorful faience since the eighteenth century. Nearby, the **Verdon River Canyon** offers untamed, breathtaking landscapes.

The eastern boundary, the Italian border, was set by the treaty of 1860. **Menton**, which snuggles up to the frontier, is friendly and picturesque, with an ocher-tinted old town, a lively market, and a lemon festival in February. The sheltered Bay of Garavan at Menton benefits from one of Europe's mildest climates, a boon for the city's famed Belle Époque gardens.

The southern limit of Provence alone poses no problems: it is the great inland sea—*media terra*. Major ports like **Marseille** and **Toulon** brim with bustling energy, but there are dozens of smaller fishing villages such as **Cassis** (famous for its white wine), **Le Lavandou**, or **Saint-Tropez** which has lured so many generations of artists and film-makers. Despite problems of overfishing and pollution, the Mediterranean continues to supply an amazing variety of seafood and fish: sea bass (bar or more commonly loup de mer), red mullet (rouget barbet), and sculpin (rascasse, indispensable in bouillabaisse), sea bream (dorade), and the "poor man's lobster," the densely fleshed monkfish or anglerfish (baudroie or lotte).

Enchanted landscapes

Though the coast has much to offer, inland Provence above all has charmed the world with its legendary scenery: "the familiar prospects of vines, olives, cypresses" as British writer Lawrence Durrell puts it, "enchanted landscapes of the European heart."

In the backcountry of course, there is little fresh fish, but dried salt cod has been a staple for centuries, used in dishes like the grand aïoli still served in most villages on feast days: platters of poached salt cod surrounded by colorful vegetables with a garlicky mayonnaise. Codfish also appears at Christmas Eve supper...followed by the Thirteen Desserts of Provence, which symbolize Christ and the twelve apostles.

These inland regions where wild limestone ridges contrast with manicured farms and small cities have much diversity: the Var *département* between Nice and Marseille produces charming wines, and is still largely unexplored. On **Mont Ventoux**, north of Avignon, lavender fields melt into the sky in mid-summer. The lower slopes are decked with vineyards, cherry and apricot orchards, fields of wheat and the winter wheat known as *épeautre*, which local chefs turn into a gourmet treat. The Ventoux is also famous for its truffles, sold at the market town of **Carpentras**.

Between **Saint-Rémy-de-Provence** and Arles rise Van Gogh's beloved **Alpilles hills**. Here a patchwork of irrigation canals and cypress hedging enclose plots of artichokes, oak-leaf and batavia lettuce, early strawberries, zucchini, tomatoes and eggplant, artichokes, melons, asparagus, or pear and apple cordons. On the scrubby hills, redolent of thyme, rosemary, and sage, placid sheep still graze. Today the opulent country life of these vivid valleys proves so attractive to footloose cosmopolitans that Saint-Rémy has recently supplanted the Riviera and the Luberon hills as the most fashionable place to live in southern France.

The keynote of life in Provence today is rustic refinement, a sensual ideal of good yet simple living which has inspired a whole generation of cooks all over France. Chefs from Alsace, Lille, and Brittany are slipping little rougets aux olives in among their local specialties, catering to a clientele more and more insistent on the fresh fish, herbs, and young vegetables which have characterized Provençal cuisine for centuries. Olive oil often replaces butter and cream in Lyon, goose fat in Alsace and the Southwest, as the most elegant—and above all most healthful—enrichment. At a time when many Americans consider French cooking over-elaborate, looking rather to Italy for inspiration, Provence offers the best of both worlds: it combines Mediterranean country roots with French *savoir vivre.*

RESTAURANTS & HOTELS

PROVENCE

AIX-EN-PROVENCE   13090
Paris 770 - Avignon 75 - Marseille 31   B./Rhône

 L'Aixquis

22, rue Victor-Leydet
04 42 27 76 16, fax 04 42 93 10 61
*Closed Sun, Mon lunch, Feb school hols, Aug 1-20.
Open until 10:30pm. Air cond.*
New chef Benoît Strohm has brought this restaurant back to life. He wraps salmon and san-
guin sausages in a crêpe for a tasty first course,
which you could follow with lamb noisettes in a
wild-thyme jus. Don't overlook the game dishes
offered in season—they go beautifully with the
cellar's powerful Provençal reds. Beautifully
presented food and fresh products may help you
forget almost sterile service. C 380. M 97-138
(lunch), 189-326, 80 (children).

 L'Amphitryon

2-4, rue Paul-Doumer
04 42 26 54 10, fax 04 42 38 36 15
Closed Sun, Mon lunch. Terrace dining. Air cond.
The spirit of Provence inhabits Bruno Ungaro's
enticing and generous cuisine, which you can
savor in this airy restaurant, graced with an indoor garden and an inviting bar. Co-owner
Patrice Lesne helps guests navigate the tempting
list of regional wines, while he oversees their
comfort in the dining room. M 100 (lunch), 140-
300, 80 (children).

 **Hôtel
des Augustins**

3, rue Masse - 04 42 27 28 59, fax 04 42 26 74 87
*Open year-round. 29 rms 500-1,200. Air cond. Bkfst
65. No pets.*
This beautifully restored twelfth-century convent houses fully renovated rooms with understated furnishings. Magnificent lobby.

 Les Bacchanales

10, rue de la Couronne
04 42 27 21 06, fax 04 42 27 21 06
Closed Wed, Thu lunch. Open until 11pm. Air cond.
In an old, charming house right in the heart of
a group of streets line with century-old trees. The
chef may be from Picardy, but he knows
Mediterranean cooking backwards and for-
wards. For the very reasonable price of 85 F, you
can eat a crispy red mullet with tapenade, veal
stew with Provençal herbs and a honey

blancmange, an almond cream dessert. C 250. M
55 (weekday lunch), 85 (weekday lunch), 135-
285, 75 (children).

12/20   Le Bistro Latin

18, rue de la Couronne
04 42 38 22 88, fax 04 42 38 36 15
*Closed Sun, Mon lunch. Open until 10:30pm. Priv
rm 20. Air cond.*
An addition to the Ungaro-Lesne team's list of
successes (see L'Amphitryon above). A novel
atmosphere with its neo-Greek/Roman decor
filled with the scents of Provence. Difficult to
find a better menu than their *Menu du Marché*,
using the best and most seasonal products found
on the market on any particular day and going
for less than 100 F. M 99, 160, 75 (children).

 Bleu Marine

Route de Galice - 04 42 95 04 41, fax 04 42 59 47 29
*Open year-round. 87 rms 420-490. Bkfst 50. Rms
for disabled. Restaurant. Rm scr. Air cond. Conf.
Pool. Pkg.*
A rotunda-shaped building near the center of
town, with well-equipped, soundproof rooms,
mahogany furniture, and generous breakfasts.
Very friendly welcome. Piano bar.

 La Caravelle

29, bd du Roi-René
04 42 21 53 05, fax 04 42 96 55 46
Open year-round. 32 rms 200-420. Bkfst 35. Pkg.
Half of the rooms (the more expensive ones)
give onto a lovely succession of indoor gardens.
Rooms are renovated regularly.

Château de la Pioline

Pôle commercial de la Pioline
04 42 20 07 81, fax 04 42 59 96 12
*Open daily until 10pm. Priv rm 130. Garden
dining. Air cond. Heated pool. Valet pkg.*
Encroaching warehouses don't exactly add to
the charm of this beautifully restored *bastide*, but
they are kept at bay by the estate's broad lawns.
A smoothly professional staff glides through the
dining room, delivering sophisticated cuisine
with bright Provençal overtones from new chef
Christophe Gilino. He has arrived too close to
printing time, we haven't had a chance to try the
cuisine. We'll keep you posted... Seductive cellar. C 350. M 180 (weekdays lunch), 230 (exc
Sun), 250 (Sun), 370.

*Please excuse us... (and the chefs). Menus
are subject to the winds of change, and the
dishes we've described may no longer be
available when you visit.*

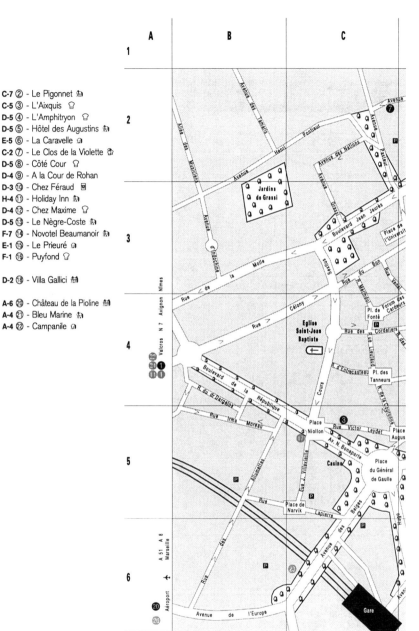

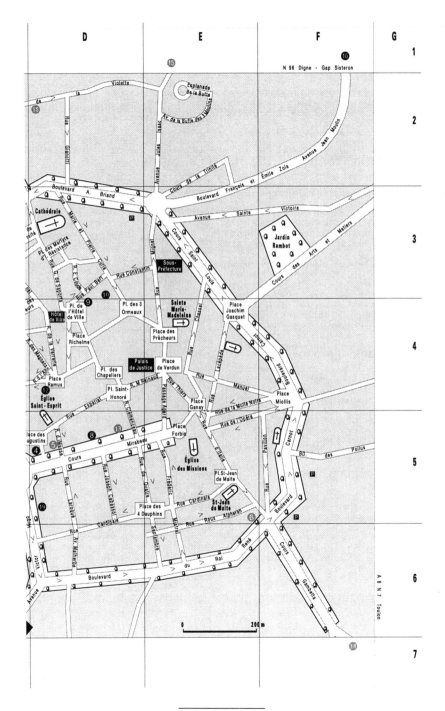

Château de la Pioline

(See restaurant above)
Open year-round. 3 stes 1,300-1,600. 18 rms 750-1,100. Bkfst 90-120. Rms for disabled. Half-board 645-810. Rm ser. Air cond. Heated pool. Valet pkg.
The luxurious guest rooms are faultlessly appointed and decorated with restrained elegance; all have pleasant views, either of the courtyard and fountain or the formal gardens. Exceptional breakfasts.

 ## Le Clos de la Violette

10, av. de la Violette
04 42 23 30 71, fax 04 42 21 93 03
Closed Sun, Mon lunch. Open until 9:30pm. Priv rm 20. Garden dining. Air cond. No pets.
Jean-Marc Banzo's sun-drenched, inventive cooking fairly sings of Provence, and every note is pure and true. Just the thought of his irresistible menu (tiny stuffed vegetables barigoule, fennel ravioli, a golden pissaladière topped with mullet and bottarga, a mellow rabbit terrine redolent of fresh herbs, peppery sea bass with fava beans and chickpeas, etc.) is enough to have us reaching for the phone to book a table! Banzo's desserts are inspired—don't miss his hazelnut sponge cake with creamy sheep cheese or delectable strawberry pain perdu. The eminently affordable cellar hews to the regional line with lots of Côtes-du-Rhône and Provençal wines. C 450. M 230 (lunch), 400, 500.

11/20 Chez Féraud

8, rue du Puits-Juif - 04 42 63 07 27
Closed Sun, Mon lunch, Aug. Open until 10:30pm. Terrace dining. Air cond. Pkg.
In a delightful Provençal setting you can lunch or dine on uncomplicated regional fare, washed down with pitchers of tasty house wine. Family-style welcome and fast service. C 170. M 100, 128.

 ## Holiday Inn

5-7, route de Galice
Open year-round. 4 stes 850-900. 90 rms 470-520. Bkfst 60. Rms for disabled. Restaurant. Half-board 639-858. Air cond. Conf. Pool. Pkg.
A functional member of the famous chain, offering well-equipped, air conditioned rooms not far from the city center. Non-smoking rooms available. Pool with a snack bar. Professional service (including room service).

 ## Chez Maxime

12, pl. Ramus - 04 42 26 28 51, fax 04 42 26 74 70
Closed Sun, Mon lunch, Jan 15-31. Open until 10:30pm (Fri & Sat 11pm). Priv rm 34. Terrace dining. Air cond. No pets.
It would be hard to find more for your money: excellent meat cooked to perfection, cut right in front of you if you request it. Excellent homemade desserts and an impressive wine list with over 500 bottles to choose from, including

the best from around the Coteaux-d'Aix region. Jean-François Canot has earned two extra points; he's certainly put a tiger in his tank in the recent past with dishes like his saffron-flavored mussel and custard tart, a duck's breast cooked to perfection, and his homemade noisettine à l'orange, a short pastry filled with orange and hazelnut cream. Extra-warm welcome. C 220. M 75-95 (lunch), 125-260.

Le Nègre Coste

33, cours Mirabeau
04 42 27 74 22, fax 04 42 26 80 93
Open year-round. 1 ste 700. 36 rms 350-650. Bkfst 50. Air cond. Garage pkg.
The oldest (eighteenth century) of Aix's historic hotels in the town center. Most of the rooms have been tastefully modernized and soundproofed. Nicely furnished, with a wonderful old-fashioned elevator and a garage service.

Novotel Beaumanoir

Résidence Beaumanoir
04 42 27 47 50, fax 04 42 38 46 41
Open year-round. 102 rms 420-470. Bkfst 52. Rms for disabled. Restaurant. Rm ser. Air cond. Conf. Pool. Pkg.
The hotel is near the superhighway, a couple of miles from the city center. It offers all the advantages of the chain: modern, airy, and regularly refurbished rooms. Newly renovated bar, lobby, and reception area.

Le Pigonnet

5, av. du Pigonnet
04 42 59 02 90, fax 04 42 59 47 77
Open year-round. 1 ste 1,500-2,000. 52 rms 500-1,500. Bkfst 65-100. Restaurant. Half-board 850-1,100. Rm ser. Air cond. Conf. Pool. Garage pkg.
A charming Provençal house right in the town center but in an agreeably leafy setting. There's a splendid, shaded terrace and a flower-filled garden. Pleasing, up-to-date rooms.

Le Prieuré

Route des Alpes
04 42 21 05 25, fax 04 42 21 60 56
Open year-round. 23 rms 190-410. Bkfst 39-50. No pets. Garage pkg.
This exquisitely comfortable, handsomely decorated seventeenth-century hotel was once a priory. Admirably situated opposite Lenfant park, which boasts gardens designed by Le Nôtre. Breakfast is served on the flower-decked terraces.

Puyfond

7 km N on N 96 & D 13, Rte de Saint-Canadet
04 42 92 13 77
Closed Sun dinner, Mon, Jan 2-10, Feb school hols, Aug 15-Sep 10. Open until 9:30pm. Priv rm 40. Garden dining. Pkg.
Anne Carbonel's cooking wants a bit of polish, but it's forthright and sincere, accompanied by well-chosen wines. It is served in an ocher-hued

dining room decorated with modern furnishings and antique mirrors and paintings or (weather permitting) on a lovely shaded terrace. C 250. M 130-160 (exc Sun), 190 (Sun lunch), 60 (children).

Villa Gallici

Av. de la Violette
04 42 23 29 23, fax 04 42 96 30 45
Open year-round. 5 stes 1,950-2,800. 14 rms 900-1,750. Bkfst 70-100. Rms for disabled. Restaurant. Half-board 900-1,700. Rm ser. Air cond. Conf. Pool. Valet pkg.
Set in a landscaped garden of over two acres dotted with olive trees, oleanders, and cypresses, this exquisite Provençal *bastide* is a highly polished jewel of a hotel. Gilles Dez decorated the interior with verve and style in a manner inspired by the eighteenth century. The rooms are done up with ravishing fabrics and furniture; the bathrooms are dreamy. In fine weather, a lunch buffet is served poolside. Fitness center. Relais et Châteaux.

And also...

Our selection of places for inexpensive, quick, or late-night meals.
À la Cour de Rohan (04 42 96 18 15 - Pl. de l'Hôtel-de-Ville. Open until 10pm, 1:30am in Jul.): With assets like a soothing Provençal décor, a roster of fresh, simple dishes (especially yummy pastries), and a warm ambience, it's no wonder the locals flock here for lunch, tea, and supper. Minuscule cellar of inexpensive wines (200).
Trattoria Chez Antoine (04 42 38 27 10 - 3, rue Georges-Clemenceau. Open until 12:30am.): Mediterranean specialties are featured, in a jolly, convivial ambience (100-150).

ANGLES (LES)	30133
Paris 701 - Nîmes 37 - Avignon 6	Gard

L'Ermitage Meissonnier

Av. de Verdun (route de Nîmes) - 04 90 25 41 68 (R), 04 90 25 41 02 (H), fax 04 90 25 11 68
Closed Sun dinner, Mon (exc lunch in seas). Open until 9:30pm. Priv rm 60. Garden dining. Pool. Pkg.
Given a choice, we always prefer a table on the garden-terrace, far more inviting than the rather fusty dining room. But wherever you sit, you're sure to enjoy Michel Meissonnier's fine cooking. This year, he's created a delicious lobster minestrone, a novel medley of cod and duck, and local peaches roasted with fresh tarragon. Adjoining the restaurant is a Lyonnais-style bistro where 100 F buys a very attractive meal. C 350-400. M 100-400.

Hostellerie L'Ermitage

(See restaurant above)

Closed Jan-Feb. 16 rms 230-480. Bkfst 55. Half-board 410-460. Rm ser. Air cond. Pool. Pkg.
Each of the extremely comfortable, soundproofed rooms here has a fine bathroom and minibar. Guests congregate around the pool, where quick meals and, in the evening, a cocktail buffet is served.

APT	84400
Paris 732 - Avignon 52 - Aix-en-P. 55	Vaucluse

Relais de Roquegure

Roquefure - 04 90 04 88 88, fax 04 90 74 14 86
Closed Jan 5-Feb 15. 15 rms 210-350. Bkfst 36. Restaurant. Half-board 250-320. Conf. Pool. Garage pkg.
In a ten-acre estate, a country hotel offering a warm welcome. For a holiday far from the madding crowd. Near riding stables.

ARLES	13200
Paris 621 - Marseille 92 - Avignon 40	B./Rhône

Hôtel d'Arlatan

26, rue du Sauvage
04 90 93 56 66, fax 04 90 49 68 45
Open year-round. 7 stes 950-1,350. 33 rms 450-695. Bkfst 60. Air cond. Conf. Valet pkg.
Near Place du Forum, this ancient town house groans with history (parts date from the fifth, twelfth, fifteenth, and seventeenth centuries). The rooms are charming and well appointed, with antique Provençal furniture. Garden. Bar.

Brasserie Nord Pinus

Rue du Palais - 04 90 93 02 32, fax 04 90 93 34 00
Closed Wed off-seas, Feb. Open until 10pm (10:30pm in summer). Terrace dining. Pkg.
If there has ever been an homage to bullfighting, this is it. The décor of owner Jean-André Charial's brasserie is a heartfelt dedication to the "art"—it's enough to make you a fan if you're not already. And chef Philippe Lepeltier's cuisine is inspired by his love and respect for something quite different: fresh, high-quality products which he treats with tender loving care, keeping his creative whims well under control. Noteworthy are his pan-fried sea perch, free-range chicken with foie gras and fresh pasta, and tasty raspberry clafoutis. The excellent service and reasonable prices are just one more positive point. C 200. M 140-180.

Grand Hôtel Nord Pinus

Pl. du Forum - 04 90 93 44 44, fax 04 90 93 34 00
Open year-round. 5 stes 1,500. 18 rms 700-900. Bkfst 65-85. Restaurant. Half-board 892-1,752. Rm ser. Air cond. Valet pkg.
Wrought-iron details and Venetian candelabra flank handsome Provençal antiques in this gorgeous hotel, part of which is a registered historic landmark. As the many bullfight posters sug-

gest, this is a favorite haunt of local matadors and show-biz celebrities.

10/20 Lou Caleu

27 rue Porte-de-Laure
04 90 93 44 44, fax 04 90 93 34 33
Open daily until 10pm. Priv rm 38. Air cond. Pkg.
It may not be fancy, but it's good home cooking as you dine in this elegant Renaissance manor house overlooking the city. Pleasant staff and reasonably priced. C 220. M 85-220.

Lou Marquès

Bd des Lices - 04 90 93 43 20, fax 04 90 93 33 47
Closed Nov 2-Dec 23. Open until 9:30pm. Priv rm 120. Terrace dining. Heated pool. Valet pkg.
This seventeenth-century former Carmelite convent is now a truly elegant, comfortable, and cheery eating house. Chef Pascal Renaud offers sunny dishes inspired by the Provençal terroir—rack of lamb with summer savory, riz au lait made with rice from the Camargue—that go capitally well with the cellar's regional bottles. The choice of whiskies, coffees, and teas is excellent. An annex called Le Cloître serves good, low-price meals. C 300-450. M 150 (lunch), 195-380, 65 (children).

Hôtel Jules César

(See restaurant above)
Closed Nov 2-Dec 23. 5 stes from 1,500. 49 rms 700-1,150. Bkfst 75-130. Rms for disabled. Half-board 870-1,705. Rm ser. Air cond. Conf. Heated pool. Valet pkg.
Some fine pieces of Provençal furniture grace the huge, comfortable rooms of this former convent, which sits in a garden on the edge of the old town. Lots of effort to create a quiet atmosphere. Large pool. Charming reception, service, and hospitality are provided in this Relais et Châteaux establishment.

Mas de la Chapelle

Petite-Route de Tarascon
04 90 93 23 15, fax 04 90 96 53 74
Closed Feb. 1 ste 600. 15 rms 400. Bkfst 50. Rms for disabled. Restaurant. Half-board 400. Conf. Pool. Tennis. Pkg.
This is a charming old farmhouse hidden in a pretty park (close to a not-so-pretty area). The large, comfortable rooms attest to the generous *tradition camarguaise*, and the service and reception are excellent. The restaurant is housed in a Renaissance chapel.

Mas de Peint

Le Sambuc - 04 90 97 20 62
Closed beg Jan-mid Mar. 2 stes 1,750-1,980. 8 rms 990-1,500. Bkfst 85. Restaurant. Pool. Pkg.
Lucille and Jacques Bon welcome you to their rustic seventeenth-century farmhouse, just outside the village of Sambuc, as if you were old friends they hadn't seen in years. Stone floors, wooden beams: character is not lacking. Food is made with products grown right there on the farm. The cowherd organizes walks across the countryside making up this 1,200-acre farm. But watch out for those 300 bulls roaming the same paths as you...

Mireille

Quartier de Trinquetaille, 2, pl. St-Pierre
04 90 93 70 74, fax 04 90 93 87 28
Closed mid Nov-mid Mar. 34 rms 320-620. Restaurant. Half-board 375-495. Air cond. Conf. Pool. Valet pkg.
Fully remodeled, functional rooms (those in the annex near the swimming pool are less grand), and an outstandingly warm welcome make Mireille a great place to stay. Dining tables are set up on the patio for lunch when the weather is fine. Nearby tennis courts are open to guests, and there's a lovely pool.

L'Olivier

1 bis, rue Réattu - 04 90 49 64 88
Closed Sun, Mon (exc hols), Nov 3-Dec 23. Open until 9:30pm. Priv rm 20. Garden dining. Air cond.
In a relaxing environment with plenty of pretty Provençal touches, patrons enjoy Jean-Louis Vidal's red-mullet velouté garnished with asparagus tips, pike perch roasted with virgin olive oil, and lamb tian à la provençale. The 128 F set meal brings a bracing tuna tartare, followed by roast saddle of rabbit and a choice of dessert. Intelligent wine list, mostly from the region, with many offerings by the glass. C 300-450. M 128-218.

12/20 La Paillote

28, rue du Docteur-Fanton
04 90 96 33 15, fax 04 90 96 56 14
Closed Thu lunch in summer, Sat lunch, Nov 15-Dec 15. Open until 9:30pm (10pm in summer). Terrace dining.
One less toque: the cooking needs to be "modernized"; people just don't like all that fat any more. It's a shame, because the hostess is as gracious and attentive as ever. The bill could be leaner too; service so-so. Good choice of wines from the region. C 160. M 77-142, 50 (children).

12/20 Les Saveurs Provençales

62, rue Amédée-Pichot
04 90 96 13 32, fax 04 90 96 54 35
Closed Sun dinner & Mon off-seas, Jan 20-30, Feb 14-22. Open until 9:30pm. Terrace dining. Air cond.
A good place to try the specialities of the region without emptying your pockets. On the 105 F Provençal menu, you can try the bull's-meat sausage (yes, I said bull) with fresh mâche salad; the mouthwatering brouffade de taureau, a bull's-meat stew cooked in white wine; and the crème caramel maison, truly the kind your grandma would make. Numerous good wines available by the glass. C 180. M 105-195.

*Looking for a hotel? Refer to the **Index**.*

Le Vaccarès

Pl. du Forum, entrance rue Favorin
04 90 96 06 17, fax 04 90 96 24 52
Closed Sep-Jun: Sun dinner, Mon; Jul-Aug: Sun, Mon lunch; Jan 15-Feb 15. Open until 9:30pm (10pm in summer). Air cond. Terrace dining.
Chef Bernard Dumas proposes clever, ably crafted dishes full of sunny regional flavors in his (air conditioned!) dining room which overlooks the picturesque Place du Forum. Dominique Dumas greets guests with genuine Southern hospitality, and there is an enticing list of Rhône Valley and Var wines. M 98 (lunch, exc Sun), 145, 195, 255, 65 (children).

And also...

Our selection of places for inexpensive, quick, or late-night meals.
Poisson Banane (04 90 96 02 58 - 6, rue du Forum. Open until 12:30am.): Times may be a changin' but some things just don't. Not the cooking, not the aquarium, and not the vine-covered terrace where you can get a quite decent meal until 12:30am (70-150).

AUBAGNE	13400
Paris 811 - Aix-en-P. 36 - Marseille 17	B./Rhône

12/20 **La Ferme**

Quartier La Font-de-Mai, chemin Ruissatel
04 42 03 29 67
Lunch only (exc Fri, Sat), Mon, Aug. Open 9:30pm. Terrace dining. No pets. Pkg.
This self-taught chef has a special place in his heart for Provençal cuisine. Try his Marseille-style pigs' feet, Provençal-style lamb's kidneys, baby squids with fennel, and the fish of the day, always cooked to perfection. C 250. M 180 (lunch, Sat dinner), 80 (children).

 Hostellerie de la Source 🌲♨

Saint-Pierre-lès-Aubagne
04 42 04 09 19, fax 04 42 04 58 72
Closed Sun, Mon, Feb school hols, Oct. 25 rms 300-1,000. Bkfst 60. Rms for disabled. Restaurant. Half-board 510-1,100. Rm ser. Conf. Heated pool. Tennis. Pkg.
This seventeenth-century manor was restored inside and out a few years back. The discreetly modern rooms are well equipped. In addition to a bar and salon, the hotel boasts leafy grounds and a shaded terrace.

AVIGNON	84000
Paris 701 - Aix-en-P. 75 - Marseille 100	Vaucluse

🏠 **Bristol**

44, cours Jean-Jaurès
04 90 82 21 21, fax 04 90 86 22 72
Closed Feb 15-Mar 9. 2 stes 800-932. 65 rms 469-786. Bkfst incl. Rms for disabled. Air cond. Conf.
Recently renovated, this is a fine hotel with comfortable rooms. Sauna.

 Brunel

46, rue de la Balance
04 90 85 24 83, fax 04 90 86 26 67
Closed Sun, Mon, Jul 15-Aug 15. Open until 9:30pm. Air cond.
Located under the arcades of a street just steps from the Palais des Papes, Brunel's elegantly simple dining room is a favorite with local gastronomes attracted by the friendly service, fine wines, and, most of all, by the invigorating cuisine proposed by André Brunel and Antoine Tameclo. Vaucluse asparagus dressed with local olive oil, garlicky cod aïoli, tapenade tart accented with basil, and red mullet anchoïade are all redolent of the region's voluptuous aromas and savors, but the helpings seem to be a little lighter, even though what's in your plate is cooked skillfully. Remember to save room for the artful desserts, and don't overlook the worthwhile 170 F prix-fixe meal. C 300-400. M 120 (lunch), 170-300.

 Cité des Papes

1, rue Jean-Vilar - 04 90 86 22 45, fax 04 90 27 39 21
Open year-round. 61 rms 420-540. Bkfst 50. Rm ser. Air cond. Pkg.
Situated near the Palais des Papes, this hotel boasts large, comfortable, air conditioned rooms in a big, modern building.

 Cloître Saint-Louis 🌲♨

20, rue du Portail-Boquier
04 90 27 55 55, fax 04 90 82 24 01
Open year-round. 3 stes 950-1,090. 77 rms 450-900. Bkfst 65. Rms for disabled. Restaurant. Rm ser. Pool. Garage pkg.
The dignified beauty of this sixteenth-century Jesuit novitiate has been scrupulously respected, in spite of the modern "design" furnishings in the lobby and bar. The rooms are lovely and quiet, with many attractive amenities (cable TV, safes, minibar). A sun lounge has been fitted out on the roof. Delicious breakfasts (and so they should be, at the price).

12/20 **Les Domaines**

28, pl. de l'Horloge
04 90 82 58 86, fax 04 90 86 26 31
Open daily until 11pm. Terrace dining. Air cond.
This anthracite-and-white dining room in the heart of old Avignon is an intelligent compromise between a wine bar and a family-style restaurant. The menu is simple and generous. Interesting cellar, but patrons are left to choose on their own. C 200-300.

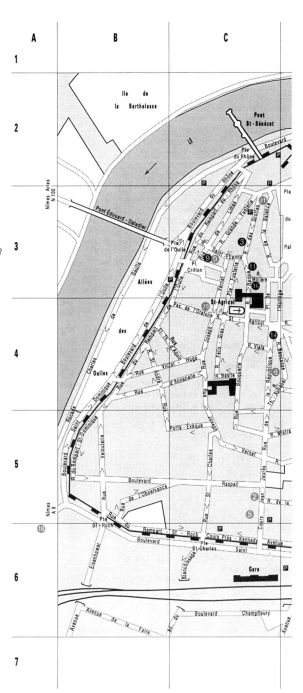

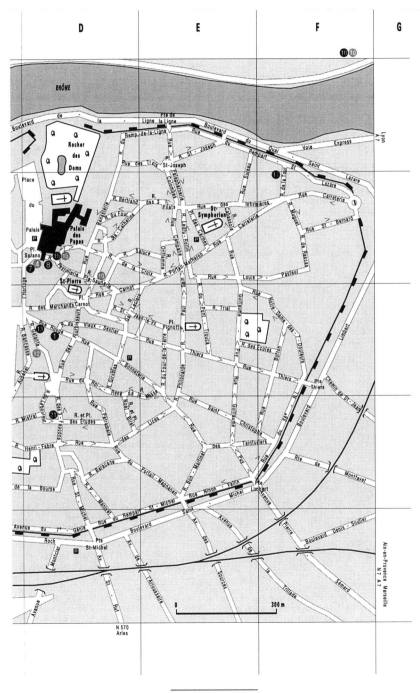

Christian Étienne

10-12, rue de Mons
04 90 86 16 50, fax 04 90 86 67 09
Closed Sat lunch, Sun. Open until 9:30pm. Priv rm 50. Terrace dining. Air cond.
Installed in the former residence of the town bailiff, Christian Étienne enjoys what may be the best location in Avignon, facing the Palais des Papes, with a panorama of the eponymous *place*. Étienne regales his guests with dishes based on choice raw materials. We liked a delicate terrine of oysters in aspic, an extraordinary sautéed red mullet with an artichoke croustillant, and a fine médaillon de veau. Superb cellar. Étienne is often on hand to greet his guests. C 400-500. M 160-480.

12/20 La Ferme

Chemin du Bois (Ile de la Barthelasse)
04 90 82 57 53, fax 04 90 27 15 47
Closed Sat lunch, Nov 4-Mar 4. Open until 9:30pm. Terrace dining. Pkg.
This old-fashioned Provençal farmhouse with a monumental fireplace and shaded courtyard, is an inviting spot for a generous, inexpensive lunch. The owner serves forth honest, regional cooking (marinated anchovies, lamb blanquette with cumin, etc.), and there's a small but engaging wine list. Charming welcome. M 110-210.

La Ferme

(See restaurant above)
Closed Nov 4-Mar 4. 20 rms 320-440. Bkfst 40. Rms for disabled. Half-board 305-495. Pool. No pets. Pkg.
Pleasant hotel on an island in the Rhône River. Cozy, attractive rooms. Must take half-board in month of July.

La Fourchette

17, rue Racine - 04 90 85 20 93, fax 04 90 85 57 60
Closed Sat, Sun, Feb 22-Mar 3, Aug 10-25. Open until 9:30pm. Air cond.
There's feeling put into the cooking here, and that's why they've just earned their first toque. Try the fresh thyme ravioli with sweet red pepper and capers, or the delicious skate with a slightly acidic ravigote sauce, or the whipped cream-covered rum cake. Walls decorated with—you guessed it!—forks and porcelain crickets. Watch out for the wine list. C 150. M 100 (weekday lunch), 150 (weekdays).

Hôtel de Garlande

20, rue Galante - 04 90 85 08 85, fax 04 90 27 16 58
Open year-round. 12 rms 200-430. Bkfst 40. Rm ser.
The Garlande occupies a well-restored, handsome old house in the center of town. All rooms are redecorated regularly, and have good bathrooms. Convivial atmosphere.

Le Grangousier

17, rue Galante - 04 90 82 96 60, fax 04 90 85 31 23
Closed Sun dinner & Mon off-seas (exc hols), Feb school hols, Aug 15-30. Open until 9:30pm.

Chef Philippe Buisson can celebrate his second toque in the unique setting he has created: an old cobbled courtyard of a medieval town house, now covered by a glass roof, giving it a distinctly modern appearance and located not far from Place de l'Horloge. There is also a distinctly modern side to his cooking: endive and oysters marinated in shallots, green asparagus with black truffle butter, pigeon perfectly roasted in brine with an exquisite au jus, and a very appetizing caramel ice cream with a Madeleine butter cookie made with honey and bitter chocolate. The menu just under 200 F is a good buy. Excellent choice of Rhône Valley wines. M 153 (lunch, exc Sun), 193-306, 100 (children).

Hiély-Lucullus

5, rue de la République
04 90 86 17 07, fax 04 90 86 32 38
Closed Mon & Tue lunch off-seas, Jun 23-Jul 2. Open until 9:45pm. Air cond.
Hiély has always offered diners excellent value for their money. Now that Pierre Hiély has retired from the kitchen, his successor, André Chaussy, maintains that laudable tradition. Timeless classicism is the hallmark of Chaussy's repertoire. The single-price menus are admirably crafted from ingredients chosen with obvious care: just taste his suave flan de foie gras or vigorously flavorful quail pie. The cellar holds an exhaustive collection of Châteauneufs as well as affordably priced white Côtes-du-Rhônes. M 150, 250, 90 (children).

L'Isle Sonnante

7, rue Racine - 04 90 82 56 01
Closed Sun, Mon, hols, 1 wk in Feb, Aug. Open until 9pm. Air cond. No pets.
A warm and lively ambience, and Jérôme Gradassi's full-flavored, aromatic cooking: that's what we call a recipe for success! Value-packed set meals in this little dining room embellished with light-wood wainscotting and flowery curtains. The 220 F one is probably the best deal in town. A refined cooking fined down to no excess: lamb brain millefeuille with spinach, artichoke and oxtail terrine with beet sauce, braised turbot with candied shallots, and Sisteron lamb cutlet in crust. Freshly baked bread, remarkable selection of cheeses, delicious little house wine, and well-stocked cellar. M 220.

12/20 Le Jardin de la Tour

9, rue de la Tour - 04 90 85 66 50, fax 04 90 27 90 72
Closed Sun dinner, Mon, 2 wks in Aug. Open until 10:30pm. Priv rm 100. Terrace dining.
The postmodern dining room opens onto a courtyard planted with olive trees: it's a setting that captures the spirit of Avignon in the '90s. The chef takes considerable care with his Provençal repertoire, but his efforts are sometimes betrayed by ingredients that are less than first class. Good regional cellar; attentive welcome. C 320-400. M 135 (weekday lunch), 395 (wine incl), 165-315, 85 (children).

Hôtel du Lavarin

1715, chemin du Lavarin
04 90 89 50 60, fax 04 90 89 86 00
Open year-round. 44 rms 300-410. Bkfst 48. Rms for disabled. Restaurant. Half-board 410. Pool. Garage pkg.
A recently built hotel located outside the city walls, just off the road to Arles, the Lavarin offers quiet, well-equipped though rather aseptic rooms. Pleasant, shaded garden.

 Hôtel Médiéval

15, rue de la Petite-Saunerie
04 90 86 11 06, fax 04 90 82 08 64
Open year-round. 35 rms 195-295. Bkfst 33.
Despite the name, this is actually a seventeenth-century town house near the Palais des Papes, with smartly turned out little salons surrounding a flower-filled patio. Rooms are spacious but not very bright.

 Mercure Palais des Papes

Quartier de la Balance, rue Ferruce
04 90 85 91 23, fax 04 90 85 32 40
Open year-round. 87 rms 365-565. Bkfst 52. Air cond. Conf. Garage pkg.
Situated within the city walls, the rooms of this hotel are comfortable, functional, modern, and well soundproofed, although not long on charm. The buffet breakfast is a better choice than the one delivered by room service and can be taken in the garden.

 Hôtel de la Mirande

4, pl. de l'Amirande
04 90 85 93 93, fax 04 90 86 26 85
Open daily until 9:45pm. Priv rm 80. Garden dining. Air cond. Valet pkg.
Set in a superb town house restored to life with pride and conviction, La Mirande is one of France's most beautiful small hotels. In the dining room (a masterpiece of refined luxury), patrons savor Alain Davi's fresh and fragrant cooking. We made a splendid meal of his John Dory with laurel, his thoroughly exceptional sautéed Bresse chicken with baby vegetables and an admirable tiramisù. Excellent bread, impeccable service, and the prodigious cellar spotlights the best bottles Provence has to offer. C 350-460. **M** 135 (weekday lunch), 210-380.

 Hôtel de la Mirande ⚔

(See restaurant above)
Open year-round. 1 ste 2,800. 19 rms 1,400-2,100. Bkfst 95-120. Rms for disabled. Rm ser. Air cond. Conf. Valet pkg.
Nestled in the heart of Avignon, this stunning little luxury hotel is graced with a delicious secret garden, richly decorated salons, and good-sized rooms whose varied decoration and refined details evoke the luxury and comfort of a bygone era. Views embrace the rooftops of the *vieille ville* and the Palais des Papes. Royal bathrooms.

 Les Trois Clefs

26, rue des Trois-Faucons
04 90 86 51 53, fax 04 90 85 17 32
Closed beg Nov, Feb school hols. Open until 9:30pm (10pm during the Festival). Air cond. No pets.
Even though the pissaladière is great, the scallops in verjuice, which was a good idea, were a real disappointment and the pan-fried Angus steak in balsamic sauce had simply lost its fighting spirit, even though the garnishes were excellent. We therefore have no choice but to lower the mark, but we feel sure that the sincerity of effort will bring back the good old days in this little haven that keeps its character evening during the Festival. Brief wine list but reasonably priced. **M** 145 (wine incl), 115-188.

 La Vieille Fontaine

12, pl. du Crillon - 04 90 14 76 76, fax 04 90 85 43 66
Closed Sun, Mon lunch. Open until 10pm. Priv rm 100. Terrace dining. Air cond. Valet pkg.
The cool, shaded courtyard, graced by a mossy fountain, is *the* place to dine on a summer's night; the rose-and-white dining room, stuffed with antiques and landscape paintings, is a bit short on charm for some tastes. Jean-Pierre Robert offers us a Provençal cuisine to which he adds his own little touch of originality, and a touch we like, thus earning him his second toque. Try his tasty pink sea bream served with artichokes in tomato, olive and zucchini matignon, a sort of vegetable fondue seasoned with olive oil, or his delicious lamb tian with fresh goat's cheese and crispy vegtables. Service for a king. Magnificent cellar, but don't bother looking for bargains. C 320. **M** 160 (lunch), 280-380.

🏰 Hôtel d'Europe

(See restaurant above)
Open year-round. 3 stes 2,100-2,450. 44 rms 620-1,700. Bkfst 90. Rm ser. Air cond. Conf. Valet pkg.
This luxurious, seductively splendid hotel is replete with Aubusson tapestries, precious *objets*, antique paintings, and artwork. The rooms are grand, with marble bathrooms. Two elegant, spacious rooftop suites have private terraces overlooking the town and the Palais des Papes (which is illuminated by night). Patio-terrace. Excellent breakfast.

And also...

Our selection of places for inexpensive, quick, or late-night meals.
Le Cintra (04 90 82 29 80 - 44, cours Jean-Jaurès. Open until 10:30pm, midnight in summer.): Old-fashioned brasserie, with a menu that includes grilled meats, duck breast confit, choucroute (160).
Entrée des Artistes (04 90 82 46 90 - 1, pl. des Carmes. Open until 10:30pm.): Chummy, Parisian-bistro atmosphere. Solid sustenance, low prices, and right downtown (120.
Les Félibres (04 90 27 39 05 - 14, rue du Limas. Lunch only.): Bookshop–tea room à la

provençale serving honest traditional fare and delicious homemade pastries (130).

Le Petit Bidon (04 90 82 33 98 - 70, rue Joseph-Vernet. Open until 10pm.) Better reserve ahead of time if you want to try these tempting regional specialities (100-150).

Simple Simon (04 90 86 62 70 - 26, rue Petite-Fusterie. Open until 7pm, 2am in Jul.): Thoroughly British restaurant and tea room. Delicious cakes, but also Indian meat loaf, seafood rolls, cottage pies, crumbles and cheesecakes (180).

See also: **Baux-de-Provence (Les), Noves**

BARCELONNETTE	04400
Paris 740 - Nice 209 - Briançon 84	Alpes/H.-P.

 La Mangeoire

Pl. des Quatre-Vents
04 92 81 01 61, fax 04 92 81 01 61
Closed Tue, May-Jun 15, Oct-Dec. Open until 9:30pm. Priv rm 70. Terrace dining. Pkg.

Built in the seventeenth century, travellers stopped here to pay duties before attacking the mountain pass. You don't have to pay duties today, just the price of an honest meal, and a good one too. New chef Loïc Balanec is still practicing, but some good practicing it is, classic but teeming with flavors. Cheerful décor. Good wine list, but short on half-bottles. C 250-350. M 98 (weekdays, Sat lunch), 140-240, 55 (children).

BAUX-DE-PROVENCE (LES)	13520
Paris 714 - Avignon 31 - Arles 19	B./Rhône

 La Benvengudo

On D 78 F - 04 90 54 32 54, fax 04 90 54 42 58
Closed end Oct-beg Mar. 3 stes 800-930. 17 rms 530-680. Bkfst 60. Restaurant. Half-board 1,090-1,240. Air cond. Conf. Pool. Tennis. Garage pkg.

A superb Provençal setting and magnificent antique furnishings make this vine-covered country manor a delightful stop. Rooms are well equipped (air conditioning was recently installed) and offer excellent value for money.

 La Cabro d'Or

Val d'Enfer - 04 90 54 33 21, fax 04 90 54 45 98
Closed Mon, Tue lunch, Nov 11-Dec 20. Open until 9:30pm. Priv rm 150. Garden dining. Pool. Pkg.

The little sister of the grand Oustau de Baumanière (see below) is blessed with a colorful garden and a terrace shaded with mulberry trees; the farmhouse also has an absolutely immense fireplace for cool winter evenings. It's a luxurious spot to sample new chef Sandro Gamba's cookery which is well crafted and full of ideas, but lacking proper follow-up in the kitchen. We waited an hour and a half for what turned out to be two excellent plates of food, served with no shame; at the prices he charges, he can't justify this knot in the rope. Seductive wine list. C 450-500. M 180 (weekdays lunch & Sat), 250, 420, 90 (children).

 La Cabro d'Or

(See restaurant above)
Closed Mon, Nov 11-Dec 20. 8 stes 1,300-1,700. 23 rms 630-1,100. Bkfst 75. Half-board 1,390. Rm ser. Air cond. Conf. Pool. Tennis. Pkg.

In a dramatic setting of rocks and bright flowers, this hotel offers guests good food, a charming welcome, children's activities, and riding. Rooms vary in size and in quality of equipment and furnishings, but were recently redone. The suites are quite new. Relais et Châteaux.

 Mas de l'Oulivié

04 90 54 35 78, fax 04 90 54 44 31
Closed Nov-Mar 20. 20 rms 585-1,050. Bkfst 70. Rms for disabled. Restaurant. Air cond. Conf. Pool. Tennis. Garage pkg.

Here is a newly constructed *mas* in the heart of the Vallée des Baux, with bright but smallish rooms, gaily decorated in pure Provençal style. Beautiful landscaped pool site, where grilled dishes and salads are served.

 L'Oustau de Baumanière

Val d'Enfer - 04 90 54 33 07, fax 04 90 54 40 46
Closed Wed & Thu lunch off-seas, mid Jan-beg Mar. Open until 9:30pm. Priv rm 25. Garden dining. Air cond. Pool. Tennis. Valet pkg.

This uniquely charming spot, in what may be the most beautiful village in France, embodies the very essence of Provence. The intense perfumes, colors, and flavors of this land come together in Baumanière's classic carte: red mullet au pistou, truffle and leek ravioli, and beef tenderloin emboldened with anchovies. Yet the kitchen could easily dispense with many of the butters, sauces, and flourishes that showcase technical skill, but which interfere, somehow, with the ingredients' pristine character. Legendary cellar, where you'll find owner Jean-André Charial's delicious Château Romanin, a wealth of fine Côtes-du-Rhônes, and a cache of vintage Bordeaux collected by Baumanière's founder, Raymond Thuilier. C 500-700. M 480-740.

 L'Oustau de Baumanière

(See restaurant above)
Closed Wed off-seas, mid Jan-beg Mar. 8 stes 1,900-2,200. 12 rms 1,250-1,300. Bkfst 120. Half-board 2,850-3,800. Rm ser. Air cond. Conf. Pool. Tennis. Valet pkg.

The captivating beauty of Provence is on full parade here from the swimming pool (which doesn't look like one) surrounded by flowers to the patrician fifteenth-century *mas* itself, with its rooms of varying sizes, some of which are vast suites. For even more peace and quiet, Le Manoir nearby offers just two suites and two rooms in a lovely garden setting. Tennis and riding at the nearby Cabro d'Or; nine-hole golf course two kilometers away. Relais et Châteaux.

La Riboto de Taven

Val d'Enfer - 04 90 54 34 23, fax 04 90 54 38 88
Closed Tue dinner & Wed off-seas, Jan 5-Mar 15.
Garden dining. Pkg.
The divine setting of this country manor built into the cliffside at the foot of this charming village, the elaborate, refined cooking of Pierre Novi and Philippe Thème might make you think you're in heaven. Don't worry, this is not heaven, but you're on your way. Take off with the well-prepared, unique slice of foie gras with carrots and shallots cooked in honey, the seafood sausage or the amusing caramelized fennel tart. The wine goes well with the menus, the price is right and the service a dream. C 380. M 200 (wine incl), 300-450.

 La Riboto de Taven 🌲🍴

(See restaurant above)
Closed Tue & Wed off-seas, Jan 5-Mar 15. 3 rms 800-1,000. Bkfst 85. Half-board 700-800. Rm ser. Pkg.
This old manor house rises right out of the cliffs. The troglodytic rooms are huge and breathtaking, and all have everything you could dream of for comfort, including extra-large bathrooms.

BEAUCET (LE) | 84210
Paris 715 - Avignon 29 - Carpentras 12 | Vaucluse

 Auberge du Beaucet

04 90 66 10 82, fax 04 90 66 00 72
Closed Sun dinner, Mon, Jan 13-Feb 1, Oct 13-31. Open until 9pm. Terrace dining.
Don't even think about dining (or lunching) here unless you've booked your table in advance. Brigitte Pizzecco can serve only 30 patrons at a time in her exquisite Provençal inn, and her fame is already such that every seat invariably has a taker. Hers is a heartfelt, finely crafted cuisine full of brawny flavors and heady perfumes, set off by house-baked bread and a wonderful regional cellar. Excellent set-price menu with oodles of choices. M 165.

BEAURECUEIL | 13100
Paris 783 - Marseille 37 - Aix-en-P. 10 | B./Rhône

 Relais Sainte-Victoire 🔆

04 42 66 94 98, fax 04 42 66 85 96
Closed Sun dinner, Mon, 2 wks in Jan, Feb school hols, 1 wk in Nov. Open until 9:30pm (10pm in summer). Air cond. Terrace dining. Pkg.
The vigorous, expressive cuisine of René Bergès sums up the gustatory pleasures of Provence, with superb, sun-gorged vegetables and the perfumes of green-gold olive oil and fresh herbs. Notable on the menu are a limpid leek terrine enriched with foie gras, and veal tongue in a concise, aromatic jus. This unique family inn at the heart of Cézanne country is constantly filled with happy customers, who

bask in the warm solicitude of Madame Bergès and her staff. Exhaustive regional cellar. C 350. M 195 (weekdays), 290-450, 135 (children).

 Relais Sainte-Victoire 🌲🍴

(See restaurant above)
Closed Sun & Mon (exc summer), 2 wks in Jan, Feb school hols, 1 wk in Nov. 6 stes 650-900.4 rms 450-600. Bkfst 70. Half-board 600-750. Air cond. Conf. Pool. Pkg.
At the foot of Mont Sainte-Victoire—so often painted by Cézanne—this hotel provides large, recently renovated and air conditioned rooms with terraces. Some are equipped with Jacuzzis.

BOUC-BEL-AIR | 13320
Paris 780 - Marseille 24 - Aix-en-P. 10 | B./Rhône

 L'Étape Lani

D 6, exit Gardanne on A 51
04 42 22 61 90, fax 04 42 22 68 67
Closed Sun dinner, Mon, Aug 15-Sep 5, Dec 23-31. Open until 9:30pm. Priv rm 60. Air cond. Pool. Pkg.
It's easy to zip right by this comfortable inn, but that would be a shame. The entire Lani family lavishes attention on their customers as they enjoy Lucien Lani's light, delicate dishes prepared with seasonal ingredients. If it's on the menu, do try his farm-raised squab with a tian (casserole) of winter wheat. Extensive cellar of excellent wines. C 300. M 138-255, 85 (children).

CARPENTRAS | 84200
Paris 683 - Cavaillon 26 - Apt 12 - Avignon 23 | Vaucluse

 L'Atelier

30, rue des Halles - 04 90 60 20 15, fax 04 90 67 11 56
Closed Sun. Open until 10:30pm. Terrace dining. Air cond.
A charming old blue-façade house serves as setting to Maurice Barnaba's well-mastered but inventive Provence-style cooking. We feasted on spinach and cèpe caillette, scallops with chanterelle mushrooms, stuffed partridge with white beets and foie gras, divine fresh goat's cheeses and real Italian tiramisù. Good buy. C 150-350. M 89 (weekday lunch), 130-240.

 Fiacre 🌲🍴

153, rue Vigne - 04 90 63 03 15, fax 04 90 60 49 73
Open year-round. 20 rms 190-460. Bkfst 40. Half-board 340-440. Garage pkg.
Quiet, yet centrally located in an eighteenth-century town house, the Fiacre boasts spacious rooms and a charming atmosphere. Beautiful garden.

*Looking for a town or restaurant? A winery? A gastronomic specialty or a celebrated chef? Consult the **alphabetical index** to locate them quickly and easily.*

Safari Hôtel

Av. Jean-Henri-Fabre
04 90 63 35 35, fax 04 90 60 49 99
Closed Jan-Feb. 42 rms 280-380. Bkfst 55. Rms for disabled. Restaurant. Half-board 370-535. Rm ser. Conf. Pool. Garage pkg.
Set in pleasant grounds outside of the town's center, this hotel offers recently remodeled, perfectly equipped rooms. There are also studios to rent with kitchenettes. "Made in Africa" décor.

 ## Le Vert Galant

12, rue de Clapies - 04 90 67 15 50
Closed Sat lunch, Sun, 3 wks in Aug. Open until 9:30pm. Air cond.
In seven years, Jacques Mégean has added five points to his rating. Why? Because he never lets up. He put his creative talents to work with the region's fragrant truffles, and came up with a novel bœuf dissocié aux truffes (the white showered with chopped tuber, the yolk whipped into a sabayon), a ragoût of baby vegetables infused with pounded truffles, and duck breast accompanied by sublime whipped potatoes flavored with—you guessed correctly! The short but pertinent wine list offers an excellent selection of local bottlings. Décor bland except for paintings by regional artists. **M** 130 (lunch), 200-270.

CARRY-LE-ROUET   13620
Paris 768 - Aix-en-P. 40 - Marseille 27   B./Rhône

 ## L'Escale

Promenade du Port
04 42 45 00 47, fax 04 42 44 72 69
Closed Sun dinner, Mon (exc dinner Jul-Aug), Nov-Jan. Open until 9:30pm. Terrace dining. Pkg.
Despite the rhetoric from doom-mongers, the sea hereabouts still swims with fabulous fish. Just ask chef Gérard Clor, who likes nothing better than to haggle at the market for flipping-fresh sculpin and John Dorys that beckon with their little fins. His bounteous 320 F set meal changes monthly, keeping pace with the seasons. You might get to taste Clor's rockfish soup, or monkfish and artichoke terrine with a lovely herbal aspic, roast turbotin, or rabbit sausages accented with sage (Clor handles meat and poultry as deftly as fish). The deep, delightful cellar is full of finds. **C** 450-550. **M** 320, 450.

CASSIS   13260
Paris 803 - Toulon 44 - Marseille 23   B./Rhône

 ## Le Jardin d'Émile

Bestouan beach - 04 42 01 80 55, fax 04 42 01 80 70
Open daily until 10:30pm. Terrace dining. Pkg.
Romantic terrace giving on to the beach, lovely dining room in yellow and ochre tones, and a winding drive through the corniches to arrive at this lovely red house resting peacefully on the hillside. Olivier Randon puts the "Cuisine of the Sun" before you with his tomato and fresh ar-

tichoke heart stew perfumed with fresh herbs, his scallop brochette served on a sprig of rosemary, his delightful stuffed vegetables, and his rich honey-sweetened orange soup. Skip the store-bought chocolate ice cream. The wine cellar is improving and the selection of local wines is small but good. **C** 220. **M** 98 (lunch, wine incl), 165-185, 50 (children).

 ## Le Jardin d'Émile

(See restaurant above)
Open year-round. 6 stes 400-600. Bkfst 50. Rm ser. Air cond. Conf. Garage pkg.
This old house, beautifully renovated, is perched over a deep creek. The Provencal-style rooms are small but full of charm. Friendly, young staff.

12/20 Nino

1, quai Barthélemy - 04 42 01 74 32, fax 04 42 01 74 32
Closed Sun dinner & Mon off-seas, Dec 15-Feb 1. Open until 11pm. Terrace dining.
Lie back and relax, listen to the waves lapping against the boats in the port, and let yourself partake of a dream Provençal-style menu based on only the best of products. Your appetite will be whetted whether you take the grilled bell peppers with anchovy paste served with stuffed Mediterranean gurnard, the Provençal fish soup or the fish stew. Local Cassis wines are featured. **C** 250-300. **M** 100-150 (lunch, exc Sun), 200.

 ## La Presqu'île

Quartier de Port-Miou
04 42 01 03 77, fax 04 42 01 94 49
Closed Sun dinner & Mon off-seas. Open until 10pm. Terrace dining. Air cond. Tennis. Pkg.
Charmingly nestled between Port-Miou, the bay of Cassis, and Cap Canaille, La Presqu'île features elaborate dishes with many a fanciful touch, crafted by Marcel Ricard. Typical of his painstaking style are an *éventail*, or fan, of aromatic rabbit meat on a bed of fava beans and almonds, braised sea bass escorted by pasta stuffed with crabmeat mousse, and a triple-chocolate dessert with cocoa sauce. Good local wines. **C** 450. **M** 165 (weekdays), 245-380.

 ## Les Roches Blanches

Route des Calanques
04 42 01 09 30, fax 04 42 01 94 23
Closed Dec-Jan. 5 stes 1,100. 20 rms 450-900. Bkfst 75. Rms for disabled. Restaurant. Half-board 695-1,145. Rm ser. Conf. Pool. Valet pkg.
A dreamy, remarkably well-situated establishment on the Cassis headlands with fully renovated rooms and enchanting views. Lovely multi-tiered terraces; sun room; private beach.

 ## Royal Cottage

6, av. du 11-Novembre
04 42 01 33 34, fax 04 42 01 06 90.
Open year-round. 25 rms 580-950. Bkfst 55. Rms for disabled. Rm ser. Air cond. Conf. Heated pool. No pets. Garage pkg.

A modern building overlooking the town. Pleasant garden with a pool and a Jacuzzi in the middle. Rooms are spacious and full of light; air conditioned and equipped with everything you need for your comfort and well-being and with private terraces.

CAVAILLON	84300
Paris 704 - Avignon 27 - Aix-en-P. 52	Vaucluse

12/20 La Fin de Siècle

46, pl. du Clos - 04 90 71 12 27
Closed Tue dinner, Wed, Aug 8-Sep 10. Open until 9:30pm. Air cond. Pkg.
The 99 F set menu is one of the best deals around and has something to please everyone. As for the dining room, you get the impression they are waiting for the return of the Belle Époque, and why not? You'll savor the best of the Côtes-du-Rhônes here. C 250-350. M 89-200, 50 (children).

 Fleur de Thym

91, rue Jean-Jacques Rousseau
04 90 71 14 64, fax 04 90 71 14 64.
Closed Sun, Mon lunch, Jul. Open until 10pm.
Jean-Yves Benoît is from Provence, and everything in his restaurant lets you know it, from the attractive décor to the food full of the accents of the region. This pretty 2-storey house, located on a quiet street right in the middle of town, has two dining rooms: one with a vaulted ceiling in the basement and another with a large fireplace. The 145 F prix-fixe menu offers a good selection of Benoît's light, original cooking, with dishes such as a thick, highly spiced spinach cream soup with Danish lobsters, tasty scallops and risotto with Mimolette cheese, a wonderful veal chop with goat's cheese served with chilled green lentils cooking in the jus of the meat. Worth setting room aside for homemade desserts. Small but interesting wine cellar. M 100-145.

 Prévot ♧

353, av. de Verdun
04 90 71 32 43, fax 04 90 71 97 05
Closed Sun dinner, Mon. Open until 9:30pm. Priv rm 30. Garden dining. Air cond.
Passionately fond of his trade, chef Jacques Prévot is a perfectionist. Every detail of his dainty dining room—the fine china, the Louis XVI décor, the attentive service—reflects the same care that goes into his savory Provençal cuisine. Excellent wine cellar, especially strong in Côtes-du-Rhônes. C 295. M 160 (weekday lunch), 225-420, 100 (children).

CHÂTEAU-ARNOUX	04160
Paris 717 - Sisteron 14 - Manosque 38	Alpes/H.-P.

 La Bonne Étape ♧

Chemin du Lac - 04 92 64 00 09, fax 04 92 64 37 36
Closed Sun dinner & Mon off-seas, beg Jan-mid Feb. Open until 9:30pm. Priv rm 60. Air cond. Heated pool. Valet pkg.

Pierre and Jany Gleize are passionate about Provence; they know every farmer and grower who provides the kitchen with its superb local ingredients. Unfortunately, the chef has lost his touch of genious and seems to be repeating the same old repertoires year after year and from one menu to another. The new bistro annex seems to be of more interest to Jany Gleize than keeping the "mother" alive and kicking. The cellar holds a notable cache of Provençal wines, as well as a splendid Sancerre from Lucien Crochet. C 400-500. M 599 (wine incl), 225-599.

 La Bonne Étape

(See restaurant above)
Closed Sun eve & Mon off-seas, beg Jan 3-mid Feb. 8 stes 900-1,500. 10 rms 550-1,100. Bkfst 85. Air cond. Conf. Heated pool. Valet pkg.
Tranquility awaits you in your rustic Provençal-style room giving onto a beautiful swimming pool or a garden abound with lavender and olive trees. Charming reception and delightful breakfasts with exquisite homemade jams! Relais et Châteaux.

CHEVAL-BLANC	84460
Paris 724 - Avignon 32 - Cavaillon 5	Vaucluse

 Alain Nicolet

Route de Pertuis - 04 90 78 01 56, fax 04 90 71 91 28
Closed Sun dinner & Mon off-seas. Open until 9:30pm. Priv rm 25. Garden dining. Pkg.
The charms of Provence abound in this spot at the foot of the Luberon. Patrons are welcomed warmly into the intimate, beamed dining rooms, and are served by a charming staff. The menu changes with the seasons so there are always well-crafted surprises to be had (good ones, too). Last time we had the honor of a flaky pastry with lobster and sea perch and spring-fetched red mullet stuffed with spinach and served with basil sauce. To drink, the cellar provides delicious Luberon and Côtes-du-Rhône wines (some served by the glass). C 400-450. M 180 (weekday lunch), 225-300, 100 (children).

CORNILLON-CONFOUX	13250
Paris 753 - Marseille 54 - Salon-de-P. 41	B./Rhône

Le Devem de Mirapier ♣♠

5 km N on D 19 on D 70
04 90 55 99 22, fax 04 90 55 86 14
Closed Oct-Mar: weekend; Dec 14-Jan 15. 1 ste 650-1,150. 14 rms 400-700. Bkfst 60. Rms for disabled. Restaurant. Half-board 500-650. Air cond. Conf. Pool. Tennis. Pkg.
The surrounding *garrigue* and pine wood make a lovely backdrop for this farmhouse-style hotel. The air conditioned rooms are comfortable and very bright, though a trifle small. Sumptuous suite just added.

CRILLON-LE-BRAVE 84410
Paris 704 - Carpentras 14 - Avignon 43 Vaucluse

 Hostellerie de Crillon-le-Brave

Pl. de l'Église - 04 90 65 61 61, fax 04 90 65 62 86
Closed weekday lunch, Jan-Mar 14. Open until 9:30pm. Garden dining. Pool. Valet pkg.
Philippe Monti is back on his native turf after gaining credentials in such lofty establishments as Pic and Taillevent. His repertoire makes excellent use of local ingredients: chicken livers en brochette, pumpkin soup with parsley, a delicious lamb and eggplant gâteau, and a yummy walnut tart. Courteous welcome and service in a charming restaurant with a pretty terrace that looks out on Mont Ventoux. C 310. M 160 (lunch), 240, 290, 100 (children).

 Hostellerie de Crillon-le-Brave

(See restaurant above)
Closed Jan-Mar 14. 6 stes 1,250-2,300. 17 rms 750-1,650. Bkfst 85. Half-board 660-1,435. Rm ser. Conf. Pool. Valet pkg.
Overlooking Mont Ventoux and the Comtat vineyards, these rooms are decorated with charming fabrics and Provençal furniture. Luxurious fittings, beautiful bathrooms, and expensive but exceptionally delicious breakfasts. Personalized service. Relais et Châteaux.

DIGNE 04000
Paris 760 - Aix-en-P. 110 - Sisteron 40 Alpes/H.-P.

 Le Grand Paris

19, bd Thiers - 04 92 31 11 15, fax 04 92 32 32 82
Closed Sun dinner & Mon off-seas, Dec 20-Mar 1. Open until 9:30pm. Garden dining. Valet pkg.
Jean-Jacques Ricaud is noted for his gossamer sauces and his knack with game and wild mushrooms (his restaurant is invariably packed in autumn, at the height of the hunting season). Madame Ricaud puts patrons at ease in a spacious yet cozy dining room enlivened by a *volière* of twittering birds, whose happy chirps can even be heard out on the shaded terrace. Try the red or white Côtes-du-Ventoux from Domaine Aymard at only 85 F a bottle. Impeccable service C 360. M 150 (weekday lunch, Sat), 195-430.

 Le Grand Paris

(See restaurant above)
Closed Dec 20-Mar 1. 4 stes 600-800. 25 rms 380-500. Bkfst 57. Half-board 440-500. Rm ser. Valet pkg.
The hotel is housed in a seventeenth-century convent, once the home of the Frères de la Trinité. The large rooms are handsomely decorated, and protected from street noise by the terrace's leafy plane trees. Centrally located but quiet.

See also: **Château-Arnoux**

ENTRECHAUX 84340
Paris 694 - Avignon 50 - Carpentras 26 Vaucluse

 La Manescale

Route de Faucon, D 205
04 90 46 03 80, fax 04 90 46 03 89
Closed Nov-Easter. 2 stes 550-900. 3 rms 425-620. Bkfst 65. Restaurant. Half-board 425-625 (oblig in seas). Pool. Garage pkg.
Pretty, cheerful, and well-maintained rooms are provided in this charmingly converted sheepfold. Efficient service in a family atmosphere. Ideal for a restful holiday, but reserve well in advance!

EYGALIÈRES 13810
Paris 715 - Avignon 28 - Cavaillon 13 B./Rhône

12/20 Bistrot d'Éygalières

Rue de la République - 04 90 90 60 34
Closed Sun dinner & Mon off-seas, Mon & Tue lunch in seas, end Feb-beg Mar, end Nov-beg Dec. Open until 10pm (11pm in summer). Terrace dining.
Flemish chef Jacques Wout-Bru stimulates your tastebuds with a mixture of his native Flemish cooking and Mediterranean-style cooking. The menu changes daily depending on what inspiration he finds at the market on any particular day. Located in a quaint old grocer's shop.

Mas de la Brune

04 90 95 90 77, fax 04 90 95 99 21
Closed Dec 15-Jan 15. 1 ste 1,500. 9 rms 750-1,350. Air cond. Pool. Valet pkg.
Behind their mullioned windows, the ten rooms of this listed château have real character and are decorated with style. They boast sumptuous bathrooms and perfect appointments; service is exceptional, too. Outside you'll find a Roman-style pool and a garden fragrant with lavender. Take care to confirm your arrival time if you run late (the management has a thing about punctuality). Refined meals available only to hotel guests in the evening.

FONTVIEILLE 13990
Paris 745 - Avignon 30 - Arles 10 B./Rhône

La Peiriero

Av. des Baux - 04 90 54 76 10, fax 04 90 54 62 60
Closed Nov 1-Mar 15. 36 rms 290-660. Bkfst 45. Restaurant. Half-board 490-650. Rm ser. Pool. Pkg.
A traditional Provençal homestead with big rooms that open onto the surrounding hills. An annex houses studios and apartments with kitchen facilities.

This **symbol** *signifies hotels that offer an exceptional degree of peace and quiet.*

La Regalido ❂

Rue Frédéric-Mistral
04 90 54 60 22, fax 04 90 54 64 29
Closed Mon (exc dinner Jul-Sep), Jan 2-31. Open until 9:30pm. Garden dining. Air cond. Valet pkg.
Jean-Pierre Michel presents an immutable roster of perennial favorites—innovation is not his style. But his performance never flags. He was ahead of his times when he dedicated an entire menu (260 F) to olive oil: olive butter, which consists of black locally-grown Fontvielle olives and tapenade; Provence-style omelette with Maussane olive oil; fish fillets "oven-steamed" with vegetables and cooked in the local Fontvielle olive oil and fresh pasta with basil; shepherd's salade (with olive oil, of course); and even Provençal apple pie with a sugar glaze and, yes, Mouriès olive oil! Vaulted dining room (nice and cool in summer) or pretty garden. And we know we'll always find a warm welcome and a terrific list of the region's best wines. C 400. M 160 (Sat lunch, wine incl), 260-400, 130 (children).

 La Regalido

(See restaurant above)
Closed Jan 2-31. 2 stes 1,490-1,510. 13 rms 450-1,160. Bkfst 95. Rms for disabled. Half-board 900-1,500. Rm scr. Air cond. Conf. Valet pkg.
The delightful rooms of this turn-of-the-century hostelry look out over the Alpilles. Breakfast may be taken on the charming terraces. An old oil mill, lost among the ivy and the lavender, a pure delight to both eye and nose. Relais et Châteaux.

FORCALQUIER   04300
Paris 790 - Aix-en-P. 66 - Manosque 23   Alpes/H.-P.

 Charembeau 🌲

Route de Niozelles, 3.5 km on N 100
04 92 75 05 69, fax 04 92 75 24 37
Closed Dec-Jan. 13 rms 280-450. Bkfst 42. Pool. Tennis. Pkg.
Meadows and hills surround this lovely Provençal dwelling, where intelligently designed rooms (some with kitchenettes) look out over the rugged Montagne de Lure. The breakfasts are worth waking up for!

FUSTE (LA)   04210
Paris 773 - Digne 52 - Manosque 7   Alpes/H.-P

 Hostellerie de la Fuste ❂

04 92 72 05 95, fax 04 92 72 92 93
Closed Sun dinner & Mon (exc hols), Oct 1-Apr 15. Open until 10:30pm. Garden dining. Heated pool. Pkg.
Set in a luminous Provençal landscape, this *auberge de charme* wears a décor that could be qualified as a mite overloaded. The tabs are pretty top-heavy, too: asparagus and stuffed morels tariffed at 250 F tend to spoil our appetite, so

we're tempted to skip dessert after the very good and picture-perfect tomato stuffed with stewed rabbit and mild onions. A special treat for vegetable lovers: chef Dominique Bucaille has prepared a wonderful vegetable-based set meal brought to life with oodles of fresh herbs. Despite the à la carte prices, the welcome and service are as sunny as the cellar's delightful Luberon wines. C 600-700. M 250-350.

Hostellerie de la Fuste 🌲

(See restaurant above)
See restaurant for closings. 2 stes 1,000-1,400. 12 rms 550-800. Bkfst 90. Rms for disabled. Half-board 940-1,190 (oblig in seas). Air cond. Conf. Heated pool. Pkg.
Here's a heavenly place to stay, with huge, immaculate rooms and memorably beautiful grounds overflowing with ever-Provençal scents of lavender and rosemary. Warm reception.

GARGAS   84400
Paris 750 - Avignon 57 - Carpentras 51   Vaucluse

 Bernard Mathys

Au chêne - 04 90 04 84 64, fax 04 90 74 69 78
Closed Tue, Wed, mid Jan-mid Feb. Open until 9:30pm. Terrace dining. Pkg.
Bernard Mathys delights guests with innovative cuisine crafted exclusively from market-fresh ingredients. Mathys underscores their vigorous Southern flavors in brilliantly balanced dishes that also show off his precise, rock-solid technique. If it's on offer, do taste his lush nougat glacé studded with local candied fruits (Apt is the *"fruits confits* capital" of France!). You can partner your meal with one of the cellar's many regional bottlings. Patrons are warmly greeted, sometimes by the chef himself. C 300-450. M 160-350.

GIGONDAS   84190
Paris 677 - Avignon 37 - Vaison 15   Vaucluse

Les Florets ❂

Route des Dentelles-de-Montmirail
04 90 65 85 01, fax 04 90 65 83 80
Closed Tue dinner & Wed off-seas, Jan-Feb. Open until 9pm. Priv rm 25. Garden dining. Pkg.
In the inviting dining room or on a terrace overlooking an adorable garden, sample fresh and flavorful regional dishes crafted by Jean-Pierre Martin: fresh foie gras and bread pudding, tiny Provençal snails, beef braised in Gigondas wine, or squab on a bed of spelt. The owner, a winemaker himself, has assembled a fine selection of Gigondas and other local wines. C 260-370. M 120-220, 60 (children).

Some establishments change their closing times without warning. It is always wise to check in advance.

GORDES 84220
Paris 734 - Avignon 38 - Cavaillon 17 Vaucluse

 La Bastide de Gordes

Le Village - 04 90 72 12 12, fax 04 90 72 05 20
*Closed Nov 15-Mar 15. 1 ste 1,150-1,350. 17 rms
520-1,150. Bkfst 80. Rms for disabled. Air cond.
Pool. Pkg.*
Nearly a score of spacious and inviting rooms in a noble Renaissance dwelling, filled with art works and fine furniture. The lodgings are totally comfortable and unostentatious, done up in Provençal style. Gym, sauna, and a little swimming pool on the terrace that faces a splendid view. Breakfast under twelfth-century Roman-style arches.

 Les Bories

2 km NW on D 177, route de l'Abbaye de Sénanque
04 90 72 00 51, fax 04 90 72 01 22
*Closed Mon, Tue lunch, mid Nov-mid Feb. Open
until 9:30pm. Priv rm 20. Air cond. Heated pool.
Tennis. Pkg.*
You get lost in the scents of provence in the bungalow of a noble room overlooking the village or on the terrace surrounded by fig and olive trees, scattered with lavender and rosemary. When you add the regional cookery of chef Laurent Suaudeau, you approach pure hedonism. We dined on his basil-flavored lamb's tongue lasagne with pea and baby bean vinaigrette, a real tongue-tingler. His sautéed chicken wings and Nice-style socca are lighter than the usual one in these parts and his saddle of lamb cooked in an earthenware dish is the star of the day. Regional wines. C 350. M 180 (weekday lunch), 220-390, 95 (children).

 Les Bories

(See restaurant above)
*Closed Mon (exc hols & summer), mid Nov-mid Feb.
1 ste 1,400-2,200. 17 rms 550-1,900. Bkfst 85. Rms
for disabled. Half-board 310. Air cond. Conf.
Heated pool. Tennis. Pkg.*
A marvelous spot in a magical corner of Provence. Ten rooms are housed in a little *mas*, the rest are in authentic dry-stone bungalows (*bories*). Lavender and cypress trees grow in the garden, and there are two pretty pools.

 Comptoir du Victuailler

Pl. du Château - 04 90 72 01 31, fax 04 90 72 14 28
*Closed Tue dinner (exc Jul-Aug), Wed, Jan 15-Apr
1, Nov 15-Dec 15. Upon reservation only. Terrace
dining.*
Easy, convivial dining in the Schmitt family's bistro set in the heart of the village, opposite the Renaissance château which houses the Vasarely Foundation. Joëlle Chaudat serves forth such graceful, homestyle dishes as herbed rabbit compote, turbot with salicornes (edible seaweed), and guinea hen with raspberries. Superb wine list. Inquire for the smoking policy. C 300-350 (dinner only). M 175 & 190 (lunch).

 Domaine de l'Enclos

Route de Sénanque
04 90 72 71 00, fax 04 90 72 03 03
*Closed Nov 15-Dec 20. 8 stes 1,180-2,060. 9 rms
680-1,080. Bkfst 55-65. Rms for disabled. Restaurant. Half-board 1,440. Air cond. Conf. Pool.
Garage pkg.*
Just outside of Gordes you'll find this group of bungalows with airy, comfortable rooms furnished in true Provençal spirit (the bathrooms are decorated with locally fired tiles). Extras include a fine terrace, a garden, and magnificent views. Courteous welcome, unobtrusive service.

11/20 **La Gacholle**

Route de Murs - 04 90 72 01 36, fax 04 90 72 01 81
*Closed Nov 12-Mar 15. Open until 9:30pm. Terrace
dining. Heated pool. Tennis. No pets. Pkg.*
The spectacle of the Luberon lends considerable charm to La Gacholle's dining room and covered terrace. Don't go here if you're famished. Although the Provence-inspired cooking is good for the money, the helpings fall short of generous. Regional wines. C 270-350. M 165-380, 55 (children).

 La Gacholle

(See restaurant above)
*Closed Nov 12-Mar 15. 12 rms 390-450. Bkfst 60.
Half-board 425-585 (oblig in seas). Heated pool.
Tennis. Pkg.*
Set in glorious surroundings, this cozily appointed *bastide* houses well-kept, peaceful rooms with splendid views, as well as a lovely terrace where guests may take their breakfast. Facilities include a very pretty swimming pool and tennis courts. Friendly reception.

Le Mas Tourteron

Chemin de Saint-Blaise, Les Imberts
04 90 72 00 16, fax 04 90 72 09 81
*Closed Sun dinner, Mon, Nov 15-Mar 1. Open until
9:30pm. Garden dining. Pkg.*
Nestled at the foot of Gordes, the Mas is a delightful spot, with its pretty, Provençal décor and charming walled garden where you can dine under the trees. Élisabeth Baiques-Bourgeois handles sun-gorged ingredients with a skilled, inventive touch. To complement her menu, the cellar provides an attractive selection of local wines. Quick light lunches are served at Le Petit Comptoir, in a light-hearted bistro setting. M 150 (weekday lunch), 200-280, 100 (children).

Le Moulin Blanc

Chemin du Moulin, Beaumettes
04 90 72 34 50, fax 04 90 72 25 41
*Open daily until 10pm. Priv rm 60. Pool. Tennis.
Pkg.*
The extremely classic style of cooking goes hand in hand with the traditional-style architecture of this house sitting amidst its own private

grounds. We liked the vegetable "mosaic" with fresh raspberry sauce and the pan-fried sea bream fillet with bell peppers and potatoes à la boulangère. Local wines in the 100 F range. M 160-280.

Le Moulin Blanc

(See restaurant above)
Open year-round. 18 rms 485-975. Bkfst 65. Half-board 455-685. Rm ser. Conf. Pool. Tennis. Pkg.
This house has a history: once a pony-express-type post office, then a flour mill, now a beautiful residence turned hotel. Pretty, well-appointed rooms, some of which give onto the grounds and the stunning pool. Well-furnished sitting room with vaulted ceiling and stone walls.

Les Romarins

Route de l'Abbaye de Sénanque
04 90 72 12 13, fax 04 90 72 13 13
Closed Jan 12-Feb 15. 10 rms 450-750. Rms for disabled. Pool. No pets. Pkg.
A fine, traditional *bastide* that overlooks the village of Gordes and its château. Fresh, pleasant rooms are furnished with attractive nineteenth-century antiques. Charming reception.

ISLE-SUR-LA-SORGUE (L')	84800
Paris 698 - Avignon 23 - Apt 32 - Carpentras 17	Vaucluse

12/20 Mas de Cure Bourse

Carrefour de Velorgues
04 90 38 16 58, fax 04 90 38 52 31
Closed Mon, Tue lunch, 2 wks in Jan, 2 wks in Oct. Open until 9:30pm. Priv rm 60. Garden dining. Pool. Garage pkg.
Real home cooking in a rustic setting or on the shady terrace. We enjoyed the "packet" of crawfish tails with artichokes, the quails stuffed with foie gras, and the pistachio crème brûlée. Well-selected wine list. C 230. M 165-260.

Mas de Cure Bourse

(See restaurant above)
Open year-round. 13 rms 290-550. Bkfst 45. Half-board 220. Conf. Pool. Garage pkg.
This eighteenth-century postmaster's station is just undergoing renovation...thank goodness! Like that, you can take better advantage of the peace and charm of the rooms and general atmosphere.

Le Mas des Grès

Route d'Apt
04 90 20 32 85, fax 04 90 20 21 45
Closed Jan 5-Feb 28. 3 stes 950-1,250. 11 rms 430-590. Bkfst 55-75. Rms for disabled. Half-board 415-495. Rm ser. Conf. Pool. No pets.
There's plenty to charm the eye and soothe the spirit in this fully renovated *mas*, where guests are lodged in large, prettily appointed rooms. The atmosphere exudes simplicity and refinement, and patrons are welcomed as if they were old friends.

 ## La Prévôté

4, rue Jean-Jacques-Rousseau - 04 90 38 57 29
Closed Sun dinner & Mon off-seas, Feb 17-28. Open until 9:30pm.
Set in a flower-filled courtyard adjoining the church, this handsome restaurant—the best in town—is built of hewn stone and bare beams warmed by tapestries. Roland Mercier is already a polished pro with more than a little imagination, evident in his deservedly popular 195 F menu. Small but well chosen wine list. M 125 (weekday lunch), 195-300.

JOUCAS	84220
Paris 738 - Avignon 46 - Carpentras 39	Vaucluse

Le Mas des Herbes Blanches

Route des Murs - 04 90 05 79 79, fax 04 90 05 71 96
Closed Jan 2-Mar 6. 6 stes 1,460-2,100. 13 rms 820-1,495. Bkfst 90. Restaurant. Half-board 790-1,490. Rm ser. Air cond. Conf. Heated pool. Tennis. Garage pkg.
The rooms were ravishingly renovated not long ago. Most of the lodgings give onto the Luberon and the hotel's extensive grounds, where stipas—the "white grasses" which gave the place its name—grow in profusion. Relais et Châteaux.

 ## Le Phébus

Route de Murs - 04 90 05 78 83, fax 04 90 05 73 61
Closed Oct 15-Easter. Open until 10pm. Priv rm 20. Terrace dining. Heated pool. Tennis. Valet pkg.
The enticing, creative cooking of Xavier Mathieu is applauded with another point and another toque. He pulls delicious surprises out of his bag at every turn, such as his anchovy ice cream with crystallized-vegetable terrine and squash, tomato and fennel sherbet: only the courageous would venture such combinations of taste. Don't worry, there are more conventional selections, such as the pot-roasted pigeon, cooked to perfection, and garnished with diced semolina and soya-tomato jam. Short wine list, but still a good selection. C 260-380. M 160-345.

 ## Le Phébus

(See restaurant above)
Closed Oct 15-Easter. 5 stes 1,395-1,645. 17 rms 665-1,080. Bkfst 95. Rms for disabled. Half-board 685-1,300. Air cond. Conf. Heated pool. Tennis. Valet pkg.
Five hugely comfortable suites (two have private pools) have joined the lovely, freshly renovated rooms, many of which boast stupendous views. The Phébus pampers guests with period furniture, dainty floral arrangements, an alluring terrace, good breakfasts, and efficient service. Extremely quiet.

L'Agneau Gourmand

"Restaurant de Guilles," route de Vaugines
04 90 68 21 04 (R), 04 90 68 30 55 (H),
fax 04 90 68 11 97 (R), 04 90 68 37 41 (H)
*Closed Wed (exc dinner in summer), Thu lunch,
Nov-end Feb. Open until 9:30pm. Priv rm 20. Terrace dining. Pool. Pkg.*
The vaulted dining room of this delightful old
bastide is the scene of elegant repasts featuring
the refined, nicely presented cuisine of Jean-
Pierre Vollaire. A small but select list of regional
wines complements the local ingredients that
Vollaire handles with admirable delicacy and
skill. His wife, Christiane, welcomes guests with
a friendly smile. C 290-390. M 145 (lunch, exc
Sun), 85-320.

 Hôtel de Guilles

(See restaurant above)
*Closed Nov-end Feb. 28 rms 400-620. Bkfst 65. Rms
for disabled. Half-board 450-560. Conf. Pool. Tennis. Pkg.*
Tuscan-like atmosphere and *art de vivre*, complete with crickets who chirp in the garden of
aromatic herbs and flowers, to underscore the
total silence. Many excursions and leisure activities can be arranged.

 La Fenière

9, rue du Grand-Pré
04 90 68 11 79, fax 04 90 68 18 60
*Closed Mon, Jan 6-31. Open until 9:30pm. Priv 14.
Air cond. Terrace dining. Pool. Garage pkg.*
In a setting of rustic refinement (La Fenière was
once a hayloft) Reine Sammut celebrates the
pleasures of the table, with a repertoire that captures all the savors and scents of Provence.
There's no bluff or showiness in Reine's beautifully balanced cuisine: we swear you can taste
the sincerity of her respectful approach to fine
ingredients. It comes through in the exquisite
chaud-froid of roasted sea bass with wee violet
artichokes and preserved lemons; in her extraordinary cream of green asparagus perfumed with
chervil; in a truffled timbale of macaroni, calf's
foot, and sweetbreads that had us aswoon with
delight; and in the mesmerizing craquant of
crisp angel's hair pasta and berries, swirled with
mascarpone sabayon. From his fabulous trove of
the region's finest wines, Guy Sammut will ex-
tract just the right partner for your meal. C 460.
M 190-490, 120 (children).

 **Le Moulin
de Lourmarin** ♻

Rue du Temple - 04 90 68 06 69, fax 04 90 68 31 76
*Closed Tue & Wed lunch off-seas, mid Jan-mid Feb.
Open until 10pm. Priv rm 80. Terrace dining. Air
cond. Valet pkg.*
If you're ready to play by his rules and accept
(or overlook) the theatrical service and the

menu's pretentious terminology, Édouard
Loubet will dazzle you with cooking of rare
virtuosity. Start off with his duo of foies gras, one
lightly cooked and served with a green-tomato
relish that adds just the right tart note, the other
pan-seared and set on a caramelized arbutus-
berry jus. You could then proceed to turbot
roasted in a verbena infusion, escorted by
crushed cooked apples and lemon (a fabulous
dish), and finish, as we did, with a dark-chocolate dessert that's crunchy outside and molten
within, enhanced by an anise-flavored jus and
amandine custard sauce. The intelligently composed cellar, rich in Southern wines, supports
the food's assertive flavors. C 450-500. M 195
(exc Sat dinner & Sun lunch), 280-420.

 **Le Moulin
de Lourmarin**

(See restaurant above)
*Closed mid Jan-mid Feb. 2 stes 1,600-2,600. 18 rms
500-1,200. Bkfst 80. Half-board 700-950 (oblig in
seas). Rm scr. Air cond. Conf. Valet pkg.*
A futuristic elevator ferries guests to their
luxurious and comfortable lodgings (though the
single beds, we find, are too narrow and the
modern windows are just plain ugly). Magnificent bathrooms; incomparable breakfasts.
Note, however, that the pool, sauna, and park
are three kilometers away. Good base for jaunts
around the Luberon countryside.

 René Alloin

8th arr. - 8, pl. de l'Amiral-Muselier
04 91 77 88 25, fax 04 91 77 76 84
*Closed Sat lunch, Sun dinner. Open until 10pm.
Terrace dining. Air cond.*
In his cheerful neo-classic-décor restaurant accented with bright colors, chef René Alloin performs lively interpretations of the
Mediterranean repertoire: try the marinated sardines, the extra-large helping of sole with
seaweed, the delicious chicken fricassée with
garlic and vinegar, and the real homemade
Provence-style desserts. Clumsy service. Exemplary selection of regional wines. C 280-350.
M 135 (weekday lunch), 195-270.

**L'Ambassade
des Vignobles**

1st arr. - 42, pl. aux Huiles
04 91 33 00 25, fax 04 91 54 25 60
*Closed Sat lunch, Sun, Aug. Open until 10:30pm.
Priv rm 50. Air cond. Garage pkg.*
This winegrowers' embassy near the city's
dockyards presents the rare opportunity to taste
perfectly partnered food and wine. The 300 F
menu changes every two or three months, to
showcase the specialties of a particular region
with the wines that match them best—the pair-
ings are most instructive! The cellar is superb,
with bottles in every price range. But the food is

not always up to par. The vegetable-anchovy paste we had was delicious, but the celery root salad was not fresh. The thyme crackers were tasty, but the cheese was a real disappointment. **M** 120-300 (wine incl).

 ## Les Arcenaulx

1st arr. - 25, cours d'Estienne-d'Orves
04 91 54 77 06, fax 04 91 54 76 33
Closed Sun, wk of Aug 15. Open until 11:30pm. Priv rm 60. Terrace dining. Air cond.
Raymond Rosso presides over the kitchens of this famous restaurant-cum-bookshop run by the Laffite sisters. He turns out passable renditions of Mediterranean specialties, like his mouthwatering though heavy winter squash cream soup with anchovy cream, but other dishes, like his baby rabbit tart with its soggy crust and boiled-meat tastes are just down right pretentious. Well-chosen wines with good advice from wine waiter Jacques Lenoir. **C** 220-310. **M** 135-280, 50 (children).

 ## L'Assiette Marine

8th arr. - 142, av. Pierre-Mendès-France
04 91 71 04 04
Closed Sun dinner. Open until 10pm. Terrace dining. Garage pkg.
It's hard to find a quiet spot on the terrace of Jean-Luc Sellam's beachfront restaurant, located in a rather brash new shopping district. But the blue-and-yellow dining room is comfortable, and conducive to enjoying Sellam's light, zesty cuisine. He's a solid technician who knows how to inject a touch of whimsy into the most classic dishes. Seafood is the specialty, but he handles poultry and meat with equal success. **C** 300. **M** 135-220.

 ## Maurice Brun

"Aux Mets de Provence,"
7th arr. - 18, quai Rive-Neuve - 04 91 33 35 38
Closed Sun, Mon lunch, 2 wks in Aug. Open until 10:30pm. Priv rm 20.
Raoul Solamito has relaunched one of Marseille's best-known culinary institutions, giving it the most beautiful interior of any restaurant in town. The menu evolves with the seasons, but every dish is authentically regional and adroitly executed. Jolly ambience; smiling welcome and service. **C** 310. **M** 200 (lunch), 260 (dinner).

 ## Capitainerie des Galères

1st arr. - 46, rue Sainte
04 91 54 73 73, fax 04 91 54 77 77
Open year-round. 137 rms 260-300. Bkfst 36. Rms for disabled. Restaurant. Half-board 380. Air cond. Conf. Garage pkg.
Just steps from the Old Port, this hotel provides functional (soundproof and air conditioned) rooms (some are on the small side), perfectly suited to an overnight stop. Cheerful reception.

 ## Le Carré d'Honoré

1st arr. - 34, pl. aux Huiles
04 91 33 16 80, fax 04 91 33 54 81
Closed Sat lunch, Sun dinner, 2 wks in Aug. Open until 10pm. Priv rm 70. Terrace dining.
Chef Jean-Marc Rutano offers fresh, nicely crafted seafood in the pleasant, Provençal décor of his two-level dining room: give the fisherman's platter or the bouillabaisse a try. Well-chosen wines; friendly service. **C** 105-270. **M** 65-180.

 ## Concorde Palm Beach

8th arr. - 2, promenade de la Plage
04 91 16 19 00, fax 04 91 16 19 39
Open year-round. 1 ste 1,680. 145 rms 675. Bkfst 65. Restaurant. Conf. Pool. Beach. Pkg.
This huge, modern hotel complex offers spacious, recently redecorated rooms that all look out to sea. Auditorium for business meetings.

 ## Les Échevins ۞

1st arr. - 44, rue Sainte - 04 91 33 08 08
Closed Sat lunch, Sun, Jul 14-Aug 15. Open until 10:30pm. Priv rm 40. Air cond.
Take a seat under the 1637 cathedral ceiling of this antique-filled dining room, to savor Jeanne Moreni's polished cooking. She presents a happy blend of her native Southwest and sunny Provence. In particular, don't miss the open-air pigeon, raised the old-fashioned way by Edouard Lamonica, so tender and tasty you want to cry for joy. Her forté is however the high quality of the ingredients she uses and the love with which she prepares them. Nicely balanced cellar with some fine Armagnacs and a good variety of half-bottles. Warm reception and service. **C** 250-330. **M** 160-335.

 ## La Ferme

1st arr. - 23, rue Sainte - 04 91 33 21 12
Closed Sat lunch, Sun, Aug. Open until 10:15pm. Air cond.
The elegant Italianate décor is unlike anything we've ever viewed in a farmhouse, on either side of the Alps. Seated amid columns and frescoes in this, one of the city's finer restaurants, patrons delight in Pascal Maufroy's cooking, although we found his food a little heavy on the sauce this year. His style is displayed to advantage on the generous 215 F prix-fixe meal. Admirably stocked cellar with monthly specials. **C** 300. **M** 215.

11/20 Chez Fonfon

7th arr. - 140, rue du Vallon-des-Auffes
04 91 52 14 38, fax 04 91 59 27 32
Closed Dec 24-Jan 8. Open until 10pm. Air cond.
Do people come to this homey restaurant tucked away in a rocky inlet for the food, or to pay homage to the patriarch of Marseille's chefs? Both, decidedly. For the bouillabaisse and bourrides are plentiful and authentic, the fish luminously fresh (monkfish with julienned vegetables, lobster and scallop ravioli). **C** 300. **M** 190-250 (exc Sun).

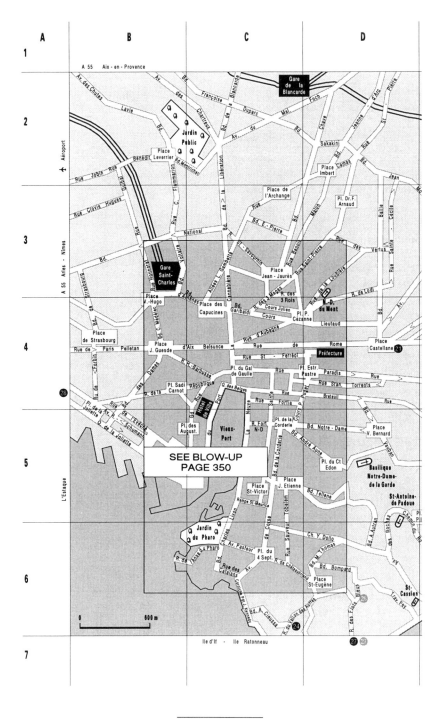

SEE BLOW-UP
PAGE 350

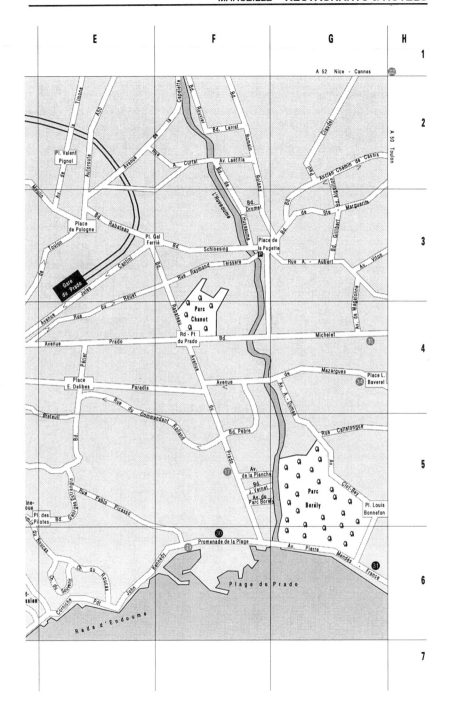

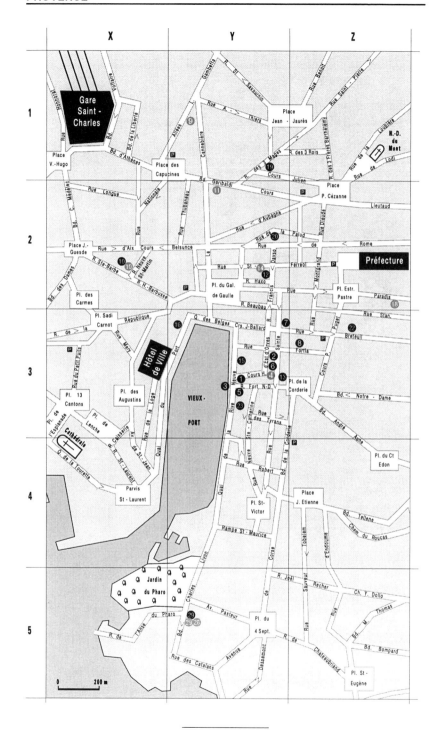

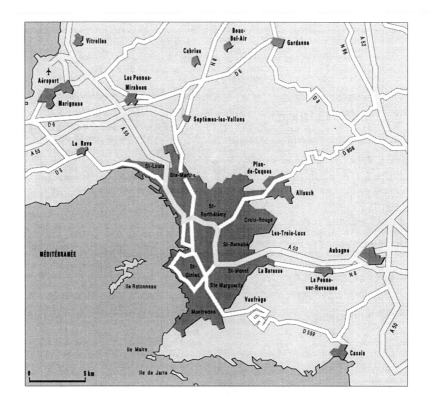

Y-3 ① - L'Ambassade
des Vignobles ♀
Y-3 ② - Les Arcenaulx ♀

Y-3 ④ - Capitainerie des Galères ♨
Y-3 ⑤ - Le Carré d'Honoré ♀
Y-3 ⑥ - Les Echevins ♀
Y-3 ⑦ - La Ferme ♀

X-2 ⑩ - L'Oursinade ♀
X-2 ⑩ - Mercure ♨
Y-2 ⑪ - New Hotel Astoria ♨

Y-3 ⑬ - Patalain ♨
Y-2 ⑭ - Saint-Ferreol's ♨

Y-3 ⑯ - Miramar ♀
F-5 ⑰ - Holiday Inn ♨

Y-2 ⑳ - Au Jambon de Parme ♀
D-4 ㉑ - Au Pescadou ♀

Y-3 ㉓ - Maurice Brun ♀
C-6 ㉔ - Chez Fonfon 🔳

D-6 ㉕ - New Hotel Bompard ♨
Y-5 ㉖ - Novotel Vieux-Port ♨
D-7 ㉗ - Passédat 🏠
D-7 ㉗ - Le Petit Nice ♨

Y-5 ㉙ - Sofitel Vieux-Port ♨
Y-5 ㉙ - Les Trois Forts ♨
F-6 ㉚ - René Alloin ♀
G-6 ㉛ - L'Assiette Marine ♀
H-1 ㉜ - Novotel-Est ♨
F-6 ㉝ - Concorde Palm Beach ♨

Plan to travel? *Look for GaultMillau/Gayot's other Best of guides to Chicago, Florida, Germany, Hawaii, Hong Kong, Italy, London, Los Angeles, New England, New Orleans, New York, Paris, Paris & the Loire Valley, San Francisco, Thailand, Toronto, Washington, D.C., and more to come...*

Holiday Inn

6th arr. - Marseille City Center, 103, av. du Prado
04 91 83 10 10, fax 04 91 79 84 12
*Open year-round. 4 stes 700-950. 115 rms 430-610.
Bkfst 55. Rms for disabled. Restaurant. Half-board
430-530. Rm ser. Air cond. Conf. Garage pkg.*
This recent addition to the famous chain is
right in the heart of the city; you'll spot it by its
smoked-glass façade. Perfectly equipped, air
conditioned rooms with neo-Hellenic décor.

 ## Maris Caupona

6th arr. - 11, rue G.-Ricard - 04 91 33 58 07
*Closed Sat lunch, Sun, Aug. Open until 10pm. Air
cond.*
Pascal Peltier offers surprising combinations
using top-quality ingredients and adding his
special touch. He's got a bright future. A distinct
preference for seafood. We savored the
pétoncles, a type of scallop, marinated with five
spices, but thought the sardines bleues with
olive oil would be better without the cream
cheese mousse. Worthy desserts. Preferable to
take a set menu; à la carte prices are over the top.
Cellar improving. C 300-350. M 160 (wine incl)

Mercure Euro-Centre

See restaurant L'Oursinade

 ## Miramar

2nd arr. - 12, quai du Port
04 91 91 10 40, fax 04 91 56 64 31
*Closed Sun, 3 wks in Aug, 3 wks in winter. Open
until 10pm. Terrace dining. No cards. Pkg.*
A strategic address on the Vieux-Port,
Miramar is not what it used to be. Only their
delicious bouillabaisse, a Marseille classic, keeps
it worthwhile. Both the waiters and the décor are
tired and need resuscitation. Interesting selection of regional and Bordeaux wines, but you
pay for them. C 350-500.

 ## New Hotel Astoria

1st arr. - 10, bd Garibaldi
04 91 33 33 50, fax 04 91 54 80 75
Open year-round. 58 rms 310. Bkfst 38.
Near the Canebière, this turn-of-the-century
hotel has been thoroughly and pleasantly modernized. It has huge, sunny, well-equipped
rooms, and an attractive lobby.

 ## New Hotel Bompard ♠♥

7th arr. - 2, rue des Flots-Bleus
04 91 52 10 93, fax 04 91 31 02 14
*Open year-round. 46 rms 370-400. Bkfst 45. Rms
for disabled. Rm ser. Air cond. Pool. Garage pkg.*
Set in quiet grounds just minutes from the Old
Port and the town center, the Bompard houses
bright, large rooms that are both functional and
comfortable (just avoid those that give onto the
parking lot). The balconies massed with flowers
are a nice touch. Studios with kitchenettes available.

 ## Novotel Est

CD 2, St-Menet - 04 91 43 90 60, fax 04 91 27 06 74
*Open year-round. 131 rms 415-460. Bkfst 50. Rms
for disabled. Restaurant. Rm ser. Air cond. Conf.
Pool. Tennis. Garage pkg.*
A modern hotel close to the superhighway,
with all of the chain's usual amenities, plus a
playground for the children.

 ## Novotel Vieux-Port

7th arr. - 36, bd Charles-Livon
04 91 59 22 22, fax 04 91 31 15 48
*Open year-round. 90 rms 510-600. Bkfst 50. Rms
for disabled. Restaurant. Rm ser. Air cond. Conf.
Pool. Garage pkg.*
Well situated in the Vieux-Port area, this hotel
is newly renovated. All rooms comfortable, functional, and especially spacious, with fine views.
Good location for a walking tour of the city.

 ## L'Oursinade

1st arr. - Centre Bourse, 1, rue Neuve-St-Martin
04 91 39 20 00, fax 04 91 56 24 57
*Closed Sat lunch, Sun, Aug. Open until 10:30pm.
Terrace dining. Air cond. Valet pkg.*
Efforts to keep prices down have taken a toll
on the quality of the food here, though the chef
does his darnedest to come up with fresh ideas
(salad of green-tomato confit, sea bass en croustillant). The scatter-brained service doesn't help
much, either. C 180. M 150-200, 90 (children).

 ## Mercure Euro-Centre

(See restaurant above)
*Open year-round. 1 ste 990. 198 rms 399-650. Bkfst
65. Rms for disabled. Half-board 450-580. Rm ser.
Air cond. Conf. Garage pkg.*
Ask for an upper-floor room with an enchanting view of the bay. All are comfortable and well
equipped. First-class service, gargantuan breakfasts.

 ## Passédat

7th arr. - Corniche Kennedy,
Anse de Maldormé
04 91 59 25 92, fax 04 91 59 28 08
*Closed Sat lunch & Sun off-seas. Open until 10pm
(10:30pm in summer). Garden dining. Air cond.
Terrace dining. Pool. Valet pkg.*
Nestled in a fold of the corniche with a breathtaking view of the islands across the way (at
sunset, it looks like paradise!), this is a most
romantic place to dine. The kitchen works exclusively with the freshest ingredients, which are
used to best advantage in novel, personalized
ways: sea bass Lucie Passédat, for instance, or
pan-roasted shellfish with stuffed macaroni. A
sumptuous bouillabaisse can be prepared if you
order in advance (and if the right fish jump into
the fisherman's nets). You should also remember
to sell a T-bond or two before you reserve your
table: the cellar posts dizzying prices, most
starters cost over 200, and main courses hover
around 300. C 700-1,000. M 310 (lunch, wine
incl), 590-700, 250 (children).

Le Petit Nice

(See restaurant above)
Open year-round. 2 stes 2,900-3,900. 13 rms 1,000-1,900. Bkfst 41-115. Half-board 1,055-2,605. Rm ser. Air cond. Conf. Pool. Valet pkg.
Set in a stunningly beautiful and peaceful spot overlooking the sea, Le Petit Nice has a handful of lovely, comfortable, and extremely expensive rooms and suites done in "designer" style (which you'll either love or hate), and superbly equipped bathrooms. Amenities include a salt-water swimming pool, sun room, water skiing, and sea fishing. A nearby villa houses two additional rooms and an opulent suite with a private terrace and sauna. Relais et Châteaux.

 ## Patalain

1st arr. - 49, rue Sainte
04 91 55 02 78, fax 04 91 54 15 29
Closed Sat lunch, Sun, Jul 14-Sep 4. Open until 11pm. Priv rm 14. Air cond.
Many a Marseillais considers this the best address in town, and Suzanne Quaglia's sincere, full-flavored cooking has convinced us that there's more than a little truth in what they say! She offers authentic dishes like fish soup with firey rouille, rock-lobster ravioli, potato salad with mussels and tapenade, daube provençal, and state-of-the-art pieds et paquets (lamb's tripe and trotters, a Marseille specialty). Fine choice of regional wines. C 350. M 150 (weekday lunch, wine incl), 180-370, 110 (children).

 ## Au Pescadou

6th arr. - 19, pl. de Castellane
04 91 78 36 01, fax 04 91 83 02 94
Closed Sun dinner, Jul 21-Aug 31. Open until 10:30pm. Priv rm 50. Air cond.
Here's an elegant bistro where you can down huge platters of fresh shellfish, red mullet en salade, or scallop ravioli anointed with truffle jus, irrigated by a cool white wine from the appealing cellar. Zealous service. C 280-300. M 158-198.

Le Petit Nice

See restaurant Passédat

 ## Pullman Beauvau

1st arr. - 4, rue Beauvau
04 91 54 91 00, fax 04 91 54 15 76
Open year-round. 1 ste 1,500. 71 rms 400-950. Bkfst 65. Rm ser. Air cond. Conf.
This deluxe hotel has welcomed no less than Chopin and George Sand. Exquisite location on the Vieux-Port, this hotel now offers modern facilities. Sunny, quiet rooms furnished tastefully with antiques.

 ## Saint-Ferréol's Hotel

1st arr. - 19, rue Pisançon
04 91 33 12 21, fax 04 91 54 29 97
Closed Aug 1-21. 19 rms 300-480. Bkfst 40. Air cond.

Here's a hotel with quirky charm in a traffic-free street just 200 yards from the Vieux-Port. The mid-sized rooms sport personalized furnishings; all are efficiently soundproofed. Warm welcome; bar; Jacuzzis.

 ## Les Trois Forts

7th arr. - Vieux-Port, 36, rue Charles-Livon
04 91 15 59 00, fax 04 91 31 46 52
Open daily until 10:15pm. Air cond. Pool. Valet pkg.
You would come here for the superb view of the Old Port, even if there were no other attraction. But Dominique Frérard's menu bursts with bold Provençal flavors, enhanced by a capital cellar of regional wines. Sample her scrambled eggs brightened with zesty bottarga and tapenade, sea bream baked with crisp bacon and garnished with chard ravioli, and caramelized pear tourte accented with a tightly reduced licorice sauce. One of the best buys in town. C 250-280. M 105-210, 95 (children).

 ## Sofitel Vieux-Port

(See restaurant above)
Open year-round. 3 stes 1,850-2,400. 127 rms 660-960. Bkfst 75. Rms for disabled. Rm ser. Air cond. Conf. Pool. Garage pkg.
The view of the town across the Old Port is superb. The Sofitel's fine, large rooms offer functional comfort and modern equipment. Excellent breakfast buffet, and a pleasant bar. Good service, too.

And also...

Our selection of places for inexpensive, quick, or late-night meals.
La Coupole (04 91 54 88 57 - 1st arr., 5, rue Haxo. Open until 10pm.): Brasserie fare and plats du jour in the heart of the shopping district (160-190).
Ducs de Gascogne (04 91 33 87 28 - 1st arr., 39 rue de Paradis. Open until 3pm.): Duck is king here, in every shape and fashion, but there is also some fish. Wine tastings every Friday night (90-215).
Toinou (04 91 33 14 94 - 1st arr., 3, cours St-Louis. Open until midnight.): In this pleasant atmosphere resembling an auction house, young waiters and waitresses serve the choicest oysters in the region. Good prices on wine (65-240).

MAUSSANE-LES-ALPILLES   13520
Paris 717 - Marseille 85 - Arles 18 - Salon 28   B./Rhône

 ## La Petite France

15, av. de la Vallée-des-Baux
04 90 54 41 91, fax 04 90 54 52 50
Closed Wed, Thu lunch, Jan 3-31, 1 wk in Nov. Open until 9:30pm. Priv rm 15. Air cond. Pkg.
Chef Thierry Maffre-Bogé wins another point for his fragrant Provençal repertoire, featuring ravioli stuffed with green olives or (in season) with potato and truffle, a famously tasty tarte de

brandade (puréed codfish) anointed with fruity olive oil, and lamb with thyme sauce and garlic confit. Kudos also goes to his wife, Isabelle, who oversees the service in the pretty dining room of this former bakery, which dates back to the eighteenth century. Highly competent young wine waiter who looks over an excellent cellar specializing in Provence and Côtes-du-Rhône wines. C 250. M 165-350, 70 (children).

 ## Le Pré des Baux

Rue du Vieux-Moulin
04 90 54 40 40, fax 04 90 54 53 07
Closed Oct 15-Mar 15 (exc Christmas-New Year).
10 rms 480-690. Bkfst 60. Rms for disabled. Pool.
Garage pkg.
In a quiet setting, this intimate, modern hotel has sunny, modern rooms with terraces that give onto a swimming pool. Walled garden; attentive service.

 ## Ou Ravi Provençau ○

34, av. de la Vallée-des-Baux
04 90 54 31 11, fax 04 90 54 41 03
Closed Tue, Nov 20-Dec 20. Open until 9:30pm
(10:30pm in summer). Priv rm 15. Terrace dining.
No pets.
Jean-François Richard's cheerily decorated Provençal restaurant is warm and welcoming. So is his cuisine, which the locals flock to sample. Try his truffled pumpkin soup, ragoût of artichokes à la barigoule, veal sweetbreads with fava beans and tiny peas, rabbit sautéed with thyme, and pieds et paquets (lamb's tripe and trotters) that regular customer Jean-Pierre Dennery, president of Souleïado fabrics, says are the best in the region. (We agree.) Nothing goes better with this food than the cellar's excellent, affordable local wines: don't miss the fine Trévallon 1990. M 190-380, 80 (children).

MEYREUIL	13590
Paris 779 - Marseille 33 - Aix-en-P. 5	B./Rhône

 ## Auberge Provençale ○

On N 7 - 04 42 58 68 54, fax 04 42 58 68 05
Closed Tue dinner, Wed, Feb school hols. Open until
9:30pm. Priv rm 25. Terrace dining. Air cond. Pkg.
Wedged between a busy road and the motorway, this charming inn is warmed by a huge fireplace and a profusion of bouquets. Gabriel Astouric's authentic, robustly flavored Mediterranean menu is based on prime local ingredients, prepared with an expert touch. And the regional cellar provides perfect foils for the food. Expect a warm welcome from host Jean-Marie Jacquême. C 300. M 100 (weekday lunch), 125-240, 75 (children).

MONTEUX	84170
Paris 708 - Avignon 19 - Carpentras 8	Vaucluse

 ## Blason de Provence

Route de Carpentras
04 90 66 31 34, fax 04 90 66 83 05

Closed Dec 20-Jan 20. 20 rms 270-390. Bkfst 50.
Restaurant. Half-board 315-370. Rm ser. Conf.
Pool. Tennis. No pets. Garage pkg.
A pleasant family-style Provençal establishment set in extensive grounds, featuring comfortable, personalized rooms. Breakfast buffet; meals on trays are served in the rooms on request.

 ## Le Saule Pleureur ○

Quartier Beauregard, 145, route d'Avignon
04 90 62 01 35, fax 04 90 62 10 90
Closed Sun dinner, Mon, Mar 1-20, Nov 1-15. Open
until 9pm. Priv rm 30. Garden dining. Pkg.
Garlic, basil, thyme, olives, sun-dried tomatoes: Michel Philibert's lilting repertoire makes lavish use of Provençal flavors, and he well deserves an extra point. His in-depth knowledge of the region's resources combines with a gift for putting them together, in dishes like a savory oxtail papeton, tuna tartare dressed with olive oil, and lamb tourte perfumed with summer savory. Peaceful setting. Note the well-designed set meals, and the concise but intelligently composed wine list. C 380-480. M 160-250, 80 (children).

MONTFAVET	84140
Paris 694 - Avignon 7	Vaucluse

 ## Le Jardin des Frênes

645, av. des Vertes-Rives
04 90 31 17 93, fax 04 90 23 95 03
Closed Nov-end Mar. Open until 9:30pm. Garden
dining. Air cond. Pool. Valet pkg.
Antoine Biancone lets his inspiration guide him, as he turns out adroit and flavorful variations on the Provençal repertoire. Accompany his aromatic dishes with one of his good Rhône Valley wines (a bit weak on the local wines), and savor the experience (weather permitting) on the leafy terrace that looks out onto lush lawns and a garden abloom with roses. Hervé Biancone greets guests with genuine warmth. C 350. M 195 (weekday lunch), 295-495.

Les Frênes

(See restaurant above)
Closed Nov-end Mar. 4 stes 1,650-2,500. 16 rms
595-1,590. Bkfst 90. Half-board 980-1,325. Rm ser.
Air cond. Conf. Pool. Valet pkg.
A gorgeous, supremely comfortable hotel, set in a wooded park with a garden and splashing fountains. The rooms are spread about in various outbuildings set round a superb swimming pool. The décor ranges from Louis XIII to Empire. Most rooms have been redecorated tastefully and equipped with luxurious baths and hydromassage. Capacious parking lot, peerless reception and service. Relais et Châteaux.

Remember to call ahead to reserve your table, and please, if you cannot honor your reservation, be courteous and let the restaurant know.

MOUSTIERS-SAINTE-MARIE   04360
Paris 875 - Digne 62 - Manosque 48   Alpes/H.-P.

 **La Bastide
de Moustiers** 🔾

Quartier Saint-Michel
04 92 70 47 47, fax 04 92 70 47 48
*Closed end Nov-mid Mar. Open until 9:45pm. Priv
rm 10. Terrace dining. Heated pool. Garage pkg.*
Alain Ducasse put his prize pupil, Benoît Witz, in charge of his irresistible country inn. It's the height of perfection in its category. There's no formal menu, but instead a choice of two or three courses plus cheese and dessert for either 195 F or 260 F, according to how many dishes you choose. Witz's simple, generous style makes the most of the region's sun-kissed foodstuffs. For example: firm young asparagus with mousseline sauce (tender and edible from tip to butt), local vegetables à la grecque with tapenade-topped toast points, farm-bred rabbit à la moutarde, tip-top cheeses from nearby producers, and a pluperfect lemon tart with a short, buttery crust. The wine list has special sections devoted to half-bottles and grands crus. M 195 (weekdays), 260.

 **La Bastide
de Moustiers** 🌲🍴

(See restaurant above)
*Closed end Nov-beg Mar. 7 rms 800-1,300. Bkfst 75.
Rms for disabled. Air cond. Conf. Heated pool. No
pets. Garage pkg.*
This unspoiled spot must be one of the most delicious in all of Europe. Here you'll discover the quintessential *hôtel de charme*, where elegant hospitality meets ideal accommodations (personalized rooms, fabulous baths, splendid breakfasts).

 Les Santons 🔾

Pl. de l'Église - 04 92 74 66 48, fax 04 92 74 63 67
Closed Mon dinner & Tue (exc in summer), Dec-Jan. Open until 9:30pm. Terrace dining.
Next to the town's Romanesque church you'll find this inviting restaurant, with an arbor that overlooks the valley and a swift-flowing stream. André Abert, assisted in the kitchen by Christophe Morant, produces regional dishes that are a treat for both the palate and the eye. Appetizing cheese board; alluring Provençal cellar. C 380. M 160 (exc Sun), 200-300, 80 (children).

NOVES   13550
Paris 700 - St-Rémy-de-P. 16 - Avignon 14   B./Rhône

 Auberge de Noves

2.5 km NW on D 28
04 90 94 19 21, fax 04 90 94 47 76
*Open daily until 10:15pm. Priv rm 60. Garden
dining. Air cond. Heated pool. Tennis. Valet pkg.*
This *auberge* set high on a hilltop dominates a gorgeous Provençal landscape. On balmy days the garden beckons, while winter feasts take place around the fireplace in a dining room with huge bay windows. Robert Lalleman, son of the chef who put this establishment on the culinary map, interprets a regional cuisine that is more flavorful than refined. His lobster bouillon with quenelles is excellent, but his turbot approaches the level of fast food and his truffle/potato combination is just too heavy with the ham. No longer merits three toques. The Côtes-du-Rhône wines are priced to buy. C 495. M 225-495, 275 (wine incl), 180 (weekday & Sat lunch).

 Auberge de Noves 🌲🍴

(See restaurant above)
*Open year-round. 8 stes 1,900-2,200. 12 rms 1,250-
1,300. Bkfst 100. Rms for disabled. Rm ser. Air
cond. Conf. Heated pool. Tennis. Valet pkg.*
The recent renovation has exposed the handsome timbers and stone façade of this dreamy inn lost among tall pines and cypresses. It is now less austere, and the lovely rooms are more comfortable and spacious than ever. Fabulous breakfasts; terrific weekend packages offered in the off-season. Relais et Châteaux.

ORANGE   84100
Paris 678 - Avignon 31 - Carpentras 23   Vaucluse

Arène 🌲🍴

Pl. des Langes - 04 90 11 40 40, fax 04 90 11 40 45
*Closed Nov 1-Dec 15. 30 rms 340-500. Bkfst 44. Air
cond. Valet pkg.*
Right in the historic city center, on a square shaded by plane trees. Rooms are well equipped. There's a nice lounge and terrace, but no elevator. Impeccable welcome and service.

Le Mas des Aigras

East Russamp, Chemin des Aigras
04 90 34 81 01, fax 04 90 34 05 66
*Open year-round. 11 rms 380-460. Bkfst 50. Pool.
Tennis. Pkg.*
Let the old stones of this lovely Provence-style farmhouse lost in the vines and the orchards seduce you. The new, comfortable rooms offer you a peacful, restful sleep (we hop!e).

12/20 Le Parvis

3, cours Pourtoules - 04 90 34 82 00
*Closed Sun dinner & Mon off-seas, Jan 19-27, Nov
11-Dec 3. Open until 9:30pm. Terrace dining. Air
cond.*
The dining room is slightly somber (not to say solemn), but the service cheers one, as does the food: asparagus flan with fava beans, eel stewed in red wine à la vigneronne, and hot-chocolate soup with gingerbread ice cream. C 250. M 98 (weekdays, Sat lunch), 128-225, 65 (children).

Note that (most) telephone numbers in France have ten digits, beginning with a zero. The initial zero must be omitted if you are calling France from abroad. Within France, dial the entire ten digits.

PONTET (LE)
84130
Paris 703 - Avinon 5   Vaucluse

 ### Auberge de Cassagne
Avignon North exit on A 6
04 90 31 04 18, fax 04 90 32 25 09
Open daily until 9:30pm. Priv rm 40. Garden dining. Air cond. Pool. Valet pkg.
Philippe Boucher's cooking is modern, yet full of temptations we've already tasted: hot oysters on a bed of spinach, served with a cream sauce with crispy shallots; guinea fowl pie with a Côtes-du-Rhône wine sauce; or black chocolate pie with citrus fruit sauce. The dining room is elegance itself, but it is awfully old worldish to sit under the plane trees on the terrace. Good, elegant service, but take your blood pressure pills before you ask for the check. You can reduce the effects by choosing your wine carefully, for instance a Saint-Gervais de Steinmaier or one of the cairannes de Corinne Couturier's Cairannes. C 500-600. M 230-460, 110 (children).

 ### Auberge de Cassagne
(See restaurant above)
Open year-round. 5 stes 1,380-1,780. 25 rms 420-1,180. Bkfst 95. Rms for disabled. Half-board 720-1,065 (oblig in seas). Rm ser. Air cond. Conf. Pool. Tennis. Valet pkg.
Belongs to a group of hotels called literally "post of tranquility", so peace and quiet are on the menu here. Refined is the word for the Provençal décor of the huge rooms, full of flowers but yet toned down in color. Comfort is the word for this newly renovated swimming pool hidden among the verdure, more inviting than ever.

 ### La Table des Agassins
In Le Pigeonnier - 04 90 32 42 91, fax 04 90 32 08 29
Closed Jan. Open until 10pm. Priv rm 30. Terrace dining. Air cond. Heated pool. Valet pkg.
A little out-of-the-way haven, just the place to slow down the pace and spend some time lounging by the pool and roaming the park abound with ancient trees. No pretense here, just fine craftsmanship to create a cuisine that is profoundly of its region: Vaucluse asparagus, goat's cheese ravioli with chervil sabayon, freshwater cod's tail served with herb butter, duckling breast with gentian au jus. Delicious desserts, especially the very original citrus fruit and lavender honey macaroons. Good selection on the prix-fixe menus, but some of the wine is embarrassingly overpriced for what it is. C 165-380. M 100 (wine incl), 185-380, 90 (children).

 ### Hostellerie des Agassins
(See restaurant above)

Closed Jan. 4 stes 950-1,300. 26 rms 450-850. Bkfst 75-110. Rms for disabled. Half-board 590-750. Rm ser. Air cond. Conf. Heated pool. Valet pkg.
A bit of Provence under the pines and the cypresses. Modern Provence-style rooms, all with air conditioning. Tastefully decorated, modern farmhouse that makes you feel right at home.

PRA-LOUP
04400
Paris 749 - Gap 59 - Barcelonnette 9   Alpes/H.-P

 ### Auberge du Clos Sorel
Village de Clos Sorel
04 92 84 10 74, fax 04 92 84 09 14
Closed Apr 11-Jul 1, Sep-Dec 15. 11 rms 400-800. Bkfst 50. Restaurant. Half-board 400-525. Conf. Heated pool.
This fine old house in a mountain village offers charming, comfortable rooms and an extraordinary view across the valley. Warm welcome.

ROCHEGUDE
26790
Paris 663 - Valence 84 - Orange 31   Drome

 ### Château de Rochegude
04 75 97 21 10, fax 04 75 04 89 87
Closed Mon & Tue am off-seas, mid Jan 15-mid Mar. 4 stes 1,800-2,500. 25 rms 650-1,500. Bkfst 95. Restaurant. Air cond. Conf. Heated pool. Tennis. Valet pkg.
Mont Ventoux and the Montmirail peaks stare back as you wander in the château's extensive grounds. This extremely elegant and charming hotel offers huge rooms furnished with rare antiques. Exemplary staff. Relais et Châteaux.

ROUSSILLON
84220
Paris 742 - Avignon 45 - Bonnieux 12   Vaucluse

 ### Mas de Garrigon
Route de St-Saturnin-d'Apt, D 2
04 90 05 63 22, fax 04 90 05 70 01
Closed Mon, Tue lunch, Nov 15-Mar 15. Open until 9:15pm. Terrace dining. Pool. No pets. Pkg.
Roussillon's beautiful ocher cliffs stand in full view of this delightful Provençal *mas* surrounded by pine groves. Sylvain Bourlet, a student of Loiseau and Maximin, is getting better every year and his love for Provençal ingredients is shining through. The 185 F menu puts before you fish as pre-appetizer, a spicy rabbit galantine with candied tomatoes, a generous portion of lamb tian with spinach, an impressive assortment of cheeses, and a taste-tingling homemade waffle with licorice ice cream. Sweet but short wine list. C 360-460. M 140 (lunch), 185-330.

Mas de Garrigon

(See restaurant above)
Open year-round. 1 ste 560-800. 8 rms 500-800. Bkfst 85. Rms for disabled. Half-board 545-700 (oblig in seas). Conf. Pool. Pkg.
This hotel features delightful, Provençal-style rooms with splendid views of Roussillon and the Luberon. Pleasant fireside lounge and library; sheltered swimming pool; riding lessons.

SAINT-RÉMY-DE-PROVENCE   13210
Paris 730 - Marseille 91 - Avignon 21   B./Rhône

 ## Alain Assaud

Le Marceau, 13, bd Marceau - 04 90 92 37 11
Closed Wed, Thu lunch, Jan 15-Feb 1. Open until 10pm. Air cond.
The long, tall, Provençal dining room is a comfortable place in which to sample Alain Assaud's sunny, market-fresh cooking. Once the pastry chef at the Oustau de Baumanière, Assaud is an ace when it comes to desserts. Decent regional cellar; slow-coach service. C 210. M 100 (lunch, exc Sun), 130-280, 70 (children).

12/20 Le Bistrot des Alpilles

15, bd Mirabeau - 04 90 92 09 17
Closed Sun, 10 days end Jan-beg Feb, 3 wks in Nov-Dec. Open until 10pm. Terrace dining.
This charming little address has it all together: a jolly atmosphere, fresh, simple food (artichoke barigoule, sardines à l'escabèche, tartare, and lemon tart), and unbeatable prices. Lots of good local wines are on hand, too. C 170-225. M 75 (lunch), 160.

 ## Château de Roussan

2 km on N 99, route de Tarascon
04 90 92 11 63, fax 04 90 92 50 59
Open year-round. 21 rms 460-750. Bkfst 60. Restaurant. Half-board 640-930. Garage pkg.
A delightful eighteenth-century residence surrounded by a huge park dotted with rare trees, flower beds, and ponds. Large, attractively furnished guest rooms; bare-bones bathrooms. Excellent breakfasts.

 ## Château des Alpilles

D 31 - 04 90 92 03 33, fax 04 90 92 45 17
Closed Nov 12-Dec 21, Jan 6-mid Feb. 5 stes 1,290-2,000. 15 rms 860-1,080. Bkfst 78. Rms for disabled. Restaurant. Rm ser. Air cond. Conf. Pool. Tennis.
Serene and lovely, this early nineteenth-century château is surrounded by majestic trees. The rooms are huge and have been redecorated in impeccable taste. One of the most refined hotels in Provence. Sauna. Poolside grill in summer.

 ## Domaine de Valmouriane

Petite route des Baux
04 90 92 44 62, fax 04 90 92 37 32
Open daily until 10pm. Terrace dining. Heated pool. Tennis. Garage pkg.

Chef since 1994, Stéphane Bettinelli cooks in a classic vein, with a few Provençal dishes to add local color to the menu. Try his 270 F prix-fixe menu: oysters poached with nettles, finnan haddie and smoked salmon in a coriander marinade, English-style rack of lamb, and caramel-apple tart. The beautiful, bright dining room opens onto a pretty terrace. C 300-450. M 105 (weekday lunch), 270, 90 (children).

 ## Domaine de Valmouriane

(See restaurant above)
Closed year-round. 2 stes 1,160-1,550. 12 rms 590-1,310. Bkfst 70. Rms for disabled. Half-board 875. Rm ser. Air cond. Conf. Heated pool. Tennis. Garage pkg.
This luxurious little hotel has spacious rooms (some with sun rooms and terraces), equipped with all modern amenities and decorated with rare attention to detail. Guests may enjoy billiards, tennis, archery, take a Turkish bath, or practice their putting.

Le Jardin de Frédéric

8 bis, bd Gambetta - 04 90 92 27 76
Closed Wed, Feb school hols. Open until 10pm. Terrace dining. Air cond.
Simone Caloux loves the tastes and smells of Provence and her à la carte set meal, which she calls simply "Provence", will win you over too. Even if you want to avoid the extra charges for certain dishes, you can still eat a perfectly good meal with the puréed cod soufflé with thin strips of smoked salmon, saffron-flavored Provençal fish soup, saddle-of-rabbit cutlets seasoned with garlic and tarragon, and strawberry soup. All this can be savored on the terrace under the leafy plane trees. C 230. M 140-170.

 ## La Maison Jaune

15, rue Carnot - 04 90 92 56 14
Closed Sun dinner & Mon in seas, Tue lunch off-seas, Jan 22-Mar 8. Open until 9:30pm (10:30pm). Priv rm 10. Terrace dining.
Some people get better with age, and François Perraud is proving to be one of them. He is reaching toward heaven, and we think he'll continue to do so. We were particularly impressed with the well-crafted prix-fixe menus. You'll understand the addition of this second toque when you taste his light, full-flavored sweet-garlic soup, the utter precision of a dish like the fricassée d'artichauts violets with parsley oil, the marvellous simplicity of the grilled sardine fillets with raw fennel and citron confit, the cooked-to-perfection roast pigeon with Baux wine sauce. Extremely affordable regional wines. M 100 (weekday lunch, wine incl), 165-275, 80 (children).

12/20 Restaurant des Arts

30, bd Victor-Hugo
04 90 92 08 50, fax 04 90 92 55 09
Closed Tue, Feb, Nov-Dec. Open until 9:30pm. Pkg.

The old village brasserie is now a local institution, where area artists exhibit their work. In summer, Saint-Rémy's entire population seems to throng en masse on the terrace to enjoy sautéed cuttlefish à la provençale, bull stewed in wine à la camarguaise, and tasty house-baked pastries. C 220. M 110 (exc Sun), 120, 140 (Sun).

 ## Vallon de Valrugues 🎖🎖

Chemin de Canto Cigalo
04 90 92 04 40, fax 04 90 92 44 01
Open year-round. 18 stes 1,380-4,200. 35 rms 600-1,080. Bkfst 85-115. Rms for disabled. Restaurant. Half-board 680-910. Rm ser. Air cond. Conf. Heated pool. Tennis. Garage pkg.
Quiet, handsomely appointed, and graced with terraces overlooking olive groves or the Alpilles, the rooms here were enlarged and renovated (marble baths) not long ago. One suite is like a country house, perched on the roof with a spectacular view and complete with a private pool and a kitchen. Leisure facilities include satellite TV, billiards, a sauna, and Jacuzzi. Peerless service.

And also...

Our selection of places for inexpensive, quick, or late-night meals.
L'Assiette de Marie (04 90 92 32 14 - 1, rue Jaune-Roux. Open until 11pm.): Amusing mixture of decorative objects picked up at secondhand fairs here and there. Max shows you in and Marie takes care of your tastebuds with her Corsican fare; she even comes to say hello when she has the time (125-169).
Le Café du Lézard (04 90 92 59 66 - 12 bis, bd Gambetta. Open until 10pm.): The hot spot in town, this wine bar lets you feast on such goodies as foie gras, the specialty of the day and a superb Saint-Marcellin cheese (75-150).
Chez Xa (04 90 92 41 23 - 24, bd Mirabeau. Open until 10pm.): Italian-inspired cooking in this pleasant little restaurant with its youthful staff. Good red mullet filets (guaranteed to have no bones) or lemon picatta (200).
Sette e Mezzo (04 90 92 59 27 - 34, bd Mirabeau. Open until 10pm, 11pm in summer.): Best Italian pizza in town. All you can eat of pizza, pasta or meat: you choose which. Another hot spot (120-150).

STES-MARIES-DE-LA-MER (LES)   13460
Paris 794 - Marseille 129 - Arles 38   B./Rhône

12/20 Auberge Cavalière

Route d'Arles - 04 90 97 88 88, fax 04 90 97 88 88
Open daily until 10pm. Priv rm 60. Terrace dining. Pool. Tennis. No pets.
Regionally-inspired cookery with innovations using prestige ingredients. Eat with the cowboys in this traditional décor equipped for every cowboy's needs. Try the 120 F menu putting before you sunset shellfish in aïoli sauce and bull's meat stew. C 130. M 120-300, 70 (children).

 ## Auberge Cavalière

(See restaurant above)
Open year-round. 42 rms 450-1,000. Bkfst 50. Half-board 450-700. Pool. Tennis. Pkg.
The rooms in the main building give onto a courtyard and garden and are nicer than the "cowboy's cabins" on the mezzanine. Satellite TV and mosquito net as well as air conditioning. Competent service and eager welcome.

 ## L'Estelle

4 km on D 38, route du Petit-Rhône
04 90 97 89 01, fax 04 90 97 80 36
Closed Nov 16-Mar 21 (exc Jan 1). 17 rms 580-840. Bkfst 60. Rms for disabled. Restaurant. Half-board 490-550. Rm ser. Conf. Pool. Tennis. Garage pkg.
Set on the edge of the Camargue marshes on the site of an old farmhouse, these pretty bungalows done up in regional style boast private terraces and fine appointments. Splendid pool with a waterfall. Horseback riding.

 ## L'Étrier Camarguais 🎖🌲

2 km N on N 570, chemin bas des Launes
04 90 97 81 14, fax 04 90 97 88 11
Closed mid Oct-Apr 1. 27 rms 540. Bkfst 50. Restaurant. Half-board 660-760 (oblig in seas). Conf. Pool. Tennis. Pkg.
A group of small houses in a verdant setting outside Les Saintes-Maries. The nicely furnished rooms are spacious and decorated in bold colors. All have fine terraces opening onto a garden.

🍽 L'Impérial

Pl. des Impériaux
04 90 97 81 84, fax 04 90 97 74 25
Closed Tue off-seas, Nov-end Mar. Open until 10pm. Terrace dining. Pkg.
Unpretentious food prepared just right by Pierre Jay, a former grill room owner. Good quality ingredients are his forté. The menu lists every possible traditional preparation imaginable for sole, turbot, beef, lamb and much more. A few good Provence-style dishes such as basil-flavored vegetable soup and telline shellfish. Fixed-price menus a good buy. Reasonbly priced local wines. Lovely terrace under the archway. C 180-200. M 98-170.

12/20 Le Kahlua

Pl. des Gitans - 04 90 97 98 56, fax 04 90 97 98 56
Closed Tue, mid Jan-mid Feb. Open until 10pm. Terrace dining. Pkg.
Interesting mix of traditional and exotic dishes. Located in center of city. We savored the tapas, West Indian blood pudding and cod fritters. Good potatoes au gratin with the broiled foods Not a lot of choice in wine. C 210-250. M 85-220.

🍽 Lou Mas doù Juge 🎉

D 85, route du Bac-du-Sauvage, quartier Pin-Fourcat
04 66 73 51 41, fax 04 66 73 51 42
Open daily until 8:30pm. Priv rm 4. Terrace dining. Air cond. No pets. HOTEL: 2 stes 500-800. 5 rms

450-500. Bkfst 30-50. Half-board 800-850 (oblig in seas). Air cond. Conf. No pets. Pkg.
Renée Granier's set menus attract hearty eaters, with such robust offerings as tourtes filled with meat or cheese, fish grilled over a wood fire, seasonal game, and capon with morels. You'll like the charming welcome, the convivial atmosphere, and picturesque décor of this old Camargue farmhouse. **M** 300-350 (wine incl), 370 (Sat dinner, Sun lunch, wine incl), 450 (wine incl).

 Mas de la Fouque 🌲🍴

Route d'Aigues-Mortes, 4 km
04 90 97 81 02, fax 04 90 97 96 84
Closed Tue off-seas, Nov 2-Mar 25. 2 stes 2,000-2,800. 12 rms 980-2,200. Bkfst 75-120. Rms for disabled. Restaurant. Half-board 985-1,320 (oblig in seas). Rm ser. Air cond. Conf. Heated pool. Tennis. Garage pkg.
Enjoy your breakfast on a sheltered poolside patio or a terrace facing the Étang des Launes. The rooms have an original, elegant décor and dreamy bathrooms. We've had warmer welcomes, though. Leisure pursuits include golf (on a practice green), shooting, and riding on the large estate.

 Mas du Tadorne

3 km N on N 570, Chemin Bas
04 90 97 93 11, fax 04 90 97 71 04
Closed Jan-Feb. 4 stes 650-1,300. 11 rms 650-850. Bkfst 65. Rms for disabled. Restaurant. Half-board 450. Conf. Pool. Pkg.
The lodgings are on the small side, but are refined and charming, with balconies overlooking the garden and pool. Contemporary amenities, including VCRs.

And also...

Our selection of places for inexpensive, quick, or late-night meals.
Les Alizés (04 90 97 71 33 - 36 bis, av. Aubanel. Open until 10:30pm.): Shellfish and fish have the seat of honor at this restaurant frequented by tourists and locals alike (75-150).

 Abbaye de Sainte-Croix 🌀

3 km NE on D 16, route du Val-de-Cuech
04 90 56 24 55, fax 04 90 56 31 12
Closed Mon lunch (exc hols), Nov 3-mid Mar. Open until 9:30pm. Priv rm 150. Terrace dining. Pool. No pets. Pkg.
An ancient abbey in a spectacular setting, with a lovely terrace shaded by mulberry trees. Pascal Morel, who trained under Roger Vergé and Georges Blanc, takes a simple yet inventive and delicate approach to his fine ingredients. The 265 F single-price menu offers lots of interesting

options (and no supplements, even for lobster or foie gras). The cassoulet is rich with house-made confit, and delicious grilled pig's tail claims a place beside the "nobler" calf's liver or John Dory a la plancha. Distinguished cellar, with plenty of local bottlings. **C** 385. **M** 200 (lunch, exc Sun), 280 (Sun lunch), 265-410, 535.

 Abbaye de Sainte-Croix 🌲🍴

(See restaurant above)
Closed Nov 3-mid Mar. 5 stes 1,370-2,250. 19 rms 625-1,315. Bkfst 77-113. Half-board 440 (oblig in seas). Rm ser. Air cond. Conf. Pool. Pkg.
The modern additions to this ancient abbey are remarkably faithful to the original. The rooms are furnished with fine antiques, and offer eye-popping views (and all are air conditioned). Leisure pursuits include riding and swimming. Perfect place if you need to get away from absolutely all. Relais et Châteaux.

 Francis Robin 🌀

"Le Mas du Soleil," Le Pilon-Blanc, 38, chemin St-Côme - 04 90 56 06 53, fax 04 90 56 21 52
Closed Sun dinner, Mon. Open until 9:30pm. Priv rm 25. Garden dining. Air cond. Pool. Garage pkg.
Jovial Francis Robin follows his inspiration wherever it leads, producing delicious variations on traditional themes. Even if his lobster and zucchini ravioli lack the divine spark, his rabbit terrine with garlic confit, honey-lime glazed duck breast, and remarkable fillets of red mullet warmed in olive oil show how an expert chef can exalt and accent the flavors of prime ingredients. Sunny, generous cooking that is definitely worth a detour. Local wines at reasonable prices. **C** 360-500. **M** 220 (lunch, exc Sun, wine incl), 400.

 Francis Robin 🌲🍴

(See restaurant above)
Open year-round. 1 ste 850-950. 9 rms 480-750. Bkfst 65. Rms for disabled. Half-board 1,100-1,500. Rm ser. Air cond. Conf. Pool. Garage pkg.
Though not far from the town center, these new, very comfortable and charming rooms (grouped around the pool or the patio) have a distinctly bucolic feel, owing to the large, shady garden. Guests may expect a kindly welcome.

 Alp' Hôtel 🌲🍴

04 92 81 05 04, fax 04 92 81 45 84
Closed Apr 10-May 19, Oct 10-Dec 18. 10 stes 420-1,135. 24 rms 320-470. Bkfst 50. Restaurant. Half-board 290-550. Rm ser. Conf. Heated pool. Pkg.
This modern complex ideally located near the ski lifts boasts simple, pretty rooms with mountain views, a garden, terrace, and heated pool as well as a bar and a fitness center. Suites have kitchenettes.

SÉGURET 84110
Paris 690 - Avignon 41 - Vaison-la-Romaine 10 Vaucluse

 Domaine de Cabasse

04 90 46 91 12, fax 04 90 46 94 01
Closed Mon & Tue off-seas, Mar 1-24, Nov 12-Dec 31. 12 rms 300-650. Bkfst 50. Restaurant. Half-board 655-515. Conf. Pool. No pets. Garage pkg.
This establishment is an agreeable stopover in the wine country, at the foot of the Montmirail peaks, with pleasant rooms overlooking a terrace and swimming pool.

 La Table du Comtat ✪

Le Village - 04 90 46 91 49, fax 04 90 46 94 27
Closed Tue dinner & Wed off-seas, Feb, Nov 23-Dec 4. Open until 9pm. Priv rm 60. Air cond. HOTEL: 8 rms 480-600. Bkfst 70. Half-board 620-700. Pool. Pkg.
The sweeping view framed by this fifteenth-century hospice is typically Provençal, and Franck Gomez makes excellent use of the region's bounty in his full-flavored, colorful cooking. If they're on the menu, do try his cold lobster soup with asparagus tips or the rabbit fricassée with peas and artichokes. Interesting selection of Côtes-du-Rhône vintages, with several wines available by the glass. Friendly welcome in a vaguely rustic, slightly over-decorated dining room (but what a view!). C 390-460. M 160 (exc hols), 260-450, 110 (children).

TARASCON 13150
Paris 710 - Arles 18 - Marseille 106 B./Rhône

 Les Mazets des Roches ♠♣

Route de Fontvieille
04 90 91 34 89, fax 04 90 43 53 29
Closed Nov-Apr. 38 rms 300-700. Bkfst 50. Restaurant. Half-board 320-495. Air cond. Pool. Tennis. Pkg.
Set in a 33-acre park at the foot of Les Baux, this agreeable hostelry features comfortable, perfectly equipped, air conditioned rooms with beautiful bathrooms.

VAISON-LA-ROMAINE 84110
Paris 687 - Avignon 46 - Carpentras 28 Vaucluse

12/20 **Le Bateleur**

1, pl. Théodore-Aubanel - 04 90 36 28 04
Closed Sun dinner, Mon, Nov 15-Dec 15. Open until 9pm (9:30pm in summer). Air cond.
Pretty bouquets add a colorful touch to this quiet dining room, where you can settle down to a homestyle meal with a fresh, Provençal touch. Short list of wines, mainly from the Côtes-du-Rhône. C 180. M 98 (lunch), 140, 68 (children).

 La Fête en Provence

Pl. du Vieux-Marché
04 90 36 36 43, fax 04 90 36 21 49
Closed Wed off-seas, Nov 15-Christmas, beg Jan-Feb. Open until 10pm. Priv rm 25. Terrace dining.
A self-taught Scandinavian chef, Niels Christensen, has created a lovely, tranquil restaurant where patrons can savor his unpretentious, regionally rooted cuisine. We tried (and liked) his warm asparagus with foie gras, rabbit confit in a mellow sauce flavored with balsamic vinegar, and almond crème brûlée. Worthwhile wine list, presented by a charming and competent *sommelière*. C 260-420. M 100 (lunch), 150.

 Hostellerie Le Beffroi

Rue de l'Évêché - 04 90 36 04 71, fax 04 90 36 24 78
Closed Feb 15-Mar 20, Nov 11-Dec 20. 22 rms 330-655. Bkfst 45. Restaurant. Half-board 495-605. Conf. Pool. Pkg.
Here's a beautiful Renaissance dwelling, in the heart of old Vaison. Rooms are immense, and furnished with antiques; there are terraced gardens and lovely views. Half the rooms are housed in an equally handsome seventeenth-century annex.

 Le Logis du Château ♠♣

Les Hauts-de-Vaison
04 90 36 09 98, fax 04 90 36 10 95
Closed Sun, Wed, end Oct-beg Apr. 45 rms 235-430. Bkfst 42. Rms for disabled. Restaurant. Half-board 250-340. Conf. Pool. Tennis. Pkg.
A rambling hotel in a verdant setting, with nice big rooms. Some have terraces with views of the town and surrounding vineyards.

 Le Moulin à Huile

Quai du Maréchal-Foch
04 90 36 20 67, fax 04 90 36 20 20
Closed Sun dinner, Mon, Jan 15-Feb 15. Open until 10pm (9:30pm off-seas). Priv rm 40. Terrace dining. No pets. Pkg.
We tip our hat to Robert Bardot who has proven himself as adept with the ingredients of sunny Provence as he was with the products of his native Flanders (formerly at Flambard in Lille, where he had three toques). His *haute cuisine* does justice to this old restored millhouse full of character in the ancient nucleus of Vaison-La-Romaine. We were delighted with his well-mastered stuffed zucchini blossoms, broiled sea perch steak, saddle of rabbit with prunes and mouthwatering desserts. Rare to find such quality at this price. C 240-350. M 120 (lunch, exc Sun), 160-240, 400 (wine incl).

VENASQUE 84210
Paris 717 - Avignon 31 - Carpentras 14 Vaucluse

Auberge la Fontaine

Pl. de la Fontaine - 04 90 66 02 96, fax 04 90 66 13 14
Dinner only. Closed Wed, mid Nov-mid Dec. Open until 9pm. Priv rm 12. Pkg.

Housed in a massive eighteenth-century manor in the heart of an old papal village, this charmingly furnished *auberge* presents a generous single menu full of robust country Provençal flavors, by chef Christian Sœhlke. A recent visit yielded poached foie gras, pike perch terrine, leg of local lamb, and tarte tatin. Game dishes are featured in season. Good wine cellar; affable reception and service. At Le Bistrot annex, simpler fare is offered at very friendly prices. M 220, 30 (children).

Auberge la Fontaine ⚐♦

(See restaurant above)
Closed mid Nov-mid Dec (exc upon reserv). 5 stes 800. Bkfst 50. Rm ser. Air cond. Pkg.
Centrally located and pleasantly furnished, with five new perfectly equipped, air conditioned suites that include kitchens, dining and living rooms, fireplaces, and terraces. Charming atmosphere. Mountain bikes are available for use, and cooking lessons are given, too. For those who like a décor that is a little different from the run of the mill.

VILLENEUVE-LÈS-AVIGNON	30400
Paris 706 - Nîmes 42 - Avignon 6	Gard

 ## Aubertin ⚙

1, rue de l'Hôpital
04 90 25 94 84, fax 04 90 26 30 71
Closed Mon, Sun. Open until 10pm. Terrace dining. Air cond.
Just 30 guests can gather in this smartly understated dining room to feast on Jean-Pierre Aubertin's simple yet refined cuisine. Split-second timing, well-harmonized flavors, and a passion for Provençal ingredients produce roast lotte and langoustines perfumed with rosemary, scallop and zucchini ravioli lavished with thyme butter, and red mullet with ratatouille and a zesty garnish of olives and pistou. Like the food, the regional wines are clemently priced. Attractive set meals. He's almost got that third toque in his grasp... C 350-400. M 100 (Sun lunch), 160-240.

Fabrice

3, bd Pasteur - 04 90 25 52 79
Closed Sun dinner, Mon, 1 wk in Feb, 3 wks in Sep. Open until 10pm. Terrace dining. No pets.
Fabrice Guisset likes fish, but he certainly doesn't do injustice to meat with his chicken liver mousse, Charollais beef fillet and mutton stew with potatoes and turnips. And his inventive fish preparations may be enough to tempt even the most die-hard meat-lovers: Italian-style stuffed squid dusted with light fresh-herb breadcrumbs; orange-flavored eggplant pâté, referred to as tian in these parts, served with sardine fillets; and tomato and tapenade toast with red mullet fillets. We thought his wine list was well-balanced and reasonably priced, just like the menu itself. C 205. M 120.

 ## La Magnaneraie

37, rue Camp-de-Bataille
04 90 25 11 11, fax 04 90 25 46 37
Open daily until 9:30pm. Priv rm 80. Garden dining. Air cond. Pool. Tennis. Valet pkg.
Superlative ingredients handled with respect and skill: that's Gérard Prayal's culinary credo. It results in dishes that brim with pure, direct flavors: warm local asparagus dressed in a vinaigrette loaded with fresh herbs, lamb noisettes cooked in smoked caul fat then enhanced with a garlic jus, and caramelized apples flambéed with Calvados were recently featured one of the prix-fixe meal (which is revised twice a month). Stylish dining on the terrace, under the palms and parasols, or in the beauty of a dining room, under the glass roof, amid the columns. Magnificent cellar, with an unparalleled collection of Châteauneuf-du-Papes. Quality service and excellent fixed-price meals. C 450. M 170-450.

 ## La Magnaneraie ⚐♦

(See restaurant above)
Open year-round. 3 stes 1,000-1,800. 25 rms 500-1,200. Bkfst 70. Rms for disabled. Rm ser. Conf. Pool. Tennis. Valet pkg.
Where silkworms once munched mulberries, spacious, freshly decorated rooms with nineteenth-century furniture now offer modern comfort and the charm of yore. Beautiful garden and pool.

 ## Le Prieuré

7, pl. du Chapitre
04 90 25 18 20, fax 04 90 25 45 39
Closed mid Mar 22-mid Apr: Wed; May 1; Nov 2-mid Mar. Open until 9:15pm. Priv rm 20. Garden dining. Air cond. No pets. Pool. Tennis. Garage pkg.
Thriving under the smiling sun of Provence, in what must be one of the most charming spots on earth, chef Serge Chenet marries Provençal flavors in delicate, beguiling ways. Examples? Try his green asparagus napped with a rich jus de daube, or cream of fresh pea soup embellished with a poached egg and truffles, John Dory studded with bay leaves (a splendid dish), and grapefruit roasted with lavender honey. Seductive cellar; perfect service. C 430. M 265 (wine incl), 200-460, 110 (children).

Le Prieuré

(See restaurant above)
Closed Nov 2-mid Mar. 10 stes 1,500-1,800. 26 rms 550-1,300. Rms for disabled. Half-board 910-1,650. Rm ser. Air cond. Conf. Pool. Tennis. Garage pkg.
Whether you book in the old priory, next to the church (smallish rooms), or in the annex by the swimming pool (large rooms with a fine view of the grounds or patios), you'll find the same grand style and luxury, far from prying eyes and the madding crowd. Impeccable reception and service. Relais et Châteaux.

THE RIVIERA

ANTIBES 06600
Paris 913 - Nice 22 - Cannes 11 Alpes-Mar.

 La Baie Dorée

579, bd de la Garoupe
04 93 67 30 67, fax 04 92 93 76 39
Closed Nov. 1 ste 2,100-2,400. 16 rms 600-2,400. Bkfst 70. Restaurant. Rm ser. Conf. Air cond. Beach. Garage pkg.
This old bastide, with its smart new Provence-Italian dress, looks dreamily out onto the sea. All rooms have a terrace and are tastefully decorated. Quite attractive but rather expensive. Breakfast brings you delicious pastries.

 Beau Site

141, bd Kennedy
04 93 61 53 43, fax 04 93 67 78 16
Closed Nov-Dec. 30 rms 270-650. Bkfst 45. Rms for disabled. Conf. Pool. Pkg.
Country house located on the road between Antibes and Eden Roc. Tree-filled garden protects it from busyness of the road. Freshened-up rooms in true Provence style. Breakfast *sur l'herbe.*

 La Bonne Auberge

On N 7, quartier La Brague
04 93 33 36 65, fax 04 93 33 48 52
Closed Sun, Mon, Tue lunch, mid Nov-mid Dec. Open until 10pm (10:30pm in summer). Priv rm 30. Air cond. Terrace dining. Pkg.
Philippe Rostang has finally heard his own drummer. It's difficult when you're following in the footsteps of one so grand, but he managed and *voilà* a second toque. Well earned with his tuna Béarnaise with green asparagrus, scorpion-fish pastry served with green cabbage in an olive oil vinaigrette, and ever-so-light, "old-fashioned" millefeuille. Priced to warm your heart with his à la carte prix-fixe menu at 200 F. The wine list may be short in size but don't think it's lacking in reflection. Delphine Cussac still greets you with her sunny smile. M 200.

11/20 Chez Olive

Square Albert-1er - 04 93 34 42 32
Closed Sun, Mon dinner, Dec 17-Jan 4. Open until 10:45pm. Air cond. Terrace dining. Pkg.
With a name like "Olive" you couldn't do any other kind of cooking than the Provence-style cooking she lays before you. Try the stuffed mussels with basil, the stuffed salmon paupiettes, or the cod with garlic purée. Blend it with a wine from her wine list which gives you a vivid description of each bottle offered. C 200-250. M 82 (lunch, wine incl), 116 (wine incl), 144-176.

 La Jarre

14, rue Saint-Esprit - 04 93 34 50 12
Open daily until 10:30pm. Terrace dining.
Charming atmosphere: this is really Old Provence. Good food though a little on the high side. We enjoyed the young pigeon terrine with baby spinach, freshwater cod sauté with veal au jus, and chocolate-morello cherry fondant. Pleasant dining under the fig trees in the summer. C 180-320.

12/20 Le Marquis

4, rue de Sade - 04 93 34 23 00
Closed Mon, Tue lunch, Jul. Open until 9:30pm.
A hard core of habitués regularly fills the Marquis's little dining room, to see what chef Francis Zany has whipped up that day. Good Provençal homestyle cooking, accompanied by an appetizing choice of local wines. C 250-350. M 90-280, 50 (children).

11/20 Oh! Tour du Monde

5, rue Frédéric-Isnard - 04 93 34 31 61
Closed Mon. Open until 10:30pm.
Formerly a wine bar, the speciality has now changed dramatically: ostrich in every shape and form: terrine, finely sliced, or as a steak, with a multitude of sauces to choose from. If you don't like flying "objects," try the shark, kangaroo, crocodile or some of the other classics... C 200. M 95 (lunch), 80-240.

 Les Vieux Murs

Av. de l'Amiral-de-Grasse
04 93 34 06 73, fax 04 93 34 81 08
Closed Mon off-seas. Open until 10:30pm. Priv rm 50. Terrace dining. Air cond. No pets. Valet pkg.
While other restaurateurs fret over half-empty dining rooms, Georges and Suzanne Romano have to turn would-be patrons away. Sure, the lovely covered terrace with its view of the port has something to do with it. The biggest attraction however has long been the excellent 200 F single-price menu, but of late George has become a bit lax on overseeing the preparation. Perhaps he should prepare some of the food in the kitchen instead of putting on the entire act in front of the customers in the dining room. A dried-out salmon puff pastry and an over-cooked, pan-fried sea bream with balsamic vinegar forced us to drop a toque. Charming old-world atmosphere. C 300-450. M 200.

And also...

Our selection of places for inexpensive, quick, or late-night meals.
Le Relais du Postillon (04 93 34 20 77 - 8, rue Championnet. Open until 10pm.): Opposite the post office in old Antibes, a reliable spot for classic dishes such as seafood stew, baby lamb chop in cream sauce, and Grand Marnier soufflé. Good wine list (75-380).

ARCS (LES)   83460
Paris 854 - Draguignan 10 - St-Raphaël 29   Var

 Bacchus Gourmand

"La Maison des Vins,"
N 7 - 04 94 47 48 47, fax 04 94 47 55 13
*Closed Sun dinner & Mon off-sease, 2 wks in Jan,
Dec 23-29. Open until 10pm. Priv rm 35. Garden
dining. Air cond. Garage pkg.*
Philippe Rousselot's delectable cooking (displayed to advantage in the two least expensive set meals) has turned this table into one of the region's most popular restaurants. The menu, designed by megachef Jacques Chibois, is full of sunny touches and accented with light, delicate sauces. Magnificent cellar of Côtes-de-Provence; swift, smiling service. C 380-540. M 150-250, 80 (children).

 Le Logis du Guetteur

Pl. du Château - 04 94 73 30 82, fax 04 94 73 39 95
*Closed Jan 15-Feb 15. Open until 9:30pm. Garden
dining. Pool. Garage pkg.*
This ancient house perches high above a medieval village, affording a lovely view of the Argens Valley and the Maures massif. Max Callegari is a proficient chef, who presents a host of appetizing dishes. Try his cassolette of escargots and foie gras en croûte, braised veal kidney with pearl onions, and red-mullet croustillant with zucchini in tarragon vinaigrette. Dessert brings lavender sorbet with candied fruit. Generous cellar, reasonably priced; friendly welcome. C 340. M 135-280, 50 (children).

Le Logis du Guetteur ⚑

(See restaurant above)
*Closed Jan 15-Feb 15. 10 rms 350-450. Bkfst 48.
Half-board 440 (oblig in seas). Conf. Pool. Garage
pkg.*
Ten spacious and pleasant rooms with fabulous views in this eleventh-century fortified castle, perfect for a romantic weekend break. Horseback riding; kayaks for rent nearby.

 Relais des Moines

Route de Sainte-Roseline
04 94 47 40 93, fax 04 94 47 52 51
*Closed Feb 17-28, Oct 27-Nov 1. Open until 9:15pm.
Terrace dining. Pool. Pkg.*
If you haven't yet earned your third or fourth million, don't even think of ordering à la carte here; stick strictly to the prix-fixe menus, where for 169 F, for example, you can sample the langoustines with eggplant, lemon, garlic and olive oil purée and tomates confites, or the pan-fried angler with two-pepper (bell peppers) sauce and herb-flavored polenta, cheese and dessert. If you're a die-hard fan and of foie gras or lobster and your pocket permits, you may let yourself stray with their clever half-portions. Small but good selection of wines. C 320-380. M 169-300.

Looking for a celebrated chef? Refer to the Index.

AURIBEAU-SUR-SIAGNE   06810
Paris 926 - Cannes 16 - Grasse 8   Alpes-Mar.

 Auberge Nossi-Bé

Pl. du Portail - 04 93 42 20 20, fax 04 93 42 33 08
*Closed in seas: Mon lunch & Wed lunch; off-seas: Tue
dinner & Wed; Nov 15-30. Open until 9:30pm.
Terrace dining. Pkg.*
Set in the last village near Cannes that hasn't been turned into a craft colony, this welcoming inn serves honest cooking based on fine ingredients: order the house-made foie gras terrine, lamb stew à l'avignonnaise with polenta, and all-chocolate assiette gourmande for dessert. A real find in this *frou-frou* region! M 145 (weekday lunch, wine incl), 170 (weekday dinner & Sun, wine incl), 70 (children).

BANDOL   83150
Paris 842 - Marseille 49 - Toulon 17 - Aix-en-P. 74   Var

Augerbe du Port

9, allée Jean-Moulin
04 94 29 42 63, fax 04 94 29 44 59
*Open daily until 10pm (11pm in summer). Air
cond. Terrace dining. Garage pkg.*
A real taste of the Mediterranean, in every form of the word: seafood, simply broiled, or more dressed-up versions with seafood couscous (semolina topped with a sort of fish stew) and red mullet "cake" with an eggplant tian. Well-respected for classics like bouillabaisse and fish paella. Pleasant terrace but must reserve ahead. Wash it down with one of their fine Bandol wines. C 330-450. M 120-250, 70 (children).

Le Clocher

1, rue de la Paroisse - 04 94 32 47 65
*Closed Sun dinner. Open until 9pm. Priv rm 25.
Terrace dining.*
Admire the produce of Bandol's open-air market as you head over to the small, sundrenched dining room of Le Clocher. Alain Gantel's cuisine is uncluttered and precise: he served us thin slices of raw scallops showered with matchsticks of fresh ginger, and lotte poached in court-bouillon with julienned zucchini, green tomatoes, and tiny pearl onions, lushly accented with garlicky aïoli. Dessert brought a gossamer-light green-apple feuilantine spiced with nutmeg. Fine regional cellar; sunny welcome from Martine Gantel. C 200-380. M 110, 190.

 Délos

Ile de Bendor - 04 94 32 22 23, fax 04 94 32 41 44
*Closed Jan-Feb. 55 rms 410-1,080. Bkfst 65. Restaurant. Half-board 220 (oblig in sea). Conf. Pool.
Beach. Tennis.*
Comfortable rooms, decorated in a variety of styles, enjoy an idyllic view of the sea in this neo-Medieval manor house. Peaceful. Numerous sporting activities.

**Master Ker
Mocotte Hôtel**

103, rue Raimu - 04 94 29 46 53, fax 04 94 32 53 54
*Open year-round. 20 rms 230-820. Restaurant.
Half-board 290-540. Conf. No pets. Pool. Pkg.*
A big white house nestled in the pine trees. The
famous 1930s actor Raimu had it built in search
of some peace and quiet between movies. Lovely
rooms looking out over the Renecros Bay. Some
of the bathrooms are a bit too old-fashioned.

Les Oliviers

17, bd Louis-Lumière
04 94 29 33 00, fax 04 94 29 49 49
*Open daily until 10pm (10:30pm in summer). Air
cond. Terrace dining. Pool. Beach. Tennis. Valet
pkg.*
Anchored near the yacht basin, Les Oliviers'
big dining room sports a bright, understated
Mediterranean décor with a great view of the
sea. Chef Laurent Chouviat gives local ingredients an original spin: sample his scallops
paired with chestnut mousseline, lobster stewed
in lightly spiced Bandol wine, rack of Sisteron
lamb with sheep-cheese ravioli, and braised
peaches with buttery brioche. But the drop in
business is made evident in the cool welcome
and even in the cooking, which has lost a bit of
its spark. Terrific selection of local wines. C 250-
450. M 165-400, 75 (children).

L'Ile Rousse

(See restaurant above)
*Open year-round. 2 stes 945-1,240. 53 rms 350-
1,130. Half-board 578-1,389. Bkfst 65. Air cond.
Conf. Pool. Beach. Tennis. Valet pkg.*
The building designed by Fleury Linossier in
Provençal style has huge, sunny, well-maintained and modernized rooms, some with views
of the sea. Full breakfast. In summer, a buffet is
served on the beach. Health center. Excellent
welcome and service.

BEAULIEU-SUR-MER 06310
Paris 943 - Menton 20 - Nice 10 - Cannes 43 Alpes-Mar.

Le Métropole

15, bd du Général-Leclerc
04 93 01 00 08, fax 04 93 01 18 51
*Closed Oct 20-Dec 20. Open until 10pm. Priv rm
30. Garden dining. Air cond. Pool. Beach. Valet pkg.*
This Italianate villa is a dreamy spot, one
where moneyed patrons find the soul-stirring
beauty, distinguished service, and elegant ambience they seek. But Gilbert Roubaud seems to
have lost contact with the muses, so we have no
choice but to drop his second toque. Mushy
smoked salmon, thoroughly uninspired beet
and endive salad with oysters as well as young
turbot with champagne sauce, what's going on?
C 600. M 400, 500, 250 (children).

Le Métropole

(See restaurant above)

*Closed Oct 20-Dec 20. 3 stes 2,500-5,300. 50 rms
840-2,800. Bkfst 120-180. Half-board 880-1,975
(oblig in sea). Air cond. Rm ser. Pool. Beach. Pkg.*
All the exquisite comforts of a luxury hotel are
lavished on guests at this huge white villa set in
over two acres of opulent gardens. Rooms are
bright and handsomely decorated, and the service is peerless: no detail is too small for attention. Le Métropole draws a wealthy clientele that
is anything but flashy. Prices lower off season.
Relais et Châteaux.

La Réserve de Beaulieu

5, bd du Général-Leclerc
04 93 01 00 01, fax 04 93 01 28 99
*Closed Oct 31-Apr 15. Open until 10:30pm. Priv rm
60. Terrace dining. Air cond. Heated pool. No pets.
Valet pkg.*
La Réserve is the sort of place where guests can
sip cocktails in a Venetian-style dining room
suspended over the sea, and admire a Riviera
sunset while a pianist plays Chopin in the background. And new chef Guillaume Sourrieu has
added a new flair with his Marseille-inspired
touch. He favors the tastes of the sun and is high
on spices, for example, with his zucchini risotto,
his Cape fish en bouillabaisse or his shellfish
cappuccino with threads of saffron. Magnificent
wine list with good explanations. C 550-600. M
400.

La Réserve de Beaulieu

(See restaurant above)
*Closed Oct 31-Apr 15. 10 stes 2,800-7,500. 27 rms
1,600-4,000. Bkfst 125. Half-board 2,425-4,525.
Rm ser. Air cond. Conf. Heated pool. Valet pkg.*
This lovely, newly renovated Belle Époque
villa fairly oozes with 1950s-style luxury. The
swimming pool looks onto the beach and a
small, private harbor.

See also: **Saint-Jean-Cap-Ferrat**

BIOT 06140
Paris 922 - Antibes 8 - Nice 22 - Cagnes 10 Alpes-Mar.

Auberge du Jarrier

30, passage de la Bourgade
04 93 65 11 68, fax 04 93 65 50 03
*Closed Mon dinner, Tue, mid Jan-mid Feb. Open
until 9:30pm. Terrace dining. Air cond.*
The Auberge boasts a warm, countrified décor
and a devoted following among locals and touring gourmets. Christian Métral's cuisine has lots
of character, and even when it gets complicated,
the ingredients (all local, all prime) are beautifully balanced. The bread rolls are baked on the
premises and the cellar is awash in affordable
regional wines. But the tabs are up and climbing,
and the service, though professional, can be snif-
fy at times. C 230. M 260 (wine incl), 230-300, 90
(children).

Domaine du Jas

625, route de la Mer
04 93 65 50 50, fax 04 93 65 02 01
Closed Jan. 2 stes 700-1,200. 15 rms 350-800. Bkfst 50. Pool. No pets. Garage pkg.
Everything you could possibly need for a restful stay by the seaside. Efficient service.

 ## Les Terraillers

11, route du Chemin-Neuf
04 93 65 01 59, fax 04 93 65 13 78
Closed Wed & Thu lunch (exc Jul-Aug). Open until 10pm. Priv rm 10. Terrace dining. Air cond. Pkg.
Planted at the foot of the village since the sixteenth century, this elegantly restored pottery is now a restaurant, where Claude Jacques presents (rather elaborate) cuisine with a Mediterranean accent. Our most recent meal was a savory success from start to finish, but the rising prices are on the verge of stifling our enjoyment. Delightful welcome and service. C 380-500. M 180-490, 100 (children).

And also...

Our selection of places for inexpensive, quick, or late-night meals.
Galerie des Arcades (04 93 65 01 04 - 16, pl. des Arcades. Open until 9:30pm.): This fifteenth-century setting offers you generous helpings in a jovial yet well-polished atmosphere (170).

BORMES-LES-MIMOSAS 83230
Paris 890 - Toulon 40 - St-Tropez 35 - Le Lavandou 5   Var

12/20 Chez Sylvia

"Restaurant-Pizzéria-Sauveur,"
872, av. Lou Mistraou - 04 94 71 14 10
Closed Wed (exc school hols), Dec-Jan. Open until 10:30pm. Garden dining. Pkg.
Sylvia serves Sicilian pizzas, savory brochettes, and sweet cannoli on her shady terrace. C 180-260. M 120 (Sun lunch).

12/20 L'Escoundudo

2, ruelle du Moulin - 04 94 71 15 53
Closed Mon & Tue off-seas. Open until 11pm. Terrace dining.
Take time out on this flower-filled terrace right in the heart of this medieval village. Max and Dandine's open-arm reception and the simple but good cooking using products from the region are just one more reason to stop here. We were partial to the bell pepper salad and tomatoes with littles slices of bread spread with anchoïade (anchovy paste). Local wines. C 200. M 100 (lunch), 150.

 ## Le Mirage

38, rue Vue-des-Iles
04 94 05 32 60, fax 04 94 64 93 03
Closed Nov 1-Dec 31. 1 ste 850-1,250. 35 rms 395-820. Bkfst 67. Rms for disabled. Restaurant. Rm ser. Air cond. Conf. Pool. Tennis. Pkg.
The well-equipped rooms have mezzanines and superb views of the bay. Great breakfasts. Children will love the game room and garden; business types will be happy to find complete conference facilities.

 ## Les Palmiers

6 km S on D 559, in Cabasson, 240, chemin du Petit-Fort - 04 94 64 81 94, fax 04 94 64 93 61
Closed Nov. 2 stes 1,000-1,280. 18 rms 380-590. Bkfst 50-60. Rms for disabled. Restaurant. Half-board 450-520 (oblig in seas). Rm ser. Conf. Tennis. Pkg.
Surrounded by greenery and five minutes' walk from the sea, this holiday hotel proposes quiet, attractive rooms.

11/20 La Tonnelle des Délices

Pl. Gambetta - 04 94 71 34 84
Closed Wed, Nov-mid Jan. Open until 10pm. Terrace dining. No pets.
Take a seat on the hanging garden-terrace or in the dining room filled with pretty bric-a-brac to sample Alain Pasetto's fresh Provençal cooking: mussels with garlic and parsley, fish soup, anchoïade, rabbit with pistou, daube à l'ancienne. The execution is more and more often marred by missteps—a little more care is in order! C 250. M 100 (lunch, exc Sun), 120-250, 75 (children).

CADIÈRE D'AZUR (LA) 83740
Paris 821 - Marseille 46 - Toulon 22 - Aix-en-P. 63   Var

 ## René Bérard

Rue Gabriel-Péri - 04 94 90 11 43, fax 04 94 90 01 94
Closed Sun dinner, Mon, Jan 10-Feb 20. Open until 9:30pm. Priv rm 10. Air cond. No pets. Garage pkg.
René Bérard is holding hands with the muses, inspired by the ingredients around him to create classics in the manner of the masters as well as truly original works of art, such as his divine nougat de bœuf, perfectly-prepared foie gras with roasted figs, and tiny red mullets with pistou. Some disillusionment with the overcooked veal chop, but made up for with the fruits rouges fritters. Second toque well merited. Good selection of local Bandol wines. Splendid welcome. C 270. M 95 (weekdays, wine incl), 175-420.

Hostellerie Bérard

(See restaurant above)
Closed Sun, Mon, Jan 10-Feb 20. 4 stes 750-1,100. 36 rms 440-760. Bkfst 70. Half-board 500-765. Air cond. Conf. Heated pool. No pets. Garage pkg.
This Renaissance-era hostelry provides thoughtfully decorated rooms in neo-Provençal style. A recent annex overlooks the garden and swimming pool. Flanked by vineyards and olive trees.

CAGNES-SUR-MER 06800
Paris 920 - Cannes 22 - Nice 13 - Antibes 11   Alpes-Mar.

 Le Cagnard

Haut-de-Cagnes, rue du Pontis-Long
04 93 20 73 21, fax 04 93 22 06 39
Closed Thu lunch, end Oct-mid Dec. Open until 10:30pm (11pm in summer). Terrace dining. Air cond. Valet pkg.
This ravishing medieval dwelling affords a stupendous view of the coast all the way to Antibes. You can enjoy that sweeping panorama from a terrace equipped with a sliding paneled ceiling, which protects you from bad weather or opens to let you admire the stars. Supplied with superb raw materials and uncommon skill, Jean-Yves Johany can turn a simple *poulet grand'mère*, stuffed vegetables à la niçoise, or *soupe au pistou* into a feast of rare refinement. But the carte is devilishly expensive, what with the kitchen's lavish use of foie gras, caviar, and truffles (even a green salad costs 110 F). Divine desserts. The wines will add further freight to an already hefty bill. **C** 350-600. **M** 275 (lunch, wine incl), 300-500, 150 (children).

 Le Cagnard

(See restaurant above)
Open year-round. 4 stes 1,300-1,500. 23 rms 750-1,100. Bkfst 80. Half-board 785-1,010. Conf. Valet pkg.
Some of the rooms and suites are situated in beautifully renovated village houses. The balconies and private terraces look out to sea. Inside, you'll find flawless appointments and gorgeous marble bathrooms. Delightful staff. Relais et Châteaux.

 Les Collettes

Chemin des Collettes
04 93 20 80 66, fax 04 93 20 61 04
Closed Nov-Dec 27. 13 rms 298-301. Bkfst 33. Pool. Tennis. Pkg.
This simple hotel-motel overlooking the sea has plain, pleasantly decorated rooms. The Musée Renoir is close by.

 Josy Jo

Haut-de-Cagnes, 8, pl. du Planastel
04 93 20 68 76
Closed Sat lunch, Sun. Open until 10pm. Terrace dining. Air cond.
For more than 25 years Jo and Josy Bandecchi have been serving seasonal Provençal fare to appreciative customers. There are artichokes à la barigoule, stuffed zucchini blossoms, charcoal-grilled meats and fish, and delectable fresh-fruit tarts. Not to mention friendly service and an adorable terrace massed with flowers. **C** 270.

 Picadero ☻

3, bd de la Plage - 04 93 22 32 84
Closed Sun dinner, Mon, Jan 2-13, Jul 1-15. Open until 10pm. Air cond.

Gérard Ferri's bright, air conditioned dining room is a wonderful place to linger over a feast of generous Provençal and Niçois dishes, full of intense, direct flavors and lively, unexpected touches. Dream of a dish in his oyster bouillon with leeks in watercress cream sauce; well-crafted breast of cockerel with walnuts served with a diable sauce (a peppery brown sauce) and dried-fruit rice. The terrace, too, is pleasant, though not out of earshot of traffic. One slip-up: the wine list is rather too concise and hard on the pocket. **M** 180.

CALLAS 83830
Paris 870 - Draguignan 15 - Castellane 61   Var

 Les Gorges de Pennafort

In Perroport, route du Muy
04 94 76 66 51, fax 04 94 76 67 23
Closed Sun dinner & Mon lunch off-seas, Feb-Mar 15. Open until 10pm. Priv rm 20. Terrace dining. Air cond. Pool. Tennis. Pkg.
The site is sensational (magnificent gorges just opposite), the restaurant is comfortable (it boasts a broad, shaded terrace), and Philippe da Silva's cooking is polished to a high sheen: cannelloni stuffed with shellfish and vegetables in lobster coulis, crisp-skinned sea bass with fennel purée, wonderful braised sweetbreads with morels, and a yummy vanilla millefeuille with made-to-order vanilla ice cream. Lots of top local wines fill the cellar, and the service is *simpatico*. **C** 350-400. **M** 195-260.

 Les Gorges de Pennafort

(See restaurant above)
Closed Sun eve & Mon off-seas, Feb-Mar 15. 4 stes 800-950. 12 rms 480-630. Bkfst 65. Rms for disabled. Half-board 550-700. Rm ser. Air cond. Conf. Pool. Tennis. Pkg.
Welcoming, air conditioned rooms and small, well-appointed marble bathrooms. An annex offers four very attractive larger rooms. Charming welcome; excellent service.

CANNES 06400
Paris 910 - Marseille 165 - Nice 33   Alpes-Mar.

Amarante

78, bd Carnot - 04 93 39 22 23, fax 04 93 39 40 22
Open year-round. 1 ste 590-1,660. 70 rms 380-950. Rms for disabled. Restaurant. Half-board 295-395. Rm ser. Air cond. Conf. Pool. Beach. Garage pkg.
A modern hotel decorated in Provençal style, with smallish but very well equipped and soundproofed rooms. Sun room and outdoor pool. Restaurant serves regional specialities.

*Some establishments change their **closing times** without warning. It is always wise to check in advance.*

11/20 **Athènes**

18, rue des Frères-Pradignac - 04 93 38 96 11
Closed Sun lunch (exc hols & Aug-Sep), Wed, 2 wks in Jun, Dec 15-25. Open until 10:30pm. Terrace dining. Air cond.
The chef once lived in Istanbul and knows how to mix both Turkish and Greek cuisine. Delicious skewered meats, authentic moussaka and stuffed vegetables. Friendly service. **C** 200-300. **M** 98 (weekday lunch, Sat, Sun dinner), 150, 190.

The Beaches

Lunch only.
Long Beach (04 93 38 17 47 - 8, bd de la Croisette.): Family and friends gather for fish soup, salmon with basil, and mussel casserole at this popular beachside restaurant opposite the Noga Hilton (180-240).
Martinez (04 92 98 74 22 - 73, bd de la Croisette.): Not only does the Martinez occupy the largest strip of beach in Cannes, it lays on a lavish Provençal-style buffet in a setting dotted with parasols and a plethora of plants. Dessert buffet open all afternoon (195-260).
Miramar Beach (04 93 94 24 74 - 67, bd de la Croisette.): Up-market ambience. The beach mat is free after a meal of fine langoustine salad or grilled fish (250-300).
Ondine (04 93 94 23 15 - 15, bd de la Croisette.): Facing the sea, near the Carlton, a perfect spot for a ridiculously expensive lunch with friends. Get them to treat... (350-500).
Plage des Dunes (04 93 94 14 99 - 15, bd de la Croisette.): A convivial spot with a pretty terrace, where you can feast on typical Mediterranean specialties (155-250).

 Beau Séjour

5, rue des Fauvettes
04 93 39 63 00, fax 04 92 98 64 66
Open year-round. 45 rms 330-750. Bkfst 65. Restaurant. Half-board 110. Rm ser. Air cond. Pool.
A modern, perfectly equipped residence 300 yards from the beach. All rooms have terraces leading into the garden and swimming pool. Efficient service. Good value, for Cannes.

 La Belle Otéro

Carlton Inter Continental,
58, bd de la Croisette
04 93 68 00 33, fax 04 93 39 09 06
Closed Sun & Mon (exc dinner Jul-Aug), Jun 8-Jul 7, Oct 27-Nov 11. Open until 10:30pm (midnight in summer). Terrace dining. Air cond. Valet Pkg.
Beneath the low wood-paneled ceiling of a Louis XV dining room that could hardly be less Mediterranean, Francis Chauveau imparts his professional touch to dishes that make the most of premium Provençal produce. There's a flawless navarin d'agneau printanier, grilled turbot with smoked bacon and fried onions, and a very attractive sauté of crustaceans and vegetables layered with potatoes to make an unusual millefeuille. The patrons are obviously unfazed by four-figure tabs—that's fortunate, since the cheapest item on the menu (pan-roasted duck liver) is 220 F. The money-conscious should stick with the 290 F set price meal, which includes wine. High-class service, of course, and the wine list posts dizzying prices. **C** 600-750. **M** 290 (lunch, wine incl), 390 (dinner), 590.

11/20 **Le Bouchon d'Objectif**

10, rue de Constantine - 04 93 99 21 76
Closed Mon, Nov 15-Dec 15. Open until 10:30pm. Terrace dining. No pets.
This restaurant-cum-photo gallery serves unpretentious, low-priced dishes like crab and marinated salmon tartare with blinis, aïoli, fish soup, monkfish bourride, and tiramisù. **M** 85, 130, 50 (children).

12/20 **La Brouette de Grand-Mère**

Rue d'Oran - 04 93 39 12 10
Dinner only. Closed Sun, Jul 1-14, Nov 1-Dec 15. Open until 11pm. Terrace dining. Air cond. Pkg.
This legendary bistro continues to draw enthusiastic crowds with its single menu: an apéritif with a few pre-dinner tidbits, followed by potatoes à la brouette with a pop of iced vodka, California salad, roast quail with grape sauce, then grilled goat cheese, dessert, and coffee. You may drink as much house wine as you like. **M** 195 (wine incl).

 La Côte

Carlton Inter Continental, 58, La Croisette
04 93 06 40 06, fax 04 93 06 40 25
Closed Tue, Wed, Nov-Mar. Open until 10:30pm (midnight in summer). Terrace dining. Air cond. No pets. Pool. Beach. Valet pkg.
Not what it was. Take advantage of the "business lunch" at La Côte because the rest might drain your savings. The prix-fixe meal does however provide an overview of chef Sylvain Duparc's once zestful cooking. We were disappointed in the squab rémoulade: the young pigeon was sumptuous but the pastry "leaf" on top made it too heavy and we never managed to taste the truffles we had been promised. The John Dory was overcooked, they forgot to include the citron confit announced on the menu, and it was more or less drowning in celery. The apple pie was good enough but the vanilla ice cream was straight out of a box. One point less and justifiably so. **C** 600-750. **M** 275 (weekday lunch, Sat, wine incl), 350, 460.

 Carlton Inter Continental

(See restaurant above)
Open year-round. 34 stes 7,000-45,000. 320 rms 1,990-3,890. Bkfst 105-145. Rms for disabled. Rm ser. Air cond. Conf. Pool. Beach. Valet pkg.
The constantly renovated, luxurious rooms are extremely comfortable, and the hotel's thirteen-room penthouse is unquestionably the most "Imperial Suite" on the Riviera. Superb service; perfectly equipped fitness center.

D-1 ① - Amarante 🏠
D-3 ② - Athènes 🗒
B-3 ③ - Beau Séjour ◔
E-4 ④ - La Belle Otéro 👨‍🍳
E-4 ④ - Carlton
         Inter-Continental 🏨
E-4 ④ - La Côte ◔
F-5 ⑤ - Palace Hôtel 🏨
D-1 ⑥ - Côté Jardin 🍽
E-3 ⑦ - Cristal 🏨
E-3 ⑧ - Fouquet's 🏠
E-4 ⑨ - Grand Hôtel 🏨
D-3 ⑩ - Gray d'Albion 🏨
E-4 ⑪ - Horset-Savoy 🏨
E-3 ⑫ - La Libera 🗒
D-3 ⑬ - Majestic 🏨
F-4 ⑭ - Martinez 🏨
F-4 ⑭ - La Palme d'Or ◔
E-3 ⑮ - Molière ◔
E-4 ⑯ - Noga Hilton 🏨
E-4 ⑯ - La Scala 🍽
G-3 ⑰ - Novotel-Montfleury 🏨

A-3 ⑲ - Sofitel-le Méditérrannée 🏨
E-4 ⑳ - Pulmann Beach 🏠

F-5 ㉒ - Le Restaurant Arménien 🗒
E-3 ㉓ - Victoria 🏠
E-3 ㉔ - Le Bouchon d'Objectif 🗒
E-3 ㉕ - La Brouette de Grand- Mère 🗒
E-2 ㉖ - Hôtel de Paris 🏠

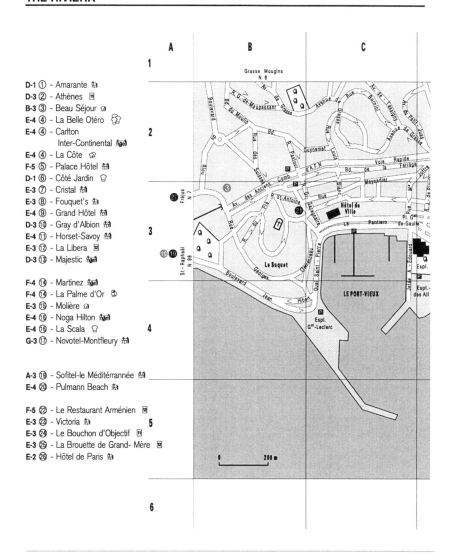

 ## Côté Jardin

12, av. St-Louis - 04 93 38 60 28, fax 04 93 38 60 28
*Closed Sun & Mon off-seas, Feb. Open until 10pm.
Priv rm 25. Garden dining. Air cond.*
Guests can take their ease in the newly renovated and enlarged dining room, where Alexandre Walger presents his imaginative cooking. The cheapest menu is an excellent deal, but the 185 F set meal also has its charms, offering a constantly renewed list of appealing dishes (eggplant fritters with chive cream, lamb stew with spring vegetables, meringues filled with ice cream and coulis). C 200-220. M 105 (lunch, wine incl), 185, 60 (children).

*The **ratings** are based solely on the restaurants' cuisine. We do not take into account the atmosphere, décor, service and so on; these are commented upon within the review.*

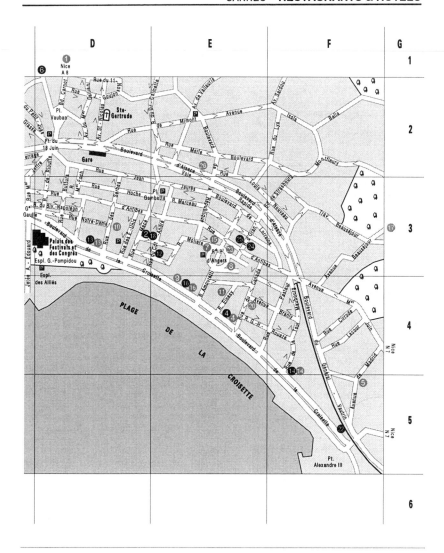

 Cristal

13, rond-point Duboys-d'Angers
04 93 39 45 45, fax 04 93 38 64 66
*Open year-round. 7 stes 950-3,000. 44 rms 550-
1,750. Bkfst 72-95. Rms for disabled. Restaurant.
Half-board 445-620. Rm ser. Air cond. Valet pkg.*
    This candy-colored luxury hotel, with its
elegantly decorated interiors, provides rather
small, but well-designed rooms with comfortable, modern furniture. The sixth floor boasts a
panoramic restaurant and bar, as well as a swimming pool, Jacuzzi, and veranda. Centrally located near the Croisette.

 Fouquet's

2, rond-point Duboys-d'Angers
04 93 38 75 81, fax 04 92 98 03 39
*Closed Nov-Mar 28. 10 rms 440-1,400. Bkfst 60.
Rm ser. Air cond. Garage pkg.*

Strategically situated about 100 yards off the Croisette, this uncommonly comfortable hotel offers irresistible rooms with boudoirs and little balconies.

 ## Grand Hôtel

45, bd de la Croisette
04 93 38 15 45, fax 04 93 68 97 45
Closed Nov 1-Dec 10. 2 stes 2,600. 74 rms 500-1,580. Bkfst 70. Restaurant. Half-board 670. Rm ser. Air cond. Beach. Valet pkg.
A remarkable little luxury hotel set amid verdant gardens. Among the assets are large, perfectly comfy rooms with terraces, high-quality reception and service, and a private beach. Panoramic restaurant.

Gray d'Albion

See restaurant Le Royal Gray

 ## L'Horset Savoy

5, rue Fr.-Einesy · 04 92 99 72 00, fax 04 93 68 25 59
Open year-round. 5 stes 2,000-5,000. 101 rms 370-1,900. Bkfst 98. Rms for disabled. Restaurant. Half-board 490-2,180. Air cond. Pool. Valet pkg.
The lobby displays a disconcerting mix of styles, with its colorful antique columns and deep, 1930s-style armchairs. As for the rooms, they are smaller than one would expect, but thoroughly soundproofed, with marble baths, sea views, Art Deco décor and irreproachable service.

11/20 La Libera

17, rue du Commandant-André · 04 92 99 00 19
Open daily until 11pm (2am in summer). Terrace dining. Air cond. No pets.
Come here for a relaxed meal of Italian food in a convivial atmosphere: fresh scampi salad with balsamic vinegar, carpaccio, fritto misto, gnocchi, delicious cod à la vicentina. Nice selection of Piedmontese wines. Friendly welcome. **C** 220.

Majestic

See restaurant La Villa des Lys

Martinez

See restaurant La Palme d'Or

 ## Le Méditerranée

Plage du Midi, 2 bd Jean-Hibert
04 92 99 73 10, fax 04 2 99 73 29
Closed Nov 25-Dec 26. Open until 10:30pm. Air cond. Heated pool. Valet pkg.
Sublime, jutting view of the bay of Cannes from the seventh-floor terrace. Business-like atmosphere with precision on the agenda: complete comfort, perfectly-timed service, and a cuisine lacking perhaps great leaps of imagination, yet prepared in generous amounts and with high regard for good-quality ingredients. We relished the quail breast salad with shallot jus; the extra-tender saddle of rabbit with leg cooked

in rosemary; and the chocolate chaud-froid with vanilla ice cream. No pleasant surprises in the wine selection, but still a respectable assortment. **C** 160-180. **M** 125, 65 (children).

 ## Sofitel Le Méditerranée

(See restaurant above)
Closed Nov 25-Dec 26. 6 stes 1,380-2,260. 143 rms 715-1,630. Bkfst 90-100. Half-board 850-1,120. Rm ser. Air cond. Conf. Heated pool. Valet pkg.
There's an admirable view of the harbor and bay from the bright and comfortable colonial-style rooms. Splendid heated swimming pool on the seventh-floor terrace. Warm welcome; numerous services, including baby-sitting.

 ## Molière

5, rue Molière · 04 93 38 16 16, fax 04 93 68 29 57
Closed Nov 15-Dec 20. 45 rms 350-520. Bkfst 40. Rms for disabled. Air cond. No pets.
A conveniently located hotel, not too far from the center of town, offering bright rooms with balconies. Pleasant garden.

Noga Hilton

See restaurant La Scala

 ## Novotel Montfleury

25, av. Beauséjour
04 93 68 91 50, fax 04 93 38 37 08
Open year-round. 1 ste 1,500-3,500. 180 rms 450-1,100. Bkfst 60. Restaurant. Half-board 100-130. Rm ser. Air cond. Conf. Heated pool. Tennis. Pkg.
Set in the heart of the ten-acre François-André Park, with a view of the bay, this contemporary luxury hotel has unusually spacious rooms, with terraces from the fourth story up. Fitness center on the premises.

 ## Palace Hôtel

14, av. de Madrid · 04 93 43 44 45, fax 04 93 43 41 30
Closed Nov 20-Dec 20. 3 stes 1,000-1,690. 98 rms 525-1,490. Bkfst 75-95. Restaurant. Half-board 415-580. Rm ser. Air cond. Conf. Pool. Pkg.
This modern hotel stands in a quiet residential district 200 yards from the beach. The spacious rooms are perfectly equipped and air conditioned. Coolish service. Numerous facilities; garden.

 ## La Palme d'Or

73, bd de la Croisette
04 92 98 74 14 (R), 04 92 98 73 00 (H), fax 04 93 39 67 82
Closed Mon, Tue (exc dinner mid May-mid Sep), mid Nov-mid Dec. Open until 10:30pm. Terrace dining. Air cond. Pool. Valet pkg.
Alsatian by birth, Christian Willer has the soul of a Southerner, and a native's affinity for the pungent, sun-soaked flavors of the Riviera. And he's got connections: after ten years at the Martinez, Willer's Rolodex is crammed with the names of all the best local growers, breeders, and fishermen. So book a table by the huge bay win-

dow overlooking the Croisette, to savor fresh vegetables dressed in premium olive oil, with shrimp beignets in a snappy ratatouille jus; or tiny squid and red mullet anointed with rosemary-scented oil; or mesclun salad with cumin-spiced lamb croquettes; or a creamy risotto embellished with wee purple artichokes, crushed truffles, and grilled pancetta. A other good point: Willer's light, brilliant menu is far from being on the Riviera among the priciest! The worthwhile 295 F lunch includes both wine and coffee. Sensational cellar (try the rich Domaine de Saint-Baillon '90). C 600-800. M 295 (lunch, exc Sun, wine incl), 350, 580.

 ## Martinez

(See restaurant above)
Open year-round. 12 stes 5,760-14,900. 418 rms 800-4,120. Bkfst 115-160. Rm ser. Air cond. Conf. Pool. Beach. Tennis. Valet pkg.
After a period of decline, the world-famous Martinez, which in the 1930s was a world-renowned hotel with a glittering guest list, has undergone a total renovation. Now the equal of the Carlton and Majestic hotels, it boasts refined and luxuriously comfortable rooms decorated in "Roaring Twenties" style. In the garden is a sumptuous swimming pool, while on the other side of the Croisette an elegant private beach is reserved for hotel guests. General manager Patrick Sicard has infused the hotel with a dynamic new attitude (now if he could just improve the breakfasts, all would be perfect).

 ## Hôtel de Paris

34, bd d'Alsace - 04 93 38 30 89, fax 04 93 39 04 61
Closed Nov 21-Dec 29. 5 stes 800-1,200. 45 rms 450-720. Bkfst 55. Air cond. Conf. No pets. Pool. Garage pkg.
A beautiful, classic dwelling, just 300 yards from the beach. The nicest rooms look onto the elegant garden and swimming pool. Effective soundproofing. Sauna, Jacuzzi.

Pullman Beach

13, rue du Canada
04 93 94 50 50, fax 04 93 68 35 38
Closed mid Nov-mid Dec. 7 stes 1,200-1,900. 67 rms 525-1,494. Bkfst 90. Rms for disabled. Rm ser. Air cond. Conf. Pool. Pkg.
The Pullmann used to enjoy a prestigious reputation, but the accommodations here have aged rather ungracefully. Though they offer many amenities, the rooms and bathrooms are not as well kept as they might be (we noticed peeling paint on the ceilings).

 ## 12/20 Le Restaurant Arménien

"Lucien et Christian," 82, bd de la Croisette
04 93 94 00 58, fax 04 93 94 56 12
Closed Wed off-seas. Open until 10pm. Terrace dining. Air cond.
Charles Aznavour's favorite restaurant, featuring authentic Armenian specialties. Try the eg-

gplant caviar, cracked-wheat salad, grilled meatballs with fresh herbs, and mint ravioli. Good choice of wines from the Var. M 240.

 ## Le Royal Gray

38, rue des Serbes - 04 92 99 79 79, fax 04 93 99 26 10
Open daily until 10:30pm. Terrace dining. Air cond. Beach. Valet pkg.
Polished wood, brass, copper: dressed up and fitted out, just like a ship! Simple cooking with well looked-after traditional dishes at prices that don't boggle the mind. Quite decent young-rabbit terrine served with a delicious mesclun salad with aged Parmesan, worthy lobster fricassée with fresh morel mushrooms in a light shellfish jus, and delightful lamb sauté with spring vegetables. Heavenly desserts. Bordeaux-dominated wine cellar. C 350-430. M 190-265.

 ## Gray d'Albion

(See restaurant above)
Open year-round. 14 stes 2,500-6,200. 172 rms 590-1,650. Bkfst 97-128. Rms for disabled. Rm ser. Air cond. Conf. Beach. Tennis. Valet pkg.
Although it isn't on the Croisette, the Gray d'Albion affords pleasant views of the hills (from the upper floors) or of the sea from the ninth floor where there is a suite with a huge balcony. The rooms are spacious and well equipped, with modern furnishings. Direct access to a shopping mall; very chic discothèque ("Jane's") on the premises, piano bar, underground parking. Lovely private beach with a restaurant.

 ## La Scala

50, bd de la Croisette
04 92 99 70 00, fax 04 92 99 70 11
Open daily until 10:30pm (11pm in summer). Garden dining. Air cond. Pool. Beach. Pkg.
One of the nicest terraces in town awaits you here, as well as a classically done up dining room. Wherever you're seated, you'll be served unpretentious but deftly handled Italian dishes, delivered by a swift, professional staff. Our stuffed zucchini and peppers wanted a spot more flavor, but we give high marks to the calf's liver in a balsamic vinegar sauce. Alluring Provençal cellar. C 350-500. M 168-195 (lunch), 295 (dinner).

 ## Noga Hilton

(See restaurant above)
Open year-round. 47 stes 3,690-24,500. 182 rms 1,450-3,290. Bkfst 135. Rms for disabled. Rm ser. Air cond. Conf. Beach. Pkg.
The new Hilton offers absolutely comfortable accommodations in a building that sports a splendid modernist façade. Every conceivable amenity has been provided, including wonderful marble bathrooms. Also on the premises are restaurants, a piano bar, a shopping arcade, and a rooftop swimming pool with a panoramic view. Private beach.

*Looking for a restaurant? Refer to the **index**.*

Sofitel Le Méditerranée

See restaurant Le Méditerranée

 Victoria

Rond-point Duboys-d'Angers
04 93 99 36 36, fax 04 93 38 03 91
Closed end Nov. 25 rms 410-1,150. Bkfst 60. Restaurant. Rm ser. Air cond. Conf. Pool. Valet pkg.
A modern hotel with quiet, comfortable, tastefully decorated rooms, located next to the former Palais des Festivals. Pleasant English bar and tea room; stylish service. Lovely terrace.

 La Villa des Lys

14, bd de la Croisette
04 92 98 77 00, fax 04 93 38 97 90
Closed mid Nov-Dec. Open until 10:30pm. Terrace dining. Heated pool. Beach. Tennis. Valet Pkg.
Bruno Oger officiates in the kitchen of the Majestic's comfortable and spectacular restaurant. After seven years with Georges Blanc, the man knows a thing or two about mixing and matching flavors. We made a capital meal of red mullet and fennel en salade, subtly spiced lacquered duck, bitter-chocolate soufflé with cocoa sorbet, and a medley of citrus fruits. Simple and tasty. Service so-so. Fine cellar, overseen by an alumnus of the Moulin de Mougins, but could be more affordable if filled in with more local wines. C 525. M 230 (lunch), 350, 460.

 Majestic

(See restaurant above)
Closed beg Nov-beg Jan. 23 stes 3,150-22,000. 264 rms 1,050-3,600. Bkfst 120. Half-board 1,300-2,210. Rm ser. Air cond. Conf. Heated pool. Beach. Tennis. Valet pkg.
The Majestic has long been a symbol of luxury and refinement in Cannes. Movie stars love to stay here during the film festival, and soak up the sumptuous atmosphere. Gorgeous rooms look out on the garden and pool or on the Croisette and the hotel's private beach. Roaring Twenties-style décor. Five tennis courts.

And also...

Our selection of places for inexpensive, quick, or late-night meals.
La Mère Besson (04 93 39 59 24 - 13, rue des Frères-Pradignac. Open until 10:30pm.): The scent of garlic emanates perpetually from the kitchen of this well-known restaurant. Unvarying *plats du jour* include frogs' legs à la provençale, fish soup, Niçois monkfish, veal kidney in aigrelette sauce. Good choice of Provençal wines (95-300).

CAP-D'ANTIBES   06600
Paris 905 - Nice 22 - Antibes 2   Alpes-Mar.

 Don César

46, bd de la Garoupe
04 93 67 15 30, fax 04 93 67 18 25

Closed Dec-Jan. 1 ste 1,750-2,900. 18 rms 800-1,550. Bkfst 80. Rms for disabled. Restaurant. Half-board 240. Air cond. Conf. Heated pool. Beach. Garage pkg.
This modern hotel with a Greek-style colonnade provides functional, well-kept rooms with views over the garden or terrace.

 Restaurant de Bacon

Bd de Bacon - 04 93 61 50 02, fax 04 93 61 65 19
Closed Mon (exc dinner Jul-Aug), Nov-Jan. Open until 10pm. Terrace dining. Air cond. No pets. Valet pkg.
Since the Sordello brothers shell out top dollar (or franc...whatever) for their locally caught seafood, patrons, too, pay a pretty penny (centime?) for the ultrafresh sea bass, sea bream, and other Mediterranean fish offered here. These prize specimens will be brought to your table for you to inspect, then prepared as you wish: grilled, steamed, baked en papillote... We're fond of the tiny red mullet cooked whole and ungutted, and of the justly celebrated bouillabaisse. To drink, why not uncork a cool bottle of white Cassis or Bandol wine? Reservations necessary. C 500-600. M 250, 400.

COLLE-SUR-LOUP (LA)   06480
Paris 943 - Nice 18 - St-Paul-de-Vence 3   Alpes-Mar.

 Le Diamant Rose

Route de St-Paul - 04 93 32 82 20, fax 04 93 32 69 98
Open daily until 10pm (11pm in summer). Terrace dining. Air cond. Pool. Valet pkg.
Antoine Versini transformed a sumptuous villa at the foot of Saint-Paul-de-Vence into a restaurant with a princely dining room and a luxurious panoramic terrace. Chef Daniel Ettlinger takes immense pains with his classic cuisine—just look at the clever layers of vegetables and cheeses that make up his millefeuille starter; or the perfect slices of roast baby veal paired with new fava beans in a refreshing main-course salad; or the beautifully crafted thin tart topped with caramelized pears. All the best Provençal wines are represented in the costly cellar. C 250-600.

 Domaine du Diamant Rose

(See restaurant above)
Open year-round. 15 stes 960-2,500. Bkfst 120. Rm for disabled. Half-board 1,460-3,000 (oblig in seas). Rm ser. Air cond. Pool. Valet pkg.
The accommodations are housed in a cluster of independent Provençal-style villas, all impeccably equipped and luxuriously decorated in the best of taste. The peace and quiet of a golden pond. Gorgeous swimming pool.

 La Strega

1260, route de Cagnes - 04 93 22 62 37
Closed Sun dinner off-seas, Mon, Tue lunch in summer, Jan-Feb. Open until 9:30pm (10pm in summer). Garden dining. Pkg.

Summer is the best time to savor Gilbert Stella's cooking, served on an enchanting garden terrace. He gives a contemporary touch to such satisfying dishes as a mellow warm duck tourte with red-wine jus or salmon with a fresh-tasting vegetable compote. Short but pertinent wine list; warm-hearted welcome from Madame Stella. M 100 (lunch, exc Sun), 150.

CROIX-VALMER (LA)	83420
Paris 879 - Toulon 62 - St-Tropez 12 - Grimaud 12	Var

La Brigantine

Plage de Gigaro - 04 94 79 67 16 (R)
04 94 79 60 35 (H), fax 04 94 54 37 05
Dinner only. Closed beg Oct-beg May. Open until 10pm (10:30pm in summer). Garden dining. Pkg.
Enjoy a lazy, holiday atmosphere on this shady seaside patio, with its restful view of beach umbrellas and Cavalaire Bay. The single set menu (which can be modified in a variety of ways, for less money) offers vivacious dishes made from ultrafresh ingredients. C 250. M 260.

Hôtel de Gigaro

(See restaurant above)
Closed end Sep-mid Apr. 38 rms 550-1,070. Bkfst 70. Half-board 560-840. Conf. Pool. Tennis. Pkg.
Airy, comfortable rooms (some can accommodate two parents and two children) in a pleasant hotel that sits in verdant grounds. The leisure center includes both a bar and a reading room. Just 150 yards away is a private beach.

Château de Valmer

Route de Gigaro - 04 94 79 60 10, fax 04 94 54 22 68
Closed Nov-Mar. 2 stes 1,670-1,855. 41 rms 750-1,325. Bkfst 85. Rms for disabled. Restaurant. Half-board 675-965. Air cond. Conf. Pool. Beach. Tennis. Garage pkg.
For a quiet stay even at the height of the season, choose this old Provençal farmhouse situated at the far end of a splendid palm grove, on a working wine-growing concern. Direct access to the beach.

Souleias

Plage de Gigaro - 04 94 79 61 91, fax 04 94 54 36 23
Closed mid Oct-end Mar. Open until 9:30pm. Garden dining. Heated pool. Tennis. No pets. Garage pkg.
What a gorgeous place this is: a splendid *mas* clinging to a remote hillside, set amid flowers and olive trees. And what a success story for the owner, a former chemical engineer who in record time turned Souleias into one of the most sought-after hotels on the Var coast. On the stunning terrace which juts out over the Gigaro beach, chef Franck Brunel is sharpening his already good quality knife. A la carte makes the pocket burn, but the 240 F menu lets you explore his talent full of the flavors of the South of France. We savored the beautifully presented pan-fried tuna and bell pepper gazpacho pre-appetizers, liked less the overcooked (barely!) assortment of

fish in tasty bouillon, but found the cod with green aïoli flawless. The waiters and waitresses were rather omnipresent; we prefer to hold our own handkerchief when we sneeze... Cellar rich in variety, with some excellent Côtes-de-Provence between 100 and 290 F, but light on the half-bottles in our opinion. C 400-550. M 240, 350.

Souleias

(See restaurant above)
Closed mid Oct-end Mar. 7 stes 1,370-2,300. 39 rms 400-1,470. Bkfst 72. Half-board 360. Air cond. Conf. Heated pool. Tennis. Garage pkg.
Large, sunny, amazingly comfortable rooms are housed in little cottages nestled in foliage and flowers, with heavenly views of the sea and coastline. The hotel's catamaran takes guests to the Iles d'Or for outings and picnics.

CROS-DE-CAGNES	06800
Paris 938 - Nice 24 - Antibes 4	Alpes-Mar.

La Bourride

Port de Cros-de-Cagnes
04 93 31 07 75, fax 04 93 31 07 75
Closed Wed, Feb school hols. Open until 8:30pm. Garden dining. Air cond. Pkg.
A dreamy summer restaurant with a pine-shaded patio opposite the port is a perfect setting for a leisurely lunch or dinner. Hervé Kobzi's bracing seafood repertoire is absolutely in tune with the scenery: tender sautéed squid à la provençale, excellent lobster in warm vinaigrette, and lusty versions of the region's traditional seafood soups, bourride and bouillabaisse. The 195 F prix-fixe menu a good buy. Friendly welcome and efficient service. C 300-350. M 150-295, 80 (children).

CUERS	83390
Paris 856 - Toulon 22 - Hyères 25	Var

Le Lingousto

Route de Pierrefeu
04 94 28 69 10, fax 04 94 48 63 79
Closed Sun dinner & Mon (exc Jun-Sep), Jan-Feb. Open until 9:30pm. Priv rm 25. Terrace dining. Garage pkg.
Alain Ryon's light, expertly wrought cooking is worth a trip to the hill country behind Toulon, to this imposing *bastide* surrounded by vineyards. Ryon wins full marks for his crackling crisp langoustine tempura, impeccably cooked lamb tenderloin with a sprightly wild-thyme jus and garlicky potatoes, and a dessert assortment that features no fewer than five scrumptious sweets. The intelligently composed cellar needs some half-bottles (only one was available when last we checked). C 320. M 180 (weekdays), 230-380, 80 (children).

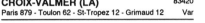
Prices for rooms and suites *are per room, not per person. Half-board prices, however, are per person.*

EZE 06360
Paris 959 - Nice 11 - Menton 18 - Monaco 7 Alpes-Mar.

 Auberge du Troubadour

Rue du Brec - 04 93 41 19 03
Closed Sun, Mon lunch, Feb school hols, 1 wk beg Jul,
Nov 25-Dec 15. Open until 9:30pm.
So winsome an inn is naturally clogged with
tourists in the high season, but the crush has no
adverse effects on the kitchen. Gérard Vuille is
an accomplished *saucier* who enhances his classic cooking with wonderfully well wrought jus,
essences, and emulsions. Costly cellar, with a
few affordable wines from the region. C 250-320.
M 118 (lunch), 165, 245.

 Château de la Chèvre d'Or

Moyenne-Corniche, rue du Barri
04 92 10 66 66, fax 04 93 41 06 72
Closed Wed off-seas, Dec-Feb. Open until 10:30pm.
Terrace dining. Air cond. Pool. Tennis. Valet pkg.
Nature has provided a breathtaking panorama
for this eyrie perched more than 1,300 feet above
the sea, and chef Élie Mazot furnishes additional
pleasures, sure to beguile the most jaded palate.
Join the (very) rich and famous who dine here on
his classic pan-roasted langoustines with
ratatouille, cod with crisp potatoes, spring
onions, and truffles, or Challans duck breast in a
vigorous jus with lentils, puréed artichokes, and
wee stuffed cabbage leaves. Alluring desserts,
and an exciting, expensive cellar with a few bargain bottles from Provence. C 500-600. M 250
(lunch, exc Sun), 360 (lunch), 560.

 Château de la Chèvre d'Or 🌲🍴

(See restaurant above)
Closed Dec-Feb. 8 stes 2,600-4,000. 21 rms 1,300-
2,600. Bkfst 110-180. Rm ser. Air cond. Conf. Pool.
Tennis. Valet pkg.
The jet set makes up the clientele of this neo-
Gothic refuge (which might be more aptly
named "the Golden Calf"), built in the 1920s. The
hotel is made up of several delightful houses that
cling to the cliff; inside are personalized rooms
and luxurious fittings. Superb swimming pools,
simple meals at the Café du Jardin, and a private
parking lot. Relais et Châteaux.

 Château Eza

04 93 41 12 24, fax 04 93 41 16 64
Closed Nov-Mar. Open until 10pm. Priv rm 22.
Terrace dining. Valet pkg.
The site is as spectacular as ever, the building
(where William of Sweden once dwelled) has
lost none of its seductive charm. The arrival of a
new chef, Thierry Bagnis, who formerly worked
under Le Stanc, has helped this restaurant make
a turnaround since last year. True South-of-
France cuisine, light with flavors abound, so we

salute the young chef from Nice by giving back
the second toque oh so dear. Some other good
news: the prices are on the way down from their
throne on high. C 550. M 250 (lunch, wine incl),
350 & 490 (dinner).

 Château Eza

(See restaurant above)
Closed Nov-Mar. 5 stes 2,250-3,500. 5 rms 1,600-
3,000. Bkfst incl. Air cond. Valet pkg.
This cluster of medieval dwellings was made
into a "château" by Prince William of Sweden.
The luxurious rooms were recently renovated,
and they afford mind-boggling views of the sea.
Prices are as lofty as the site.

 Les Terrasses d'Eze

Route de La Turbie
04 93 41 24 64, fax 04 93 41 13 25
Open year-round. 6 stes 1,000-2,800. 75 rms 550-
950. Bkfst 65. Rms for disabled. Restaurant. Half-
board 790-1,090. Rm ser. Air cond. Pool. Tennis.
Valet pkg.
A pretty, contemporary residence built in to
the mountainside and facing out to sea. Large,
sunny rooms with pretty decoration. Newly
done, luxurious bathrooms. Extremely attentive
staff.

FRÉJUS 83600
Paris 890 - Cannes 40 - Ste-Maxime 21 - Hyères 76 Var

Aréna

139, rue du Général-de-Gaulle
04 94 17 09 40, fax 04 94 52 01 52
Closed Sat lunch, Mon lunch. Open until 10:30pm.
Priv rm 25. Garden dining. Air cond. Pool.
Hubert Bluntzer and Catherine Bouchot welcome you into their sunny establishment with
open arms, and cheerfully serve you the light,
delicious dishes prepared by Bruno Masselin:
ginger-spiced scampi, sea bass croustillant accented with star anise, braised sweetbreads in a
garlic cream sauce. In summer, you can dine in
a charming garden abloom with flowers. Short
but interesting list of Provençal wines. C 300-350.
M 120, 165, 195, 215, 60 (children).

 Aréna

(See restaurant above)
Open year-round. 1 ste 600-1,200. 22 rms 300-600.
Bkfst 45. Rms for disabled. Half-board 300-450.
Rm ser. Air cond. Conf. Pool. No pets. Garage pkg.
What used to be a bank in the center of the old
town is now a tastefully restored hotel just five
minutes from the beaches. The rooms are not all
large, but they are cozy and beautifully outfitted,
soundproofed and provided with attractive
bathrooms. Good value; delightful service.
Breakfast is served in a garden by the pool.

Port Royal

In Port-Fréjus - 04 94 53 09 11, fax 04 94 53 75 24
*Closed Wed, mid Jan-mid Feb. Open until 9:30pm
(10:30pm in summer). Priv rm 12. Terrace dining.*
  Fréjus's brand-new yacht port seems to want
to remain a secret; there are no signs directing
you there! But if you manage to find it, your
reward is this friendly restaurant offering the
flavorful, generous cooking of Marcel
Chavanon. His repertoire is traditional,
prepared with sincerity: try the John Dory with
eggplant caviar or sweetbreads paired with
oyster mushrooms in a luscious sauce. Good
cellar. C 300-350. M 120-195.

12/20 Les Potiers

135, rue des Potiers - 04 94 51 33 74
Open daily until 10pm. Air cond.
  It's worth the trek through the charmless old
town to fetch up in this pretty dining room. New
owners Jeanne and Hubert Guillard are moving
in the right direction: original, unpretentious
cooking using market-fresh products from
Provence. We liked the pumpkin soup with
mussels and the burbot with bell pepper sauce.
Admirable 165 F prix-fixe menu. Short but well-
balanced wine list. C 220-320. M 165.

GASSIN	83580
Paris 877 - Le Lavandou 33 - St-Tropez 8	Var

 La Verdoyante

866, VC de Coste-Brigade
04 94 56 16 23, fax 04 94 56 43 10
*Closed Wed off-seas, Oct-Mar. Open until 9:30pm
(10pm in summer). Garden dining. Pkg.*
  Soft vineyard breezes and the gentle pace of
another era stir this exquisite terrace where
yesterday, today, and—we are certain—tomor-
row patrons feed on an unvarying menu of mussels and spinach au gratin, Provençal beef stew,
garlicky sautéed rabbit, iced nougat, and other
perennial favorites. Wash them down with a
Château de Minuty, made right nearby. C 215.
M 135, 180.

GIENS	83400
Paris 875 - Toulon 27 - Hyères 12 - Carqueiranne 13	Var

12/20 L'Eau Salée ✪

Port Niel - 04 94 58 92 33
*Closed Sun dinner, Mon, mid Jan-mid Feb. Open
until 10pm. Terrace dining. Pkg.*
  Enjoy luminously fresh seafood and other
treats like scallop stew with baby vegetables or
a textbook rendition of pieds et paquets (lamb's
tripe and trotters), followed by homey desserts,
all served on the most wonderful terrace imaginable, overlooking the beach and the harbor.
C 250-350. M 95 (lunch, exc Sun), 120, 180.

 Le Provençal

Pl. St-Pierre - 04 94 58 20 09, fax 04 94 58 95 44
*Closed Nov-Apr 25. 45 rms 270-650. Bkfst 65. Res-
taurant. Half-board 395-600. Pool. Tennis. Pkg.*
At the tip of the peninsula you'll find this hotel
with simple rooms and sumptuous sea views
(that same sea water, by the way, feeds the swimming pool).

GOLFE-JUAN	06350
Paris 929 - Nice 27 - Cannes 6 - Antibes 5	Alpes-Mar.

12/20 Le Bistrot du Port

53, bd des Frères-Roustan - 04 93 63 70 64
*Closed Mon, Jan. Open until 9:30pm. Terrace
dining. Air cond. No pets.*
  The attractions here are a series of small
glassed-in rooms overlooking the port, an enjoyable summer terrace, and simple cuisine based
on fresh seafood and fine meats. Decent cellar. C
200. M 80 & 100 (lunch, exc Sun), 125, 170.

GRASSE	06130
Paris 938 - Nice 39 - Draguignan 56	Alpes-Mar.

11/20 Pierre Baltus

15, rue de la Fontette - 04 93 36 32 90
*Closed Mon, mid Feb-mid Mar, Jul 1-13. Open until
10pm. Terrace dining. No cards.*
  The cozy dining room can hold only fourteen
guests—the rest of the space is given over to a
large bar and an upright piano. Traditional but
passé cuisine full of heavy sauces, but good-
priced set meals. Quite reasonable prices on
wines. Pleasant, efficient service. C 220-350. M
95, 130, 150, 65 (children).

 **La Bastide
Saint-Antoine** ✪

48, av. Henri-Dunant
04 93 09 16 48, fax 04 93 42 03 42
*Open daily until 10pm. Terrace dining. Air cond.
Pool. Valet pkg.*
  Although his fifteen years at the Gray d'Albion
hotel in Cannes were crowned by enviable success and endless accolades, it was inevitable that
Jacques Chibois would one day want to open a
place of his own. He bided his time until he
found the perfect site: an eighteenth-century
homestead set amid century-old olive trees, in
surroundings that sum up the sweet, unspoiled
charms of Provence. Chibois is a virtuoso who
orchestrates the region's vivacious tastes and
aromas to create endlessly fascinating flavor harmonies. Consider these compositions: a lively
piccata of tuna with olives and anchovies in a
vinaigrette based on roasted bell peppers; or
John Dory with zucchini in a delicate leek jus; or
squab in a fresh fondue of Southern vegetables.
More elaborate but just as enticing are a salad of
squid with asparagus and anise-flavored olives,
and local sea bass in a fragrant reduction of
onion and fennel. For dessert, don't miss the
strawberries improbably (but delectably!) combined with basil, rose petals, and black olives.
Wonderful Provençal cellar. C 450-600. M 210
(weekday & Sat lunch), 380 (dinner), 550.

Hôtel du Patti

Pl. du Patti - 04 93 36 01 00, fax 04 93 36 36 40
Open year-round. 50 rms 330-420. Bkfst 40. Rms for disabled. Restaurant. Half-board 420. Rm ser. Air cond. Conf. Garage pkg.
Marvelously situated in the heart of the old town, this charmless modern hotel houses small, quiet rooms with individual heating and good bathrooms. There's an adorable terrace on the little square out front.

See also: **Mougins**

GRIMAUD	83310
Paris 857 - Hyères 45 - Saint-Tropez 10	Var

 ## Athénopolis

Quartier Mouretti - 04 94 43 24 24, fax 04 94 43 37 05
Closed Nov-Easter. 11 rms 490-660. Bkfst 48. Rms for disabled. Half-board 380-470. Rm ser. Conf. Pool. Tennis. Pkg.
On the outskirts of town but well worth the detour. Fine, large rooms, well equipped and modern. Charming, heartfelt welcome. The sea is five minutes away by car.

 ## La Boulangerie 🌲🌶️

Route de Collobrières
04 94 43 23 16, fax 04 94 43 38 27
Closed Oct 10-Easter. 1 ste 1,300-1,420. 10 rms 580-820. Bkfst 60. Rms for disabled. Rm ser. Air cond. Conf. Pool. Tennis. Pkg.
An attractive and cozy hotel with a capital view of the Massif des Maures. Video library. In fine weather, lunch is served to guests (many are return visitors) around the superb swimming pool.

 ## La Bretonnière

Pl. des Pénitents - 04 94 43 25 26
Closed Sun dinner & Mon off-seas. Open until 10:30pm (midnight in summer). Air cond.
A new restaurant overflowing with old Provence-style furniture and paintings and offering a magnificent view of the Grimaud vineyards. Marcel Mannoy's inventive cuisine is based on market-fresh ingredients with well-mastered cooking times that bring out a maximum of the flavors. The wine list could use a little "development"... **C** 250. **M** 190 & 390 (lunch), 155 (dinner), 85 (children).

 ## Le Coteau Fleuri

Pl. des Pénitents - 04 94 43 20 17, fax 04 94 43 33 42
Closed Tue (exc Jul-Aug), Jan 6-31, Dec 1-18. Open until 9:30pm (10:30pm in summer). Terrace dining. No pets. HOTEL: 14 rms 275-550. Bkfst 45. Half-board 220. Conf. Pkg.
Flowers, flowers everywhere engulf this wonderful villa next to the Penitents' Chapel. From the terrace you'll discover a mind-blowing view of the Massif des Maures and the Provençal hill country. Chef Jean-Claude Paillard favors local ingredients for his always flavorful cook-ing, which he's finally learned to simplify to take better advantage of the natural flavors. **C** 350-400. **M** 150 (lunch), 190, 215 (Sun), 95 (children).

 ## Les Santons

Route Nationale - 04 94 43 21 02, fax 04 94 43 24 92
Closed Wed, Jan 2-Mar 15, Nov 2-Dec 23. Open until 10:30pm. Priv rm 50. Air cond. Pkg.
Santons—those terracotta figurines which adorn the Christmas crèche—fill this Provençal dining room, the fief of gentle giant Claude Girard. Here's a chef who goes in for classic cuisine with lots of Mediterranean flavor, characterized by prime ingredients, rigorous technique, and delicate sauces. You'll love his artichokes barigoule, saddle of Sisteron lamb with thyme blossoms, sea bass roasted with fennel, bourride (garlicky fish soup), and Bresse chicken sauce velours. Girard is a winemaker himself, so trust his choices when it comes to picking a winning bottle. **C** 400-560. **M** 215 (lunch, wine incl), 260, 420, 110 (children).

HYÈRES	83400
Paris 866 - Fréjus 76 - Toulon 18	Var

 ## La Colombe

La Bayorre - 04 94 65 02 15
Closed Sat lunch, Sun dinner & Mon off-seas. Open until 9:45pm. Air cond.
Youthful and bursting with energy, chef Pascal Bonamy purchases market-fresh ingredients, then turns them into exciting dishes with a distinctive Provençal flavor. The regularly revamped menu features the likes of scallops in truffle vinaigrette and red mullet in crisp phyllo pastry, accented with a creamy sea-urchin sauce. Don't overlook the remarkable 135 F set meal (salmon tartare, rack of lamb in an herbal crust, and almond-coffee malakoff with gingerbread ice cream). Seductive regional cellar; charming welcome from Nadège Bonamy. **C** 250. **M** 135.

 ## Les Jardins de Bacchus

32, av. Gambetta - 04 94 65 77 63
Closed Sun dinner, 2 wks in Jun. Open until 10pm (10:30pm in summer). Terrace dining. Air cond.
Bacchus beams benevolently down from the huge mural that adorns the dining room, and he inspires the wine list (rich in local treasures) that Claire Santioni has put together. Jean-Claude Santioni's bracing menu takes its cue from the culinary traditions of the Rhône and the Mediterranean. Though the food is sometimes too complicated, his rock-solid technique saves the day. **C** 270-380. **M** 210 (weekdays, wine incl), 300 (dinner), 145-190, 60 (children).

*This **symbol** stands for "Les Lauriers du Terroir", an award given to chefs who prepare traditional or regional recipes.*

ISSAMBRES (LES) 83380
Paris 884 - Toulon 32 - Hyères 15   Var

 Chante-Mer

Village provençal - 04 94 96 93 23
*Closed Sun dinner & Mon (exc in summer). Open
until 9pm. Air cond. Terrace dining.*
The name tells all. Mario Battaglia has a love
affair with the sea and your tastebuds will prove
it to you. His sea perch, sea bream and bass with
fennel are faultless. His steamed salmon simply
makes you want to stay and savor more. Enjoyable lemon-tree terrace. Not a large selection of
wines, but all the sought-after "gems" of
Provence are available. C 300. M 130, 210.

 Villa Saint-Elme

N 98, at L'Arpillon
04 94 49 52 52, fax 04 94 49 63 18
*Open until 9:30pm (10:30pm in seas). Terrace
dining. Air cond. HOTEL: 16 rms 850-3,100. Bkfst
incl. Half-board 225. Pool. Beach. Sauna. Garage
pkg.*
This white villa from the 1930s, standing between the superhighway and the sea, offers a
splendid view of the Golfe de Saint-Tropez
through large bay windows overlooking the terrace. Locals flock here (especially in the evening)
to indulge in Thibault Peyroche's enticing
seafood menu. If they're on hand, try his gambas
in gazpacho or tuna with a vegetable marmalade. After imbibing a bottle of good
Provençal wine, you might want to book one of
the three lovely air conditioned suites (the rooms
in the more modest annex are a bit noisy). C 350.
M 230, 350.

JUAN-LES-PINS 06160
Paris 920 - Nice 22 - Cannes 9   Alpes-Mar.

 Ambassadeur

50-52, chemin des Sables
04 93 67 82 15, fax 04 93 67 79 85
*Open year-round. 6 stes 1,900-2,000. 235 rms 750-
1,200. Bkfst 95. Rms for disabled. Restaurant. Half-
board 545-715. Air cond. Conf. Pool. Beach. Valet
pkg.*
Not far from the pine grove you'll find this
luxurious modern hotel, where cozily decorated
rooms boast balconies and the very best
bathrooms. All the usual amenities are on hand,
as well as some delightful extras. Zealous,
professional service.

 Belles Rives

Bd du Littoral - 04 93 61 02 79, fax 04 93 67 43 51
*Closed Oct 5-Mar. Open until 10:30pm. Garden
dining. Air cond. Beach. No pets. Valet pkg.*
Formerly a holiday villa occupied by the likes
of Scott and Zelda Fitzgerald, for the last 60 years
Belles Rives has been a family-run luxury hotel,
with a guest register signed by the Windsors,
Édith Piaf, Josephine Baker, Miles Davis, and
loads of other celebrities. A breath of new life

with Bordeaux native Pascal Silman, who recently arrived in the kitchen after working with the
likes of Jacques Maximin and others from whom
he picked up that South-of-France influence.
He's a real revelation offering an exact, modern
cooking with dishes such as the exquisite
vegetable fricassée or the broiled John Dory with
baby beans served with a rich meat jus. Conventional wine selection. Exquisite Art Deco dining
room with views of the sea. C 300-450. M 190
(lunch), 290 & 360 (dinner), 95 (children).

 Belles Rives

(See restaurant above)
*Closed Oct 10-Mar. 4 stes 1,680-4,300. 41 rms 700-
2,450. Bkfst 110-150. Half-board 390 (oblig in
seas). Air cond. Conf. Beach. Valet pkg.*
With superb views over the bay, these 1930s–
style rooms are all different and extra comfortable (not to mention expensive), with lovely
marble bathrooms. Some rooms have views of
the sea. Business services available, as well as a
private beach and landing dock.

 Bijou Plage

Bd Charles-Guillaumont
04 93 61 39 07, fax 04 93 67 81 78
*Open daily until 9:30pm (midnight in summer).
Terrace dining. Air cond. Beach. Valet pkg.*
Here's a rarity: a real "bijou" of a Riviera beach
restaurant, open year round to boot. The
Japanese chef deftly selects and prepares utterly
fresh fish for a gilt-edged clientele: salmon and
asparagus terrine, grouper au pistou, and tarragon-scented fricassée of monkfish and scampi
with smoky bacon are excellent choices. Appealing Provençal cellar. If you just want a quick bite,
head for the beachside terrace. C 350. M 100
(weekday lunch), 165, 280, 50 (children).

 Garden Beach Hotel

La Pinède, 15-17, bd Baudoin
04 92 93 57 57, fax 04 92 93 57 56
*Open year-round. 16 stes 1,000-3,300. 159 rms 600-
1,800. Bkfst 105. Rms for disabled. Restaurant.
Half-board 475-855. Rm ser. Air cond. Conf.
Beach. Valet pkg.*
Housed in a modernist cube constructed on the
site of the former casino, this luxurious hotel
offers every comfort and service. The rather chilly interior of red and black marble and granite is
warmed by photos of jazz greats who have
graced the local festival, and by the great sea
views from the rooms. Impeccable service.
Lunch buffet and dinner grill service in summer
on the lovely private beach.

 Hélios

3, av. du Docteur-Dautheville
04 93 61 55 25, fax 04 93 61 58 78
*Closed Nov-Mar. 5 stes 1,600-3,000. 60 rms 500-
1,400. Bkfst 60-90. Rms for disabled. Restaurant.*

Half-board 560-860. Rm ser. Air cond. Beach. Valet pkg.

Another luxurious hotel, this one with its own private beach (meals are served by the water). Some of the lovely, large, modern rooms have splendid balconies, while others are smaller with plain-vanilla furniture and only the merest sliver of a sea view. Piano bar.

 ## Les Mimosas

Rue Pauline - 04 93 61 04 16, fax 04 92 93 06 46
Closed Oct-mid Apr. 34 rms 470-650. Bkfst 50. Pool. No pets. Pkg.

An agreeable white house with a garden in a residential area 500 yards from the sea. The bright rooms all have balconies and have just been refurbished. Huge swimming pool.

 ## Pré Catelan

22, av. des Lauriers (corner av. des Palmiers)
04 93 61 05 11, fax 04 93 67 83 11
Open year-round. 18 rms 250-500. Bkfst 40. Restaurant. Half-board 400-450. Air cond. Conf. Pkg.

A little house in a quiet, palm-shaded garden 200 yards from the sea. Good, traditional rooms.

 ## La Terrasse

La Pinède, av. Georges-Gallice
04 93 61 20 37 (R), 04 93 61 08 70 (H),
fax 04 93 61 76 60
Closed Tue (exc in summer), Nov-Easter. Open until 10pm (10:30pm in summer). Garden dining. Heated pool. Beach. Valet pkg.

Christian Morisset shuns the limelight: he prefers to stick close to his stoves, working away on a dazzling *carte*. Glistening Mediterranean fish, perfumed Provençal vegetables and herbs, and prime foodstuffs from all over the map are transformed into triple-toque dishes like green Pertuis asparagus combined with Normandy scallops and Breton langoustines in a briny shellfish jus; roast breast and confit of Challans duckling with baby spinach and mango in a sweet-sour jus; and saddle of Pauillac lamb cooked to ineffable juiciness in a mantle of clay, and presented with delicate zucchini blossoms. This is the work of a perfectionist: disciplined, precise cooking that defines and enhances each nuance of flavor. Cooking of this caliber doesn't come cheap, of course, but there's always the 270 F lunch, which is as carefully crafted as the rest. Pascal Paulze supervises the captivating cellar (he introduced us to a fabulous pure Syrah from the Domaine Gavoty). C 600-800. M 270 (lunch), 410-630.

 ## Juana

(See restaurant above)
Closed Nov-Easter. 5 stes 1,600-3,500. 45 rms 650-2,050. Bkfst 95-160. Rms for disabled. Half-board 355-495. Rm ser. Air cond. Conf. Heated pool. Beach. Valet pkg.

On the edge of the lovely pine grove that marks the border between Juan-the-chic and Juan-the-crass, this small luxury hotel with a splendid pavillon-swimming pool attracts a cosmopolitan clientele. Beautiful, ultracomfortable rooms; inviting cocktail bar.

LAVANDOU (LE)   83980
Paris 887 - Toulon 41 - St-Tropez 38 - Cannes 104   Var

 ## L'Algue Bleue

62, av. du Général-de-Gaulle
04 94 71 05 96, fax 04 94 71 20 12
Closed Wed off-seas. Open until 10pm. Air cond. Garden dining. Pool. Pkg.

The view is positively appetizing: the dining room's arched windows frame a dreamy perspective of the port and the Hyères Islands beyond. New chef Bernard Roger takes his profession seriously, and his updated, Mediterranean-style food is full of his heart and soul. The set meals are the best buy, letting you partake of red mullet confit with tapenade, a thick paste made from capers, anchovies, ripe olives, olive oil and lemon juice; burbot steak with truffles; or white fish cooked in bouillabaisse. Well-rounded wine list with lots of local wines. C 280-380. M 200-360, 100 (children).

 ## Auberge de la Calanque

(See restaurant above)
Closed Nov 11-Dec 15, Jan 2-Feb 15. 2 stes 950-1,200. 35 rms 500-750. Bkfst 60-100. Half-board 425-780. Rm ser. Air cond. Conf. Pool. Pkg.

This handsome, post-war building, set before the moorings, is fully modernized. The guest rooms are decorated in good taste and all have sea views. Boat trips, diving, hikes, and tuna fishing can be arranged.

 ## Belle Vue

In Saint-Clair, bd du Four-des-Maures
04 94 71 01 06, fax 04 94 71 64 72
Closed Nov-Easter. 19 rms 290-600. Bkfst 55. Restaurant. Half-board 350-600 (oblig in seas). Conf. No pets. Pkg. No cards.

Overlooking the sea and coast, this quiet, charming hotel offers rustic but comfortable rooms. You'll love the beautiful flower garden and the genial reception.

 ## Le Club

Plage de Cavalière - 04 94 05 80 14, fax 04 94 05 73 16
Closed Oct-May 10. Open until 10pm. Terrace dining. Air cond. Heated pool. Beach. Tennis. Valet pkg.

Le Club was remodeled from stem to stern last year, and the improvements have given new vigor to Marc Dach's Mediterranean cuisine. This is truly one of the most exquisite spots in all the Riviera (with the exception of the grandest of grand hotels, which are not in the same category, after all). You'll understand why both the hotel and restaurant are full all summer long... But the location is just one reason; Marc Dach's cooking is certainly another. The menu is abound with tasty morsels: Vichyssoise with summer truffles and John Dory with olives from Nice and Parma ham, and pappardelle pasta tossed with pistou and dried tomatoes. Are you hungry yet? The desserts are particularly well crafted and obviously hold a place of importance for this chef. The second toque we are adding is well-earned, but some days the ingredients were fresher than others; this could weaken the threads of the toque in the future if consistency of quality is not attended to. Adorable welcome. **C** 380. **M** 350-440, 100 (children).

 ### Le Club 🎄🍴

(See restaurant above)
Closed Oct-May 10. 3 stes 1,700-2,750. 39 rms 1,050-2,400. Bkfst incl. Rms for disabled. Half-board 1,200-2,550 (oblig in seas). Air cond. Conf. Heated pool. Beach. Tennis. Valet pkg.
One of the rare luxury hotels on the coast with a private sandy beach. All of the rooms are freshly renovated in beautiful Provence style, and boast terraces where breakfast is served. Wonderful location, between Cap Bénat and the rocky spur of Cap Nègre.

 ### Les Roches 🎄🍴

In Aiguebelle, 1, av. des Trois-Dauphins
04 94 71 05 07, fax 04 94 71 08 40
Closed Jan-Feb. 8 stes 2,600-3,270. 45 rms 1,500-2,600. Restaurant. Half-board 375 (oblig in seas). Air cond. Conf. Pool. Valet pkg.
Les Roches is unquestionably one of the most refined recent constructions on this stretch of coast. The sunny, antique-filled rooms, with terraces overlooking the sea, are furnished with taste, the bathrooms are clad with marble and Salerno tiles. Shady footpaths wind through a garden planted with cactus and rare trees, leading to the private beach and freshwater swimming pool. Tennis and boating facilities are close at hand, and there's a golf course nearby. Relais et Châteaux.

 ### Les Tamaris

"Chez Raymond," plage de Saint-Clair
04 94 71 07 22, fax 04 94 71 88 64
Closed mid Nov-mid Dec, mid Jan-beg Feb. Open until 10:30pm. Air cond. Terrace dining. Pkg.
Lounge a while under the rose laurels on the terrace just off the beach, fall into one of those comfortable armchairs. The locals call it "Raymond's place," how suitable. Unpretentious fare cooked with care by a chef who did his "internship" in the best of the Riviera hotels. Wide selection, from broiled lobster or sardine fritters, to spaghetti with meat sauce or fried fish mix. Good-priced Côte-de-Provence wines for around 100 F. **C** 250-400.

See also: Bormes-les-Mimosas, Porquerolles (Ile de), Port-Cros (Ile de)

 ## La Brise Marine 🎄🍴

Pl. du Village - 04 94 05 91 15, fax 04 94 05 93 21
Closed Nov-Apr 15. 20 rms 295-460. Bkfst 35. Restaurant. Half-board 475-890 (oblig in seas). Conf. Pool.
Situated at the high point of the island, overlooking the sea, the Brise boasts handsome, comfortable, well-equipped rooms set round a delightful, flower-filled patio. Superb swimming pool and sun-terrace.

 ## Hôtel Gaétan

04 94 05 91 78, fax 04 94 36 77 17
Closed mid Nov-Mar. 14 rms 220-260. Restaurant. Half-board 290-310 (oblig in seas). Conf.
Set in a pleasant garden, the Gaétan's rooms are very simple (all have showers, not all have toilets) and are quite well kept. Solarium, bar.

 ## Chez Bruno 🕄

Route de Vidauban
04 94 73 92 19, fax 04 94 73 78 11
Closed Sun dinner & Mon. Open until 10pm. Garden dining. Pkg.
The phrase *bon vivant* seems to have been coined just for Bruno Clément, a generous, sensual chef with a passion for truffles. Now mind, these are not the Périgord variety, but the summer truffles found in the earth of the Haut-Var. Bruno's single menu, priced at 270 F, is constantly revamped, but it offers the likes of a whole truffle enveloped in puff pastry, crayfish poached in Champagne with truffled scrambled eggs, and a fudgy chocolate cake with almond-milk ice cream. We still recall the haunting flavors of Bruno's grilled truffle toasts and an unforgettable sorbet spiked with truffled brandy! The wine list features the pride of Provence's vineyards, chosen with care by Bruno himself. He just added three rooms if you need a nap after all that! **M** 270, 135 (children, free under 11).

 ## Acadia

681, av. de la Mer - 04 93 49 28 23, fax 04 92 97 55 54
Closed Nov 19-Dec 25. 6 stes 450-820. 29 rms 250-440. Bkfst 35. Rms for disabled. Heated pool. Tennis. No pets.
This pleasant villa, recently built on the banks of the Siagne, was built with your vacation in mind. Sunny, comfortable rooms, a quiet garden, and good sports facilities. Package deals include hotel and green fees on the numerous golf courses in the area.

Domaine d'Olival

778, av. de la Mer - 04 93 49 31 00, fax 04 92 97 69 28
Closed Nov-mid Jan. 11 stes 680-1,780. 7 rms 435-925. Bkfst 58. Air cond. Conf. Tennis. Pkg.
For the past fourteen years the hotel's blooming garden has won first prize in the *Jardins Fleuris* competition. The accommodations are tastefully decorated, with kitchen facilities and lots of amenities. Boating excursions can be arranged.

 ## L'Oasis

La Napoule - Rue Jean-Honoré-Carle
04 93 49 95 52, fax 04 93 49 64 13
Closed Sun dinner & Mon off-seas. Open until 10pm. Garden dining. Air cond. Valet pkg.
Stéphane Raimbault took time to give his own twist to Outhier's signature mix of Mediterranean and Asian flavors—hot, herbal, highly perfumed dishes that require every element to be in perfect balance—but now he's found the right note. The scales tip slightly more toward the Mediterranean side, with dishes like the Danish lobster marinière (cooked in white wine and herbs) served with zucchini blossoms and pistou oil or the daurade royale (the king of breams!) risotto with clams and lemon thyme. Outhier's principles are sound; the kitchen's raw materials are as always of the highest quality. **C** 500-700. **M** 275 (lunch, wine incl), 390-620.

 ## Royal Hôtel Casino

605, av. du Général-de-Gaulle
04 92 97 70 00, fax 04 93 49 51 50
Open year-round. 30 stes 1,700-6,000. 180 rms 725-1,660. Bkfst 95. Restaurant. Half-board 1,020-1,440 (oblig). Rm ser. Air cond. Conf. Heated pool. Tennis. Valet pkg.
The contemporary rooms with sea views sport a fresh, attractive look. The hotel provides an hourly shuttle service to Cannes and excellent facilities for business meetings, but the soundproofing is not up to par on the street side. Piano bar and many deluxe services.

See also: **Cannes**

MENTON	06500
Paris 961 - Nice 31 - Cannes 63	Alpes-Mar.

 ## L'Aiglon

7, av. de la Madone
04 93 57 55 55, fax 04 93 35 92 39
Closed beg Nov-mid Dec. 3 stes 640-900. 28 rms 270-640. Bkfst 40. Restaurant. Half-board 360-530. Air cond. Heated pool. Tennis. Pkg.
A beautiful nineteenth-century mansion situated not far from the center of Menton, and just 50 yards from the sea, presents big, well-outfitted rooms and delightful gardens. The furniture, though, is oddly mismatched.

 ## Ambassadeurs

2, rue du Louvre - 04 93 28 75 75, fax 04 93 35 62 32

Closed Jan 12-Feb 7. 9 stes 1,200-1,400. 40 rms 495-930. Bkfst 70. Rms for disabled. Restaurant. Rm ser. Air cond. Valet pkg.
Modern comforts in a romantic, nineteenth-century hotel (note the beautiful wrought-iron staircase). The rooms are large and tastefully decorated, with all the amenities one might require. Piano bar; excellent welcome and service.

 ## Chambord

6, av. Boyer - 04 93 35 94 19, fax 04 93 41 30 55
Open year-round. 4 stes 500-900. 32 rms 211-522. Bkfst 35. Air cond. Tennis. Pkg.
Close to the sea, this hotel features fairly spacious, sunny rooms next to the municipal gardens and casino.

11/20 La Coquille d'Or

1, quai Bonaparte - 04 93 35 80 67
Open daily until 10:30pm. Terrace dining. Pkg.
Ignore the menu and choose one of the reliable daily specials (the ones that are scrawled on a blackboard) offered at this likable Italian restaurant. **C** 100-200. **M** 140-250.

 ## Napoléon

29, porte de France
04 93 35 89 50, fax 04 93 35 49 22
Closed Nov-Dec 18. 40 rms 350-600. Bkfst 40. Restaurant. Half-board 315-425. Conf. Pool.
You will enjoy a view either of the mountains or the sea, depending on which of these well-outfitted rooms you occupy. Panoramic restaurant.

 ## Le Royal Westminster

1510, promenade du Soleil
04 93 28 69 69, fax 04 92 10 12 30
Closed Nov. 92 rms 310-720. Bkfst 36. Rms for disabled. Restaurant. Half-board 370-610. Rm ser. Air cond. Conf. No pets. Pkg.
A turn-of-the-century luxury hotel with pleasant, bright rooms and Pompeian bathrooms! The blooming garden looks out to sea. Peace and quiet assured.

MONACO (PRINCIPALITY OF)	98000
Paris 955 - Nice 18 - Menton 9 - San-Remo 44	Monaco

 ## Abela Hôtel

Quartier Fontvieille, 23, av. des Papalins
(377) 92 05 90 00, fax (377) 92 05 91 67
Open year-round. 18 stes 1,100-1,340. 174 rms 650-1,120. Bkfst 90-110. Rms for disabled. Restaurant. Rm ser. Conf. Air cond. Pool. Garage pkg.
The very attractive and comfortable rooms overlook the Princess Grace rose garden and the harbor. Excellent service and equipment; delicious breakfasts.

Balmoral

12, av. Costa
(377) 92 16 20 20, fax (377) 92 16 38 58

Closed Nov. 9 stes 1,200-1,500. 55 rms 450-850. Bkfst 75. Restaurant. Rm ser. Air cond. Conf. No pets. Garage pkg.
This hotel, facing the marina, just turned one hundred, and unfortunately you can tell. Even though the sitting room is old-fashioned, you'll admire the tasteful period antiques.

Beach Plaza

See restaurant La Pergola

12/20 Café de Paris

Pl. du Casino
(377) 92 16 20 20, fax (377) 93 25 46 98
Open daily until 2am. Garden dining. Air cond. Garage pkg.
A wide, sun-washed terrace opens in front of this enormous brasserie decorated in Belle Époque style. Despite the crowds, the service is smiling and the cooking fresh and good. Some decent Provençal wines are also on hand. C 285-495. M 210.

Côté Jardin

Pl. du Casino
(377) 92 16 68 44, fax (377) 92 16 38 40
Closed Jul 11-Aug. Open lunch only until 3pm. No pets. Air cond. Terrace dining. Valet pkg.
For those who like to eat among the stars... But fortunately there's more reason than that to come. Delicious Provençal classics laid before you by a kitchen crew trained by none other than Alain Ducasse himself: aïoli, lamb fricasée, porchetta...the list goes on! Every day dawns a different regional speciality. C 300.

La Coupole

1, av. Princesse-Grace
(377) 92 16 65 65, fax (377) 93 50 84 85
Closed Aug. Open until 10pm. Terrace dining. Air cond. Heated pool. Beach. No pets. Valet pkg.
Prices here are as dizzying as ever, but the six-course 300 F set meal gives an excellent overview of chef Joël Garault's considerable skills. It starts with fish goujonnettes and glazed vegetables in sauce vierge, then on to foie gras, fish in a ginger-spiced broth or chicken fricassée with apples, followed by a selection of cheeses and desserts. With the cellar's lowest-priced half-bottle (a Beaujolais-Villages, 100 F) you'll have yourself a real feast in a dreamy setting with service of the highest caliber—for 400 F! C 550-700. M 300, 430.

Mirabeau

(See restaurant above)
Open year-round. 10 stes 3,000-4,000. 83 rms 1,000-2,300. Bkfst 140-195. Half-board 1,050-2,050. Air cond. Conf. Heated pool. Beach. Tennis. Valet pkg.
The well-equipped rooms have individual air conditioning and terraces overlooking the sea. Heated swimming pool. Free access to activities sponsored by the *Société des Bains de Mer*, reduced prices on tennis and golf fees. Note that the Coupole restaurant closes in July and

August, but the Café Mirabeau is open for lunch, and the Terrasse de La Coupole is open at night.

Hermitage

Square Beaumarchais
(377) 92 16 40 00, fax (377) 92 16 38 52
Open year-round. 34 stes 4,200-10,000. 197 rms 1,250-2,800. Bkfst 140-150. Restaurant. Air cond. Conf. Heated pool. Valet pkg.
A stunning Belle Époque hotel perched on a cliff and doting a dome built by none other than Eiffel of Eiffel Tower fame: stay here and you'll be just a few yards from the beach and a minute from the casino. Some of the huge rooms were just renovated, as well as the terrace of the restaurant and bar. Splendid swimming pool; seawater spa.

L'Hirondelle

2, av. de Monte-Carlo, Thermes Marins
(377) 92 16 49 47, fax (377) 92 16 49 49
Closed Sun dinner. Open until 10pm. Terrace dining. Air cond. Pool. No pets. Valet pkg.
A cuisine overflowing with new ideas and clever conception using good-quality ingredients with muse-inspired arrangement of food on plates that makes you want to eat whether you're hungry or not. Tucked into the new seawater baths with a view on the port and The Rock, this new addition to the guide lets you savor such delights as tender "heart" (i.e. the tenderest, middlemost part) of salmon fillet served on a scrumptious potato salad, the beautifully presented turbot steak cooked simply but perfectly with Jamaica pepper, or the unctuous chocolate pudding with caramelized almond meringue. Professional is the only word to describe this reception and service. C 310-398. M 260.

Hôtel Loews

Av. de Spélugues
(377) 93 50 65 00, fax (377) 93 30 01 57
Open year-round. 105 stes 2,900-7,500. 472 rms 1,200-1,850. Bkfst 110-140. Rms for disabled. Restaurant. Rm ser. Air cond. Conf. Pool. Valet pkg.
As well as its luxurious suites and bright, welcoming rooms and broad terraces, this prestigious hotel offers a host of facilities: five restaurants, bars, cabaret, casino, boutiques, swimming pool, and a fitness club with unparalleled equipment.

Le Louis XV

"Alain Ducasse," pl. du Casino
(377) 92 16 30 01 (R),
(377) 92 16 30 00 (H)
fax (377) 92 16 69 21 (R), (377) 92 16 38 50 (H)
Closed Tue, Wed (exc in seas), 2 wks in Feb, Dec. Open until 10pm. Priv rm 50. Terrace dining. Air cond. Heated pool. No pets. Valet pkg.
Now that Alain Ducasse has won the gold medal in the City of Light, what's happening with the Louis XV, his great conquest in the Riviera and his launching pad? We have been happy to state that quality is still on the menu in

Monaco. Firstly, because Alain Ducasse spends several days here each week and secondly, because he is being strongly supported by his second, the excellent Franck Cerutti. The precision-trained staff executes the brilliant, keen-flavored cuisine that Ducasse created, and is now admired and copied the world over. Here at the Louis XV, Mediterranean savors continue to dominate the menu. Since prices for each dish start at 280 F and soar up from there, Ducasse can afford the most sublime ingredients on earth. Still, his technique is what transforms and exalts them: we've never tasted anything like his thin tart topped with flash-seared herbs, greens, and baby vegetables; or the incredibly bracing seafood salad composed of shrimp from the Gulf of Genoa combined with cockles, baby squid, arugula, and red basil. The rest is equally dazzling: who could forget his half-wild duck rubbed with Indonesian pepper and cardamom then spit-roasted with apples and turnips? The food is not the whole show at the Louis XV, of course: there's the extravagant, theatrical setting, the impressively orchestrated service, the 250,000-bottle cellar. Yes, one does spend a fortune for these pleasures—but it's better than losing it at the casino across the way! C 800-1,400. M 780, 890.

 Hôtel de Paris

(See restaurant above)
Open year-round. 59 stes 3,000-10,600. 141 rms 1,800-3,100. Bkfst 150-180. Air cond. Conf. Heated pool. Beach. Tennis. Valet pkg.
The last of Europe's really grand hotels has been welcoming the rich and famous since it opened in 1865. Now completely modernized, it has divinely comfortable rooms, a chic bar, and a lovely indoor pool. But don't expect a warm reception unless you roll up in a...Rolls. The hotel shops are less classy than they seem to think, and the breakfasts are quite ordinary.

12/20 La Maison du Caviar

1, av. Saint-Charles
(377) 93 30 80 06, fax (377) 93 30 23 90
Closed Tue dinner, Sat lunch off-seas, 3 wks in Jul. Open until 10:30pm. Air cond. Terrace dining.
Caviar is the speciality, but this friendlystyle bar offers a variety of other taste-tinglers: smoked salmon, curried chicken, sweet and sour calf's liver are just a few. Pretty good food at pretty good prices. C 235. M 120 (weekday lunch), 150-250 (exc weekday lunch).

 La Pergola

22, av. Princesse-Grace
(377) 93 30 98 80, fax (377) 93 50 23 14
Closed Sun, Mon, Dec. Open until 11pm. Terrace dining. Pool. Beach. No pets. Valet pkg.
The full flavors of the South of France enlightened by the touch of Rafaele Lauria: mouthwatering risotto wrapped in country ham and first-rate osso-buco (an Italian veal shank and vegetable stew) cooked in Dolcetto red wine. Meanwhile in the dining room, the pleasant

Italian staff has a good eye for who's who. C 350. M 395 (dinner).

 Beach Plaza

(See restaurant above)
Open year-round. 9 stes 1,600-5,500. 304 rms 800-2,500. Bkfst 125. Rms for disabled. Restaurant. Half-board 750-1,600. Rm ser. Air cond. Conf. Heated pool. Beach. Valet pkg.
This elegant hotel has a private beach, three swimming pools, and a "sea club" offering a range of sporting activities. The rooms are spacious and prettily decorated. Private beach. Just undergone complete renovation, including swimming pools.

 Sans Soucis

42, bd d'Italie - (377) 93 50 14 24
Closed Sun off-seas. Open until 11pm. Terrace dining.
Join the many Italians who flock to this convivial bistrot for uncontrived dishes made with luminously fresh ingredients. Frisky Italian wines accompany assorted frittatas, risotto with cèpes, pasta with poutargue (dried mullet roe) and *tutti quanti*. Good selection of Italian wines. Jolly, swift service. C 250-400. M 160, 200.

And also...

Our selection of places for inexpensive, quick, or late-night meals.
Le Pinocchio ((377) 93 30 96 20 - 30, rue Comte-Félix-Gastaldi. Open until 11pm, 2pm in summer.): The tiny terrace, near a small square, provides an attractive setting for supping on freshly-made ravioli with sage or carpaccio with Parmesan (200-250).
Polpetta ((377) 93 50 67 84 - 2, rue du Paradis. Open until 11pm): Everybody who's anybody shows up here to taste this simple but carefully prepared, Italian-inspired cooking. You can eat on the terrace or in the rather small vaulted-ceiling dining room (150-250).
Pulcinella ((377) 93 30 71 61 - 17, rue du Portier. Open until 11pm.): An appetizing menu and fair prices make this one of Monaco's most popular trattorias (150-250).
Il Triangolo ((377) 93 30 67 30 - 1, av. de la Madonne. Open until 1am.): The only real trattoria up on The Rock, offering such fare as basil spaghetti, tagliatelle pasta with cèpe mushrooms and gorgonzola gnocchi. Smiling staff and a lively time to be had by all (100-200).

See also: Roquebrune-Cap-Martin

MOUANS-SARTOUX	06370
Paris 910 - Nice 35 - Cannes 13 - Grasse 7	Alpes-Mar.

12/20 Le Palais des Coqs

By CD 409, 107, chemin Plan-Sarrain
04 93 75 61 57, fax 04 92 92 91 71
Closed Mon. Open until 9:30pm (10:30pm in seas). Terrace dining. Pkg.

Family tradition is still the dictum here after Honoré Boulicaut took over the family operation: you still can't beat the coq au vin offered on a very respectable 138 F set-price menu, and you're still sure to have a lively evening, because the Boulicauts think that a good time and good eating go hand in hand. Authentic cooking using good ingredients. The dance parties on Saturday nights liven up the place even more than usual. C 150-200. M 98 (weekday lunch, wine & coffee incl), 175 (Sat dinner, wine & coffee incl), 138-250, 70 (children).

12/20 **Le Relais de la Pinède**
Route de la Roquette - 04 93 75 28 29
Closed Feb. Open until 9:30pm. Terrace dining. Pkg.
A modest log cabin in a pine grove, with a simple, savory menu of inexpensive dishes: try the veal sweetbreads in mushroom cream sauce, beef fillet with cèpes, and nougat glacé with peach coulis. Tiny wine list. M 99 (exc Sun lunch), 149-170, 70 (children).

MOUGINS	06250
Paris 902 - Nice - Cannes 8 - Grasse 11	Alpes-Mar.

12/20 **Clos Saint-Basile**
351, av. St-Basile - 04 92 92 93 03, fax 04 92 92 19 34
Closed Wed, Mar. Open until 10pm. Priv rm 50. Terrace dining. Pkg.
Charming restaurant-art gallery combined where Claude Muscatelli expresses his origins with tasty dishes like fresh cod with tomate confite and saddle of rabbit with goat's cheese and thyme—enough to tingle the tastebuds of even the tiredest of tourists. Flower-embellished terrace, real Provence-style décor. Refreshing choice of wines. C 200. M 100 (weekday lunch, wine incl), 185, 100 (children).

La Ferme de Mougins
10, av. St-Basile - 04 93 90 03 74, fax 04 92 92 21 48
Closed Sun dinner & Mon off-seas. Open until 9:30pm (10pm in summer). Terrace dining. Pkg.
The 380 F prix-fixe menu is an alluring introduction to Thierry Thiercellin's delicate, flavorful repertoire. It treats you to a lush crème de parfait de foie gras aux chanterelles, sea bream with a lusty pistou sauce, roast lamb, and chocolate cake studded with dried fruit and nuts. The well-priced cellar is just as fascinating as ever. C 400-600. M 195 (lunch), 250 (weekday, wine incl), 260, 380.

12/20 **Le Manoir de l'Étang**
66, allée du Manoir, route d'Antibes
04 93 90 01 07, fax 04 92 92 20 70
Closed Nov. Open until 10:30pm. Garden dining. Pool. Pkg.
Picture a luxurious poolside terrace next to a splendid manor house. Makes you want to take a holiday? This is the place for it. Much to our dismay, eating in this splendid setting is not what it was in days of yore, the service is moving in the same direction, so a toque will simply have

to drop. C 250-350. M 150 (weekday lunch & Sat, wine incl), 145, 190, 80 (children).

Le Manoir de l'Étang
(See restaurant above)
Closed Nov. 2 stes 1,200-1,500. 15 rms 600-900. Bkfst 55. Half-board 500-650. Conf. Pool. No pets. Pkg.
This sumptuous Provençal dwelling dates from the nineteenth century; it is set in handsomely groomed grounds and offers airy rooms (some are huge) with personalized décor and antique furniture. Golf course nearby.

12/20 **Le Mas Candille**
Bd Rebuffel - 04 93 90 00 85, fax 04 92 92 85 56
Closed Tue & Wed lunch (exc Jul-Aug), Nov-Mar. Open until 10pm. Priv rm 25. Air cond. Terrace dining. Heated pool. Tennis. No pets. Garage pkg.
Although this eighteenth-century farmhouse offers an irresistible charm, the cooking didn't quite live up to our expectations. The dishes are well-crafted though uninspired, but the wine list, full of variety, only offers one half-bottle under 90 F. Too bad. C 280-450. M 185-250.

Le Mas Candille
(See restaurant above)
Closed Nov-Mar. 2 stes 1,900-2,300. 21 rms 680-1,050. Bkfst 85. Restaurant. Half-board 970-1,270. Rm ser. Air cond. Conf. Heated pool. Tennis. Garage pkg.
Bright, comfortable rooms with excellent facilities look out onto a delightful green landscape dotted with cypresses, olive trees, and umbrella pines. Absolute, blessed quiet. Heated pool; tennis courts. Rather stiff welcome.

Le Moulin de Mougins
Quartier Notre-Dame-de-Vie, 424, chemin du Moulin - 04 93 75 78 24, fax 04 93 90 18 55
Closed Thu lunch, Mon (exc dinner Jul 15-Aug 31), mid Feb-mid Mar, Dec 1-18. Open until 8:45pm. Priv rm 40. Terrace dining. Air cond. Valet pkg.
The "cuisine of the sun" that earned Roger Vergé an international reputation still stars on the menu of his Moulin, though the dishes don't generate quite the same excitement anymore. Still, the repertoire turned out under Serge Chollet's supervision continues to please the gilt-edged gastrotourists who come to taste Vergé's stuffed zucchini blossoms studded with Valréas truffles, or steamed Pegomas asparagus in a vivid herb coulis perfumed with Maussane olive oil, John Dory grilled on a single side and presented with fennel fondue, and the joconde, a lush dessert that brings together apricots and preserved ginger in a hazelnut-chocolate coating. Courteous reception; impeccable service (but given the prices, that's the least one should expect). C 1,000. M 315 (lunch, wine incl), 615, 700.

Le Moulin de Mougins

(See restaurant above)
Closed mid Feb-mid Mar, Dec 1-18. 4 stes 1,300-1,500. 3 rms 800-900. Bkfst 75. Air cond. Valet pkg.
The three rooms and two small suites are delightful and much cheaper than a grand hotel, but harder to book than a place in Paradise. Relais et Châteaux.

Les Muscadins

18, bd Courteline - 04 93 90 00 43, fax 04 92 92 88 23
Closed Tue off-seas, mid Feb-mid Mar, 1 wk in Dec. Open until 10pm. Priv rm 40. Terrace dining. Pkg.
The flower-massed terrace of Les Muscadins looks out on the bay of Cannes—what a dreamy spot for dining deliciously on Noël Mantel's Italo-Provençal cuisine. The 165 F set menu merits your close attention: it brings asparagus risotto, sautéed lamb's trotters, guinea hen stuffed with olives, and a chocolate-cherry croustillant. If you're feeling particularly flush, go for the even better 290 F prix-fixe meal. Appealing cellar; smiling young staff. C 350. M 165, 290, 110 (children).

Les Muscadins

(See restaurant above)
Closed mid Feb-mid Mar, 1 wk in Dec. 1 ste 1,200. 7 rms 750-950. Bkfst 60. Half-board 900-1,100. Rm ser. Air cond. Pkg.
Eight delightful rooms, each one individually decorated and attractively furnished. Sensational marble bathrooms. Charming, intimate bar and lounge.

NANS-LES-PINS   83860
Paris 811 - Toulon 61 - Aix-en-P. 43 - Marseille 41   Var

Domaine de Châteauneuf

N 560, Logis de Nans
04 94 78 90 06, fax 04 94 78 63 30
Closed beg Dec-beg Mar. Open until 10pm. Priv rm 80. Garden dining. Heated pool. Tennis. Valet pkg.
Beware of the charm: once you arrive, the attraction may be so strong that you might have trouble leaving this eighteenth-century *bastide*, hidden away in its mass of luxuriant peace and quiet. The spell doesn't seem to have any effect on the chefs however, who seem to follow one after the other. The newest chef, Bruno Gazagnaire, hadn't quite finished hanging up his utensils when we arrived, and we weren't too impressed with the commonplace dishes we tried. The pastry chef did however produce a good apple pie with honey ice cream. Splendid cellar. Warm ambience; elegant setting; attentive service. C 400. M 170 (weekday lunch, exc Sun), 230 (dinner & Sun), 380.

Domaine de Châteauneuf

(See restaurant above)

Closed beg Dec-beg Mar. 5 stes 1,270-2,300. 25 rms 580-1,210. Bkfst 75. Half-board 590-880. Rm ser. Conf. Heated pool. Tennis. Valet pkg.
Surrounded by wooded grounds and a superb eighteen-hole golf course, this eighteenth-century residence is decorated in infinite taste with clear, bright colors and fine antiques. Excellent breakfasts and perfect reception. Relais et Châteaux.

NICE   06000
Paris 943 - Lyon 475 - Marseille 188   Alpes-Mar.

Abela Regency Hôtel

223, promenade des Anglais
04 93 37 17 17, fax 04 93 71 21 71
Open year-round. 12 stes 1,600-6,000. 321 rms 720-1,200. Bkfst 90. Air cond. Conf. Pool. Valet pkg.
The huge, extremely comfortable rooms of this seafront palace on the Baie des Anges boast loggias with superb views.

12/20 L'Allégro

4, pl. Guynemer - 04 93 56 62 06, fax 04 93 56 38 28
Closed Wed lunch, Sun, Aug. Open until 10:45pm. Air cond. Pkg.
Frescoes depicting the Commedia dell'Arte grace this eating house near the port. No pizzas here: L'Allegro specializes in "real" Italian food. Good, but not to die for, and the prices have leapt up the ladder, so use a calculator when you order if you want to avoid (unpleasant) surprises. C 250. M 130 (lunch).

12/20 L'Auberge des Arts

9, rue Pairolière - 04 93 85 63 53
Closed Sun & Mon lunch (exc hols). Open until 11pm. Air cond. Terrace dining. Garage pkg.
For those evenings when you're up to the full-of-life atmosphere where one night you are entertained by magicians, another by what the French call "theme evenings"—springtime, Mardi Gras, Twelfth Night—depending on the season. Tucked into the heart of Nice, this pretty little restaurant whets your appetite with respectably-prepared dishes like petits farcis niçois (see explanation in glossary) and fattened pullet's leg confite with morel mushrooms, foie gras terrine and market-of-the-day fish. The cellar has a variety of good but reasonably priced wines as well as grands crus. C 200-270. M 98 (wine incl), 148, 168, 65 (children).

Beau Rivage

24, rue Saint-François-de-Paule
04 93 80 80 70, fax 04 93 80 55 77
Open year-round. 10 stes 1,300-1,800. 108 rms 500-1,200. Bkfst 95. Rms for disabled. Restaurant. Half-board 680-1,930. Rm ser. Air cond. Conf. Beach.
Near the opera and favored by prima donnas. The rooms are charming, air conditioned, and soundproof, and have lovely marble bathrooms. Very warm welcome.

12/20 Boccaccio

7, rue Masséna - 04 93 87 71 76
Open daily until 11pm. Terrace dining. Air cond.
An effervescent mood reigns at this big brasserie in downtown Nice. On offer are splendid shellfish assortments and uncomplicated but tasty seafood dishes. Appealing little cellar of Mediterranean wines. C 300-350. M 140 (lunch).

 ## Hôtel Brice

44, rue du Maréchal-Joffre
04 93 88 14 44, fax 04 93 87 38 54
Open year-round. 58 rms 360-640. Bkfst 40. Restaurant. Half-board 345-491. Rm ser. Valet pkg.
At nightfall, this centrally situated, fully redecorated hotel lights up like a Christmas tree. Guests may enjoy a verdant garden-terrace as well as spacious rooms (for the most part) with country-style furniture. New elevator. Friendly welcome.

12/20 Café de l'Horloge

12, av. Félix-Faure - 04 93 80 62 52, fax 04 93 80 40 02
Open daily until 11pm. Terrace dining. Air cond. Pkg.
Good brasserie fare with a personal touch from time to time, located in the Aston hotel. Luxury furnishings and decorated in rich, warm colors. Highly admirable wine list with good selection of half-bottles and varied price range. C 160. M 120, 170.

 ## Grand Hôtel Aston

(See restaurant above)
Open year-round. 155 rms 450-1,300. Bkfst 60. Half-board 575-1,425. Air cond. Conf. Pkg.
Some of the rooms of this plush, modern hotel overlook a square with floodlit fountains. Among the Aston's assets are a beautiful lobby, richly decorated public rooms, and well-equipped (though slightly noisy) accommodations, as well as a rooftop terrace that affords a view of the Mediterranean.

 ## Chantecler

37, promenade des Anglais
04 93 16 64 00, fax 04 93 88 35 68
Closed mid Nov-mid Dec. Open until 10:30pm. Priv rm 50. Air cond. Terrace dining. Valet pkg.
Alain Llorca, trained by Alain Ducasse, was recently fetched up to wake up the Chantecler's kitchens. He's a remarkable young chef whose repertoire glows with intelligence, generosity, and the sunny savors of Provence. As you admire the hotel's extravagant interior—which includes wainscotting that is registered as an artistic landmark along with the world's biggest rug—your palate is teased by such delights as upside down zucchini tart with honey butter and crayfish sprinkled with fresh rosemary, pan-fried sea perch with fried and pureed artichokes, and squab casserole with foie gras in a honey and balsamic vinegar jus. All this is topped off by fine desserts like creamy mascarpone and strawberries with guava and passion fruit sherbet. C 600. M 395, 440, 500, 560.

 ## Negresco

(See restaurant above)
Open year-round. 21 stes 3,750-7,500. 122 rms 1,300-2,350. Bkfst 120-190. Rms for disabled. Rm ser. Air cond. Conf. Beach. Valet pkg.
Witness to turn-of-the-century wealth and extravagance, the Negresco still oozes luxury and style. The fine old paintings and period furniture would fill an auction room several times over, and there's even a huge chandelier that is listed as a historic monument (its twin hangs in the Kremlin). The 6,000 square meters of rooms and suites require constant maintenance, and the owners spare no efforts to keep them freshly decorated. The riot of color in the guest rooms may not be to everyone's taste but these opulent lodgings provide a glimpse of a more leisured era (as does the much-photographed car attendant in his jaunty plumed hat). It's worth noting that this is the last great palatial hotel along the Côte d'Azur to still remain in private (Niçois) hands.

 ## Château des Ollières

39, av. des Baumettes
04 92 15 77 99, fax 04 92 15 77 98
Open year-round. 4 stes 1,100-2,800. 4 rms 800-1,650. Bkfst 90. Rm ser. Air cond. Conf. No pets. Garage pkg.
If you want to go back in time, say to the Belle Époque, stay at this château, nestled snuggly into its two and one half-acre park, among its multitudinous rare species of trees. It was bought by Prince Lobanov-Rostowsky in 1885 and converted to a hotel in 1990 by current owner Robert Fontana. Overflowing with exquisite wainscotting, silk, ceilings decorated with Pompeii-style frescoes, objets d'art, the only word to describe this setting is grandiose. Each of the eight rooms are unique and some of the bathrooms resemble theatre decor more than bathrooms. Unfortunately, some of the secret enchantment of the park is ruined by the noise from the expressway. Centrally located around the corner from the Chéret museum.

 ## Le Ciel d'Azur

Nice Airport (2nd floor)
04 93 21 36 36, fax 04 93 21 35 31
Lunch only. Open until 3pm. Priv rm 24. Air cond. Pkg.
Look up: no azure sky in sight, just metal beams and sheeting. Though the restaurant doesn't live up to its name, the menu keeps its promises. Chef Francis Dulucq's cooking is deft and delicious, perfectly complemented by the cellar's delightful Provençal wines. Stylish, attentive welcome and service. M 170-300.

11/20 Coco Beach

2, av. Jean-Lorrain
04 93 89 39 26, fax 04 92 04 02 39
Closed Sun dinner, Mon. Open until 9:30pm. Terrace dining. Pkg.
So what if the grilled langouste costs 700 F? You'll be eating it in the company of movie stars

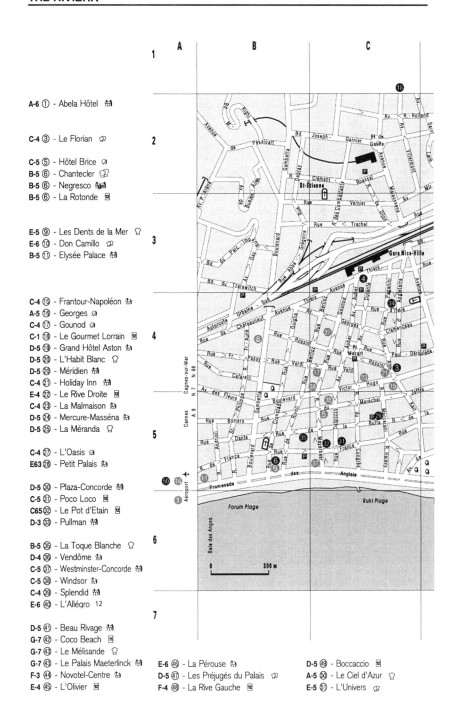

A-6 ① - Abela Hôtel

C-4 ③ - Le Florian

C-5 ⑤ - Hôtel Brice
B-5 ⑥ - Chantecler
B-5 ⑥ - Negresco
B-5 ⑥ - La Rotonde

E-5 ⑨ - Les Dents de la Mer
E-6 ⑩ - Don Camillo
B-5 ⑪ - Elysée Palace

C-4 ⑮ - Frantour-Napoléon
A-5 ⑯ - Georges
C-4 ⑰ - Gounod
C-1 ⑱ - Le Gourmet Lorrain
D-5 ⑲ - Grand Hôtel Aston
D-5 ⑳ - L'Habit Blanc
D-5 ⑳ - Méridien
C-4 ㉑ - Holiday Inn
E-4 ㉒ - Le Rive Droite
C-4 ㉓ - La Malmaison
D-5 ㉔ - Mercure-Masséna
D-5 ㉕ - La Méranda

C-4 ㉗ - L'Oasis
E63 ㉘ - Petit Palais

D-5 ㉚ - Plaza-Concorde
C-5 ㉛ - Poco Loco
C65 ㉜ - Le Pot d'Etain
D-3 ㉝ - Pullman

B-5 ㉟ - La Toque Blanche
D-4 ㊱ - Vendôme
C-5 ㊲ - Westminster-Concorde
C-5 ㊳ - Windsor
C-4 ㊴ - Splendid
E-6 ㊵ - L'Allégro 12

D-5 ㊶ - Beau Rivage
G-7 ㊷ - Coco Beach
G-7 ㊸ - Le Mélisande
G-7 ㊸ - Le Palais Maeterlinck
F-3 ㊹ - Novotel-Centre
E-4 ㊺ - L'Olivier

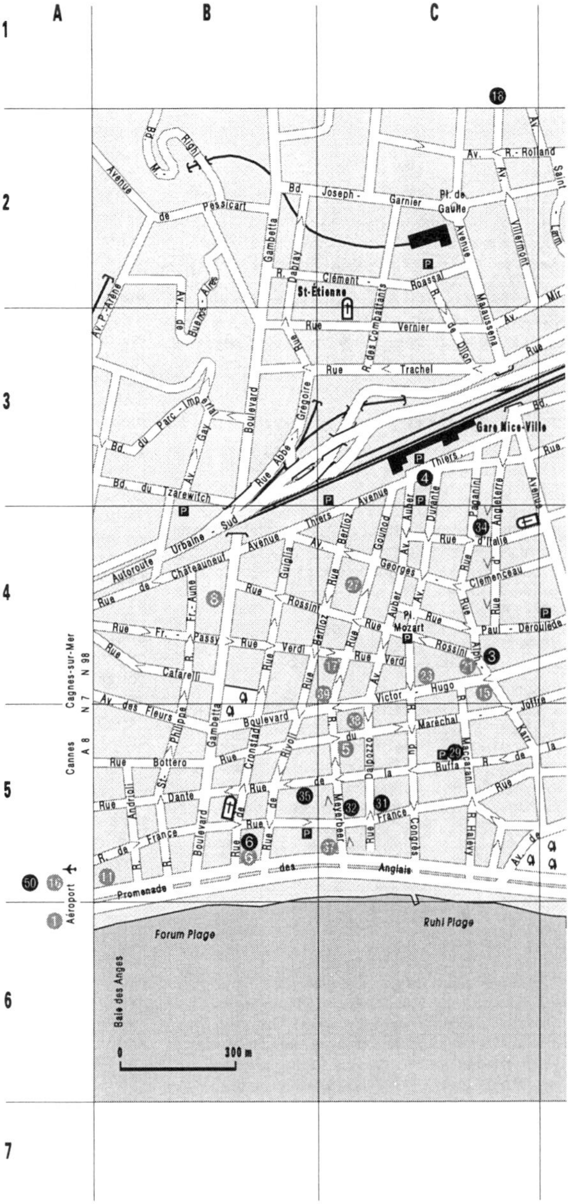

E-6 ㊻ - La Pérouse
D-5 ㊼ - Les Préjugés du Palais
F-4 ㊽ - La Rive Gauche

D-5 ㊾ - Boccaccio
A-5 ㊿ - Le Ciel d'Azur
E-5 (51) - L'Univers

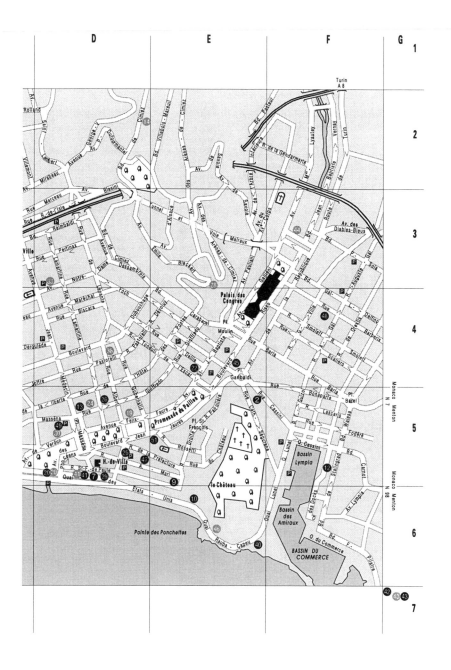

and celebrities both pseudo and real, with a spectacular view of Nice (and for the latter there's no extra charge). C 265. M 220 (lunch).

 ### Les Dents de la Mer

2, rue Saint-François-de-Paule
04 93 80 99 16, fax 04 93 85 05 78
Open daily until 11pm. Terrace dining. Air cond. Pkg.
A cool terrace shaded by an awning, an up-turned boat, and tanks full of fish compose the décor of this chic, popular restaurant serves lively Mediterranean fare: spaghetti with clams, bouillabaisse, and sea bream with eggplant are typical of the house style. Concise, well-composed wine list, but rather dear, as the English say. C 280-360. M 148, 199.

 ### Don Camillo   ✪

5, rue des Ponchettes
04 93 85 67 95, fax 04 93 13 97 43
Closed Sun, Mon, mid Nov-mid Dec. Open until 9:30pm. Air cond.
Here in the chic Ponchettes district near Nice's flower market, you'll discover a bright, unassuming restaurant that has become one of the best in the city. Franck Cerutti's graceful yet assertively flavored cuisine is firmly rooted in the traditions of Italy and Provence: stuffed veal breast with sun-dried tomatoes, lamb's tripe and trotters with chickpea crêpes, and a tart topped with fresh local anchovies, marinated peppers, capers, and olives are lusty dishes crafted with the disciplined skill one would expect from a chef trained by Maximin and Ducasse. Few half-bottles in the cellar, but a small selection of wines is offered by the glass. C 330-400. M 200, 320.

 ### Élysée Palace

59, promenade des Anglais
04 93 86 06 06, fax 04 93 44 50 40
Open year-round. 22 stes 1,650-3,300. 121 rms 800-1,300. Bkfst 95. Restaurant. Half-board 790-1,050. Rm ser. Air cond. Conf. Pool. Beach. Valet pkg.
The façade features a female giant, 26 meters tall and 15 across, fashioned in bronze by the sculptor Sosno. Inside there are deluxe rooms, a piano bar, gym, sauna, and conference rooms. And on the roof, a swimming pool.

 ### Frantour Napoléon

6, rue Grimaldi - 04 93 87 70 07, fax 04 93 16 17 80
Open year-round. 2 stes 700-1,100. 81 rms 450-890. Bkfst 60. Rms for disabled. Air cond.
This imposing 1930s hotel a stone's throw from the Promenade des Anglais offers good-sized, fairly quiet renovated rooms and a wide array of services.

 ### Georges

3, rue Henri-Cordier
04 93 86 23 41, fax 04 93 44 02 30
Open year-round. 18 rms 300-430. Bkfst 33-58. Rms for disabled. Air cond. Garage pkg.

Just 100 yards from the sea, with a family atmosphere and trim, tidy rooms. You can have breakfast and admire the view from the third-floor terrace. You get your money's worth.

 ### Gounod

3, rue Gounod - 04 93 88 26 20, fax 04 93 88 23 84
Closed mid Nov-mid Dec. 6 stes 500-790. 42 rms 335-590. Bkfst 35-60. Air cond. Pool. Garage pkg.
This pink Belle Époque hotel provides huge, nicely equipped rooms, but the ambience is melancholy and the hallways gloomy. Friendly reception; a certain old-fashioned charm lingers still.

12/20 Le Gourmet Lorrain

7, av. Santa-Fior - 04 93 84 90 78, fax 04 92 09 11 25
Closed Sat lunch, Sun dinner, Mon, Jan 1-7, mid Jul-mid Aug. Open until 9:30pm. Terrace dining. Air cond.
Come into the spacious, tidy dining room of this old-fashioned villa for traditional country cooking based on first-rate ingredients. The cheese board and wine list are sensational, and the welcome is friendly. C 300. M 95 (weekday lunch), 155, 165, 175, 195.

Grand Hôtel Aston

See restaurant Café de l'Horloge

 ### L'Habit Blanc

1, promenade des Anglais - 04 93 82 69 16 (R), 04 93 82 25 25 (H), fax 04 93 88 91 29
Open daily until 10:30pm. Air cond. Terrace dining. Pool. Valet pkg.
Even if you normally flee hotel restaurants, give this one a chance. The light and airy dining room looks out to sea, the staff coddles guests with unobtrusive attentions, and the chef makes inventive use of superfresh market ingredients. Taste his langoustine salad flavored with vanilla seeds, zucchini blossoms stuffed with salmon and strewn with baby fava beans, and finish up with a strawberry croustillant enlivened with lemon and thyme. Wine overpriced. C 300-350. M 160, 240, 80 (children).

 ### Méridien

(See restaurant above)
Open year-round. 24 stes 2,500-3,300. 290 rms 950-1,150. Bkfst 95-125. Rm ser. Air cond. Conf. Pool. Valet pkg.
The very modern, well-furnished rooms all boast sea views. There's a piano bar, tea room, admirably appointed fitness center—and the service is perfect.

 ### Holiday Inn

20, bd Victor-Hugo
04 93 16 55 00, fax 04 93 16 55 55
Open year-round. 2 stes 1,400-1,900. 129 rms 580-1,090. Bkfst 65-85. Rms for disabled. Restaurant. Half-board 120-200. Rm ser. Air cond. Valet pkg.

This hotel of recent vintage stands on a broad boulevard in the heart of Nice. It offers fine, thoughtfully equipped rooms (satellite television, minibar, air conditioning) furnished with wicker pieces. Steam bath; sauna.

La Malmaison

48, bd Victor-Hugo
04 93 87 62 56, fax 04 93 16 17 99
Closed mid Nov-mid Dec. 2 stes 600-800. 50 rms 300-650. Bkfst 50. Restaurant. Half-board 390-490. Air cond. Conf. Beach. Garage pkg.
A late-nineteenth-century ,corner building with up-to-date facilities. The rooms are comfortable, with soundproofing and air conditioning, and are redecorated regularly. Satellite television.

Le Mélisande

Basse corniche, 30, bd Maeterlinck
04 92 00 72 00, fax 04 92 04 18 10
Closed Sun dinner & Mon off-seas, Jan-mid Mar. Open until 10pm. Terrace dining. Air cond. Pool. Valet pkg.
This Babylonian-style building with its columns and fake marble offers a cuisine as pretentious as its architecture. Marc Thivet fails to add his own touch of life to the good regional ingredients he uses. Stiff and stuffy reception and service. When all is said, we just have to drop this resaurant a point. In addition, the excellent wine list is awfully expensive. C 470-600. M 190 (weekday lunch), 240 (weekday dinner).

Le Palais Maeterlinck

(See restaurant above)
Closed Jan-mid Mar. 22 stes 1,950-10,000. 14 rms 1,450-2,500. Bkfst 160-130. Rm for disabled. Half-board 290. Rm ser. Air cond. Conf. Pool. Beach. Valet pkg.
Designed by a Swiss financier for his friends and the occasional wealthy traveler bored by the average luxury hotel. Here you can admire a profusion of murals and *trompe-l'œil* paintings by Serge Megter. Huge terraces, and a private beach, landing stage, and helipad. The superb swimming pool is surrounded by Ionic columns; the amenities include private safes, minibars, VCRs, and satellite TV. Pricey.

Mercure Masséna

58, rue Gioffredo - 04 93 85 49 25, fax 04 93 62 43 27
Open year-round. 116 rms 420-795. Bkfst 70. Rms for disabled. Conf. Pkg.
This fine traditional hotel 500 yards from the sea boasts newly renovated bathrooms. Modern facilities, plenty of amenities, and meals served in the rooms at all hours. Many deluxe services.

La Merenda

4, rue de la Terrasse
Closed Sat, Sun, Feb, Aug. Open until 9:30pm. Air cond. Pkg.

You can't book a table here because there's no telephone, the bar-stool seating is uncomfortable, and there's only one type of wine (available in red, white, or rosé). Nonetheless, Dominique Le Stanc's small restaurant is packed all year with customers eager to taste the best zucchini-blossom fritters in the world, the earthy Niçois blood sausage called trulle, pasta with basil-bright pistou, and a famous chocolate mousse. Authentic cooking at bargain prices. C 180-230.

Méridien

See restaurant L'Habit Blanc

Negresco

See restaurant Chantecler

Novotel Centre

8-10, esplanade du Parvis-de-l'Europe
04 93 13 30 93, fax 04 93 13 09 04
Open year-round. 2 stes 800. 171 rms 400-690. Bkfst 52. Restaurant. Half-board 500-790. Rm ser. Air cond. Conf. Pool. Garage pkg.
Situated in the city's new shopping and cultural center. The rooms have just been redone, along with the bar and terrace. Pleasant reception, eager service, and a free shuttle service to the airport.

L'Oasis

23, rue Gounod - 04 93 88 12 29, fax 04 93 16 14 40
Open year-round. 38 rms 300-430. Bkfst 38. Restaurant. Rm ser. Garage pkg.
An oasis of greenery in the center of Nice. The little rooms are clean, somewhat faded, but quiet and comfortable. Very pretty terrace for relaxing after a long day.

12/20 L'Olivier

2, pl. Garibaldi - 04 93 26 89 09
Closed Wed dinner, Sun, Aug. Open until 9:30pm. Terrace dining. Air cond. No pets.
The neighborhood is certainly not glamorous, and the dining room is remarkable more for its tidiness than its charm. Still, we keep coming back to L'Olivier for the warm-hearted welcome, cheery ambience, and fresh, generous, family-style cooking. C 150-200.

Le Palais Maeterlinck

See restaurant Le Mélisande

La Pérouse

11, quai Rauba-Capeu
04 93 62 34 63, fax 04 93 62 59 41
Open year-round. 3 stes 1,640-2,200. 61 rms 405-1,325. Bkfst 85. Restaurant. Rm ser. Air cond. Conf. Pool. Valet pkg.
One of the most pleasant hotels in Nice, La Pérouse has magnificent rooms with loggia or terrace and sea views. Sun room with panoramic views, sauna, and hydrotherapy pool. Grill in

summer. But for the price, we expect a better breakfast!

 ## Petit Palais

10, av. Emile-Bieckert
04 93 62 19 11, fax 04 93 62 53 60
Open year-round. 1 ste 990-1,290. 25 rms 390-780. Bkfst 50-75. Rm ser. Garage pkg.
This Petit Palais sits majestically on a hilltop overlooking Nice. The interior décor follows the lead of the building's handsome Belle Époque architecture: the attractive, well-equipped rooms—with terrace or private garden—boast fine paintings, comfortable armchairs, and superb bathrooms. Very attentive service. Near museums.

 ## Plaza Concorde

12, av. de Verdun - 04 93 16 75 75, fax 04 93 82 50 70
Open year-round. 10 stes 1,300-2,500. 176 rms 650-1,300. Bkfst 80. Restaurant. Half-board 150. Rm ser. Air cond. Conf. Beach.
Wonderful rooftop terrace and well-equipped, air conditioned conference rooms. Rooms just redecorated in contemporary style. Bar, grill, and various shops and services are on the premises.

12/20 Poco Loco

2, rue Dalpozze - 04 93 88 85 83
Closed Sat & Sun lunch, May 1. Open until 11:30pm (midnight in summer). Terrace dining. Air cond. No pets.
Sip expertly mixed tequila cocktails in a convivial atmosphere, then order from the Mexican menu: enchiladas, nachos, and fajitas are all tasty and inexpensive. C 160. M 50-75 (weekday lunch), 52 (children).

12/20 Le Pot d'Étain

12, rue Meyerbeer
04 93 88 25 95, fax 04 93 87 75 04
Open daily until 11pm. Terrace dining. Air cond. Garage pkg.
Éric Régnier uses tip-top ingredients for a traditional menu crafted with considerable care. And patrons can count on a warm welcome at this friendly restaurant decorated with warm wood paneling and mirrors. Decent cellar. C 175-270. M 90.

 ## Pullman

28, av. Notre-Dame
04 93 13 36 36, fax 04 93 62 61 69
Open year-round. 1 ste 1,000-1,500. 200 rms 525-695. Bkfst 75. Rm ser. Air cond. Pool. Valet pkg.
A remarkably soundproofed modern hotel in the center of town. The comfortable, newly decorated rooms have various amenities that can be conveniently operated by remote control from the bed. The rooftop terrace hosts a bar, swimming pool, and sauna, with a poolside grill from May to October.

12/20 Le Rive Droite

29, rue Saint-Jean-Baptiste - 04 93 62 16 72

Open daily until 11pm. Terrace dining. Air cond.
Authentic Niçois dishes—socca, air-dried beef, onion pizza, great gnocchi, daube and polenta—are featured on a copious 180 F set meal. C 150-285. M 180.

11/20 La Rive Gauche

27, rue Ribotti - 04 93 89 16 82, fax 04 93 89 16 82
Closed Sun dinner. Open until 10pm. Air cond.
Generous Provençal cooking in a cheerful, bistro atmosphere. A generous set menu priced at 134 F brings stuffed cabbage, basil-scented cod fillet, and orange bavarian cream. Affordable cellar; speedy service. C 200-250. M 134.

12/20 La Rotonde

Hôtel Negresco, 37, promenade des Anglais
04 93 16 64 00, fax 04 93 88 35 68
Open daily until midnight. Terrace dining. Air cond. Beach. Valet pkg.
This is the place to go in the Riviera and what a place with its merry-go-round décor where wooden horses circle round you as you dine. If you miss speaking English, you'll most certainly find a willing party here. Southern cooking with a tidbit of inventiveness. Richly-stocked wine cellar but this is not the place for bargains. C 200. M 115-155.

 ## Sofitel

2-4, parvis de l'Europe
04 92 00 80 00, fax 04 93 26 27 00
Open year-round. 15 stes 1,100-2,000. 137 rms 810-1,600. Bkfst 90. Rms for disabled. Restaurant. Rm ser. Air cond. Conf. Pool. Garage pkg.
This six-story building just opposite the exhibition center dons a swimming pool and rooftop bar overlooking Nice. High-grade service and comfort, offering in addition a workout room and sauna.

 ## Splendid

50, bd Victor-Hugo
04 93 16 41 00, fax 04 93 87 02 46
Open year-round. 12 stes 950-1,500. 115 rms 580-790. Bkfst 48-75. Restaurant. Half-board 650-780. Air cond. Conf. Pool. Garage pkg.
The smallish rooms are air conditioned and well equipped, decorated in apricot tones, and with smallish bathrooms. Friendly service, mediocre breakfasts, and Riviera prices.

 ## La Toque Blanche

40, rue de la Buffa
04 93 88 38 18, fax 04 93 88 38 18
Closed Sun dinner, Mon. Open until 9:30pm. Priv rm 30. Air cond.
Alain Sandelion's good cooking helps us overlook the noise of passing buses and the dining room's boring décor. He turns out a delicious salmon gâteau with lobster sauce, basil-scented sculpin cooked with split-second timing and served with fresh pasta, and an appetizing dessert buffet that features a lush chocolate fondant. Tempting cheese board; short but balanced wine list. C 300-400. M 145 (exc Sun), 160, 290.

L'Univers

54, bd Jean-Jaurès - 04 93 62 32 22
Closed Sat lunch. Open until 11:30pm. Priv rm 45. Terrace dining. Air cond.
A genial welcome puts guests in a receptive mood for Christian Plumail's delectable rabbit confit perfumed with rosemary, Parmesan-coated cod in a red-wine sauce with fennel, pinenut macaroons, and berries swathed in rich mascarpone cream. The cellar is still young, but we enjoyed a heady Crozes-Hermitage Petite-Ruche '93. The good-humored atmosphere at this new center-city venue is simply delightful. C 270-320. M 160 (weekday lunch, Sat, wine incl), 170.

 Vendôme

26, rue Pastorelli - 04 93 62 00 77, fax 04 93 13 40 78
Open year-round. 5 stes 495-695. 51 rms 315-560. Bkfst 40-65. Rm ser. Air cond. Conf. Garage pkg.
This former town house with its superb staircase, built in the nineteenth century, has been restored in the best of taste. The pleasant rooms are decorated in attractive colors and have handsomely designed furniture. Room service (including meal trays); garden.

 Westminster-Concorde

27, promenade des Anglais
04 93 88 29 44, fax 04 93 82 45 35
Open year-round. 5 stes 1,000-1,200. 100 rms 500-1,000. Bkfst 80. Restaurant. Half-board 120. Rm ser. Air cond. Conf. No pets.
Ideally located on the Promenade des Anglais, the majestic Westminster has plenty of character and charm, as well as all the modern conveniences. The service has remained soothingly old-fashioned. Bar.

 Windsor ▲♥

11, rue Dalpozzo - 04 93 88 59 35, fax 04 93 88 94 57
Open year-round. 60 rms 400-670. Bkfst 40. Restaurant. Half-board 465-640. Air cond. Conf. Pool. Pkg.
A lovely tropical garden and moderate prices make the Windsor a standout. This elegant hotel with superb frescoes in some rooms also boasts modern facilities such as offices for business meetings and a fitness club. Very pleasant bar.

And also...

Our selection of places for inexpensive, quick, or late-night meals.
L'Auberge de Théo (04 93 81 26 19 - 52, av. Cap-de-Croix. Open until 11pm.): Close to the Matisse and Chagall museums, a charming restaurant that served robustly flavorful Italian food (150-200).
Chez Pipo (04 93 55 88 82 - 13, rue Bavastro. Dinner only. Open until 10pm.): A 70-year-old institution serving socca (chickpea pizza), baked in a wood-fired oven and washed down with a

glass of red. Picturesque (160).
Choupette (04 93 80 28 69 - 20, rue Barillerie. Open until 10:30pm.): An appealing little place in Old Nice with a fine fixed-price menu (served until 10pm) and Niçois dishes (120-250).
Le Vendôme (04 93 16 18 28 - 1, pl. Grimaldi. Open until 7pm.): An authentic bistro serving tasty homestyle cooking (120-125).

PEILLON	06440
Paris 953 - Nice 18 - Contes 13	Alpes-Mar.

 L'Authentique

04 93 79 91 17, fax 04 93 79 99 36
Closed Wed, Jan 7-24, Oct 20-Dec 20. Open until 9pm (or upon reserv). Priv rm 40. Terrace dining. Pkg.
After an appetite-rousing trek among the *villages perchés* of the Niçois hill country, here is a delightful place to regather your strength. At their adorable *auberge* set in a blooming garden, the Millo family welcome walkers with open arms. Sample the chicken liver terrine with onion confit, red mullet fillet with new potatoes, sea bass with wild fennel and a vegetable fondue, and thyme-scented roast lamb. Good cellar, too. C 300. M 135 (lunch, exc Sun), 185 (exc Sun), 230-300, 80 (children).

Auberge de la Madone ▲♥

(See restaurant above)
See restaurant for closings. 3 stes 800-1,200. 17 rms 440-800. Bkfst 58-80. Half-board 480-700. Rm ser. Conf. Tennis. No pets. Pkg.
Discover superb scenery at this comfortable country inn, where rooms are attractively decorated with Provençal fabrics. Perfect peace and quiet are assured.

PORQUEROLLES (ILE DE)	83400
	Var

 Auberge des Glycines

Pl. des Armes - 04 94 58 30 36, fax 04 94 58 35 22
Closed Jan-mid Feb. 12 rms 400-600. Bkfst 50. Restaurant. Half-board 450-850 (oblig in seas). Garage pkg.
Sprightly, refined country décor, in the true style of Provence, set off with dainty fabrics and light-colored woodwork. All rooms give onto a delight of a patio, shaded by a single fig tree; as you enjoy the comfort of your room, you'll appreciate that someone has thought of not only your every desire, but your every need.

Mas du Langoustier ۞

04 94 58 30 09, fax 04 94 58 36 02
Closed mid Oct-end Apr. Open until 9pm. Garden dining. Tennis. Garage pkg.
Day trippers seldom venture here, for the Mas du Langoustier shelters behind a screen of umbrella pines and eucalyptus trees. This magical site is the preserve of the hotel's residents and

moneyed mariners from Le Lavandou or Saint-Tropez, whose yachts weigh anchor in the turquoise-tinted creek below. But you can join them, if you book ahead, on the Mas's lovely terrace or in the big, bright, newly decorated dining room, to savor Joël Guillet's sun-struck cuisine. The menu is a rhapsody of barely tamed Mediterranean flavors, with tiny red mullet set atop eggplant and glazed tomatoes, grilled sea bream with a fondue of spring onions, zucchini blossoms with mushrooms in a garlicky persillade, and fresh-caught grouper dabbed with ginger oil. These savors marry beautifully with wines made right here on the island, by the owner's brother-in-law. C 400. M 320 (wine incl), 400-500.

 Mas du Langoustier 🌲🍷

(See restaurant above)
Closed mid Oct-end Apr. 3 stes 1,446-1,534. 50 rms 1,193-1,271. Bkfst 80. Half-board oblig. Conf. Tennis. Garage pkg.
An island of edenic tranquility, pierced only by the murmur of the wind in the pines or the cicadas' creaking song. The 50-odd rooms and suites have been further refurbished; those on the ground floor have private terraces overlooking the water. Air conditioning is provided by the sea breezes, and there's a sandy beach instead of a pool. Two tennis courts; and a heliport, of course.

12/20 **La Plage d'Argent**

04 94 58 32 48
Closed mid Sep-Easter. Open until 9:30pm. Priv rm 140. Terrace dining.
The touch of the fairy godmother turned this former beach hut into a charming but wee restaurant. Appetizing seafood dishes that you can wash down with the local island wine. C 200-250. M 95 (lunch), 55 (children).

PORT-CROS (ILE DE)   83145
                                        Var

12/20 **Le Manoir**

04 94 05 90 52, fax 04 94 05 90 89
Closed Oct-Apr. Open until 9pm. Priv rm 20. Terrace dining. No pets.
Gérard Ré offers sunny specialties like a fricot of langoustines, simple grilled meats and fish, and chocolate profiteroles. The garden facing the bay is a lovely sight, with its huge white parasols, eucalyptus trees, and dancing butterflies. M 250-290, 130 (children).

 Le Manoir 🌲🍷

(See restaurant above)
Closed Oct-Apr. 23 rms 700-1,100. Bkfst 60. Half-board 700-1,100 (oblig). No pets.
A charming white colonial-style hotel with large, quiet rooms (cars are banned on the island). Some rooms have private terraces.

PORT-GRIMAUD   83310
Paris 884 - Toulon 32 - Le Lavandou 13   Var

 L'Amphitrite

Grand-Rue - 04 94 56 31 33, fax 04 94 56 33 77
Closed mid Oct-Easter. Open until 10pm. Terrace dining. Air cond. Heated pool. Beach. Valet pkg.
The lizard has a new skin—a new chef, Laurent Carlier, a new assistant chef and a new maître d'hôtel—but warm reception and top-quality food are still on the menu. Only the best ingredients go into the preparation of his baked duck liver, spicy red mullet, simmered duck with sherry vinegar, and gently steamed John Dory fish. C 300. M 135 (lunch), 180 & 250 (dinner).

 Giraglia

(See restaurant above)
Closed mid Oct-Easter. 7 stes 1,615-2,065. 42 rms 600-1,965. Bkfst 60. Rm ser. Air cond. Valet pkg.
A very attractive set of Provençal-style buildings which blend in well with the village. Rooms are spacious, comfortable, and remarkably well appointed. A fine sandy beach, water sports, and excursions into the hills are additional attractions. Magnificent swimming pool and terrace.

RAMATUELLE   83350
Paris 892 - Hyères 54 - St-Tropez 10   Var

The Beaches

Lunch only.
Le Bar du Soleil (04 94 97 65 12 - Plage de Tahiti.): You've not been to Saint-Tropez if you've not been here. Go for the atmosphere, the service and to see who's who. Worth the trip.
Tahiti Plage (04 94 97 18 02 - Le Pinet.): Watch the Paris movie stars as you dangle your toes in the water. Interesting enough food too (230-280).

 Les Bergerettes 🌲🍷

Route des Plages, quartier des Marres
04 94 97 40 22, fax 04 94 97 37 55
Closed Oct-Easter. 29 rms 560-980. Bkfst 70. Restaurant. Rm ser. Air cond. Pool.
This charming hotel, which looks rather like a Provençal *bastide*, is set in a pine wood, facing the beach. The rooms are very appealing, and some have terraces.

 Les Bouis 🌲🍷

Route de la Plage de Pampelonne
04 94 79 87 61, fax 04 94 79 85 20
Closed Oct 30-Mar 20. 4 stes 750-1,150. 13 rms 600-1,150. Bkfst 70. Rms for disabled. Air cond. Pool. Garage pkg.
A group of luxurious buildings in a pine grove dotted around the swimming pool. The attractive rooms have rattan furniture, tiled floors, and private terraces with a sea view. All are now air conditioned and have satellite TV.

Dei Marres

Route des Plages - 04 94 97 26 68, fax 04 94 97 62 76
*Closed mid Oct-mid Mar. 2 stes 550-1,400. 22 rms
350-1,100. Bkfst 45. Conf. Pool. Tennis. Garage pkg.*
Comely modern structure with sunny, well-appointed rooms. Pleasant setting among the cypresses and the olive trees, and just 500 yards from the Lices beach. Some rooms have terraces. Reasonably priced.

12/20 Chez Camille

Quartier de Bonne-Terrasse - 04 94 79 80 38
*Closed Tue (exc dinner in summer), Oct 10-Apr 1.
Open until 9:30pm. Terrace dining. Pkg.*
An excellent bouillabaisse (order it in advance) and perfectly good grilled fish are sufficient reason to stop for a meal and a view of the Bonne-Terrasse Bay. It's not great gastronomy, but the holiday crowd eats it right up. M 185-420.

12/20 Chez Madeleine

Route de Tahiti - 04 94 97 15 74
Closed Oct 15-Easter. Open until 10:30pm. Garden dining. Pkg.
Madeleine Serra's children somehow manage to grab the best of the catch from their fishermen friends, even at the height of summer. Wonderful bouillabaisse (order in advance) and bourride, and the freshest fish in town. Saint-Tropez prices, but an institution worth visiting. C 300. M 160.

 La Ferme d'Hermès

Route de l'Escalet - 04 94 79 27 80, fax 04 94 79 26 86
*Closed Jan 10-Mar 31, Nov 3-Dec 27. 1 ste 950-
1,050. 8 rms 600-850. Bkfst 70. Pool. Pkg.*
A charming little *mas* in wine country, offering rooms with kitchenettes and a swimming pool set amid the vineyards.

 La Figuière

Le Pinet, route de Tahiti
04 94 97 18 21, fax 04 94 97 68 48
*Closed Oct-end Mar. 41 rms 430-950. Bkfst 65. Rms
for disabled. Restaurant. Air cond. Pool. Tennis.
Garage pkg.*
An old farmhouse set among vineyards, just 300 yards from the sea. Peace, comfort, and an elegant clientele of regulars.

 La Garbine

Route de Tahiti - 04 94 97 11 84, fax 04 94 97 34 18
*Closed mid Oct-Dec 25, Jan 3-Mar. 20 rms 450-950.
Bkfst 55-75. Rms for disabled. Air cond. Conf. Pool.
Tennis. Garage pkg.*
Nice setting: 500 yards from the beach with a little stream running alongside it. With the tile roof and the olive grove, you really get the feeling you're in Provence, even though all the rooms are air conditioned and have a private terrace giving onto the pool.

 L'Hacienda

Quartier des Marres
04 94 56 61 20, fax 04 94 97 05 24

*Open year-round. 8 rms 600-1,200. Bkfst 65-85.
Restaurant. Rm ser. Conf. Pool. Pkg.*
An attractive Provençal house and veritable oasis of luxury and calm, right near Saint-Tropez and the beaches. The rooms are very comfortable and tastefully furnished. Meals are served only upon request (they're good) in the lovely poolside garden. Very warm welcome and service.

 Mooréa

Route de Tahiti - 04 94 97 18 17, fax 04 94 97 24 72
*Lunch only. Closed mid Nov-Mar. Open until 4pm.
Terrace dining. Garage pkg.*
So you want to eat a real meal on the beach? Here's the place to come for tomatoes and mozzarella, Niçoise salad, broiled sea bream, sea perch or lamb chops, on the most sought-after beach in Europe. You even get to sit under a red umbrella... Not a lot of thought put into the wine list, but the local wines are good enough. C 250-350.

Tahiti

Le Pinet - 04 94 97 18 02, fax 04 94 54 86 66
*Closed mid Oct-Easter. 8 stes 1,150-1,280. 13 rms
640-1,180. Bkfst 70. Restaurant. Air cond. Pool.
Beach. Tennis. No pets. Garage pkg.*
Leftover hippies will relish this darling little hotel. The owner Félix will greet you in his most graphic manner. Muscle building, boutiques, you name it: everything you need to take you back a few decades.

La Terrasse

Av. Gustave-Étienne
04 94 79 20 48, fax 04 94 79 28 36
*Closed Nov-mid Mar. Open until 9:30pm. Terrace
dining. Heated pool. Pkg.*
Sylvain Humbert is climbing the ladder toward another toque he lays before us such exquisite dishes as his oh-so-fresh-and-firm roasted langoustines or his young Pyrénées leg of lamb. Quality ingredients are king in his cuisine so very Southern and yet fit to lay before royalty or presidents alike, such as the extra-light sardine turnover with ratatouille and heaven-sent arugula salad. Sky-high score for his little farcis niçois (squash, eggplant, tomatoes and onions filled with their own pulp mixed with chopped pork or veal, eggs and garlic, then baked in oven with oil). The pleasant terrace looks out over the hilltops, vineyards and sea and makes an ideal stop for a dinner in the cool of the evening far from the maddening crowd. The wine list may be short, but it is brimming with good taste, especially for the local Provence wines. Good choice of half-bottles. M 180-270.

Hostellerie Le Baou

(See restaurant above)
*Closed Nov-mid Mar. 2 stes 1,350. 39 rms 500-
1,250. Bkfst 65-100. Half-board 731-1,131. Conf.
Heated pool. Pkg.*
On summer nights, you can eat grilled foods around the beautiful swimming pool. This

modern hotel—sitting smack on the edge of a hillside covered in olive trees, cypresses and aromatic herbs, located at the foot of the old village of Ramatuelle—proposes comfortable, sunny, spick-and-span rooms, all with a terrace.

 La Vigne de Ramatuelle

Quartier Audrac, route des Plages
04 94 79 12 50, fax 04 94 79 13 20
Closed Nov-Mar. 14 rms 600-1,500. Bkfst 75. Air cond. Conf. Pool. Garage pkg.
The sweet smells of the pine forest envelop you from your private terrace, and all you see round you are vineyards and lawn. This hilltop hotel, a mile and a half from the beach, proposes small but luxurious rooms with relaxing décor. Efficient, charming reception.

ROQUEBRUNE-CAP-MARTIN	06190
Paris 953 - Nice 26 - Menton 5	Alpes-Mar.

12/20 La Dame Jeanne

1, chemin Sainte-Lucie - 04 93 35 10 20
Closed Sun, Feb-Mar. Open until 10:30pm.
Century-old arches put you in the mood for Claude Nobbio's good downhome, Provence-style eating in this house full of old-world character and charm. Try the cèpes risotto, the beef fillet with garlic cream sauce, or the rabbit with rosemary essence on a starry night on the terrace and wash it down with one of the many wines from his well-rounded cellar. C 220-280.

12/20 Les Deux Frères

Pl. des Frères
04 93 28 99 00, fax 04 93 28 99 10
Closed Thu & Fri lunch off-seas, Mar 7-15, Nov 15-Dec 15. Open until 10:15pm. Terrace dining. Pkg.
A smiling staff will efficiently serve you delights such as a three-foie gras sampler, a roast turbot served as a flat sausage with marrow and red wine, or roasted, caramelized white-fleshed peaches. When weather permits, sit on the marvellous terrace overhanging Monaco; when warmth and coziness are of necessity, sit by the fireplace in the lovely dining room literally crawling with flowers. C 350. M 145 (weekday lunch), 285-345, 85 (children).

Les Deux Frères

(See restaurant above)
Open year-round. 10 rms 385-495. Bkfst 45. Rm ser. Pkg.
This old village schoolhouse has now been turned into a pleasant spot langorously lounging on the edge of the crag. From your room you'll see Monaco and the coastline 300 yards away (look straight down!).

12/20 Au Grand Inquisiteur

18, rue du Château - 04 93 35 05 37
Closed Mon, Tue lunch, Nov-Dec 26. Open until 10pm. Terrace dining. Pkg.

The name promises torture, but the only torture you'll find here is having to choose from among Max Valente's tempting dishes, such as squash and mussel casserole, knuckle of ham with mushroom cream sauce, or red mullet with liver and anchovies. Respectable enough wine cellar. Village sheep-fold converted into restaurant, charming is the only word for the décor. C 200. M 148-220.

Monte-Carlo Beach Hotel

Av. Princesse-Grace
04 93 28 66 66, fax 04 93 78 14 18
Open year-round. 4 stes 2,400-5,500. 41 rms 2,350-2,550. Rms for disabled. Restaurant. Rm ser. Air cond. Conf. Heated pool. Beach. Tennis. Valet pkg.
Billionaires lurk behind the splendid curved façade of this luxury hotel with its Olympic-sized swimming pool and service reminiscent of a more leisurely age. The magnificently restored rooms all have loggias overlooking the sea. The luncheon buffet is served on the "La Vigie" covered terrace which affords glorious sweeping views of the Riviera.

Le Roquebrune

100, Corniche-Inférieure
04 93 35 00 16, fax 04 93 28 98 36
Closed Jun-Aug: lunch Mon-Thu; Sep-May: Tue, Wed lunch; Nov. Open until 10:15pm, and upon reservation. Terrace dining. Valet pkg.
From the terrace or the spacious dining room, well-heeled patrons ooh and aah over the view of Roquebrune Bay. Daniel Tessier handles his magnificent seafood and produce with respect, creating dishes with intense, well-balanced flavors. Warm welcome and excellent service. The cellar is distinguished, but the à la carte prices are crippling. C 500-800. M 170-360.

Le Vistaero

Grande-Corniche - 04 92 10 40 20 (R)
04 92 10 40 00 (H), fax 04 93 35 18 94
Closed Nov 15-Dec 22. Open until 10:15pm. Priv rm 230. Terrace dining. Air cond. Heated pool. No pets. Valet pkg.
Jean-Pierre Pestre's richly fragrant, expertly crafted cuisine gets better every year, from sardines layered with roasted tomatoes and thyme blossoms, slow-roasted shoulder of lamb with marjoram fumet, to ultrasmooth vanilla ice cream with a roasted peach in vanilla-butter sauce: and that's just the 200 F set meal! Other, more costly pleasures are in store if you choose à la carte; and the wine list is ever so pricey! But the heart-stopping view from the panoramic dining room may well be worth the price of admission. Polished reception and service. C 600. M 200 (weekday lunch), 300 (dinner), 560.

Vista Palace

(See restaurant above)
Closed Nov 15-Dec 22. 26 stes 1,250-6,000. 42 rms 1,050-1,600. Bkfst 100-130. Rms for disabled. Half-

board 370. Rm ser. Air cond. Conf. Heated pool. Valet pkg.

This exquisitely luxurious hotel pampers guests with large, bright rooms and suites and with what just might be the best view in the Riviera; some have private swimming pools and Jacuzzis. Divine nine-acre garden "suspended" over the sea. Charming, experienced staff; fitness center. The Mont Agel golf course is within easy reach.

SAINT-JEAN-CAP-FERRAT	06230
Paris 945 - Nice 14 - Monaco 11	Alpes-Mar.

 Brise Marine

58, av. Jean-Mermoz
04 93 76 04 36, fax 04 93 76 11 49
Closed Nov-beg Feb. 16 rms 570-730. Bkfst 55. Air cond.

This hotel, 100 yards from the beach, has large, rather antiquated rooms, a garden, and terraces for summer breakfasts. Some rooms look out to sea. Pricey.

 Grand Hôtel du Cap-Ferrat

Bd du Général-de-Gaulle
04 93 76 50 50, fax 04 93 76 04 52
Closed Jan-Feb. Open until 9:45pm (10:15pm in summer). Terrace dining. Air cond. Pool. Beach. Tennis. No pets. Valet pkg.

This beautiful establishment, with its glorious veranda and terrace, is one of the last remaining grand hotels dating from the Riviera's heyday. Chef Jean-Claude Guillon pampers guests with fresh, light dishes that are luxurious but still identifiably Southern: langoustines au foie gras et aux ravioles de ricotta, grilled sea bass, squab à l'ancienne. Magnificent desserts, and a capital cellar, administered by Daniel Delcassé. Impressive service. C 500. M 420, 490, 120 (children).

 Grand Hôtel du Cap-Ferrat

(See restaurant above)
Closed Jan-Feb. 11 stes 2,800-10,000. 48 rms 950-5,200. Bkfst incl. Rms for disabled. Half-board 520. Rm ser. Air cond. Pool. Beach. Tennis. Valet pkg.

This grand hotel from the Belle Époque is hidden away in fifteen acres of lawns, copses, and flower beds, but overlooks the sea. The Sazale group, a Japanese concern, invested plenty of yen to turn this into one of the Riviera's top luxury hotels, complete with an Olympic-sized swimming pool. The British decorators who embellished the lounges and rooms have done a bang-up job, creating an atmosphere that is elegant yet relaxed. Rooms offer heavenly comfort with a dream of a balcony. The clientele is younger and less flashy than one might expect. The Le Dauphin restaurant offers poolside dining. Piano bar.

 Jean-Jacques Jouteux

"Le Provençal," 2, av. Daniel-Semeria
04 93 76 03 97, fax 04 93 76 05 39
Closed Mar-Apr: Mon; Nov-Dec 29, Jan 10-Feb. Open until 11pm. Priv rm 40. Air cond. Terrace dining.

There are those times in life when you are moved by what you see before you because never in your wildest dreams did you think such things could become reality. It takes a visionary, a magician, an artist not bound by the limits of convention to create the food you'll relish here: that is our label for Jean-Jacques Jouteux. Need more adjectives? Overcome with emotion at the wild but successful juxtaposition of ingredients we partook in this lovely dining room adorned with walls painted in classic Italian style. God touched his hand when he cooked our barely-crunchy langoustines accompanied by a hefty stack of fine green asparagus and gossamer-like tapenade tuiles, made truly sublime with a jus au café; was still present when he prepared our John Dory fillet roasted in a fig leaf served with a spellbounding honey and Modena vinegar bigarade sauce; and was certainly still hovering over him when he crafted the melt-in-your-mouth chocolate, caramel and walnut macaroon; the cinnamon-flavored baked apples and the glorious crème brulée. Turning dreams into reality never comes cheap though... The cellar you dream of owning. C 450-510. M 150, 280, 300.

 Panorama

3, av. Jean-Monnet - 04 93 76 31 00, fax 04 93 01 23 07
Closed Dec-Feb. Open until 10pm. Garden dining. Air cond. Pool. Beach. Tennis. No pets. Valet pkg.

The views of the bay and the Villa Kerylos are so spectacular, especially at night, that it is easy to be distracted from your food. Which would be a pity, because Yves Merville's cooking is a marvel of harmony and balance. A recent feast here brought a thin tart topped with apples and foie gras and a caramelized glaze of balsamic vinegar, baby lamb baked on a bed of potatoes strewn with rosemary, and a gossamer cappuccino mousse with cocoa sabayon. The cellar holds a trove of fine regional wines, amassed by sommelier Philippe Cronenberger. Top-flight welcome and service. C 400-600. M 220, 265.

 Royal Riviera

(See restaurant above)
Closed Jan-Feb. 5 stes 3,400-5,030. 72 rms 800-2,575. Bkfst 110-140. Rms for disabled. Half-board 350-400. Rm ser. Air cond. Conf. Pool. Beach. Tennis. Valet pkg.

This superb Belle Époque hotel has been impeccably renovated and is now one of the choicest on the coast. The best of these luxuriously appointed rooms overlook the garden and the magnificent pool. Private beach.

For a complete guide to our restaurant rank- ing system, see "Symbol Systems" page 7.

Le Sloop

At the marina - 04 93 01 48 63
Closed Wed off-seas, Nov 15-Dec 15. Open until 9:30pm (10:30pm in summer). Priv rm 60. Terrace dining. Pkg.

The cooking isn't the world's most creative, but it's based on flavorful ingredients prepared with precision and presented with flair. The wine list is worth perusing, for its choice of Provençal bottlings. You can look forward to a cheerful greeting from the energetic *patronne*, who oversees the pretty blue-and-white dining room with a portside terrace. C 300-450. M 155.

 La Voile d'Or

At the marina
04 93 01 13 13, fax 04 93 76 11 17
Closed Nov-Mar. Open until 10:30pm. Priv rm 30. Garden dining. Air cond. Pool. Beach. Valet pkg.

This restaurant, which became an institution under the twenty-year chefdom of Jean Crépin, is now transfused with the new blood of chef Denis Labonne. He had the good sense to reduce the size of the menu and maintain the good quality ingredients of the past. His 250 F set meal is a truly good buy; in the past, one never came to this "institution" with that as objective. The wine list has moved in the same direction, offering some wines at under 150 F a bottle. C 400. M 250 (lunch), 360.

 La Voile d'Or

(See restaurant above)
Closed Nov-Mar. 4 rms 4,260. 41 rms 580-2,660. Bkfst 120. Half-board 360. Air cond. Conf. Pool. Beach. Valet pkg.

An Italian villa and its luxuriant gardens overlooking the harbor. The interior is highly decorative, with *trompe-l'œil* paintings, fine fabrics, and marble everywhere you look. Countless services and amenities.

See also: Beaulieu

ST-MARTIN-DU-VAR   06670
Paris 970 - Nice 27 - Antibes 34   Alpes-Mar.

 Issautier

3 km S on N 202 - 04 93 08 10 65, fax 04 93 29 19 73
Closed Sun dinner & Mon off-seas, mid Feb-mid Mar, 2 wks in Oct. Open until 9:30pm. Air cond. Pkg.

Sun-gorged seasonal produce from the hilly Niçois hinterland is the keynote of Jean-François Issautier's full-bodied cooking. An extremely affable staff served us delectable ravioli stuffed with herbs and truffles, roast fillet of pageot (a kind of sea bream) set atop a vivid sweet-pepper coulis and flanked by silken celery mousseline and a heap of crisp artichoke chips, and an ineffably light, crackling strawberry croustillant. The accessibly priced cellar holds a wonderful cache of Provençal wines. C 435-585. M 250 (lunch, wine incl, exc Sun & hols), 320, 515.

SAINT-PAUL-DE-VENCE   06570
Paris 925 - Cannes 27 - Nice 20 - Antibes 16   Alpes-Mar.

 La Brouette

"Chez les Danois,"
830, route de Cagnes - 04 93 58 67 16
Closed Sun dinner, Mon, 2 wks in Feb, 2 wks in Oct. Open until 11pm. Priv rm 12. Garden dining. Air cond. Garage pkg.

Ole and Brigitte Bornemann serve authentic Danish specialties in a lively, pleasant atmosphere. Opt for a seat near the fireplace in winter, or in the garden when the weather warms, for its great view of the village and a barbecue where fish are smoked. Sample the tasty liver terrine with cucumber confit, trout smoked with dill, and leg of Greenland reindeer. Expansive welcome. C 220. M 95 (lunch), 120-188 (dinner), 148.

12/20 La Colombe d'Or

Pl. du Général-de-Gaulle
04 93 32 80 02, fax 04 93 32 77 78
Closed beg Nov-Dec 20. Open until 10pm. Priv rm 40. Terrace dining. Heated pool. Valet pkg.

Picture a paradise for art lovers, with works by Picasso, Rouault, Léger, Miró and others adorning the walls. Come here to enjoy the leafy terrace and garden, and some very simple but pricey Provençal food (rack of lamb, chicken fricassée with morels, almond tart spiked with sweet Beaumes-de-Venise wine). C 370-480.

 La Colombe d'Or

(See restaurant above)
Closed beg Nov-Dec 20. 10 stes 1,500. 16 rms 1,300. Rms for disabled. Half-board 1,700. Air cond. Heated pool. Sauna. Valet pkg.

This warmly welcoming Provençal hotel is very tastefully decorated. The rooms are delightful. Superb swimming pool.

 La Grande Bastide

1350, route de la Colle
04 93 32 50 30, fax 04 93 32 50 59
Closed Jan 15-Feb 15. 4 stes 750-950. 6 rms 650. Bkfst 50. Air cond. Conf. Heated pool. Pkg.

This bastide sits happily on the hilltop on the road leading into the village. Beautifully renovated, it offers rooms of varying sizes, all decorated with bright Provence-style fabrics. Some have mezzanines. Friendly welcome. Too bad the pool and garden are so small.

 Hostellerie des Messugues

Domaine des Gardettes, impasse des Messugues
04 93 32 53 32, fax 04 93 32 94 15
Closed Oct-Mar. 15 rms 450-650. Bkfst 50. Rms for disabled. Pool. Beach. Tennis.

Just outside the village, deep in a pine grove, stands this comfortable, attractively decorated hotel. Good rooms, pretty baths.

Mas d'Artigny

Route de La Colle
04 93 32 84 54, fax 04 93 32 95 36
Open daily until 10pm. Garden dining. Heated pool. Tennis. Valet pkg.
The largest dining room in this huge, rambling building now sports a warm and colorful Provençal décor. All the better to put diners in the mood for Francis Scordel's subtle, sunny cooking: if it's on the menu, try his rabbit terrine with foie gras "Grand Maman," or the fillet of sea bass with persillade in an anise jus. Prices, predictably, remain stratospheric, especially those charged for the cellar's premium wines. C 450-600. M 290, 395.

 Mas d'Artigny

(See restaurant above)
Open year-round. 29 stes 1,585-2,680. 53 rms 575-1,830. Bkfst 100-140. Half-board 690-1,315. Rm ser. Air cond. Conf. Heated pool. Tennis. Valet pkg.
The rooms and poolside suites have all it takes to make you feel like a millionaire. There are several marvelous multi-room villas scattered among the twenty acres of pines. Relais et Châteaux.

 Le Saint-Paul

86, rue Grande - 04 93 32 65 25, fax 04 93 32 52 94
Closed Wed & Thu lunch off-seas. Open until 10pm. Priv rm 20. Terrace dining. Air cond. Valet pkg.
The time-worn stones and frescoes of this charming Provençal house look even better after their full-dress renovation a couple years ago. But unfortunately, pretty surroundings don't necessarily make for good food. Too many botched dishes and blunders this year in Frédéric Buzet's personalized repertoire of sun-drenched dishes; a point just has to drop. Nevertheless, his cheese is as good a quality as you find and the wine cellar is chock-full of good bottlings. Perfect service but you wonder who programmed the robots. Pleasant terrace. C 350. M 185 (lunch), 290-380, 130 (children).

 Le Saint-Paul

(See restaurant above)
Open year-round. 3 stes 1,300-2,500. 15 rms 750-1,500. Bkfst 90. Rms for disabled. Half-board 390. Rm ser. Air cond. Conf. Valet pkg.
This delightful hotel dates from the Renaissance. Its freshly refurbished rooms are most attractive and comfortable (those with a view of the countryside are the best), and the service is very good indeed. There's also a library, and a bar. Relais et Châteaux.

SAINT-RAPHAËL   83700
Paris 892 - Cannes 44 - Toulon 96   Var

 L'Arbousier

6, av. de Valescure
04 94 95 25 00, fax 04 94 83 81 04
Closed Tue dinner & Wed off-seas, Dec 10-Jan 3. Open until 10pm. Priv rm 8. Terrace dining. Air cond.
Happily ensconced in a pretty town house with a garden and terrace, Philippe Troncy combines keen flavors with inventive flair: his is a resolutely modern version of Provençal cuisine. Although it costs 200 F on Sundays and holidays, the 170 F prix-fixe meal is a very good deal: truffled rabbit and vegetables served with a little salad dressed with balsamic vinegar, famously good lobster ravioli in a concentrated jus, a perfectly wrought fricassée of sweetbreads and duck breast, and an ethereal berry millefeuille. Capital cellar, fairly priced, with many half-bottles. C 300-330. M 140 (lunch, exc Sun), 170 (exc Sun & hols), 200 (Sun & hols), 300.

 Golf-Hôtel de Valescure

Valescure Golf course, av. Paul-Lhermite
04 94 52 85 00, fax 04 94 82 41 88
Closed Jan 7-31, Nov 15-Dec 22. 40 rms 460-910. Bkfst incl. Rms for disabled. Restaurant. Half-board 470-795. Air cond. Conf. Pool. Tennis. Pkg.
Comfortable, sunny rooms (some facing the golf course) are available here. Golf and tennis lessons.

 Le Jardin de Sébastien

595, av. des Golfs - 04 94 44 66 56, fax 04 94 82 40 55
Closed Sun dinner & Mon off-seas, 2 wks in Jan, 2 wks in Nov. Open until 10:30pm. Terrace dining. Garage pkg.
On a starry summer's night, reserve a table on the terrace by the fountain and dine to the soothing sound of the water. Chef Sébastien Arfeuillère has grounded himself here after a long stay in one of the finer kitchens of France. He is following in his master's footsteps by offering you market-fresh ingredients crafted with the tenderest of loving care: red mullet fillet risotto or loin of milk-fed lamb with baby vegetables. Good service. C 280. M 125-250.

 Pastorel

54, rue de la Liberté
04 94 95 02 36, fax 04 94 95 64 07
Closed Sun dinner, Mon lunch in Aug. Open until 10pm. Priv rm 40. Terrace dining.
Take a terrace table if you can. There you'll enjoy even more Charles Floccia's updated traditional dishes from the Provençal repertoire, available on a variety of well-designed, fairly priced set meals. Lots of customers in season, but the welcome is always cordial. Good selection of local wines. M 160, 190, 90 (children).

La Potinière

5 km E on N 98, Boulouris
04 94 95 21 43, fax 04 94 95 29 10
Open year-round. 4 stes 550-870. 24 rms 290-760. Bkfst 50-70. Restaurant. Half-board 295-520 (oblig in seas). Conf. Heated pool. Garage pkg.
A large villa lazing in the middle of eucalyptus and umbrella pines. Peace and quiet are on the agenda in this little corner a little away from the seaside. The major renovation has made this into a pleasant place.

SAINT-TROPEZ	83990
Paris 890 - Cannes 75 - Toulon 69	Var

 Les Arcades

Av. Paul-Signac - 04 94 56 68 00, fax 04 94 56 68 01
Closed mid Oct-mid Mar. Open until 10:30pm (11:30pm in summer). Priv rm 120. Terrace dining. Air cond. Heated pool. Valet pkg.
Perfect place to get away from the hustle and bustle of the crowd with the 180 F lunch special around the swimming pool. Dinner is another matter. The Caves du Roy downstairs draws the cream of the Saint-Tropez crop—Paris-based stars congregate there—so don't go there expecting the haven you found at lunchtime. The cuisine is to be taken seriously, although we find it's been on the downslide for a few years now: therefore we have to take away a point. We won't be too hard on them though: the Bresse chicken with pure salt and the almond milk pudding full of surprising sweet/acidic/bitter flavors all gloriously melted into each other were certainly more than noteworthy. Fine selection of rosés to dry up your thirst. C 450-550. M 180 (lunch), 290-410.

 Byblos

(See restaurant above)
Closed mid Oct-mid Mar. 55 stes 1,980-5,800. 47 rms 700-2,380. Bkfst 120-160. Half-board 1,100-3,300. Rm ser. Air cond. Conf. Heated pool. Valet pkg.
A mythical venue, where everyone who's anyone in Saint-Trop' eventually shows up, either at the magnificent pool or the trendy disco. The hotel's layout is so skillful that customers are not bothered by the bustling attendance of Saint-Tropez's gilded set. Extremely luxurious appointments, incredibly high rates.

12/20 L'Astragale

N 98, chemin de Gassine
04 94 97 48 98, fax 04 94 97 16 01
Closed mid Oct-beg May. Open until 10:30pm. Terrace dining. Air cond. Pool. Tennis. Pkg.
Oddly decorated chalets (the Swiss Alps meet Louisiana bayou) surround a glorious swimming pool. There or in a pretty pavilion patrons enjoy chestnut gnocchi, pan-roasted foie gras, spiced duck served with a tomato tarte Tatin, and walnut croustillant with cappuccino sauce. C 250-350. M 190 (dinner, wine incl), 290.

 L'Astragale

(See restaurant above)
Closed mid Oct-beg May. 34 rms 1,100-2,220. Bkfst 95. Rms for disabled. Half-board 1,420. Rm ser. Air cond. Conf. Pool. Beach. Tennis. Pkg.
Luxurious accommodations set in beautiful grounds around the pool; rooms on the upper floor have balconies, while those below give directly onto the garden. Access to the private Bouillabaisse beach and restaurant.

Auberge des Maures

4, rue du Docteur Boutin
04 94 97 01 50, fax 04 94 97 18 35
Open daily until 11pm. Terrace dining.
Modern, light cooking in this lovely little inn with simple but well prepared dishes such as steamed burbot with a really fine-tuned aïoli sauce, a first-rate broiled sea bass (although a touch overcooked) and a velvety frozen nougat. Pleasant straightforward service. C 200-300. M 130.

Bastide de Saint-Tropez

See restaurant L'Olivier

La Bastide des Salins

Route des Salins - 04 94 97 24 57, fax 04 94 54 89 03
Open year-round. 1 ste 1,200-2,300. 14 rms 750-1,600. Bkfst 50. Air cond. Rm ser. Pool. Garage pkg.
This is one of the most pleasant hotels in town. A fortified farmhouse built during the last century, it has huge, handsome rooms and superb grounds.

The Beaches

Generally open from Easter to October, for lunch only.
Bora-Bora (04 94 97 19 75 - Plage de Pampelonne.): A relaxed atmosphere where you can eat a hearty lunch on La Mandarine's private beach as you twitter your toes in the water...(160-180).
Club 55 (04 94 79 80 14 - Plage de Pampelonne.): Fried fish combo plates and broiled fish. Local wines. Lost in the pine trees behind the bamboo arbor (200-350).
Tropicana (04 94 79 83 96 - Plage de Pampelonne.): Wide selection of regional specialities at reasonable prices (considering where you are!) in this simple little restaurant full of good cheer (250).
La Voile Rouge (04 94 79 84 34 - Plage de Ramatuelle.): This restaurant serves well-prepared food made from market-fresh ingredients and served by a youthful (and beautiful) staff. Salads, artichokes with parsley sauce, etc. (300 and up).

*Remember to call ahead to **reserve your table**, and please, if you cannot honor your reservation, be courteous and let the restaurant know.*

Aux Bigorneaux

"Yvan," pl. de la Garonne - 04 94 97 89 65
Open daily until midnight. No pets.
This is as about as typical a Saint-Tropez atmosphere as you can get. Yvan's house may be simple in décor and the service may be slow, but don't let that fool you. The sun-drenched food is artfully prepared and handled with the utmost care, yet it remains simple and light. Some examples: tuna carpaccio with basil or crispy curried cod steak. Nothing can be done but to give him a toque! **M** 208.

 Bistrot des Lices

3, pl. des Lices
04 94 97 29 00, fax 04 94 97 76 39
Closed Sun dinner & Wed off-seas, Jan 10-Easter, Nov 15-Dec 15. Open until 10:30pm (11:30pm in summer). Garden dining.
From the terrace, diners can admire the skill of local *boules* players; inside, there's an intimate dining room that leads out to a walled garden and tables shaded by parasols. Breton native Laurent Tarridec presides over this smart, *très tropézien* scene, and though we had a few doubts about the three-toque rating after our first visit, successive experiences prove that Tarridec is still a great chef. From his garden vegetable soup with a scallion infusion and tiny clams, or roast baby veal with carrots and gratinéed marrow, to the gnocchi ragoût with grilled belly bacon and roasted langoustines, or lamb's trotter stew with white beans au jus, each dish displays precise yet expansive flavors that only a gifted craftsman can contrive. The generous 185 F lunch is a fine introduction to Tarridec's direct, virile cuisine, for which the cellar's Provençal wines are ideal partners. **C** 500. **M** 185 (lunch), 295.

Le Byblos

See restaurant Les Arcades

 Château de la Messardière

Route de Tahiti - 04 94 56 76 00, fax 04 94 56 76 01
Closed Nov-end Mar. Open until 10:30pm. Terrace dining. Air cond. Heated pool. Valet pkg.
Once shipwrecked on the shoals of ambition, this curious, enormous turn-of-the-century villa is now seaworthy again. The cuisine served in the chintz-decked dining room (and on the terrace with a splendid view of the Bay of Pampelonne) is the work of Jean-Louis Vosgien, whose eclectic menu harmonizes flavors from Provence, the West Indies, and Southeast Asia. Try his lively gingered shrimp, codfish tart, sea bream with spicy tomato sauce, and saffron-tinged peach gratin. Fine choice of Provençal wines at a wide range of prices. Chic clientele. **C** 500-600. **M** 240-420 (dinner), 280, 150 (children).

 Château de la Messardière

(See restaurant above)

Closed Nov-end Mar. 20 stes 2,400-12,000. 70 rms 800-3,000. Bkfst 100-150. Rms for disabled. Half-board 380. Rm ser. Air cond. Conf. Heated pool. Valet pkg.
Despite vast sums already spent on the place, more buckets of money were needed to bring guest rooms and terraces up to par. Irreprochable comfort now reigns in this hotel set in twenty acres of grounds, with awe-inspiring views of the bays of Saint-Tropez and Pampelonne. The suites are vast; the rooms less so, but they're also much cheaper. Magnificent pool.

12/20 **Chez Fuchs**

7, rue des Commerçants
04 94 97 01 25, fax 04 94 97 81 82
Closed Tue, Nov 15-Dec 15. Open until 11:30pm. Air cond.
The cigar cellar gives this restaurant a chic atmosphere that the locals like a lot. The simple, well-crafted regional dishes include ravioli, beef stew, fresh fish, and mesclun salad. **C** 200-350.

 Ermitage

Av. Paul-Signac - 04 94 97 52 33, fax 04 94 97 10 43
Open year-round. 1 ste 590-990. 25 rms 390-890. Bkfst 48. Valet pkg.
From the garden of this white 1930s villa on Place de Lices at the foot of the citadel, guests enjoy a sweeping view of old Saint-Tropez. The smallish rooms are decorated in a plush, comfortable style.

12/20 **Le Girelier**

Quai Jean-Jaurès - 04 94 97 03 87, fax 04 94 97 43 86
Closed Oct 10-Mar. Open until 10:30pm. Terrace dining. Air cond.
With its lovely navy-blue terrace, Le Girelier is the best restaurant on the port, with an uncomplicated repertoire devoted to nicely turned out seafood and homestyle dishes. There are half-bottles galore in the worthwhile cellar of regional wines, and you can expect a most affable welcome. **C** 280. **M** 185.

 Les Lauriers

Rue du Temple - 04 94 97 04 88, fax 04 94 97 21 87
Closed mid Jan-mid Feb. 18 rms 275-575. Bkfst 40.
Here's a quiet little establishment near Place des Lices, with a garden and freshly redecorated rooms. Their new satellite dish may encourage you to take refuge in the garden.

 Le Levant

Route de Salins - 04 94 97 33 33, fax 04 94 97 76 13
Closed Oct 15-Mar 15. 28 rms 395-875. Bkfst 57. No pets. Pool. Garage pkg.
Sweet little bungalows offering charming, tastefully renovated rooms and located on a country road. Direct access to the sea.

> Remember to call ahead to **reserve your room**, and please, if you cannot honor your reservation, be courteous and let the hotel know.

Lou Troupelen

Chemin des Vendanges
04 94 97 44 88, fax 04 94 97 41 76
Closed end Oct-Easter. 45 rms 330-499. Bkfst 50. No pets. Pkg.
These two roomy neo-Provençal buildings are located between the shore and the town center. Lodgings are comfortable and pleasantly decorated, with attractive views. Breakfast is served in the quiet, shady garden.

 La Maison Blanche

Pl. des Lices - 04 94 97 52 66, fax 04 94 97 89 23
Open year-round. 1 ste 500-1,800. 7 rms 500-1,800. Bkfst 90-110. Rm ser. Air cond. Valet pkg.
This turn-of-the-century residence in the center of town is flanked by a tiny garden, where a bar is set up in summer. Pleasant, tasteful décor and atmosphere, antique furniture. Very attentive service.

12/20 La Maison de Marie

26, rue des Charrons - 04 94 97 09 99
Closed Mon off-seas, Jan. Open until 10pm. Terrace dining.
A typically Saint-Tropez style house with its two magnolias in the yard, although the prices are not all so typical as that. A must. Savor this totally Mediterranean cooking made from only the highest quality ingredients: soupe au pistou (vegetable soup flavored with basil), stuffed squids, lasagne, garlic chicken, honey and almond cake. And it's so inviting, you might forget whether you're in a restaurant or at home in your own kitchen. C 200 (wine incl). M 160.

 La Mandarine

Route de Tahiti - 04 94 76 06 66, fax 04 94 97 33 67
Closed mid Oct-beg May. 4 stes 2,100-2,940. 39 rms 930-2,310. Bkfst 85. Restaurant. Half-board 345. Rm ser. Air cond. Pool. Beach. Pkg.
Accommodations consist of several pink neo-Provençal bungalows scattered around five acres of idyllic grounds. Luxurious rooms, impeccably tended, with views of vineyards and mountains. Pool on the premises; the hotel's private beach is Bora-Bora (see *The Beaches*), at nearby Pampelonne.

12/20 Le Migon

"Bonne Terrasse," route de Ramatuelle
04 94 79 83 68, fax 04 94 79 83 68
Closed Oct-Apr. Open until 10:30pm. Priv rm 50. Terrace dining. Pkg.
This little country cottage right on the beach serves unpretentious meals made from market-fresh ingredients. Try the good-quality ratatouille or the interesting zucchini au gratin cooked over a wood fire, or again the tasty broiled fish. Good selection of local wines to wash it down. C 200-300. M 180, 60 (children).

 Nioulargo et Kailargo

Bd Patch - 04 94 79 82 14, fax 04 94 79 90 42
Closed mid Oct-Mar. Open until 10:30pm. Priv rm 150. Terrace dining. Pkg.
Exotically-inspired cooking in a restaurant you can drive right up to in your boat. Sample the shrimp and green mango salad, the shrimp and squids sautéed in hot-pepper basil, or the ginger-spiced fish broiled in a banana leaf. Located on the Pampelonne beach, with a pontoon serving as entrance bridge. C 280-350.

L'Olivier

Route des Carles, 1 km
04 94 97 58 16, fax 04 94 97 21 71
Closed Feb 16-Apr 28 (exc Easter weekend) & Oct 6-Dec 23: Mon & Tue lunch; Jan 5-Feb 13. Open until 11pm. Garden dining. Heated pool. Valet pkg.
Just minutes away from Place des Lices you find yourself among verdant fields and vineyards, in a lush garden planted with palm, olive, and fig trees. This is the realm of new young chef, Franck Putelat, who worked one year at Taillevent and four years at Blanc. The change comes a little too close to printing time for us to have a chance to try out the cuisine. We can tell you, however, that the classical repertoire of the menu we looked at offers promising dishes like confit vegetable ravioli with olive oil, sea bream and fennel with a light parsley sauce, and two-chocolate hot and cold soufflé. The wine list is short but *à propos*. C 350. M 220 (lunch), 290 (dinner).

 Bastide de Saint-Tropez

(See restaurant above)
Closed Jan 6-Feb 15. 8 stes 2,200-3,500. 18 rms 980-2,350. Rms for disabled. Half-board 1,330-2,700. Rm ser. Air cond. Conf. Heated pool. Valet pkg.
Well away from the buzzing crowds of Saint-Tropez, in an enchanting garden, you can stay in delightful rooms and suites, all of which have either a terrace or a private garden where you can invite your friends in to lunch or dine just as if you were at L'Olivier. Gorgeous pool; really perfect service overseen by the young general manager, Pascal Lambert.

 Les Palmiers

Pl. des Lices, 26, bd Vasselot
04 94 97 01 61, fax 04 94 97 10 02
Open year-round. 23 rms 390-600. Bkfst 50. Rms for disabled.
The rooms are unexceptional, but pretty inexpensive by local standards. What's more, the garden is a delight. You can take your breakfast there, amid orange trees and jasmine.

 Le Petit Charron

6, rue des Charrons - 04 94 97 73 78
Closed Wed, Sun dinner off-seas, 2 wks in Feb, 2 wks in Oct. Open until 10:30pm. Air cond. Terrace dining.

A pearl of a place in Saint-Tropez. Violaine and Christian Benoît welcome guests into their tiny dining room and serve them simple, eminently satisfying food: a crisp-crusted tomato and sweet-pepper tart, tiny red mullet given a quick turn on the grill and served with their briny juices intact, and a rich crème brûlée perfumed with lavender. The cellar's prices are as friendly as the service. C 210-270. M 145-175.

12/20 La Ponche

Port des Pêcheurs, 3, rue des Remparts
04 94 97 02 53, fax 04 94 97 78 61
Closed Nov-Mar. Open until midnight. Priv rm 30. Terrace dining. Air cond. Valet pkg.
A cosmopolitan crowd haunts La Ponche's terrace overlooking the old fishing port, to sample seafood salads, turbot with tomato-butter sauce, and simple Provençal dishes prepared with obvious care. Regional cellar; attentive staff. C 280. M 120-180.

La Ponche

(See restaurant above)
Closed Nov-Mar. 5 stes 700-2,300. 13 rms 500-1,700. Bkfst 60-80. Half-board 680-1,780. Rm ser. Air cond. Valet pkg.
Charming, remodeled, well-equipped rooms with sea views. You'll find elegant décor and excellent comfort. Breakfast is served on the terrace that overlooks the port.

11/20 Le Relais des Caves du Roy

Hôtel Le Byblos, av. Paul-Signac
04 94 56 68 20, fax 04 94 56 68 01
Closed Mon off-seas, Oct-beg May. Open until 1:20am. Terrace dining. Air cond. Valet pkg.
If you're itching to see and be seen, here's the place to go. For night owls only. A charming bistro where you can dine with as well as under the stars if you choose the terrace. Standards such as tomato and mozzarella, risotto, and even pizza, but all done with care and precision. C 200. M 180 (dinner).

Résidence de la Pinède

Plage de la Bouillabaisse
04 94 97 04 21, fax 04 94 97 73 64
Closed mid Oct-end Mar. Open until 10:30pm. Terrace dining. Air cond. Pool. Beach. Valet pkg.
Hervé Quesnel is versatile. He can come up with a deluxe poolside snack for a billionaire guest who's feeling peckish, while he turns out a vegetable fricassée (a pastoral poem!), a red mullet with potatoes in a concisely finished jus, or a duck perfumed with a balanced blend of spices. Now that's a professional! Innovation isn't his strong suit, but he knows how to get a bead on culinary trends (like the current fashion for Latino-rustic flavors) and use them to enliven his repertoire. Excellent service; enticing cellar, rich in regional wines and fine Bordeaux. C 500-700. M 150, 380, 550, 150 (children).

Résidence de la Pinède

(See restaurant above)
Closed mid Oct-end Mar. 7 stes 2,100-5,100. 44 rms 1,300-2,985. Bkfst 115. Rms for disabled. Half-board 1,650. Rm ser. Air cond. Heated pool. Beach. Tennis. Valet pkg.
A screen of greenery keeps road noise out, and the Bay of Saint-Tropez spreads seductively below (direct access to the beach). Umbrella pines shade the huge, extremely comfortable rooms, all of which were recently remodeled and redecorated. Kidney-shaped swimming pool, private beach, and spectacular views from the balconies of each room and suite overlooking the sea. Exemplary service. Relais et Châteaux.

Résidence des Lices

Av. Augustin-Grangeon
04 94 97 28 28, fax 04 94 97 59 52
Closed Jan-Feb. 41 rms 300-1,600. Bkfst 60-100. Air cond. Pool. Valet pkg.
All-new bathrooms, a freshly renovated terrace, a brand-new Jacuzzi, solarium, and outdoor bar, and soon-to-be-renovated rooms add to the attractions of this impeccably kept hotel just steps away from Place des Lices.

Hôtel Sube

On the harbor - 04 94 97 30 04, fax 04 94 54 89 08
Open year-round. 30 rms 390-1,500. Bkfst 65. Air cond. Conf. Valet pkg.
Behind the recently renovated façade are some expensive, though pleasant little rooms with views of Saint-Tropez's quays, yachts, and crowds.

La Tartane

Route de la plage des Salins
04 94 97 21 23, fax 04 94 97 09 16
Closed Oct 15-Mar 15. 13 rms 350-900. Bkfst 68. Restaurant. Rm ser. Air cond. Heated pool. Beach. Tennis. Garage pkg.
La Tartane's thirteen handsome bungalows, nestled in a verdant setting, form a sort of hamlet, with superb, well-equipped rooms and comfortable terraces. The beach is 800 yards away.

Le Yaca

1, bd d'Aumale - 04 94 97 11 79, fax 04 94 97 58 50
Closed Oct 15-Mar 27. 1 ste 3,400. 24 rms 1,400-2,400. Bkfst 85-99. Restaurant. Rm ser. Air cond. Heated pool. Valet pkg.
In the heart of Saint-Tropez, Le Yaca is an elegant, expensive hotel with a score or so of rooms (the nicest are on the upper floors). There's also a lovely enclosed garden.

And also...

Our selection of places for inexpensive, quick, or late-night meals.
Bar à Vins (04 94 97 46 10 - 13, rue des Féniers. Open until 9pm.): Wine by the glass, and a con-

vivial atmosphere in the *salle de billard*. Tanned guests sample pleasant dishes at marble tables (100-150).

See also: Gassin, Grimaud, Port-Grimaud, Ramatuelle

SAINTE-MAXIME	83120
Paris 880 - St-Raphaël 23 - Cannes 61	Var

Calidianus

Bd des Hortensias
04 94 96 23 21, fax 04 94 49 12 10
Open year-round. 33 rms 790-930. Bkfst 80. Restaurant. Conf. Pool. Tennis. Pkg.
Nestled in leafy grounds near the sea, the Calidianus comprises a group of small buildings in the local style. The rooms are spacious and well furnished; most have balconies or terraces giving onto the swimming pool. All have minibars.

Hostellerie de la Belle Aurore

4, bd Jean-Moulin
04 94 96 02 45, fax 04 94 96 63 87
Closed Wed lunch off-seas, end Sep-Apr 1. Open until 10pm. Priv rm 10. Terrace dining. Air cond. Pool. Beach. Tennis. Garage pkg.
Get away from it all in this rotunda-shaped dining room with large bay windows giving onto the bay, with Saint-Tropez as backdrop. The chefs just keep changing here, but the quality remains the same. Christophe Lesbats is well versed in the sunny flavors of the South of France, and awards us with admirable efforts like old-fashioned upsidedown tomato tart, turbot with lemon grass, zucchini risotto, delicate scampi ravioli, and pan-fried hog fish with truffles and celery tatliatelle pasta. His 198 F fixed-price meal is a good value, but read the price of the Provence wines carefully before you order. C 400. M 198, 80 (children).

Hostellerie de la Belle Aurore

(See restaurant above)
Closed Oct 10-25, Nov 15-Dec 20, Jan 2-Mar 1. 1 ste 1,300-2,200. 16 rms 600-1,800. Bkfst 70. Rms for disabled. Half-board 700-1,300. Rm ser. Air cond. Conf. Pool. Beach. Tennis. Pkg.
Dawn's rosy fingers reach across the bay into the rooms of this Riviera inn perched above the sea. Provençal-style furniture, handsome fabrics, cane chairs. Swimming pool with diving board.

Hostellerie La Croisette

2, bd des Romarins - 04 94 96 17 75, fax 04 94 96 52 40
Closed Nov-Mar 1. 17 rms 400-980. Bkfst 50. Rms for disabled. Air cond. Conf. Garage pkg.
The Provençal-style rooms are attractively decorated and well equipped, with views either of the sea or the charming garden out back. Cheerful reception.

12/20 La Maison Bleue

24 bis, rue Paul-Bert
04 94 96 51 92, fax 04 94 96 71 69
Closed Sun dinner & Mon off-seas, Tue, Jan 10-Feb school hols, Nov-Dec 26. Open until 10pm (11pm in summer). Terrace dining. Air cond.
This little restaurant is almost lost among the many bars and coffee houses of this pedestrian street, but has kept its head up over the years thanks to good-quality downhome cooking using fresh ingredients. Warm reception. Small wine cellar, but still a respectable selection. C 240. M 90, 125, 55 (children).

Parc-Hôtel du Jas Neuf

71, route du Débarquement
04 94 96 51 88, fax 04 94 49 09 71
Open year-round. 23 rms 300-790. Bkfst 45. Half-board 365-610. Restaurant. Air cond. Conf. Pool. Pkg.
Several modern, Provence-style buildings arranged in stairsteps around the fresh-water swimming pool. Pleasant rooms with Provence-style décor, most of which give onto the pool and garden. Located on the Nartelle beach.

Hôtel de la Poste

7, bd Frédéric-Mistral
04 94 96 18 33, fax 04 94 96 41 68
Closed Oct 15-May 15. 24 rms 300-620. Bkfst 45. Pool. Pkg.
Just 100 yards from the harbor, in the center of town, this outstanding modern hotel is elegant and bright, with handsome rooms (some connecting, for families). Breakfast is served on the poolside terrace.

Le Relais de Provence

"Hotel Country Club," Golf de Sainte-Maxime
04 94 56 66 66, fax 04 94 56 66 00
Open dinner only until 10:15pm. Priv rm 80. Air cond. Terrace dining. Pool. Tennis. Pkg.
Luckily you can't see the hulking façade of the Golf Plaza hotel from the dining room here, but you do note that the coast is mostly covered with high-rise buildings these days. There's a nice view of the sea to compensate, and chef Michel Réthoré now offers us more authentic regional cooking than in the past with taste-tinglers like socca pancakes, lamb with thyme, rabbit and lamb's sweetbread "mosaic" with tomates confites and ricotta polenta au gratin. The fixed-price meals have greatly improved. Respectable selection of Provence wines. C 200-300. M 195.

Golf Plaza

(See restaurant above)
Open year-round. 13 stes 1,500-3,100. 93 rms 740-1,300. Bkfst 75. Rms for disabled. Half-board 900. Rm ser. Air cond. Conf. Pool. Tennis. Pkg.
This hotel with its garish façade, a developer's dream, dominates the Sainte-Maxime golf

course. The attractive, super-comfortable rooms are nicely equipped, with south-facing terraces that look out onto the Bay of Saint-Tropez. Lots of sporting facilities: eight tennis courts, fitness club, private beach. Panoramic restaurant.

SOPHIA-ANTIPOLIS	06560
Paris 919 - Nice 20 - Valbonne 7	Alpes-Mar.

 L'Arlequin

"Country Club," 3550, route des Dolines
04 92 96 68 78, fax 04 92 96 68 96
Open daily until 10:15pm. Terrace dining. Air cond. Garage pkg.
From your seat in the dining room or on the broad terrace, you can enjoy a view of the hotel's pool and grounds, while sampling Thierry Maynier's partly classic, partly informal repertoire. The 180 F "Parfums de Provence" set-price menu offers tasty morsels such smoked red mullet fillets with thyme and apples in cream sauce, salt cod risotto in sour cream sauce, fresh fruit pistou, and mascarpone ice cream. You can even afford to order à la carte, with such interesting offerings as the original chilled salt cod brandade served with a light lemon-flavored sauce or the saffron-laced bourride of the day. Tiny but well-composed wine list. C 200-260. M 90 (weekday lunch, wine incl), 160 & 180 (weekdays, Sun dinner), 75 (children).

 Grand Hôtel Mercure

(See restaurant above)
Open year-round. 2 stes 800-1,600. 105 rms 565-700. Bkfst 70. Rms for disabled. Rm ser. Air cond. Conf. Pool. Pkg.
An immense leisure complex set in extensive grounds just a few minutes from the sea (free shuttle bus to the beach). Guest rooms are well appointed, soundproofed, and have private balconies. Among the many services on tap are a masseur, exercise classes, a beauty salon, gift shop, and car-rental agency. Piano bar.

TOULON	83000
Paris 833 - Nice 152 - Aix-en-P. 81 - Marseille 66	Var

 La Chamade

25, rue Denfert-Rochereau - 04 94 92 28 58
Closed Sat lunch, Sun, Aug 1-15. Open until 9:30pm. Priv rm 20. Air cond.
Véronique Bonneau's warm welcome adds to the charm of La Chamade's brand-new décor. Her husband Francis, an alumnus of Taillevent, has composed a very up-to-date menu based on top-quality ingredients: taste his lusty brochette of snails and lamb's tongue à la provençale, grouper roasted with rashers of smoky bacon and a touch of rosemary, and delectable date craquelin spiked with gentian liqueur. Charming service. C 320-420. M 130 (lunch), 175, 290, 60 (children).

 La Corniche

17, littoral Frédéric-Mistral
04 94 41 35 12, fax 04 94 41 24 58
Open year-round. 3 stes 400-550. 19 rms 350-450. Bkfst 50. Rms for disabled. Restaurant. Half-board 450-700. Air cond. Conf. No pets. Pkg.
This hotel provides well-equipped, distinctive, comfortable rooms, half of which have balconies or terraces overlooking the sea. All are air conditioned and offer cable TV.

 Le Gros Ventre

Corniche du Mourillon, opposite Fort St-Louis
04 94 42 15 42, fax 04 94 31 40 32
Closed Wed & Thu lunch (exc Jul-Aug). Open until 11pm. Terrace dining.
Alain Audibert's specialty is puff pastry: he wraps truffles, fish, and beef in buttery, golden layers of the stuff, creating rich, traditional masterpieces that invite one to indulge. His salads of wild greens are full of authentic flavor, and he even cooks up the yummy jams and preserves that adorn many of his desserts. The cellar, full of modestly priced surprises, is worth a wine lover's careful attention. C 250. M 95 (lunch), 148, 224, 60 (children).

 Holiday Inn Garden Court

1, av. Rageot-de-la-Touche
04 94 92 00 21, fax 04 94 62 08 15
Open year-round. 7 stes 600. 74 rms 375. Bkfst 45. Rm for disabled. Restaurant. Half-board 415. Air cond. Conf. Pool. Garage pkg.
Central location just around the corner from the train station. Good quality hotel with prettily decorated, big rooms. Efficient reception and service. The rooms cost the same for up to four people.

 Le Jardin du Sommelier

20, allée Courbet - 04 94 62 03 27, fax 04 94 09 01 49
Closed Sat lunch, Sun. Open until 11pm. Priv rm 35. Terrace dining. Air cond. Pkg.
This little dining room is elegance itself with its exquisite floral compositions. In this prime location right next to the Place d'Armes, Gilles Oliviero tempts you with his skillfully executed cooking full of inventiveness and ingenuity. Let yourself be seduced by the first-rate, cooked-to-perfection lobster pistou served with a delectable stuffed-squid salad. Surprise yourself with the duck tournedos with girolle (a type of chanterelle) mushrooms served with potatoes in oil. The owner used to be a sommelier, thus the name, and thus the cleverly selected wines of his ever-evolving wine list. Professional, attentive service. Keep your eye on this restaurant; the future looks bright. C 250. C 60 (children).

Au Sourd

10, rue Molière - 04 94 92 28 52, fax 04 94 91 59 92
*Closed Sun lunch, Mon, Jul. Open until 10:30pm.
Terrace dining.*
The exuberant citizens of Toulon love to pile in here for scallop brochettes, sea bass simmered in Noilly-Prat vermouth, lusty bouillabaisse, and tasty house-made pastries. Frisky wines from Bandol and Cassis flow freely, and the evenings often end in song. Jean-Pierre Martellotto is a genial, attentive host. C 260-410. M 140 (exc Sun), 60 (children).

12/20 **Les Terrasses**

Bd de l'Amiral-Vence
04 94 24 41 57, fax 04 94 22 42 25
Open daily until 10:30pm. Terrace dining. Air cond. Pool. Pkg.
This comfortable modern dining room with its panoramic harbor view and its impeccable though rather "mechanical" service offers a seafood-based cooking with an ebullient Southern accent, but we noted a certain slack in the food preparation this year. There was also a total lack of atmosphere. All this together makes us drop a toque. Balanced, fairly priced cellar. C 210-270. M 90 (wine incl), 150, 50 (children).

 New Hotel Tour Blanche 🌲🍽

(See restaurant above)
Open year-round. 3 stes 495. 89 rms 395. Bkfst 50. Rms for disabled. Half-board 420. Rm ser. Air cond. Conf. Pool. Pkg.
Bright, very nicely equipped, air conditioned rooms and comfortable bathrooms (some with a balcony overlooking the sea).

And also...

Our selection of places for inexpensive, quick, or late-night meals.
Chez Mimi (04 94 92 79 60 - 83, av. de la République. Open until 11pm.): If you've always been curious about spices, here's the place to come to enhance your knowledge. Traditional dishes such as deep-fried egg turnovers (*brick à l'œuf*), couscous and tagines (Moroccan meat and chicken stews) served with a smile (160).
La Corniche (04 94 41 35 12 - 17 - Littoral Frédéric-Mistral. Open until 10:30pm.): If you're in the mood for seafood, the freshest in town is to be found here. Exquisite panoramic view. Young, attentive service (120-280).

TOURTOUR   83690
Paris 860 - Draguignan 20 - Aups 10 - Salernes 11   Var

 Bastide de Tourtour 🌲🍽

04 94 70 57 30, fax 04 94 70 54 90
Closed Nov-Mar 1. 25 rms 320-1,200. Bkfst 70. Rms for disabled. Restaurant. Half-board 550-1,000

(oblig in seas). Rm ser. Conf. Pool. Tennis. Garage pkg.
You can take in a hundred kilometers of magnificent Var scenery from this luxurious mountain fastness among the pines. Jacuzzi, exercise room.

 Les Chênes Verts ⚙

2 km on route de Villecroze
04 94 70 55 06, fax 04 94 70 59 35
Closed Tue dinner, Wed, Jan-Feb 10. Open until 9:15pm. Priv rm 10. Garage pkg.
Can a chef follow the same path for twenty years, yet continue to improve? Paul Bajade shows that it is indeed possible: he refines his beautifully designed set menus year by year, adding ever more full-flavored regional dishes. On a recent visit, the 250 F market menu brought local melon laced with Sauternes followed by zucchini with morel cream sauce, a galette of lobster and green asparagus, and rack of Sisteron lamb with baby vegetables (though we might have chosen farm-bred pigeon with polenta). To close, we devoured a tangy farmhouse chèvre and a vibrant raspberry tian. Washed down with a half-bottle of county wine, it was an hour of pure gastronomic bliss! C 450. M 200, 250, 390.

TRIGANCE   83840
Paris 818 - Draguignan 44 - Grasse 72 - Castellane 20   Var

12/20 **Château de Trigance**

04 94 76 91 18, fax 04 94 85 68 99
Closed Wed lunch off-seas, Nov 2-Mar 21. Open until 9:30pm. Tennis. Garage pkg.
Unless you have X-ray vision, you'll miss the breathtaking panorama of the Verdon Valley on the other side of these stout, windowless ninth-century walls. Concentrate instead on the fresh cuisine based on excellent ingredients: if they're on the menu, try the sea trout en homardine, squab à la provençale, or grilled sea bream with red cabbage. C 250-400. M 150 (lunch, exc Sun), 200, 270.

 Château de Trigance 🌲🍽

(See restaurant above)
Closed Nov 2-Mar 21. 2 stes 900. 8 rms 550-900. Bkfst 68. Half-board 550-720 (oblig). Garage pkg.
These beautiful rooms are handsomely furnished (canopied beds), and equipped with excellent bathrooms. Relais et Châteaux.

VALBONNE   06560
Paris 913 - Cannes 13 - Grasse 9 - Nice 30   Alpes-Mar.

🏠 **Les Armoiries**

Pl. des Arcades - 04 93 12 90 90, fax 04 93 12 90 91
Open year-round. 16 rms 450-800. Bkfst 50. Air cond.
This hotel, on the national register of historical monuments, goes back a long way—to the seventeenth century, to be exact. Located on a most bewitching square and offering simple but well-appointed rooms.

L'Auberge Fleurie

1016, route de Cannes
04 93 12 02 80, fax 04 93 12 22 27
Closed Sun dinner, Mon, Dec 15-Jan 30. Open until 9:30pm. Terrace dining. Pkg.
Jean-Pierre Bataglia's traditional cuisine is polished and precise. Sample his à la carte specialties, or choose a set menu, accompanied by one of the well-chosen wines from the regional cellar. Guests are welcomed with a smile into the comfortable, modern dining room (in fine weather, ask for a terrace table). C 230. M 115-190.

12/20 Bleu Lavande

28, chemin de Pinchinade - 04 93 12 28 01
Closed Tue. Open until 10pm. Priv rm 25. Terrace dining. Garage pkg.
Delightfully executed dishes with a heavy emphasis on local spices, with dishes such as the tender spring salad with tapenade, jumbo shrimp flambéed in pastis, the local aniseed apéritif, or mouthwatering fresh-fig pie. Lovely welcome and efficient service; take their advice on which local wine suits your needs. C 200. M 135-180, 60 (children).

Novotel

Rue Dostoïevski - 04 93 65 40 00, fax 04 93 95 80 12
Open year-round. 97 rms 450-600. Bkfst 52. Rms for disabled. Restaurant. Half-board 410. Rm ser. Air cond. Conf. Pool. Tennis. Pkg.
In front of the big Sophia-Antipolis park, this is an excellent hotel for conferences.

12/20 Relais de la Vignette

Route de Cannes - 04 93 12 05 82
Open daily until 10:30pm. Terrace dining. Garage pkg.
A good sign in these parts: local business people frequent this pleasant little restaurant as much as the tourists! Good fixed-price meals where you can try such delicacies as ravioli au pistou or calf's sweetbread chartreuse. Couldn't ask for better service. C 280-400. M 135, 180, 70 (children).

12/20 La Gousse d'Ail

11, av. de Grasse - 04 93 64 10 71
Closed Mon dinner & Tue (exc in summer), Nov 12-Dec 12. Open until 10pm. Air cond.
A fetching little Provençal restaurant that serves a zesty roster of fresh, generous seafood dishes as well as regular brasserie fare, cooked with skill and obvious care. Charming welcome and service. C 200. M 110-180, 72 (children).

Le Manuscrit

224, chemin Lintier - 04 93 64 56 56
Closed Mon & Tue off-seas, mid Jan-beg Feb, mid Nov-beg Dec. Open until 9:45pm. Garden dining. Garage pkg.
Once a perfume distillery, Le Manuscrit offers simple, bountiful meals at prices unheard-of for Cannes and its environs. Just 95 F buys pistachioed rabbit terrine, veal kidney and sweetbreads en cassolette, and a refreshing fruit gratin. Moderately tariffed cellar; smiling staff—what more could you ask? C 160. M 95 (weekday lunch, Sat), 120-245, 40 (children).

Château Saint-Martin

Av. des Templiers - 04 93 58 02 02, fax 04 93 24 08 91
Closed end Oct-beg Apr. Open until 9:30pm. Garden dining. Air cond. Heated pool. Tennis. No pets. Valet pkg.
The Knights Templar, who founded this castle, rode two to a horse as a sign of poverty. Saint Martin is said to have cut his mantle in two to share with a beggar here. The patrons of Château Saint-Martin have plenty of horsepower under the hoods of their fancy cars, and they are also willing to sacrifice half the price of a mink coat to spend a weekend admiring the Château's stupendous views while gorging on Dominique Ferrière's impeccable, classic cuisine. Starchy service; excellent cellar, supervised by René Leroux. C 450-650. M 300 (weekday lunch), 430, 490.

Château Saint-Martin

(See restaurant above)
Closed end Oct-beg Apr. 10 stes 2,700-4,000. 24 rms 1,370-3,000. Bkfst 120. Air cond. Conf. Heated pool. Tennis. Valet pkg.
Guests are housed in little villas whose richly decorated rooms have an unimpeded view over the hills. Lovely swimming pool; beautiful grounds. Relais et Châteaux.

11/20 La Farigoule

15, rue Henri-Isnard - 04 93 58 01 27
Closed Fri (exc lunch in seas), Sat lunch, Nov 10-Dec 15. Open until 9:15pm (10pm in summer). Terrace dining. No cards.
Georgette Gastaud entices you with large helpings of downhome Provençal cooking. From her farigoule rabbit (farigoule is the word in these parts for "thyme"), her Niçois veal sauté, to her roasted herb-coated duckling, you will taste all the sunny flavors of the South. We really like the prices. C 120-150. M 120, 145.

Hôtel Floréal

440, av. Rhin-et-Danube
04 93 58 64 40, fax 04 93 58 79 69
Closed Oct 15-Mar. 43 rms 350-490. Bkfst 50. Conf. Pool. Garage pkg.
A modern building set in pretty grounds. The rooms are bright and cozy, with tasteful decoration and a view over the countryside. Snacks are

served round the swimming pool. Garden with exotic plants.

 ### Maximin ✪

689, chemin de la Gaude
04 93 58 90 75, fax 04 93 58 22 86
Closed Sun dinner & Mon (exc hols), Jan 12-Feb 12. Open until 10:30pm. Terrace dining. Air cond. Valet pkg.
Jacques Maximin made his reputation by shaking up sleepy hotel kitchens and turning them into hotbeds of culinary innovation. Now he's had enough of working *chez les autres* and is happily ensconced in a house of his own, a beautiful villa near Vence set in grounds planted with palms and olive trees. The comfortable dining room displays works of contemporary art (sculpture by César, glass by Novaro...), and holds just a dozen round tables. (Seats are hotly contested, by the way, so remember to book yours in advance.) On the menu are clever renditions of classics such as chicken vol au vent or succulent Lauragais squab served with tender little lentils. Guests are welcomed with a smile by Josie Maximin and the veteran maître d'. Tempting cellar of Southern wines. M 240.

 ### Relais Cantemerle 🏨♟

258, chemin Cantemerle
04 93 58 08 18, fax 04 93 58 32 89
Closed mid Oct-beg Apr. 19 stes 950-1,030. 1 rm 600. Bkfst 70. Restaurant. Half-board 560-775. Rm ser. Air cond. Pool. Garage pkg.
A gorgeous Provençal garden surrounds the Relais with tranquility. Inside, you'll find a 1930s–style bar and lounge, and bright guest rooms with private terraces.

 ### Le Vieux Couvent

37, av. Alphonse-Toreille - 04 93 58 78 58
Closed Wed. Open until 9:15pm (10pm in summer).
You might dine in the former chapel of a seventeenth-century convent, but Jean-Jacques Bissières's fine cooking is the furthest thing possible from monastic. In fact, this chef is about to enter "chefs' heaven". His ingredients are so lovely you could display them in a showcase. His cooking times clearly approach perfection; he just gets better with age (men do, they say). Just dare to taste his duck foie gras, most likely the best in the entire Riviera. Tempt your buds with his veal "topskirt" with chive cream (talk about melting in the mouth) or about the thinnest apple pie you've ever seen. A well-deserved second toque. C 280. M 150-280.

VIDAUBAN   83550
Paris 846 - Cannes 65 - Fréjus 29 - Toulon 64   Var

 ### Château Les Lonnes 🏨♟

3 km NW on D 84, chemin des Moulins-d'Entraigues
04 94 73 65 76, fax 04 94 73 14 97

Open year-round. 2 stes 1,400-3,600. 12 rms 550-1,650. Bkfst 100. Rms for disabled. Conf. Pool. Tennis. Garage pkg.
Set in 55 acres of woodland, this luxury hotel is admirably appointed. There are leather armchairs and solid-wood furniture in the rooms; marble in the bathrooms. Facilities include a library with reading room, a sauna, a massage room, and a beauty salon. The staff, alas, is not on its toes.

12/20 Le Concorde

9, pl. Georges-Clemenceau
04 94 73 01 19, fax 04 94 73 11 01
Closed Tue dinner & Wed off-seas. Open until 9:30pm (10:30pm in summer). Priv rm 15. Terrace dining. Pkg.
The Concorde seems to have revved its engine and be taking off again now that Alain Bœuf's son has joined him; it is already full of locals savoring the farcis provençaux, garlic-and-rosemary kid and farm-raised young guinea fowl, and we noted joyful looks on the faces of all who partook. A food truly of its region. C 230-360. M 140-360, 40 (children).

VILLEFRANCHE-SUR-MER   06230
Paris 935 - Monaco 16 - Nice 6   Alpes-Mar.

 ### Le Saint-Pierre

1, quai de l'Amiral-Courbet - 04 93 76 93 93 (R), 04 93 76 76 93 (H), fax 04 93 01 88 81
Closed Mon, Nov. Open until 10pm (11pm in summer). Terrace dining. Air cond.
The sheltered terrace in the heart of the port is the main attraction at this sunny restaurant, but the seafood-oriented cooking also merits attention. Unfortunately the 140 F menu is on the dull side with its avocado and shrimp salad, mussels and French fries, grilled sirloin and John Dory fillet with sorrel sauce. You'd probably be more satisfied with the Provence-style stuffed artichokes with basil mousseline or the country-style sea perch cooked in a crust of salt. Modest cellar, with some good local wines. Highly professional welcome and service. C 160-400. M 140-255.

 ### Welcome

(See restaurant above)
Closed Nov 20-Dec 20. 32 rms 400-920. Bkfst 40. Half-board 393-610. Rm ser. Air cond. Conf. Pkg.
This former convent where writer Jean Cocteau liked to stay was recently modernized, adding bedside quotations from Cocteau to serve as food for your dreams. The rooms are comfortable and air conditioned, with some spectacular ones on the fifth floor overlooking the sea.

***See also:* Beaulieu-sur-Mer**

REGIONAL FOODS

Here in the land of the sun, the air and light have a singular character. The locals have plenty of character, too, and a lilting accent that is a joy to hear. When in the South, do as the Southerners do: take the time to enjoy life and appreciate nature's bounteous gifts: aromatic olive oil, taut-skinned vegetables, luscious fruits, a glass of cool pastis served on a shaded terrace, sweets made from local fruits and almonds...

• *CHOCOLATE & CANDY*

AIX-EN-PROVENCE   13100 – B./Rhône

Calissons du Roy René

La Pioline, rue Guillaume du Vair,
13290 Les Milles - 04 42 39 29 89
 Calissons are a famed local specialty: a tender, aromatic sweet based on almond paste.

Chocolaterie de Puyricard

7, rue Rifle-Rafle - 04 42 21 13 26
Also in Arles, Avignon, Marseille, Nice, Toulon
 Good chocolates, with classic and unusual varieties on offer. Delicious calissons, too.

CANNES   06400 – Alpes-Mar.

Bruno

50, rue d'Antibes - 04 93 39 26 63
 A rainbow of gorgeous candied fruits. We particularly recommend the Vaucluse apricots and the sweet local tangerines.

CARPENTRAS   84200 – Vaucluse

Confiserie Bono

282, allée Jean-Jaurès - 04 90 63 04 99
 Fruits candied the old-fashioned way, over low heat for a long time. The most succulent (in our estimation) are the Provençal figs, Alpine pears, the local plums, melons, tangerines, and lemons. The delicious fruit jams are also worth trying.

MARSEILLE   13004 – B./Rhône

Facor

4th arr. - 13-15, rue Xavier-Progin - 04 91 49 38 07

It would be hard to find better candied chestnuts (marrons glacés): these are succulent, aromatic little morsels!

MONACO   98000 – Principality of Monaco

Jean-Marie Canet

4, bd de France - 04 93 30 82 94
 Very good fruit jellies (pâtes de fruits) and excellent chocolates.

Chocolaterie de Monaco

7, rue Biovès - 04 93 15 00 55
 Refined, very well crafted chocolates, filled with delicately flavored ganaches.

NICE   06300 – Alpes-Mar.

Confiserie Auer

7, rue Saint-François-de-Paule - 04 93 85 77 98
 Come to this charming Rococo shop for toothsome fruits confits, candied by hand the old-fashioned way.

Confiserie du Vieux Nice

14, quai Papacino - 04 93 55 43 50
 Watch as fruits confits are candied before your eyes by experts. An enormous variety to choose from.

SAULT   84390 – Vaucluse

André Boyer

Porte des Aires - 04 90 64 00 23
 What could be more Provençal than nougat? here you'll find white nougat, black (because it's caramelized) nougat, as well as crunchy pralines, candied fruits, marzipan, and a host of other sweet indulgences. An excellent address.

SORGUES   84700 – Vaucluse

Au Petit Prince

52, pl. de la République - 04 90 83 00 29
 A typically Provençal sweet shop, stocked with nougat, pralines, candied fruit, and candies made with almond paste. Everything's delicious, so just follow your fancy!

• *GOURMET SPECIALTIES*

Honey & Jams

Les Ruchers du Bessillon

2, rue des Naïs - 04 94 04 60 39
Provençal honeys in an array of subtly nuanced flavors: acacia, lavender, orangeflower, linden-blossom... Also on offer are candies, gingerbread, and other honey-based delicacies.

La Roumanière

Pl. de l'Église - 04 90 76 61 21
The luscious fruit jams (many original varieties) are all made by hand, and are prettily presented in jars capped with Provençal print fabrics.

Olive Oil

Coopérative Oléicole

3, rue Alphonse-Daudet - 04 42 52 06 81
This is the source for a fruity, mild olive oil obtained with an ancient granite olive press.

Moulin Jean-Marie Cornille

Coopérative Oléicole de la Vallée des Baux, rue Charloun-Rieu - 04 90 54 32 37
This is truly one of the region's best olive oil producers.

Alziari

14, rue Saint-François-de-Paule - 04 93 85 76 92
Stop at this pretty, old-fashioned shop to purchase wonderfully fragrant olive oil, excellent tapenade, and other interesting condiments.

Escale en Provence

7, rue du Marché - 04 93 85 23 90
Here's an interesting shop, stocked with top-quality, handmade Provençal sweets and condiments: olive oil, Niçois olives, jams, honeys, vinegars (flavored or not).

Pastis

Distilleries et Domaines de Provence

04 92 75 00 58
This distillery produces Pastis Bardouin, the most refined and subtly flavored of all the anise-flavored spirits on the market. Also on hand is a selection of Provençal wine- and spirit-based specialties (wine punch, walnut wine, peach wine, almond cordial, fruits preserved in brandy) that make wonderful gifts.

• *PASTRY & COOKIES*

Croquettes Aujoras

Route de Saint-Saturnin - 04 90 32 21 40
Here we discovered crunchy cookies with true almond flavor, as well as lemon croquettes, delicious macarons, and all manner of tempting treats.

WINE

In Provence, winemaking is a tradition rooted deep in antiquity. Grapes flourished here even before the Greeks landed in what is now Marseille, around 600 BC. Wine and its culture are woven into the fabric of daily life in Provence, and the vine has indelibly marked the countryside: even now vineyards carpet the hillsides, from the southern Rhône Valley downriver to the delta, and east to the Italian border.

Though they are actually situated in Provence (and so will be included in this chapter), Châteauneuf-du-Pape, Gigondas, Tavel, and several other prestigious *appellations* are considered Rhône Valley wines—for reasons that have as much to do with "image" as with geography and grape varieties!

In official terms, the wine-growing region of **Provence** covers the coast and the mountainous hinterland between **Arles** and **Nice**. The region's two largest AOCs, the Coteaux-d'Aix and the gigantic Côtes-de-Provence area, are surrounded by a string of more or less smaller cousins: the Coteaux Varois (recently promoted to AOC status), Cassis, Bandol, and the tiny AOCs of Palette (near Aix) and Bellet (next to Nice). Many different types of grapes are cultivated, but lately the Southern workhorse varieties—Carignan for red, Cinsault for rosé, and Ugni for white—are yielding to Grenache, for powerful, fruity reds; Tibouren for deeply colored and flavorful rosés; Bourboulenc and Rolle for clean, aromatic whites. Bellet is planted with its own distinctive varieties (Braquet, Folle Noire...), and Bandol's long-lived red wines owe their velvety texture and inky hue to the Mourvèdre grape. Marsanne and Syrah (white and red varieties, respectively) recently migrated from the northern Rhône, and are thriving in Provence.

Provence still suffers from an out-dated image as a wellspring of highly alcoholic, slightly oxidized rosés. In fact, since the mid-'80s the region's most talented vintners have concentrated on producing premium reds. The results are impressive: certain red wines from the Coteaux-d'Aix and Côtes-de-Provence can rival many a fine bottle from Bordeaux or the northern Rhône. First-rate white wines are less common, but they do exist; and the newly established Institut du Rosé in Vidauban is dedicated to refurbishing the image of Provençal rosés.

SOUTHERN RHÔNE VALLEY

CHÂTEAUNEUF-DU-PAPE   84230 – Vaucluse

Château Mont-Redon

04 90 83 72 75, fax 04 90 83 77 20
Open daily 8am-7:30pm.
Here, all thirteen traditional grapes varieties are cultivated for an always distinguished Châteauneuf-du-Pape. Notable white Châteauneuf as well, and a spectacular Côtes-du-Rhône AOC produced with as much care as a Grand Cru.

COURTHÉZON   84350 – Vaucluse

Château de Beaucastel

J.-P. et F. Perrin - 04 90 70 41 00, fax 04 90 70 41 19
Open Mon-Fri 9am-11:30am & 2pm-5:30pm.
Beaucastel continues to cultivate all thirteen of the grape varieties that traditionally compose Châteauneuf-du-Pape (elsewhere Syrah, Mourvèdre, and Grenache predominate); and each variety is vinified separately. Come here for consistently superb, concentrated Château-neufs, and a lovely second wine, Le Coudoulet de Beaucastel.

GIGONDAS   84190 – Vaucluse

Cave des Vignerons de Gigondas

04 90 65 86 27, fax 04 90 65 80 13
Open Mon-Sat 8am-noon & 2pm-6pm, Sun 10am-6:30pm.
This coop is one of the very few that offers wines as interesting as those of a top-quality individual producer. The secret? Rigorous selection. Look for the Vieilles Vignes cuvées: brawny, but balanced and fragrant Gigondas from older vines.

TAVEL   30126 – Gard

Château d'Aquéria

04 66 50 04 56, fax 04 66 50 18 46
Open Mon-Fri 8am-noon & 2pm-6pm & by appt.
Tavel is the only Grand Cru of rosé, yielding a spicy, solid, aromatic wine that can stand up to

food. Vincent and Bruno de Bez, a devoted pair of winemakers, produce one of the *appellation*'s most consistently remarkable wines: brimming with fruit and menthol nuances that evolve into resinous aromas with age. Also: splendid white and red Liracs.

VACQUEYRAS
84190 – Vaucluse

Domaine Le Clos des Cazaux

Maurice et Jean-Michel Vache
04 90 65 85 83, fax 04 90 65 83 94
Open Mon-Sat 9am-noon & 2pm-6:30pm.
Tannic by definition, Vacqueyras (now a cru, like Gigondas and Châteauneuf) is a quality wine for long keeping. Maurice and Jean-Michel Vache's firmly structured Cuvée des Templiers fits the description. Also: a charming white Vacqueyras redolent of ferns and almonds.

PROVENCE

BAUX-DE-PROVENCE (LES)
13520 – B./Rhône

Mas Sainte-Berthe

04 90 54 39 01, fax 04 90 54 46 17
Open daily 9am-noon & 2pm-7pm.
At a site long famed for its pure spring water, Louis and Hélène David cultivate old Grenache vines along with newer plantings of Syrah and Rolle to make their Cuvée Louis David, a superb red Coteaux-d'Aix with heady aromas of fruit, spice, and herbs.

CADIÈRE-D'AZUR (LA)
83740 – Var

Château de Pibarnon

04 94 90 12 73, fax 04 94 90 12 98
Open Mon-Sat 8am-noon & 2pm-6:30pm.
Bandol produces mostly rosés, but true wine buffs really get excited over the *appellation*'s spicy, intense, and long-lived red wines (dominated by the Mourvèdre grape), perfect partners for red meats and game. Pibarnon is one of Bandol's top estates, with exceptional soil (the owner, Count Henri de Saint-Victor, is particularly proud of his land's blue marl). The wonderfully powerful red wines are aged for nearly two years in wood before bottling, and require several more years in the cellar. Memorable rosés, too.

CASSIS
13260 – B./Rhône

Clos Sainte-Magdeleine

Av. du Revestel - 04 42 01 70 28, fax 04 42 01 15 51
Open Mon-Fri 10am-noon & 3pm-7pm.
Only a dozen growers work the Cassis AOC region, making famous white wines that are lively and fresh, ideal companions to seafood and bouillabaisse. This estate, perched in a dreamy setting above the Mediterranean, makes one of France's greatest white wines, from a blend of grapes dominated by Marsanne, along with Ugni and Clairette. Excellent rosé, too.

FLASSANS-SUR-ISSOLE
83340 – Var

Domaine de Saint-Baillon

N 7 - 04 94 69 74 60, fax 04 94 69 80 29
Open Mon-Sat 8am-1pm & 2pm-7pm.
Hervé Goudard, a former lawyer, is now one of the top winemakers in the Côtes-de-Provence region. He only makes his Cuvée du Roudaï (60 percent Cabernet, 40 percent Syrah) in ideal years. But what a wine! Powerful, smoky, full-bodied, and long... The rosé Orpale is also a winner, and his pure Rolle white wine (aged in oak) will be appearing soon!

LONDE-LÈS-MAURES (LA)
83250 – Var

Château Sainte-Marguerite

04 94 66 81 46, fax 04 94 66 51 05
Open Mon-Sat.
The estate's Ugni Blanc vines are over 100 years old. They yield exceptional white Côtes-de-Provence wines, particularly the Cuvée M de Marguerite and the floral, supple Grande Réserve. Jean-Pierre Fayard also presents vivacious, full-bodied rosés and reds that benefit from a few years in the cellar.

LUC (LE)
83340 – Var

Domaine La Bernarde

04 94 60 71 31, fax 04 94 47 96 04
Open Sat 8:30am-noon & 1:30pm-5:30pm.
Guy Meulnart's Côtes-de-Provence wines don't come cheap, but they compare favorably in quality to some of Médoc's Crus Bourgeois. The reds (made from Cabernet, Syrah, Mourvèdre, Grenache) are splendid: Le Clos La Bernarde is undoubtedly one of the region's top wines. Sémillon grapes give his whites a heady perfume, and his rosés are ripe and spicy (Guy serves them with caviar...).

Plan to travel? Look for GaultMillau/Gayot's other Best of guides to Chicago, Florida, Germany, Hawaii, Hong Kong, Italy, London, Los Angeles, New England, New Orleans, New York, Paris, Paris & the Loire Valley, San Francisco, Thailand, Toronto, Washington, D.C., and more to come...

MEYREUIL 13590 – B./Rhône

Château Simone

René Rougier - 04 42 66 92 58, fax 04 42 66 80 77
Open Mon-Sat 8am-noon & 2pm-6pm.
Palette is a minuscule AOC near the city of Aix, and Château Simone is Palette's best-known estate, whose very old vines benefit from a favorable microclimate. The red wines are bottled only after three years in wood and should age another ten years before they are uncorked. Even the whites and rosés can reach a ripe old age, with no danger of oxidation. No need to worry about vintage years here: the wines are always wonderful.

NICE 06000 – Alpes-Mar.

Château de Bellet

Quartier Saint-Roman de Bellet
04 93 37 81 57, fax 04 93 37 93 83
Open by appt only.
Just a few hundred yards (straight up!) from Nice's Promenade des Anglais, the AOC vineyards of Bellet produce a small quantity of estimable wine. Ghislain de Charnacé, owner of this estate, makes his white wines from Rolle grapes, which seem to have more character here than elsewhere in Provence. The cuvée aged in new oak is remarkable, but the finest of all is the white Cuvée Baron G, made from a single vineyard.

PLAN-DU-CASTELLET (LE) 83330 – Var

Domaine Tempier

GAEC Peyraud - 04 94 98 70 21, fax 04 94 90 21 65
Open Mon-Sat 9am-noon & 2pm-6pm (exc Sat pm & hols).
Jean-Marie Peyraud is the grand master of the historic Tempier estate. Peyraud isn't interested in making popular wines; in the past eight years he's reduced yields to obtain more concentrated, richer wines with a strong regional character. Five different cuvées of red Bandol are elaborated—none is cheap, and none is for early drinking!

ROQUEBRUNE-SUR-ARGENS 83520 – Var

Domaine des Planes

04 94 82 90 03, fax 04 94 82 94 76
Open Mon-Sat 9am-noon & 2pm-6:30pm.
Come here to taste a red Côtes-de-Provence made from 100 percent Mourvèdre grapes, and an array of delicious white wines. The new tast-ing cellar is most welcoming (regional specialties are also on sale), and there is a furnished rental (*gîte*) on the property.

ROQUEBRUSSANNE (LA) 83136 – Var

Domaine du Loou

04 94 86 94 97, fax 04 94 86 80 11
Open Mon-Sat 9am-noon & 2:30pm-6:30pm, Sun 11am-noon & 4:30pm-6:30pm.
The Coteaux Varois is a small, new AOC area in the center of the Var *département*. Unlike most of the red wines made in this area, Daniel di Placido's are structured, powerful, and destined for a stint in the cellar before they reach the table. He also makes a fine rosé firm enough to stand up to food, and a fresh, aromatic white.

ST-RÉMY-DE-PROVENCE 13210 – B./Rhône

Château de Romanin

04 90 92 45 87, fax 04 90 92 24 36
Open Mon-Fri 8:30am-1pm & 2pm-6:30pm, Sat-Sun 11am-7pm.
The château's spectacular cellars are carved out of solid rock. Therein you may sample elegant Coteaux-d'Aix wines made with state-of-the-art methods and equipment. The Château Romanin Rouge is typical of the region's new wave of spicy, well-crafted reds.

Domaine des Terres Blanches

D 99 - 04 90 95 91 66, fax 04 90 95 99 04
Open daily 10am-1pm & 2pm-6pm.
Organically grown vines and the vintners' know-how produce super Coteaux-d'Aix-les-Baux wines. Try the red Taven '91, dominated by the deep flavors of the Mourvèdre grape. Also: a delicious Coteaux-d'Aix rosé.

VILLECROZE 83690 – Var

Domaine de Saint-Jean

04 94 70 63 07, fax 04 94 70 67 41
Open daily 8am-noon & 2pm-5pm.
The estate's American owner leaves the winemaking chores to Marilène Merlin and Elphège Bailly. Most of the property's Coteaux Varois are meant to be consumed in their youth, but the Cabernet Sauvignon de Saint-Jean is a keeper, with wonderful aromas of truffles and thyme.

THE RHÔNE VALLEY & THE ALPS

Olive trees
and edelweiss

The land that lies between the tumultuous Rhône—a river the historian Michelet called "a raging bull"—and Europe's loftiest peaks, a land that embraces glaciers and olive trees, ancient cities and untamed wilderness, is still in the process of forging its modern identity. Comparable in size to Switzerland or Belgium, Rhône-Alpes is France's second-largest region. It forms a counterweight in the nation's southeastern sector to Paris–Ile-de-France in the north. Though it is swiftly becoming a major European crossroads, Rhône-Alpes is more a political construct than a coherent cultural or geographic entity—the **Région Rhône-Alpes** is a very recent creation. Paradoxically, perhaps, the stunning diversity of the region's topography counts among its prime assets, and is surely its primary attraction for travelers.

Follow the course of the Rhône River, and look east to majestic **Mont-Blanc**, as it surveys the **Chablais**, **Faucigny**, and **Aravis** massifs. Climb still higher to the **Vanoise**, **Belledonne**, and **Chartreuse** massifs, to **L'-Oisans** and **Le Vercors**: you are enveloped in infinite blue. Listen to the fury of torrents rushing down the mountain at the **Rouget** waterfall (called "Queen of the Alps"), or the 30 thundering cascades that come alive in summer at the **Fer-à-Cheval** near **Sixt** in Haute-Savoie. Then hear the sudden stillness as these mountain waters spread silently into **Lake Geneva**, **Lake Annecy**, the lakes of **Le Bourget, Aiguebelette, Monteynard, Nantua, Paladru**... The water stretches out and lies in lake and riverbeds down in the plains as far as Dauphiné, giving the Rhône-Alpes more shoreline than any other region. Travel farther south now, still following the Rhône. Endless vineyards and orchards promise huge harvests of fruit. The Drôme wears a mantle of lavender. Everywhere gnarled olive trees spread their low branches, and in the fragrant herb-filled scrub of Ardèche cicadas chirrup at the sun.

The Rhône Valley and the Alps preserve thousands of acres of unspoiled nature. Sure-footed chamois skitter through Alpine pastures dotted with edelweiss, hide under pines or behind a rhododendron, then skip upward to join their ibex cousins on the snowy peaks. Beavers busy themselves by mountain streams while otters tease and frolic. The four national and regional parks of the **Écrins**, **Vanoise**, **Vercors**, and **Pilat**, as well as 28 nature reserves, including the **Ardèche Gorges** and the **Aiguilles Rouges** mountains, invite you to discover forests, lakes, high pastures, craggy peaks, and austere plateaus.

Sports
for every season

In winter 3,700 miles of manicured, well-marked ski runs show why the Rhône-Alpes region was chosen three times to host the Olympic Games, at **Chamonix**, **Grenoble**, and **Albertville**. With 220 ski resorts ranging in style from chic—**Courchevel**, **Méribel**, **Megève**, or **Alpe-d'Huez**—to *rustique* (**Gex**, **Vars** in the beautiful Queyras), there are plenty of opportunities for Alpine and cross-country skiing. The *département* of Savoie alone boasts well over 500 miles of ski trails that thread through the awesome mountain scenery of **La Maurienne** and **La Tarentaise**. Resorts at **Corrençon**, **Autrans**, and **Villard-de-Lans** provide fabulous cross-country terrain for novices and veterans alike.

In summer the mountains are a paradise for climbers and hikers. At **Chamonix**, where alpinism was born in the eighteenth century, the history of the pioneers who first scaled Mont-Blanc is retold at the Musée Alpin. No one should leave Chamonix without making an excursion to the enormous glacier known as **La Mer de Glace**, but only the daring will want to climb 12,000 feet in a cable car to the Aiguille du Midi peak. The Isère River, which rises in the Alps and flows down to the Rhône, challenges whitewater rafters to descend its turbulent rapids, but these trout-filled waters also invite anglers to try out their fly-fishing techniques.

Mountain air rouses the appetite, whetting it for hearty Alpine fare. While the tonier spas and ski resorts boast world-class tables (see **Évian** and Courchevel, for example), simple *auberges* also have their charm. Their menus feature mountain charcuteries (Pormonier sausage), raclette—melted cheese with potatoes—and fondue, both convivial après-ski favorites, and such local fish as trout, pike, and lake char, often accented with wild mushrooms. The cheese course is always worthwhile in the French Alps, where superb Beaufort, Reblochon, Tomme de Savoie, and crumbly Bleu de Gex are made.

An age-old artistic legacy

The art and architecture of the Rhône Valley and the Alps tell a mesmerizing story of the region's past. An artistic legacy built up over thousands of years still bears the visible signatures of the civilizations who crafted it. The wall paintings of the recently discovered **Chauvet Cave** in Ardèche reveal the talents of Magdalenian artists who lived 20,000 years BC. The **Orgnac Caves** lead spelunkers into a spectacular subterranean maze; above ground, the Prehistory Museum illustrates early humans' workshops, shelters, and tombs. At the **Marzal Caves** a prehistoric "zoo" recreates the huge monsters that roamed this land long ago. Down in the shivery **Choranche Grottoes** of the Vercors, an underground lake and amazing stalactites await, along with the ghosts of Resistance fighters who launched guerilla attacks against the Nazis from these caves and hills. The huge Gaulish fortress of Larina at **Hières-sur-Amby** near Grenoble was occupied from Neolithic times until the eighth century of our era. The archaeological park on the site documents the life of the Gauls—Allobroges, Ambarres, Segusiaves, Helvians—who passed through the region, paving the way for settlements of the kind the Romans discovered when they came to conquer. The Temple of Augustus and Livia in **Vienne**, the Temple of Diana and the Baths at **Aix-les-Bains** still speak of the glory that was Rome. On a smaller scale, and perhaps more moving because of it, are the second-century Roman villas of **Saint-Romain-en-Gal** not far from Vienne. Set amid fountains and colonnades, the dwellings were decorated with vivid polychrome mosaics of seascapes and floral motifs—the latter were copied throughout the empire. An instructive Archaeology Museum just opened on the site. The vigorous spirituality of the Middle Ages still radiates from the abbey church at **Cruas** on the Rhône, the Alpine cathedral of **Saint-Jean-de-Maurienne**, and the cathedral of **Saint-Paul-Trois-Châteaux** in the Rhône Valley near Grignan. The Gothic style made few inroads in the region, but the austere elegance of the Romanesque reaches a pinnacle of perfection at the monastery of **La Grande Chartreuse** (which does not admit visitors), at the abbey of **Talloires**, in its splendid site on Lake Annecy, the Cistercian abbey of **Léoncel**, and at the Chartreuse du Reposoir in the **Aravis massif**. On the western shore of

Lac du Bourget, in a sublime, isolated site stands the abbaye of **Hautecombe**, founded in 1125 by Saint Bernard. A community of Benedictine monks continues to lead a life of meditation inside this abbey, the burial place of the dukes of Savoie.

As heir to disputed borderlands and to the powerful medieval states of Savoie and Dauphiné, Rhône-Alpes bristles with a legion of fortresses and châteaux. Just as Savoie's ducal castle watches over **Chambéry**, Annecy is guarded by the twelfth-century fortress of the counts of Geneva. Viewing the ramparts built in the 1600s by Vauban at the **Forts de Maurienne**, one can easily imagine the onslaught of an invading army... A less bellicose spirit imbues the Renaissance châteaux of **Grignan** (immortalized by Madame de Sévigné), **Tournon** (in a ravishing town), and **Vogüé**.

The venerable urban centers of the Rhône Valley and the Alps preserve notable examples of civil architecture. With **Pérouges**, in the nearby Bresse region, **Crémieu** is one of the finest medieval villages in France, rivaled perhaps for sheer loveliness by **Viviers** on its perch above the Rhône. Early Renaissance town houses in the old quarters of **Vienne**, **Valence**, and **Romans-sur-Isère** irresistibly evoke Italian exuberance. So, in a more stately fashion, does **Grenoble**'s Palais de Justice, built under Louis XII. As you travel through the upper Maurienne and Tarantaise massifs, don't be fooled by the sober façades of the churches and chapels in **Valloire**, **Lanslevillard**, **Peisey-Nancroix**, **Saint-Nicolas-de-Véroce**: inside, the Baroque explodes in an orgy of gilt, twisting columns, and polychrome altars.

A huge fruit basket

Industry developed early in this part of France. As far back as the fifteenth century **Romans-sur-Isère** prospered from a booming trade in clogs and shoes. Still the capital of French footwear, it honors the shoemaker's art in its unique Musée de la Chaussure. Hats have their own museum in **Chazelles-sur-Lyon**, where they have been manufactured since the Renaissance (though the industry is in steep decline), and **Sévrier** on Lake Annecy hosts a museum that commemorates the famous bells cast at the Paccard foundry. The silk industry that flourished in nearby Lyon until the nineteenth century fostered the spinning, weaving, and printing factories that once were scattered throughout the Vivarais and Dauphiné. Today pharmaceuticals, chemicals, and nuclear energy fuel the economy of the Rhône Valley, while the Alps, with their immense hydroelectric resources, raw industries (steel, aluminum, ⸻) that require tremendous reserves ⸗ energy.

Heavy industry isn't the whole story, of course. Grenoble still employs watchmakers and leatherworkers. Quality handcrafts abound: the pottery of **Dieulefit** in the Drôme is renowned, but all over the region you can visit glass blowers, stained-glass artists, and wood carvers who open their workshops to the public. And skilled cabinetmakers perpetuate the traditional country furniture for which Savoie, in particular, is noted. Farmers and winemakers, cheese-makers and sheep herders account for a cheering proportion of the population. From vineyards around **Ampuis** and **Tain-l'Hermitage** come the mightiest of the northern Côtes-du-Rhône wines—Hermitage, Côte-Rôtie, Cornas. Ardèche also produces delectable little country wines, and the herb-fed lamb and tangy goat cheeses that partner them so well. The Drôme supplies local markets with honey and truffles, as well as olives and their gloriously perfumed oil pressed in the mills of **Nyons**. In fact the entire Rhône Valley is one huge fruit basket, overflowing with strawberries, cherries, melons, raspberries, blueberries, peaches...

Charming towns and cities

The exceptionally beautiful cities that grace the Rhône Valley and the Alps are a pleasure to explore. Rising mountains surround **Grenoble** like the tiers of an amphitheater: *"au bout de chaque rue, une montagne"* ("at the end of each street, a mountain") is how Stendhal, the novelist who is Grenoble's most famous son, described the city where he was born in 1783. Ride a cable car up to the Fort de la Bastille, a citadel set above the Isère River, and take in the heart-stopping view. You'll understand why Grenoble is called the "Gateway to the Alps." Recover from your

emotion at a café on Place Grenette, then make time for a visit to the distinguished Musée de Grenoble, an art museum that opened in 1994 on Place de la Lavalette in the city's historic center, with collections that range from Egyptian antiquities to Pop Art.

Noble **Chambéry**, the heart of Savoie, still beats with the glory of its ancient dukes, whose (heavily restored) château gazes down on Place Saint-Léger and old Chambéry. In this artfully refurbished *vieille ville* shoppers and strollers amble through narrow, winding streets unimpeded by traffic, among Italianate houses that date from the Middle Ages to the Empire. Jean-Jacques Rousseau made his home in Chambéry. His spirit lingers at **Les Charmettes**, just outside of town, where he lived with Madame de Warens in idyllic happiness.

Chambéry's eternal rival, **Annecy** admires its reflection in the limpid mirror of its lake. The city's pride is understandable: the exquisite harmony of mountains and pure, blue water make Annecy resemble a jewel poised in a setting of snowy peaks. Masses of flowers brighten the quays along the canal, and the old town's cobbled streets brim with charm. The best way to see the lake is by boat (cruises leave from Quai du Thiou), for fabulous views of castles at **Duingt** and **Menthon-Saint-Bernard**, or fabulous meals at **Talloires** (L'Auberge du Père Bise) and **Veyrier-du-Lac** (Marc Veyrat, see *Restaurants*).

From the feudal fastness of **Aubenas** in Ardèche to the bustling market town of **Valence** on the Rhône and the Alpine crossroads of **Gap**, charming and historic towns are scattered throughout the region: romantic **Aix-les-Bains**, **Vienne** with its summer jazz festival staged in a Roman theater, the nostalgic spa towns of **Thonon** and **Évian** on the shores of Lake Geneva... The Rhône Valley and the Alps offer more varied sources of wonder and excitement than a traveler could exhaust in several lifetimes.

RESTAURANTS & HOTELS

THE RHÔNE VALLEY

AMPUIS   69420
Paris 495 - Vienne 6 - Condrieu 5 - Lyon 36   Rhône

Le Côte Rôtie

Pl. de l'Église - 04 74 56 12 05, fax 04 74 56 00 20
*Closed Sun dinner, Mon, 1st wk of Jan, last wk of
Aug-Sep 15. Open until 9:30pm. Terrace dining.
Pkg.*
You can't miss this pretty restaurant in the
center of the village; behind its blue façade is a
dining room that opens onto a garden with a
view of the vineyards. So pull up a chair and
prepare for a feast, because Manuel Viron's
cooking is as generous as it is inventive. How's
this for a 160 F menu: a slice of goat cheese on a
bed of tomatoes sautéed in olive oil; gazpacho
with mint jus and little Nice violine sandwiches;
farm-raised hen stuffed with candied turnips
and grapefruit and served with braised endives
and a Beaumes-de-Venise sweet-wine jus. Be
prepared for smells and flavors abound, never
interfering with each other, peeking their heads
and blending into each other to infinity; smells
and flavors that whet your taste buds and strike
your curiosity. Some compare him to Gagnaire,
but for us, he's just Viron in all his splendor.
Delightful welcome by Marie. Another point
well deserved. M 108-340, 70 (children).

BAIX   07210
Paris 591 - Valence 33 - Privas 16   Ardèche

La Cardinale

Quai du Rhône - 04 75 85 80 40, fax 04 75 85 82 07
*Closed Apr & Nov 1-15: Mon, Nov 15-Mar 7. Open
until 10pm. Terrace dining. Pool. Pkg.*
We have wished some changes on this
Provençal *bastide* on the banks of the Rhône.
Some changes have indeed been going on back-
stage: the pastry chef was promoted to *chef de
cuisine* and a young crew, not yet run in, has
come on the scene. The storm will have to calm
before we really start to enjoy its pretty dining
room with its old tiled floors or its leaf-covered
terrace again. Let's hope the changes are for the
better! C 350-450. M 160 (weekday dinner, Sat &
Sun lunch), 220 (weekday lunch, wine incl), 260-
395, 100 (children).

La Cardinale

(See restaurant above)

*Closed Nov 15-Mar 7. 4 stes 1,500-1,950. 10 rms
800-1,200. Bkfst 100. Half-board 1,140-2,140. Rm
ser. Air cond. Pool. Pkg.*
Luxury and nature are close companions in
this seventeenth-century mansion with a superb
view of the Rhône Valley. Four rooms are in the
mansion itself, with the others in La Résidence,
an annex three kilometers away. Some of the
rooms looked in need of a brush-up, but there is
a gorgeous pool and the breakfasts are
sumptuous. Charming welcome. Relais et
Châteaux.

GRIGNAN   26230
Paris 630 - Montélimar 28 - Valence 71   Drôme

Manoir de la Roseraie

Route de Valréas - 04 75 46 58 15, fax 04 75 46 91 55
*Closed Mon off-seas, Jan 6-Feb 12. Open until
9:15pm. Terrace dining. Air cond. Pool. Tennis.
Pkg.*
After a ramble around the manor's sumptuous
rose garden, you can sit down to such traditional
Southern specialties as poulet aux saveurs
provençales, beef tenderloin with lovely fresh
vegetables, and a creditable apple tart with apple
sorbet. Wines are charitably priced than the
food. Courteous welcome and service. C 300. M
185-235, 100 (children).

Manoir de la Roseraie

(See restaurant above)
*Closed Mon off-seas, Jan 6-Feb 12. 2 stes 1,550-
1,650. 13 rms 660-1,130. Bkfst 90. Rms for disabled.
Half-board 660-1,130. Air cond. Conf. Heated pool.
Tennis. Pkg.*
Standing at the foot of Grignan's château
(where Madame de Sévigné penned her witty
letters), this manor house provides guests with
bright rooms gaily decorated in the Provençal
style. Lovely bathrooms.

PONT-DE-l'ISÈRE   26600
Paris 580 - Valence 8 - Tournon 12   Drôme

Chabran

Av. du 45e-Parallèle (N 7)
04 75 84 60 09, fax 04 75 84 59 65
*Open daily until 10pm. Garden dining. Air cond.
Garage pkg.*
The recent renovation gave birth to a successful
mixture of country and refined quite in keeping
with the tone of the cuisine: whole loaves of
bread cut in front of you when it's served and
first-rate Provençal and Rhône Valley in-

gredients (including the most fantastic lamb!) abound with clear-cut flavors. It's well-concieved simplicity, but we'd still like to see the addition of a pastry chef. Chabran's admirable cellar can provide the mature Hermitage of your dreams, or a simple Côtes-du-Rhône that is the equal in finesse of many a more prestigious label. C 550. **M** 215 (lunch, exc Sun, wine incl), 290, 415, 655, 100 (children).

 ## Chabran

(See restaurant above)
Open year-round. 12 rms 350-690. Bkfst 80. Rm ser. Terrace dining. Air cond. Conf.
A new extension is on the way, with far more luxurious rooms. But as things are, the warm welcome and decent comforts help one ignore the tiny bathrooms. And the breakfasts are delicious (orchard-fresh fruit, homemade jam, just-baked rolls, etc.). Relais et Châteaux.

RUY   38300
Paris 509 - Grenoble 63 - Lyons 41   Isère

 ## Laurent Thomas

Vie-de-Boussieu - 04 74 93 78 00, fax 04 74 28 60 90
Closed Sun dinner, Mon, dinner on hols, Aug. Open until 9:30pm. Terrace dining. Air cond. Pool. Garage pkg.
This Italianate house in its immense green park dotted with sequoias is home to an amiable-priced restaurant. Solid technique is the cornerstone of Laurent Thomas's fine cooking: his jus are taut and concise, his dishes are timed with unfailing accuracy, to keep flavors pure and true. Taste for yourself: order his tiny chèvre-stuffed ravioli afloat in a sapid chicken bouillon, or veal sweetbreads with a black-olive jus under a blanket of whipped potatoes, or pinkly roasted local squab. The prices charged are almost philanthropic (the 140 F lunch is a steal), and the cuisine is classic, granted, but brimming with life—so much that we flirted with a third toque! The wine list includes many regional Balmes Dauphinoise wines at attractive prices, as well as some excellent Burgundies. C 250-350. **M** 140 (weekday lunch), 200-360.

 ## Les Séquoias

(See restaurant above)
Closed Sun, Mon, hols, Aug. 5 rms 550-750. Bkfst 55. Conf. Pool. Garage pkg.
Guests have the run of a huge, wooded estate with a pool and a lovely terrace. A superb stone staircase leads to just five huge, remarkably comfortable rooms decorated with pretty fabrics.

This **symbol** stands for "Les Lauriers du Terroir", an award given to chefs who prepare traditional or regional recipes.

SERRIÈRES   07340
Paris 540 - Privas 93 - St-Etienne 53   Ardèche

 ## Schaeffer

Quai Jules-Roche
04 75 34 00 07, fax 04 75 34 08 79
Closed Sun dinner & Mon (exc Jul-Aug), Jan 2-15, Nov school hols. Open until 9:30pm. Terrace dining. Air cond. Pkg.
Why not pull off the highway at the Chanas exit, and treat yourself to an inexpensive feast? Bernard Mathé's 120 F and 168 F menus are exemplary! But the *carte* is worth exploring too, what with foie gras poised atop a savory spice poundcake, or lobster consommé with Chinese cabbage and a tonic touch of ginger, or a gâteau of wild mushrooms and escargots... Mathé also has a rare gift for creating irresistible desserts, and his cellar is a dream, with Côte-Rôties from Guigal, Jasmin, and Gaillard, and Cornas from Voge and Clape. C 350. **M** 120 (exc Sun), 168.

 ## Schaeffer

(See restaurant above)
See restaurant for closings. 12 rms 260-330. Bkfst 40-50. Air cond. Pkg.
A great stopover, no more expensive than a chain hotel. Tastefully decorated rooms with excellent beds.

VALENCE   26000
Paris 560 - Lyon 100 - Grenoble 99   Drôme

Pic

285, av. Victor-Hugo
04 75 44 15 32, fax 04 75 40 96 03
Closed Sun dinner, 2 wks in Aug. Open until 9:30pm. Garden dining. Air cond. Valet pkg.
From his late father, Jacques, Alain Pic inherited rock-solid classic technique, a gift for saucery, and an unerring eye for premium ingredients. Pic's 560 F *Menu Tradition* showcases his talents with a splendid procession of dishes: escalope of salmon showered with sesame seeds segues into a remarkably bracing lobster in caviar vinaigrette with lentils, tabbouleh, and fresh peas. On to the main course: veal sweetbreads paired with morels and a delicate artichoke purée, followed by a sugar-free sorbet of marc de l'Hermitage. Do indulge in the cheese tray's irresistible local chèvres, because the desserts, frankly, are a letdown. And their sheer quantity only make us long the more for a single, superlative sweet on a par with the rest. This restaurant—with its total comfort, upper middle class furnishings, spacious rooms and lovely gardens—is somehow a relic of the past, and it is high time that the kitchen get its act together. The current renovation of the premises should perhaps be accompanied by a renovation of the general state of mind: one cannot live forever on past glories. The cellar, though, is sumptuous, a landmark for lovers of Côtes-du-Rhône wines. C 680. **M** 290 (weekday lunch), 480 (lunch, exc Sun), 560, 660.

Pic

(See restaurant above)
Closed 2 wks in Aug. 2 stes 950-1,000. 3 rms 750-1,000. Bkfst 100. Terrace dining. Air cond. Conf. Valet pkg.
The house offers a grand total of two suites and three guest rooms (a new wing of rooms is in the works, though). Expect to spend a very comfortable night and to waken to birdsong and a fabulous breakfast. Relais et Châteaux.

VIENNE   38200
Paris 488 - Grenoble 86 - Lyon 31   Isère

 ## La Pyramide

Fernand Point, 14, bd Fernand-Point
04 74 53 01 96, fax 04 74 85 69 73
Closed Wed & Thu lunch off-seas. Open until 9:30pm. Garden dining. Air cond. Valet pkg.
Patrick Henriroux is now in full charge of La Pyramide, heading a motivated, talented team. Though the shadow of the legendary Fernand Point still hovers, Henriroux has transformed La Pyramide from a culinary museum into a model of what a modern restaurant should be. His vivid, vibrantly flavored cuisine harmonizes the best of the Rhône Valley with the Mediterranean. Taste his zesty ragoût of tiny violet artichokes, frogs' legs, and escargots; a fragrant fish minestrone; or pan-roasted red mullet with smothered herbs and greens, flanked by a savory potato tart flecked with bacon and Saint-Marcellin cheese. In the pink-and-ivory dining room or on the terrace overlooking a garden of boxwood and roses, patrons are pampered by an attentive staff. And Jean-Claude Ruet supervises a fabulous cellar awash in the best Rhône Valley wines. C 550-800. M 275 (weekday lunch, wine incl), 430-630, 105 (children).

 ## La Pyramide

(See restaurant above)
Closed Wed & Thu off-seas. 4 stes 1,350-1,450. 20 rms 780-970. Bkfst 85-105. Rms for disabled. Rm ser. Air cond. Conf. Valet pkg.
The 21 rooms and 4 suites overlooking the garden provide the perfect place to stop halfway between Paris and the Riviera. The décor is bright and modern, renovated in Provençal style with hand-painted grapevines, olive trees, and mimosa. Bathrooms are on the small side. Breakfast, coffee, and the wonderful collection of old Port and liqueurs are served in the airy conservatory.

 Plan to travel?

Look for GaultMillau/Gayot's other Best of guides to Chicago, Florida, Germany, Hawaii, Hong Kong, Italy, London, Los Angeles, New England, New Orleans, New York, Paris, Paris & the Loire Valley, San Francisco, Thailand, Toronto, Washington, D.C., and more to come...

 # THE ALPS

ALBERTVILLE   73200
Paris 592 - Chambéry 50 - Grenoble 86   Savoie

Million

8, pl. de la Liberté - 04 79 32 25 15, fax 04 79 32 25 36
Closed Sun dinner, Mon. Open until 9:30pm. Garden dining. Air cond. Pkg.
The signature dish on Philippe Millon's fascinating menu of Savoyard specialties is grilled-to-perfection féra (a delicate lake fish) served with ground wheat. But Millon also looks out to sea for inspiration: witness the seductive oyster velouté with a lush caviar charlotte, succulent lobster ravioli, or sole paupiettes strewn with fresh shellfish. Sublime desserts; you'll be tempted to scrape the plate so as not to miss a bite of the Savoie cake with quince sauce and the pan-fried pineapple with vanilla syrup. The extensively annotated wine list will please oenophiles no end, with many bottles priced under 100 F and a wealth of half-bottles, too. C 360. M 150-550.

Million

(See restaurant above)
Closed Sun eve, Mon. 26 rms 350-650. Bkfst 55-125. Half-board 450-550. Air cond. Conf. Garage pkg.
A convenient stopover on the way to the area's ski resorts, this hotel, with its comfortable, nicely appointed rooms, is the perfect place to bed down after a feast at the adjoining restaurant. Generous breakfasts.

ANNECY   74000
Paris 547 - Lyon 142 - Geneva 43   H.-Savoie

12/20 Les Écuries du Pré Carré

Cour du Pré-Carré, 10, rue Vaugelas
04 50 45 59 14
Closed Sun, Mon lunch. Open until 11pm. Terrace dining.
Walk into a quiet courtyard in the center of Annecy to find this spacious, convivial dining room, where hefty portions of bistro cooking await your hearty appetite. To drink, order one of the pleasant little wines offered by the carafe. C 190-270. M 85 (weekday lunch), 110.

L'Impérial Palace

32, av. d'Albigny - 04 50 09 30 00, fax 04 50 09 33 33
Open year-round. 7 stes 1,600-4,000. 91 rms 800-1,500. Bkfst 100. Rms for disabled. Restaurant. Half-board 660-755. Air cond. Conf. Valet pkg.
Huge, deliciously comfortable rooms with unusual contemporary furnishings (lots of chrome and blond wood) overlook manicured grounds and the lake. Facilities include a beauty and fit-

ness institute, and a terrific heated swimming pool.

BOURGET-DU-LAC (LE)
Pais 656 - Chambéry 12 - Voiron 59

73370
Savoie

 ## Ombremont

"Jean-Pierre Jacob," 2 km N on N 504
04 79 25 00 23, fax 04 79 25 25 77
Weekly closings not available. Closed beg Nov-end Apr. Open until 10pm. Terrace dining. Pool. Pkg.
Formerly a triple-toque chef, Jean-Pierre Jacob moved to Ombremont in summer 1995, and wasted no time in putting his inimitable stamp on this enchanting establishment perched above the lake. The fish is still exceptionally fresh in all its simplicity, but the other things we tried this time were more tempting than satisfying: rather over-spiced langoustines, overcooked pancakes with the veal sweetbreads, inane enough foie gras. The desserts were more than up to par however. The pastry chef is a technical wizard who hovers over every minute detail. May the overall quality of the past set foot here again. A distinguished cellar, of course, and faultless service. C 470. M 195, 350, 510.

 ## Ombremont

(See restaurant above)
Closed beg Nov-end Apr. 5 stes 1,420-1,700. 12 rms 800-1,420. Bkfst incl. Half-board 1,300-2,200 (2 per). Air cond. Conf. Pool. Pkg.
The spacious rooms and suites are perfectly comfortable, with views of the lake and mountains. The professional, obliging personnel makes sure that guests are duly pampered. Enjoy skiing and boating on the lake, or relax by the beautiful pool overhanging the lake. Relais et Châteaux.

 ## L'Orée du Lac

La Croix-Verte - 04 79 25 24 19, fax 04 79 25 08 51
Closed Nov 10-Feb 1. 3 stes 950-1,300. 9 rms 615-950. Bkfst 65. Rms for disabled. Restaurant. Half-board 535-650. Rm ser. Air cond. Pool. Tennis. Pkg.
A distinguished lakeside hotel set in five acres of grounds of inspirational beauty. The huge, comfortable rooms and suites are attractively decorated; there's a pretty winter garden, too. Restaurant service is available to residents.

CHAMONIX
Paris 619 - Annecy 96 - Albertville 67

74400
H.-Savoie

 ## Albert Ier

119, imp. du Montenvers
04 50 53 05 09, fax 04 50 55 95 48
Closed Wed, May 4-15, Oct 19-Dec 4. Open until 9:30pm. Terrace dining. Heated pool. Valet pkg.
Since there's no such thing as an off-season in Chamonix, Pierre and Martine Carrier keep their newly decorated dining room filled with happy gourmets all year round. Pierre continues to refine and expand his already extensive repertoire, but who could complain about having the choice of a melting foie gras "cooked" in a salt marinade, or fricassée of Breton lobster with parsnips fresh from the kitchen garden, or farm-bred chicken braised in a fragrant bed of hay and wild thyme? Still, we're partial to Carrier's "Kingdom of Savoie" menu (the realm included Nice and Piedmont, too), which features féra (local salmon trout) in an herbed sesame crust, served with polenta and a veal-based jus perfumed with wild caraway. To hold the regional note (and to hold the line on the tab!) uncork a Roussette de Seyssel or a red Mondeuse Vieilles Vignes from the remarkable cellar chock-full of the best growers from all over the country. C 400. M 195 (lunch), 215 (dinner, Sun), 295-470, 130 (children).

 ## Albert Ier

(See restaurant above)
Closed May 4-15, Oct 19-Dec 4. 12 stes 1,000-1,700. 17 rms 700-900. Bkfst 80. Half-board 580-995. Rm ser. Conf. Heated pool. Valet pkg.
A friendly, family-style hotel that stands out among Chamonix's finest, with a recently renovated Alpine look (lots of natural wood paneling). The charming rooms are remarkably well equipped, the reception is warm, and the breakfasts (hot rolls, homemade yogurt, mountain honey) are simply delicious. Cute chalets for rent year-round in the hotel's park. Relaxation room with sauna and Jacuzzi; driving range with putting green; lovely flowered grounds.

 ## Auberge du Bois Prin

69, Chemin de L'Hermine, Les Moussoux
04 50 53 33 51, fax 04 50 53 48 75
Closed 2 wks in Apr, Oct 27-Dec 4. 11 rms 740-1,000. Bkfst 70. Rms for disabled. Restaurant. Half-board 590-765 (oblig in seas). Rm ser. Conf. Pkg.
This top-of-the-line Savoyard chalet is perched on the sunny side of the Chamonix Valley facing Mont Blanc, just down the street from the ski station. The spacious rooms are tastefully decorated and open onto balconies. Relais et Châteaux.

 ## Le Matafan

Allée du Majestic
04 50 53 05 64, fax 04 50 55 89 44
Closed Oct 11-Dec 13. Open until 9:30pm. Garden dining. Heated pool. Tennis. Pkg.
The handsome dining room is spacious and well-lit, the service and reception are warm, and the chef, Alain Corvi—who has worked with the likes of Bocuse, Nandron and Léon de Lyon—knows how to hit the right notes. He ventures to offer Savoyard cooking as well as seafood-inspired dishes: jumbo shrimp chutney cooked in lard, Matafan sole and scallops, and veal chops simmered with morel mushrooms. Good local wines are proposed en carafe, but the cellar also holds exciting possibilities from Chile, Australia, and beyond! Extremely attentive service. C 360-440. M 140 (lunch), 180, 320, 80 (children).

Hôtel Mont-Blanc

(See restaurant above)
*Closed Oct 11-Dec 13. 20 stes 994-1,174. 22 rms
397-974. Bkfst 80. Half-board 637-737. Conf.
Heated pool. Tennis. Pkg.*
A beautiful hotel with majestic public rooms,
right at the heart of Chamonix. The standard
rooms are decorated in a pleasing Alpine style,
while the deluxe accommodations are huge and
done up in gay colors and fabrics. In addition,
there is a pretty garden, a swimming pool with
a view of Mont Blanc (you can breakfast on the
poolside terrace), and a sauna.

12/20 **Le Rosebud**

Le Lavancher, 705, route du Chapeau
04 50 54 03 76, fax 04 50 54 10 75
*Closed May 15-Jun 15, mid Nov-Dec 15. Open until
9:30pm. Terrace dining. Heated pool. Tennis. No
pets. Valet pkg.*
Seated on the summer terrace or in the pretty
dining room you can savor the fresh flavors of
Bruno Borton's good cooking: try the pasta
tossed with wild mushrooms and country ham,
the grilled salmon, or the chicken breast in a
verbena infusion. C 200-280. M 245-295 (lunch),
165-380, 80 (children).

 Jeu de Paume

(See restaurant above)
*Closed May 15-Jun 15, mid Nov-Dec 15. 4 stes
1,190-1,390. 18 rms 690-1,080. Rms for disabled.
Half-board 580-930. Rm ser. Conf. Heated pool.
Tennis. Valet pkg.*
In the adorable village of Lavancher, Élyane
Prache has fitted out a comfortable, intimate
chalet on the edge of a larch grove. The cozy,
pine-paneled rooms have tile and terra-cotta
bathrooms, and balconies that look out over the
Balme pass or the Aiguille Verte peak. Sauna;
shuttle to Chamonix.

And also...

*Our selection of places for inexpensive,
quick meals.*
Le Chaudron (04 50 53 40 34 - 79, rue des
Moulins. Open until 11pm.): Sample good fondues and other local treats in a setting of stone
and mellow wood (150).
L'Impossible (04 50 53 20 36 - 9, chemin Cry.
Open until midnight.): Rustic décor, regional
costumes, and, of course, hearty Savoyard fare
served around a huge central fireplace; warm
welcome (180-200).
Le Sarpé (04 50 53 29 31 - 30, passage Mottets.
Open until 9:30pm.): Good regional classics and
other traditional fare in a country-style setting
(130-280).

COURCHEVEL   73120
Paris 653 - Chambéry 99 - Annecy 96   Savoie

 Les Airelles

Jardin Alpin - 04 79 09 38 38, fax 04 79 08 38 69
*Closed mid Apr-mid Dec. Open until 10:30pm.
Terrace dining. Heated pool. No pets. Valet pkg.*
The wood-paneled dining room has acquired
a mellow patina, and looks less like something
out of an Enchanted Forest fantasy. Michel
Renaud's cooking, so in touch with the times, is
gradually moving toward the halls of greatness.
The duck pâté en croute on his lavish Sunday-
lunch Savoyard buffet can easily compete with
that of Léon de Lyon and even that of Greuze at
Tournus. But his turn of hand doesn't stop with
such resolute classics; he also invents more
modern fare such as truffle and red-skin potato
"corolla," impeccable minute-grilled turbot with
pepperoni and anchovy sauce, and frog salad
with baby broad beans. Owner André Fenestraz
will guide you through his cellar of fine Savoie
and Bordeaux wines. First-rate service without
too much to-do. The prices? Ah yes, the prices...
C 500-700. M 310 (lunch), 440 (dinner).

 Les Airelles

(See restaurant above)
*Closed mid Apr-mid Dec. 4 stes 8,000-14,000. 52
rms 2,400-5,600. Bkfst 150-180. Rms for disabled.
Half-board 1,500-2,900. Rm ser. Conf. Heated
pool. No pets. Valet pkg.*
The Fenestraz family's opulent hotel is
decorated in a cheery Austrian style (so is the
staff, attired in lederhosen, no less). The beautiful rooms are admirably equipped (they look out
over a parking lot, though), and guests enjoy a
host of amenities, including sauna, Jacuzzi,
heated garage, and more. Don't miss the spectacular pool! Good (expensive) breakfasts with
regional specialities and pastries including
Saint-Genix brioche.

 **Alpes Hôtel
Pralong 2000**

Courchevel 1850, route de l'Altiport
04 79 08 24 82, fax 04 79 08 36 41
*Closed Apr 14-Dec 20. 8 stes 1,800-2,750. 56 rms
785-1,690. Restaurant. Half-board 785-2,650
(oblig in seas). Rm ser. Conf. Heated pool. Valet pkg.*
A very special hotel set atop Courchevel 1850
opposite the ski lifts. Rooms are huge, comfortable, and attractively decorated. There's a superb buffet breakfast, an indoor swimming pool
and golf practice green (to help work off those
calories), a leisure center, tanning bed, sauna,
and a hairdresser. You can rent your skis at the
hotel. Lots of television channels, too! Relais et
Châteaux.

Annapurna

Courchevel 1850, route de l'Altiport
04 79 08 04 60, fax 04 79 08 15 31
Closed Apr 20-Dec 15. 4 stes 4,880-5,840. 60 rms 1,080-1,770. Bkfst 120. Restaurant. Half-board 1,150-1,770. Rm scr. Air cond. Conf. Heated pool. Valet pkg.
This is one of the best hotels of the resort, indeed in all the French Alps. The terraced rooms are spacious, remarkably well appointed, and face full south toward the mountains and the slopes. Amenities and services galore, including a fitness club, masseur, swimming instructor, manicurist, and a piano bar.

 ## Le Bateau Ivre

04 79 08 36 88, fax 04 79 08 38 72
Closed mid Apr-mid Dec. Open until 10pm. Terrace dining. Air cond. Garage pkg.
This is assuredly the best view you'll find of the slopes, but you'll be thinking of other things as you taste the fare of Jean-Pierre Jacob, who has been cooking in the Bateau's kitchen for more than twenty years now. In all those years, his inspired technique hasn't aged a whit. The 350 F set menu offers an excellent overview of the pricier *carte*. It kicks off with a beautifully balanced warm salad of scallops, potatoes, and salmon roe set atop a wreath of artichoke slices. Then comes a splendid John Dory braised in olive oil escorted by a cohort of vegetables: fresh fava beans, glazed pearl onions, mild garlic, and cracked olives exalt the briny flavor of the fish. Ready for more? How about a pigeon roasted with split-second accuracy to tender, rosy perfection, in a red-wine sauce hinting of pear brandy. The feast winds up with well-matured cheeses (we found the selection somewhat succinct) and a luscious chocolate tart with bittercocoa sorbet. The cellar is full of premium bottles, and is less costly than you might expect. C 480. M 195 (lunch), 350-510, 100 (children).

 ## La Pomme de Pin

(See restaurant above)
Closed mid Apr-mid Dec. 49 rms 1,620. Bkfst 60. Rms for disabled. Half-board 760-1,090. Rm scr. Conf. Garage pkg.
An excellent hotel with rooms that are spacious, bright, and thoughtfully equipped. Comfortable beds and super breakfasts.

Byblos des Neiges

See restaurant La Clairière

 ## Caravelle

Jardin Alpin - 04 79 08 02 42, fax 04 79 08 33 55
Closed Apr 15-Dec 15. 3 stes 750-1,110. 57 rms 600-875. Restaurant. Half-board 500-1,110 (oblig). Rm scr. Air cond. Conf. Heated pool. No pets. Valet pkg.
Here's an attractive and welcoming chalet: rooms have been cozily decorated and there are loads of extras: sauna, massage, squash courts, gym, and game room.

Carlina

Courchevel 1850 - 04 79 08 00 30, fax 04 79 08 04 03
Closed Apr 15-Dec 15. 8 stes 1,770-2,250. 56 rms 600-875. Restaurant. Half-board 1,110-1,790 (oblig). Rm scr. Conf. Heated pool. Valet pkg.
Even more splendid after its recent facelift, this magnificent resort hotel offers untold comfort and every imaginable service: sauna, massage, UVA, and plenty more.

Chabichou

Courchevel 1850, quartier Les Chenus
04 79 08 00 55, fax 04 79 08 33 58
Closed May 1-end Jun, beg Sep-end Nov. Open until 10pm. Terrace dining. Valet pkg.
In one of Courchevel's handsomest chalets, owner-chef Michel Rochedy presents an original, appetizing repertoire. On a recent occasion, the amuse-bouche—a parsleyed clam, a cheese croûton, and a subtle shrimp cream—provided an enticing taste of things to come. Like a duck breast in a hauntingly spiced sauce, flanked on one side by a fig quenelle underscored with prune compote, and on the other by a light potato and wild-mushroom gratin. We're glad we saved room for dessert: a splendiferous millefeuille layered with gingerbread ice cream and lavished with banana cream. Served with a tot of amber rum, it was a fitting finish to the meal. The cellar harbors many mature vintages at accessible prices, with a good selection of half-bottles tariffed around 100 F. Stylish but unstuffy service. C 500-600. M 240-550.

Chabichou

(See restaurant above)
Closed May 1-end Jun, beg Sep-end Nov. 20 stes 1,900. 20 rms 780. Bkfst 70-100. Rms for disabled. Half-board 780-1,900 (oblig in seas). Rm scr. Conf. Valet pkg.
Chabichou is a handsome white chalet with plush accommodations, ideally located near center of the resort and the ski runs. After a generous buffet breakfast, guests can repair to the hotel's workout room.

Le Chalet de Pierres

Courchevel 1850, Piste des Verdont, Jardin Alpin
04 79 08 18 61, fax 04 79 08 38 06
Closed May-Dec 1. Open until 10pm. Terrace dining. Valet pkg.
This chalet is jammed with Courchevel's smart set day and night (400 to 600 people served at lunch), but the quality doesn't suffer. The secret? Simple dishes made with prime ingredients. Try the warm Beaufort cheese tart, a fresh Biollay salad, tartares, veal scallops, beef fillet, and the dizzying dessert assortment. It's expensive, but it works! C 260-310. M 295, 120 (children).

La Clairière

Jardin Alpin - 04 79 00 98 00, fax 04 79 00 98 01
Closed Apr 15-Dec 18. Open until 10:30pm. Terrace dining. Heated pool. No pets. Valet pkg.

There's no better buffet in Courchevel: the dishes are uniformly fresh and appealing, and there are baronial roasts and hearty potées to be savored as well. The more elaborate à la carte dishes are crafted with evident care, and the (expensive!) set meals are oft revised. La Clairière's sun-drenched terrace surrounded by pines is one of the resort's most popular rendez-vous. C 460. M 330 (lunch).

 Byblos des Neiges

(See restaurant above)
Closed Apr 15-Dec 18. 11 stes 5,070-8,670. 66 rms 1,650-3,780. Bkfst 125-190. Rms for disabled. Half-board 1,400-2,400 (oblig in seas). Conf. Heated pool. Valet pkg.
A real snow palace, with sinfully luxurious rooms, saunas, Jacuzzi, Turkish baths, gym, pool, a piano bar, and lots of boutiques. Sunny terraces and spectacular interiors. Friendly, relaxed ambience. Gives right onto the slopes.

 L'Orchidée

Courchevel 1850 - 04 79 08 03 77, fax 04 79 08 18 70
Closed Apr 15-Dec 15. Open until 10pm. Terrace dining. No pets. Pkg.
Yet another new chef is in the Orchidée's kitchen, but he seems to have the house repertoire under control. He served us a flawless sea bass with artichokes, followed by a wonderful banana crème brûlée; still, we're eager to see what original ideas he can come up with when he presents his own *carte*. Stay tuned! C 320-400. M 300 (lunch), 355 (dinner).

 Hôtel des Neiges

(See restaurant above)
Closed Apr 13-Dec 14. 5 stes 1,700-2,280. 37 rms 815-2,630. Rms for disabled. Half-board 1,190-1,780 (oblig in seas). Rm ser. Conf. No pets. Pkg.
This large and immensely comfortable chalet is situated at the foot of the slopes, within walking distance of the village center. The rooms are lovely, bright and quiet, with white walls and floral drapes. A lively atmosphere is assured thanks to the film-world clientele. Entertainment nightly in the piano bar. Relais et Châteaux.

And also...

Our selection of places for inexpensive, quick, or late-night meals.
Bel Air (04 79 08 00 93 - Altitude 2000.): At the top of the Montriond lift you'll find a fresh, family-style set meal featuring tarragon chicken, braised ham and the like (120).
Les Peupliers (04 79 08 41 47 - Le Praz. Open until 9pm.): Traditional cooking and Savoyard specialties, including marvelous mountain charcuterie, served in a rustic setting (100-210).

DIVONNE-LES-BAINS 01220
Paris 502 - Geneva 19 - Nyons 13 Ain

 Château de Divonne

Route de Gex
04 50 20 00 32, fax 04 50 20 03 73
Closed mid Jan-beg Mar. Open until 10pm. Terrace dining. Tennis. Pkg.
Michel de Mattéis heads the kitchen at this nineteenth-century manor house overlooking Lake Geneva. Entrust him with your appetite, which he'll tempt, whet, tease, and satisfy with langoustine ravioli in a snappy herbal jus; or a luxurious take on lasagne, filled with frogs' legs and shellfish; or sea bass emboldened with black olives and an ink-stained fricassée of baby squid. The "tout tomate" extravaganza sings with sunny flavors: it presents pressed tomato with mozzarella and basil, gazpacho andalou, tiny stuffed tomatoes, and tomatoes glazed with honey and spices. What's more, there's a staggering cellar, and everything's served with style. The panoramic terrace affords a breathtaking view of Mont Blanc. C 500. M 270 (weekday lunch, Sat, wine incl), 270-490, 145 (children).

 Château de Divonne

(See restaurant above)
Closed mid Jan-beg Mar. 11 stes 1,140-1,700. 14 rms 730-1,270. Bkfst 85-130. Half-board 975-1,280. Rm ser. Air cond. Conf. Tennis. Pkg.
Enjoy a gorgeous view of Lake Geneva and the Mont Blanc range from this nineteenth-century manor set in immense, wooded grounds. The interior design is nothing special, but you'll love the spacious rooms, modern bathrooms, exquisite breakfasts, and perfect service. There's an eighteen-hole golf course, casino, sailing, and summer music festivals for your entertainment. Relais et Châteaux.

 La Terrasse

Av. des Thermes
04 50 40 34 34, fax 04 50 40 34 24
Closed Sun dinner, Mon, Feb. Open daily until 9:30pm (10pm in summer). Terrace dining. Air cond. Heated pool. Tennis. No pets. Valet pkg.
No, this isn't the most swinging spot in Divonne-les-Bains (we're not sure there is one...) but Jean-Marc Delacourt will make your taste buds do the boogaloo with his earthy braised oxtail in a superb sauce, lake char from Lake Geneva quickly sautéed to point up its delicate savor, and succulent breast of grain-fed pigeon wrapped in leaves and roasted to juicy perfection. For dessert, don't miss the symphonie tout chocolat. In addition to the expected lordly vintages, the cellar also harbors many lesser-known wines that are a treat to discover. C 400-500. M 200-370, 100 (children).

Domaine de Divonne

(See restaurant above)
Closed Feb. 8 stes 2,500-7,000. 119 rms 700-1,600. Bkfst 95. Rms for disabled. Air cond. Conf. Heated pool. Tennis. Pkg.
Charmingly old-fashioned (not wildly cheerful), this 1930s luxury hotel provides rooms overlooking either the manicured grounds and the Jura Mountains, or Lake Geneva and the Alps. Night club; casino.

ÉVIAN 74500
Paris 589 - Annecy 81 - Geneva 42 H.-Savoie

 ## Le Gourmandin

Royal Club Évian, South shore of Lake Geneva 04 50 26 85 00, fax 04 50 75 61 00
Closed Nov 11-Feb 7. Open until 9:30pm (10pm Fri, Sat & in summer). Terrace dining. Heated pool. Tennis. No pets. Valet pkg.
Filtered light and flowered curtains embellish the pretty, Directoire-style dining room of the Hôtel Ermitage. Come here to savor fine regional foodstuffs, deftly prepared: smoked ham, air-dried beef, lake trout, lake char with bacon, rack of lamb with green thyme, and sabayon with brilliant blue bilberries. Appealing and (all in all) affordable cellar, run by a competent sommelier. **C** 310-430. **M** 270 (Sun), 170-340, 80 (children).

 ## Hôtel Ermitage

(See restaurant above)
Closed Nov 11-Feb 7. 4 stes 1,980-3,500. 87 rms 530-2,900. Bkfst 90. Rms for disabled. Half-board 630-1,670. Rm ser. Conf. Heated pool. Tennis. Valet pkg.
This lovely Belle Époque hotel recently underwent a thorough overhaul; it offers complete comfort and a relaxed atmosphere in a tranquil rural setting. Numerous sporting and leisure activities are proposed, including a newly enlarged fitness center.

 ## Les Prés Fleuris sur Évian

D 24 - 04 50 75 29 14, fax 04 50 70 77 75
Closed beg Oct-mid May. Open until 8:30pm. Garden dining. No pets. Valet pkg.
A fairytale view over Lake Geneva with mountain pastures in the foreground is the main attraction here these days, because although chef Roger Frossard uses flawless ingredients, creativity and originality are missing these days (thus the dropping of a toque). You'll still have a good meal: broiled Dublin bay prawns, lake fish with beurre blanc, or Bresse poultry with tarragon cream. Unfortunately, the wine list blatantly fails to cite any growers' names... **C** 410-550. **M** 280-420.

 ## Les Prés Fleuris sur Évian

(See restaurant above)

Closed beg Oct-mid May. 12 rms 850-1,400. Bkfst 80-100. Half-board 850-1,300 (oblig in seas). Valet pkg.
A delightfully relaxed atmosphere pervades the quiet, huge, comfortable rooms (with balconies offering spectacular views) of this hotel perched high above Lake Geneva. Relais et Châteaux.

 ## Hôtel Royal

Domaine du Royal Club Évian, South shore of Lake Geneva - 04 50 26 85 00, fax 04 50 75 61 00
Closed Dec 1-Feb 5. 29 stes 1,480-7,580. 127 rms 680-3,120. Bkfst 105. Restaurant. Half-board 810-1,820. Rm ser. Conf. Heated pool. Tennis. Valet pkg.
The owners aim to make this luxury hotel one of the best in Europe. Not a modest ambition, but a realistic one, considering the peerless setting on the wooded slopes above Lake Geneva, the hotel itself, with its gorgeous Art Nouveau frescoes, and the wide-open corporate purse that finances it all. Other advantages include lovely, faultlessly appointed rooms; one of the most effective health and beauty institutes in Europe; indoor and outdoor swimming pools; a world-renowned eighteen-hole golf course; six tennis courts; a heliport; a club for children; the casino, of course, and the famous spring chamber-music festival, directed by Russian cellist and composer Mstislav Rostropovich.

 ## La Toque Royale

Domaine du Royal Club Évian, South shore of Lake Geneva - 04 50 75 03 78, fax 04 50 75 48 40
Closed Sun, Jan 5-26. Open until 10pm. No pets. Valet pkg.
This lakeside restaurant with its *fin-de-siècle* interior attracts gamblers, families, and Swiss gourmets who come for Michel Lentz's well-designed *carte*. The actual cooking is performed by Patrick Frenot: among the modern, regionally inspired offerings are scrambled quails' eggs with celery and celery root, féra (lake fish) with bacon, omble chevalier (another lake fish) à la matouille, beef tenderloin with ratte potatoes, and truffled squab. You're sure to find just the ideal partner for these good things in the vast cellar. Too bad, though, that the décor lacks warmth, and that the staff feels compelled to indulge in all manner of unnecessary (even irritating) flourishes. **C** 480. **M** 160 (weekday lunch), 250 (weekdays, exc Fri dinner), 360-480.

La Verniaz

Neuvecelle-Église - 04 50 75 04 90, fax 04 50 70 78 92
Closed Nov 23-Feb 7. Open until 9:30pm. Garden dining. Pool. Pkg.
On the slopes above Évian stands an idyllic dwelling, on grounds dotted with adorable guest chalets. When you finally locate the immense dining room, you might well believe that you're still in the garden, as you luxuriate in the flood of light and riot of flowers. Charcoal-grilled and spit-roasted meats are chef Christian Métreau's specialty, but he also turns out some interesting dishes based on féra and omble

chevalier from Lake Geneva. Relaxed, friendly service. Wide selection of wines. C 330. M 210-350, 130 (children).

La Verniaz

(See restaurant above)
Closed Nov 23-Feb 7. 6 stes 850-1,500 and up. 34 rms 500-1,100. Bkfst 75. Half-board 580-900 (oblig in seas). Rm ser. Conf. Pool. Tennis. Golf. Pkg.
The pleasant chalet rooms scattered around the peaceful grounds command a view of Lake Geneva and an Alp or two. Perfect amenities (billiards, covered putting green) and service. Relais et Châteaux.

FAVERGES-DE-LA-TOUR   38110
Paris 530 - Lyon 65 - Chambéry 37   Isère

Château de Faverges de la Tour

10 km E on N 516 & D 145
04 74 97 42 52, fax 04 74 88 86 40
Closed Oct-May. 3 stes 2,100. 35 rms 750-1,800. Bkfst 95. Rms for disabled. Restaurant. Half-board 1,670-2,920. Rm ser. Air cond. Conf. Heated pool. Tennis. Valet pkg.
An authentic château flanked by a tall tower, furnished with superb antiques. The guest rooms are decorated in bold style and are impeccably appointed. Beautiful terraces. Relais et Châteaux.

GRENOBLE   38000
Paris 562 - Lyon 104 - Chambéry 57   Isère

L'Escalier

6, pl. Lavalette - 04 76 54 66 16, fax 04 76 63 01 58
Closed Sat lunch, Sun. Open until 10pm.
In this prime location across from the Grenoble museum, Boris Roginski doesn't stray totally away from Grenoble's traditional dishes, yet adds original dishes like roast asparagus with zucchini flowers and sautéed scallops and sour cream with dried fruit. His refined 190 F *minceur* or "slimming" meal is a shining example of modern cuisine. Well-crafted desserts and excellent management by Alain Girod. C 240-350. M 140 (lunch), 190-450.

12/20 Le Madelon

55, av. d'Alsace-Lorraine - 04 76 46 36 90
Closed Sat lunch, Sun. Open until 10pm. Priv rm 12. Terrace dining.
Catherine and Philippe Cartillier compose a menu that looks toward Lyon and Provence for inspiration. Among the highlights are chicken terrine enriched with foie gras and cèpes, fish poached in a fragrant broth thickened with aïoli, and raspberry feuillantine. Small but pertinent cellar; obliging service. The brasserie menu on the bistro side is more affordable than the menu on the restaurant side, but both offer carefully prepared, imaginative cooking. C 220-350. M 94-200.

Park Hotel

10, pl. Paul-Mistral
04 76 85 81 23, fax 04 76 46 49 88
Closed Jun 26-Aug 18, Dec 20-Jan 5. 10 stes 1,600. 40 rms 1,000-1,300. Bkfst 65-95. Restaurant. Conf. Valet pkg.
Grenoble's top hotel, with highly trained staff, comfortable rooms and central location, is across from a verdant park. Conference facilities offering up-to-date technology (video projection, PC for Internet) and fitness center. The rooms boast warm furnishings and inlaid woodwork in a wide variety of styles. Private rooms for business lunches.

MEGÈVE   74120
Paris 613 - Annecy 60 - Chamonix 35 - Lyon 197   H.-Savoie

Chalet du Mont d'Arbois

Route du Mont-d'Arbois
04 50 21 25 03, fax 04 50 21 24 79
Closed mid Apr-mid Jun, mid Oct-mid Dec. Open until 10pm. Terrace dining. Heated pool. Tennis. Pkg.
The split-level dining room is done up to resemble a deluxe hunting lodge; beyond the window is a picture-postcard view of Megève. Young and brilliant Alexandre Faix has recently taken over the kitchen. He quickly adapted to the style of this Rothschild-owned restaurant with its stayed upper middle class refinement and well-to-do authenticity, bringing with him all the serious-minded technical skills he learned from Robuchon. Savor a chilled foie gras that is perfection pure, a sole with a full-flavored baby shrimp cream sauce, a runny-in-the-middle bitter cocoa cake with vanilla ice cream. Wash down the excellent cheese with one of the fine wines from the cellar's collection, presented by a highly competent wine waiter. Expect a rather too formal welcome and stylish service in this luxurious décor. C 270-360. M 200-280.

Chalet du Mont d'Arbois

(See restaurant above)
See restaurant for closings. 1 ste 3,280-4,780. 20 rms 840-1,900. Bkfst 80. Half-board 1,180-2,620 (oblig in seas). Rm ser. Heated pool. Tennis. Pkg.
A lovely mountain chalet, tastefully decorated in Alpine style by Nadine de Rothschild, with uncommonly pretty furnishings. Gorgeous heated pool; truly excellent breakfasts. Ultracomfortable rooms. Relais et Châteaux (a very aristocratic one).

La Chaumine

36, chemin des Bouleaux
04 50 21 37 05, fax 04 50 21 37 21
Closed Apr 15-Jun 28, Sep 15-Dec 15. 11 rms 300-510. Bkfst 35. No pets. Garage pkg.
Blond-wood paneling, pretty fabrics and furnishings contribute to the charm of this adorable

chalt, and so does the owner's heartwarming welcome.

 ## Les Fermes de Marie ♻

Chemin de Riante-Colline
04 50 93 03 10, fax 04 50 93 09 84
Closed mid Apr-Jun, mid-Apr-mid Sep. Open until 10pm. Garden dining. Heated pool. Garage pkg.
Chef Nicolas Le Bec is a newcomer to this geranium-spangled chalet which Guillaume Sourrieu made into a major attraction for Megève's food lovers. The young Breton prepares a pork chop the likes of which you've never eaten, and is successfully learning to integrate Savoie-inspired dishes into his cuisine. Mountain picnics are still organized at the Pré-Rosset chalet for those staying in the hotel. A grill room is soon to be added to the cheese-theme restaurant. C 360-420. M 220 (wine incl), 380 (dinner, exc weekdays), 140 (children).

 ## Les Fermes de Marie ⚑

(See restaurant above)
See restaurant for closings. 3 stes 1,290. 52 rms 795-1,560. Rms for disabled. Half-board 795-1,560 (oblig in seas). Rm ser. Heated pool. Garage pkg.
For a storybook winter holiday in Megève: a hamlet of ten rustic yet utterly refined farmhouses has been restored as a luxury resort. The interiors are all done up with floral fabrics, regional antiques, folk art, etc. Slimming and beauty facilities are on hand, as well as a magnificent swimming pool. Individual chalets for families. Wonderful welcome and service.

 ## Hôtel du Mont-Blanc

Rue Amboise-Martin, pl. de l'Église
04 50 21 20 02, fax 04 50 21 45 28
Closed Apr 21-May. 11 stes 2,010-2,640. 28 rms 910-1,630. Bkfst 80. Restaurant. Conf. Heated pool. Valet pkg.
Jean-Louis and Jocelyne Sibuet have renovated this luxurious establishment from stem to stern, in a warm, welcoming English style. Fabulous rooms with every amenity, public lounges in perfect taste. The tea room is sure to become Megève's smartest society rendezvous.

 ## Parc des Loges ⚑

100, rue d'Arly - 04 50 93 05 03, fax 04 50 93 09 52
Closed Apr 15-Jun, Sep 15-Dec 15. 11 stes 1,200-3,000. 42 rms 700-2,000. Bkfst 80. Rms for disabled. Restaurant. Half-board 930-1,230 (oblig in seas). Rm ser. Conf. Heated pool. Valet pkg.
A true "snow palace" from the 1930s, sumptuously restored to its Art Deco glory, right down to the authentic room furnishings, but the rooms sometimes lack some of the fittings you might expect. The opulent amenities even include the rarest of all: sun-lit bathrooms. Non-alcoholic beverages in the mini-bar are free. Fitness center, Jacuzzi and sauna. A jazz bar provides evening entertainment.

Looking for a restaurant? Refer to the **Index.**

And also...

Our selection of places for inexpensive, quick, or late-night meals.
L'Alpette (04 50 21 03 69 - Rochebrune. Open until 3pm.): The terrace is definitely a place to be seen; order the boudin sausage with apples and whipped potatoes, or leek terrine followed by poulet grand'mère (65-135).
Le Delicium (04 50 21 37 15 - Le Sporting de Rochebrune. Open until 10:30pm.): A good pizzeria that also serves osso buco, pasta, and tiramisù (130).

MÉRIBEL-LES-ALLUES	73550
Paris 637 - Chambéry 93 - Albertville 45	Savoie

 ## Allodis

Le Belvédère - 04 79 00 56 00, fax 04 79 00 59 28
Closed Apr 25-Jun, Sep 15-Dec 15. Open until 10:30pm. Terrace dining. Heated pool. No pets. Pkg.
Alain Plouzane has moved into the ranks of Méribel's leading chefs with consistently fine cooking that highlight the essential flavors of excellent ingredients. His use of spices is particularly à propos. You'll be courteously welcomed into the elegant dining room, which boasts a stunning coffered ceiling. Good wine list (but why so few half-bottles?); competent service. C 400-500. M 170 (lunch), 240-340 (dinner).

 ## Allodis ⚑

(See restaurant above)
Closed Mar 24-Jun, Sep 15-Dec 15. 12 stes 1,900-2,200. 31 rms 900-1,900. Bkfst 60. Rms for disabled. Half-board 890-1,100. Rm ser. Conf. Heated pool. No pets. Pkg.
On the slopes above the resort area, these spacious wood-paneled rooms enjoy a great view of the Olympic runs. Wonderfully convivial atmosphere; gym, half-court and sauna.

 ## Cassiopée

04 79 23 28 23, fax 04 79 23 28 18
Closed Apr-Jul, Sep-Dec. Open until 10pm. Priv rm 40. Terrace dining. Heated pool. Valet pkg.
Chef Christian Farenasso, a native of Provence, infuses his menu with the forthright flavors of the Mediterranean. Always refined and precisely rendered for such fresh, fragrant offerings as a salad of crisp-cooked vegetables and langoustines in an anchoïade dressing, or red mullet with olive caviar and potatoes topped with aïoli, and a sumptuous opéra cake with pear jus, a masterpiece of pâtisserie. Showy wine list. The youthful staff is energetic and stylish, in tune with the elegant but unstuffy setting. Prices that match the smartness of the place. C 380. M 180 (lunch), 310-460, 90 (children).

 ## L'Antarès ⚑

(See restaurant above)
Closed Apr-Jul, Sep-Dec. 16 stes 2,350-4,350. 47 rms 1,500-2,460. Bkfst 120. Rms for disabled. Half-

board 1,220-2,770 (oblig in seas). Rm ser. Conf. Heated pool. Valet pkg.

The electronic equipment and bath fixtures found in these huge, beautiful rooms may take some getting used to! The fitness center and swimming pool are superb; the reception and service are excellent. You pay for it though...

 Le Grand Cœur

04 79 08 60 03, fax 04 79 08 58 38
Closed Apr 7-Dec 13. Open until 10pm. Terrace dining. Valet pkg.

Marc Dach's proficient cooking grows more attractive each year (he invites Grand Véfour chef Guy Martin every year at the end of January for the Soupers Des Ducs de Savoie, which allows him to increase his knowledge of Savoie cooking), with a few bright Mediterranean notes now added to his regionally rooted repertoire. After a day on the slopes, it's a treat to sit down to farmhouse ravioli in a creamy sauce of Vacherin cheese or to a crackling-good croustillant of pig's trotter with Chambéry mustard. Work well done, so a second toque it will be. Remarkable welcome and service. All the best local wines are on hand in the cellar. C 350-400. M 170 (lunch), 340 (dinner).

 Le Grand Cœur

(See restaurant above)
Closed Apr 7-Dec 13. 3 stes 1,375-2,050. 38 rms 700-1,300. Bkfst 90. Half-board 350. Conf. Valet pkg.

A magnificent chalet in the heart of Méribel, with spacious, well-designed rooms that give onto the Vanoise summits. Six rooms were refurbished last year as every year. Excellent fitness equipment is featured, along with a Jacuzzi, sauna, and Turkish bath. Delightful reception; fabulous buffet breakfasts. Relais et Châteaux.

12/20 L'Orée du Bois

Rond-point des Pistes
04 79 00 50 30, fax 04 79 08 57 52
Closed Easter-Jul 1, Aug 31-Dec 20. Open until 9pm. Priv rm 30. Terrace dining. HOTEL: 35 rms 470. Half-board 370-720 (oblig in seas). Rm ser. Conf. Heated pool. No pets. Pkg.

Settle down in this bright, airy dining room to enjoy full-flavored Alpine cooking. The menu proposes a robust salad of Belgian endive and morsels of smoked duck breast, roast rib steak with an exemplary gratin dauphinois, and a pluperfect crème caramel. Small cellar dense in regional choices, but light on others. C 200. M 190-210 (dinner), 65 (children).

■ **In Le Mottaret 73550**   *6 km S*

 Mont Vallon

04 79 00 44 00, fax 04 79 00 46 93
Closed Apr 16-Dec 21. 6 stes 1,400-1,800. 86 rms 790-1,250. Bkfst 90. Rms for disabled. Restaurant.

Half-board 790-1,250. Rm ser. Conf. Heated pool. Valet pkg.

An immense, sumptuous chalet with intimate, warmly elegant decor. Wonderfully comfortable rooms (the suites even have fireplaces) and superb facilities (fitness club, squash, solarium, etc.).

 Château de Coudrée

04 50 72 62 33, fax 04 50 72 57 28
Closed mid Dec-mid Apr. Open until 9pm. Terrace dining. Pool. Tennis. Pkg.

This elegant twelfth-century château offers updated classic cuisine. The "François I" fixed-price meal lets you sample burbot jaw and langoustine salad, sea bream fillet with candied lemons and veal jus, and an almond-cream millefeuille with a roast peach. The wine list is good, but short on half-bottles. Courteous welcome. C 300-400. M 150, 290, 380.

 Château de Coudrée

04 50 72 62 33, fax 04 50 72 57 28
Closed mid Dec-mid Apr. 5 stes 1,480-1,850. 14 rms 680-1,480. Bkfst 85-135. Half-board 725-1,075 (oblig in seas). Conf. Heated pool. Tennis. Pkg.

The quiet of the well-groomed grounds, a fine view of Lake Geneva, and sumptuously decorated rooms are some of the reasons this hotel is one of the most pleasant Relais et Châteaux. Sauna; disco; private beach.

 L'Abbaye

Chemin des Moines
04 50 60 77 33, fax 04 50 60 78 81
Closed Jan-Feb. 4 stes 960-1,395. 28 rms 675-1,195. Bkfst 70-85. Restaurant. Half-board 595-865. Conf. Valet pkg.

The Abbaye de Talloires is a fief of elegant good taste on the shore of Lake Annecy. Marvelously appointed rooms look out onto the cloister (it dates from the seventeenth century) and are adjoined by fabulous bathrooms. The Prior's Room (said to be haunted by a long-gone *prieur*) is a registered landmark. Relais et Châteaux.

 Auberge du Père Bise

Route du Port - 04 50 60 72 01, fax 04 50 60 73 05
Closed Tue & Wed lunch off-seas, Nov-mid Feb. Open until 9pm. Terrace dining. Valet pkg.

Père Bise is an honest-to-god "temple of gastronomy," of the sort one only finds in France. It's a perfect place to celebrate a special occasion, when money is no object and only a dreamy setting will do. You won't be disappointed. Across the handsome garden winks lovely Lake Annecy; the personnel, overseen by Charlyne Bise, performs flawlessly; and from her kitchen Sophie Bise sends forth opulent, festive dishes: extra-big Dublin Bay prawn ice cream feathered with basil, marinated red mullet with stewed baby squids, "red-foot" crayfish risotto, and a lavishly truffled upside-down tart of potatoes and foie gras. The first set-price meal is well-balanced with François Bise-style salmon trout with ginger, lobster gratin, cheese and dessert of the day. Since even a Chinon fetches 220 F, you may as well splurge on a *grand cru* from a cellar awash in mature growers' wines. C 600-850. M 490-790, 180 (children).

 ### Auberge du Père Bise

(See restaurant above)
See restaurant for closings. 9 stes 2,500-3,000. 25 rms 1,100-1,600. Bkfst 100-150. Rms for disabled. Half-board 1,250-1,950. Conf. Tennis. Valet pkg.

Perched on the edge of the lake, this delightfully romantic hotel provides ideal comfort in an ultraclassic setting. Book a room in the beautiful new Villa des Roses annex. Superb views of lake and mountains, first-class breakfasts. The newly added boutique sells homemade gastronomic specialties such as foie gras, smoked salmon, sweetmeats and chocolate, as well as linens and dishes with the famous Père Bise signature. Relais et Châteaux.

TIGNES	73320
Paris 690 - Bourg-St-Maurice 30	Savoie

12/20 La Calèche

Galerie du Palafour
04 79 06 50 80, fax 04 79 06 45 92
Closed May 10-Jun, Sep 5-Oct 20. Open until 10pm. Terrace dining.

Famished skiers devour huge portions of better-than-average fondues, raclette, and charcoal grills, all diligently served in this bright wood-paneled eating house. C 160-260. M 95, 138, 55 (children).

 ### Le Ski d'Or

2 km SW, in Le Val-Claret
04 79 06 51 60, fax 04 79 06 45 49
Closed May-Dec 1. Open until 9:30pm. Pkg.

With assets like a handsome dining room and splendid view, it's a shame that the Ski d'Or closes in summer. This season's chef proffers a relatively inventive and spicy cuisine: ginger-flavored hot-oyster Parmentier, steamed bass and marrow dumplings with fines herbes, lamb fillet panoufle with tarragon, and regional Savoyard cheeses. Fully-stocked cellar. C 300. M 135-245, 100 (children).

 ### Le Ski d'Or

(See restaurant above)
Closed May-Dec 1. 22 rms 800-1,150. Half-board 1,030 (oblig in seas). Rm ser. Conf. Pkg.

A picturesque and charming hotel in the Val-Claret, with panoramic mountain views. The bright, adorably decorated rooms boast big beds and many amenities. Cheerful personnel. Relais et Châteaux.

URIAGE	38410
Paris 572 - Grenoble 10	Isère

 ## Les Terrasses d'Uriage
04 76 89 10 80, fax 04 76 89 04 62
Closed Sep-Jun: Sat lunch, Sun dinner, Mon; Jan. Open until 9:30pm. Priv rm 50. Garden dining. Heated pool. Valet pkg.

Philippe Bouissou is fulfilling his promise as one of the most gifted chefs of his generation. Backed up by a first-class brigade and faultless service, he heads up greater Grenoble's top-rated table. We don't usually make much ado about cocktail snacks, but his are works of art. Some are even brought to you in a silver spoon! Imagine: mini oyster and mushroom bouillon, saddle of rabbit, lobster crisp, fried paprika-coated mixed herbs or herb fritters. Your taste buds will be more than ready to taste what comes next! Just look at the 205 F menu: herbed white tuna cooked with impeccable precision is followed by roast tenderloin of lamb in a rich, full-bodied sauce, an extraordinary cheese board (it features a memorable blue-veined persillé de Tignes), and a procession of enticing desserts. The sommelier, a real pro, presides over a wide-ranging cellar with lots of growers' wines. And the good news is that the prices are still accessible to mere mortals. C 350. M 205 (weekday lunch, wine incl), 185 (weekday lunch), 260-360.

 ### Le Grand Hôtel

(See restaurant above)
Closed Jan. 44 rms 395-560. Bkfst 65. Half-board 385-435. Rm ser. Conf. Heated pool. Valet pkg.

Spacious, comfortable accommodations, fine bathrooms, and excellent breakfasts draw patrons to this handsomely renovated Second Empire hotel. Facilities include a hydrotherapy institute and a heated pool. Excellent value for money.

VAL-D'ISÈRE	73150
Paris 690 - Chambéry 133 - Albertville 85	Savoie

 ### Christiana
04 79 06 08 25, fax 04 79 41 11 10
Closed May-Dec. 11 stes 2,274-4,268. 59 rms 1,047-1,814. Bkfst 60-95. Rms for disabled. Restaurant. Rm ser. Heated pool. Pkg.

Here is Val-d'Isère's most concentrated glitter. Lovely rooms, with fine appointments; the whole place has just been totally renovated, with everything from beds to bathrooms, balconies to bars done in natural pine for an authentically Alpine look. The runs are just outside the door. Sauna and steam bath.

12/20 Le Pré d'Aval

Le Solaise building, rue Principale
04 79 41 14 05.
*Weekly closings not available. Closed May 10-Jun 20,
Sep 30-Nov 15. Open until 10pm.*
The Pré d'Aval sports a rustic, Scandinavian
look, but the menu is pure Savoie: raclette, fondue, tartiflette, diots (local sausages) au vin
blanc, and polenta are the mainstays. Wash them
down with one of the pleasant regional wines
served by the carafe. Don't neglect the tasty desserts. C 180-280. M 75, 90, 50 (children).

 ## Savoyarde

04 79 06 01 55, fax 04 79 41 11 29
*Closed May 5-Aug 8, Aug 23-Nov. 2 stes 1,470-
2,050. 44 rms 500-1,100. Bkfst 60. Rms for disabled.
Restaurant. Half-board 560-810 (oblig in seas).
Pkg.*
Here's a traditional mountain chalet, just 100
yards from the lifts, with attractive rooms, pine
furnishings, and wood-paneled bathrooms. Fitness center offering sauna, Turkish bath, Jacuzzi
and massage service.

 ## Tsanteleina

04 79 06 12 13, fax 04 79 41 14 16
*Closed May 4-Jun, end Aug 30-Nov. Open until
9:30pm. Terrace dining. HOTEL: 40 stes 800-
1,300. 29 rms 600-1,000. Bkfst 80. Half-board 520-
980 (oblig in seas). Rm ser. Pkg.*
Ask the excellent maître d' to usher you to a
table by a bay window. You'll be served a curried
langoustine millefeuille, rack of lamb in a mustardy crust, prime Savoyard cheeses, and some
fantastic desserts. The principally regional cellar
is short on growers' wines for other regions, and
needs more half-bottles. C 300. M 150 (lunch),
230 (dinner), 100 (children).

VAL-THORENS   73440
Paris 670 - Albertville 70 - Moûtiers 36   Savoie

 ## La Table du Roy

04 79 00 04 78, fax 04 79 00 06 11
*Closed May 10-Dec 1. Open until 10:30pm. Terrace
dining. Air cond. Heated pool. No pets. Valet pkg.*
François Prudent is a self-taught chef, one who
never stops learning if we're to judge by his
refined, balanced cuisine. His repertoire evokes
the Mediterranean and Savoie, and is full of
bright ideas (great chestnut-flour bread) that are
mostly well executed (we encountered some
overcooked tuna). The sommelier is a real pro,
so ask his advice on choosing from the wide-
ranging cellar. And you can count on a courteous
welcome and flawless service. C 350. M 220-500
(dinner), 280 (lunch), 120 (children).

 ## Fitz Roy

(See restaurant above)
*Closed May 10-Dec 1. 7 stes 900-1,700. 30 rms
900-1,350. Bkfst 120. Rms for disabled. Half-board*

*1,000-1,700 (oblig). Rm ser. Air cond. Conf.
Heated pool. Valet pkg.*
A huge, modern, deluxe chalet with spacious,
cozily paneled rooms. Panoramic lift. Fitness
buffs will love the swimming pool, brand-new
Turkish baths, and superb exercise and slimming equipment. Lots of services; impeccable
staff. Relais et Châteaux.

VEYRIER-DU-LAC   74290
Paris 545 - Annecy 7   H.-Savoie

 ## Marc Veyrat

13, Vieille Route des Pensières
04 50 60 24 00, fax 04 50 60 23 63
*Closed Mon. Open until 9:30pm. Terrace dining.
Air cond. Valet pkg.*
His posing and pronouncements can get on
our nerves, but we have to forgive Marc Veyrat.
The man may be mad, but he's a brilliant chef,
and a brave one at that—while others prudently
put their creativity on hold, Veyrat gives full rein
to his inventive powers. He's inspired by
Savoie's native bounty and by the precious herbs
and rare roots that he gathers himself in Alpine
meadows. You've surely never tasted anything
like his "beggar's purse" of heirloom vegetables
in a whey-based emulsion ennobled with truffles; or duck roasted in fragrant spruce bark and
juniper branches; or a simple citrus-fruit salad
transformed by the perfumes of wild caraway
and fennel. Yes, the price of admission to
Veyrat's "decorator" dining room is stunningly
steep. But he gives unstintingly: just look at the
carts laden with loaves of bread, lordly roasts,
farm cheeses, and rare brandies that waiters
wheel about the room, and we thought cellars
like this only existed in dreams—it's a vision of
opulence that harks back to a more generous,
hospitable age. C 700-1,000. M 365 (weekday
lunch), 595-995, 200 (children).

 ## Auberge de l'Éridan

(See restaurant above)
*Open year-round. 2 stes 4,300-4,850. 9 rms 1,500-
3,400. Bkfst 150-195. Rms for disabled. Air cond.
Conf. Valet pkg.*
Veyrat's magnificent 1930s villa offers guest
rooms and suites that overlook a sloping garden
and Lake Annecy. The lavender-colored façade
is bit of a shock, but turns out to be a traditional
local hue. Neither effort nor expense has been
spared (au contraire). The bathrooms are among
the most luxurious in France (some have double
Jacuzzis). Prices are high, but rooms are extraordinarily vast, elegant, and luxurious. After a
sumptuous breakfast, wander down to the landing and pick up the Auberge's private boat.
Relais et Châteaux.

REGIONAL FOODS

The Rhône Valley and the Alps encompass areas as diverse as the rugged Ardèche, mountainous Savoie, and the Drôme, which is practically Provence. Rich in game, the Ardèche still cultivates a thrifty peasant tradition of curing and preserving the meats that the hunter brings home. Chestnuts, too, from the trees that grow thickly on the area's hillsides, are a staple in Ardèche. Other specialties worth seeking out are Alpine cheeses (Beaufort and Reblochon in particular); honey, olives, and olive oil from the Drôme; rustic Picodon and Pélardon cheeses from the Vivarais; Montélimar's renowned nougat, Tricastin's truffles, and aromatic cherry liqueur from the Dauphiné.

• *CHARCUTERIE & FOIE GRAS*

GRAND BORNAND (LE)   74450 – H.-Savoie

Maison Bozon

La Fordaz - 04 50 02 32 13
Like most Alpine charcuterie, the hams and sausages offered here have a typical smoky savor. A worthwhile address.

MAGLAND   74300 – H.-Savoie

Charcuterie Pineau

915, rue Nationale - 04 50 34 71 13
Another reliable source for smoked sausages and excellent country hams.

• *CHEESE*

ANNECY   74000 – H.-Savoie

Crémerie du Lac

3, rue du Lac - 04 50 45 19 31
Savoie's cheeses have pride of place here: sample the sublime farmhouse Reblochon, Beaufort, earthy Tomme de Savoie, and blue-veined cheeses from Tignes and the Aravis massif.

GRENOBLE   38000 – Isère

Laiterie Bayard

17, rue Bayard - 04 76 44 36 25

This reputed cheese shop features a wonderful aged Beaufort and a tangy blue-veined Persillé de Tignes.

THONON-LES-BAINS   74200 – H.-Savoie

Fromagerie Boujon

7, rue Saint-Sébastien - 04 50 71 07 68
Some 30 Savoie cheeses are on display *chez* Boujon: Tommes from Chablais, Mont-Cenis, Bauges, etc., as well as Alpine Beaufort, Bleu de Gex, and an unusual Tomme made with goat milk.

• *CHOCOLATE & CANDY*

ANNECY   74000 – H.-Savoie

Bernard Laurent

6, rue du Lac - 04 50 45 04 70
Chocolates filled with a delectable variety of ganaches. Among the most appealing specialties are Roseaux du Lac ("lake reeds," chocolate sticks filled with mocha cream) and Marrons Bleus filled with marzipan.

MONTÉLIMAR   26200 – Drôme

Maison Chabert et Guillot

9, rue Charles-Chabert - 04 75 01 03 95
Hard nougat (preferred by connoisseurs) and soft, delicious tender nougat can be purchased here, alongside an array of nougat-based specialties.

Le Gavial

6, chemin de Gery - 04 75 01 67 19
Hard or soft nougat, almond croquettes, and other sweet treats. Le Gavial's soft nougat placed first in a recent competition judged by Gault Millau.

VALENCE   26000 – Drôme

Maison Giraud

5, pl. de la République - 04 75 43 05 28
Some 40 different chocolates, hand-dipped by the owner. By all means try his delicious G de Giraud, stuffed with guanaja (chocolate-hazelnut) ganache.

• *GOURMET SPECIALTIES*

Chesnuts

Domaine de Lavenant

04 75 58 21 82
There's a tempting array of artisanal jams here, but the house specialty is a smooth and delectable sweetened chestnut purée.

Clément Faugier

Le Logis du Roi - 04 75 64 07 11
Chestnuts in all their glory: try the lush crème de marron (sweetened purée), the succulent glazed chestnuts, and tins of preserved chestnuts perfect for stuffing a turkey.

Oil & Olives

Maison Bayle

Moulin Bayle, route de Vinsobres - 04 75 27 17 22
Delicately fruity olive oil with a lovely golden color and green highlights.

Coopérative Agricole du Nyonsais

Pl. Olivier-de-Serres - 04 75 26 03 44
The olive oil sold here is the only one that can boast an AOC (Appellation d'Origine Contrôlée) label. And you'll understand why, when you see its green-glinting golden color and taste its elegant fruitiness. Also excellent olives and exquisite tapenade.

Truffles

Maison de la Truffe du Tricastin

04 75 96 61 29
The Tricastin is France's foremost truffle-producing region. At this promotional center you can obtain the addresses of local suppliers who sell truffles to the public.

• *PASTRY & COOKIES*

Établissements Pitot

23, rue Paul-Bourret - 04 75 08 60 69
Many of the stellar cakes and pastries presented here are based on walnuts (Grenoble's walnuts are the only ones to boast an AOC label). Try the cake filled with walnut jam (it keeps very well), or the pastries enhanced with raspberry, apricot, and blueberry preserves.

WINE

THE RHÔNE VALLEY

The vineyards of the **northern Rhône Valley** unwind in a narrow ribbon along the river's banks from Vienne to Valence. The vines are planted on terraced hillsides that must be worked by hand, for the steep terrain foils the use of labor-saving machinery. Still, the growers' efforts are richly rewarded by stupendous (and at the moment, wildly fashionable) red wines that command premium prices. Voluptuous Hermitage, lordly Côte-Rôtie, and dark, long-lived Cornas are the most sublime expressions of the Syrah grape.

White wines are produced in far smaller qualities, but what there is, is choice: Château-Grillet, Condrieu (from the violet-scented Viognier grape), and white Hermitage (based on Roussane and Marsanne vines). On a less exalted—and less costly—level, the red and white wines of Crozes-Hermitage and those of Saint-Joseph are well worth discovering, especially the examples sold at the estate by quality-conscious growers.

The Ardèche, to the **west of the Rhône**, rewards devotees of country wines with fresh, frankly flavorful varietals that represent excellent value. The region's poor, granitic soil fosters splendid Merlots, excellent Syrahs, and even some interesting Cabernet Sauvignons. In the Rhône Valley's eastern reaches, a handful of districts in the *département* of the Drôme produce Côtes-du-Rhône-Villages, which are a good cut above plain Côtes-du-Rhône. Certain growers in Vinsobres, for instance, are making some truly superb wines.

- *NORTHERN RHÔNE VALLEY*

AMPUIS
69420 – Rhône

Bernard Burgaud
Le Champin · 04 74 56 11 86, fax 04 74 56 13 03
Open Mon-Sat.
Burgaud's Côtes-Rôties possess an inimitable style composed of refined tannins and rich, concentrated fruit touched with vanilla (from aging in small oak barrels).

CONDRIEU
69420 – Rhône

Guy & Frédéric Bernard
Tupin Semons · 04 74 59 54 04, fax 04 74 59 54 04
Open daily 8am-7pm.
Ridiculously low yields (half that of a Chablis Premier Cru) are the rule at the Bernards' estate. In addition to richly colored, riotously fragrant Côte-Rôtie, the Bernards produce a tiny quantity of lovely Condrieu.

Robert Niero
20, rue Cuvillière · 04 74 59 84 38, fax 04 74 56 62 70
Open afternoons (all day Sat).
Unless you are very lucky indeed, you probably won't find any Côte-Rôtie for sale at Robert Niero's winery. But you may be able to persuade him to sell you a bottle or two of his golden, delightfully floral Condrieu.

CORNAS
07130 – Ardèche

Alain Voge
Rue de l'Equerre · 04 75 40 32 04, fax 04 75 81 06 02
Open daily.
Cornas is a tiny AOC opposite Valence that produces tannic, inky-dark wines that take years to soften and bloom. The best are well worth waiting for: when mature, they exhale a distinctive aroma of bilberries, cranberries, and blackcurrants. Alain Voge's Cornas from old vines is an exemplary wine, whatever the vintage. Voge's current project is to restore the reputation of white Saint-Péray wines. His are made from old Marsanne vines and require a few years in the cellar.

SARRAS
07370 – Ardèche

Cave de Sarras
Pl. Jean-Moulin · 04 75 23 14 81, fax 04 75 23 38 36
Open daily 8am-noon & 2pm-6pm.
This coop situated in the center of the Saint-Joseph *appellation* presents a fine array of quality wines. Not only Saint-Josephs, either (though they are well represented, notably by the Cuvée Champtenaud, pure Syrah aged in oak), but Vins de Pays (look for the white Viognier varietal), and Condrieu as well.

Looking for a town or restaurant? A winery? A gastronomic specialty or a celebrated chef? Consult the alphabetical index to locate them quickly and easily.

Marc & Michel Chapoutier

18, av. du Docteur-Paul-Durand
04 75 08 28 65, fax 04 75 08 81 70
Open Mon-Fri 10am-7pm.
This venerable family-run firm presents a legendary white Hermitage (Chante-Alouette), reliable red Hermitage that is a splendor in any vintage year, and a most attractive red Crozes-Hermitage (Cuvée Petite Ruche). Also: a variety of wines from other *appellations*, including Châteauneuf-du-Pape.

Cave Coopérative de Tain-l'Hermitage

22, route de Larnage
04 75 08 20 87, fax 04 75 07 15 16
Open daily 8am-noon & 2pm-6pm.
Quality is the credo of this well-run coop, which represents 534 growers. In poor years, the directors have been known to vinify only half the crop as AOC wine, declassifying the rest into Vin de Table (a financial blow, as you can imagine, for the growers but it's the price they pay for an impeccable reputation). The Cave has members with holdings in Hermitage, Crozes-Hermitage, Saint-Joseph, and Cornas.

• *ARDÈCHE & THE DRÔME*

Vignerons Ardéchois

Quartier de Chaussy
04 75 39 98 00, fax 04 75 39 69 48
Open Mon-Fri 8am-noon & 2pm-6pm.
A coop that has developed a reputation for fine varietals, including a lovely white Viognier (also available in a special wood-aged cuvée Prestige), a tasty Syrah, and a ripe-flavored Cabernet Sauvignon "Collection." All are excellent value.

Domaine du Rieux Frais

Jean-Yves Liotaud, quartier Rieux Frais
04 75 27 31 54, fax 04 75 27 34 47
Open daily 8am-noon & 2pm-7pm.
An attractive range of varietals (Chardonnay, Syrah, Viognier, Cabernet Sauvignon) with distinctive flavors. Some wines, like the '92 Syrah, have proved to be keepers that improve with a few years in the cellar. Jean-Yves Liotaud is a hard-working vintner who deserves your support—if you're in the area, swing by and visit his winery.

Domaine de Vigier

F. & J. Dupré, Vallée de l'Ibie
04 75 88 01 18, fax 04 75 37 18 79
Open Mon-Sat 8am-noon & 2pm-6pm, Sun 2pm-6pm.
Francis and Jacqueline Dupré planted their estate with Syrah vines to produce laudably structured red wines (the '92 Syrah was mistaken by our testers for a Cornas). Taste the Duprés' delicious and very inexpensive Côtes-du-Vivarais and their wonderfully fruity Coteaux-de-l'Ardèche.

Domaine du Moulin

Denis Vinson - 04 75 27 65 59, fax 04 75 27 63 92
Open Mon-Sat 8am-noon & 2pm-7pm.
Denis and Frédérique Vinson are passionately committed winemakers. He takes particular care over the Grenache vines, while she watches over the Syrah. Blended together, the two varieties produce the remarkable Cuvée Charles Joseph, a red Vinsobres Côtes-du-Rhône-Villages. The couple's "plain" Vinsobres displays attractive fruit and supple tannins.

Cave de la Vinsobraise

P. Monier & R. Faure
04 75 27 64 22, fax 04 75 27 66 59
Open daily 8am-noon & 2pm-6pm.
While you can purchase bulk wines here that cost under 6 F per liter, the more interesting offerings are bottles in the 30 to 40 F range. For that sum, you can come away with a red Vinsobres Sélection du Terroir (Grenache blended with 15 percent Syrah) or a Cuvée Rustica (urbane, polished flavors, despite the name).

THE ALPS

Savoie's vineyards occupy the well-exposed slopes of the lower Alps, which sweep down toward Grenoble from the shores of Lake Geneva. Their production is popular not only with the natives (the Savoyards are proud of their wines and very much attached to their winemaking traditions) but with vacationers, too, who clamor for light, fruity Crépy as a refreshing après-ski tipple, and order bottles of Seyssel, Mondeuse, or Roussette to wash down the hearty local cuisine. In Savoie a whole string of villages are recognized as particular *crus*, and have the right to add their name to the *appellation* Savoie (Savoie-Ripaille, Savoie-Chignin, Savoie-Arbin, etc.). The region's red wines are based on Gamay, Pinot-Noir, or Mondeuse grapes. The Mondeuse varietal may remind you of American Zinfandel, though it is a typically Savoyard grape; it yields a vigorous wine of great character. The whites are made from Chasselas, Jacquère, and Altesse grapes. Altesse is perhaps the most distinctive of these; it forms the basis of the remarkably elegant Roussette de Savoie. Owing to a cool climate and chalky subsoil, Savoie's white wines are lively and fresh, with fairly high acidity. The local sparklers are surprisingly good, and rarely found outside of the region—by all means give them a try.

ARBIN   73800 – Savoie

André & Daniel Genoux

Chemin des Moulins
04 79 84 24 30, fax 04 79 65 24 32
Open daily 8am-noon & 2pm-8pm.
No weed killers, insecticides, or chemical fertilizers ever touch the Genouxs' vineyards. Their vigorous red Mondeuse-d'Arbin comes in two different cuvées: Tradition, which is pleasantly rustic and explosively fruity; and Prestige, a more complex and tannic wine that will improve for several years.

FRÉTERIVE   73250 – Savoie

Gilbert & Guillaume Bouvet

Le Villard - 04 79 28 54 11, fax 04 79 28 51 97
Open daily 8am-noon & 2pm-8pm.
A full range of very well made wines: red, white, rosé, and sparkling. Try the tasty, easy-drinking Gamay, or the solidly fruity yet tannic Mondeuse, and a delicious, peachy-litchi white Chignin-Bergeron that spritzes lightly on the tongue. Best of all is the opulent, complex Roussette de Savoie-Monterminod made with all Altesse grapes from old vines (the '94 vintage sells for just over 30 F).

RUFFIEUX   73310 – Savoie

Cave de Chautagne

04 79 54 27 12, fax 04 79 54 51 37
Open Mon 2pm-7pm, Tue-Sat 9am-noon & 2pm-7pm.
High standards prevail at this little coop set in the center of a region famed for its fine red wines, based on Gamay and Pinot Noir grapes. The pick of the crop is the Gamay-based Chautagne. Among the whites, we like the Roussette de Savoie, made with 100 percent Altesse grapes.

SCIEZ   74140 – H.-Savoie

Bernard Canelli-Suchet

Château La Tour de Marignan
04 50 72 70 30, fax 04 50 72 36 02
Open daily 9am-7pm.
The oldest wine cellar in Savoie dates from the eleventh century. Within these fortified walls, you can sample Bernard Canelli-Suchet's Savoie-Marignan, a very slightly sparkling ("perlant") wine from the Chasselas grape. Attractively floral and spicy, when it is aged in wood the wine takes on an astonishing richness that complements exotic or highly spiced foods.

THONON-LES-BAINS   74200 – H.-Savoie

Château de Ripaille

Domaine de Ripaille
04 50 71 75 12, fax 04 50 71 72 55
Open daily 9am-noon & 2pm-7pm.
From this magnificent château near Lake Geneva (be sure to visit the kitchens and refectory where Carthusian monks once dined) comes Savoie's best Chasselas-based wine. The estate's Savoie-Ripaille boasts a brilliant golden color and a complex, very seductive aroma of fruit and flowers.

THE SOUTHWEST

From Cro-Magnon's caves to Bordeaux's châteaux

Somehow, life seems just a bit more intense in the Southwest of France than in other parts of the country: the food is richer, the wine heartier, the history more tumultuous—even the grass is greener.

Descending from the north, the verdant valleys and rolling hills of Périgord give way to the peaceful agricultural lands of Gascony and Quercy, then to the peaks of the Pyrenees, populated by grazing sheep and isolated Basque hamlets. In the northwest is the city of Bordeaux, surrounded by the region's renowned château vineyards. Farther south are the beaches, sand dunes, and pine forests of the Landes, and, in the southwest corner of the country near the border with Spain, the glitzy port town of **Biarritz**, a magnet for the international jet set.

Throughout the Southwest, the homegrown cuisine features rich, full-flavored delicacies like foie gras (the liver of a fattened goose or duck) and confit de canard (duck preserved in its own fat). Although the health-conscious might scold that these dishes are a recipe for a heart attack, studies have shown that Southwesterners actually have a low rate of heart disease and that foie gras may even play a positive role. The region is, of course, awash in red wine, which is also thought to be beneficial for the heart.

The Dordogne (or Périgord, as the area has traditionally been known) is the land of ancient cave dwellings decorated with early man's sophisticated and mysterious paintings; of beautifully preserved villages like **Monpazier**, **La Roque-Gageac**, **Collonges-la-Rouge**, and **Domme**, with its stunning views over the Dordogne Valley; and of fortified castles and *bastides*, or walled towns, that were captured and recaptured between the twelfth and fifteenth centuries by the English and French as they fought for control of the territory. Périgord first fell into English hands when Eleanor of Aquitaine married Henry Plantagenet in the middle of the twelfth century, handing over to him as her dowry the lands of Aquitaine, which in addition to Périgord includes the present-day French administrative *départements* of the Gironde, the Landes, the Pyrénées-Atlantique, and Lot-et-Garonne.

Neanderthal havens

It is both an advantage and a drawback that Périgord is not served by a superhighway. It takes longer for visitors to reach their destinations, but they are rewarded by increasing beauty around every twist and turn of the road: beyond one bend awaits the stunning château of **Beynac**, once the stronghold of Richard the Lionheart, perched on its clifftop; around another, a view of the lush, cultivated valley of the winding Dordogne River. Across the river from Beynac is **Castelnaud**, a château held by Simon de Montfort during the Albigensian Crusade.

The caves of the Dordogne provided havens for Neanderthal and Cro-Magnon man. Wall paintings and engravings, mostly of animals, can be seen at **Les-Eyzies-de-Tayac** and at **Lascaux II**, an amazingly exact replica of the original **Lascaux** cave, which is no longer open to the public because a surfeit of visitors were causing damage to the prehistoric paintings. A smaller, lesser-known cave at **Saint-Cirq-Lapopie**, a village on the Vézère River, displays engravings of bison, horses, mysterious symbols, and rare representations of human beings.

The English and French are still fighting for control of Périgord, but this time without arms. As the French countryside empties of its natives and gradually loses its agricultural vocation, many of its charming blond-stone houses are being snapped up as vacation, retirement, or even permanent homes by British citizens, who are reminded of the green countryside at home, where property costs are much higher than in Périgord. This recent colonization has produced some interesting consequences: in one small area near **Ribérac**, no fewer than five restaurants have English owners, and some villages are almost exclusively inhabited by invaders from across the Channel.

In addition to foie gras and confits from farmers' flocks of ducks and geese, the earthy flavors of Périgord include locally pressed walnut oil, truffles and wild mushrooms from the forests, and tangy Cabécou goat cheese. The region's purple plums are distilled into potent eau-de-vie de prune. Although Périgord is not primarily known as a wine-growing region, a few worthwhile offerings can be tracked down. While many Bergeracs are undistinguished, some of the Pécharmants can be delightful. The sweet white wine of Monbazillac is a popular accompaniment to foie gras, and the tannic "black" wine of Cahors stands up to the region's robust cuisine.

In Gascony to the south and Quercy to the east, the culinary specialties are much the same as in Périgord. But Quercy prides itself on cassoulet, a satisfying stew of beans, sausage, and confit; and tourtière quercinoise, a flaky tart filled with apples and prunes. Gascony, of course, is Armagnac country. This quiet area of rolling hills and peaceful farms is blessedly free of tourist traffic and is a fine place for relaxing vacations that involve biking, hiking, eating, drinking, and visiting *bastide* villages like **Mirande** or the town of **Condom**, which claims a Gothic cathedral as well as an Armagnac museum.

The Pyrenees are the domain of the French Basques, a proud people with a unique culture and a language of obscure origins which, owing to the isolating influence of the high mountains, has developed into several mutually incomprehensible dialects. In these rough, mist-shrouded mountains slashed by rushing streams, the Basques traditionally lived in villages and lonely farmhouses, some of which were accessible only by footpaths until quite recently. However small, each village has its fronton, a court on which locals play *pelote*, a form of handball that is the regional passion.

In Basque towns like **Ascain** and **Aïnhoa** the bright whitewashed exteriors of the houses, set against the lush green of the mountainsides, sparkle in the sunshine when the mists rise—a beautiful sight. The country folk tend their farms and their sheep, which provide mutton and brebis, a cheese made from ewes' milk. The Basques are also avid hunters of *palombes*, the wood pigeons that fill the skies during their autumn migration; and along the coast, they are skillful fishermen of tuna and hake. Black cherries are grown hereabouts to provide the preserves that fill buttery gâteaux basques. Chili peppers cultivated around **Espelette** lend fire to the typical piperade—scrambled eggs with peppers, tomatoes, onions, and garlic—or are dried and rubbed into the famous hams of Bayonne.

Bordeaux: a city for Anglophiles

Farther up the Atlantic coast is **Bordeaux**. To the entire world Bordeaux means wine, but Bordeaux is also a provincial capital and busy river port on the Garonne. Among the architectural treasures worth visiting in old Bordeaux are the graceful Place de la Bourse,

the late Gothic church of Saint-Michel, noble Renaissance mansions and narrow stone houses with wrought-iron balconies and ornate door knockers, and the seventeenth-century Grande Cloche, whose bell proclaimed the start of the grape harvest. Other must-sees are the Grand Théâtre, recently restored to its original eighteenth-century splendor; the Musée d'Art Contemporain, housed in the Entrepôt Lainé, a converted warehouse on the old port; and the cathedral of Saint-André, a Gothic wonder built between the eleventh and sixteenth centuries.

Caught between hedonistic Spain to the south and the more austere north, Bordeaux combines elements of both cultures. The locals flock to bullfights and dance the flamenco while maintaining a very British reserve. Indeed the British, with whom the wine trade has always been important, have left their mark on Bordeaux as they have on much of the French Southwest. This is a city of Anglophiles, who take their Burberry raincoats seriously and know how to keep a stiff upper lip, which perhaps explains their reputation as rather haughty burghers.

The wine trade brought wealth to the city, for centuries an active port from which the region's red gold was shipped to the rest of the world. The fabled wines of Médoc, Graves, Saint-Émilion, Pomerol, Fronsac, Bordeaux, and Côtes de Bordeaux come from the more or less flat countryside around the city. A good starting point for château visits is the town of **Saint-Émilion**, to the east of Bordeaux, with its cloisters, views of the surrounding wineries, and curious church carved out of rock. The names of the winegrowing estates to the north of Bordeaux resonate around the world: Château-Lafite, Château Mouton-Rothschild, and Château-Margaux among them. Itineraries for visiting the region's wine-producing châteaux can be obtained from Bordeaux's Tourist Office.

Below Bordeaux stretch the beaches and pine forests of the **Landes**, known as the **Côte d'Argent**, or Silver Coast. Home to the largest forest in Europe, planted in the eighteenth and nineteenth centuries to prevent the coastal sand dunes from overwhelming the interior sand plain, the Landes has miles of fine sandy beaches and dramatic sand dunes, including the 375-foot-high Dune du Pilat at **Pyla-sur-Mer** south of **Arcachon**. Parts of this once wild landscape, where towns and abbeys sank from view beneath invading dunes, have been marred by the construction of tacky vacation villages (like the one at **Mimizan-Plage**), but if they wander off the beaten track, adventurous visitors will find their reward.

RESTAURANTS & HOTELS

BORDELAIS

AIRE-SUR-L'ADOUR   40800
Paris 708 - Tarbes 69 - Mont-de-Marsan 31   Landes

 Chez l'Ahumat 🙂

2, rue des Écoles - 05 58 71 82 61
Closed Wed, 2 wks in Mar, 2 wks in Sep. Open until
9:30pm. HOTEL: 13 rms 103-185. Bkfst 22. Half-
board 170-185 (oblig in seas). No pets. Pkg.
Located on a little street in the center of town,
this restaurant has two dining rooms, one of
which is more intimate than the other. The
owner likes to tease his customers before serving
them with great professionalism, and they appreciate the cuisine with a country accent. We
tried a salad of white asparagus and house-
smoked salmon, luscious flambéed scampi, and
a delicious caramel ice cream. A well-stocked
cellar. C 140. M 85-140, 52 (children).

See also: Eugénie-les-Bains (Michel
Guérard), Villeneuve-de-Marsan

ARCACHON   33120
Paris 627 - Biarritz 183 - Bordeaux 60   Gironde

 Aquamarina

82, bd de la Plage
05 56 83 67 70, fax 05 57 52 08 26
Closed Dec 21-Jan 5. 33 rms 198-565. Bkfst 45. Rms
for disabled. Rm ser. Pkg.
A modern hotel just next to the yacht harbor.
The rooms are sunny and decorated in a pretty
nautical style in pastel blue and have very
pleasant private terraces.

 Arc Hôtel sur Mer

89, bd de la Plage
05 56 83 06 85, fax 05 56 83 53 72
Open year-round. 3 stes 1,120-2,100. 30 rms 398-
920. Bkfst 52. Rm ser. Air cond. No pets. Pool. Valet
pkg.
The exterior is modern and the interior has
been carefully decorated to emulate the warm
ambience of seaside guest houses and hotels. The
well-soundproofed rooms have terraces overlooking the sea or gardens. Sauna, Jacuzzi.

12/20 L'Écailler Diego Plage

Beach front - 05 56 83 84 46, fax 05 56 54 28 20
Open daily until 11pm. Terrace dining. Air cond.
Pkg.
Ideally located next to the beach, this restaurant has a terrace where you can delight in
seafood platters, grilled fish, and incomparable
oysters. Jean-Pierre Diego creates a warm atmosphere with a Spanish flair, complete with
flamenco evenings. The upstairs dining room
offers views of the town and of the magnificent
sunsets. C 250. M 90, 140 (wine incl).

 Grand Hôtel Richelieu

185, bd de la Plage
05 56 83 16 50, fax 05 56 83 47 78
Closed Nov 3-Mar 15. 43 rms 300-650. Bkfst 50. Rm
ser. Conf. Garage pkg.
A grand old seaside hotel facing the docks and
set in a fairly quiet pedestrian zone in the center
of town. Time has taken its toll, and the rooms
are sometimes a bit dilapidated, but at least they
have views of the Atlantic.

 Mercure

4, rue du Professeur-Jolyet
05 56 83 99 91, fax 05 56 83 87 92
Closed Nov 15-Dec 15. 3 stes 950-1,200. 54 rms
365-770. Bkfst 58. Rms for disabled. Rm ser. Air
cond. Conf. Garage pkg.
The former Hôtel Deganne has been "converted" into a Mercure. Good location near
casino and beach. Impeccable, air-conditioned
rooms, room service and very pleasant reception.

 Le Nautic

20, bd de la Plage - 05 56 83 01 48, fax 05 56 83 04 67
Open year-round. 1 ste 320-655. 43 rms 199-450.
Bkfst 38. Conf. Pkg.
Just around the corner from the fishing port
and marina, this Spanish-style hotel has comfort-
able rooms.

 Les Ormes

77, bd de la Plage - 05 56 83 09 27, fax 05 56 54 97 10
Open year-round. 28 rms 290-750. Bkfst 54. Res-
taurant. Half-board 280-610 (oblig in seas). Rm
ser. Conf. Pkg.
A modern building near the marina offering
comfortable rooms. On the sea side of the hotel,
the rooms have either a balcony or a garden.
Numerous sports facilities.

 Le Patio

10, bd de la Plage - 05 56 83 02 72, fax 05 56 54 89 98
Closed Tue (in winter), 2 wks in Feb, 2 wks in Nov.
Open until 10pm (11pm in summer). Priv rm 16.
Garden dining. Pkg.
This rustic restaurant, decorated with bric-à-
brac, charms both locals and visitors, not only
with its waterfall, but also—and especially—

with Bruno Falgueirette's cuisine: shellfish feuilleté with leeks, fried sole and squid, and profiteroles. Commonplace wine list. Attentive service. C 300-400. M 160 (wine incl).

12/20 Chez Pierre

Beach front, 1, bd Veyrier-Montagnères
05 56 22 52 94, fax 05 56 22 53 11
Open daily until 10:30pm (11:30pm in summer). Terrace dining. Air cond. Pkg.
You can partake of immense seafood platters and broiled fish on this terrace just off the wharf. Totally unpretentious and laid back. Finish off with a classic such as strawberries with Melba sauce. C 150-200. M 98, 148, 50 (children).

Point France

1, rue du Grenier - 05 56 83 46 74, fax 05 56 22 53 24
Closed Nov-Feb. 34 rms 295-650. Bkfst 55. Air cond. Conf. Valet pkg.
A few steps from the beach and the casino, this hotel has a 1970s-style contemporary décor. The large salon has lacquered walls. Rooms open onto private terraces, some of them overlooking the sea.

Les Vagues

9, bd de l'Océan - 05 56 83 03 75, fax 05 56 83 77 16
Open year-round. 30 rms 360-796. Bkfst 58. Restaurant. Half-board 421-624. Rm ser. Conf. Pkg.
An astonishing blue building that overhangs the sea. First-floor rooms boast good-sized terraces and those on the fourth large windows—both have superb views of the sea. Modern décor and pleasant welcome.

ARCINS	33460
Paris 543 - Bordeaux 41 - Margaux 6	Gironde

12/20 Le Lion d'Or

"Chez Barbier,"
Pl. de la République - 05 56 58 96 79
Closed Sun, Mon, Jul, Dec 23-Jan 1. Open until 9:45pm. Terrace dining. Pkg.
Wine lovers sit at the wooden bar and debate the merits of various vintages in this provincial bistro where the owner offers sincere, flavorful cuisine, made of the good, local ingredients. Nice cellar. C 200. M 64 (exc Sat dinner, wine incl).

BORDEAUX	33000
Paris 566 - Angoulême 116 - Périgueux 120	Gironde

L'Alhambra

111 bis, rue Judaïque - 05 56 96 06 91
Closed Sat lunch, Sun. Open until 9:45pm. Priv rm 20. Air cond.
The welcome is amiable, the service smiling and efficient. The two dining rooms, one with a cozy décor and 1930s paintings, and the other bright and Italianate, are fitting settings for the cuisine of Michel Demazeau. Based on seasonal ingredients, the menu includes grilled scallops with red butter, a deboned farm squab with garlic wrapped in pastry, and a gratin of local

strawberries. Even the cheapest fixed-price menus are delicious. The well-balanced wine list focuses on Bordeaux. C 250-280. M 105 (lunch), 160, 220.

L'Arène Catherine

34, rue Sainte-Colombe - 05 56 44 76 08
Closed Sat lunch, Sun, 1 wk in Aug. Open until 11:30pm. Terrace dining. Air cond. Pkg.
Alain and Catherine Moretti like bright colors, striped banquettes, and Baroque light fixtures. We like them, too. Especially since the young chef's cooking gets straight to the point, as is shown by the fried ham on toasted bread, the tuna steak with onions and bacon bits, and the hot and cold cherries for dessert. All the first courses cost 35 F, the main courses 75 F, and the desserts 35 F, which also helps to keep things simple. There are inexpensive Bordeaux on the wine list. C 160-220. M 65 (weekday lunch), 135 (dinner, exc Sun, wine incl).

Hôtel de Bayonne

4, rue de Martignac
05 56 48 00 88, fax 05 56 52 03 79
Open year-round. 36 rms 390-695. Bkfst 55. Rms for disabled. Air cond. Conf. No pets.
In the heart of the city, in an eighteenth-century building, this hotel has guest and public rooms decorated in a 1930s style and equipped with all the contemporary comforts, including good soundproofing.

12/20 Bistro du Sommelier

163, rue Georges-Bonnac
05 56 96 71 78, fax 05 56 24 52 36
Closed Sat lunch, Sun. Open until 11pm. Terrace dining. Air cond.
The sign outside this modern building decorated with lively abstract paintings indicates that wine takes first place here, especially the excellent Bordeaux offered at prices that beat out all the competition. The cuisine is pleasantly simple. C 170. M 96.

Au Bonheur du Palais

74, rue Paul-Louis-Lande
05 56 94 38 63, fax 05 56 31 32 32
Closed Sun, Aug. Open until 10:30pm. Priv rm 60. Air cond.
It must be said: the setting lacks charm, the façade lacks allure, and the décor, consisting of paper garlands with ghostly lighting, is more than a bit disturbing. But then there is the authentic Cantonese and Szechuan cuisine, with surprising and flavorful dishes that are hard to find anywhere else. The desserts, however, are totally uninteresting. A nice cellar, and a friendly welcome from the owner. C 220-280. M 135-250.

> **Please excuse us... (and the chefs.)** *Menus are subject to the winds of change, and the dishes we've described may no longer be available when you visit.*

D-2 ① - L'Alhambra ♨
C-5 ② - L'Arène Catherine ♟
D-3 ③ - Hôtel de Bayonne ♨
C-3 ④ - Bistro du Sommelier ▥
C-4 ⑤ - Au Bonheur du Palais ♟
D-2 ⑥ - Hôtel Burdigala ♨
E-5 ⑦ - Le Café du Musée ♟
D-3 ⑧ - Le Café Gourmand ♟
E-5 ⑨ - La Cave de Bigoudy ♟
D-3 ⑩ - Le Chalut ▥
D-3 ⑪ - Le Chapon Fin ♟

B-6 ⑬ - Le Clavel Saint-Jean 12
D-3 ⑭ - Clemenceau ♨
D-3 ⑮ - Continental ♨
C-3 ⑯ - La Coquille d'Œuf ▥
C-5 ⑰ - Le Croc Loup ▥

D-5 ⑲ - Didier Gélineau ♨
D-5 ⑳ - Chez Gilles ▥
D-3 ㉑ - Grand Hôtel Français ♨
E-5 ㉒ - Gravelier ♟
C-5 ㉓ - Jean-Jacques ▥
D-5 ㉔ - Hôtel Majestic ♨
C-5 ㉕ - Malabar ▥
B-5 ㉖ - Meson Andaluz ▥
D-5 ㉗ - Normandie ♨
G-4 ㉘ - Mercure-Le Lac ♨
G-4 ㉙ - Novotel-Le Lac ♨
B-6 ㉚ - One Star Hotel ♨
E-2 ㉛ - Pavillon des Boulevards ♨
B-2 ㉜ - La Pelouse ♨
E-5 ㉝ - La Petite Sirène ♟
D-5 ㉞ - Chez Philippe ♟
C-5 ㉟ - Les Plaisirs d'Ausone ♨
C-5 ㊱ - Le Plat dans l'Assiette ▥
B-7 ㊲ - Le Port de la Lune ▥

D-5 ㊳ - Quality Hotel
          Sainte-Catherine ♨
D-5 ㊵ - Hôtel des Quatre-Sœurs ♨
D-5 ㊶ - Jean Ramet ♟

D-3 ㊸ - Studio ♨
C-5 ㊹ - La Tupina ♟
C-5 ㊺ - Le Vieux Bordeaux ♟
E-2 ㊻ - La Villa Carnot ♨
E-5 ㊼ - Claret ♨

F-6 ㊾ - Le Doris ▥

G-4 ㊿ - Sofitel -Le Lac ♨

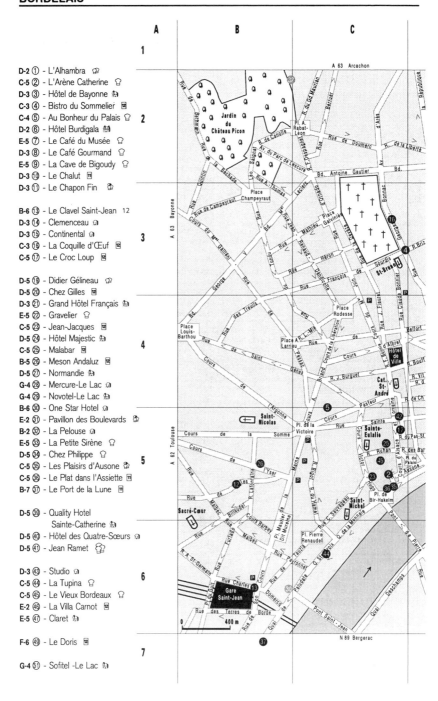

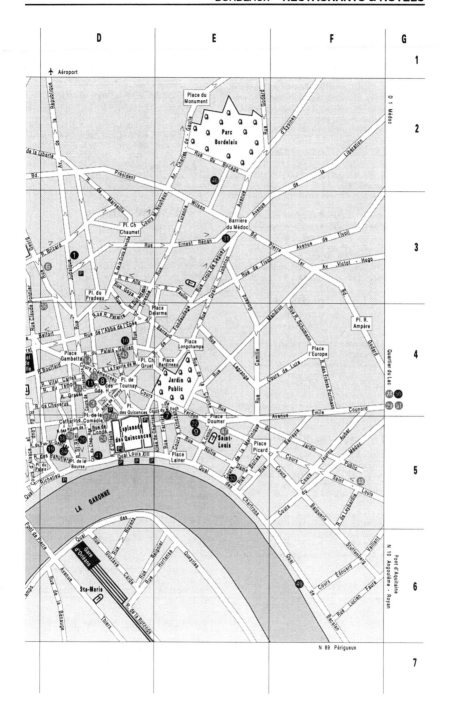

Hôtel Burdigala

115, rue Georges-Bonnac
05 56 90 16 16, fax 05 56 93 15 06
*Open year-round. 15 stes 1,290-2,200. 68 rms 860-
1,500. Bkfst 80. Rms for disabled. Conf. Valet pkg.*
This hotel has both the advantages (business
district, stores, museums) and the inconvenien-
ces (noise, traffic, etc.) of a city center location.
Rooms are functional and soundproofed. Very
good buffet breakfast and a charming reception.

 ## Le Café Gourmand

3, rue Buffon - 05 56 79 23 85, fax 05 56 52 03 45
*Closed Sun. Open until 11pm. Priv rm 30. Terrace
dining. Air cond. Pkg.*
Bruno Oliver is always having a good time in
the dining room and in the kitchen of his brasserie, filled with a mixed clientele at lunch and
dinner time. They all enjoy the fixed-priced
menu and à la carte offerings that make use of
both family and regional traditions. His veal
shank braised with lime, scallop stew, artichoke
stuffed with Brie, Pauillac lamb, and delicious,
homey desserts are now classics. C 160. M 120.

 ## Le Café du Musée

7, rue Ferrère - 05 56 44 70 60, fax 05 56 44 12 07
*Closed Mon. Open until 10pm. Terrace dining. Air
cond.*
You might think you have walked into a contemporary art museum, with an intelligent décor
and staff dressed in creations by fashion designer Azzedine Alaïa. Philippe Pelhate's irreproachable cuisine gets the best out of
excellent ingredients: lamb aspic with orange,
lobster pot-au-feu with broad beans, and peppery fruit soup. C 170. M 160, 70 (children).

 ## La Cave de Bigoudy

36, rue Tourat - 05 56 51 69 43
*Closed Sat lunch & Sun off-seas, 2 wks in Aug. Open
until 11pm. Terrace dining. Air cond. Pkg.*
You can bring your own bottle of wine, choose
one from the restaurant's boutique, or let the
friendly, mustachioed owner recommend one.
The lively ocher-colored dining room with rustic
furnishings has an adjoining terrace. The cuisine
is simple and generous, making use of high-
quality meat and poultry and fresh fish, grilled
in the fireplace on vine shoots. C 140-250. M 95,
135, 35 (children).

11/20 Le Chalut

59, rue du Palais-Gallien - 05 56 81 43 51
*Closed Sun, Mon, hols, 1 wk in Aug. Open until
11pm. Terrace dining.*
The sea is the source of inspiration in this
friendly restaurant. Good choice of regional
wines. C 190. M 75 (wine incl), 60-165.

 ## La Chamade 💠

20, rue des Piliers-de-Tutelle
05 56 48 13 74, fax 05 56 79 29 67
*Closed Sat lunch, Jul-Aug. Open until 10:30pm.
Priv rm 70. Air cond.*

A lovely little stone staircase leads down to the
dining room of this charming house right in the
heart of town. The principal assistant of Michel
Carrère has just taken over the burners, and is
continuing in the same line as his mentor with
an interesting brand of Southwest cuisine. For
example, the 120 F set-price meal offers a duck
liver savarin with Madeira sauce, a veal knuckle
salad with vinaigrette and cabbage, and a
fricassée of rabbit cooked in white wine with
pearl onions. We loved the lamb sweetbreads,
simply cooked with parsley, as well as the perfectly cooked stewed pigeon. Bordeaux-
dominated wine list offering good prices. These
two toques are more than holding their own. C
350-400. M 120-190, 75 (children).

 ## Le Chapon Fin

5, rue Montesquieu
05 56 79 10 10, fax 05 56 79 09 10
*Closed Sun. Open until 9:45pm. Priv rm 15. Garden
dining. Air cond.*
Francis Garcia is a hot-blooded chef, and his
cooking reflects his nature. His dishes are exuberant, unpredictable, more intuitive than
thought-out, and have a touch of Spanish influence. When he doesn't pay attention, they can
slip into sloppiness or excess. That is what came
close to happening over the past few years, and
we have made a point of saying so. But the chef
of this Bordeaux institution, which has seen the
likes of Sarah Bernhardt and Alphonso XIII, has
demonstrated more than once that he is capable
of bouncing back, and for the moment, we hold
our critiques of his perfect-quality vegetable tart
with sautéed duck liver, lamprey fish à la Bordelaise (which was however difficult to digest),
young pigeon chop à la grand'mère, and respectable raspberry puff pastry. The third toque is just
barely holding on; if it weren't for the fabulous
wine cellar, this restaurant might just drop down
to two. We'll let you be surprised by the Belle
Époque décor, one of the most amazing in
France. C 400-500. M 160 (lunch), 270-400.

 ## Claret

18, parvis des Chartrons
05 56 01 79 79, fax 05 56 01 79 00
*Open year-round. 97 rms 495-550. Bkfst 65. Rms
for disabled. Restaurant. Conf. Pkg.*
Part of the new "wine city" complex, the Claret
has quiet, comfortable rooms. Excellent business
services and facilities are offered. Guests may
enjoy the buffet breakfast served on a panoramic
terrace.

12/20 Le Clavel Saint-Jean

44, rue Charles-Domercq
05 56 92 63 07, fax 05 56 92 91 52
*Closed Sat lunch, Sun, 2 wks in Aug. Open until
10pm. Air cond.*
Convenient location opposite the train station,
but depressing décor. We've had to drop the
toque. The cooking shows signs of some good
ideas, but the execution doesn't manage to follow on. We must be fair, however: the desserts

are still worth a toque, even if the quality of the rest has slipped. Smiling, impeccable reception. Good wine list, with, yes, mostly Bordeaux wines. C 300. M 160-205, 120 (weekday lunch, wine incl), 60 (children).

 ## Clemenceau

4, cours Georges-Clemenceau
05 56 52 98 98, fax 05 56 81 24 91
Open year-round. 45 rms 150-220. Bkfst 25. Air cond. Pkg.
Near Place Tourny, an eighteenth-century hotel with simple, modern rooms. Tastings of Bordeaux wines are held in the cellar.

 ## Continental

10, rue Montesquieu
05 56 52 66 00, fax 05 56 52 77 97
Open year-round. 50 rms 300-433. Bkfst 35. Pkg.
In the pedestrian district, an eighteenth-century mansion with a refined entrance hall. The flowery decoration of the rooms is a bit much.

12/20 Le Croc Loup

35, rue du Loup - 05 56 51 61 11
Closed Sun, Mon, Aug. Open until 10:30pm.
One of those rare places where quality comes at good prices. Try the 107 F menu, which includes exquisite squid ravioli with coriander, perfect lamb, a chèvre feuilleté with salad, and an unusual crème brûlée with honey and licorice. What could be better? C 160-200. M 67 (lunch), 107-135, 48 (children).

12/20 Le Doris

52, quai Bacalan - 05 56 39 42 30
Closed Sat lunch, Sun, Aug 15-Sep 1. Open until 10pm.
An authentic seaman's bistro, where the regulars enjoy simple, flavorful cuisine straight from the sea: smoked or marinated salmon, and lobster-stuffed crêpes carefully prepared by Jacques Guinaud. C 190-250. M 85.

 ## Dubern

42, allées Tourny - 05 56 52 27 32, fax 05 56 51 60 38
Closed Sat lunch, Sun. Open until 10:30pm. Priv rm 40. Terrace dining. Air cond.
We once again have the honor of passing the threshold of this exquisite mansion after two years of it being closed for renovation. The quality of food in this temple of Bordeaux gastronomy remains as in the past. Under the gilt of the Louis XV drawing rooms, so exquisitely renovated, you can savor wonders such as the morel mushroom ravioli or the lobster and ratte tart with confit garlic, as well as desserts with variations around a single fruit. Things are working their way in the right direction, if only the service would stop being so prissy and clumsy. C 300-350. M 150, 170 (dinner), 250.

 ## Didier Gélineau

26, rue du Pas-St-Georges
05 56 52 84 25, fax 05 56 51 93 25
Closed Sat lunch, Sun, 2 wks in Aug. Open until 10pm. Air cond.
In the heart of the historic center of the city, near Place du Parlement, Didier Gélineau pampers his customers with culinary attentions and never treats them as cash cows. His standards can be seen in the quality and presentation of his basic ingredients, demonstrated by the duck foie gras and veal sweetbreads with fried celery, the squab roasted with chestnut flowers, or the dark-chocolate soufflée with chicory cream. The wine list is well-chosen but is short on half-bottles. C 250-350. M 120, 260.

12/20 Chez Gilles

6, rue des Lauriers - 05 56 81 17 38
Closed Sat lunch, Sun. Open until 11pm. Terrace dining.
The charming pastel dining room might make you think you are in Louisiana. Customers are welcomed with great attention, then sit down to interesting cuisine made with quality ingredients, judiciously flavored with herbs and spices, and prepared with skill. The cellar is mostly stocked with Bordeaux. C 200-300. M 89 (weekday lunch, wine incl), 110-250.

 ## Grand Hôtel Français

12, rue du Temple
05 56 48 10 35, fax 05 56 81 76 18
Open year-round. 35 rms 370-640. Bkfst 60. Rms for disabled. Pkg.
This hotel in a nineteenth-century mansion in the city center is purely traditional. Rooms are well appointed.

 ## Gravelier

114, cours de Verdun
05 56 48 17 15, fax 05 56 51 96 07
Closed Sat lunch, Sun, Feb school hols, Aug 5-25. Open until 10pm. Priv rm 30. Air cond.
Chef Yves Gravelier's repertory is limited but mouthwatering. It exhibits plenty of imagination and occasionally a touch of exoticism, and always shows his skill. Smiling Anne-Marie Troisgros, the daughter of chef Pierre Troisgros, offers competent advice on the wine list, dominated by Burgundies, and watches out for the well-being of her customers. Strategically located near the antique district, the restaurant has a contemporary décor. C 250. M 90 (weekday lunch), 135, 195, 70 (children).

12/20 Jean-Jacques

11, rue Teulière - 05 56 51 20 67
Closed Sat lunch, Sun, Aug. Open until midnight. No pets.
In this lovely medieval setting, Jean-Jacques Guichard offers bistro fare at prices you can afford: ramekins of escargots with cèpe mushrooms, boned, stuffed pigeon with...you guessed it, cèpes. You can also taste standard regional dishes. The 100 F set-price menu is absolutely

splendid and includes wine. Cellar offering almost exclusively selections from region. C 200-220. M 100 (wine incl), 135-180, 50 (children).

 ## Hôtel Majestic

2, rue de Condé - 05 56 52 60 44, fax 05 56 79 26 70
Open year-round. 1 ste 900. 49 rms 390-520. Bkfst 50. Rms for disabled. Air cond. Garage pkg.
This eighteenth-century manor house, thoroughly in the style of the Bordeaux region, and now a hotel, is conveniently situated. Tastefully-decorated, sunny rooms are well-appointed. Minibar and room service available.

12/20 Malabar

7, rue des Ayres - 05 56 52 18 19
Closed Sun, Mon, Aug. Open until 10:30pm.
Nicole Taillade charges low prices for a meal that might include raïta with potatoes and onions, Goa-style sole, and lime-flavored cheesecake. Be daring and try the ginger liqueur, rose petal grain alcohol, or coconut liqueur. Charming welcome. C 150. M 45 & 65 (lunch, wine incl), 72 & 124 (dinner).

 ## Mercure Bordeaux-Le Lac

Quartier du Lac, rue du Petit-Barail
05 56 11 71 11, fax 05 56 43 07 55
Open year-round. 3 stes 900. 108 rms 310-360. Bkfst 60. Rms for disabled. Restaurant. Half-board 380. Conf. Pkg.
Only 50 yards from the lake and near the Palais des Congrès and the trade-fair grounds, a hotel with well-appointed rooms and bathrooms. Special weekend packages include golf lessons and vineyard tours.

12/20 Meson Andaluz

43, rue La Fontaine - 05 56 92 21 58
Closed Sun, Aug. Open until 11pm. No pets. No cards.
The Gonzales family invites you to discover specialties like seafood paella, zarzuela, lomo, and boquerones, all simply served in a modern bistro décor. Generous, authentic cuisine. M 110, 130.

 ## Normandie

7-9, cours du 30-Juillet
05 56 52 16 80, fax 05 56 51 68 91
Open year-round. 100 rms 310-680. Bkfst 47. Rm ser. Air cond. Conf.
The vast lobby with marble columns and a high ceiling is impressive, but the rooms are much less so, although they are pleasant and have a superb view of Place des Quinconces.

 ## Novotel Le Lac

Quartier du Lac, av. Jean-Gabriel-Domergue
05 56 50 99 70, fax 05 56 43 00 66
Open year-round. 176 rms 430-470. Bkfst 50. Rms for disabled. Restaurant. Rm ser. Air cond. Conf. Pool. Pkg.

At the foot of the Aquitaine bridge and not far from the Palais des Congrès, this hotel is right next to the lake. Rooms are functional and very well equipped. Bar, seminar rooms, restaurant.

 ## L'Oiseau Bleu

65, cours de Verdun - 05 56 81 09 39
Closed Sat lunch, Sun, 3 wks in Aug, 1 wk in Dec. Open until 9:45pm. Priv rm 12. Air cond. Pkg.
The Bordelais call Vincent Poussard the "president's chef" because he used to cook in the Élysée Palace. But he has found his true niche in Bordeaux, with a surprising menu that includes duck liver salad with chanterelles, blood sausage parmentier, and seasonal dishes like Marennes oyster profiteroles, Noilly scallops, etc. Reasonably-priced menu that changes with the seasons. C 250-300. M 102.

 ## One Star Hotel

34, rue Tauzia - 05 56 94 59 00, fax 05 56 94 21 27
Open year-round. 62 rms 230. Bkfst 30. Rms for disabled. Pkg.
A charmless modern building in the city center. The small, pleasant rooms are decorated in nautical style. The bathrooms and soundproofing are not perfect. Nice reception.

 ## Pavillon des Boulevards

120, rue de la Croix-de-Seguey
05 56 81 51 02, fax 05 56 51 14 58
Closed Sat lunch, Sun, 1 wk in Jan, Aug 10-20. Open until 10pm. Garden dining. Air cond.
Denis Franc is a hardworking craftsman who does not tolerate compromise in his cooking, which is straightforward, unaffected by the latest trends, and blessed with an elegant sense of detail. His sauces are carefully prepared to bring out their flavors and enhance each ingredient. The simple sole, served with sautéed artichokes and ham, bursts with flavor on the palate. The caviar with chestnut cream has absolutely no affectations. Located near the border with Médoc, the restaurant has a soothing décor. Bordeaux wines dominate the cellar. C 400-500. M 220 (weekday lunch), 270, 320, 420.

 ## La Pelouse

65, rue Pelouse-de-Douet
05 56 93 17 33, fax 05 56 24 66 71
Closed 2 wks in Aug, Dec 22-Jan 3. 36 rms 250-300. Bkfst 34. Pkg.
Near the Hôpital Pellegrin, with small, quiet rooms.

 ## La Petite Sirène

28-29, quai des Chartrons
05 56 51 22 60, fax 05 56 51 92 81
Closed Sat lunch. Open until 10:30pm (midnight Fri & Sat). Air cond.
The hostess who welcomes you to the dining room in this large stone building has all the charms of Copenhagen's Little Siren. The buffet also offers the best of Denmark, with superb

dill-marinated or home-smoked salmon, four types of herring, nicely grilled veal meatballs, and lovely roast pork. There is also a Danish apple tart. The dry white Château Bonnet is refreshing. **C** 160. **M** 52 (lunch), 152.

 ## Chez Philippe

1, pl. du Parlement
05 56 81 83 15, fax 05 56 79 19 36
Closed Sun, Mon, Aug. Open until 11pm. Terrace dining. Air cond. No pets.
A favorite meeting place of the beautiful people of Bordeaux, who cross the marvelous Place de la Bourse and take their seats on the pleasant terrace of this eighteenth-century house. The small, low-ceilinged dining rooms have stone walls and a nautical décor. Diners partake of magnificent seafood platters and high-quality, super-fresh fish, prepared with simplicity. The cellar is short on white wines, apart from regional offerings. Attentive service. **C** 380-600. **M** 125 (lunch), 180, 250.

 ## Les Plaisirs d'Ausone

10, rue Ausone
05 56 79 30 30, fax 05 56 51 38 16
Closed Sat lunch, Sun, Mon lunch, Jan 2-10, 2 wks in Aug. Open until 10pm. Priv rm 40.
In an old stone stable located in the heart of eighteenth-century Bordeaux, Philippe Gauffre has finally attained his goal: to offer cuisine that is as good as that of his top local competitors—not easy with so many of them around—at lower prices. In a way, he was ahead of his time, not only in terms of lowered prices, but also in the range of his cooking, which assimilates all the latest trends without getting stuck in any of them. In the past, we weren't always fully satisfied with his creations: he sometimes had too light or too heavy a hand with spices. But now he seems to have found the right balance, and his flavorings show a sinewy elegance, in both simple and rich dishes: lobster salad with rabbit, ox jowls with carrots, foie gras, and shad à la gribiche. The cheerful, motivated staff also merits three toques. The prices are right on the wine list as well. But the welcome blows hot and cold. **C** 350-500. **M** 160, 250 (lunch, wine incl), 310.

11/20 Le Plat dans l'Assiette

8, rue Ausone - 05 56 01 05 01, fax 05 56 49 27 05
Closed Sat lunch, Sun, Mon lunch, 1 wk in Mar, 3 wks in Aug. Open until 11pm. Pkg.
The foods of the Southwest and Lyon come together successfully here, with dinner platters at prices that won't empty your wallet. **C** 150-190. **M** 85, 95.

11/20 Le Port de la Lune

59, quai de Paludate
05 56 49 15 55, fax 05 56 49 29 12
Open daily until 2am. Terrace dining. Air cond. Pkg.
A restaurant with a jazzy ambience that is open till 2am. Night owls partake of oysters, herb-

marinated salmon, eel persillade, and clafoutis with seasonal fruits. **C** 120-300. **M** 100 (wine incl).

 ## Quality Hôtel Sainte-Catherine

27, rue Parlement-Ste-Catherine
05 56 81 95 12, fax 05 56 44 50 51
Open year-round. 1 ste 1,200. 83 rms 530-900. Bkfst 60. Rms for disabled. Restaurant. Half-board 660-1,030. Rm ser. Air cond. Conf. Garage pkg.
Set on the longest pedestrian street in Europe, a handsome 1900s hotel. Rooms are air conditioned and soundproofed.

 ## Hôtel des Quatre-Sœurs

6, cours du 30-Juillet
05 57 81 19 20, fax 05 56 01 04 28
Open year-round. 34 rms 240-500. Bkfst 40. Air cond.
Wagner once slept in this hotel with a remarkable flowered façade. The three magnificent salons and the bar are decorated in the Napoléon III style.

 ## Jean Ramet

7-8, pl. Jean-Jaurès
05 56 44 12 51, fax 05 56 52 19 80
Closed Sat lunch, Sun, 3 wks in Aug. Open until 10pm. Priv rm 10. Air cond. Valet pkg.
Located between the stock exchange and Place des Quinconces, Jean Ramet's marvelous bistro enjoys unflagging success. His ingredients are super-fresh and selected when they are in perfect form. His cuisine has strong flavors and a classic, unpretentious slant. There is a perfect accord between the place and its décor, which is impeccably modest but a bit stiff. We particularly enjoyed a good foie gras cassoulet, and lovely French toast. Certainly things have improved and deserve another toque. **C** 450-600. **M** 160 (lunch), 250 (dinner), 300.

Sofitel Le Lac

Quartier du Lac, bd J.-G.-Domergue
05 56 50 83 80, fax 05 56 39 73 75
Closed Dec. 7 stes 1,000-1,200. 184 rms 700-850. Bkfst 80. Restaurant. Rm ser. Air cond. Pool. Pkg.
Large, functional rooms and impeccable bathrooms. Highly professional (maybe too professional) reception. But they do carry your luggage, a service that is becoming rare.

Studio

26, rue Huguerie - 05 56 48 00 14, fax 05 56 81 25 71
Open year-round. 40 rms 98-135. Bkfst 20. Pkg.
This hotel was recently renovated, and its rooms are of excellent quality for the price. The quietest ones are in the back.

For a complete guide to our hotel **ranking system**, see "Symbol Systems", page 8.

La Tupina

6, rue de la Porte-de-la-Monnaie
05 56 91 56 37, fax 05 56 31 92 11
Closed Sun. Open until 11pm. Valet pkg.
The small dining rooms are pleasantly rustic in this old restaurant that serves the capably prepared regional cuisine of Jean-Pierre Xiradakis. Give yourself over to the délice de foie gras and the poularde roasted in the picturesque fireplace. Save a little room for the magnificent assortment of homey desserts like French toast. The Médocs and Greek wines will help you wash it all down. **C** 300. **M** 100 (lunch), 220.

 Le Vieux Bordeaux

27, rue Buhan - 05 56 52 94 36, fax 05 56 44 25 11
Closed Sat lunch, Sun, hols, 2 wks in Feb, 3 wks in Aug. Open until 10:30pm. Priv rm 20. Garden dining. Air cond.
An old house with two comfortable dining rooms. The brighter one is more pleasant, with its flowery enclosed terrace and illustrations of local grape varieties. All this bodes well for the attractive wine list, dominated by Bordeaux, of course. Michel Bordage never compromises on the quality of his ingredients, many of them noble, from which he prepares delicate and inventive dishes that are interesting and tasty. Warm welcome. **C** 220-280. **M** 165-270.

12/20 La Villa Carnot

2, av. Carnot - 05 56 08 04 21
Closed Sat lunch, Sun, Aug 1-17. Open until 11pm. Garden dining.
In an elegant décor that could have been a set for "Out of Africa," Serge Belvisotti offers cuisine that makes you think you are vacation. Near the fireplace or on the terrace, his lobster gazpacho, cassolette of snails and bacon, grilled fish, and beef carpaccio with Parmesan take you on a pleasant voyage in an elegant ambience. **C** 330-450. **M** 100, 185.

And also...

Our selection of places for inexpensive, quick, or late-night meals.
Baud et Millet (05 56 79 05 77 - 19, rue Huguerie. Open until midnight.): Gérard Baud, a passionate cheesemaker, explains to his customers the 200 cheeses on the menu and the wines from around the world to go with them (160).
Brasserie du Sud-Ouest (05 56 92 03 06 - 275, cours de la Somme. Open until midnight.): Bruno and his team have brought back the luster of yesteryears to this brasserie. Friendly prices in a friendly atmosphere where you can taste the best of the Southwest (65-240).
Restaurant du Musée des Arts Décoratifs (05 56 52 60 49 - 39, rue Bouffard. Lunch only until 2:30pm.): Cooking based on the products that inspire the chef on the day's market. Short menu with lots of pleasant surprises. Perfect place to meet friends at lunchtime (80-120).
Le Rital (05 56 48 16 69 - 3, rue des Faussets. Open until 11pm.): For the best fresh, homemade pasta

around with the most surprising and delicate flavors: basil, foie gras, seafood, and many more. Probably the best osso-buco in town (50-150).
Viandocks (05 56 49 52 69 - 52, quai de Paludate. Open until 1am.): An old meat warehouse that has been minimally renovated. You order your meat by weight, and it is grilled in front of you (80-150).

BOULIAC   33270
Paris 577 - Bordeaux 10   Gironde

Amat

3, pl. Camille-Hosteins
05 57 97 06 00, fax 05 56 20 92 58
Open daily until 10pm. Garden dining. No pets. Heated pool. Tennis. Pkg.
Jean-Marie Amat no longer controls this establishment, but we were happy to find him back in the kitchen again, preparing his precise, purely flavored dishes. He has had his ups and downs in the past few years, but things are now back on track, including the prices of both menu and wine list. Amat does his own cooking, contrary to what some people are saying, and charges prices that are about the same as those of a Paris bistro: first courses at about 100 F, main courses around 140 F, and a filling fixed-price menu at 180 F. We liked an asparagus ragoût and sublime Serrano ham, and a rightly cooked sole. The Pauillac lamb, slow-cooked for seven hours, is bewitching. We are also very fond of the top-flight sommelier. **C** 380-500. **M** 180 (exc Sun lunch, wine incl), 255, 360.

Saint James ♠♥

(See restaurant above)
Open year-round. 3 stes 900-1,300. 15 rms 600-800. Bkfst 80. Rms for disabled. Half-board 1,340-1,540. Rm ser. Air cond. Conf. Heated pool. Tennis. No pets. Pkg.
You don't often get the chance to sleep with a Harley Davidson, but in Jean-Marie Amat's hotel, it is can be done. Everything here is surprising, including the asymmetric shape of the rooms and the rusty exterior of the building. Sleeping here is an adventure, and everyone loves the peace and quiet and the view over the Gironde River. Relais et Châteaux.

CARBON-BLANC   33560
Paris 567 - Bordeaux 11 - Arcachon 83   Gironde

Marc Demund

5, av. de la Gardette
05 56 74 72 28, fax 05 56 06 55 40
Closed Sun dinner, Mon, 2 wks in Aug. Open until 10pm. Priv rm 14. Garden dining. Pkg.
You might get lost on the highway ramps trying to find this pleasant restaurant with a comfortable modern décor in ocher tones and a charming terrace-garden. Marc Demund, who learned the art of cooking from Guérard and Girardet, does not compromise on the quality of his ingredients and treats traditional themes

with a great deal of personality and remarkable technique. The majestic cellar contains prestigious Bordeaux, including some finds at decent prices. C 310-420. M 130 (exc Sun & hols), 260, 350.

DAX   40100
Paris 706 - Biarritz 57 - Pau 78   Landes

 L'Amphitryon

38, cours Gallieni - 05 58 74 58 05
Closed Sun dinner, Mon, Jan 2-15, Aug 17-Sep 3. Open until 9:30pm.
The personalized cuisine of Éric Pujos, who sometimes uses regional recipes, confirms the high level of his establishment. In a fresh, restful décor, he sends out from the kitchen copious portions of eggplant gâteau with fresh chèvre, bass with anise served with squid ravioli, and a soft Toblerone-like dessert made with two kinds of chocolate. The wine list includes one or two vintages from each region of France. One quibble: the prices need to be revised downward. C 175. M 75 (weekdays), 100-200.

 Grand Hôtel

Rue de la Source - 05 58 90 53 00, fax 05 58 90 52 88
Open year-round. 7 stes 330-464. 130 rms 221-304. Restaurant. Half-board 264-353. Rm ser. Conf. Garage pkg.
Part of the thermal spa, a hotel that mixes styles: pseudo–Louix XV and contemporary. The décor, the soundproofing, and the welcome all leave something to be desired.

12/20 La Renardière

Route de Bayonne, La Pince, 40990 Saint-Paul
168, av. de la Résistance - 05 58 91 57 30
Closed Wed, Sun dinner, Feb 7-17. Open until 9pm (9:30pm in summer). Garden dining. Pkg.
While the children play in the large garden behind this pretty restaurant, their parents enjoy the comfortable pink décor chock-full of hunting trophies and copper pots. The fresh, straightforward cuisine is prepared by chef-owner Serge Panzolato, whose repertory has a traditional base, with dishes such as foie gras. But some of the dishes were just too bland and uninteresting to merit a toque, so we've had to drop this restaurant a point. The cellar is full of nice regional bottles. A charming welcome from the *patronne*. C 150-180. M 85 (lunch, exc Sun), 130 & 180 (weekdays), 40 (children).

 Splendid Hotel

2, cours de Verdun
05 58 56 70 70, fax 05 58 74 76 33
Closed Dec-Feb. 6 stes 540-650. 157 rms 340-460. Bkfst 55. Restaurant. Half-board 360-510. Rm ser. Air cond. Conf. Heated pool. Pkg.
Art Deco style reigns in the vast rooms with magnificent bathrooms and in the public rooms of this grand old hotel with its own thermal spa and beauty-treatment center.

EUGÉNIE-LES-BAINS   40320
Paris 726 - Pau 53 - Mont-de-Marsan 25 - Dax 69   Landes

 Auberge de La Ferme aux Grives   🍴

At Les Charmilles - 05 58 51 19 08, fax 05 58 51 10 10
Closed Mon dinner & Tue (exc mid Jul-mid Sep & hols), beg Jan-beg Feb. Open until 10:30pm. Priv rm 14. Terrace dining. Air cond. Pool. Tennis. Pkg.
Michel Guérard deserves credit for having managed to attract not only tourists but locals to this farm in the Landes, complete with bunches of corn hanging from the ceiling of the gallery, thrushes (grives) in cages, a henhouse, vegetable garden, bread oven, logs, barrels, a rustic cart, and even an outhouse. But, as in paintings of peasant feasts, people also come here to eat. For 175 F, you can sample tripe simmered in Armagnac, spit-roasted poultry, succulent pork, lamb shoulder, or beef gratin with cèpes, all washed down by Gascon wines at 68 F. M 175.

11/20 L'Auberge du Vieux Moulin

05 58 51 12 27, fax 05 58 51 10 14
Closed Mon. Open until 9pm. Terrace dining. Pkg.
An old millhouse lost in the greenery about two miles from the pomp of Eugénie. On the terrace overhanging the river you can savor simple, healthy food as the geese and ducks promenade before you. C 180-350. M 65 (weekday lunch), 89, 130, 150.

 Michel Guérard   🍴

05 58 05 06 07 (R),
05 58 05 05 05 (H), fax 05 58 51 10 10
Closed Wed & Thu lunch (exc mid Jul-mid Sep & hols), Dec-Feb. Open until 10:15pm. Priv rm 16. Garden dining. Air cond. Heated pool. Tennis. No pets. Valet pkg.
It's hard to believe that any other place in France approaches the refinement and perfection of Christine and Michel Guérard's little Second Empire kingdom. In the magnificent kitchens—there are two—Guérard, far from resting on his laurels, continues to experiment. Yet he remains modest and makes adjustments in response to the slightest criticism. He was the first to prepare gourmet low-fat meals, which remain faithful to the joyous harmonies of Southwestern cuisine. His fine sensibilities and his matchless technique account for the refinement—without excessive sophistication—and the vivid flavors in dishes like grilled langoustine aspic with a warm salad of spring onions and a crunchy Parmesan galette, truffles à la tartoufle accompanied by a divine vegetable risotto, chicken breast grilled with bacon in the fireplace, and slow-cooked ox jowl pot-au-feu with a powerful truffle sauce. Like the desserts, the wines harmonize perfectly with the cuisine, with a preference for Madirans and Jurançons, and the white Tursan "Baron de Bachen" from Guérard's own vineyards. This is a restaurant that is as much a feast for the eyes as for the taste

buds, with its handsome Colonial–style country décor, fine paintings, and white-painted wood-work. Service is provided by charming waitresses dressed in old-fashioned costumes. C 480-670. M 550, 690, 100 (children).

 ## Les Prés d'Eugénie

(See restaurant above)
Closed Dec-Feb. 9 stes 1,000-2,000. 32 rms 800-1,650. Bkfst 95-110. Rm ser. Air cond. Conf. Heated pool. Tennis. Valet pkg.

In Empress Eugénie's time, Mexico was all the rage, which explains the Colonial style of this white building with wrought-iron balconies, patio with luxuriant exotic plants, gurgling fountain, and an alluring statue of Venus. All of the highly comfortable rooms incite pleasant dreams, but the ones in the back that look out on the garden and the swimming pool are the most desirable. The luckiest guests sleep in the eighteenth-century Couvent des Herbes, with its superb décor: old paving stones and exposed beams, a fire in the hearth ready to be lit, fabrics by Frey and Canovas, dried-rose sachets for the bath, and so on—pure voluptuousness. There are all sorts of package deals: off-season, fitness, relaxation, nature, and diet cuisine. Thermal spa. Beauty treatments. Relais et Châteaux.

 ## La Maison Rose

05 58 05 06 07, fax 05 58 51 10 10
Closed Jan 5-Feb 9, Dec 1-20. 5 stes 550-850. 27 rms 400-580. Bkfst 60. Restaurant. Conf. Pool. Tennis. No pets. Pkg.

In an oak grove next to the old–style kitchen garden of the Ferme aux Grives, an English–style inn with spruce rooms and small suites with kitchenettes. Thermal spa and package deals for those taking the cure.

GRENADE-SUR-L'ADOUR   40270
Paris 720 - Aire-sur-l'Adour 18 - Mont-de-Marsan 15   Landes

12/20 Hôtel de France ☺

Pl. des Tilleuls - 05 58 45 19 02, fax 05 58 45 11 48
Closed Sun dinner & Mon (exc Jul-Aug & hols), 2 wks in Jan. Open until 9:30pm. Terrace dining.

Jean-Jacques Bernardet is no longer at the fires, but his team is trying its hardest to keep up the spirit of their mentor by continuing to offer well-filled plates for hearty appetites. In the rustic décor of this old restaurant, you can tickle your taste buds with fresh salmon with lemongrass, beef fillet with ginger, duck cooked in Port, and caramelized custard with walnuts. Nice choice of Armagnacs. Wine cellar lacking subtlety but moderately priced. C 230. M 68 (exc Sun dinner), 130, 205, 45 (children).

 ## Pain, Adour et Fantaisie

7, pl. des Tilleuls
05 58 45 18 80, fax 05 58 45 16 57
Closed Sun dinner, Mon (exc dinner in Jul-Aug & hols). Open until 10:30pm. Terrace dining. Pkg.

This handsome seventeenth-century restaurant's customers were dismayed when Didier Oudill left for Biarritz, but they have been consoled by the cuisine of his replacement and former assistant, 37-year-old Philippe Garret. The restaurant sits on the village square and has a rustic yet elegant dining room and a wonderful sunny terrace with palm trees and parasols, overlooking the Adour River. The fixed-price menu at 175 F is full of mouthwatering ideas, offering dishes with both Gascon and Italian influences: minestrone with mussels, tuna and artichokes with Pecorino, duck-stuffed cabbage accompanied by blood sausages and chicken wings, and chestnut-flour crêpes with honey ice cream. The friendly sommelier offers a fruity Madiran from Le Couvent du Château Peyros. This menu is so good that the more expensive one can be bypassed. C 300. M 175 (wine incl), 200-250, 80 (children).

 ## Pain, Adour et Fantaisie

(See restaurant above)
Open year-round. 1 ste 1,200. 9 rms 380-700. Bkfst 75. Rms for disabled. Half-board 440-650. Rm ser. Air cond. Conf. Pkg.

Plain, bright rooms with romantic names, some of which overlook the river from a small terrace. Modern furniture inspired by the 1930s. Most bathrooms have Jacuzzis. Some guests love the Egyptian room.

HOSSEGOR   40150
Paris 755 - Biarritz 28 - Bayonne 20   Landes

 ## Beauséjour ☘

Av. de la Tour-du-Lac
05 58 43 51 07, fax 05 58 43 70 13
Closed Oct 16-May 6. 2 stes 1,000-1,200. 45 rms 300-770. Bkfst 65. Restaurant. Half-board 400-700 (oblig in seas). Rm ser. Conf. Pool. Pkg.

There is plenty of light and fresh air in this hotel set in a pine forest between Hossegor Lake and the Atlantic. The spacious, cozy, peaceful rooms are tastefully decorated and give onto a shady garden.

Hortensias du Lac ☘

Av. de la Tour-du-Lac
05 58 43 99 00, fax 05 58 43 42 81
Closed Nov-Feb. 31 rms 290-430. Bkfst 40. Rms for disabled. Conf. No pets. Pkg.

A large, beautiful hotel in the pine forest, with terraces overlooking a saltwater lake. Pleasant, well-equipped rooms, some with mezzanines.

12/20 Les Huîtrières du Lac

1187, av. du Touring-Club
05 58 43 51 48, fax 05 58 41 73 11
Closed Mon, 3 wks in Jan. Open until 10:15pm. Priv rm 30. Terrace dining. HOTEL: 9 rms 260-380. Bkfst 45. Half-board 320-400 (oblig in seas). Pkg.

If you're not careful, you'll make this old inn on the Hossegor Lake a regular stop. The owners make you feel right at home and the good-quality ingredients are selected with care and treated the same way in the kitchen. Lively, pleasant atmosphere. C 200-300. M 95, 135.

LANGON	33210
Paris 604 - Bordeaux 47 - Marmande 37	Gironde

 Claude Darroze ❀

95, cours du Général-Leclerc
05 56 63 00 48, fax 05 56 63 41 15
Closed Jan 5-25, Oct 15-Nov 5. Open until 9:30pm. Priv rm 60. Garden dining. Valet pkg.
Just half an hour from Bordeaux, this beautiful, peaceful restaurant provides a good excuse for an excursion. We awarded chef Claude Darroze an extra point for his refined, intelligent cuisine, and we may not stop there. His cèpe brouillade is a work of art in rustic guise and nearly deserves three toques with its warm, soft eggs and perfectly cooked mushrooms. His roasted wood pigeon is admirable: cooked to perfection and accompanied by vegetables in a light wine sauce. The large cellar offers Bordeaux and wines of other regions, with some rare finds and good deals. C 380-400. M 210-450, 80 (children).

 Claude Darroze

(See restaurant above)
Closed Jan 5-25, Oct 15-Nov 5. 1 ste 450-550. 15 rms 280-450. Bkfst 70. Half-board 450-550. Pkg.
The dream you started at dinner continues on through breakfast. In between the two, you'll snooze in prettily decorated rooms with everything you need to make your stay comfortable. Impeccable service.

LIBOURNE	33500
Paris 542 - Périgueux 89 - Bordeaux 31	Gironde

12/20 **Le Bistrot Chanzy**

16, rue Chanzy - 05 57 51 84 26, fax 05 57 51 84 89
Closed Sun, Mon dinner. Open until 9pm. No pets.
The former sommelier of the Chapon Fin in Bordeaux has resuscitated an authentic bistro near the train station, where he offers his wine-loving customers an impressive fixed-price menu at 85 F and à la carte choices that change with the seasons. High-quality ingredients are prepared with seriousness and simplicity. The result is a restaurant you can count on, with reasonable prices, in a city where it's not enough to know how to appreciate a glass of wine. C 130. M 60 (wine incl), 85.

MAGESCQ	40140
Paris 698 - Soustons 10 - Bayonne 42 - Castets 12	Landes

 Relais de la Poste

05 58 47 70 25, fax 05 58 47 76 17
Closed Mon dinner, Tue, Nov 11-Dec 20. Open until 9:30pm. Priv rm 40. Air cond. HOTEL: 2 stes

900-920. 10 rms 450-650. Bkfst 60-90. Half-board 650-850. Rm ser. Conf. Heated pool. Tennis. Pkg.
If you want to discover the real cuisine of the Landes, pay a visit to the Coussau family's restaurant, located on the edge of the pine forest. The chef serves the best confit imaginable with pommes cocotte cooked in goose fat: a sinful experience! Equally tasty are the wood pigeon with cèpes, and the fresh lamprey eel with leeks. If you really want to overindulge, try the country ham. Excellent Southwestern wines, not all of them as expensive as the Madiran or the Tursan. C 450-480. M 290, 395, 100 (children).

MARGAUX	33460
Paris 598 - Bordeaux 22 - Lesparre-Médoc 20	Gironde

 Le Relais de Margaux ♣♥

Chemin de l'Ile-Vincent
05 57 88 38 30, fax 05 57 88 31 73
Open year-round. 5 stes 1,200. 26 rms 700-800. Bkfst 75-90. Restaurant. Rm ser. Air cond. Conf. Pool. Tennis. Pkg.
In the heart of the Margaux vineyards, this hotel has a truly superb setting, with a park and swimming pool. Spacious, well-equipped rooms. Jazz-brunch on Sundays.

MIMIZAN	40200
Paris 676 - Bordeaux 108 - Dax 73 - Arcachon 65	Landes

 Au Bon Coin du Lac

34, av. du Lac - 05 58 09 01 55, fax 05 58 09 40 84
Closed Sun dinner, Mon, Feb. Open until 10pm. Garden dining. Air cond. Pkg.
This restaurant lives up to its name. The tile-roofed chalet overlooks the lawns bordering the lake. In this rustic setting, Jean-Pierre Caule cooks up equally rustic yet classic cuisine. Cèpes served with Charollais beef, eels simmered in Graves wine, and squab with cabbage are dishes that are as calming and reassuring as the lake. Admirable wine list, with a good selection of half-bottles and interesting finds from the Southwest, like the Jurançon from Clos Uroulat or the Madiran from Domaine d'Aydie, at 160 F and 150 F, respectively. C 350-400. M 160-350.

 Au Bon Coin du Lac ♣♥

(See restaurant above)
Closed Feb. 4 stes 580-700. 4 rms 360-490. Bkfst 65. Rms for disabled. Half-board 570-650. Conf. No pets. Pkg.
Enormous, bright rooms in which you can sleep peacefully after boating on the lake or biking in the forest. Robust breakfasts. Windsurfing.

---

*The **C** (A la carte) restaurant prices given are for a complete three-course meal for one, including a half-bottle of modest wine and service. **M** (Menu) prices are for a complete fixed-price meal for one, excluding wine (unless otherwise noted).*

MONT-DE-MARSAN	40000
Paris 686 - Bordeaux 123 - Bayonne 97	Landes

Auberge
des Clefs d'Argent

333, av. des Martyrs-de-la-Résistance
05 58 06 16 45, fax 05 58 06 23 03
Closed Sun dinner & Mon (exc hols), Oct 20-30. Open until 10pm. Priv rm 60. Terrace dining. No pets. Pkg.
Try to ignore the gloomy décor and just enjoy the cuisine of Jacques Porte, an old–style professional who has perfect respect for and knowledge of his ingredients. The repertory is classic, with, for example, a divine mushroom sauce that simmers for no less than three days. His technique is faultless, and the portions are generous. Most dishes are served without any unnecessary trimmings. Cellar rich in local wines as well as great Bordeaux and Armagnacs. C 230-310. M 75 (weekdays, Sat lunch, wine incl), 100, 130, 160, 170, 230.

Le Renaissance

Route de Villeneuve
05 58 51 51 51, fax 05 58 75 29 07
Closed Sat lunch, Sun dinner. Open until 10pm. Garden dining. Pool. Garage pkg.
While the restful décor is resolutely contemporary, the cuisine is rooted in regional tradition. The "Menu du Dauphin" (155 F) includes Chinese cabbage tourte, saddle of rabbit, and a potato tart. Nice Bordeaux priced at around 90 F. Professional service. In nice weather, you can sit on the terrace and watch the ducks and swans flitter about on the lake. C 240-330. M 105-155.

Le Renaissance

(See restaurant above)
Open year-round. 1 ste 550-570. 28 rms 250-420. Bkfst 35-50. Rms for disabled. Half-board 250-350. Rm ser. Pool. Garage pkg.
This neoclassic white manor house is set among shady lawns, and there are lakes nearby. Huge, pleasant rooms with modern appointments and good equipment. Sports activities available in the vicinity. Bar.

See also: Eugénie-les-Bains

PAUILLAC	33250
Paris 570 - Bordeaux 50 - Lesparre-Médoc 20	Gironde

Château
Cordeillan-Bages

Route des Châteaux
05 56 59 24 24, fax 05 56 59 01 89
Closed Sat lunch, Mon, Dec 8-Jan. Open until 9:30pm. Priv rm 16. Garden dining. Valet pkg.
In the heart of Médoc wine country, an area with few gastronomic choices, this restaurant provides a welcome exception. In this handsome, seventeenth-century château, everything

possible has been done to make visitors comfortable. Alain Rabier, who used to work at the Château d'Artigny, treats everyone like a VIP. In the kitchen, Thierry Marx shows a mastery of excellent ingredients, including superb Pauillac lamb. During our last visit, we were impressed by his Marennes oyster flan, a perfect turbot served with a balsamic and honey sauce, and irreproachable side dishes of tomato crépinette and marble-sized potatoes. The desserts would satisfy even the most demanding customer. The 50-page wine list contains some of the best bottles available. The verdict: pure joy among the vineyards. C 400-500. M 150-290, 180 (wine incl), 235 (weekday lunch & Sun), 380 (Sat & Sun).

Château
Cordeillan-Bages

(See restaurant above)
Closed Dec 8-Jan. 1 ste 915-1,100. 24 rms 720-930. Bkfst 65-95. Rms for disabled. Half-board 675-910. Rm ser. Valet pkg.
Set in a pretty park surrounded by vineyards, a gorgeous seventeenth-century château built of blond stone. The modern, light-filled rooms and suites are tastefully decorated and impeccably equipped. Guests can take courses on the wines of Bordeaux. Relais et Châteaux.

PEYREHORADE	40300
Paris 727 - Pau 71 - Bayonne 36 - Dax 22	Landes

Le Central

Pl. Aristide-Briand
05 58 73 03 22, fax 05 58 73 17 15
Closed Sun dinner & Mon (exc Jul-Aug), Mar 10-26, Dec 23-31. Open until 9:30pm. HOTEL: 2 stes 500-600. 15 rms 280-320. Bkfst 40. Rms for disabled. Half-board 340. Pkg.
Many tourists stop at this pleasant and restful restaurant decorated in contemporary style. Éric Galby's dishes are generous, flavorful, and interesting, expertly made from good products and enhanced with excellent sauces. Judiciously chosen wine list with many regional finds. Friendly welcome and good service in a pleasant atmosphere. C 300-420. M 110 (weekdays), 140, 160, 190, 220, 57 (children).

SAINT-ÉMILION	33330
Paris 549 - Bordeaux 38 - Libourne 7	Gironde

Château Grand Barrail

Route de Libourne
05 57 55 37 00, fax 05 57 55 37 49
Closed Sun dinner off-seas, Mon. Open until 9:30pm. Terrace dining. Heated pool. Valet pkg.
In the heart of the most prestigious vineyard in the Bordelais and set in a handsome, peaceful park, this spectacularly restored château seems to have popped out of a fairy tale. Philippe Etchebest has dusted off the classic repertory and offers harmonious, perfectly cooked cuisine that charms from beginning to end of the meal. The wine list goes all out for Saint-Émilions,

listing no fewer than 500. A friendly welcome and service in the huge dining room inspired by Moorish architecture and fitted out with handsome classical furnishings. C 300-350. M 160 (weekday lunch), 230, 320.

Le Clos du Roy

12, rue de la Petite-Fontaine
05 57 74 41 55, fax 05 57 74 45 13
Closed Sun dinner, Feb school hols, 1 wk in Nov. Open until 9:30pm.
This restaurant is hard to find in the streets of the old village, but it is nevertheless always full thanks to the cuisine of Patrick Hugueny: pastry boats with a cargo of baby vegetables and Serrano ham, lobster with mead and lime, apple tart with Calvados. It goes without saying that the cellar contains nearly only Bordeaux (with a 1990 Moulin Saint-Georges at 190 F) with a good selection of half-bottles. Irreproachable welcome and service. C 200-320. M 98-260.

Francis Goullée

27, rue Guadet - 05 57 24 70 49, fax 05 57 74 47 96
Closed Sun dinner, end Nov-beg Dec. Open until 9:30pm. Air cond.
Behind the pretty façade of painted wood with its mullioned windows, it is always a pleasure to rediscover, in the warm ambience created by old furniture and copper pots, the charming smile of Annie Goullée and the delicious food of Francis Goullée. They describe the seductive cuisine with Gascon accents (such as bean terrine with duck foie gras), prepared with great sincerity by Francis and Fabrice Beylot. Wine list far too short and hardly any half-bottles. C 250. M 130 (exc Sun), 180 (wine incl), 200, 230.

Hostellerie de Plaisance

Pl. du Clocher - 05 57 24 72 32, fax 05 57 74 41 11
Closed Jan 2-31. Open until 9:15pm. Air cond. Pkg.
Up in the hills of the town, Louis Quilain offers honest cuisine in a beautiful stone house. Spiny lobster roasted in the shell with ginger, beef fillet with bone marrow, and monkfish with saffron pistils go down very well in the classic, luminous décor. M 145 & 165 (exc Sun), 195, 275.

Hostellerie de Plaisance

(See restaurant above)
Closed Jan 2-31. 2 stes 950-1,350. 10 rms 500-790. Bkfst 58. Air cond. Conf. Pkg.
Right next to the bell tower, a hotel with bright, well-kept rooms that have either a terrace or mini-garden.

Palais Cardinal

Pl. du 11-Novembre
05 57 24 72 39, fax 05 57 74 47 54
Closed Dec-Mar. 17 rms 325-390. Half-board 361-548. Rm ser. Conf. Heated pool. Garage pkg.

This eighteenth-century manor house with its old white stones and old-world charm is roosted on a hillside in the outskirts of the city. Its highly pleasurable terrace and swimming pool look out over some of the world's most famous vineyards. Spacious rooms, decorated with the height of taste, and high-quality bathrooms. A reception fit for royalty.

SAINT-LOUBÈS — 33450
Paris 571 - Bordeaux 19 - Libourne 19 — Gironde

12/20 Au Vieux Logis

57, av. de la République
05 56 78 92 99, fax 05 56 78 91 18
Closed Sun dinner, Mon lunch, 1 wk in Aug. Open until 10pm. Priv rm 15. Terrace dining. Air cond. HOTEL: 6 rms 225-285. Bkfst 40. Half-board 320-350. Air cond. Conf. Heated pool. Pkg.
Recently relocated a few yards down from the old restaurant in a big private house. The good quality of Chantal Belot's reception is not accompanied by good quality cooking in the kitchen, however, so we are forced to drop the toque. C 280-380. M 125-250, 60 (children).

SAINT-MACAIRE — 33490
Paris 640 - Bordeaux 51 - Marmande 35 — Gironde

L'Abricotier

2, rue François-Bergœing
05 56 76 83 63, fax 05 56 76 28 51
Closed Tue, 3 wks in Nov. Open until 9:30pm. Terrace dining. Pkg.
The way Alain Zanette's cuisine deals with regional recipes is truly charming thanks to the freshness of the foodstuffs and his skillful hand in the kitchen. Whether his dishes are simple or ambitious, he knows how to bring out the best in them. The small wine list is rich in Bordeaux. Excellent welcome in the light-filled dining room hung with watercolors. The apricot tree that gives the restaurant its name grows on the adjacent terrace. C 250. M 80 (weekday lunch), 105-200, 45 (children).

SAINT-SEVER — 40500
Paris 705 - Orthez 37 - Mont-de-Marsan 16 — Landes

Patio des Jacobins

11, pl. Verdun - 05 58 76 32 04, fax 05 58 76 38 84
Closed Sun dinner, Mon. Open until 10pm.
During our last visit, this little dining room with a light-gray décor, bright and full of flowers, was jam-packed. Each year, more diners are attracted by Éric Costedoat's cuisine, which treats regional ingredients with a great deal of inventiveness, precise cooking times, and a harmonious mingling of flavors. Small but complete wine list. Irreproachable welcome and service. Reasonable prices. C 160. M 70-130.

SAUTERNES   33210
Paris 613 - Langon 11 - Villandrau 11   Gironde

 Le Saprien

Le Bourg - 05 56 76 60 87, fax 05 56 76 68 92
Closed Sun dinner, Mon, 2 wks in Feb, Nov 15-Dec 15. Open until 9:30pm. Terrace dining. Pkg.
Sauternes now has a restaurant on a par with its wines. Over a period of a few years, Jean-Luc Garrigues and his young wife have succeeded in maintaining laudable standards. The fixed-price menus are generous, varied, and offer a nice choice of regional products (duck, duck's liver, Pauillac lamb), and the à la carte dishes delight visitors to one of the most celebrated wine-growing areas in the world. The local wine growers are regular customers. Superb scallop salad, sweetbreads accompanied by a subtle curry and Sauternes sauce, tasty desserts. Fine cellar. **C** 270. **M** 109-299.

SÉGOS   32400
Paris 750 - Auch 88 - Mont-de-Marsan 47   Landes

 Domaine de Bassibé ✪

05 62 09 46 71, fax 05 62 08 40 15
Closed Tue & Wed lunch off-seas, beg Jan-end Mar. Open until 10pm. Priv rm 25. Garden dining. Pool. Valet pkg.
The cuisine at this adorable ivy-covered farmhouse not far from the road to Compostella stays close to the land. The talented chef, Ricardo Thomis, offered us lentils with pig's feet and fried onions; stuffed, stewed chicken; and orange gratin with ginger sabayon. Excellent cellar. Expect a warm welcome in the pretty, bright dining room in a former wine storehouse. **C** 240. **M** 160-240, 80 (children).

Domaine de Bassibé ▲♥

(See restaurant above)
Closed beg Jan-end Mar. 7 stes 980-1,100. 11 rms 500-800. Bkfst 75. Half-board 1,200-1,800. Rm ser. Conf. Pool. Valet pkg.
Renovated rooms in a complex of lovely buildings in the countryside. In the main house, some rooms have exposed beams and mansard roofs. Relais et Châteaux.

See also: Eugénie-les-Bains (Michel Guérard), Villeneuve-de-Marsan

TESTE-DE-BUCH (LA)   33260
Paris 649 - Bordeaux 65 - Arcachon 4   Gironde

12/20 **Chez Diego**

Centre Captal - 05 56 54 44 32, fax 05 56 54 28 20
Closed 10 days in Dec. Open until 11pm. Priv rm 80. Garden dining. Air cond. Pkg.
The Diegos and their chef, Denis Belliard, offer regional cooking in a bodega-like setting. The oysters come from the restaurant's own beds (the family has been cultivating oysters for four generations). The hake is served with a green

sauce, and the bass is grilled and served with vinaigrette. Good-natured service. **C** 250-350. **M** 90, 140, 180, 48 (children).

VILLENEUVE-DE-MARSAN   40190
Paris 690 - Mont-de-Marsan 17 - Aire-sur-l'Adour 21   Landes

 Hélène Darroze

Grand-Rue - 05 58 45 20 07, fax 05 58 45 82 67
Closed Sun dinner & Mon (exc Jul-Sep & hols), Jan 2-24. Open until 10pm. Priv rm 30. Garden dining. Pool. Garage pkg.
Now that the elder Darroze has retired, it is only fitting that his daughter, Hélène, should take up the torch after a stint with Ducasse. This restaurant has a 100-year-old tradition, and the food is still as good as it ever was. Hélène has updated the family recipes without depriving them of any of their charm: a crispy potato millefeuille, fried langoustines, superb squab, and French toast with spiced and roasted pears. Sublime cellar, marvelous Armagnacs. The service is a little too stiff, which is a shame because it affects the overall impression. **C** 320. **M** 290-420.

 Hélène Darroze

(See restaurant above)
Closed Jan 2-24. 1 ste 980. 13 rms 580-750. Bkfst 80-110. Half-board 680-880. Rm ser. Conf. Pool. Garage pkg.
Well-kept, well-equipped, tastefully decorated rooms. Great breakfast that includes some specialties of the Landes. Newly added herb and flower garden behind hotel gives an added note of charm. Relais et Châteaux.

 L'Europe   ▲♥

Pl. de la Boiterie - 05 58 45 20 08, fax 05 58 45 34 14
Open year-round. 2 stes 600. 10 rms 300-500. Bkfst 60-90. Restaurant. Half-board 250-475. Rm ser. Conf. Pool. Valet pkg.
A welcoming hotel located on a shady square with well-equipped rooms and attractive décor. Organizes day-long tours of the region. Friendly, professional service.

THE BASQUE COUNTRY & WESTERN PYRENEES

AHETZE   64210
Paris 781 - Pau 125 - Bidart 5   Pyrénées-A.

12/20 **L'Épicerie d'Ahetze**

Pl. du Fronton - 05 59 41 94 95
Closed Sun dinner & Mon off-seas. Open until 10:30pm. Garden dining. Pkg.
Decorative hens and cocks watch over the pleasant dining room of this former grocery store. The atmosphere is soothing, and the

cuisine exhibits a rustic refinement, carefully and seriously prepared with good-quality ingredients at modest prices. Wine list could use improvement. Amiable welcome, attentive service. C 220-260. M 100 (lunch exc Sun, wine incl), 130, 60 (children).

AINHOA   64250
Paris 768 - St-Jean-de-Luz 23 - Bayonne 26   Pyrénées-A.

 Argi Eder   🌣
Route Notre-Dame-de-l'Aubépine
05 59 93 72 00, fax 05 59 29 72 13
Closed Sun dinner & Wed off-seas, Nov 15-end Mar. Open until 9pm. Priv rm 120. Terrace dining. Air cond. Pool. Tennis. Pkg.
Chef Jean-Pierre Dottax prepares regional specialties with care and delicacy. The excellent cellar is particularly strong on Bordeaux, but also offers good Spanish vintages and an interesting assortment of liquors. A charming welcome and gracious service in a large Basque chalet with terracotta-tiled floors and comfortable, traditional décor. Meals can also be enjoyed on the poolside terrace. C 310-360. M 125 (exc Sun), 150 (wine incl), 190-225 (exc Sun), 195 & 230 (Sun), 75 (children).

 Argi Eder
(See restaurant above)
See restaurant for closings. 4 stes 680-860. 32 rms 610-820. Bkfst 54. Half-board 610-670 (oblig in seas). Air cond. Conf. Pool. Tennis. Pkg.
Set in a tree- and flower-filled park in the countryside, with huge (although not well soundproofed) rooms that are well equipped and have modern bathrooms with bathtubs. A warm welcome is assured. Half the rooms were redecorated last year.

 Ithurria   🌣
05 59 29 92 11, fax 05 59 29 81 28
Closed Wed (exc in Jul-Sep), beg Nov-end Mar. Open until 9pm. Air cond. Pool. Tennis. Pkg.
You can't get any more Basque than this. Maurice Isabal is a true Basque chef, and he shows it off in his anchovy salad à l'escabèche, perfectly prepared and seasoned fish, Basque cassoulet with kidney beans, and wonderful homemade charcuterie, all available on the 165 F menu. The wine list is fairly eclectic, with a good selection of local products. C 280. M 165, 245, 260.

 Ithurria
(See restaurant above)
Closed Wed (exc in Jul-Sep), beg Nov-end Mar. 27 rms 400-600. Bkfst 48. Half-board 520-560. Conf. Pool. Tennis. Pkg.
This hotel, located in what must be the loveliest village in the Labourd (a stop on the road to Compostella), offers pleasant, rustic rooms.

 Ohantzea
05 59 29 90 50

Closed Sun, Mon, Nov 15-Feb 15. 9 rms 245-325. Bkfst 35. Restaurant. Half-board 310-325. Pkg.
A typical Basque *auberge* in the Pyrenees with handsome, rustic furnishings. Children are welcome to play in the garden. A truly warm welcome.

ANGLET   64600
Paris 748 - Biarritz 4 - Bayonne 3   Pyrénées-A.

 Atlanthal   ⚑♠
153, bd des Plages
05 59 52 75 75, fax 05 59 52 75 13
Open year-round. 4 stes 1,030-1,360. 95 rms 525-1,030. Bkfst 65. Restaurant. Half-board 780-1,430 (oblig in seas). Air cond. Conf. Heated pool. Tennis. Pkg.
Spacious, well-equipped rooms with plain modern décor look out on a flowered patio, the swimming pool, or the sea. Studio apartments are available in this complex , which also houses a sea-water spa and fitness center.

 Château de Brindos   🌣
Route de l'Aviation
05 59 23 17 68, fax 05 59 23 48 47
Closed Tue off-seas. Open until 10pm. Pool. Tennis. Pkg.
There is much to dazzle the eye here, with views of a lily-dotted lake and the rich décor of the vast rotunda dining room, adorned with lake and tapestries and lit by majestic copper candelabra. We are more than pleased to see the return of chef Lhabid Bouderba, producing dishes illustrating true inspiration and craftsmanship while remaining light: goose consommé in jelly, succulent calf's sweetbread lasagna with fresh broad beans, and a fruity horn of plenty with unctuous pastry cream (a sort of thick egg custard). A second toque is a must! Divine wines and splendid selection of Armagnacs. The price is quite another matter unless you take the 170 F fixed-price meal. C 370-500. M 150-400.

 Château de Brindos
(See restaurant above)
Open year-round. 2 stes 1,300-1,850. 12 rms 650-1,200. Bkfst 75-100. Rms for disabled. Half-board 1,000 (oblig in seas). Conf. Pool. Tennis. Pkg.
The décor of this spectacular neo-Renaissance home in a green, flower-filled setting bristles with armor but is softened by tapestries. Well-equipped rooms offer a charming view of lake.

12/20 L'Orangerie
104, bd des Plages - 05 59 58 48 48, fax 05 59 63 57 84
Closed Sun dinner off-seas. Open until 10pm. Priv rm 200. Terrace dining. Pool. Tennis. Garage pkg.
A friendly little estate near the pine forest bordering the golf course. An up-to-date, well-measured cuisine that remains constant in quality from one year to another. Try the calf's sweetbread and escargot soup with confit garlic or the truffled burbot fillet à la bayonnaise. Smil-

ing service. Small but varied wine cellar. C 240-280. M 140, 70 (children).

Hôtel de Chiberta et du Golf

(See restaurant above)
Open year-round. 3 stes 830-1,230. 55 rms 310-920. Bkfst 58. Rms for disabled. Half-board 380-663. Rm ser. Pool. Tennis. Garage pkg.
Right on the grounds of the golf course, a laid-back haven for golfers and conference-goers alike. Excellent equipment: sauna, muscle building, beauty treatments, sports gear. Charming reception. Sunny, comfortable rooms.

ARGELÈS-GAZOST	65400
Paris 812 - Cauterets 17 - Lourdes 13	H.-Pyrénées

12/20 Le Casaou

Av. des Pyrénées - 05 62 97 01 26, fax 05 62 97 56 67
Closed beg Nov-mid Dec. Open until 9pm. Priv rm 15. Air cond. No pets. Pkg.
A lovely house with enormous bay windows overlooking a flower garden right next to the Tour-Argelès. No one could resist being pampered by the friendly staff and tasting chef Pierre Pucheu's succulent scallop salad with ham or generous helping of lamb stew. Needless to say, a reservation is necessary. C 210-300. M 75 (exc Sun), 125-215.

Le Miramont

(See restaurant above)
Closed beg Nov-mid Dec. 2 stes 400-450. 25 rms 250-340. Bkfst 37. Rms for disabled. Half-board 250-300 (oblig in seas). No pets. Pkg.
An elegant, all-white Art Deco hotel filled with flowers and located near the spa. The large, harmoniously decorated rooms are hard to leave. The convivial welcome makes you feel like you are staying with friends.

Hôtel du Lac d'Estaing

05 62 97 06 25
Closed Oct 15-May 1. Open until 9:30pm. Terrace dining. Pkg.
On a beautiful day, you will be tempted to move from the charming little dining room with its country décor to the immense terrace with its flowers and magnificent view of the lake. Chef Christian Houerie's cuisine is often inspired by regional products and recipes, but he doesn't hesitate to leave the well-worn path to try out new ideas. Well-stocked cellar. Friendly welcome. C 220-330. M 85-160, 60 (children).

BARCUS	64130
Paris 831 - Pau 49 - Oloron-Ste-Marie 16	Pyrénées-A.

Chez Chilo

05 59 28 90 79, fax 05 59 28 93 10
Closed Sun dinner & Mon off-seas, Jan 15-Feb 10, last wk of Mar. Open until 10pm. Terrace dining. Pool. Pkg.

Faithful customers regularly make the trek from Biarritz or Pau to this lively inn located in a charming village nestled at the foot of the Pyrenees. They take their seats on the flowered terrace or in the large dining room with rustic décor. They are attracted by the sunny cuisine of Pierre Chilo and Éric Dequin, composed of rich country dishes, dexterously prepared. Good cellar. Friendly welcome. C 300. M 88 (weekdays), 110-320, 50 (children).

Chez Chilo

(See restaurant above)
See restaurant for closings. 12 rms 170-500. Bkfst 45. Rms for disabled. Half-board 300-450. Pool. Pkg.
Pretty rooms with antique furniture and modern, well-equipped bathrooms in a comfortable inn. There is a garden with a view of snow-topped mountains. Delicious breakfast.

BAYONNE	64100
Paris 744 - Bordeaux 176 - Pau 107	Pyrénées-A.

12/20 El Asador

Pl. Montaut - 05 59 59 08 57
Closed Sun dinner & Mon (exc hols), end Dec-beg Jan. Open until 10:30pm. Air cond. Pkg.
The owner recreates the atmosphere of his birthplace in the middle of the city. Quality and freshness characterize cuisine that is faithful to country recipes and is guaranteed to charm: haricot beans with clams, stuffed peppers, stuffed crab, and lovely prime rib. A little work on the wine list would round out the pleasure. C 160-250. M 118 (wine incl).

Cheval Blanc

68, rue Bourgneuf
05 59 59 01 33, fax 05 59 59 52 26
Closed Sun dinner & Mon (exc in summer). Open until 10pm. Priv rm 25. Air cond. Pkg.
Jean-Claude Tellechea keeps on improving his cooking while maintaining good quality at reasonable prices. Don't miss the Ibaïona ham with lambs' lettuce leaves (the ham itself is a masterpiece), the galette de pommes de terre, the delicious sheep cheese, and the chocolate assortment (Bayonne provided a haven for Portuguese chocolate makers chased out of their country by the Inquisition). Good, eclectic, fairly reasonably priced wine list. Warm welcome in the pure Basque tradition. C 300. M 115 (weekdays, Sat lunch), 185, 250, 50 (children).

Le Grand Hôtel

21, rue Thiers - 05 59 59 14 61, fax 05 59 25 61 70
Open year-round. 3 stes 650. 54 rms 370-520. Bkfst 45. Rms for disabled. Restaurant. Half-board 500-650. Rm ser. Pkg.
Near the cathedral on a commercial street. Well-equipped and -soundproofed rooms with serviceable bathrooms. Terrace.

> Some establishments change their **closing times** without warning. It is always wise to check in advance.

François Miura   ۞

24, rue Marengo - 05 59 59 49 89
*Closed Wed, Sun dinner. Open until 10pm. Air
cond.*
The décor is as minimal as François Miura's
concise menu. The limited choices allow the chef
to master his rather ambitious dishes. The delicately roasted scallops with butter sauce are delicious, and the fried striped bass works perfectly
with a cabbage paupiette with pork shank. A fine
dessert choice is the pear eau-de-vie soufflé
served with warm chocolate. Fine selection of
prix-fixe menus. Good choice of regional wines
and plenty of half-bottles. **C** 300. **M** 100, 175.

12/20 **Le Saint-Simon**

1, rue des Basques - 05 59 59 27 71
*Closed Sun dinner, Mon, mid Jan-mid Feb. Open
until 10pm. Terrace dining. Air cond. Pkg.*
Ludovic Marginet recently set up shop in this
old house with a fresh, rustic décor. France's best
apprentice offers a neoclassic menu that displays
the mastery he has over his good ingredients.
The wine cellar needs to be expanded. The
patronne provides a warm welcome, and the service is efficient. **C** 190-340. **M** 69 (weekday
lunch), 97, 187, 50 (children).

And also...

*Our selection of places for inexpensive,
quick, or late-night meals.*
Le Chistera (05 59 59 25 93 - 42, rue Port-Neuf.
Open until 10pm, 10:30pm in summer.): A
beautiful country-style décor in one of the most
picturesque streets in town. Regional cooking
using local products prepared with utmost care.
The crowd sometimes breaks into Basque songs
at dessert time (85-150).
Le Trinquet Moderne (05 59 59 05 22 - 60, av.
Dubrocq. Open until 10:30pm.): Everybody
who's anybody comes here; this is also the "head
office" of the Basque game pelota's national
federation. Simple, local cooking. Enormous
choice. Regional wines. A good time is assured
to all (90-120).

BIARRITZ	64200
Paris 747 - Dax 57 - Bayonne 8	Pyrénées-A.

12/20 **L'Auberge**

22, rue du Maréchal-Harispe - 05 59 41 01 41
*Closed Tue off-seas, Jun 15-30, Oct 12-15. Open
until 11pm. Terrace dining.*
This charming, country-style inn offers the essence of well-being, whether you're seated by
the fireplace or on the patio (depending on the
season). The prices are what you call right and
the high-quality ingredients are handled in pure
Basque tradition. Carefully selected wine list
with a distinct preference for the Southwest. **C**
160. **M** 100, 138.

 Auberge du Relais

44, av. de la Marne
05 59 24 85 90, fax 05 59 22 13 94
*Closed Tue off-seas, 2 wks in Dec, 3 wks in Jan. Open
until 10pm. Terrace dining. Pkg.*
Located on a busy street, this amiable inn offers
a comfortable, bright, rustic dining room
warmed by a large fireplace. The kindly welcome and service match the integrity of René
Lacam's cuisine. The fixed-price menu at 154 F
provides a good example. The wine list offers a
wide choice of regional wines. **C** 240-310. **M** 95,
154.

12/20 **Bistrot Bellevue**

5, pl. Bellevue
05 59 24 19 53, fax 05 59 24 18 20
*Closed Tue & Wed lunch off-seas, Feb-Apr 1. Open
until 10:30pm. Terrace dining.*
In the bistro of the Café de Paris, with its a
1930s–style décor, diners sit elbow-to-elbow
while sampling asparagus with horseradish
mousse, nicely flavored tuna carpaccio, and almond tart with chocolate sauce. Limited wine
list. **C** 200-280. **M** 165.

 Café de Paris   ۞

5, pl. Bellevue
05 59 24 19 53, fax 05 59 24 18 20
*Closed Tue & Wed lunch (exc Jul-Sep & hols),
Jan-Mar. Open until 10:30pm. Priv rm 30. Air
cond. Garden dining.*
This *fin-de-siècle* restaurant was once a Biarritz
hot spot. Today, the Café de Paris, with its light-
colored walls, large bay windows, and sleek furnishings, has found the chef it deserves: Didier
Oudill, who practices the art of combining rus-
ticity with refinement, paying attention to the
slightest details. He is a master of herbs and
spices. The flavors of his fresh morels stuffed
with crab explode in the mouth with a springlike elegance. A completely different dish, hog
jowls stuffed with black truffles, represent the
earthy flavors of the Southwest. The pyramid of
ice cream served on warm apricots with French
toast, the fruit brochettes, and the pineapple
chips all demonstrate astounding virtuosity. The
wine list is highly discriminating, with only the
best Bordeaux, the rare Burgundies of Morey,
the Muscat of Desbœufs, and exceptional Ports.
Hardly any half-bottles. **C** 450. **M** 270, 360.

🏠 **Café de Paris**

(See restaurant above)
*Closed Jan-Mar. 1 ste 1,100. 18 rms 500-1,050.
Bkfst 85. Rms for disabled. Half-board 675-950.
Rm ser. Air cond.*
There's no parking garage and no swimming
pool, but there are terraces with unobstructed
views of the ocean (on the third floor), tasteful
furnishings, excellent service and reasonable
prices. The breakfast still needs some work, and
we wonder why the narrow bathtubs are inver-
sely proportionate to the size of the bathrooms.

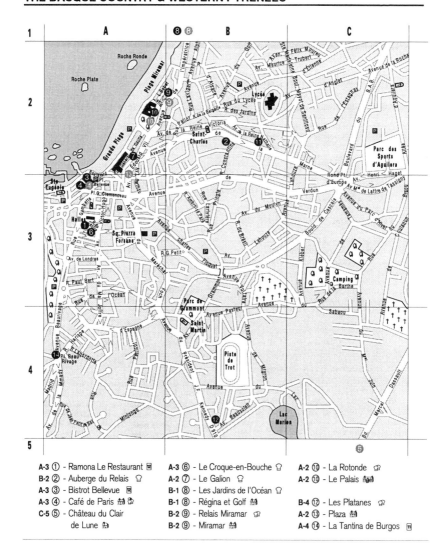

A-3 ① - Ramona Le Restaurant 🍴

B-2 ② - Auberge du Relais 🍷

A-3 ③ - Bistrot Bellevue 🍴

A-3 ④ - Café de Paris 🏨🍷

C-5 ⑤ - Château du Clair
        de Lune 🛏

A-3 ⑥ - Le Croque-en-Bouche 🍷

A-2 ⑦ - Le Galion 🍷

B-1 ⑧ - Les Jardins de l'Océan 🍷

B-1 ⑧ - Régina et Golf 🏨

B-2 ⑨ - Relais Miramar 🍷

B-2 ⑨ - Miramar 🏨

A-2 ⑩ - La Rotonde 🍷

A-2 ⑩ - Le Palais 🏨

B-4 ⑫ - Les Platanes 🍷

A-2 ⑬ - Plaza 🏨

A-4 ⑭ - La Tantina de Burgos 🍴

 ## Campagne et Gourmandise

Route d'Arbonne - 05 59 41 10 11, fax 05 59 43 96 16
*Closed Sun dinner, Wed. Open until 10pm. Priv rm
15. Terrace dining. Pkg.*
  The name says it all: country and gourman-dism. This superb site, located just a few minutes from downtown Biarritz, offers a breathtaking view of the Pyrenees in an atmosphere of country-style simplicity of the most pleasant type. There's only one "formula": you choose from among eight hors d'œuvres, eight main dishes and eight desserts. You might choose from chilled vegetable gazpacho with grilled shrimp and confites tomatoes, or chilled ar-tichokes stuffed in Provençal manner and served with langoustines and bacon bits, or a cod steak roasted in parsley-threaded breadcrumbs. **M** 175, 190, 90 (children).

Looking for a city or a locality? Refer to the index.

**Château
du Clair de Lune**

Route d'Arbonne, 48, av. A.-Seeger
05 59 41 53 20, fax 05 59 41 53 29
*Open year-round. 1 ste 600-800. 14 rms 450-680.
Bkfst 50. Pkg.*
This turn-of-the-century hunting lodge in
colonial style is set on splendid grounds and
approached via a mimosa-lined alley. The
refined, flower-decorated rooms have an old-
fashioned charm.

12/20 **Le Clos Basque**

12, rue Louis-Barthou - 05 59 24 24 96
Open daily until 10:30pm. Terrace dining.
Good homemade cooking right off the main
shopping street. The menu may be brief, but so
are the prices. The only place in town where you
can buy a plate of food for 45 F! Good cream of
cauliflower soup and fresh cod with fennel. A
few wines could be added to the cellar. They're
so nice it makes you think it's your grandmother
serving you. C 138.

 Le Croque-en-Bouche

5, rue du Centre - 05 59 22 06 57
*Closed Sun dinner off-seas, Mon & Tue lunch in
summer. Open until 10pm.*
The sober, elegant décor and charming welcome from Marie-Hélène Bergès add up to a
pleasant dining experience when combined with
the technically flawless cuisine of Bernard
Olasagasti. Prices are reasonable. Don't miss the
pepper-flavored fig jam tart and the duck foie
gras, the roasted hake with Bayonne ham, or the
warm caramelized apple feuillantine served
with apricot sauce. Well-selected wine list. C 175.
M 140.

 Le Galion

17, bd du Général-de-Gaulle
05 59 24 20 32, fax 05 59 24 67 54
*Closed Sun dinner & Mon off-seas, Nov. Open until
11pm. Terrace dining. Air cond.*
The Atlantic Ocean is on show here from the
large bay windows in the comfortable dining
room with dark woodwork. The full-flavored
cuisine of Monique Lissar, which shows its
Southwestern origins, concentrates on seafood,
which she treats with originality and flair. The
small wine list is well chosen, with good
Jurançons direct from the growers. Warm welcome from the owners. C 260. M 150.

 Les Jardins de l'Océan

52, av. de l'Impératrice
05 59 41 33 00, fax 05 59 41 33 99
*Closed Dec-Feb. Open until 10pm (10:30pm in sum-
mer). Air cond. No pets. Valet pkg.*
This imposing hotel sits on a cliff facing a
lighthouse. The décor is Second Empire, and
there is a large patio with trees and a winter
garden. The quail salad, a bit overcooked, was
served with the bird's tiny egg and a celeriac
cream. The lemon tart was fine. The wine list

offers a wide choice, with many bottles from
Spain and Bordeaux, and a good selection of
Champagnes. We wondered why the prices
were not listed on the menu posted outside. C
250-350. M 230.

 Régina et Golf

(See restaurant above)
*Closed Dec-Feb. 10 stes 1,100-1,650. 68 rms 620-
1,385. Rms for disabled. Half-board 745-1,745. Rm
ser. Air cond. Conf. Heated pool. Valet pkg.*
Perched on a cliff overlooking the sea, a handsome hotel with spacious, bright rooms that are
air conditioned and very well equipped. Enormous but to-be-improved breakfasts. Weekend
packages include golf and a sea-water spa.

Miramar

See restaurant Relais Miramar

 L'Operne

17, av. Édouard-VII
05 59 24 30 30, fax 05 59 24 37 89
*Open daily until 11pm. Priv rm 70. Terrace dining.
Air cond. No cards.*
A toque standing firmly on its feet. Don't let
the outside fool you: the view from the terrace
will make you float on the clouds (if there happen to be any). Good assortment of seafood as
well as regional Southwest dishes with a
pleasant touch of imagination. Wine available by
the glass. C 250-300. M 135, 160, 175, 255.

Le Palais

See restaurant La Rotonde

 Les Platanes

32, av. Beausoleil - 05 59 23 13 68
Closed Mon, Tue lunch. Open until 10pm.
Slowly but surely, Arnaud Daguin is on the
way to making us forget his famous father as he
forges his own reputation based on solid culinary values. In an unpretentious suburban villa,
he works hard at his task, and to good effect,
bringing out the flavors of his high-quality ingredients without attempting risky combinations. The ingredients themselves are what
counts, and the customer leaves satisfied by his
good foie gras, sea bream with onions and mushrooms, and minted custard with fruit. The wine
list features a good selection of regional wines,
judiciously chosen by Véronique Daguin. C 350.
M 150 (lunch, exc Sun), 240, 290.

Plan to travel?

Look for GaultMillau/Gayot's other Best of
guides to Chicago, Florida, Germany,
Hawaii, Hong Kong, Italy, London, Los Angeles, New England, New Orleans, New York,
Paris, Paris & the Loire Valley, San Francisco,
Thailand, Toronto, Washington, D.C., and
more to come...

Plaza

Av. Édouard-VII - 05 59 24 74 00, fax 05 59 22 22 01
Open year-round. 60 rms 315-860. Restaurant.
Half-board 364-880. Rm ser. Air cond. Conf. Pkg.
Near the beach and the casino, a well-preserved luxury hotel dating from the 1930s. Rooms are pleasant and well equipped.

12/20 **Ramona Le Restaurant**

5, rue du Centre - 05 59 24 34 66
Closed Mon dinner, Tue, 2 wks in Feb. Open until 10:30pm. Air cond.
Jean-Claude Bucau opened his restaurant right next to his fish shop, so it's not surprisingly that his cuisine is redolent of the sea: fried scampi flambéed with whiskey, striped bass supreme, and nougat ice cream soufflé with pistachio cream. Good wine cellar. Pleasant welcome and service. C 190. M 98 (lunch, exc Sun, wine incl), 150.

 Relais Miramar

13, rue Louison-Bobet
05 59 41 30 00, fax 05 59 24 77 20
Open daily until 10pm. Terrace dining. Air cond.
No pets. Heated pool. Beach. Valet pkg.
Newcomer Patrice Demangel knows all the right places to go to find the best ingredients: local farms and fishermen, in other words, you'll find here all the best products of the Southwest. The décor has recently undergone a facelift to make it more in keeping with the artfully-crafted cooking. We savored the surprising confit lobster cooked in goose grease, the thin piperade tart with a round slice of stuffed cuttlefish and served with an acidulous Basquaise jus, and the superb sole with a "minstrel" of season's vegetables and parsley juice. Make sure to save room for dessert; it's well worth it! We salute the selection of wines by the glass; it's rare in restaurants of this caliber. C 400-450. M 280.

 Miramar

(See restaurant above)
Open year-round. 17 stes 1,490-3,230. 109 rms 760-2,705. Bkfst 100. Half-board 740-1,625. Rm ser.
Air cond. Conf. Heated pool. Beach. Valet pkg.
Directly linked to the sea-water spa—The famous Louison Bobet Biarritz Thalassotherapy Institute—the hotel Miramar offers to those taking and cure—and other—all the earthly consolations they could wish for, with top-level comfort, to make you feel better, and look your best.

Régina et Golf

See restaurant Les Jardins de l'Océan

 La Rotonde

1, av. de l'Impératrice
05 59 41 64 00, fax 05 59 41 67 99
Closed Feb. Open until 10:30pm. Garden dining.
Air cond. Heated pool. No pets. Valet pkg.
Its different menus and fixed-priced offerings can cause confusion in the restaurant of the

legendary Hôtel du Palais, which tries to maintain nostalgia for the Empire without discouraging those enjoying a seaside holiday. On the gigantic menu decorated with crowns, we find hake cooked with clams and green asparagus at 150 F, while on the small menu, hake is cooked *à la plancha* and served with steamed potatoes at 95 F. Both dishes pay tribute to regional tradition, with chipirons (squid), Serrano ham, or Landes poultry. The extravagant wine list has prices to match. A few wines are served by the glass. C 380-400. M 280.

 Le Palais

(See restaurant above)
Closed Feb. 20 stes 2,000-6,250. 132 rms 1,155-2,755. Bkfst 120-190. Rms for disabled. Half-board 1,550-2,400. Air cond. Conf. Heated pool. Beach. Valet pkg.
Set on the edge of the beach, this superb palace still plays the role of the *grande dame*, with its gilt, chandeliers, and terraces overlooking the sea, but it is equipped with all the modern luxuries. The swimming pool, with its solarium, restaurant and grill, and private cabins, is straight out of a Hollywood set. Sea-water therapy available.

11/20 **La Tantina de Burgos**

2, pl. Beau-Rivage - 05 59 23 24 47
Closed Sun off-seas. Open until 11pm. Air cond. Pkg.
A joyous atmosphere reigns in this Iberian country–style dining room, where diners enjoy fresh, simple Basque and Spanish cuisine, nicely prepared and reasonably priced, washed down by a small selection of wines from Bordeaux and the other side of the Pyrenees. C 180-200.

BIDART   64210
Paris 755 - Biarritz 6 - Bayonne 12   Pyrénées-A.

 Bidartea Best Western

N 10 - 05 59 54 94 68, fax 05 59 54 83 82
Closed Oct 15-Apr 1. 32 rms 332-480. Bkfst 48. Rms for disabled. Restaurant. Half-board 380-525. Rm ser. Pool. Pkg.
Large, rustic-style rooms with a view of the pool or the natural scenery. Lovely bathrooms. Breakfast buffet almost enough to last all day.

 Les Frères Ibarboure

Chemin de Ttalienia
05 59 54 81 64, fax 05 59 54 75 65
Closed Wed (exc Jul-Sep), mid Nov-beg Dec. Open until 9:30pm. Priv rm 80. Garden dining. Air cond. Pkg.
Surrounded by luxuriant greenery, with a view of the Atlantic behind the hills, the restaurant's interior goes a bit overboard on pink. There is also a bit too much color in the cooking: Philippe Ibarboure would do better to simplify his dishes and strengthen their flavors. That is the only advice we are going to offer. For the rest, every member of the family gives his or her best, exhibiting a love for their work and

pride in giving pleasure. We particularly enjoyed a sensational turbot braised with vegetables and served with robustly flavored cèpe ravioli. We have one more wish: a few half-bottles of wine for those eating alone. C 390-420. M 200-350, 120 (children).

11/20 La Tantina de la Playa

Plage du Centre - 05 59 26 53 56
Closed Sun dinner, Mon, 1 wk beg Jun, last 2 wks of Oct. Open until 10pm (11pm in summer). Pkg.
New owner and cook. The crisp nautical décor and the pretty waitresses don't distract diners' attention from the quality of the seafood, including grilled sea bream in vinegar sauce with garlic and peppers, and fish parrillada with stuffed peppers. For dessert: chocolate fondant with vanilla cream. Remarkable view. C 180-250.

BIRIATOU   64700
Paris 801 - Pau 143 - Hendaye 4   Pyrénées-A.

Bakéa

05 59 20 76 36, fax 05 59 20 58 21
Closed Jan 26-Feb 14. Open until 9:30pm (10:30pm in summer). Priv rm 60. Terrace dining. Pkg.
Between the sea and the Spanish border on a mountain road, this chalet has a somewhat austere aspect, but guests quickly learn to relax by the fireside in a comfortably rustic décor or, even better, on the shaded terrace overlooking the gorgeous valley. Éric Duval puts his own twist on a basically classic cuisine. We liked the perfectly prepared Adour shad steak and the melt-in-your-mouth veal salami with duck liver and cèpes, both perfect balances of classic and modern. He works with excellent ingredients, an undeniable professionalism, and an occasional touch of fantasy, so another toque is well merited. Judicious choice of Bordeaux. Corine Duval offers a charming welcome. C 280. M 155-205.

CAMBO-LES-BAINS   64250
Paris 787 - Pau 118 - Bayonne 20   Pyrénées-A.

Errobia

Av. Chantecler - 05 59 29 71 26, fax 05 59 29 96 36
Closed Nov-May 1 (exc Easter). 3 stes 450-500. 15 rms 170-400. Bkfst 30. Rms for disabled. Heated pool. Pkg.
A pretty house overlooking a valley and set in extensive grounds. The large, comfortable rooms have either Basque or period furnishings.

Le Relais de la Poste

Pl. de la Mairie - 05 59 29 73 03, fax 05 59 29 86 00
Closed Sun dinner, Mon, Open until 10pm. Terrace dining. HOTEL: 10 rms 190-250. Bkfst 80. Half-board 300-350. Rm ser. Pkg.
Bruno Ranouil has been offering his accomplished cuisine in Cambo since the end of 1994. He manages to respect local traditions

while remaining inventive. The remarkable choice of ingredients, the passionate attention of the young chef, and his subtle taste for plants grown in his kitchen garden all contribute to the diner's pleasure. His à la carte prices are reasonable, and there is a fixed-price menu at 95 F that lets you eat a finely prepared meal, or a "gourmet" menu at 160 F offering duck foie gras with fruit, panaché of seafood with vegetable vermicelli, cheese and a super-thin apple pie. The wine list is well-balanced and the impeccable service friendly. This is a must stop. C 270-350. M 95-220, 50 (children).

CIBOURE   64500
Paris 792 - Pau 134 - St-Jean-de-Luz 2   Pyrénées-A.

Chez Dominique

Quai Maurice-Ravel - 05 59 47 29 16
Closed Sun dinner, Mon, Feb. Open until 9:30pm. Terrace dining. Air cond.
Over the years, this restaurant has continued to offer excellent fish and shellfish. Add to this the delicacy of the desserts, the discreet service, and the pleasing décor of the dining room with its adjacent terrace overlooking the port, and you have a highly pleasurable dining experience. C 250. M 140 (weekday lunch).

ESPELETTE   64250
Paris 761 - Bayonne 22 - Pau 123   Pyrénées-A.

Euzkadi

Rue Principale - 05 59 93 91 88, fax 05 59 93 90 19
Closed Mon & Tue off-seas, Nov 5-Dec 15. Open until 9pm. Pool. Tennis. Pkg.
In the country of *pottiok* and pimentos, the sound of Basque songs echoes off the rafters of the immense dining room and reaches as far as the garden. This is a bastion of regional traditions, orchestrated by André Darraidou, who tempts our taste buds with veal sausage, Espelette axoa (veal with chili peppers), and homemade koka (crème caramel). The *patronne* offers a warm welcome. C 190-250. M 95-175.

GAN   64290
Paris 795 - Pau 8   Pyrénées-A.

Le Tucq

4 km on route de Laruns - 05 59 21 61 26
Closed dinner Mon-Wed, Oct. Open until 9pm (9:30pm in summer). Terrace dining. Pkg.
A welcoming inn with a terrace bordered by a rushing stream. Michel Rances, a lover of regional products, offers a set menu at 70 F: Béarnais stew, trout meunière, and custard. C 270. M 70 (weekdays, exc Sat lunch & Sun dinner), 105.

♣♥
*This **symbol** signifies hotels that offer an exceptional degree of peace and quiet.*

HENDAYE   64700
Paris 777 - Biarritz 28 - St-Jean-de-Luz 13   Pyrénées-A.

 Enbata

76, av. des Mimosas
05 59 48 88 88, fax 05 59 48 88 89
Closed Sun dinner & Mon off-seas, Feb, Nov. Open until 9:30pm (10pm in summer). Priv rm 50. Terrace dining. Air cond. Pool. Pkg.
On the new pleasure port, this restaurant with a blue-and-white contemporary décor and a poolside terrace takes full advantage of a magnificent view of Fuenterrabia's old town. Scott Serrato's cuisine, based on the best products of the sea and land, is light, perfectly cooked, and full of sunny, harmonious flavors. The wine list include some Spanish selections. Friendly welcome and even friendlier prices. C 285-390. M 90 (weekdays, Sat lunch, wine incl), 160 (wine incl), 220, 70 (children).

 Ibaïa

(See restaurant above)
Closed Feb, Nov. 1 ste 945-1,300. 60 rms 480-685. Bkfst 55-70. Rms for disabled. Half-board 455-557. Rm ser. Air cond. Pool. Pkg.
Facing the yacht harbor and near all the sporting activities available in a seaside town, this establishment has comfortable and perfectly equipped rooms. Their vast balconies let you take full advantage of the beautiful setting.

 Thalasso Serge Blanco

125, bd de la Mer - 05 59 51 35 00 (R)
05 59 51 35 35 (H), fax 05 59 51 36 00
Closed 1 wk in Dec. Open until 9:30pm. Garden dining. Air cond. Heated pool. Garage pkg.
How do you satisfy a clientele made up of spa-goers, tourists, and businesspeople? The cuisine here makes the attempt with an attractive repertory, excellent ingredients, and interesting interpretations, and although it remains light, we found it far too complicated. You'll nevertheless enjoy the young lamb charlotte in tomato jelly with its curry-flavored marinière sauce or the arthichoke stew with duck sweetbreads served with foie gras salpicon. The wine list, with its many Bordeaux, also seemed banal. Warm welcome and good service in a discreetly decorated contemporary dining room hung with lithographs and overlooking the estuary. C 340-400. M 180-250, 80 (children).

Thalasso Serge Blanco

(See restaurant above)
Closed 1 wk in Dec. 14 stes 495-748. 76 rms 430-980. Bkfst 50. Rms for disabled. Half-board 650-970. Rm ser. Conf. Heated pool. Garage pkg.
On the beach, a pleasant, neo-Basque–style establishment with roomy, elegant, well-equipped rooms with balconies. Low-calorie or traditional breakfast. Thalassotherapy (sea-water cure) institute.

JURANÇON   64110
Paris 789 - Pau 2   Pyrénées-A.

Castel du Pont d'Oly

2, av. Rausky - 05 59 06 13 40, fax 05 59 06 10 53
Open daily until 10pm. Priv rm 30. Terrace dining. Pool. Pkg.
Christian Marcoux is headed toward the top; in our opinion, a second toque is by no means out of reach. A modern yet rich style of cooking without forgetting local ingredients, where he incorporates little surprises such as chorizo cream soup, Jurançon zabiglione, or piperade. Accuracy and detail win over ostentatiousness when it comes to the prix-fixe menus, in particular the dégustation (tasting) menu where you choose seven courses from the main menu! The desserts offer few surprises but they are still good. The wine cellar displays a distinct love of the region. C 310-410. M 120 (Sun lunch), 165-395, 60 (children).

Castel du Pont d'Oly

(See restaurant above)
Open year-round. 6 rms 350-450. Bkfst 50. Half-board 550. Rm ser. Conf. Pool. Pkg.
Immense, modern rooms decorated in pretty pastels. The charming building was just repainted. Garden.

Ruffet

3, av. Charles-Touzet - 05 59 06 25 13
Closed Sun dinner, Mon. Open until 10pm. Pkg.
The décor of this inviting restaurant, enhanced by bouquets of flowers, evokes the good life in the country. Vigorous and flavorful, the cuisine of Milou Larrouy sticks to regional ingredients and treats these excellent ingredients with great care: terrine of cèpes with morels and asparagus, goose confit à l'ancienne. Attractive cellar of regional wines. Charming welcome. C 230-350. M 100.

LESTELLE-BÉTHARRAM   64800
Paris 812 - Pau 25 - Lourdes 16   H.-Pyrénées

12/20   Le Vieux Logis

Route des Grottes - 05 59 71 94 87, fax 05 59 71 96 75
Closed Nov-mid Feb. Open until 9pm. Priv rm 100. Terrace dining. Pool. Pkg.
Whether you eat in the rustic dining room that looks out on a large park and a swimming pool or on the terrace, the cuisine of father-and-son team Pierre and Francis Gaye always pleases with its authenticity. Try the carpaccio of marinated trout, sole with cèpes served with a dry Jurançon, and the orange crêpes. The wine list is eclectic and reasonably priced. Homey atmosphere. C 250-300. M 75 (exc Sun lunch), 110-210, 45 (children).

Le Vieux Logis

(See restaurant above)
Closed Nov-mid Fev. 40 rms 210-270. Bkfst 35. Rms for disabled. Half-board 360-410. Conf. Pool. Pkg.
Adjacent to an old farm, this well-kept, modern white building has functional bathrooms and private balconies with views of the countryside and nearby valleys. The breakfast is robust.

LOURDES	65100
Paris 828 - Pau 43 - Tarbes 20	H.-Pyrénées

 Adriatic Palace Hôtel

4, rue du Baron-Duprat
05 62 94 31 34, fax 05 62 42 14 70
Closed Dec 19-Feb 4. 87 rms 250-400. Bkfst 35. Rms for disabled. Restaurant. Half-board 230-420. Garage pkg.
A stone house in the old town with light-filled rooms decorated in pastel tones and with a view of the château. A pleasant welcome and relative quiet.

 Gallia Londres

26, av. Bernadette-Soubirous
05 62 94 35 44, fax 05 62 42 24 64
Closed mid Oct-Mar. 90 rms 900-1,600. Bkfst 50-85. Rms for disabled. Restaurant. Half-board 600-650. Rm ser. Air cond.
This venerable monument dating from the end of the Second Empire has been completely renovated. Spacious rooms with balconies, Louis XVI furnishings, and modern bathrooms that manage to retain period charm.

 Hôtel de la Grotte

66, rue de la Grotte
05 62 94 58 87, fax 05 62 94 20 50
Closed Oct 25-Mar 24. 3 stes 1,000-1,200. 80 rms 330-930. Bkfst 60. Rms for disabled. Restaurant. Half-board 365-699. Rm ser. Conf. Air cond. Pkg.
An immense, all-white hotel, very well kept up, overlooking the Pau River and the basilica. Bright, spacious, handsomely decorated rooms, and smiling personnel.

 Impérial

3, av. du Paradis
05 62 94 06 30, fax 05 62 94 48 04
Closed end Oct-beg Apr. 6 stes 530. 93 rms 335-530. Bkfst 55-85. Rms for disabled. Restaurant. Half-board 415-456. Rm ser. Conf. Garage pkg.
This pretty Arts Déco façade has a great location. The rooms are pretty and well-equipped. 1930s-style furniture, plush woolly carpet, sunny bathrooms. Small breakfast buffet is so-so but not expensive.

11/20 Le Magret

10, rue des Quatre-Frères-Soulas
05 62 94 20 55, fax 05 62 94 71 91
Closed Mon, Sat lunch, Jan 6-20. Open until 10pm. Priv rm 20. Terrace dining. Air cond.
You'll always find duck breast on the menu in one form or another, along with escargot ramekins, loin of mutton, gâteau à la broche (a regional specialty) and Armagnac pudding. C 200. M 80-350, 60 (children).

 Paradis

15, av. du Paradis
05 62 42 14 14, fax 05 62 94 64 04
Closed end Oct-1 wk before Easter. 2 stes 1,000. 300 rms 440-500. Bkfst 45-87. Rms for disabled. Restaurant. Half-board 460. Rm ser. Air cond. Conf. Garage pkg.
This large, peaceful white hotel near the Pau River has a friendly staff and bright, modern rooms that are perfectly equipped.

LURBE-SAINT-CHRISTAU	64660
Paris 795 - Lourdes 60 - Oloron-Ste-Marie 9	Pyrénées-A.

Au Bon Coin

05 59 34 40 12, fax 05 59 34 46 40
Closed Sun dinner & Mon off-seas. Open until 9:30pm. Garden dining. Pool. Pkg.
This big pile of a building houses a rustic dining room with a terrace surrounded by green countryside. An ideal place to savor the cuisine of Thierry Lassala: lasagna with mousserons (wild mushrooms); red mullet fillets fried with Madiran, savarin (a ring-shaped cake soaked in a sweet syrup) with fruits and fruit purée. The wine cellar is rich in Bordeaux and local vintages. Cordial, smiling welcome and service. C 300. M 85-235, 40 (children).

Au Bon Coin

(See restaurant above)
Closed Sun eve & Mon off-seas. 18 rms 280-380. Bkfst 35. Rms for disabled. Half-board 540. Rm ser. Conf. Pool. Pkg.
Filled with white-painted wood furniture, this hotel's rooms are soundproofed and overlook the park, the swimming pool, and the countryside. A 300 F package includes dinner, a one-night stay, and breakfast. Packages are also available for those taking the cure.

MADIRAN	65700
Paris 700 - Tarbes 40 - Maubourguet 13	H.-Pyrénées

Le Prieuré

05 62 31 92 50, fax 05 62 31 90 66
Closed Sun dinner & Mon off-seas. Open until 9:30pm. Terrace dining. Pkg.
Michel Cuénot's cuisine has everything going for it. It is firmly rooted to the region's soil and seasons, and is served in an impeccable décor that successfully marries the old with the new, or on an attractive terrace giving onto a park. The 95 F fixed-price menu includes duck giblets, milk-fed-lamb stew, and a chocolate marquise. Smiling welcome and professional service. C 250-350. M 95 (exc Sun), 165-235, 65 (children).

Le Prieuré

(See restaurant above)
See restaurant for closings. 10 rms 230-290. Bkfst 30-50. Half-board 255-335. Rm ser. Conf. Pkg.

In the heart of a vineyard, this former Benedictine abbey dating from the eleventh century has well-equipped rooms decorated in excellent taste. Copious breakfasts.

NESTIER   65150
Paris 840 - Lannemezan 14 - St-Gaudens 24   H.-Pyrénées

 Relais du Castéra   ✪

05 62 39 77 37, fax 05 62 39 77 29
Closed Sun dinner & Mon off seas, Jan 4-20, 1 wk in Jun. Open until 9:30pm. Terrace dining. Priv rm 30. Pkg.

In an old house with a terrace, Serge Latour has set himself the task of promoting the cuisine of his native region. He is succeeding, with cooking that breathes sincerity and respect for his ingredients and their flavors. He enchants his customers with broad-bean soup with poultry breast and morels, polenta with cèpes, and a savarin à la folle blanche and red-fruit compote. The *terroir* menu will having you licking your fingers, and the others are just as attractive, offering high quality at reasonable prices. This chef never stops surprising us with his creativity, his lust for all that is good in life, his freshness and his *joie de vivre*, which are all evident in everything he puts before you. Another point, with absolutely no hesitation. The prices are also right on the well-chosen wine list. Smiling, efficient service. C 200-260. M 110 (lunch, exc Sun), 140-250, 55 (children).

 Relais du Castéra

(See restaurant above)
See restaurant for closings. 7 rms 200-250. Bkfst 35-45. Half-board 230-260. Rm ser. No pets. Pkg.

A simple little hotel known for its eleven chapels! All the rooms were renovated last fall. An extremely quiet and comfortable stopover.

ORTHEZ   64300
Paris 751 - Pau 41 - Dax 37   Pyrénées-A.

 Auberge Saint-Loup

20, rue du Pont-Vieux
05 59 69 15 40, fax 05 59 67 13 19
Closed Sun dinner & Mon off-seas. Open until 10pm. Terrace dining. Priv rm 35.

On the route to Compostella, this fifteenth-century building houses, behind its pretty half-timbered façade, a beautiful old-style dining room, warmed in winter by an imposing fireplace, and an adorable inner courtyard where an abundance of flowers bloom as soon as the weather turns nice. Patrick Brosse, the owner-chef, has a distinct preference for regional ingredients, and his cooking shows an admirable ability to combine technique with personal inspiration. Good regional wine list. C 250. M 98 (exc Sun), 125-145.

PAU   64000
Paris 759 - Bordeaux 195   Pyrénées-A.

 Au Fin Gourmet   ✪

24, av. Gaston-Lacoste
05 59 27 47 71, fax 05 59 82 96 77
Closed Sun dinner, Mon. Open until 10pm. Terrace dining. Pkg.

It looks rather like a pagoda and has bay windows, a rustic décor, and a terrace bordered with hedges. The Fin Gourmet lives up to its name thanks to Patrick Ithurriague, who offered langoustine salad with orange zest, cassolette of squid stuffed with ratatouille and served with a Catalan sauce, and pear millefeuille. The wine list is especially strong in regional offerings and Bordeaux. C 250-340. M 85 (exc Sun), 160.

 Gramont

3, pl. Gramont - 05 59 27 84 04, fax 05 59 27 62 23
Open year-round. 3 stes 495-700. 33 rms 200-495. Rms for disabled. Bkfst 35-45. Restaurant. Half-board 295-475. Rm ser. Air cond. Conf. Pkg.

In the heart of the historic quarter, an old post house has been transformed into a refined hotel with elegant rooms furnished with period pieces. Some of them overlook the garden of the Château Henri IV.

 Le Majestic

9, pl. Royale - 05 59 27 56 83
Closed Sun dinner, Mon lunch. Open until 10pm. Priv rm 14. Terrace dining.

Everyone in the area wants to have a reserved seat at this cozy, quiet restaurant with a terrace and a lovely green and salmon-pink décor, located at the end of linden-tree-lined lane. Why? Because Jean-Marie Larrère knows how to make regional flavors sing in his interesting, well-conceived dishes. The 118 F menu is always a good deal, and the prices on the good wine list will not overinflate the bill. Charming welcome. C 250. M 85 (lunch), 118.

 Paris

80, rue Émile-Garet
05 59 82 58 00, fax 05 59 27 30 20
Open year-round. 41 rms 350-380. Bkfst 35. Conf. Garage pkg.

A few steps from the Beaumont park in the center of town, the rooms here are fairly quiet.

 Pierre

16, rue Louis-Barthou
05 59 27 76 86, fax 05 59 27 08 14
Closed Sat lunch & Sun (exc hols), Jan 2-9, Aug 10-17. Open until 10pm. Priv rm 30. Air cond.

A British pub in the heart of Pau whose cuisine doesn't bear much resemblance to that of the country across the Channel. This is a meeting place for businesspeople and others where regional products are prepared with taste and talent by Raymond Casau: red-mullet fillet with a vegetable tartare, Béarn-style cassoulet with

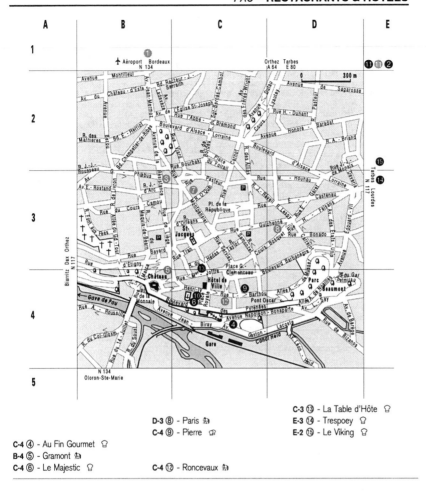

corn beans, and good desserts. The cellar offers some fine Bordeaux. Friendly welcome and service. **C** 350-450.

 ## Roncevaux

25, rue Louis-Barthou
05 59 27 08 44, fax 05 59 82 92 79
Open year-round. 40 rms 280-390. Bkfst 40. Pkg.
  Between the château's park and the casino, a handsome bourgeois residence in the center of town. Three rooms now have four-poster beds.

*Some establishments change their **closing times** without warning. It is always wise to check in advance.*

 ## La Table d'Hôte

19, rue des Cordeliers & 1, rue du Hédas
05 59 27 56 06
Closed Sat lunch, Sun. Open until 10pm. Terrace dining. Priv rm 12.
  Pierre Bruneteau knows how to delight both business executives and tourists who have the luck to enjoy a meal in the cozy Béarnais décor, warmed by a brick fireplace. Langoustine fricassée with foie gras, lamb sweetbreads with cèpes and Espelette peppers, and a fine apple tart with Armagnac-flavored whipped cream. The intelligent wine list is modest and concentrates on regional offerings. Warm welcome. **C** 210-290. **M** 80 (weekday lunch), 105-149.

Trespoey

71, av. du Général-Leclerc
05 59 30 64 77, fax 05 59 02 62 64
Closed Fri dinner, Dec 20-Jan 10, Aug. Open until 9:30pm. Air cond. Pkg.
In a classic register that has been amiably updated and renewed by seasonal offerings, the cuisine of Pascal Montmayeur offers diners a pleasant experience amid the restaurant's bright contemporary décor. He serves as regional "ambassador" with his *Terroir* fixed-price meal at 140 F offering seafood served in pumpkin cream soup, rabbit stew cooked in country wine, and Barbary duck in Balsamic vinegar. Good desserts and daily specials. A limited wine list with too few half-bottles is explained by owner Jean Peyrou. C 250-360. M 75 (weekday dinner), 140.

 Le Viking

33, bd Tourasse - 05 59 84 02 91
Closed Sat, Sun, hols, Feb school hols, Jul 14-Aug 15. Open until 9:15pm. Terrace dining. No pets. Garage pkg.
This little restaurant nestled in a garden is difficult to find, but Hubert David's cooking and the family ambience makes it worth looking for. In this cozy atmosphere, you can savor warm oysters à la Nantaise (invented by the chef), tournedos "Sainte-Anne," or the warm Normandy tart flambéed with Calvados. A nice little wine list. Excellent welcome and service. C 320-450. M 160.

And also...

Our selection of places for inexpensive, quick, or late-night meals.
Le Berry (05 59 27 42 95 - 4, rue Gachet. Open until 11pm, 11:30pm Fri & Sat.): This jolly, totally Bearn atmosphere offers fresh fish and melt-in-your-mouth meat as well as Southwest specialties (50-120).
La Trotte-Vieille (05 59 27 54 43 - 18, rue Henri-IV. Open until 10:30pm, 11pm in summer.): Near the castle. Traditional fare such as duck liver, sole meunière with cèpes, duck breast and much more. Fixed-priced meal offering regional specialties (85-200).

SAINT-JEAN-DE-LUZ   64500
Paris 790 - Biarritz 19 - Pau 133   Pyrénées-A.

12/20 **L'Atlantique**

Pl. Maurice-Ravel
05 59 51 51 51, fax 05 59 51 51 54
Closed 2 wks in Dec. Open until 10pm. Priv rm 120. Terrace dining. Air cond. No pets.
A restaurant with a splendid, unobstructed view of the bay from the bright, elegant Art Deco dining room or the large, parasol-shaded terrace. The cuisine remains in the most classic category, with an interpretation that is serious and respectful of the flavors of the ingredients. A nice wine list. C 350. M 135 (lunch), 195.

 Hélianthal

(See restaurant above)
Closed 2 wks in Dec. 6 stes 900-1,400. 94 rms 450-1,200. Rms for disabled. Bkfst 70. Restaurant. Half-board 645-1,395. Rm ser.
Next to the beach and set amid a garden, a pleasant contemporary hotel decorated in the Art Deco spirit, with well-equipped but not very well air conditioned rooms, most with balconies or loggias. Buffet-style breakfast. Sea-water spa.

 La Devinière

5, rue Loquin - 05 59 26 05 51, fax 05 59 51 26 38
Open year-round. 8 rms 500-650. Bkfst 50.
An old family pension with vast, tastefully decorated rooms. The most peaceful look out on the garden. There is a pretty tea room. Pleasant welcome.

11/20 **L'Écailler**

"L'Alcalde," 22, rue de la République
05 59 26 89 44, fax 05 59 26 38 43
Open daily until 10:30pm (midnight in summer). Terrace dining. No pets. No cards.
A meal prepared by Michel Bordagaray is worth a stop on this touristy street where most of the restaurants don't live up to their promises. Try the Serrano ham, fish parillada or generous seafood platters, and tarte Tatin, washed down with Txakoli. C 180-300. M 95, 130, 200.

12/20 **Kaïku**

17, rue de la République
05 59 26 13 20, fax 05 59 51 07 47
Closed mid Sep-mid Jun: Wed; mid Jun-mid Sep: Mon lunch; mid Nov-Dec 20. Open until 11:15pm. Terrace dining.
The enormous success of this venerable restaurant, with its huge stone-walled dining room, is well deserved. The serious cuisine concentrates on top-notch seafood (the shellfish is superb), but is somewhat lacking in finesse. Good cellar. Smiling, dynamic welcome and service. C 250-300. M 145, 190, 250.

 Madison

25, bd Thiers - 05 59 26 35 02
Closed Jan. 2 stes 400-750. 23 rms 230-460. Bkfst 39. Conf.
Near the beach and the city center, a hotel whose nice, cool rooms are decorated in a comfortable provincial style. Sauna, gym, currency exchange.

 La Marisa

16, rue Sopite - 05 59 26 95 46, fax 05 59 51 17 06
Closed Jan 10-Feb 10. 16 rms 400-480. Bkfst 40. Rms for disabled. Garage pkg.
Located near both the beach and the city center. Comfortable rooms.

 Le Parc Victoria

5, rue Cépé - 05 59 26 78 78, fax 05 59 26 78 08
Closed Nov 15-Mar 15. 2 stes 1,250-1,600. 10 rms 800-1,300. Bkfst 80. Rms for disabled. Restaurant.

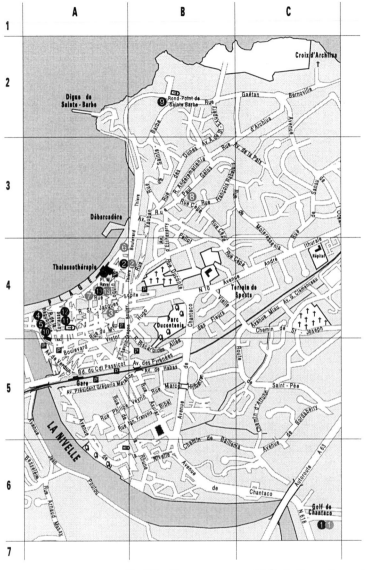

A-4 ③ - La Devinière ♀
A-4 ④ - L'Ecailler ▣

A-4 ⑤ - Kaïku ▣
A-4 ⑥ - Madison ♀
A-4 ⑦ - La Marisa 🏨
B-3 ⑧ - Parc Victoria 🏨
B-2 ⑨ - La Réserve ♀

A-4 ⑩ - La Taverne Basque ▣
A-4 ⑪ - Le Tourasse ♀
A-4 ⑫ - La Vieille Auberge ▣
A-4 ⑬ - L'Atlantique ▣
A-4 ⑬ - Hélianthal 🏨

Half-board 950-1,350 (oblig in seas). Rm ser. Conf. Air cond. Heated pool. Garage pkg.
Away from the beach, this town house inhabits its own park. Its well-equipped rooms look out on leafy scenery and have marble bathrooms. Relais et Châteaux.

 ## La Réserve

Rond-point Sainte-Barbe
05 59 26 04 24, fax 05 59 26 11 74
Closed Nov 15-Mar 30. Open until 9:30pm. Terrace dining. Heated pool. Tennis. Garage pkg.
A handsome white building with small pink dining rooms and a terrace. Diners can enjoy the green landscape while supping new chef Cyril Arrouard's up-to-date yet regionally-inspired cuisine: escargot in puff pastry with thin slices of Serrano country ham, local milk-fed lamb in its own jus flavored with piperarde (tomato, sweet pepper and olive oil sauce), or suckling pig roasted in Espelette spices and herbs. The set-price menus give you good quality for the money; even the à la carte prices won't kill you. The wine cellar won't stimulate your taste buds but it's passable. C 250-350. M 160-250, 180 (Sun).

12/20 La Taverne Basque

5, rue de la République - 05 59 26 01 26
Closed Mon dinner & Tue (exc Jul-Aug), Jan, Feb. Open until 9:30pm. Terrace dining.
The chef's son has just taken over the kitchen of this likable eatery situated in a touristy pedestrian street where there are too many restaurants to count, and is continuing in the spirit of his father. Typical décor and a pleasant terrace is worth a stop for regional cuisine, handled with a good deal of finesse: pan-fried cuttlefish with onions, herb cod, sheep's cheese and much more. Charming welcome. C 240-300. M 97-165.

 ## Le Tourasse

25, rue Tourasse - 05 59 51 14 25
Closed Tue dinner & Wed off-seas (exc school hols), Jan 15-Feb 15. Open until 10pm (10:30pm in summer).
Pascal Basset has not fallen into a rut even after ten years in the kitchen. As starters, we liked the summer-vegetable salad with crawfish and black truffles and the thin tuna pissaladière with Espelette hot peppers. As main dish, try the Saint-Jean tuna tart with local hot peppers and cuttlefish ink and the stuffed pan-fried cuttlefish with pigs' feet. For dessert, try the red fruit roasted with vanilla or the chocolate sorbet capuccino with frozen espresso. A nice little wine cellar. Véronique Basset offers a charming welcome. C 260. M 90.

12/20 La Vieille Auberge

22, rue Tourasse - 05 59 26 19 61, fax 05 59 51 08 11
Closed off-seas: Tue dinner & Wed; Jul-Aug: Tue lunch; beg Nov-end Mar. Open until 10pm. Priv rm 100. Terrace dining.
This appealing inn has a rustic dining room with exposed beams where holidaymakers enjoy unpretentious food, skillfully prepared from quality ingredients. Limited wine list and local cider. C 250. M 72-125.

SAINT-JEAN-PIED-DE-PORT   64220
Paris 819 - Pau 120 - Bayonne 54   Pyrénées-A.

 ## Les Pyrénées

19, pl. du Général-de-Gaulle
05 59 37 01 01, fax 05 59 37 18 97
Closed Tue (exc Jul-Sep & hols), Jan 6-28, Nov 20-Dec 22. Open until 9pm. Terrace dining. Air cond. Heated pool. Tennis. No pets. Garage pkg.
The Pyrénées provide the backdrop for this classically decorated restaurant. Firmin Arrambide's cuisine, however, is far from classic. Its base is regional tradition, which he reinterprets according to his inspirations. Thanks to his light and talented hand, the results are most seductive. Delicious pibales (baby eels), lightly cooked and sprinkled with olive oil and served on spinach mousse. Superb fresh morels, perfectly cooked and stuffed with veal sweetbreads and foie gras, make a top-level composition. A clever and exotic duck variation is a breast fried with spices (ginger, cinnamon, and saffron) and fruits (mangoes, apples, figs). Then there is the tasty country lamb fillet with garlic: tender, perfectly grilled, and accompanied by baby broad beans with a creamy white bean sauce. Excellent regional cheeses are matured in-house. Fine desserts. The superb cellar concentrates on the Southwest, including the best Irouléguys and Jurançons, and Spanish wines (excellent Riojas). C 450. M 240-500.

Les Pyrénées

(See restaurant above)
See restaurant for closings. 2 stes 1,000-1,100. 18 rms 560-900. Bkfst 85. Restaurant. Half-board 650-780. Air cond. Heated pool. No pets. Garage pkg.
A lovely terrace overlooks the pink-sandstone pool. Comfortable, pleasantly decorated rooms with luxurious bathrooms. The best view is from the gallery approaching the entrance. Breakfasts are nothing special. Relais et Châteaux.

SAINT-SAVIN   65400
Paris 873 - Tarbes 39- Lourdes 19   H.-Pyrénées

Le Viscos

05 62 97 02 28, fax 05 62 97 04 95
Closed Mon (exc school hols), 2 wks in Dec. Open until 9:30pm. Terrace dining. HOTEL: 16 rms 260-320. Bkfst 36. Half-board 260-290. Pkg.
The beauty of this mountain village on the edge of the Pyrenees National Park competes with the restaurant's simple pastel décor. Yet chef Jean-Pierre Saint-Martin's refined cooking, inspired by regional specialties, will manage to hold your attention. You will immediately be won over by his cod salad with gizzards, the rabbit spring roll with rosemary gravy, and the remarkable sturgeon with a spicy caviar purée. The dessert and the wine cellar both need some work. Atten-

tive, efficient service. C 200-340. M 108, 156, 240, 275, 55 (children).

TARBES 65000
Paris 806 - Toulouse 155 - Pau 42 H.-Pyrénées

 ## L'Ambroisie

38, rue Larrey - 05 62 93 09 34, fax 05 62 93 09 24
Closed Sun, Mon. Annual closings not available. Open until 9:30pm. Air cond. No pets.
When he decorated his restaurant, located across from the covered market, in delicate, pale colors, chef-owner Daniel Labarrère was thinking of the food he prepares: aromatic, flavorful, market-fresh cuisine. A few examples: leek royale with truffle vinaigrette, crispy turbot stuffed with salmon mousseline, guanaja chocolate ice cream with a flambéed pear. The cellar is a wine buff's delight. Friendly welcome. C 300-350. M 98 (weekday lunch), 150-280.

 ## Henri-IV

7, av. Bertrand-Barrère
05 62 34 01 68, fax 05 62 93 71 32
Open year-round. 2 stes 550. 21 rms 270-360. Bkfst 40. Rm ser. Conf. Garage pkg.
This well-situated, pretty little hotel offers comfortable, well-appointed rooms. The colors of the décor are perfectly matched. Good breakfast.

 ## Le Petit Gourmand

62, av. Bertrand-Barrère - 05 62 34 26 86
Closed Sat lunch, Mon, Aug. Open until 9:30pm. Terrace dining.
The charming *patronne* offers a warm welcome that prepares you for the delights of Guy Espagnacq's cuisine. Its regional accents can be found in the duck breast persillé and foie gras accompanied by a lentil salad seasoned with wine vinegar, or the sautéed monkfish with clams and curry. The crème anglaise (egg custard sauce) with coffee beans concludes a meal that can be washed down by a 1988 Haut-Médoc from Château Potensac (150 F). C 250-300. M 98-160, 40 (children).

URT 64240
Paris 758 - Pau 121 - Bayonne 14 Pyrénées-A.

 ## Auberge de la Galupe

Pl. du Port
05 59 56 21 84, fax 05 59 56 28 66
Closed Sun dinner & Mon (exc Jul-Aug), Jan 19-Mar 3. Open until 10pm. Priv rm 30. Air cond. Pkg.
In this seventeenth-century sailors' inn on the Adour River, the ambience is as warm as the cooking of Christian Parra is excellent. The perfectly seasoned salmon tartare with basil is exquisite, and the salmon steak just caught from the Adour has a remarkable flavor. Real blood sausage from Gaves is accompanied by a gorgeous potato purée (mashed potatoes!), and the pork pot-au-feu is memorable. The chef's mother, Anna, prepares a creamy plum pudding

and prune ice cream for dessert. The well-chosen wine list offers an interesting selection of Southwestern vintages, including a pleasant 1992 Madiran from Frédéric Laplace, priced at 140 F. C 310-420. M 245, 360, 550.

USTARITZ 64480
Paris 777 - Pau 119 - Bayonne 9 Pyrénées-A.

 ## La Patoula

05 59 93 00 56, fax 05 59 93 16 54
Closed Sun dinner & Mon off-seas, Jan 5-Feb 15. Open until 10pm. Priv rm 25. Terrace dining. HOTEL: 9 rms 350-470. Bkfst 60. Rms for disabled. Half-board 350-410. Pkg.
Patoula has a lovely covered terrace, a true winter garden with big bay windows overlooking the river. Pierre Guilhem has taken over the kitchen again, and his enthusiasm mixed with his incredible *savoir-faire* give excellent results. He follows the seasons like a mother follows here child's every sniffle. In the spring, he gives you the first salmon from the Adour river; in the summer, he buys his fish from the Saint-Jean-de-Luz fishermen; in the winter, the hunters provide his source of inspiration. What he puts before you is done with loving care, total lack of pretentiousness, and generosity (and generous helpings, too!). The cellar may be on the small side, but you'll find something for every occasion. C 220-300. M 100 (weekday lunch, wine incl), 130, 180, 240, 80 (children).

GASCONY & PÉRIGORD

AGEN 47000
Paris 647 - Bordeaux 142 - Toulouse 108 Lot/Garonne

 ## Château des Jacobins

1 ter, pl. des Jacobins
05 53 47 03 31, fax 05 53 47 02 80
Open year-round. 15 rms 400-650. Bkfst 75. Rm ser. Garage pkg.
A handsome early-nineteenth-century town house with a garden. The rooms have period furnishings and well-equipped bathrooms. Meals on trays are available.

 ## Michel Latrille

66, rue Camile-Desmoulins
05 53 66 24 35, fax 05 53 66 77 57
Closed 2 weeks in Jun. Open until 9:30pm. Air cond.
Michel Latrille distinguishes himself from the multitude of restaurants lining this street by his pretty, well-lit façade as well as by his well-crafted cooking fine-tuned in relation to the top-quality ingredients he uses. The scallops with

caviar are both elegant and scrumptuous; the burbot tail with black olive brunoise (mixture of finely chopped vegetables) is full of flavors yet subtle; the farm-raised veal chop, bought from Nicolas, the best butcher in town, can only be described as delicious. The 105 F prix-fixe menu is a steal and quite impressive in terms of quality. The wine list does not fall short in any way and has numerous prestigious bottles to offer. C 350. M 105 (weekdays), 155-310.

12/20 La Malmaison

36, cours Gambetta - 05 53 47 25 46
Closed Sat lunch, Sun, Aug. Open until 9:30pm. Priv rm 50. Air cond. Pkg.
If you're in the mood for a romantic walk along the Garonne, venture toward this pretty stone house with its big, elegant dining room. Jacques Porcel is particularly gifted with seafood; don't hesitate to try the squid or skate. Good little wine list. The third fixed-price menu is a particularly good deal. C 230-350. M 89 (weekdays), 125-225.

Le Petit Vatel

52, rue Richard-Cœur-de-Lion - 05 53 47 66 00
Closed Sat lunch, Mon, Aug. Open until 10pm. Priv rm 15. Terrace dining. Air cond.
The owner moves around the small dining room with its warm ambience giving advice and explaining the very inventive cuisine, which favors fish over meat. The escargot croquettes with garlic and licorice approach perfection, the fish fricassée with herbs is beautifully cooked and presented, and the feuilletés filled with vanilla ice cream rival any profiterole. The choice of wines has been expanded. Every dish here is a discovery, as is chef Christophe Meret. C 250. M 120, 65 (children).

Le Provence

22, cours du 14-Juillet
05 53 47 39 11, fax 05 53 68 26 24
Open year-round. 23 rms 275-330. Bkfst 35. Air cond. Conf.
Good central location for this hotel with its own goodtime bar. Most rooms have good air conditioning even though the reception is sometimes hot and uncomfortable.

Stim'Otel

105, bd Carnot - 05 53 47 31 23, fax 05 53 47 48 70
Open year-round. 58 rms 290. Bkfst 35. Rms for disabled. Restaurant. Rm ser. Conf. Air cond. Pkg.
Functional, well-equipped rooms in the city center, a few steps from the Garonne. The breakfast buffet is quite a spectacle and you can eat as much as you want! Impersonal but efficient enough service.

ANTONNE-ET-TRIGONANT   24420
10 km NE on N 21   Dordogne

12/20 Les Chandelles   🔾

Le Parc - 05 53 06 05 10, fax 05 53 06 07 33
Closed Sun dinner & Mon off-seas, Jan-Feb. Open until 10pm. Terrace dining. Pool. Tennis. Pkg.
The owner's regional cuisine is worth tasting: croustade d'escargots, sole à la julienne, and crème brûlée with bergamot orange. Well-chosen cellar; professional service. Watch what you order if you're counting pennies. C 280-380. M 85 (lunch, exc Sun), 115 (lunch), 145-225, 55 (children).

AUCH   32000
Paris 716 - Toulouse 77 - Tarbes 72 - Agen 71   Gers

Daguin   🔾

2, pl. de la Libération
05 62 61 71 71, fax 05 62 61 71 81
Closed Sun dinner & Mon (exc in summer & hols), 2 wks in Jan. Open until 9:30pm (10pm in summer). Priv rm 100. Air cond. Valet pkg.
Regulars and newcomers mingle in the Napoléon III–style dining room. Chef André Daguin does all he can to keep his guests coming back, especially if they like the foie gras with its truffle sauce, which we still dream about. What we like best are the magrets (duck breast) and the confits, washed down with the local wines that Daguin knows so well. Go here when you're famished. Fabulous cellar full of choice wine and Armagnacs. C 400-600. M 185-505, 80 (children).

Hôtel de France

(See restaurant above)
Open year-round. 2 stes 1,500-2,500. 27 rms 290-970. Bkfst 80. Half-board 480-565. Rm ser. Air cond. Valet pkg.
Handsome, pleasant, well-equipped rooms for the most part, but be sure to insist on a nice room, because some of them are downright commonplace for a place of this caliber. The boutique sells regional products, including the owner's foie gras. The hotel is also home to a cooking school. Magnificent breakfasts. Relais et Châteaux.

Claude Laffitte   🔾

34-38, rue Dessoles
05 62 05 04 18, fax 05 62 61 86 85
Closed Sun dinner & Mon off-seas. Open until 10pm. Priv rm 20. Terrace dining.
It's rare to find such an esthetically pleasing rustic décor. The chef, Alain Grazide, is a master at choosing his ingredients, and he willingly explains his Gascon cuisine. Nice choice of game. The cellar has a fine collection of regional offerings, as well as of Bas-Armagnacs. Too bad that the high prices cast a chill over the warm atmosphere of the restaurant. C 230-500. M 75 (exc Sun), 125-350, 60 (children).

Le Papillon

6 km on N 21, toward Agen, Montaut-les-Créneaux
05 62 65 51 29, fax 05 62 65 54 33
Closed Wed, 1 wk in Feb, 2 wks end Aug-beg Sep. Open until 9:30pm. Priv rm 80. Terrace dining. Pkg.
There is a terrace off the contemporary dining room where you can sample interesting, down-to-earth cuisine, including stuffed sole, and puff pastry with raspberries for dessert. The wine cellar needs work, but includes lots of local wines at reasonable prices. C 260-360. M 75 (lunch, exc Sun, wine incl), 95-245, 54 (children).

 ## Le Relais de Gascogne

5, av. de la Marne - 05 62 05 26 81
Open year-round. 32 rms 260-400. Conf. No pets. Garage pkg.
This comfortable hotel, right as you go into town, offers hospital-clean, soundproofed rooms with everything you need. Highly professional, efficient service. A little indulgence is nice from time to time...

BARBOTAN-LES-THERMES　　　32150
Paris 714 - Mont-de-Marsan 43 - Condom 37　　Gers

 ## La Bastide Gasconne ❁

05 62 08 31 00, fax 05 62 08 31 49
Closed end Oct-end Mar. Open until 9:30pm. No pets. Terrace dining. Pool. Garage pkg.
This *bastide* with eighteenth-century arcades has a cozy flagstone dining room. The restaurant is a favorite with people taking the cure, who love the menu of Arnaud Lindivat, a disciple of Michel Guérard. His interesting cuisine with regional, countrified accents shows equal doses of character and know-how. The short wine list concentrates on regional offerings and Bordeaux and is wisely priced. C 150.

 ## La Bastide Gasconne ▲♥

(See restaurant above)
Closed end Oct-end Mar. 2 stes 780-1,350. 20 rms 380-690. Bkfst 66. Half-board 493-898. Rm ser. Pool. No pets. Garage pkg.
Near the spa, with pretty rooms decorated in warm, soft tones, and spacious bathrooms. The rooms overlook the park and the swimming pool of this charming old manor house. Friendly welcome.

 ## Cante Grit

51, av. des Thermes
05 62 69 52 12, fax 05 62 69 53 98
Closed Nov-Apr 10. 22 rms 165-295. Bkfst 35. Restaurant. Half-board 215-322. Conf. Pkg.
An adorable vine-covered country house. The sunny rooms look out on a marvelous flower garden with palm trees. The only thing you'll hear are the birds singing.

BEAUPOUYET　　　24400
Paris 548 - Bergerac 37 - Périgueux 37　　Dordogne

 ## Le Clos Joli

N 89 - 05 53 81 10 01
Closed Fri off-seas, Sun dinner, Feb. Open until 10:15pm. Priv rm 20. Garden dining. Pkg.
A pretty enclosed flower garden with hundred-year-old boxwood trees adds to the charms of this tastefully restored former presbytery. In the huge, comfortable dining room, Jean-Jacques Martin is a thoughtful host, and meanwhile back in the kitchen, his wife cooks up rich, authentic traditional dishes such as duck breast stuffed with cèpes, beef fillet with Pinot Noir sauce and mint and chocolate profiteroles. Not much excitement in this fare, but carefully prepared, which is enough for the moment. Interesting cellar of local wines. C 200-300. M 85 (weekdays, Sat lunch, wine incl), 115-195.

BON-ENCONTRE　　　47240
Paris 736 - Agen 4　　Lot/Garonne

 ## Mariottat ❁

41, rue de la République
05 53 96 17 75, fax 05 53 96 29 05
Closed Sun dinner, Mon. Open until 9:30pm. Priv rm 15. Terrace dining. Air cond. Pkg.
The region's gourmets frequent this lovely farmhouse-cum-restaurant with a comfortable mixutre of modern and rustic décor that manages to be romantic and charming, and a pleasant shady terrace. Every meal here provides a moment of happiness, thanks to the inspired cuisine of Éric Mariottat, which brings the best local products to life. A judiciously chosen cellar, dominated by good Southwestern vintages. Christiane Mariottat offers a wonderful welcome. C 365. M 100 (weekdays), 150-250.

Le Parc ▲♥

(See restaurant above)
Closed Sun off-seas. 10 rms 195-255. Bkfst 28. Half-board 395-420. Rm ser.
A few attractive rooms just upstairs from the restaurant decorated in country style and overflowing with charm. Superb breakfasts priced to steal. Charming reception and highly professional service.

BRANTÔME　　　24310
Paris 500 - Périgueux 27 - Angoulêmes 60　　Dordogne

 ## Les Frères Charbonnel ❁

57, rue Gambetta - 05 53 05 70 15, fax 05 53 05 71 85
Closed Sun dinner & Mon (exc hols), Feb 3-21, Nov 15-Dec 15. Open until 9pm. Priv rm 20. Terrace dining. HOTEL: 20 rms 260-400. Bkfst 45. Half-board 360-460. Conf.
The Dronne River provides inspiration for the fresh cuisine of Jean-Claude and Bernard Char-

bonnel. Based on both regional and traditional recipes, it is precise in its execution and opulent on the plate. Really good selection of fixed-price menus. The wine cellar is fit for a king and exhibits a preference for Bordeaux; the prices are far from regal—incredibly affordable. It is truly pleasant to sit here looking out at the river. C 260-500. **M** 160-210 (exc Sun), 230-400.

Moulin de l'Abbaye

1, route de Bourdeilles
05 53 05 80 22, fax 05 53 05 75 27
Closed Mon lunch, Nov 3-Apr 25. Open until 10pm. Garden dining. Garage pkg.
It might be a photo for an interior decoration magazine: a watermill with its wheel dripping with moss, a crooked bridge, weeping willows, and, in the background, a majestic abbey. Régis Bulot obviously cares about creating a model of the good life in France in every respect (he's the president of the prestigious Relais et Châteaux): service, welcome, decoration, and, of course, cuisine, which treats with equal ease both regional and international recipes. So he has carefully choosen the new chef, Jean-Christophe Perrin, who has worked with Troisgros and Rostang in the past. But the change comes too close to printing time, we haven't had a chance to try the cuisine. We'll keep you posted... **M** 220, 290, 450.

 Moulin de l'Abbaye

(See restaurant above)
Closed Nov 1-Apr 25. 3 stes 1,100-1,350. 17 rms 650-800. Bkfst 75. Rms for disabled. Half-board 800-950. Rm ser. Air cond. Garage pkg.
Cross the bridge to find this riverside hotel whose beautiful rooms have exposed beams and pretty furnishings. There are also rooms in the Moulin and the Maison du Meunier, where you will feel right at home. The absolute summit of waterside hotels. The garage is in former cave dwellings. Relais et Châteaux.

BRAX	47310
Paris 735 - Agen 8	Lot/Garonne

 ## La Renaissance de l'Étoile 🖸

Route de Mont-de-Marsan
05 53 68 69 23, fax 05 53 68 62 89
Closed 1 wk at Feb school hols. Open until 9:30pm. Garden dining. Garage pkg.
Set in a lovely park, this restaurant in a manor house has a cheerful, well-kept décor and a flower-filled garden. Unfortunately, Yves Gruel has passed away and Pascal Friedly is trying to continue in his footsteps with a generous market cuisine that reinterprets regional specialties in interesting, light dishes with delicate flavors such as veal sweetbread fricassée served with bay scallops and morels, and burbot steak with a thin pancake chiffonade served with chicory-flavored soya. The cheese platter is a work of art, and the impressive wine list is rich in the *grands*

crus of the Southwest. The atmosphere and service are both suffering from the loss, but that is understandable. C 300-350. **M** 105 (exc Sat lunch & Sun), 169 (Sat lunch), 195, 305.

CAHORS	46000
Paris 590 - Agen 91 - Montauban 60	Lot

 ## Le Balandre

5, av. Charles-de-Freycinet
05 65 30 01 97, fax 05 65 22 06 40
Closed Sun dinner & Mon (exc Jul-Aug). Open until 10pm. Terrace dining. Priv rm 15. Air cond. No pets. Garage pkg.
Wainscoting and stained-glass windows form the perfect high-style setting for a gastronomic rest stop. Diners here are treated like old friends. Gilles Marre is one of those chefs for whom respect for his customers goes hand-in-hand with respect for his ingredients. He takes a few detours from his classic, traditional cuisine, as in the melon gazpacho with duck "ham" and almond oil, or the beef fillet with lime. Lovely desserts, including crème cuite with three flavorings. The well-stocked cellar is rich in local vintages, namely Cahors. Everything here is designed to please. C 280-300. **M** 150 (dinner), 170 (weekday lunch, Sat, wine incl), 240-350.

Hôtel Terminus

(See restaurant above)
Open year-round. 1 ste 800-950. 21 rms 300-600. Bkfst 50-90. Rm ser. Conf. No pets. Garage pkg.
The rooms, bar, and reception area of this hotel were completely renovated in 1995, and the result is pleasant and unpretentious. Rooms are well appointed and equipped. Family-run with a sense of tradition. Good quality for the price.

CARDAILLAC	46100
Paris 569 - Cahors 71 - Figeac 9	Lot

12/20 Chez Marcel 🖸

05 65 40 11 16
Closed Mon. Open until 8:30pm. Priv rm 150.
Every Sunday a long line of cars parks outside this bar-restaurant furnished with handsome antiques, paintings, and religious objects. The friendly owner offers traditional dishes followed by uninteresting desserts. Good Cahors wines at reasonable prices. Good C 80. **M** 120, 80-170 (exc Sun lunch), 55 (children).

CARENNAC	46110
Paris 534 - Cahors 94 - Brive 37	Lot

11/20 Auberge du Vieux Quercy

05 65 10 96 59, fax 05 65 10 94 05
Closed Sun dinner & Mon off-seas, Nov 15-Mar 15. Open until 9:30pm. Priv rm 50. Terrace dining. Pool. Pkg.
Contemporary paintings lend charm to this large modern dining room, where the *patronne*

welcomes hungry regular customers and tourists. They are soon restored with generous servings of classic and local cuisine that is not always perfectly executed but is sincere and reasonably priced. C 180-300. M 90-195.

 ## Auberge du Vieux Quercy

(See restaurant above)
Closed Sun & Mon off-seas, Nov 15-Mar 15. 22 rms 260-350. Bkfst 40. Half-board 310-330 (oblig in seas). Rm ser. Conf. Pool. Pkg.
Most of the simply decorated and comfortably equipped rooms with handsome lithographs have a superb view of the beautiful old village. Perhaps a little too modern for the medieval setting, but peace reigns. Thoughtful service.

CASTÉRA-VERDUZAN	32410
Paris 774 - Toulouse 100 - Auch 23 - Agen 60	Gers

 ## Le Florida

05 62 68 13 22, fax 05 62 68 10 44
Closed Sun dinner & Mon off-seas, Wed, Feb. Open until 9:30pm. Priv rm 60. Terrace dining. HOTEL: 25 rms 178-230. Bkfst 32. Half-board 182-192. Conf. Pkg.
An attractive white building with a dining room warmly decorated in country style and a shady, flower-filled terrace. Don't hesitate to ask Bernard Ramounéda about the history of Gascony. This local boy is also a highly professional chef, who turns out regional dishes that are tasty and sincere and so cherished by the locals. Fine local wines and Armagnacs. Friendly welcome. We're awarding him another point. C 250-350. M 70-135 (weekdays, Sat lunch), 140-190 (Sat dinner, Sun), 200, 70 (children).

CASTILLONNÈS	47330
Paris 585 - Agen 66 - Bergerac 27	Lot/Garonne

 ## Hôtel des Remparts

Rue de la Paix - 05 53 36 80 97, fax 05 53 36 93 87
Closed Sun dinner & Mon off-seas, Jan, Nov. Open until 9:30pm. Priv rm 45. Terrace dining. Pkg.
On the ramparts of this gorgeous village, Anne-Marie Gœrn's lovely old house with a pleasant terrace has been restored and decorated in sunny colors. The friendly staff creates a homey atmosphere. Her husband Ulrich took over the cooking two years ago; he produces a Mediterranean-influenced cuisine full of subtle flavors: tuna carpaccio, salmon and zucchini ramekins, Pyrenees lamb served with rosemary-flavored jus, and cherry soup with cinnamon and blackcurrant liqueur. Passable wine list. C 280-300. M 150 (weekday lunch, Sat), 160, 195.

 ## Hôtel des Remparts

(See restaurant above)
Closed Sun & Mon off-seas, Jan, Nov. 10 rms 320-480. Bkfst 50. Half-board 330-375. Rm ser. Pkg.

Near the twelfth-century *bastide* in a little park with hundred-year-old trees, this venerable hotel has spacious, well-kept rooms, most of which have a pretty view of the valley and the rooftops of the old town.

CAZAUBON	32150
Paris 739 - Auch 63 - Barbotan-les-Thermes 3	Gers

Château Bellevue

Rue Jean-Cappin - 05 62 09 51 95, fax 05 62 09 54 57
Closed Jan 2-Feb 15. Open until 9:30pm. Priv rm 40. Terrace dining. Pool. No pets. Garage pkg.
The terrace and the peaceful, luminous dining room, with its polished furniture and elegant draperies, both have lovely views of the château's park. Ms. Consolaro offers high-quality food with an original touch, with offerings such as zucchini terrine with lamb's sweetbreads and shrimp and salmon trout fillet roll with olives or tasty Pyrenees lamb. Lovely desserts. Nice local vintages in the cellar. Friendly welcome and highly professional service. A toque well earned. C 250. M 100-155.

 ## Château Bellevue

(See restaurant above)
Closed Jan 2-Feb 15. 2 stes 700. 21 rms 550. Bkfst 50-75. Rms for disabled. Half-board 300-420. Conf. Pool. No pets. Garage pkg.
In its beautiful, peaceful park, a splendid nineteenth-century residence with huge, well-equipped, tastefully decorated rooms that give onto the park, pool, or courtyard. Bar, sitting rooms. Many sporting activities nearby.

CHANCELADE	24650
Paris 523 - Périgueux 6	Dordogne

 ## Château des Reynats

Av. des Reynats - 05 53 03 53 59, fax 05 53 03 44 84
Closed Mon lunch in summer, Tue lunch off-seas, Feb-Mar 9. Open until 9:30pm. Terrace dining. Pool. Tennis. Garage pkg.
Régis Chirozas must be feeling tired, or in any case uninspired. Even the exquisite light fixtures and the thoroughly bourgeois décor are not enough to make this meal seem up to par. Everything is not lost however: the assorted broiled fish platter was perfection itself, even though the pigeon cooked in honey was bland. The most deceptive part was the 180 F fixed-price menu which is, frankly, not worth more than a very small toque. Brigitte Chiorozas looks over the service with the same professionalism and good humor as always, but the kitchen doesn't parallel this. Respectable selection of wines with some well-priced local ones. C 330. M 135 (exc Sun, wine incl), 180-350.

Château des Reynats

(See restaurant above)
*Closed Feb-Mar 9. 5 stes 750. 32 rms 450-590. Bkfst
50-85. Rms for disabled. Half-board 460-610. Conf.
Pool. Tennis. Garage pkg.*
A stone's throw from the golf course, a lovely
nineteenth-century château that has been carefully renovated. Spacious rooms. Tennis court
and swimming pool in the shade of the park's
trees. In-room meal trays on request.

CONDOM	32100
Paris 680 - Auch 43 - Agen 38 - Toulouse 110	Gers

 ## Le Logis
des Cordeliers

2 bis, rue de la Paix
05 62 28 03 68, fax 05 62 68 29 03
Closed Jan. 21 rms 260-330. Bkfst 38. Pool. Pkg.
Far from the madding crowds, a charming
Gascon hotel set within the walls of an abbey. Its
rooms have sheltered loggias next to the swim-
ming pool. Meals are served in the shady garden.
Lovely breakfasts.

12/20 Le Moulin
du Petit Gascon

Route d'Eauze - 05 62 28 28 42
*Closed Mon (exc Jul-Aug), Dec-Mar. Open until
9:30pm (10:30pm in summer). Terrace dining. Pkg.*
Pleasure boats cruise through the water as
diners watch from the two lovely covered terraces of this light-filled restaurant. In this not-al-
ways friendly ambience, they savor fresh,
pleasing traditional dishes inspired by regional
recipes. Good local wines, especially the
Madirans from Brumont. C 180-280. M 70 (weekday lunch, wine incl), 90 (exc Sat dinner, Sun),
115-180, 50 (children).

 ## Hôtel des Trois Lys

38, rue Gambetta
05 62 28 33 33, fax 05 62 28 41 85
*Closed Feb. 10 rms 260-560. Bkfst 42. Rms for
disabled. Restaurant. Half-board 332-422. Conf.
Pool. Pkg.*
In the center of town, a superb eighteenth-century town house with spacious, extremely comfortable, beautifully decorated rooms. Friendly
service and perfect breakfasts. Unbeatable value.

DOMME	24250
Paris 555 - Périgueux 75 - Sarlat 12	Dordogne

 ## L'Esplanade

05 53 28 31 41, fax 05 53 28 49 92
*Closed Mon lunch (May-Jun & Sep-Oct), Nov 3-Feb
14. Open until 9:15pm. Terrace dining.*
The marvelous panoramic view of the Dordogne River from this elegant, antique-furnished dining room will make you forget the
food for a little while. But you will soon be
distracted by the recipes perfected by René Gillard and prepared by Pascal Bouland, who treat

rich regional ingredients with great delicacy.
Unfortunately these costly products also inflate
the bill. The first fixed-price menu is a good bet.
A well-diversified wine list, especially rich in
Cahors and Bergeracs. C 350-550. M 160-350.

 ## L'Esplanade

(See restaurant above)
*Closed Nov 3-Feb 14. 1 ste 800. 24 rms 300-590.
Bkfst 50. Half-board 380-525.*
In the heart of the medieval village, a homey
hotel with quiet rooms that are regularly
renovated. Some have gorgeous views over the
park and the Dordogne Valley.

EYZIES-DE-TAYAC (LES)	24620
Paris 550 - Périgueux 50 - Sarlat 20	Dordogne

17 Le Centenaire

Le Rocher de la Penne
05 53 06 68 68, fax 05 53 06 92 41
*Closed Tue lunch, Nov-Mar. Open until 9:30pm.
Garden dining. Air cond. Heated pool. Tennis. Pkg.*
At the entrance to the village, behind a stone
wall, sits an old inn with a bright dining room
and a courtyard for summer meals. Chef Roland
Mazère has rethought the cuisine of the
Périgord. His fixed-price menu at 295 F is a god-
send; starters include salmon tartare, and goose
sausages and rillettes. There is also a pleasing
vegetable terrine with foie gras and goose confit.
The flavors of a just-caught sole blossom in its
lightly spiced bouillon, which rivals the delicate
and original composition of hake poached with
chestnuts and oysters. The rabbit coated with
powdered cèpes is tender, highly flavorful, and
perfectly cooked. The cheese platter included
many regional chèvres, and the dessert cart offered a well-executed, classic selection. You'll
think you've found true happiness in this atmosphere full of *joie de vivre* The stellar wine list is
commented by an impressive British sommelier,
Tim Harrison, but you can't go wrong with the
very good 1990 Château Richard Bergerac, at
160 F. Wide selection of half-bottles. C 400-500.
M 155 (lunch, exc hols), 295, 420, 520.

Le Centenaire

(See restaurant above)
*Closed Nov-Mar. 4 stes 900-1,300. 20 rms 450-700.
Bkfst 80. Half-board 565-820. Rm ser. Air cond.
Conf. Heated pool. Tennis. Pkg.*
The village is most enjoyable in the evening,
when the hordes of tourists have left and you can
finally take advantage of the comfort of this well-
renovated old inn with its pretty rooms or take
a lovely walk along the river. Relais et Châteaux.

14 Cro Magnon

05 53 06 97 06, fax 05 53 06 95 45
*Closed Wed lunch, Oct 10-beg May. Open until
9:15pm. Priv rm 20. Garden dining. HOTEL: 4 stes*

650-800. 18 rms 350-550. Bkfst 50. Half-board 380-505. Heated pool. Pkg.

Our famed ancestor, Cro-Magnon man, was first discovered at this very site. He would probably have preferred the cozy charm of this antique-furnished, softly lit dining room to his cold, rocky cave. The delicate, precise, traditional cuisine of Xavier Davoust makes intelligent use of the flavors of fresh ingredients. Particularly nice choice of Bordeaux at affordable prices. Warm, courteous welcome from the Leyssales. **M** 140-350, 60 (children).

 Au Vieux Moulin

05 53 06 93 39, fax 05 53 06 98 06
Closed Tue lunch, Jan 2-beg Mar. Open until 9:30pm. Terrace dining. Pkg.

This old mill at the foot of a cliff, with views of the Beune River from its pretty terrace, has charm to spare. The sober modern décor of the dining room is not unpleasant, but the real enjoyment is provided by what is on your plate. Georges Soulié's interesting cuisine is dominated by clever flavor associations, but remains influenced by his region. Incredibly large selection à la carte, but the fixed-price menus are rather skimpy in comparison. Small, well-diversified cellar with emphasis on Cahors and Bergeracs at reasonable prices. **C** 290-430. **M** 170 (wine incl), 95-280, 50 (children).

 Moulin de la Beune

05 53 06 94 33, fax 05 53 06 98 06
Closed end Nov-beg Apr. 20 rms 260-400. Bkfst 40. Half-board 320-420. Rm ser. Pkg.

Next the Museum of Prehistory, a pleasant hotel with large, prettily decorated rooms that look out on greenery and the river.

FIGEAC	46100
Paris 559 - Cahors 71 - Aurillac 67 - Tulle 103	Lot

 La Dînée du Viguier

4, rue Boutaric - 05 65 50 08 08, fax 05 65 50 09 09
Closed Oct-Apr: Sun dinner & Mon; May-Sep: Mon lunch. Annual closings not available. Open until 9:30pm. Terrace dining. Air cond. No pets.

This medieval structure, finished only in the eighteenth century, and listed as a national landmark, is full of charm. The conversion into a hotel has produced both a piece of architecture and an atmosphere which are harmonious. The reception and service are friendly and natural, in full Quercy tradition. The food is sometimes lacking in precision but is clearly working toward improvement. We liked the duck liver cooked in a cauldron served with a lamb compote, the scallop and Dublin bay prawn puff pastry with asparagus, and the pigeon and morel mushroom tourte. Cellar needs work. **C** 300. **M** 130, 195, 60 (children).

Prices for rooms and suites *are per room, not per person. Half-board prices, however, are per person.*

 Château du Viguier du Roy

Rue Droite - 05 65 50 05 05, fax 05 65 50 06 06
Open year-round. 4 stes 1,350-3,750. 17 rms 570-1,250. Rms for disabled. Restaurant (see above). Air cond. Conf. Pool. Valet pkg.

A marvelous twelfth-century complex with a Gothic chapel, cloister, and interior gardens. Immense, medieval–style rooms have stone walls, period woodwork, and four-poster beds.

 La Puce à l'Oreille

5, rue Saint-Thomas - 05 65 34 33 08
Closed Sun dinner & Mon off-seas. Open until 9:30pm. Terrace dining.

In the old town, a venerable restaurant on a narrow street. The cuisine warms the hearts of the locals with salmon charlotte, duck brochettes, and prune mousse. Judicious choice of regional wines. Friendly welcome and service. A winner! **C** 200. **M** 85 (exc Sun), 130-250, 50 (children).

FRANCESCAS	47600
Paris 731 - Agen 31 - Condom 21	Lot/Garonne

 Le Relais de la Hire

11, rue Porte-Neuve
05 53 65 41 59, fax 05 53 65 86 42
Closed Sun dinner, Mon. Open until 10pm. Priv rm 20. Terrace dining. Tennis. Pkg.

This handsome 200-year-old manor house has two beautiful dining rooms and a terrace. Step into chef Jean-Noël Prabonne's world of herbs and condiments where he treats regional products with ingenuity. His basic premise is to produce authentic dishes brimming over with flavor and "truffled" with fascinating ideas. Examples are the sumptuous Albret artichoke with its foie gras soufflé or the multi-flavored fish served in bouillon. The chocolate-based desserts are a real wonder. The fine 165 F fixed-price menu is recommended. Delightful welcome and irreproachable service. All this adds up to an extra point. Superb wine list with a majority of local offerings. There is a wide choice of wines by the glass, but not enough half-bottles. **C** 215. **M** 115 (weekdays), 165-255, 70 (children).

GIMONT	32200
Paris 820 - Toulouse 51 - Auch 24	Gers

Château de Larroque

Route de Toulouse
05 62 67 77 44, fax 05 62 67 88 90
Closed Sun & Mon off-seas, Jan-Feb. 1 ste 1,300. 14 rms 480-1,080. Bkfst 70. Restaurant. Half-board 580-800 (oblig in seas). Rm ser. Conf. Pool. Tennis. Garage pkg.

In a peaceful 50-acre park, a sumptuous Second Empire château with stylish, comfortable, contemporary rooms. All have terraces and marble bathrooms. Fishing on a private pond.

GRAMAT 46500
Paris 524 - Figeac 35 - Cahors 57 - Brive 56 Lot

 Le Lion d'Or

8, pl. République
05 65 38 73 18, fax 05 65 38 84 50
*Closed Dec 15-Jan 15. Open until 9:15pm. Priv rm
20. Terrace dining. Air cond. Pkg.*
Some people never get away from their roots.
I think we can safely say this about René Mommejac now that he's turned sixty! His Quercy-inspired fixed-price menu is proof of this: escargots stewed with cèpes, confit duck leg with sorrel chiffonade, artisanal cabécou (the local goat's cheese), and frozen nougat with walnut praline and aged prune alcohol. It's lovely to sit on the terrace among the wisteria covering the lovely stone façade when the weather permits. C 250-300. M 100-300.

 Le Lion d'Or

(See restaurant above)
*Closed Dec 15-Jan 15. 15 rms 270-420. Bkfst 45.
Half-board 300-330 (oblig in seas). Air cond. Pkg.*
Arbors and old stones: that's what you find at this old pony-express station. You can't beat the charm of the rooms, but the functional aspect is a bit on the light side.

LACAVE 46200
Paris 540 - Cahors 65 - Rocamadour 10 Lot

 **Château
de la Treyne**

05 65 27 60 60, fax 05 65 27 60 70
*Closed Tue lunch & Wed lunch (exc Jul-Aug), Nov
15-end Mar. Open until 10pm. Priv rm 40. Garden
dining. Air cond. Heated pool. Tennis. Valet pkg.*
This is a real château, built between the fourteenth and seventeenth centuries and splendidly renovated. Laurent Clément's cooking, however, is very up to date, with an astounding variety of flavors. Fennel, tomatoes, and star anise bring out the best in pike perch. Try the cod with mild Cantal cheese, the Provençal vegetable gratin, and lamb fillet with juniper berries. The real standout on the menu is pigeon stuffed with endives and walnuts, served with stewed lentils and calamari. The well-chosen wine list includes both rare vintages and more affordable offerings, as well as a good choice of half-bottles. C 390-500. M 180 (lunch, wine incl), 120-220 (lunch), 280-380, 80 (children).

 **Château
de la Treyne** 🌲🌷

(See restaurant above)
*Closed Nov 15-end Mar. 2 stes 1,600-1,800. 12 rms
700-1,600. Bkfst 80. Half-board 360 (oblig in seas).
Rm ser. Air cond. Heated pool. Tennis. Valet pkg.*
Surrounded by greenery, this château is built on a rock overlooking the Dordogne River. Each room has its own special charm and the

bathrooms are purely and simply a dream! None of the modern comforts have been forgotten: you can have a meal served to you while you recline in your four-poster bed, take a dip in the pool, or enjoy an invigorating tennis game. Romanesque chapel, beautiful walks in the woods, fireplace in the drawing rooms: is this reality? Relais et Châteaux.

 Pont de l'Ouysse 😃

05 65 37 87 04, fax 05 65 32 77 41
*Closed Mon lunch (& dinner off-seas), Jan-beg Mar,
mid Nov-Dec 15. Open until 9:30pm. Priv rm 40.
Garden dining. Heated pool. Pkg.*
A the foot of the Château de Belcastel, between the cliff and the river and near the Lacave grottoes, this is one of the most enchanting places in Haut Quercy. Daniel Chambon's cooking is full of flavors and imagination: homemade foie gras is offered in an artichoke millefeuille with truffle sauce or in a Monbazillac aspic; eels come in sauce poulette or with verjuice and corn bread; kid fricassée is accented with garlic, parsley, and baby vegetables; and a chocolate tart is lavished with barley-sugar cream. Good choice of Bergeracs and Cahors. The service is good in the pale-pink dining room or under the chestnut trees on the terrace. C 400. M 160-490.

 Pont de l'Ouysse 🌲🌷

(See restaurant above)
*Closed Jan-beg Mar, mid Nov-Dec 15. 2 stes 600-
750. 12 rms 350-600. Bkfst 60. Half-board 650-700.
Heated pool. Pkg.*
Rooms decorated in spring colors, with bright bathrooms. The mornings are lovely above the Ouysse River, which has newly installed walking trails along its banks.

LALINDE 24150
Paris 574 - Cahors 90 - Périgueux 60 Dordogne

 Hôtel du Château

1, rue de Verdun - 05 53 61 01 82, fax 05 53 24 74 60
*Closed Sun dinner off-seas, Mon (exc lunch Jul-
Aug), Jan, 3rd wk of Sep. Open until 9pm. Terrace
dining. Pool. Pkg.*
Once used as a prison, this little château built in the thirteenth century and rebuilt in the nineteenth has been turned into a pleasant stopping place, thanks to the efforts of Guy Gensou. The traditional cuisine with regional inspirations is ably prepared and full of honest flavors. The small cellar concentrates on local offerings. In the summer, there are poolside barbecues. C 300-400. M 105 (weekday lunch), 165-220.

 Hôtel du Château

(See restaurant above)
*Closed Sun off-seas, Jan, 3rd wk of Sep. 1 ste 850. 6
rms 270-670. Bkfst 65. Half-board 320-620 (oblig
in seas). Pool. Pkg.*
Some rooms have a pretty view over the Dordogne River, and all have been recently redecorated in good taste. Well-equipped

bathrooms. Weekend packages. Friendly welcome.

LAMAGDELAINE   46090
Paris 594 - Cahors 7   Lot

 Marco   𝄐

05 65 35 30 64, fax 05 65 30 31 40
Closed Sun dinner & Mon off-seas, Jan 6-Mar 6, Oct 20-29. Open until 9:30pm. Terrace dining. Pool. Pkg.
Claude Marco offers his customers a cuisine full of flavors and aromas. His refined classicism is enriched with a touch of originality. In the handsome vaulted cellar of his ivy-covered restaurant, sample the superb and perfectly cooked line-caught bass with saffron, the subtly delicious artichoke braised with cèpes and served with pan-fried foie gras, the very good cheeses, and the large dessert platter that will have you licking your fingers. The wine list is nothing special, aside from a good selection of local vintages. The welcome and service are friendly and efficient. **C** 300-430. **M** 130 (weekdays), 200, 220, 75 (children).

Marco   🌲🎐
(See restaurant above)
Closed Sun & Mon off-seas, Jan 6-Mar 6, Oct 20-29. 1 ste 650. 3 rms 480-550. Bkfst 50. Pool. Pkg.
A few large rooms full of the sweet things in life. Bathrooms all have hydrotherapy equipment. An inn away from the hustle and bustle of this touristic region, and that welcomes you warmly.

LASCABANES   46800
Paris 612 - Cahors 18 - Moissac 45   Lot

12/20 La Petite Auberge   𝄐

Domaine de Saint-Géry
05 65 31 82 51, fax 05 65 22 92 89
Closed Mon, Tue, Jan 10-Mar 15. Open until 10:30pm. No pets. HOTEL: 1 ste 680. 5 rms 200-450. Bkfst 70. Half-board 360-600. Conf. Heated pool. Pkg.
A seventeenth-century hamlet that is coming back to life thanks to this old farmhouse with its gardens, antique bread oven, and regional foods boutique. The same ingredients go into the flavorful regional cuisine prepared by the owner with skill and imagination. **M** 120 (exc Sun lunch), 165, 350.

LECTOURE   32700
Paris 700 - Agen 36 - Condom 23 - Toulouse 94   Gers

 Hôtel de Bastard   𝄐

Rue Lagrange - 05 62 68 82 44, fax 05 62 68 76 81
Closed Jan. Open until 9:30pm. Priv rm 60. Terrace dining. Pool. Pkg.
A serene, luxurious atmosphere emanates from this beautiful eighteenth-century town house. Its dining room, with a charming, refined

pastel décor, still has its original flooring. The terrace looks out on the countryside. Good regional produce inspires the generous cuisine of Jean-Luc Arnaud, who marries delicate flavors in unusual ways. A comprehensive wine list. Smiling welcome. **C** 300. **M** 85-24.

 Hôtel de Bastard   🌲🎐
(See restaurant above)
Closed Jan. 2 stes 550-650. 27 rms 190-350. Bkfst 40. Half-board 260-350 (oblig in seas). Rm ser. Conf. Pool. Pkg.
Some of the well-kept rooms in this superb town house were renovated last year, and the ones on the second floor have mansard roofs. Terrace and garden. Friendly welcome. Good breakfasts.

MARMANDE   47200
Paris 684 - Agen 58 - Bordeaux 89   Lot/Garonne

 Le Trianon

Route d'Agen, N 113 - 05 53 20 80 94 (R)
05 53 64 16 14 (H), fax 05 53 20 80 18
Closed Sat lunch, Sun, 1st week Jan. Open until 9:30pm (10pm in summer). Priv rm 60. Terrace dining. Air cond. HOTEL: 34 rms 260-280. Rms for disabled. Closed 2 wks end Dec-beg Jan. Half-board 220-320. Rm ser. Air cond. Pool. Garage pkg.
Escape from the drab modern neighborhood into the pleasant dining room decorated in pastel colors, where you will receive a warm welcome from Patricia Arbeau. Her husband, Thierry, skillfully prepares his sauces and vegetables, but he seems to have lost his golden thumb when it comes to the rest. The crab sauce for the fish fricassée was delicious; the broiled quail was cooked to perfection and its herb cream sauce was a pure delight; but the little red peppers simply overwhelmed the lobster salad, and the apples in the apple pie were highly acidic. The real advantage to this restaurant is the quantity you get for your money. We probably don't know a place that gives more generous helpings than this. In addition, some dishes can be ordered in half-portions for half-price! Reasonably priced cellar. **C** 220. **M** 78 (weekdays), 98-220.

MERCUÈS   46090
Paris 583 - Toulouse 102 - Cahors 7   Lot

 **Château de Mercuès**   𝄐

05 65 20 00 01, fax 05 65 20 05 72
Closed Wed (exc Jul-Aug), Nov-Easter. Open until 10pm. Priv rm 80. Terrace dining. Pool. Tennis. No pets. Valet pkg.
Philippe Combet continues to enjoy his culinary explorations, which show his love for quality ingredients. Try the creamy crab soup, spider crab with cèpe ravioli, and scallops with truffles. The chef, who learned his trade at L'-Oasis, also serves local products like tender farm ham, goose, and lamb with garlic cream. Excellent list of local Cahors wines, including one belonging to the owner Georges Vigouroux. The

service is on a par with the majestic setting. We hear that Dussau is to take over the Pont-Napoléon in Moissac. C 380. M 180-200 (exc Sun, wine incl), 195-420, 120 (children).

Château de Mercuès

(See restaurant above)
Closed Nov-Easter. 6 stes 1,350-1,950. 24 rms 700-1,500. Bkfst 80. Rms for disabled. Half-board 990-1,790. Rm ser. Conf. Pool. Tennis. Valet pkg.

How can we describe in a few lines the grandeur of the site and the architecture, with all their charms and refinement? Perched on a cliff overlooking the Lot Valley, where the bishops of Cahors once lived, this hotel has sumptuously furnished rooms, a covered walkway, and a watchtower. The rooms have four-poster beds, sumptuous bathrooms and antique furniture. Suspended pool and tennis court tucked into the verdure. Relais et Châteaux.

MEYRONNE	46200
Paris 532 - Cahors 76 - Rocamadour 14	Lot

La Terrasse

05 65 32 21 60, fax 05 65 32 26 93
Closed Nov 15-Mar 1. Open until 9:30pm. Priv rm 50. Terrace dining. HOTEL: 2 stes 500. 15 rms 260-400. Bkfst 40. Half-board 270-350. Pool. Pkg.

Overlooking the Dordogne Valley, a small château where chef Gilles Liebus reigns. He stays firmly in the tradition of the Quercy region with his duck- and truffle-based dishes. Too bad that only the 180 F fixed-price meal is worth the money. You'll immediately be given to ordering à la carte, which will give you a good sampling of regional dishes but also a hefty bill. Charming welcome and helpful, friendly service. The cellar holds a good selection of Cahors wines and some very good old Bordeaux. C 200-260. M 75 (lunch, exc Sun), 100-260, 50 (children).

MONPAZIER	24540
Paris 573 - Périgueux 80 - Sarlat 50	Dordogne

La Bastide

52, rue St-Jacques - 05 53 22 60 59, fax 05 53 22 09 20
Closed Mon off-seas, Feb 1-Mar 1. Open until 10pm.

One of the 100 most beautiful villages in France is the home of this marvelous thirteenth-century *bastide* built by the English. Gérard Prigent, the jovial owner, is from Brittany, but Périgord inspires the dishes served in the huge rustic dining room. He cooks with as much enthusiasm as skill and serves in generous portions specialties like chopped liver infused with truffles, and duck with apples and green grapes. C 250-350. M 80 (wine incl), 140-240, 40 (children).

Looking for a town or restaurant? A winery? A gastronomic specialty or a celebrated chef? Consult the alphabetical index to locate them quickly and easily.

MONTIGNAC	24290
Paris 525 - Brive 38 - Sarlat 25 - Limoges 102	Dordogne

Château de Puy Robert

1.5 km S on D 65 - 05 53 51 92 13, fax 05 53 51 80 11
Closed Wed lunch, Oct 17-May 1. Open until 9:30pm. Priv rm 20. Air cond. Pool. Garage pkg.

A fifteen-minute walk from Lascaux 2 (the replica of the original Lascaux caves), a Napoléon III-era château furnished with antiques. Olivier Pons offers dishes that are neither too refined nor too ordinary, influenced by regional tradition but sparked with original ideas: chicken with pinenuts and mixed greens with sesame seeds, pan-fried mullet and duck foie gras. Fine cellar, with a wide range of vintages and prices. C 450-500. M 190-415.

Château de Puy Robert

(See restaurant above)
Closed Oct 17-May 1. 5 stes 1,300-1,700. 33 rms 650-1,050. Bkfst 80. Half-board 750-1,260 (oblig in seas). Air cond. Conf. Pool. Garage pkg.

You can pretend you are the lord of the manor in these rooms with varied décor. In the modern building, balconies overlook the swimming pool. Comfort is on the agenda, the staff is always there when you need them and never when you don't, and what a dream to behold, the breakfasts. Tasteful as well. Relais et Châteaux.

Le Relais du Soleil d'Or

16, rue du 4-Septembre
05 53 51 80 22, fax 05 53 50 27 54
Closed Sun & Mon off-seas. 4 stes 540-820. 28 rms 250-405. Bkfst 55. Rms for disabled. Restaurant. Half-board 345-540 (oblig in seas). Rm ser. Conf. Pool. Pkg.

In a superb park with age-old trees, huge, pleasantly decorated, comfortable rooms. Charming welcome.

MUSSIDAN	24400
Paris 549 - Bergerac 25 - Angoulême 84	Dordogne

Le Chaufourg

05 53 81 01 56, fax 05 53 82 94 87
Open year-round. 2 stes 1,400-1,550. 8 rms 630-1,150. Bkfst 75. Conf. Heated pool. Pkg.

Set next to a romantic island, this pretty house has been transformed into an extremely refined hotel by a former fashion photographer, Georges Dambier. The elegant rooms have big white beds, and the magnificent garden is graced with rose bushes and hundred-year-old trees. Music room. Mosaic swimming pool. Calm and harmony.

PÉRIGUEUX 24000
Paris 528 - Bordeaux 120 - Limoges 101   Dordogne

12/20 Les Berges de l'Isle

2, rue Pierre-Magne - 05 53 09 51 50
Closed Sat lunch, Sun. Open until 10pm. Terrace dining. Air cond.
A charmless hotel hides a discreetly warm dining room with a pretty view of the old town. New owner Jean-François Parisis owns another well known restaurant in the region (L'Auberge du Coq Rouge), and he has brought the same repertory here. The problem is that some of the dishes are completely botched; he just can't seem to get things together in this new kitchen for the moment. A beautiful but costly slice of pan-fried foie gras, good veal tripes and an original lavender-flavored crème cuite still make us forget the blandness of the oversalted three-meat cassoulet and the other dishes that were overcooked. C 220-380. M 87 (lunch), 98-230, 72 (children).

 Le 8

8, rue de la Clarté - 05 53 35 15 15
Closed Sat lunch, Sun, Jul. Open until 9:30pm. Priv rm 20. Terrace dining.
Near the Saint-Front cathedral, the gray and blue tones of the windows of this restaurant give a welcoming look to the stone façade. After the highly professional welcome by Madame Delpey, you will savor dishes like the most wonderfully-textured two-foie gras plate or the cod steak, cooked to absolute perfection, and served with delicious hot oysters. The latter dish encouraged us to look toward a second toque. Very interesting assortment of cheeses and an excellent crème brûlée. Short wine list selected by the woman of the house. C 250-300. M 100 (weekday lunch, wine incl), 150-400.

POUDENAS 47170
Paris 738 - Agen 55 - Monts-de-Marsan 67   Lot/Garonne

 Moulin
de la Belle Gasconne 🕄

05 53 65 71 58, fax 05 53 65 87 39
Closed Sun dinner & Mon (exc Jul-Aug & hols), Jan 6-Feb 12. Open until 9:30pm (exc by reserv). Garden dining. Pool. Pkg.
An ancient mill on the Gélise River that is irresistible in itself. The lovely dining room has stone walls and views over the river and the Roman bridge, and the flower-bedecked tables are set around the millstone. The most important charm of the place, however, is the cuisine of Marie-Claude Gracia. Her creamy leek and mushroom pie is light yet rustic, the roast pigeon with vegetables is rich in flavor, and the pork stew with sauce noire (made of wine and blood) gives off a heavenly aroma. Charming, efficient welcome and service, an unbeatable atmosphere and *savoir-vivre*. This girl is destined to be a star. Priced to please. The only drawback is the lack

of half-bottles on the wine list. C 300-400. M 180-285.

A la Belle Gasconne 🏮

(See restaurant above)
Closed Jan 6-Feb 12. 1 ste 650. 6 rms 380-570. Bkfst 55. Half-board 590-660. Conf. Pool. Pkg.
There are only a few rooms in this charming refuge. Try to get one that has a view on the Gélise River. All the rooms are personalized and equipped with remarkable bathrooms.

PUJOLS 47300
Paris 620 - Agen 33 - Villeneuve-sur-Lot 4   Lot/Garonne

Auberge Lou Calel

05 53 70 46 14, fax 05 53 70 49 79
Closed Tue dinner, Wed (exc Aug), Jan 3-17, Oct 16-30. Open until 9:45pm. Terrace dining. Pkg.
This pleasant annex of La Toque Blanche has two terraces with a splendid view of the valley and a bright dining room decorated with antique country furniture. The young chef, Jean-Bernard Jugnon, serves attractive, generous helpings of his personalized traditional cuisine. Everything's fine here, don't change a thing! The cellar holds interesting Bordeaux and regional wines. Professional welcome and service. C 260. M 85 (weekdays), 120-200, 70 (children).

La Toque Blanche

05 53 49 00 30, fax 05 53 70 49 79
Closed Sun, Mon (exc lunch in Aug), Feb 17-Mar 3, Jun 23-30. Open until 9:45pm. Priv rm 50. Garden dining. Air cond. Pkg.
Last year, Bernard Lebrun celebrated his fifteenth anniversary as the chef at this pretty village restaurant, where he settled down after working in restaurants all over France. His highly developed cuisine has found a perfect home in this region with its generous flavors. In season, cèpes and other wild mushrooms can be found on the menu, and the veal fillets, sweetbreads, and kidneys are eternal favorites. Add to that an impressive cellar that is rich in regional wines, including a Buzet (Château de Gueze) or a Duras (Domaine de Durand) at 130 F and 140 F respectively, and you have everything you need for a pleasurable meal. C 360. M 145 (weekdays), 195-450, 80 (children).

PUYMIROL 47270
Paris 748 - Agen 17 - Moissac 42   Lot/Garonne

L'Aubergade 🕄

"Michel Trama," 52, rue Royale
05 53 95 31 46, fax 05 53 95 33 80
Closed Sun dinner & Mon off-seas (exc hols), Feb school hols. Open until 9:30pm. Priv rm 50. Garden dining. Air cond. Valet pkg.
Michel and Maryse Trama have a vision and that is why they have succeeded through the bad times and the good. They have made this exquisite fortified *bastide*, formerly the seat of the Counts of Toulouse, into a crown jewel. The

décor is the most fine-tuned balance of old and modern you'll find, with utmost respect for the old stones of the bastide and minimal touches of modern and artistic to highlight them. When you walk into L'Aubergade, you walk into a world they've created especially for you, a labor of love, that they offer you with the generosity, irreproachable standards and years of dedication it takes to create a work of genius. Every detail is taken into consideration, and the experience touches all your senses, but of course especially your tastebuds. Some of Michel Trama's creations, such as his hot foie gras "hamburger" served with cèpes and his pigeon roasted with spices, have become classics. But new ideas are never what's lacking for this self-taught master of the art who never gets stuffy even after all his success and amuses himself with such creations as polenta French fries with escargots in simple parsley butter, or marvellous spring vegetables with pure salt essence. Desserts are yet again a marvel. You must *always* save room! Dream of vanilla-flavored thyme-honey jelly with berries, crystallized green apples, and his most original of original desserts, inspired by his passion for Havana cigars: the double corona of nougatine stuffed with spiced cream and served with its pepper-flavored "tobacco leaf". Just the thing to slip down before you recline in the cigar room under the Giotto-inspired star-studded ceiling. Enough to make you think you're in heaven... Reasonable wine prices to soften the shock. So make the trip to Puymirol, for a dining experience that is pure hedonism. C 500-700. M 180 (weekdays lunch), 280-680, 120 (children).

Les Loges de l'Aubergade

(See restaurant above)
Closed Sun pm & Mon off-seas, Feb school hols. 10 rms 750-1,410. Bkfst 90. Rms for disabled. Half-board 1,800-2,100. Rm ser. Air cond. Valet pkg.
Here is the perfect marriage of old stone and Italian design. Maryse and Michel Trama have decorated this ancient *bastide*, built for the Counts of Toulouse, in a charming personal style. The beautiful, huge, bright rooms open onto one of two courtyard gardens. Guests who have come for one or two nights often ask to stay longer, which is not always possible. Dip your feet in the Jacuzzi pool while sipping a drink. Tennis and golf nearby. VCRs, babysitting, and tours of the region available. Relais et Châteaux.

RIGNAC	46500
Paris 539 - Cahors 69 - Gramat 5	Lot

Château de Roumégouse

05 65 33 63 81, fax 05 65 33 71 18
Closed Tue (exc Jul-Aug), Oct 25-Mar 28. Open until 10pm. Garden dining. Pool. Valet pkg.
A predominantly English clientele frequents this turreted manor house whose bright, elegant dining room looks out on a pretty garden. Truf-

fles, foie gras, and duck confits take first place in Jean-Louis Laîné's repertory, but he also knows what to do with the vegetables and herbs from his kitchen garden to produce fresh, savory dishes with rustic accents. Well-balanced cellar. C 350. M 105 (lunch), 180-225 (wine incl), 185-330, 95 (children).

Château de Roumégouse

(See restaurant above)
Closed Oct 25-Mar 28. 2 stes 1,200-1,500. 13 rms 650-980. Bkfst 65-80. Rms for disabled. Half-board 735-900 (oblig in seas). Air cond. Conf. Pool. Valet pkg.
Overhanging the limestone cliff of Rocamadour, a small, romantic medieval-inspired castle with cozy rooms furnished with antiques. Rooms have air conditioning and modern bathrooms. Drawing rooms tastefully decorated and brimming with flowers. Relais et Châteaux.

ROCAMADOUR	46500
Paris 522 - Figeac 46 - Gramat 9 - Cahors 61	Lot

Domaine de la Rhue

N 140 - 05 65 33 71 50, fax 05 65 33 72 48
Closed Oct 15-end Mar. 12 rms 380-580. Bkfst 45-65. Rms for disabled. Pool. Pkg.
The stables of this large, beautiful house have been converted into a hotel. Built of gray Quercy stone, it has bright, rustic, tastefully decorated rooms. The surrounding countryside is so calm that you will find total peace here. Enjoy the good breakfast next to the fireplace in the sitting room.

Jehan de Valon

Cité Médiévale
05 65 33 63 08, fax 05 65 33 65 23
Closed Nov 12-Feb 12. Open until 9pm (10pm in summer). Terrace dining. No pets. Valet pkg.
The pretty flower-filled dining room may be sunny, but the sun seems to have gone down on the kitchen (but we feel sure that it will come up again!). We liked the soft-boiled egg with truffles, the braised lamb, and the walnut and caramel ice cream, but disliked the taste of the grill on the grilled steak and found several of the desserts incredibly ordinary. We hesitated about whether to keep the toque, but we'll wait for the sunrise... Excellent service. C 220-380. M 98-290.

Le Beau Site

(See restaurant above)
Closed Nov 12-Feb 12. 2 stes 590-660. 42 rms 290-490. Bkfst 49. Half-board 290-560. Rm ser. Conf. Valet pkg.
At the foot of the legendary rock, you will find bright, clean rooms in this hotel in the medieval town. The welcome and service are affable and diligent. Buffet breakfast.

11/20 Sainte-Marie

Pl. des Senhals - 05 65 33 63 07, fax 05 65 33 69 08
Closed Oct 15-end Mar. Open until 9:15pm. Terrace dining. No pets. HOTEL: 22 rms 180-275. Bkfst 34. Half-board 200-250. Rm ser. Pkg.
In the heart of medieval Rocamadour, this beautiful establishment has plans to renovate. While waiting, enjoy the view of the valley while regaling your taste buds with croustillant d'escargots, herbed leg of lamb, and nougat ice cream with walnuts. C 200. M 70-250.

ROQUE-GAGEAC (LA)	24250
Paris 550 - Périgueux 70 - Sarlat 13	Dordogne

 ## La Plume d'Oie

D 703 - 05 53 29 57 05, fax 05 53 31 04 81
Closed Sep-Jun: Mon & Tue lunch; Jul-Aug: lunch Sat & Mon; end Nov-end Dec; mid Jan-Feb. Open until 9:15pm. Priv rm 35. Pkg.
There is a good fixed-price menu at 195 F, but the prices of à la carte offerings have soared. True, chef Marc-Pierre Walker uses only the best of products, but there are limits to everything. It's too bad, because this is truly a lovely place, with its stone and wood décor, located between the cliff and the Dordogne River. There are four hotel rooms reserved for customers of the restaurant who have had a little too much Bergerac with their truffle and polenta lasagna, pigeon with cèpes or shoulder of lamb with garlic and rosemary. Good choice of regional wines at under 100 F a bottle. C 300-400. M 195-295.

 ## La Plume d'Oie

(See restaurant above)
Closed end Nov-end Dec, mid Jan-Feb. 4 rms 275-380. Bkfst 55.
Perfect location for visiting the nearby châteaux. Delightful welcome to these four charming rooms where you can stop off to listen to the constant flow of the river. Personalized decoration and very attentive service.

SAINT-CÉRÉ	46400
Paris 521 - Cahors 76 - Tulle 58 - Figeac 45	Lot

 ## France

Av. François-de-Maynard
05 65 38 02 16, fax 05 65 38 02 98
Closed Fri, Sat lunch, Nov 1-Easter. Open until 9:30pm. Priv rm 20. Terrace dining. Heated pool. No pets. Pkg.
You can count on Patrick Lerhm to make good use of regional ingredients in a highly professional manner. The proof is there, from the beginning of the meal to the end, in perfectly cooked dishes with rich, balanced flavors, enhanced by excellent sauces. Diverse, reasonably priced wine list. Rapid, efficient service in the huge, rustic dining room decorated with Lurçat tapestries. C 270. M 150 (exc Sun), 90-125 (weekdays), 190-240, 60 (children).

 ## France

(See restaurant above)
Closed Nov 1-Easter. 22 rms 300-400. Bkfst 45. Half-board 340-400. Heated pool. Pkg.
In a modern hotel, vast, comfortably equipped rooms with some antique furnishings and sparkling-clean bathrooms. Small terraces overlook the park and the swimming pool. Good breakfasts.

 ## Les Trois Soleils de Montal

Les Prés-de-Montal
05 65 38 20 61, fax 05 65 38 30 66
Closed Oct-Mar: Sat lunch, Sun dinner, Mon lunch; Jan 1-20. Open until 9:30pm. Priv rm 14. Terrace dining. Pool. Tennis. No pets. Garage pkg.
You will know you are on vacation as soon as you take a seat on the terrace looking out on greenery and flowers, or in the salmon-hued dining room with its elegant white-painted furniture and nineteenth-century landscapes. The intelligent, very good cuisine of Frédéric Bizat shows its Provençal origins without neglecting regional ingredients, such as the whole foie gras en cocotte with pears and spices. Good cellar with affordable offerings. Lovely welcome. C 280. M 120-295, 75 (children).

 ## Les Trois Soleils de Montal

(See restaurant above)
Open year-round. 2 stes 550-650. 26 rms 300-450. Bkfst 48. Rms for disabled. Half-board 330-530 (oblig in seas). Pool. Tennis. Garage pkg.
Near the golf course and the Château de Montal, and surrounded by greenery, an attractive modern hotel with pretty, bright, well-equipped rooms with terraces. Gym, miniature golf, and poolside barbecues.

SAINT-CIRQ-LAPOPIE	46330
Paris 628 - Cahors 33 - Villefranche-de-Rouergue 36	Lot

 ## Auberge du Sombral

05 65 31 26 08, fax 05 65 30 26 37
Closed Tue, Wed, Nov 15-Apr 1. 8 rms 300-400. Bkfst 48. Restaurant.
A pretty village house with bright, comfortable, well-kept rooms and spotless bathrooms. Amiable welcome. Bar, restaurant.

 ## La Pelissaria

05 65 31 25 14, fax 05 65 30 25 52
Closed Nov 15-Apr 1. 2 stes 650. 8 rms 400-650. Bkfst 50. Rms for disabled. Restaurant. Heated pool. Pkg.
Facing the medieval village on the peaceful river, an old house built into the hillside, with its own garden.

SAINT-MARTIN-D'ARMAGNAC   32110
Paris 740 - Agen 90 - Auch 80 - Tarbes 59   Gers

 Auberge du Bergerayre

05 62 09 08 72, fax 05 62 09 09 74
Closed Wed. Open until 8pm (9pm in summer). Priv rm 50. Terrace dining. Pool. Tennis. Pkg.
   This spruce little farmhouse is a temple of Gascon traditions, right down to the décor of the dining rooms, which are filled with family furnishings. Pierrette Sarran's fresh, flavorful cuisine uses regional foods in traditional recipes, augmented by a few successful inventions of her own, but we found her less inspired this year, offering us a slightly-salted cod and a boiled chicken that were downright boring. Her smoked foie gras terrine is still her mark of success, and still merits a second toque. The rest forced us to drop her a toque. Small cellar considering the region you're in. Friendly welcome and service. C 270-360. M 80-200, 50 (children).

 Auberge du Bergerayre   ♣♥

(See restaurant above)
Closed Wed. 6 stes 300-680. 8 rms 300-480. Bkfst 35. Half-board 255-445. Rm ser. Pool. Tennis. Pkg.
   Get away to the farm. Newly done farmhouse façade, with rooms in the outbuildings! Rooms give onto the garden or pool.

SAINT-SAUD-LACOUSSIÈRE   24470
Paris 460 - Limoges 57 - Périgueux 69   Dordogne

 Hostellerie Saint-Jacques   ✪

05 53 56 97 21, fax 05 53 56 91 33
Closed Sun dinner, Mon (exc residents Jul-Aug), Oct 15-Apr 1. Open until 9pm (9:30pm in summer). Terrace dining. Heated pool. Tennis. Pkg.
   In the heart of "green" Périgord, an ivy-covered eighteenth-century establishment with a cozy dining room and a terrace. Try the succulent cèpe and morel flan, a light salad of bay scallops and green asparagus, and the fine selection of cheeses. They use good ingredients, but perhaps they try a little too hard to dress them up; simplicity and respect for the element might be more in the calling in this family-run restaurant. Good fixed-price meals. Well-chosen but costly wine list. C 250-340. M 97-297.

Hostellerie Saint-Jacques   ♣♥

(See restaurant above)
Closed Sun & Mon (exc Jul-Aug), Oct 15-Apr 1. 3 stes 750. 16 rms 300-550. Bkfst 50. Half-board 260-390. Rm ser. Heated pool. Tennis. Pkg.
   This stopping place on the road to Compostella is located in a well-preserved natural environment. Some of the nicely equipped rooms look out on a shady park.

SAINT-SYLVESTRE-SUR-LOT   47140
Paris 625 - Agen 29 - Villeneuve-sur-Lot 8   Lot/Garonne

 Château Lalande   ♣♥

05 53 36 15 15, fax 05 53 36 15 16
Open year-round. 4 stes 1,300-1,600. 18 rms 850-1,200. Bkfst 75. Rms for disabled. Restaurant. Half-board 690-1,865. Rm ser. Conf. Heated pool. Tennis. No pets. Garage pkg.
   This fairytale castle, built in the thirteenth and eighteenth centuries and set in a huge, beautifully-kept park, has spacious, pretty, individually decorated rooms with fine bathrooms. Gym and steam bath. Excellent welcome.

SARLAT-LA-CANÉDA   24200
Paris 535 - Périgueux 67 - Brive 50 - Cahors 62   Dordogne

 La Hoirie

2 km S, La Canéda
05 53 59 05 62, fax 05 53 31 13 90
Closed Nov 15-Mar 15. Open until 9pm. Terrace dining. Pool. No pets. Pkg.
   Arlette de Vienne composes the menu of this warm country restaurant, a good place to savor the local traditions. The duck, cassoulet, panfried foie gras with figs, and red mullet with creamed lentils are served in generous portions, as are the homey desserts like gingerbread with walnuts. Wash all this down with a Bergerac or Pécharmant. C 230-420. M 120-195.

 La Hoirie   ♣♥

(See restaurant above)
Closed Nov 15-Mar 15. 4 stes 570. 13 rms 370-570. Bkfst 55. Half-board 350-450. Rm ser. Pool. Pkg.
   In the midst of a peaceful park, a hotel in a former hunting lodge with neo-rustic rooms that are well kept. Friendly, competent welcome and service. Bar.

12/20 La Madeleine

1, pl. de la Petite-Rigaudie
05 53 59 10 41, fax 05 53 31 03 62
Closed Mon lunch (exc hols & Aug), Nov 15-Apr 15. Open until 9:30pm. Priv rm 15. Terrace dining.
   If the "wing" that is being added to the hotel doesn't change the tendency, you can eat dishes made with local ingredients like calf's sweetbread and mushroom pie and black-chocolate and orange fondant. Good wine selection with mostly Bordeaux and Southwest wines. C 280. M 100-260, 65 (children).

 La Madeleine   ♣♥

(See restaurant above)
Closed Nov 15-Mar 15. 39 rms 295-395. Bkfst 45. Half-board 340-365. Air cond. Conf.
   A few steps away from the historic quarter of Sarlat, with its 77 monuments, this establishment was built in 1840 and is the oldest in Sarlat. The rooms are adequately equipped and comfortable. Seventeen new rooms have just been added.

Saint-Albert

10, pl. Pasteur - 05 53 31 55 55, fax 05 53 59 19 99
*Closed Sun eve & Mon off-seas. 6 stes 420-520. 55
rms 280-320. Bkfst 35. Restaurant. Half-board
290-320. Air cond. Conf. No pets.*
Behind this pretty façade you'll find simple but
functional rooms. You can have your breakfast
on the covered terrace in nice weather. Just a step
away from downtown.

SORGES	24420
Paris 480 - Périgueux 24 - Limoges 77	Dordogne

12/20 Auberge de la Truffe

On N 21 - 05 53 05 02 05, fax 05 53 05 39 27
*Closed Sun dinner off-seas. Open until 9:30pm.
Terrace dining. HOTEL: 26 rms 220-315. Bkfst 35.
Half-board 275. Rm ser. Air cond. Conf. Heated
pool. Pkg.*
Truffles, foie gras, sole, and duck are prepared
in every possible way in this regional repertory.
Several fixed-price menus at attractive prices
provide a good sampling of the chef's generous,
well-prepared cuisine. A nice selection of wines
in carafes. Warm welcome in the restful, salmon-
painted dining room. C 190-350. M 75 (weekdays, Sat lunch), 100 (exc Sun), 145-260, 50
(children).

SOUILLAC	46200
Paris 525 - Cahors 67 - Sarlat-la-Canéda 29	Lot

Le Redouillé

28, av. de Toulouse
05 65 37 87 25, fax 05 65 37 09 09
*Closed Tue off-seas. Open until 10pm. Priv rm 45.
Terrace dining. Air cond. Garage pkg.*
This chef may be young but he's already a
master at his trade, and no wonder, since he was
trained by none other than Maximin and Bardet.
Recent may be his arrival, but he has immediately and lovingly absorbed the essence of this
regional cuisine to which he has already added
his gifted and innovating touch. He's making
waves around here with his obvious talent, keen
spirit and sincere approach. Other than his highly classic but well-crafted cassoulet aux trois
confits, he's enveloped a good number of other
Quercy classics and added his own special twist.
We savored his absolutely superb rendition of
local river fish and his exquisite oxtail tournedos
with marrow. The cheese board could be perfected, but the iced walnut and prune fondant
with caramel sauce is divine. Well-stocked cellar
but rather on the young side, and far too few
half-bottles. We're giving this second toque and
hoping that the prices won't go sky high as a
result. C 160-350. M 95-165 (weekdays), 350.

La Vieille Auberge

1, pl. de la Minoterie
05 65 32 79 43, fax 05 65 32 65 19
*Closed Sun dinner & Mon (off-seas). Open until
9:30pm. Priv rm 20. Air cond. HOTEL: 19 rms*

*240-350. Bkfst 40. Half-board 280-380 (oblig in
seas). Rm ser. Conf. Heated pool. Pkg.*
Forget about your surroundings in this vast,
charmless dining room and concentrate on the
regional cuisine. We enjoyed the copious serving
of delicious veal sweetbreads sautéed with truffles and morels, and the perfectly cooked potato
estouffade with fabulous truffles. The unusual
wine list includes bottles from New Zealand and
Australia. C 250. M 100-350, 55 (children).

TRÉMOLAT	24510
Paris 530 - Périgueux 54 - Bergerac 34	Dordogne

Le Vieux Logis

05 53 22 80 06, fax 05 53 22 84 89
*Closed Tue lunch & Wed off-seas. Open until
9:30pm. Garden dining. Pool. Tennis. Valet pkg.*
In a bend of the Dordogne River, a magnificent
house filled with little corners, gardens, and outbuildings. The bright, comfortable dining room
is the perfect setting for Pierre-Jean Duribreux's
refined cuisine, full of good ideas and the flavors
of the region. His admirable potato stuffed with
veal sweetbreads and truffles alone is worth a
visit. If you spend the night there, you can order
in advance the hare à la royale, roast duckling,
or a whole veal shank (for four persons). The
desserts are enough to make you melt. A well-
rounded cellar from many regions, with a selection of half-bottles and Southwestern wines at
soothing prices. C 250-400. M 180-380.

Le Vieux Logis

(See restaurant above)
*Closed Tue & Wed am off-seas. 6 stes 1,590. 19 rms
760-1,320. Bkfst 80-95. Rms for disabled. Rm ser.
Conf. Pool. Tennis. Valet pkg.*
A little group of buildings that almost forms its
own village, with a garden, a stream, and a lake
with water-sports facilities. Top-class service
and comfort, and oh what a joy to open your
windows onto such heavenly countryside every
morning when you wake to partake of their
scrumptious breakfast. Good location for visiting châteaux in the region. Relais et Châteaux.

VÉZAC	24220
Paris 558 - Sarlat 10 - Saint-Cyprien 11	Dordogne

Relais des Cinq Châteaux

D 47, exit Beynac toward Sarlat, Le Bourg
05 53 30 30 72, fax 05 53 31 19 39
*Closed Wed off-seas, Feb 3-28. Open until 9pm
(9:30pm in summer). Terrace dining. HOTEL: 10
rms 260-280. Bkfst 35. Half-board 285-295. Conf.
Pool. Pkg.*
This Perigord-style house has a huge dining
room with veranda that boasts a view of the
Château de Castelnaud. For four years now,
Jacky Vasseur has been treating diners to his
reasonably-priced cuisine based on regional
products, including rabbit salad with warm lan-

goustines, pike perch with leek fondue, and pears with strawberry sauce. The fixed-price meals are one of the best examples of such that we know: they are reasonably priced and delicious. Too bad others don't follow his example. Well-balanced wine list with incredibly accessible Bergeracs. C 270. M 78 (weekdays, Sat lunch), 90-175, 45 (children).

VIEUX-MAREUIL	24340
Paris 500 - Périgueux 45 - Angoulême 45	Dordogne

 ## Château de Vieux-Mareuil

05 53 60 77 15, fax 05 53 56 49 33
Closed Sun dinner & Mon off-seas, beg Jan-Mar 15. Open until 9:30pm. Garden dining. Pool. Pkg.
A beautiful fifteenth-century building set in a park with shady lanes and fields. When the parasols are up on the terrace, you have an idyllic country scene. The arrival of a new manager and a new chef do not seem to have made waves. Chef Pascal Nebout's modern cooking maintains respect for classic cuisine in dishes like hot foie gras upside down tart with truffled caramel, pan-fried pike perch served with frogs' leg and mushroom aumônières (literally means "almspurse"!), and baby lamb chops stuffed with snail Duxelles. The desserts are rather more conventional and the wines a bit young. C 280. M 150-250, 60 (children).

 ## Château de Vieux-Mareuil

(See restaurant above)
Closed beg Jan-Mar 15. 2 stes 700. 12 rms 550-650. Bkfst 60. Rms for disabled. Half-board 550-650. Rm ser. Air cond. Conf. Pool. Pkg.
A cobblestone road leads to this peaceful haven set around an attractive rectangular swimming pool. The rooms are somewhat impersonal, as is the rest of the establishment. Prices are nearly prohibitive.

VILLENEUVE-SUR-LOT	47300
Paris 614 - Bergerac 60 - Agen 29	Lot/Garonne

 ## Aux Berges du Lot

3, rue de l'Hôtel-de-Ville
05 53 70 84 41, fax 05 53 70 43 15
Closed Sun dinner, Mon, 2 wks in Nov. Open until 9:45pm. Priv rm 55. Terrace dining. Air cond.
It's hard to believe that a former police station could have so much charm! The décor is warm and filled with flowers, and the lovely terrace garden overlooks the River Lot. The generous and very appealing cuisine of Laurent Carlier, who handles traditional themes with fantasy, energy, and precision, is highly appreciated by both local and visiting gourmets. Dishes like the salmon steak with verjuice and verbena herb tea,

the braised burbot with Pécharmant wine or the duckling fricassée with cumquats and prunes breathe of creativity, yet don't stray all that far from regional tradition. Complete cellar predominantly from Southwest, some wine by the glass. Charming welcome and faultless service. C 275. M 75 (weekday lunch), 110-320.

 ## Hostellerie du Roy

Chemin de la Labourdette
05 53 70 48 48, fax 05 53 49 17 74
Closed Sun dinner, Mon, Sep. Open until 10pm. Terrace dining.
This alluring old house with its heavenly, arbor-covered terrace serves as pleasant setting for a cuisine predominantly of regional inspiration using top-quality ingredients. One point more, while waiting for some inspiration at dessert time. C 230-350. M 98, 130, 135, 190, 230.

VITRAC	24200
Paris 550 - Périgueux 77 - Sarlat-la-Canéda 10	Dordogne

 ## Domaine de Rochebois

Route de Montfort
05 53 31 52 52, fax 05 53 29 36 88
Closed Nov-mid Apr. Open until 9:30pm. Priv rm 130. Terrace dining. Air cond. Pool. Garage pkg.
Golfers and well-off tourists have adopted this restaurant with a huge, bright dining room, a charming, refined décor, and a view of the valley. Chefs come and chefs go, especially here. The new one is doing nothing to rock the boat with his pan-fried duck liver with verjuice, carmelized sweet-onion strudel and saddle of sea bass roasted in Brive violet mustard. C 400-530. M 190-250, 80 (children).

 ## Domaine de Rochebois

(See restaurant above)
Closed Nov-mid Apr. 2 stes 1,150-1,500. 38 rms 525-1,690. Bkfst 80. Rms for disabled. Half-board 540-1,060. Rm ser. Air cond. Pool. Garage pkg.
In a wonderful location above the Dordogne River, a large nineteenth-century hotel with huge, prettily decorated, perfectly equipped rooms in the Mediterranean style, with large bathrooms.

12/20 La Ferme

Caudon-de-Vitrac - 05 53 28 33 35
Closed Sun dinner & Mon off-seas, Oct, Dec 15-Jan 25. Open until 9pm. Priv rm 80. Air cond. Pkg.
This rustic little restaurant on the banks of the river offers local dishes using market-fresh ingredients. Try the excellent rye-bread soup, the brow-raising confit de canard and the absolutely delicious walnut pie. Short wine list. Smiling service. C 250. M 85-165, 50 (children).

REGIONAL FOODS

France's Southwest embraces the ancient lands of Périgord, Quercy, Aquitaine... Bucking the modern trend toward "liteness," it remains the realm of rich, rib-sticking country fare. Hearty appetites are solicited by home-prepared foie gras, fragrant truffles (the aromatic Périgord truffle, however, is growing rare), and slow-simmered confit. If you're seeking gastronomic souvenirs, think of walnut oil, perfect in a garlicky vinaigrette; or plump local prunes: first imported by Crusaders in the twelfth century, the prunes produced nowadays in Agen and Villeneuve-sur-Lot are France's very best. Look, too, for Rocamadour's famous Cabécou cheese, or the less familiar Bleu du Quercy. Farther south, in Gascony, Béarn, and the Basque Country, traveling gourmands can ferret out small producers of Bayonne ham, Armagnac, or AOC Pyrenees sheep cheeses, as well as farm-based suppliers of foie gras, confit, and garbure (cabbage and bean soup).

• *ARMAGNAC*

LABASTIDE-D'ARMAGNAC   40240 – Landes

Domaine Boingnères

05 58 44 80 28
    For a wide choice of refined Armagnacs, with aromas of quince, prune, violet, grapes...visit this reliable producer.

LAVARDAC   47230 – Lot/Garonne

Maison Castarède

Pont de Bordes - 05 53 65 50 06
    This venerable firm was founded around 1830, and boasts an impressive collection of vintage Armagnacs.

NOGARO   32110 – Gers

Cave des Producteurs Réunis

Les Hauts de Montrouge - 05 62 09 01 79
    A cooperative with a remarkable catalog of Armagnacs, including some interesting old vintages.

• *CHARCUTERIE & FOIE GRAS*

ALDUDES   64430 – Pyrénées-A.

Pierre Oteiza

Route Urepel - 05 59 37 56 11
    Splendid hams from free-range Basque porkers, fiery chorizo (spiced with hot Espelette chilis), and a Basque version of smoked jésus sausages.

BEUSTE   64800 – Pyrénées-A.

Biraben

05 59 61 01 08
    Peerless foie gras in a multitude of preparations, as well as cassoulet, poached chicken, sausages, and more, all packaged for traveling.

DONZACQ   40360 – Landes

Ferme La Place

05 58 89 88 17
    Come here to stock up on expertly prepared duck foie gras and confit (made from free-range, grain-fed birds), as well as stuffed duck necks—a noted local delicacy—giblets, and duck rillettes (a rich spread of shredded duck meat and fat).

GUICHE   64520 – Pyrénées-A.

Montauzer

05 59 56 84 04
    Jacques Montauzer and his two associates produce a wonderfully flavorful Basque ham, according to old-fashioned methods. The result bears comparison with Parma's famous prosciutto or Spain's Serrano ham.

SALIGNAC-EYVIGNES   24590 – Dordogne

Crouzel

05 53 28 80 83
    Just steps away from the Lascaux caves is this quality producer of foie gras and other Southwestern specialty foods.

---

*Looking for a town or restaurant? A winery? A gastronomic specialty or a celebrated chef? Consult the **alphabetical index** to locate them quickly and easily.*

SOUPROSSE

40250 – Landes

Dupérier

Route de Saint-Sever - 05 58 44 23 23
Stop here to purchase excellent foie gras, confit, sausages, and prepared Southwestern dishes.

• *GOURMET SPECIALTIES*

SADIRAC

33670 – Gironde

Domaine de Belloc

05 56 30 62 00
Old-fashioned "heirloom" vegetables, either cooked or preserved au naturel. Don't overlook the bottled Périgord verjuice, which you can use in lieu of vinegar to season a salad or deglaze a pan.

Honey & Jams

PAU

64000 – Pyrénées-A.

Musée de la Confiture

48, rue du Maréchal-Joffre - 05 59 27 69 51
Yes, there is such a thing as the Museum of Jam, and it's right here in Pau. You can view the 800 exhibits relating to the history of jam-making, or you can head straight for the gift shop, where an array of delectable jams is on sale.

SAINT-FAUST

64110 – Pyrénées-A.

La Cote des Abeilles

Chemin des Crêtes - 05 59 83 04 60

Featured here are powerfully flavored mountain honeys as well as milder honeys from the plains. Also on offer are royal jelly, pollen, and specialty items made with honey.

• *PASTRY & COOKIES*

BORDEAUX

33000 – Gironde

Pâtisserie Antoine

19, cours Portal - 05 56 81 43 19
The recipe for cannelés de Bordeaux (tiny cakes baked in a distinctive mold) was invented 300 years ago by local nuns. The cannelés sold here count among the best in the city.

DAX

40100 – Landes

Maison Cazelle

6, rue de la Fontaine-Chaude - 05 58 74 26 25
The same family has been baking fat, buttery madeleines since the dawn of the century. Don't leave town without trying them!

SAINT-JEAN-DE-LUZ

64500 – Pyrénées-A.

Maison Adams

6, pl. Louis-XIV - 05 59 26 03 54
The almond-flavored macarons produced by the Maison Adams (since the sixteenth century!) are crispy on the outside, tender within.

Maison Pariès

9, rue Gambetta - 05 59 26 01 46
You must try the smooth, rich Kanouga caramels sold at this shop: they're soft, creamy, and chocolaty.

WINE

BORDEAUX

The subject of Bordeaux is an intimidating one, even for the most earnest and devoted student of wine. The sheer size of the Bordeaux AOC area is staggering: 100,000 hectares (270,000 acres), which roughly correspond to the Gironde *département*. And consider this: in certain bountiful years, Bordeaux's 20,000 growers can produce close to a billion bottles of wine! Among those battalions of "high-shouldered" Bordeaux bottles are some of the most prestigious Grands Crus on earth, as well as vast quantities of excellent to very good wine from Crus Bourgeois and *petits châteaux*. Bordeaux owes its preeminent status in the wine world to this unique combination of high volume and high quality.

The wine region of Bordeaux is defined by three rivers: the Gironde estuary, which empties into the Atlantic, and the Garonne and the Dordogne rivers, which flow into the Gironde. The **Médoc** is the strip of land that lies between the estuary and the ocean (its name comes from the Latin *medio aquae*, "in the middle of the water"). The famous *appellations communales* of Saint-Estèphe, Saint-Julien, Pauillac, and Margaux are situated in the Médoc, along the left bank of the Gironde. To the south, on the Garonne's left bank, is the **Graves** district, which encompasses the *appellation* of Pessac-Léognan (where all sixteen of the Graves's Crus Classés are located), as well as the vineyards of Sauternes and Barsac, known for their ambrosial sweet wines. The broad **Entre-Deux-Mers** district lies between the Garonne and Dordogne rivers. Most familiar for its dry white wines, this area is a vast reservoir of straight Bordeaux AOC and Bordeaux Supérieur in red, white, and rosé. On the right bank of the Dordogne is the city of **Libourne** (created by the British as a shipping port in the thirteenth century) and the **Libournais**. This is the realm of the Merlot grape, which in Pomerol, Fronsac, and Saint-Émilion yields seductive, silky red wines of incomparable finesse. To the north, still on the Dordogne's right bank and directly across from the Médoc, the **Côtes de Bourg** and **Côtes de Blaye** are sources of reliable, underestimated wine that often represent exceptional value.

The same group of grape varieties is cultivated all over the Bordeaux region: Cabernet Sauvignon, Merlot, and Cabernet Franc for the reds (sometimes with a little Malbec and Petit-Verdot); Sémillon with Sauvignon Blanc and a bit of aromatic Muscadelle for whites. But the distinctive soils they spring from, and the varying proportions in which they are used, produce wines of widely differing styles. Merlot, as we mentioned, dominates the wines of the Libournais (Pomerol's celebrated Château Pétrus is virtually 100 percent Merlot), while the more tannic Cabernet Sauvignon contributes to the structure and depth of Médoc's *appellations communales*.

You won't find the addresses of any Grands Crus listed below, since they are not sold at the château but through retailers and *négociants*. We have included only the names of growers who welcome the public and sell their wines directly at the property.

• *MÉDOC*

BÉGADAN   33340 – Gironde

Château La Tour de By
05 56 41 50 03, fax 05 56 41 36 10
Open winter: 8am-noon & 2pm-4:30pm; summer: 11am-5pm.
There's practically never a bad year at La Tour de By, one of the most reliable Crus Bourgeois in Bordeaux, owned and overseen by Marc Pagès.

LAMARQUE   33460 – Gironde

Château Malescasse
Route du Moulin-Rose
05 56 58 90 09, fax 05 56 58 97 89
Open Mon-Fri 9am-noon & 2pm-5pm.
This Haut-Médoc estate occupies an exceptional piece of land, but until quite recently the wine was an underachiever. Visitors can tour the estate, and are warmly welcomed in the tasting cellar.

LISTRAC-MÉDOC   33480 – Gironde

Château Fourcas Dupré
05 56 58 01 07, fax 05 56 58 02 27
Open Mon-Fri 8am-noon & 2pm-6pm.
This estate occupies one of the two highest points in Médoc. Visitors are invited into the

tasting room to sample recent vintages of the château's traditionally vinified, barrel-aged Listrac.

MARGAUX   33460 – Gironde

Château Larruau

4, rue de la Trémoille - 05 56 88 35 50
Open daily 9am-8pm.
Bernard Château is justly proud of his splendid Margaux, which he sells exclusively to individual clients.

MOULIS-EN-MÉDOC   33480 – Gironde

Château Poujeaux

05 56 58 02 96, fax 05 56 58 01 25
Open Mon-Sat 9am-noon & 2pm-6pm.
This Cru Exceptionnel is the most consistently successful wine in Moulis. The estate is run with great competence and high standards by the Theil brothers.

Château Maucaillou

Quartier de la Gare
05 56 58 01 23, fax 05 56 58 00 88
Open daily 10am-noon & 2pm-7pm. Table d'hôte at lunch & dinner.
Not only are Maucaillou's wines consistently balanced and seductive, the estate also instructs and entertains visitors with a wine museum, table d'hôte meals, and a wine school open to amateurs and professionals. A most hospitable château.

SAINT-CHRISTOLY-MÉDOC   33340 – Gironde

Château Les Grands Chênes

9, route de Lesparre
05 56 41 53 12, fax 05 56 41 35 69
Open Mon-Fri 9am-6pm, Sat & Sun by appt.
Jacqueline Gauzy runs this minuscule estate with a passionate devotion that is reflected in her wine. It was recently awarded a Certificate of Excellence from the British Masters of Wine Institute.

SAINT-ESTÈPHE   33180 – Gironde

Château Ségur de Cabanac

05 56 70 10, fax 05 56 59 73 94
Open daily, appts preferred.
Guy Delon is the sole man in charge of this estate. Vinified like Crus Classés, his Saint-Estèphe (Ségur de Cabanac) and Saint-Julien (Moulin de la Rose) can be had for half the price a classed growth would command.

Château Tour de Pez

Pez - 05 56 59 31 60, fax 05 56 59 71 12
Open Mon-Fri 9am-noon & 2pm-5:30pm.
This estate is of recent vintage, so to speak: the current owner joined two properties formerly run by growers who sold their production to the local cooperative. Today, Château Tour de Pez proudly puts its own label on a distinctively fragrant Saint-Estèphe.

VALEYRAC   33340 – Gironde

Château Sipian-Méhaye

28, route du port de Goulée
05 56 41 56 05, fax 05 56 41 35 36
Open daily.
Frédéric Méhaye grows an unusually large proportion (ten percent) of Petit-Verdot to give his fine Médoc extra flavor and color.

• *GRAVES*

BARSAC   33720 – Gironde

Château Simon

05 56 27 15 35, fax 05 56 27 24 79
Open Mon-Fri 8am-noon & 2pm-6pm.
Under the Château Simon label this estate produces red and white Graves, and a Sauternes that is a model of richness and concentration. The '90 vintage is destined for a long, long life.

Château de Nairac

05 56 27 16 16, fax 05 56 27 26 50
By appt. Rooms available.
Nairac is a Cru Classé de Sauternes, a spectacular wine in great years, but impressive even in lesser vintages. The delicate, fruity '94 is one of the most successful Sauternes from that difficult year.

LANGON   33210 – Gironde

Château Brondelle

Roland Belloc - 05 56 62 38 14, fax 05 56 62 23 14
Open Mon-Sat 8am-noon & 2pm-7pm.
The estate's gravelly soil and the know-how of vintner Roland Belloc and his team combine to produce a white and a red Graves both well worth your attention. The red is particularly dense, with an elegant, fruity bouquet.

LÉOGNAN   33850 – Gironde

Château Haut Bergey

05 56 64 05 22, fax 05 56 64 06 98
Open Mon-Fri 8am-noon & 2pm-6pm.
While Haut-Bergey does not (yet!) belong to the *appellation's* elite, it's an estate that has recently attained a most respectable level, with

worthwhile red and white wines bearing the Pessac-Léognan AOC.

Château Grand Ormeau

Château de Chantegrive

05 56 27 17 38, fax 05 56 27 29 42
Open Mon-Fri 8am-noon & 2pm-6pm, Sat by appt.
Chantegrive's white Cuvée Caroline is a straight Graves that can rival many a high-hat Pessac-Léognan. These are wines that require some bottle age—don't be tempted to open them too soon. The estate's red Graves is full of delicious fruit touched with wood.

Lalande-de-Pomerol
05 57 25 30 20, fax 05 57 25 22 80
Open Mon-Sat 9am-6pm.
The estate's owner made his fortune selling orange soda; today, he produces a consistently admirable Lalande-de-Pomerol (the '93 is fantastic) that appeals to more mature tastes!

Château Les Justices

05 56 76 28 44, fax 05 56 76 28 43
Open Mon-Thu 9am-noon & 2pm-6pm, Fri until 5pm.
Christian Médeville also owns Château Gilette, an excellent source of Sauternes, and Château Respide-Médeville, which produces reliably good red and white Graves. Les Justices merits your attention for its '93 Sauternes: a fine bottle in a minor year.

Château de Roquefort

05 56 23 97 48, fax 05 56 23 51 44
Open Mon-Fri 9am-noon & 2pm-5pm.
Bordeaux and Bordeaux Supérieur in all three colors. The white Bordeaux aged in oak barrels is especially long and aromatic. Excellent value.

Château Garraud

05 57 55 58 58, fax 05 57 25 13 43
Open Mon-Fri 9am-6pm.
Harvard alumnus Jean-Marc Nony is not a conventional wine grower. He's put a crack team in charge of his Lalande-de-Pomerol estate, which since 1990 has produced an enviable series of fine wines (the '93 won high marks from our tasters—it's a keeper). Reasonable prices.

• *ENTRE-DEUX-MERS*

Castenet Greffier

05 56 61 40 67, fax 05 56 61 38 82
Open Mon-Fri 8am-7pm.
Individual buyers are welcome at this estate, where you can sample a delightful Bordeaux rosé and an elegant, wood-aged red Bordeaux AOC.

Château Bellegrave

Château Lesparre

Michel Gonet - 05 57 24 51 23, fax 05 57 24 03 99
Open Mon-Fri 8am-11am & 2pm-5:30pm. Table d'hôte meals.
The Gonets take infinite pains with their red Bordeaux AOC, limiting yields and maturing a portion of the wine in wood. A straight Bordeaux that could easily be mistaken for a classed growth Graves!

Jean-Marie Bouldy, at the place called "René"
05 57 51 20 47, fax 05 57 51 23 14
Open Mon-Fri 8am-noon & 2pm-7:30pm, Sat & Sun by appt.
We almost hate to give away this address. After all, how many Pomerols are sold at the estate? And for such reasonable prices (around 80 F)?

Domaine de Bouillerot

Thierry Bos - 05 56 71 46 04, fax 05 56 71 46 04
Open Mon-Sat 8am-noon & 2pm-7pm.
Over the years, Thierry Bos has presented consistently elegant red Bordeaux Supérieur, wines with unusual complexity and concentration. Fine rosés, too.

Château La Rousselle

05 57 24 96 73, fax 05 57 24 91 05
Open daily 8:30am-12:30pm & 2:30pm-6pm.
From vines grown in soil similar to that of Saint-Émilion, the Davaus produce an always impressive Fronsac AOC. Note that there is a furnished rental (*gîte*) on the estate.

SAILLANS

Château Villars

05 57 84 32 17, fax 05 57 84 31 25
Open Mon-Fri 9am-noon & 2pm-5pm, Sat & Sun by appt.
Thierry Gaudrie regrets that Fronsac does not yet enjoy the reputation it deserves. Indeed, there are certain Fronsacs that we wouldn't trade for a Pomerol! Gaudrie's Château Villars 1990, for example. If it's still available, we advise you to buy.

SAINT-ÉMILION

Château Destieux

05 57 40 25 05, fax 05 57 40 37 42
Open Mon-Fri, Sat & Sun by appt.
Christian Dauriac's Saint-Émilion, made from handpicked, handsorted grapes, is matured in handmade oak barrels. The man is a perfectionist! His stock includes some fabulous older vintages of Château Destieux.

Château La Couspaude

05 57 40 15 76, fax 05 57 40 10 14
Open by appt: weekdays 8am-noon & 2pm-6pm (summer: daily 9am-8pm). Table d'hôte meals.
The Aubert family has been making wine since 1750. That heritage is apparent in La Couspaude's reliably rich, dense Saint-Émilions.

• *CÔTES DE BLAYE & CÔTES DE BOURG*

CUBNEZAIS

Château Haut Bertinerie

05 57 68 70 74, fax 05 57 68 01 03
Open Mon-Fri 9am-noon & 2pm-6pm, Sat & Sun by appt.
Vinified with infinite care, Haut Bertinerie's aromatic, expressive red wines are regular fixtures on yearly "best of" lists. Wines from the Côtes de Blaye often represent good value, but these are truly exceptional bargains.

SAINT-PAUL

Château Les Jonqueyres

7 Courgeau - 05 57 42 34 88, fax 05 57 42 93 80
Open Mon-Sat 9am-noon.
Low yields, meticulous winemaking methods, and new oak barrels for aging combine to produce consistently superior Côtes de Blaye. Pascal Montaut also presents a remarkable Côtes de Bourg, Le Clos Alphonse Dubreuil (the '93 is reminiscent of a Pauillac).

SAINT-TROJAN

Château Mercier

05 57 64 92 34, fax 05 57 64 82 37
Open daily 8am-6pm.
Founded in 1698, this estate is a source of fine-quality red Côtes de Bourg. Note that there is a furnished rental (*gîte*) for six on the premises.

TAURIAC

Château Nodoz

05 57 68 41 03, fax 05 57 68 37 34
Open Mon-Fri 8am-noon & 2pm-7pm.
The estate's elegant, fruity Côtes de Bourg always seem to come up trumps in comparative tastings. The château is situated in a picturesque, historic site, and there is a furnished rental (*gîte*) on the property.

THE SOUTHWEST

The winegrowing region known as the Southwest is a scattered and diverse—indeed motley—group of *appellations*, which includes some of France's most venerable vineyards. Côtes de Duras, for example, was the court wine of Renaissance monarch François I. And drops of Jurançon were touched to the lips of future King Henri IV at his baptism. Yet the wines of the Southwest gradually fell into a long decline, overshadowed by the quality wines of Bordeaux and overwhelmed by the gushing vineyards of Languedoc. Wine continued to be made, but on a much smaller scale, principally for local consumption. Because they had no reason to abandon local grape varieties for more commercially popular types, Southwestern growers continued to cultivate such indigenous varietals as Malbec, Tannat, Négrette, and Fer Servadou for red wines, and Gros-Manseng, Petit-Manseng, Barroque, Courbu and for whites. This loyalty to tradition has turned out to be an asset in today's market. The wines of the Southwest display an authenticity and a distinctive, often rustic character that consumers find most attractive. The Southwest also produces some elegant, highly polished wines: a mature Cahors or Madiran from a top producer can be a revelation. In our estimation, these wines never taste better than when savored with the region's hearty cooking. Why not sip a sweet Pacherenc or Monbazillac with a terrine of locally raised foie gras? Or uncork a bottle of Pécharmant or Irouléguy to partner a confit de canard?

• *GASCONY, PÉRIGORD & QUERCY*

winemaking estate, where Bertrand-Gabriel Vigoroux produces consistently remarkable Cahors.

Domaine du Haut Pécharmant

Michel Roches, Peyrelevade
05 53 57 29 50, fax 05 53 24 28 05
Open daily (exc Sun morning).
Pécharmant, Périgord's finest red wine, hails from a tiny AOC district on the right bank of the Dordogne. Michel Roches makes some of the best: just remember that these rich, tannic wines require several years in the cellar (the '89 is ready now).

Clos des Verdots

Fourtout Family
05 53 58 34 31, fax 05 53 57 82 00
Open daily (Sun by appt).
Cattle and grain are raised on this huge farm in Périgord, but wine is the passion of father and son Jean-Guy and David Fourtout. They produce two different types of red Bergerac: one straight up (Clos des Verdots) and one matured in oak (Tour des Verdots). A furnished rental *(gîte)* is available on the property.

Domaine de Laulan

Gilbert Geoffroy
05 53 83 73 69, fax 05 53 83 81 54
Open daily.
Côtes de Duras is a little-known *appellation* that produces delicious wines in all three colors, as well as tempting sweet wines (when the weather cooperates). Gilbert and Claudie Geoffroy offer fresh, tasty whites based on Sauvignon Blanc grapes, and intensely fruity reds. There is a furnished rental *(gîte)* on the property.

Château de Mercuès

Georges Vigouroux, route de Toulouse
05 65 20 80 80
Open daily 9am-6pm.
Cahors, in the old province of Quercy, boasts vineyards that date back to Gallo-Roman times. Planted on either bank of the winding Lot River, Cahors's vines (mostly Malbec, locally referred to as Auxerrois, with some Tannat and Merlot) furnish a robust "black" wine that should be drunk quite young, on its fruit, or else with several years of bottle age. Château Mercuès is not only a gorgeous Relais et Châteaux establishment (see *Restaurants*), but also a first-class

Comte de Bosredon

Château de Bélingard Chayne
05 53 58 28 03, fax 05 53 58 38 39
Open Mon-Sat 10am-noon & 2pm-6pm.
The Count presents a full range of wines— sweet and dry, red, white, and rosé—but the best are his Tête de Cuvée Blanche de Bosredon, a rich, red Bergerac, and his beautifully balanced sweet Monbazillac.

Château La Coustarelle

Michel & Nadine Cassot
05 65 22 40 10, fax 05 65 30 62 46
Open daily 8am-1pm & 2:30pm-8pm.
The Cassots are happy to show visitors around their cellars, and invite them to taste their Cuvée Prestige (a Cahors aged in wood for one year) and Cuvée Tradition (eighteen months in wood).

Domaine Le Gouyat

Vignobles Dubard Frères et Sœurs
05 53 82 48 31, fax 05 53 82 47 64
Open daily 8am-noon & 2pm-7pm.
Just a stone's throw away from the tower where Michel de Montaigne penned his immortal *Essays*, this large estate produces an exemplary red Bergerac and a distinctively aromatic white Montravel.

• *THE BASQUE COUNTRY & WESTERN PYRENEES*

Vignobles Laplace

Château d'Aydie
05 59 04 03 96, fax 05 59 04 01 53
Open daily 9am-1pm & 2pm-7pm.
The Laplaces were among the movers and shakers who revived Madiran's reputation. The château's muscular Madiran, dominated by the local Tannat grape, is always concentrated, full, and rich. If you enjoy dessert wines, do try their sweet version of Pacherenc: floral, fruity, and round.

Château de Bachen

Michel Guérard
05 58 05 06 41, fax 05 58 71 77 77
By appt only.
Michel Guérard is not only a chef *extraordinaire*, he is a vintner, the proud owner of a former barony with extensive old vineyards. Visitors are requested to make an appointment to taste his range of dry yet rich and complex white Tursans (a blend of Sauvignon, Manseng, and Barroque grapes). Top of the line: Baron de Bachen, aged in new oak barrels. Four rooms are available for rent at the property.

Château Bouscassé

Alain Brumont, Montus-Bouscassé
05 62 69 74 67, fax 05 62 69 70 46
Open daily 9am-noon & 2pm-6pm.
Twenty years ago, the Madiran *appellation* was on the brink of extinction. Today, it is one of the most dynamic in France. Madiran's brawny, dark-hued wines have achieved international renown, thanks largely to Alain Brumont, the first to make a superb oak-aged Madiran from 100 percent Tannat grapes. Brumont is also noted for a glorious white Pacherenc that exhales honey and citrus—don't miss it!

Domaine Bru-Baché

Rue Barada - 05 59 21 36 34, fax 05 59 21 32 67
Open Mon-Fri 9am-noon & 2pm-6pm, Sat by appt.
Like Madiran, Jurançon is an ancient wine region which very nearly fell into oblivion. And as in Madiran, a small corps of dedicated growers—among them Georges Bru-Baché—brought this *appellation* back to life. Dry or sweet, Jurançon is made from indigenous white grape varieties: Gros-Manseng, Courbu, and Petit-Manseng. Sweet Jurançon draws its honeyed flavor from extra-ripe, late-harvested grapes (not from "noble rot," which does not exist here). This estate produces superb dry and sweet Jurançons.

Domaine Cauhapé

Henri Ramonteu, quartier Castet
05 59 21 33 02, fax 05 59 21 41 82
Open Mon-Sat 9am-7pm & by appt.
To be first in Jurançon means to be the last to gather in your grapes. Henri Ramonteu, one of the region's "godfathers," (with Bru-Baché and Charles Hours) has proved pretty much unbeatable when it comes to timing his harvest. The proof is in the bottle: sweet or dry, his are fabulous Jurançons.

Cave d'Irouléguy

Route de Saint-Jean-Pied-de-Port
05 59 37 41 33, fax 05 59 37 47 76
Open daily 9am-noon & 2pm-6pm.
A small coop that concentrates on quality. Irouléguy in all three colors: white (try the lively, spicy Xuri d'Ansa cuvée), red (blended from equal parts of Tannat, Cabernet Sauvignon, and Cabernet Franc), and a delicious rosé that is perhaps too drinkable!.

Domaine Brana

3 bis, av. du Jaï-Alaï
05 59 37 00 44, fax 05 59 37 14 28
Open weekdays (May, Jun, Sep); daily (Jul-Aug).
Irouléguy is a Basque country *appellation* that yields aromatic, tannic red wines based on Tannat and Cabernet grapes, and a little white Irouléguy as well. Jean Brana's reds are usually jammy, supple, with elegant tannins. They're perfect partners to the region's hearty cooking.

FOOD NOTES

MENU SAVVY

A

Agneau: lamb
Aïoli: garlicky mayonnaise
Américaine or armoricaine: sauce of white wine, Cognac, tomatoes, and butter
Ananas: pineapple
Andouille: smoked tripe sausage, usually served cold
Anglaise (à l'): boiled meats or vegetables
Anguille: eel
Asperges: asparagus

B

Bar: bass
Ballottine: boned, stuffed, and rolled poultry
Béarnaise: sauce made of shallots, tarragon, vinegar, and egg yolks, mixed with butter
Béchamel: sauce made of flour, butter, and milk
Beurre blanc: sauce of wine and vinegar boiled down with minced shallots, then thickened with butter
Beurre noisette: lightly browned butter
Bière: beer
Bigarade: bitter orange used in sauces and marmalade
Bisque (crayfish, lobster, etc.): rich, velvety soup, usually made with crustaceans, flavored with white wine and Cognac
Blinis: small, thick crêpes made with eggs, milk, and yeast
Bœuf: beef
Bœuf bourguignon: beef stewed with red wine, onions, and lardoons
Bombe glacée: molded ice cream dessert
Bordelaise: fairly thin brown sauce of shallots, red wine, and tarragon
Boudin noir: blood sausage
Brioche: a soft, often sweet yeast bread or roll enriched with eggs and butter
Brochet: pike
Brochette: on a skewer
Biscuits: cookies

C

Caille: quail
Calvados: distilled apple cider
Canard: duck
Carbonnade: pieces of lean beef, first sautéed then stewed with onions and beer
Carrotte: carrot
Carré d'agneau: rack of lamb
Cèpe: prized wild mushroom, the same as the Italian porcini
Cerise: cherry
Champignon: mushroom
Chanterelle: prized wild mushroom, trumpet-shaped
Charlotte: dessert of flavored creams and/or fruit molded in a cylindrical dish lined with ladyfingers (if served cold) or strips of buttered bread (if served hot)
Chasseur: brown sauce made with shallots, white wine, and mushrooms

Chèvre (fromage de): goat (cheese)
Chevreuil: venison
Chou: cabbage
Choucroute: sauerkraut; often served with sausages, smoked bacon, pork loin, and potatoes
Citron: lemon
Citron vert: lime
Chou-fleur: cauliflower
Clafoutis: a dessert of fruit (usually cherries) baked in an eggy batter
Confit: pork, goose, duck, turkey, or other meat cooked and sealed in its own fat
Coquilles St-Jacques: scallops
Côte d'agneau: lamb chop
Coulis: thick sauce or purée, often of vegetables or fruits
Court-bouillon: stock in which fish, meat, and poultry are cooked
Crème chantilly: sweetened whipped cream
Crêpes Suzette: crêpes stuffed with a sweetened butter mixture and ground almonds, Grand Marnier, tangerine juice, and peel
Crevette: shrimp
Croque-monsieur: grilled ham and cheese sandwich
Croûte (en): in pastry crust
Crudités: raw vegetables
Crustacé: shellfish

D

Daube: beef braised in red wine
Daurade: sea bream

E

Écrevisse: crayfish
Entrecôte: beef rib steak
Épinards: spinach
Escalope: slice of meat or fish, flattened slightly and sautéed
Escargots (à la bourguignonne): snails (with herbed garlic butter)

F

Faisan: pheasant
Financière: Madeira sauce enhanced with truffle juice
Fish: poisson
Florentine: with spinach
Foie: liver
Foie gras: liver of a specially fattened goose or duck
Forestière: garnish of sautéed mushrooms and lardoons
Fraise: strawberry
Framboise: raspberry
Frangipane: almond pastry cream

G

Galantine: boned poultry or meat, stuffed and pressed into a symmetrical shape, cooked in broth and coated with aspic
Gâteau: cake
Gelée (en): in aspic; gelatin usually flavored with meat, poultry, or fish stock

Génoise: sponge cake
Gibier: game
Glace: ice cream
Granité: lightly sweetened fruit ice
Gratin dauphinois: sliced potatoes baked in milk, sometimes with cream and/or grated Gruyère
Grenouille: frog (frogs' legs: cuisses de grenouilles)

H

Hollandaise: egg-based sauce thickened with butter and flavored with lemon
Homard: lobster
Huître: oyster

J

Jambon: ham
Julienne: shredded vegetables; also a consomme garnished with shredded vegetables
Jus: juice; also a reduction or essence used as a sauce

L

Lait: milk
Langouste: rock or spiny lobster
Langoustine: saltwater crayfish
Lapereau: young rabbit
Lapin: rabbit
Lièvre: hare
Lotte: monkfish or anglerfish; sometimes called "poor man's lobster"

M

Magret (Maigret): breast of fattened duck, cooked with the skin on; usually grilled
Médaillon: food, usually meat, fish, or foie gras, cut into small, round "medallions"
Mirabelle: yellow plum
Morue: salt cod
Moules (marinière): mussels (cooked in the shell with white wine, shallots, and parsley)

N

Nantua: sauce of crayfish, white wine, butter, and cream with a touch of tomato
Navets: turnips
Noisettes: hazelnuts; also, small, round pieces of meat (especially lamb or veal)
Nougat: sweet made with roasted almonds, egg whites, honey, and sugar

O

Œuf: egg

P

Pain: bread
Parfait: sweet or savory mousse; also a layered ice cream dessert
Parisienne: garnish of fried potato balls
Pâtisserie: pastry
Paupiette: thin slice of meat stuffed with forcemeat and shaped into rolls
Pêche: peach
Pigeonneau: squab
Pintade: guinea hen
Poireau: leek
Poire: pear
Pomme: apple
Pomme de terre: potatoe
Poulet: chicken

Provençale (à la): with garlic or tomato and garlic
Prune: Plum

Q

Quiche: savory tart filled with a mixture of eggs, cream, and various fillings (such as ham, spinach, or bacon)

R

Raisin: grape
Ratatouille: stew of eggplant, tomatoes, bell peppers, zucchini, onion, and garlic, all sautéed in oil
Rémoulade: tangy cold sauce often flavored with capers, onions, parsley, gherkins, or herbs
Ris de veau: sweetbreads
Rissole: type of small pie filled with forcemeat
Rognon: kidney
Rouget: red mullet
Rouille: a Provençal sauce, so called because of the red chiles and sometimes saffron which give it a "rust" color; chiles are pounded with garlic and breadcrumbs and blended with olive oil; the sauce being served with bouillabaisse, boiled fish or octopus

S

Sabayon: fluffy, whipped egg yolks, sweetened and flavored with wine or liqueur and served warm
Saint-Pierre: John Dory; a white-fleshed fish
Salade niçoise: salad of tomatoes, hard-boiled egg, anchovy fillets, tuna, sweet peppers, celery, and olives (also can include green beans, potatoes, basil, onions, and/or broad beans)
Sandre: pikeperch
Saumon: salmon
Soissons: garnished with white beans
Sole meunière: sole dipped in flour and sautéed in butter, served with parsley and lemon
Steak au poivre: pepper steak; steak covered in crushed peppercorns, browned in a frying pan, flambéed with Cognac, often served with a cream sauce
Steak tartare: chopped raw steak mixed with onion, anchovy, seasonings, and egg yolk; called "cannibale" in Belgium

T

Tapenade: a paste of black olives, often with capers and anchovies, crushed in a mortar with lemon juice and pepper
Tartare: cold sauce for meat or fish: mayonnaise with hard-boiled egg yolks, onions, and chopped olives
Tarte: tart, round cake or flan; can be sweet or savory
Tarte Tatin: upside-down apple tart invented by the Tatin sisters
Tortue: turtle, also, a sauce made with various herbs, tomato, Madeira
Tourteau: large crab
Truffe: truffle; highly esteemed subterranean fungus, esp. from Périgord
Truite: trout

V

Vacherin: ice cream served in a meringue shell; also, creamy, pungent cheese from Switzerland or eastern France
Viande: meat
Volaille: poultry

REGIONAL SPECIALTIES

A

Aïgo bouido or boulido or bullido (Provence): garlic soup with oil served over slices of bread

Aïoli or aïlloli (Provence): sauce (mayonnaise with garlic) has lent its name to this dish of dried cod, various vegetables, snails, and hard-boiled eggs

Aligot (Auvergne): mashed potatoes combined with garlic and Cantal or fresh Tomme cheese; has a very elastic consistency

Anchoïade (Provence): purée of anchovy fillets combined with garlic and olive oil; accompanies crudités

Andouille de Guémené (Brittany): andouille (tripe sausage) with a characteristic marking of concentric rings

Andouille de Vire (Calvados): andouille (pork tripe sausage) with irregular marbling

Andouillette de Troyes (Champagne): small andouille made of pork in rather broad and alternating strips

Anguille au vert (Lille): eel in a green sauce flavored with thirteen herbs

B

Baba (Lorraine): a small yeast cake soaked in a rum syrup; said to have been invented by King

Bæckeoffe (Alsace): hot terrine made with alternating layers of beef, mutton, and pork, marinated in wine with sliced potatoes and onions

Beignets de fleurs de courge (Provence, Nice): squash blossoms (pistils removed) dipped in batter and deep fried

Beurre blanc nantais (Nantes, Loire, Anjou): sauce consisting of minced shallots cooked in a reduction of Muscadet and/or vinegar, with butter whisked in until the consistency is perfectly creamy; most often accompanies pike. The sauce often lends its name to the dish itself

Bireweck (Alsace): sweet, moist bread studded with dried fruit, flavored with Kirsch and spices

Bœuf gardiane (Camargue): marinated beef stewed with bacon, onions, garlic, tomatoes, olives, and red wine

Boles de picoulat (Roussillon): meatballs made of minced beef, pork, garlic, and eggs, accompanied by parsleyed tomatoes

Boudin blanc (Normandy and all of France): sausage of pork fat, milk, eggs, bread, starch, and rice flour; often includes truffles, trimmings or leftover fowl

Bouillabaisse (Provence): various fish (including scorpionfish) in a soup of olive oil, tomatoes, garlic and saffron

Bouilleture or bouilliture (Anjou, Aunis): eel stewed in red wine with onions or shallots, prunes, and (optionally) garlic and egg yolk

Bouillinade (Roussillon): a sort of bouillabaisse made of pieces of fish (lotte, turbot, John Dory, sea bass) with potatoes, oil, onions, and garlic; the broth is thickened with egg yolk and oil

Bourdelot (Normandy): a whole apple baked in a pastry crust

Bourride (Provence): a sort of bouillabaisse usually made with large white fish (lotte, turbot); the creamy broth is thickened with aïoli and poured over slices of bread

Boutifare or boutifaron (Catalonia, Roussillon): boudin with bacon and herbs

Brandade de morue (Nîmes): salt cod puréed with olive oil, truffles (optional) and milk or cream

Broufado (Provence): layers of thin slices of marinated beef and chopped onions with vinegar, capers, and anchovies

Bugnes (Lyonnais, Burgundy): a sweet dessert fritter

C

Cabassol (Languedoc): lamb tripe

Cagouille or luma (Charentes): local name for snail; (cagouillard, the nickname for natives of the Charentes, comes from cagouille)

Caillette (Ardèche, Drôme): chopped spinach, chard, onion, parsley, garlic, bread, minced pork, and egg formed into fist-sized balls, baked, and served hot or cold

Carbonnade (Flanders): pieces of lean beef, first sautéed then stewed with onions and beer

Cargolade (Languedoc, Roussillon): snails simmered in wine, or cooked over charcoal, with salt and pepper, flavored with bacon fat

Casserons en matelote (Ile de Ré, Charente-Maritime): squid in a sauce of red wine (from the island), garlic, shallots, a bit of sugar, and butter

Cassoulet (Toulouse, Castelnaudary and other regions): white Cazères or Pamiers beans and various meats (mutton, preserved goose or duck, sausage, salt brisket, pig's trotters) cooked at length in an earthenware casserole

Caudière or chaudrée (Flanders): fish soup with potatoes, for which there are numerous recipes(it is the origin of American chowder)

Cervelas de Lyon (Lyonnais): fat, short pork sausage, often flavored with truffles or pistachios and placed in a brioche crust

Cervelas de Strasbourg (Alsace): sausage in a red-colored casing, eaten hot or cold (in a salad)

Cervelle de canut (Lyonnais): white cheese mixed with shallots, herbs, and chives, cream, white wine, and a bit of oil

Chaudrée (Poitou, Saintonge, Aunis): soup or stew of various fish cooked in white wine, with shallots, garlic, and butter

Chipirons à l'encre (Pays Basque): cuttlefish stuffed with onions, bread, and cuttlefish meat, served in a sauce of its own ink with tomatoes

Confit (Périgord, Quercy, Béarn): wings, thighs, and other pieces of duck, pork, or goose (or, rarely, turkey or chicken), cooked in their own fat and stored in a stoneware jar

Cornics (Brittany): type of croissant

Cotriade (Brittany): fisherman's soup, infinitely variable, composed of delicate fish simmered with potatoes, onions, garlic, parsley, and butter; served over croûtons

Cou d'oie farci (Périgord): mixture of sausage meat, duck liver, and a small amount of minced truffle, stuffed in the skin of a fatted goose. The whole is cooked in boiling fat, like a confit, and eaten hot or cold, accompanied by a salad dressed with walnut oil

Cousina or cousinat (Vivarais, Auvergne): chestnut soup made with cream, butter, onions, and leeks, or sometimes with prunes or apples

Cousinat (Pays Basque): a stew of Bayonne ham, small artichokes, beans, carrots, tomatoes and various other vegetables

Craquelot (Flanders): herring smoked over walnut leaves

Crémet (Loire): whipped cream and stiffly beaten egg whites placed in a mold lined with muslin; served with cream and sprinkled with sugar

Crémet (Nantes): molded cheese covered with sweetened whipped cream; Normandy has an almost identical recipe for white cheese that bears the same name

Crêpes dentelle (Brittany): crêpes that are extremely thin, almost like lace (dentelle), and flaky, served rolled up. Originally from Quimper

Criques (Vivarais): grated potatoes mixed with eggs and fried like pancakes. Related to the râpée and grapiau (Morvan) and truffiat (Berry)

D

Daube (Provence, Languedoc): beef or mutton marinated in red wine with oil and onions, then braised in an earthenware pot

Diots (Savoie): sausages made with chard, spinach, cabbage, and leeks, mixed with pork and pork fat; they are preserved in oil and are often cooked in white wine with shallots and minced onions

Douillon (Normandy): a whole pear baked in a pastry crust

E

Éclade de moules or fumée or térée (Saintonge): mussels laid out on a board with their tips up, roasted over a fire of pine needles

Escargots à la bourguignonne (Burgundy): snails stuffed with butter, garlic, and parsley

F

Farci poitevin (Poitou): pâté of greens (spinach, chard, sorrel, cabbage) mixed with bacon and eggs, wrapped in cabbage leaves and cooked in bouillon; eaten hot or cold

Farcis niçois (Nice): squash, eggplant, tomatoes, and onions stuffed with their own pulp mixed with chopped pork or veal, eggs, and garlic, then baked in the oven with oil

Farçon (Auvergne): large pancake made of sausage meat, sorrel, onions, eggs, flour, and white wine

Farçon (Savoie): potatoes, bacon, prunes, and eggs, or mashed potatoes, milk, and eggs, mixed and gratinéed in the oven

Ficelle picarde (Picardie): crêpe rolled with ham, mushrooms, and grated cheese, gratinéed in the oven

Flamique or flamiche (Picardie): sort of tart-flan with leeks, onion, or squash

Flammekueche or tarte flambée (Alsace): a rectangle of bread dough with raised edges, filled with cream, bacon, onions, and (sometimes) white cheese, then baked

Flamusse (Nivernais, Morvan): fruit (often apple) omelet

Flognarde or flaugnarde (Auvergne): a type of flan

Fougassette (Provence): oval-shaped bread made with oil and flavored with orange or lemon rind and orangeflower water

G

Galettes and crêpes (Brittany): galettes are made of buckwheat flour and are usually savory; crêpes are made of wheat flour and are usually sweet

Garbure (Southwest): soup prepared with fat (sometimes with streaky bacon and sausage), green beans, thinly sliced cabbage, beans, garlic, marjoram, thyme, and parsley; a piece of preserved duck, turkey, goose, or pork (tromblon or trébuc) is added and the soup is served over slices of bread

Gâteau basque (Pays Basque): thick torte stuffed with pastry cream

Gâteau breton (Brittany): type of pound cake or a large, somewhat hard and crumbly cake

Gaufres (Flanders, Artois): waffles

Grattons (Lyonnais): rillettes; browned but not molded cubes of bacon

Grillons (Périgord): bits of goose (or pork) meat left over from preparation of confit

H

Hochepot (Flanders): sort of pot-au-feu made with oxtails

Huîtres à la bordelaise (Bordelais): oysters accompanied by sausages with optional truffles

J

Jambon persillé (Burgundy): ham cooked in white wine, cut into pieces, and mixed with aspic and parsley; served cold molded in a salad bowl

Jésus de Morteau (Franche-Comté): large pork sausage with a small wooden peg at one end—a sign that it has been smoked over pine and juniper

K

Kouing amann (Douarnenez, Brittany): a rich, buttery cake

Kugelhopf (Alsace): a sort of brioche with raisins and almonds, cooked in a characteristic fluted mold

L

Langues d'avocat (Bordelais): "lawyer's tongues"—the local name for small sole

M

Madeleine de Commercy (Lorraine): small, fluted, and domed cake; said to have been created by King Stanislaw Leszczynski's cook, Madeleine

Millia (Périgord): a pumpkin-and-cornflour flan; a very similar dish is made in the Limousin

Mogette or mojette, Mougette, Mohjette (Angoûmois): a small bean that reminds natives of Charente of the humble, curled-up posture of a nun (mougette) at prayer

Mouclade (Charentes): mussels cooked with cream, egg yolks, white wine, and butter, to which Pineau des Charentes can also be added

P

Panisses (Provence): chickpea flour made into a porridge, then fried in oil

Pastis (Pays Basque): cake flavored with orangeflower water

Pissaladière (Nice): tart topped with onions, black olives, and anchovy fillets

Pogne (Dauphiné): brioche loaf studded with candied fruit

Pommes de terre sarladaise (Périgord): raw potatoes cut into thin slices and baked with goose fat and (optional) truffles

Pompe (Auvergne, Nivernais, Morvan): sort of torte or turnover filled with fruit (such as apples)

Pompe de Noël or gibassié (Provence): bread made with oil and orange rind or lemon, perfumed with orangeflower water

Porchetta (Nice): a small pig stuffed with its offal mixed with herbs and garlic, then roasted on a spit

Potée (multiregional): various vegetables and meats boiled together

Potjevfleisch (Dunkirk, Nord): terrine of veal, pork, and rabbit

Pounti (Auvergne): meatloaf made with ground pork and chard; eggs or cream can also be added, or grapes, prunes, and herbs

Poutargue (Provence): red or gray mullet roe, salted, pressed and served in the form of slightly flattened sausages

Presskopf or tête roulée (Alsace): cubes of pig's head or veal and pieces of pork in wine aspic with (optionally) shallots and gherkins. Often served with an herbal vinaigrette

Q

Quenelles (Lyonnais, Bugey, Alsace): fowl or pike made with a mousseline stuffing thickened with eggs and shaped into small cylinders

R

Raisiné (Aunis, Saintonge, Burgundy): jam made with grape juice or must, reduced until it has the consistency of jelly or marmalade

Ravioles (Dauphiné): pasta stuffed with goat cheese

Ravioli à la niçoise (Nice): pasta stuffed with meat (veal, pork, or beef), poached and minced chard, and a bit of grated cheese

Rillettes du Mans (Sarthe): shredded pork spread with some rather large bits left in

Rillettes de Tours (Touraine): darker in color than the previous type, with a rather delicate texture; often contain pork liver

Rillons or rillauds (Touraine, Anjou): pieces of pork brisket and shoulder cut into large cubes and cooked in pork fat

Rosette (Lyonnais): large dry sausage of pure pork (usually wrapped in a net)

Rouille (Provence): rust-colored mayonnaise flavored with chilis, garlic, bread soaked in bouillon, olive oil, and saffron; often accompanies bouillabaisse

S

Saladier lyonnais (Lyonnais): salad of sheep's trotters, chicken Spätzle (Alsace): round noodles, sometimes made with egg

T

Tablier de sapeur (Lyonnais): pieces of tripe browned and cut into triangles, dipped in beaten eggs, then breaded; often served with snail butter or with mayonnaise containing shallots and tarragon

Tapenade (Provence): black olives from Nice, capers, and anchovies, crushed in a mortar with lemon juice and pepper. Can be eaten as an hors d'œuvre on toast, or used as a stuffing for hard-boiled eggs

Tergoule or teugoule, torgoule, terrinée (Normandy): rice cooked with sweetened milk, a dash of cinnamon, baked for a long time in an earthenware dish

Tourin or tourain (entire Southwest): onion soup made with bacon and a small clove of garlic, thickened with egg yolk and a dash of vinegar, then poured over thin slices of bread

Touron (Languedoc, Roussillon): sort of almond paste, with different flavors, containing pistachios, hazelnuts, or candied fruit

Tourteau fromagé (Poitou): a round cheese-flavored cake with a very dark brown top

Tripes à la mode de Caen (Caen, Calvados): beef tripe cooked (for about twelve hours) with calf's feet, onions, carrots, herbs, and (optionally) Calvados, in a clay pot

Tripoux or tripous (Auvergne, Rouergue, Cévennes): mutton or calf's tripe in the shape of small bundles, stuffed with meat from the trotters, cloves, and lots of pepper

Truffade (Auvergne): a large pancake of sautéed potato, with or without bits of bacon, and Tomme cheese; another recipe calls for the Tomme to be served separately, cut into cubes

Truffiat (Berry): grated potato mixed with flour, eggs, and butter, then baked. Related to criques and râpée (Vivarais) and grapiau (Morvan)

Trulet (Nice): blood sausage typical of Nice, made with pork's blood, chard, onion, sweetbreads, and bacon

Ttoro (Pays Basque): slices of various fish baked or fried with minced onion, tomato, and garlic

W

Waterzooï or waterzoï de poulet (or poisson) (Flanders): chicken (or fish) braised with whites of leek, bouillon, cream, and egg yolk

RESTAURANT-SPEAK

Breakfast: petit déjeuner
Lunch: déjeuner
Dinner: dîner

The menu, please: la carte, s'il vous plaît
The wine list: la carte des vins
Waiter: serveur
Waitress: serveuse
Tip included: service compris
The check, please: l'addition, s'il vous plaît
To reserve a table: réserver une table

Dish: plat
Prix fixe: menu
Appetizer: entrée
Main course: plat principal
Children's menu: menu enfant
Tip: pourboire
Today's special: plat du jour
Dessert: dessert
Cheese: fromage

Fork: fourchette
Spoon: cuillère
Knife: couteau
Plate: assiette
Glass: verre
Napkin: serviette

Beverage: boisson
Wine steward: sommelier
Wine cellar: cave

Pre-dinner drink: apéritif
White wine: vin blanc
Rosé: vin rosé
Red wine: vin rouge
Vin de table: a plain red or white table wine
Mineral water: eau minérale
Ice water: eau glacée
Carbonated water: eau gazeuse
Draft beer: bière à la pression
A (glass of) beer: un demi
After-dinner drink: digestif

Salt: sel
Pepper: poivre
Mustard: moutarde
Oil: huile
Vinegar: vinaigre
Bread: pain
Butter: beurre

Rare: saignant
Medium rare: à point
Well-done: bien cuit
Steamed: à la vapeur
Cold: froid
Hot: chaud

Coffee: café
Tea: thé
Sugar: sucre
Milk: lait
Honey: miel

A FINAL NOTE

We have made a herculean effort to provide as much practical information as possible: phone numbers, hours, daily and annual closings, fax numbers, specific amenities and special features, prices, credit cards accepted, and more. We've also done our utmost to keep all the information current and correct. But establishments change such things with alarming speed, so please forgive us if you come across incorrect or incomplete information.

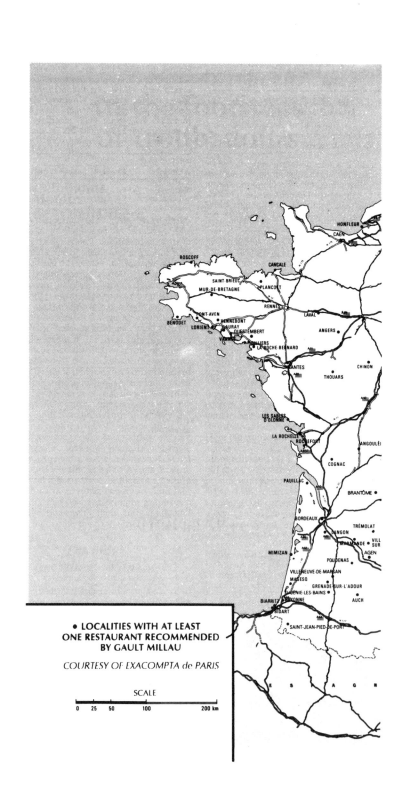

**• LOCALITIES WITH AT LEAST
ONE RESTAURANT RECOMMENDED
BY GAULT MILLAU**

COURTESY OF EXACOMPTA de PARIS

SCALE

0   25   50   100   200 km

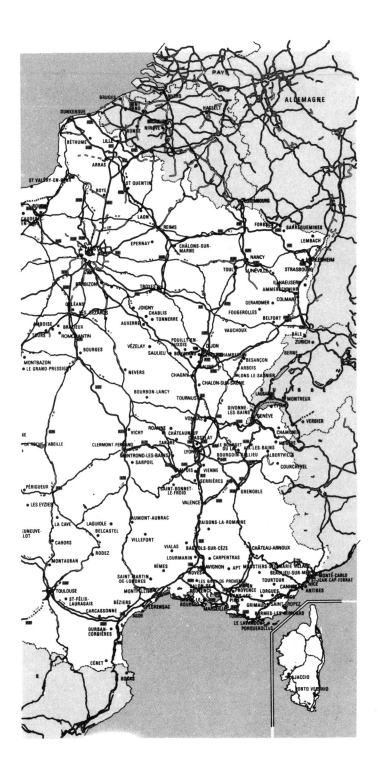

FRANCE ADMINISTRATIVE

50 **MANCHE** Département
● **Caen** Chef-lieu de Région
● Saint-Lô Préfecture
○ Cherbourg Sous-Préfecture

REGIONS

A ALSACE
B AQUITAINE
C AUVERGNE
D BOURGOGNE

E BRETAGNE
F CENTRE
G CHAMPAGNE
H CORSE

I FRANCHE-COMTÉ
J LANGUEDOC ROUSSILLON
K LIMOUSIN
L LORRAINE

M MIDI-PYRÉNÉES
N NORD
O BASSE-NORMANDIE
P HAUTE-NORMANDIE
Q RÉGION PARISIENNE

R PAYS DE LA LOIRE
S PICARDIE
T POITOU-CHARENTES
U PROVENCE CÔTE-D'AZUR
V RHÔNE-ALPES

INDEX

Entries in CAPITALS are names of cities and localities.
Entries in **bold print** are regional food specialties.

GAYOT PUBLICATIONS

RECEIVE A
FREE
SUBSCRIPTION TO

(A $30 VALUE)

BY FILLING OUT THIS QUESTIONNAIRE, YOU'LL RECEIVE A COMPLIMENTARY ONE-YEAR SUBSCRIPTION TO "TASTES," OUR INTERNATIONAL NEWSLETTER.

NAME _____

ADDRESS _____

CITY _____ STATE _____

ZIP _____ COUNTRY _____

PHONE (   )   –

The Gayot/GaultMillau series of guidebooks reflects your demand for insightful, incisive reporting on the best that the world's most exciting destinations have to offer. To help us make our books even better, please take a moment to fill out this anonymous (if you wish) questionnaire, and return it to:

GaultMillau, Inc., P.O. Box 361144, Los Angeles, CA 90036;
Fax: (213) 936-2883.

1. How did you hear about the Gayot guides? Please specify: bookstore, newspaper, magazine, radio, friends or other.

2. Please list in order of preference the cities or countries which you would like to see Gayot cover.

3. Do you refer to the AGP guides for your own city, or only when traveling?

A. (Travels) ....   B. (Own city) ....   C. (Both) ....

(Please turn)

4. Please list by order of preference the three features you like best about the Gayot guides.

A. ....

B. .... C. ....

5. What are the features, if any, you dislike about the Gayot guides?

6. Please list any features that you would like to see added to the Gayot guides.

7. If you use other guides besides Gayot, please list below.

8. Please list the features you like best about your favorite guidebook series, if it is not Gayot/GaultMillau.

A. ....

B. .... C. ....

9. How many trips do you make per year, for either business or pleasure?

Business: International .... Domestic ....

Pleasure: International .... Domestic.........................

10. Please check the category that reflects your annual household income.

$20,000–$39,000 .... $40,000–$59,000 ....
$60,000–$79,000 .... $80,000–$99,000 ....
$100,000–$120,000 .... Other (please specify) ....

11. If you have any comments on the AGP guides in general, please list them in the space below.

12. If you would like to recommend specific establishments, please don't hesitate to list them:
   Name   **City**   **Phone**

We thank you for your interest in the Gayot guides, and we welcome your remarks and recommendations about restaurants, hotels, nightlife, shops, services and so on.

THE WORLD DINING & TRAVEL CONNECTION

Want to keep current on the best bistros in Paris? Discover that little hideaway in Singapore? Or stay away from that dreadful and dreadfully expensive restaurant in New York? André Gayot's *Tastes* newsletter gives you bi-monthly news on the best restaurants, hotels, nightlife, shopping, airline and cruiseline information around the world.

Please enter/renew my subscription to TASTES newsletter for:

☐ Six bi-monthly issues at the rate of $30 per year & $35 outside U.S./Canada.

☐ 12 bi-monthly issues at the rate of $55 for two years US & $60 outside US/Canada.

Name _____

Address _____

City _____ State _____

ZIP _____ Country _____

Phone ( ) –

☐ Enclosed is my check or money order made out to Gault Millau, Inc.

☐ $_____

☐ Charge to: _____ VISA _____ AMEX _____ MASTERCARD Exp. _____

Card# _____ Signature _____

 FOR FASTER SERVICE CALL 1 (800) LE BEST 1

"Gault Millau
is provocative
and frank."
—*Los Angeles
Times*

"You will enjoy
their prose."
—*US News &
World Report*

"Gault Millau
is the toque
of the town."
—*San Francisco
Examiner*

Please send me the "The Best of" books checked below:

❑ Chicago $18.00
❑ Florida $17.00
❑ France $25.00
❑ Germany $20.00
❑ Hawaii $18.00
❑ Italy $20.00

❑ London $20.00
❑ Los Angeles $18.00
❑ LA Restaurants $10.00
❑ New Orleans $17.00
❑ New York $18.00
❑ NYC Restaurants .. $12.00

❑ Paris $20.00
❑ Paris &
 Il-de-France $15.00
❑ San Francisco $18.00
❑ SF Restaurants $12.00
❑ Wineries of North
 America $18.00

Mail to:
Gault Millau, Inc., P.O. Box 361144, Los Angeles, CA 90036

Order toll-free:
1 (800) LE BEST 1 • FAX: (213) 936-2883 • *E-mail:* **gayots@aol.com**
In the U.S., include $4 (shipping charge) for the first book, and $3 for each
additional book. Outside the U.S., $7 and $5.

❑ Enclosed is my check or money order made out to Gault Millau, Inc.
 for $ _____.

❑ Please charge my credit card: ❑ VISA   ❑ MC   ❑ AMEX

Card # _____ Exp. ___ / ___

Signature_____ Telephone _____

Name _____

Address _____

City _____ State_____ ZIP_____

Country _____